PAGE
44

ON THE
ROAD

YOUR COMPLETE DESTINATION GUIDE
In-depth reviews, detailed listings
and insider tips

PAGE
513

SURVIVAL
GUIDE

VITAL PRACTICAL INFORMATION TO
HELP YOU HAVE A SMOOTH TRIP

Transport

GETTING THERE
& AWAY

THIS EDITION WRITTEN AND RESEARCHED BY
Regis St Louis
Jayne D'Arcy, Sarah Gilbert, Paul Harding, Catherine Le Nevez,
Virginia Maxwell, Olivia Pozzan, Penny Watson

welcome to East Coast Australia

Spectacular Scenery

With nearly 18,000km of coastline, Australia's East Coast has some of the most captivating scenery on the planet. The most famous attraction is the colourful aquatic wonderland of the Great Barrier Reef, which stretches for more than 2000km and contains an astonishing array of marine life. Both on and off the reef, you'll encounter hundreds of islands – from craggy windswept nature reserves to rainforest-covered isles. Richly hued fringing coral, mesmerising beaches and ruggedly beautiful shorelines offer endless variety. Tear yourself away from the ocean, and you'll find bewitching national parks, with lush rainforests (temperate, subtropical and tropical), rolling mountains, pristine lakes and a staggering array of wildlife that rates from cute and cuddly (koalas) to downright fearsome (crocs).

Big Adventures

The great outdoors holds endless possibilities in Australia. You can don a mask and fins and explore some of the most stunning underwater landscapes on earth. There's adrenalin-charged white-water rafting and scenic kayaking on peaceful seas and forest-lined rivers. Bushwalking and hiking is first-rate, whether you opt for a challenging trek on one of Australia's famous multi-day routes, or tackle a shorter trail through bush, up mountains or along gorges, rushing rivers and mirrorlike lakes. You can go sailing

Beautiful beaches, cosmopolitan cities, wildlife-filled rainforests and the Great Barrier Reef are just a few reasons why so many have fallen under the spell of Australia's enchanting East Coast.

(left) Sydney Opera House (p53) and Sydney Harbour Bridge (p49) at sunset
(below) Blue Mountains (p97), New South Wales

through the turquoise waters of the Whitsundays, stopping at powdery white-sand beaches along the way; hire a car and explore quaint coastal towns and wild landscapes from Victoria to northern Queensland; or go on a 4WD adventure, plying the 'beach highway' of Fraser Island, jostling past giant dunes and verdant forest growing right from the sand.

Eat, Drink & Celebrate

Sydney and Melbourne are gateways to Australia's rich culinary experience, with fantastic cafe scenes, sprawling food markets and award-winning restaurants serving temptations from every corner of the globe. After dark, wine bars, nightclubs and good old-fashioned Aussie pubs provide memorable settings to raise a glass. Brisbane, ever on the rise, also has a great dining and drinking scene. But you don't have to stay in the city to savour the great Australian bounty. You'll find culinary rewards big and small, from seafood feasts along the coast to gourmet meals in the Gippsland Lakes district, Newcastle, Byron Bay, Noosa, Townsville, Port Douglas and countless other places. The vineyards of the Hunter Valley set the stage for a bacchanalian feast, with luscious wines, celebrated restaurants and gourmet produce of every flavour and texture. Wineries here and in Victoria's Mornington Peninsula make for some rewarding tasting tours. The hardest part is deciding where to begin...

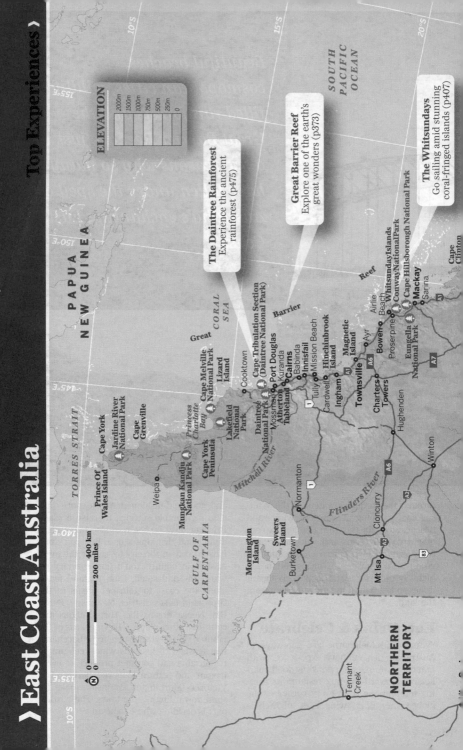

The Daintree Rainforest
Experience the ancient rainforest (p475)

Great Barrier Reef
Explore one of the earth's great wonders (p373)

The Whitsundays
Go sailing amid stunning coral-fringed islands (p407)

ELEVATION

2000m
1500m
1000m
750m
500m
250m
0

SOUTH
PACIFIC
OCEAN

PAPUA
NEW GUINEA

CORAL
SEA

Great Barrier Reef

TORRES STRAIT

GULF OF
CARPENTARIA

Cape York

Prince Of
Wales Island

Jardine River
National Park

Cape
Grenville

Weipa

Mungkan Kandju
National Park

Cape York
Peninsula

Mitchell River

Princess
Charlotte
Bay

Lakefield
National
Park

Cape Melville
National Park

Lizard
Island

Cooktown

Cape Tribulation Section
(Daintree National Park)

Mossman
Port Douglas
Daintree National Park
Kuranda
Atherton
Cairns
Tableland
Babinda
Innisfail
Tully
Mission Beach
Cardwell
Hinchinbrook
Island
Ingham
Magnetic
Island
Townsville
Ayr
Charters
Towers
Bowen
Proserpine
Airlie Beach
Whitsunday Islands
Conway National Park
Eungella
National Park
Cape Hillsborough National Park
Mackay
Sarina

Cape
Clinton

Normanton

Sweers
Island

Mornington
Island

Burketown

Flinders River

Cloncurry

Hughenden

Winton

Mt Isa

Tennant
Creek

NORTHERN
TERRITORY

400 km
200 miles

N

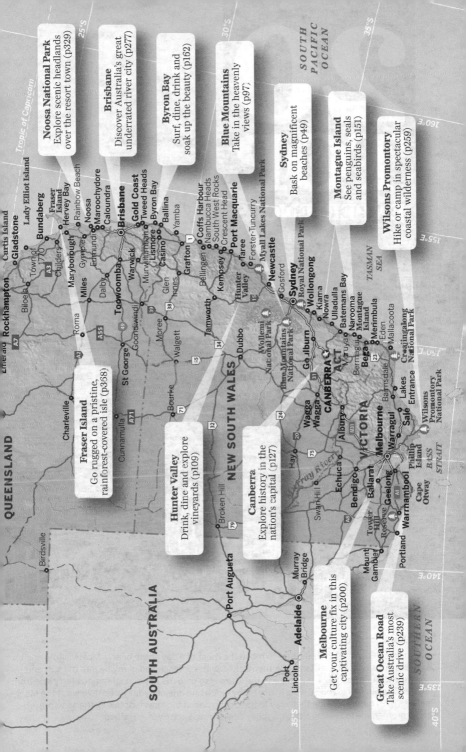

Noosa National Park
Explore scenic headlands over the resort town (p329)

Brisbane
Discover Australia's great underrated river city (p277)

Byron Bay
Surf, dine, drink and soak up the beauty (p162)

Blue Mountains
Take in the heavenly views (p97)

Sydney
Bask on magnificent beaches (p49)

Montague Island
See penguins, seals and seabirds (p151)

Wilsons Promontory
Hike or camp in spectacular coastal wilderness (p259)

Fraser Island
Go rugged on a pristine, rainforest-covered isle (p368)

Hunter Valley
Drink, dine and explore vineyards (p109)

Canberra
Explore history in the nation's capital (p127)

Melbourne
Get your culture fix in this captivating city (p200)

Great Ocean Road
Take Australia's most scenic drive (p239)

QUEENSLAND

NEW SOUTH WALES

SOUTH AUSTRALIA

VICTORIA

CANBERRA
ACT

SOUTH PACIFIC OCEAN

TASMAN SEA

SOUTHERN OCEAN

BASS STRAIT

Tropic of Capricorn

Murray River

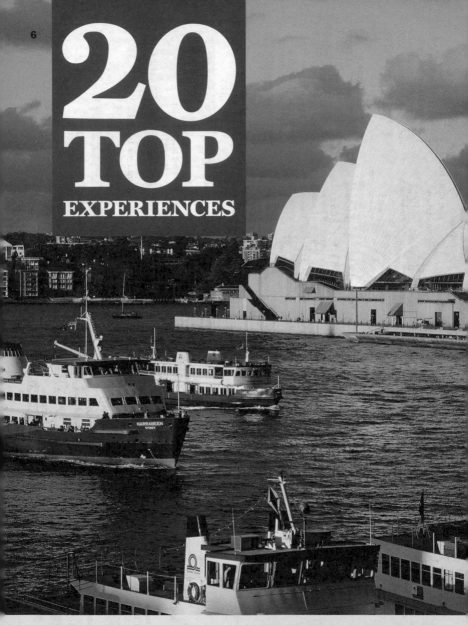

20 TOP EXPERIENCES

Sydney

1 Sydneysiders certainly know how to make the most of a day at the beach. Most visitors end up laying out a beach towel, lathering themselves with sunblock and plunging into the surf and social scene at Bondi (p62), but those in the know also take the city's most famous ferry ride from Circular Quay to Manly (p63), where they enjoy lunch and one of Sydney's best views at the Manly Pavilion (p79) before making their way to the ocean beach for a swim or taking the sea-sprayed scenic promenade to Shelley Beach. Sydney Opera House and Sydney Harbour

BOB HALSTEAD/LONELY PLANET IMAGES ©

The Great Barrier Reef

2 Stretching more than 2000km up the Queensland coastline, the awe-inspiring Great Barrier Reef (p373) is one of the world's great wonders. Among the best ways to experience it is to don a mask and fins and delve into the vivid undersea kingdom for a close-up view of dazzling corals, sea turtles, sharks, rays and tropical fish of every colour and size. You can also explore the reef by sailboat, take a scenic flight, gaze at marine life through a glass-bottomed semisubmersible, and linger in a resort (or camp) on a remote coral-fringed island.

The Daintree Rainforest

3 Fan palms, ferns and mangroves are just some of the 3000 or so plant species in the ancient, World Heritage–listed Daintree Rainforest (p476), which is alive with a chorus of birds, insects and frogs. Guided day walks, wildlife spotting night tours, mountain treks, interpretive board-walks, canopy walks and self-guided walking trails, 4WD trips, horse riding, kayaking, croc-spotting cruises, and tropical-fruit orchard tours and tastings are among the many ways to experience one of the most extraordinary ecosystems on the planet.

RICHARD I'ANSON/LONELY PLANET IMAGES ©

Melbourne

4 Head down the bluestone-lined laneways in Melbourne (p200) to find hidden restaurants and bright, bold street art that encapsulates the alternative vibe that Melburnians carry so well. Take a seat in Degraves St and let a local barista change the way you think about coffee, then window-shop for quirky 'only in Melbourne' craft and clothes. Watch evening's arrival by the Yarra River then, almost blindly, head up some stairs or along a graffiti-covered lane to find a smooth drinking establishment serving up quality Victorian wine and beer along with home-grown music.
Centre Place, Melbourne

RACHEL LEWIS/LONELY PLANET IMAGES ©

Sailing the Whitsunday Islands

5 Sailing across the shimmering blue water of the Coral Sea, lounging beside the pool in a luxury island resort, playing castaway on a secluded beach...there are so many ways to enjoy the beautiful Whitsunday Islands (p398). One of the best ways is from the deck of a sailing boat, basking in the warm sunshine and balmy sea air, savouring the dramatic tropical sunsets and star-studded night skies. Sailing through this island paradise brings the romance of the sea to life.

RICHARD I'ANSON/LONELY PLANET IMAGES ©

Byron Bay

6 Vibrant, laid-back and offbeat are words oft used to describe this small-time, big-hearted, beachside destination. At first encounter, it might seem too touristy, too packed – but no matter how many bronzed shoulders you rub up against, Byron Bay (p161) tends to soften even the harshest critic. Long lazy stretches of beach and a cute undeveloped town centre help; so too the eclectic food scene, where cheap, cheerful takeaway joints sit comfortably next to hip bars and restaurants. The town's infectious, upbeat vibe will put a smile on your dial.
Tallow Beach, Byron Bay

RICHARD I'ANSON/LONELY PLANET IMAGES ©

Noosa National Park

7 Covering the headland beside the stylish resort town of Noosa, the Noosa National Park (p329) has a string of perfect bays fringed with sand and lined with pandanus trees. Surfers come for the long, rolling waves, nature-buffs for the unspoilt landscape. Fine walks criss-cross the park but on the scenic coastal trail to Hell's Gates you might spy sleepy koalas in the trees around Tea Tree Bay, and dolphins swimming off the rocky headland.

RICHARD I'ANSON/LONELY PLANET IMAGES ©

CHRISTOPHER GROENHOUT/LONELY PLANET IMAGES ©

Fraser Island

8 Fraser Island (p368) is an ecological wonderland created by drifting sand, where wild dogs roam free and lush rainforest grows on sand. It's a primal island utopia, home to a profusion of wildlife including the purest strain of dingo in Australia. The best way to explore the island is in a 4WD – cruising up the seemingly endless Seventy-Five Mile Beach and bouncing along sandy inland tracks. Tropical rainforest, pristine freshwater pools and beach camping under the stars will bring you back to nature.

Brisbane

9 Queensland's cultural capital, Brisbane (p277) is an arts-loving city with a calendar packed with food and music festivals, dance and theatre performances, exhibitions and concerts. There's great sport (cricket, rugby league, Aussie Rules football) and many ways to enjoy the subtropical climate year-round. The river city also boasts open-air markets, boutiques and a great cafe scene, while award-winning restaurants and burgeoning nightlife means you'll never run out of options when the sun goes down. Grand Arbour (designed by Denton Corker Marshall), Brisbane

RICHARD I'ANSON/LONELY PLANET IMAGES ©

Blue Mountains

10 The views from the scenic lookouts at Katoomba's Echo Point and Blackheath's Govetts Leap in the Blue Mountains (p98) are so sensational that you'll find yourself pushing the limits of your camera's memory card. So, shut down the photo shoot and follow one of the signed walking tracks into the magnificent Jamison and Grose Valleys instead. You'll be accompanied on your bushwalk by the scent of eucalyptus oil, a fine mist of which issues from the dense tree canopy and gives this World Heritage–listed landscape its name. Three Sisters and Mt Solitary, Blue Mountains, New South Wales

ANDREW BAIN/LONELY PLANET IMAGES ©

Far North Queensland

11 Big adventure comes in many forms in Queensland's wild tropics. You can take in breathtaking views of rainforest and reef from 9000ft on a skydive over Mission Beach (p440), ride the rapids on the Tully River (p440) or swim into the technicolour underwater world of the Great Barrier Reef (p373). There's magnificent snorkelling and diving, and the opportunity for downtime in pristine settings like Green Island (p463), just off Cairns. A wide array of tour operators in Far North Queensland can get you above, in and under the water. Rafting the Tully River

Great Ocean Road

12 Jutting out of turbulent waters, the Twelve Apostles (p248) are one of Victoria's most vivid sights, but it's the 'getting there' road trip that doubles their impact. Take it slow while driving along roads that curl beside Bass Strait beaches, then whip inland through rainforests and past quaint towns. The Great Ocean Road (p239) doesn't stop at the Twelve Apostles; further along is maritime treasure Port Fairy (p251) and hidden Cape Bridgewater (p253). For the ultimate in slow travel, walk the Great Ocean Walk from Apollo Bay to the Apostles. Twelve Apostles, Victoria

Sydney Nightlife

13 Sydney's glistening beaches and scenic harbour offer undeniable allure. But for many, it's after dark (p82) when the city comes to life. You can find your tribe amid the mix of stylish lounges, buzzing nightclubs, old-fashioned pubs and indie-rock bars scattered around town. Or escape the crowds by squeezing in stage-side at an underground jazz club or sinking into a low-key wine bar overlooking the water. There are art-gallery bars, grassy backyard lounges, restaurants with hidden dance floors and mod-Asian watering holes. The only way to experience it is to dive in.

MITCH REARDON/LONELY PLANET IMAGES ©

Wildlife-Watching

14 Furry, cuddly, ferocious: you can find all this and more on a wildlife-watching journey along Australia's East Coast. Head south for penguins and fur seals and north for otherworldly cassowaries and dinosaur-like crocodiles. In between, you'll find extraordinary animals found nowhere else on earth: koalas, kangaroos, wombats and platypuses. There's whale-watching along the coast, and the awe-inspiring sight of nesting sea turtles (and later hatchlings) on Queensland beaches. Penguins, Montague Island, New South Wales

St Kilda

15 With its beachside ambience, fairground appeal and somewhat seedy undertones, St Kilda (p212) has long been one of Melbourne's most charismatic inner-city suburbs. Acland St is the place to go for cakes, while the Esplanade Hotel (the Espy) has been melding live music with sticky carpet and pots of beer for decades. There are some not-so-obvious secrets: a penguin colony, an outdoor spot to catch a movie and some fine waterfront restaurants.

Lady Elliot Island

16 This ecofriendly resort island (p388) is one of the loveliest and most peaceful places to experience the Great Barrier Reef. Snorkel straight off Lady Elliot's white sands – the living reef that surrounds the tiny coral cay is teeming with tropical fish, turtles and the island's resident manta rays. At hatching time (January to April) you can see baby turtles scamper across the sand, and humpback whales pass by from June to October. Getting to the island is equally memorable – with a scenic flight over the turquoise reef-filled waters.

Wilsons Promontory

17 For sheer natural beauty, Wilsons Promontory (p259) has it all. Jutting out into Bass Strait, this national park boasts sublime ocean beaches and some of the best wilderness hiking and camping in coastal Australia. Just grab a map and permit, strap on a pack and head into the wilds. The overnight walk across 'the Prom' from Tidal River to Sealers Cove and back is a great way to get started, but serious hikers should tackle the three-day Great Prom Walk, staying a night in the gloriously isolated lighthouse keepers' cottages. Whale Rock, Tidal River, Wilsons Promontory

OLIVER STREWE/LONELY PLANET IMAGES ©

Hunter Valley Wineries

18 Picture this: a pavilion made of glass overlooking gently rolling hills covered with row after row of vines, all laden with grapes. Inside, you're sipping a glass of golden-hued Semillon and pondering the delectable lunch menu, which showcases top-quality local produce. All you have to do is make your choice, settle back, move onto a glass of earthy Shiraz and enjoy a leisurely lunch. It's the stuff of which lasting travel memories are made, and it's on offer in New South Wales' premier wine district, the Hunter Valley (p109).

Canberra

19 If there's one thing Canberra (p127) has got going for it, it's museums. Whether your passion is art, history, film or big guns, you'll find it in spades in the bush capital. The highlights include the National Gallery of Australia, with its magnificent collections of Aboriginal and Torres Strait Islander, Australian and Asian art; the National Museum of Australia, whose imaginative exhibits provide insights into the Australian heart and soul; and the War Memorial, with its moving Hall of Memory and fascinating displays. National Museum of Australia, Canberra

ROSS BARNETT/LONELY PLANET IMAGES ©

Montague Island

20 It's a sign of more ecofriendly times when tourists pay to get their hands dirty rather than have them manicured. Nine kilometres offshore from Narooma, in Batemans Marine Park, this spectacular nature reserve (p151) is home to fur seals, little penguins and birdlife, along with sacred Aboriginal sights. Tours are a must-do, but the best experience is to stay overnight in the lighthouse keepers' cottages. Guests are expected to do conservation work and help with the cooking. Although not cheap, this can end up being the experience of a lifetime. Crested-tern breeding colony, Montague Island

MITCH REARDON/LONELY PLANET IMAGES ©

need to know

Currency
» Australian dollar ($)

Language
» English

When to Go

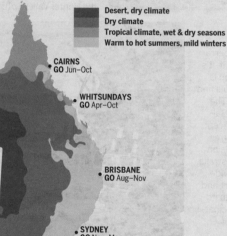

Desert, dry climate
Dry climate
Tropical climate, wet & dry seasons
Warm to hot summers, mild winters

CAIRNS
GO Jun–Oct

WHITSUNDAYS
GO Apr–Oct

BRISBANE
GO Aug–Nov

SYDNEY
GO Nov–Mar

MELBOURNE
GO Nov–Mar

Dec–Mar

» High season in the south, with higher accommodation prices

» Hot and humid with abundant rainfall in the north

» Stinger season (officially November to May) makes swimming unsafe north of Agnes Water

Oct–Nov & Mar–May

» Generally pleasant temperatures and fewer crowds in the south and the north

» Blooming spring flowers (October); autumn colours in Victoria (April)

Jun–Sep

» Cold, wet wintry days and the lowest accommodation prices in the south

» High season in the north, with higher accommodation prices.

» Warm temperatures in the north; good visibility on Great Barrier Reef

Your Daily Budget

Budget less than

$100

» Dorm beds: $20–30; camping: from $5.50

» Free activities (beach days, free concerts)

» Youth cards save on sights, lodging, transport

Midrange

$100– 250

» Double room in midrange hotel: $100–180

» Decent restaurant dinner: $50–80 for two

» Car hire from $35 per day

Top End more than

$250

» Lodging in a resort: from $250

» Dining in top restaurants: $100 per person

» Adventure activities: sailing the Whitsundays (from $300 per night), diving course ($650)

Money

» ATMs widely available. Credits cards accepted at most lodgings, restaurants and shops.

Visas

» All visitors except for New Zealanders need a visa (available online through www.immi.gov.au).

Mobile Phones

» Local SIM cards can be used in Australian and European phones. Of the main providers, Telstra has the most extensive network.

Driving

» Drive on the left; steering wheel is on the right side of the car.

Websites

» **Lonely Planet** (www.lonelyplanet.com/australia/queensland) Destination information, hotel bookings, travel forum, photos.

» **Australian Tourist Commission** (www.australia.com) Nationwide visitor info.

» **Queensland Holidays** (www.queenslandholidays.com.au) Queensland coverage.

» **Tourism New South Wales** (www.visitnsw.com.au) NSW information.

» **Tourism Victoria** (www.visitvictoria.com) Victoria's official site.

Exchange Rates

Canada	C$1	A$0.98
Euro zone	€1	A$1.36
Japan	¥100	A$1.14
New Zealand	NZ$1	A$0.75
UK	UK£1	A$1.54
USA	US$1	A$0.93

For current exchange rates see www.xe.com.

Important Numbers

Emergency	☑000
Country code (Australia)	☑61
Directory assistance	☑1223
Reverse-charge call	☑1800-REVERSE (/38 3773)
International access code	☑0011

Arriving in Australia

» **Sydney Kingsford Smith Airport**
Airport Link train – from $15
KST shuttle bus – from $14
Taxis – from $45 to Circular Quay
See details (p95)

» **Melbourne Tullamarine Airport**
Skybus (to Southern Cross Station) – 24 hours a day, $16
Taxis – from $40
See details (p233)

» **Brisbane Airport**
Airtrain – $15
Coachtrans shuttle bus – $15
Taxis – around $40
See details (p277)

Top Travel Tips

» Browse accommodation online to save cash: try www.wotif.com.au, www.quickbeds.com and www.lastminute.com.au.

» Don't forget to try out all the great Aussie sweets: Lamington (chocolate and coconut sponge cake), Pavlova (meringue), Tim Tams (chocolate biscuits), chocolate crackles (rice bubbles with chocolate).

» Avoid driving between dusk and dawn, when wildlife might cross your path.

» Take care in the water and swim between the flags; surf can be strong with dangerous currents.

» Remember to bring sunscreen, a hat and sunglasses to deflect fierce UV radiation.

» Bring a lightweight rain jacket for unexpected downpours.

» Make sure you have travel insurance for any adrenalin-charged activities, such as bungee jumping, white-water rafting or rock climbing.

if you like...

Beaches

With nearly 18,000km of coastline, East Coast Australia has a dazzling array of beaches, from hedonistic, people-packed sands to remote tropical beauties. You'll find sun-kissed shores of every type: picture-perfect white powdery strips fronting azure seas, magnificent surf spots and wild, idyllic seafront inviting endless walks.

Bondi Beach The famous Sydney icon is a melting pot of sun-seekers from every corner of the globe (p62)

Squeaky Beach This white-sand beauty is one of many gems along Wilsons Promontory (p261)

Hyams Beach This Jervis Bay beauty has snow-white sands and crystal-clear waters, with whales frolicking offshore from May to November (p144)

Noosa Main Beach One of the glittering stars of the Sunshine Coast, Noosa has lovely sands backed by a lush, lighthouse-topped national park – where you can sometimes spot koalas (p329)

Whitehaven Beach The jewel of the Whitsundays, and one of Australia's loveliest beaches, with powdery white sand and crystal-clear waters (p421)

Islands

Home to hundreds of islands, Australia has some spectacular getaways of the powdery sand and palm-fringed variety. Magical bushwalks, magnificent wildlife, deserted beaches and cinematic aquatic beauty (colourful coral reefs, whale- and dolphin-watching) are just a few draws...

Montague Island Seabirds, little penguins and fur seals live on this small but impressive island in NSW; you can visit for the day on guided tours or stay overnight in the lighthouse keepers' cottage (p151)

Fraser Island An ideal setting for 4WD adventure, the world's largest sand island has giant sand dunes, freshwater lakes and abundant wildlife (p368)

Whitsundays Book in at one of the islands' top resorts, or board a sailboat and explore as many of these amazingly pristine islands as you can (p407)

Lady Elliott Island Ringed by the Great Barrier Reef and reachable by light aircraft, this remote island is a great place to play castaway (p388)

Fitzroy Island One of a handful of lovely islands off Cairns, Fitzroy is a magical combination of enticing beaches, rich coral and a hilly tropical interior (p463)

Aquatic Adventures

Endless beaches, surf-pounded islands and the magnificent Great Barrier Reef provide countless opportunities for aquatic adventure. Surfing, diving, snorkelling, kayaking, reef walks and marine wildlife-watching – few places on earth can compete with Australia's enormous bounty.

Swim with seals You can swim with seals, dolphins and check out coral habitats on a cruise off Queenscliff (p235)

Diving the Great Barrier Reef Book passage out to this vast marine kingdom and dive or snorkel amid some of the most striking underwater scenery on the planet (p376)

Surfing Grab a board and hit the amazing breaks all along the coast; for the unskilled, Byron Bay is an ideal spot to learn (p163)

Paddling the Everglades Noosa's Everglades are a serene setting for a canoe trip – and unlike in Florida, these waters are alligator-free (p331)

HOLGER LEUE/LONELY PLANET IMAGES ©

» Koala, Cairns, Queensland

Nightlife

Sydney and Melbourne may vie for top honours in the nightlife stakes, but there are hundreds of other spots to spend a sleepless night, tinny in hand, from fun-loving beachside towns to remote wilderness pubs, with a great live music scene all along the coast.

Venue 505 Sydney's best little jazz bar features top-notch performers in an edgy underground space (p83)

Northcote Social Club One of Melbourne's best live music spots, with a buzzing front bar and a spacious deck in the back (p229)

Fortitude Valley When the sun sets, Brisbane's nightlife-loving 'hood comes to life, with eye-catching lounges, rock-filled bars and dance-loving mega-clubs all within easy stumbling distance of one another (p295)

Railway Friendly Bar This sprawling indoor-outdoor pub features live music most nights and is a requisite stop in easy-going Byron Bay (p170)

Full moon parties For a memorable all-night fest, Base Backpackers draws hundreds of revellers to the sand during its wild monthly party on Magnetic Island (p433)

Wildlife Encounters

Home to bouncing kangaroos, cuddly koalas and cackling kookaburras – not to mention crocs, spiders and snakes – Australia has a treasure chest of wildlife. You'll find creatures great and small, with regional differences adding spice, from penguins and seals in the south to coral riches (and those lovable crocs) in the north.

Penguins aplenty Phillip Island is home to the world's largest little penguin colony; catch them at sunset marching up from the sea (p254)

Whale-watching In season (July to October), you can see whales on a scenic cruise from Hervey Bay (p353)

Sea turtles Get an awe-inspiring view of loggerheads – adults and hatchlings – at Mon Repos (p365)

Koala cuddling Outside Brisbane, Lone Pine Koala Sanctuary is a great place to have a one-on-one with a soft, furry marsupial (p283)

Croc spotting Have a look at saltwater crocs on a river cruise along the Daintree (p480)

Outdoor Adventures

Nature lovers and adrenalin junkies will be high-fiving over the staggering choices when it comes to bushwalking, birdwatching, white-water rafting and skydiving. For other ways to get your heart racing, see p31

Exploring Croajingalong National Park With superb birdwatching, bushwalking and beach frolicking, this extraordinary coastal wilderness is a Unesco World Biosphere Reserve (p274)

White-water rafting Queensland's mighty Tully River has 44 rapids and makes for one great (and very wet) white-water journey (p439)

Fraser Island Great Walk This magnificent six- to eight-day walk takes in rainforest canopies, picturesque lakes and shifting dunes (p369)

Jungle surfing through the rainforest In Cape Tribulation's ancient rainforest, you can whiz through a jungle canopy on a flying fox (p479)

Skydiving over Mission Beach For an unforgettable rush, head 9000ft skyward, step out of a plane and enjoy the ride (p440)

» Wet'n'Wild theme park (p318), Gold Coast, Queensland

Indigenous Culture

There are some fine ways to experience the age-old culture of the first Australians. You can take a Dreaming tour through spiritually rich native sites, gaze upon ancient rock art or hit the Brisbane galleries where a new generation of Aboriginal artists are making their mark.

Ku-Ring-Gai Chase National Park This sprawling reserve north of Sydney shelters hundreds of important Aboriginal sites, including rock engravings and cave paintings (p64)

Unearthing the past in Melbourne The Koorie Heritage Trust is a great place to discover southeastern Aboriginal culture, with contemporary and traditional art on display and tours on offer (p206)

National Gallery of Australia This superb Canberra museum houses over 7500 works by Aboriginal and Torres Strait Islander artists, including the moving *Aboriginal Memorial* (p127)

Kuku-Yalanji Dreamtime Walks Take a guided walk through lush Mossman Gorge, learning about bush tucker sources and Dreaming legends from knowledgeable Indigenous guides (p474)

Festivals & Events

No matter the season, Aussies find cause for celebration. Big music festivals, New Year's Eve bashes, horse races, the return of the whales – just a few reasons to break out the bubbly. You'll find more causes for carousing on p20.

Melbourne Cup Don your fanciest hat, place your bets and celebrate with Melburnians on this high-spirited and festive race day (p215)

New Year's Eve Seeing midnight fireworks over the world's loveliest harbour is pure magic (p68)

Blues & Roots Festival Byron Bay's big jam fest is reason enough to venture to this lovely, chilled-out surf town (p166)

Brisbane Festival Brisbane's biggest celebration features fireworks over the river and three weeks of concerts, theatre, dance and other events in September (p287)

Hervey Bay Whale Festival The seductive town celebrates the reappearance of the whales with live concerts, a street parade and kids fest (p356)

Food & Drink

Temptation comes in many forms when it comes to food and drink in Australia. Front and centre is the vast coastline, which yields a seafood bounty. You'll also find award-winning wines, food festivals and a plethora of great restaurants. For more on the culinary scene, see p505.

Cutler & Co *Gourmet Traveller's* Restaurant of the Year (2011) is a Melbourne legend (p222)

Icebergs This Sydney classic is equal parts fantastic cuisine (seafood and northern Italian), celeb spotting and magnificent sea views (p78)

Hunter Valley Home to over 140 wineries, this verdant region is pure heaven for lovers of a good drop (p109)

Oskars Perched over the beach, this Gold Coast charmer is the place to sample some of Queensland's finest seafood (p320)

Noosa Food & Wine Festival The lovely Sunshine Coast town serves up a gluttonous eat-drink-and-be-merry fest in May (p332)

If you like... rugged adventures, ferry your 4WD to Fraser Island for a trip along the beach 'highway', backed by towering dunes, lakes and rainforest (p368)

Family Fun

Australia has a wealth of options to keep both kids and adults amused when travelling the country. Top picks include high-action theme parks, whale-watching cruises, aquariums and a world-class zoo. For big-city attractions for children, see Sydney (p67), Melbourne (p214) and Brisbane (p287).

Whale & dolphin encounters Eden on NSW's South Coast is the go-to place for heady encounters with migrating humpback and southern right whales – plus dolphins and seals (p158)

Theme parks There's non-stop adventure in Gold Coast theme parks, with refreshing water parks, aquatic shows and plenty of heart-racing roller coasters (p314)

Underwater World The largest oceanarium in the southern hemisphere is a great place to see sharks, stingrays, dazzling fish and more (p339)

Australia Zoo Allow a full day to spend at the massive Australia Zoo, Queensland's temple to the world's wondrous wildlife (p336)

Daydream Island Resort Unlike many Whitsunday Island resorts, this one welcomes children with open arms, offering heaps of activities for the kids (p418)

Scenic Journeys

In Australia, getting from point A to point B often entails lovely scenery and big adventure. You can plan an itinerary by train, sailboat or bicycle, taking in some awe-inspiring views along the way.

The Lakes Way Scenic Drive If you're heading up the NSW coast, skip the Pacific Hwy and take this picturesque drive that passes Myall Lakes and Booti Booti National Parks (p117)

East Gippsland Rail Trail Hop on a bicycle or walk the scenic 97km former railway line in East Gippsland, Victoria. With luggage transfers available and towns along the way, you won't even have to rough it (p266)

Sailing the Whitsundays This stunning archipelago is one of Australia's most magical places to sail. You can hire a bareboat or join a multi-day tour (p410)

Train to Cairns The *Sunlander* keeps the golden era of train travel alive on its scenic 30-hour journey between Brisbane and Cairns (p302)

Seaplane to Lizard Island The journey to this spectacular island – home to campgrounds and a five-star resort alike – is memorable, with a seaplane landing on Watson's Bay (p484)

A Touch of Luxury

If you've got money to burn, Australia would be quite interested in making your acquaintance. A growing number of first-rate hotels and resorts compete for top honours when it comes to guest pampering.

Park Hyatt Sydney Drink in the majestic views at this opulent hotel facing the harbour (p69)

Kingfisher Bay Resort Ecofriendly Kingfisher makes a splendid base for beach-combing, wildlife-watching and exploring Fraser Island's captivating scenery (p369)

Daintree Eco Lodge & Spa This splendid rainforest retreat has it all – boutique villas, a high-end spa and guided walks led by members of the Kuku-Yalanji community (p480)

Mouses House In Gold Coast's Springbrook National Park, these charming cedar cottages set in the misty forest seem like something out of a fairy tale (p324)

Paradise Bay This eco-resort has just 10 beautifully sited bungalows, and manages to deliver a heavy dollop of luxury while still doing good by the environment (p417)

month by month

January

Heat and humidity are hallmarks everywhere on the East Coast, while north Queensland experiences monsoonal rains (and remains largely closed for business). Holidaying families head to the beach.

Big Day Out

This huge open-air music concert tours Sydney, Melbourne and the Gold Coast, stopping over for one day in each city. It attracts big-name international acts and dozens of local bands. Buy tickets well in advance (www.bigdayout.com).

Australia Day

Australians celebrate the arrival of the First Fleet (in 1788) over the barbie with plenty of good cheer. Big towns often host events, with live concerts on outdoor stages, followed by fireworks. It all happens on 26 January.

Sydney Festival

Over three weeks in January, Sydney Festival hosts some 80 events held at different venues across town, from the realms of dance, theatre, music, visual arts and multimedia. Free outdoor concerts on the Domain kick things off (www.sydneyfestival.org.au).

Midsumma

Melbourne's gay, lesbian and transgender festival starts in mid-January with the music- and dance-filled outdoor party of Midsumma Carnival followed by three weeks of revelry and events, including theatre, exhibitions, cabaret, film screenings, live music and socio-political debates (www.midsumma.org.au).

Australian Open Tennis Championships

Held in Melbourne Park in late January, the Australian Open brings tennis fanatics front and centre as the world's best players battle it out on the court. The Australia Open is the first of four annual Grand Slam tennis events (www.australianopen.com).

February

High temperatures and blessed sunshine (in the south) make for fine outdoor activities and steamy beach days. Up north, the big Wet continues, and Queensland swelters.

Tropfest

The world's largest short film festival is a free one-day extravaganza of film screenings and live performance. It's held at Sydney's Domain in the Royal Botanic Gardens, with live satellite links to outdoor locations in Melbourne, Canberra, Brisbane and Surfers Paradise (www.tropfest.com).

Sydney Gay & Lesbian Mardi Gras

One of Australia's biggest and wildest festivals, the 17-day Mardi Gras has an amazing street parade down Oxford St and a riotous Mardi Gras party (www.mardigras.org.au).

March

Heat and humidity eases off in the south, crowds dissipate and prices drop a bit in resort areas. Meanwhile, high temperatures and general irritability prevail in the north.

☆ Australian Formula One Grand Prix

Normally peaceful Albert Park Lake is dominated by four days of rev-head action in late March. The 5.3km street circuit around the lake is known for its smooth, fast surface (www.grandprix.com.au).

April

Autumn brings fiery colours to parts of Victoria. All along the coast, you'll find cooler, mild temperatures. In the north, the end of the wet season brings smiling faces outdoors for warm, pleasant weather.

☆ Byron Bay Bluesfest

There's an explosion of sound over the long Easter weekend when around 20,000 festival-goers come to hear blues and roots bands hailing from all over the world. It's held on 120-hectare Tyagarah Tee Tree farm, 11km north of Byron Bay. Some folks camp (www.bluesfest.com.au).

☆ Nimbin Mardi Grass

The alternative community of Nimbin swells for this mother-of-all-hippy-festivals, with music, hemp products, costumed ganja faeries and sporting events of a sort (bong throwing, joint rolling etc). Pitch a tent and join very chilled festival-goers as they pay tribute to their favourite weed (www.nimbinmardi grass.com).

May

Days grow noticeably cooler in the south; beach days are unlikely south of Queensland, but still a possibility from the Gold Coast northwards. You can find good deals on accommodation all around.

Noosa Food & Wine Festival

One of the Australia's best regional culinary fests happens in food-loving Noosa, with cooking demonstrations, wine tasting, cheese exhibits and plenty of feasting on gourmet fare. There are live concerts at night. It happens over three days in mid-May.

☆ Wintermoon Festival

In a pretty, bush setting north of Mackay, this family friendly music fest features three stages, with musicians playing folk and world music. Most people camp, which adds to the appeal – as impromptu performances happen around the grounds. On Labour Day weekend (www.wintermoonfestival.com).

★ Sydney Writers Festival

For one week in May, Sydney hosts some 300-plus novelists, essayists, poets, historians and philosophers – from Australia and beyond – who read from their works, lead writing workshops and host edifying panel discussions (www.swf.org.au).

◉ Biennale of Sydney

Held in even-numbered years, Sydney's Biennale showcases the work of hundreds of contemporary artists in the country's largest visual arts event. It runs from May to August, with tours, artist talks, film screenings and cutting-edge exhibitions all on the menu; most events are free (www.biennaleofsydney.com.au).

June

The south shivers in the cold, while tourist season kicks into high gear in the warm, clear tropical north, with now-stinger-free beaches. Migrating whales are sighted off the coast (until November).

★ Cooktown Discovery Festival

This weekend event commemorates Captain Cook's landing in 1770, with a lively re-creation by local costumed performers, both of Aboriginal and European ancestry. Highlights include fireworks, garden parties and indigenous heritage – 'campfire yarns', performances and food stalls, including bush tucker (www.cooktowndiscoveryfestival.com.au).

August

It's still winter in the south, with brisk days and long nights. August remains peak season in Queensland, particularly in the north, where temperatures are mild and rainfall minimal.

Cairns Festival

Running three weeks from late August to early September, this massive art-and-culture fest brings a stellar program of music, theatre, dance, comedy, film, indigenous art and public exhibitions. Outdoor events make good use of Cairns' tropical setting (www.festivalcairns.com.au).

⭐ Hervey Bay Whale Festival

One of the world's best whale-watching towns pays homage to its favourite cetacean in this popular early August event. Attractions include an illuminated evening street parade, a kids' festival and free concerts on the seafront (www.hervey baywhalefestival.com.au).

September

With the end of winter, spring returns, bringing wildflowers and brighter spirits in the south. Weather generally remains mild across the country.

⭐ Brisbane Festival

One of Australia's largest and most diverse arts festivals runs through 22 days in September and features an impressive menu of concerts, plays, dance performances and fringe events. It kicks off with 'Riverfire', an elaborate fireworks show over the river (www.bris banefestival.com.au).

⭐ Valley Fiesta

Fortitude Valley, Brisbane's buzzing nightlife district, hosts this weekend-long arts event with free outdoor concerts, craft and designer markets, fashion parades, art exhibitions and other events that showcase the city's more creative side (www.valleyfiesta.com).

☆ Noosa Jazz Festival

Lovely Noosa becomes a music mecca during this long-running jazz festival held in early September. Over 90 different performances come to town, showcasing the talents of national and international artists alike in both indoor and outdoor venues. Some events are free.

October

Temperatures are on the rise, though it's still jacket weather in the south. October heads towards the tail end of the dry season up north.

⭐ Melbourne International Arts Festival

This annual festival offers some of the best of opera, theatre, dance and the visual arts from around Australia and the world. It starts in early October and runs to early November (www.mel bournefestival.com.au).

November

Stinger season arrives in November and runs through to May in northern Queensland (swimming is unwise from Agnes Water north).

◉ Melbourne Cup

Australia's premier horse race is in Melbourne, but the whole country watches (and Victorians get a public holiday!). For many Australians, race day is pure merriment, complete with fancy clothes (a posh hat is essential for gals) and cel-

ebrations at the pub (www.melbournecup.com.au).

December

Summer arrives, bringing longer days and warmer weather (hotter the further north you go). The wet season gets underway in northern Queensland, making travel unpleasant there. Summer holidays bring hordes to beach areas.

☆ Woodford Folk Festival

One of the Sunshine Coast's biggest gatherings, the Woodford Folk Festival stages a diverse collection of performers playing folk sounds from across the globe. There's also dance, food, performance art, workshops, discussions and more; it runs from 27 December to 1 January (www.woodfordfolkfestival.com).

◉ Sydney to Hobart Yacht Race

Pack a picnic and join the Boxing Day (26 December) crowds along Sydney's waterfront as they cheer on sailing vessels of all shapes and sizes setting off on this multi-day race (http://rolex-sydneyhobart.com).

◉ Sydney Harbour Fireworks

A fantastic way to ring in the New Year is to join the festive crowds overlooking the harbour as a brilliant fireworks display lights up the night sky. There's a family fireworks show at 9pm, with the main event erupting at the stroke of midnight.

Your Reef Trip

Best Wildlife Experience

Watching protected sea turtles hatch and make their first daring dash to the water on **Lady Elliot Island** or **Heron Island**, then, while snorkelling or diving, watching their older relatives glide gracefully through the ocean.

Best Snorkelling Experience

Taking a fast catamaran from Airlie Beach out to **Knuckle Reef** or a seaplane to **Hardy Reef** and immersing yourself in some of the word's best snorkelling spots.

Best View from Above

Soaring above the Reef on a **scenic flight** from Cairns and watching its huge and vivid mass carpet the sea beneath you.

Most Tranquil Experience

Exploring the pristine southern end of the Great Barrier Reef, especially **Fitzroy Reef Lagoon**, one of the least-touristed areas of the Reef.

Best Sailing Experience

Sailing from Airlie Beach through the **Whitsunday Islands** and exploring exquisite fringing reefs on the islands' perimeters.

The Great Barrier Reef is one of Australia's World Heritage areas and one of nature's richest realms. Stretching over 2000km from just south of the tropic of Capricorn (near Gladstone) to just south of Papua New Guinea, it is the most extensive reef system in the world, and made entirely by living organisms.

There is a multitude of ways to see the magnificent spectacle of the Reef. Diving and snorkelling are far and away the best methods of getting up close and personal with the menagerie of marine life and dazzling corals. Immersing yourself in the sea furnishes you with the most exhilarating appreciation of just how wonderful and rich this community is. The unremarkable surface of the water belies the colourful congestion less than a metre or so beneath.

You can also surround yourself with fabulous tropical fish without getting wet on a semi-submersible or glass-bottomed boat, which provides windows to the underwater world below. Alternatively, you can go below the ocean's surface inside an underwater observatory, or stay up top and take a reef walk.

Another spectacular way to see the Reef while staying dry is on a scenic flight. Soaring high provides a macroperspective of the Reef's beauty and size and allows you to see the veins and networks of coral connecting and ribboning out from one another.

When to Go

High season on the Great Barrier Reef is from June to December. The best overall visibility is from August to January.

From December to March **northern Queensland** (north of Townsville) has a distinct wet season, bringing oppressive heat and abundant rainfall (from July to September it's drier and cooler). Cyclones can occur from November to March but are not common and shouldn't prevent you from going (an effective cyclone warning system is in place in the Pacific).

Anytime is generally good to visit the **Whitsundays**. Winter (June to August) can be pleasantly warm, but you will occasionally need a jumper during the day and a light jacket at night. South of the Whitsundays, summer (December to March) can be hot and humid, but the wet season doesn't extend as far south as the Whitsundays.

Southern and **central Queensland** experience mild winters (June to August) – pleasant enough for diving or snorkelling in a wetsuit.

Picking Your Spot

It's said you could dive here every day of your life and still not see all of the Great Barrier Reef. Individual chapters in this book provide in-depth information, but the following are some of the most popular and remarkable spots from which to access the Reef. Bear in mind that individual areas change over time, depending on the weather or any recent damage.

Mainland Gateways

There are several mainland gateways to the Reef, all offering slightly different experiences or activities. Deciding which to choose can be difficult – so here's a brief overview, ordered from south to north.

Agnes Water & Town of 1770 (p382) are small towns and good choices if you want to escape the crowds. From here tours head to Fitzroy Reef Lagoon, one of the most pristine sections of the Reef, where visitor numbers are still limited. The lagoon is excellent for snorkelling but also quite spectacular viewed from the boat.

Gladstone (p385) is a slightly bigger town but still a relatively small gateway. It's an excellent choice for avid divers and snorkellers, being the closest access point to the southern or Capricorn reef islands and innumerable cays, including Lady Elliot Island.

Airlie Beach (p412) is a small town with a full rack of sailing outfits. The big attraction here is spending two or more days aboard a boat and seeing some of the Whitsunday Islands' fringing coral reefs. The surrounding scenery is sublime, but you'll only see the edges of the Reef. There are, however, a number of fast-catamaran operators that zoom across 60km to reach reefs that provide outstanding snorkelling, swimming and diving.

Airlie is also friendly to all wallets, so whether you're a five- or no-star traveller, there'll be a tour to match your budget.

Townsville (p425) is a renowned gateway among divers. Whether you're learning or experienced, a four- or five-night onboard diving safari around the numerous islands and pockets of the Reef is a great choice. In particular, Kelso Reef and the wreck of the SS *Yongala* are teeming with marine life. There are also a couple of day-trip options on glass-bottomed boats, but for more choice you're better off heading to Cairns. **Reef HQ** (p425), which is basically a version of the Reef in an aquarium, is also here.

Mission Beach (p440) is closer to the Reef than any other gateway destination. This small, quiet town offers a few boat and diving tours to sections of the outer reef. Although the choice isn't huge, neither are the crowds, so you won't be sharing the experience with a fleet of other vessels.

Cairns (p449) is undeniably the main launching pad for Reef tours: there is a bewildering number of operators here. You can do anything from relatively inexpensive day trips on large boats to intimate five-day luxury charters. The variety of tours covers a wide section of the Reef, with some operators going as far north as Lizard Island. Inexpensive tours are likely to travel to inner reefs, ie those close to the mainland, which tend to be more damaged than outer reefs. Scenic flights also operate out of Cairns. Bear in mind, though, that this is the most popular destination, so unless your budget stretches to a private charter you'll be sharing the experience with many others.

Port Douglas (p468) is a swanky resort town and a gateway to the Low Isles and Agincourt Reef, an outer ribbon reef featuring crystal-clear water and particularly stunning corals. Although Port Douglas is smaller than Cairns, it's very popular and has a wealth of tour operators. Diving, snorkelling and cruising trips tend to be classier, pricier and less crowded than in Cairns. You can also take a scenic flight from here.

Cooktown (p482) is another one for divers. The town's lure is its close proximity to Lizard Island (see p484). Although you can access the island from Cairns, you'll spend far less time travelling by boat if you go from here. Cooktown's relatively remote location means there are only a handful of tour operators and small numbers of tourists, so your experience is not likely to be rushed or brief. The only drawback is that the town and its tour operators shut down between November and May for the wet season.

Islands

Speckled throughout the Reef is a profusion of islands and cays that offer some of the most stunning access to the Reef. Here is a list of some of the best islands, travelling from south to north.

For more information on individual islands, see the Whitsunday Coast (p398), Capricorn Coast & the Southern Reef Islands (p381), Townsville to Innisfail (p423) and Cairns & the Daintree Rainforest (p448) chapters.

The coral cay of **Lady Elliot Island** (p388) is the most southerly of the Reef islands. It's awe-inspiring for birdwatchers, with some 57 species living on the island. Sea turtles also nest here and it's possibly the best location on the Reef to see manta rays. It's also a famed diving spot. There's a simple, pricey camping resort here, but you can also visit Lady Elliot on a day trip from Bundaberg.

Heron Island (p388) is a tiny coral cay sitting amid a huge spread of reef. It's a diving mecca, but the snorkelling is also good and it's possible to do a reef walk from here.

Heron is a nesting ground for green and loggerhead turtles and home to some 30 species of birds. It's an exclusive, utterly tranquil place, and the sole resort on the island charges accordingly.

Hamilton Island (p418), the daddy of the Whitsundays, is a sprawling resort laden with infrastructure. While this doesn't create the most intimate atmosphere, there is a wealth of tours going to the outer reef. It's also a good place to see patches of the Reef that can't be explored from the mainland. Families are extremely well catered for.

USEFUL WEBSITES

» **Dive Queensland** (www.dive-queensland.com.au) Queensland's dive tourism association, with info on dive locations, dive operators, liveaboards and diving schools.

» **Tourism Queensland** (www.queenslandholidays.com.au) Official state tourism portal with listings for accommodation and attractions.

» **Great Barrier Reef Marine Park Authority** (www.gbrmpa.gov.au) Reef-related info on climate change, conservation, tourism and fisheries.

» **Queensland Parks & Wildlife Services** (www.derm.qld.gov.au) Info, including permits and how to get there, for all national parks.

» **Australian Bureau of Meteorology** (www.bom.gov.au) The latest info (and annual statistics) on rainfall, temperatures and weather conditions.

Hook Island (p417) is an outer Whitsunday Island surrounded by fringing reefs. There is excellent swimming and snorkelling here, and the island's sizeable bulk provides plenty of good bushwalking. There's affordable accommodation on Hook and it's easily accessed from Airlie Beach, making it a top choice for those on a modest budget.

Orpheus Island (p430) is a national park and one of the Reef's most exclusive, tranquil and romantic hideaways. This island is particularly good for snorkelling – you can step right off the beach and be surrounded by the Reef's colourful marine life. Clusters of fringing reefs also provide plenty of diving opportunities.

Green Island (p463) is another of the Reef's true coral cays. The fringing reefs here are considered to be among the most beautiful surrounding any island, and the diving and snorkelling are quite spectacular. Covered in dense rainforest, the entire island is national park. Bird life is abundant, with around 60 species to be found. The resort on Green Island is well set up for reef activities; several tour operators offer diving and snorkelling cruises and there's also an underwater observatory. The island is accessible as a day trip from Cairns.

TOP SNORKELLING SITES

Some nondivers may wonder if it's really worth going to the Great Barrier Reef 'just to snorkel'. The answer is a resounding yes. There are some fantastic sites for snorkellers – in fact, much of the rich, colourful coral lies just underneath the surface (as coral needs bright sunlight to flourish) and is easily accessible. Here's a round-up of the top snorkelling sites:

» Fitzroy Reef Lagoon
» Heron Island
» Keppel Island
» Lady Elliot Island
» Lady Musgrave Island
» Hook Island
» Hayman Island
» Lizard Island
» Border Island (Whitsundays)
» Hardy Reef (Whitsundays)
» Knuckle Reef (Whitsundays)
» Michaelmas Reef (Cairns)
» Hastings Reef (Cairns)
» Norman Reef (Cairns)
» Saxon Reef (Cairns)
» Opal Reef (Port Douglas)
» Agincourt Reef (Port Douglas)
» Mackay Reef (Port Douglas)

Lizard Island (p484) is remote, rugged and the perfect place to escape civilisation. It has a ring of talcum-white beaches, remarkably blue water and few visitors. It's also world-renowned as a superb scuba-diving location, with what is arguably Australia's best-known dive site at Cod Hole (p453) where you can swim with docile potato cod, weighing as much as 60kg. Pixie Bommie is another highly regarded dive site on the island.

Snorkellers will also get an eyeful of marine life here all around the island, with giant clams, manta rays, barracudas and dense schools of fish abundant in the waters just offshore.

If you're staying overnight you need to have deep pockets or no requirements whatsoever – it's either five-star or luxury bush camping.

Diving & Snorkelling the Reef

Much of the diving and snorkelling on the Reef is boat-based, although there are some excellent reefs accessible by walking straight off the beach of some islands scattered along the Great Barrier. Free use of snorkelling gear is usually part of any cruise to the Reef and you can typically fit in around three hours of underwater wandering. Overnight or 'live-aboard' trips obviously provide a more in-depth experience and greater coverage of the reefs. If you want to do more than snorkel but don't have a diving certificate, many operators offer the option of an introductory dive, which is a guided dive where an experienced diver conducts an underwater tour. A solid lesson in safety and procedure is given beforehand and you don't require a five-day Professional Association of Diving Instructors (PADI) course or a 'buddy'.

Boat Excursions

Unless you're staying on a coral-fringed island in the middle of the Great Barrier Reef, you'll need to join a boat excursion – either on a day trip or on a multi-day live-aboard – to experience the Reef's real beauty. Day trips leave from many places along the coast, as well as from island resorts (see p24 for prime gateways) and typically include the use of snorkelling gear, snacks and a buffet lunch, with scuba diving an optional extra. Many boats also offer an introductory scuba dive on the Reef, escorted by a divemaster, which can be a great way to get a taste of diving. On some boats a naturalist or marine biologist presents a talk on the Reef's ecology.

Boat trips vary dramatically in passenger numbers, type of vessel and quality – which is reflected in the price – so it's worth getting all the details before committing to a particular trip. When selecting a tour, consider the vessel (motorised catamaran or sailing ship), the number of passengers (from six to 400), what extras are offered and the destination. The outer reefs are usually more pristine. Inner reefs often show signs of damage from humans, coral bleaching and coral-eating crown-of-thorns starfish. Some companies that are only licensed to visit the inner reef have cheaper tours; in most cases you get what you pay for. Some operators offer the option of a trip in a glass-bottomed boat or semi-submersible.

Many boats have underwater cameras for hire – although you'll save money by hiring these on land (better yet, purchase an underwater housing case for your digital camera if you plan to take a lot of pictures). Some boats also have professional photographers on board who will dive with you and take high-quality shots of you in action.

Live-Aboards

If you're eager to do as much diving as possible, a live-aboard is an excellent option. This allows reef-goers the chance to make around three dives per day, plus the ocassional night dive, and visit more remote parts of the Great Barrier Reef. Trip lengths vary from one to 12 nights. The three-day/three-night voyages, which allow up to 11 dives (nine day and two night dives) are among the most common. Some go on exploratory trips, others run a set route and may use fixed moorings or pontoons, while others are more impromptu. It is worth checking the various options as some boats offer specialist itineraries following marine life and events such as minke whales or coral spawning, or offer trips to more remote spots like the far north-

ern reefs, Pompey Complex, Coral Sea Reefs or Swain Reefs.

It's recommended to go only with operators who are Dive Queensland members: this ensures they follow a minimum set of guidelines. See www.dive-queensland.com. au for the latest membership list. Ideally, they are also accredited by the Ecotourism Association of Australia (www.ecotourism. org.au).

Here's a list of popular departure points for live-aboard dive vessels, along with the locales they visit:

» **Bundaberg** – the Bunker Island group, including Lady Musgrave and Lady Elliot Islands, possibly Fitzroy, Llewellyn and rarely visited Boult Reefs or Hoskyn and Fairfax Islands.

» **1770** – Bunker Island group.

» **Gladstone** – Swains and Bunker Island group.

» **Mackay** – Lihou Reef and the Coral Sea.

» **Airlie Beach** – the Whitsundays, Knuckle Reef and Hardy Reef.

» **Townsville** – Yongala wreck, plus canyons of Wheeler Reef and Keeper Reef.

» **Cairns** – Cod Hole, Ribbon Reefs, the Coral Sea and possibly far northern reefs.

» **Port Douglas** – Osprey Reef, Cod Hole, Ribbon Reefs, Coral Sea and possibly the far northern reefs.

KEY DIVING DETAILS

Diving & Flying
Remember that your last dive should be completed 24 hours before your flight – even in a balloon or for a parachute jump – in order to minimise the risk of residual nitrogen in the blood that can cause decompression injury. On the other hand, it's fine to dive soon after arriving by air.

Insurance
Find out whether or not your insurance policy classifies diving as a dangerous sport and excludes it. For a nominal annual fee, the **Divers Alert Network** (DAN; www. diversalertnetwork.org) provides insurance for medical or evacuation services required in the event of a diving accident. DAN's hotline for diving emergencies is ☑800 088 200.

Visibility
Coastal areas: 1m to 3m
Several kms offshore: 8m to 15m
Outer edge of the Reef: 20m to 35m
Coral Sea: 50m and beyond

Water Temperature
In the north, the water temperature is warm all year round, from around 24°C to 30°C. Going south it gradually gets cooler, dropping to 20°C to 28°C in winter.

MAKING A POSITIVE CONTRIBUTION TO THE REEF

The Great Barrier Reef is incredibly fragile and it's worth taking some extra time to educate yourself on responsible practices while you're there. Here are a few of the more important sustainable practices, but this is by no means an exhaustive list.

» Whether on an island or in a boat, take all litter with you – even biodegradable material like apple cores – and dispose of it back on the mainland.

» Remember that it is an offence to damage or remove coral in the marine park.

» Don't touch or harass marine animals and be aware that if you touch or walk on coral you'll damage it. It can also create some nasty cuts. Never rest or stand on coral.

» If you have a boat, be aware of the rules in relation to anchoring around the reef, including 'no anchoring areas'. Be very careful not to damage coral when you let down the anchor.

» If you're diving, check that you are weighted correctly before entering the water and keep your buoyancy control well away from the reef. Ensure that equipment such as secondary regulators and gauges aren't dragging over the reef.

» If you're snorkelling (and especially if you are a beginner) practice your technique away from coral until you've mastered control in the water.

» Hire a wetsuit rather than slathering on sunscreen, which can damage the reef.

» Watch where your fins are – try not to stir up sediment or disturb coral.

» Do not enter the water near a dugong, including when swimming or diving.

» Note that there are limits on the amount and types of shells that you can collect.

Dive Courses

In Queensland, there are numerous places where you can learn to dive, take a refresher course or improve your skills. Dive courses in Queensland are generally of a high standard, and all schools teach either PADI or Scuba Schools International (SSI) qualifications. Which certification you choose isn't as important as choosing a good instructor, so be sure to seek local recommendations and meet with the instructor before committing to a program.

One of the most popular places to learn is Cairns, where you can choose between courses for the budget-minded (four-day courses from around $450) that combine pool training and reef dives, to longer, more intensive courses that include reef diving on a live-aboard (five-day courses including three-day/two-night live-aboard are around $825).

Other places where you can learn to dive, and then head out on the Reef include the following:

» Bundaberg

» Mission Beach

» Townsville

» Airlie Beach

» Hamilton Island

» Magnetic Island

» Port Douglas

For more details on dive courses, see p454.

Safety Guidelines for Diving

Before embarking on a scuba-diving, skin-diving or snorkelling trip, carefully consider the following points to ensure a safe and enjoyable experience:

» If scuba diving, make sure you have a current diving certification card from a recognised scuba-diving instructional agency.

» Make sure you are healthy and feel comfortable diving.

» Obtain reliable information from a reputable local dive operation about the physical and environmental conditions at the dive site, such as water temperature, visibility and tidal movements and find out how local divers deal with these considerations.

» Be aware that underwater conditions vary significantly from one region, or even site, to another. Seasonal changes can significantly alter any site and dive conditions. These differences influence the way divers dress for a dive and what diving techniques they use.

» Be aware of local laws, regulations and etiquette with regards to marine life and the environment.

» Dive only at sites within your realm of experience. If available, engage the services of a competent, professionally trained dive instructor or divemaster.

Diving for Nondivers

Several operators from Cairns use systems that allow nondivers to 'dive' using surface-supplied air systems. With helmet diving, hoses provide fresh surface air to divers via astronaut-like helmets so you can breathe normally and your face and hair stay dry (you can even wear glasses). There's also no need to know how to swim as you'll be walking on a submerged platform, 4m to 5m below the surface. Walks typically last 15 to 20 minutes, and are conducted under the guidance of a qualified dive instructor. Prices start at around $140. Anyone older than 12 and over 140cm tall can participate, although as with scuba diving, certain medical conditions will prohibit participation (asthma, heart disease, pregnancy, epilepsy). For operators, see p453.

Picking the Right Resort

The Great Barrier Reef is home to over a dozen island resorts, offering varying levels of comfort and style. Although most options sit squarely in the luxury category, there are some affordable stays for those who are seeking a beautiful setting, but don't mind middle-of-the-road accommodation, like that offered on Lady Elliot Island.

Where to stay depends not only on your budget, but also what sort of activities you have in mind. Some resorts are small and secluded (and don't allow children), which can be ideal for a tropical getaway doing little more than swinging in a hammock, basking on powdery sand beaches and sipping tropical cocktails. If this sounds ideal, try Orpheus or Hayman Islands. Other resorts have a busier vibe and offer a wide range of activities, from sailing and kayaking to helicopter joy rides, plus restaurants and even some nightlife. If this is more to your liking, try Hamilton Island.

You'll find the widest selection of resorts in the Whitsundays (p407). For an overview of resort options, see p25.

Camping on the Great Barrier Reef

Pitching a tent on an island is a unique and affordable way to experience the Great Barrier Reef. If you don't mind roughing it a bit, you can enjoy an idyllic tropical setting at a fraction of the price of the five-star island resort that may be located down the road from the camping ground. Campsite facilities range from virtually nothing to showers, flush toilets, interpretive signage and picnic tables. Most islands are remote, so ensure you are adequately prepared for medical and general emergencies. Wherever you stay, you'll need to be self-sufficient, bringing your own food and drinking water (5L per day per person is recommended). Weather can often prevent planned pickups, so have enough supplies to last an extra three or four days in case you get stranded.

As a general reminder, all the islands have fragile ecosystems, so camp only in designated areas, keep to marked trails and take out all that you brought in. Fires are banned so you'll need a gas stove or similar.

You'll need to reserve camp sites well in advance. National park camping permits can be reserved online through **QPWS** (⏎13

TOP REEF DIVE SPOTS

The Great Barrier Reef is home to some of the world's best diving sites. Here are a few of our favourite spots to get you started:

» **SS Yongala** – a sunken shipwreck that has been home to a vivid marine community for more than 90 years.

» **Cod Hole** – go nose-to-nose with a potato cod.

» **Heron Island** – join a crowd of colourful fish straight off the beach.

» **Lady Elliot Island** – with 19 highly regarded dive sites.

» **Pixie Bommie** – delve into the after-five world of the Reef by taking a night dive.

74 68; www.derm.qld.gov.au). Here are our top camping picks.

Whitsunday Islands (p409) Nearly a dozen beautifully sited camping areas, scattered on the islands of Hook, Whitsunday and Henning.

Capricornia Cays Camping available on three separate coral cays, including Masthead Island, North West Island and Lady Musgrave Island (p388) – a fantastic, uninhabited island that's limited to a maximum 40 campers.

Dunk Island (p445) Equal parts resort and national park with good swimming, kayaking and hiking.

Fitzroy Island (p463) Resort and national park with short walking trails through bush, and coral just off the beaches.

Frankland Islands (p463) Coral-fringed islands with white-sand beaches off Cairns.

Lizard Island (p484) Stunning beaches, magnificent coral and abundant wildlife; you must arrive by plane.

Orpheus Island (p430) Secluded island (accessible by air) with pretty tropical forest and superb fringing reef.

East Coast Australia Outdoors

Best Wildlife-Spotting

Fur seals and penguins on Montague Island
Whales off Eden and Hervey Bay
Koalas at Cape Otway
Cassowaries in the Daintree Rainforest
Sea turtles at Mon Repos
Crocodiles in the Daintree River

Top Aquatic Activities

Diving and snorkelling the Great Barrier Reef
Surfing at Bondi Beach, Byron Bay and Noosa
Sailing the Whitsundays
Kayaking at North Stradbroke Island, Noosa and Airlie Beach

Best Activities for Daredevils

Canyoning in the Blue Mountains
Rock climbing at Wilsons Promontory
Skydiving over Mission Beach
Bungee jumping in Cairns
White-water rafting on the Tully River

Best Bushwalking

Blue Mountains
Dorrigo National Park
Wilsons Promontory
Croajingolong National Park
Wooroonooran National Park
Springbrook National Park

Home to ancient rainforests, magnificent islands, rugged mountains and the stunning Great Barrier Reef, East Coast Australia has some outstanding settings for outdoor adventure. Scuba diving and snorkelling among the rich aquatic life off the coast are extremely popular, while surfing here is world-class; there's also great whale-watching, sailing, fishing and loads of other waterside activities. Islands come in hundreds of varieties, from sparkling, reef-fringed beauties to massive sand-dune-laden national parks whose interiors are accessible only by 4WD. You can camp on deserted beaches, surf amazing breaks or paddle a kayak through dense mangroves. Heading inland, you'll find superb bushwalking in rainforests, trekking and rockclimbing around craggy peaks, and white-water rafting on rushing rivers. Those looking for something a little different can go abseiling, bungee jumping or skydiving.

Bushwalking & Trekking

The East Coast of Australia has an array of landscapes and coastline that are laced with amazing bushwalks of every length, standard and difficulty imaginable. Coastal and hinterland national parks and state forests – many of which are easily accessible from the city – provide some of the best places for walking.

GREAT WALKS OF QUEENSLAND

WALK	DIFFICULTY	DISTANCE	DURATION	SCENERY
Fraser Island	Hard	90km	up to 8 days	rainforests, coloured sands, picturesque lakes, towering sand dunes
Gold Coast Hinterland	Moderate	55km	3 days	palm-filled valleys, mist-covered mountains, cliff-top views, waterfalls, crystal-clear rivers
Mackay Highlands	Moderate	50km	4-6 days	rainforest, gorges, steep escarpments, rolling farmlands
Sunshine Coast Hinterland	Moderate	58km	4 days	winds through the scenic Blackall Range with waterfalls, eucalypt forest, subtropical rainforest and fine views
Wet Tropics	Moderate	100km	6 days	waterfalls, gorges, views and World-Heritage-listed rainforest at Girringun National Park
Whitsunday	Hard	30km	3 days	lowland tropical rainforest, rocky creeks, lush palm valleys and views, amid rugged Conway Range inside Conway National Park

When to Go

Bushwalking is enjoyed year-round along the East Coast. Summer is the most popular time in the southeast. In north Queensland (above the Capricorn Coast), the best time to go is from April to September as things can get pretty hot and sticky over summer, particularly in the wet season between November and February (many trails are closed then). Bushfires are a serious hazard in summer and hot conditions shouldn't be taken lightly. Inquire locally before setting out.

Regardless of what time of year it is and no matter how short the walk, you should go well prepared, and always take plenty of drinking water.

New South Wales

Opportunities for bushwalking abound in coastal NSW, with a variety of standards, lengths and terrains. In Sydney, the breathtaking Bondi to Coogee Coastal Walk combines coastal panoramas with opportunities for a surf or a coffee. Beyond the city, you'll find outstanding bushwalks in the Blue Mountains (p99), Ku-ring-gai Chase (p64) and Royal National Park (p138).

For superb coastal vistas, wildflowers and short but rugged hikes, the ascents of Pigeon House Mountain (p146), on the NSW south coast, and Mt Warning (p177), on the NSW north coast, can't be beaten. The verdant valleys of Dorrigo National Park (p193) are ideal for walkers and boast many beautiful waterfalls.

Victoria

In Victoria's national parks and state forests, walkers enjoy everything from short walks through cool temperate rainforests to more challenging hikes that climb mountains or trace the wilderness coastline.

For coastal treks, head down to Wilsons Promontory National Park (p261) in Gippsland, with marked trails from Tidal River and Telegraph Saddle that can take anywhere from a few hours to a couple of days. Expect squeaky white sands and clean aquamarine waters, pristine bushland and stunning coastal vistas. Further east, and almost tipping over into NSW, the Croajingolong National Park (p274), near Mallacoota in East Gippsland, offers rugged inland treks and easier coastal walks past historic lighthouses and over sand dunes.

Queensland

There are some celebrated tracks for experienced walkers in Queensland. In northern Queensland the 32km ungraded Thorsborne

Trail (p439) on Hinchinbrook Island traverses remote beaches, lush rainforests and crystal-clear creeks.

National parks favoured by bushwalkers include Springbrook (p324) in the Gold Coast hinterland, and D'Aguilar Range National Park (p283), which is a popular escape from the city. More good parks for bushwalking include the Cooloola section of Great Sandy National Park (p346), just north of the Sunshine Coast, and Wooroonooran National Park (p446), south of Cairns, which contains Queensland's highest peak, Mt Bartle Frere (1622m).

The Great Walks of Queensland is a $16.5 million project to create a world-class set of walking tracks. For complete details, including walk descriptions, mapping details and camp-site bookings, visit **QPWS** (www. derm.qld.gov.au). Of the featured Great Walks, the best known is the 87km rainforest and coastal path on Fraser Island (p369).

Bushwalking Books

» Lonely Planet *Walking in Australia:* 60 detailed countrywide walks of varying lengths.

» *Take a Walk in Victoria's National Parks:* 3000km of walking tracks in 35 national parks.

» *Take a Walk in a National Park Sydney to Port Macquarie:* 1000km of tracks, including Sydney Harbour, aboriginal rock art and ancient forests.

» *Take a Walk in South-East Queensland:* 170 hikes in 22 Queensland national parks.

» *Tropical Walking Tracks:* Excellent coverage of the tropical north.

Bushwalking Resources

Local bushwalking clubs and information:

Bushwalking NSW (www.bushwalking.org.au)

Bushwalking Victoria (www.bushwalkingvictoria. org.au)

Bushwalking Queensland (www.bushwalkingqueensland.org.au)

Diving & Snorkelling

Even if the Great Barrier Reef weren't here, the diving would still be world-class along Australia's East Coast. Coral reefs, a rich array of marine life (temperate, subtropical and tropical species) and thousands of shipwrecks to explore contribute to the enchanting diving scene.

Diving is generally good year-round although in Queensland you'll want to avoid the wet season (December to March) when floods can wash mud out into the ocean, impairing visibility. Also, all water activities are affected by stingers (box jellyfish), which are found on the Queensland coast from Agnes Water north from November to May.

You can snorkel all along the coast; it requires minimum effort and anyone can do it. Many diving locations mentioned here are also popular snorkelling sites.

For details on diving and snorkelling in the Great Barrier Reef, see p373 .

Diving Courses

Every major town along the coast has one or more diving schools, but standards vary, so it's worthwhile doing some research before signing up. When choosing a course, look carefully at where much of your open-water experience will take place. Budget outfits tend to only offer shore dives, while pricier outfits may take place on a live-aboard boat for several days. Normally you have to show that you can tread water for 10 minutes and swim 200m before you can start a course. Most schools also require a medical, which usually costs extra (around $55 to $80). A four- or five-day **PADI** (Professional Association of Diving Instructors; www.padi.com) open-water course costs anything from $275 to $800 (the Bundaberg area is among the cheapest places to learn).

For certified divers, trips and equipment hire are available just about everywhere. You'll need evidence of your qualifications, and some places may also ask to see your logbook. Renting gear and going on a two-tank day dive generally costs between $75 and $190. You can also hire a mask, snorkel and fins from a dive shop for around $30 to $50.

Popular Diving & Snorkelling Sites

New South Wales

Sydney Dive Centre Bondi (www.divebondi. com.au; p65); cave systems, schooling fish, Port Jackson sharks, blue gropers

Byron Bay Dive Byron Bay (www.byronbaydivecentre.com.au; p163); spectacular marine-rich sites with turtles, rays and 400 fish species

Solitary Islands Marine Park Jetty Dive Centre (www.jettydive.com.au; p188); impressive marine life, with tropical and subtropical fish and hard and soft corals

Jervis Bay Dive Jervis Bay (www.divejervisbay.com; p145); more than 30 dive sites with fur seals, grey nurse sharks, sea dragons

Montague Island Island Charters Narooma (www.islandchartersnarooma.com; p151); tropical, subtropical and cold-water species, including two seal colonies, wreck of SS *Lady Darling*

Victoria

Bunurong Marine Park Seal Diving Services (www.sealdivingservices.com.au; p259); rock reefs, colourful seaweeds, seals, sting rays, 87 fish species

Arches Marine Sanctuary Port Campbell Boat Charters (www.portcampbellboatcharters.com.au; p249) Kelp forests, canyons, arches and tunnels, plus wreck dives and diverse marine life

Queensland

North Stradbroke Island Manta Lodge (www.mantalodge.com.au; p304); manta rays, leopard and grey nurse sharks, humpback whales, turtles, dolphins, hard and soft corals

Moreton Island Tangatours at Tangalooma (www.tangalooma.com; p306); Tangalooma Wrecks, good snorkelling site

Mooloolaba Scuba World (www.scubaworld.com.au; p339); dive with sharks and rays at Underwater World; or wreck dive a sunken warship off the coast

Rainbow Beach Wolf Rock Dive Centre (www.wolfrockdive.com.au; p359); one of Australia's top diving destinations, with grey nurse sharks, turtles, manta rays and giant groupers amid volcanic pinnacles

Bundaberg Bundaberg Aqua Scuba (www.aquascuba.com.au; p366); wreck dives, groupers, turtles, rays, live-aboard dive boat

Surfing

The southern half of the East Coast is jam-packed with sandy surf beaches and point breaks. North of Agnes Water in Queensland, the waves disappear thanks to the Great Barrier Reef shielding the coast from the ocean swells. Many travellers who come to the East Coast want to learn to surf, and you'll find plenty of good waves, board hire and lessons available all along the coast.

Two-hour lessons cost around $40 to $65 and five-day courses for the really keen go for around $180 to $250.

New South Wales

Those endless NSW beaches are battered by beautiful waves much of the year and there are simply so many places to surf that crowds at all but the trendiest spots are rare.

» Bondi Beach (p79) The famed (and often packed) surf mecca.

» Manly Beach (p79) Gentler waves, good place to learn.

» Batemans Bay (p148) Several decent surf beaches, particularly Pink Rocks.

» Booderee National Park (p144) Best at the Pipeline, an A-grade reef break with periodic 3.5m tubes.

» Newcastle (p106) Great options all around.

» Crescent Head (p198) Fabled waves ideal for longboarders.

» Coffs Harbour (p188) Fine swells averaging 1.5m to 2m.

» Lennox Head (p178) Excellent surf off Seven Mile Beach.

» Byron Bay (p161) Wide range of breaks, with surf culture to rival Bondi.

Queensland

From a surfer's point of view, Queensland's Great Barrier Reef is one of nature's most tragic mistakes – a 2000km-long breakwater! Mercifully, there are some great surf beaches in southern Queensland.

» Coolangatta (p321) Popular surfing haunt for Gold Coast locals, particularly at Kirra Beach.

» Burleigh Heads (p319) Serious waves that require experience.

» Caloundra (p337) to Mooloolaba (p339) A good strip with fine breaks.

» Noosa (p329) Popular among longboarders.

» North Stradbroke Island (p304) Harder to reach, but good surf beaches and fewer crowds than the Gold and Sunshine Coasts.

Victoria

With its exposure to the relentless Southern Ocean swell, Victoria's rugged southern coastline provides plenty of quality surf, while the southeast coast is a little gentler. The usually chilly water (even in summer) has the hardiest surfer reaching for a wet-

BOATING

After surfing, boating is the number one-ocean activity on the East Coast. It has its own distinct marina culture that you'll find in towns with large ports and even its own migratory patterns: during the southern winter, boaties and yachties migrate towards the warmer north.

New South Wales

The simplest boating activity would have you resting your bum on a harbour cruise (p67), but Sydney's greatest natural asset is an ideal setting to learn to sail (p66). South and north of Sydney you'll find enticing harbours bursting with activity, including Port Stephens (p113) and Jervis Bay (p143). In the north, Ballina is good for boat hire (p179).

Queensland

Queensland's waters teem with mariners of all skills, with some of the most stunning sailing locations in the world. The postcard-perfect Whitsunday Islands (p407) are magical for a sail. You can join a full- or multiday cruise, or charter your own craft in Airlie Beach (p412).

You can also explore the Great Barrier Reef and some of the islands off the Far North Queensland coast on board a chartered boat or cruise from Cairns (p453) or Port Douglas (p469), where the yacht club offers free sailing on Wednesdays.

Victoria

Victoria's southeast coast boasts a couple of expansive bays and some pretty estuaries where boating is popular. City-based yachties tend to gravitate to the many sailing clubs around Port Phillip Bay. Other popular boating areas include the sprawling Gippsland Lakes (see Metung, p266) and the lovely Mallacoota Inlet (p271) near the NSW border.

---

suit. A full-length, up-to-7mm-thick wetsuit is the standard for winter.

» Phillip Island (p255) Eastern Victoria's best surf, especially at Woolami Beach.

» Torquay (p242) The undisputed capital of Australian surfing, with surf schools, a surf museum and good surf beaches nearby.

» Bells Beach (p243) Inconsistent but famed surf beach, which hosts the Rip Curl Pro competition every Easter.

Kayaking & Canoeing

Kayaks and canoes let you paddle into otherwise inaccessible areas, poking in and out of dense mangroves and estuaries, river gorges, secluded island beaches and remote wilderness inlets.

New South Wales

You can go seakayaking right in Sydney Harbour (p65); although it is busy and can be challenging for a novice, instruction and guiding is easily arranged. Many of the state's numerous rivers are suitable for canoeing and kayaking, with adventurous swift-flowing runs, and long, lazy paddles.

Port Stephens Blue Water Sea Kayaking (www.kayakingportstephens.com.au; p114); dolphins, whales, sunsets

Coffs Harbour Liquid Assets (www.surfrafting.com; p188); rushing surf-rafting, gentle sea kayaking and flat-water kayaking amid wetlands and littoral rainforest of Bongil Bongil National Park

Yamba Yamba Kayak (http://angourie.me; p182); idyllic scenery on Clarence River and Lake Wooloweyah

Byron Bay Cape Byron Kayaks (www.capebyronkayaks.com; p164); dolphins, migrating whales, sea turtles

Jervis Bay Jervis Bay Kayaks (www.jervisbaykayaks.com; p145); sea kayaking in a pristine marine park, overnight camping/kayaking trips

Victoria

Melbourne's Yarra River is popular with paddlers, with its gentle lower reaches suitable for families while more exciting rapids of about grade three can be found in the higher reaches. Melbourne-based **Sea Kayak Australia** (www.seakayakaustralia.com.au) offers a wide range of tours, from half-day city tours spying penguins and other wildlife off St Kilda, full-day trips off Phillip Island, and multiday trips around Wilsons Promontory, Gippsland Lakes and other areas. Two other recommended outfits:

Melbourne Kayak Melbourne (www.kayakmelbourne.com.au; p213); day and moonlight paddle trips along the Yarra River

Apollo Bay Apollo Bay Surf & Kayak (www.apollobaysurfkayak.com.au; p246); fur seal colony, pristine coastline

Queensland

There are numerous outfits along the Queensland coast that offer paddling expeditions along idyllic waterways and lakes, or out through the calm Barrier Reef waters – sometimes from the mainland to offshore islands. There are also companies that operate guided tours off the Gold and Sunshine Coasts.

North Stradbroke Island Straddie Adventures (www.straddieadventures.com.au; p304); mangroves and lovely coastline, dolphins, sea turtles, rays

Whitsunday Islands Salty Dog (www.saltydog.com.au; p408); one-day and multiday trips exploring Molle Islands, amid coral reefs, dolphins, turtles and sea eagles

Noosa Noosa Ocean Kayak Tours (www.noosakayaktours.com; p330); sea kayak tours amid dolphins, turtles on Laguna Bay; river kayaking on Noosa River

Magnetic Island Magnetic Island Sea Kayaks (www.seakayak.com.au; p433); exploring the picturesque bays of the island

Mission Beach Coral Sea Kayaking (www.coralseakayak.com.au; p441); day paddles to and around Dunk Island, multiday trips to stunning Hinchinbrook Island

White-Water Rafting

In Queensland, the mighty Tully, North Johnstone and Russell Rivers between Townsville and Cairns are renowned white-water-rafting locations, benefiting from the very high rainfall in the area. The Tully is the most popular of the three and has 44 rapids graded 3 to 4. Full-day rafting trips cost about $130 on the Russell River and $185 on the Tully, including transfers. See the Cairns and Tully sections for details. Rafting is good year round.

In Victoria, the Snowy River offers a range of white-water adventures, from easy-going day trips on class 2 rapids to more challenging two- and four-day excursions with towering gorges, rainforest-covered gullies and open valleys. It's best from November to March.

In New South Wales, you can go white-water rafting on class 2 and 3 rapids on the scenic Goolang River near Coffs Harbour. Trips are offered by Liquid Assets.

Bungee Jumping & Skydiving

Adrenalin-loving Cairns has bungee jumping (from $140) and 'minjin swings' (from $90) – multiperson jungle plummets for those not wanting to go alone.

Tandem skydiving provides one of the most spectacular ways to get an eyeful of the Australian landscape. Prices depend on the height of your jump. Most folk start with a jump of 9000ft, which provides up to 28 seconds of freefall and costs around $250. You can also do 11,000ft or even 14,000ft, which affords 60 seconds of freefall, reaching speeds up to 200kph; this one costs around $350.

Popular locations for skydiving are Byron Bay (p164), Caloundra (p337), Surfers Paradise (p313), Brisbane (p286), Airlie Beach (p412), Mission Beach (p440) and Cairns (p454).

Abseiling, Canyoning & Rock Climbing

NSW's Blue Mountains, especially around Katoomba, are fantastic for abseiling (rappelling) and canyoning, with numerous professionals able to set you up with equipment and training.

With a name like Wilsons Promontory, you just know there are going to be some rock faces to abseil (see First Track Adventures, p261). Another good place in Victoria is around the beautiful and legendary Snowy River (see Karoonda Park, p272).

itineraries

Whether you've got six days or 60, these itineraries provide a starting point for the trip of a lifetime. Want more inspiration? Head online to lonelyplanet. com/thorntree to chat with other travellers.

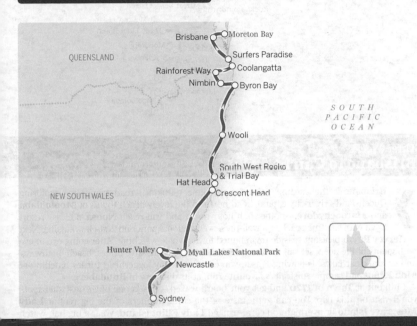

Two Weeks
Sydney to Brisbane

> Start in **Sydney**, taking in iconic sights, headland walks and great restaurants, shopping and nightlife. After a few days head north to the arts- and surf-loving city of **Newcastle**, then inland to the idyllic vineyards of **Hunter Valley**. Back on the coast, explore the stunning scenery and pristine beaches of **Myall Lakes National Park**.
> Northern NSW basks in subtropical glory. Surf excellent breaks at **Crescent Head**, take in the views at **Hat Head**, and frolic in the waves at pretty **South West Rocks** and nearby **Trial Bay**. Further up, you pass some sensational, untouched beaches like those near little wild **Wooli**. **Byron Bay** is inescapable: don't resist this mellow yet groovin' beach town where surfers, hipsters and hippies all share the sands. Meditating in Byron's verdant hinterland is the once-alternative, still-delightful **Nimbin**. Continue inland through lush national parks on the **Rainforest Way**. The Gold Coast is next with stops in laid-back beach **Coolangatta** and party-loving **Surfers Paradise**. End your journey in riverside **Brisbane** with great drinking, dining, nightlife and cultural goings-on. If time allows, tack on a few days exploring the islands of **Moreton Bay**.

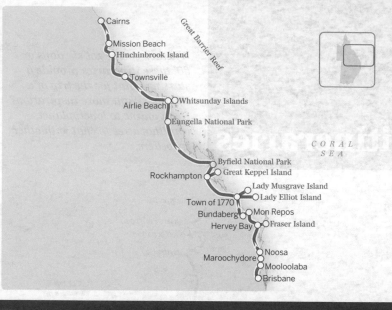

Three Weeks
Brisbane to Cairns

Brisbane is the starting point for this epic 1800km(!) road trip. After exploring Queensland's river-city capital, head north to the lovely beach towns of **Mooloolaba** and **Maroochydore**. Another half-hour north and you reach **Noosa**, a classy resort town with sublime beaches, a well-preserved national park and first-class cuisine. Next is **Hervey Bay**, a pleasant seaside town famed for its whale-watching. After going eye-to-eye with giants of the deep, set sail for **Fraser Island**, home to massive dunes, beach 'highways' and crystal-clear lakes. Following Fraser, you can watch tiny loggerhead turtles hatching at **Mon Repos** and sample Australia's favourite rum at its distillery in **Bundaberg**.

Chill out at **Town of 1770** and get your board waxed – this is one of the last surf spots you'll visit on this trip. You can get a taste of the coral wonders of the big reef at **Lady Musgrave Island** or overnight on coral-fringed **Lady Elliot Island**. Wear a big hat, watch someone riding a bull or join them devouring a steak at beef city, **Rockhampton**. Explore the trails and sample the beaches of **Great Keppel Island**; it's pure tropical beach bliss. Get even more remote slightly further north at **Byfield National Park**, where streams flow with water so clear you don't even realise it's there. And it may be the official mammal of NSW, but the best place to spot platypuses is at peaceful **Eungella National Park**.

Your next stop is bustling **Airlie Beach**, gateway to the magical **Whitsunday Islands**, where you can sail, dive, snorkel and bask in luxury (or camp on uninhabited islands), all against a backdrop of picture-perfect azure waters and powdery white-sand beaches. Vibrant **Townsville** is next, with a surprising eating and drinking scene, an excellent aquarium and live-aboards heading out to pristine sections of the **Great Barrier Reef**. Next up, walkers should not miss the Thorsborne Trail on magnificent **Hinchinbrook Island**. More adventure awaits on the rushing white water of the mighty Tully River. Recover on charming **Mission Beach**, where the rainforest meets the sea. End your grand road trip in the tourist town of **Cairns**, and shout yourself a trip to the reef and a seafood feast. You'll find no shortage of fellow travellers here whom you can one-up with your coastal tales of adventure.

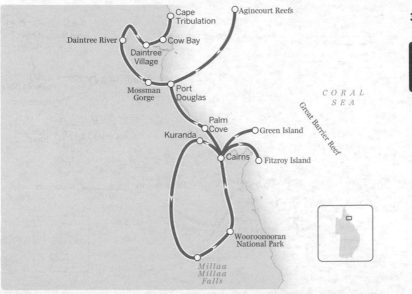

One to Two Weeks
Rainforest & Reef

Australia's reef-diving capital and gateway to the ancient tropical rainforests to the north, **Cairns** is an obligatory stop on almost any itinerary through Queensland. Spend a few days in the buzzing town, visiting its lush botanic gardens, enjoying good meals and getting a taste of the town's brash nightlife. Take day trips to **Green** and **Fitzroy Islands**, with reef-trimmed shores, verdant vegetation and lovely beaches. Book a snorkelling or dive trip to the **Great Barrier Reef** (ideally the outer reef) or plan a few days on a live-aboard expedition to **Cod Hole**, one of Australia's best dive spots. You can also plan adventure activities like white-water rafting and skydiving.

After a few days in Cairns, head inland via gondola cableway or scenic railway to **Kuranda** for rainforest walks and browsing the popular markets. Spend a few days exploring the region (though you'll need your own wheels), visiting picturesque **Millaa Millaa Falls** and hiking in spectacular **Wooroonooran National Park**.

Head back to the coast and treat yourself to a night in a peaceful resort in lovely **Palm Cove**, just north of Cairns. Continue an hour further north to **Port Douglas**, a peaceful holiday town with a beautiful beach. It's also a base for boat trips to the outer reef with first-rate catamarans heading to **Agincourt Reefs**.

After a few nights eating, drinking and relaxing in Port Douglas, hit the road. The first stop is **Mossman Gorge**, where lush lowland rainforest surrounds the photogenic Mossman River. Sign up for a memorable **Kuku-Yalanji Dreamtime walk**, run by the indigenous Kuku-Yalanji.

Go north to the **Daintree River**. Take a crocodile-spotting cruise and stop for lunch in the **Daintree Village**. Afterwards, continue back to the river, where you'll cross by vehicle ferry to the northern side. From here continue driving north (carefully, as this is cassowary country). Stop at the **Daintree Discovery Centre** to learn about this magnificent area. The lovely beach at nearby **Cow Bay** is also worth a detour. Continue north, taking a bit of refreshment at the **Daintree Ice Cream Company**. The last stop is **Cape Tribulation**, a magnificent meeting of rainforest and reef. Spend a few nights taking in the splendour at one of the fine lodges tucked in the rainforest.

Great Ocean Road
Melbourne to Sydney

One to Two Weeks
Melbourne to Sydney

Begin in **Melbourne**, with some live music, fashion and cafe culture, before heading to **Phillip Island**, where penguins, seals and surfers frolic in the bracing briny. Next stop is **Wilsons Promontory**, where you can hike, spot wildlife and relish beautiful beaches. Head northeast through the forests, farms and the Gippsland Lakes district to Victoria's loveliest seaside town, **Mallacoota**. Entering the warmer climes of south-coast NSW, pay a visit to the sleepy town of **Eden**, which is famed for its whale-watching, and have a wander through picture-perfect **Central Tilba**. Continue on to **Narooma**, with its pretty beaches and good surf. From here, catch a ferry to **Montague Island**, an important Aboriginal site and a stunning nature reserve. Heading north, detour inland at **Bateman's Bay** to **Canberra** and visit some of Australia's best museums. Back on the coast, **Jervis Bay** is a scenic spot with white-sand beaches, frolicking dolphins and national parks. Continue along the coast, taking in the dramatic cliffs and rainforest of **Royal National Park**, before reaching the dazzling lights of **Sydney**. Get your dose of urban exploring, but leave time for the awe-inspiring scenery of the **Blue Mountains**.

One to Two Weeks
Great Ocean Road

The Great Ocean Road is one of the most popular touring routes in the country, and it's worth the hype. Start in the surfing mecca of **Torquay** by checking out the waves at **Bells Beach**, then head to family-friendly **Anglesea** to see the kangaroos at its golf course and take a break by its river. **Aireys Inlet** is next; tour the lighthouse before a beach walk at **Fairhaven** and a coffee and overnight stay in the resort town of **Lorne**. The Great Ocean Road is in its element now, but you can break up the sea views with a detour up into the rainforests of the **Otway Ranges**. Back on the Great Ocean Road, head to the fishing village of **Apollo Bay** for a day or two then continue west into the koala and lighthouse zone of **Cape Otway**. It's quite a stretch to **Port Campbell National Park** and its famed **Twelve Apostles**; take the time to count them and spend a night in **Port Campbell** to get a real feel for the area. Look for whales off **Warrnambool**'s coast then continue west to quaint, and very Irish, **Port Fairy**. If there's time, head to tiny **Cape Bridgewater**.

regions at a glance

Sydney & the Central Coast

Beaches ✓✓✓
Food ✓✓✓
History ✓✓

Beaches
Australia claims to be 'world's best' in a number of fields (sport and beer drinking being two of the more credible), but we think there's one claim that is indisputable – Aussie surf beaches can't be beaten, particularly those in Sydney.

Food
Sydney used to come second to Melbourne in the culinary stakes, but in recent years a thoroughbred line-up of chefs, restaurateurs and artisan producers have made the dining scenes in Sydney, the Blue Mountains and the Hunter Valley the most exciting in the country – make sure you celebrate their ascendancy.

History
There are two different historical narratives here – that of the convicts and soldiers who arrived here in 1788, and of the Indigenous people they dispossessed.

p46

Canberra & Southern NSW

Beaches ✓✓✓
Food ✓✓✓
History ✓✓

Beaches
Kangaroos hang out at South Coast beaches; that's how good they are. Elsewhere, choose your white sand or your surf break and go it alone. Explore inlets and mangrove swamps by kayak.

Food
Politicos rub shoulders with journalists in Canberra and food and wine are the great pacifiers. On the coast, restaurants tend to open seasonally but when they do, fresh seafood, local produce and Sydney flair combine for memorable feasts.

History
Canberra's galleries showcase a wealth of Indigenous and post-colonial art. On the coast, Aboriginal middens nod to ancient times; so too the Indigenous stories of natural wonders.

p125

Byron Bay & Northern NSW

Nightlife ✓✓✓
Beaches ✓✓✓
Parklife ✓✓✓

Nightlife
Byron Bay has the bars and pubs for every taste, be it boozing with beer, styling it with sauvignon blanc, or getting messy with margaritas. Name your poison and, in the spirit of Byron, share it with everyone else.

Beaches
Whether you're after a spectacular sunset, fish and chips on the sand or great surf, you'll find it all in Byron Bay. If it's quiet time you're after, head for the idyllic and isolated white sands along the north coast of NSW.

Parklife
The far north hinterland has three of the biggest and best national parks in the country. One has a volcano and another a forest of trees over 2000 years old.

p160

Melbourne & Coastal Victoria

Hiking ✓✓
Food ✓✓✓
Beaches ✓✓✓

Hiking
The Great Ocean Road offers short or multiday treks, Wilsons Promontory has heaps of marked trails and scenic camping, while Croajingolong National Park offers inland treks and coastal walks.

Food
Buy fresh seafood from a coastal wharf, dine in award-winning Melbourne restaurants and sample cool-climate wines on the Mornington Peninsula.

Beaches
From Bells Beach to Ninety Mile Beach, Victoria has the pick of sandy scapes. You'll find family-friendly bay beaches along the Mornington Peninsula, beach horse riding in Gunnamatta and Fairhaven, and countless great surfing spots.

p200

Brisbane & the Gold Coast

Theme parks ✓✓
Food ✓✓✓
Nightlife ✓✓✓

Theme Parks
The Gold Coast offers something totally different: aside from being a surfer's nirvana, it's home to Australia's best theme parks.

Food
First-rate chefs, delectable ingredients from the fertile countryside and lovely riverside settings combine for exquisite dining in Queensland's capital. No matter your craving, you'll find it in Brisbane.

Nightlife
Nights out in Brisbane entail open-air riverside bars, nightlife-loving mayhem in Fortitude Valley, lounges with DJs and live jazz and rock. Après-surf, the Gold Coast kicks into overdrive with loud al fresco eateries, street music and throbbing nightclubs.

p275

Noosa & the Sunshine Coast

Surfing ✓✓✓
Beaches ✓✓✓
Nature ✓✓✓

Surfing
Blonde, bronzed and waxed-down – the relaxed surfer ethos of the Sunny Coast permeates the street and the beach. With good surf breaks all along the coast, there are plenty of waves, breaks, smiles and zinc cream for everyone.

Beaches
Noosa's beach is an idyllic bay of calm blue water. Further south, Mooloolaba is a popular swimming beach, especially for kiddies. You'll have the beach to yourself between Coolum and Peregian.

Nature
Bathed by the South Pacific, the splendid beaches of the Sunshine Coast merge into native bushland, subtropical rainforest and the forested folds of the hinterland – perfect for bushwalking.

p327

Fraser Island & the Fraser Coast

Nature ✓✓✓
Whales ✓✓✓
Island life ✓✓✓

Nature
Known for its long sandy beaches and spectacular national parks, the Fraser Coast is home to egg-laying sea turtles, migrating whales, wild dingoes and dolphins.

Whales
Migrating humpback whales are like giant, playful sea puppies – breaching, blowing, fin-waving and tail-slapping. And when they roll up beside the boat with one eye clear of the water, you've got to wonder who's doing the eyeballing.

Island Life
Fashioned by the wind and sea, Fraser Island hosts a unique subtropical ecosystem that's as close to paradise as you can get. A day tour merely whets the appetite; camp overnight and wish upon a thousand shooting stars.

p351

Capricorn Coast & the Southern Reef

Scenery ✓✓✓
Islands ✓✓
Diving ✓✓✓

Scenery
Great Keppel Island has powdery white-sand beaches and dense bushland, the Capricorn Caves provide a labyrinthine glimpse of the ancient past, while Byfield has deserted beaches and sublime canoeing.

Islands
Tiny, coral-ringed Lady Elliot has superb snorkelling, as does densely vegetated Heron Island, Lovely Great Keppel Island has fantastic bushwalking.

Diving
You'll find spectacular diving and snorkelling in the Great Barrier Reef's southern reaches. You can board a day cruise or live-aboard dive vessel from Town of 1770 or base yourself on one of the islands for full immersion in the technicolour underwater world.

p381

Whitsunday Coast

Islands ✓✓✓
Sailing ✓✓✓
Snorkelling ✓✓✓

Islands
With 74 tropical beauties to choose from, the Whitsunday Islands is Utopia for beach castaways. Whether bushwalking, kayaking or lounging, all island trips eventually lead to the stunning sugar-white sands of Whitehaven Beach.

Sailing
Surrounding the Whitsunday Islands, translucent blue seas seem incomplete without the snow-white yacht sailing into the picture. The Whitsundays is sailing and island-hopping heaven.

Snorkelling
Snorkel along the fringing reefs to see tropical fish flit through a vibrantly coloured landscape of coral, polyps, anemones and other weirdly wonderful marine life.

p398

Townsville to Innisfail

Beaches ✓✓✓
Architecture ✓✓
Parklife ✓✓

Beaches
Between Townsville's palm-shaded Strand and Flying Fish Point, next to Innisfail, this stretch of coastline shelters vast, sandy expanses such as Mission Beach through to intimate coves like Etty Bay.

Architecture
Historic architecture in the region includes the grand, gold-rush era streetscapes of Charters Towers, beautiful 19th-century buildings in Townsville, and Australia's highest concentration of art deco architecture in Innisfail.

Parklife
Hiking, camping, swimming and picnicking opportunities abound in the region's national parks, as well as wildlife such as flightless prehistoric-looking cassowaries roaming the rainforest.

p423

Cairns & the Daintree Rainforest

Diving ✓✓✓
Food ✓✓✓
Cultural tours ✓✓

Diving
Every day, boats ferry passengers from Cairns and Port Douglas to the dazzling Great Barrier Reef. Serious dive lovers can join a live-aboard vessel to explore more remote sections of the reef.

Food
Many of the Atherton Tableland's farms, orchards and plantations can be visited on tours, including tropical fruit wine producers – or simply taste the delicious local produce at restaurants throughout the region.

Cultural Tours
A number of Aboriginal-led tours can take you on a spiritual journey through this ancient rainforest region, offering an insight into its rich Indigenous culture.

p448

Look out for these icons:

TOP CHOICE Our author's recommendation

A green or sustainable option

FREE No payment required

See the Index for a full list of destinations covered in this book.

On the Road

Sydney & the Central Coast

Best Places to Eat

» Icebergs Dining Room & Bar (p78)
» Bécasse (p75)
» Solitary (p101)
» Margan (p112)
» Bent on Food (p119)

Best Places to Stay

» Sydney Harbour YHA (p68)
» Bondi Beach House (p73)
» Tower Lodge (p111)

Why Go?

Sydney is special. Its traditional owners, the Eora people, have always known this. In 1770 they watched Captain James Cook recognise their land's huge potential and covet it for Britain, and now they welcome nearly three million international visitors every year who seem to instantly and unanimously emulate Cook's positive assessment. The city's spectacular harbour setting, gorgeous climate and sophisticated sheen make it unique among the Australian states, and its fun-loving local population endows it with a confident charm that every city yearns for but few achieve.

It would seem reasonable to assume that the areas surrounding Sydney should be content to bask in the reflected and undeniably golden glow of their neighbour, but that's not the case. Destinations such as the Blue Mountains, Hunter Valley and Central Coast have more than enough accolades and attractions of their own, including pristine beaches, picture-perfect vineyards and magnificent mountain ranges.

When to Go

Sydney

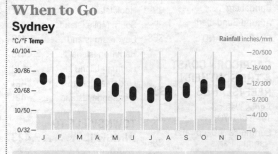

January The year kicks off with a spectacular firework display over Circular Quay.

February Summer's party season culminates with the decadent Gay & Lesbian Mardi Gras.

July Wood fires, wine and winter menus are on offer at the Blue Mountains and Hunter Valley.

Indigenous Culture

The Indigenous people of NSW have had a complex and mutually supportive relationship with the landscape for millennia and gaining an insight into their ancient heritage can be a highlight of any visit – to do so, book a place on an Aboriginal Heritage Tour of the Royal Botanic Gardens (p52), an Aboriginal Culture Tour around Sydney Harbour (p52) or a Blue Mountains Walkabout (p100).

For more information on the region's Aboriginal culture, see p65.

AUSTRALIAN CONVICT SITES

The most recent Australian additions to the World Heritage List are 11 sites that are collectively known as the Australian Convict Sites (www.environment.gov.au/heritage/places/world/convict-sites). Four of these sites are in or around Sydney: Old Government House and Domain in Parramatta; Hyde Park Barracks Museum in Sydney (p57), Cockatoo Island, at the junction of the Parramatta and Lane Cove Rivers in Sydney; and the Old Great North Rd, which you can visit on your way to the Hunter Valley.

These sites are among many in Sydney and on the Central Coast dating back to early colonial times. In Sydney, many of them are maintained and opened to the public by the Historic Houses Trust – purchasing one of its 'Tickets through Time' (p49) gives discounted entry to the sites while at the same time supporting the trust's program of ongoing maintenance and interpretation. And not everything is in Sydney; Port Macquarie's main street has a number of convict-constructed buildings, making it a popular heritage promenade.

Great Surfing Spots

» Northern Beaches, Sydney (p64) – a 20km stretch of amazing urban surf

» Bar and Merewether Beaches, Newcastle (p106 & p106) – world-famous beach breaks

» Boomerang Beach, Pacific Palms (p118) – catch a wave with the local dolphins

» Lighthouse Beach, Seal Rocks (p117) – epic waves when the south swell comes in

» One Mile Beach, Anna Bay (p113) – for experienced and novice surfers alike

» North Haven (p118) – magical rights on the breakwall

Fast Facts

» Population 4.2 million

» Area 800,642 sq km

» Telephone Area Code ☑02

» Number of patrolled surf beaches 405

Planning Your Trip

» Visit when regions hold annual festivals: Hunter Valley (p109) during June, the Blue Mountains (p97) in winter, and Newcastle's beaches (p103) in March.

» Book accommodation well in advance, particularly for summer.

» Fine dining restaurants are often fully booked on weekends and closed early in the week – call for reservations.

Resources

» Visit NSW (www.visitnsw.com.au) has information about Sydney and NSW.

» Department of Environment, Climate Change & Water (www.environment.nsw.gov.au/nationalparks) provides information about NSW National Parks

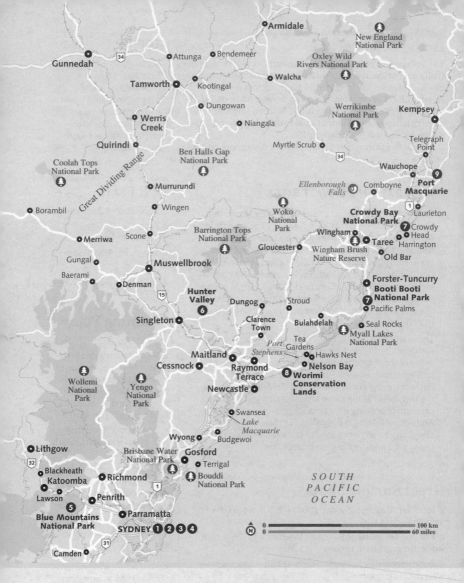

Sydney & the Central Coast Highlights

❶ Hopping aboard one of Sydney's iconic **harbour ferries** (p96)

❷ Eating and drinking your way along Crown St in **Surry Hills** (p77)

❸ Enjoying scenery and sculpture on the **Bondi to Coogee Clifftop Walk** from Bondi to Coogee (p62)

❹ Attending a performance at the **Sydney Opera House** (p53)

❺ Meditating under dense and ancient forest canopies in the **Blue Mountains** (p97)

❻ Broadening your palate and waistline in the **Hunter Valley** (p109)

❼ Colonising an empty stretch of beach in the **Booti Booti** (p118) and **Crowdy Bay National Parks** (p118)

❽ Traversing the **Worimi Conservation Lands** (p114) sand dunes

❾ Taking in **Port Macquarie** (p120) beach and cafe culture

SYDNEY

POP 4,200,000

Sydney is the capital that every other Australian city loves to hate, but what that really means is that they all want to be just like her; sun-kissed, sophisticated and supremely self-confident. Built around one of the most beautiful natural harbours in the world, she has three of Australia's major icons – the Harbour Bridge, the Opera House and Bondi Beach – and her attractions definitely don't stop there. This is the country's oldest, largest and most diverse city, home to magnificent museums, even more magnificent beaches and an edgy multiculturalism that injects colour and vitality into her inner neighbourhoods and outer suburbs.

History

The Sydney region is the ancestral home of the Eora (the Guringai, Birrabirragal and Gadigal peoples), who possessed an intimate understanding of environmental sustainability, spoke three distinct languages and maintained sophisticated sacred and artistic cultures. In 1788 Captain Arthur Phillip established Australia's first European settlement, and the Eora were soon stripped of the legal rights to their land, and systematically incarcerated, killed or driven away by force.

Early Sydney bumbled through near starvation and rum-fuelled political turmoil, and the boom didn't arrive until the 1850s gold rush, when the population doubled in a decade.

In the 20th century, post-WWII immigrants from the UK, Ireland and the Mediterranean brought spirit and prosperity to the city. These qualities have endured as the immigrant pool has expanded to include Asia (especially Vietnam and China), the Middle East and Africa. Hosting the 2000 Olympic Games thrust Sydney into the global limelight for celebratory reasons and its glitzy vibe keeps it there.

Sights

Sydney will keep you busy. If you plan on seeing an exceptional number of museums, attractions and tours, check out the discount passes offered by Australian Travel Specialists (ATS; ☑1800 355 537; www.atstravel.com.au; ticket booths at Wharf 6, Circular Quay & Harbourside Shopping Centre, Darling Harbour). These include the See Sydney & Beyond Pass (with/without travel on public transport adult

from $183/149, child $122/109), but be sure to work out whether purchasing the pass will really save you money. Other discount cards include the Explore 4 Pass (adult/child $50/30), which gives access to the Sydney Aquarium, Sydney Tower, Oceanworld in Manly and Sydney Wildlife World; and the excellent Ticket Through Time (☑02 8239 2211; www.hht.net.au/visiting/ticket_through_time; adult/concession & child $30/15), which gives access to 11 properties opened to the public by the Historic Houses Trust.

SYDNEY HARBOUR

Stretching 20km inland from the South Pacific Ocean to the mouth of the Parramatta River, this magnificent natural harbour is the city's shimmering soul and the focus of every visitor's stay. Providing a serene and picture-perfect backdrop to Sydney's fast-paced urban lifestyle, the harbour's beaches, coves, bays, islands and wildlife-filled pockets of national park offer locals innumerable options for recreation, relaxation and rejuvenation. Exploring this vast, visually arresting area by ferry (p96) is one of Sydney's great joys.

Forming the gateway to the harbour from the ocean are North Head and South Head. The former fishing village of Watsons Bay nestles on South Head's harbour side, and the city's favourite day-trip destination, Manly, occupies a promontory straddling harbour and ocean near North Head. Into the harbour and roughly equidistant from the heads is the North Shore's Middle Head, characterised by sheltered coves and upmarket residential suburbs.

The focal point of the inner harbour and the city's major transport hub is Circular Quay (Map p54), presided over by the city's flamboyant visual signatures, the Sydney Harbour Bridge and Sydney Opera House. From here, you are able to access the central business district (CBD) and catch ferries to destinations along both shores of the harbour and to some of the harbour islands.

Sydney Harbour Bridge   LANDMARK

Whether they're driving over it, climbing up it, rollerblading across it or sailing under it, Sydneysiders adore their 'giant coathanger' (Map p54). Opened in 1932, this majestic structure links the CBD with North Sydney, spanning the harbour at one of its narrowest points.

The best way to experience the bridge is on foot – don't expect much of a view crossing

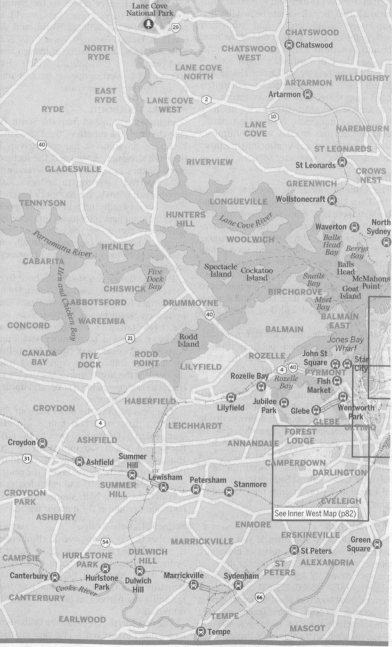

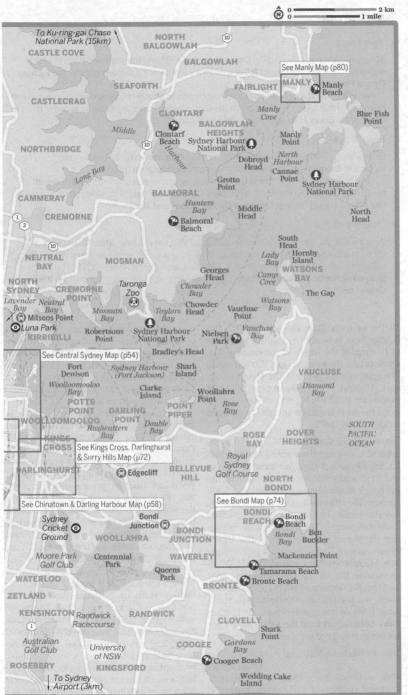

SYDNEY IN...

Two Days

Start your first day by exploring **Circular Quay** (p53) and then follow the harbourside walkway to the **Art Gallery of NSW** (p57). At night, enjoy a performance at the **Sydney Opera House** (p53).

Next day, board a ferry and sail past the Heads to **Manly** (p63), where you can swim at the beach, have a long lunch or brave the 9km Manly Scenic Walkway. That night, head to fashionable **Surry Hills** (p77) for drinks and dinner.

Four Days

On day three, energise yourself with yum cha in **Chinatown** (p76) before catching a ferry to genteel **Balmain** (p62) or shopping in pretty **Paddington** (p93).

On day four, it's time to spend the day soaking up the sun and the scene at **Bondi** (p62). Be sure to take the Bondi to Coogee Clifftop Walk before making your way back to Bondi for a sunset drink at **Icebergs Dining Room and Bar** (p78).

One Week

With a week, you can spare a couple of days to visit the majestic **Blue Mountains** (p97), fitting in a full day of bushwalking before rewarding yourself with a gourmet dinner. Back in Sydney, get out on the water on a yacht (p66), explore the Rocks (p53) or take a tour of **Sydney Harbour National Park** (p52). On your last night, explore infamous **Kings Cross** (p60).

by car or train. Staircases climb up to the bridge from both shores, leading to a footpath running the length of the eastern side. Cyclists take the western side. You can climb the southeastern pylon to the **Pylon Lookout** (Map p54; www.pylonlookout.com.au; adult/child/senior $9.50/4/6.50; ☺10am-5pm), or ascend the great arc on an adrenaline-charged **bridge climb** (p67).

Royal Botanic Gardens   GARDEN
(Map p54; www.rbgsyd.nsw.gov.au; Mrs Macquaries Rd; admission free; ☺7am-sunset) One of the most accessible ways to appreciate the harbour's magnificence is by taking a walk through the city's lush, 30-hectare botanical reserve, established in 1816 as the colony's vegetable patch. The highlight is following the signed walkways from the Opera House around Farm Cove, past picturesque Mrs Macquaries Point and alongside Woolloomooloo Bay to the **Domain** (Map p54) and the **Art Gallery of NSW** (p57). Alternatively, you can take an **Aboriginal Heritage Tour** (p65) or free **guided walk** (☺10.30am daily). Both depart from the Palm Grove Centre in the middle of the gardens.

Sydney Harbour National Park

                              NATURE RESERVE
This **national park** (Map p50) protects scattered pockets of harbourside bushland incorporating walking tracks, scenic lookouts, Aboriginal engravings and historic sites. Its southern side incorporates **South Head** and **Nielsen Park** in Vaucluse. On the North Shore, the park includes **North Head**, **Dobroyd Head**, **Middle Head**, **Georges Head** and **Bradleys Head**.

The park also includes five harbour islands: **Clark Island** off Darling Point, **Shark Island** off Rose Bay, **Rodd Island** in Iron Cove near Birkenhead, **Goat Island** off Balmain, and the small, fortified **Fort Denison** off Mrs Macquaries Point. All can be visited: Rodd and Goat by private vessel or water taxi ($7 landing fee per person, payable at the Sydney Harbour National Park Information Centre, p94) or via its website or telephone information service; Fort Denison on a package including ferry transport, day pass and 30-minute **guided history tour** (adult/concession $27/22; ☺12.15pm & 2.30pm & 10.45am Wed-Sun), also booked through the Sydney Harbour National Park Information Centre; Clark on a two-hour **Aboriginal culture tour** (☎02 9206 1111; www.captaincook.com.au/tribal; adult/concession/child $60/45/40; ☺Wed-Sun) run by the Tribal Warriors Association; and Shark on a ferry operated by **Captain Cook Cruises** (bookings ☎9358 1999, www.captaincook.com.au; adult/child $20/17; ☺five ferries daily from 9.45am-3pm). There is a cafe and restaurant on Fort Denison offering morning teas and lunches and the other islands have facilities for BYO picnickers.

CIRCULAR QUAY

Sydney Opera House LANDMARK

(Map p54; www.sydneyoperahouse.com; Bennelong Pt, Circular Quay E) Designed by Danish architect Jørn Utzon, this World Heritage Listed–building is Australia's most recognisable landmark. Visually referencing the billowing white sails of a seagoing yacht (but described by some local wags as more accurately resembling the sexual congress of turtles), it's a commanding presence on Circular Quay.

The complex comprises five performance spaces hosting dance, music, theatre and opera – the most spectacular is the Concert Hall. Program details and an online booking facility can be found on the website.

The best way to experience the opera house is, of course, to attend a performance, but you can also take a **guided tour** (☑9250 7250). The one-hour **Essential Tour** (adult/ concession $35/24.50; ☺every 30 min from 9am to 5pm) is an interactive audiovisual presentation that tells the story of the building's design and construction and visits one performance space. Tour tickets are cheaper if booked online. The two-hour **Backstage Tour** ($155; ☺7am) gives access to areas normally reserved for performers and production crews and includes a breakfast in the Green Room. Note that children 12 years and under are not permitted on the Backstage Tour. There are also special access tours for those with limited mobility at noon daily – bookings are essential for this and for the Backstage Tour. To purchase tickets on the spot, go to the Guided Tours desk in the Box Office Foyer.

Locals and visitors alike flock to the **Opera Bar** (p81) and fine-dining restaurant **Guillaume at Bennelong** (p76). Both venues offer extraordinary harbour views.

Customs House LANDMARK

(Map p54; www.cityofsydney.nsw.gov.au/library; 31 Alfred St; admission free; ☺8am-midnight Mon-Fri, 10am-midnight Sat, noon-5pm Sun, library 10am-7pm Mon-Fri, 11am-4pm Sat & Sun) Opposite the unforgivably dishevelled Circular Quay transport hub, this handsome 1885 building reopened to the public in 2005 after a major renovation. It now houses a branch of the Sydney City Libraries where it's possible to access the internet via free wi-fi or on the

library's own terminals ($2 per 30 minutes plus initial purchase of $1 access card), read a huge selection of international newspapers and magazines, use toilet facilities and admire a 1:500 model of Sydney displayed under the foyer's glass floor. The upmarket Cafe Sydney occupies the building's top floor, but its harbour view is considerably more impressive than its menu, so locals tend to patronise the ground-floor indoor/outdoor **Young Alfred Cafe** (☑9251 5192; cnr Alfred & Young Sts, Circular Quay; pizzas $24-32, pastas $22/26; ☺7am-11pm Mon-Sat) instead.

FREE Museum of Contemporary Art

MUSEUM

(Map p54; www.mca.com.au; 140 George St; admission free except for touring exhibitions; ☺10am-5pm) This spectacularly sited showcase for Australian and international contemporary art occupies a stately Art Deco building fronting Circular Quay West – the view from its ground floor cafe is an artwork in itself. The constantly changing exhibition program has a particularly strong multimedia focus, but painting and sculpture also feature prominently. The annual 'Primavera' show, held in spring, showcases Australian visual artists under the age of 35 and offers a fascinating survey of the local art scene.

THE ROCKS

The site of Sydney's first European settlement, this historically rich enclave at the foot of the Harbour Bridge's southern pylon has evolved unrecognisably from the days when its residents sloshed through open sewers and squalid alleyways. Here, sailors, whalers and rapscallions boozed and brawled shamelessly in countless harbourside pubs and nearly as many brothels and opium dens.

The Rocks remained a commercial and maritime hub until shipping services left Circular Quay in the late 1800s. A bubonic plague outbreak in 1900 continued the decline. Construction of the Harbour Bridge in the 1920s brought further demolition, entire streets disappearing under the bridge's southern approach.

It wasn't until the 1970s that the Rocks' cultural and architectural heritage was recognised. The ensuing tourism-driven redevelopment saved many old buildings, but has turned the area east of the bridge highway into a tourist trap where kitsch cafes

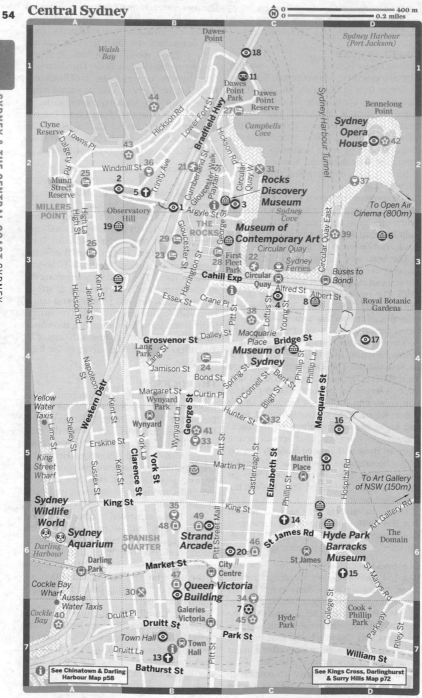

N 0 ———— 400 m
0 ———— 0.2 miles

Sydney Harbour
(Port Jackson)

Walsh
Bay

Dawes
Point

18

11
Dawes
Point
Park

27

Dawes
Point
Reserve

Bennelong
Point

Sydney-Harbour Tunnel

Sydney
Opera
House 42

Clyne
Reserve

Campbells
Cove

Towns Pl

Dalgety Rd

44

Hickson Rd

Lower Fort St

Bradfield Hwy

Hickson Rd

37

Munn
Street
Reserve

MILLERS
POINT

25

43

Windmill St

36

2

5

21

Trinity Ave

Cumberland St

Gloucester St

Playfair St

Circular Quay W

31

Rocks
Discovery
Museum

To Open Air
Cinema (800m)

High La

High St

19

Observatory
Hill

1

Argyle St

George St

3

Sydney
Cove

THE
ROCKS

Museum of
Contemporary Art

39

6

Kent St

Jenkins St

Hickson Rd

26

29

23

28

First
Fleet
Park

22

Circular Quay

Sydney
Ferries

Circular Quay East

Royal Botanic
Gardens

12

Harrington St

Cahill Exp

Circular
Quay

Alfred St

Albert St

Buses to
Bondi

Napoleon St

Essex St

Crane Pl

Pitt St

38

Loftus St

Young St

4

8

Western Dstr

Kent St

Grosvenor St

Lang
Park

Lang St

Dalley St

Macquarie
Place

Bridge St

17

Jamison St

24

Bond St

Spring St

O'Connell St

Bent St

Phillip St

Phillip La

Museum of
Sydney

Margaret St

Wynyard
Park

Curtin Pl

Bligh St

Macquarie St

16

Shelley St

Lime St

Yellow
Water
Taxis

Erskine St

Sussex St

Kent St

York St

Clarence St

Wynyard

George St

Wynyard La

York La

41

33

Hunter St

32

King
Street
Wharf

Martin Pl

Pitt St

Castlereagh St

Elizabeth St

Phillip St

Martin
Place

10

Hospital Rd

To Art Gallery
of NSW (150m)

King St

35

King St

9

Art Gallery Rd

Sydney
Wildlife
World

Sydney
Aquarium

Darling
Harbour

SPANISH
QUARTER

48

49

Strand
Arcade

Pitt Street Mall

46

20

14

St James Rd

St James

Hyde Park
Barracks
Museum

The
Domain

Darling
Park

Market St

City
Centre

47

Queen Victoria
Building

Cockle Bay
Wharf

Aussie
Water Taxis

30

Druitt Pl

Galeries
Victoria

34

7

45

Hyde
Park

College St

St Marys Rd

Cook +
Phillip
Park

Cockle
Bay

40

Druitt St

Town Hall

Town
Hall

13

Bathurst St

Druitt La

Pitt St

Park St

15

Parkway

Riley St

William St

See Chinatown & Darling
Harbour Map p58

See Kings Cross, Darlinghurst
& Surry Hills Map p72

and shops hocking stuffed koalas and ersatz didgeridoos reign supreme.

Cadmans Cottage HISTORIC BUILDING
(Map p54; ☎9247 5033; www.nationalparks.nsw. gov.au; 110 George St; ⊙9.30am-4.30pm Mon-Fri, 10am-4.30pm Sat & Sun) Built on a buried beach, Cadmans Cottage is Sydney's oldest house (1816). Its namesake, John Cadman, was Government Coxswain. Water police detained criminals here in the 1840s and it was later converted into a home for retired sea captains. Today it functions as an information centre for the NSW National Parks and Wildlife Service.

Sydney Observatory MONUMENT
(Map p54; www.sydneyobservatory.com; Watson Rd; free entry to bldg & grounds, daytime show adult/ child & concession $7/5, night viewings adult/child/ concession $15/10/12; ⊙10am-5pm) This Italianate building, built from Sydney sandstone

and sporting a copper-domed roof, sits atop Observatory Hill. You can visit the building and grounds, enjoy a celestial show in the 3D theatre or see the stars and planets through the telescopes at night (note that the hours of night viewings vary and that booking for these is essential). Sessions for the daytime shows are at 2.30pm and 3.30pm on weekdays and at 11am, noon, 2.30pm and 3.30pm on weekends.

SH Ervin Gallery   GALLERY

(Map p54; ✆9258 0173; www.nsw.nationaltrust.org. au/ervin.html; Watson Rd; adult/child over 11 years $7/5; ◷11am-5pm Tue-Sun) In the old military hospital building is the state headquarters of the National Trust as well as the trust's SH Ervin Gallery, which exhibits historical and contemporary Australian art.

Rocks Discovery Museum   MUSEUM

(Map p54; www.therocks.com; 2-8 Kendall Lane, The Rocks; admission free; ◷10am-5pm) This museum digs deep into the area's artefact-laden history and provides interactive insights into the lives of its people, including the original Indigenous inhabitants.

Beyond the **Argyle Cut** (Map p54), an impressive tunnel excavated by convicts, is **Millers Point**, a charming district of early colonial homes; stroll here to enjoy everything the Rocks is not. **Argyle Place** (Map p54) is an English-style village green overlooked by **Garrison Church** (Map p54), Australia's oldest house of worship (1848).

The wharves around Dawes Point are rapidly emerging from prolonged decay. Walsh Bay's Pier 4 houses the renowned **Sydney Theatre Company** (p84) and several other performance troupes. The impressive **Sydney Theatre** (p84) is across the road.

CITY EAST

Narrow lanes lead southeast from Circular Quay up the hill towards Sydney's historic parliament precinct on Macquarie Street.

Museum of Sydney   MUSEUM

(Map p54; www.hht.net.au; cnr Bridge & Phillip Sts; adult/child/family $10/5/20; ◷9.30am-5pm) Janet Laurence and Fiona Foley's evocative *Edge of the Trees* sculptural installation occupies pride of place in the forecourt of this sleek museum, marking the site of first contact between the British colonisers and Sydney's original inhabitants, the Gadigal people. It's one of a number of important artworks here, including Gordon Bennett's

1991 painting *Possession Island*, which greets visitors as they enter the foyer and presents a very different interpretation of Captain Cook's 1770 arrival and claim of British sovereignty from that presented in most history books. Built on the site of Sydney's first Government House (1788), the foundations of which can be spotted through panels of glass in the floor, the museum also offers a modest array of permanent exhibits documenting Sydney's early colonial history – brought to life through oral histories, artefacts and state-of-the-art interactive installations – as well as a changing exhibition program in its two temporary galleries.

Justice & Police Museum   MUSEUM

(Map p54; www.hht.net.au; cnr Albert & Phillip Sts; adult/child & concession $8/4; ◷10am-5pm) Occupying the old Water Police Station building (1858) opposite Circular Quay East, this small museum documents the city's dark and disreputable past through a constantly changing series of exhibitions.

Macquarie Street   HISTORIC PRECINCT

A swath of splendid sandstone colonial buildings graces this street, defining the central city's eastern edge. Many of these buildings were commissioned by Lachlan Macquarie, the first NSW governor with a vision of Sydney beyond its convict origins. He enlisted convict architect Francis Greenway to help realise his plans, and together they set a gold standard for architectural excellence that the city has – alas – never since managed to replicate.

Government House

(Map p54; ✆9931 5222; www.hht.net.au; admission free; ◷10.30am-3pm Fri-Sun, grounds 10am-4pm daily) Built between 1837 and 1845, this Gothic Revival building is just off Macquarie St in the Royal Botanic Gardens. The interior can only be visited on a tour, and bookings are essential.

Sydney Conservatorium of Music

(Map p54; www.usyd.edu.au/conmusic; Macquarie St) At the top of Bridge St, this was the Greenway-designed stables and servants' quarters designed to service an earlier government house. Governor Macquarie was usurped as governor before the house could be finished, partly because of the project's extravagance.

State Library of NSW

(Map p54; www.sl.nsw.gov.au; ◷9am-8pm Mon-Thu, 9am-5pm Fri, 10am-5pm Sat & Sun) Further south, the State Library holds over five million tomes and hosts innovative exhibitions in its galleries. If you are travelling with a laptop, the State Reference Library is a great place to access free wi-fi – just ask for the day's password at the desk.

Mint & Parliament House
(Map p54; www.hht.net.au, www.parliament.nsw. gov.au; admission free; ⊘9am-5pm Mon-Fri) Next to the library are the deep verandahs, formal colonnades and ochre tones of these twin 1816 buildings, originally wings of the infamous Rum Hospital, built by two Sydney merchants and the colony's principal surgeon in 1816 in return for a three-year monopoly on the rum trade. At the rear of the Mint building is one of central Sydney's most thoughtful and attractive contemporary architectural interventions, the headquarters of the Historic Houses Trust, designed by FJMT Architects and built in 2002.

Hyde Park Barracks Museum
(Map p54; www.hht.net.au; adult/child/family $10/5/20; ⊘9.30am-5pm) Built in 1819, the barracks functioned as quarters for Anglo-Irish convicts (aka Oz pioneers) from 1810 to 1848, an immigrant depot (1848–86) and government courts (1887–1979) before its current incarnation as a museum offering an absolutely fascinating insight into everyday convict life through installations and exhibits.

St James Church
(Map p54) Sydney's oldest church, built in 1819.

AROUND HYDE PARK
At the southern end of Macquarie Street, Hyde Park (Map p54), a much-loved civic space, has a grand avenue of trees and a series of delightful fountains. Its dignified Anzac Memorial (Map p72; www.rslnsw.com. au; admission free; ⊘9am-5pm) has an interior dome studded with one star for each of the 120,000 NSW citizens who served in WWI, and the pines near the entrance grew from seeds gathered at Gallipoli. St Mary's Cathedral (Map p54) overlooks the park from the east, while the 1878 Great Synagogue (Map p54; www.greatsynagogue.org.au; 187a Elizabeth St; adult/child & senior $8/5; ⊘tours noon Tue & Thu) is located off the park's western flank.

Australian Museum   MUSEUM
(Map p72; www.australianmuseum.net.au; 6 College St; adult/child/concession $12/6/8; ⊘9.30am-

5pm) Occupying a prominent position opposite Hyde Park, on the corner of William Street, this natural history museum stuffed its first animal just 40 years after the First Fleet dropped anchor and its curatorial philosophy and exhibits don't appear to have changed much in the intervening centuries. The only exceptions are the changing exhibits in the Indigenous Australians gallery, which often showcase contemporary Aboriginal issues and art.

TOP CHOICE ⟩ Art Gallery of NSW   ART GALLERY
(Map p54; www.artgallery.nsw.gov.au; Art Gallery Rd, The Domain; admission free, varied costs for touring exhibitions; ⊘10am-5pm Thu-Tue, to 9pm Wed) Highlights at this impressive gallery include 19th- and 20th-century Australian art, and Aboriginal and Torres Strait Islander art. There's also an excellent program of touring exhibitions from interstate and overseas. The controversial, much-discussed Archibald Prize (www.thearchibaldprize. com.au) exhibits here annually, with portraits of the famous and not-so-famous bringing out the art critic in everyone.

While here, consider having a drink in the cafe or eating in the restaurant, which has a lovely view across to Woolloomooloo Bay. See the website for details about guided tours, lectures, film screenings and the kids' program.

CENTRAL SYDNEY
Martin Place   MALL
(Map p54) Sydney lacks a true civic centre but Martin Place comes close. This grand pedestrian mall extends from Macquarie St to George St, and is lined with monumental financial buildings and the Victorian colonnaded General Post Office. There's a cenotaph commemorating Australia's war dead, an amphitheatre for lunchtime entertainment and plenty of places to sit and watch the weekday crowds. On weekends it's as quiet as a graveyard.

Town Hall   HISTORIC BUILDING
(Map p54) This impressive building (1874) is a few blocks south of Martin Place on the corner of George and Druitt Sts. The elaborate chamber room and concert hall inside match the fabulously ornate exterior.

Sydney Tower   TOWER
(Map p54; 86-100 Market St; adult/child/concession $25/15/20; ⊘9am-10.30pm) Accessed from the Westfield Sydney shopping mall, this observation tower allows you

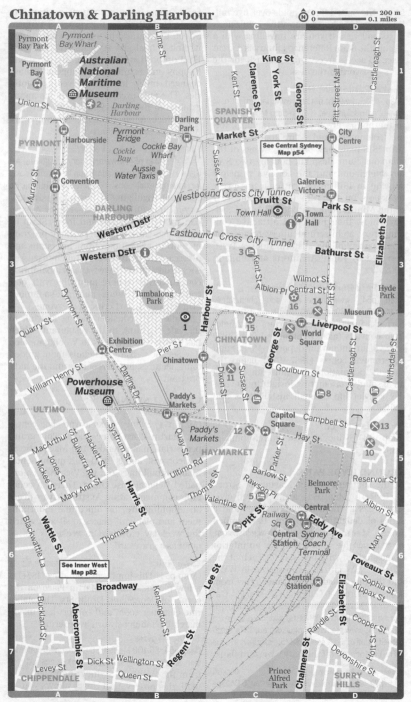

to enjoy a stunning 360-degree view of the city.

St Andrew's Cathedral CHURCH
(Map p54), Located next door to the Town Hall, this Anglican church was built around the same time and is Australia's oldest cathedral.

Next to St Andrew's, occupying an entire city block, the **Queen Victoria Building** (p93) is Sydney's most sumptuous shopping complex and a real highlight. Running a close second is the elegant **Strand Arcade** (p93) between Pitt St Mall and George St, which has a strong representation of Australian designer fashion. The newly opened **Westfield Sydney** is the city's glitziest shopping mall (Map p54) and has an excellent food hall on its fifth level.

Breathing life into the southwestern zone are Sydney's modest **Spanish Quarter** (Map p58) and thriving **Chinatown** (Map p58), an always-busy district of restaurants, shops and aroma-filled alleyways around Dixon St. Chinatown parties hard during Chinese New Year in late January/early February – streets throng with sideshows, digitally accompanied musicians and stalls selling everything from good-luck tokens to black-sesame ice-cream burgers (fear not: seeing jaunty, fire-breathing paper dragons after eating these is not a hallucinogenic effect).

DARLING HARBOUR
Cockle Bay on the city's western edge was once an industrial dockland full of factories, warehouses and shipyards. These days it's a sprawling and exceptionally tacky water-

front tourist development (www.darlinghar bour.com), and the only redeeming features are an excellent aquarium and maritime museum.

Visitors are confronted with an architectural spoil of grotesque flyovers, an ugly convention centre, chain hotels and overpriced eateries and shops – none will entice you to linger. If you're keen to find somewhere for a coffee or meal, we suggest skipping the overpriced and underwhelming outlets on **Cockle Bay Wharf** (Map p58) and **King St Wharf** (Map p54), instead making your way to **Jones Bay Wharf**, home to the excellent Flying Fish restaurant and reliable Café Morso. Both have great views.

Alternatively, stroll across the restored **Pyrmont Bridge** (Map p58), which cuts over this mess with a timeless dignity. It leads to **Pyrmont** home of the Sydney Fish Market (p60).

Darling Harbour and Pyrmont are serviced by ferry, monorail and Metro Light Rail (MLR).

Sydney Aquarium AQUARIUM
(Map p54; www.sydneyaquarium.com.au; Aquarium Pier; adult/child $35/18; ⏰9am-8pm) Celebrating the richness of Australian marine life, this phenomenally popular tourist attraction has three 'oceanariums' moored in the harbour: sharks, rays and humungous fish are in one; Sydney Harbour marine life and seals in the other two. Don't miss the kaleidoscopic colours of the Great Barrier Reef exhibit, platypuses and crocodiles at the Southern and Northern Rivers exhibits and

ⓘ MOËT & CHANDON BAR

Instead of paying the steep admission price to visit the Sydney Tower's viewing platform, make your way to its **Moët & Chandon Bar** (☑8223 3800; www.sydneytowerrestaurant.com.au; flute of Moët & 4 canapés $26; ☺from 4.30pm). The view is the same, but for roughly the same amount of money you'll also get a glass of champagne and some canapés, enabling you to enjoy the sunset in style. Note: booking is advised and a strict dress code applies (no trainers, shorts or flip-flops). Sunset is around 5pm in winter and 7.30pm in summer.

Also located here are the **360 Restaurant** (2-/3-course dinner excl drinks $85/90) and **Sydney Tower Buffet** (meals $49.50-85), both of which – like the bar – rotate 360 degrees over one hour.

the cute penguins in the Southern Oceans section.

Sydney Wildlife World ZOO
(Map p58; www.sydneywildlifeworld.com.au; Aquarium Pier; adult/child $35/18; ☺9am-5pm) This indoor wildlife zoo next to the aquarium offers the chance to get up close to local critters including koalas, red kangaroos, rock wallabies and scrub pythons. The displays of ants and other industrious bugs are unexpectedly intriguing.

Australian National Maritime Museum
MUSEUM
(Map p58; www.anmm.gov.au; 2 Murray St; general admission free; ☺9.30am-5pm) Beneath an Utzon-like roof, this museum examines Australia's strong relationship with the sea through exhibits arranged thematically. Exhibitions range from Aboriginal canoes to surf culture and the Navy. You'll need a **Big Ticket** (adult $32, child & concession $17, cheaper limited options available) to explore the destroyer HMAS *Vampire*, submarine HMAS *Onslow*, tall ship *James Craig* and replica of Captain Cook's *Endeavour*, all docked here.

Powerhouse Museum MUSEUM
(Map p58; www.powerhousemuseum.com; 500 Harris St, Ultimo; adult/child under 4/child 4-15yr & student card holders $10/free/5, additional costs for

special exhibits; ☺9.30am-5pm) Housed in the former power station for Sydney's defunct tram network, this sensational showcase for science and design is thought by many to be Australia's best museum. Visitors are encouraged to discover and be inspired by human ingenuity through exhibits that are always thoughtfully curated and often interactive.

Sydney Fish Market MARKET
(Map p50; ☑9004 1122; www.sydneyfishmarket.com.au; cnr Pyrmont Bridge Rd & Bank St, Pyrmont; ☺7am-4pm) With over 15 million kilograms of seafood shipped through here annually, the city's cavernous fish market is the place for a bewildering array of mud crabs, Balmain bugs, lobsters, oysters, mullet, rainbow trout and more. There are plenty of fishy restaurants, including an excellent yum cha venue, a deli, a wine centre, a sushi bar and an oyster bar. You can also picnic on the water. This is the world's second-largest fish market after Tokyo, and the early morning auctions are exciting to watch – but the only way you can do so is on a **Behind the Scenes Tour** (adult/child 6-12yr $20/10; ☺6.55-8.30am Mon & Thu). Note that reservations for this tour are essential and participants must wear closed-toe shoes. You can also book yourself in for a cooking class at the **Sydney Seafood School** (☑9004 1111; classes from $85), many conducted by local celebrity chefs.

The market is west of Darling Harbour on Blackwattle Bay, accessible on the MLR.

Chinese Garden of Friendship GARDEN
(Map p58; www.chinesegarden.com.au; adult/Australian student & child under 12yr $6/3; ☺9.30am-5.30pm) Built according to the balanced principles of Yin and Yang, this garden is an oasis of tranquillity in the otherwise hectic Darling Harbour.

KINGS CROSS
Riding high above the CBD under the big **Coca-Cola sign** (Map p72) – as much a Sydney icon as LA's Hollywood sign – 'the Cross' is a bizarre, densely populated dichotomy of good and evil. Strip joints, tacky tourist shops and backpacker hostels bang heads with trendy restaurants, funky bars and sybaritic guesthouses. If you visit, you'll quickly realise that, although it retains a sleazy and often tragically exploitative aura, the sense of menace here is more imaginary than real. Sometimes the razzle-dazzle has a sideshow appeal, sometimes walking up

Darlinghurst Rd promotes pity. Either way, it's never boring.

The gracious, tree-lined enclaves of **Potts Point** and **Elizabeth Bay** have been popular residential enclaves ever since Alexander Macleay, colonial secretary of New South Wales, built the Greek revival–style **Elizabeth Bay House** here between 1835 and 1839. Once set in 54 acres of land, his charming residence overlooks the harbour and is now open to the public as a **house museum** (www.hht.net.au; 7 Onslow Ave, Elizabeth Bay; adult/concession $8/4; ⊙Fri-Sun 9.30am-4pm).

Possibly the only word in the world with eight 'o's, **Woolloomooloo**, down **McElhone Stairs** from the Cross, was once a slum full of drunks and sailors (a fair few of whom were drunken sailors). Things are begrudgingly less pugilistic these days – the pubs are relaxed and **Woolloomooloo Wharf** is now home to the self-consciously hip **Blue Hotel** (www.tajhotels.com/sydney) and a swathe of upmarket restaurants. Outside the wharf is the famous **Harry's Cafe de Wheels**, where generations of Sydneysiders have stopped to sober up over a late-night 'Tiger' (beef pie served with mushy peas, mashed potato and gravy) on the way home from a big night at the Cross.

It's a 15-minute walk to the Cross from the city, or you could hop on a train. Buses 323-7, 324-5 and 333 from the city also pass through here.

INNER EAST

Once the heart of Sydney's entertainment and shopping scenes, **Oxford Street** (Map p72) is now sadly tawdry. Most shopping action has moved onto side streets such as Glenmore Rd in Paddington and Queen Street in Woollahra, while bars and restaurants have migrated to neighbouring **Surry Hills**. Despite this, the area around **Taylor Square** (Map p72) is still the decadent nucleus for the city's gay community. The **Sydney Gay & Lesbian Mardi Gras** (see p68) famously gyrates through here every February, and gay-centric pubs and clubs do a brisk trade every weekend. From the CBD, walk from Hyde Park or catch bus 378 from Railway Sq and buses 380, 389 and L82 from Circular Quay.

Wedged between Oxford and William Sts, the boho neighbourhood of Darlinghurst is home to cafes, boutique hotels and the **Sydney Jewish Museum** (Map p72; www.sydneyjewishmuseum.com.au; 148 Darlinghurst Rd;

adult/child/concession $10/6/7; ⊙10am-4pm Sun-Thu, to 2pm Fri, closed Jewish holidays).

Paddington, aka 'Paddo', is an upmarket residential suburb of restored Victorian-era terrace houses, many with attractive iron 'lace' detailing. The best time to explore its jacaranda-lined streets and laneways is on Saturday, when the **Paddington Market** (p93) is held. After braving the market's crowds, you can easily wander over to Surry Hills for lunch and a visit to the **Brett Whiteley Studio** (Map p50; www.brettwhiteley.org; 2 Raper St, Surry Hills; admission free; ⊙10am-4pm Sat & Sun), where works by the talented and famously drug-addicted Sydney artist (1939–92) are on show. The streets around here are home to a raffish mishmash of style-conscious urbanites and plenty of great pubs – be sure to sink a few schooners while you're in the area. Surry Hills is a short walk east of Central Station or south from Oxford St. Catch buses 301, 302 or 303 from Circular Quay.

Just southeast of Paddington, at the top end of Oxford Street, is the 220-hectare **Centennial Park** (Map p50), which has running, cycling, skating and horse-riding tracks, duck ponds, barbecue sites and sports pitches.

Near Moore Park, much of the former Sydney Showgrounds has been converted into the private **Fox Studios**. Nearby are the Aussie Stadium and Sydney Cricket Ground (Map p50).

EASTERN SUBURBS

Handsome **Rushcutters Bay** is about a five-minute walk east of Kings Cross; its harbourside park is a lovely spot for a walk or jog. The eastern suburbs extend out from here – a conservative conglomeration of European sedans, overpriced boutiques and heavily mortgaged waterside mansions. The harbour-hugging New South Head Rd passes through **Double Bay** and **Rose Bay**, and then climbs east into the gorgeous enclave of **Vaucluse**, where shady **Nielsen Park** is home to one of Sydney's best harbour beaches, complete with a netted swimming enclosure, crescent-shaped stretch of sand, picnic facilities and a popular cafe/restaurant. It's an idyllic spot to spend a day, preferably during the week as crowds are inevitable on weekends.

From the park, you can take an easy 10-minute loop walk along Bottle and Glass Rocks or make your way to the public park in the grounds of nearby **Strickland House**, built in 1856. The harbour views from here are wonderful. Alternatively, you can visit Vaucluse House (www.hht.net.au; Wentworth Rd, Vaucluse; adult/child/family $8/4/17; ☺9.30am-4pm Fri-Sun), an imposing, turreted specimen of Gothic Australiana set in gorgeous gardens. Explorer and political sabrerattler William Charles Wentworth lived here from 1828 to 1862.

At the entrance to the harbour is Watsons Bay, where you can enjoy blissful, briny breezes and a postcard-perfect view of the city skyline while eating takeaway fish and chips at Doyle's on the Wharf (☺10am-6pm; fish & chips $11.80-17.50) at Fisherman's Wharf. Nearby Camp Cove (Map p50) is one of Sydney's best harbour beaches, and there's a mostly male nude beach near South Head at Lady Bay. South Head has great views across the harbour entrance to North Head and Middle Head. The Gap is an epic cliff-top lookout where sunrises, sunsets, canoodling and suicide leaps transpire with similar frequency.

Buses 324 and 325 from Circular Quay service the eastern suburbs via Kings Cross (grab a seat on the left heading east to snare the best views). The Watsons Bay ferry leaves from Wharf 4 at Circular Quay, stopping at Double Bay and Rose Bay en route.

BONDI

Flanked by rugged rocks and multimillion-dollar apartments, Bondi lords it over every other beach in the city, despite the crowds, the crass boardwalk, the often-treacherous rips and the less-than-consistent surf breaks. The famous golden crescent attracts a daily cast of sunburned backpackers, bronzed locals, botoxed mini-celebs and body-worshipping Sydneysiders who swarm over the sand, surrounding clifftop paths and beachfront park. Perhaps it's the contradictions of the place that make it so compelling – everyone fits into the Bondi scene as long as they're wearing swimmers, sunblock and a smile. The suburb itself has a unique atmosphere due to its eclectic mix of traditional Jewish community members, dyed-in-the-wool Aussies, tourists who never went home and socially aspirational young professionals.

The simply sensational 5.5km Bondi to Coogee Clifftop Walk leads south from Bondi Beach along the cliff tops to Coogee via Tamarama, Bronte and Clovelly, interweaving panoramic views, patrolled beaches, sea baths, waterside parks and plaques recounting local Aboriginal myths and stories.

In Bondi, most of the decent pubs, bars and restaurants are found at the northern end of Campbell Pde, on Bondi Rd or on Glenayr Ave. Sunday's laid-back Bondi Markets (p93) are held in the grounds of the primary school on Campbell Parade, and the famous Bondi Icebergs Swimming Club, with its beachfront pool (p66), is at the southern end of the beach where the Eastern Beaches Walk starts.

Catch bus 380 or 333 from Circular Quay to get to North Bondi (note that this service doesn't stop at Bondi Beach, which is a five-minute walk from the bus interchange at Brighton Blvd) or take a bus or train to the transport interchange at Bondi Junction, from where bus 389 or 333 will take you straight to the beach.

INNER WEST

West of the centre is the higgledy-piggledy peninsula suburb of Balmain, once a notoriously rough neighbourhood of dockyard workers but now an arty enclave flush with beautifully restored Victorian houses, welcoming pubs, cafes and trendy shops. The Saturday market (p93) is a popular drawcard, particularly when combined with a stop at Sydney's most famous patisserie, Adriano Zumbo (p79). Catch a ferry from Wharf 5 at Circular Quay or bus 441/2 from the QVB.

Once a bohemian hotspot, the now-somnolent suburb of Glebe (Map p82) lies just southwest of the centre, close to Sydney University. There are a number of good budget accommodation options here, as well as one of the city's best-loved bookshops, Gleebooks (Map p82; www.gleebooks.com.au; 49 Glebe Point Rd; ☺9am-9pm). On Saturdays, Glebe markets (p93) overrun Glebe Public School. Glebe is a 10-minute walk from Central Station along side streets – avoid smoggy Broadway. Buses 431 and 433 run via George St along Glebe Point Rd; the 433 continues to Gladstone Park at the western end of Balmain. The MLR also stops here.

South of Sydney University is Newtown (Map p82), a melting pot of social and sexual subcultures. King St, its relentlessly urban main drag, is full of funky clothes stores, bookshops and cafes. Take the train, or bus 422, 423, 426 or 428 from Circular Quay or Castlereagh St to King St.

Southwest of Glebe is the predominantly Italian **Leichhardt**. Norton St is the place for pizza, pasta and debates about the relative merits and demerits of the Ferrari 430 Spider. Buses 436, 438 and 440 from Circular Quay service Leichhardt.

NORTH SHORE

At the northern end of the Harbour Bridge are the unexpectedly tranquil waterside suburbs of **Milsons Point** and **McMahons Point**. Both command astonishing city views as well as overlooking the shimmering waters of **Lavender Bay**. Situated here is one of Sydney's hidden treasures, **Wendy Whiteley's Secret Garden** (Map p50; admission free). This public garden was created by the widow of artist Brett Whiteley (an artist in her own right) on an old railway siding and is accessed through Clark Park, off Lavender St.

On the eastern shore of Lavender Bay is **Luna Park** (Map p50; www.lunaparksydney.com; 1 Olympic Pl, Milsons Point; admission free, multiride passes from $20; ⊙hours vary), a classic carnival in the Coney Island mould. Operating since 1935, it boasts a Ferris wheel, Rotor, Flying Saucer, Tumble Bug and other rides.

Just east of the bridge is the stately suburb of **Kirribilli**, home to **Admiralty House** and **Kirribilli House**, the Sydney residences of the governor general and prime minister respectively.

You can walk across the bridge to access Milsons Point, McMahons Point, Lavender Bay and Kirribilli, or take the short ferry ride from Wharves 4 and 5 at Circular Quay.

East of here are the upmarket residential suburbs of **Neutral Bay**, **Cremorne** and **Mosman**, known for their coves, harbourside parks and 'ladies who lunch'. On the northern side of Mosman is pretty-as-a-picture **Balmoral**, its beach fronting Hunters Bay. There's a netted swimming enclosure here, as well as the much-loved **Bather's Pavilion** (www.batherspavilion.com.au) restaurant, cafe and kiosk. The best way to visit all of these North Shore suburbs is by catching a ferry from Wharf 4 at Circular Quay.

Taronga Zoo   ZOO
(Map p50; www.taronga.org.au/taronga-zoo; Bradleys Head Rd, Mosman; adult/child 4-15/concession $43/21/30; ⊙9am-5pm) Sydneysiders often joke that the animals here are housed on the best tract of real estate in the city. Unfortunately, the zoo's knock-'em-dead views

and glorious profusion of trees go hand-in-hand with sadly cramped enclosures for the residents.

Twilight concerts take place during summer and you can even sign up for a 'Roar and Snore' overnight stay. Families can save money by taking advantage of the family tickets on offer.

Zoo ferries depart Circular Quay's Wharf 2 twice every hour – note that the entrance near the ferry stop doesn't open until 11am on weekdays. After alighting from the ferry, head to the ticket office and then to the nearby **Sky Safari cable car** (ticket included in admission), which will take you up the steep slope to the zoo's highest point. You'll look down onto a number of enclosures during the short trip. A **ZooPass** (adult/child 4-15 $49.50/24.50), sold at Circular Quay and elsewhere, includes return ferry rides and zoo admission and usually represents a 10% saving.

MANLY

Refreshingly relaxed **Manly** occupies a narrow isthmus between ocean and harbour beaches near North Head. It's the only place in Sydney where you can catch a harbour ferry to swim in the ocean. The scene here is radically different from that at Bondi: locals outnumber foreign tourists, and body boards are considered far more important accessories than designer bikinis or show-off 'budgy smugglers' (tight fitting men's swimsuits).

The helpful **Manly visitors centre** (Map p80; ⊕9977 1430; www.manlytourism.com; Manly Wharf; ⊙9am-5pm Mon-Fri, 10am-4pm Sat & Sun) is just outside the ferry wharf.

There's an array of slightly tacky cafes, pubs and restaurants at the wharf, the best of which is **Hugos Manly** (p79). For something special, make your way to the nearby **Manly Pavilion** (p79), which offers a glorious view of the harbour and is a wonderful spot to enjoy a leisurely lunch or sunset drinks. Next to the pavilion is **Oceanworld** (Map p80; www.oceanworld.com.au; W Esplanade; adult/child/concession $20/10/14; ⊙10am-5.30pm), a tired 1980s aquarium with underwater transparent tubes where you can see 3m sharks.

A somewhat scruffy pedestrian mall known as the **Corso** connects the suburb's ocean and harbour beaches. There are plenty of burger joints, juice bars and cafes along this stretch, but the quality is underwhelming and you're much better off buying a takeaway burger from **BenBry Burgers** (Map p80; www.benbryburgers.com.au; 5 Sydney Rd; burgers $7.50-14; ⊘7am-late), fish and chips from **Manly Fish Market** (Map p80; 11-27 Wentworth St; fish & chips $11.50; ⊘8am-8pm) or truly excellent coffee from **Barefoot Coffee Traders** (Map p80; cnr Sydney Rd & Whistler St; ⊘6.30am-5.30pm Mon-Fri, from 7.30am Sat & Sun) to enjoy on the beach.

One of the most popular activities in Manly is strolling along the **Manly Scenic Walkway**. This has two major components: the western stretch between Manly Cove and Spit Bridge, and the eastern stretch from Manly Cove to North Head.

The western walkway tracks around North and Middle Harbours, past waterside mansions, harbour beaches and viewpoints, an Aboriginal engraving site and through rugged Sydney Harbour National Park. It ends at Spit Bridge on Fisher Bay, from where you can catch bus 160, 179 or 189 into the CBD.

The eastern walkway follows Eastern Esplanade and Stuart St to Spring Cove, heads into the North Head section of Sydney Harbour National Park, and makes its way through the bush to the spectacular Fairfax Lookout on North Head. If you're here in the middle of the year, you may see migrating whales from this vantage point. From the lookout, walk the Fairfax Loop and then head back to the ferry wharf via the Cabbage Tree Bay Coastal Walk, which follows the sea-sprayed shoreline back to Manly via tiny **Fairy Bower Beach** and picturesque **Shelly Beach**.

To get to Manly, take the ferry from Circular Quay's Wharf 3 – it's one of Sydney's best-loved journeys.

NORTHERN BEACHES

The 20km-stretch of coast between Manly and well-heeled Palm Beach (where TV soap *Home and Away* is filmed) is often described as the most impressive urban surfing landscape in the world, and the locals who swim and catch the waves at Manly, Collaroy, Freshwater, Dee Why, North Narrabeen, Mona Vale, Newport, Bilgola, Avalon, Whale and Palm Beaches would be quick to agree.

To get to Collaroy, North Narrabeen, Mona Vale, Newport, Bilgola, Avalon, Whale and Palm Beaches from the CBD, catch bus No L90 from Railway Sq. From Manly Wharf, bus 136 goes to Chatswood via Curl Curl and Dee Why; bus 156 goes to McCarrs Creek via Dee Why, North Narrabeen and Mona Vale.

Ku-ring-gai Chase National Park PARK

(Map p50; www.nationalparks.nsw.gov.au; admission per car $11) This spectacular 14,928-hectare park, 24km from the city centre, forms Sydney's northern boundary. It's a classic mix of sandstone, bushland and water vistas, taking in over 100km of coastline along the southern edge of Broken Bay, where it heads into the Hawkesbury River.

Ku-ring-gai takes its name from its original inhabitants, the Guringai people, who were all but wiped out just after colonisation through violence at the hands of British settlers or introduced disease. It's well worth reading Kate Grenville's Booker-nominated *The Secret River* for an engrossing but harrowing telling of this story.

Remnants of Aboriginal life are visible today thanks to the preservation of more than 800 sites, including rock paintings, middens and cave art. To learn more, enter the park through the Mt Colah entrance and visit the **Kalkari Discovery Centre** (☑9472 9300; Ku-ring-gai Chase Rd; admission free; ⊘10am-4pm Mon-Fri, to 5pm Sat & Sun), which has displays and videos on Australian fauna and Aboriginal culture. There is a self-guided walk on which you can see swamp wallabies, bush turkeys, native ducks and goannas.

From the Resolute picnic area at **West Head** you can amble 100m to **Red Hands Cave**, where there are some very faint ochre handprints. About another 500m along **Resolute Track** (after a short steep section) is an Aboriginal engraving site. You can turn around or continue to one more site and make a 3.5km loop that takes in **Resolute Beach**. The view from the **West Head Lookout** is truly spectacular – don't miss it.

Less than 3km west of the picnic area along West Head Rd is the **Basin Track**, which offers an easy stroll to a good set of engravings. Approximately 2.5km further along the track is **the Basin** (day visit adult/child $3/2), a shallow round inlet where there is a **camping area** (☑9974 1011; www.basincampground.com.au; sites per adult/child $14/7) with barbecues, showers and toilets. Access is via the Basin Track or by ferry or water taxi from Palm Beach.

For information about the park, stop at the **Bobbin Head Information Centre** (☑9472 8949; Bobbin Inn, Bobbin Head; ⊘10am-4pm), operated by the NSW Parks & Wildlife Service. Also here are a marina, picnic areas,

Sydney is a good place for an introduction to Aboriginal culture and life.

For information on the ancient Aboriginal rock paintings and engravings around Sydney Harbour, check with the Sydney Harbour National Parks Information Centre (p94). You can see rock engravings up close on the **Manly Scenic Walkway** (p64) and in the **Ku-ring-gai Chase National Park** (p64).

The **Australian Museum** (p57), **Art Gallery of NSW** (p57), **Museum of Sydney** (p56), **Powerhouse Museum** (p60) and **Royal Botanic Gardens** (p52) all have exhibits and programs relating to Aboriginal life and culture.

Unfortunately, there are very few companies offering tours concentrating on Aboriginal culture. If you're lucky, you may be able to book a place on an **Aboriginal heritage tour** (☑9231 8134; adult/concession $28/13; ☺10am Fri) run in the Sydney Royal Botanic Gardens. Another option is to take an **Aboriginal culture cruise** out on Sydney Harbour (p52).

Many of the city's shops sell Indigenous-made artworks, artefacts and products, but it's sadly common to encounter Chinese-made fakes, works that breach the cultural copyright of Indigenous artists and galleries that exploit artist poverty by buying their art unreasonably cheaply. Try looking for products that are being produced and/or marketed by Indigenous-owned, not-for-profit operators. If buying from a gallery, make sure that it's a member of the Australian Indigenous Art Trade Association or the Australian Commercial Galleries Association. Art and artefacts should be properly documented (ie, by a certificate of authenticity from a reputable source, by photographs or by other evidence) and their provenance should be clearly stated (ie, where, when and by whom was it made? How has it come onto the market?).

---

a cafe and a boardwalk leading through mangroves.

Access to the park is by car or the **Palm Beach Ferry** (☑9974 2411; www.palmbeachferry.com.au; adult/child $6.90/3.50; ☺9am-7pm Mon-Fri, to 6pm Sat & Sun) that is run by Fantasea. This runs hourly from Palm Beach to Mackerel Beach, via the Basin. To get to Palm Beach from the CBD, catch bus L90 from Railway Sq or Bus 156 or 169 from Manly Wharf.

If you are arriving by car, enter Ku-ring-gai Chase Rd off Pacific Hwy, Mt Colah; Bobbin Head Rd, North Turramurra; or McCarrs Creek Rd, Terrey Hills.

🏃 Activities

Canoeing & Kayaking

Natural Wanders   BRIDGE TOURS
(☑0427 225 072; www.kayaksydney.com; per person from $65) Offers exhilarating morning tours around the harbour bridge, Lavender Bay, Balmain and Birchgrove.

Cycling

Bicycle NSW   CYCLING
(www.bicyclensw.org.au) Publishes *Cycling Around Sydney*, which details city routes and paths. It also sells Bicycle Australia's *Where to Ride Sydney* and the NRMA's *Great Cycling Rides in NSW* from its online store.

Sydney City Council   CYCLING
(www.cityofsydney.nsw.gov.au) Has information about inner city maps and routes on its website, provides links to cycling information offered by other councils and publishes the hard-copy, free-of-charge *Sydney Cycling Guide + Map*.

Centennial Park Cycles   CYCLING
(www.cyclehire.com.au; per day/week from $50/110; ☺9am-5pm) Branches in Randwick and Centennial Park.

Diving

Sydney's best shore dives are at Gordons Bay, north of Coogee; Shark Point, Clovelly; and Ship Rock, Cronulla. Popular boat-dive sites are Wedding Cake Island off Coogee, Sydney Heads, and off Royal National Park.

Dive Centre Bondi   DIVING
(Map p74; ☑9369 3855; www.divebondi.com.au; 198 Bondi Rd, Bondi; ☺8.30am-6pm Mon-Fri, from 7.30am Sat & Sun) One-day PADI Discover Scuba course $225; shore and boat dives; rentals.

Dive Centre Manly   DIVING
(Map p80; ☑9977 4355; www.divesydney.com.au; 10 Belgrave St, Manly; ☺9am-6pm Mon-Wed & Fri,

to 8pm Thu, 8am-6pm Sat & Sun) PADI Discover Scuba course $155, shore and boat dives, and rentals.

Horse Riding

Centennial Parklands Equestrian Centre
HORSE RIDING

(☎9332 2809; www.cpequestrian.com.au; Lang Rd, Paddington; ⊙9am-5pm) Several stables at the centre conduct lessons and rides for adults and children in tree-lined Centennial Park, Sydney's favourite urban green space (one-hour, 3.6km horse rides $70 to $80, one-hour lessons $100 to $135).

In-Line Skating

The beach promenades at Bondi and Manly and the paths of Centennial Park are the favoured spots for skating.

Rollerblading Sydney
SKATING

(☎0411 872 022; www.rollerbladingsydney.com.au; lessons per hr $50) Rentals, lessons and tours.

Skater HQ
SKATING

(Map p80; www.skaterhq.com.au; 2/49 North Steyne, Manly; hire per hr adult/child $20/15; ⊙10am-7pm Mon-Thu, 10am-8pm Fri, 9am-8pm Sat, 9am-6pm Sun) Hires rollerblades, scooters and skateboards.

Sailing

Sydney has dozens of yacht clubs and sailing schools, including the following:

EastSail Sailing School
SAILING

(☎9327 1166; www.eastsail.com.au; d'Albora Marina, New Beach Rd, Rushcutters Bay; cruises per adult/child from $119/89, 2-day 'start yachting' course $575; ⊙9am-6pm) A sociable outfit offering 'Start Yachting' courses, more advanced outings and morning/sunset cruises.

Sydney by Sail
SAILING

(Map p58; ☎9280 1110; www.sydneybysail.com.au; Festival Pontoon, National Maritime Museum, Darling Harbour) Daily harbour sailing tours (three hours, adult/child $150/$75), introductory weekend sailing courses ($495), whale-watching cruises (six hours, $175) and plenty of other options.

Surfing

On the South Shore, get tubed at Bondi, Tamarama, Coogee, Maroubra and Cronulla. The North Shore is home to a dozen gnarly surf beaches between Manly and Palm Beach, including Curl Curl, Dee Why, Narrabeen, Mona Vale and Newport.

Let's Go Surfing
SURFING

(Map p74; ☎9365 1800; www.letsgosurfing.com.au; 128 Ramsgate Ave, Bondi; 2hr group lesson incl. use of board & wetsuit adult/child from $89/79; ⊙9am-5pm, later in summer) Also offers board and wetsuit hire ($30 for two hours).

Manly Surf School
SURFING

(Map p80; ☎9977 6977; www.manlysurfschool.com; North Steyne Surf Lifesaving Club, Manly; 2hr group lesson incl. use of board & wetsuit adult/child $60/50; ⊙9am-6pm) Lessons cater to all levels of fitness, ability and age.

Swimming

There are 100-plus public swimming pools in Sydney, and many beaches have protected rock pools. Harbour beaches offer sheltered and shark-netted swimming, but nothing beats Pacific Ocean waves. Just remember: always swim within the flagged lifeguard-patrolled areas, and never underestimate the surf.

Andrew 'Boy' Charlton Pool
SWIMMING

(www.abcpool.org; 1C Mrs Macquaries Rd, The Domain; adult/child/locker $5.60/2/3; ⊙6am-7pm Sep-Apr, 1hr later in daylight saving time) A 50m outdoor saltwater pool and harbour-view cafe.

Bondi Icebergs Swimming Club
SWIMMING

(Map p74; http://icebergs.com.au; ⊙6am-6.30pm Mon-Wed & Fri, 6.30am-6.30pm Sat & Sun; adult/child & senior $5/3) Sydney's most famous swimming pool commands the best view in Bondi and has a cute little cafe.

Dawn Fraser Baths
SWIMMING

(www.lpac.nsw.gov.au/Dawn-Fraser-Baths.html; Elkington Park, Glassop St, Balmain; adult/child & student/senior $4/2.80/2.10; ⊙7.15am-6.30pm Oct-Nov & Mar-Apr, 6.45am-7pm Dec-Feb) This magnificently restored late-Victorian tidal-flow seawater pool (1884) offers a small beach at low tide and yoga classes ($12.20) during summer.

North Sydney Olympic Pool
SWIMMING

(www.northsydney.nsw.gov.au; 4 Alfred St South, Milsons Point; adult/child/senior $6.50/3.20/5.20; ⊙5.30am-9pm Mon-Fri, 7am-7pm Sat & Sun) Next to Luna Park, right on the harbour. A place of legends – many world records have been set here. For $18 you can also use the gym, sauna and spa.

Wylie's Baths
SWIMMING

(www.wylies.com.au; Neptune St, Coogee; adult/child/senior $4/0.50/1.50; ⊙7am-7pm daylight saving time, to 5pm rest of year) Superb seawater pool built in 1907. After your swim,

Organised kids' activities ramp up during school holidays (December/January, April, July and September). Check www.sydneyforkids.com.au, www.kidfriendly.com.au and the free *Sydney's Child* magazine for listings.

Most kids love the **Sydney Aquarium** (p59), **Sydney Wildlife World** (p60), **Australian National Maritime Museum** (p60) and **Powerhouse Museum** (p60) at Darling Harbour. Elsewhere, **Taronga Zoo** (p63) and **Luna Park** (p63) are sure-fire entertainers. Visits to swimming pools (p66), surfing lessons (p66), and horse or pony rides in Centennial Park (p66) should please even the most exacting under-ager, and **Nielsen Park** (p67) in Vaucluse is the perfect choice if the younger members of your entourage need to stretch their legs and burn up some energy. It's also a great spot for sandcastle building!

take a yoga class ($14), enjoy a massage or have a coffee at the kiosk, which has magnificent views of the Pacific Ocean.

☞ Tours

There are countless tours available in Sydney. You can book most of them at the visitors' centres (p94).

City Bus Tours

City Sightseeing CITY TOUR
(www.city-sightseeing.com) This company operates two sightseeing buses around Sydney. One ticket (adult/child/student/senior 24-hour ticket $35/20/30/25, 48-hour ticket $56/32/48/40; open every 20 minutes from 8.30am to 7.30pm) covers both. Buses leave Central Station every 15 to 20 minutes and can be boarded at any stop. Buy your ticket on the bus. One of the two services is **Sydney Tour**, which has a 90-minute, 23-stop hop-on, hop-off loop from Central Station through Pyrmont, Darling Harbour, the Rocks, Circular Quay, the city centre, Kings Cross, the Domain and Macquarie Street. The other tour offered is **Scenic Bondi & Bay Tour**, a 90-minute nine-stop hop-on, hop-off loop starting at Central Station and stopping at Sydney Tower, Paddington, Bondi Beach, North Bondi, Rose Bay, Double Bay and the Australian Museum.

Harbour Cruises

Captain Cook Cruises CRUISES
(Map p54; ☎9206 1111; www.captaincook.com.au; Wharf 6, Circular Quay) Offers a 1¼-hour 'Harbour Highlights' cruise (adult/child 5-14 years/student $30/16/26) and a 24-hour 'hop-on hop-off' 'Harbour Express' pass with entry to Fort Denison, Shark Island and Taronga Zoo (adult/child/student $58/32/36). Also at Aquarium Wharf, Darling Harbour.

Sydney Ferries FERRIES
(Map p54; www.sydneyferries.nsw.gov.au) Visit the website or Circular Quay ticket booth to find out everything there is to know about touring the harbour by ferry.

Scenic Flights

Sydney Seaplanes SCENIC FLIGHTS
(☎9974 1455; www.seaplanes.com.au; 15-/30-min scenic flights $170/235, flight & lunch packages $460 555) Take a seaplane flight from Rose Bay to the Berowra Waters Inn on the Hawkesbury or Jonah's at Whale Beach on Sydney's Northern Beaches. It also offers flights around Sydney Harbour and 30-minute flights to Newcastle ($175 to $225).

Walking Tours

Sydney Architecture Walks WALKS
(☎bookings 8239 2211; www.sydneyarchitecture.org; adult/concession $35/25) These two-hour, architect-led tours run from September to May, departing from the Museum of Sydney. There's a tour of the city on most Wednesdays at 10.30am, one concentrating on the Opera House on Saturdays at 10.30am and an occasional tour focusing on the industrial heritage of the Rocks (various times).

BridgeClimb BRIDGE CLIMBS
(Map p54; ☎9240 1100; www.bridgeclimb.com; 5 Cumberland St, The Rocks; adult $188-268, child aged 10-15 $128-188; ⊙3½hr tours around the clock) Don a headset, an umbilical cord and a naff grey jumpsuit and you'll be ready to embark on the climb of your life! Book well in advance.

✸ Festivals & Events

Sydney has plenty of festivals and special goings-on year-round. Visitor centres will be able to advise you what's on when you're in town.

January

Big Day Out   LIVE MUSIC
(www.bigdayout.com) Open-air concert in
January featuring many local and international performers and bands.

Sydney Festival   ARTS
(www.sydneyfestival.org.au) This massive
event in January floods the city with art
and includes free outdoor concerts in the
Domain.

February

Chinese New Year   CULTURAL
(www.cityofsydney.nsw.gov.au/cny) Colourful
celebration featuring food, fireworks and
much more. Actual dates vary according
to the phases of the moon.

Sydney Gay & Lesbian Mardi Gras
                                            GAY PRIDE
(www.mardigras.org.au) The highlight of this
world-famous festival is the over-the-top,
sequined Oxford St parade that culminates
in a bacchanalian party at the Entertainment Quarter.

Tropfest   FILM
(www.tropfest.com) The world's largest short-
film festival takes over the Domain for
one night.

March/April

Royal Easter Show   AGRICULTURE
(www.eastershow.com.au) Twelve-day agricultural show and funfair at Homebush Bay.

May

Sydney Writers' Festival   LITERATURE
(www.swf.org.au) The country's pre-eminent
literary shindig is held at various venues,
including Pier 4/5 at Walsh Bay.

June

Biennale of Sydney   ARTS
(www.biennaleofsydney.com.au) High-profile
festival of art and ideas held every even-
numbered year.

September

Rugby League Grand Final   SPORT
(www.nrl.com) The two teams left standing
in the National Rugby League (NRL) meet
to decide who's best.

December

Sydney to Hobart Boat Race   SPORT
(www.rolexsydneyhobart.com) On 26 December, Sydney Harbour is a sight to behold
as hundreds of boats crowd its waters

to farewell the yachts competing in this
gruelling race.

New Year's Eve   FIREWORKS
(www.cityofsydney.nsw.gov.au/nye) The biggest
party of the year, with a flamboyant firework display on the Harbour Bridge.

🛏 Sleeping

You'll sleep well (though not cheaply) in
Sydney. The winter months sometimes deliver bargains, but between November and
February you should expect prices to jump
by as much as 40%. The reality is that the
city is busy all year – we advise you to book
ahead and shop around for the best price.

Read up on Sydney's neighbourhoods before you decide where to stay: party animals
should head for Kings Cross, Potts Point,
Darlinghurst, Surry Hills or Bondi; keen
sightseers should shoot for the Rocks, the
CBD, Darling Harbour or Chinatown. If you
want to feel like a local, try Glebe, Manly or
Newtown.

In this chapter, a budget room ($) is
classified as costing under $110 per night.
Midrange rooms ($$) cost between $110
and $200, and top-end rooms ($$$) start at
$200 a night. The prices we have given don't
apply during the busy Christmas/New Year
period, when rates skyrocket.

CIRCULAR QUAY & THE ROCKS

TOP CHOICE Sydney Harbour YHA   HOSTEL $
(Map p54; ☏8272 0900; www.yha.com.au/
hostels/nsw/sydney-surrounds/sydney-harbour;
110 Cumberland St, The Rocks; dm $44-59, d $148-
170, d with harbour view $165-185; ❄@🛜) The
view from the rooftop terrace and deluxe
rooms at this recently opened and exceptionally well-run YHA hostel is fabulous –
right over Circular Quay to the Opera House.
The modern dorms and private rooms are
neat, comfortable and air-conditioned; all
have private bathrooms. The building was
designed to be environmentally sustainable
and incorporates an archaeology education
centre that reflects its location amid the archaeological remnants of the early colony.

The Russell   BOUTIQUE HOTEL $$$
(Map p54; ☏9241 3543; www.therussell.com.au;
143a George St, The Rocks; d with private bathroom
$199-245, with shared bathroom $130-199) A re-
cent renovation has seen this long-standing
favourite divest itself of frills and furbelows
and achieve some contemporary style as
well as a downstairs wine bar. The rooftop

Gay and lesbian culture forms a vocal, vital part of Sydney's social fabric. **Taylor Square** (Map p72) on Oxford St is the centre of what is arguably the second-largest gay community in the world after San Francisco, while Newtown is home to Sydney's lesbian scene.

Sydney's famous **Gay & Lesbian Mardi Gras** (www.mardigras.org.au) draws over 700,000 spectators, and the Mardi Gras also runs the annual **Sleaze Ball**, held in late September/early October at the **Horden Pavilion** in Moore Park.

Free gay media includes *SX*. Online resources include www.ssonet.com.au (Sydney's main gay newspaper), www.lotl.com (Sydney's monthly lesbian magazine) and the G&L pages of the monthly *Time Out* magazine.

Most accommodation in and around Oxford St is very gay-friendly. For frolicking, go for a wander along the city end of Oxford Street or check out the following:

ARQ
NIGHTCLUB

(Map p72; www.arqsydney.com.au; 16 Flinders St, Darlinghurst; cost varies; ⊙9pm-7am Thu, to 9am Fri-Sun) This flash megaclub has a cocktail bar, a recovery room and two dance floors with high-energy house music and drag shows. The Moist night for gay girls is held on the last Friday of every month.

Imperial Hotel
CABARET VENUE

(Map p82; www.theimperialhotel.com.au; 35 Erskineville Rd, Erskineville; public bar/cabaret bar/cellar dance club free/$10/$5; ⊙3-11.30pm Mon, to midnight Tue & Wed, to 4am Thu, to 6am Fri & Sat, 1pm-midnight Sun) The drag shows at this Art Deco pub inspired *Priscilla, Queen of the Desert* (the opening scene was filmed here), and there's a Priscilla tribute show every Saturday night ($10). Any drag queen worth her sheen has played the Cabaret Bar.

Midnight Shift
NIGHTCLUB/BAR

(Map p72; www.themidnightshift.com.au; 85-91 Oxford St, Darlinghurst; video bar free, club cover varies; ⊙noon-4am Mon-Wed, to 6am Thu & Fri, 2pm-6am Sat & Sun) The grande dame of the Oxford Street scene, the Shift has two quite distinct venues. The downstairs video bar attracts an unpretentious mix of blokes, twinks and bears. Upstairs, there's a club with grinding beats and lavish drag productions.

Oxford Hotel
BAR

(Map p72; www.theoxfordhotel.com.au; 134 Oxford St, Taylor Sq, Darlinghurst; admission free; ⊙10am-late) Another year, another owner, another refit...another panic that this treasured venue might (shudder) go straight. Fortunately, so far, so gay. Three very different floors await.

Finally, if you simply must bring home a gift, the **Tool Shed** (Map p72; www.toolshed.com.au; Level 1, 81 Oxford St; ⊙24hr) has sex toys that will both fascinate and horrify airport screeners.

garden and location just minutes from Circular Quay are major drawcards, but only a few rooms have air-con.

Lord Nelson Brewery Hotel
BOUTIQUE HOTEL **$$**

(Map p54; ☎9251 4044; www.lordnelson.com.au; 19 Kent St, The Rocks; d $190, without bathroom $130; ✲🛜) Built in 1841, this boutique sandstone pub has its own brewery (try a pint of 'Nelson's Blood') and offers elegantly understated rooms, many with walls of the original exposed stone. Bathrooms are regal – even the shared ones.

Park Hyatt
HOTEL **$$$**

(Map p54; ☎9241 1234; www.sydney.park.hyatt.com; 7 Hickson Rd, The Rocks; r $695-1045; ✲@🛜☀) Luxury meets location at Sydney's most expensive hotel. Bookending Circular Quay with the Opera House, the rooms, service levels and facilities are second to none, although the building itself lacks architectural grace (and then some).

Observatory Hotel
HOTEL **$$$**

(Map p54; ☎9256 2222; www.observatoryhotel.com.au; 89-113 Kent Street, The Rocks; r $315-615; ✲@🛜☀) Giving the Park Hyatt a run for its money in the luxury stakes, this sleek operation is housed in an undistinguished building in the Rocks, but more than makes amends with its extremely elegant and comfortable rooms. There's a day spa, restaurant, gym, indoor pool and tennis court.

B&B Sydney Harbour   B&B **$$-$$$**
(Map p54; ☎9247 1130; www.bedandbreakfast sydney.com; 140-142 Cumberland St, The Rocks; s $165-214, without bathroom $140-165, d $178-260, without bathroom $155-178; ❄) Rooms at this century-old guesthouse in the Rocks sport a pleasant, traditional decor with an Australiana flavour; some have harbour views. The lavish breakfast can be enjoyed in the pretty courtyard. Not all rooms have air-con.

CITY CENTRE

Vibe Hotel   HOTEL **$$**
(Map p58; ☎9282 0987; www.vibehotels.com.au; 111 Goulburn St; d $165-220, ste $220-300; ❄@☞≋) The rooms are spacious and extremely well priced at this excellent choice near Central Station. All have a seating area, flat-screen TV, work desk and enormous closet. There's a ground-floor cafe and a gym, a sauna and a good-sized pool on the outdoor deck. Breakfast costs an extra $22 to $28.

Westend Backpackers   HOSTEL **$**
(Map p58; ☎9211 4588; http://legendhasitwestend. com.au; 412 Pitt St; dm $19-35, s with private bathroom $85-95, d $87-97; ❄@☞) For the cheapest sleep in Sydney, check into the 32-bed 'Church' dorm at this well-run hostel. You'll save even more money by taking advantage of the free pasta and rice supplied in the excellent communal kitchen, and the free wine and cheese served in the welcoming communal lounge on Friday nights. Plus it's clean, comfortable and secure.

Y Hotel   HOSTEL **$-$$$**
(Map p72; ☎9264 2451; www.yhotel.com.au; 5-11 Wentworth Ave; dm $35-65, s $70-202, d $70-250; ❄@☞) Package tourists are more in evidence than party animals at this popular budget hotel. Perfectly located in a quiet pocket of the city close to Hyde Park, Oxford St, train stations and bus stops, it offers simple, well-maintained and extremely clean sleeping options that span the gamut from small dorms to spacious studios with en suites and kitchenettes.

Establishment Hotel   BOUTIQUE HOTEL **$$$**
(Map p54; ☎9240 3100; www.merivale.com; 5 Bridge Lane; r $445-800; ❄@☞) Through this door pass discreet celebrities, style-

conscious couples and execs hoping for a nooner with their assistant. What the hotel lacks in facilities is more than made up for in glamour, although light sleepers should beware – the hotel is in Sydney's most happening (and noisiest) entertainment complexes.

Wake Up!   HOSTEL **$**
(Map p58; ☎9288 7888; www.wakeup.com.au; 509 Pitt St; dm $32-40, d or tw $112-132, without bathroom $98-118; ❄☞≋) This converted 1900 department store on top of Sydney's busiest intersection is a convivial, colourful, professionally run hostel with a tour desk, 24-hour check-in, sunny cafe, bar and pronounced party atmosphere. Dorms have four to 10 beds.

Sydney Central YHA   HOSTEL **$**
(Map p58; ☎9218 9000; www.yha.com.au/hostels/ nsw/sydney-surrounds/sydney-central; 11 Rawson Pl; dm $36-45, d with private bathroom $108-132; ❄@☞≋) Near Central Station, this 1913 heritage-listed 556-bed monolith was renovated in recent years and is a safe if somewhat utilitarian choice. Rooms are brightly painted and the kitchens and cinema room are great, but the highlight is lazing in the heated rooftop pool.

CHINATOWN & DARLING HARBOUR

Pensione Hotel   BOUTIQUE HOTEL **$$**
(Map p58; ☎9265 8888; www.pensione.com.au; 631-635 George St; s/d from $100/135; ❄@☞) This tastefully reworked post office features 68 smart, neutrally shaded rooms. There's also a communal lounge with kitchenette. Mark Rothko prints and a wooden staircase warm the simple, restrained surrounds. Aim for a rear room away from traffic noise. Breakfast is an extra $10.

Medina Grand Sydney   APARTMENTS **$$**
(Map p58; ☎9211 8633; www.rydges.com/ capitolsquare; cnr George & Campbell Sts; studio $160-430, 1-bed apt $210-500, 2-bed apt $280-650; ❄☞≋) Near both Chinatown and Darling Harbour but with double-glazed windows to ensure a good night's sleep, this apartment hotel offers spacious, fully equipped apartments and smaller studio rooms with kitchenettes. The apartments offer the best value.

KINGS CROSS & POTTS POINT

The Original Backpackers   HOSTEL **$**
(Map p72; ☎9356 3232; www.originalbackpack ers.com.au; 160-162 Victoria St, Kings Cross; dm

$25-32, d with private bathroom $90-95, d with shared bathroom $80-85; @☎) Operating for over three decades, this exceptionally well-run hostel occupies two character-filled Victorian houses filled with contemporary art (the owners also run an art gallery). A new wing hosts double rooms with en-suite bathrooms, fridge, TV and DVD; dorms and doubles with shared bathroom are in the original houses and feature polished floorboards and high ceilings. Smack-bang in the middle of the party precinct, it runs a busy activities program and has a convivial courtyard area and excellent communal kitchen with food lockers.

Diamant Hotel
HOTEL $$-$$$
(Map p72; ☎9295 8888; www.8hotels.com/diamant-boutique-hotel-sydney-welcome.html; 14 Kings Cross Rd, Kings Cross; d $165-350, ste $305-375; ❋@☎) Standing as proudly tall as the nearby Coca-Cola sign, this super-sleek member of the 8 Hotels chain offers a choice of room styles, many complete with views and courtyards. King-size beds and quality linen feature in a seriously sophisticated package, with the only disappointment being the lack of wi-fi access in rooms. The popular Time to Vino wine bar is on the ground floor. No breakfast.

Simpsons of Potts Point
B&B $$$
(☎9356 2199; www.simpsonspottspoint.com.au; 8 Challis Ave, Potts Point; r $235-335, ste $325-385; ❋@☎) An 1892 red-brick villa at the quiet end of a busy cafe strip, the perennially popular Simpsons looks towards Laura Ashley and her ilk for decorative flourishes. The downstairs lounge and breakfast room are lovely, and rooms are both comfortable and impeccably clean. An excellent, albeit conservative, choice.

Eva's Backpackers
HOSTEL $
(☎9358 2185; www.evasbackpackers.com.au; 6-8 Orwell St, Kings Cross; dm $30-34, d $80-92; ❋@☎) This long-running favourite offers a friendly communal kitchen, rooftop terrace and free wi-fi/internet. Though basic, the rooms and bathrooms are clean and well-maintained. A few of the upstairs dorms have air-con, but the rest of the building gets hot in summer.

Victoria Court Hotel
B&B $$
(Map p72; ☎9357 3200; www.victoriacourt.com.au; 122 Victoria St, Potts Point; s $99-132, d $110-280; ❋@☎) Chintzy charm reigns supreme at this faded but well-run B&B, which has 25 rooms in a pair of three-storey 1881 brick terrace houses. The more-expensive rooms are larger and have balconies.

INNER EAST

Kirketon
BOUTIQUE HOTEL $$
(Map p72; ☎9332 2011; www.8hotels.com; 229 Darlinghurst Rd, Darlinghurst; r $145-239; ❋@) The Kirketon's 40 designer rooms are as impeccably turned out as its hip clientele and hot staff. The stylishly sparse standard rooms are cramped – upgrade to premium, executive or superior if possible. If not, never fear: you can always hang out in the glam Eau de Vie bar.

Hotel Altamont
BOUTIQUE HOTEL $$
(Map p72; ☎9360 6000; www.8hotels.com; 207 Darlinghurst Rd, Darlinghurst; r from $135; ❋@☎) The Rolling Stones have stayed in this Georgian pile, hence the name. It's been given a postmodern makeover since their stay, with the rooms now more Zen than rock and roll grunge. The foyer bar/breakfast room is a great spot to sit and watch the daily Darlinghurst parade go by. Excellent value.

TOP CHOICE Adina Apartment Hotel Sydney
APARTMENTS $$$
(Map p72; ☎9212 1111; www.adinahotels.com.au; 359 Crown St, Surry Hills; 1-bed apt $250-350, 2-bed apt $350-460; ❋@☎❄) In the heart of the Surry Hills entertainment precinct, the recently renovated Adina offers 85 exceptionally stylish and well-equipped apartments. Bill's, one of Sydney's most famous cafes, is in the same building and will provide room service dinners on request. Ask for an upper-floor apartment, as the lower floors can be noisy.

150 Apartments
APARTMENTS $$$
(Map p72; ☎1300 246 835; www.apartmenthotel.com.au; 150 Liverpool Street, Darlinghurst; $249-599; ❋☎) Designed by minimalist masters Engelen Moore, these ferociously fashionable two-bedroom apartments near Hyde Park are fully equipped with designer furniture and appliances. There are discount rates for long-terms stays.

Medusa
BOUTIQUE HOTEL $$$
(Map p72; ☎9331 1000; www.medusa.com.au; 267 Darlinghurst Rd, Darlinghurst; r $310-420; ❋☎) There's not a serpent in sight at this theatrically decorated designer hotel. Eighteen seductive rooms open onto a tranquil courtyard with a reflection pool or onto tree-lined Darlinghurst Road. Staff will happily welcome your chihuahua, but aren't crazy about kids.

City Crown Motel   MOTEL **$$**

(Map p72; [9331 2433; www.citycrownmotel.com.au; 289 Crown St, Surry Hills; r $110-150, f $140-177; ❄@) In an unbeatable Surry Hills location, this nondescript three-storey motel has basic rooms with a bright colour scheme and so-so beds. Escape to the balcony (every room has one) or to the streetside cafe to plan your next fun foray. Breakfast costs extra.

Hughenden   GUESTHOUSE **$$-$$$**

([9363 4863; www.hughendenhotel.com.au; 14 Queen St, Woollahra; r $148-328, apt $228-288; ❄@🖢) This 1870s Italianate guesthouse is owned by a writer of children's novels, and has a cheerfully bohemian ambience that comes to the fore during the Thursday and Friday jazz nights. The well-worn rooms feature eclectic furnishings; some are small and dark but the best have balconies overlooking pretty Queen Street. Pet friendly.

Manor House   BOUTIQUE HOTEL **$$$**

(Map p72; [9380 6633; www.manorhouse.com.au; 86 Flinders St, Paddington; r $175-350, ste $400; ❄@🖢) Step off busy Flinders St and step back in time to 1850 as you enter this grand mansion, complete with extravagant chandeliers, moulded ceilings, Victorian tiling and enough brocade for a queen (many of whom stay here, especially during Mardi Gras).

Arts Hotel   HOTEL **$$**

(Map p72; [9361 0211; www.sullivans.com.au; 21 Oxford St, Paddington; r $140-195; ❄🖢🏊) Another choice popular with gay travellers, this well-run 64-room motel in 'Paddinghurst' has bland but comfortable rooms that could do with a makeover. On the positive side, there's free car parking, bicycles are available for guest use and the garden courtyard has a good-sized solar-heated pool. Breakfast costs an extra $15 to $20.

BONDI

Bondi Beach House GUESTHOUSE $$

TOP CHOICE (Map p74; 0417 336 444; www.bondi beachhouse.com.au; 28 Sir Thomas Mitchell Rd; s $95-135, without bathroom $80-110, d $170-300, without bathroom $120-215, ste $185-325; ❄🖅) Tucked away in a tranquil pocket behind Campbell Pde, this charming place offers a real home-away-from-home atmosphere. Though only a five-minute walk from the beach, you may well be tempted to stay in all day – the rear courtyard and front terrace are great spots for relaxing, and the rooms (particularly the suites) are conducive to long sleep-ins. No children under 12, and DIY breakfast.

Bondi Beachouse YHA HOSTEL $

(Map p74; 9365 2088; www.yha.com.au; 63 Fletcher St; dm $33-50, d or tw $100-130, without bathroom $78-110; @🖅) A short stroll from the beach, this 95-bed art deco hostel is the best in Bondi. Dorms sleep between four and eight, and some of the double or twin rooms have ocean views – all are clean and well maintained. Facilities include a table-tennis table, games room, air-conditioned TV room, barbecue, free body board and snorkel use, and a rooftop deck with views over

to Bronte Beach. It's the sort of place where you can tell the staff 'another night please'. Bus 380 from Circular Quay stops nearby.

Ravesi's BOUTIQUE HOTEL $$$

(Map p74; 9130 3271; www.hotelbondi.com.au; 178 Campbell Pde; r $249-399 weekdays, $269-429 weekends; ❄🖅) To enjoy a sybaritic Bondi sojourn, claim one of the 12 spacious and stylish rooms above the famous Campbell Parade bar. Those celebrating a big occasion should consider booking the Deluxe Penthouse, which has a large private terrace overlooking the beach. No breakfast.

COOGEE

Coogee Sands Hotel & Apartments HOTEL $$-$$$

(9665 8588; www.coogeesands.com.au; 161 Dolphin St; r $155-295; ❄🖅) The golden sands of Coogee Beach are across the street from this apartment hotel on Dolphin Street (love that name!). The pick of the accommodation is a terrace studio with ocean view.

Dive Hotel HOTEL $$-$$$

(9665 5538; www.divehotel.com.au; 234 Arden St; r $150-310; ❄🖅) It seems strange to be recommending a hotel that's a dive, but so be it. Here's your chance to live the cheap-chic

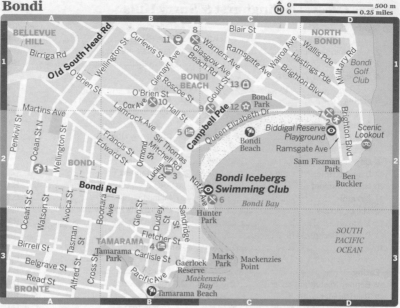

IKEA lifestyle without having to screw your furniture together. The smart and simple rooms have kitchenettes and blue-tile bathrooms; some have balconies with beach views.

GLEBE & NEWTOWN

Billabong Gardens   HOSTEL $
(Map p82; ☎9550 3236; www.billabonggardens.com.au; 5-11 Egan St, Newtown; dm $26-28, s/d $95, without bathroom $55; @☲) This enduring motel/hostel near Sydney university offers a richer experience than most backpacker joints, with travellers, touring rock bands and anonymous others mixing by the jellybean of a pool. Rooms and six-bed dorms come with or without bathrooms; dorms have up to six beds. Internet is free (wi-fi is charged).

Glebe Point YHA   HOSTEL $
(☎9692 8418; www.yha.com.au; 262-264 Glebe Point Rd, Glebe; dm $28-32, s $64, d $76.50; @☎) A good example of what architect Robin Boyd called the great *Australian Ugliness*, this utilitarian hostel on leafy Glebe Point Rd is best seen from the inside looking out. Rooms, dorms and shared bathrooms are basic but clean; a few dorms have no external windows. There's a large and well-equipped communal kitchen and a rooftop where barbecue night are held.

Glebe Village   HOSTEL $
(☎9660 8878; www.glebevillage.com; 256 Glebe Point Rd, Glebe; dm $23-27, s/d $65/$90; @☎) The dorms here are hot and stuffy, the private rooms are basic and the place isn't as clean as the nearby YHA, but management is friendly, prices are low and there's a great garden entertainment area with table tennis, meaning that the party vibe is strong.

NORTH SHORE

Lane Cove River Tourist Park
CAMPGROUND $
(☎9888 9133; www.lcrtp.com.au; Plassey Rd, North Ryde; d unpowered/powered sites $35/37, cabins from $121, d luxury ecotent $390-450; ❋@☲) This cheery place in the Lane Cove National Park lies 14km north of the city and has excellent facilities. The CBD is a 25-minute trip away by train or bus.

MANLY

Manly Pacific   HOTEL $$$
(Map p80; ☎9977 7666; www.accorhotels.com.au; 55 North Steyne; d $209-419; ❋@☎☲) Right on Manly's ocean beach, this recently refurbished midrise hotel is managed by resort-

Bondi

brand, Novotel. Its 214 rooms may be a quick ferry ride from the CBD but they are closer in holiday spirit to Coffs Harbour or even the Gold Coast. Lounge by the rooftop pool or on your ocean-view balcony.

101 Addison Road   B&B $$
(☏9977 6216; www.bb-manly.com; 101 Addison Rd; s $150, d $170) Owner Jill Caskey offers a B&B in the true sense of the word – two rooms of her charming Victorian cottage are available, but only one guest booking is accommodated. The private lounge comes complete with books, TV, DVD and grand piano. There are even beach towels and umbrellas for guests' use.

Boardrider Backpacker   HOSTEL $
(Map p80; ☏9977 6077; www.boardrider.com.au; Rear 63, The Corso; dm $26-47, d with private bathroom $90-162, d with shared bathroom $65-132; @⊛) The best of the two hostels in Manly (by a long shot), Boardriders has a range of dorms and private rooms; the best options are the female-only eight-bed dorm and the deluxe en-suite doubles. Be warned: cleanliness doesn't appear to be high on the priority list and the location right on the Corso will make noise a problem for light sleepers.

✖ Eating

Abundant fresh produce, innovative chefs and a multicultural melange all combine to make eating out in Sydney an extremely pleasurable and popular activity – book ahead wherever possible.

In this chapter, budget options ($) are those offering main courses for under $20; midrange options ($$) charge between $20 and $50, and top-end options ($$$) over $50. Inclusion of a telephone number means that booking is advisable.

CITY CENTRE, THE ROCKS & CIRCULAR QUAY

Bécasse   MODERN AUSTRALIAN $$
(Map p54; ☏9283 3440; www.becasse.com.au; Level 5, Westfield Sydney, cnr Pitt St Mall & Market St, Sydney; 3/5/9-course tasting menu $120/150/190; ⊙lunch & dinner Mon-Sat) Acclaimed chef Justin North constructs modern European dishes with a deft and delicious touch. Recently, he took the bold step of relocating his flagship restaurant to a new space that seats a mere 25 diners. Those who can't score a table can instead try another of his new ventures, the adjacent **Quarter 21** (⊙lunch daily, dinner Mon-Sat), a more casual and less pricey option (mains $34 to $39, seven-course tasting menu $90).

Rockpool Bar & Grill   MODERN AUSTRALIAN $$
(Map p54; ☏8078 1900; www.rockpool.com.au/sydney/bar-and-grill; cnr Hunter & Blight Sts, Sydney; mains $21-110; ⊙lunch Mon-Fri, dinner Mon-Sat) You'll feel like a pampered 1930s Manhattan stockbroker when you dine at this sleek operation in the Art Deco City Mutual Building. The bar is famous for its dry-aged, full-blood wagyu hamburger (make sure you also order a side of the hand-cut fat chips), but carnivores will be equally enamoured with the succulent steaks served in the grill. Both go down well with an expertly made martini. Owner-chef Neil Perry also runs the darkly atmospheric **Spice Temple** (☏8078 1088; www.rockpool.com.au/sydney/spice-temple; dishes $16-85) in the basement, which specialises in Chinese provincial dishes and has the same opening hours.

Quay   MODERN AUSTRALIAN $$$
(Map p54; ☏9251 5600; www.quay.com.au; upper level, International Passenger Terminal, Circular Quay; 3-course lunch/dinner $105/155, degustation menu $210; ⊙lunch Tue-Fri, dinner daily) One of the big guns of the Sydney dining scene,

Quay is known for its extraordinary harbour views, solicitous service and exquisitely presented dishes. Those who baulk at the prospect of the city's heftiest bill should instead purchase a copy of chef Peter Gilmore's cookbook, which discloses the secrets of the utterly extraordinary sea-pearls entrée and snow-egg dessert that grace the menu here.

Guillaume at Bennelong   MODERN AUSTRALIAN

(Map p54; ☑9241 1999; www.guillaumeatbenne long.com.au; mains $40-80; lunch Thu & Fri, dinner Mon-Sat) For special occasions, this supremely stylish restaurant is hard to beat. Award-winning chef Guillaume Brahimi offers a mod Oz menu with classical French influences. Dine beneath Jørn Utzon's vaulted concrete 'ribs' and enjoy spectacular views of Sydney Harbour, the Harbour Bridge, the Royal Botanic Gardens, Circular Quay and the city.

Le Grand Cafe   FRENCH $

(Map p54; ☑9283 3440; www.becasse.com.au; 257 Clarence St, Sydney; breakfast $4-12, lunch $9-12; ⊙breakfast & lunch Mon-Sat) All we can say about Justin North's cafe in the foyer of the Harry Seidler–designed Alliance Française building is *ooh la la*. The classic French snacks (think rich soups, quiche and croque-monsieur) are delicious, and the surrounds are extremely smart. No bookings and cash only.

CHINATOWN & DARLING HARBOUR

Din Tai Fung   TAIWANESE $

(Map p58; www.dintaifungaustralia.com.au; Level 1, World Square, 644 George St, Haymarket; dumplings $8.80-17.80, noodles $4.80-16.80; ⊙lunch & dinner) Din Tai Fung's crabmeat, crab roe and pork dumplings deliver an explosion of fabulously flavoursome broth when you bite into their delicate casing. And the delights of this place don't stop there, with a huge choice of noodles, dumplings and buns to choose from. Come early, come hungry, come prepared to share your table.

Sydney Madang   KOREAN $

(Map p58; 371A Pitt St, Sydney; ⊙11.30am-1am daily) Hidden away in a somewhat dingy laneway off Pitt Street, Sydney Madang serves spicy steam bowls, killer kimchi dishes and lavish barbecue arrays to a loyal coterie of locals and an appreciative cast of visiting Korean nationals. No reservations, so arrive early or expect to queue.

Mamak   MALAYSIAN $

(Map p58; www.mamk.com.au; 15 Goulburn St, Haymarket; satay $8-14, roti $5-10.50, mains $13-18; ⊙lunch & dinner, to 2am Fri & Sat) Get here early (from 5.30pm) if you want to score a dinner table without queuing, because this eat-and-run Malaysian joint is one of the most popular cheap eateries in the city. The satays are cooked over charcoal and are par-

THE CULT OF THE CELEBRITY CHEF

Many Sydneysiders consider a sprinkling of celebrity to be an essential ingredient when it comes to dining out – whether it be courtesy of a star-studded roll-call of regulars, or a celebrity chef at the restaurant's helm. Restaurants such as Armando Percuoco's Buon Ricordo (www.buonricordo.com.au) in Paddington fit perfectly into the former category, and there is a veritable constellation of chefs cooking around town who have attained local and international stardom courtesy of TV cooking programs or cookbooks. These include:

» **Bill Granger**: Bills (p78) Lifestyle chef and author of 12 cookbooks whose food and style are thought by many to be quintessentially Sydney.

» **Kylie Kwong**: Billy Kwong (p77) Presents her own TV programs (*My China* etc) and has written a number of cookbooks.

» **Luke Nguyen**: Red Lantern (p77) Has his own TV program (*Luke Nguyen's Vietnam*) and wrote the *Songs of Sapa* cookbook.

» **Neil Perry**: Rockpool Bar & Grill (p75), Rockpool and Spice Temple (www.rockpool. com.au) The city's original rock-star chef (with ponytail to match) has three restaurants and a long list of cookbooks and appearances on TV cooking programs to his credit.

» **Adriano Zumbo**: Adriano Zumbo (p79) Everyone who watched the TV series about Sydney's hip pastry chef knows that Mr Zumbo takes his role as a celebrity chef very seriously – fortunately, his sweet concoctions live up to their hype.

ticularly delicious when accompanied by a flaky golden roti. No bookings are taken and and you can BYO alcohol.

Marigold Restaurant   CHINESE $-$$
(Map p58; ✆9217 6090; www.marigold.com.au; Levels 4 & 5, 683-689 George St, Haymarket; 4-5 serves yum cha $15-25, set lunch & dinner menus $33-48; ☺10am-3pm & 5.30pm-midnight) This vast yum cha palace is a constant whirl of trolley dollies in cheongsams, waiters in bow ties and up to 800 diners tucking into some of the best dumplings in town.

SURRY HILLS

Bird Cow Fish   MODERN AUSTRALIAN $$
(off Map p72; ✆9380 4090; www.birdcowfish.com. au; shops 4 & 5, 500 Crown St, Surry Hills; brunch $15.50-18.50, mains $36-37; ☺lunch daily, dinner Mon-Sat, brunch Sat & Sun from 9am) The name of this terrific Surry Hills bistro sums up the ingredient list, but gives no hint of the excellence of the produce, dishes, wine list and service on offer. Brunch is a delight, particularly as the coffee is among the best in Sydney.

Spice I Am   THAI $
(Map p58; www.spiceiam.com.au; 90 Wentworth Ave; mains $14-26; ☺lunch & dinner Tue-Sun) The signature dishes at this mega-popular BYO eatery on the city edge of Surry Hills are fragrant, flavoursome and cheap, meaning that queues are inevitable. Service is speedy, but if the tables aren't turning over fast enough, you can always try the nearby House (202 Elizabeth St), a courtyard eatery in the Triple Ace Bar that is run by the same crew and serves Thai street food.

Porteño   SOUTH AMERICAN $$
(✆8399 1440; 358 Cleveland St, St, Surry Hills; share dishes $4-48; ☺dinner Mon-Sat) The attitude-laden boys who made their mark with the wildly popular Bodega tapas bar in Commonwealth St have decided to move their robust homage to the foods of South America to the western edge of Surry Hills, and they've taken loads of fans along for the gastronomically wild ride. Bring a huge appetite and at least four friends if possible, as you can only book for five or more. And don't miss the roast suckling pig – it's truly magnificent.

Bourke Street Bakery   BAKERY $
(off Map p72; www.bourkestreetbakery.com.au; 633 Bourke St, Surry Hills; pastries & cakes $2.80-4.80, pies $4-5.30, sandwiches $7.50; ☺7am-6pm Mon-Fri, 8am-5pm Sat & Sun) Surry Hill's much-loved corner bakery makes wonderful sandwiches with its sourdough, soy loaves and crusty white ficelles. And the cakes, pastries, pies and quiches are equally delicious. Grab one of the hotly contested seats and enjoy your choice with a coffee.

Marque   MODERN AUSTRALIAN $$$
(Map p72; ✆9332 2225; www.marquerestaurant. com.au; 4-5 Crown St, Surry Hills; meals 3-course/degustation $95/150; ☺lunch Fri, dinner Mon-Sat) Mark Best's cooking style is global in inspiration but has superbly executed French cuisine at its heart – after eating here you'll understand why Marque won the 2011 *Sydney Morning Herald Good Food Guide* restaurant of the year. There's an excellent-value, three-course set lunch on Fridays ($45).

Red Lantern   VIETNAMESE $$
(off Map p72; ✆9698 4355; www.redlantern. com.au; 545 Crown St, Surry Hills; mains $28-38; ☺lunch Tue-Fri, dinner daily) At the Cleveland St end of the gourmet mile-and-a-bit that is Crown St, this atmospheric eatery is run by TV presenters Luke Nguyen (*Luke Nguyen's Vietnam*) and Mark Jensen (*Ready Steady Cook*), and Pauline Nguyen (Mark's wife, Luke's sister and author of the excellent *Secrets of the Red Lantern* cookbook-autobiography). It serves modern takes on classic Vietnamese dishes, and is deservedly popular.

Bentley Restaurant & Bar
  MODERN AUSTRALIAN $$-$$$
(Map p72; ✆9332 2344; Crown St, Surry Hills; mains $33-40; ☺lunch & dinner Tue-Sun) Almost as fashionable as Surry Hills itself, this converted corner pub has a down-to-earth bar where you can enjoy tasty tapas, but its main drawcard is the highly regarded restaurant, which serves beautifully presented and carefully prepared food in – alas – tiny portions. The eight-course tasting menu ($120) is the way to go, particularly with the $70 wine match.

Billy Kwong   CHINESE $$
(Map p72; shop 3, 355 Crown St, Surry Hills; mains $26-48; ☺dinner) We're in two minds as to whether to recommend Kylie Kwong's phenomenally popular eatery. The business strives hard to be sustainable, serving organic, seasonal and local produce wherever possible, and the results can be truly inspired (on our most recent visit, the crispy skin duck with orange was truly magnificent). However, the cramped, noisy and uncomfortable seating, sometimes lackadaisical

service, lack of desserts and no-bookings policy don't seem to tally with the high prices. Make up your own mind.

Pizza e Birra
PIZZA $$
(500 Crown St, Surry Hills; pizza $22-25, pasta $20-24; ⊘lunch Thu-Sun, dinner Mon-Wed) Authentic, Neapolitan-style pizza goes down a treat with a well-chilled beer or excellent glass of wine at this perennially popular pizzeria. No bookings.

POTTS POINT & DARLINGHURST

TOP CHOICE Fratelli Paradiso
ITALIAN $-$$
(16 Challis Ave, Potts Point; mains $20-33; ⊘7am-11pm Mon-Fri, to 6pm Sat & Sun) Challis Ave is one of the city's cafe hubs, and this bakery-bistro is in the thick of the action. The menu and atmosphere are 100% Italian, a theme maintained with great espresso and sexily solicitous service. Dishes change daily, and everything is delicious.

Café Sopra
ITALIAN $-$$
(81 Macleay St, Potts Point; mains $16-24, panini $10.50, salads $16-22; ⊘lunch & dinner) Attached to the mighty impressive Fratelli Fresh providore, Sopra is quite possibly the most popular eatery in Sydney and for good reason. It serves no-fuss, perfectly prepared Italian food in a bustling, friendly atmosphere. The huge menu changes seasonally, but some favourites (eg the fabulous *rigatoni alla bolognese*) are constants. There are other branches in Danks St, Waterloo and at Walsh Bay (Map p54).

Fish Face
SEAFOOD $$
(Map p72; 132 Darlinghurst Rd, Darlinghurst; mains $36-45; ⊘dinner daily, lunch Sun) This sardine-sized hole-in-the-wall is the place to come for fish so fresh it's almost wriggling. Plate after plate of exquisite preparations emerge from the constant drama of the open kitchen – the sushi and sashimi are particularly noteworthy.

Bills
CAFE $
(Map p72; www.bills.com.au; 433 Liverpool St, Darlinghurst; breakfast $5.50-18.50, lunch $7.50-26; ⊘7.30am-3pm Mon-Sat, 8.30am-3pm Sun) Bill Granger almost single-handedly introduced the Sydney craze for stylish brunch. His two most famous dishes – ricotta hotcakes and sweetcorn fritters – have legions of fans, but we wish the coffee served at his three Sydney cafes was better. The other branches are in Woollahra and Surry Hills (Map p72).

PADDINGTON & WOOLLAHRA

Four in Hand
FRENCH $$
(☎9362 1999; 105 Sutherland St, Paddington; mains $36-42; ⊘lunch & dinner Tue-Sun) You can't go far in Paddington and Woollahra without tripping over a beautiful old pub with amazing food. In this case, you'll be tripping over some of the best pub grub in Sydney. The restaurant here is famous for its slow-cooked meat dishes, and also offers fabulously fresh seafood dishes and a limited but delectable array of desserts. The bar menu (mains $15 to $18) is also a winner.

Bistro Moncur
FRENCH $$
(116 Queen St, Woollahra; mains $30-43; ⊘dinner daily, lunch Tue-Sun) For the city's best *steak frites*, you need look no further than the famous ground-floor bistro at the upmarket Woollahra Hotel. Its blue swimmer crab and sweet-corn omelette is pretty fabulous, too. There's live rock on Thursday nights from 7.45pm to 10.45pm and live jazz on Sunday from 6.30pm to 9.30pm. No bookings.

Jackie's Cafe
JAPANESE/MODERN AUSTRALIAN $$
(Map p72; 1C Glenmore Rd, Paddington; sandwiches $13-18, sushi from $15; ⊘7.30am-4pm) Join the air-kissing, perennially dieting local ladies who lunch at this, their favourite cafe. The sushi is excellent, the sashimi salad looks lavish but is low-cal and the coffee is consistently good. The surrounding boutiques offer tempting après-lunch credit-card workouts.

BONDI

TOP CHOICE Icebergs Dining Room & Bar
ITALIAN $$$
(Map p74; ☎9365 9000; www.idrb.com; 1 Notts Ave; mains $36-97; ⊘lunch & dinner Tue-Sun) The magnificent view sweeps over Bondi Beach, making Icebergs Australia's most glamorous restaurant – bar none. The menu doesn't disappoint either, offering modern and delicious takes on classic Italian dishes and a choice of aged beef, perfectly cooked. Come for lunch so as to make the most of the view, or arrive in time to enjoy a sunset cocktail at the bar before your meal.

Pompei's
PIZZA $$
(Map p74; ☎9365 1233; www.pompeis.com.au; 126-130 Roscoe St, Bondi Beach; pizzas $19-23, pasta $24-26; ⊘11am-late Fri-Sun, 3pm-late Tue-Thu) Locals and visitors alike devour simply sensational Roman-style pizzas, homemade pasta and the best gelato in the city at Bondi's busiest eatery. There's indoor and outdoor seating, but no views.

Organic Republic   BAKERY $
(Map p74; cnr Glenayr & Warners Ave, Bondi Beach; sandwiches $7-10, pastries $3-4; ☺5am-6pm) Its motto 'let the bread speak' says it all. Fabulous sandwiches on slabs of home-baked organic bread (including spelt) are the signature at this bakery-cafe in a peaceful pocket of Bondi, but you can also enjoy delicious cakes, pastries, pies and biscuits accompanied by a free-trade coffee made with organic milk.

North Bondi Italian Food   ITALIAN $$
(Map p74; www.idrb.com/northbondi; 118-120 Ramsgate Ave, North Bondi; pasta/mains $27/$29; ☺dinner daily) As noisy as it is fashionable, this trattoria in the North Bondi RSL building has a casual vibe, simple but *molto delizioso* food and a democratic no-booking policy. Come early to snaffle a table overlooking the beach.

Sabbaba   FAST FOOD $
(Map p74; 80-82 Hall St, Bondi Beach; falafel roll $8.50, kebab roll 49.50, kebab with dips & salad $17; ☺11am-10pm) There are more boardshorts than black coats on view at this friendly Middle Eastern joint in Bondi's main Hasidic strip. Choose from falafels and kebabs in pitta, vegetarian Moroccan soup, dips and salads. Everything's fresh, well priced and tasty.

EASTERN BEACHES

Bronte Road Bistro   FRENCH $$
(☎9389 3028; www.bronteroadbistro.com; 282 Bronte Rd, Charing Cross; mains $31; ☺dinner Tue-Sat, lunch Thu-Sat) This friendly neighbourhood bistro is the perfect reward/draw for the lovely clifftop walk from Bondi. The casual, always-bustling interior (half-indoor, half-outdoor) and the menu of French favourites are true crowd pleasers.

INNER WEST

Adriano Zumbo   PATISSERIE $
(http://adrianozumbo.com; 296 Darling St; ☺8am-6pm Mon-Sat, to 5pm Sun) Look for the queue, and you'll find Sydney's most famous patisserie. Pastry chef Adriano Zumbo became an overnight star when he appeared on the *MasterChef* reality TV show, and he now leads a sugar-fuelled celebrity lifestyle. Try his signature macaroons (the passionfruit and basil ones are divine) and any of the cakes. Take away only here and at his shop in Manly (Map p80; cnr East Esplanade & Wentworth St; ☺7am-7pm Mon-Fri, 8am-5.30pm Sat & Sun), although there's a cafe in nearby Rozelle (114 Terry St; ☺6.30am-4pm Mon-Fri, 7.30am-4pm Sat & Sun).

Manly Pavilion   ITALIAN $$
(Map p80; ☎9949 9011; West Esplanade; mains $40-45; ☺lunch & dinner) Lingering over lunch on the waterfront terrace or water-facing dining room of Manly's best restaurant is one of the quintessential Sydney dining experiences. The 1930s building (an old bathing pavilion) has been stylishly restored, and the view, modern Italian cuisine, wine list and service are all impressive. It's also a great choice for a sunset *aperitivo* with delectable *stuzzichini* (snacks, $10 to $15) or antipasti ($26 to $30).

Hugos Manly   PIZZA $$
(Map p80; ☎8116 8555; www.hugos.com.au; Shop 1, Manly Wharf, East Esplanade; pizzas $20-28; ☺noon-late Mon-Fri, from 11.30am Sat & Sun) Glamour counts a lot in this town, and nowhere is this more the case than at Hugos. The location at the wharf is great and the pizzas are good, but the waiters often display more attitude than aptitude. There's another branch in Kings Cross (☎9332 1227; 33 Bayswater Rd; ☺5pm-late Tue-Sat, 3pm-late Sun).

PALM BEACH

Barrenjoey House   MODERN AUSTRALIAN $$
(☎9976 2051; www.barrenjoeyhouse.com; 1108 Barrenjoey Rd, Palm Beach; mains $25-39; ☺lunch & dinner) Overlooking picturesque Pittwater from its location opposite the ferry wharf, Barrenjoey House is the perfect location for a leisurely weekend lunch. The menu is casual but assured, with a selection that will please most palates, even junior ones. To get here from the CBD, catch bus L90 from Railway Sq or Bus 156 or 169 from Manly Wharf.

The Boathouse   CAFE $-$$
(www.theboathousepb.com.au; Governor Phillip Park, Palm Beach; breakfast $5.50-15.50, lunch $12.50-34; ☺7.30am-4pm) Sit on the timber deck suspended over Station Beach or take a picnic blanket so that you can stretch out on the grass – either option is alluring at Palm Beach's most popular cafe. The food and coffee here are nearly as impressive as the views, and that's really saying something.

🍺 Drinking

Pubs are a crucial part of the Sydney social scene, and you can down a glass or schooner (NSW term for a large glass) of amber nectar at elaborate 19th-century affairs, cavernous Art Deco joints, modern and minimalist recesses, and everything in-between. Bars are generally more stylish and urbane, sometimes with a dress code.

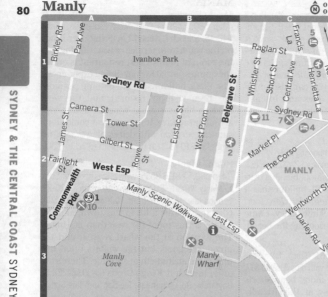

Manly

CITY CENTRE, THE ROCKS & CIRCULAR QUAY

Grasshopper BAR

(Map p54; Temperance Lane; ☺noon-1am Mon-Fri) The first of what is bound to be many grungy laneway bars in the inner city (Ash Street Cellar doesn't count, as the laneway was created anew), Grasshopper is about as cool as the city centre gets. The food served in the upstairs restaurant is good, but the heart of the operation is the downstairs bar.

Bambini Wine Room WINE BAR

(Map p54; www.bambinitrust.com.au; 185 Elizabeth St; ☺from 3pm Mon-Fri, from 5.30pm Sat) This tiny dark-wood-panelled room with a huge chandelier is the sort of place where you might expect to see Oscar Wilde holding court in a corner. There's an extensive wine list and a classy array of bar food ($8 to $40). The excellent Bambini Trust restaurant is in the same building.

Ash Street Cellar WINE BAR

(Map p54; www.merivale.com; 1 Ash St; tapas $8-32; ☺11am-late Mon-Fri) Part of the frighteningly fashionable Ivy complex, this European-flavoured wine bar in a pedestrianised laneway located off George St largely caters to suits but makes everyone feel welcome. There's excellent coffee during the day and even better tapas and wine at night. Other bars in the complex include the Ivy Bar and Ivy Lounge.

Hero of Waterloo PUB

(Map p54; http://heroofwaterloo.com.au; 81 Lower Fort St; ☺9am-midnight Mon-Sat, noon-10pm Sun) Enter the roughly hewn stone interior, meet some of the boisterous locals and enjoy the nightly music (piano, folk, jazz or Irish tunes) at this historic, old-time bar.

Lord Nelson Brewery Hotel PUB
(See p69) Built in 1841, the 'Nello' claims to be Sydney's oldest pub, and the on-site micro-brewery produces some of Sydney's best ales.

Opera Bar BAR
(Map p54; ⊙11.30am-midnight Sun-Thu, to 1am Fri & Sat) Located in the Opera House's lower concourse, this is the perfect spot to enjoy a drink or pre-performance bar meal accompanied by live jazz.

KINGS CROSS, DARLINGHURST & SURRY HILLS

Shakespeare Hotel PUB
(200 Devonshire St; ⊙11am-11pm) Surry Hills' best-loved pub is everything a neighbourhood boozer should be, with ice-cold beer, cheap bar meals and laconic locals watching the gee-gees and chewing the fat.

Mille Vini WINE BAR
(Map p72; 397 Crown St; ⊙6-11pm Tue-Thu, to midnight Fri, 2pm-2am Sat & 2-10pm Sun) Claim a seat at the downstairs bar or on the pavement, choose a glass of wine from a huge list of tipples (the name means 1000 wines), order a plate of antipasto and settle back for an hour or two of Italian-style R&R.

Aperitif BAR
(Map p72; 7 Kellett St, Kings Cross; ⊙6pm-3am Mon & Wed-Sat, to midnight Sun) Like a gently sloping mini–Bourbon St, Kellett St is a snaky, sexy laneway with as many bars as brothels. Intimate Aperitif elevates the tone with an expertly constructed all-European wine list and a late-night kitchen (last orders 2am) serving fabulous French and Spanish food.

Shady Pines Saloon BAR
(Map p72; Shop 4, 256 Crown St, Darlinghurst; ⊙4pm-midnight) There's a boho buzz about 'Surryhurst' (the border of Darlinghurst and Surry Hills) at the moment, largely due to drinking dens like this one. Expect American pioneer memorabilia and Willie Nelson on the sound system. Yes, really.

Old Fitzroy Hotel PUB
(Map p72; 129 Dowling St; ⊙11am-midnight Mon-Fri, from noon Sat, from 3pm Sun) The Old Fitzroy has 13 beers on tap in the downstairs bar (six in the more-intimate upstairs bar), a smokers' verandah and a resident theatre company that stages regular performances (http://rocksurfers.org).

Green Park Hotel PUB
(Map p72; www.greenparkhotel.com.au; 360 Victoria St, Darlinghurst; ⊙10am-2am Mon-Sat, noon-midnight Sun) This dolled-up corner pub is popular with Darlo locals and staff from the nearby St Vincent's Hospital. There's live music on Thursday nights.

Beresford Hotel PUB
(Map p72; www.theberesford.com.au; 354 Bourke St; ⊙noon-1am) A venue with attitude rather than a classic pub, the Beresford has a sleek public bar, Italian trattoria and beer garden where flicks are screened on occasional summer evenings.

Clock PUB
(Map p72; www.clockhotel.com.au; 470 Crown St; ⊙11.30am-midnight) The balcony bar at this iconic Surry Hills pub is always packed, as is the pool bar, which comes complete with pool table, lounges and big-screen TV screening sporting matches.

PADDINGTON & WOOLLAHRA

TOP CHOICE Wine Library WINE BAR
(Map p72; ⊘9331 2604; 18 Oxford Street, Woollahra; ⊙9am-10pm Mon-Sat, to 6pm Sunday) This place has an impressive range of wines by the glass and a stylish but casual feel. If you want to eat, you can choose from the Mediterranean-inclined bar menu or consider sauntering around the corner to **Buzo** (www.buzorestaurant.com.au; mains $26-35; ⊙dinner Mon-Sat) in Jersey Rd, a much-loved local trattoria run by the same team.

Royal Hotel PUB
(⊘9331 2604; 237 Glenmore Rd, Five Ways, Paddington; ⊙11am-midnight) One of the points on the star-shaped junction, this fine pub is spread over three floors. At the top, the Elephant Bar has views over the city skyline.

NEWTOWN & GLEBE

Courthouse Hotel PUB
(Map p82; 202 Australia St, Newtown; ⊙10am-midnight Mon-Sat, to 10pm Sun) Your drinking companions here are a multifaceted lot: everyone from uni students enjoying a cheap meal in the beer garden to ferals hanging around the jukebox and nuggety locals who have propped up the front bar for half a century.

Friend in Hand Hotel PUB
(Map p82; www.friendinhand.com.au; 58 Cowper St, Glebe; ⊙8am-midnight Mon-Sat, 10am-10pm Sun) Don't be surprised when poetry readings and crab racing distract you from trying the 11 local beers on tap.

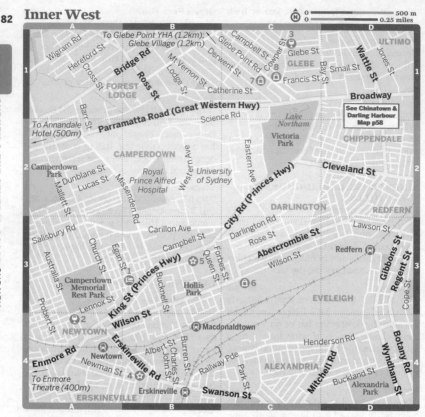

BONDI & COOGEE

Beach Road Hotel PUB

(Map p74; www.beachroadbondi.com.au; 71 Beach Rd, Bondi; ☺10am-11pm Mon & Tue, to midnight Wed-Fri, 9am-midnight Sat, 10am-10pm Sun) Weekends at this big, boxy pub see Bondi types (bronzed, buff and often brooding) sharing bar space with out-of-towners playing pool, drinking beer and partying to live bands and DJs. It's much better than the backpacker-only Shack behind Noah's hostel.

Coogee Bay Hotel PUB

(www.coogeebayhotel.com.au; cnr Coogee Bay Rd & Arden St, Coogee; ☺10am-late) The rambling, rowdy Coogee Bay complex has live music, a beer garden and views across the water.

☆ Entertainment

Sydney has an eclectic and innovative arts, entertainment and music scene. Outdoor cinemas and sports stadiums cater to fami-

Inner West

☺ Sleeping
1 Billabong Gardens B3

☺ Drinking
2 Courthouse Hotel A4
3 Friend in Hand Hotel C1

☺ Entertainment
4 Imperial Hotel B4
5 Vanguard B3

☺ Shopping
6 Eveleigh Market C3
7 Glebe Markets C1
8 Gleebooks C1

lies, the city's theatre scene is healthy and dynamic and live music is everywhere.

Pick up the 'Metro' section in Friday's *Sydney Morning Herald* for comprehensive entertainment details. Free weekly street magazines including *The Brag* and *The Drum* specialise in gig and club information. Tickets for most shows can be purchased directly from venues or through the **Moshtix** (☑1300 438 849; www.moshtix.com.au) or **Ticketek** (Map p54; ☑132 849; www.ticketek.com.au) ticketing agencies.

Cinemas

First-run cinemas abound; tickets generally cost $15 to $18 for an adult, $13 to $14 for a student and $10 to $12 for a child. Most cinemas have a cheap night when tickets are discounted by around a third. Sydney also has a huge following of indie and foreign films.

Open Air Cinema   CINEMA
(Map p54; www.stgeorgeopenair.com.au; Mrs Macquaries Point, Royal Botanic Gardens; adult/concession $30/28; ⊙box office 6.30pm, screenings 8.30pm Jan & Feb) Right on the harbour, the outdoor three-storey screen here comes with surround sound, sunsets, skyline and swanky food and wine. Most tickets are purchased in advance, but a limited number of tickets go on sale at the door each night at 6.30pm – check the website for details.

Bondi Open Air Cinema   CINEMA
(Map p74; ☑1300 438 849; www.bondiopenair.com.au; Bondi Pavilion, Bondi; ⊙dusk-late Jan–early Mar) Enjoy open-air screenings at the ocean's edge, with live bands providing pre-screening entertainment. Bookings essential.

Dendy Opera Quays   CINEMA
(Map p54; www.dendy.com.au; Shop 9, 2 Circular Quay East) A plush cinema screening first-run independent films from around the world.

Moonlight Cinema   CINEMA
(www.moonlight.com.au; Belvedere Amphitheatre, cnr Loch & Broome Aves, Centennial Park; adult/child/concession $18/14/16; ⊙box office 7pm, screenings 8-8.30pm Dec-Mar) Take a picnic and enjoy a new-season release under the stars in magnificent Centennial Park. Enter via Woollahra Gate on Oxford St.

Nightclubs

GoodGod Small Club   LIVE MUSIC VENUE, CLUB
(Map p58; www.goodgodgoodgod.com; 53-55 Liverpool St, Chinatown; cover charge varies, front bar free; ⊙10pm-late Wed-Sat) In a defunct underground taverna in the Spanish Quarter, GoodGod's rear dancetaria hosts everything from live indie bands to Jamaican reggae, '50s soul, rockabilly and tropical house mu-

sic. Its success lies in the focus on great music rather than glamorous surrounds.

Home   CLUB
(Map p54; www.homesydney.com; Cockle Bay Wharf, Darling Harbour; admission varies; ⊙Thu-Sat) Welcome to the pleasure dome: a three-level, 2000-capacity timber-and-glass extravaganza, home to a huge dance floor, countless bars, outdoor balconies and an amazing DJ booth. Top-name international DJs spin house; live bands amp it up.

Ivy   CLUB
(Map p54; www.merivale.com; 330 George St, Sydney) Celebrities and wannabes flock to Justin Hemmes' Ivy complex to see and be seen. The main bar features a spacious dance floor and hosts Saturday's **Pure Ivy** ($20; ⊙6pm-late), **Tank** (Fri from 10pm, Sat from 9pm) dance floor, which glitters on weekends, and the infamous rooftop **Pool Club** (⊙Mon 4pm-late, Tue-Fri noon-late), which provides a place to aqua-boogie when the weather gets too hot. You'll need to finagle your way onto the guest list for all three.

Oxford Art Factory   BAR
(Map p72; www.oxfordartfactory.com; 38-46 Oxford St, Darlinghurst; cover charge & hours vary) The Darlo set parties against an arty backdrop in a two-room multipurpose venue modelled on Warhol's New York creative base. There's a gallery, bar and performance space that often hosts international acts and DJs. Check the website for a program.

Live Music

Sydney Opera House   CLASSICAL
(p53) Yes, it's more than a landmark. As well as theatre and dance, the Opera House hosts performances by **Opera Australia** (tickets ☑9318 8200; www.opera-australia.org.au) and the **Sydney Symphony** (tickets ☑8215 4600; www.sydneysymphony.com).

TOP CHOICE **Venue 505**   JAZZ
(http://venue505.com; 280 Cleveland St, Surry Hills; cover varies; ⊙Mon-Sat from 7.30pm) Focusing on jazz, world and classical music, this small and relaxed live venue is artist-run and thoughtfully programmed. The space features comfortable couches and murals by local artist Benjamin Yarrad.

Basement   JAZZ
(Map p54; www.thebasement.com.au; 7 Macquarie Pl, Circular Quay; admission varies; ⊙noon-1.30am Mon-Thu, to 2.30am Fri, 7.30pm-3am Sat, 7pm-1am Sun) Sydney's premier jazz venue

presents headline touring acts and big local talent. A broad musical mandate also sees funk, blues and soul bands performing. Book a table by the stage.

Vanguard
ROCK

(Map p82; ☎9550 3666; www.thevanguard.com.au; 42 King St, Newtown; ⊙6.30pm-midnight Tue-Sun) The UK's *Independent* newspaper rates the Vanguard as one of the world's 10 best live music venues, and the city's boho set would probably agree. An intimate, purpose-built space, it showcases everything from burlesque to blues, country to world. Most seats are reserved for dinner-and-show ($40 to $45) patrons; door entry is $15.

Annandale Hotel
ROCK

(Map p82; www.annandalehotel.com; 17 Parramatta Rd, Annandale) 'F*ck this – I'm going to the Annandale!' is the motto at Sydney's premier rock venue. Loads of regulars follow its advice, enjoying live music most Wednesdays to Sundays and cult movies on Tuesdays – check the website for the program.

Enmore Theatre
ROCK

(Map p82; ☎9550 3666; www.enmoretheatre. com.au; 118-132 Enmore St, Newtown) Newtown is the centre of Sydney's music scene and the Enmore is its mainstream heart, hosting big-name local and international acts.

Metro Theatre
ROCK

(Map p58; ☎9550 3666; www.metrotheatre.com. au; 624 George St) Big-name indie acts grace the Metro's stage. It has theatre-style tiers, air-conditioning, super sound and good visibility.

Spectator Sports

On any given Sydney weekend there'll be all manner of balls being hurled, kicked and batted around. Sydneysiders are passionate about the **National Rugby League** (NRL; www. nrl.com.au; tickets through Ticketek from $25), the season transpiring at suburban stadia and the **ANZ Stadium** (Map p50; ☎9360 6601; www.anz stadium.com.au; Sydney Olympic Park, Olympic Blvd, Homebush Bay), with September finals.

From March right through to September, hometown favourites the **Sydney Swans** (www.sydneyswans.com.au) play in the **Australian Football League** (AFL; www.afl.com.au; tickets $20-40) at the **Sydney Cricket Ground** (SCG; www.sydneycricketground.com.au; Driver Ave, Moore Park). In 2012 they will be joined by a second Sydney-based team, Greater Western Sydney (The Giants), which will probably be based at the Sydney Showgrounds.

The **cricket** (http://cricket.com.au) season runs from October to March, the SCG hosting interstate Sheffield Shield and sell-out international test, Twenty20 and 50-over matches.

Theatre

Sydney Theatre Company
THEATRE

(Map p54; ☎9250 1777; www.sydneytheatre.com. au; level 2, Pier 4, Hickson Rd, Walsh Bay; tickets $60-65) Sydney's premier theatre company performs at its Walsh Bay base and in the Drama Theatre at the Sydney Opera House. Artistic directors Cate Blanchett and Andrew Upton program work by local and international playwrights and draw actors and directors from around the world. There are heavily discounted tickets for under '30s.

Company B
THEATRE

(☎9699 3444; www.belvoir.com.au; 25 Belvoir St, Surry Hills; tickets from $39) Stars such as Geoffrey Rush regularly perform at this innovative theatre space.

Sydney Theatre
THEATRE

(Map p54; ☎9250 1999; www.sydneytheatre.org. au; 22 Hickson Rd, Walsh Bay; tickets $40-79) The resplendent Sydney Theatre at the base of Observatory Hill puts 850 bums on seats for specialist drama and dance.

🔒 Shopping

Most stores are open from 9.30am to 6pm Monday to Wednesday, Friday and Saturday and until 9pm Thursday. Sunday trading is common but expect shorter hours, such as noon to 4pm or 5pm. Exceptions are noted in reviews.

CITY CENTRE

Sydneysiders head cityward if they have something special to buy or when serious retail therapy is required. The central city's diverse range of mainly upmarket stores – centred on Pitt St Mall, Market St and George St – offers plenty of choice for gifts and treats.

David Jones
DEPARTMENT STORE

(Map p58; www.davidjones.com.au; cnr Market & Castlereagh Sts, Sydney; ⊙9.30am-7pm Mon-Wed, to 9pm Thu & Fri, 9am-9pm Sat & 10am-7pm Sun) DJs is Sydney's premier department store. The Market St store has menswear; Castlereagh St has women's and children's wear and a friendly concierge to point you in the right direction. The Australian designer fashion and the food halls in the Market St basement are particularly impressive.

continued on page 93

This is Sydney

Sydney Harbour »
Beaches »
After Dark »
National Parks »

Sydney Harbour Bridge (p49)

Sydney Harbour

It's called the Harbour City for good reason. Few places on earth are as defined by their geographical form as Sydney, and none are blessed with such a spectacular natural landscape.

Visitors have been writing odes to the harbour's beauty ever since the First Fleet landed here on 26 January 1788. Few have done it justice, though. After all, how can any writing match the exultation of a ferry trip across shimmering blue waters or the satisfaction of an afternoon spent lazing in a sheltered sandy cove?

Everything here revolves around this huge body of water – suburbs, recreation, traffic, even the collective consciousness.

The somewhat stolid North Shore is the location of choice for the city's conservative middle classes, whose leafy villas stretch from Neutral Bay to Manly. Traffic snarls are the norm here, as is the residents' aspiration to own a sailboat for weekends on the water.

Across the iconic Sydney Harbour Bridge is an altogether different Sydney. A ring of gregarious inner-city neighbourhoods surround the central business district and give the city its urban edge, albeit one with a magnificent harbour view around every corner.

ANDREW WATSON/LONELY PLANET IMAGES ©

To the east a genteel ribbon of suburbs unfurls, characterised by mansions, money and mindsets that are often as old as the colony itself. Harking west, towards the Parramatta River, are former working-class neighbourhoods that in recent years have been reinvented as arty residential enclaves.

At the centre of all this is Circular Quay, home to Sydney's two signature sights – the Opera House (p53) and Harbour Bridge (p49). From here, the city's famous flotilla of green-and-yellow ferries do five-minute dashes across to Milsons Point and Kirribilli, speedy sails to the Middle Harbour and majestic processions past the Heads to Manly.

The harbour's attractions are as entrancing as they are accessible – a rare and wonderful combination. Ferry trips are relatively inexpensive; and there's no charge to explore the scenic walking paths and bushwalking tracks scattered throughout Sydney Harbour National Park (p52), swim in a harbour cove or marvel at an extraordinary water view. When you're here, make sure you take advantage of them all.

TOP FIVE HARBOUR ACTIVITIES

» Take the ferry to **Manly** (p63)
» Enjoy a harbour view with your meal at **Quay** (p75), **Manly Pavilion** (p79) or the **Bather's Pavilion** (p63)
» Swim at **Nielsen Park** (p61), **Balmoral Beach** (p63) or **Camp Cove** (p62)
» Follow the **Manly Scenic Walkway** (p64)
» Explore the **harbour islands** (p52)

Clockwise from top left
1. Sydney Opera House (p53) **2.** Sydney Harbour Bridge climb (p67) **3.** Fishing, Sydney Harbour

Beaches

Here, nothing beats a day at the beach. Sun, sand and surf dominate the culture for six months of every year, and locals wouldn't have it any other way.

The city's magnificent string of ocean beaches stretches north from the Royal National Park to Palm Beach, luring surfers, scenesters, swimmers and sunbathers onto their golden sands and into the powerful waves of the South Pacific Ocean.

There's none of that horrible European habit of privatising the beach here. Lay down a towel and you've claimed a personal patch of paradise for as long as you want it. Some locals enjoy a quick dip before or after work, while the lucky ones stay on the sand for the whole day – everyone makes the most of what time they have.

Serious surfers head to Cronulla in the south; Maroubra, Bronte, Tamarama and North Bondi in the east; and Narrabeen, Queenscliff, Harbord (Freshwater) and Manly on the Northern Beaches. Of these, Bronte and Manly are also popular with swimmers, joining Coogee, Clovelly, Bondi, Whale and Palm as regular entries on 'Best Beaches' lists. Each of these beaches has a devoted crew of regulars – families flock to Clovelly, Bronte and Whale Beach, while bronzed singles strut their stuff at Coogee and Palm Beach. The best-known beaches – Bondi and Manly – host an incongruous mix of pasty-skinned foreigners, weatherwizened surf gurus, grommets (beginner surfers), camera-savvy minor celebrities and geriatric locals who have been perfecting their body-surfing techniques for more than half a century. Always crowded, these two beaches showcase the most endearing and eclectic aspects of Sydney's character, and shouldn't be missed.

Those who find surf off-putting have two excellent alternatives: ocean pools and harbour beaches. Of the many pools on offer, the most popular are the Bondi Icebergs Swimming Club (p66), the historic Wylie's Baths in Coogee (p66) and the

Clockwise from top left
1. Surfers, Manly (p63) **2.** Looking out to Bondi Beach (p62), from Bronte **3.** Coogee Beach

ocean pools at Bronte, Avalon, Bilgola, Newport, Freshwater, Manly, Palm and Whale beaches. In the harbour, there are netted swimming enclosures or pools at Cremorne Point, Nielsen Park and Balmoral Beach.

And the choices don't stop there. Aspiring skinny-dippers should make their way to Lady Bay near Watsons Bay; Obelisk and Cobbler's beaches in the Middle Harbour; and Werrong Beach in the Royal National Park (p138), all of which are official nudist beaches.

Our advice? Plunge in and enjoy yourself, regardless of whether you're wearing a swimsuit or not!

BONDI TO COOGEE CLIFF-TOP WALK

This 5.5km, 2.5-hour walk follows a cliff-top path from Bondi Beach to Coogee, and is one of the city's most exhilarating experiences. Start at the Bondi Icebergs Swimming Club and follow the signposts south towards the small reserve known as Mark's Park. Along the route there are scenic vantage points (look out for whales and dolphins) as well as plaques recounting local Aboriginal myths and stories.

Continue to diminutive Tamarama Beach. Walk around the grassed reserve and con-tinue onto charming Bronte Beach with its Norfolk Island pines, picnic ground and popular children's playground.

Follow the cliff-top and continue along the boardwalk edging picturesque Waverley Cemetery, which will lead you to Clovelly (a popular snorkelling spot), Gordon's Bay and Coogee Beach.

The best time of year to do the walk is between late October and mid-November, when the wildly popular Sculpture by the Sea (www.sculpturebythesea.com) transforms the route between Bondi and Tamarama.

After Dark

Sydneysiders love nothing more than shimmying and shaking their way from performance to party, makin' plenty of friends along the way. And who's to blame them?

After all, the city has come a long way in the leisure stakes since its foundation as a penal colony. Back then, a beaker or two of rum was the only type of partying available to soldiers, convicts and emancipists. These days, the situation couldn't be more different.

The festival calendar is a good case in point. The year kicks off with a frenzy of fireworks over Circular Quay and doesn't calm down for months. No sooner has the Sydney Festival, with its associated openings and events, finished than the biggest party of all kicks off: the famous Gay & Lesbian Mardi Gras (p69). Winter brings fashion, literature, film and art to the fore, with opening nights, cocktail parties and literary soirées dominating everyone's datebooks. And then there's a slight hiatus until summer works its magic and everyone takes to the city's streets to make the most of daylight savings' long days and blissfully balmy nights.

Whatever your inclination, Sydney will indulge it. You can attend the theatre or the opera, take in a jazz performance or a drag show, watch films under the stars or club late into the night. Sexy, sweaty and solipsistic, the social scene here is bigger and way better than those in the other states; ignore anyone who tries to convince you otherwise.

And lest you think that the only way to kick up your heels is to take to the dance floor or attend a star-studded concert, think again. For many locals, the best evening entertainment comes courtesy of the city's huge range of bars and restaurants – there truly is something for every budget and palate here.

Put simply, this is a town that well and truly lives up to its hype when it comes to partying. Enjoy!

(image credit: GREG ELMS/LONELY PLANET IMAGES ©)

DON'T MISS

» The restaurant and bar scene on **Crown Street, Surry Hills** (p71 and p72)
» Attending a performance at the **Sydney Opera House** (p53)
» Camping it up during the **Gay & Lesbian Mardi Gras** (p69)
» Spending a hot night chillin' to some **cool jazz** (p83)
» Watching a movie under the stars at an **open air cinema** (p83)

Clockwise from top left
1. City skyline from Darling Harbour 2. Mardi Gras (p69)
3. New Year's Eve fireworks, Sydney Harbour

National Parks

Sampling Sydney's sybaritic menu of sights, activities and entertainments can lead to sensory overload. When this happens it pays to escape to one of the four national parks in the immediate area.

The most accessible of these is the Sydney Harbour National Park (p52), which includes islands and foreshore areas in and around the harbour. Rich in remnant bushland and cultural heritage, the park is one of the city's great – and refreshingly understated – tourist attractions.

A bit harder to access, but worth the effort, is Ku-ring-gai Chase National Park (p64), 150 sq km of forest located where the Hawkesbury River meets the South Pacific Ocean. A repository for millennia-old Aboriginal rock art, it also protects a wide array of native wildlife and plants.

Incongruously but wonderfully located in the midst of residential development on the North Shore, the Lane Cove National Park extends from East Ryde to Pennant Hills, protecting bushland and freshwater sections of the Lane Cove River. It's the city's largest and best-loved suburban back garden.

The greatest escape of all is the Royal National Park (p138). The world's second-oldest national park (after Yellowstone in the USA), it offers magnificent surf beaches, walks through cliff-top heathland and innumerable leisure activities.

TOP FIVE NATIONAL PARK ACTIVITIES

» Enjoying a picnic, walk and swim at **Nielsen Park** (p52)
» Viewing Aboriginal rock paintings and engravings in the **Ku-ring-gai Chase National Park** (p64)
» Camping overnight at the **Lane Cove River Tourist Park** (p74)
» Surfing at **Garie Beach** (p138)
» Walking the Coast Track in the **Royal National Park** (p138)

Resolute Beach, Ku-ring-gai Chase National Park (p64)

continued from page 84

Queen Victoria Building
SHOPPING CENTRE

(QVB; Map p54; www.qvb.com.au; 455 George St, Sydney) This high-Victorian masterpiece occupies an entire city block opposite the Town Hall, and though there are some inspiring retail offerings, they run a distant second to the magnificent wrought-iron balconies, stained-glass shopfronts and mosaic floors.

RM Williams
CLOTHING

(Map p58; www.rmwilliams.com.au; 389 George St, Sydney) Urban cowboys and country folk can't get enough of this hard-wearing outback gear. Favourites include oilskin jackets, Akubra hats, moleskin jeans and leather boots. There are other outlets scattered throughout the city.

Strand Arcade
SHOPPING CENTRE

(Map p54; www.strandarcade.com.au; 412 George St & 193-195 Pitt St Mall, Sydney) Constructed in 1891, the Strand competes with the QVB for the title of most gorgeous shopping centre in Sydney. It has a particularly strong range of Australian designer fashion, and is home to the famous Strand Hatters (www.strandhatters .com.au), which blocks and steams hats to customers' cranial requirements.

Westfield Sydney
SHOPPING CENTRE

(Map p54; http://westfield.com.au/sydney; cnr Pitt St Mall & Market St, Sydney) The city's newest and largest shopping mall hosts main street retailers such as Zara, as well as designer boutiques and an excellent food court.

PADDINGTON & WOOLLAHRA

Glenmore Rd in Paddington and Queen St in Woollahra are Sydney's premier fashion en-

MARVELLOUS MARKETS

Sydneysiders enjoy going to local markets nearly as much as going to the beach (and that's really saying something). Many inner-city suburbs host weekend markets in the grounds of local schools and churches, and these sell everything from organic food to original designer clothing. You'll inevitably encounter some tragic hippy paraphernalia, appalling art and overpriced tourist tat, but there are often exciting purchases to be made, too.

The best markets include the following:

Balmain Market
MARKET

(www.balmainmarket.com.au; cnr Darling St & Curtis Rd, Balmain; ☺8.30am-4pm Sat) A small market set in the shady grounds of St Andrews Congregational Church. Stalls sell arts, crafts, books, clothing, jewellery, plants, and fruit and veg.

Bondi Markets
MARKET

(Map p74; www.bondimarkets.com.au; Bondi Beach Public School, cnr Campbell Pde & Warners Ave, Bondi; ☺10am-4pm Sun) Filled with Bondi characters rummaging through tie-dyed second-hand clothes and books, beads and earrings, aromatherapy oils, candles, old records and more. There's a farmers' market in the school grounds on Saturdays between 9am and 1pm.

Eveleigh Market
MARKET

(Map p50; www.eveleighmarket.com.au; 243 Wilson St, Darlington; ☺farmers market 8am-1pm Sat, artisans' market 1st Sun of every month 10am-3pm, closed 1st half of Jan) Over 70 regular stallholders sell their home-grown produce at Sydney's best farmers' market, which is held in a heritage-listed railway workshop in the Eveleigh Railyards. When here, you can also visit the CarriageWorks arts and cultural precinct (www.carriageworks.com.au).

Glebe Markets
MARKET

(Map p82; www.glebemarkets.com.au; Glebe Public School, cnr Glebe Point Rd & Derby Pl, Glebe; ☺10am-4pm Sat) The best of the west; Sydney's dreadlocked, shoeless, inner-city contingent beats an aimless course to this crowded hippyish market.

Paddington Markets
MARKET

(Map p72; www.paddingtonmarkets.com.au; St John's Church, 395 Oxford St, Paddington; ☺10am-4pm Sat) Sydney's most popular weekend market dishes up vintage clothes and hip fashions, jewellery, books, massage and palmistry. Just as your spirits flag, you'll find something special under a little awning.

claves. There are several options if you need to source a fetching outfit or two:

Akira Isagowa CLOTHING
(12A Queen St, Woollahra) Meticulously tailored ensembles featuring gorgeous fabrics. There's another store in the Strand Arcade.

Collette Dinnigan CLOTHING
(www.collettedinnigan.com.au; 104 Queen St, Woollahra) The queen of Aussie couture delivers fabulously feminine frocks with exquisite trimming.

Dinosaur Design JEWELLERY
(www.dinosaurdesigns.com.au; 339 Oxford Street, Paddington) Fabulous jewellery and homewares made from richly coloured polyester resin. There's another store in the Strand Arcade.

Easton Pearson CLOTHING
(Map p72; 30 Glenmore Rd, Paddington) Brisbane designers who popularised ethnochic in Australia and are particularly beloved by women of a slightly fuller figure.

Willow CLOTHING
(Map p72; www.willow.com.au; Glenmore Rd, Paddington) Local designer Kit Willow Podgornik has made it big around the globe with her gorgeous clothes and lingerie.

Zambesi CLOTHING
(Map p54; www.zambesi.co.nz; 5 Glenmore Rd, Paddington) New Zealand outfit stocking an exciting range of men's and women's clothing.

Zimmermann CLOTHING
(Map p72; http://zimmermannwear.com; Shop 2, 2-16 Glenmore Rd, Paddington). Chic and cheeky street clothes and swimwear from Nicky and Simone Zimmermann. There's another store in Westfield Sydney.

❶ Information

Emergency
In the event of an emergency, call ☑000 to contact the police, ambulance and fire authorities.

Lifeline (☑13 11 14; www.lifeline.com.au) Over-the-phone counselling services, including suicide prevention.

Police Stations For a searchable list of all police stations in NSW, go to www.police.nsw.gov.au/about_us/structure/operations_command/local_area_commands.

Rape Crisis Centre (☑1800 424 017) 24hr counselling.

Internet Access
Internet cafes are common in Sydney, especially in Kings Cross, Chinatown and Bondi. Rates are around $3 an hour. Hostels tend to use providers such as **Global Gossip** (http://globalgossip.com) for their guest wi-fi and broadband access; these charge approximately $3 per hr. The more-expensive hotels can use providers charging up to $20 per hour. For a list of free wi-fi hotspots, go to www.unwired.com.au/get/storefinder.php?p=3.

Medical Services
Kings Cross Travellers Clinic (☑9358 3066; www.travellersclinic.com.au; 13 Springfield Ave, Kings Cross; standard consultation $65; ⊙9am-1pm & 2-6pm Mon-Fri, 10am-noon Sat) General and travel medical services, vaccinations; bookings advised.

St Vincent's Hospital (☑8382 1111; www.stvincents.com.au; 390 Victoria St, Darlinghurst; ⊙24hr emergency)

Sydney Hospital (☑9382 7111; www.sesahs.nsw.gov.au/sydhosp; 8 Macquarie St, Sydney; ⊙24hr emergency)

Money
There are plenty of ATMs throughout Sydney; foreign exchange offices are found in Kings Cross and around Chinatown, Circular Quay and Central Station.

American Express City Centre (☑1300 139 060; 296 George St, Sydney; ⊙9am-5pm Mon-Fri); Haymarket (☑1300 139 060; 296 George St, Sydney; ⊙9am-5pm Mon-Fri)

Post
General Post Office (GPO; Map p54; ☑13 13 18; www.auspost.com.au; 1 Martin Pl; ⊙8.15am-5.30pm Mon-Fri, 10am-2pm Sat)

Tourist Information
Sydney City Council Information Kiosks (www.cityofsydney.nsw.gov.au) Circular Quay (Map p54; cnr Pitt & Alfred Sts; ⊙9.30am-3.30pm); Town Hall (Map p54; George St; ⊙9.30am-3.30pm) Extremely friendly and helpful staff supply maps, brochures and information, including the free *Sydney Guide*, which includes information and discount vouchers and is available in English-, Chinese-, Japanese- and Korean-language editions.

Sydney Harbour National Parks Information Centre (Map p54; ☑9247 5033; Cadmans Cottage, 110 George St, The Rocks; ⊙9.30am-4.30pm Mon-Fri, 10am-4.30pm Sat & Sun) Has maps of walks in different parts of the park and information on tours of the harbour islands.

Sydney Visitor Centres (☑9240 8788; www.sydneyvisitorcentre.com) The Rocks (Map p54; 1st fl, cnr Argyle & Playfair Sts; ⊙9.30am-5.30pm); Darling Harbour (Map p54; Palm

Grove, behind Imax; ☺9.30am-5.30pm) Both branches have a wide range of brochures and staff can book accommodation, tours and attractions. The Rocks location is part gift shop.

Websites

For more information on Sydney, check out the following websites:

www.art-almanac.com.au Comprehensive public and private gallery listings.

www.cityofsydney.nsw.gov.au Visitor information, disabled access, parking, history and downloadable walking tours.

www.realsurf.com Local surf reports.

www.shfa.nsw.gov.au Links to dedicated websites about three Sydney Harbour Foreshore Authority precincts: The Rocks, Darling Harbour and soon-to-be-developed Barangaroo.

www.smh.com.au Good for upcoming events, restaurant and bar reviews, and to take the pulse of the city.

www.timeoutsydney.com.au Listings and articles from the monthly magazine.

🛈 Getting There & Away

Air

Sydney Airport (code: SYD; Map p50; www.sydneyairport.com.au) is Australia's busiest, so don't be surprised if there are delays. It's only 10km south of the city centre, making access relatively easy. The T1 (international) and T2 and T3 (domestic) terminals are a 4km bus ($5.50; 10 minutes) or train ($5; 2 minutes) ride apart (the airport is privately run so transferring terminals – a service that's free in most of the world – is seen as a profit opportunity). If you are transferring from a Qantas international flight to a Qantas domestic flight (or vice versa), free transfers are provided by the airline. Virgin Blue offers a similar service.

You can fly into Sydney from all the usual international points and from within Australia. **Qantas** (☏13 13 13; www.qantas.com.au), **Jetstar** (☏13 15 38; www.jetstar.com.au), **Virgin Blue** (☏13 67 89; www.virginblue.com.au) and **Tiger Airways** (☏03-9335 3033; www.tigerairways.com/au/en) have frequent flights to other major cities. Smaller Qantas-affiliated airlines fly to smaller Oz destinations.

For further details on air travel within Australia, see p527. For air travel to/from Australia, see p526.

Bus

All private interstate and regional bus travellers arrive at **Sydney Coach Terminal** (Map p58; ☏9281 9366; Central Station, Eddy Ave; ☺6am-6pm Mon-Fri, 8am-6pm Sat & Sun). Sample destinations include Brisbane (from $88, 16 hours), Byron Bay (from $85, 12½

hours), Canberra (from $15, 3½ hours) and Melbourne (from $60, 14 hours). There are lots of discounted fares.

The government's CountryLink rail network is also complemented by coach services. Most buses stop in the suburbs on the way in and out of Sydney. The major bus companies using the depot:

Australia Wide (☏9516 1300; www.austwidecoaches.com.au) Orange and Bathurst.

Busways (☏9625 8900; www.busways.com.au) Central Coast.

Firefly (☏1300 730 740; www.fireflyexpress.com.au) Wagga Wagga, Albury, Melbourne and Adelaide.

Greyhound (☏1300 473 946; www.greyhound.com.au) Canberra, Melbourne, Byron Bay.

Murrays (☏13 22 51; www.murrays.com.au) Canberra and the South Coast.

Port Stephens Coaches (☏4982 2926; www.pscoaches.com.au) Newcastle and Nelson Bay.

Premier (☏13 34 10; www.premierms.com.au) Coffs Harbour, Byron Bay, Brisbane and Cairns.

Train

Sydney's main rail terminus for CountryLink interstate and regional services is the huge **Central Station** (Map p58; ☏bookings 13 22 32, 24hr transport information 13 15 00; www.countrylink.info; Eddy Ave; ☺staffed ticket booths 6.15am-8.45pm, ticket machines 24hr). CountryLink discounts often nudge 40% on economy fares – sometimes cheaper than buses.

Sample train fares (without discount) include Brisbane ($92, 14½ hours) and Melbourne ($92, 11 hours).

🛈 Getting Around

Your transport options may be many in Sydney but your journey may not be easy. Spend more than a day in town and you won't be able to miss stories about the dire state of the overpatronised, underfunded system. Ferries, trains and many buses are operated by the same government department but each mode seems to operate in blissful ignorance of the others, with only one integrated ticket, the MyMulti pass, available. And even this doesn't include the privately owned tram and monorail.

For information on government buses, ferries and trains try the **Transport Infoline** (☏13 15 00; www.131500.com.au).

To/From the Airport

One of the easiest ways to get to and from the airport is with a shuttle company such as **Kingsford Smith Transport** (KST; ☏9666 9988; www.kst.com.au; one way/return from $12.60/20.70; ☺5am-7pm), which services central Sydney hotels. **Airport Shuttle North**

(📞1300 505 100; www.airportshuttlenorth.com; one way from $35; ⏱5am-11pm) and **Manly Express** (📞8065 9524; www.manlyexpress.com.au; one way from $30; ⏱3am-11.30pm) service the North Shore and Northern Beaches. Bookings are essential for all.

Airport Link (📞13 15 00; www.airportlink.com.au; one way/return from Central Sydney adult $15/25, child $10/15.50, ⏱4.30am-12.40am) is a strange service: it's a normal commuter line (with dirty cars) but you pay through the nose to use the airport stations (punters going to Wolli Creek, the next stop *beyond* the airport, pay $3.20).

Taxi fares from the airport are approximately $39 to the City Centre ($51 between 10pm and 6am), $43 to Bondi ($55 between 10pm and 6am) and $80 to Manly ($106 between 10pm and 6am).

Boat

FERRY Harbour ferries and RiverCats (to Parramatta) operated by **Sydney Ferries** (www.sydneyferries.info) depart from Circular Quay. Most ferries operate between 6am and midnight; those servicing tourist attractions operate shorter hours.

A one-way inner-harbour ride on a regular ferry costs adult/concession $5.30/2.60. A one-way ride to Manly or Parramatta costs $6.60/$3.30. Seniors are eligible for a $2.50 all-day excursion ticket and on Sundays families can take advantage of the 'Family Funday' ticket, which gives all-day travel on all Sydney transport for $2.50 per person (minimum one adult and one child).

The privately owned **Captain Cook Ferries** (www.captaincook.com.au) operates ferry services to Manly from Circular Quay (return adult/child $17/8.50) and Darling Harbour (return adult/child $24/12). It also runs a Zoo Express service to Taronga Zoo from Circular Quay and Darling Harbour (return adult/child $49.50/24.50 including entrance fee).

For information about harbour cruises, see p49.

WATER TAXI Water taxis ply dedicated shuttle routes; rides to/from other harbour venues can be booked.

Aussie Water Taxis (Map p54; 📞9211 7730; www.aussiewatertaxis.com; Cockle Bay Wharf, Darling Harbour; ⏱9am-10pm) Darling Harbour to Circular Quay adult single/return $15/25, child $10/15; Darling Harbour to Taronga Zoo adult single/return $25/40, child $15/25; 45-minute Harbour and Nightlights Tours $35/25 adult/child.

Yellow Water Taxis (Map p54; 📞1300 138 840; www.yellowwatertaxis.com.au; King St Wharf, Darling Harbour; ⏱7am-midnight) Circular Quay to Darling Harbour is $15/10 per adult/child; a 45-minute Harbour 'Hop On, Hop Off' Tour stopping at Sydney Aquarium, Luna Park, Taronga Zoo and Sydney Opera House costs $40/20 per adult/child.

Bus

Sydney Buses (www.sydneybuses.info) has an extensive network; you can check routes and timetables online. Nightrider buses operate after regular services cease around midnight. The main city bus stops are Circular Quay, Wynyard Park (York St) and Railway Sq. Many services are prepay only during the week – buy tickets from newsagents or Bus TransitShops.

On weekends, you can usually purchase your ticket on the bus. There are three fare zones: $2/3.30/4.30. There's a **Bus TransitShop booth** (www.sydneybuses.info; cnr Alfred & Loftus Sts; ⏱7am-7pm Mon-Fri, 8.30am-5pm Sat & Sun) at Circular Quay, and there are others at the Queen Victoria Building (Map p54), Railway Sq (Map p54) and Wynyard Station (Map p54).

Bus routes starting with an 'X' indicate limited-stop express routes; those with an 'L' have limited stops. A free CBD shuttle (555) departs every 20 minutes between 9.30am and 3.30pm Monday to Wednesday and Friday, to 9pm on Thursday and between 9.30am and 6pm Saturday and Sunday. It travels between Circular Quay and Central Station, stopping at Martin Pl, St James and Museum stations, Chinatown, Town Hall, QVB and Wynyard station en route.

Car & Motorcycle

Cars are good for day trips out of town, but driving one in the city is like having an anchor around your neck. Heavy traffic, elusive and very expensive parking (even at hotels, expect to pay$30 per day) and the extra costs just aren't worth the stress.

BUYING OR SELLING A CAR The secondhand car industry is a minefield of mistrust and dodgy wheelers and dealers, but with a bit of research you can still land yourself a decent deal. Parramatta Rd is lined with used-car lots, and the *Trading Post* (www.tradingpost.com.au), a weekly rag available at newsagents, lists secondhand vehicles. For more information on buying or selling a vehicle, see p531.

The **Kings Cross Car Market** (📞1800 808 188; www.carmarket.com.au; 110 Bourke St, Woolloomooloo; ⏱9am-5pm) is a good spot to buy or sell a car. It can be hit and miss, but always busy.

RENTAL Major rental agencies with offices in Sydney:

Avis (📞13 63 33; www.avis.com.au)

Budget (📞13 27 27; www.budget.com.au)

Europcar (📞1300 13 13 90; www.europcar.com.au)

Hertz (📞13 30 39; www.hertz.com.au)

Thrifty (📞1300 367 227; www.thrifty.com.au)

The **Yellow Pages** (www.yellowpages.com.au) lists many other car-hire companies, some specialising in renting clapped-out wrecks at rock-bottom prices – read the fine print! For campervan hire, head towards William St in the Cross, where companies such as **Jucy** ([📞]1800 150 850; www.jucy.com.au) are located.

ROAD TOLLS There's a $4 southbound toll on the Sydney Harbour Bridge and Tunnel; a $5.50 northbound toll on the Eastern Distributor; a $2.10 toll on the Cross City Tunnel; and a $2.83 toll on the Lane Cove Tunnel. Sydney's main motorways (M2, M5 and M7) are also tolled ($2.50 to $7). There are a few cash booths at toll gates, but the whole system is electronic, meaning that it's up to you to have organised an electronic tag or visitor's pass through any of the following websites: www.roamcom.au, www.roamexpress.com.au or www.myRTA.com.au. For info, try www.sydneymotorways.com.

Monorail & Metro Light Rail (MLR)

The privately operated **Metro Monorail** (www.metromonorail.com.au; single circuit $4.90, day pass $9.50; ⊘every 5min, 7am-10pm Mon-Thu, 8am-10pm Sat & Sun) travels in a loop from Galleries Victoria on the corner of Pitt and Park Sts through Chinatown and Darling Harbour.

Run by the same outfit, the **Metro Light Rail** (MLR; www.metrolightrail.com.au; Zone 1 adult/concession $3.40/2.20, Zone 1 & 2 adult/concession $4.40/3.40, day pass adult $9; ⊘24hr, every 10-15min 6am-midnight, every 30min midnight-6am) is a tram service that runs between Central Station and Pyrmont via Chinatown and Darling Harbour. The Zone 2 service beyond Pyrmont to Lilyfield via the Fish Markets, Glebe and Rozelle operates from 6am to 11pm Monday to Thursday and Sunday and till midnight Friday and Saturday.

Taxi

Taxis and taxi ranks proliferate in Sydney. Flag fall is $3.30, then it's $1.99 per kilometre (plus 20% from 10pm to 6am). The waiting charge is $0.86 per minute. Passengers must pay bridge, tunnel and road tolls (even if you don't incur them 'outbound', the returning driver will incur them 'inbound').

The major taxi companies offering phone bookings ($2.20 fee):

Legion ([📞]13 14 51; www.legioncabs.com.au)

Premier Cabs ([📞]13 10 17; www.premiercabs.com.au)

Taxis Combined ([📞]13 33 00; www.taxiscombined.com.au)

Train

Sydney's suburban rail network is operated by **CityRail** ([📞]13 15 00; www.cityrail.info). Lines radiate from the underground City Circle (seven

city-centre stations) but don't service the northern and southern beaches Balmain or Glebe. All suburban trains stop at Central Station, and usually one or more of the other City Circle stations.

Trains run from around 5am to midnight. After 9am on weekdays you can buy an off-peak return ticket, valid until 4am the next day, for little more than a standard one-way fare.

Twenty-four-hour ticket machines occupy most stations, but humans are usually available if you need help with the fares. If you have to change trains, buy a ticket to your ultimate destination, but don't exit the transfer station en route or your ticket will be invalid.

For train information, visit the helpful **CityRail Information Booth** (Circular Quay; ⊘9.05am-4.50pm).

BLUE MOUNTAINS

POP 77,784

A region with more gorges, gum trees and gourmet restaurants than seem viable, the spectacular Blue Mountains (Map p99) was an obvious contender when Unesco called for Australian nominations to the World Heritage List, and its inclusion was ratified in 2000. The slate-coloured haze that gives the mountains their name comes from a fine mist of oil exuded by the huge eucalyptus gums that form a dense canopy across the landscape of deep, often-inaccessible valleys and chiselled sandstone outcrops. The landscape has an extraordinary beauty and biodiversity, making the area one of Australia's most popular bushwalking destinations.

The foothills begin 65km inland from Sydney, rising to an 1100m-high sandstone plateau riddled with valleys eroded into the stone over thousands of years. There are eight connected conservation areas in the region, including the **Blue Mountains National Park** (www.environment.nsw.gov.au/nationalparks), which has some truly fantastic scenery, excellent bushwalks, Aboriginal engravings and all the canyons and cliffs you could ask for. It's the most popular and accessible of the three national parks in the area. Great lookouts include the Evan's and Govett's Leap lookouts near Blackheath and Echo Point in Katoomba.

Wollemi National Park (www.environment.nsw.gov.au/nationalparks), north of the Bells Line of Rd, is NSW's largest forested wilderness area, stretching all the way to Denman in the Hunter Valley.

Six Aboriginal language groups treasure connections with the area that reach back into ancient time: the Dharawal and Gundungurra people in the south, the Wiradjuri in the west and northwest and the Wanaruah, Darkinjung and Darug in the northeast.

Although it's possible to visit on a day trip from Sydney, we strongly recommend that you stay at least one night so that you can explore a few of the towns, do at least one bushwalk and enjoy a dinner at one of the excellent restaurants in Blackheath or Leura.

After the beaches of Bondi, you may find the hills surprisingly cool, so bring a coat or wrap.

⊙ Sights

Arriving from Sydney, the first of the Blue Mountains towns you will encounter is Gembrook. From here, you can drive or walk into the **Blue Mountains National Park** (Map p99)$7 per car, walkers free; ⊙8.30am-6pm, to 7pm during daylight savings). Six kilometres from the park entrance gate is the Mt Portal Lookout with panoramic views into the Glenbrook Gorge, over the Nepean River and back to Sydney.

Further up the mountain, the town of **Wentworth Falls** commands views to the south, out across the majestic Jamison Valley. Wentworth Falls themselves launch a plume of fraying droplets over a 300m drop – check them out from Falls Reserve. This is also the starting point for a network of walking tracks into the sublime Valley of the Waters, which has waterfalls, gorges, woodlands and rainforests. Many of these walks start from the **Conservation Hut** (www.conservationhut.com.au; Fletcher St; mains $23-30; ⊙9am-4pm Mon-Fri, to 5pm Sat & Sun), where you can enjoy a coffee or meal on a deck overlooking the valley.

Nearby **Leura** (Map p99) is a genteel town of undulating streets, heritage houses and lush gardens. At its centre is The Mall, a tree-lined main street with boutiques, galleries and cafes. The National Trust–owned property **Everglades** (www.everglades.org.au; 37 Everglades Ave; adult/child/concession $8/4/6; ⊙10am-5pm Oct-Mar, to 4pm Apr-Sep) was built in the 1930s and has one of the country's foremost heritage gardens.

From Leura, it's only 2km to **Katoomba** (Map p99), the region's main town, whose often-misty steep streets are lined with Art Deco buildings. The population here is an odd mix of working-class battlers and hippyish refugees from the big smoke (Sydney), all of whom seem to cope with the huge numbers of tour buses and tourists who come here to ooh-and-aah at the spectacular view of the Jamison Valley and **Three Sisters** rock formation towers from the **Echo Point** viewing platforms. There are a number of short walks from Echo Point that allow you to escape the bulk of the crowds. Parking is expensive ($3.80 for first hour, $4.40 for subsequent hours); if you're walking here from the town centre, Lurline St is the most attractive route.

Three kilometres from the centre of Katoomba you'll find **Scenic World** (www.scenicworld.com.au; cnr Cliff Dr & Violet St; return adult/child $21/10; ⊙9am-5pm), with a megaplex vibe and an 1880s railway and modern cable car descending the 52-degree incline to the valley floor. Also here is the glass-floored **Scenic Skyway** (adult/child $16/8), a cable car floating out across the valley.

The next town to the west is **Blackheath** (Map p99) where you can enjoy amazing views from Perrys Lookdown, Pulpit Rock, Govetts Leap and Evans Lookout. Crowds here aren't as oppressive as at Echo Point. Blackheath is also the gastronomic centre of the region, with some excellent restaurants operating between Thursday and Sunday.

🏃 Activities

Bushwalking

Explorers Wentworth, Blaxland and Lawson set off a craze for exploring the area when they became the first Europeans to traverse these majestic mountains in 1813. Fortunately, there are walks of every possible duration and level of difficulty on offer, so everyone can participate. The two most popular bushwalking areas are the Jamison Valley, south of Katoomba, and the Grose Valley, northeast of Katoomba and east of Blackheath. The area south of Glenbrook is also good. One of the most rewarding walks is the 45km, three-day 'Six Foot Track' from Katoomba along the Megalong Valley to Cox's River and on to the Jenolan Caves. It has camp sites along the way.

The NPWS centre in Blackheath can help you pick a hike; for shorter walks, ask at the Echo Point visitors centre. Note that the bush here is dense and that it can be easy to become lost – there have been deaths as a consequence. Always leave your name and walk plan with the Katoomba Police, at the NPWS office or at one of the visitor centres; the Katoomba police station, Echo Point visitor information centre and NPWS office also offer free use of personal locator beacons.

Also remember to carry clean drinking water with you – the mountain streams are polluted due to their proximity to urban areas.

A range of NPWS walks pamphlets and maps ($3 to $6) are available from the NPWS office and from the visitor information centres at Glenbrook and Katoomba. All three also sell the Heama *Blue Mountains* walking map ($8.95) and Veechi Stuart's well-regarded *Blue Mountains: Best Bushwalks* ($29.95) book.

Cycling

The mountains are also a popular cycling destination, with many people taking their bikes on the train to Woodford and then cycling downhill to Glenbrook, a ride of two to three hours. Cycling maps ($7) are available from the visitor information centres at Glenbrook and Katoomba.

Driving

The **Greater Blue Mountains Drive** (www.greaterbluemountainsdrive.com.au) is a 1200km tour linking Sydney with the Blue Mountains region; it incorporates 18 'discovery trails' (stand-alone scenic drives), the most popular being the 36km, one hour 'Blue Mountains Drive Discovery Trail' that starts in Katoomba and finishes at the Valley of the Waters picnic area at Wentworth Falls.

The best driving maps are Gregory's *Blue Mountains Touring Map* ($7.95) and the *Greater Blue Mountains Drive Touring Map* ($7.95). Both are available at the visitor information centres.

Adventure Activities & Tours

Most operators have offices in Katoomba – competition is steep, so shop around for the best deal.

Australian School of Mountaineering
MOUNTAINEERING
(ASM; Map p99; ☑4782 2014; www.asmguides.com; 166 Katoomba St, Katoomba) Rock climbing/abseiling/canyoning from $175/145/175.

Blue Mountains Adventure Company
ADVENTURE SPORTS
(Map p99; ☑4782 1271; www.bmac.com.au; 84A Bathurst Rd, Katoomba) Abseiling from $110,

abseiling and bushwalking combo from $180, canyoning from $165, bushwalking from $100 and rockclimbing from $180.

Blue Mountains Walkabout
ABORIGINAL TREKS
(☑0408 443 822; www.bluemountainswalkabout.com) Seven-hour or half-day Aboriginal owned and guided adventurous treks with Aboriginal and spiritual themes ($95/75). Meets at Faulconbridge train station.

Tread Lightly Eco Tours
ECO TOURS
(☑4788 1229; www.treadlightly.com.au) Has a wide range of day and night walks ($65 to $135) that emphasise the region's ecology.

🛏 Sleeping

There's a good range of accommodation in the Blue Mountains, but you'll need to book ahead during winter and for every weekend during the year (Sydneysiders love coming here for romantic weekends away). Backpackers tend to stay in Katoomba, where the hostels are, but those with their own transport prefer Leura and Blackheath, where the restaurants and cafes are better.

Note that the famous **Hydro Majestic Hotel** (www.hydromajestic.com.au), an Art Deco extravaganza at Medlow Bath, was undergoing a major renovation when this book was being researched and was due to re-open in 2012.

TOP CHOICE Glenella Guesthouse
GUESTHOUSE $$
(Map p99; ☑4787 8352; www.glenellabluemountainshotel.com.au; 56-60 Govetts Leap Rd, Blackheath; r $100-160, f $200-240; 🐾) Gorgeous Glenella has been functioning as a guesthouse since 1912 and is now operated with enthusiasm and expertise by a young British couple who make guests feel very welcome. There are seven comfortable bedrooms, an attractive lounge and a stunning dining room where a truly excellent breakfast is served.

Flying Fox
HOSTEL $
(Map p99; ☑4782 4226; www.theflyingfox.com.au; 190 Bathurst Rd, Katoomba; dm $29, d with shared bathroom $79, tent sites $19pp; @🐾) Owners Ross and Wendy, travellers at heart, have endowed this unassuming hostel with an endearing home-away-from-home feel. There's no party scene here – just glühwein and Tim Tams in the friendly lounge and a free pancake breakfast in the well-equipped communal kitchen. Internet and wi-fi are free, but there aren't many bathrooms.

Blue Mountains YHA
HOSTEL **$**

(Map p99; ☑4782 1416; www.yha.com.au; 207 Katoomba St, Katoomba; dm $29.50-31.50, d with/without bathroom $98.50/$88.50, f with/without bathroom $140/$126; @☎) Behind the austere Art Deco exterior of this popular 200-bed hostel is a selection of dorms and family rooms that are comfortable, light and spotlessly clean. Highlights include a lounge with open fire, central heating, a huge TV room, pool table, excellent communal kitchen and outdoor space with barbecues. You can organise plenty of activities from here. A DIY breakfast costs $6.50.

Greens of Leura
B&B **$$**

(Map p99; ☑4784 3241; www.thegreensleura.com.au; 24-26 Grose St, Leura; r from $145/175 weekdays/weekends; @☎) On a quiet street parallel to The Mall, this pretty timber house set in a lovely garden offers five rooms named after English writers (Browning, Austen etc). All are individually decorated; some have four-poster beds and spas.

Leura House
GUESTHOUSE **$$**

(Map p99; ☑4784 2035; www.leurahouse.com.au; 7 Britain St, Leura; s $145, d $170-190, ste $190-230; @☎) Occupying an 1880s mansion set in a splendid garden, this sprawling place has functioned in the past as a convent but has been a guesthouse for the past few decades. The 13 rooms are comfortable and clean, if a tad faded (opt for number 11, which has a great view). Breakfast could be better.

Carrington Hotel
HOTEL **$$-$$$**

(Map p99; ☑4782 1111; www.thecarrington.com.au; 15-47 Katoomba St, Katoomba; r with private bathroom $205-315, r with shared bathroom $129-149, ste $340-490; ✿@☎) The Carrington, Katoomba's social and architectural high-water mark, has been accommodating travellers since 1880. Though much of the building has been refurbished, its historical character remains intact. Amenities include a library, a billiards room and stately gardens.

No 14
HOSTEL **$**

(Map p99; ☑4782 7104; www.numberfourteen.com; 14 Lovel St, Katoomba; dm $25-28, d with bathroom $75-85, d with shared bathroom $65-75; @☎) Resembling a cheery share house, this small hostel has a friendly vibe but suffers from a lack of bathrooms (three showers for 30 beds). Dorms have three or four beds; attic-style doubles are comfy. A basic breakfast is included in the price and internet access on the in-house computer is free; wi-fi costs $5 per 24 hours.

✖ Eating

Despite being the major town in the mountains, Katoomba has a lacklustre array of restaurants and cafes – if you have transport you are better off eating elsewhere.

TOP CHOICE Solitary
MODERN AUSTRALIAN **$$**

(Map p99; ☑4782 1164; www.solitary.com.au; 90 Cliff Drive, Leura Falls; lunch $14-33.50, dinner $26-33.50; ☺lunch daily, dinner Sat, closed 2 wks Jan) The magnificent views to Mt Solitary are the main event here, but the seasonally driven and totally delicious food lives up to this elegant restaurant's setting atop the Leura Cascades. Also serves Devonshire teas ($10).

Whisk & Pin Store & Cafe
CAFE **$**

(Map p99; www.whiskandpin.com; 1 Railway Pde, Medlow Bath; breakfast $7-17.50, sandwiches $9.50-16.50, light lunch dishes $15.50-17.50; ☺8.30am-4pm Mon-Fri, to 5pm Sat & Sun) This cafe is set in a store selling gourmet pantry products and stylish gifts. Claim a seat on a couch or at the communal table and enjoy the freshly prepared and deliciously healthy food on offer. You'll find it opposite the railway station on the northern side of the highway.

Ashcrofts
MODERN AUSTRALIAN **$$**

(Map p99; ☑4787 8297; www.ashcrofts.com; 18 Govetts Leap Rd, Blackheath; 2/3 courses $68/85; ☺dinner Wed-Sun, lunch Sun, closed Feb & 1st half of Mar) Chef Corinne Evatt has been wooing locals and visitors alike with her flavoursome, globally inspired dishes for the past decade. The wine list is possibly the best in the mountains and service is exemplary.

Escarpment
MODERN AUSTRALIAN **$$**

(Map p99; ☑4787 7269; www.escarpmentblackheath.com; 246 Great Western Highway, Blackheath; mains $28-34.50; ☺dinner Thu-Mon, lunch Sat & Sun) The decor at this recently opened bistro near the railway station features attractive artwork and an old-fashioned espresso machine. There's nothing old-fashioned or overly arty about the menu, though – it changes with the season and makes the most of local produce.

Fresh Espresso & Food Bar
CAFE **$**

(Map p99; www.freshcafe.com.au; 181 Katoomba St, Katoomba; breakfast $4.50-14.90, lunch $12.90-15.90; ☺8am-5pm Mon-Sat, to 4pm Sun) The organic, rainforest alliance and fair-trade coffee served at Fresh attracts a devoted local following. Excellent all-day breakfasts are popular, too. The Katoomba branch is small but the new cafe/roastery on the corner of Megalong St and The Mall in Leura has plenty of seats.

Silk's Brasserie MODERN AUSTRALIAN **$$**
(Map p99; ☎4784 2534; www.silksleura.com; 128 The Mall, Leura; mains $24-37; ☺lunch & dinner) The decor and staff are equally welcoming at Leura's long-standing fine diner. Dishes can sometimes be overworked, but serves are generous and flavours harmonious.

Blue Mountains Food Co-op
GROCERY STORE **$**
(Map p99; www.bluemtnsfood.asn.au; Shops 1 & 2, Ha'penny Lane, Katoomba; ☺9am-6pm Mon-Wed & Fri, to 6.30pm Thu, 8.30am-5pm Sat & 10am-4.30pm Sun) The perfect stop for hard-core self-caterers and bushwalkers in need of goodies for their backpacks, the Co-op stocks organic, vegan and gluten-free local foods and produce.

Drinking

Station Bar BAR
(Map p99; http://stationbar.com.au; 287 Bathurst Rd, Katoomba; ☺till late) This new bar next to the train station is the town's most popular drinking hole, but our experience would indicate that the pizzas are best avoided. There's live music on Sunday nights from 7pm.

The Old City Bank Bar & Brasserie BAR
(Map p99; Katoomba St, Katoomba; ☺7am-2am Mon-Thu, to 3am Fri & Sat, 10am-10pm Sun; ☐) This popular place has a bar on the ground floor and a dining room upstairs serving decent pub grub and pizzas (mains $14 to $24). There's live music most Friday and Saturday nights.

Information

For more information on the national parks (including walking and camping) contact the **NPWS Visitors Centre** at Blackheath (Map p99; ☎4787 8877; www.nationalparks.nsw.gov.au; Govetts Leap Rd, Blackheath; ☺9am-4.30pm), about 2.5km off the Great Western Hwy and 10km north of Katoomba.

There are **Visitor Information Centres** (☎1300 653 408 or 1800 641 227; www.visit bluemountains.com.au) on the Great Western Highway at **Glenbrook** (☺9am-4.30pm Mon-Fri, 8.30am-3.30pm Sat & Sun) and at Echo Point in **Katoomba** (Map p99; ☺9am-5pm). Both can provide plenty of information and will book accommodation, tours and attractions.

Getting There & Around

To reach the Blue Mountains by road, leave Sydney via Parramatta Rd. At Strathfield detour onto the toll-free M4, which becomes the Great Western Hwy west of Penrith and takes you to all of the Blue Mountains towns. It takes approximately 1½ hours to drive from central Sydney to Katoomba.

The scenic Bells Line of Rd is north of the Great Western Hwy. It twists and turns through the mountains and can be combined with the Great Western Hwy for a circle route. To reach it, head out on Parramatta Rd, and from Parramatta drive northwest on Windsor Rd to Windsor. Richmond Rd from Windsor becomes the Bells Line of Rd west of Richmond.

Blue Mountains Bus (☎4751 1077; www.bmbc. com.au) Local buses travel from Katoomba to Wentworth Falls (685 and 690K), Scenic World (686), Leura (690K) and Blackheath (698). Fares cost between $2 and $4.30.

Blue Mountains Explorer Bus (☎1300 300 915; www.explorerbus.com.au; 283 Main St, Katoomba; adult/child $36/18; ☺9.45am-4.54pm) Offers hop-on hop-off service on a Katoomba–Leura loop. Leaves from Katoomba station every 30 minutes to one hour.

Blue Mountains ExplorerLink (☎13 15 00; www.cityrail.info; 1-day pass adult/child from $46.80/23.40, 3-day pass adult/child from $66.80/33.40) Gives return train travel from Sydney to the Blue Mountains, plus access to the Explorer Bus service.

CityRail (☎13 15 00; www.cityrail.info) Runs to the mountains from Sydney's Central Station (one way adult/child $7.80/3.90, two hours, hourly).

Trolley Tours (☎4782 7999, 1800 801 577; www.trolleytours.com.au; 285 Main St, Katoomba; adult/family $20/60; ☺9.45am-5.42pm) Runs a 'hop-on, hop-off' bus barely disguised as a trolley. Twenty-nine stops in Katoomba and Leura.

SYDNEY TO NEWCASTLE

After struggling through the traffic of Sydney's northern suburbs, you can choose whether to motor straight up the freeway to Newcastle or meander along the coast. Truth be told, neither route will be a highlight of your trip, but if you've got time to kill there are some pleasant diversions along the coastal road.

The largest town in the area is hilly **Gosford**, an uninspiring place that serves as the transport and services hub for the surrounding beaches. The best place to access tourist information about the area is the **Central Coast Visitor Centre** (☎4343 4444; www.visitcentralcoast.com.au; The Avenue, Kariong;

⊙9am-5pm Mon-Fri, 9.30am-3.30pm Sat & Sun) just off the F3 freeway at the entrance to town, but there's also a smaller, volunteer-manned **visitors centre** (☑4343 4444; 200 Mann St; ⊙9.30am-4pm Mon-Fri, to 1pm Sat) near the train station and a **National Parks & Wildlife Service (NPWS) office** (☑4320 4200; 207 Albany St N; ⊙8.30am-4.30pm Mon-Fri) behind the Gosford Town Centre Shopping Centre.

The **Australian Reptile Park** (☑4340 1022; www.reptilepark.com.au; adult/child/concession $24.50/12.50/17; ⊙9am-5pm), well sign-posted from the freeway exit, offers a chance to get up close to koalas and pythons, watch funnel-web spiders being milked (for the production of antivenin) and learn about the plight of the Tasmanian devil (the park serves as a breeding ark). There's also a wonderfully craptastic *Lost Kingdom of Reptiles* Disney-style enclosure.

Southwest of Gosford, rambling trails run through rugged sandstone in **Brisbane Water National Park** (www.nationalparks.nsw.gov.au), which borders the Hawkesbury River and is known for its wildflowers. The **Bulgandry Aboriginal Engraving Site** is situated 3km south of the Central Coast Hwy on Woy Woy Rd.

A favourite retreat for actors, writers and other luvvies is the pretty village of **Pearl Beach**, on the eastern edge of the park. It has plenty of cafes and restaurants including **Pearls on the Beach** (☑4342 4400; www.pearlsonthebeach.com.au; 1 Tourmaline Ave; mains $30-36; ⊙lunch & dinner Thu-Sun), a stylish beach shack right on the water.

Southeast of Gosford, **Bouddi National Park** (www.environment.nsw.gov.au/national parks) extends from the north head of Broken Bay to MacMasters Beach, 12km south of Terrigal. Vehicle access is limited but there are short walking trails leading to isolated beaches, including lovely **Maitland Bay**. The park is in two sections on either side of **Putty Beach**, which has vehicle access ($7). There are camp sites at **Little Beach** (site per adult/child $14/7), **Putty Beach** (site per adult/child $14/7) and **Tallow Beach** (site per adult/child $10/5); book through the NPWS office in Gosford. Only the Putty Beach site has drinkable water and flush toilets.

East of Gosford, the coast is heavily populated. The crescent-shaped beach at **Terrigal** is pleasant and the surf's good, so it's worth a pit-stop. You can enjoy a meal or drink overlooking the water at **Cove Cafe** (http://covecafe.com.au; The Haven; mains $15.90-33.90; ⊙breakfast & lunch daily, dinner Fri & Sat in summer) or grab some fish & chips to eat on the beach from **Haven Seafoods** on the waterfront or **Snapper Spot** on The Esplanade. Attractive accommodation options are thin on the ground – try the cramped but clean **Terrigal Beach YHA** (☑4384 1919; www.yha.com.au; 9 Ocean View Dr; dm $30, d with private/shared bathroom $85/75; ☎).

A series of saltwater 'lakes' spreads north up the coast between Bateau Bay and Newcastle, the largest of which, **Lake Macquarie**, covers four times the area of Sydney Harbour.

⊙ Getting There & Away

Gosford has numerous CityRail connections to Sydney (adult/child $7.80/3.90, 1½ hours) and Newcastle (adult/child $7.80/3.90, 1½ hours). From Gosford station, **Busways** (☑9625 8900; www.busways.com.au) and **Redbus** (☑4332 8655; www.redbus.com.au) run services to Terrigal and neighbouring towns and beaches; these are less frequent on weekends.

CityRail trains stop at Wondabyne train station inside Brisbane Waters National Park upon request (rear carriage only). To access Bouddi National Park via public transport, take Busways bus 61 from Gosford.

NEWCASTLE

POP 540,796

Sydney may possess the glitz and the glamour, but the state's second-largest city has down-to-earth larrikin charm instead. Newcastle is the kind of place where you can grocery shop barefoot, go surfing in your lunch hour and quickly become best buddies with the Novocastrian sitting next to you in any bar.

This easygoing, 'no worries' attitude has been shaped by Newcastle's rough-and-tumble past, shaped by a cast of convicts and coal miners. Today it continues to be the largest coal-export harbour in the world, but the city is undergoing something of a renaissance. Wharf rejuvenation projects are breathing new life into the harbour and an eclectic and innovative arts scene is injecting colour and culture into the streets.

Swim or surf at the popular beaches and soak in ocean baths, explore the outstanding heritage architecture in the CBD and window shop along funky Darby St. Dine on fish and chips, watch the tankers chug along the

Newcastle

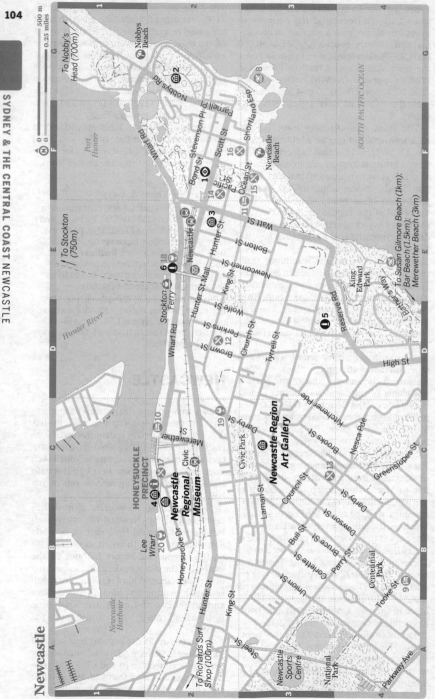

500 m
0.25 miles

To Nobby's Head (700m)

Nobbys Beach

Port Hunter

To Stockton (750m)

Hunter River

HONEYSUCKLE PRECINCT

Newcastle Harbour

Lee Wharf

Newcastle Regional Museum

Stockton Ferry

Hunter St Mall

Nobbys Rd

Parnell Pl

Stevenson Pl

Scott St

Shortland Esp

Bond St

Pacific St

Ocean St

Wall St

Bolton St

Hunter St

King St

Wolfe St

Perkins St

Church St

Brown St

Newcomen St

Tyrrell St

Reserve Rd

High St

Kitchener Pde

Darby St

Brooks St

Nesca Pde

Greenslopes St

Laman St

Council St

Darby St

Dawson St

Bull St

Corlette St

Bruce St

Parry St

Union St

Tooke St

King St

Steel St

Hunter St

Parkway Ave

Merewether St

Honeysuckle Dr

Wharf Rd

Civic Park

Centennial Park

National Park

Newcastle Sports Centre

Newcastle Region Art Gallery

Civic

Newcastle Beach

SOUTH PACIFIC OCEAN

King Edward Park

Bathers Way

To Susan Gilmore Beach (1km);
Bar Beach (1.5km);
Merewether Beach (3km)

To Richards Surf Shop (100m)

horizon and catch some live music – Newcastle is easily worth a day or two of your time.

Sights
Museums, Galleries & Historical Sites

FREE **Lock Up** CULTURAL CENTRE
(www.thelockup.info; 90 Hunter St; ☺10am-4pm Wed-Sun) These days, artists in residence are incarcerated in this former police station (1861) rather than prisoners. There's a contemporary art gallery, artists' studios and an interesting law-and-order museum within the creepy, cramped cells of the heritage-listed prison cells.

Newcastle Regional Museum MUSEUM
(www.newcastle.nsw.gov.au/about_newcastle/newcastle_museum; Workshop Way, Honeysuckle Precinct; admission free; ☺10am-5pm Tue-Sun) Opened in August 2011, the city's flagship museum occupies the restored Honeysuckle rail workshops on the foreshore and focuses on the people, activities and places of the city and region.

Fort Scratchley HISTORIC SITE
(www.fortscratchley.org.au; Nobby's Rd; admission to top area free, guided tour of site & tunnels adult/child/concession $15/7.50/8; ☺Wed-Mon 10am-4pm, guided tours weekends or by appointment) Originally constructed during the Crimean War to protect the city from possible invasion, this recently restored fort, perched high above Newcastle Harbour, was one of the few gun installations in Australia to fire in anger during WWII. On 8 June 1942, a Japanese submarine suddenly surfaced, raining shells on the city. Fort Scratchley returned fire, eliminating the threat after just four rounds. Learn all about it on a guided tour.

The Newcastle Maritime Centre MUSEUM
(Lee Wharf, 3 Honeysuckle Dr; adult/child/concession $10/5/7; ☺10am-4pm Tue-Sun) Learn all about Newcastle's nautical heritage at this new museum in a restored harbourfront wharf building.

FREE **Newcastle Region Art Gallery**
ART GALLERY
(www.newcastle.nsw.gov.au/nag; 1 Laman St; ☺10am-5pm Tue-Sun) This gallery has a permanent collection of works by revered Australian artists (Drysdale, Nolan, Whiteley) and hosts exciting temporary exhibitions.

Wildlife Reserves

FREE **Blackbutt Reserve** NATURE RESERVE
(www.newcastle.nsw.gov.au/recreation/blackbutt_reserve; Carnley Ave, Kotara; ☺9am-5pm) Sitting in a tract of bushland with plenty of walking trails and picnic areas, this council-run reserve has enclosures of native critters: koalas, kangaroos, wallabies and wombats and a cacophonic chorus of native birds. Take bus 224 or 317 (30 minutes) to the park's edge then walk 1km to the entrance.

Hunter Wetlands Centre NATURE RESERVE
(www.wetlands.org.au; Sandgate Rd, Shortland; adult/child/concession $10/5/6.50; ☺9am-4pm Mon-Fri, to 5pm Sat & Sun) This swampy wonderland is home to over 200 bird and animal species. You can explore via canoe ($14.90 for two hours) or dip in a net and examine the results under a magnifying glass. Bring mosquito repellent if you don't want to contribute to the ecosystem in ways you hadn't intended. Take the Pacific Hwy towards

Maitland and turn left at the cemetery, or catch bus 106 or 107 (40 minutes) from the train station.

Other Attractions

Queens Wharf Tower, on the waterfront, and the **obelisk** above King Edward Park provide commanding views of the city and the water. Across the river (about five minutes by ferry) is **Stockton**, a modest settlement with striking views back towards Newcastle and exposed shipwrecks in its waters.

Nobby's Head used to be an island until it was joined to the mainland in 1846 to create a singularly pretty sand spit; it was twice its current height before being reduced to 28m above sea level in 1855. The walk along the spit towards the lighthouse and meteorological station is exhilarating, with waves crashing about your ears and joggers jostling your elbows.

🏃 Activities

Swimming & Surfing

At the East End, the needs of surfers and swimmers are sated at **Newcastle Beach**, but if you're irrationally paranoid about sharks, the concrete **ocean baths** are a mellow alternative, encased in wonderful multicoloured 1922 architecture. There's a shallow pool for toddlers and a compelling backdrop of heaving ocean and chugging cargo ships. Surfers should goofy-foot it to **Nobby's Beach**, just north of the baths – the fast left-hander known as the Wedge is at its northern end.

South of Newcastle Beach, below King Edward Park, is Australia's oldest ocean bath, the convict-carved **Bogey Hole**. It's an atmospheric place to splash about when the surf's crashing over its edge.

The most popular surfing break is at **Bar Beach**, 1km south. If your swimsuit is chafing, scramble around the rocks at the northern end to the (unofficial) clothing-optional **Susan Gilmour Beach**, which is only accessible at low tide. At nearby **Merewether Beach**, the opening of the winter swimming season is heralded at its ocean baths, where blocks of ice are dumped into the water so that the cold-blooded freaks from the Merewether Mackerels Winter Swimming Club can strut their stuff. Frequent local buses from the CBD run as far south as Bar Beach, but only buses 201, 225 and 310 continue to Merewether.

For surfing supplies, head to **Richards Surf Shop** (☏4961 3088; 755 Hunter St). The

Jye Byrnes Surf School (☏0409 227 407; jyebyrnes@hotmail.com; 80-min group lesson per person $40, private lesson $70) specialises in individual coaching and small-group tuition.

The city's famous surfing festival, **Surfest** (www.surfest.com), takes place in March each year.

Walking Tours

The visitors centre has a map-brochure outlining two self-guided themed walking tours of the city. **The Bather's Way** leads between Nobby's and Merewether Beaches, with signs describing Indigenous, convict and natural history in between swims. The **Newcastle East Heritage Walk** heads past colonial highlights including, the **Convict Lumber Yard** opposite the Newcastle train station.

The *Newcastle by Design* brochure available at the visitors centre outlines a short stroll down and around Hunter St covering some of the inner city's interesting architecture.

👉 Tours

Hunter Valley Day Tours   WINERY TOURS
(☏4951 4574; www.huntervalleydaytours.com.au) Visits four or five Hunter Valley vineyards, the Hunter Valley Cheese Company and the Hunter Valley Chocolate Company; prices vary according to group numbers (from $95 per person).

Tex Tours   WINERY TOURS
(www.textours.com.au; ☏0410 462 540) Offers entertaining full-day Hunter Valley winery tours ($65, backpacker discounts available) as well as dolphin and 4WD dune tours to Port Stephens ($75).

🛏 Sleeping

Newcastle Beach YHA   HOSTEL $
(☏4925 3544; www.yha.com.au/hostels/details. cfm?hostelid=134; 30 Pacific St; dm $33, s $55, d $80; @🛜) This heritage-listed building is a bikini strap away from Newcastle Beach. Inside, it's a bit like an English public school (without the humiliating hazing rituals), featuring grand spaces and high ceilings. There's also free body board use, surfboard hire, free pub meals and a free barbecue on Thursday nights.

Stockton Beach Tourist Park   CAMPGROUND $
(☏4928 1393; www.stocktonbeach.com; Pitt St, Stockton; unpowered site $24-37, powered site $29-46, d bunkhouse $59-86, d cabins $97-176; @🛜) The beach is at your doorstep (or should that be tent flap?) at this tourist park behind

the dunes in Stockton. There are barbecues, a camp kitchen, kids' playground areas, a fully equipped laundry, and free wi-fi and internet access. You'll need to hire linen if you stay in a bunkhouse.

Hamilton Heritage B&B
B&B $$

(☑4961 1242; colaine@iprimus.com.au; 178 Denison St, Hamilton; s $95-110, d $135-165; ✻☎) It's all florals and frills in this Federation-era home near the Beaumont St cafe strip. Three rooms are reasonably sized and have en suites; one 'hobbit' room uses a shared bathroom (s/d $60/80). Child and pet friendly.

Backpackers Newcastle
HOSTEL $

(☑1800 33 34 36, 4969 3436; www.backpackersnewcastle.com.au; 42-44 Dennison St; dm $26-29, d/tw $60-65, camp site $15pp; @✉☎) It's not a patch on the YHA but it's cheap and offers free surfing lessons (board and wetsuit hire $25 for two hours), free dinners on Monday and Wednesday and free pick-up from the train station.

Crowne Plaza
HOTEL $$$

(☑4907 5000; www.crowneplaza.com.au/newcastle; cnr Merewether St & Wharf Rd; r $248-374; ✤☎☐✻☎) It's a large, beige, modern hotel, but it's right on the waterfront and easily the best in town. Service is excellent and the pool is a real plus. Breakfast costs $40.

Cooks Hill Cottage
RENTAL HOUSE $$$

(☑0401 269 863; www.cookshillcottage.com.au; 102 Dawson St, Cooks Hill; rates on application; ✻) Relax in the five-person hot tub on the deck or cook up a storm in the gourmet kitchen in this stylishly renovated two-bedroom house near Centennial Park.

🍴 Eating

Darby and Beaumont are the main eat streets. There are also plenty of cafes and restaurants around Honeysuckle Wharf and along the foreshore.

Bacchus
MODERN AUSTRALIAN $$

(☑4927 1332; www.bacchusnewcastle.com.au; 141 King St; lunch 2/3 courses $48/60, dinner mains $44-49, degustation $110-120; ☉lunch Thu & Fri, dinner Tue-Sat) A decadent Roman god has transformed this former Methodist mission into a very atmospheric place to splurge (not purge – this isn't Ancient Rome, after all). The surrounds are extremely elegant, dishes are assured and the wine list is excellent.

Jonah's on the Beach
MODERN AUSTRALIAN $$

(☑4929 5181; cnr Shortland Esplanade & Zara St; mains $35-57, set 2-/3-course lunch $38/45; ☉breakfast, lunch & dinner) In a four-star hotel overlooking Newcastle Beach, Jonah's offers magnificent views and a menu full of robustly flavoured delights. The wine list has a strong representation of Hunter Valley drops and there's live music on Thursday, Friday and Saturday evenings.

East End Enoteca
ITALIAN $-$$

(☑4925 2244; www.eastendenoteca.com; 14 Pacific St, Newcastle East; ☉lunch Thu & Fri, spuntini & dinner Tue-Sat; spuntini $4-22, lunch mains $15, dinner mains $23-35) Yep, it's got that casual Italian thang happening in spades. The food is great and there's a decent choice of wines by the glass.

Estabar
CAFE $

(61 Shortland Esplanade; ☉7am-8pm) Start the day with an excellent coffee or Spanish-style hot chocolate at this sun-drenched cafe overlooking Newcastle Beach. When the temperature soars, stop in for the best gelato in town.

Silo
MODERN AUSTRALIAN $$

(www.silolounge.com.au; 1 Honeysuckle Wharf; lunch mains $19-25, dinner mains $32-39; ☉breakfast Sat & Sun, lunch & dinner daily) One of the many places to have opened in the restored wharf precinct in recent times, Silo is a popular bar-restaurant with outdoor seating and pretensions to glamour. Pop in between 4pm and 6pm for $10 pizzas and $3.50 glasses of beer or sparkling wine.

Delucas Pizza
PIZZA $$

(☑4929 3555; 159B Darby St, Cooks Hill; pizzas $18-25; ☉dinner Tue-Sun 5pm-late) Delicious pizza and an endearingly old-school decor make this Newcastle's most popular pizzeria. The pasta's good, too.

🌿 3 Bean
CAFE $

(103 Tudor St, Hamilton; breakfast $7-16, lunch $18-21; ☉7am-5pm Mon-Fri, to 3pm Sat) Serious foodie attention has been paid to the menu here, including notes on the provenance of the produce, much of which is biodynamic and organic. Enter off Beaumont St.

🍷 Drinking & Entertainment

Finnegans
PUB

(www.finneganshotel.com.au; 21-23 Darby St; ☉Mon-Sat) The place for backpacker meals, trivia, pool competitions and, on the weekends, live bands and DJs.

Brewery
MICROBREWERY

(http://qwb.com.au; 150 Wharf Rd) Perched on Queens Wharf, with views and outdoor tables sought after by both Novocastrian office workers and uni students. Has regular live music Wednesday to Sunday and decent food.

Honeysuckle Hotel
PUB

(www.honeysucklehotel.com.au; Lee Wharf, Honeysuckle Drive; ⊗Mon-Thu 10am-11pm, Fri & Sat to midnight, Sun to 10pm) The deck at this waterfront place located in the trendy Honeysuckle precinct is a perfect spot for a sundowner. A DJ takes centre stage on summer Sundays between 4 and 9pm.

Cambridge Hotel
CLUB

(www.yourcambridge.com; 789 Hunter St, Newcastle West) This backpacker favourite launched Silverchair, Newcastle's most famous cultural export, and continues to showcase touring national bands and local acts in gigs from Wednesday to Sunday.

ⓘ Information

If you've got a laptop with wireless capability, head to Beaumont St in Hamilton where there's free wi-fi broadband between Tudor and Donald Sts. The airport also offers free wireless connections. You'll find banks and ATMs in Hunter St Mall. Most have foreign exchange.

John Hunter Hospital (☑4921 3000; Lookout Rd, New Lambton) Has 24-hour emergency care.

Post office (☑13 13 18; 1 Market St)

Visitors centre (☑4974 2999; www.visitnewcastle.com.au; Lee Wharf, 3 Honeysuckle Dr; ⊗10am-4pm Tue-Sun) Volunteer operated and well intentioned, but not particularly useful.

ⓘ Getting There & Away
Air

Newcastle Airport (☑4928 9800; www.newcastleairport.com.au) is at Williamtown, 23km north of the city.

Virgin Blue (☑13 67 89; www.virginblue.com.au) and **Jetstar** (☑13 15 38; www.jetstar.com) both fly to Brisbane, the Gold Coast and Melbourne. **Brindabella Airlines** (☑1300 66 88 24; www.brindabellaairlines.com.au) services Brisbane, Coffs Harbour, Port Macquarie and Canberra. **Aeropelican** (☑13 13 13; www.aeropelican.com.au) flies to Sydney. **Norfolk Air** (☑1300 669 913; www.norfolkair.com) has a weekly link to its island home.

Sydney Seaplanes (☑1300 732 752; www.seaplanes.com.au) operates a twice-daily weekday service between Honeysuckle Wharf and Sydney's Rose Bay ($175 to $225; 45 minutes).

Bus

Nearly all long-distance buses stop behind the Newcastle train station. **Greyhound** (☑1300 473 946; www.greyhound.com.au) heads to Forster ($39, three hours, daily) and Port Macquarie ($59, four hours, three daily). **Premier Motor Service** (☑13 34 10; www.premierms.com.au) has a daily bus to/from Sydney ($34, 2½ hours) and Brisbane ($76, 14 hours).

Rover Coaches (☑4990 1699; www.rovercoaches.com.au) heads to Cessnock ($4.30, 1½ hours) in the Hunter Valley. **Port Stephens Coaches** (☑4982 2940; www.pscoaches.com.au) has regular buses between Nelson Bay and Newcastle ($4.30, 1¾ hours). **Busways** (☑1800 043 263; www.busways.com.au) operates services to/from Hawks Nest via Tea Gardens ($23, 90 minutes, three daily).

Train

A better option than the buses, **CityRail** (☑13 15 00; www.cityrail.info) has frequent trains to Sydney (adult/child $7.80/3.90, three hours) via Gosford (adult/child $7.80/3.90, 90 minutes). A line also heads to Branxton (adult/child $7.80/3.90, 55 minutes) in the Hunter Valley.

ⓘ Getting Around
To/From the Airport

Port Stephens Coaches (☑4982 2940; www.pscoaches.com.au) heads to Williamtown airport frequently ($4.30, 40 minutes) en route to Nelsons Bay.

Shuttle bus services from the airport to Newcastle cost approximately $35 per person ($45 for two people). To book these or shuttles to other destinations in the area, contact **Newcastle Airport Information Services** (☑4928 9822; ⊗7am-7pm).

Taxi to Newcastle city centre costs about $65.

Bus

Newcastle has an extensive and reasonably priced network of **local buses** (☑13 15 00; www.newcastlebuses.info). There's a fare-free bus zone in the inner city between 7.30am and 6pm. Other fares are time-based (one-hour/four-hour/all-day $3.30/6.40/9.80). The main depot is next to Newcastle train station.

Ferry

The Stockton ferry (adult/child $2.30/1.10) leaves every half-hour from Queens Wharf, 5.15am to midnight on Friday and Saturday, to 11pm Monday to Thursday and to 10pm on Sunday.

Train

Services terminate at Newcastle station after stopping at Broadmeadow, Hamilton, Wickham and Civic.

HUNTER VALLEY

POP 50,834 (CESSNOCK SHIRE), 14,043 (UPPER HUNTER SHIRE)

A filigree of narrow country lanes criss-crosses this verdant valley, but a pleasant country drive isn't the main motivator for visitors – sheer decadence is. The Hunter is one big gorge fest: fine wine, boutique beer, chocolate, cheese, olives, you name it. Bacchus would surely approve.

Going on the philosophy that good food and wine will inevitably up the odds for nookie, the region is a popular weekender for Sydney couples. Every Friday they descend, like a plague of Ralph Lauren–polo-shirt-wearing locusts. Prices leap up accordingly.

The oldest wine region in Australia, the Hunter is known for its Semillon and Shiraz. Vines were first planted in the 1820s and by the 1860s there were 20 sq km under cultivation. However, the wineries gradually declined, and it wasn't until the 1960s that winemaking again became an important industry. If it's no longer the crowning jewel of the Australian wine industry, it still turns in some excellent vintages.

The Hunter has an important ace up its sleeve: these wineries are refreshingly attitude-free and welcoming of viticulturists and novices alike. Staff will rarely give you the evil eye if you leadenly twirl your glass once too often, or don't conspicuously savour the bouquet. Even those with only a casual interest in wine should be sure to tour around – it's a lovely area, and a great direction to turn to if the weather drives you from the beaches.

⊙ Sights & Activities

Most attractions lie in an area bordered to the north by the New England Hwy and to the south by Wollombi/Maitland Rd. The main town serving the area is Cessnock, to the south. Wine Country Dr heads straight up from Cessnock to Branxton, where there's a train station. To confuse matters, the bottom half of this route is sometimes labelled Allandale Rd and the top end Branxton Rd.

To the northwest, there are further vineyards around Broke and Singleton.

Wineries

The valley's 140-plus wineries range from small-scale, family-run affairs to massive commercial operations. Most offer free tastings, although a couple of the glitzier ones charge a small fee. Remember that the vineyards don't offer this service out of the goodness of their hearts. It's poor form if you don't buy at least the occasional bottle.

Grab a vineyard map and plot your course or just follow your nose, hunting out the tucked-away small producers. The majority are located on or around Broke Rd in Pokolbin. Here are a few picks to get you started:

Audrey Wilkinson Vineyard WINERY
(www.audreywilkinson.com.au; DeBeyers Rd, Pokolbin; ⊙9am-5pm Mon-Fri, 9.30am-5pm Sat & Sun) One of the oldies (first planted in 1866), it's worth visiting more for its interesting historic display and excellent views (bring a picnic) than for its overcrowded and touristy tasting room.

Brokenwood WINERY
(www.brokenwood.com.au; 401-427 McDonalds Rd, Pokolbin; ⊙9.30am-5pm) One of the Hunter's most acclaimed wineries.

Hungerford Hill WINERY
(www.hungerfordhill.com.au; 2450 Broke Rd, Pokolbin; ⊙10am-5pm Sun-Thu, 9am-6pm Fri & Sat) Shaped like a big barrel, with its 'lid' permanently propped open, this winery stands sentinel at the entry to Broke Rd. It's home to the highly regarded **Muse restaurant** (⊙lunch daily, dinner Wed-Sat; lunch mains $28-36, dinner mains $39-44, 5-course tasting menu $110).

Macquariedale Estate WINERY
(☑6574 7012; www.macquariedale.com.au; 170 Sweetwater Rd, Rothbury; ⊙10am-5pm) A boutique winemaker that's certified organic and biodynamic. It also grows garlic.

Margan WINERY
(www.margan.com.au; 1238 Millbrodale Rd, Broke; ⊙10am 5pm) Gorgeous setting, classy tasting room and the valley's best restaurant (see p112).

McWilliams Mount Pleasant Estate WINERY
(www.mountpleasantwines.com.au; 401 Marrowbone Rd, Pokolbin; ⊙10am-5pm) Guided wine tours ($5) at 11am.

Moorebank Vineyard WINERY
(www.moorebankvineyard.com.au; 150 Palmers Lane, Rothbury; ⊙10am-5pm) Sustainable winemaking practices and delicious homemade condiments.

Pooles Rock Wines WINERY
(www.poolesrock.com.au; DeBeyers Rd, Pokolbin; ⊙9.30am-5pm) A big player, producing the midpriced Cockfighter's Ghost range as well as its excellent flagship wines. Fabulous cafe-restaurant (see p112).

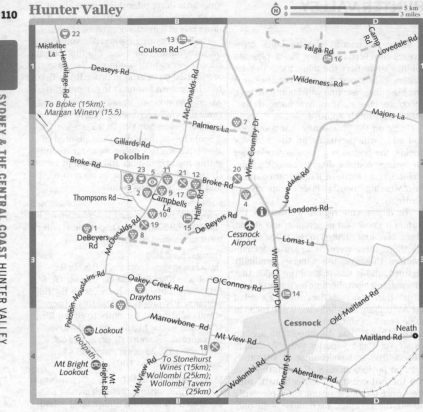

Small Winemakers Centre   WINERY
(www.smallwinemakerscentre.com.au; McDonalds Rd, Pokolbin; ☺10am-5pm) Acts as a cellar door for six boutique winemakers.

Stonehurst Cedar Creek   WINERY
(www.cedarcreekcottages.com.au; 1840 Wollombi Rd, Wollombi; ☺10am-5pm) One of the six wineries in the picturesque Wollombi Valley. Uses organic practices and offers basic cabin accommodation.

Tamburlaine   WINERY
(www.tamburlaine.com.au; 358 McDonalds Rd, Pokolbin; ☺9am-5pm) An excellent producer focusing on sustainable viticulture.

Tempus Two   WINERY
(www.tempustwo.com.au; cnr McDonalds & Broke Rds, Pokolbin; ☺9am-5pm) This huge place is a favourite with tour buses, which descend upon its Korean and Japanese restaurants and purchase gourmet goodies from its Smelly Cheese Shop (see p112).

Tower Estate   WINERY
(www.towerestatewines.com.au; cnr Halls & Broke Rd, Pokolbin; ☺10am-5pm) Established by one of Australia's major wine experts, the late Len Evans, this is the classiest winery in the valley and also offers a sophisticated accommodation option (see p111).

Other Attractions

Hunter Valley Gardens   GARDEN
(www.hvg.com.au; Broke Rd; adult/child/concession $23.50/12/18; ☺9am-5pm) Although there's something a little Disney about it, this relatively young 24-hectare garden has impressive floral and landscape displays. It's the home of the valley's famous **Christmas Lights Spectacular** (mid-Nov–early Jan), Australia's biggest Christmas lights display.

☞ Tours
If no-one's volunteering to stay sober enough to drive, there are plenty of winery tours available. Some operators will collect you in

Hunter Valley

Sydney or Newcastle for a lengthy day trip. Staff at visitors centres and accommodation providers should be able to arrange a booking that suits your needs. These are a few of the local operators:

Floveda Tours WINERY TOUR
(☑0402 909 090; www.aussiewinetours.com.au) You can determine your own itinerary if you take one of these private, chauffeur-driven tours.

Hunter Valley Tours WINERY TOUR
(☑4990 8989; www.huntervalleytours.com.au) Boutique tours for small groups; from $65 per person for a half-day tour and from $99 for a full-day tour including lunch.

Wine Rover WINERY TOUR
(☑4990 1699; www.rovercoaches.com.au) Coaches connect at Morriset in the morning with trains coming from Sydney ($55) and drop passengers back at the station after a day of visiting wineries and attractions. They also pick up passengers at Newcastle (weekdays/weekends $60/70) and Cessnock (weekdays/weekends $45/55).

✦ Festivals & Events

During the warm months superstars regularly drop by for weekend concerts at the bigger vineyards. If there's something special on, accommodation books up well in advance. Check what's on at www.winecountry.com.au.

A Day on the Green MUSIC FESTIVAL
(www.adayonthegreen.com.au) At Bimbadgen Estate during summer.

Lovedale Long Lunch FOOD FESTIVAL
(www.lovedalelonglunch.com.au) In May, seven wineries and chefs produce gut-bursting lunches served with music and art.

Hunter Valley Wine & Food Month WINE FESTIVAL
(www.hvwineandfood.hvva.com.au) In June.

Jazz in the Vines MUSIC FESTIVAL
(www.jazzinthevines.com.au) At Tyrrell's Vineyard, October.

Opera in the Vineyards MUSIC FESTIVAL
(www.4di.com.au) At Wyndham Estate, October.

🛏 Sleeping

Prices shoot up savagely on Friday and Saturday nights and two-night minimum stays are common. It's best to time your trip for midweek.

TOP CHOICE **Tower Lodge** HOTEL $$$
(☑4998 7022; www.towerlodge.com.au; Halls Rd, Pokolbin; d midweek/weekends from $720/810; ❀@🌐☀) There are 12 luxurious rooms to choose from at this vineyard hotel, each furnished with antiques, artworks and the biggest bathrooms in the world (or at least the Hunter). After a day spent touring the valley, you can enjoy a complimentary afternoon tea or aperitif in the magnificent lounge before kicking onto dinner in the intimate **Nine Restaurant** (degustation menu $180, $250 with matched wines). The anti-children policy attracts some visitors while putting some offside.

Buffs at Pokolbin   CABINS **$$**
(☑4998 7636; www.buffsatpokolbin.com.au; 47 Coulson Rd, Pokolbin; 1-bedroom cottage midweek/weekend $180/225, 2-bedroom cottage $250/350; ✱✱) Set on a tranquil 100-acre property where kangaroos hop under the gum trees and gentle cooling breezes come off the dam, Buffs's four spotlessly clean, self-contained cottages are as comfortable as they are keenly priced. A fantastic choice for families and couples alike.

Peppers Convent   BOUTIQUE HOTEL **$$$**
(☑07-5665 4450; www.peppers.com.au; Halls Rd; r from $372; ✱@🛜) Recently taken under the wing of the crew who run the luxe Tower Lodge, this grand former nunnery has been moved hundreds of kilometres, planted among the vineyards and thoroughly renovated in a French provincial style. It makes for a lovely, lavish retreat. Don't get it mixed up with the far-less-impressive Peppers Guest House.

Tonic   BOUTIQUE HOTEL **$$$**
(☑4930 9999; www.tonichotel.com.au; 251 Talga Rd, Lovedale; d incl breakfast $425; ✱@✱) Sydney style-meisters adore this boutique hotel, which has six double rooms and a two-bedroom apartment. The decor is avowedly anti-chintz, with polished concrete floors, a vivid colour scheme and contemporary furnishings; toiletries are from Aesop. It's another anti-child venue.

Hunter Valley YHA   HOSTEL **$**
(☑4991 3278; www.yha.com.au/hostels/details.cfm?hostelid=235; 100 Wine Country Dr; site per person $10, dm $27-34, d with private bathroom $85.50-95, d with shared bathroom $73.50-82; @✱) In late summer this newish, custom-built hostel is packed to the rafters with working holidaymakers picking fruit on the vineyards. The reward at the end of a long day is a welcoming pool, clean facilities and plenty of bonhomie; on weekends the hostel's winery tours are popular. Be warned that the rooms can get stiflingly hot.

✗ Eating

It seems that everyone expects wine lushes to also be gluttons and millionaires, as the Hunter is stuffed full of expensive restaurants offering huge set menus.

TOP CHOICE **Margan**   MODERN AUSTRALIAN **$$**
(☑6579 1372; 1238 Milbrodale Rd, Broke; mains $22-36; ⊙breakfast Sun, lunch Fri-Sun, dinner Fri & Sat) Live up to the area's name and go for broke when it comes to ordering from the tempting array of dishes on offer at this vineyard restaurant. Much of the produce is sourced from the vineyard's kitchen garden; the rest comes from local provedores whenever possible. Views are across the vines to the Brokenback Range.

Firestick Cafe & Rock Restaurant
    MODERN AUSTRALIAN **$$-$$$**
(☑4998 6968; www.rockrestaurant.com.au; Pooles Rock Wines, DeBeyers Rd; lunch mains $36-39, pizzas $23-25, dinner mains $59-60; ⊙lunch daily, dinner Thu-Fri) By day, the restaurant at picturesque Poole Rock winery functions as the casual Firestick; at night, it morphs into the award-winning Rock. The delicious daytime-only crispy pizzas are an affordable route to sampling the Hunter's top foodie destination, although you run the risk of caving in once you peruse the innovative Mod Oz mains on the menu.

Cafe Enzo   CAFE **$**
(www.enzohuntervalley.com.au; Peppers Creek, cnr Broke & Ekerts Rds, Pokolbin; breakfast dishes $8.50-22.50, lunch mains $22.50-36; ⊙breakfast & lunch) Claim a table by the fireside in winter or in the garden in summer to enjoy the rustic, generously sized dishes served at this popular place in the Pepper Creek Village. There's a tempting produce shop next door.

Bistro Molines   FRENCH **$$**
(☑4990 9553; www.tallaveragrove.com.au; 749 Mount View Rd, Mount View; mains $40-45; ⊙lunch Thu-Mon, dinner Fri & Sat) Set in the Tallavera Grove winery, this French restaurant has a sensational, seasonally driven menu that is nearly as impressive as the view over the vines.

Provedores

Hunter Valley Smelly Cheese Shop   DELI **$**
(www.huntervalleysmellycheeseshop.com.au; Tempus Two Winery, 2144 Broke Rd, Pokolbin; ⊙9am-5.30pm) A hugely popular place full to the rafters with produce from local suppliers and elsewhere. The climate-controlled cheese room is stacked with smelly desirables, and you can also buy bread, relishes, meats and olives for Wine Country picnics. There's another branch at Pokolbin Village, 2188 Broke Rd.

Hunter Valley Cheese Company
    PRODUCER **$**
(www.huntervalleycheese.com.au; McGuigans Complex, McDonalds Rd; platters $28; ⊙9am-5.30pm) 'Blessed are the cheesemakers' quote the staff T-shirts, and the people inside those shirts will chew your ear about cheesy co-

SENSIBLE SUPPING

If driving, remember that to stay under the blood-alcohol limit of 0.05, men can generally have two standard drinks in the first hour and one every hour after. Women can have one standard drink per hour. Wineries usually offer 20mL tastes of wine – five of these equals one standard drink.

mestibles all day long, especially during the daily 11am cheese talk. There's a bewildering variety of styles available for purchase.

For other yummy stuff:

Hunter Valley Chocolate Company
PRODUCER $
(www.hvchocolate.com.au; Peterson's Champagne House, cnr Broke & Branxton Rds; ⊙9am-5pm) All manner of cacao derivatives.

Hunter Olive Centre PRODUCER $
(www.pokolbinestate.com.au; Pokolbin Estate Vineyard, 298 McDonalds Rd; ⊙10am-5pm) Dozens of things to try on little squares of bread – oil, tapanade, *dukkah* (a blend of ground nuts and spices), chutney etc. If you're shameless, you could make it lunch.

⚑ Drinking

Wollombi Tavern PUB
(www.wollombitavern.com.au; Old North Rd, Wollombi; ⊙10am-late) Strategically located at the Wollombi crossroads, this fabulous little pub is the home of Dr Jurd's Jungle Juice, a dangerous brew of port, brandy and wine. The less adventurous (or should that read foolhardy?) can opt for a glass of excellent locally produced wine, including Stonehurst's Chambourcin and Undercliff's Semillon and Shiraz. On weekends, the tavern is a favourite pit-stop for motorbike clubs (the non-scary sort).

Bluetongue Brewery BREWERY
(www.Hunter Valley.com.au/bluetongue; Hunter Valley Resort, Hermitage Rd; ⊙10am-late) Sample the creative and refreshing brews using the Tasting Paddle (six beers for $12). Also on offer are pies, sandwiches, cheese plates and a pool table.

Harrigan's PUB
(☑4998 4000; Broke Rd) A comfortable Irish pub with beef-and-Guinness pies on the menu, live bands most weekends and plenty of opportunities for the craic.

❶ Information

Visitors centre (☑4990 0900; www.winecountry.com.au; 455 Wine Country Dr; ⊙9am-5pm Mon-Sat, to 4pm Sun)

❶ Getting There & Away

CityRail has a line heading through the Hunter Valley from Newcastle (adult/child $6/3, 55 minutes). From Sydney (adult/child $7.80/3.90, 3¾ hours), you'll need to catch a train to Hamilton and then change for Branxton, the closest station to the vineyards.

Greyhound (☑1300 473 946; www.greyhound.com.au) runs a daily bus from Sydney ($65, 4½ hours) to Branxton, departing outside Central Station at 6.30pm. **Rover Coaches** (☑4990 1699; www.rovercoaches.com.au) has regular services between Cessnock and Newcastle ($4.30, 1½ hours). **Hunter Valley Day Tours** (☑4951 4574; www.huntervalleydaytours.com.au) operates a shuttle service from Newcastle Airport to Hunter Valley hotels ($125 for one to two people).

❶ Getting Around

Exploring without a car can be challenging. The YHA hostel hires bikes, as do **Grapemobile** (☑0418 404 039; www.pokolbinbrothers.com.au/grapemobile.htm; Pokolbin Brothers Vineyard, Palmers Lane; $25 per day) and **Hunter Valley Cycling** (☑0418 281 480; www.huntervalleycycling.com.au; $45 for two day).

The **Vineyard Shuttle** (☑4991 3655; www.huntervalleyclassiccarriages.com.au) offers a door-to-door service from $15 per person per trip, perfect for trips to and from restaurants.

NEWCASTLE TO TAREE

From Newcastle, you can choose to zoom north along the Pacific Hwy or enjoy a far more pleasant trip by making a series of meandering diversions along the coast.

Port Stephens

POP 27,531

This stunning sheltered bay is about an hour's drive north of Newcastle, occupying a submerged valley that stretches more than 20km inland. Framing its southern edge is the narrow **Tomaree Peninsula**, blessed with near-deserted beaches, national parks and an extraordinary sand-dune system.

The main centre, **Nelson Bay**, is home to both a fishing fleet and an armada of tourist vessels, capitalising on its status as the 'dolphin capital of Australia'.

Just east of Nelson Bay, and virtually merged with it, is the slightly smaller **Shoal Bay**, with a long beach that's great for swimming (but only in the morning, as winds come up in the afternoon). The road ends a short drive south from here at **Fingal Bay**, with another lovely beach on the fringes of **Tomaree National Park**. The park stretches west around clothing-optional **Samurai Beach**, a popular surfing spot, and **One Mile Beach**, a gorgeous semicircle of the softest sand and bluest water favoured by those in the know: surfers, beachcombers, idle romantics.

The park ends at the somnolent surfside village of **Anna Bay**, which has as a backdrop the incredible **Worimi Conservation Lands**. Gan Gan Rd connects Anna Bay, One Mile Beach and Samurai Beach with Nelson Bay Rd.

◉ Sights

Worimi Conservation Lands   SAND DUNES
Located at Stockton Bight, these are the longest moving sand dunes in the southern hemisphere, stretching over 35km. The tourist board claims the dunes are *Mad Max*-style, but if you want to talk films, think *Lawrence of Arabia* – it's more Sahara than outback. In the heart of it, it's possible to become so surrounded by shimmering sand that you'll lose sight of the ocean or any sign of life. In short, it's incredibly evocative. At the far west end of the beach, the wreck of the *Sygna* founders in the water.

Thanks to the generosity of the Worimi people (see boxed text, p119), whose land this is, you're able to roam around (provided you don't disturb any Aboriginal sites), camp within 100m of the high tide mark (you'll need a portable toilet), drive along the beach (4WD only; permit required) and mash up the sand dunes within the designated recreational vehicle area. Get your permits ($10 for three days) from the Port Stephens Visitors Centre or NPWS offices in Nelson Bay (p116) or by telephoning ☑4984 8200 (allow seven days for the pass to be mailed to you).

Tomaree National Park   NATIONAL PARK
(www.environment.nsw.gov.au/nationalparks; vehicle admission $7) This wonderfully wild expanse harbours several threatened species, including the spotted-tailed quoll and powerful owl. If you keep your eyes peeled, you're bound to spot a koala or wallaby. At the eastern end of Shoal Bay there's a short walk to the surf at unpatrolled **Zenith Beach** (beware of rips and strong undercurrents), or you can tackle the strenuous **Tomaree Head Summit Walk** (1km and one hour return) and be rewarded by stunning ocean views. Longer walks are detailed in *Bushwalks around Port Stephens* ($5.95), a pamphlet available from the NPWS and visitors information offices.

Heritage Light House Cottage   LIGHTHOUSE
(☑4984 2505; admission free; ⊙10am-4pm) This restored (1875) building at Nelson Head has a small museum with displays on the area's history and a tearoom. The views of Port Stephens are suitably inspiring.

⌖ Tours

There are dozens of operators offering various action-packed ways to spend your day. Book at the visitors centre in Nelson Bay.

Wet Stuff

Imagine Cruises   CRUISES
(☑4984 9000; www.imaginecruises.com.au; Dock C, d'Albora Marinas, Nelson Bay) Eco-accredited trips, including the 3½-hour Sail, Swim & Snorkel (adult/child/concession $50/30/45; December to March), two-hour Dolphin Watch cruises ($30/15/25; December to March), three-hour Whale Watch cruises ($60/25/50; May to November); two-hour Seafood Dinner cruises ($35/20/30; December to April); and 3½-hour Swim with the Dolphins experience ($229; weekends only).

Anna Bay Surf School   SURFING
(☑0411 419 576; www.annabaysurfschool.com.au; Hannah Pde, One Mile Beach Holiday Park; introductory $75, 2/3 days $110/165) Surf lessons and board hire (per hour/day $17/50).

Blue Water Sea Kayaking   KAYAKING
(☑0405 033 518; www.kayakingportstephens. com.au) Offers a range of paddle-powered excursions, including hour-long beginner tours (adult/child $25/20), 90-minute champagne sunset tours ($35/25) and 2½-hour discovery tours ($45/35).

Moonshadow   DOLPHIN-WATCHING
(☑4984 9388; www.moonshadow.com.au; Shop 3, 35 Stockton St, Nelson Bay) Dolphin-watching (adult/child/concession $23/11.50/18), whale-watching ($51/22/43; May to November) and dinner cruises ($65/21.50/59). Eco-accredited.

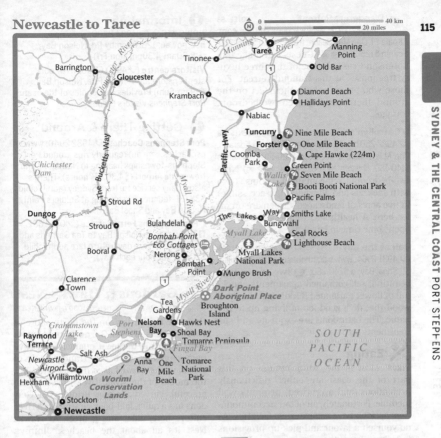

Sandy Stuff

Oakfield Ranch CAMEL RIDES
(☑0429 664 172; www.oakfieldranch.com.au;
Birubi Pt car park, James Patterson Dr, Anna
Bay) Twenty-minute camel rides along the
beach on Sundays and school holidays.

Port Stephens 4WD Tours BEACH TOURS
(☑4984 4760; www.portstephens4wd.com.
au; Shop 3, 35 Stockton St, Nelson Bay) Offers a 1½-hour beach and dune tour
(adult/child/concession $49/29/46) and
a sandboarding experience (adult/child
$26/19).

🛏 Sleeping

Accommodation in both Nelson Bay and
Shoal Bay is generally characterless and
expensive. Consider staying at Anna Bay or
One Mile Beach instead so that you can take
advantage of their tranquil settings near
great beaches.

TOP CHOICE **Port Stephens YHA Samurai
Beach Dungalows** HOSTEL $
(☑4982 1921; www.samuraiportstephens.com;
Frost Rd, Anna Bay; dm $31-50-37, d with private
bathroom $102-159, d with shared bathroom $82-
117; @🛜🗷) Thcsc attractively furnished,
wooden-floored cabins are arranged around
a swimming pool and set in koala-populated
bushland dotted with Asian sculpture.
There's a bush kitchen with BBQs and a
ramshackle games shed with pool table.
Fabulous.

Melaleuca Surfside Backpackers HOSTEL $
(☑4981 9422; www.melaleucabackpackers.com.
au; 2 Koala Pl, One Mile Beach; camp sites $18-20pp,
d $30-40, d with private bathroom $80-100; @🛜)
Architect-designed wooden cabins are set
amid peaceful scrub inhabited by koalas
and kookaburras at this friendly, well-run
place. There's a welcoming lounge area and
kitchen and the owners offer dune surfing
and other day trips. Equally fabulous.

Wanderers Retreat
HOTEL $$

(☑4982 1702; www.wanderersretreat.com; 7 Koala Pl, One Mile Beach; treehouse d $195-270, d cabin $125-250; ❋❋) Guests can make like Robinson Crusoe in one of the three luxury treehouses at this tranquil retreat. For those who prefer to keep their feet on the ground, there are also seven two-bedroom cottages.

O'Carrollyn's
APARTMENTS $$

(☑4982 2801; www.ocarrollyns.com.au; 5 Koala Pl, One Mile Beach; d weekdays $120-140, weekends $140-180, children each $15 extra; ❋❋❋) Nine two-bedroom, self-contained cabins (two with Jacuzzis and all wheelchair-accessible) in five acres of landscaped garden are on offer here. A health and wellness centre will open some time in late 2011.

Bali at the Bay
APARTMENTS $$$

(☑4981 2964; www.baliatthebay.com.au; 1 Achilles St, Shoal Bay; d $240-260; ❋) Two exceedingly beautiful, self-contained apartments chock-full of flower-garlanded Buddhas and carved wood that do a good job of living up to the name. The bathrooms are exquisite and spa treatments are available.

✕ Eating

Yikes! Most of the eating options on this part of the coast are either ridiculously pretentious (and overpriced) or pretty well inedible. Fortunately, all of our accommodation options have self-catering facilities, so do yourself a favour and pick up provisions in Nelson Bay so that you can eat well.

Point
MODERN AUSTRALIAN $$

(☑4984 7111; www.thepointrestaurant.com.au; Soldiers Point Marina, Sunset Blvd, Soldiers Point; mains $34-38; ⊙lunch & dinner Tue-Sun) When locals celebrate romantic milestones, this restaurant on the marina at Soldiers Point is their number-one choice. Views from the balcony and glassed dining room are lovely, and the menu has loads of tempting seafood dishes. It's 9km west of Nelson Bay.

Red Ned's Pies
FAST FOOD $

(www.redneds.com.au; Shop 3/17-19 Stockton St, Nelson Bay; pies $5.50-7; ⊙6am-5pm) Pie-maker Barry Kelly learnt his trade in top-shelf international hotels and his philosophy is simple: he gets a kick out of watching people stare at his specials board, goggle-eyed (anyone for crocodile in parsley, shallot and white-wine sauce?).

❶ Information

NPWS office (☑4984 8200; www.npws.nsw.gov.au; 12B Teramby Rd, Nelson Bay; ⊙8.30am-4.30pm Mon-Fri)

Visitors centre (☑4980 6900; www.portstephens.org.au; Victoria Pde, Nelson Bay; ⊙9am-5pm) Provides free copies of the useful *Port Stephens Visitors Guide*.

❶ Getting There & Around

Port Stephens Coaches (☑4982 2940; www.pscoaches.com.au) regularly zips around Port Stephens' townships heading to Newcastle and Newcastle Airport ($4.30, 1¾ hours). There's also a daily service to/from Sydney (adult/child $38/31, four hours) stopping at Soldiers Point, Nelson Bay and Shoal Bay.

Port Stephens Ferry Service (☑0412 682 117) chugs from Nelson Bay to Tea Gardens and back three times a day (return fare adult/child $20/10, one hour each way).

Tea Gardens & Hawks Nest

☑02 / POP 2094 (TEA GARDENS), 1030 (HAWKS NEST)

Opposite Nelson Bay, on the north shore of Port Stephens, are **Tea Gardens** and **Hawks Nest**. Sporting the most quaintly evocative names on the coast, this tranquil pair of towns in the Great Lakes district straddles the mouth of the Myall River, linked by the graceful, curved Singing Bridge. Tea Gardens has a quiet, laid-back charm; it's a river culture here, older and genteel. At Hawks Nest it's all about the beaches. **Jimmys Beach** fronts a glasslike stretch of water facing Nelson Bay, while stunning **Bennetts Beach** looks to the ocean and Broughton Island.

⟟ Sleeping & Eating

Tea Gardens Boat Shed
CAFE $-$$

(110 Marine Dr, Tea Gardens; breakfast dishes $5-16.50, sandwiches $7.50, mains $15-24.95; ⊙8.30am-9pm) You'll have to cope with a few shrieks from the local pelicans when you choose to devour your meal at this former boat shed right on the water rather than sending the food their way. And it's no wonder they're miffed – everything's delicious. The coffee is good and the deck is a lovely spot for a sunset drink.

Nicole's
CAFE $$

(81 Marine Dr, Tea Gardens; breakfast & lunch $5-17, dinner $15-27; ⊙breakfast & lunch daily, dinner Mon-Sat) Housed in a Victorian cottage, this seriously sweet cafe doubles as an art gallery

and gift shop. The garden is seductive, with trickling water features, bird baths, much greenery and statues.

Tea Gardens Hotel Motel HOTEL **$**
(2 4997 0203; www.teagardenshotelmotel.com.au; cnr Marine Dr & Maxwell St; r from $55; ☎) On the riverfront, this popular watering hole offers basic rooms set around a rear garden.

❶ Information

Tea Gardens Visitors Information Centre
(2 4997 0111; www.greatlakes.org.au; Myall St; ☺10am-4pm) Near the bridge.

❶ Getting There & Around

While only 5km from Nelson Bay as the cockatoo flies, the drive necessitates returning to the Pacific Hwy via Medowie and then doubling back – a distance of 81km. The alternative is the Port Stephens Ferry Service (p116).

If you're continuing north, take the stunning scenic route through Myall Lakes National Park, which involves a short ferry crossing at Bombah Point.

Busways (2 1800 043 263; www.busways.com.au) has services to/from Newcastle ($23, 90 minutes, three daily).

Myall Lakes National Park

On an extravagantly pretty section of the coast, this large **national park** (www.environment.nsw.gov.au/nationalparks; vehicle admission $7) incorporates a patchwork of lakes, islands, dense littoral rainforest and beaches. The lakes support an incredible quantity and variety of bird life, including bowerbirds, white-bellied sea eagles and tawny frogmouths. There are paths through coastal rainforest and past beach dunes at **Mungo Brush** in the south, perfect for spotting wildflowers and dingoes.

The best beaches and surf are in the north around beautiful, secluded **Seal Rocks**, a bushy hamlet hugging Sugarloaf Bay. It has a great beach, with emerald-green rock pools, epic ocean views and golden sand. Take the short walk to the **Sugarloaf Point Lighthouse**, where the views are sublime. There's a water-choked gorge along the way and a detour to lonely **Lighthouse Beach**, a popular surfing spot. The path around the lighthouse leads to a lookout over the actual Seal Rocks – islets that provide sanctuary for Australia's northernmost colony of Australian fur seals. During summer breeding, the seals are out in abundance and you'll do well to bring binoculars. **Humpback whales** swim past Seal Rocks during their annual migration and can sometimes be seen from the shore.

About a half-hour by boat from Nelson Bay, **Broughton Island** is uninhabited except for muttonbirds, little penguins and an enormous diversity of fish species. The diving is tops and the beaches are incredibly secluded.

There are plenty of accommodation options in the park, the most atmospheric of which are the three historic stone **lighthouse keepers cottages** (2 4997 6590; www.sealrockslighthouseaccommodation.com.au; $300-450) at Sugarloaf Point. These self-contained cottages are fully refurbished and sleep between six and eight people each. Equally desirable are the architect-designed self-contained **Bombah Point Eco Cottages** (2 4997 4401; www.bombah.com.au; 969 Bombah Pt Rd; d $220-275; ☎).

The park is well served with **camp sites** (www.npws.nsw.gov.au; sites per adult $7.50-10, child $3.50-5), most of which have composting toilets and water for boiling; none can be booked ahead of your visit. Also here is the excellent **Seal Rocks Holiday Park** (2 4997 6164; www.sealrocksholidaypark.com.au; Kinka Rd, Seal Rocks; unpowered campsites $26-33, powered camp & caravan sites $30-37, cabins $70-185), offering a range of budget accommodation styles including grassed camping and caravan sites that are right on the water.

At Bombah Broadwater, the **Bombah Point ferry** (per car $5; five minutes) crosses every half-hour from 8am to 6pm. A 10km section of Bombah Point Rd heading to the Pacific Hwy at Bulahdelah is unsealed.

The Lakes Way

A scenic alternative to the Pacific Hwy, this lovely drive starts just after the small town of Bulahdelah and twists through Myall Lakes and Booti Booti National Parks, passing popular Pacific Palms en route. It then continues through the built-up regional centre of Forster-Tuncurry before rejoining the Pacific Hwy at Rainbow Flat, an 80km journey all up.

If you need to refuel your vehicle before veering off the highway, do so at Bulahdelah. And if you're hungry, grab one of the fabulous meat pies sold at the **Bulahdelah Bakery** (65 Stroud St).

Pacific Palms

POP 680

Hidden away between Myall Lakes and Booti Booti National Parks, Pacific Palms is one of those places that well-heeled city dwellers slink off to on weekends – which sounds perfectly dreadful, but is actually something that we'd all like to do if we had the chance. It's a hell of a lot nicer than Forster and Tuncurry up the road, which is best avoided. If you're camping in either of the parks you might find yourself here when the espresso cravings kick in – there are a couple of excellent cafes.

Most of the houses cling to Blueys Beach or Boomerang Beach, both long stretches of golden sand that are popular with surfers. Elizabeth Beach, just inside Booti Booti National Park, is the nicest and is patrolled during peak holiday times.

The volunteer-run visitors centre (6554 0123; Boomerang Dr; 10am-3pm) has internet access ($2.50 per 15 minutes) and some arts and crafts for sale.

Sleeping & Eating

Mobys Beachside Retreat APARTMENTS $$-$$$
(6591 0000; www.mobysretreat.com.au; 4 Red Gum Rd, Boomerang Beach; 1-bedroom apt $170-225, 2-bedroom $210-275, 3-bedroom $290-365;) Directly opposite Boomerang Beach, this holiday resort crams 75 self-contained holiday apartments with sleek decor and excellent amenities into a relatively small area. There's a tennis court, swimming pool and children's playground on site, as well as the extremely popular M Bistro (6554 0766; www.mbistro.com.au; set lunch $17.50, dinner mains $22-29; lunch & dinner Wed-Sun).

Buddha on the Lake INTERNATIONAL $$
(6554 0877; www.thebuddhaonthelake.com.au; cnr The Lakes Way & Kookie Ave; breakfast dishes $5-15, mains $25-27; breakfast Sat & Sun, lunch Wed-Sun, dinner Wed-Sat) You've gotta love any place that's located on Kookie Ave! Guests are greeted by Balinese statues and the evocative scent of spices when they arrive at this laid-back place located five minutes' drive east of Blueys Beach. There's a dedicated vegetarian menu and $10 kids' meals. BYO alcohol.

Recky PUB $
(6554 0207; The Lakes Way; mains $14-21; 11am-late) If you want to be formal, it's the Pacific Palms Recreation Club. Yep, it's one of those sign-in clubs with cheap booze, a bistro and occasional live music. And be warned: its slogan is 'Get wrecked at the Recky'.

Twenty by Twelve CAFE $
(Shop 8, 207 Boomerang Dr; breakfast dishes $4-13, wraps $9.50, burgers & pies $14.50; 7.30am-3pm) Camping is all very well, but try getting a coffee like this out of a billycan! It also sells light meals, local organic produce and delicious deli treats.

Getting There & Around

Busways (1800 043 263; www.busways.com.au) stops at Blueys Beach on its journey between Taree/Forster and Newcastle.

Booti Booti National Park

This 1567-hectare national park (www.environment.nsw.gov.au/nationalparks; vehicle admission $7) stretches along a skinny peninsula with Seven Mile Beach on its eastern side and Wallis Lake on its west. The northern section of the park is swathed in coastal rainforest and topped by 224m Cape Hawke. At the Cape Hawke headland there's a viewing platform, well worth the sweat of climbing the 420-something steps.

You won't really be darkening the door of a church if you visit the Green Cathedral, as there is no door. This interesting space (consecrated in 1940) consists of wooden pews under the palm trees, looking to the lake.

There's self-registration camping at the Ruins (camping per adult $10-14, child $5-7), at the southern end of Seven Mile Beach, with an NPWS office (6591 0300; 8.30am-4.30pm) nearby.

Avoid Forster's motel mania at Lakeside Escape B&B (6557 6400; www.lakesideescape.com.au; 85 Green Point Dr, Green Point; s $140-155, d $165-195;), seven minutes out of town in the Green Point fishing village. The ensuite rooms overlook Wallis Lake and there's a spa. Breakfast is included.

TAREE TO PORT MACQUARIE

From Forster-Tuncurry the Pacific Hwy swings inland to Taree (population 20,000), a large town serving the farms of the fertile Manning Valley. The helpful Taree visitors centre (1800 182 733, 02-6592 5444; 21 Manning River Dr; 9am-5pm Sep-May, 9am-5pm Mon-Fri, to 4pm Sat & Sun Jun-Aug) is at the northern end of town.

Further west into the valley is **Wingham Brush Nature Reserve**, a patch of idyllic rainforest that is home to giant, otherworldly Moreton Bay figs and flocks of flying foxes. The nearby town of **Wingham** combines English county cuteness with a rugged lumberjack history. Consider stopping here for two reasons: to eat at **Bent on Food** (sandwiches & salads $12-16; ⊘8am-5pm Mon-Fri, to 3pm Sat, 9am-3pm Sun), one of the best cafes in rural NSW, and to stay overnight at **Bank Guesthouse** (☑6553 5068; www. thebankandtellers.com.au; 48 Bent St; s $155-175, d $165-185, cottage $110-120; ✽☎), a friendly place offering stylishly decorated rooms in a 1920s bank manager's residence, as well as a self-catering guesthouse cottage in the rear garden.

CountryLink (☑8202 2000; www.country link.info) trains from Sydney stop at Taree and Wingham ($47, 5½ hours, two daily). The train continues to Coffs Harbour ($32, 3½ hours, two daily).

Back on the Pacific Hwy, a half-hour drive north will bring you to the turn-off to the fishing village of **Harrington**, sheltered by a spectacular rocky breakwater and watched over by pelicans. It's a leisure-orientated hamlet popular with both holidaymakers and retirees – 30% of the population is over the age of 65. When not playing golf or fishing, the locals hang out at the **Harrington Hotel** (☑6556 1205; 30 Beach St; s/d $45/55), a spacious pub with a popular bistro and large waterside terrace.

Crowdy Head is an even smaller fishing village 6km northeast of Harrington at the edge of **Crowdy Bay National Park** (www. environment.nsw.gov.au/nationalparks; vehicle admission $7). It was supposedly named when Captain Cook witnessed a gathering of Aborigines on the headland in 1770. The views from the 1878 **lighthouse** are absolutely breathtaking – out to the limitless ocean, down to the deserted beaches and back to the apparent wilderness of the coastal plain and mountains. It's as if Cook had never arrived at all.

Known for its rock formations and rugged cliffs, the 100-sq-km national park here backs onto a long and beautiful beach that sweeps from Crowdy Head north to **Diamond Head**. There's a lovely 4.8km (two-hour) loop track over the Diamond headland.

The roads running through the park are unsealed and full of potholes, but the dappled light of the gum trees makes it a lovely drive. There are basic **camp sites** (☑6582 3355; site per adult/child $10/5) at Diamond Head, Indian Head, Kylie's Hut and Kylie's Beach, as well as in the southern part of the park at **Crowdy Gap** (☑6552 4097; site per adult/child $10/5). You'll need to bring water in for all of them.

Leaving the national park via Diamond Head Rd, continue through to Laurieton and then on to the tiny town of Kew, from where you can veer off the highway and follow Ocean Dr all the way through to Port Macquarie. Along the way, you will pass **Dooragan National Park**, which is dominated by **North Brother Mountain** with lookouts and incredible views. Nearby is **Camden Haven**, a cluster of sleepy villages around the wide sea entrance of **Queens Lake**, and **North Haven**, an absolute blinder of a surf beach. North of here, the road passes **Lake Cathie** (which is pronounced cat-eye), a shallow body of water that is perfect for kiddies to have a paddle in.

WORIMI COUNTRY

The area from the Tomaree Peninsula to Forster and as far west as Gloucester is the land of the Worimi people, who have lived in this region for thousands of years. Very little of it is now in their possession, but in 2001 the sand dunes of the Stockton Bight were returned to them, creating the Worimi Conservation Lands (p114). The Worimi people in turn entered an agreement to co-manage it with the NPWS.

Sacred places and occupation sites are scattered throughout the region. **Dark Point Aboriginal Place** in Myall Lakes National Park has been significant to the Worimi for around 4000 years. Local lore has it that in the late 19th century it was the site of one of many massacres of Aboriginals at the hands of white settlers, when a group was herded onto the rocks and pushed off.

For more information, look out for the *Worimi Conservation Lands* brochure published by the NSW Department of Environment and Climate Change.

ELLENBOROUGH FALLS

If you're fond of country drives, the 40km route from Wingham to the **Ellenborough Falls** shouldn't be missed. About 17km of it is unsealed and full of potholes, but the countryside is bucolic. As the road climbs steeply to the Bulga Plateau, farms give way to native bush once exploited for its cedar. The falls plunge 200m in one dramatic drop into a gorge below. The best view is from The Knoll, an easy short bushwalk. A more strenuous walk leads to the base, taking about 30 minutes down but 45 minutes back up.

PORT MACQUARIE

POP 39,220

Pleasure has long replaced punishment as the main purpose of Port Macquarie. Formed in 1821 as a place of hard labour for those convicts who reoffended after being sentenced to Sydney, it was the third town to be established on the Australian mainland. These days, though, Port, as it's commonly known, is overwhelmingly holiday-focused, making the most of its position at the entrance to the subtropical coast, its beautiful surf beaches and its laid-back coffee culture.

◉ Sights

Beaches

Port is blessed with nine awesome beaches. Surfing is excellent at **Town**, **Flynns** and **Lighthouse Beaches**, all of which are patrolled in summer. The rainforest runs down to the sand at **Shelly** and **Miners Beaches**, the latter an unofficial nude beach.

It's possible to walk all the way from the Town Wharf to Lighthouse Beach. Along the way, the **breakwater** at the bottom of town has been transformed into a work of community guerrilla art. The elaborately painted rocks range from beautiful memorials for lost loved-ones to 'party hard'–type inanities.

Wildlife

Koala Hospital   NATURE RESERVE
(www.koalahospital.org.au; Lord St; admission by donation; ⊙8am-4.30pm) Koalas living near urban areas are at risk from traffic and domestic animals, and more than 200 each year end up in this shelter. You can walk around the open-air enclosures any time of the day,

but you'll learn more during the tours (3pm). Some of the longer-term patients have signs detailing their stories. Check the website for details of volunteer opportunities.

Sea Acres Rainforest Centre   NATURE RESERVE
(www.nationalparks.nsw.gov.au; Pacific Dr; adult/child $8/4; ⊙9am-4.30pm) This 72-hectare pocket of coastal rainforest (a candidate for national park status) is alive with birds, goannas, brush turkeys and, so as to be truly authentic, mosquitoes (insect repellent is provided). While there's no charge for wandering through most of the paths here, it's worth paying the admission to the ecology centre and wheelchair-accessible 1.3km-long boardwalk. Fascinating one-hour guided tours by knowledgeable volunteers are included in the price. Call ahead for times of bush-tucker tours led by Aboriginal guides.

Billabong Koala & Wildlife Park
NATURE RESERVE
(61 Billabong Dr; adult/child $18/11; ⊙9am-5pm) For more koala action, head just west of the intersection of the Pacific and Oxley Hwys and make sure you're there for the 'koala patting' (10.30am, 1.30pm and 3.30pm). The park has a koala-breeding centre, although if this facility is anything to go by, koala dating requires a lot of sitting around looking stoned. There are heaps of other Australian critters here, too.

FREE **Kooloonbung Creek Nature Park**
NATURE RESERVE
(cnr Gordon & Horton Sts) Home to many bird species, this park close to the town centre encompasses 50 hectares of bush and wetland that can be explored via walking trails and wheelchair-accessible boardwalks. It includes the **Port Macquarie Historic Cemetery** (Gordon St).

Historic Buildings & Museums

St Thomas' Anglican Church   CHURCH
(Hay St; adult/child $2/1; ⊙9.30am-noon & 2-4pm Mon-Fri) This 1824 convict-built church is one of Australia's oldest still-functioning churches. It still has its box pews and crenulated tower, echoing the Norman churches of southern England.

Roto House   HISTORIC BUILDING
(Lord St; admission by gold-coin donation; ⊙10am-4pm subject to availability of volunteer staff) Located next to the Koala Hospital in Macquarie Nature Reserve, this is a lovely Victorian villa (1890) with interesting displays about its original owners.

Garrison Building
HISTORICAL BUILDING

(cnr Clarence & Hay Sts) This building is camouflaged by an uninspiring array of fast-food shops.

Port Macquarie Historical Society Museum
MUSEUM

(22 Clarence St; adult/child $5/2; ⏱9.30am-3pm Mon-Sat) Next door to the Garrison Building, this 1836 museum has fared better; its labyrinth of rooms includes a costume gallery.

Courthouse
HISTORICAL BUILDING

(adult/child $2/0.50; ⏱10am-3.30pm Mon-Fri, to 1pm Sat) Located opposite the Port Macquarie Historical Society Museum is this courthouse, built in 1869.

Tacking Point Lighthouse
LIGHTHOUSE

This little lighthouse (1879) commands a headland offering immense views along the coast. It's a great spot to watch the waves rolling in to the beautiful stretch of Lighthouse Beach.

Maritime Museum
MUSEUM

(⏱6583 1866; 6 William St; adult/child $5/2; ⏱10am-4pm) The old pilot house above Town Beach has been converted into this small museum. There's an even smaller extension of the museum in the 1890s Pilots Boatshed at the Town Wharf.

Observatory
OBSERVATORY

(⏱6584 9164; www.pmobs.org.au; William St; adult/child $8/7; ⏱7.30-8.30pm Wed & Sun, 8.15-9.15pm during daylight saving) Stargazers will enjoy this small observatory located in Rotary Park.

Glasshouse Cultural Centre
CULTURAL CENTRE

(www.glasshouse.org.au; cnr Clarence & Hay Streets; ⏱9am-5.30pm Mon-Fri, to 4pm Sat & Sun) Recently opened, the Centre was built on the site of convict overseers' cottages and many archaeological artefacts from the original buildings are on display in the foyer.

FREE Newcastle Regional Art Gallery
GALLERY

(⏱10am-5pm Tue-Fri, to 4pm Sat & Sun) Housed in the Glasshouse Cultural Centre, this is a 600-seat theatre, the tourist information centre and a shop selling local arts & crafts.

🏃 Activities

Port Macquarie Surf School
SURFING

(⏱6585 5453; www.portmacquariesurfschool. com.au; lessons from $40) Offers a wide range of lessons and prices.

Port Sea Kayak Adventures
KAYAKING

(⏱0409 776 566; www.portkayak.com.au; Buller St Bridge) Runs a two-hour River & Mangrove trip ($35) and a six-hour Freshwater Rapids trip ($70).

Port Macquarie Camel Safaris
CAMEL SAFARIS

(⏱0437 672 080; www.portmacquariecamels. com.au; Matthew Flinders Dr; ⏱9.30am-1pm Sun-Fri) Thirty-minute camel rides (adult/ child $30/25) on the southern end of Lighthouse Beach.

🧭 Tours

Port Macquarie Cruise Adventures
CRUISES

(⏱1300 555 890; www.cruiseadventures.com.au; 74 Clarence St, Town Wharf; adult/child/concession from $25/10/22) Offers dolphin-watching, whale-spotting, oyster-guzzling, lunch, sunset, river and everglades tours.

🛏 Sleeping

Port offers options ranging from a clutch of tidy hostels to a multitude of apartment-style resorts.

TOP CHOICE Observatory
HOTEL $$

(⏱6586 8000; www.observatory.net.au; 40 William St; r $129-199, apts $159-329; ⚹❄️🖥) A friendly welcome is the norm at this excellent modern hotel opposite Town Beach. Rooms and apartments are comfortable and well equipped; many have balconies overlooking the water. The close proximity to the beach, good cafes and the Stunned Mullet restaurant (p122) means that you won't have to stray far from your room. Everyone loves the indoor pool, spa and sauna.

Port Macquarie Backpackers
HOSTEL $

(⏱6583 1791; www.portmacquariebackpackers. com.au; 2 Hastings River Dr; dm $26-30, d with shared bathroom $60-80; @❄️🖥) This heritage-listed house has pressed-tin walls, comfy bunks, a new shower/toilet block and an enthusiastic owner/manager who sometimes takes guests on three-day camping/surfing trips to Crowdy Bay National Park ($195). Traffic can be noisy, but the freebies (including breakfast) compensate.

Ozzie Pozzie Backpackers
HOSTEL $

(⏱/fax 6583 8133; 36 Waugh St; dm $26-33, s with shared bathroom $45-65, d with shared bathroom $65-90; @🖥) In a somewhat strange compound made up of three converted suburban houses, this hostel offers clean rooms,

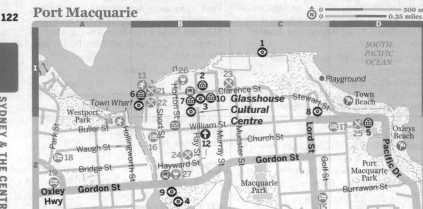

uncomfortable beds and a definite party atmosphere. There's a range of activities on offer, along with pool and table-tennis tables, free internet, free body boards, bike hire ($5 per day) and surfboard/wetsuit hire ($20 per day).

Mantra Quayside APARTMENTS **$$**
(☎6588 4000; www.mantraquayside.com.au; cnr William & Short Sts; studios/apts from $135/170; ✳@✿✖) This place joins the newly opened **Mercure Centro Hotel** (☎1300 786 989; www.centrohotel.com.au; 103 William St; r from $169) in being as slick as Port gets. It's a favourite with visitors wanting a self-contained bolthole close to both the beach and the cafe strip.

South Pacific Apartments APARTMENTS **$$**
(☎6583 8033; www.southpacificpm.com.au; 37 Pacific Dr; apt $99-320; ✳✿✖) The upstairs apartments at this somewhat characterless block opposite Flynn's Beach have sea views and those downstairs have a small terrace;

all sleep between four and six people and are clean and bright.

Eastport Motor Inn MOTEL **$$**
(☎6583 5850; www.hwmotel.com.au; cnr Lord & Burrawan Sts; s $95-105, d $130-140; ✳✿✖) At the cheaper end of the non-hostel scale, this place has smallish, clean and well-equipped rooms with comfortable beds and crisp linen. Wi-fi is free.

✖ Eating

Port punches above its weight when it comes to food and coffee – you'll eat and drink well here.

TOP CHOICE **Stunned Mullet** MODERN AUSTRALIAN **$$**
(☎6584 7757; www.thestunnedmullet.com.au; 24 William St; mains $26-49; ☉lunch & dinner) Australian idiom lesson: to 'look like a stunned mullet' is to wear an expression of bewilderment. It's exactly the sort of look you might adopt while struggling to choose

between the delicious Mod Oz menu items and extensive wine-list offerings at Port's best restaurant.

Corner Restaurant Cafe   CAFE **$$**
(cnr Clarence & Munster Sts; breakfast dishes $6-19, baguettes $16, dinner mains $27-34; ☺breakfast, lunch & dinner) On the ground floor of the Macquarie Waters Boutique Apartment Hotel, this sleek operation has a definite Sydney-ish sheen and good cafe fare that could hold its own in Surry Hills (and that's a real compliment).

Milkbar Town Beach   CAFE **$$**
(Shop 2, 40 William St; breakfast dishes $4.50-11.50, lunch dishes $9.50-14.50; ☺breakfast & lunch Mon-Fri, breakfast & brunch Sat & Sun) Another casually chic cafe on the ground floor of a modern apartment block (this time the Observatory), Milkbar is known for its homemade icy poles, Single Origin coffee and surfer clientele.

Fusion 7   MODERN AUSTRALIAN **$$**
(✆6584 1171; www.fusion7.com.au; 124 Horton St; mains $28-34; ☺dinner Tue-Sat) Chef Lindsey Schwab worked with the father of fusion cuisine, Peter Gordon, in London but returned to Port to be closer to his family. Despite this pedigree and the restaurant's

name, the food is more Mod Oz than fusion. Desserts are particularly delicious.

Cedro   CAFE **$**
(72 Clarence St; breakfast $6-18, lunch $12-18; ☺breakfast & lunch Mon-Sat) On a sunny day, you can sit on the street between the palm trees, order the generous house breakfast, sip a good coffee and plan your next move: the beach or another coffee stop?

Boardwalk   TAPAS **$$**
(75 Clarence St; tapas dishes $8-22; ☺breakfast, lunch & dinner Sat & Sun, lunch & dinner Mon-Fri) Commanding lovely views over the Hastings River, this recently opened tapas and wine bar is just a castanet click away from Town Wharf. Locals love it.

🍺 Drinking & Entertainment

Finnian's   PUB
(97 Gordon St; ☺11am-late) The backpacker's boozer of choice, this Irish tavern near the new bus depot offers raffles and trivia nights midweek but cranks up the party atmosphere on Fridays and Saturdays with live music from 8pm.

Beach House   PUB
(Horton St; ☺11am-late) The enviable position right on the grassy water's edge makes this

beautiful pub perfect for lazy afternoon drinks. As the wee hours draw near, folk fasten their beer goggles and mingle on black-leather couches inside.

ℹ️ Information

Port Macquarie Base Hospital (☎6581 2000; Wrights Rd)

Post office (Palm Court, cnr Short & William Sts)

Visitors centre (☎6581 8000; www.port macquarieinfo.com.au; Glasshouse Cultural Cenre, cnr Hay & Clarence Sts; ⊙9am-5.30pm Mon-Fri, to 4pm Sat & Sun)

ℹ️ Getting There & Around
Air

Port Macquarie Airport (☎6581 8111; Boundary St) is 5km from the centre of town ($17 in a taxi).

Both **Qantas** (☎13 13 13; www.qantas.com.au) and **Virgin Blue** (☎13 67 89; www.virginblue.

com.au) have daily flights to Sydney. **Brinda-bella Airlines** (☎1300 66 88 24; www.brinda bellaairlines.com.au) has services to Brisbane, Coffs Harbour and Newcastle.

Bus

Greyhound (☎1300 473 946; www.greyhound. com.au) stops three times daily on its way between Sydney ($49 to $81, 6½ hours) and Brisbane ($55 to $110, 9½ hours).

Premier Motor Service (☎13 34 10; www. premierms.com.au) heads daily to Sydney ($60, 6½ hours), Newcastle ($47, four hours) and Brisbane ($67, 8½ hours).

ℹ️ Getting Around

Busways (☎6559 7712; www.busways.com.au) runs local bus services.

The **Settlement Point Ferry** (per car $3) operates 24 hours. A 10-minute trip on a flat punt gives you access to North Beach.

Canberra & Southern NSW

Why Go?

The textbook 20th-century architecture and town planning of Canberra and the Australian Capital Territory (ACT) couldn't be further removed from the luscious natural green and blue meanderings of the NSW South Coast. But in many ways the extremes make these two destinations ideal bedfellows.

One day visitors can be rubbernecking in museums and art galleries, strolling around manmade lakes and marvelling at the powers that be and the fabulous buildings they inhabit. The next they can find themselves in the natural world with its unpolluted and spectacularly clear waters, dolphin and whale populations, vast tracts of national park and kangaroos that wander down to the shore for an evening stroll. Being able to enjoy both of these quintessential Australian experiences with relative ease adds another dimension to any East Coast odyssey.

Best Places to Eat

- » River (p150)
- » Ottoman Cuisine (p131)
- » Zanzibar (p157)
- » Bannisters (p146)
- » Hungry Duck (p141)

Best Places to Stay

- » Montague Island (p151)
- » Paperbark Camp (p145)
- » Pebbly Beach (p147)
- » Hyatt Hotel (p131)

When to Go

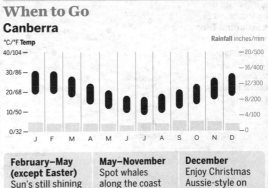

Canberra

February–May (except Easter)
Sun's still shining and kids are back at school

May–November
Spot whales along the coast

December
Enjoy Christmas Aussie-style on the coast – seafood for lunch and beach cricket

Canberra & Southern NSW Highlights

1 Having kangaroos call in at your camp site in **Murramarang National Park** (p147)

2 Sounding your barbaric yawp atop stunning **Pigeon House Mountain** (p146).

3 Hanging out with the seals and penguins at **Montague Island** (p151)

4 Leaving snowy white footprints on the brilliant sands of **Jervis Bay** (p143)

5 Ogling at the architectural splendour of **Parliament House** (p127)

6 Eating ice cream as the sun sets on one of the eye-blinkingly beautiful urban beaches at **Wollongong** (p133)

7 Watching **Eden's** whale-human reconciliation play itself out (p158)

8 Experiencing village life with the 'quaint' quotient at max in **Central Tilba** (p153)

9 Negotiating the network of Australiana in the **National Museum of Australia** (p127)

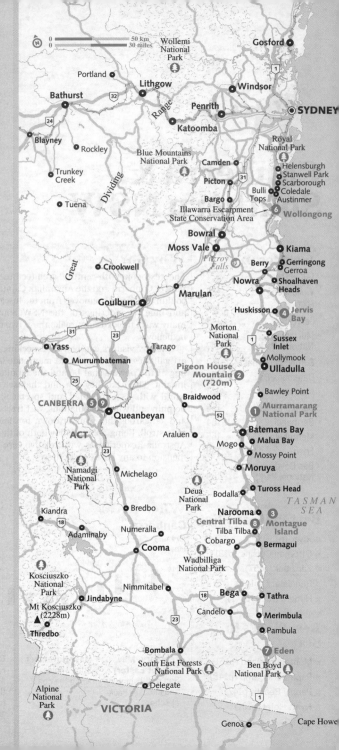

ℹ️ Getting There & Around

Air

An international airport is in Canberra and smaller airports are at Moruya and Merimbula.

Bus

Coaches run between Canberra and the capital cities, and from the capital cities along the coast.

Car & Motorcycle

The quickest route between Canberra and the coast is the Kings Hwy. The Princes Hwy winds its way from Wollongong in the north to Eden in the south and is the main route for exploring the coast no matter which direction you're coming from. It passes through the bigger towns of Batemans Bay, Narooma and Merimbula. Smaller roads that bypass sections of the highway are a good way of accessing coastal and hinterland villages.

Train

Trains run to/from Canberra and Sydney. There are no direct trains to Melbourne. See p133 for more information.

CANBERRA

⚹02 / POP 323,000

Known fondly as the 'bush capital', mild-mannered Canberra might seem sleepy, but it boasts delightful natural surroundings, the country's best museums and a growing food and wine scene.

In 1901 Australia went from colony to modern federated democracy, and Sydney and Melbourne duked it out for the honour of becoming the new nation's capital. Neither prevailed, and a compromise was reached when a brand spanking new city – built to Walter Burley Griffin's masterful design – was plonked down among the Brindabella Hills.

A hyperplanned city, Canberra occasionally makes you feel like you're wandering about in an architectural model but if you want a crash course in Australian history, culture and politics, this is your town. Its fine art galleries and wonderful museums offer a window into the Australian soul, and its political institutions provide fascinating insights into how this marvellous modern democracy works.

◉ Sights

Most of Canberra's significant buildings, museums and galleries are scattered around Lake Burley Griffin. You can easily walk here from Civic, Manuka or Kingston.

Parliament House   NOTABLE BUILDING
(☑6277 5399; www.aph.gov.au; admission free; ⊙9am-5pm) The four-legged, 81m flagpole atop Capital Hill marks the location of Parliament House, an accomplished piece of modern architecture in harmony with its environment. The public spaces contain informative displays, an excellent collection of Aboriginal art and a 1297 edition of the *Magna Carta*.

Frequent and free guided tours (45 minutes on nonsitting days, 20 minutes otherwise) are held daily, but you're welcome to find your own way around. Tickets for question time (2pm on sitting days) are free, but must first be booked through the **Sergeant at Arms** (☑6277 4889); get them by midday or you may miss out. Tickets aren't required for other sessions in either house.

National Gallery of Australia   ART GALLERY
(☑6240 6502; www.nga.gov.au; Parkes Pl, Parkes; permanent collection free; ⊙10am-5pm) This excellent gallery showcases Australian art, including important paintings by Arthur Boyd, Sidney Nolan and Grace Cossington Smith. Aboriginal works include the wonderful *Aboriginal Memorial* (1988), a forest of 200 burial logs painted by 43 Arnhem Land artists for the bicentenary of colonisation. Of the international pieces featured, perhaps the most famous is Jackson Pollock's *Blue Poles: Number 11, 1952*.

There are free daily guided tours (check the website for current times), with overviews of the gallery's highlights as well as tours focusing on Australian and Australian Indigenous art.

National Museum of Australia   MUSEUM
(☑6208 5000; www.nma.gov.au; Lawson Cres, Acton Peninsula; admission free; ⊙9am-5pm) This museum, a modern construction on the northern shore of the lake, showcases the land, nation and people of Australia through Australian eyes and with the aid of interactive gizmos. There are attendants on hand to help you navigate exhibitions on environmental change, Indigenous culture, national icons and more, and you can take one-hour guided tours (adult/child $7.50/5.50).

Bus 34 from Civic runs here.

Australian War Memorial   MUSEUM
(☑6243 4211; www.awm.gov.au; Treloar Cres, Campbell; admission free; ⊙10am-5pm) The colossal war memorial is set in beautiful grounds at the foot of Mt Ainslie, littered with mature trees, sculptures and big

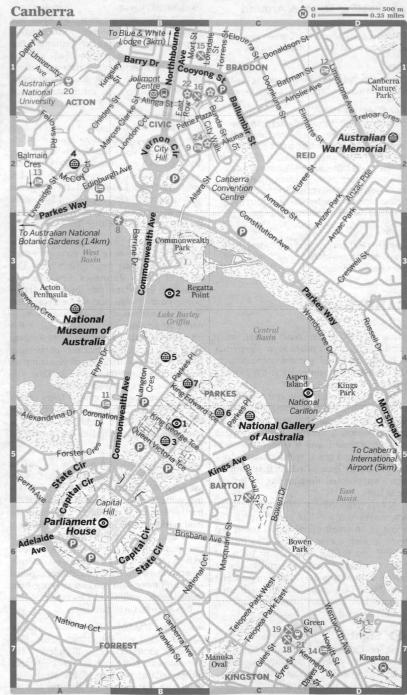

guns. It houses an interesting collection of dioramas, paintings, artefacts and exhibitions. Free 90-minute guided tours are held throughout the day.

Entombed in the glorious **Hall of Memory** is the **Unknown Australian Soldier**, whose remains were returned from a WWI battlefield in 1993. The hall itself is steeped in symbolism, with churchlike stained glass and an exquisite 1958 mosaic with over six million Italian tiles covering the roof and walls. It's here that the cult of the Anzac (Australian and New Zealand Army Corps) reaches its apotheosis – but even pacifists will be impressed.

The view down Anzac Parade across the lake to Parliament shows Canberra at its most planned, geometric and grandiose.

To get to the War Memorial catch bus 33 from Civic.

Museum of Australian Democracy at Old Parliament House
MUSEUM

(☎6270 8222; www.moadoph.gov.au; King George Tce, Parkes; adult/concession $2/1; ⊙9am-5pm) This museum is housed in the venerable Old Parliament House, which was the seat of government from 1927 to 1988 and is a great place to get a whiff of bygone parliamentary activity. As well as preserving the old senate and house of representative chambers, the museum's exhibits place Australia's tradition in the context of the broader history of democracy, spanning the globe over two millennia. The restaurant and cafe here are both excellent.

Parked on the lawn in front of Old Parliament House is the **Aboriginal Tent Embassy** – an important site in the struggle for equality and representation for Indigenous Australians.

National Portrait Gallery
ART GALLERY

(www.portrait.gov.au; King Edward Tce, Parkes; admission free; ⊙10am-5pm) This gallery tells the story of Australia through its faces. The several hundred works on show also tell the story of the evolution of portraiture, from wax cameos of Aboriginal tribespeople to a DayGlo Nick Cave. The gallery's beautiful new building is a treat in itself – it's made from wood and stone from every state and territory.

National Film & Sound Archive
MUSEUM, CINEMA

(☎02-6248 2000; www.nfsa.gov.au; McCoy Circuit, Acton; admission free; ⊙9am-5pm Mon-Fri, 10am-5pm Sat & Sun) This excellent archive, set in a delightful art deco building, preserves Australia's rich history of film, TV and radio. The small theatrette screens gems from the collection, while the larger **Arc Cinema** (⊙screenings 2pm & 7pm Thu, 2pm & 4:30pm Sat & Sun plus 7:30pm Sat; adult/concession $11/9) shows classics and new international cinema.

A LONG WEEKEND IN CANBERRA

SATURDAY After checking into your digs, get your fill of Australian art, stopping by the **National Gallery of Australia** (p127) and the **National Portrait Gallery** (p129). Wander west along Lake Burley Griffin's foreshore, past the High Court and **National Library** (p130), ending your walk with high tea at the historic **Hyatt Hotel** (p131). Take in a classic or a modern masterpiece at the **Arc Cinema** (p129) before a late dinner at **Ottoman Cuisine** (p131) or **Italian & Sons** (p132). For something livelier, try a few rounds of tapas and drinks at the swish **Parlour Wine Room** (p132).

SUNDAY Have brunch at **Silo Bakery** (p132) or **Urban Pantry** (p132) then head to the **National Museum of Australia** (p127), where you'll learn all you need to know about the country's fascinating Indigenous and post-colonial histories. If you have a car, take the afternoon to explore some of the region's excellent wineries (see www.canberrawines. com.au for details). Otherwise, jump on a bicycle and cycle around the **lake** (p130) before exploring nearby Yarralumla, with its collection of quirky embassy buildings. Reward yourself with dinner at **Portia's Place** (p132).

MONDAY If today's a sitting day, book a ringside seat at the only game in town – **Parliamentary Question Time** (p127). On your way to the 2pm session, drop into the **Museum of Australian Democracy at Old Parliament House** (p129) and bone up on some political history before lunching in the pleasant courtyard cafe. Before leaving town, be sure to visit the moving and informative **War Memorial** (p127).

Lake Burley Griffin
LANDMARK

Named after Canberra's architect, Lake Burley Griffin was created by damming the Molonglo River in 1963. Swimming is not recommended, but the lake is suitable for boating and great to cycle around. Boats, bikes and in-line skates are available for hire at Acton Park ferry terminal, on the northern shore.

Around the lake's 35km shoreline are many places of interest. The most visible is the **Captain Cook Memorial Water Jet**, built in 1970 for the bicentenary of Captain Cook's landfall.

Australian National Botanic Gardens
GARDEN

(✆6250 9540; www.anbg.gov.au/anbg; Clunies Ross St, Acton; admission free; ☺8.30am-5pm) Spreading over 90 hectares of the lower slopes of Black Mountain, Australian National Botanic Gardens is devoted to the growth, study and promotion of Australian plants. Dedicated trails take in the highlights of the gardens, including sections of rainforest and themed plantings.

Its **visitor centre** (☺9am-4.30pm) has maps and is the departure point for free guided walks.

Bus 81 from Civic will take you directly to the gardens on weekends, public holidays and school holidays. If you're feeling fit, it's a pleasant walk to the gardens through the grounds of the Australian National University.

National Library of Australia
NOTABLE BUILDING

(✆6262 1111; www.nla.gov.au; Parkes Pl, Parkes; admission free; ☺main reading room 9am-9pm Mon-Thu, 9am-5pm Fri & Sat, 1.30-5pm Sun) The National Library of Australia is one of the most elegant buildings in Canberra, and holds more than six million items, including rare books, paintings, early manuscripts, photographs, oral histories and maps. Book ahead for the free, 45-minute **Behind-the-Scenes Tour** (✆6262 1271; ☺tours 12.30pm Thu). The **Exhibition Gallery** (admission free; ☺9am-5pm) presents engaging displays from the library's diverse collections.

National Zoo & Aquarium
ZOO

(✆6287 8400; www.zooquarium.com.au; Lady Denman Dr, Yarralumla; adult/child $30/19; ☺10am-5pm) This impressive zoo is near Scrivener Dam at the western end of Lake Burley Griffin.

Bus 81 from Civic heads to the zoo before stopping at the Botanic Gardens, but only on weekends, public holidays and school holidays.

Questacon – National Science & Technology Centre
MUSEUM

(✆6270 2800; www.questacon.edu.au; King Edward Tce, Parkes; adult/child $20/15; ☺9am-5pm) This hands-on museum is educational and great fun. The 200-plus interactive exhibits show how science and technology work in everyday life.

★ Festivals & Events

National Multicultural Festival CULTURAL
(www.multiculturalfestival.com.au) Celebrated
over 10 days in February.

Royal Canberra Show AGRICULTURAL
(www.rncas.org.au/showwebsite/main.html) The
country meets the city (it's not that far to
travel) at the end of February.

Celebrate Canberra Festival CULTURAL
(www.celebratecanberra.com) Canberra's extended birthday party, held mid-March.

National Folk Festival FOLK MUSIC
(www.folkfestival.asn.au) Held Easter weekend.

Floriade GARDENS
(www.floriadeaustralia.com) A month-long
celebration of spring flowers, held from
mid- September to mid-October.

🛏 Sleeping

This is a government town. There are very
few bargains and even shoddy choices dry
up when Parliament is sitting. It pays to
book ahead, and booking online through
sites like www.lastminute.com.au and www.
wotif.com can mean large discounts.

TOP CHOICE Hyatt Hotel Canberra HOTEL $$$
(6270 1234; www.canberra.park.hyatt.
com; Commonwealth Ave, Yarralumla; r from $250;
❋@≋) Staff zing to attention in plus-fours
at this Gatsby-esque, art deco hotel. You can
almost smell the whiff of past power-plays in
the diplomatic suites. The illusion fades in
the newer wing, where it's back to the Hyatt
world of comfortable normality.

University House HOTEL $$
(6125 5211; www.anu.edu.au/unihouse; 1 Balmain
Cres, Acton; s without bathroom $90, r $134-$149;
❋@❋) Restored rather than renovated,
this glorious 1950s building (with fabulous
furniture to match) is soothingly positioned
amid the rambling university grounds. The
rooms are actually minisuites; many have
balconies.

Diamant BOUTIQUE HOTEL $$
(6175 2222; www.8hotels.com/dia-can; 15 Edin-
burgh Place, Civic; r/ste from $160/295; ❋@❋)
The rooms are super hip (think printed wall-
paper and miniature fishscale bath tiles) at
this boutique hotel not far from the National
Museum. It boasts a great wine bar (p132).

Canberra City YHA HOSTEL $
(6248 9155; canberracity@yhansw.org.au;
7 Akuna St, Civic; dm $29-39, d/tw $89/99;
❋@≋) This large, bright complex offers

plenty of potential to mingle, with its
rooftop barbecue area, bar, indoor swim-
ming pool, spa, pool tables and comfort-
able lounge.

Olims Hotel Canberra HOTEL $$
(6243 0000; www.olimshotel.com; cnr Ainslie &
Limestone Aves, Braddon; r $85-350; ❋@❋)
This 1927 heritage-listed building surrounds
a lovely courtyard. The 1st-floor, 'loft' rooms
are self-contained, more spacious and have
balconies overlooking the garden.

Victor Lodge GUESTHOUSE $
(6295 7777; www.victorlodge.com.au; 29 Dawes
St, Kingston; s/d & tw without bathroom, incl
breakfast $89/106; ❋@❋) Far from flash yet
quite presentable, this large house offers
clean rooms with shared facilities and a
communal kitchen.

Blue & White Lodge B&B $$
(6248 0498; http://blueandwhitelodge.com.
au; 524 Northbourne Ave, Downer; s/d $110/130;
❋) Somewhere between a brick-and-tile
home and the Parthenon (Ionian columns
and pediments), this family-run B&B is
a short bus ride north of the centre and
offers cooked breakfasts and comfortable,
clean rooms.

Tall Trees Motel MOTEL $$
(6247 9200; www.bestwestern.com.au/talltrees;
21 Stephen St, Ainslie; r $150; ❋) The green
grounds of this motel and its location in
leafy Ainslie, an easy distance from the
centre, lend it a relaxed air.

Canberra Motor Village
CARAVAN PARK, CABINS $$
(6247 5466; www.canberravillage.com; Kunzea
St, O'Connor; camp sites unpowered/powered
$23/28, powered sites for caravans $35, cabins
$115-195; ❋≋) Dozing in peaceful bush
6km northwest of the centre, the orderly
arrangement of tidy cabins and camp sites
mirrors Canberra itself.

✖ Eating

Most restaurants are in Civic, Kingston,
Manuka and Griffith, and there's a fantastic
Asian strip in Dickson. Many of the city's
sights have excellent eateries – try the War
Memorial, Old Parliament House and the
National Film & Sound Archive.

TOP CHOICE Ottoman Cuisine TURKISH $$$
(6273 6111; cnr Broughton & Blackall
Sts, Barton; mains $29-35; ◷lunch Tue-Fri, dinner
Tue-Sat) A real sense-of-occasion restaurant,
Ottoman is to Turkish what Mod Oz is to

meat-and-two-veg. The service is impeccable, there's a good wine list and the mezze plates are amazing.

Italian & Sons   ITALIAN $$
(☑6162 4888; 7 Lonsdale St, Braddon; mains $23-32; ☺lunch Tue-Fri, dinner Mon-Sat) This friendly new restaurant on the edge of Civic serves hearty mains along with delicious pastas and woodfired pizzas (with good vegetarian options), all made from top ingredients – it also has great wine and cheese lists.

Silo Bakery   BAKERY, CAFE $
(☑6260 6060; 36 Giles St, Kingston; mains $6-19; ☺7am-4pm Mon-Sat, closed Christmas–31 Jan) Popular to the point of insanity, this legendary bakery and cheese shop has cafe seating and an excellent breakfast menu.

Portia's Place   CHINESE $$
(☑6239 7970; 11 Kennedy St, Kingston; mains $22-35; ☺lunch Sun-Fri, dinner daily) The effervescent Portia is very much the host at this popular and accomplished traditional Chinese restaurant. It's a good place to spot politicians.

Milk & Honey   CAFE $
(☑6247 7722; Garema Pl, Civic; breakfast $5-16, lunch & dinner $16-32; ☺breakfast, lunch & dinner) There are several cafes on this alley but this place has the most interesting food. Try the breakfast trifle or for something heartier, the gypsy breakfast with eggs, chorizo and beans.

Urban Pantry   MODERN AUSTRALIAN $$
(☑02-6162 3556; 5 Bougainville St, Manuka; mains $12-38; ☺8am-late Mon-Sat, 8am-4pm Sun) This chic and popular brunch spot sells homemade breads and cakes, serves excellent meals, and hosts Friday-night jazz outside during summer.

🍷 Drinking & Entertainment

For entertainment listings, see the 'Fly' section of Thursday's *Canberra Times* and the free monthly street mag *bma*. **Ticketek** (☑132 849; www.ticketek.com.au; 11 Akuna St, Civic) sells tickets to major events.

TOP CHOICE **Parlour Wine Room**   WINE BAR
(☑02-6162 3556; www.parlour.net.au; 16 Kendall Lane, Civic; ☺noon-late Tue-Thu, to 3am Fri & Sat, to midnight Sun) This contemporary take on the Victorian smoking lounge serves excellent wines, sumptuous tapas and killer cocktails. The sunny terrace overlooking the lake is perfect for afternoon drinks, while

the leather-studded lounges and plush banquets make this a very inviting option for late-night snacking and sipping.

Filthy McFadden's   PUB
(☑6239 5303; www.lovefilthys.com; Green Sq, Kingston; ☺noon-late) There's a suitably dingy ambience at this better-than-average Irish pub with a big selection of beer flowing on tap.

ANU Union Bar   PUB
(☑6125 3660; www.anuunion.com.au; Union Court, Acton; ☺gigs 8pm) Has energetic live music up to three times a week during semester; usually around $10 for local bands, but cover charges can climb to $50.

Academy   NIGHTCLUB
(☑6257 3355; www.academyclub.com.au; Bunda St, Civic; admission $5-25; ☺9pm-late Thu-Sat) The original movie screen of this former cinema dominates the crowded dance floor with frenetic, larger-than-life visuals.

Dendy Canberra Centre   CINEMA
(☑6221 8900; www.dendy.com.au; 148 Bunda St, Civic; adult/child $15/11) A flash art-house cinema complex.

ℹ️ Information

The YHA (p131) has a reliable, central internet cafe.

Canberra Hospital (☑6244 2222, emergency 6244 2611; Yamba Dr, Garran)

General post office (☑13 13 18; 53-73 Alinga St, Civic) Mail can be addressed: Poste Restante Canberra GPO, Canberra City, ACT 2601.

National Library Bookshop (☑6262 1424; Parkes Pl, Parkes) Superb selection of Australian books.

Visitors centre (☑1300 554 114; www.visitcanberra.com.au; 330 Northbourne Ave, Dickson; ☺9am-5pm Mon-Fri, 9am-4pm Sat & Sun) Maps of bicycle routes, local hikes and bushwalks.

NRMA (☑6222 7000; Canberra Centre, City Walk, Civic) Information for motorists and road maps.

ℹ️ Getting There & Away

Air

Canberra International Airport (☑6275 2222; www.canberraairport.com.au) is serviced by four airlines:

Brindabella Airlines (☑1300 66 88 24; www.brindabellaairlines.com.au) Services Newcastle (70 minutes) and Albury (45 minutes).

Qantas (☑13 13 13; www.qantas.com.au; Jolimont Centre, Northbourne Ave, Civic) Heads to Brisbane (95 minutes), Sydney (50 minutes), Melbourne (one hour), Adelaide (1¾ hours) and Perth (four hours).

Tiger Airways (☑03-9335 3033; www.tigerairways.com) Services to/from Melbourne.

Virgin Blue (☑136 789; www.virginblue.com.au) Also has services to Sydney, Melbourne and Adelaide, plus the Gold Coast (90 minutes).

Bus

The interstate bus terminal is the **Jolimont Centre** (Northbourne Ave, Civic), which has free phone lines to the visitor centre.

Greyhound (☑1300 473 946; www.greyhound.com.au; Jolimont Centre, Northbourne Ave & Alinga St; ⊙7am-6pm) has frequent services to Sydney ($25 to $40, 3½ hours) and Melbourne ($50 to $80, nine hours).

Murrays (☑13 22 51; www.murrays.com.au; Jolimont Centre, Northbourne Ave & Alinga St; ⊙7am-6pm) has daily services to Sydney ($37, 3½ hours), Batemans Bay ($24, 2½ hours), Narooma ($37, 4½ hours) and Wollongong ($31, 3½ hours), as well as the ski fields.

Car & Motorcycle

The quickest route between Canberra and the coast is the Kings Hwy, passing through grazing land before descending the nearly sheer cliffs of the escarpment in a steep, winding, but extremely beautiful road through Mongo National Park to Batemans Bay (150km).

If you're fast-tracking it to Sydney (280km), take the Federal then the Hume Hwy. For Melbourne (660km), take the Barton Hwy and then the Hume. For the Victorian Coast, take the Monaro Hwy to Lakes Entrance (420km).

Train

Kingston train station (Burke Cres, off Wentworth Ave) is the city's rail terminus (take bus 35 or 39 from Civic). Seats are booked at the station's **CountryLink travel centre** (☑13 22 32; www.countrylink.info; ⊙6am-4.45pm Mon-Fri). Trains run to/from Sydney ($56, 4½ hours, two daily). There are no direct trains to Melbourne – instead you take a CountryLink coach to Yass and transfer to the train, but the trip takes a couple of hours longer than a direct bus with Murrays or Greyhound.

① Getting Around

To/From the Airport

Canberra International Airport is 7km southeast of the city. A taxi to the city costs around $35. The **Airliner bus** (☑6299 3722; www.airliner.com.au) runs between the airport and the city (one-way/return $9/15, 20 minutes).

Bus

Canberra's public transport provider is **Action** (☑13 17 10; www.action.act.gov.au), with routes that criss-cross the city.

You can purchase single-trip tickets (adult/concession $4/2), but a better deal is a daily ticket (adult/concession $7.60/3.80). Prepurchase tickets from Action agents (including the visitor centre and some newsagents) or buy them from the driver.

Taxi

Cab Express (☑6260 6011)
Canberra Cabs (☑13 22 27)

WOLLONGONG

☑02 / POP 93,849

Hemmed in by the majestic Illawarra Escarpment, Wollongong sprawls along the coast from Lake Illawarra in the south, to within spitting distance of the Royal National Park. It's a city that gets progressively nicer as you head north, with the southern end dominated by the biggest steelworks in Australia at Port Kembla. The town centre isn't about to be crowned Miss Australia either, but a string of ever prettier surf beaches to the north compensate somewhat, as does the ever-present backdrop of those immense cliffs.

The region is part of the traditional lands of the Dharawal people, which continue north to Botany Bay. It was explored by Europeans in the early 19th century, but apart from timber cutting and dairy farming there was little development until the escarpment's coalfields attracted miners in the mid-19th century. By the turn of the 20th century Wollongong was a major coal port. Steelworks were developed in the 1920s and today the region is one of Australia's major industrial centres and Wollongong its ninth-biggest city.

The Gong's surf ethos is a happy contrast to its blue-collar grit, and the result is genuine locals and a laid-back lifestyle. The city's cuisine measures up to that of any major city and the robust student population ensures that bar staff are never bored for long.

◉ Sights & Activities

Belmore Basin   NATURE RESERVE

Wollongong's fishing fleet is based here at the southern end of the harbour. The Basin was cut from solid rock in 1868. There's a fishing cooperative and an 1872 lighthouse

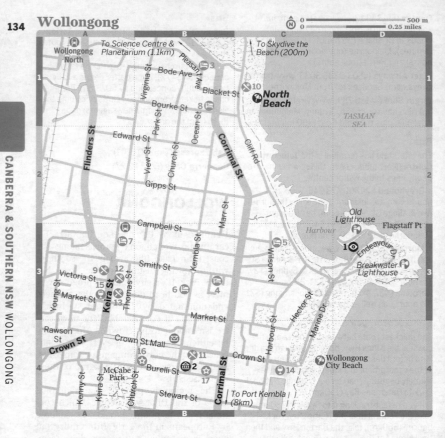

on the point. Nearby, on the headland, is the newer **Breakwater Lighthouse**.

Beaches BEACH
North Beach generally has better surf than Wollongong City Beach and you can't see the mill. The harbour itself has beaches that are good for children. Others run north up the coast, including the surfer magnets of Bulli, Sandon Point, Thirroul (where DH Lawrence lived during his time in Australia; the cottage where he wrote *Kangaroo* still stands) and pretty Austinmer.

Jumbulla Aboriginal Discovery Centre
CULTURAL CENTRE
(www.jumbulla.com.au; visitor centre, Pacific Hwy, Bulli Tops, adult/child $15/10.50) Brand new, Jumbulla explores the social history and culture of the Illawarra Aboriginal people with the latest technology including four theatre narrations. Follow signs to Southern Gateway Centre.

Science Centre & Planetarium MUSEUM
(http://sciencecentre.uow.edu.au/; Squires Way, Fairy Meadow; adult/child $11/8; ◷10am-4pm) Quizzical kids of all ages can indulge their senses here. It's operated by the University of Wollongong and covers everything from dinosaurs to electronics. Planetarium shows run through the day (per person $4).

Wollongong Botanic Gardens GARDEN
(61 Northfields Ave, Keiraville; admission free) Utterly serene and beautiful, this is a great spot to wind down with a picnic lunch. The gardens represent a range of habitats including tropical, temperate and woodland.

Nan Tien Temple TEMPLE
(www.nantien.org.au; Berkeley Rd, Berkeley; admission free; ◷9am-5pm Tue-Sun) Just south of the city, Nan Tien is the largest Buddhist temple in the southern hemisphere. The custodians encourage visitors to contemplate the 10,000 Buddhas and participate in medita-

Wollongong

◎ Top Sights
North Beach...C1

◎ Sights
1 Belmore Basin...................................D3
2 Wollongong City Gallery.....................B4

⊜ Sleeping
3 Beach Park Motor Inn........................B1
4 Belmore All-Suite Hotel.....................B3
5 Boat Harbour Motel...........................C3
6 Keiraleagh..B3
7 Keiraview Accommodation.................A3
8 Novotel Northbeach..........................B1

✕ Eating
9 Caveau...A3
10 Diggies...C1
Educated Palate.........................(see 11)
11 Lee & Me..B4
12 Lorenzo's Diner...............................A3
13 Old Siam Style................................A3

◐ Drinking
14 Five Islands Brewing Company..........C4
15 Hotel Illawarra................................A3

◉ Entertainment
16 Greater Union.................................B4
17 Illawarra Performing Arts
Centre...B4

tions and cultural activities. Dress appropriately (no shorts, singlets or flip-flops) and remove your shoes before entering.

Wollongong City Gallery   MUSEUM
(www.wollongongcitygallery.com; cnr Kembla & Burelli Sts; admission free; ☉10am-5pm Tue-Fri, noon-4pm Sat & Sun) An excellent place displaying a permanent collection of modern Australian, indigenous and Asian art, and diverse temporary exhibits.

Cockatoo Run   HERITAGE TRAIN
(☎1300 653 801; www.3801limited.com.au; adult/child/family $50/40/140; ☉10.50am, mostly Sun & Thu) Board a heritage tourist train that travels inland across the Southern Highlands to Moss Vale. The route traverses the escarpment, coursing through dense rainforest along the way.

Skydive the Beach   SKYDIVING
(☎4225 8444; www.skydivethebeach.com; Stuart Park; tandem jumps $285-339; ☉any day, any time) More adrenalin? Skydive from 14,000ft and land in the sand.

🛌 Sleeping

Many of Wollongong's motels seem to have been time-warped in from the 1970s or earlier. Prices leap by 20% to 30% on weekends.

The council runs three **tourist parks** (http://touristparks.wollongong.nsw.gov.au; camp sites per 2 people $22-28) on popular beaches: **Windang** (☎4297 3166; Fern St; cabins $63-168), **Corrimal** (☎4285 5688; Lake Pde; cabins $84-168) and **Bulli** (☎4285 5677; 1 Farrell Rd; cabins $68-200).

TOP CHOICE **Coledale Beach Camping Reserve**   CAMPGROUND $
(☎4267 4302; Beach Rd, Coledale; unpowered/powered sites from $22/28) Small and right on the beach about 20 minutes north of the city centre, this is one of the best urban camping spots on the coast. Campers can wake to great surf, with a chance of having dolphins, southern right and humpback whales for company. It's beautiful in its simplicity.

Keiraleagh   HOSTEL $
(☎4228 6765; www.backpack.net.au; 60 Kembla St; dm $20-25, s/d $43/70) This rambling heritage house is clogged with atmosphere, with pressed-metal ceilings, roses in the cornices and festively painted rooms. The basic dorms are out the back, along with a sizeable patio and a barbecue.

Keiraview Accommodation   HOSTEL $
(☎4229 1132; www.yha.com.au/hostels; 75-79 Keira St; dm/d/tw $33/110/82; @) Modern and clinically clean, this complex contains the YHA hostel, which caters to students and backpackers in tidy four-bed dorms. It's also home to Keiraview, which has pricey double and family rooms with verandahs and kitchenettes.

Boat Harbour Motel   MOTEL $$
(☎4228 9166; www.boatharbour-motel.com.au; cnr Campbell & Wilson Sts; s $110-129, d $120-145; ❈) Dressed like a sailor in white and navy-blue trim, this older style motel has nice balconies, a palm-cluttered inner courtyard and comfortable if unmemorable decor. The better rooms overlook the water (and the road).

Novotel Northbeach   HOTEL $$$
(☎4226 3555; www.novotelnorthbeach.com.au; 2-14 Cliff Rd; r incl breakfast from $209; ❈@❈) Wollongong's flashiest joint has spacious and comfortable rooms featuring balconies with ocean or escarpment views.

Beach Park Motor Inn   HOTEL $$
(☎4226 1577; 16 Pleasant Ave, North Beach; s $82-99, d $88-120; ❈) The friendly owners

LOCAL KNOWLEDGE

TAMAHRA PROWSE – SKYDIVER

I started skydiving when I was 19 after being challenged by an ex-airforce uncle to do a jump. One freefall later I was hooked! My partner Anthony and I were travelling through Mexico a couple of years later and did a jump onto the beach in Playa del Carmen; after a few too many tequilas we decided to open Skydive the Beach in Wollongong.

How often do you skydive?

While the guys who instruct here jump up to 12 times a day, I am currently grounded as I am expecting my second child in six months' time!

What's the best bit?

For me the best part about jumping is the split second my feet leave the plane. I love the feeling of complete freedom and the rush I still get (even after hundreds of skydives).

Must see

The view from Bald Hill Lookout (Stanwell Tops) over Wollongong and the South Coast.

Hidden gem

Wombarra beach is my favourite of many great stretches of golden sand.

keep the slightly twee rooms in this white brick establishment spick-and-span. It's in an urban setting, a short walk from the beach.

Pleasant Heights B&B   B&B $$$
(☑4283 3355; www.pleasantheights.com.au; 77 New Mt Pleasant Rd; r $250-450) Eccentrically but stylishly furnished, these three very different rooms are luxe indeed. Some have awesome views while others have opulent spa baths. All smell very nice.

Belmore All-Suite Hotel   HOTEL $$
(☑4224 6500; www.belmore.net; 39 Smith St; apt $139-219; ❋) All the units (ranging from studios to two-bedroom apartments) are spacious in this gracious, conservatively decorated building near the beaches. There are kitchenettes and attractive patios.

✖ Eating

North of the mall, Keira St is jammed with eateries of all types and budgets. (The Thai places are more reliably authentic than the Vietnamese). Other places are spread across town.

TOP CHOICE **Lee & Me**   CAFE $$
(www.leeandme.com.au; 87 Crown St; ⊙breakfast & lunch) A cafe and art and clothing store in a two-storey heritage building. There's nothing quite like dining on a mushroom and goat's-cheese omelette on the sunny balcony, then shopping in the boutique on a full stomach.

Diggies   CAFE, BAR $$
(www.diggies.com.au; 1 Cliff Rd, North Beach; tapas $7-11; ⊙breakfast & lunch daily, dinner Fri & Sat, cocktails from 4pm Sun) Sunny service matches the views at this informal cafe on the beach. Keep an eye on the surf while ordering from the foodie-friendly breakfast menu or just listen to it roar over a few drinks.

Caveau   MODERN AUSTRALIAN $$$
(☑4226 4855; www.caveau.com.au; 122-4 Keira St; 2-/3-/7-course degustation menu $60/77/95; ⊙dinner Tue-Sat) This is the top-rated restaurant on the south coast – even with its hip corrugated-iron trim Caveau shrieks 'formal'! The menu offerings are all 'champagne *veloute*' this and 'perigord truffle' that, promising memories that will live on after the credit-card pain subsides. Bookings are recommended.

Educated Palate   CAFE, DELI $
(rear 87 Crown St; mains $7-20; ⊙breakfast & lunch) Forgive the seriously pretentious name and raid the deli counter for provisions, or let the cooks put in the hard yards over, say, the grilled haloumi and chorizo omelette. The coffee is excellent.

Lorenzo's Diner   ITALIAN $$
(☑4229 5633; www.lorenzosdiner.com.au; 119 Keira St; mains $19-34; ⊙lunch Thu & Fri, dinner Tue-Sat) Seriously nice people run this upmarket modern Italian restaurant. The food matches the excellent service. Bookings recommended.

Austibeach MODERN AUSTRALIAN $
(www.austibeach.com.au; 104 Lawrence Hargrave Dr, Austinmer; breakfast $4-17, lunch $13-20, tapas $10-14; ☺breakfast & lunch daily, dinner Sat & Sun) Drop in for brunch or a homemade gelato as you're heading up the coast. The views from the terrace look to heaven via Austinmer Beach. Dinner is tapas-style Australian.

Old Siam Style THAI $
(157 Keira St; mains $14; ☺lunch & dinner) One of the better restaurants on the Keira St strip, this spacious place with all the trimmings serves up exquisite authentic Thai dishes, orchids and all.

🍸 Drinking

Hotel Illawarra PUB
(www.hotelillawarra.com.au; Cnr Keira & Market St) Modernised into the city's swankiest pub complex, the Illawarra has a bistro, pool tables, regular DJs and a waterfall constantly tinkling in the beer garden.

Five Islands Brewing Company BAR
(www.fiveislandsbrewery.com; WIN Entertainment Centre, cnr Crown & Harbour Sts; ✸) Its 10 signature draughts lubricate the crowd, which bursts at the seams on weekends. There's a great patio overlooking the sea.

☆ Entertainment

Illawarra Performing Arts Centre THEATRE
(IPAC; ☎4226 3366; www.ipac.org.au; 32 Burelli St) This busy venue presents an excellent and continuous stream of theatre, dance and music. It's home to the impressive Merrigong Theatre Co.

Greater Union CINEMA
(☎4228 4888; www.greaterunion.com.au; 68 Burelli St) Multiple screens showing Hollywood blockbusters.

❶ Information

The **Wollongong visitor centre** (☎4227 5545; www.tourismwollongong.com) has moved to purpose-built premises inconveniently located 20 minutes from the CBD on the Princes Hwy at Bulli Tops.

There's a post office and banks with ATMs on Crown St Mall.

NPWS office (☎4223 3000; ground fl, State Government Office Block, Market St; ☺9am-3pm Mon-Fri)

❶ Getting There & Away

All long-distance buses leave from the **long distance bus station** (☎4226 1022; cnr Keira & Campbell Sts). **Premier** (☎13 34 10; www.premierms.com.au) has buses to Sydney ($18, two hours) and Eden ($69, eight hours). **Murrays** (☎13 22 51; www.murrays.com.au) travels to Canberra ($33, 3½ hours). **CountryLink** (☎13 22 32; www.countrylink.info) runs buses to Moss Vale ($7.80, 1½ hours) from outside the train station, and links with **CityRail** (☎13 15 00; www.cityrail.info) to Sydney's Central Station ($8, 1½ hours). CityRail also runs south to Kiama, Gerringong and Bomaderry/Nowra.

❶ Getting Around

Two local bus companies, **Premier Illawarra** (☎4271 1322; www.premierillawarra.com.au) and **Dions** (☎4254 4888; www.dions.com.au), service the local area. The main stops are on Marine Dr, and the corner of Crown and Keira Sts. Bringing a bike on the train from Sydney is a great way to get around; a cycle path runs from the city centre north to Bulli and south to Port Kembla.

Gong Green Shuttle (No 55; www.131500.com.au/tickets/fares/cbd-shuttle; ☺7am-10pm Mon-Fri & 7am-6pm Sat & Sun) is a free bus shuttle that runs every 10 minutes from 7am to 6pm weekdays and every 20 minutes at other times.

For **taxis**, call ☎4229 9311.

Around Wollongong
SOUTH OF THE CITY

Just south of Wollongong, Lake Illawarra is popular for water sports, including windsurfing. There are good ocean beaches on the Windang Peninsula to the east of

---

DON'T MISS

HERE'S TO THE VIEW

Built in 1886 and now heritage listed, the grand old **Scarborough Hotel** (www.scarboroughhotel.com.au; 383 Lawrence Hargrave Dr, Scarborough; mains $12-33) has recently been renovated, reopened and reinvigorated so that punters can once again take advantage of one of the best beer gardens in NSW, if not Australia. The ocean view from the wooden bench seats and tables is so spectacular it wouldn't matter if the beer was warm. It's not, thankfully, and the gastro food gets thumbs up to too.

the lake. Further south is **Shellharbour**, a popular holiday resort, and one of the oldest towns along the coast. Its name comes from the number of shell middens (remnants of Aboriginal occupation) that the European colonists found here.

ILLAWARRA ESCARPMENT STATE CONSERVATION AREA

Rainforest hugs the edge of the ever-eroding sandstone cliffs of the escarpment, which rise to 534m at their peak at **Mt Kembla**. This discontinuous conservation area protects much of it. For wonderful views of the coast, you can drive up to the **Mt Keira lookout** (464m); take the freeway north and follow the signs. There are other lookouts at **Bulli** and **Sublime Point**.

The park is accessible from several roadside car parks; grab the excellent pamphlet from NPWS (p137), with maps and details of walks.

NORTH OF THE CITY

On the road to the Royal National Park, the **Lawrence Hargrave Lookout** at Bald Hill above Stanwell Park is a superb cliff-top viewing point. Hargrave, a pioneer aviator, made his first attempts at flying in the area early in the 20th century. His obsession has since been picked up by avid hang-gliders. To join in, **HangglideOz** (☎0417 939 200; www.hangglideoz.com.au) and **Sydney Hang Gliding Centre** (☎0400 258 258; www.hanggliding.com.au) offer tandem flights from $220.

Symbio Wildlife Gardens (☎4294 1244; www.symbiozoo.com.au; 7-11 Lawrence Hargrave Dr, Stanwell Tops; adult/child $22/12; ☉9.30am-5pm) has more than 1000 cute and furry critters. Some are native, some are exotic and some are farm animals, but all are popular with kids.

You can hit the trails on the back of a horse at **Darkes Forest Riding Ranch** (☎4294 3441; www.horseriding.au.com; 84 Darkes Forest Rd, Darkes Forest; per hr from $48).

Royal National Park

The only thing preventing Wollongong from becoming a suburb of Sydney is this wonderful coastal park, which protects 15,091 hectares stretching inland from 32km of beautiful coast. Encompassing dramatic cliffs, secluded beaches, scrub and lush rainforest, it's the second-oldest national park in the world having been gazetted in 1879.

⊙ Sights & Activities

The **park** (per car $11, pedestrians & cyclists free) has a large network of **walking tracks**, including a spectacular 26km (two-day) Coast Track.

There are lots of beautiful beaches, but most are unpatrolled and rips can make them dangerous. **Garie, Era, South Era** and **Burning Palms** are popular surf beaches and **Werrong Beach** is 'clothing-optional'. The side roads to the smaller beaches are closed at 8.30pm. Cycling is popular but stick to the trails to avoid a fine.

The sizeable town of **Bundeena**, on the southern shore of Port Hacking opposite Sydney's southern suburb of Cronulla, is surrounded by the park. From here you can walk 30 minutes towards the ocean to **Jibbon Head**, which has a good beach and interesting Aboriginal rock art. Bundeena is the starting point out of the coastal walk.

The **visitor centre** (☎9542 0648) is at Audley, 2km inside the northeastern entrance, off the Princes Hwy.

🛏 Sleeping

Bush camping is allowed in several other areas, but you must obtain a permit (adult/child $5/3) from the visitor centre, where you can get information about current usable camp sites.

Bonnie Vale   CAMPGROUND **$**
(☎9542 0648; camp sites per adult/child $14/7) Near Bundeena, this is the only park camping ground accessible by car.

Weemalah Cottage   COTTAGES **$$**
(☎9542 0648; cottage winter/summer $190/220) NPWS also rents out this gorgeous place by the river at Warumbul. Once kept for visiting dignitaries, this fully self-contained house has wide verandahs and sleeps eight.

Beachhaven B&B   B&B **$$$**
(☎9544 1333; www.beachhavenbnb.com.au; 13 Bundeena Dr, Bundeena; r $275; ❄@) Shaded by palms and with direct access to gorgeous Hordens Beach, this place has two swank rooms. Amenities include DVD players, antiques and a spa overlooking the sand.

❶ Getting There & Away

Cronulla National Park Ferries (☎9523 2990; www.cronullaferries.com.au; adult/child $5.70/2.85; ☉hourly 8.30am-5.30pm) travels to Bundeena from Cronulla, which you can reach by train from Sydney. Hours are longer on weekdays and in summer.

Kiama & Around

♪02 / POP 12,290

Kiama's a large town with fine old buildings, magnificent mature trees, numerous beaches and crazy rock formations, but it's the blowhole that's the clincher.

◉ Sights & Activities

Blowhole Point   LANDMARK

At its most dramatic when the surf's up, the water pounding the cliff explodes out of a gaping fissure in the headland. It's been drawing visitors for a century and is now floodlit at night. It's just off the main street.

The **visitor centre** (☑4232 3322; www.kiama.com.au) is nearby, beside the small **Pilot's Cottage Museum** (☑4232 1001; adult/child $3/2; ⊘11am-3pm Fri-Mon).

Little Blowhole   LANDMARK

(off Tingira Cres, Marsden Head) It's only a couple of feet wide, but it rivals its big brother, shooting water in a jet like a dragon snorting. There's a small enclosed surf beach right in town and Bombo Beach, 3km north of the centre, has a great beach and a CityRail stop near the sand.

Saddleback Mountain   NATURE RESERVE

From the top you get a great view of the Illawarra Escarpment, the massive sandstone rampart that separates the coastal plain from the Southern Highlands. From Manning St, turn right on to Saddleback Mountain Rd, keeping an eye out for the historic dry-stone walls lining the road.

Minnamurra Rainforest Centre
NATURE RESERVE

(☑4236 0469; car $11; ⊘9am-5pm, last entry 4pm) In the same vicinity as the Illawarra Fly, this centre is on the eastern edge of **Budderoo National Park**, about 14km inland from Kiama. From the NPWS visitor centre you can take a **1.6km loop walk** on a boardwalk through the rainforest following a cascading stream. Keep an eye out for water dragons and some of the most sociable lyrebirds in the country. A secondary 2.6km walk on a beautiful, but sometimes steep, track leads to the **Minnamurra Falls**. The visitor centre has a cafe.

Coastal Walk   WALKING

The new 6km trail, with the requisite boulders, beaches, sea caves and cliff faces, stretches from Love's Bay in Kiama Heights to the north end of Werri Beach.

Illawarra Fly   NATURE RESERVE

(☑1300 362 881; www.illawarrafly.com.au; 182 Knights Hill Rd, Knights Hill; adult/child/family $22/9.50/55; ⊘9am-5pm) There are spectacular views from this 500m viewing tower above the rainforest canopy at the top of the escarpment, 25km west of town.

Jamberoo   NOTABLE BUILDING

On the way to Minnamurra, this lovely old village has a nice pint-worthy **pub**.

ᕦ Sleeping & Eating

Kiama Harbour Cabins   APARTMENTS $$

(☑4232 2707; Blowhole Point, Kiama; 1-/2-/3-bedroom cabins from $205/220/280) In the best position in town, these cute cottages are neat-as-pins and well equipped with barbecues on front verandas that overlook the beach and the ocean pool.

Kendalls on the Beach Holiday Park
CARAVAN PARK $

(☑4232 1790; www.kiama.net/holiday/kendalls; Bonaira St; sites per 2 people $35-40, cottages $100-300; ❄) Perched on one of Kiama's loveliest beaches, this upmarket holiday park has flash cottages facing the beach and good clean facilities for campers.

Bellevue Accommodation   GUESTHOUSE $$

(☑4232 4000; www.bellevueaccommodation.com.au; 21 Minnamurra St; units from $180; ❄) Six large modern units with wide porches and town views have been carved out of this lovely 1890 house. Plush units have DVD players and kitchen facilities.

Chachi's   ITALIAN $$$

(☑4233 1144; 32 Collins St; mains $14-34; ⊘dinner Mon-Sat, Sun during summer) Located in a historic strip of terraced houses, Chachi's is well loved among locals for its casual Italian alfresco dining. The smells wafting onto the pavement are hard to resist.

Seafood Co-op   SEAFOOD $$

(☑4233 1800; Kiama Harbour) Fresh from the trawlers, this locals-love-it hidey-hole sells local tiger prawns (per kg $25) and oysters (per two dozen $20).

Hanoi on Manning   VIETNAMESE $$

(10 Manning St; mains $15-24; ⊘lunch & dinner Wed-Mon) Spot the Viet 333 beer on the menu and be assured this place delivers on authenticity. Old faves such as rice-paper rolls and *pho* are improved by fresh local ingredients.

Kiama Produce Market MARKET $
(132 Black Beach; ⊙8am-1pm Sat) Every fourth Saturday, an array of local organic produce, unusual baked goods and prepared foods is on offer.

ℹ Getting There & Around

Premier (☑13 34 10; www.premierms.com.au) buses run twice daily to Berry ($18, 30 minutes), Eden ($69, 7½ hours) and Sydney ($25, 2½ hours). **Kiama Coachlines** (☑4232 3466; www.kiamacoachlines.com.au) runs to Gerroa, Gerringong and Minnamurra (via Jamberoo).

Frequent **CityRail** (☑13 15 00; www.cityrail.info) trains run to Wollongong, Sydney and Bomaderry/Nowra.

If you're driving, take the beach detour via Gerringong and Gerroa and rejoin the highway either in Berry or just north of Nowra.

Gerringong & Gerroa
☑02

The lesser of the coast's two Gongs, Gerringong (population 3588) is a pleasant little town surrounded by farmland above the impressive sweep of Werri Beach. It's popular with both retirees and surfies. Next door, is Gerroa (population 497) an even sleepier huddle of houses overlooking Crooked River inlet and stunning Seven Mile Beach. **Just Gifts** (cnr Fern & Belinda Sts, Gerringong) acts as the visitor centre.

◉ Sights & Activities

Boolarng Nangamai CULTURAL CENTRE
(☑0414 322 142; www.boolarng-nangamai.com; 5/9 Bergin St, Gerringong; ⊙10.30am-3.30pm Sat & Sun) An Aboriginal art and culture studio that runs workshops and acts as a gallery for local artists. Take the first left after the train station.

Heritage Centre MUSEUM
(10 Blackwood St, Gerringong; ⊙1-4pm Sat & Sun) Gives an insight into the local dairying industry and history.

Seven Mile Beach Holiday Park WATER SPORTS
(200 Crooked River Rd, Gerroa) Has bikes, surfboards and kayaks for rent ($15).

Surf Camp Australia SURFING
(☑1800 888 732; www.surfcamp.com.au; 2 days $275) Gives surf lessons on Seven Mile Beach.

🛏 Sleeping & Eating

Seven Mile Beach Holiday Park
CARAVAN PARK $
(☑4234 1340; www.kiamacoast.com.au/Sevenmile_Beach/index.html; 200 Crooked River Rd, Gerroa; sites $23-65, cabins $85-285; ☒) Straddling both sides of the Crooked River, this serene spot has good cabins and facilities, and lots of leafy outdoor play space. The northern side has direct access to 7 miles of beach.

Bellachara Boutique Hotel
BOUTIQUE HOTEL $$$
(☑4234 1359; www.bellachara.com.au; 1 Fern St; r midweek from $145; ✸✸) An old motel in the town has been given quite a makeover to turn it into this luxurious complex. The rooms are smartly furnished and the day spa is suitably glam. The room rates double in peak season.

TOP CHOICE **Seahaven Cafe** MODERN AUSTRALIAN $$
(☑4234 3796; 19 Riverleigh Ave, Gerroa; mains $18-35; ⊙breakfast & lunch daily, dinner Sat & Sun) One of the South Coast's perennially good cafe-cum-restaurants, with gourmet food, tasteful decor and a seaside setting. From the breakfast menu, try the watermelon and strawberry fruit salad with rose water, yoghurt and pistachios.

Gerringong Deli & Café DELI, CAFE $
(133 Fern St; breakfast $5-17, lunch $10-20) Housed in a nice old wooden building with lots of art on the walls, this deli cafe has plenty of vego choices, along with sandwiches, wraps, burgers and pasta.

ℹ Getting There & Away

From **Gerringong station** (☑4234 1422; Grey St) regular **CityRail** (☑131 500; www.cityrail.info) trains go to Wollongong ($6, 56 minutes) and Berry ($4, nine minutes), with connections to Sydney.

SHOALHAVEN COAST

The coastal beauty is undiminished in this region, with its great beaches, state forests and numerous national parks, including the huge (190,751-hectare) Morton National Park in the westerly ranges. You're still in striking distance of Sydney, so expect holiday spots to fill up and prices to explode on weekends and during school holidays.

Berry

📱 02 / POP 1485

Berry has metamorphosed from a small re-
tiree kind of town into a popular inland stop
on the South Coast. Is the chintz outweigh-
ing the heritage character these days? You
decide. In any case, it has a plethora of great
eating venues, an overdose of cafes (some
good, some average), two pubs fit for shout-
ing a round or two, and a smattering of National Trust–classified buildings. The main
tourist info centre is about 17km southwest
in Nowra or try www.berry.net.au.

◉ Sights & Activities

Founded in the 1820s, Berry remained a
private town on the Coolangatta Estate
(p144) until 1912. The town's short main
street is worth a stroll for its National Trust–
classified buildings and a multitude of gift
shops and cafes.

Treat Factory
(📱4464 1112; www.treatfactory.com.au; Old
Creamery Lane; ⊘9.30am-4.30pm Mon-Fri, 10am-
4pm Sat & Sun) An old-school place chock-
full of nostalgic lollies such as rocky road
and liquorice.

Berry Museum
(135 Queen St; admission free; ⊘11am-2pm Sat,
11am-3pm Sun) Near the post office, in an
interesting 1884 bank building.

VINEYARDS
There are some good-quality vineyards in
the rolling countryside around Berry.

Hotel Berry   HOTEL
(📱4464 1011; 120 Queen St; ⊘tours 11am Sat)
Runs a short and sweet wine tour ($30),
but you need to book ahead.

Jasper Valley Wines   VINEYARD
(📱152 Croziers Rd; ⊘10am-4pm Fri-Sun) Located 5km south of Berry, and offers tastings and lunches.

Silos Estate   VINEYARD
(www.thesilos.com; B640 Princes Highway, Jaspers
Brush; starters $20, mains $27-33; ⊘lunch & dinner Thu-Sun) Offers tastings along with an
acclaimed restaurant and boutique accommodation ($195 to $395).

🎉 Festivals & Events

Berry Country Fair   AGRICULTURAL
This popular fair is held on the first Sun-
day of the month at the showgrounds.

Berry Celtic Festival   CULTURAL
(www.berrycelticfestival.org.au; Berry Showground;
adult/child $10/5) On the last Saturday in
May the peace is shattered by the caber-
tossers, haggis-hurlers and bagpipes.

🛏 Sleeping

Conjuring up images of cosy wood fires, Berry is a popular weekender in winter as well.

Berry Hotel   HOTEL $
(📱4464 1011; www.berryhotel.com.au; 120 Queen
St; s/d without bathroom $50/80) This country
pub is a rarity – it caters to weekending city
slickers without losing its status as a local
watering hole. The rooms are standard pub
bedrooms with bathrooms down the corri-
dor, but they are large and well presented.

Bellawongarah at Berry   B&B $$
(📱4464 1999; www.accommodation-berry.com.
au; 869 Kangaroo Valley Rd, Bellawongarah; r/ste/
cottage per two nights $400/520/500; 🌀) Misty,
magical rainforest surrounds this wonder-
ful place, 8km from Berry on the mountain
road leading to Kangaroo Valley. Asian art
features in the main house, while nearby
an 1868 Wesleyan church has been given a
French provincial makeover and is rented as
a self-contained cottage for two.

Posthouse   GUESTHOUSE $$$
(📱4464 2444; www.berryposthouse.com.au; 137
Queen St; s/d incl breakfast $190-260) At the end
of the main street, this is an excellent place
in one of the town's more impressive buildings. There are two exquisite rooms, one
with a four-poster bed and open fire. Breakfast is served downstairs, in the award-winning **restaurant** (⊘breakfast Sat & Sun, lunch &
dinner Thu-Sun).

Berry Village Boutique Motel   MOTEL $$
(📱4464 3570; www.berrymotel.com.au; 72 Queen
St; r $155-235; 🌀🌀) Large, comfortable
rooms are the go at this upmarket place at
the edge of the main strip. The tiny pool,
just off reception, seems to work more as
a water feature.

🍴 Eating

TOP CHOICE **Hungry Duck**   MODERN ASIAN $$$
(📱4464 2323; www.hungryduck.com.au;
85 Queen St; tapas $8-30; ⊘dinner Wed-Sun,) This
chic little red-and-black dining room is paired
nicely with a contemporary Asian menu
served tapas-style. There's a rear courtyard
and kitchen garden where herbs are plucked
direct to the plate. Fresh fish and meat are

WORTH A TRIP

FITZROY FALLS

Water falling 81m makes a big roar and that's what you hear at this stunning spot in **Morton National Park** (per vehicle $3). Even more spectacular is the view down the Yarrunga Valley from the sheer cliffs of the escarpment. There are various walks in the vicinity where, if you're very lucky, you might spot a platypus or a lyrebird. The **visitor centre** (4887 7270) has a cafe and good displays.

From either Nowra or Berry the road is a delight, heading through pretty Kangaroo Valley where the historic town is hemmed in by the mountains. Then it's over castlelike Hampden Bridge, an ostentatious 1898 sandstone affair, before taking the steep climb up the escarpment.

sourced locally and the eggs are from the chef's own chooks. An ever-changing menu might include tempura zucchini flowers with aged soy and citrus. Five- and seven-course degustation menus also available. Also open Wednesday to Monday in summer.

Coach House Restaurant PUB FARE $
(120 Queen St; mains $15-25; ⊗10am-late) The restaurant at the Berry Hotel offers a nice ambience and meals a cut above usual pub grub. Sit in the large covered beer garden or grab a table in the 1860 Kangaroo Inn, a single room brick building at the back.

Berry Woodfired Sourdough Bakery
BAKERY, CAFE $
(Prince Alfred St; mains $5-17; ⊗breakfast & lunch Wed-Sun) Stock up on delicious bread or sit down for a light meal at this highly esteemed bakery that attracts foodies from far and wide.

ℹ Getting There & Away

Frequent **CityRail** (131 500; www.cityrail. info) trains go to Wollongong ($6, 75 minutes) and Nowra ($4, 10 minutes) from **Berry station** (4464 1022; Station Rd), with connections to Sydney.

There are scenic roads from Berry to pretty Kangaroo Valley. **Premier** (13 34 10; www. premierms.com.au) has buses to Kiama ($18, 30 minutes), Nowra ($18, 20 minutes) and Sydney ($25, three hours, twice daily).

Nowra

02 / POP 27,480

From a traveller's perspective, Nowra's more of a means to an end rather than an end in itself. It may be the largest town in the Shoalhaven area but it doesn't have the charm of Berry, 17km northeast, or the beaches of Jervis Bay, 25km southeast. It is, however, the southernmost point that the train from Sydney stops on the East Coast. There are some good eateries and when Jervis Bay fills up you can stop here and commute.

◉ Sights & Activities

Nowra Wildlife Park ANIMAL PARK
(www.nowrawildlifepark.com.au; Rock Hill Rd; adult/child $16/8; ⊗9am-5pm) The 6.5-hectare park on the north bank of the Shoalhaven River, is where you can kiss a cockatoo and meet other native animals. Head north from Nowra, cross the bridge and immediately turn left, then follow the signs. It has a fully catered **camp site** (adult/child $10/6).

Fleet Air Arm Museum
(www.navy.gov.au/faam/; 489a Albatross Rd; adult/child $10/free; ⊗10am-4pm) If you're interested in military planes and helicopters, there's a great display here, 10km south of Nowra. Nearby **Nowra Hill lookout** offers expansive views over the plains to the escarpment.

Meroogal MUSEUM
(www.hht.net.au/museums/meroogal/; cnr West & Worrigee Sts; adult/child $8/4; ⊗1-5pm Sat, 10am-5pm Sun) Intriguingly, this historic 1885 house contains the artefacts accumulated by four generations of women who lived there. Also open Fridays in January.

Nowra Museum MUSEUM
(Cnr Kinghorne & Plunkett Sts; adult/child $1/50c; ⊗1-4pm Sat & Sun) Has heaps of old stuff.

Shoalhaven River Cruises BOAT TOUR
(0429 981 007; www.shoalhavenrivercruise. com) Two-hour tours ($26) or fish and chip tours ($39) on the beautiful Shoalhaven River, leaving from the wharf just east of the bridge. Call ahead for times.

WALKING

The visitor centre produces a handy compilation of walks in the area. The relaxing **Ben's Walk** starts at the bridge near Scenic

Dr and follows the south bank of the Shoalhaven River (6km return). North of the river, the circular 5.5km **Bomaderry Creek Walking Track** runs through sandstone gorges from a trailhead at the end of Narang Rd.

🛏 Sleeping & Eating

White House Heritage Guest House

B&B $$

(☑4421 2084; www.whitehouseguesthouse.com; 30 Junction St; s $98-123, d $98-151, tr/f $139/$152; ✽) A friendly family runs this beautifully restored guesthouse with comfortable en suite rooms, some with spas. The light breakfast out on the wide verandah is a great way to start the day.

Boatshed MODERN AUSTRALIAN $$

(☑4421 2419; 10 Wharf Rd; breakfast $5-12, lunch $13-15, dinner $19-24; ☺breakfast & lunch Sat & Sun, dinner Thu-Sat) Nowra's most atmospheric eating option is right by the river, almost under the bridge. Enjoy weekend brunch on the terrace or settle into a more formal experience in the dining room.

Tea Club CAFE $

(☑4422 0900; www.teaclub.com.au; 46 Berry St; breakfast $7, lunch $11; ☺breakfast & lunch Mon-Sat) Nowra's bohemian set hangs out at this comfortable little vegetarian cafe with art on the walls and a vast back garden. Try the chai and check its website for interesting live gigs.

George Bass Motor Inn MOTEL $$

(☑4421 6388; www.georgebass.com.au; 65 Bridge Rd; s $109-129, d $124-144; ✽) An unpretentious but well-appointed single-storey motor inn, the George Bass has clean and sunny rooms. The more expensive ones are slightly newer.

River Deli CAFE $

(84 Kinghorne St; meals $5-15; ☺breakfast & lunch Mon-Sat) Pore over the stacks of newspapers and savour the array of deli items, including filled baguettes and salads.

Red Raven ITALIAN $$

(☑4423 3433; 55 Junction St; lunch $13-20, dinner $20-28; ☺lunch Tue-Fri, dinner Tue-Sat) Occupying the 1908 fire station, this BYO restaurant serves interesting Italian-influenced dishes, including pizza, with plenty of vegetarian options.

ℹ Information

NPWS office (☑4423 2170; 55 Graham St; ☺8.30am-4.30pm Mon-Fri)

Post office (59 Junction St)

Visitor centre (☑4421 0778; www.shoalhaven. nsw.gov.au; cnr Princes Hwy & Pleasant Way) Internet is available ($1 per 15 minutes).

ℹ Getting There & Around

The **train station** (☑4423 0141; Meroo St) is 3km north of town at Bomaderry. Frequent **CityRail** (☑131 500; www.cityrail.info) trains go to Wollongong ($7.80, 75 minutes) via Berry ($4, 10 minutes), with connections to Sydney. Local buses link Nowra to the train station on weekdays, with only limited services on Saturdays. Or take a **taxi** (☑4421 0333).

Premier (☑13 34 10; www.premierms.com. au) coaches stop on the run between Sydney ($25, three hours) via Berry ($18, 20 minutes), and Melbourne ($82, 14 hours) via Ulladulla ($19, one hour).

Ulladulla to Jervis Bay

Milton, on the highway 6km north of Ulladulla, is this area's original town, built to serve the nearby farming communities. In a sign of how values have changed, note that Milton, like so many early towns in this coastal region, was built several kilometres inland, away from the cold and stormy coast.

There are several cafes and a few antique shops on the main street (Princes Hwy) and it gets pretty busy here on weekends. **Pilgrims Wholefoods** (☑4455 3421; Princes Hwy; meals $5-12; ☺breakfast & lunch) has interesting vegetarian lunches (six types of vegie burger!), along with organic supplies.

The highway passes **Conjola National Park** before skirting **St Georges Basin**, a large body of water that has access to the sea through narrow **Sussex Inlet**. The north shore of the basin has succumbed to housing developments reminiscent of the suburban sprawl on the central coast.

Jervis Bay

One of the most stunning spots on the south coast, this large, sheltered bay is a magical amalgamation of snow-white sand, crystalline waters, national parks and frolicking dolphins. Seasonal visitors include hordes of Sydney holidaymakers (summer and most weekends) and migrating whales (May to November).

In 1995 the Aboriginal community won a land claim in the Wreck Bay area and now jointly administers Booderee National Park

SURF & TURF

East of Nowra, the Shoalhaven River meanders through dairy country in a system of estuaries and wetlands, finally reaching the sea at Crookhaven Heads, aka Crooky, where there's good surf. **Greenwell Point**, on the estuary about 15km east of Nowra, is a quiet, pretty fishing village specialising in **fresh oysters**. The little kiosk near the pier has fresh fish and chips.

On the north side of the estuary is **Shoalhaven Heads**, where the river once reached the sea but is now blocked by sandbars. Just north of the surf beach here is stunning **Seven Mile Beach National Park** (admission free) stretching up to Gerroa. It's an idyllic picnic spot.

Just before Shoalhaven Heads you pass through **Coolangatta**, the site of the earliest European settlement on NSW's south coast. **Coolangatta Estate** (☑4448 7131; www. coolangattaestate.com.au; s/d $120/140; ☺winery 10am-5pm) is a slick winery with a golf course, a good restaurant and accommodation in convict-built buildings. Prices nearly double on the weekends.

at the southern end of the bay. By a strange quirk this area is actually part of the ACT, not NSW.

Most of the development in Jervis Bay is on the western shore, around the settlements of Huskisson and Vincentia (combined population 3391). The northern shore has less tourist infrastructure. Callala Bay (population 2717), despite its close proximity to Huskisson, is cut off by the Currambene Creek – you have to drive back to the highway and head south (which is just the way the locals like it). Beecroft Peninsula forms the northeastern side of Jervis Bay, ending in the dramatic sheer wall of appropriately named Point Perpendicular. Most of the peninsula is navy land but is usually open to the public.

◉ Sights & Activities

Huskisson (Huskie to her friends) is the centre for most tourist activities. South of Huskisson, **Hyams Beach** is an attractive stretch of sand that is said to be the whitest in the world. It's a little like walking on warm snow.

Booderee National Park   NATURE RESERVE
Occupying Jervis Bay's southeastern spit, this sublime national park offers good swimming, surfing and diving on both bay and ocean beaches. Much of it is heath land, with some forest, including small pockets of rainforest.

Booderee means 'plenty of fish' and it's easy to see what a bountiful place this must have been for the indigenous people. For personalised tours with an Aboriginal focus, talk to Wreck Bay identity **Uncle Barry** (☑0402 441 168).

There's a good **visitor centre** (☑4443 0977; www.booderee.gov.au; ☺9am-4pm) at the park entrance with walking-trail maps and information on camping. Inside the park is **Booderee Botanic Gardens** (☺8.30am-4pm), which is a branch of the Australian National Botanic Gardens in Canberra and includes some enormous rhododendrons.

There are many walking trails around the park. Keep an eye out for the 206 species of bird, 27 species of land mammal and 23 species of reptile. Amphibian enthusiasts can thrill to the 15 species of frogs.

Entry to the park costs $10 per vehicle per 48 hours, or you can buy an unlimited annual pass for $40 (NPWS passes are not valid). There are idyllic camping grounds at **Green Patch** (camp sites $20-45, plus $10/5 per adult/child) and **Bristol Point** (camp sites $20-52, plus $10/5 per adult/child). For a more secluded experience try the basic camping at **Caves Beach** (camp sites $11). Book through the visitors centre or via the internet up to three weeks in advance at peak times. If you haven't booked, it's worth dropping by, as no-shows are common. There's a 24-hour self-registration system at the entrance to the park.

Surfing is good at Caves Beach, but the real drawcard is the **Pipeline** (aka Black Rock, Wreck Bay or Summercloud Bay), an A-grade reef break that produces 12ft tubes in optimal conditions.

The park is also home to the naval training base HMAS *Creswell*, which is off-limits to the public.

Jervis Bay National Park
NATURE RESERVE

(www.environment.nsw.gov.au) To reach Callala Bay, you have to pass through sections of Jervis Bay National Park, 4854 hectares of low scrub and woodland, which shelter the endangered eastern bristlebird. The bay itself is a marine park.

Lady Denman Maritime Museum
MUSEUM

(www.ladydenman.asn.au; cnr Woollamia Rd & Dent St; adult/child $8/4; ☺10am-4pm) Take a peek at the interesting historic collection as well as the 1912 Lady Denman ferry. Also, **Timbery's Aboriginal Arts & Crafts** sells work produced by one family of artisans. There's also a small **visitor centre**.

Dive Jervis Bay
DIVING

(☑4441 5255; www.divejervisbay.com; 64 Owen St) The marine park is popular with divers, offering the chance to get close to grey nurse sharks and fur seals. This place charges $100 for two boat dives, plus equipment hire ($150 with full gear).

Jervis Bay Kayaks
KAYAKING

(☑4441 7157; www.jervisbaykayaks.com; 13 Hawke St) These guys do rentals (two hours/day $39/69) or guided half-day paddling trips ($96). Adventurers will appreciate the self-guided camping expeditions.

Huskisson Sea Pool
SWIMMING

(admission free; ☺7am-6pm Mon-Fri, 10am-5pm Sat & Sun) Behind the pub, the pool has saltwater but is more like an Olympic pool than the usual ocean pools.

Hire Au Go-Go
CYCLING

(☑4441 5241, www.hireaugogo.com.au; 1 Tomerong St; 1hr/day $18/60) Pathways around the water's edge can be explored on an electric bike.

Dolphin Watch Cruises
BOAT TOURS

(☑4441 6311; www.dolphinwatch.com.au; 50 Owen St) Offers several dolphin- ($35/20) and whale-watching ($65/35) trips on its custom catamaran.

Husky Hire-A-Boat
BOAT HIRE

(☑4441 6200; Wollamia Boat Ramp; 1-4hr $40-100) Leases boats for use on lovely Currambene Creek.

🛏 Sleeping

There's plenty of accommodation in Huskisson and Vincentia but it still pays to book ahead. Prices skyrocket on weekends. Hyams Beach is a relaxing place to stay, but options are limited to mainly private rentals; try **Hyams Beach Real Estate** (☑4443 0242; www.hyamsbeachholidays.com.au; 76 Cyrus St, Hyams Beach).

TOP CHOICE **Paperbark Camp**
ECO TENTS $$$

(☑4441 6066; www.paperbarkcamp.com.au; 59 Woollamia Rd; tent $350) Camp in eco-friendly style in one of 12 luxurious solar-powered safari tents, with comfy beds, gorgeous en suites and wraparound decks. It's set in dense bush 3.5km from Huskisson; you can borrow kayaks to paddle up the creek to the bay.

Jervis Bay Guesthouse
B&B $$$

(☑4441 7658; www.jervisbayguesthouse.com.au; 1 Beach St; r incl breakfast $235-255; ❇@) This beautifully restored wooden guesthouse is opposite the beach, surrounded by tropical gardens. Most rooms have a beach view and wide verandahs. Fully cooked breakfast.

Huskisson Beach Tourist Resort
CAMPGROUND $

(☑4441 5142; www.holidayhaven.com.au; Beach St; sites per 2 people $38-76, cabins $95-190; ❇) Run by the Shoalhaven Council, this well-equipped camping ground has flash cabins and a great location right on the beach.

Jervis Bay Motel
MOTEL $$

(☑4441 5781; www.jervisbaymotel.com.au; 41 Owen St; r $99-139; ❇❇) An old-fashioned motel that's been tarted up; you'll find pleasant decor and quality furnishings, as well as lovely views from the (more expensive) upstairs rooms.

🍴 Eating

TOP CHOICE **Seagrass Brasserie**
MODERN AUSTRALIAN $$$

(☑4441 6124; www.seagrass.net.au; 13 Currambene St, Huskisson; starters $20, mains $34; ☺dinner) With its wooden louvre windows and white tablecloths, this delightful beachy-but-classy restaurant combines indoor and outdoor deck dining. The seafood dishes with Asian ingredients stand out on the top-notch menu as do the bloody mary oyster shots.

Gunyah Restaurant
MODERN AUSTRALIAN $$$

(☑4441 7299; www.paperbarkcamp.com.au; 59 Woollamia Rd; mains $29-32; ☺breakfast & dinner) Sit under the canopy and watch the light change through the trees from the balcony of this acclaimed restaurant at Paperbark Camp (p145). The focus is on local ingredients, although ordering 'roo has less appeal when there's a possibility of a live one walking past.

Supply

CAFE $

(1/54 Owen St, Huskisson; mains $5-15; ⊗breakfast & lunch) The best of Huskisson's cafes, Supply doubles as a deli. Grab a newspaper and settle into the smart surroundings for a satisfying breakfast.

🍷 Drinking & Entertainment

Husky Pub

PUB

(☑4441 5001; www.thehuskypub.com.au; Owen St) The funnest place in town has fabulous bay views from indoors and outside at the many picnic tables. There's live music most weekends.

Huskisson Pictures

CINEMA

(☑4441 6343; www.huskipics.com.au; cnr Sydney & Owen Sts; tickets $8.50-9.50) This lovely old picture house leans towards the art house.

ℹ Getting There & Around

Jervis Bay Territory (☑4423 5244) Runs a bus around Jervis Bay communities, and from Huskisson to Nowra three times every weekday and once on Saturday and Sunday.

Nowra Coaches (☑4423 5244; www. nowracoaches.com.au) Runs a bus (route 733) around Jervis Bay and to Nowra (70 minutes) on Tuesdays and Fridays.

Ulladulla

🕭 02 / POP 10,298

The harbour is the centre of life in this fishing-focused town that lets its hair down at Easter for the Blessing of the Fleet ceremony. While Ulladulla can be a bit, well, dull, it does have some beautiful beaches.

⊙ Sights & Activities

Have a stab at climbing **Pigeon House Mountain**.

Coastline

BEACH

North of the centre, gorgeous **Mollymook** stretches to over 2km of golden sand. **Narrawallee Beach**, the next one up, ends at a pretty kayak-friendly inlet. Both have beach breaks, although the serious surfers head for **Collers Beach** below the golf course, which offers left- and right-hand reef breaks and decent barrels. Immediately south of the harbour is a small beach with a large **ocean pool**.

Coomee Nulunga Cultural Trail

WALKING

This is a 700m walking trail established by the local Aboriginal Land Council. It begins near Lighthouse Oval (take Deering St east of the highway) and follows a path forged by the Rainbow Serpent (an important being in Aboriginal mysticism) from the headland through native bush to the beach.

Ulladulla's Oldest House

HISTORIC BUILDING

(☑4455 6996; www.somethingsbrewing.org.au; 275 Green St; admission free; ⊗9am-5pm Mon & Wed-Fri, 9am-4pm Sat, 10am-3pm Sun) In comparison to the trail, this house is a youngster, having been built in 1850. It's now a speciality teashop but gawkers are welcome.

🛏 Sleeping

For holiday home rentals try **First National** (☑4455 3999; www.firstnationalulladulla.com.au; The Plaza, 107 Princes Hwy).

Ulladulla Headland Tourist Park

CARAVAN PARK $

(☑4455 2457; www.holidayhaven.com.au; South St; camp sites $30-42, cabins $75-235; 🛜🏊) Not skimping on the 'park' part of the tourist park equation, this headland property has a lovely, leafy setting with ample ocean views. Facilities are good and well kept.

Mollymook Shores

HOTEL $$

(☑4455 5888; www.mollymookshores.com. au; cnr Golf Ave & Shepherd St; d/ste/apt from $110/140/170; 🛁) If a leafy low-rise hotel right on Mollymook Beachfront sounds like your cup of tea, here it is. The owners are friendly, the suites have spas and the restaurant is well regarded (dinner Tuesday to Saturday).

Southcoast Backpackers

HOSTEL $

(☑4454 0500; www.southcoastbackpackers. com.au; 63 Pacific Hwy; dm/d/tw $30/$65/$65) Known as the Traveller's Rest Accommodation, this guesthouse-style place attracts a mix of travellers, old and young alike. It's clean and comfy and guests have access to bikes, surfboards and bodyboards.

Bannisters

HOTEL $$$

(☑4455 3044; www.bannisters.com.au; 191 Mitchell Pde, Mollymook; r $250-395, ste $540-895; 🛁@🛜🏊) The ultimate extreme makeover: the bones of a 1970s concrete-block motel provide the basis of this hip, unassumingly luxurious place. Splash to the lip of the infinity pool for sublime views up the coast, or enjoy them from your balcony.

🍴 Eating

TOP CHOICE **Bannisters Restaurant**

(☑4455 3044; 191 Mitchell Pde; breakfast $15, dinner $28-48; ⊗breakfast & dinner daily, lunch Wed, Sat & Sun) Elegantly situated on Bannister's Point, 1km north of town; famed

UK chef Rick Stein's seafood fare matches the fine views. The catch of the day determines the menu.

Cupitt's Winery & Restaurant
MODERN AUSTRALIAN $$$
(☑4455 7888; www.cupittwines.com.au; 60 Washburton Rd; starters $16, mains $32-37; ⊙lunch Wed-Sun, dinner Fri & Sat) For a little piece of Provence make a pit stop at this glorious spot and enjoy some of the most respected cuisine this side of Sydney and wine tasting in the restored 1851 creamery. There's boutique accommodation in the vineyard.

Hayden's Pies
CAFE $
(☑4455 7798; 166 Princes Hwy; pies $3-5; ⊙6.30am-5.30pm Mon-Fri, 7am-4.30pm Sat & Sun) From the traditional to the gourmet (Moroccan lamb or salmon and prawn) and vegetarian, this little pie shop is filled with crusty goodness and delicious smells.

Jasper Peel Breads
BAKERY $
(☑4454 7969; shop 16, 10 Wason St) Sourdough bread is the speciality here but the pastries and pizzas are worth stopping for too.

❶ Information
Post office (Princes Hwy)
Visitor centre (☑4455 1269; www.shoalhaven holidays.com.au; Princes Hwy) Has internet access (per half hour $1).

❶ Getting There & Away
Premier (☑13 34 10; www.premierms.com.au) coaches stop on the run between Sydney ($35, five hours) and Melbourne ($82, 12 hours) via Batemans Bay ($16, 45 minutes) and Nowra ($19, one hour).

Ulladulla Bus Lines (☑4455 1674; www. ulludullabus.com.au) services the local area, including Milton, Narrawallee and Mollymook.

Murramarang National Park

This beautiful 12,386-hectare **coastal park** (per car $7) begins just above Batemans Bay and extends to within 20km of Ulladulla. If you haven't seen a kangaroo in the wild yet, here's your chance. At dawn and dusk large numbers of them wander out of the gum- and rainforests to the edges of lovely **Durras Lake**, while colourful parrots fill the trees.

Wasp Head, Depot, Pebbly and **Merry Beaches** are all popular with surfers and **Myrtle Beach** with nudists. We're not sure where nude surfers go. There are numerous walking trails snaking off from these beaches and a steep but enjoyable walk up **Durras Mountain** (283m).

At the north of the park, **Murramarang Aboriginal Area** encompasses the largest midden on the south coast, its remains suggesting 12,000 years of continual occupation. A self-guided walking track has been laid out with interpretive displays.

🛏 Sleeping
NPWS has idyllic **camp sites** (www.environ ment.nsw.gov.au/NationalParks/; powered sites per adult/child $14/7, unpowered sites per adult/child $10/5) with showers, flushing toilets and barbecues at **Depot Beach** (☑4478 6582), **Pebbly Beach** (☑4478 6023) and **Pretty Beach** (☑4457 2019). Sites are scarce during school holidays; book ahead. It also

---

PIGEON HOUSE MOUNTAIN

Climbing Pigeon House Mountain (720m), or as it is now known, **Didthul**, the name given to it by the Indigenous people, in the far south of Morton National Park might be the kind of upper-thigh workout that isn't called for on holiday, but the rewards make any huffing and puffing worthwhile.

The main access road leaves the highway about 8km south of Ulladulla, then it's a rough and rocky 26km drive to the picnic area at the start of the track. The return 5km walk takes three to four hours, but plan for longer; the summit is barbaric-yawp territory where the rest of the world rolls out from under your feet in all directions.

On a clear day, Gulaga (Mt Dromedary) sticks its head towards the south and to the northwest is Point Perpendicular. In between, a canopy of stunning national park vegetation spreads out like a blanket, occasionally making creases in the steep gorges carved by the Clyde River and flattening out over the elongated plateaus of Byangee Walls and the Castle.

People with a fear of heights should avoid the final section, and be sure to take water as there is none available.

rents tidy, self-contained forest and beach-side cabins (forest/beach $100/120) at Depot Beach and Pretty Beach, sleeping between four and six people.

EcoPoint Murramarang Resort RESORT $$$
(☑4478 6355; www.murramarangresort.com.au; Mill Beach, Banyandah St, South Durras; camp sites per 2 people $34-74, villas $120-350; ⌨) This is another favourite hangout of the marsupial mob. It is a big, modern place that has a row of Norfolk pines running between it and the beach. Posh extras such as camp sites with en suites and cabins with spa tubs are the norm.

Durras Lake North Holiday Park
CARAVAN PARK $$
(☑4478 6072; www.durrasnorthpark.com.au; 57 Durras Rd, Durras North; camp sites per 2 people $20-50, cabins $60-215) This friendly holiday park has shady camp sites and cute cabins. It's very popular with kangaroos.

❶ Getting There & Away
The Princes Hwy forms the park's western edge, but it's 10km from the beaches. Many of the roads are pretty rough, but those to Durras, Durras Lake, Depot Beach and Durras North are all sealed, as is Mt Agony Rd to Pebbly Beach (but not Pebbly Beach Rd).

EUROBODALLA COAST

Meaning 'Land of Many Waters', this southern section of coast continues to celebrate all things blue. A fair bit of green gets a look in too, with segments of the disjointed Eurobodalla National Park spreading much of its length.

It's an area of sweet little townships, lakes, bays and inlets backed by spotted-gum forests and home to much native wildlife. Part of the Yuin homelands, it includes their sacred mountain, Gulaga (see p155).

Batemans Bay
🎵02 / POP 10,845
Although Canberra is located 150km away, Batemans Bay is effectively its beach, which explains why it is one of the south coast's largest holiday centres. The suburban sprawl along the beaches located south of the town centre has rendered it charmless in comparison to the beautiful coast surrounding it.

◉ Sights & Activities
Beaches BEACH
The closest beach to the town centre is **Corrigans Beach**. South of this a series of small beaches dot the rocky shore. There are longer beaches along the coast north of the bridge, leading into **Murramarang National Park**. Surfers flock to **Surf Beach, Malua Bay**, small **McKenzies Beach** (just south of Malua Bay) and **Bengello Beach**, which has waves when everywhere else is flat. For the experienced, the best surfing is at **Pink Rocks** (near Broulee) when a north swell is running. Locals say the waves are sometimes 6m high. Broulee itself has a wide crescent of sand, but there's a strong rip at the northern end.

Old Courthouse Museum MUSEUM
(Museum Place; adult/child $5/1; ⊙noon-3pm Tue & Thu, 9am-noon most Sun) Just off Orient St, this has displays relating to local history. Just behind the museum is the small **Water Garden Town Park** and a boardwalk through wetlands.

Merinda Cruises BOAT TOURS
(☑4472 4052; www.southcoast.com.au/tickets/merinda; Boatshed, Clyde St; adult/child $27/14; ⊙tours 11.30am) Three-hour trips up the Clyde River to Nelligen.

Bluefin Adventures BOAT TOURS
(☑0427 220 238; www.bluefinadventures. com.au Main Wharf; adult/child $55/29) Sea tours where you might see dolphins and penguins at the Tollgate Islands Nature Reserve in the bay and, in season, whales.

Region X KAYAKING
(☑0400 184 034; www.regionxrivers.com.au) Three-hour sea kayak ($75), and morning or evening ($99) tours.

Bay & Beyond KAYAKING
(☑4478 7777; www.bayandbeyond.com.au) Has a similar gig.

✴ Festivals & Events
Great Southern Blues & Rockabilly Festival MUSIC
(www.bluesfestival.tv) Grease up your quiff on the last weekend of October.

⛏ Sleeping
Holiday apartments are profuse; letting agents include **Nola Debney Real Estate** (☑4472 1218; www.beachfrontholidays.com.au). Rates go up in summer.

Batemans Bay 🧭 0 ▭ 200 m / 0 ▭ 0.1 miles

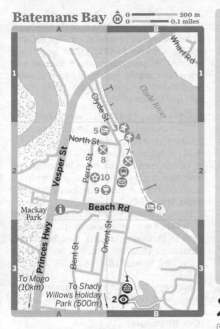

Alternatively, gather your mates and hire a houseboat. **Bay River Houseboats** (☑4472 5649; www.bayriverhouseboats.com.au; Wray St) and **Clyde River Houseboats** (☑4472 6369; www.clyderiverhouseboats.com.au) lease six-/10-berth boats from $840 for four nights (Monday to Friday).

Esplanade Motor Inn HOTEL $$
(☑4472 0200; www.esplanade.com.au; 23 Beach Rd; d $130-230; ❄) If it's river views you want, you can't beat this hotel at the end of the promenade in the centre of town. It's flashy in an '80s kind of way and the rooms are clean and comfortable.

Shady Willow Holiday Park HOTEL $
(☑4472 6111; www.shadywillows.com.au; cnr South St & Old Princes Hwy; dm/d $27/57; ❄❅☲) Set amid static caravans and shady palms located close to the centre of town, this YHA has a rather boho ambience, which can attract or detract from the place depending on your disposition. Doubles sleep in a caravan and there is a cabin that accommodates groups of four.

Clyde River Motor Inn HOTEL $$
(☑4472 6444; www.clydemotel.com.au; 3 Clyde St; s $90-136, d $100-157, f $136; ❄) An older motel on the river in the centre of town, this one's bathed in the sweet smell of jasmine. Rooms are clean and some have views.

✖ Eating

TOP CHOICE **On the Pier**
SEAFOOD, MODERN AUSTRALIAN **$$$**
(☑4472 6405; www.onthepier.com.au; 2 Old Punt Rd; mains $31; ⊙lunch & dinner) With a view of the Clyde River and the houseboats gliding under the bridge, this former heritage punt house, now daubed in blue, is the pick for a treat-yourself lunch. It's on the water on the north side of town (for a change). You'll spot it from the bridge. Good idea to book.

Monet's MEDITERRANEAN **$$**
(www.monetscafe.com.au; 2/5 Orient St; mains $20; ⊙breakfast & lunch daily, tapas Thu-Sat) One of the more homely local establishments that manages to combine inventive food and a great atmosphere. Oh and there's an upstairs bar with water views too. Organic produce and free-range eggs are the norm, as are vegetarian options.

North St Café & Bar
(5 North St; mains $8-20; ⊙breakfast & lunch) A beacon of modernity – from its cool counter to its organic and gluten-free treats.

🍷 Drinking & Entertainment

Bayview Hotel PUB
(20 Orient St; ⊙10am-midnight) The only real pub in town offers a lively roster of bands, DJs and trivia nights.

Bay City Cinemas CINEMA
(☑4472 6009; www.baycitycinemas.com.au; Perry St; tickets $10.50-11.50) Blockbusters for rainy days.

❶ Information

Post office (7 Orient St)

Visitor centre (☑4472 6900; cnr Beach Rd & Princes Hwy) Has internet access ($2 per 15 minutes).

❶ Getting There & Away

The scenic Kings Hwy climbs the escarpment and heads to Canberra from just north of Batemans Bay. **Murrays** (☑13 22 51; www.murrays.com.au) services this route with daily runs to Canberra ($22, 2½ hours), Moruya ($16, one hour) and Narooma ($24, two hours).

Premier (☑13 34 10; www.premierms.com.au) coaches stop on the run between Sydney ($45, six hours) and Melbourne ($73, 11 hours) via Ulladulla ($16, 45 minutes) and Moruya ($11, 30 minutes).

Mogo

☑02 / POP 257

Mogo is a historic strip of wooden shops and houses almost entirely devoted to Devonshire teas, crafts and antiques.

Just off the highway is **Gold Rush Colony** (☑4474 2123; www.goldrushcolony.com.au; 26 James St; adult/child $15/8; ☺10am-5pm), a rambling recreation of a pioneer village, complete with free gold-panning. You can stay in **miners' cabins** (dm/s/d/f $30/105/120/110, ste s/d $60/75; ❈) inside the colony, giving you a good opportunity to play pioneer after dark.

Mogo Zoo (www.mogozoo.com.au; 222 Tomakin Rd; adult/child $23/12), 2km east off the highway, is a small but interesting zoo where you can get terrifyingly close to the big cats. The stars of the show are the playful and rare white lions.

Blue Fox Cafe (15 Sydney St; meals $9-15; ☺brunch & lunch) is also a sourdough bakery and organic grocery, so the focus is on delicious sandwiches stuffed full with salad and deli ingredients.

Moruya

☑02 / POP 2432

Its name means black swan but this town is no ugly ducking, with a pleasant collection of Victorian buildings gathered around a broad river. There's a popular weekly **market** (☺9am-noon Sat) on the south side of Moruya Bridge. The best place to stay is **Post & Telegraph B&B** (☑4474 5745; www.southcoast.com.au/postandtel; cnr Page & Campbell Sts; s/d from $100/135), the beautifully restored old post office, which features polished floorboards, iron beds and verandahs overlooking gardens. Of the three rooms only one has an en suite.

TOP CHOICE River (☑44745505; www.theriver moruya.com.au; 16b Church St; mains $26-34; ☺lunch Wed-Sun, dinner Wed-Sat; ❈) is right on the...you guessed it. The food is proof that rural doesn't mean bumpkin: fresh local ingredients mix liberally with international flavours on the ever-changing menu. It's popular, so book.

Moruya Airport (☑4474 2095; George Bass Dr) is 7km from town, near North Head. **Rex** (☑13 17 13; www.rex.com.au) flies here from Merimbula ($75, 30 minutes, two to three daily) and Sydney (from $125, 50 minutes, daily).

Murrays (☑13 22 51; www.murrays.com.au) buses head to Canberra ($26, 3½ hours), Sydney ($49, nine hours) and Melbourne ($69, 10½ hours).

Moruya to Narooma

From Moruya the highway stays on its inland path, leaving a long stretch of little-visited coast to sections of **Eurobodalla National Park**. Nearly any left-hand turn along here can be rewarding, especially if you're a surfer.

At **Moruya Heads**, there's a good surf beach and views from Toragy Point. From here it's a 7km drive west along the river to Moruya. Or south, a dirt road heads through beautiful forest to **Congo**, a pretty and peaceful spot, where there's a **camp site** (☑4476 0800; per adult/child $10/5) between the estuary and the surf beach. Congo is also the end of the **Bingi Dreaming Track**, a 14km walk following a spiritually significant Aboriginal route (pick up a brochure from NPWS in Narooma). Keep an eye out for kangaroos, wallabies, bandicoots and goannas. It starts further south at the incredible rock formations at **Bingi Point**.

North of Narooma the highway skirts a series of saltwater lakes (inlets, lagoons...call them what you will). The council operates **Dalmeny camp site** (☑44 768 596; powered/unpowered sites $23/20), close to **Brou Beach**. There's a free, basic **camp site** within the park at **Brou Lake**. **Potato Point** has a decent surf break.

Narooma

☏ 02 / POP 3100

Sitting at the mouth of a large, tree-lined inlet and flanked by surf beaches, Narooma is exceedingly pretty. While the commercial centre on the hill is nothing special, the ocean views more than compensate. The locals are a friendly bunch, but with all that pristine water to relax them, why wouldn't they be?

◉ Sights & Activities

TOP CHOICE Montague Island (Baranguba)

NATURE RESERVE

Nine kilometres offshore from Narooma, this small, pest-free island is a spectacular nature reserve, home to many seabirds (shearwaters, sea eagles and peregrine falcons) and hundreds of fur seals. Little penguins nest here and although some remain year-round, there are more than 10,000 at their peak between September and February.

Baranguba, its Aboriginal name, translates as Big Brother (see p155), predating both the TV franchise and Orwell by around 8000 years. Sacred sites remain on the island, which only the local Yuin people may access.

The only way to see the island is via extremely interesting three-hour **guided tours** (☏4476 2881; www.montagueisland.com. au; adult/child/family $130/99/430) conducted by NPWS rangers, which include climbing up the granite **lighthouse** (1881). Trips are dependent on numbers and weather conditions, so book ahead through the visitor centre. The boat voyage takes about 30 minutes and circumnavigates the island if the water's not too choppy. Take the afternoon tour for a better chance of seeing penguins.

NPWS offers the unforgettable opportunity to stay in the solar-powered **lighthouse keepers' cottages** (www.conservationvolun teers.com.au/volunteer/montague.htm; 2 nights s/d per person $690/810, 3 nights per room $1318-2058) on the proviso that you take part in conservation work while you're there. That might entail counting and weighing penguins, weeding or planting trees. The cottages are beautifully renovated and very comfortable. Meals are included, but you'll be expected to help with the preparation. Rates slightly cheaper out of whale season. Book well ahead.

The clear waters around the island are good for **diving**, especially from February to June. **Island Charters Narooma** (☏4476 1047; www.islandchartersnarooma.com) offers diving (double dive $85), snorkelling ($75), whale-watching (adult/child $80/55) and other tours. Attractions in the area include grey nurse sharks, seals and the wreck of the SS *Lady Darling*.

Beaches

BEACH

The water surrounding Narooma is so exceptionally clear that it's a constant struggle to resist leaping in. The best place for a sheltered swim is over the bridge in the **netted swimming area** at the south end of Bar Beach, below the breakwall. There's a surf club at **Narooma Beach**, but the breaks are better at **Bar Beach** when a southeasterly blows.

Bar Rock Lookout

LANDMARK

If you fancy a stroll, there's a nice walk from Riverside Dr along the inlet to the ocean, and here you'll find excellent views. Just below the lookout is **Australia Rock**, a boulder with a bloody great hole in it that vaguely resembles the country (minus Tasmania, of course).

Wagonga Princess

BOAT TOURS

(☏4476 2665; www.wagongainletcruises.com; Rivorcido Dr; tours 1pm Sun, Wed & Fri Feb Dec, daily Jan; adult/child/family $33/22/100), A century old, this electric ferry takes a three-hour cruise up the inlet, departing from Taylor's Boatshed.

Kayaking Narooma

KAYAKING

(☏0407 705 371; www.kayakingnarooma.com.au) If you enjoy setting your own pace, hire single and double kayaks (half/one hour $12/20).

✵ Festivals & Events

Oyster Festival

FOOD

(www.narooma.org.au) Narooma has a shucking good time during this festival in mid-May.

🛏 Sleeping

Narooma Real Estate (☏4476 3887; www. naroomaholidays.com.au; 78 Princes Hwy) deals in the myriad private holiday accommodation options.

Whale Motor Inn

HOTEL $$

(☏4476 2411; www.whalemotorinn.com; 104 Wagonga St; r $120-205; ❋❄) Spot whales from your balcony (binoculars to hand) at this upmarket motel with terrific views and nicely renovated rooms (though some of the bathrooms are a little last century). You can even make like a whale in the spa suites.

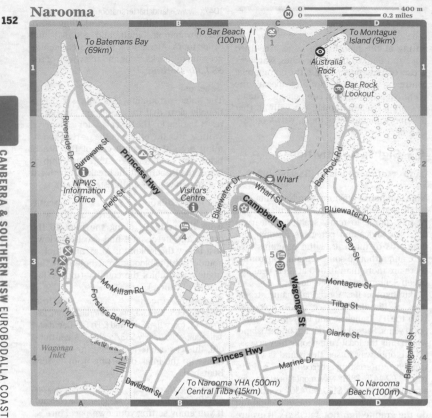

0 — 400 m
0 — 0.2 miles

To Bar Beach (100m)

To Montague Island (9km)

To Batemans Bay (69km)

Australia Rock

Bar Rock Lookout

Riverside Dr

Burrawang St

Princess Hwy

NPWS Information Office

Field St

Visitors Centre

Bluewater Dr

Wharf

Wharf St

Campbell St

Bluewater Dr

Bay St

Wagonga St

Montague St

Tilba St

Clarke St

McMillan Rd

Forsters Bay Rd

Wagonga Inlet

Ballingalla St

Princes Hwy

Marine Dr

Davidson St

To Narooma YHA (500m)
Central Tilba (15km)

To Narooma Beach (100m)

Narooma YHA   HOSTEL $
(☑4476 4440; www.yha.com.au; 243 Princes Hwy; dm/tw $26/69, d $68-72; @) Although it was obviously once an old-style motel, this superfriendly establishment makes a great hostel. Each room has a bathroom for starters. Free bikes and bodyboards are the icing on the stripper-sized cake.

Easts Narooma Shores Holiday Park
                                    CARAVAN PARK $$
(☑4476 2046; www.easts.com.au; Princes Hwy; sites $28-60, cabin $90-195; ❄@🛜🏊) More than 260 camp sites and 43 cabins occupy this lovely spot by the inlet. The friendly managers look after the place well and there's a big pool under the palm trees.

✕ Eating

The most evocative eating options are on the marinas of Riverside Dr. They all have heart-melting views over the still, clear waters of the inlet – particularly romantic at sunset.

TOP CHOICE **Whale Restaurant**
                          MODERN AUSTRALIAN $$$
(☑4476 2411; www.whalemotorinn.com; 104 Wagonga St; mains $34) It might seem unlikely, but this hotel restaurant with its simple decor punches above its weight in the gourmet department. Treat yourself to eye fillet steak or a rack of lamb – beautifully presented – while enjoying views of the coast. BYO wine.

Quarterdeck Marina   SEAFOOD $
(13 Riverside Dr; mains $22; ⊘breakfast & lunch Thu-Mon) The only place on the inlet where the decor is even more captivating than the views. Enjoy the excellent breakfasts and seafood lunches under the gaze of dozens of tikis, Chairman Maos and autographed photos of 1950s TV stars.

Taylor's Seafood Café   SEAFOOD $
(12B Riverside Dr; meals $7-16; ⊘lunch & dinner Tue-Sun) The takeaways are a little cheaper, but why miss out on the chance to consume the grilled fish and nongreasy chunky chips while gazing at paradise?

Narooma

Activities, Courses & Tours
1 Netted Swimming Area......................C1
2 Wagonga Princess............................A3

🛏️ 🏊 Sleeping
3 East's Narooma Shores Holiday
  Park...B2
4 Narooma Real Estate.......................B3
5 Whale Motor Inn..............................C3

✖️ Eating
6 Quarterdeck Marina..........................A3
7 Taylor's Seafood Café.......................A3
  Whale Restaurant........................(see 5)

☕ Entertainment
8 Narooma Cinema..............................C2

☆ Entertainment

Narooma Cinema   CINEMA
(📞4476 2352; 94 Campbell St; tickets adult/child
$12/11) A good rainy-day option, this picture palace began showing flicks in 1926 and hasn't changed much since.

ℹ️ Information

Library (Field St; ⊙10am 5pm Mon Fri, 9.30am-2pm Sat) Free internet access.
NPWS office (📞4476 2888; Burrawang St)
Post office (106 Wagonga St)
Visitor centre (📞4476 2881; www.eurobod alla.com.au; Princes Hwy) Has a small museum.

ℹ️ Getting There & Away

Premier (📞13 34 10; www.premierms.com. au) has buses to Melbourne ($67, 10 hours) via Eden ($27, 2½ hours), and Sydney ($58, seven hours) via Wollongong ($56, five hours). Buses stop outside Lynch's Hotel. **Murrays** (📞13 22 51; www.murrays.com.au) runs to Moruya ($17, one hour), Batemans Bay ($22, two hours) and Canberra ($33, 4½ hours).

Tilba Tilba & Central Tilba

📞02 / POP 500
The coastal road from Bermagui rejoins the Princes Hwy just before the loop road leading to these outrageously cute National Trust villages in the shadow of Gulaga.

Tilba Tilba is half the size of its singularly named neighbour, 2km down the road. Central Tilba sits in a nook of a valley that has remained virtually unchanged since the 19th century when it was a gold-mining

boomtown – except now the main street is jammed with visitors' cars on weekends. Strolling along Bate St, you'll find a string of shops selling the sort of things you'd expect to find in National Trust villages: fudge, boiled lollies, cheese, speciality teas, ice cream, crafts and cafes. Behind the pub, there's a short walk up to a water tower where boulders provide terrific views of Gulaga.

There's information, including a handy town guide, at the **Bates Emporium** (Bates St; ⊙8am-5pm), which also serves as the petrol station, internet cafe and post office.

⊙ Sights & Activities

Foxglove Spires   GARDEN
(www.foxglovespires.com.au; Corkhill Dr; admission $7.50; ⊙10am-4pm) Gardening freaks will love this magical 3½-acre private garden with lots of hidden avenues and bowers.

🛏️ Sleeping & Eating

Dromedary Hotel   HOTEL $
(📞4473 7223; 5 Bate St, Central Tilba; d $60) There's clean, basic accommodation upstairs in this nice old pub. The walls downstairs are lined with old photos and pictures of prize pumpkins. The bistro is a rare after-dark eating option.

Green Gables   B&B $$
(📞4473 7435; www.greengables.com.au; 269 Corkhill Dr, Tilba Tilba; r $150; 📶) Try to resist the word 'delightful' when describing this gay-friendly B&B. The 1879 cottage offers three attractive rooms with either en suites or private bathrooms and views over the fields.

Two Story B&B   B&B $$
(📞4473 7290; www.tilbatwostory.com; Bate St, Central Tilba; d $140) This atmospheric 1894 former postmaster's residence has plenty of charm and a cosy log fire in winter. Some rooms have en suites. Cooked breakfast included.

Rose & Sparrow Café   CAFE $
(3 Bate St; mains $5-15; ⊙breakfast & lunch) Serves generous portions of healthy food, including delicious lentil burgers with homemade hot mango chutney.

🎉 Festivals & Events

Tilba Easter Festival   ARTS FESTIVAL
(www.tilba.com.au) The streets are all blocked off for this festival, which has lots of music, entertainment and several thousand visitors.

WORTH A TRIP

MAGICAL MYSTERY BAY TOUR

South of Narooma, just before the turn-off to the Tilbas take the road to gorgeously un-developed **Mystery Bay** and the first pocket of **Eurobodalla National Park**. At the south end of the main surf beach, a rock formation forms an idyllic **natural swimming pool**. There's a council-run **camp site** (☑0428-622 357; www.mysterybaycampground.com; sites off-peak/peak $15/25) under the trees. It's so close to the beach you could boil a billy with your tootsies in the sand – well, almost.

Cobargo Folk Festival　　　　　　MUSIC
(www.cobargofolkfestival.com) The other big event is this acclaimed festival, held in historic Cobargo, 20km towards Bega.

❶ Getting There & Away

Premier (☑13 34 10; www.premierms.com. au) buses serve the Tilbas daily on the route between Sydney ($59, eight hours) via Narooma ($9, 25 minutes), and Eden ($25, two hours) and Merimbula ($23, 90 minutes).

SAPPHIRE COAST

Not to be outdone by Queensland's Gold Coast, the southernmost part of NSW considers itself precious too. The moniker is apt, with the coast's pristine water revelling in every shade of blue. You won't see a lot of it from the Princes Hwy, but you can feel confident that taking just about any road east will yield a bit of mostly unblemished coast set in rugged surrounds. This is the start of the traditional lands of the Yuin people.

Bermagui

☑02 / POP 1300
South of the beautiful bird-filled Wallaga Lake and off the Princes Hwy, Bermagui is a pretty fishing port with a main street that hums to the sound of small-town contentment. The vibe is probably due to the eclectic mix of fisherfolk, surfers, alternative lifestylers and Indigenous Australians who call it home. In typical Aussie parlance it's invariably referred to as Bermie.

The purpose-built **information centre** (☑6493 3054; www.bermagui.net; Bunga St; ◷10am-4pm) with its museum and discovery centre was the first sign that tourists had cottoned on to the place. Now there's a new whiz-bang **Fishermen's Wharf** (Lamont St), designed by renowned architect and resident Philip Cox, with all the tempters city visitors expect.

◎ Sights & Activities

There are several walks around Bermagui including a 6km trail north along the coast to **Camel Rock** and a further 2km to **Wallaga Lake**. The route follows **Haywards Beach**, a good surfing spot.

There's also good surfing at Camel Rock and Cuttagee beaches, or you could toss a mullet from the shops and hit **Shelly Beach**, a child-friendly swimming spot. A kilometre's wander around the point will bring you to the **Blue Pool**, a dramatic ocean pool built into the base of the cliffs.

⛌ Sleeping

For lettings, see **Julie Rutherford Real Estate** (☑6493 3444; www.julierutherford.com. au; Fisherman's Wharf).

TOP CHOICE **Bermagui Beach Hotel**
　　　　　　　　　　　BOUTIQUE HOTEL **$$**
(☑6493 4206; www.bermaguibeachhotel.com.au; 10 Lamont St; r $110-135; ❄) At the beach end of the main street, this gorgeous old pub built in 1895 has nine suites, four of them with balcony views towards the beach and Mt Gulaga. Stay here to tap into the local scene. The suites have spas.

Bermagui Motor Inn　　　　　　HOTEL **$**
(☑6493 4311; www.acr.net.au/~bmi/; 38 Lamont St; s/d $89/99; ❄) Right in town, this motel may be a classic but it's got new carpets, comfy beds and very friendly owners.

Zane Grey Tourist Park
　　　　　　CAMPGROUND, CARAVAN PARK **$**
(☑6493 4382; www.zanegreytouristpark.com. au; Lamont St; sites $27, cabins $47-95) From its prime position on Dickson's Point, you could throw a frisbee from here into Horseshoe Bay.

✗ Eating

TOP CHOICE **Bluewave Seafoods**　FISH & CHIPS **$**
(Fishermen's Wharf; ◷lunch & dinner) Overlooking the marina, this smart takeaway joint is the reincarnation of the original fishermen's co-op. It has deck seats with a view

to the trawlers and the lightly battered fish-and-chip box is the South Coast's best. Watch the seagulls!

Mister Jones
ESPRESSO BAR $

(1/4 Bunga St; www.misterjones.com.au; ☉from 7am Tue-Sat) This anonymous little art studio-cum-cafe would go unnoticed if it weren't for the caffeine fiends sitting outside. Mister Jones (or the man purporting to be him) tops his cappuccinos with big chunks of chocolate. The art's cool too.

il Passaggio
ITALIAN $$

(Fishermen's Wharf; mains $29; ☉lunch Fri-Sun & dinner Tue-Sun) This suitably hip place with green felt walls and red leather seating dishes up a short but authentic Italian menu. There are specials like veal saltimbocca alla Romana, but simpler dishes such as linguini with prawns, chilli, rocket and lemon prevail.

❶ Getting There & Away

Premier (☎13 34 10; www.premierms.com.au) stops here once a day on the run between Sydney ($60, 10 hours) via Narooma ($13, 40 minutes), and Eden ($24, 1¾ hours) via Merimbula ($20, 45 minutes)

Bermagui to Merimbula

Mimosa Rocks (5802 hectares) is a wonderful coastal park with dense and varied bush, sea caves, lagoons and 20km of beautiful coastline. Check out car-based **camp sites** (☎4476 2888; per adult/child $10/5) at Gillards Beach, Picnic Point and Aragunnu Beach. Walk-in camping at Middle Beach is especially lovely, passing under a canopy of tall eucalypts and palms to the deserted surf beach.

Sapphire Coast Ecotours (☎6494 0283; www.sapphirecoastecotours.com.au; tours adult $30-60, child $15-30) runs highly regarded walks exploring the park's varied ecosystems and may include an Aboriginal guide.

South of the main beach at **Cuttagee**, Kullaroo St leads to secluded, bush-lined **Armands Bay**, the only clothing-optional beach on the Sapphire Coast.

Tathra (pop 1622) is a sweet little beach town with the Bega River forming a dreamy, undeveloped lagoon at its north end. Dating from 1862, **Tathra Wharf** is the last remaining coastal steamship wharf in the state and a popular place for fishing. It houses a small **Maritime Museum** (adult/child $2/1; ☉10am-4pm). **Tathra Beach Pickle Factory** (35 Andy Poole Dr; snacks $3-8; ☉breakfast & lunch) is a very worthy grab-and-run deli-cafe, with disposable cups and gourmet-food mags.

The 2654ha **Bournda National Park** (per car $7) has beautiful empty surf beaches, rugged headlands and walking trails through heath, eucalyptus forests and tea tree.

TOP CHOICE Hobart Beach (☎6495 5000; camp sites per adult/child $10/5), in the park on the southern shore of peaceful **Wallagoot Lake**, is a great bush-cum-break camp spot.

Merimbula

☎02 / POP 3850

Spread around the top end of a gorgeous long golden beach and an appealing inlet (which locals insist on calling a lake), Merimbula is in thrall to holidaymakers and retirees. Not big enough to be interesting and yet weighed down with development, it's hard to muster much enthusiasm for the town centre, except that the inlet is rather fabulous. As the numerous holiday

---

THE MOTHER'S STORY

In Yuin tradition, Gulaga (Mt Dromedary, 806m) is the mother and Barunguba (Montague Island) and Najanuga (Little Dromedary) are her two sons. The sons wanted to head out exploring, but Gulaga thought that Najanuga was too young and kept him at her feet. Barunguba went out alone and was eventually cut off by the water.

These places are highly sacred and in 2006 the mountain was designated the first Area of Aboriginal Significance in Australia. The mountain now forms **Gulaga National Park** (4768 hectares) and is jointly managed by the Indigenous community and NPWS. Its walking tracks are open to all people who treat the mountain with respect. Beginning at Pam's Store in Tilba Tilba you can follow an old **pack-horse trail**. The 11km return walk takes about five hours, but don't miss the loop walk at the summit. There's often rain and mist on the mountain, so come prepared. She's a woman's mountain and local lore has it that it's scornful men that get lost or return with grazes and sprained ankles.

Merimbula

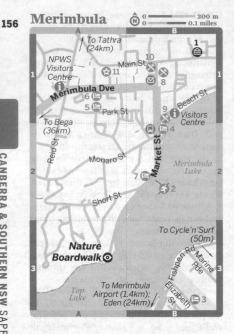

Merimbula

apartments would suggest, this is one of the few places on the far south coast that really heaves during summer school holidays.

◎ Sights

Nature Boardwalk NATURE RESERVE
Make sure you don't miss this gorgeous addition to the town's natural highs. It follows the estuary 1.75km southwest of the causeway around mangroves, oyster farms and melaleucas. A plethora of birds, mammals and crustaceans are visible as you make your way along the boardwalk.

Merimbula Aquarium AQUARIUM
(www.merimbulawharf.com.au; Lake St; adult/child $11.50/6.50; ☉10am-4pm) It might be small but this friendly aquarium displays the sorts of fish you'll find in the bay. Mum and Dad might nod off but the kids will love it. It's at the dead end of Lake St.

Old School Museum MUSEUM
(Main St; adult/child $3/free; ☉2-4.30pm Tue, Thu & Sun) It isn't dedicated to ageing rappers, rather it's one of those volunteer-run museums featuring knick-knackery and displays on local history.

⚡ Activities

Grab your bathers; most activities around Merimbula are water-based.

True Blue DOLPHIN WATCHING
(www.merimbulamarina.com; Merimbula Marina; adult/child $30/20) Bargain-priced dolphin-watching cruises in the bay, along with whale-watching from mid-September to November.

Coastlife Adventures SURFING, KAYAKING
(☑6494 1122; www.coastlife.com.au) Morning surf ($55) and stand-up paddle ($30) lessons as well as marine kayak tours ($55).

Top Lake Boat Hire BOAT HIRE
(☑64951987; Lakewood Dr; ☉8am-1pm Mon & Tue, to 4pm Wed-Sun) Near the end of the boardwalk, rents out motor boats, pedal boats, kayaks, canoes and rowing boats.

Cycle'n'Surf CYCLING, SURFING
(1b Marine Pde) South of the lake, hires out bikes (per hour $7), bodyboards (half day $10) and surfboards (per hour $10) as well as carrying out bike repairs.

DIVING

With several wrecks in the area including the large *Empire Gladstone*, which sank in 1950, diving is popular.

Merimbula Divers Lodge TOURS
(www.merimbuladiverslodge.com.au; 15 Park St) Offers basic instruction and one/two shallow dives from $77/99, plus $55 for

equipment. It also does snorkelling trips ($44).

🛏 Sleeping

The isthmus between the beach and the lake is completely overrun with motels and holiday apartments. Self-contained apartments are usually let on a weekly basis, particularly in summer when rates take a hike. See **Fisk & Nagle** (☑6495 2000; www.getawaymerimbula.com.au; The Promenade, Market St).

Merimbula Lakeview Hotel   HOTEL $$
(☑6495 1202; www.merimbulalakeviewhotel.com.au; Market St; r from $79) This waterfront establishment has stylish rooms with all the motel trimmings. Come summertime, they're close to the beer garden...which may be good or bad. The Lakeview bistro (mains $12 to $30) has upmarket pub food and an open fire in winter.

Coast Resort   APARTMENTS $$$
(☑6495 4930; www.coastresort.com.au; 1 Elizabeth St; 1-/2-/3-bedroom apt from $160/$180/$240; ❄❄) You could describe the decor of this huge upmarket apartment-style complex as ultramodern, although stark might be more apt. Still, comfort's not a problem and the two pools, tennis court and proximity to the beach are all very appealing.

Wandarrah YHA Lodge   HOSTEL $
(☑6495 3503; www.yha.com.au; 8 Marine Pde; dm/s/d from $30/55/73) This clean place, with a good kitchen and hanging-out areas, is near the surf beach and the bus stop. Pick-ups by arrangement or let the staff know if you're arriving late.

Merimbula Beach Holiday Park
          CAMPGROUND, CARAVAN PARK $$
(☑6495 3381; www.merimbulabeachholidaypark.com.au; 2 Short Point Rd; camp sites $31-67, cabins $75-185; ❄❄) Away from the town centre, but it's close to the surf action and vistas of Short Point Beach. Choose a leafy camping spot or kid-friendly area by the pool.

Merimbula Gardens Motel   MOTEL $
(☑6495 5900; 36 Merimbula Dr; r from $75; ❄@❄) Though there are no gardens to speak of, this old-school motel is one of the cheaper options in the heart of town. Rooms are basic but clean and comfortable.

Merimbula Divers Lodge   HOSTEL $
(☑6495 3611; www.merimbuladiverslodge.com.au; 15 Park St; dm $29) Linen (including pillows) costs an extra $10, but this central place offers clean, bunk-style accommodation split into three separate self-contained apartments, each sleeping eight.

🍴 Eating & Drinking

TOP CHOICE **Zanzibar**
          SEAFOOD, MODERN AUSTRALIAN $$$
(☑6495 4038; cnr Main & Market Sts; mains $25-33; ☺dinner Tue-Sat) Don't leave town without treating yourself at this culinary gem, which prides itself on locally caught seafood and handpicked South Coast produce. The seafood hotpot for two filled with king prawns, Eden black mussels and Balmain bugs is a menu stalwart.

Cantina   TAPAS, MEDITERRANEAN $
(56 Market St; tapas $10-16, mains $18-30; ☺lunch & dinner) This atmospheric little hidey-hole in the centre of town dishes up tasty plates of salt-and-pepper calamari, fried chorizo and lamb souvlaki. Not hungry? The bar has a good vibe also.

Waterfront Café   CAFE $
(Beach St; breakfast $5-17, lunch $18-23; ☺8am-5pm) Try this place for an excellent coffee or a snack while looking out over the, ahem, lake.

☆ Entertainment

Picture Show Man   CINEMA
(www.pictureshowman.com.au; 80 Main St; tickets $9-11) Screens a busy program of art-house and blockbuster movies.

WORTH A TRIP

COWS OR COAST?

From Tilba Tilba and Bermagui you've got the option of continuing on the Princes Hwy through Bega or heading to Merimbula taking **Sapphire Coast Drive**. While the highway leads through some pretty farmland, the latter option alternates between spectacular beaches and national parks until it rejoins the highway near Pambula. It's 5km shorter and there are a couple of galleries on the way.

ℹ️ Information

NPWS visitor centre (☎6495 5000; cnr Merimbula & Sapphire Coast Drs)

Post office (5 Merimbula Dr)

Visitor centre (☎6495 1129; www.sapphire coast.com.au; 2 Beach St)

ℹ️ Getting There & Around

Air

Merimbula Airport (MIM; ☎6495 4211; www. merimbulaairport.com.au; Arthur Kaine Dr) is 1km out of town on the road to Pambula. There are flights to Melbourne (from $143, 90 minutes, one to two daily), Moruya ($75, 30 minutes, two to three daily) and Sydney (from $143, 1¾ hours, three daily) with **Rex** (☎13 17 13; www. rex.com.au).

Bus

Buses stop outside the Commonwealth Bank on Market St. **Premier** (☎13 34 10; www.pre miermis.com.au) has two daily buses to Sydney ($69, 8½ hours) via Narooma ($25, two hours) and one to Melbourne ($58, 8¼ hours). **CountryLink** (☎13 22 32; www.coun trylink.com.au) runs a daily bus to Canberra ($33, four hours).

Deanes Buslines (☎6495 6452; www. deanesbuslines.com.au) provides the local bus service (Monday to Saturday only) that includes Bega ($10.60, one hour, six daily) and Eden ($8.80, 40 minutes, five daily). **Tathra Bus Service** (☎6492 1991; www.tathrabus.com.au) has two buses to/from Tathra ($8.40, 25 minutes) on Tuesdays and Thursdays.

Eden

☎02 / POP 3006

The first town north of the Victorian border, Eden's a little sleepy place where the only bustle you're likely to find is down at the wharf when the fishing boats come in. Pretty beaches run either side of the town's knobbly peninsula.

For possibly thousands of years this bay has been the site of extraordinary interactions that have taken place between humans and whales. Migrating humpback whales and southern right whales pass so close to the coast that whale-watching experts consider this to be one of the best places in Australia for people to observe these magnificent creatures. Often they can be seen feeding or resting in Twofold Bay during their southern migration back to Antarctic waters.

◉ Sights & Activities

Cat-Balou Cruises   WHALE-WATCHING

(☎0427 260 489; www.catbalou.com.au; Main Wharf, 253 Imlay St) This crew operates 3½-hour whale-spotting voyages (adult/child $70/60) in October and November. At other times of the year, dolphins and seals can usually be seen during the two-hour bay cruise (adult/child $32.50/20).

Sapphire Coast Marine Discovery Centre   AQUARIUM

(www.sapphirecoastdiscovery.com.au; Main Wharf; ☺1-4pm Wed-Sun) See the sea through a rocky reef aquarium at the newish addition to town and sign up for a rocky shore ramble or beachcombing walk (adult/child $5/2).

Killer Whale Museum   MUSEUM

(www.killerwhalemuseum.com.au; 94 Imlay St; adult/child $7.50/2; ☺9.15am-3.45pm Mon-Sat, 11.15am-3.45pm Sun) Established in 1931, the museum's main purpose is to preserve the skeleton of Old Tom, a killer whale and local legend.

Whale Lookout   LANDMARK

Among the many options to spot Moby and his mates is at the base of Bass St. When whales are spotted the Killer Whale Museum sounds a siren.

🎊 Festivals & Events

Eden comes alive in late October for the **Whale Festival**, with the typical carnival, street parade and stalls plus some innovative local events such as the Slimy Mackerel Throw.

🛏️ Sleeping

As you enter town from either direction, rows of run-of-the-mill motels and motor parks line the road to greet you.

Crown & Anchor Inn   B&B $$$

(☎6496 1017; www.crownandanchoreden.com.au; 239 Imlay St; r from $180) Awesomely atmospheric, this historic house (1845) has been beautifully restored and furnished with the likes of four-poster beds and claw-foot baths. There's a lovely view over Twofold Bay from the back patio.

Eden Tourist Park   CARAVAN PARK $

(☎6496 1139; www.edentouristpark.com.au; Aslings Beach Rd; camp sites per two people $26, cabins $63-171) Serenely situated on the spit separating Aslings Beach from Lake Curalo, this large well-kept park echoes with birdsong from its sheltering trees.

Great Southern Hotel

HOSTEL $

(☑6496 1515; www.greatsoutherninn.com.au; 121 Imlay St; dm/s/d/f $20/30/60/80) This friendly place has good-value shared pub rooms and nicely renovated backpacker accommodation. The pub grub downstairs is hearty and the rear deck is a winner.

Twofold Bay Motor Inn

HOTEL $$

(☑6496 3111; www.twofoldbaymotorinn.com.au; 164-166 Imlay St; r from $110; ❄☎☐) Substantial rooms, some with water views, are the norm at this centrally located motel. There's also a tiny indoor pool.

✖ Eating

The following eateries are clumped together on the Main Wharf (253 Imlay St) at the bottom of town.

Taste of Eden

SEAFOOD $$

(☑6496 1304; mains $10-28; ⊙breakfast & lunch) With decor that has been pulled straight out of Davy Jones' locker, this brightly painted cafe serves delicious local seafood (among other dishes) without any airs or graces. The menu is so fresh it has to be listed on a whiteboard.

Wharfside Café

MODERN AUSTRALIAN $$

(☑6496 1855; www.wharfsidecafe.com; mains $10-20; ⊙breakfast & lunch; ☎) Decent breakfasts, strong coffees and tables that offer views of the harbour tables make this a good place to start the day.

❶ Information

Post office (140 Imlay St)

Visitor centre (☑6496 1953; www.visiteden. com.au; cnr Imlay & Mitchell Sts) Internet access.

❶ Getting There & Away

Premier (☑13 34 10; www.premierms.com. au) has two daily bus sevices that run to Wollongong ($69, eight hours)and Sydney ($71, nine hours), and one bus service to Melbourne ($58, eight hours). **CountryLink** (☑13 22 32; www. countrylink.com.au) runs a daily bus sevice to Canberra ($35, 5¼ hours).

Deanes Buslines (☑6495 6452; www. deanesbuslines.com.au) has five buses, Monday to Saturday, to Bega ($13.20, 1¼ hours) via Merimbula ($8.80, 40 minutes).

Ben Boyd National Park

The wilderness barely pauses for breath before starting again at 10,485-hectare **Ben Boyd National Park**. Boyd was an entrepreneur who failed spectacularly in his efforts to build an empire around Eden in 1850. This park protects some of his follies, along with a dramatic coastline peppered with isolated beaches. It's split into two sections, with Eden squeezed in between.

The southern section is accessed by mainly gravel roads (per vehicle $7) leading off sealed Edrom Rd, which leaves the Princes Hwy 19km south of Eden. At its southern tip, the elegant 1883 **Green Cape Lightstation** (☑6495 5000; www.nationalparks.nsw.gov. au; Green Cape Rd; cottage midweek/weekend from $200/280) copes with its isolation by gazing out at awesome views. There are **tours** (adult/child $7/5; ⊙1pm & 3pm Thu-Mon) or if you want to share the seclusion, you can spend the night in a lavishly restored keepers' cottage (sleeps six).

Eleven kilometres along Edrom Rd there's a turn-off to the historic **Davidson Whaling Station** on Twofold Bay where you can have a picnic in the rustic gardens of **Loch Gaira Cottage** (1896). Not much whaling paraphernalia remains, but interpretive signs tell the story. It's hard to imagine that until 1929 the peace of this place was rent by the agonised groans of dying whales and the stench of boiling blubber.

Further along is the turn-off for **Boyd's Tower**, an impressive structure indulgently built in the late 1840s with sandstone shipped from Sydney. It was intended to be a lighthouse but the government wouldn't give Boyd permission to operate it.

The 31km **Light to Light Walk** links Boyd's wannabe lighthouse to the real one at Green Cape. There are **camp sites** (☑6495 5000; adult/child $10/5) along the route at **Saltwater Creek** and **Bittangabee Bay**. Both have vehicle access.

The northern section of the park can be accessed from the Princes Hwy north of Eden. From Haycock Point, where there are good views, a walking trail leads to a headland overlooking the Pambula River. Another good – if short (1km) – walk is to the **Pinnacles**.

Byron Bay & Northern NSW

Includes »

Best Places to Eat

Best Places to Stay

Why Go?

Nowhere on the East Coast conjures up the beach-cum-nature-cum-good times quite like Byron Bay. Its unique mix of leisure and energy is infectious and those who visit seldom go home complaining – if they go home at all.

But if Byron is the heartbeat, the surrounding hinterland (with its green hills and national parks) and north coast (stretching north to Tweed Heads and south almost to Port Macquarie) are the blood that keeps it pumping. Byron might bring them here, but it's the breathtaking vistas, endless white sands and blue-hued breaks that tempt travellers further afield to little coastal towns like Yamba and Crescent Head. And when the sand between your toes starts getting up your nose, national parks are scattered amid the rich deltas of mighty rivers; and villages like Bangalow and Bellingen, with sublime food and organic produce, tempt both alternative-lifestylers and city slickers. This really is the good life.

When to Go

Byron Bay

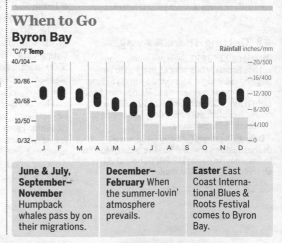

June & July, September–November Humpback whales pass by on their migrations.

December–February When the summer-lovin' atmosphere prevails.

Easter East Coast International Blues & Roots Festival comes to Byron Bay.

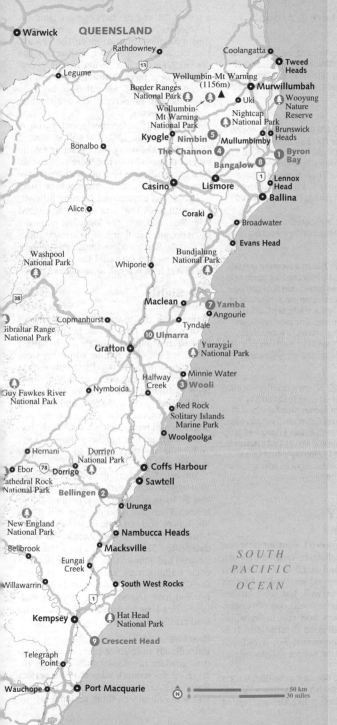

QUEENSLAND

Warwick

Rathdowney

Coolangatta

Legume

Tweed
Heads

13

Wollumbin-Mt Warning
(1156m)

Border Ranges
National Park

Murwillumbah

Uki

Wooyung
Nature
Reserve

Wollumbin-
Mt Warning
National Park

Nightcap
National Park

Brunswick
Heads

Bonalbo

Kyogle

Nimbin

Mullumbimby

Byron
Bay

The Channon

Bangalow

Casino

Lismore

Lennox
Head

1

Alice

Coraki

Ballina

Broadwater

Washpool
National Park

Whiporie

Bundjalung
National Park

Evans Head

38

Maclean

Yamba

Copmanhurst

Tyndale

Angourie

Gibraltar Range
National Park

Ulmarra

Grafton

Yuraygir
National Park

Guy Fawkes River
National Park

Halfway
Creek

Nymboida

Minnie Water

Wooli

Red Rock
Solitary Islands
Marine Park

Woolgoolga

Hernani

Dorrigo
National Park

Ebor

78

Dorrigo

Coffs Harbour

Cathedral Rock
National Park

Bellingen

Sawtell

Urunga

New England
National Park

Nambucca Heads

Bellbrook

Macksville

Eungai
Creek

SOUTH
PACIFIC
OCEAN

Willawarrin

South West Rocks

1

Kempsey

Hat Head
National Park

Crescent Head

Telegraph
Point

Wauchope

Port Macquarie

N

0
0

50 km
30 miles

ℹ️ Getting There & Around

Air

Airports along the north coast, including at Coffs Harbour, Grafton, Ballina and Lismore, attract the service of budget carriers in addition to commuter runs to Sydney. Services fluctuate all the time.

Bus

Greyhound (☑1300 473 946; www.greyhound. com.au) and **Premier** (☑13 34 10; www.pre mierms.com.au) both offer services three to five times daily linking major – and minor – towns along the Pacific Hwy. The real choice between them may come down to which one you have a bus pass with and which has the schedule you want.

Local bus services are sporadic along the coast and are often timed solely for school runs.

Road

The Pacific Hwy (Hwy 1) is an adventure in itself. Parts have been greatly improved (eg north of Byron Bay) with eased curves and dual carriageways. But other stretches remain a minefield of narrow curves, stoplights, traffic (eg Coffs Harbour) and speed cameras. One local politician has called it a 'national shame'; a little strong, perhaps. But the rotten road conditions give you yet more reasons to stop and enjoy yourself.

Train

CountryLink (☑13 22 32; www.countrylink.info) stopped its essential services to Byron Bay in 2004. Trains to/from Sydney stop far inland at the agricultural town of Casino and you have to transfer to a bus to reach Byron, Lismore et al. To the south, the train still serves Coffs Harbour, Nambucca Heads and Kempsey. Other CountryLink buses offer useful services linking towns, especially in the far north.

BYRON BAY

☑02 / POP 4980

New South Wales doesn't want for beaches. In fact, go a short distance north and south from Byron Bay and you'll find untrodden sands stretching beyond your vision. Byron's beaches are nice as well, but what makes them special is Byron itself: one of Australia's best beach towns. Low-rise, funky, walkable, relaxed are all good descriptions. It is everything that the overhyped, overdeveloped towns across the border in Queensland are not.

Of course Byron does get crowded, which is in direct conflict with its mellow charms. Jonson St can seize up like the arteries of a pie addict and the bars can get jammed. Developers would cheerfully turn Byron into a Surfers Paradise given the chance. But locals are dedicated to preserving the essential small-town soul even as everyone wants a piece. The left-wing council is constantly under assault from business interests, and property prices are sending residents packing.

The thing to remember about Byron is that under all the glitz it is still at heart a small town. The whole place is set up for the several thousand who live there year-round. So if the roads were widened and new shopping centres built, the charm would be gone.

Byron was a quiet, unassuming little village until 1963. That year surfers discovered 'The Pass' and over the following years the town became a cauldron of artistically minded people. Surfers adore the seven different beachfronts that surround the point, knowing that at least one will always have a break.

👁️ Sights

Cape Byron   NATURE RESERVE

Many think the town is the namesake of George Gordon Lord Byron, but they're off by two generations: Captain Cook named this spot for his grandfather while they were sailing past in the 1770s. (Later bureaucrats assumed it was the poet's grandson who'd been honoured and planned out streets with names such as Jonson and Shelley). Among the spectacular views, you can see dolphins and humpback whales, which pass nearby during their northern (June to July) and southern (September to November) migrations.

You can drive right up to the picturesque 1901 **lighthouse** (☺8am-sunset), but it'll cost you $7 to park (there's free parking 300m below). There are good displays and if you like it here, you can stay; for details, see the boxed text, p169. **Tours** (☑6685 5955; adult/child $8/6; ☺11am, noon & 2pm Tue & Thu, Sat in summer) are illuminating. There's a 4km circular walking track around the cape from the **Captain Cook Lookout** on Lighthouse Rd. You have a good chance of seeing wallabies, brush turkeys and feral goats in the final rainforest stretch.

Beaches   BEACH

Immediately in front of town, **Main Beach** is as good for people-watching as for swimming. At the western edge of town, perfect **Belongil Beach** avoids many of the crowds and is unofficially clothing optional. At the east end, the **Wreck** is a powerful right-hander surf break.

Clarkes Beach, at the eastern end of Main Beach, can have good surf but the best is further east, at the next few beaches. **The Pass** adjoins Clarkes. **Watego's** is a wide crescent of sand with turquoise surf. There's limited parking, so use the 1.1km walk that begins at the **Captain Cook Lookout**. Another 400m brings you to **Little Watego's**, another lovely patch of sand backed by rocks. Go another 300m east and the only option to go further is swimming: you've reached the easternmost point in Australia.

Tallow Beach extends 7km south of Cape Byron. It's quite an amazing stretch of sand, backed by **Arakwal National Park**, and fronting rugged open ocean. The rocks of Cape Byron are to the north and there are many good walks to near the beach parking area. This is the place to flee the crowds and it's only a short walk or bike ride from the centre.

Past Tallow Beach, there is a rockier stretch around **Broken Head** and the nature reserve, where a succession of small beaches dot the coast before opening onto **Seven Mile Beach**, which goes all the way to Lennox Head.

The suburb of **Suffolk Park** (with more good surf, particularly in winter) starts 5km south of town. **Kings Beach** is a popular gay beach, just off Seven Mile Beach Rd near the Broken Head Holiday Park.

🏃 Activities

Adventure sports abound in Byron Bay and most operators offer a free pick-up service from local accommodation. Surfing and diving are the biggest draws.

Surfing

Most hostels provide free boards to guests, or you can rent equipment. Half-day classes typically start at $60.

Blackdog Surfing SURFING
(⌨6680 9828; www.blackdogsurfing.com; Shop 8, The Plaza, Jonson St) Intimate group lessons and women's courses.

Byron Bay Surf School SURFING
(⌨1800 707 274; www.byronbaysurfschool.com; 127 Jonson St) Surf camps too.

Byron Surf Kool Katz SURFING
(⌨6685 5169; www.koolkatzsurf.com) Half-day lessons $49.

Mojosurf Adventures SURFING
(⌨1800 113 044; www.mojosurf.com; Marvell St) Epic surf trips.

Samudra SURFING, YOGA
(⌨6685 5600; www.samudra.com.au) Surf-and-yoga retreats.

Surfing Byron Bay SURFING
(⌨6685 7099; www.gosurfingbyronbay.com; 84 Jonson St) Has courses for kids.

Diving

About 3km offshore, **Julian Rocks** is a meeting point for cold southerly and warm northerly currents, attracting a profusion of marine species and divers alike. Much of these waters is protected by the Cape Byron Marine Park.

Dive Byron Bay DIVING
(⌨1800 243 483, 6685 8333; www.byronbaydivecentre.com.au; 9 Marvell St) Rentals, sales, PADI courses from $495, dives from $95.

Sundive DIVING, SNORKELLING
(⌨6685 7755; www.sundive.com.au; 8 Middleton St; ☉tours 8am, 10.45 & 1pm) Scuba diving plus daily snorkelling tours ($50).

Alternative Therapies

Healing hippies are just some of the many characters ready to put your mind and body at rest in Byron. Bulletin boards are awash with cards for people with titles like 'Evolutionary Facilitator'.

Abundantia HEALING
(⌨6685 8008; www.ruthsmithhealing.com; 6-7 Byron St; treatments from $125) Connect with your spirit to bring about healing.

Bikram Hot Yoga YOGA
(⌨6685 6334; www.bikramyogabyronbay.com.au; 35 Childe St; casual 90min class $20)

Buddha Gardens SPA
(⌨6680 7844; www.buddhagardensdayspa.com.au; Arts Factory Village, 21 Gordon St; treatments from $85) Balinese-style day spa.

Byron Ayurveda Centre AYURVEDA
(⌨6632 2244; www.ayurvedahouse.com.au; Shop 6, Middleton St; treatments from $45; ☉10am-5pm Wed-Sun) It's exfoliation over enemas at this restful place aimed at the masses.

Cocoon MASSAGE
(⌨6685 5711; www.cocoonbyron.com.au; 6/11 Fletcher St; massages from $65) Offers 'health retreats' from family holidays.

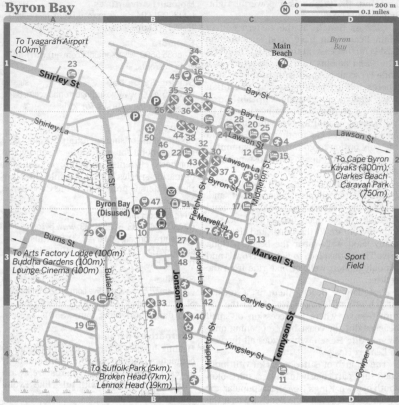

Relax Haven   MASSAGE, FLOTATION TANK
(☑6685 8304; www.belongilbeachouse.com;
Belongil Beachouse, Childe St; ☉to 8pm) Offers flotation tanks (one hour $35) and
massage sessions (one hour $45). Female
therapists.

Shambala   REFLEXOLOGY, ACUPUNCTURE
(☑6680 7791; www.shambala.net.au; 4 Carlyle
St; treatments from $50; ☉to 7pm) Massage,
reflexology and acupuncture.

Kayaking

Exhibitionist dolphins enhance scenic, half-
day kayaking tours in and around Cape Byron Marine Park. Tours go for $60 to $65 per
adult, less for children.

Cape Byron Kayaks   KAYAKING
(☑6680 9555; www.capebyronkayaks.com;
☉tours 8.30am & 1pm)

Dolphin Kayaking   KAYAKING
(☑6685 8044; www.dolphinkayaking.com.au;
☉tours 8.30am)

Gosea Kayaks   KAYAKING
(☑0416 222 344; www.goseakayakbyronbay.com.
au; ☉tours 9.30am & 2pm)

Flying

Byron Airwaves   HANG-GLIDING
(☑6629 0354; www.byronair.cjb.net) Tandem
hang-gliding ($145) and courses (from
$1500).

Byron Bay Ballooning   BALLOONING
(☑1300 889 660; www.byronbayballooning.com.
au; Tyagarah Airport; adult/child $325/175) Sun-
rise flights including gourmet breakfast.

Byron Bay Microlights
                WHALE-WATCHING, SCENIC FLIGHTS
(☑0407 281 687; Tyagarah Airport) Whale-
watching ($180) and scenic flights ($100).

Skydive Byron Bay   SKYDIVING
(☑6684 1323; www.skydivebyronbay.com; Tyagarah Airport) Tandem dives ($249 to $334)

are priced depending on altitude and time of freefall (20 to 70 seconds).

Other

Byron Surf & Bike Hire   ACTIVE-GEAR HIRE
(☑6680 7066; 1-3 31 Lawson St) Rents bikes ($20 per day), kayaks (half-day $45), surfboards ($25 per day) and other active gear.

Circus Arts   CIRCUS ARTS
(☑6685 6566; www.circusarts.com.au; 17 Centennial Circuit) About 2km west of town; Type A characters may find the juggling classes useful.

☞ Tours

Numerous operators run tours to Nimbin and other interesting places in the hinterland. Most tour companies will pick you up from where you're staying.

Aboriginal Cultural Concepts
INDIGENOUS HERITAGE
(☑0405 654 280; www.aboriginalculturalcon cepts.com; from $80; ☺10am-1pm Wed-Sat) Heritage tours exploring mythological sights along the Bundjalung Coast. Includes bush-tucker tour.

Byron Bay Wildlife Tours   WILDLIFE
(☑0429 770 686; www.byronbaywildlifetours.com; adult/child $70/35) Platypus and wildlife spottings guaranteed. Cheaper if booked online.

Happy Coach   NIMBIN
(☑6685 3996; www.happycoach.com.au; ☺10am; $25) Nimbin tours.

Jim's Alternative Tours   NIMBIN
(☑0401 592 247; www.jimsalternativetours.com; tours $40; ☺10am) Entertaining tours (with soundtrack!) to Nimbin.

Mountain Bike Tours
MOUNTAIN BIKE

(☎1800 122 504, 0429 122 504; www.mountain biketours.com.au; tours $99; ⓢ9.30am) Environmentally aware bike tours.

Night Vision Walks
WILDLIFE

(☎6687 4237; www.visionwalks.com; adult/child from $40/25) See nocturnal animals in their natural habitat.

✯✯ Festivals & Events

Splendour in the Grass music festival has decamped to Woodford in Queensland.

East Coast International Blues & Roots Music Festival
MUSIC

(www.bluesfest.com.au) Held over Easter, this international jam attracts high-calibre international performers and local heavyweights. Book early.

Byron Bay Writers Festival
LITERARY

(☎6685 5115; www.byronbaywritersfestival.com.au) In late July/early August, this gathers together top-shelf writers and literary followers from across Australia.

🛏 Sleeping

There's every kind of accommodation you could hope for in and around Byron. Just don't be a bonehead and turn up in January without a reservation or you'll join the hordes of backpackers and jet-set models milling around the visitors centre with hang-dog looks because they thought there would be just one more room.

Schoolies Week at the end of November is also one to avoid. During these periods, one-night-only bookings are rare.

Motels are clustered in town and south along Bangalow Rd. There are scores of B&Bs and apartments all along Belongil Beach. The **accommodation booking office** (☎6680 8666; www.byronbayaccom.net), run by the visitor centre, is a great service for booking in advance.

For holiday houses check out **Professionals** (☎6685 6552; www.byronbaypro.com.au; cnr Lawson & Fletcher Sts).

TOP CHOICE Byron at Byron
RESORT $$$

(☎1300 554 362, 6639 2000; www.thebyronatbyron.com.au; 77 Broken Head Rd; r from $325; ❋@☎☀) For the ultimate in luxury, this 92-suite resort is set within 45 acres of subtropical rainforest. It is a hive of wildlife and endangered species and the resort maintains its sympathy to the environment with a list of eco credentials. When you're not lounging by the infinity pool having someone cut your toenails, take the 10-minute stroll to Tallow Beach via a series of wonderful boardwalks. Online bookings attract discounts.

Arts Factory Lodge
HOSTEL, CAMPGROUND $

(☎6685 7709; www.artsfactory.com.au; Skinners Shoot Rd; dm/d from $34/80, camp sites $17; @☀) For an archetypal Byron experience, pull up stumps here. The complex has didgeridoo lessons and yoga and meditation workshops delivered in a serene hippie-esque setting on a picturesque swamp. Choose from colourful six- to 10-bed dorms, a cottage, tepees or wagons. Couples can opt for aptly titled 'cube' rooms, island retreat canvas huts (both $90) or the pricier love shack with bathroom ($100).

Atlantic
GUESTHOUSE $

(☎6685 5118; www.atlanticbyronbay.com.au; 13 Marvell St; dm/d from $25/150; ❋☎☀) What a difference a facelift makes. This little residential hub has been transformed into a shiny white weatherboard seaside haven with varying room combos to suit backpackers, singles, couples or families. Rooms are bright and cheery; the cheapest share bathrooms and kitchens, and dorm rooms are bunk-free. For something a little less ordinary, ask about sleeping in the retro polished aluminium caravan ($175).

Nomads
HOSTEL $

(☎6680 7966; www.nomadsbyronbay.com.au; 1 Lawson Lane; dm/d $30/89; @☎) Byron's newest backpacker place packs an edgy punch with its glossy designer-led decor and funky furniture. It's purpose-built, so the 10 dorm rooms are squeaky clean and comfortable, but they're not half as good as the king rooms ($140), which have bathrooms, fridges and plasma televisions. It adjoins Global Gossip in the heart of town.

Beach Hotel Resort
RESORT $$$

(☎6685 6402; www.beachhotelresort.com.au; Bay St; r incl breakfast from $260; ❋☀) Nowhere is more central than this beachfront icon, which attracts a crowd slightly more classy than that of the massive adjoining hotel beer garden next door. Ground-floor rooms open onto lush gardens and a heated pool where a family of lizards sunbakes; rooms in the upper storeys have ocean views. Rooms 3 and 4 are the biggest.

Bamboo Cottage
GUESTHOUSE $$

(☎6685 5509; www.byron-bay.com/bamboocottage; 76 Butler St; r from $99) Featuring global charm and wall hangings, Bamboo Cottage

You can get a real insight into the far north coast and hinterland at one of the myriad markets, which bring together hippies, yuppies and just about anyone else you can imagine. The food offerings are exquisite and diverse and you get a chance to experience the region firsthand (see (www.farmersmarkets.org.au).

Expect to find oodles of seasonal organic produce along with other foodstuffs such as farmhouse cheeses, honey and baked goods. There are often vendors selling crafts and it's common to hear some live folk music, especially at the weekend markets. Hours can be erratic, but you're safest aiming to arrive in the morning.

Weekly Markets

Bangalow Farmers Market (Byron St; ⊘7-11am Sat) Organic produce.

Byron Farmers Market (Butler St; ⊘7-11am Thu)

Lismore Farmers Market (Lismore Showground; ⊘8am-noon Sat)

Rainbow Region Organic Markets (Lismore Showground; ⊘7-11am Tue)

Ballina Missingham Bridge Farmers Market (Kingsford Smith Dr; ⊘6am-noon Sun)

First Weekend of the Month

Brunswick Heads (Memorial Park; ⊘7.30am-2pm Sat)

Byron Community Market (Butler St; ⊘8am-2pm Sun)

Lismore Car Boot Market (Lismore Shopping Centre; ⊘8am-2pm Sun)

Second Weekend of the Month

Alstonville Market (Apex Pavilion, Alstonville Showground; ⊘8am-12.30pm Sun)

Channon Craft Market (Coronation Park; ⊘9am-3pm Sun)

Lennox Head Lakeside Market (Lake Ainsworth Foreshore; ⊘8am-2pm Sun)

Third Weekend of the Month

Nimbin Aquarius Market (Community Centre; ⊘8am-4pm Sun) Produce and art. Live music.

Ballina Markets (Canal Rd; ⊘7am-1pm Sun)

Lismore Car Boot Market (Lismore Shopping Centre; ⊘8am-2pm Sun)

Mullumbimby Museum Market (Stuart St; ⊘7.30am-2pm Sat)

Murwillumbah Cottage Market (City centre; ⊘8am-1pm Sat)

Fourth Weekend of the Month

Bangalow Village Market (Bangalow centre; ⊘7.30am-2pm Sun)

Evans Head Riverside Market (Park St Recreation Reserve; ⊘7.30am-2pm Sat)

Fifth Weekend of the Month

Nimbin Aquarius Markets (Community Centre; ⊘8am-4pm Sun) Produce and art. Live music.

Lennox Head Lakeside Market (Lake Ainsworth Showground; ⊘8am-2pm Sun)

BYRON BAY SLEEPING

treats guests to a choice of three individually styled rooms with Asian overtones in a home-away-from-home atmosphere. It's on the quiet side of the tracks.

Rae's on Watego's   HOTEL **$$$**
(⌨6685 5366; www.raes.com.au; Marine Pde; price on application; ✷@☎✷) This dazzlingly white Mediterranean villa was once rated by *Condé Nast Traveller* one of the world's top 25 hotels. It's definitely one of Australia's. Rooms here have an artistic and casual elegance that lets the luxury sneak up on you. The restaurant alone is worth the trip.

Oasis Resort & Treetop Houses

APARTMENTS $$

(☎1800 336 129, 6685 7390; www.byronbayoasis resort.com.au; 24 Scott St; apt from $190, treetop apt from $325; ❄✿) Away from the town centre, this compact resort is engulfed by palms and has sizeable one- and two-bedroom apartments with big balconies. Even better are the apartments sitting atop the tree canopies with outdoor spas and ocean views. Longer stays attract discounts.

Aquarius

HOSTEL $

(☎6685 7663; www.aquarius-backpackers.com.au; 14-16 Lawson St; dm/d from $35/100, motel d from $200; ❄@✿) This motel-style backpacker place overflows with the comings and goings of hyperactive, excitable travellers. There's plenty of communal space – including a bar – ensuring that those going it solo can find mates. Self-contained apartments (doubles from $140) also available.

Outrigger Bay Resort

APARTMENTS $$

(☎6685 8646; www.outriggerbay.com; 9 Shirley St; 2-/3-bedroom apt $206/267; ❄✺✿) This apartment complex has one-, two- and three-bedroom units on a shady site overlooking a pool. The beach is only 50m away. The open kitchens are good for festive food fun.

Belongil Beachouse

HOSTEL $

(☎6685 7868; www.belongilbeachouse.com; Childe St; dm/d from $30/70, self-contained cottages from $160; @) Across from Belongil Beach in a parklike area, this stylish place has excellent self-contained cabins, spartan studio units and comfortable dorms. Pick of the bunch are the cosy, self-contained doubles.

Byron Bayside Motel

APARTMENTS $

(☎6685 6004; www.byronbaysidemotel.com. au; 14 Middleton St; d/f from $89/109) These spotless but basic rooms have small kitchenette and full laundry; they are ideal for campers looking for downtime. It's central, comparatively cheap and takes security seriously.

Amigos

GUESTHOUSE $$

(☎0417 732 244; www.amigosbb.com; 32 Kingsley St; s/d from $88/108) Soaked in south-of-the-border flavours, this cute TV-free B&B has three bedrooms with crisp white linen and South American spreads. The owners *habla espanole* (the author doesn't).

Bay Beach Motel

MOTEL $$

(☎6685 6090; www.baybeachmotel.com.au; 32 Lawson St; r $155-180, 2-bed apt from $235; ❄✿) Unpretentious but smart, this white-brick hotel with IKEA-esque furnishings is close to town and the beach, but not so close that partygoers keep guests awake.

Main Beach Backpackers

HOSTEL $

(☎6685 8695; www.mainbeachbackpackers.com; cnr Lawson & Fletcher Sts; dm/d from $27/70; ❄@✺✿) The staff might be a little down in the mouth but this 94-bed place near the beach and town centre, with a decent-sized pool, is hard to beat.

Also recommended:

Clarkes Beach Caravan Park

CARAVAN PARK $

(☎6685 6496; www.northcoastparks.com.au/ clarkes; off Lighthouse Rd; unpowered sites/cabins from $38/125) Tightly packed cabins and sites in a bush setting.

Hibiscus Motor Inn

MOTEL $$

(☎6685 6195; www.hibiscusmotel.com.au 33 Lawson St; d $165; ❄) A basic but central motel, right in town and near Main Beach, with friendly owners.

Waves

APARTMENTS $$$

(☎1800 040 151; www.wavesresorts.com.au; 35 Lawson St; d apt from $300; ❄✺) Cushy, boutique penthouse and studio apartments in the heart of Byron.

Cape Byron YHA

HOSTEL $

(☎1800 652 627, 6685 8788; www.yha.com.au; cnr Middleton & Byron Sts; dm/d from $34/115; ❄@✺) This two-storey complex is situated close to the town centre and has its own shops and heated pool. It's a modern and tidy place.

Glen Villa Resort

CARAVAN PARK $$

(☎6685 7382; www.glenvillaresort.com.au; Butler St; d cabin from $120; ❄@✺) Though slightly militant with its 'two people only' rule, this well-maintained cabin park is clean, comfortable and secure. It's off the main traffic route so it is last to fill up, and blissfully peaceful.

✖ Eating

You can eat well in Byron; there's a huge range of choices and many are excellent. Where phone numbers are included, booking is recommended for peak-time dining.

TOP CHOICE **St Elmo**

MEDITERRANEAN $$

(☎6680 7426; www.stelmodining.com; cnr Fletcher St & Lawson Lane; shared plates $23; ☺lunch & dinner) Kartell stools are a nod to just how much design work it takes to get bums on seats. Sit on one to be served gourmet cocktails by extremely fit bronzed and

NAPPING IN NATURE

Located right at the Byron Bay lighthouse (p161), the historic 1901 **Lighthouse Keepers Cottages** (☑6685 6552; www.byronbaypro.com.au; 3-day rentals from $900) have been renovated with polished wood floors and lovely furnishings so that guests can pull up stumps. The views are swell and you have the place to yourself after dusk. If you miss out on this one, don't sweat it. There is a booty of similar gems hidden in national parks, state conservation areas and nature reserves along the coast. You can hole up in a lighthouse, get back to nature in a beachfront cottage or bunker down in a hinterland cabin. The NPWS website (www.environment.nsw.gov.au/NationalParks) has a wealth of info.

accented barmen, or settle in for dinner; the shared plates make great date fodder.

Kinoko Sushi Bar JAPANESE $$
(7/23 Jonson St; mains $7-25; ⊘lunch & dinner) Choo-choo-choose something from the sushi train or let the Japanese chef slice up a plate of fresh sashimi. This is a lively place where the Asahi also goes down well. It's also one of the last places open for dinner.

Balcony MEDITERRANEAN $$
(☑6680 9666; www.balcony.com.au; cnr Lawson & Jonson Sts; dinners $9-39; ⊘breakfast, lunch & dinner; 🛜) The eponymous architectural feature here wraps around the building and gives you tremendous views of the passing Byron parade and the always-clogged traffic circle. The food is Mediterranean, with global influences. The drink list is long.

Petit Snail FRENCH $$$
(☑6685 8526; www.thepetitsnail.com.au; 5 Carlyle St; mains $31-39; ⊘dinner) This intimate restaurant is off the main beat and is more Bordeaux than Byron. French staff serve up traditional red, white and blue fare such as steak tartare, wild rabbit terrine, duck confit and lots of *fromage*. There's outdoor dining on the verandah.

Bay Leaf Café MODERN AUSTRALIAN $
(Marvell St; mains $10-18; ⊘breakfast & lunch daily, dinner Thu-Sat) This tiny wedge-shaped bohemian cafe has a small but excellent menu prepared in a busy open kitchen. Best meal of the day is breakfast, with fresh stewed rhubarb, yoghurt and pistachios on the menu. That is, unless fresh pasta takes your fancy. It's homemade.

Fishheads SEAFOOD $
(www.fishheadsbyronbay.com.au; 1 Jonson St; mains $6-27; breakfast, lunch & dinner 🛜) Right on the beach, this fabulous takeaway shop sells traditional battered fish and chips ($12.50), or take it up a notch with grilled

prawns and salad ($18). The restaurant is fine too, but why wouldn't you dine on the beach?

Orient Express THAI, VIETNAMESE $$$
(☑6680 8808; www.orientexpresseatery.com.au; 1/2 Fletcher St; mains $20-34; ⊘lunch Fri-Sun, dinner Tue-Sun) Easily mistaken for an Asian decorator's shop, or a teahouse, this is actually one of the best restaurants in Byron, helmed by Tippy Heng. Unlike some places, the modern menu here is fairly brief but, you guessed it, full of flavour. Expect to wait.

One One One MEDITERRANEAN $$
(☑6680 7388; 1/111 Jonson St; mains $10-25; ⊘breakfast & lunch daily, dinner Fri & Sat; 🛜☑) HQ for Slow Food devotees locally; the ingredients celebrate regional produce. The menu is mostly vegetarian, save for some superb spiced prawns and other seafood. Plates are good for sharing.

Earth 'n' Sea ITALIAN $$
(☑6685 6029; www.earthnsea.com.au; cnr Fletcher & Byron Sts; mains $14-34; ⊘lunch & dinner) The pizza list at this old favourite is long and full of flavour. Pasta is on the menu too. Beers include several excellent microbrews from the Northern Rivers Brewing Co.

Rae's on Wategos's MODERN AUSTRALIAN $$$
(☑6685 5366; www.raes.com.au; Marine Pde; mains $40-45; ⊘lunch & dinner) Exquisite cuisine on a terrace with the sound of surf providing background noise to your witticisms. The menu changes daily but always surprises with its unconventional pairings of ingredients and spices. Book ahead.

Fresh CAFE $
(☑6685 7810; www.byronfresh.com.au; 7 Jonson St; meals $13-31; ⊘breakfast, lunch & dinner) Top spot for breakfast, with excellent pancakes. At night, sit at open-air tables and chow down on a menu running the gamut of light (salads) or heavy (braised beef cheek)

dishes. Always popular, the people-watching is half the appeal.

Mongers FISH & CHIPS $
(www.byron-bay.com/mongers; Bay Lane; mains $10-20; ⊘lunch & dinner) Tucked behind the Beach Hotel, the region's best fish and chips issue forth to tables of devotees. It's a narrow, back-alley space but the quality is all high street. It's one of a handful of eateries that have popped up here.

Espressohead ESPRESSO BAR $
(shop 13, 108 Jonson St) Locals flock to this place tucked away behind Woolworths, for its excellent coffees. See if you can count the number of dodgy vans for sale on the bulletin board.

Orgasmic MIDDLE EASTERN $
(11 Bay Lane; mains $8-19; ⊘10am-10pm) Plop your bum on a cube cushion at this alley eatery that's one step above a stall. Takeaways include big mezze plates, ideal for quick picnics.

Twisted Sista CAFE
(Shop 1, 4 Lawson St; mains $9-18; ⊘breakfast & lunch) Bounteous baked goods include huge muffins, cheesy casseroles and overstuffed sandwiches on beautiful bread. Outdoor tables add to the slightly happy-hungover vibe.

Mary Ryan's CAFE $
(www.maryryans.com.au; shop 5, 21-25 Fletcher St; mains $8-18) Snuggled up to the ABC Bookshop, this literary cafe provides coffee drinkers with a caffeine high. Speaking of high, the ceilings are, leaving plenty of wall space for artworks.

Blue Olive SELF-CATERING $$
(27 Lawson St; ⊘10am-5.30pm Tue-Sat, 10am-4pm Sun) Fine cheeses and deli items; enjoy the beautiful prepared foods at shady pavement tables.

Also recommended:

Engine Room ESPRESSO BAR $
(shop 1, Lawson Lane) Hole-in-the-wall coffee sensation that opens early.

Dip MEDITERRANEAN $
(21 Fletcher St; tapas $6-18; ⊘lunch & breakfast daily) A groovy bar atmosphere with an inspired menu.

Mokha MEDITERRANEAN, MIDDLE EASTERN $
(shop 2, Lawson St; mains $6-27; ⊘breakfast, lunch & dinner daily; 🎯) Eclectic Euro-Middle Eastern menu and a wine list as long as your arm.

Lemongrass VIETNAMESE $$
(☑6680 8443; Lawson Arcade, 3/17 Lawson St; mains $15-20; ⊘dinner Mon-Sat) All your favourite Vietnamese dishes, from ricepaper rolls and beef *pho* to green pawpaw salad and prawn fried rice.

● Drinking

Byron Bay's nightlife is varied and runs late. Check the gig guide in Thursday's *Byron Shire News* or tune into Bay 99.9 FM.

TOP CHOICE **Railway Friendly Bar** PUB
(Jonson St; ⊘11am-late) This indoor-outdoor pub, aka 'The Rails', draws everyone from grey pensioners and lobster-red British tourists to acid-soaked hippies and high-on-life earth mothers. Its cosy interior is the old railway station. The front beer garden, conducive to boozy afternoons, has live music every night. The pub grub is excellent, so too the St Arnou beer on tap.

Balcony BAR
(☑6680 9666; cnr Lawson & Jonson Sts; ⊘8am-11pm) With its verandah poking out amid the palm trees, this fine bar-cum-restaurant is the place to park yourself. Choose from stools, chairs or sofas while working through a cocktail list that will make you giddy just looking at it.

Great Northern PUB
(☑6685 6454; Byron St; ⊘noon-late) You won't need your fancy duds at this brash and boisterous pub. It's loud and beery with live music most nights and even louder when hosting headline acts. Live music almost nightly. Soak up the booze with a wood-fired pizza.

Beach Hotel PUB
(☑6685 6402; cnr Jonson & Bay Sts; ⊘11am-late) The mother ship of all pubs is close to the main beach and is shot through with a fabulously infectious atmosphere that makes everyone your best mate. There's live music and DJs some nights.

St Elmo BAR
(www.stelmodining.com; cnr Fletcher St & Lawson Lane) Cocktails taken to an all-new gourmet level. Wear your heels, gals.

☆ Entertainment

Arts Factory Lounge Cinema CINEMA
(☑6685 5828; www.loungecinema.com; Skinners Shoot Rd; admission $9) The 135-seat cinema at the Arts Factory Lodge (p166) shows classic reruns and art-house flicks nightly.

Byron Theatre CINEMA, THEATRE
(☑6685 6807; www.byroncentre.com.au; 69 Jonson St) A 350-seat theatre featuring well-known Australian actors. Also a cinema showcasing art-house and foreign films and directors.

Cheeky Monkeys CLUB
(www.cheekymonkeys.com.au; 115 Jonson St; ☺7pm-3am) A backpacker's bonanza – and dare we say it, wet T-shirt comps.

Cocomangas CLUB
(www.cocomangas.com.au; 32 Jonson St; ☺9pm-late) This two-storey gay-friendly club thrashes about to indie rock, doof doof and fusion. Mondays is backpacker night.

🛍 Shopping

You can while away hours away from the beach in Byron's many shops. Broadly speaking, Fletcher St, north of Marvell St, has artsy boutiques; frock shops hover around the Lawson and Fletcher Sts traffic circle; west of here and south on Jonson St you'll find a huge range: everything from lingerie to New Age hokum.

Planet Corroboree INDIGENOUS ART
(☑6680 7884; 1/69 Jonson St) Has a huge range of Aboriginal art.

Happy High Herbs HERBS, NATURAL REMEDIES
(www.happyhighherbs.com; 1/5-7 Byron St) Adults only can explore the wonders of herbs and natural remedies.

ℹ Information

In addition to the resources listed here, the website www.byron-bay.com is helpful. The *Pink Guide* is a local publication aimed at gay and lesbian tourists; have a look at its useful website (www.byronbaypinkguide.blogspot.com).

Internet Access

Byron has many internet-access places that cram customers together in tight, sweaty little pods to stare at tiny screens. The Balcony and One One One have wi-fi.

Global Gossip (☑6680 9140; 84 Jonson St; per hr $8; @) Internet access.

Laundry

Coin Laundry (cnr Jonson & Marvell Sts; ☺7am-7pm)

Medical Services

Bay Centre Medical Clinic (☑6685 6206; www.byronmed.com.au; 6 Lawson St; ☺8am-5pm Mon-Thu, to 5.30pm Fri, 8am-noon Sat) Full-service general surgery.

Byron Bay Hospital (☑6639 6699; www.

ncahs.nsw.gov.au; cnr Wordsworth & Shirley Sts; ☺24hr) For medical emergencies.

ChemCoast Pharmacy (☑6685 6274; 20 Jonson St; ☺8am-8pm)

Money

Byron Foreign Exchange (Central Arcade, 4/47 Byron St; @) Foreign exchange, cash and money transfers, internet access.

Tourist Information

Backpackers World (☑6685 8858; www.backpackersworld.com.au; Shop 6, 75 Jonson St) Primarily a travel agent.

Byron Bus & Backpacker Centre (☑6685 5517; 84 Jonson St; ☺7.30am-7pm) Next to the coach stop; handles bus, train, accommodation and activity bookings. Has left-luggage lockers ($6).

Byron Environmental Centre (www.byronenvironmentcentre.asn.au; Mullumbimby Railway Station, 2 Prince Street, Mullumbimby) The hours are highly sporadic but the passions of these local environmentalists are not.

Visitors centre (☑6680 9279; www.visitbyronbay.com; Stationmaster's Cottage, Jonson St) Ground zero for tourist information (and when it's busy this cramped office feels like it).

ℹ Getting There & Away

Air

The closest airport is at Ballina (p180) and with its rapidly expanding service it is the best airport for Byron. It also has shuttle services and rental cars for Byron travellers.

Coolangatta airport (see p277) on the Gold Coast has a greater range of services but can involve a traffic clogged drive. **Byron Bay Shuttle** (www.byronbayshuttle.com.au) serves both Coolangatta ($37) and Ballina ($15) airports.

Bus

Long-distance buses for **Greyhound** (☑1300 473 946; www.greyhound.com.au) and **Premier** (☑13 34 10; www.premierms.com.au) stop on Jonson St. Approximate times and fares for both are as follows: Brisbane ($30, 2¾ hours), Coffs Harbour ($50, 5¼ hours) and Sydney ($90, 12 to 14 hours). Services operate several times daily. Check the boards at the bus stop for other Queensland options.

Blanch's Bus Service (☑6686 2144; www.blanchs.com.au) operates several daily services from Byron Bay to Lennox Head ($6.40, 30 minutes), Ballina (Tamar St stop $9.60, 40 minutes; Airport stop $9.60, 70 minutes) and Mullumbimby ($9.60, 35 minutes).

Train

People still mourn the loss of the popular CountryLink train service from Sydney. In fact a popular movie released in 2008, *Derailed*, documents this transport travesty. **CountryLink** (☑13 22 32; www.countrylink.info) has buses connecting to trains at the Casino train station (70 minutes). Get full details from the rather forlorn **train station** (◷10am-4pm Mon-Fri).

❶ Getting Around

Byron Bay Bicycles (☑6685 6067; The Plaza, 85 Jonson St) Hires out mountain bikes for $28 per day.

Byron Bay RentaCar (☑6685 5517; 84 Jonson St) Rents out a wide range of vehicles.

Hertz (☑6621 8855; 5 Marvell St) Ask about one-way rentals to Ballina airport.

Earth Car Rentals (☑6685 7472; www.earth car.com.au; 3a/1 Byron St) 'Australia's first carbon-neutral car rentals'.

Byron Bay Taxis (☑6685 5008; www.byron baytaxis.com.au) On call 24 hours.

FAR NORTH COAST HINTERLAND

It's not all beach. Away from the coast, the lush scenery, organic markets and alternative lifestyles inland complement places such as Byron Bay and make the far north coast region one of Australia's most appealing places – for locals and visitors alike. In fact the post-hippie rural lifestyle out here has become so mainstream that the epicentre of Nimbin is almost a theme park.

Twenty-two million years ago, an eruption of lava from Wollumbin-Mt Warning created

---

WORTH A TRIP

BYRON TO TWEED HEADS

The Pacific Hwy continues north to the Queensland border at Tweed Heads. If it's a leisurely pace you're after, take a detour through the towns of **Mullumbimby** ('Mullum'; population 3655) and **Brunswick Heads** (population 1614). The former is a serene coast-hinterland hybrid with lazy palms, typical tropical architecture and a cosmopolitan spread of cafes, bistros and pubs. Of these, one of the goodies is **Milk & Honey** (☑6684 1422; 59a Station St; mains $14-22; ◷dinner Mon-Sat), an artisan pizza joint created by chef Chris Pellen, who wood-fires thin-crust wonders with a changing line-up of toppings. Lines form early for the tables inside and out. Walk it off on a trail along the Brunswick River in town that passes through tropical forest and is lined with signs relating **Aboriginal stories**. The **Mullum Music Festival** (www.mullummusicfestival.com), at the end of November, is a prime time to visit.

Only slightly north, on the Old Pacific Hwy, beautiful Brunswick Heads reaps a bounty of fresh oysters and mud crabs from its peaceful Brunswick River inlets and beaches. The 1940s **Hotel Brunswick** (☑6685 1236; www.hotelbrunswick.com.au; Mullumbimby St; s/d/f $55/85/110) is a sight to behold and a destination unto itself, with a magnificent beer garden that unfurls beneath flourishing poincianas. It has decent pub rooms and the **Bruns** (mains $15-25; ◷lunch & dinner) serves good burgers, pasta and more; there's live music on weekends. Similarly laudable but easy to miss in a daggy motel, **FatBelly Kat** (☑6685 1100; www.fatbellykat.com; 26 Tweed St; mezze plates $4-26; ◷dinner Wed-Mon) is a celebrated Greek restaurant that brings feta fetishists and dolmades adorers from afar. You can't get food this good in the Old Country.

Keep trucking up the (newer) Pacific Hwy to the Wooyung turn. Crossing over a cool little old wooden railway bridge, the road passes through untouched coastal NSW countryside. Drive 5km east to where the sealed road turns north up the coast. You're in the **Wooyung Nature Reserve**, a suitably undeveloped place that features a long, dune-backed beach. Pull off almost anywhere for beautiful and deserted seashore. After 8km, you come to Pottsville Beach, your cue to head west back to the highway.

Tweed Heads (population 51,788) marks the southern end of the Gold Coast strip. At Point Danger, the towering **Captain Cook Memorial** straddles the state border, which can pass by unnoticed, as there is no river or landmark. Before you cross into the 'Sunshine State' check out the **Minjungbal Aboriginal Cultural Centre** (☑5524 2109; cnr Kirkwood & Duffy Sts; ◷9am-4pm Mon-Fri), set in a grove of old gum trees on the Tweed River. Displays detail how the Minjungbal people were able to live in harmony with the land and there's a Walk on Water Track and boardwalk through the mangroves.

the northern half of the hinterland, flattening the valley and enclosing it with dramatic mountain ranges. The southern end is a maze of steep hills and beautiful valleys, some still harbouring magnificent stands of rainforest. Other parts of the area have been cleared for cattle grazing as well as macadamia, avocado and coffee plantations. The area's three national parks – Border Ranges, Wollumbin (which now includes former Mt Warning National Park) and Nightcap – all have World Heritage rainforest (see the boxed text, p177).

Bangalow

☑02 / POP 1330

Boutiques, fine eateries, bookshops and an excellent pub – a mere 14km from Byron Bay. Beautiful Bangalow, with its character-laden main street, is the kind of place that turns Sydneysiders into tree-changers.

There's a good weekly **farmers market** (Byron St; ◎8-11am Sat) and a praised **cooking school** (☑6687 2799; www.bangalowcookingschool.com).

Riverview Guesthouse (☑6687 1317; www.riverviewguesthouse.com.au; 99 Byron St; d/tw from $195/150) is a stately old place that sits on the river's edge, ensuring that guests see platypuses and oversized lizards as they take on breakfast. It's the stuff of B&B dreams.

🌿**Possum Creek Eco Lodge** (☑6687 1188; www.possumcreeklodge.com.au; Cedarvale Rd; bungalows from $198; ▣), about 4km north, has views across the lush valleys. The 'eco' in the name is not green-washing – water is recycled, stored from rain and otherwise conserved. Power is partially solar.

[TOP CHOICE] **Satiate** (degustation from $75; ◎dinner Tue Sat), upstairs from Ate, does an award-winning set menu with seasonal local produce.

Ate (☑6687 1010; www.ate.net.au; 33 Byron St; mains $23-36; ◎breakfast & lunch) is great for sipping coffee on the verandah or dining in for inventive dishes.

Bangalow Dining Rooms (☑6687 1711; www.bangalowdining.com; Byron St; mains $15-32; ◎lunch & dinner) at Bangalow Hotel is a classy place with just the right amount of cool. Reserve a table in the dining room or sit on the deck and order from the cheaper menu; gourmet burgers and the like.

The interior at **Utopia** (☑6687 2088; 13 Byron St; meals $13-30; ◎breakfast & lunch daily, dinner Fri & Sat; ▣) is like the foam on a rich

latte. The long, narrow space is open and airy; piles of stylish magazines provide diversions. Desserts are to die for.

Gluten-free, organic and sublimely tasty wraps, salads, rolls and produce are up for grabs at **Pantry 29** (29 Byron St; ◎breakfast, lunch & dinner) and **Urban Café** (37 Byron St; mains $10-25; ◎breakfast & lunch), which changes its stripes at night to become **Bang Thai** (☑6687 2000; mains $20-32; ◎dinner Thu-Sat), with all the faves including Mussuman curry.

Blanch's Bus Service (☑6686 2144; www.blanchs.com.au) operates a service to Ballina ($7.60, 30 minutes) and Byron Bay ($6.40, 20 minutes).

Lismore

☑02 / POP 27,070

Lismore, the hinterland's commercial centre, appears to have been dropped into its green surroundings without ruffling the feathers of the pristine hinterland. The town itself sits on the Wilson River, though it has yet to take advantage of this, and is otherwise beautified by a liberal supply of heritage and art deco buildings, and a thriving artistic community. Students from Southern Cross University add to the town's eclecticism.

◉ Sights & Activities

Koala Care Centre   WILDLIFE REFUGE
(☑6622 1233; Rifle Range Rd; per person/family $5/10; ◎tours 10am & 2pm Mon-Fri, 10am Sat) The Koala Care Centre is home to recovering koalas and well worth a visit. To get a glimpse of platypuses, head to the northern end of Kadina St and walk up to **Tucki Tucki Creek** at dawn or sunset. You can also spot fuzzy grey bums-in-the-gums at **Robinson's Lookout** (Robinson's Ave, Girards Hill).

Walking Track   WALKING TRACK
Wilson River walking track starts in the CBD and skirts the river. Along the way you'll pass a **bush tucker garden**, nurturing the once daily diet of the Widjabal people, traditional owners of the land.

Lismore Regional Art Gallery   ART GALLERY
(☑6622 2209; www.lismoregallery.com.au; 131 Molesworth St; admission by donation; ◎10am-4pm Tue-Sat, to 6pm Thu) Lismore's diminutive gallery has just enough space for two visiting exhibitions, but the curators do it justice by showing excellent works.

🛏 Sleeping & Eating

With a couple of exceptions, Lismore is not a motel mecca. Most people stay in the hinterland's villages or closer to the coast. Its **farmers market** (☑6621 5916; ⊗8am-11am Sat) and **Organic Market** (☑6628 2391; ⊗8-11am Tue) are at the showground, off the Nimbin road.

TOP CHOICE **Howard's**   CAFE, DELI **$**
(106 Keen St; www.howardsdeli.com.au; mains $8-20; ⊗breakfast & lunch) Stop. Go no further than this deli-cum-cafe-cum-butchery, a Babette's feast of wholesome salads, meaty lasagnes, hearty frittatas and the like. For picnics, the shelves are stocked with gourmet chutney, oil and coffee, and if you're camping the house-made snags and fresh cuts of meat are fodder for the barbie.

Blue Tongue   CAFE **$**
(☑6622 0750; 43 Bridge St; mains $8-19; ⊗breakfast & lunch) One of a couple of worthy cafes on the quieter side of the river, this one is in a wonderfully worn building. Great BLATs, toasted Turkish sandwiches and fine coffee can be enjoyed in a sunny courtyard out the back.

Mecca   CAFE, BAR **$**
(☑6621 3901; 80 Magellan St; meals $8-16; ⊗7am-5pm Mon-Wed, 7am-late Thu-Sat) A stodgy old caff has been reborn as a retro-hip scenester playground. Lots of local musicians hang out at the pavement tables sipping the excellent coffee by day and jamming till late weekend nights.

Lismore Palms   CARAVAN PARK **$**
(☑6621 7067; 42 Brunswick St; camp sites/cabins from $20/70; 🐾) The best of Lismore's caravan parks, this one is right on the river and has 13 self-contained cabins.

Karinga   MOTEL **$$**
(☑6621 2787; www.karingamotel.com; 258 Molesworth St; s/d $95/105; ❄@🐾) The pick of the litter, the Karinga has had a tasteful facelift: the rooms have been fully refurbished and a funky pool and spa installed.

Lismore Pie Cart   PIES
(☑6622 2946; 11 Magellan St; ⊗6am-5pm Mon-Fri) Serves homemade pies, mashed potato, mushy peas and gravy.

Goanna Bakery & Café   BAKERY, CAFE
(☑6622 2629; 171 Keen St; mains $6-10; ⊗breakfast & lunch Mon-Sat) House-roasted coffee and enticing veggie meals at tables inside or out.

🛍 Shopping

More than a half-dozen secondhand book stores are within a block of the intersection of Carrington and Magellan Sts. Typical is **Noahs Arc** (www.noahsarcbookstore.com.au; 66 Magellan St), which has a large selection in a heritage building.

ℹ Information

Lismore visitor centre (☑1300 369 795; www.visitlismore.com.au; cnr Molesworth & Ballina Sts) Has internet, a rainforest display and local indigenous art. Kids dig the Heritage Park playground and skate park, next to the centre.

ℹ Getting There & Away

Lismore may well have the most helpful transit centre in NSW. It's right on Molesworth St by the gallery.

Kirklands (☑6622 1499; www.kirklands.com.au) runs to Byron Bay ($15, 50 minutes, two to three times daily). **Waller's** (☑6687 8550) school buses run to Nimbin ($10, 70 minutes).

Nimbin

📞02 / POP 350

A true product of the hippie era and the legendary 1973 Aquarius Festival, Nimbin works so hard at being alternative it's almost mainstream. But not too mainstream. 'Bra' is still an abbreviation for brass here even if the tattoos are still red around the edges and the didgeridoo players went to the best Sydney schools. Characters young and old prowl the streets and there are numerous businesses and community centres that attest to the unique culture found locally.

Nimbin is a study in contrasts. At noon when the hordes of bused-in day-trippers from Byron are prowling the streets in gaggles while being hectored by pot dealers it can all seem literally like a bad trip. (This scene took a hit in 2008 when a huge force of heavily armed state police made mass arrests of pot dealers.)

At other times when the true locals are dominant, you get a sense of the real Nimbin, where anyone searching for a real rainbow might just find it.

⊙ Sights & Activities

Despite the reticence of many locals to be pinned down on exact opening times, for fear of ruining Nimbin's image, generally everything is open 10am to 5pm. Every third and fifth Sunday, Nimbin has its own **market** (⊗8am-4pm), a spectacular affair of pro-

The **Rainforest Way** (www.rainforestway.com.au) is a touring route that takes in the hinterland's lovely meandering roads, national parks and charming little villages. You can see quite a bit of it by following the portion from Lismore north through the Channon, Nimbin, Uki and Murwillumbah.

If you can, time your visit to the **Channon** for the second Sunday of each month for a true classic hinterlands craft market. Other times you'll find a cafe and old pub where you can chill out and find out about the many idiosyncratic B&Bs hidden in the hills. **Eternity Springs B&B** (☑6688 6385; www.eternitysprings.com; 483 Tuntable Creek Rd; camping per person $12, s/d from $50/110) and **Havan's** (☑6688 6108; www.rainbowregion.com/havan; Lot 1, Lawler Rd; s/d $85/125) are true eco-haven options with the requisite wildlife and greenery.

Uki (uke-i) is a cute little village tucked between the surging Tweed River and the dominating peak of Wolllumbin-Mt Warning. It has a couple of galleries and a second-hand bookshop. The **visitor information centre** (☑6679 5399; ⊙10am-3pm Mon-Sat), run by volunteers, has details of the nearby national parks. Note the **memorial** at the town crossroads. The sheer number of names attests to the profound impact the 20th century's world wars had on small country towns.

The fully accessible **Uki Guesthouse** (☑6679 5777; www.ukiguesthouse.com.au; Mitchell St; s/d $110/135; @🖕🖤) is in an old weatherboard house overlooking the crossroads. The **Uki Café** (1 Rowlands Creek Rd; ⊙breakfast & lunch daily, dinner Fri & Sat), serves good food on a sweeping verandah, or by a damp-banishing potbelly stove inside.

duce, live music and art where locals revel in their culture. Plans are afoot for a **skate park**. Keep your board handy.

Hemp Embassy
MUSEUM
(☑6689 1842; www.hempembassy.net; 51 Cullen St) Opposite the museum, this place raises consciousness about marijuana legalisation, as well as providing all the tools and fashion items you'll need to get high (or at least attract police attention). The embassy leads the Mardi Gras festival each May. Smokers are welcome at the tiny Hemp Bar next door, which is like Haight-Ashbury in a bottle.

Nimbin Candle Factory
CANDLE FACTORY
(☑6689 1010; www.nimbincandles.com.au) Just 400m down the hill from town and off the Murwillumbah road, the Old Butter Factory now incubates a number of little businesses including the candle factory, redolent with wax. Thousands of hand-dipped paraffin candles are on display.

Nimbin Museum & Café
MUSEUM
(☑6689 1123; www.nimbinmuseum.com; 62 Cullen St) An interpretive and expressionistic museum that packs an eclectic collection of local art into a modest space. It's far more a work of art than of history.

Nimbin Artists Gallery
GALLERY
(☑6689 1444; 47 Cullen St; ⊙10am-4pm) Nimbin has more artists than pot dealers and you can find their work on display here.

🛏 Sleeping

Given that some locals would have a hard time answering the question 'Which came first, Nimbin or the organic farms?', it shouldn't surprise that there are nearly 100 local farms more than happy to host volunteers willing to yank weeds and perform other chores. The international Willing Workers on Organic Farms (www.wwoof. com.au) coordinates many such programs.

Nimbin Rox YHA Hostel
HOTEL $
(☑6689 0022; www.nimbinrox.com; 74 Thornburn St; dm/d from $28/60; @🖤) Rox has hammocks, permaculture gardens, craft workshops, live bands, Thai massage, yurts ($72), tepees (per person $25) and camping (per person $15) plus a heated pool. Check out the website, a trip in itself.

Rainbow Retreat Backpackers
HOSTEL $
(☑6689 1262; www.rainbowretreat.net; 75 Thorburn St; dm $20, d from $40) Very basic, but totally in the age-of-Aquarius spirit. Relax, chill out, sleep in a shack ($30), gypsy van ($30 to $50) or camp out ($13). There's a free courtesy bus from Byron Bay.

Black Sheep Farm
GUESTHOUSE $$
(☑6689 1095; www.blacksheepfarm.com.au; near Nightcap National Park; d $195) With a saltwater pool and Finnish sauna, guests might struggle to leave the self-contained cabin on the edge of a rainforest. It sleeps up to seven

people (per extra person $20). There's also a smaller and cheaper cottage available. Other recommendations:

Nimbin Hotel & Backpackers PUB ROOMS $
(☎6689 1246; www.nimbinhotelandbackpackers. com; 53 Cullen St; dm/d $30/60; @) The two- and four-bed rooms in the town's veteran pub are tidy and open onto the classic, shaded verandah.

Nimbin Caravan & Tourist Park
CARAVAN PARK $
(☎6689 1402; 29 Sibley St; camp sites from $16; ⌘) A simple place with three dozen sites next to the local swimming pool, down Cullen St past the Nimbin Hotel.

✗ Eating & Drinking

A number of coffee places tenuously exist along the pavement.

Nimbin Hotel MODERN AUSTRALIAN $
(☎6689 1246; Cullen St; meals $7-15) The classic local boozer. A vast covered porch out the back overlooks a verdant valley. Inside, artistic photos of regulars grace the walls and there's actually a slight hint of minimalist style. The fare is typical pub grub; there's live music many Friday nights.

Rainbow Café CAFE $
(☎6689 1997; 64a Cullen St; mains $6-13; ⊘breakfast & lunch) Murals cover the walls of this thumping Nimbin institution serving generous burgers, wraps, nachos and salads. The leafy courtyard has a familiar whiff.

Nimbin Trattoria & Pizzeria ITALIAN $$
(☎6689 1427; 70 Cullen St; mains $10-20; ⊘lunch Fri-Sun, dinner daily) Outstanding pizzas ($4 a slice) and delicious pastas. Live music every Thursday.

❶ Information

Nimbin is actually a tiny village, easily walked in a few minutes. Most businesses are on Cullen St. There's lots of parking out the back.

The **Nimbin Visitors Centre** (☎6689 1388; www.visitlismore.com; Cullen St; ⊘10am-4pm Mon-Sat) in the heart of town has accommodation options, bus tickets and a wealth of knowledge. The community website (www.nimbinweb. com.au) is useful. Blow your mind listening to 2NIM 102.3FM.

❶ Getting There & Around

The **Nimbin Tours & Shuttle Bus** (☎6680 9189; www.nimbinaustralia.com/nimbinshuttle/ nimbin.html) runs between Byron Bay, Nimbin and Uki with optional stops at Wollumbin-Mt Warning. The bus leaves from the visitor centre.

Several outfits run shuttles and tours for day trippers from Byron Bay (p165); some include stops in the region at natural wonders and small towns. The tours charge $25 to $40 depending on the itinerary and time of year, but most offer a lower rate if you just want to get to or from Nimbin.

Waller's (☎6687 8550) For a traditional trip (as it were), Waller's school buses run to Lismore. **Gosel's** (☎0427 149 689) school buses run to Uki, Murwillumbah (90 minutes) via Uki and the Wollumbin–Mt Warning turn-off.

Murwillumbah

⬛02 / POP 7950

Sitting on the banks of the wide Tweed River, Murwillumbah bridges the mist-shrouded hills that include Wollumbin-Mt Warning to the west and the broad, green fertile river plain to the east. It's a scenic spot and well worth the detour off the Pacific Hwy. It is also the gateway to the Border Ranges National Park and is a key point on the Rainforest Way driving tour. The compact centre is good for a stroll and a stop in a cafe.

◉ Sights

Tweed River Regional Art Gallery
ART GALLERY
(☎6670 2790; www.tweed.nsw.gov.au/artgallery; cnr Mistral Rd & Tweed Valley Way; ⊘10am-5pm Wed-Sun) This exceptional gallery is an architectural delight and home to some of Australia's finest in a variety of media.

Murwillumbah Museum MUSEUM
(☎6672 1865; 2 Queensland Rd; adult/child $2/1.50; ⊘11am-3pm Wed-Fri & 4th Sun of month) The town's small museum is housed in a beautiful old building and features a solid account of local history and an interesting radio room.

Tropical Fruit World FRUIT FARM
(☎6677 7222; www.tropicalfruitworld.com.au; Duranbah Rd; adult/child/family $37/20/85) North of town, this place has plantation safaris, tastings and a jungle cruise. Plan for at least half a day to make the most of the pricey entry.

⛱ Sleeping & Eating

Mount Warning-Murwillumbah YHA
HOSTEL $
(☎6672 3763; www.yha.com.au; 1 Tumbulgum Rd; dm/d from $32/70) This former river captain's home offers free ice cream at night, plus

Testament to its natural beauty, the far north coast hinterland has not one, not two, but three national parks, all of them home to cascading waterfalls, mystical creeks, ancient volcanos and bountiful, near-extinct flora and fauna. The World Heritage–listed Gondwana Rainforest runs through all of them in an ecological tapestry stitched 50 million years ago when it was part of the supercontinent Gondwana. It would be a crime, of sorts, to visit the area without living and breathing at least one of the parks.

Nightcap National Park

South of Murwillumbah, north of Lismore and bordering Nimbin and the Channon, **Nightcap National Park** (8080 hectares) is home to the bent-winged bat, the wompoo pigeon, the masked owl and the red-legged pademelon (a type of wallaby). The spectacular waterfalls and sheer cliff walls are perhaps expected from somewhere with the highest annual rainfall in NSW. The exposed rock pinnacles of the **Sphinx** can be seen from Lismore, and **Mt Nardi** (800m) offers a challenging climb.

The historic **Nightcap Track** (16km) passes through here and was originally used by postal workers in the late 19th and early 20th century. **Rummery Park** is not far off the road down from the falls and is a well-provided picnic spot. **Peate's Mountain Lookout**, just on from Rummery Park, gives you a great panoramic view from Jerusalem Mountain in the north, to Byron Bay in the east. There's a **platypus-viewing** platform at Rocky Creek Dam picnic area. **Alstonville NPWS office** (☑6627 0200; Colonial Arcade, 75 Main St) has more information.

Wollumbin-Mt Warning National Park

Southwest of Murwillumbah, **Wollumbin National Park** (which includes the former Mt Warning National Park and now covers 4117 hectares) is home to Wollumbin-Mt Warning (1156m), the most dramatic feature of the hinterland, towering over the valley.

Captain Cook aptly named this mountain in 1770 to warn seafarers of the offshore reefs. Today it has reverted to its Aboriginal name, Wollumbin, meaning all of these: 'cloud catcher', 'fighting chief of the mountain' and 'weather maker'.

Its peak is the first part of mainland Australia to be touched by sunlight each day, a drawcard that sees many people make the 9km, five-hour round-trip trek to the top from Breakfast Creek. You should be aware that, under the law of the local Bundjalung people, only specific people are allowed to climb the mountain and, out of respect, they ask you not to go. The 200m **Lyrebird Track** is an alternative, if not a very challenging one. The NPWS Murwillumbah visitor centre (p184) has more information.

Border Ranges National Park

West again, and covering 31,729 hectares, **Border Ranges National Park**, covers the NSW side of the McPherson Range, which runs along the NSW–Queensland border, and some of its outlying spurs. It has been estimated that a quarter of all bird species in Australia can be found here.

To set eyes on a few, try the rugged **Tweed Range Scenic Drive** – gravel and usable in dry weather – which loops through the park from Lillian Rock (midway between Uki and Kyogle) to Wiangaree (north of Kyogle on the Woodenbong road). The signposting on access roads isn't good (when in doubt take roads signposted to the national park), but it's well worth the effort of finding it.

The road runs through mountain forest, with steep hills and breathtaking lookouts over the Tweed Valley to Wollumbin-Mt Warning and the coast. The seemingly perilous walk out to the **Pinnacle** – about half an hour's walk from the road and back – is not for agoraphobics, but it is one of the best places to see the silhouette of Wollumbin-Mt Warning against a rising sun. At **Antarctic Beech** there is a forest of 2000-year-old Antarctic beeches. From here, a walking track (about 5km) leads down to lush rainforest, swimming holes and a picnic area ar **Brindle Creek**. The road leads here too. **Kyogle NPWS office** (☑6632 0000; 136 Summerland Way) has more information.

canoe and bike hire. Tours to Wollumbin-Mt Warning are reason enough to stay here.

Sugar Beat
CAFE $

(⌖6672 2330; Shop 2, 6-8 Commercial Rd; mains $15; ⊘breakfast & lunch) Park yourself by the sunny window, settle into a corner of the long bench seating or take in the scene from one of the pavement tables. There's cafe-style fusion fare and locally famous baked goods.

Murwillumbah Motor Inn
MOTEL $$

(⌖6672 2022; www.murwillumbahmotorinn.com.au; 17 Byangum Rd; s/d $96/106; ❋@✱) These clean and comfortable rooms are a great option away from the town centre. The deluxe rooms have flat-screen televisions. There's a pleasant courtyard out the back.

Imperial Hotel
PUB $

(⌖6672 2777; 115 Main St; s/d without bathroom $39/77, d $55) It's hard to miss this pink pub on the main street. The grand old pub rooms are shabby chic without even trying. Downstairs is a decent bistro.

New Leaf Café
VEGETARIAN $

(⌖6672 2667; Shop 10, Murwillumbah Plaza; meals $5-18; ⊘breakfast & lunch; ☒) The food here is creative and vegetarian, with plenty of Middle Eastern flavours and salads on offer. Dine inside, alfresco, or takeaway.

Modern Grocer
DELI $$

(⌖6672 5007; Shop 3, 1 Wollumbin St; ⊘Tue-Sat) A foodie haven to turn everyday picnics into gluttonous feasts.

❶ Information

Visitors centre (⌖6672 1340; www.tweed coolangatta.com.au; cnr Alma St & Tweed Valley Way) Has national park info and passes, a great rainforest display and a prime position on the Tweed River.

❶ Getting There & Away

Greyhound (⌖1300 473 946; www.greyhound.com.au) and **Premier** (⌖13 34 10; www.premiermerms.com.au) have services several times daily on the Sydney ($92, 14 hours) and Brisbane ($27, two hours) routes.

Gosel's (⌖0427 149 689) has school-day buses to Nimbin (90 minutes) via Uki.

FAR NORTH COAST

This is where the coast heats up in activity, hype and temperature. Byron Bay is the centre of the attention, with its nightlife, stunning location and beach. But there are places with equal beauty that are quieter. Lennox Head and its surrounds are more serene than the tourist Babylon to the north, while Yamba offers some colour on its estuary.

Coupled with the beaches and ideal subtropical climate are rivers rich in appeal. The Clarence River vies to be the most beautiful in NSW, such as its striking blueness. The Richmond and Tweed Rivers sprawl out into rich deltas and provide wide vistas. Many visitors simply come for the weather: warm winters and long, hot summers.

Lennox Head

⌖02 / POP 6620

Classified as a protected National Surfing Reserve – à la the surfing mecca of Angourie – Lennox Head is home to picturesque coastline with some of the best surf on the coast, including long right-hander breaks. Its blossoming food scene combined with a laid-back atmosphere makes it an alternative to its boisterous well-touristed neighbour Byron, 19km north, although its small main street can get crowded.

◉ Sights & Activities

Beaches
BEACH

Stunning **Seven Mile Beach** runs along parallel to the main street. The best places for a dip are at the north end near the surf club or at the southern end in the Channel. **Port Morton lookout** is a whale- and dolphin-spotting high point.

Lake Ainsworth, a lagoon just back from the surf club, is made brown by tannins from the tea trees along its banks, which also make swimming here beneficial to the skin.

Outdoor Activities
OUTDOOR ACTIVITIES

If the wind's up, **Wind & Water Action Sports** (⌖0419 686 188; www.windnwater.net; from $80) has kite-boarding, windsurfing and surf lessons, plus hire equipment. **Seabreeze Hang Gliding** (⌖0428 560 248; www.seabreezehanggliding.com; from $95) offers tandem flights off Lennox Headland.

✕ Eating & Sleeping

Professionals (⌖6687 7579; www.professionalslennoxhead.com.au; 66 Ballina St) is a good agent for holiday rentals.

Lennox Lodge
HOSTEL $

(⌖6687 7210; www.lennoxlodge.com.au; 20 Byron St; s/d $25/80; @✱) This motel-style backpacker place is daubed in mustard paint and dotted with palm trees and frangipanis. The atmosphere is relaxed, and with a maximum of four people to each room, with bathroom, it's comfortable.

Lennox Head Beach House HOSTEL $
(☑6687 7636; www.yha.com.au; 3 Ross St; dm/d $28/78) YHA-affiliated and only 100m from the beach, this place has immaculate rooms and a great vibe. For $5 you can use the boards, sailboards and bikes.

Lake Ainsworth Holiday Park
CARAVAN PARK $
(☑6687 7249; www.ballinabeachside.com.au; Pacific Pde; unpowered/powered sites $27/29, cabins from $80) The family-friendly vibe here is endearing. The park sits on flat, green grass just opposite the beach and near the lake.

O-pes MEDITERRANEAN $$
(☑6687 7388; 90-92 Ballina St; mains $25; ☺breakfast Sat & Sun; lunch & dinner daily) Comfy couches and low-slung tables mix it with a beachfront vibe and vista. The menu balances casual tapas with more formal à la carte dishes.

Lennox Bistro MODERN AUSTRALIAN $$
(☑6687 5769; 17-19 Pacific Pde; mains $22; ☺lunch & dinner) Within the Lennox Point Hotel, this local hang-out cooks up gastro-bistro fare. Its upstairs balcony is also the best place for a beer with your eye to a wave.

ⓘ Getting There & Away
Blanch's Bus Service (☑6686 2144; www.blanchs.com.au) Operates a service to Ballina ($6.40, 15 minutes), Mullumbimby ($10, one hour) and Byron Bay ($7.60, 30 minutes).

Ballina
☑02 / POP 16,480
Crossing the Richmond River marks the end of the fishing villages and the beginning of the tourist-driven economy. Ballina is a sign of the times, basing its appeal around family holidays and nature activities. Although it likes to tout itself as a quiet alternative to Byron, Ballina is fast developing along the riverfront.

The Pacific Hwy approaches from the north and turns into River St, the main drag. A bypass due for completion by 2012 will whack off the Pacific Hwy's clogged route

through Ballina to the benefit of the town and drivers.

⦿ Sights & Activities
For a good sampling of local history, stroll the length of **Norton Street**, which boasts a number of impressive late-19th-century buildings from Ballina's days as a rich lumber town. For architecture (and intrigue) of a different kind, the dilapidated **Big Prawn** is 1km west of town

Beaches BEACH
White and sandy, like all good beaches, **Shelly Beach** is patrolled. Calm **Shaws Bay Lagoon** is popular with families. **South Ballina Beach** is a good excursion option via the car **ferry** on Burns Point Ferry Rd.

Naval & Maritime Museum MUSEUM
(Regatta Ave; admission by donation; ☺9am-4pm) Behind the information centre, this museum is where you will find the amazing remains of a balsawood raft that drifted across the Pacific from Ecuador as part of the Las Balsas expedition in 1973.

Richmond River Cruises CRUISE
(☑6687 6688; Regatta Ave; 2hr trip adult/child $25/13; ☺noon & 2pm Wed, Sat & Sun) This is the most established cruise service and is wheelchair friendly. It has lunch and dinner cruises, as well as morning and afternoon tea cruises.

Aboriginal Cultural Concepts
INDIGENOUS CULTURE
(☑0405 654 280; www.aboriginalculturalcon cepts.com; ☺10am-1pm Wed-Sat; from $80) Get an Indigenous insight into the local area; these heritage tours explore mythological sights along the Bundjalung Coast. The three-hour bush-tucker tour is popular.

Cycling CYCLING
Ballina's many waterways are lined with paths. **Jack Ransom Cycles** (16 Cherry St) rents out bikes from $20 per day.
Other activities:

Ballina Boat Hire BOAT HIRE
(☑6681 6115; cnr Brunswick St & Winton Lane; per half-day $90) Has tinnies for fishing and catamarans for the more adventurous.

Ballina Ocean Tours
WILDLIFE-WATCHING, SNORKELLING
(☑0408 863 999; www.ballinaoceantours.com; tours from $45) Has whale- and dolphin-watching tours, snorkelling and various other exciting aquatic diversions.

Summerland Surf School　　　SURFING
(www.summerlandsurfschool.com.au; Pacific Hwy;
⊙9am-5pm; 2-5hr from $50) Lessons just
south of Ballina in Evans Head.

Thursday Plantation　　　TEA-TREE OIL
(www.thursdayplantation.com; Pacific Hwy;
⊙9am-5pm) Just north of Ballina, an
established vendor of products made with
tea-tree oil.

🛏 Sleeping

River St and the northern approach from
the Pacific Hwy both have many motels to
choose from. Among the local holiday-rental
agents is **Ballina Professionals** (☑6686
3511; www.professionalsballina.com.au; cnr Martin
& River Sts).

TOP CHOICE **Ballina Manor**　　　GUESTHOUSE $$$
(☑6681 5888; www.ballinamanor.com.au;
25 Norton St; r $165-375; ❄❅) One of the best
places to stay in the region, this boutique ho-
tel began in the 1920s as an Edwardian-style
girls' school. The 12 rooms have been beauti-
fully restored and boast many antiques. The
small restaurant serves dinner.

Ramada Ballina　　　HOTEL $$
(☑1800 826 181; www.ramadaballina.com.au; 2
Martin St; r from $160; ❄❅❆) Part of a flash
development right on the river, the Ramada
has large rooms that come with king-sized
bed, work desk, spa tub and balcony with
great views. One-bedroom apartments are
available. The swish cafe is popular with local scenesters.

Ballina Heritage Inn　　　HOTEL $$
(☑6686 0505; www.ballinaheritageinn.com.au;
229 River St; d $130; ❄❅) In the centre of
town, this tidy inn has neat, bright and
comfortable rooms that are a significant
leap in quality from the nearby motels.
Some rooms have spas.

Ballina Travellers Lodge　　　HOTEL $
(☑6686 6737; www.ballinatravellerslodge.com.au;
36-38 Tamar St; s/d/tw $69/92/97; ❄@❅❆)
In a quiet residential street, this lodge
combines motel and hostel guests. It is
clean and comfortable and the owners are
a good source of info.

Shaws Bay Caravan Park　　　CARAVAN PARK $
(☑6686 2326; www.ballinabeachside.com.au; 1
Brighton St; camp sites/cabins from $31/105; ❅)
Right on the lagoon, this low-key park is
an easy walk to the centre. There are 123
sites.

🍴 Eating

Evolution Espresso Bar　　　CAFE, BAR $
(☑6681 4095; Martin St; mains $12-18; ⊙break-
fast & lunch, dinner Fri & Sat; @❅) Sniff hard
enough and the fresh coffee aroma emanat-
ing from this cool little cafe might lead you
off the highway. It has light meals, cakes,
couches and a bar looking towards the Rich-
mond River.

La Cucina di Vino　　　ITALIAN $$
(☑6618 1195; cnr Martin & Fawcett Sts; mains
$15-30; ⊙lunch daily, dinner Wed-Sun) Water
views and an open corner locale make this
Italian restaurant an excellent venue for
a long lunch. Short on time? There's pizza
too. Its authenticity surprises every time.

Other recommendations:

Healthy Noodle Bar　　　ASIAN $
(☑6686 6632; 216 River St; mains $10; ⊙lunch &
dinner) One of several cheap and cheerful
takeaways on this little strip. Singapore
fried noodles with extra peppers and
garlic will have you singing.

Shelly's on the Beach　　　CAFE $
(☑6686 9844; Shelly Beach Rd; meals $9-18;
⊙breakfast & lunch) The mist from the surf
over the dunes will help perk up your
tired cheeks. The fine brekkies and lunchtime sambos will fuel your day.

Pelican 181　　　FISH & CHIPS $
(☑6686 9181; 12-24 Fawcett St; meals $6-20;
⊙breakfast, lunch & dinner) A breezy fish-and-
chips restaurant and takeaway right on
the river. Prawn baguettes are irresistible
for many.

Wicked　　　MEDITERRANEAN $$
(☑6686 2564; 37 Cherry St; mains $24-30; ⊙din-
ner Wed-Sun) Global tastes flavour the excel-
lent seafood at this chic open-air bistro.

ℹ Information

For internet access, try Evolution Espresso Bar.

Visitors centre (☑6686 3484; www.discov
erballina.com; cnr Lasbalsas Plaza & River
St) Has detailed information on surrounding
attractions.

ℹ Getting There & Around

If you're driving to Byron Bay, take the coast
road through Lennox Head. It's much prettier
than the Pacific Hwy and less traffic-clogged
as well.

Air

Ballina's airport (BNK) is the best way to reach
Byron Bay – only 30km to the north. It has car-

rental desks and plenty of local transport options. Airline service is increasing.

Jetstar (☎13 15 38; www.jetstar.com.au) Serves Sydney.

Regional Express (☎13 17 13; www.regionalexpress.com.au) Serves Sydney.

Virgin Blue (☎13 67 89; www.virginblue.com.au) Serves Melbourne via Sydney.

Bus

Greyhound (☎1300 473 946; www.greyhound.com.au) heads north to Byron ($17, 40 minutes) and Brisbane ($55, three hours) and south to Sydney ($137, 12 hours). **Premier** (☎13 34 10; www.premierms.com.au) heads south to Sydney ($97, 11 hours).

Blanch's Bus Service (☎6686 2144; www.blanchs.com.au) operates several daily services from the airport and the Tamar St bus stops to Lennox Head ($6.40, 30 minutes/15 minutes), Byron Bay ($9.60, 70 minutes/40 minutes) and Mullumbimby ($10, 85 minutes/95 minutes).

CountryLink (☎13 22 32; www.countrylink.info) has buses connecting to trains at the Casino train station (70 minutes).

Shuttles

Numerous shuttle companies meet flights and serve Ballina, Byron Bay and other nearby towns. Rates average $15 to $20.

Airport Express (☎0414 660 031; www.stevestours.com.au)

Byron Easy Bus (☎6685 7447; www.byronbayshuttle.com.au)

Yamba & Angourie

☎02

Once a sleepy little fishing town, **Yamba** (population 5514) is slowly distancing itself from this reputation by attracting a fan base that has cottoned on to the merits of beaches on three fronts, a relaxed pace and excellent food without too much encroaching development.

Its southern neighbour **Angourie** (population 169) is home to NSW's first National Surfing Reserve and has always been a hot spot for experienced surfers (the type who were born on a board, wear helmets and leap off rocks). It complements Yamba's can-do attitude by remaining a small chilled-out place. Apart from the surf, the only sign of development is the Pacific St home (mansion) of Gordon Merchant, founder of the surf brand Billabong, who grew up here (and who, by all accounts, still gets around in boardshorts).

◉ Sights & Activities

Blue Pools NATURE RESERVE
These springwater-fed water holes are the remains of the quarry used for the breakwall. Locals and the daring climb the 'chalkline', 'tree-line' or 'death-line' cliff faces and plunge to their depths. The saner can slip silently into clear water, surrounded by bush, only metres from the surf.

Beaches BEACH
Surfing for the big boys is at **Angourie Point** but Yamba's beaches have something for everyone else. When the surf is flat **Pippi's** is decent, especially when dolphins hang around. **Main Beach** is the busiest, with an ocean pool, banana palms and a grassy slope for those who don't want sand up their clacker. **Convent Beach** is a sunbaker's haven and **Turner's**, protected by the breakwall, is ideal for surf lessons.

Iluka Nature Reserve NATURE RESERVE
World Heritage–listed Iluka is a short detour off the highway or a ferry ride away; it's the southern end of **Bundjalung National Park** (per car per day $7), largely untouched and best explored with 4WD. Highlights include the literally named Ten Mile Beach and the hopefully not-literally named Hell Hole Lagoon. The passenger-only **Clarence River Ferry** (☎6646 6423; www.clarenceriverferries.com; adult/child $8/3) runs four times daily.

Yamba-Angourie Surf School SURFING
(☎6646 1496; www.yamba-angouriesurfschool.com.au; 2hr lessons $50) Classes here are run by an Australian surfing champion. To go it alone, rent boards of all shapes and sizes, including mini-mals, from the **Plank Shop** (☎6645 8362; Clarence St, Yamba).

Rockfish Cruises CRUISES
(☎0447 458 153; www.rockfish.com.au; The Marina, Yamba Rd) Lovely owners Di and Pete offer barbecue-lunch cruises on the Clarence River (11am to 2pm, budget/gourmet $55/75); passengers can swim clinging onto the boom nets. There are also romantic sunset cruises (departures at sunset; $55) and three-hour whale-watching cruises (9.30am departures from late May to mid-November; $95).

Walking & Cycling WALKING, CYCLING
A walking and cycling track winds around the peaks and troughs of Yamba's coastline. The prettiest bit is from Pippi's Beach around Lovers Point to Convent Beach. **Xtreme Cycle & Skate** (☎6645 8879;

34 Coldstream St; adult half-/full day $15/25, child $10/15) has bikes for rent.

Yamba Kayak KAYAKING

(☑6646 1137; www.yambakayak.com.au; Whiting Beach car park; 3hr adult/child $70/60) Half- and full-day adventures are a speciality, including multiday pub crawls – or pub paddles – stopping at heritage hotels along the Clarence River.

Other options:

Sunday Jazz Cruise CRUISE

(☑0408 664 556; adult/child $30/15; ⊙11am-3pm) River cruise with licensed bar. The same folk also do a **Hardwood Island cruise** (adult/child $20/10; ⊙Wed & Frid 11am-3pm).

Yuraygir Coastal Walk WALKING

Begins in Angourie; see p185.

Yamba River Markets MARKET

(www.rivermarkets.weloveyamba.com; Ford Park) Fourth Sunday of month, on the Clarence River.

Story House Museum MUSEUM

(☑6646 2316; River St; adult/child $3/50c; ⊙10am-4.30pm Tue, Wed & Thu, 2-4.30pm Sat & Sun) Photos tell the story of the once pervasive local maritime culture. Check out details of the dozens of shipwrecks.

🛏 Sleeping

TOP CHOICE **Yamba YHA** HOSTEL $

(☑6646 3997; www.yha.com.au; 26 Coldstream St; dm/d $30/80; ❄@🏊) Spankingly modern and groovy, this is a purpose-built hostel with an excellent downstairs bar and restaurant (mains $9 to $29). Upstairs there's a rooftop deck, small pool and barbecue area. It's family run and extremely welcoming. After sampling one of Shane's '10-buck' welcome tours, you're guaranteed to extend your stay.

Pacific Hotel PUB, MOTEL $

(☑6646 2466; www.pacifichotelyamba.com.au; 18 Pilot St, Yamba; dm $35, r with/without bathroom $120/60) This is a fabulous pub overlooking the ocean, with bright bunk rooms and handsome hotel rooms. It would be remiss to come to Yamba without sampling a beer with this kind of view but the food is also exceptional – a lofty step above the usual pub nosh.

Angourie Rainforest Resort RESORT $$$

(☑6646 8600; www.angourieresort.com.au; 166 Angourie Rd, Angourie; r $140-355; ❄@🏊) A little piece of paradise sidled up to 600

hectares of fauna. Luxuries include a pool, tennis court, restaurant and day spa. Extras include a pristine rainforest aroma and resident birds and lizards.

Surf Motel MOTEL $$

(☑6646 2200; 2 Queen St; r $120-300; ❄) On a bluff overlooking the main beach, this modern, seven-room place is across from a large green. Rooms are quite big and have balcony and kitchenette. It's blissfully quiet, aside from the sound of the surf.

Calypso Holiday Park CARAVAN PARK $

(☑6646 2468; www.calypsoyamba.com.au; Harbour St; camp sites from $26, cabins $77-155; ❄@) The best-located camping place, Calypso is a short walk from the town centre and all the beaches. There are 162 sites and 32 cabins, some quite posh.

🍴 Eating, Drinking & Entertainment

TOP CHOICE **Gorman's Restaurant** SEAFOOD $$$

(☑6646 2025; Yamba Bay; mains $30; ⊙dinner) Tucked away behind Calypso Holiday Park, this seafood restaurant, hanging out over the water, is a Yamba institution. The greenhouse decor is a flashback to the '70s. Happily, so is the menu – few places still do 'bugs thermidor' and 'garlic prawns' quite like this place.

El Pirata TAPAS $$

(☑6646 3276; 6 Clarence St, Yamba; ⊙dinner Tue-Sun) This is a fabulous tapas bar serving authentic hot and cold Spanish dishes including *jamon* (ham), chorizo, oily garlic prawns and cheesy stuffed peppers ($9 to $18). It's at its best during the summer months when the Sydney owners are back in town.

Yamba Bar & Grill STEAK $$$

(☑6646 1155; 15 Clarence St; mains $14-34; ⊙dinner Tue-Sun) This stylishly hip place is spacious, with a great rear deck and view. The menu is for serious steak-lovers, with sides right from the gastropub playbook: chips with aioli and rocket salad. There are a couple of other restaurants on this little strip.

Sounds Lounge Café CAFE $

(☑6646 3909; 16 Yamba Rd, Yamba; mains $5-18; ⊙breakfast & lunch; @🛜) There's a funky collection of CDs for sale at this idiosyncratic place in the centre. Smoothies, burgers, juices and coffees highlight the menu. There are tables inside and out.

Other options:

Frangipan MEDITERRANEAN $$$
(✆6646 2553; www.frangipan.com.au; 11-13 The Crescent, Angourie; mains $19-32; ⊙dinner Tue-Sat) It has won awards but local reviews are mixed.

Beachwood MIDDLE EASTERN $
(✆6646 9781; 22 High St) Tipped as the best breakfast in town.

Yamba Bowling Club CLUB
(✆6646 2305; 44 Wooli St) For regular live music, check the schedule here.

ℹ Information

There is no visitor centre (yet), but **Yamba YHA** (✆6646 3991; www.yambabackpackers.com.au; 26 Coldstream St) has the low-down on everything. Also check out http://weloveyamba.com.

ℹ Getting There & Around

Yamba is 15km east of the Pacific Hwy; turn off at the Yamba Rd intersection just south of the Clarence River.

Busways (✆1300 555 611; www.busways.com.au) buses go to Maclean ($6, 30 minutes) and Grafton ($11.20, 75 minutes, several Monday to Saturday). **CountryLink** (✆13 22 32; www.countrylink.info) buses go to Byron Bay ($14, three hours, one daily) and to Grafton, where they connect to Sydney ($75, 11½ hours). **Greyhound** (✆1300 473 946; www.greyhound.com.au) buses stop on runs south to Sydney ($127, 11½ hours) and north to Byron ($54, two hours).

Yamba to Grafton

Heading south on the Pacific Hwy the Clarence River, which meets the sea in Yamba, gives life to a beautiful and fertile valley along the way. The delta between Grafton and the coast is a patchwork of farmland in which the now sinuous and spreading Clarence River forms more than 100 islands, some very large.

The area is the end of sugar-cane country and the Queensland-style domestic architecture, wooden houses with high-pitched roofs perched on stilts to allow air circulation in the hot summers, will give way to more grounded styles. The burning of the cane fields (May to December) adds a smoky tang to the air.

Maclean (population 3245) is a picturesque little town that takes its Scottish heritage seriously. It sweeps alongside a lazy sprawl of the delta in vaguely Celtic fashion. Stroll the riverfront, check out the shops and have a cold one at one of the old hotels. The **Clarence Coast visitor centre** (✆6645 4121; Ferry Park, Pacific Hwy, Maclean), at the edge of town, can help with accommodation.

It's worth taking a small detour to **Ulmarra** (population 1586), a heritage-listed town with a river port. There's a quaint old corner **pub** (✆6644 5305; 2 Coldstream St; ⊙breakfast & lunch daily, dinner Fri & Sat) with a wrought-iron verandah, pub rooms (singles/doubles $40/65) and a greener-than-green beer garden that stretches down to the river, which can be crossed by car ferry 1km north of town.

Grafton

☑02 / POP 17,500

Grafton is a regional agricultural centre that has prominence due to its location on the Pacific Hwy. In fact it will give you a good taste of the vast NSW hinterlands and may well encourage you to keep right on driving. Still, it is pretty enough and in late October the streets are awash with the purple flowers of Brazilian jacaranda. For the road weary, there're just enough places to offer a choice.

Don't be fooled by the franchises along the highway: the main part of town is reached over an imposing 1932 double-decker (road and rail) bridge.

◉ Sights

Victoria Street HISTORIC BUILDINGS
Victoria St is the focal point of days gone by, with the **courthouse** (1862), **Roches Family Hotel** (1870), **Anglican Cathedral** (1884) and the private residence **Istria** (1899) providing glimpses of 19th-century architecture.

FREE **Grafton Regional Gallery** ART GALLERY
(✆6642 3177; 158 Fitzroy St; ⊙10am-4pm Tue-Sun) Running parallel to Victoria St, Fitzroy St is home to the town's art gallery, in a slightly grand 1880 house. With works by regional artists, it's a well-curated place and there are regular special exhibitions.

Nearby, **Schaeffer House** (1903) is where you'll find the **Clarence River Historical Society** (190 Fitzroy St; adult/child $3/1; ⊙1-4pm Tue, Wed, Thu & Sun), with its displays of treasures once littering attics across town.

INLAND FROM GRAFTON

The Clarence River is navigable as far upstream as the village of **Copmanhurst**, about 35km northwest of Grafton. Further upstream the Clarence River descends rapidly from the Gibraltar Range through the rugged **Clarence River Gorge**, a popular and challenging site for white-water canoeing.

Private property flanks the gorge. On the south side the land is owned by the Winters family, who allow day visitors and have cabin accommodation at **Winters' Shack** (✆6647 2173; camp sites per person $10, s/d $30/60). Access is via Copmanhurst. It's best to ring first to get permission and to arrange for the gates to be unlocked. On the north side, **Wave Hill Station** (✆6647 2145; www.wavehillfarmstay.com.au; camp sites $25, B&B d $80) has a homestead and accommodation plus 4WD or horse-riding trips to the gorge.

Heading southwest, there's an interesting route from Grafton to Armidale via Nymboida and Ebor, passing turn-offs to Dorrigo (p194) and the New England and Cathedral Rock National Parks. Heading west to Glen Innes, the Gwydir Hwy passes through the superb Washpool and Gibraltar Range National Parks.

✨ Festivals & Events

Horse Racing Carnival   HORSE RACING
(www.racenet.com.au/grafton-raceclub-nsw)
Every July; this is the richest horse-racing event in country Australia.

Jacaranda Festival   FLOWERS
(www.jacarandafestival.org.au) In the week joining October and November, Australia's longest-running floral festival sees Grafton come alive in an ocean of mauve.

Grafton Artsfest   ARTS
(www.artsfestgrafton.com) The local arts scene manifests itself twice yearly with workshops and exhibitions.

🛏 Sleeping & Eating

Motels line the Pacific Hwy.

Annie's B&B   B&B $$
(✆0421 914 295; www.anniesbnbgrafton.com; 13 Mary St; r $120-200; ❋🤚🐕) This beautiful big old Victorian home occupies a glorious corner block in one of Grafton's prettiest areas. Guest rooms have period furniture and are separate from the family home.

Roches Family Hotel   HOTEL $
TOP CHOICE (✆6644 2866; www.roches.com.au; 85 Victoria St; s/d $30/40) This historic old corner pub in the town centre has spruced-up rooms. Be sure to get one with doors opening onto the verandah. It's a tidy place with new bathrooms.

Georgie's Café   CAFE $$
(✆6642 6996; 158 Fitzroy St; mains $12-20; ⏱lunch Tue-Sun, dinner Tue-Sat) The food here is as artful as the location: the courtyard of the Grafton Regional Gallery. Dishes by day include lovely baked goods, creative salads, thick sandwiches and more. At night it's a serious restaurant with a changing menu depending on what's coming off the local farms.

Clocktower Hotel   PUB $
(www.clocktowerhotel.com.au; 93 Princes St; mains $11-30; ⏱lunch & dinner) Too young for old stuff? Grafton's 20-something drinking hole has maintained its heritage character but lashed out with a modern interior. It's a popular place with decent food and live music acts on weekends.

ℹ Information

Clarence River visitors centre (✆6642 4677; www.clarencetourism.com; cnr Spring & Charles Sts; ⏱9am-5pm) On the Pacific Hwy south of the town, near the turn-off to the bridge. Tellingly, it shares a parking lot with a McDonald's.

NPWS office (National Parks & Wildlife Service; ✆6641 1500; 49 Victoria St)

ℹ Getting There & Away

Busways (✆1300 555 611; www.busways.com.au) runs to Yamba ($11.20, 75 minutes, six times daily) and Maclean ($10, 45 minutes).

Greyhound (✆1300 473 946; www.greyhound.com.au) and **Premier** (✆13 34 10; www.premierms.com.au) stop at the train station on runs south to Sydney ($67, 11 hours) and north to Byron ($47, 3½ hours).

CountryLink (✆13 22 32; www.countrylink.info) stops here on its north-coast route. Sydney is served three times daily ($72, 10 hours).

MID-NORTH COAST

The best thing about the Pacific Hwy driving south from Grafton is all the chances you have to drive off it. Beachy Coffs Harbour defines 'family friendly' and there're discoveries to be made, including the natural beauty of Wooli. Further south, on the ocean, Crescent Head and South West Rocks bracket beautiful and often-deserted beaches; in the hills, the drive through delightful Bellingen and on to Dorrigo plunges into the heart of waterfall-laced rainforest.

Grafton to Coffs Harbour

From Grafton the Pacific Hwy tracks back towards the coast past the turn-off to Yuraygir National Park and the isolated beach town of Wooli. It then runs near the coast – but not in sight of it – for 30km north of Coffs. Look for turn-offs to small beaches that are often quite uncrowded.

The 53,502-hectare **Yuraygir National Park** (per car per day $7) covers the 60km stretch of coast north from Red Rock. The isolated beaches are best discovered on the **Yuraygir Coastal Walk**, a 65km signposted walk from Angourie to Red Rock following the path of the coastal emu over a series of tracks, trails, beaches and rock platforms, and passing through the villages of Brooms Head, Minne Water and Wooli.

Walkers can bush-camp at seven basic **camping areas** (per person from $17) along the route. It's best walked north to south with the sun at your back. **Grafton NPWS**

(☑6641 1500; www.environment.nsw.gov.au) has info and a downloadable map.

Wooli (population 501) is on a long isthmus, with a river estuary on one side and the ocean on the other. This only adds to its isolated charm. It hosts the **Australian Goanna Pulling Championships** (www.goannapulling.com.au). Rather than ripping the eponymous animal to shreds, participants, squatting on all fours, attach leather harnesses to their heads and engage in a cranial tug-of-war.

Solitary Islands Marine Park Resort (☑1800 003 031, 6649 7519; North St; camp sites/cabins/beach shacks from $26/82/46) here has lovely cabins in a scrubby bush setting.

Red Rock (population 274) is a sleepy village with an inlet and surrounds so gorgeous it's worth trekking 3km off the highway. It is a site sacred to the Gunawarri people. Soak up the sun or catch a fish while camping at **Red Rock Caravan Park** (☑6649 2730; www.redrock.org.au; 1 Lawson St, Red Rock; camp sites/cabins from $19/94, cottages $105). The **Yarrawarra Aboriginal Cultural Centre** (☑6640 7100; http://yarrawarra.org; 170 Red Rock Rd, Corindi Beach) has bush-medicine tours, traditional basket-weaving and art classes and a bush-tucker cafe with croc, roo and emu dishes. Ring ahead to see what's on.

About 20km north of Coffs, coastal **Woolgoolga** (also known as Woopi; population 4356), is a good small-town stop option. It's known for its surf-and-Sikh community. As you drive by on the highway you're sure to notice the impressive **Guru Nanak Temple**, a Sikh *gurdwara* (place of worship).

RUSSELL CROWE'S CURIOS

What is Russell Crowe's *Gladiator* costume doing in an old wooden barn in the tiny town of Nymboida, an hour's drive northwest of Coffs Harbour? How about Johnny Cash's gold albums and Don Bradman's caps? The answer: this is the 'Museum of Interesting Things', and Crowe owns it.

The Aussie superstar grew up in nearby Nana Glen, where his parents still live. When he bought the adjoining **Coaching Station Inn** (☑6649 4126; www.coachingstation.com; 3970 Armidale Rd, s/d $90/120), a great old roadside guesthouse, he had the old barn pimped-up to house his considerable collection of boys' toys, from music and movie memorabilia to sporting paraphernalia and vintage motorbikes. The **museum** (☉11am-3pm Wed-Fri & Sun, to 5pm Sat) also acts as a repository for artefacts from local pioneering history, a nod to the day when horse-drawn Cobb & Co coaches stopped here on the woolpack road from Armidale to Grafton.

Don't get too excited, though: aside from the photos that dot the inn's main bar, you're not likely to see the man himself. Then again, the barman reckons he sometimes pops in announced. After all, 'it's only 11 minutes by chopper from his mum and dad's house'.

Drive straight through town for a magnificent view of the group of five islands in the **Solitary Islands Marine Park**, the meeting point of warm currents and cooler southern currents, making for a great combination of corals, reef fish and seaweeds. Dive shops in Coffs Harbour organise tours.

The **Woolgoolga Beach Caravan Park** (☑6654 1373; www.coffscoastholidayparks.com. au; Beach St; unpowered sites/cabins from $27/60) right on the beach can't be beaten on position. Neither can **Bluebottles Brasserie** (☑6654 1962; cnr Wharf & Beach Sts; mains $24-28; ☺breakfast & lunch daily, dinner Fri & Sat), a happening place that serves fine seafood and hosts live jazz sessions.

Coffs Harbour

☑02 / POP 26,350

You can't help but stop in Coffs Harbour: the coagulated Pacific Hwy gives you no choice. This regional centre has protected beaches and attractions that appeal to families. Of course 'family friendly' can also mean 'dull and predictable' but this isn't necessarily so.

Originally called Korff's Harbour, the town was settled in the 1860s. The jetty was built in 1892 to load cedar and other logs; it fell into disrepair some years ago but is now restored to its former glory. Bananas were first grown in the area in the 1880s, but no one made much money from them until the railway came to town in 1918.

Banana growing reached its peak in the 1960s; these days tourism is the mainstay of the local economy.

The town is split into three areas: the jetty area, the commercial centre with its malls, and the beaches. The Pacific Hwy becomes Grafton St and then Woolgoolga Rd on its fume-ridden run through town. The city centre is around the Grafton St and Harbour Dr junction. Note that High St and Harbour Dr are one and the same, with both names used interchangeably by adjoining businesses.

The Pacific Hwy is the best way to access the beaches and resorts to the north. South of Coffs is Sawtell, a sprawl of housing developments fronting some fabulous surf beaches, which merge into Coffs Harbour.

◉ Sights

TOP CHOICE **Legends Surf Museum** MUSEUM
(☑6653 6536; Pacific Hwy; adult/child $5/2; ☺9am-4pm) Over 160 boards are on display here, including ancient ones from, like,

50 years ago, man. Owner Scott Dillon is as salty as the ocean and has a collection of tales, although as he notes: 'Everyone wants to hear shark stories'. It's 500m west of the Pacific Hwy 7km north of town (if highway construction work doesn't see it relocated).

North Coast Botanic Gardens GARDEN
(Hardacre St; admission by donation; ☺9am-5pm) Immerse yourself in the subtropical surrounds. Lush rainforest and numerous endangered species are some of the features, which also include sections devoted to places as faraway and foreign as Africa, China and Queensland. The 6km **Coffs Creek Habitat Walk** passes by, starting opposite the council chambers on Coffs St and finishing near the ocean.

Muttonbird Island NATURE RESERVE
Dramatically joined to Coffs Harbour by the northern breakwater in 1935, this eco treasure is occupied from late August to early April by some 12,000 pairs of muttonbirds, with cute offspring visible in December and January. The 500m walk to the top rewards with sweeping vistas along the coast. It marks the southern boundary of the Solitary Islands Marine Park, a meeting place of tropical waters and southern currents.

Big Banana AMUSEMENT PARK
(www.bigbanana.com; Pacific Hwy) Some see this as a national icon with plenty of appeal, others find it ripe for abuse. Admission is free, with charges for individual attractions such as the ice-skating and snow-slope combo ($16/14). Built in 1964, it actually started the craze for 'Big Things' in Australia (just so you know who to blame or praise).

Beaches

TOP CHOICE **Park Beach,** which has a picnic ground and is patrolled at busy times, is a long and lovely stretch of sand. It is backed by dense shrubbery and sand dunes, which conceal the urban blight beyond. **Jetty Beach** is somewhat more sheltered. **Diggers Beach**, reached by turning off the highway near the Big Banana, has a nude section. Surfers enjoy Diggers and **Macauleys Headland**, where swells average 1m to 1.5m.

Galleries

Coffs Harbour Regional Gallery ART GALLERY
(www.coffsharbour.nsw.gov.au; Rigby House, cnr Coff & Duke Sts; ☺10am-4pm Wed-Sat) hosts regional art and travelling shows. **Bunker Cartoon Gallery** (www.coffsharbour.nsw.gov.au; John Champion Way;

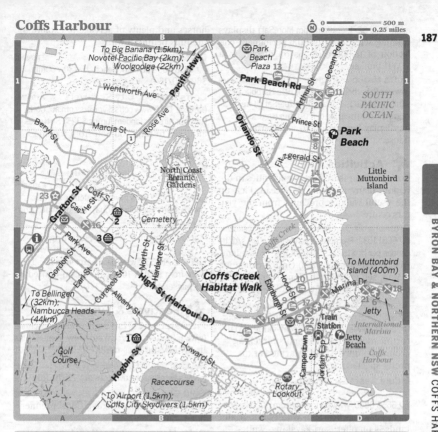

Coffs Harbour

◎ Top Sights
Coffs Creek Habitat Walk	C3
Park Beach	D2

◎ Sights
1	Bunker Cartoon Gallery	B4
2	Coffs Harbour Regional Gallery	B2
3	Coffs Harbour Regional Museum	A3

⦿ Activities, Courses & Tours
	Crying Tiger Cooking School	(see 17)
4	Jetty Dive Centre	D3
5	Lee Winkler's Surf School	D2
6	Liquid Assets Adventure Tours	D3
	Promenade Canoes	(see 19)

⬭ Sleeping
7	Aussietel Backpackers Hostel	C4
8	Bo'suns Inn Motel	D2
9	Caribbean Motel	C3
10	Coffs Harbour YHA	C3
11	Hoey Moey Pub	D1
12	Observatory Holiday Apartments	C4
13	Pacific Property & Management	C1
14	Park Beach Holiday Park	D2

⊗ Eating
15	Caffé Fiasco	D3
16	Cocoa	A2
17	Crying Tiger	C3
18	Fisherman's Co-op	D3
	Foreshore Café	(see 17)
19	Mangrove Jacks	C3
20	OP81	D1
	Urban Espresso Lounge	(see 17)
21	Yknot Bistro	D3

⦿ Drinking
	Hoey Moey Pub	(see 11)
22	Pier Hotel	C3

⦿ Entertainment
23	Plantation Hotel	A2

adult/child $2/1; ⊙10am-4pm Mon-Sat) displays rotating selections from the permanent collection of 18,000 cartoons on display in a WWII bunker.

Coffs Harbour Regional Museum MUSEUM (www.coffsharbour.nsw.gov.au; 191a Harbour Dr; adult/child $3/1; ⊙10am-4pm Tue-Sat) The region's nautical and fruit heritage are on display here in an old weatherboard house.

🏃 Activities

Coffs Harbour is a centre for activities in the region, many involving the ocean. Pick up the useful walking brochure from the visitors centre.

Promenade Canoes CANOEING (☑6651 1032; Promenade, 321 Harbour Dr; s/d/tr canoes per hr $15/22/27, 3rd hr free; ⊙9am-1pm Fri-Mon, 9am-5pm Sat & Sun) Grab a canoe for a 5km, self-guided trip along scenic Coffs Creek in the heart of town.

Jetty Dive Centre DIVING, SNORKELLING (☑6651 1611; www.jettydive.com.au; 398 Harbour Dr; double dives from $115) Great-value PADI certification; the diving and snorkelling around Solitary Islands Marine Park is pretty spectacular.

Liquid Assets Adventure Tours
WATER SPORTS (☑6658 0850; www.surfrafting.com; 328 Harbour Dr; half-day tours from $50) Watery fun of all kinds is on offer: surf-kayaking, whitewater rafting, kayaking in the marine park, platypus tours and more.

East Coast Surf School SURFING (☑6651 5515; www.eastcoastsurfschool.com.au; Diggers Beach; lessons from $55) This school is particularly female-friendly, as it is run by the noted East Coast surfer Helene Enevoldson.

Crying Tiger Cooking School COOKING (☑6650 0195; http://thecryingtiger.com; $110 per person; 382 Harbour Dr) Brush up on Thai cooking at this popular restaurant. The class (maximum four per class) starts at 10am and finishes with a sit-down feast of your own creation.

More active options:

Lee Winkler's Surf School SURFING (☑6650 0050; Park Beach; lessons from $60) Has a good reputation.

Valery Horse Trails HORSE RIDING (☑6653 4301; www.valerytrails.com.au; 758 Valery Rd, Valery; 2hr rides $50) A stable of 60 horses and plenty of acreage to explore in the hills behind town.

Coffs Jet Ski JET SKIING (☑0418 665 656; Park Beach; 15-/30-/60min $60/100/160)

Coffs Harbour City Skydivers SKYDIVING (☑6651 1167; www.coffsskydivers.com.au; Coffs Harbour airport; tandem jumps $325) Satisfies all urges to fling yourself from a plane.

👉 Tours

Spirit of Coffs Harbour Cruises
WHALE-WATCHING (☑6650 0155; www.gowhalewatching.com.au; shop 5, Coffs Harbour Marina) Whale-watching ($45) and cruises.

Pacific Explorer Whale Watching
WHALE-WATCHING (☑0422 210 338; www.pacificexplorer.com.au; 2-3hr from $30) A 10m catamaran limited to 23 passengers.

🎊 Festivals & Events

Pittwater to Coffs Yacht Race YACHTING (www.pittwatertocoffs.com.au) New Year. Starts in Sydney, finishes here.

Sawtell Chilli Festival CHILLI (www.sawtellchillifestival.com.au) Early July.

Gold Cup HORSE RACING (☑6652 1488) Early August. Coffs' premier horse race.

Coffs Harbour International Buskers' Festival MUSIC, THEATRE (www.coffsharbourbuskers.com) Late September and not to be missed.

Coffs Coast Food & Wine Festival WINE, FOOD Early November.

🛏 Sleeping

Motels cluster in two spots: out on the Pacific Hwy by the visitors centre where they can suck in road-trippers, and down by Park Beach where they can comfort beachgoers.

One of many holiday-apartment agents is **Pacific Property & Management** (☑6652 1466; www.coffsholidayrentals.com.au; 101 Park Beach Rd). The range of offerings is numbing. The visitors centre has an accommodation-booking service.

There's no real reason to stay out by the Pacific Hwy. If you're visiting during peak times, it's good to note that many hostel prices remain consistent all year, but book ahead.

Observatory Holiday Apartments

APARTMENTS $$

(☑6650 0462; www.theobservatory.com.au; 30-36 Camperdown St; apt from $130; ✳🔊) Some apartments have window spas and all have balcony with ocean view. The one-, two- and three-bedroom apartments in this attractive modern complex are bright and airy, with chef-friendly kitchen.

Caribbean Motel

MOTEL $$

(☑6652 1500; www.caribbeanmotel.com.au; 353 High St; r $100-180; ✳🔊🔊) Close to Coffs Creek and the jetty, this 24-unit motel has been tastefully renovated and features a breakfast buffet and tables outside by the pool. The best rooms have balcony, view and spa, and there are great-value one-bedroom suites with kitchenette.

Coffs Harbour YHA

HOSTEL $

(☑6652 6462; www.yha.com.au; 51 Collingwood St; dm/d/f $31/86/132; @🔊) With service and amenities like these, it's a wonder hotels don't go out of business. The dorms and doubles with bathroom are spacious and modern, and the TV lounge and kitchen are immaculate. You can hire surfboards and bikes.

Aussitel Backpackers Hostel

HOSTEL $

(☑1800 330 335, 6651 1871; www.aussitel.com; 312 Harbour Dr; dm/d $27/65; @🔊) Don't be put off by the exterior. This capacious brick house, with homely dorms and a shady courtyard, is a hub for backpackers of all shapes and sizes, codes and creeds. Diving specialists are on site (PADI courses from $295).

Hoey Moey Pub

PUB, HOSTEL $

(☑6652 3833; www.hoeymoey.com.au; 90 Ocean Pde; s/d $25/60) You can hear the waves roll in from these motel-style backpacker rooms nicely located between the pub and the main beach. You can also hear your mates in the beer garden. Renovated rooms are slightly pricier.

Aanuka Beach Resort

RESORT $$$

(☑6652 7555; www.aanuka.com.au; 11 Firman Dr; r from $123; ✳@🔊) It might be out of town, but this luxurious resort, set amid luscious foliage, has excellent studios and apartments, all with spa and dishy interior. It sits on a quiet neck of Diggers Beach and has tennis courts and an award-winning restaurant.

Novotel Pacific Bay

RESORT $$$

(☑6659 7000; www.pacificbayresort.com.au; cnr Pacific Hwy & Bay Dr; r from $185; ✳🔊🔊) Has all the features of a large resort: tennis courts, a golf course, walking trails, a kids' club, a spa and a fitness centre. The grounds are large and the 180 rooms have balconies, many with kitchen. It's 3km north of Coffs.

Bo'suns Inn Motel

MOTEL $$

(☑6651 2251; www.motelcoffsharbour.com; 37 Ocean Pde; d from $80; ✳🔊) The nautical theme here runs from the life-size seaman out the front to the scenes of frigates mounted over the beds. It's one of a few run-of-the-mill places credited for its beachside locale rather than aesthetic.

Park Beach Holiday Park

CARAVAN PARK $

(☑6648 4888; www.coffsholidays.com.au; Ocean Pde; camp sites/cabins from $27/61; @🔊) This place is massive, with 332 sites and 55 cabins; ideally located at the beach. Kids are well catered for.

✖ Eating

You can eat well down by the jetty. The strip of eateries on Harbour Dr is a hungry browser's delight. The downtown area is good for lunch, or for coffee all day, but most places are closed in the evening. The pedestrian area opposite Palm Mall (part of High St Pedestrian Mall) has a few pavement cafes.

As well as the listings here, you'll find budget Italian, Vietnamese and Indian, and fish and chips. Kitchens start closing around 8.30pm, so come early and make a reservation if you have your heart set on a particular place or a pavement table.

TOP CHOICE | **Mangrove Jacks** MODERN AUSTRALIAN $$

(☑6652 5517; www.mangrovejackscafe.com.au; Promenade Centre, Harbour Dr; mains $25; ⊙breakfast & lunch daily, dinner Tue-Sat) One of two wonderfully located restaurants overlooking a quiet bend of Coffs Creek; this one serves sultry gourmet dinners and has Coopers on tap. Brekkie and lunch are more casual.

Urban Espresso Lounge

CAFE $$

(www.urbanespressolounge.com.au; 384a Harbour Dr, Jetty; mains $8-17; ⊙breakfast & lunch) A stylish little java outpost on the strip. Pancakes, fresh fruit and yoghurt are some of the breakfast delights. Lunches include a Thai beef and prawn salad and a luscious roast-beef sandwich.

Caffè Fiasco

ITALIAN $$$

(☑6651 2006; www.caffefiasco.com.au; 368 Harbour Dr, Jetty; mains $15-30; ⊙brunch Sun, dinner Tue-Sat) It doesn't live up to its name: Caffè Wonderful is more apt. Classic Italian fare is prepared in an open kitchen surrounded by widely spaced tables that flow from inside to out. The gardens have herbs used in the dishes, which include some excellent local seafood. Bar open from 4pm.

Crying Tiger
THAI $$

(http://thecryingtiger.com; 382 Harbour Dr, Jetty; mains $19-24; ⊗dinner) Swimming in ambience and fragrant smells, the newly snazzed-up Crying Tiger keeps inquisitive diners happy with red-duck curry and king prawns in lime leaf and coconut. You can turn the chilli gauge as high or low as you like.

YKnot Bistro
BAR, RESTAURANT $$

(www.yknotbistro.com.au; 30 Marina Dr, Marina; mains $15-39; ⊗breakfast, lunch & dinner) Part of the Coffs Harbour Yacht Club, this understated eatery has a pub-style bar, huge dining room and plenty of outdoor seating. Best of all, it has an ocean view – rare in Coffs.

OP81
MODERN AUSTRALIAN $$

(81 Ocean Pde; mains $8-27; ⊗breakfast & lunch Tue-Sun, dinner Fri) One of the few eateries along hotel-cluttered Ocean Pde, OP81 has been revamped so that punters can enjoy modern decor and a big front deck. The hiss of the coffee machine should give you the tip.

Cocoa
CAFE $

(36/35 Harbour Dr; mains $8-13; ⊗breakfast & lunch) The bright and gleaming modern decor and excellent coffee make Cocoa a hot spot for Coffs' business set and pram brigade. Or maybe it's the breakfast on offer; the fruit salad and fresh yoghurt is good.

Foreshore Café
CAFE $

(394 Harbour Dr, Jetty; ⊗breakfast & lunch) Crowds flock to this spacious cafe with big wooden tables, both inside and out, and a menu to suit all tastes.

Fisherman's Co-op
FISH & CHIPS $

(www.coffsfishcoop.com.au; Cnr Marina Dr & Orlando St; mains $8-10; ⊗9am-6pm in winter, to 8pm in summer) Chips, and fresh fish such as whiting. Homemade gelato and covered picnic tables complete the joy; there's much here that would make a good picnic at Muttonbird Island.

🍷 Drinking & Entertainment

See Thursday's edition of the *Coffs Harbour Advocate* for listings. Clubs change names with the seasons.

Coast Hotel
PUB

(www.coasthotel.com.au; 2 Moonee St; ⊗11am-late) Formerly the Old Fitzroy Hotel, this place has been purpose-renovated to supply lovers of a lazy afternoon in a beer garden with a venue. It has landscaped decking and cool breakaway areas so you can kick back on a couch if the mood takes you. The food is great, too.

Hoey Moey Pub
PUB

(www.hoeymoey.com.au; Ocean Pde; ⊗10am-late) The massive inner beer 'garden' gives a good indication of how much this place kicks off in the summer months. Pool competitions, live music (from Wednesday to Sunday nights each week) and terrifying karaoke sessions are the norm.

More pub sessions and live music:

Coffs Hotel
PUB

(www.coffsharbourhotel.com; cnr Pacific Hwy & West Harbour Dr; ⊗11am-1am) Irish pub with bands, several bars, DJs and mad Friday nights.

Pier Hotel
PUB

(www.pierhotelcoffs.com.au; cnr Hood St & Harbour Dr; ⊗10am-1am) Renovated with a sunny rear terrace, this place has live music on Wednesdays.

Plantation Hotel
PUB

(www.plantationhotel.com.au; 88 Grafton St aka Pacific Hwy) The Plantation is a pub at heart, so beer, live rock and decent steak are mainstays.

❶ Information

Jetty Dive (398 Harbour Dr; per hr $4) Has internet access.

Main post office (ground fl, Palms Centre Shopping Complex) In a mall. There's another outlet at the jetty, opposite the Pier Hotel, and a third at Park Beach Plaza (the large mall off the Pacific Hwy).

Visitors centre (☑6652 1522, 1300 369 070; www.coffscoast.com.au; cnr Pacific Hwy & McLean St; ⊗8am-5pm) Has a complete rundown on accommodation, activities and tours, although it annoyingly obscures contact info on brochures with its own.

❶ Getting There & Away
Air

Coffs Harbour Airport (CFS) is just south of town. **Virgin Blue** (☑13 67 89; www.virginblue. com.au) and **QantasLink** (☑13 13 13; www.qantas.com.au) fly to Sydney ($120, 75 minutes).

Bus

Long-distance and regional buses leave from a shelter adjacent to the visitors centre.

Premier (☑13 34 10; www.premierms.com. au) has several services a day north, including Byron Bay ($50, 5¼ hours), and south to Sydney ($66, 8½ hours). **Greyhound** (☑1300 473 946; www.greyhound.com.au) offers similar services in both directions.

Busways (☑1300 555 611; www.busways. com.au) runs two or three times daily Monday to Saturday to Nambucca Heads ($9, 70 minutes) and Bellingen ($8.80, 70 minutes) via Urunga.

Train

CountryLink (☑13 22 32; www.countrylink. info) has three trains daily all the way north to the nonthriving town of Casino (where the train used to branch off to Byron Bay) and Brisbane ($59, 5½ hours), and south to Sydney ($67, nine hours).

❶ Getting Around

Hostel shuttles meet most long-distance buses and trains.

Coffs Bike Hire (☑6652 5102; cnr Orlando & Collingwood Sts; per day from $25) rents cruisers, mountain bikes and more.

Major car-rental companies are at the airport.

For a cab, **Coffs District Taxi Network** (☑13 10 08, 6658 5922) operates a 24-hour service.

Bellingen

☑02 / POP 2880

Bellingen is a charming hill town that manages to have a lot of interest without selling itself out with some of the tacky tourism vices found in other places along the coast. There's a delightfully laid-back vibe that's spiced with art and alternative lifestyles. Many of the buildings date from the early 1900s and have cast-iron details. Numerous folk musicians live in the region and bulletin boards features fliers for various forms of yoga, guinea-pig breeding, acoustic-guitar lessons and much more.

The wide Bellingen River valley here was part of the extensive territory of the Gumbainggir people until European timber-cutters arrived in the 1840s. The first settlement here was at Fernmount, about 5km east of Bellingen, but later the administrative centre of the region was moved to Bellingen. River craft were able to come up here until the 1940s, when dredging was discontinued. Until tourism boomed at Coffs Harbour in the 1960s, Bellingen was the most important town in this area.

The main road from the Pacific Hwy to Dorrigo and the Waterfall Way becomes Hyde St in town. Next to the post office, Wharf St leads across the river to North Bellingen and Gleniffer. The closest visitors centre is in Urunga, south on the Pacific Hwy.

◉ Sights & Activities

Hammond & Wheatley Emporium   SHOPPING
(Hyde St) To get a feel for the town's past, head to this magnificent building, an ode to shopping of yore. It has a range of stylish goods for sale in the restored 1909-vintage surrounds.

Music   MUSIC
Among the dozens of interesting shops, two attest to the importance of music locally: **Heritage Music** (☑6655 1611; 23 Hyde St; ⊙10am-4pm Tue-Sat) and **Heartland Didgeridoos** (☑6655 9881; www.heartlanddidgeridoos.com.au; 2/25 Hyde St; ⊙10am-4pm Mon-Sat). The former is an acoustic mecca selling and servicing guitars. You can take lessons from local luminaries and, on occasion, a few drop by to perform. The latter is the real deal, with didgeridoos from across Australia, lessons on offer and more.

Nature   NATURE
For a nature fix, from December to March there's a huge colony of flying foxes on Bat Island. It's an impressive sight when thousands head off at dusk to feed (best seen from the bridge). There's also an interesting walk to rope swings into the river, near the YHA hostel.

Markets   MARKETS
On the third Saturday of the month the **community market** (www.bellingenmarkets.com.au) in Bellingen Park is a regional sensation, with more than 250 stalls. On the second and fourth Saturday of the month there's a **growers market** at Bellingen showgrounds. Although mobbed, the markets show Bellingen in full blossom.

Old Butter Factory   ART, ARTEFACTS
(☑6655 2150; 1 Doepel Lane; ⊙9.30am-5pm) A little piece of local history, this place houses craft shops, a local art gallery, opal dealers and various New Age healers.

Bellingen Museum   MUSEUM
(☑6655 0382; Hyde St; adult/child $3/free; ⊙10am-2pm Mon-Fri) One of those places run by enthusiastic volunteers who you suspect hang out there even when it's

closed. It has a range of booklets on local walks and history.

Bellingen Canoe Adventures CANOEING
(6655 9955; www.canoeadventures.com.au; 4 Tyson St; day tours per adult/child $90/60) About 8km east of town in Fernmount; sign up for wonderful guided canoe tours on the Bellinger River, including full-moon tours (adult/child $25/20).

Festivals & Events

Camp Creative ARTS
(www.campcreative.com.au) A week-long carnival of the arts in mid-January.

Bellingen Jazz & Blues Festival MUSIC
(www.bellingenjazzfestival.com.au) Features a strong line-up of jazz names in mid-August.

Global Carnival MUSIC, ARTS
(www.globalcarnival.com) A multicultural mix of music and performances held annually in early October.

Sleeping

Much of the region's accommodation is in small B&Bs and cottages scattered across the hillsides. Breakfast is included in prices for places listed here.

Bellingen YHA HOSTEL $
TOP CHOICE (6655 1116; www.yha.com.au; 2 Short St; dm/d/tw/f from $30/98/78/98; @) Once you enjoy the rainforest views from the broad verandah or listen to the flying foxes from a hammock, it's easy to see why this hostel is always popular. A tranquil, engaging atmosphere pervades this renovated weatherboard house. There's a free shuttle to the bus stop and train station in Urunga. Camping also available.

CasaBelle B&B $$$
(6655 9311; www.casabelle.com; Gleniffer Rd; r from $235; ✱) Treat yourself to a little piece of Tuscany at this luxurious guesthouse built around a serene courtyard, with double doors that open onto vines and hedges. Added touches include luxuriously late breakfast and check-out, L'Occitane bath products and log fires.

Bellingen River Family Cabins CABINS $$
(6655 0499; www.bellingencabins.com.au; 850 Waterfall Way; cabins from $120) Two large two-bedroom cabins overlook the wide river valley on this family farm 4km east of Bellingen. The units are nicely equipped with DVDs and other extras such as complimentary canoes and fishing gear.

Rivendell GUESTHOUSE $$
(6655 0060; www.rivendellguesthouse.com.au; 12 Hyde St; s/d $115/140; ✱) Unlike many, Rivendell is right in town. The three bedrooms have verandahs fronting lush gardens surrounding a freshwater pool. Decor is restrained, always a plus with a B&B. Prices go up at peak times.

Federal Hotel PUB $
(6655 1003; www.federalhotel.com.au; 77 Hyde St; dm/s/d $40/65/80; ✱@) This beautiful old pub has refurbished weatherboard rooms that open onto a balcony with a sweeping view of the main street. Downstairs there is a lively pub scene, and popular bar and grill (meals $20) open for lunch and dinner.

Lily Pily GUESTHOUSE $$$
(6655 0522; www.lilypily.com.au; 54 Sunny Corner Rd; r from $240; ✱) Set on a knoll, this architect-designed modern complex has three bedrooms overlooking the valleys. It's a high-end place designed to pamper with champagne on arrival, lavish breakfasts served until noon, luxurious furnishings and more. It's 3km south of the centre.

Koompartoo Retreat APARTMENTS $$
(6655 2326; www.koompartoo.com.au; cnr Lawson & Dudley Sts; d $165-185; ✱) Ferns hang over the wide balconies on the four chalets at this tropical retreat close to town. Each is constructed from local hardwoods and blends right into the hillside. Kitchenettes let you show off your romantic prowess at the cooker.

Eating & Drinking

The creativity of the locals comes through in the many cafes and restaurants.

Lodge 241 CAFE, BAR $
TOP CHOICE (6655 2470; Hyde St; ⊙from 8.30am Wed-Sun, dinner Fri & Sat) A pew at this excellent cafe is golden. Chess players gather here on a Sunday to soak up the atmosphere while locals line up along a communal table and imbibe great coffee. Breakfast includes banana and coconut bread with ricotta and honey. It has recently been licensed so is good for a drink too.

Vintage Espresso CAFE $
(6655 0015; 62 Hyde St; meals $9; ⊙breakfast & lunch) Sip on excellent coffee amid the eclectic curios of this vintage shop. One side is clothes-tastic, the other is a nudge at nostalgia with old books and records, used furniture and '70s kitchenware. Thankfully

the hearty roast beef and tandoori chicken Turkish sandwiches are not preloved.

No 2 Oak St
MODERN AUSTRALIAN $$$

(☑6655 9000; 2 Oak St; mains $28; ⊙dinner Wed-Sat) The bounty of local produce is celebrated at this lauded restaurant where host Toni Urquart provides the welcome while Ray Urquart works his kitchen magic. A table on the verandah in the 1910 country house is a magical place for the evening. Open Tuesdays during holidays.

Tuckshop Bellingen
CAFE $

(☑6655 0655; www.tuckshopbellingen.com.au; 63 Hyde St; ⊙8am-5pm Mon-Fri, to 2pm Sat) If only all tuckshops were like this. This incy wincy cafe serves great coffee and a delicious line-up of breakfast and lunch options. Try the bacon, egg and roast tomato on Turkish or polenta with chargrilled vegetable, pesto, prosciutto and bocconcini.

Bean @ Bello
CAFE, BAR $

(☑0413 707 775; 7 Church St; meals under $12; ⊙9am-4pm Tue-Sun) Excellent brekkies and fresh juices fuel the tummy while the broad assortment of books and games fuel the mind. Sofas are the place to curl up when the rains fall outside.

More options:

Bellingen Gelato Bar
CAFE $

(☑6655 1870; 101 Hyde St; ⊙10am-6pm) A 1950s-America-styled cafe with sensational homemade ice cream and outdoor tables.

Little Red Kitchen
ITALIAN $

(☑6655 1551; 111 Hyde St; mains $10-32; ⊙5-9pm Thu-Mon) A pizza and pasta shop with gourmet toppings.

Kombu Wholefoods
CAFE $

(☑6655 9299; 105 Hyde St) An organic grocery-cum–community centre that speaks to the local culture by posting its business philosophy outside.

❶ Information

Bellingen Book Nook (☑6655 9372; 25 Hyde St; ⊙10am-4pm Mon-Fri, 9am-3pm Sat market) In a real nook. Lots of books are crammed into this small space. There's always a few itinerant readers lounging around while others gossip.

www.bellingen.com This community website is an excellent resource.

❶ Getting There & Away

Busways (☑1300 555 611; www.busways.com.au) runs two or three times Monday to Saturday

from Nambucca Heads ($9.80, 40 minutes) and Coffs Harbour ($8.80, 70 minutes) to Bellingen via Urunga.

Keans (☑1800 625 587) has buses west to Dorrigo and Tamworth a pitiful two times a week.

From Bellingen the Waterfall Way (p194) climbs steeply 29km to Dorrigo – it's a spectacular drive.

Around Bellingen

Explorations of Belligen's lush surrounding valleys are always rewarded. The most accessible is the tiny hamlet of **Gleniffer**, 6km to the north and clearly signposted from North Bellingen. There's a good swimming hole in the **Never Never River**, behind the small Gleniffer School of Arts at the crossroads. Then you can drive around Loop Rd, which takes you to the foot of the New England Tableland – a great drive that words cannot do justice to.

If you want to sweat, tackle the **Syndicate Ridge Walking Trail** (www.environment.nsw.gov.au/NationalParks), a strenuous 15km walk from Gleniffer to the Dorrigo Plateau following the route of a tramline once used by timber-cutters. There's a very steep 1km climb on the way up. To get to the start of the trail, take the Gleniffer road from Bellingen, turning into Adams Lane soon after crossing the Never Never River. The walking track commences at the first gate.

The **Kalang Valley**, southwest of town, and the **Thora Valley**, about 10km west of town, are also well worth exploring. Feel like you missed the 1960s? They never ended here.

Dorrigo National Park

Layered over sharp peaks and plunging valleys, this is the most accessible of Australia's World Heritage rainforests. The 11,902-hectare park is home to a huge diversity of vegetation owing to its rich soil and subtropical conditions. All those trees mean there's plenty of places for birds to perch and at last count there were over 120 species present.

The **Waterfall Way** climbs the hills between Bellingen and Dorrigo and lives up to its name by passing several plunging streams at the roadside. Near the top, 2km south of Dorrigo, the **Rainforest Centre** (Dome Rd; ⊙9am-4.30pm), at the park entrance, has information about the park's many walks and nature displays. The highlight is the short **Skywalk** walkway that arches over the rainforest and provides vistas to the valleys below. You can see right down to the ocean on a fine day. The **Wonga Walk** is a three-hour, 6km-return walk on a sealed track through the heart of the rainforest. It's well worth making the drive down to the **Never Never rest area** in the middle of the national park, from where you can walk to waterfalls or begin longer walks.

Dorrigo

☑02 / POP 970

The drowsy streets of this agricultural village atop the plateau are starting to see an upmarket outpost or two, attesting to its burgeoning popularity. It's sunny and warm up here in contrast to the often misty forests in the national park below.

The town's main attraction is the Dorrigo Rainforest Centre and **Dangar Falls**, which pound down into a swimming hole – think of it as aquatic massage.

🛏 Sleeping & Eating

Dorrigo Hotel/Motel   PUB, MOTEL **$**
(☑6657 2017; www.hotelmoteldorrigo.com.au; cnr Cudgery & Hickory Sts; dm/f $30/190, d $60-85) The charm of this almighty pub's exterior might not be echoed in the public bar or the rear dining room. Upstairs, however, the bedrooms, some with bathrooms, have been tastefully renovated to provide wholesome country hospitality. Double doors open onto the wide-girthed verandah for a sweeping main-street vista. There are motel rooms also.

Mossgrove   B&B **$$**
(☑6657 5388; http://mossgrove.com.au; Old Coast Rd; d $185) Set on six acres, 8km from Dorrigo, this lovely Federation home has two homely rooms, a guest lounge and bathroom, all tastefully renovated to suit the era. An extra $35 will get you a cooked breakfast, the perfect sustenance for a stroll around the bonsai gallery and olive grove.

33 on Hickory   ITALIAN **$$**
TOP CHOICE (☑6657 1882; www.thirtythreeonhickory.com.au; 33 Hickory St; mains $20; ⊙lunch Sun, dinner Thu-Sun) In the heart of town 'Thirty Three' is a gorgeous 1920s weatherboard cottage with stained-glass windows, tasteful antiques and a blossoming garden. The main game is organic sourdough pizza, but it's served in style with white tablecloths, sparkling silverware and a cosy wood fire. The B&B accommodation ($135 per couple) is equally as stylish.

Red Dirt Distillery   DISTILLERY, CAFE **$**
(☑6657 1373; 51-53 Hickory St; ⊙10am-4pm Mon-Fri, 10am-noon Sat) Right in the centre, owner David Scott gets creative with a range of vodka and liqueur made with, for example, potatoes grown in Dorrigo's red dirt. Buy a bottle, plus some of his deli snacks and you're talking picnic or sit in for an antipasto platter.

Dragonfly   CAFE **$**
(☑6657 2356; 18-20 Cudgery St; mains $10-20; ⊙breakfast & lunch Mon-Sat) The local foodies' hub and hangout is a cafe-cum-bookshop set in a chic minimalist space with a large sunny rear dining area. Creative salads, sandwiches and veggie specials entice even if service is a tad slow.

ℹ Information

The **visitors centre** (☑6657 2486; 36 Hickory St; ⊙10am-4pm), located in the middle of what passes for the main drag, is run by volunteers who share a passion for the area. Pick up the useful scenic drives brochure ($1).

WORTH A TRIP

FOLLOWING THE WATERFALL WAY

Once you've travelled the 41km from the Pacific Hwy through Bellingen to Dorrigo, you've gone pretty far from the coast, although there's still another 124km of the Waterfall Way to go before you reach Armidale. Should you press on, these are the highlights:

» Forty-eight kilometres past Dorrigo (2km west of Ebor) there's a turn for Ebor Falls, where the Guy Fawkes River takes a big plunge.

» A further 7km on is Point Lookout Rd, which leads to New England National Park, another World Heritage site. There are numerous walks into this misty rainforest.

» After another 30km, look for Wollomombi Falls, a highlight of the World Heritage–listed Oxley Wild Rivers National Park. Here the water plunges down 260m.

ⓘ Getting There & Away

Keans (☎1800 625 587) has buses east to Bellingen and west to Tamworth a pitiful two times a week.

Nambucca Heads

⚑02 / POP 5870

Nambucca (nam-*buk*-a) Heads has a workaday centre atop a hill. But get towards the water and you'll be rewarded with wide vistas of the coast. There's a number of nature walks and plenty of beachy walking so you can get fit while you holiday.

The Nambucca (which means 'many bends') Valley was occupied by the Gumbainggir people until European timbercutters arrived in the 1840s. There are still strong Aboriginal communities in Nambucca Heads and up the valley in Bowraville.

The town is just off the Pacific Hwy. Riverside Dr runs alongside the estuary of the Nambucca River, then climbs a steep hill to Bowra St, the main shopping street. A right turn onto Ridge St at the top of the hill leads to the bluffs and the beaches. Wellington Dr follows the river to the V-Wall.

◉ Sights & Activities

Gulmani Boardwalk NATURE TRAIL
From the **visitor centre** (☎6568 6954; cnr Riverside Dr & Pacific Hwy), this extended trail stretches 3km along the foreshore, through parks and bushland, and over pristine sand and waterways. It's the perfect introduction to the town.

Beaches BEACH
At the east end of town, 1.2km from the centre on a high bluff, **Captain Cook Lookout** is the place to ponder the swath of beaches. A road here leads down to **Shelly Beach**, which has tidepools. Going north, it blends into **Beilby's Beach** and then **Main Beach**, which has lots of parking and surf patrols. **Bellwood Park** is best for still-water swimming and paddling. For surfers **Grassy Head** is the least crowded. **Scotts Head** is best during winter.

Wellington Dr NATURE TRAIL
Turn off Bowra St and follow this road downhill to the waterfront and the **V-Wall** breakwater, with its mostly well-mannered graffiti by locals and travellers. There's a short but interesting boardwalk through the mangroves here. Various nature trails wander

WORTH A TRIP

DORRIGO TO COFFS

Forget shortcuts when there's time for a long cut. A partly sealed road continues north from Dorrigo past **Dangar Falls** and swings east into Coffs Harbour via beautiful winding rainforest roads and a **huge tallow-wood tree**, 56m high and more than 3m in diameter. Sitting at the base of this big old beauty is to fully appreciate nature. This is off-road action without getting too far off the track.

der the hillside up to the lookouts; scan the many trees for a sighting of a kookaburra.

Headland Historical Museum MUSEUM
(☎6568 6380; www.here.com.au/museum; Liston St; adult/child $2/50c; ⊙2-4pm Wed, Sat & Sun) Above Main Beach, this place has local history exhibits, including a collection of over 1000 photos and displays of maritime equipment.

Nambucca Kayaks KAYAKING
(☎0488 588 743; www.nambuccakayaks.com.au) Creek and inner-harbour tours including a sunset tour (per person $33).

🛏 Sleeping

Nambucca Heads has a loyal cadre of sunseekers, and books out in summer.

Riverview Boutique Hotel GUESTHOUSE $$
(☎6568 6386; www.riverviewlodgenambucca.com. au; 4 Wellington Dr; d $125-185; ❄) Built in 1887, this old pub (also known as Nambucca Riverview Lodge) was for many years one of the few buildings on the rise of a hill overlooking the foreshore. Today the old two-storey wooden charmer has a colourful history the owners will happily share. The eight rooms have fridges and some have stunning views.

Marcel Towers APARTMENTS $$
(☎6568 7041; www.marceltowers.com.au; Wellington Dr; d from $120; ❄@) The decor at these holiday apartments might be somewhat passé, but the balcony views over a restaurant-studded foreshore soon make up for it. Apartments are clean and available for overnight stays.

White Albatross Holiday Resort CARAVAN PARK $
(☎6568 6468; www.whitealbatross.com.au; Wellington Dr; camp sites from $35, cabins/vans from $90/45) Located near the river mouth with an adjacent lagoon to swim in, this

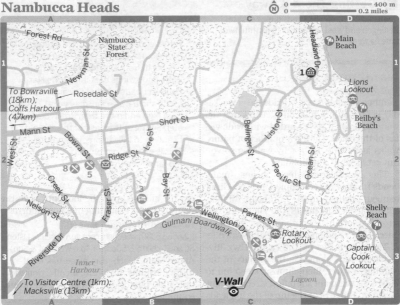

Nambucca Heads

large holiday park surrounds a sheltered lagoon. Beaches and the V-Wall Tavern are all close by.

✗ Eating & Drinking

The bracing ocean breezes here put people to bed early; the streets are mostly rolled up by 10pm weeknights.

TOP CHOICE **Matilda's** SEAFOOD **$$**
(☑6568 6024; Wellington Dr; mains $25-39; ⊘dinner Mon-Sat) Saved up for a seafood feast? Go no further. This cute little shack juggles good old-fashioned beachfront character with food and service know-how. A front porch allows diners to catch a few rays as they indulge in their favourite fish. BYO.

Ocean Chill Restaurant
MODERN AUSTRALIAN **$$$**
(☑6568 8877; http://oceanchill.com; Ridge St; mains $35; ⊘dinner Wed-Sat) Set in the bushy urban streets, this contemporary restaurant has all the telltale signs of people who know food and service. Mind the crisp white linen when you're eating the likes of roast duck with bok choy and beetroot.

V-Wall Tavern PUB, BISTRO **$$**
(☑6568 6394; 1 Wellington Dr; mains $27; ⊘lunch & dinner) A big, modern place with classic water views from its long patio on the upper floor. There's pub food and a bistro called Bluewater Brasserie with more expensive fishy fare. On weeknights the taps stop pouring their mediocre selection of beer as early as 9pm. It's family friendly.

Bookshop Café CAFE **$**
(☑6568 5855; cnr Ridge & Bowra Sts; meals $8-16; ⊘8am-5pm; @) The porch tables here

are *the* place in town for breakfast. The fruit smoothies are excellent and the local banter worthy.

Terrie Catherine's   CAFE **$**
(📞6569 4422; 5 Mann St; ⊘lunch & dinner) This BYO establishment on the main strip has gorgeous views from the back verandah and cosy couches when the weather turns.

ℹ️ Getting There & Around

Long-distance buses stop at the visitors centre. **Premier** (📞13 34 10; www.premierms.com. au) charges $63 to either Sydney or Brisbane (both eight to nine hours). **Greyhound** (📞1300 473 946; www.greyhound.com.au) charges $96 to Sydney (nine hours) and $110 for a slightly quicker run to Brisbane.

Busways (📞1300 555 611; www.busways. com.au) runs two or three times Monday to Saturday from Nambucca Heads to Bellingen ($9.80, 40 minutes) and Coffs Harbour ($9, 50 minutes) via Urunga.

CountryLink (📞13 22 32; www.countrylink. info) has three trains north to Coffs Harbour ($5, 40 minutes) and beyond, and south to Sydney ($67, eight hours).

South West Rocks

📞02 / POP 4070

Well off the Pacific Hwy, South West Rocks is a little beach town with just enough to keep you busy relaxing for days. Overlooking Trial Bay to the north, the town has a hook shape that affords views back over the water at sunset. Ignore the fringe of suburban blight and make for the centre.

Just getting to South West Rocks may be more than half the fun. The area west of the Pacific Hwy is a rich river delta lined with dense reeds, appealing old farmhouses and vintage shacks built on stilts. It's a great drive; to fully appreciate it, leave the Pacific Hwy at Seven Oaks and take the sinuous 22km road along the Macleay River, which passes through a few quaint fishing villages.

🔘 Sights & Activities

Trial Bay   HISTORIC SITE
Imposing and historic, this site occupies the east headland of South West Rocks. The area has a rather dramatic past: Sydney convicts stole a boat, the *Trial,* in 1816 but their bid for freedom ended up literally on the rocks after a storm sank it. Eventually the government decided that a breakwater was needed to protect boats – stolen or otherwise – taking

shelter in the now-named Trial Bay. As a result, **Trial Bay Gaol** was built to house convicts charged with the breakwater's construction. However, plans fizzled and except for a brief interlude in WWI when it housed Germans, the jail has been unoccupied for more than 100 years. It's now a **museum** (📞6566 6168; adult/child $8/5; ⊘9am-4.30pm). The **Arakoon State Conservation Area** surrounds the jail and has a popular campground. From South West Rocks it's a pleasant 4km dawdle to Trial Bay along the beach.

Smoky Cape Lighthouse   LIGHTHOUSE
(📞6566 6301) Southeast of South West Rocks, this lighthouse, perched high above the ocean on a bracingly breezy cape, is a landmark that shouldn't be missed. Phone ahead for tours. It also has accommodation.

Diving   DIVING
The waters off South West Rocks are great for divers, especially **Fish Rock Cave,** south of Smoky Cape. **South West Rocks** (📞6566 6474; www.southwestrocksdive.com.au; 5/98 Gregory St) and **Fish Rock** (📞6566 6614; www.fish rock.com.au; 134 Gregory St) dive centres both offer two dives for around $165. Both have accommodation.

Little Bay Beach   BEACH
This is a good spot to have a swim with kangaroos looking on. It's the start of a couple of nice walks.

🛏️ Sleeping & Eating

Smoky Cape Lighthouse   B&B **$$$**
TOP
CHOICE (📞6566 6301; www.smokycapelighthouse. com; d $198, cottages per 2 nights from $390) Romantic evenings can be spent hearing the wind whip around the sturdy white lighthouse-keeper's building just a few metres from the lighthouse itself. The views are also fuel for passion.

Horseshoe Bay Beach Park   CARAVAN PARK **$**
(📞6566 6370; www.horseshoebaypark.com. au; 1 Livingston St; powered sites/vans/cabins $39/50/90) Planted a hop and a skip from the main street and right on sheltered Town Beach, the 82 sites and 12 cabins at this fine caravan park are in understandably high demand during the summer holidays.

Seabreeze Hotel   PUB, HOTEL **$$**
(📞6566 6909; www.seabreezebeachhotel.com. au; Livingstone St; mains $8-18; ⊘lunch & dinner; 🆒@) This place serves scrubbed-up pub nosh on pleasant decks. The rooms (singles/doubles from $80/105) with balconies

WORTH A TRIP

THE RIVERS RUN

For a bit of adventure take the partly unsealed but well-kept Loftus Rd from South West Rocks to Crescent Head alongside the pretty-as-a-picture Belmore and Macleay Rivers. The road detours through gorgeous riverside Gladstone, which is worth a stop for a meal at Heritage Hotel (www.heritagehotel. net.au; 21 Kinchela St; ⊘lunch & dinner), an excellent pub on the water's edge with an oasislike beer garden. Nearby, the Old Lodge Gallery & Riverbank Café (8 Kinchela St; ⊘breakfast & lunch) does sumptuous scones.

don't have views and the rooms with views don't have balconies, but they're clean and spacious.

Trial Bay Camping Area   CAMPGROUND **$**
(✆6566 6168; camp sites per night from $27) Behind the gaol, this magnificent campground sits on the peninsula, affording generous beach views from most sites. Amenities include hot showers and coin-slot barbies.

Heritage   GUESTHOUSE **$$**
(✆6566 6625; www.heritageguesthouse.com.au; 21-23 Livingstone St; d incl breakfast from $115; ❋) This renovated 1880s house has lovely, old-fashioned rooms, some with spas. Choose from the simpler rooms downstairs or the more lavish versions upstairs with ocean views.

Geppys   MEDITERRANEAN **$$**
(✆6566 6169; cnr Livingstone & Memorial Sts; mains $30; ⊘dinner) This cosmopolitan restaurant is signed up to the Slow Food movement; tuck into veal medallions with a raspberry reduction or fresh fish with salsa verde. It's open for drinks too.

South West Woks   ASIAN **$**
(✆6566 6655; Gregory St; mains $5-23; ⊘dinner) This is a good option for a cheap night out. Take a bottle of wine (it's BYO) and choose from a varied Asian menu. Some tables are alfresco.

Surf Club   CLUB **$**
(⊘4-9pm Fri-Sun Dec-Feb) This club on Horseshoe Bay is the best place in town for a beer with an ocean view. Unpretentious meals including roasts and shepherds pie are a Sunday must.

❶ Information

South West Rocks Visitor Centre (✆1800 642 480; Boatman's Cottage) At the end of the main street.

❶ Getting There & Away

Busways (✆1300 555 611; www.busways.com. au) runs two or three times daily Monday to Saturday to/from Kempsey (Belgrave St, $11.20, 55 minutes).

Cavanaghs (✆6562 7800; www.cavanaghs. com.au) runs to Kempsey, leaving from the town bus stop at Horseshoe Bay.

Hat Head National Park

This remote coastal park of 7458 hectares runs south almost from near South West Rocks to Crescent Head. It protects wetlands and some excellent beaches backed by one of NSW's largest sand dunes. Birds are prolific. Rising up from the generally flat landscape is Hungry Hill, near Hat Head, and sloping Hat Head itself. Walking tracks include a 2½-hour loop from the Cap picnic area.

Surrounded by the national park, the village of Hat Head is minute. At the end of town, a picturesque wooden footbridge crosses the aqua-green salt marsh ocean inlet. The water is so clear you can see fish darting around. Hat Head Holiday Park (✆6567 7501; www.4shoreholidayparks.com.au; camp sites/cabins from $22/79) is close to the sheltered bay and footbridge and offers backpacker rates.

You can camp (adult/child $5/3) in the park at Hungry Gate, 5km south of Hat Head (there are pit toilets and no showers, and you'll need to take your own water) or at Smoky Cape, just below Smoky Cape Lighthouse (p197) at the north end of the park.

The park is accessible from the hamlet of Kinchela, on the pretty road between Kempsey and South West Rocks.

Crescent Head

✆02 / POP 1080
This little hideaway, 18km southeast of Kempsey, is the kind of sleepy place you'd come to write a book. Failing that, how about learning to ride a longboard? The town is the surf longboarding capital, and it's here that the Malibu surfboard gained prominence in Australia during the '60s.

Today many come just to watch the long-board riders surf the epic waves of **Little Nobby's Junction**. There's also good short-board riding off Plomer Rd. Untrammelled **Killick Beach** stretches 14km north.

Sun Worship Eco Apartments (☑1300 664 757; www.sunworship.com.au; 9 Belmore St; apt $150-300; 🖥) are new contemporary rammed-earth villas with sustainable design including flow-through ventilation, solar orientation and solar hot water. Or try **Point Break Realty** (☑1800 352 272, 6566 0306; www.pointbreakrealty.com.au; Rankine St). For shorter stays, **Wombat Beach Resort** (☑6566 0121; www.wombatresort.com.au; 30-34 Pacific St; d $95-115; ✳@≋) offers comfy rooms, lush gardens and a decent pizza restaurant.

Bush & Beach Motel (☑1800 007 873; www.surfaris.com; 353 Loftus Rd; dm/d $25/60; @≋), better known as Surfari Central, is the perfect place for keen surfers to stay. These guys started the original Sydney-Byron surf tours and have now based themselves in Crescent Head because 'the surf is guaranteed every day'. The rooms are clean and comfortable, with bathrooms and some wicked wall murals. Surf-and-stay packages are a speciality.

TOP CHOICE **Crescent Tavern** (2 Main St; mains $26; ⊙lunch & dinner) has cold beer, a sun-soaked deck and excellent food. The local Vietnamese chef dishes up rice-paper rolls on the weekend, among other authentic Asian dishes. From his front room, **'Mongrel'** (7 Main St) sells a dozen of the freshest **Sydney rock oysters** you can eat for $9 – the perfect beach snack.

Right on the beach, **Crescent Head Holiday Park** (☑6566 0261; Pacific St; camp sites/cabins from $20/87; @) is a lovely spot to pitch a tent. The reception doubles as **Creso Cafe**, with espresso coffee, wraps and sandwiches as well as a heart-starting breakfast egg-and-bacon roll for $5. It also rents out surf boards ($15/30/40 per hour/half-day/full day)

Busways (☑1800 043 263; www.busways.com.au) buses run from Crescent Head to Kempsey (25 minutes).

Kempsey

☑02 / POP 8140

Kempsey is a large agricultural town about 45km north of Port Macquarie serving the farms of the Macleay Valley. The town is the home of the **Akubra hat** (www.akubra.com.au), which screams 'Down under!' from the top of any head sporting one. Although the factory misses tourism opportunities by the busload (it's closed to visitors), the local department store will happily fit out those wanting an iconic Aussie souvenir.

The late Slim Dusty, another Oz icon, was born here and he presumably got his inspiration for country-music songs such as 'Duncan' from this unassuming town. A long-proposed **Slim Dusty Heritage Centre** (www.slimdustycentre.com.au; Old Kempsey Showgrounds) remains the attraction, with no completion date.

The **visitors centre** (☑6563 1555, 1800 642 480; Pacific Hwy) is at a rest stop on the south side of town. It shares space with a small museum that honours the sacrifice of sheep-shearers, lumber-whackers, cattle-pokers and all the others who've made Kempsey an agricultural paradise.

The turn-off to Crescent Head is near the visitor centre in Kempsey. Alternatively, from the north take the very scenic Belmore Rd, which leaves the Pacific Hwy at Seven Oaks and follows the Macleay River.

Cavanaghs (☑6562 7800; www.cavanaghs.com.au) runs buses to South West Rocks from Kempsey Medical Centre (Belgrave St).

Melbourne & Coastal Victoria

Includes »

Why Go?

From windswept beaches to cosmopolitan seaside towns and legendary surfing spots, Victoria's coastline boasts stunning vistas, cool climates and the culture-packed city of Melbourne. It's a diverse coast; fairy penguins march up and down beaches in the popular tourist destination of Phillip Island, while Victoria's west coast faces onto Bass Strait and attracts surfers and those searching for the almighty Twelve Apostles.

Heading up the southeast coast from the hiking paradise of Wilsons Promontory is a long, cruisy expanse of beach that meets up with a popular, activity-filled lakes system around Lakes Entrance (Australia's largest inland waterway system). There are more stunning national parks on the approach to the Victoria–New South Wales border.

Melbourne's culinary focus stretches the entire way along the coast, while accommodation options include luxury eco-hostels and boutique B&Bs.

Best Places to Eat

- » Metung Galley (p266)
- » Merrijig Inn (p252)
- » Cutler & Co (p222)
- » Loam (p235)

Best Places to Stay

- » Déjà Vu (p268)
- » Adobe Mudbrick Flats (p273)
- » Punthill (p219)
- » Medina Executive Flinders Street (p215)

When to Go

Melbourne

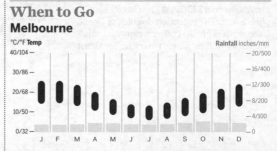

February School-holiday crowds have packed up, leaving good weather for swimming and hiking.

April Enjoy quiet beaches and the Apollo Bay Music Festival.

November It's getting warmer and hiking trails are in full colour after spring.

Regional Tours

The **Great Ocean Road** is one of the most popular touring routes in Australia, and, blow us down with a limestone outcrop, it's worth the hype. Take plenty of time – two weeks is good – to get the best from this region.

Start in the surfing mecca of Torquay by checking out the waves at **Bells Beach**, then head to family-friendly **Anglesea** to see kangaroos grazing on its golf course. **Aireys Inlet** is next; tour the lighthouse then plan an overnight stay in the resort town of **Lorne**. Break up the sea views with a detour up into the rainforests of the **Otway Ranges**. Back on the Great Ocean Road, head to the fishing village of Apollo Bay for a day or two then continue west into the koala and lighthouse zone of **Cape Otway**. It's quite a stretch to **Port Campbell National Park** and its famed **Twelve Apostles**; take the time to count them and spend a night in **Port Campbell** to get a feel for the area. Look for whales off the coast around **Warrnambool** then continue west to quaint, and very Irish, **Port Fairy**. If there's time, head to tiny **Cape Bridgewater** to meet its seal population.

DON'T MISS

Who can resist the nightly parade of cute little fairy penguins waddling out of the ocean and into their sandy burrows at **Phillip Island**? Not the three million-plus tourists who visit annually, that's for sure. This little island in Western Port Bay also has fabulous surf beaches, a moto-GP circuit and wildlife parks.

For sheer natural beauty, **Wilsons Promontory** has it all. Jutting out into Bass Strait, this national park is isolated but accessible, boasting sublime ocean beaches and some of the best wilderness hiking in the state. It has a well-maintained network of trails and bush camping areas – you just need to grab a map, strap on a pack and disappear into the wilds.

Beaches

» Surfing: try famous Bells Beach near Torquay
» Isolation: Ninety Mile Beach attracts those seeking space
» Beachside camping: camp for free by wild Johanna Beach

Fast Facts

» Population: 5,444,000
» Area: 227,500 sq km
» Telephone area code: 03
» Coastline: 2000km

Planning Your Trip

Avoid the coast from Christmas until late January, and during Easter; school holidays equate to packed beaches, booked-out accommodation and restricted access to popular hiking trails. See www.education.vic.gov.au for dates.

Resources

» Visit Victoria (www.visitvictoria.com) Official state tourism site
» Parks Victoria (www.parkweb.vic.gov.au) National park information
» The Age (www.theage.com.au) Victorian news
» Bureau of Meteorology (www.bom.gov.au/weather/vic) Weather forecasts

Melbourne & Coastal Victoria Highlights

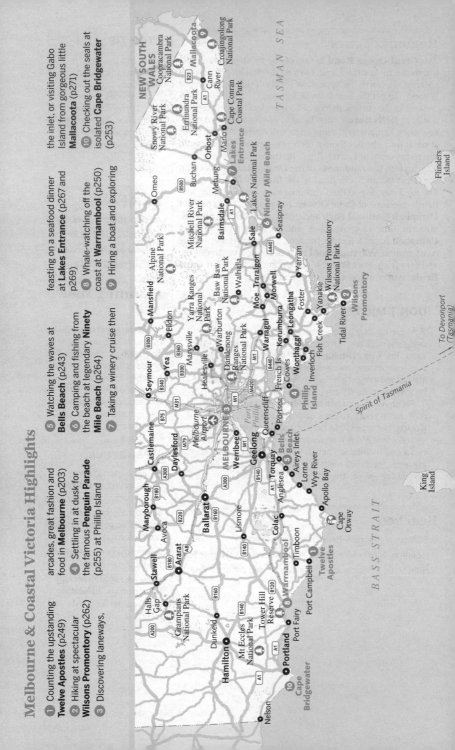

❶ Counting the upstanding **Twelve Apostles** (p249)

❷ Hiking at spectacular **Wilsons Promontory** (p262)

❸ Discovering laneways, arcades, great fashion and food in **Melbourne** (p203)

❹ Settling in at dusk for the famous **Penguin Parade** (p255) at Phillip Island

❺ Watching the waves at **Bells Beach** (p243)

❻ Camping and fishing for the beach at legendary **Ninety Mile Beach** (p264)

❼ Taking a winery cruise then

feasting on a seafood dinner at **Lakes Entrance** (p267 and p269)

❽ Whale-watching off the coast at **Warrnambool** (p250)

❾ Hiring a boat and exploring the inlet, or visiting Gabo Island from gorgeous little **Mallacoota** (p271)

❿ Checking out the seals at isolated **Cape Bridgewater** (p253)

MELBOURNE

There's a lot of fun packed into this city of some four million people. Coffee, food, art and fashion are taken mighty seriously, but that doesn't mean they're only for those in the know; all you need to eat well, go bar-hopping and/or shopping is a bit of cash and a deft ability to find hidden stairways and explore graffiti-covered laneways.

In many ways, it's the indie scene that sets Melbourne's tone – it can be spotted mainly in the CBD, St Kilda, Fitzroy, Collingwood, Brunswick and Northcote, but ekes out a living in most nooks and crannies in the city's inner suburbs.

Splitting the northern suburbs of Fitzroy, Collingwood and Carlton from its southern sisters including Prahran and South Yarra is the very brown Yarra River. There's a slight cultural divide, too, though sport knows no boundaries and Melburnians are intoxicatingly loud-voiced about AFL football (footy), horse racing or cricket, depending on the season.

◉ Sights

CENTRAL MELBOURNE

Federation Square LANDMARK
(Fed Sq; Map p216; www.federationsquare.com.au; cnr Flinders & Swanston Sts) Striking Federation Square has become the place to celebrate, protest or party. Occupying a prominent city block, the 'square' is far from square. Its undulating forecourt of Kimberley stone echoes the town squares of Europe. Here you'll find the subterranean **Melbourne Visitor Centre** (☑9928 0096; ⊙9am-6pm; tours per adult $12).

Ian Potter Centre: National Gallery of Victoria Australia ART GALLERY
(NGVA; Map p216; www.ngv.vic.gov.au; Federation Sq; ⊙10am-5pm Tue-Sun) This houses the NGV's extensive collection of Australian paintings, decorative arts, photography, prints, drawings, sculpture, fashion, textiles and jewellery.

The gallery's Indigenous collection dominates the ground floor and seeks to challenge ideas of the 'authentic'. Upstairs there are permanent displays of colonial paintings and drawings by 19th-century Aboriginal artists. There's also the work of Heidelberg School impressionists and an extensive collection of the work of the modernist 'Angry Penguins', including Sir Sidney Nolan, Arthur Boyd, Joy Hester and Albert Tucker.

Australian Centre for the Moving Image MUSEUM
(ACMI; Map p216; www.acmi.net.au; Federation Sq; ⊙10am-6pm) Educating, enthralling and entertaining in equal parts, ACMI has enough games and movies on call for days, or even months, of screen time. **Screenworld** is an exhibition that celebrates the work of mostly Australian cinema and TV and, upstairs, the **Australian Mediatheque** is a venue set aside for the viewing of programs from the National Film and Sound Archive and ACMI.

Birrarung Marr PARK
(Map p216; btwn Federation Sq & Yarra River) Featuring grassy knolls, river promenades and a thoughtful planting of indigenous flora, Birrarung Marr is a welcome addition to Melbourne's patchwork of parks and gardens. It houses the sculptural and musical **Federation Bells**.

Collins Street STREET
(Map p216; btwn Spring & Spencer Sts) The top end of Collins St (aka the 'Paris end'), between Spring and Swanston Sts, is lined with plane trees, grand buildings and luxe boutiques, giving it its moniker.

The **Block Arcade**, which runs between Collins and Elizabeth Sts, was built in 1891 and features etched-glass ceilings and mosaic floors.

Chinatown NEIGHBOURHOOD
(Map p216; Little Bourke St, btwn Spring & Swanston Sts) Chinese miners arrived in search of the 'new gold mountain' in the 1850s and settled in this strip of Little Bourke St, now flanked by red archways. Here you'll find an interesting mix of bars and restaurants, including one of Melbourne's best (see Flower Drum, p221). Come here for yum cha (dim sum) or explore its attendant laneways for late-night dumplings or cocktails. Chinatown hosts the city's vibrant Chinese New Year celebrations and the **Chinese Museum** (Map p216; www.chinesemuseum.com.au; 22 Cohen Pl; adult/child $7.50/5.50; ⊙10am-5pm).

FREE **Parliament House** HISTORIC BUILDING
(Map p216; www.parliament.vic.gov.au; Spring St) The grand steps of Victoria's parliament (c 1856) are often dotted with slow-moving, tulle-wearing brides smiling for the camera and placard-holding protesters doing the same. Inside, the exuberant use of ornamental plasterwork, stencilling and gilt are full of gold-rush-era pride and optimism. Though they've never been used, gun slits

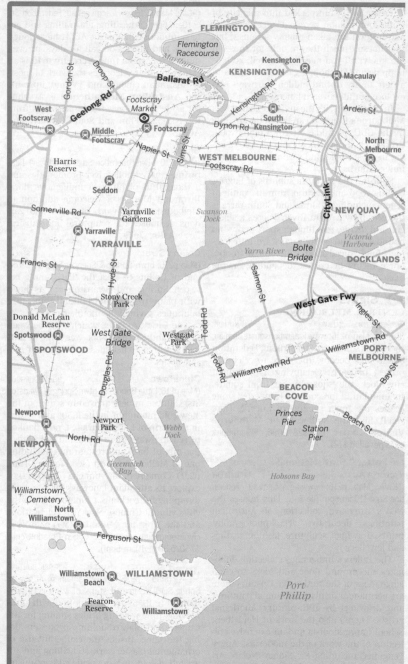

FLEMINGTON

Flemington Racecourse

Maribyrnong River

Kensington

KENSINGTON

Macaulay

Ballarat Rd

Gordon St

Droop St

Kensington Rd

Arden St

West Footscray

Geelong Rd

Footscray Market

Footscray

Dynon Rd

South Kensington

North Melbourne

Middle Footscray

Napier St

Sims St

WEST MELBOURNE

Harris Reserve

Footscray Rd

CityLink

Seddon

NEW QUAY

Somerville Rd

Yarraville Gardens

Swanson Dock

Victoria Harbour

Yarraville

Yarra River

Bolte Bridge

DOCKLANDS

YARRAVILLE

Francis St

Hyde St

Salmon St

West Gate Fwy

Ingles St

Stony Creek Park

Todd Rd

Donald McLean Reserve

Spotswood

West Gate Bridge

Westgate Park

Williamstown Rd

PORT MELBOURNE

SPOTSWOOD

Douglas Pde

Todd Rd

Williamstown Rd

Bay St

BEACON COVE

Newport

Newport Park

Princes Pier

Beach St

NEWPORT

North Rd

Webb Dock

Station Pier

Greenwich Bay

Hobsons Bay

Williamstown Cemetery

North Williamstown

Ferguson St

Williamstown Beach

WILLIAMSTOWN

Port Phillip

Fearon Reserve

Williamstown

MELBOURNE

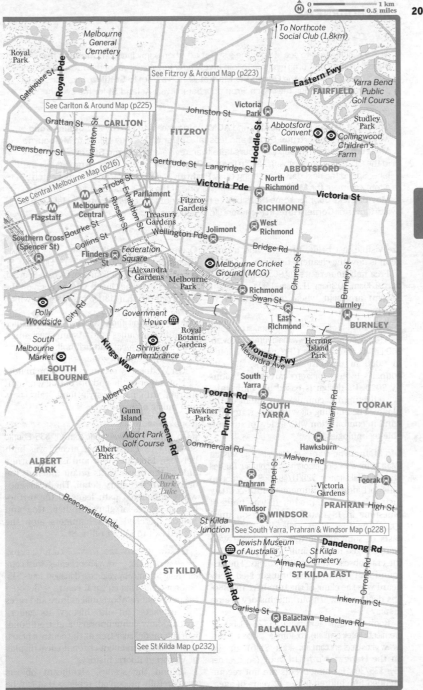

MELBOURNE & COASTAL VICTORIA

MELBOURNE IN...

Two Days

Join a walking tour to see Melbourne's street art, then enjoy lunch at **Cumulus Inc**. Chill out at a rooftop bar until it's time to join an evening kayaking tour of the Yarra River. Day two, shop your way to the **Queen Vic Market**. Catch a tram to **St Kilda**, take sunset photos and stroll along the beach. Prop up a bar in lively **Acland St** for the evening.

A Week

Check out the **Ian Potter Centre** and **ACMI** before heading **Fitzroy** and **Collingwood** way. Shop along **Gertrude Street** and feast at **Cutler & Co**. You're close to **Melbourne Museum**, so spend a couple of hours here then revive with a **Lygon Street** coffee. Back in the CBD, dine on dumplings at **HuTong** in **Chinatown**, or at **Flower Drum** across the lane. Spend the next day discovering busy **Prahran** and **South Yarra**. In winter, catch a footy game at the **MCG** before going lo-fi at one of the city's laneway bars. Pop into **Movida Next Door** for some tapas before heading out to the **Northcote Social Club** in Northcote or **Corner Hotel** in Richmond for live music.

are visible just below the roof, and a dungeon is now the cleaners' tearoom.

Free half-hour **tours** (☑9651 8911; ⊙weekdays 9.30am, 10.30am, 11.30am, 1.30pm, 2.30pm, 3.45pm) are held when parliament is in recess.

Council House 2   NOTABLE BUILDING
(CH2; Map p216; www.melbourne.vic.gov.au; 240 Little Collins St) The CH2 was completed in 2006 in response to meeting the city council's targets for zero carbon emissions by 2020. Its design is based on 'biomimicry', reflecting the complex ecosystem of the planet. The building uses the sun, water and wind in combination with a slew of sustainable technologies.

Old Melbourne Gaol   HISTORIC BUILDING, MUSEUM
(Map p216; www.oldmelbournegaol.com.au; Russell St; adult/child/family $21/11/49; ⊙9.30am-5pm) This forbidding monument to 19th-century justice is now a museum. It was built of bluestone in 1841, and was a prison until 1929. The tiny, bleak cells display plaster casts of some of the 130-plus people who were hanged here, a chilling 'by-product' of the era's obsession with phrenology. The last sound that legendary bushranger Ned Kelly heard was the clang of the trap here in 1880. His death mask, armour and history are on display.

Book through **Ticketek** (☑13 28 49; http://premier.ticketek.com.au) to join a **ghost hunt** (www.ghostseekers.com.au; adult $140) or go on the **Hangman's night tour** (adult/under 15yr $35/30). Evening events are not recommended for children under 12 years of age.

Queen Victoria Market   MARKET
(Map p216; www.qvm.com.au; 513 Elizabeth St; ⊙6am-2pm Tue & Thu, 6am-5pm Fri, 6am-3pm Sat, 9am-4pm Sun) The Queen Vic has been on the site for more than 130 years, prior to which it was a burial ground.

Melburnians shop here for fresh produce including organics and Asian specialities. There's a deli, meat and fish hall, as well as a fast food/restaurant zone.

On Wednesday evenings from the middle of November to the end of February, a night market with hawker-style food stalls, bars and music takes over.

Royal Arcade   HISTORIC ARCADE
(Map p216; www.royalarcade.com.au; 335 Bourke St Mall) This Parisian-style arcade was built between 1869 and 1870 and is Melbourne's oldest; the upper walls retain much of the original 19th-century detail. The black-and-white chequered path leads to the mythological figures of giant brothers Gog and Magog, perched with hammers atop the arched exit to Little Collins St.

Koorie Heritage Trust   CULTURAL CENTRE
(Map p216; www.koorieheritagetrust.com; 295 King St; entry by gold-coin donation, tours $15; ⊙10am-4pm) This cultural centre is devoted to southeastern Aboriginal culture and cares for artefacts and oral history. Its gallery spaces show contemporary and traditional work, a model scar tree at the centre's heart, as well as a permanent chronological display of Victorian Koorie history.

Behind the scenes, significant objects are carefully preserved; replicas that can be touched by visitors are used in the displays. There's also a shop with books, CDs, crafts and bush-tucker (food) supplies.

Immigration Museum MUSEUM
(Map p216; www.museumvictoria.com.au/immigrationmuseum; 400 Flinders St; adult/child $8/free; ⊙10am-5pm) The Immigration Museum uses personal and community voices, images and memorabilia to tell the stories of some of the nine million people who have migrated to Australia since 1788. It's symbolically housed in the old Customs House (1858–70).

Melbourne Aquarium AQUARIUM
(Map p216; ✆9923 5999; www.melbourneaquarium.com.au; cnr Queenswharf Rd & King St; adult/child/family $33/19/88; ⊙9.30am-9pm Jan, to 6pm Feb-Dec) This aquarium is home to rays, gropers and sharks, all of which cruise around a 2.2-million-litre tank, watched closely by visitors via a see-through glass tunnel. Three times a day, divers are thrown to the sharks; for between $150 and $345 you can join them.

State Library of Victoria LIBRARY
(Map p216; www.slv.vic.gov.au; 328 Swanston St; ⊙10am-9pm Mon-Thu, to 6pm Fri-Sun;) When the library opened in 1856, people entering were required to sign the visitors book, be over 14 years old and have clean hands. The only requirements today are that you leave your bags in the locker room ($1 to $2 for four hours) and maintain a bit of shush.

When the octagonal **La Trobe Reading Room** was completed in 1913, the reinforced-concrete dome was the largest of its kind in the world. The **Wheeler Centre** (www.wheelercentre.com), initially funded by Lonely Planet founders Tony and Maureen Wheeler, regularly features talks by local and international writers. It's on the Little Lonsdale St side. Refresh at **Mr Tulk** (⊙closed Sun).

FREE **Until Never** ART GALLERY
(Map p216; www.untilnever.net; 2nd fl, 3-5 Hosier Lane; ⊙11am-5pm Wed-Sat) This gallery space is run by Andrew Mac, one of Melbourne's street art masters, and highlights underground artists. It links in beautifully with the area's street art and ageing city lights project. Enter from Rutledge Lane.

Bourke Street Mall MALL
(Map p216; btwn Swanston & Elizabeth Sts) West of Swanston St marks the beginning of the Bourke St Mall. The mall is thick with trams, the sounds of Peruvian bands busking, shopfront spruikers and the general hubbub from shoppers. In a 60-year tradition, November to early January sees people lining up (sometimes for hours) to get a peek at

MELBOURNE SIGHTS

LOCAL KNOWLEDGE

FAY JUNE BALL: WIRADJURI WOMAN & EDUCATOR, KOORIE HERITAGE TRUST

I run walking tours around Melbourne, showing people the only two Indigenous river red gums left in Flagstaff Gardens, and taking them along the Birrarung (Yarra). It was misnamed the Yarra, which was actually the name of the (now gone) waterfall. Its real name is the Birrarung. People don't realise that Aboriginal language and art is specific to different regions. There are no dots in Victorian art: come to the Koorie Heritage Trust to buy real Victorian art and avoid ripping off Indigenous people.

See

The two scar trees in the MCG car park and the Corroboree Tree at St Kilda Junction (Map p232), which the St Kilda community saved.

Eat

Try Charcoal Lane in Fitzroy (Map p223).

Read

Aboriginal Melbourne: the Lost Land of the Kulin People by Gary Presland; *The Melbourne Dreaming: a Guide to the Aboriginal Places of Melbourne* by Meyer Eidelson

Did you know?

Everyone talks about Melbourne's weather, and Melbourne's Wurundjeri had the answer: there are six seasons in Melbourne, not four.

the animated displays in the **Myer Christmas windows**.

SOUTHBANK & DOCKLANDS

Southbank, once a gritty industrial site, sits directly across the Yarra from Flinders St. Behind the Southgate shopping mall is the city's major arts precinct, including the NGV International and Arts Centre. Back down by the river, the promenade stretches to the Crown Casino & Entertainment Complex, a self-proclaimed 'world of entertainment', pulling in visitors 24/7. To the city's west lies Docklands.

FREE **National Gallery of Victoria International** ART GALLERY
(NGVI; www.ngv.vic.gov.au; 180 St Kilda Rd; general admission free, fees for international exhibitions; ⊙10am-5pm Wed-Mon) Beyond the water wall you'll find international art that runs from the ancient to the contemporary. Completed in 1967, the original NGV building – Roy Grounds' 'cranky icon' – was one of Australia's most controversial but ultimately respected modernist masterpieces. Interior remodelling was undertaken from 1996 to 2003, overseen by Mario Bellini. Don't miss a gaze up at the Great Hall's stained-glass ceiling.

Eureka Tower & Skydeck 88 OBSERVATION DECK
(Map p216; www.eurekaskydeck.com.au; 7 Riverside Quay, Southbank; adult/child/family $18/9/40, The Edge extra $12/8/29; ⊙10am-10pm, last entry 9.30pm) Eureka Tower, built in 2006, has ninety-two storeys. Take a wild elevator ride to almost the top and you'll do 88 floors in less than 40 seconds. 'The Edge' – not a member of U2, but a slightly sadistic glass cube – propels you out of the building.

FREE **Australian Centre for Contemporary Art** ART GALLERY
(ACCA; www.accaonline.org.au; 111 Sturt St; ⊙10am-5pm Tue-Fri, 11am-6pm Sat & Sun) The ACCA is one of Australia's most exciting and challenging contemporary galleries. Shows include work specially commissioned for the space. The gallery shows a range of local and international artists. The building is fittingly sculptural, with a deeply rusted exterior evoking the factories that once stood on the site, and a slick, soaring, ever-adapting interior designed to house often massive installations. From Flinders Street Station, walk across Princes Bridge and along St Kilda Rd. Turn right at Grant St, then left onto Sturt.

Crown Casino & Entertainment Complex CASINO
(Map p216; www.crowncasino.com.au; Southbank) The Crown Entertainment Complex sprawls across two city blocks and includes three luxury hotels linked with Crown Casino, which has over 300 tables and 2500 gaming machines open 24/7. It's another world in its no-natural-light interior, where hours fly by.

Thrown in for good measure are waterfalls, fireballs, a giant cinema complex, a bowling alley, a variety of nightclubs and a 900-seat showroom. The complex is also home to a handful of luxury retailers, chain stores and speciality shops, as well as bars, cafes and a food hall. Restaurants here range from the perfunctory to the sublime, with several major culinary players stretched out along the river.

Polly Woodside Maritime Museum MUSEUM
(Map p204; www.pollywoodside.com.au; 2a Clarendon St, South Wharf; adult/child $15/8) A revamped interactive visitors centre tells the story of the iron-hulled merchant ship the *Polly Woodside*, which was launched in Belfast, Northern Ireland, in 1885, and now resides in what looks like a giant holding pen.

Melbourne Recital Centre/Melbourne Theatre Company MUSIC/THEATRE
(MTC; www.melbournerecital.com.au, www.mtc.com.au; cnr Southbank Blvd & Sturt St, Southbank) This new and award-winning building may look like a framed piece of giant honeycomb, but it's actually the hub (or hive) of two of Melbourne's arts companies. It's not unusual to see the likes of Geoffrey Rush performing at the MTC, while the Recital Centre's program ranges from local singer-songwriters and quartets to Babar the Elephant. From Flinders Street Station, cross the Yarra and turn right at Southbank Blvd.

Victorian Arts Centre ARTS CENTRE
(Map p216; www.theartscentre.com.au; 100 St Kilda Rd) The Arts Centre is made up of two separate buildings: the concert hall (Hamer Hall, which at the time of writing was undergoing a major redevelopment) and the theatres building (under the spire). Both are linked by a series of landscaped walkways.

The Famous Spiegeltent, one of the last of the great Belgian mirror tents, occupies the forecourt annually between February and April and is the stage for cabaret, music, comedy and circus. The George Adams Gallery and St Kilda Road Foyer Gallery are free gallery spaces with changing exhibitions.

The Arts Centre hosts a **makers' market** every Sunday from 10am to 4pm. Around 80 artisans sell everything from juggling balls to photographs.

Across the way in the Kings Domain is the **Sidney Myer Music Bowl**, a summer venue with a stage that's been graced by everyone from Dame Kiri to huge summer dance parties.

Docklands

PRECINCT

(Map p204; www.docklands.vic.gov.au) This waterfront area was the city's main industrial and docking area until the mid-1960s. In the mid-'90s a purpose-built studio complex and residential, retail and entertainment areas were built. Of most interest to travellers is the first-born, **New Quay**, with public art, promenades and a wide variety of cafes and restaurants. **Waterfront City** also has restaurants, bars, a yacht club and, if it rises again, the troublesome observation wheel, which was erected in 2010 then disassembled as structural problems became evident.

EAST MELBOURNE & RICHMOND

East Melbourne's sedate wide streets are lined with grand double-fronted Victorian terraces and Italianate mansions. It's also home to the mighty Melbourne Cricket Ground (MCG). On the other side of perpetually clogged Punt Rd/Hoddle St is the suburb of Richmond, which houses a vibrant stretch of Vietnamese restaurants along Victoria St, clothing outlets along Bridge Rd and some good drinking spots along Church St.

Melbourne Cricket Ground

SPORT STADIUM

(MCG; Map p204; www.mcg.org.au; Brunton Ave) It's one of the world's great sporting venues, and for many Australians the 'G' is considered hallowed ground.

In 1858 the first game of Australian Rules (Aussie rules) football was played where the MCG and its car parks now stand, and in 1877 it was the venue for the first Test cricket match between Australia and England. The MCG was also the central stadium for the 1956 Melbourne Olympics and the 2006 Commonwealth Games. The William Barak Bridge now links it to the CBD. MCG membership is a badge of honour for Melburnians of a particular class.

If you want to make a pilgrimage, **tours** (9657 8879; adult/child/family $20/10/50) take you through the stands, corporate and coaches' areas, the Long Room and (subject to availability) the players' change rooms and out onto the ground. They run (on non-

match days) between 10am and 3pm. Bookings are not essential but recommended. The MCG houses the **National Sports Museum**; you can incorporate both the MCG tour and entrance to the museum (adult/child/family $30/15/60).

Fitzroy Gardens

GARDEN

(Map p204; btwn Wellington Pde, Clarendon, Lansdowne & Albert Sts) The city drops away suddenly just east of Spring St, giving way to Melbourne's beautiful backyard, the Fitzroy Gardens. The stately avenues lined with English elms, flower beds, expansive lawns, strange fountains and a creek are a short stroll from town.

Cooks' Cottage (www.cookscottage.com.au; adult/child/family $4.50/2/12; ⊙9am-5pm) was shipped from Yorkshire in 253 packing cases and reconstructed in 1934 (the cottage actually belonged to the navigator's parents). Nearby is writer Ola Cohn's equally kooky carved **Fairies' Tree**. Efforts to preserve the 300-year-old stump, embellished in 1932 with fairies, pixies, kangaroos, emus and possums, include dissuading true believers from leaving notes to the fairies in the tree's hollows.

Between Cooks' Cottage and the Fairies' Tree is the Fitzroy Gardens **Scarred Tree** (now a stump), which was stripped of a piece of its bark to make a canoe by Aboriginal people.

In the centre of the gardens is a 'model' **Tudor village**. This well-meaning gift was a way of saying thanks for sending food to Britain during WWII.

FITZROY & AROUND

Fitzroy, Melbourne's first suburb, had a reputation for vice and squalor. Today, despite a long bout of gentrification, it's still where creative people meet up, though now it's more to 'do' lunch and blog about it before checking out the offerings at local 'one-off' boutiques and vintage shops.

Gertrude St, where grannies once feared to tread, is Melbourne's street of the moment. Smith St has some rough edges, though talk is more of its smart restaurants, cafes and boutiques rather than its down-and-out days of old. It's still a social spot for Aboriginal people.

To the north is the leafy residential area of North Fitzroy, which centres around the hipster hang-out of Edinburgh Gardens. When evening sets on Northcote's High St, it hums to the sound of a thousand Converse All Stars hitting the pavement in search of fun.

Abbotsford Convent
ARTS PRECINCT

(Map p204; (☑9415 3600; www.abbotsford convent.com.au; 1 St Heliers St, Abbotsford; ☺7.30am-10pm) Spread over nearly seven hectares of riverside land just 4km from the CBD, the convent dates back to 1861. The nuns are long gone – no one is going to ask you if you've been to mass lately – and there's now a rambling collection of creative studios and community offices. The **Convent Bakery** (www.conventbakery.com) supplies impromptu picnic provisions, or Steve at his 1950s-style bar **Handsome Steve's House of Refreshment** (http://houseofrefreshment. com; 1st fl) will mix you up a Campari soda to sip on the balcony while you're overlooking the ecclesiastic architecture and listening to the footy on the radio. There's a **Slow Food Market** (www.mfm.com.au; admission $2; ☺8am-1pm) every fourth Saturday and **Shirt and Skirt Market** every third Sunday. Opposite is the **Collingwood Children's Farm** (www. farm.org.au; adult/child/family $8/4/16; ☺9am-5pm), a rustic riverside retreat with a range of frolicking farm animals.

Centre for Contemporary Photography
ART GALLERY

(CCP; Map p223; www.ccp.org.au; 404 George St, Fitzroy; admission by donation; ☺11am-6pm Wed-Fri, noon-5pm weekends) This not-for-profit centre has a changing schedule of exhibitions across a couple of galleries. Shows traverse traditional technique and the highly conceptual.

CARLTON & AROUND

Lygon St reaches out through leafy North Carlton to booming Brunswick. Here you'll find a vibrant mix of students, long-established families, renovators and newly arrived migrants. The central Brunswick artery, Sydney Rd, is perpetually clogged with traffic and is packed with Middle Eastern restaurants and grocers. Lygon St, East Brunswick just keeps getting more fashionable; it has a cluster of restaurants, music venues and bars.

Melbourne Museum
MUSEUM

(Map p225; (☑13 11 02; www.museumvictoria. com.au; 11 Nicholson St, Carlton; admission adult/child $8/free, exhibitions $24/16); ☺10am-5pm) This confident postmodern exhibition space mixes old-style object displays with themed interactive display areas. The museum's reach is almost too broad to be cohesive but provides a grand sweep of Victoria's natural and cultural histories. Walk through the reconstructed laneway lives of the 1800s or become immersed in the legend of champion racehorse Phar Lap. Bunjilaka, on the ground floor, presents Indigenous stories and history told through objects and Aboriginal voices. There's also an open-air forest atrium featuring Victorian plants and animals and an **Imax cinema** (p227) next door.

Royal Exhibition Building
HISTORIC BUILDING

(Map p225; www.museumvicoria.com.au/reb; Nicholson St, Carlton) Built for the International Exhibition in 1880, and winning Unesco World Heritage status in 2004, this beautiful great hall, influenced by Byzantine, Lombardic, Romanesque and Italian Renaissance design, symbolises the glory days of the Industrial Revolution, Empire and 19th-century Melbourne's economic supremacy. Australia's first parliament was held here in 1901; more than a hundred years later everything from trade fairs to designer sales to dance parties take place here. **Tours** (☑bookings 13 11 02; adult/child $5/3.50) leave from the Melbourne Museum most days at 2pm.

Royal Melbourne Zoo
ZOO

(☑9285 9300; www.zoo.org.au; Elliott Ave, Parkville; adult/child/family $25/13/57; ☺9am-5pm) Melbourne's zoo is one of the city's most popular attractions. Walkways pass through some enclosures; you can stroll through the bird aviary, cross a bridge over the lions' park or enter a tropical hothouse full of colourful butterflies. There's also a large collection of native animals in natural bush settings, a platypus aquarium, fur seals, lions and tigers, plenty of reptiles, and an 'am I in Asia?' elephant enclosure. In summer the zoo hosts **Twilight Concerts**. **Roar 'n' Snore** (adult/child $195/145; ☺Sep-May) allows you to camp at the zoo and join the keepers on their morning feeding rounds.

Ceres
ENVIRONMENT PARK

(www.ceres.org.au; 8 Lee St, East Brunswick; ☺9am-5pm, market 9am-1pm Wed & Sat) Ceres is a 20-something-year-old community environment project built on a former tip. Stroll around the permaculture and bush-tucker nursery before refuelling with an organic coffee and cake at the pretty (and extremely popular) cafe. Children enjoy the natural miniworlds, and on market days you can buy organic and backyard-produced goodies while the kids marvel at the chooks and sheep.

ELVIS IN MELBOURNE

Given that Elvis Presley never actually performed in Melbourne, it's surprising to find out that after he died (or did he?) in 1977, his Melbourne fans erected a tribute to the King at Melbourne General Cemetery, North Carlton. Look for the large grotto (and, on his birthday and certain anniversary dates, his fans).

SOUTH YARRA, PRAHRAN & WINDSOR

This neighbourhood has always been synonymous with glitz and glamour; it might be south but it's commonly referred to as the 'right' side of the river. Its elevated aspect and large allotments were always considered prestigious.

Chapel St's South Yarra strip still parades itself as a must-do fashion destination, but has seen better days; it's been taken over by chain stores, tacky bars and, come sunset, doof-doof cars. Prahran, however, is still a gutsy and good place, with designer stores, bars and some refreshingly eclectic businesses. Commercial Rd is Melbourne's pumping pink zone, and has a diverse collection of nightclubs, bars and bookshops. It is also the home of the Prahran Market, where the locals shop for fruit, veg and upmarket deli delights. Chapel St continues down to Windsor, a hive of fun cafes and op shops.

Hawksburn Village, up the Malvern Rd hill, and High St, Armadale make for stylish shopping.

FREE **Royal Botanic Gardens** GARDEN (Map p204; www.rbg.vic.gov.au; ⊙7.30am-8.30pm Nov-Mar, to 5.30pm Apr-Oct) The Botanic Gardens are one of Melbourne's most glorious attractions. Sprawling beside the Yarra River, the beautifully designed gardens feature a global selection of plantings as well as specific Australian gardens. Along with the abundance of plant species, there's a surprising amount of wildlife, including waterfowl, ducks, swans and child-scaring eels in and around the ornamental lake, as well as cockatoos and possums. There's also an excellent, nature-based **Children's Garden**.

The gardens are encircled by the **Tan**, a 4km-long former horse-exercising track, and now used to exercise joggers. During the summer months, the gardens play host to the **Moonlight Cinema** (p229) and theatre performances.

Shrine of Remembrance MONUMENT (Map p204; www.shrine.org.au; Birdwood Ave, South Yarra; ⊙10am-5pm) Beside St Kilda Rd stands the massive Shrine of Remembrance, which was built as a memorial to Victorians killed in WWI. Thousands attend the moving Anzac Day (25 April) dawn service.

Governor La Trobe's Cottage & Government House HISTORIC BUILDING (Map p204; Kings Domain) East of the Shrine of Remembrance is **Governor La Trobe's Cottage** (www.nattrust.com.au), the original government house building that was sent out in prefabricated form from the mother country in 1840. Inside, you can see many of the original furnishings, and the servants' quarters out the back.

This modest cottage sits in stark contrast to the Italianate pile of **Government House** (☑8663 7260; Government House Dr), a replica of Queen Victoria's palace on England's Isle of Wight. It's been the residence of all serving Victorian governors since it was built in 1872. Book well in advance to take the National Trust **tour** (www.nattrust.com.au; adult/child $10/5), which includes both houses on Mondays and Wednesdays.

Herring Island PARK (Map p228; http://home.vicnet.net.au/~herring) Once an unloved dumping ground for silt, Herring Island is now a prelapsarian garden that seeks to preserve the original trees, shrubs and grasses of the Yarra and provide a home for indigenous animals such as parrots, possums and lizards, as well as sculptures.

Designated picnic areas, with barbecues, make for a rare retreat just 3km from the city centre. The island is theoretically open to visitors all year round but can only be reached by boat. **A Parks Victoria punt** (☑13 19 63; per person $2; ⊙11.30am-5pm Sat & Sun Dec-Mar) operates in summer from Como Landing on Alexandra Ave in South Yarra.

Prahran Market MARKET (Map p228; www.prahranmarket.com.au; 163 Commercial Rd, South Yarra; ⊙dawn-5pm Tue & Sat, dawn-6pm Thu & Fri, 10am-3pm Sun) The Prahran Market has been an institution for over a century and is one of the finest produce markets in the city.

FOOTSCRAY & YARRAVILLE

Head west beyond the city's remaining working docklands to Footscray and Yarraville. The area's 'capital' is the fabulously unfussy Footscray. Almost half of Footscray's population was born overseas, the majority in Vietnam, Africa, China, Italy and Greece. **Footscray Market** (Map p204; cnr Hopkins & Leeds St; ⊙7am-4pm Tue, Wed & Sat, to 6pm Thu, to 8pm Fri) is testament to the area's diversity.

From authentic ethnic cuisine to cafes with more than just the usual staples, there's no need to go hungry in the west; try **Le Chien** (5 Gamon St, Seddon) cafe in Seddon, African restaurant **Cafe Lalibela** (91 Irving St, Footscray) and pho at **Hung Vuong** (128 Hopkins St, Footscray).

Heading south from Footscray are the fashionable residential neighbourhoods of Seddon and Yarraville. Yarraville centres on its train station, with a beautifully well-preserved heritage shopping area around Anderson St.

ST KILDA & AROUND

Come to St Kilda for its sea breezes, seedy history and for a good old bit of people-watching.

St Kilda's palm trees, bay vistas, briny breezes and pink-stained sunsets are heart-breakingly beautiful. On weekends, the volume is turned up, the traffic crawls and the street-party atmosphere sets in.

Jewish Museum of Australia MUSEUM
(Map p204; www.jewishmuseum.com.au; 26 Alma Rd, St Kilda; adult/child/family $10/5/20; ⊙10am-4pm Tue-Thu, 11am-5pm Sun) Interactive displays tell the history of Australia's Jewish community from the earliest days of European settlement, while permanent exhibitions celebrate Judaism's rich cycle of festivals and holy days.

Luna Park AMUSEMENT PARK
(Map p232; www.lunapark.com.au; Lower Esplanade, St Kilda; adult/child 1-ride ticket $9.40/7.50, unlimited-rides ticket $42/32; ⊙check website for seasonal opening hours) Luna Park opened in 1912 and still retains the feel of an old-style amusement park, with creepy Mr Moon's gaping mouth swallowing you up whole on entering. There's a heritage-listed scenic railway (the oldest operating roller coaster in the world) and the full complement of gut-churning modern rides. For grown-ups, the noise and lack of greenery or shade can pall all too fast.

St Kilda foreshore BEACH
(Map p232; Jacka Blvd, St Kilda) There are palm-fringed promenades, a parkland strand and a long stretch of sand. Still, don't expect Bondi or Noosa. St Kilda's seaside appeal is more Brighton, England, than *Baywatch*, despite 20-odd years of glitzy development.

And that's the way Melburnians like it; a certain depth of character and an all-weather charm, with wild days on the bay providing for spectacular cloudscapes and terse little waves, as well as the more predictable sparkling blue of summer.

The breakwater near the **St Kilda Pier** was built in the '50s and is now home to a colony of little penguins. You can visit the penguins on an eco **stand-up paddle boarding trip**. During summer, the **Port Phillip Eco Centre** (www.ecocentre.com; 55a Blessington St, St Kilda) runs a range of tours including one that starts at a stormwater drain and ends up at the penguin colony. Contact **Earthcare St Kilda** (earthcarestkilda@gmail.com) to get involved in penguin research or rakali (water rat) watch.

SOUTH MELBOURNE, PORT MELBOURNE & ALBERT PARK

There's something boastful about these seaside suburbs and their peaceful, upmarket environment (though come Grand Prix time, the noise is ramped up big time). Head to South Melbourne for its market (famous for its dim sims), homewares shops and top cafes (seems there's a coffee competition going on). At nearby Port Melbourne is Station Pier, the passenger terminal for the ferry service between Melbourne and Tasmania (see p233).

Albert Park Lake LAKE
(Map p204; btwn Queens Rd, Fitzroy St, Aughtie Dr & Albert Rd, Albert Park) Elegant black swans give their inimitable bottoms-up salute as you circumnavigate the 5km perimeter of this man-made lake. Jogging, cycling, walking or clamouring over play equipment is the appropriate human equivalent. Lakeside Dr was used as an international motor-

racing circuit in the 1950s, and since 1996 the revamped track has been the venue for the **Australian Formula One Grand Prix** (p215) each March.

South Melbourne Market   MARKET
(Map p204; cnr Coventry & Cecil Sts, South Melbourne; ⊘8am-4pm Wed, to 6pm Fri, to 4pm Sat & Sun) The market's labyrinthine interior is packed to overflowing with an eccentric collection of stalls selling everything from carpets to bok choy (Chinese greens).

🏃 Activities
Canoeing & Kayaking

Kayak Melbourne   KAYAKING
(☑0418 106 427; www.kayakmelbourne.com.au; tours $89) Two-hour long tours take you past Melbourne city's newest developments and explain the history of the older ones. Moonlight tours are most evocative and include a fish-and-chips dinner.

Cycling
Cycling maps are available from the Melbourne Visitor Information Centre at Federation Square and **Bicycle Victoria** (☑8636 8888; www.bv.com.au). You'll not be alone on the roads; there's a large club scene, as well as a new breed of 'slow cyclists'. Wearing a helmet while cycling is compulsory in Australia. Borrow a bike from the public scheme (p234) or go vintage.

Humble Vintage   CYCLING
(☑0432 032 450; www.thehumblevintage.com) Get yourself a set of special wheels from this collection of retro racers, city bikes and ladies bikes. Rates start at $30 per day, or $80 per week and include lock, helmet and a terrific map.

Lawn Bowls
Formerly the domain of senior citizens wearing starched white uniforms, bowling clubs are inundated by younger types: barefoot, with a beer in one hand and a bowl in the other.

St Kilda Bowling Club   LAWN BOWLS
(Map p232; 66 Fitzroy St, St Kilda; ⊘noon-sunset Tue-Sun) The only dress code at this popular bowling club is shoes off. So join the many others who de-shoe to enjoy a beer and a bowl in the great outdoors.

North Fitzroy Bowls   LAWN BOWLS
(www.fvbowls.com.au; 578 Brunswick St, North Fitzroy) This centre comes equipped with lights for night bowls, barbecues and a

beer garden. Phone to make a booking and for opening times.

Windsurfing, Kitesurfing & Stand-up Paddle Boarding

RPS – the Board Store
WINDSURFING, PADDLE BOARDING
(☑9525 6475; www.rpstheboardstore.com; 87 Ormond Rd, Elwood) Offers windsurfing courses and stand-up paddle boarding (SUP) lessons in summer.

Stand Up Paddle Boarding   PADDLE BOARDING
(☑0416 184 994; www.supb.com.au; St Kilda Sea Baths; tours $89-130) Hires out SUP equipment from St Kilda for $25 per hour and runs tours.

Swimming
In summer, hit the sand at one of the city's metropolitan beaches. St Kilda, Middle Park and Port Melbourne are popular patches, with suburban beaches at Brighton (with its photogenic bathing boxes) and Sandringham. Public pools are also well loved.

Fitzroy Swimming Pool   SWIMMING
(Map p223; Alexandra Pde, Fitzroy; adult/child $4.60/2.10) Between laps, locals love catching a few rays up in the bleachers or on the lawn. The pool's Italian 'Aqua Profonda' sign was painted in 1953 – an initiative of the pool's manager who frequently had to rescue migrant children who couldn't read the English signs. The sign is heritage-listed (misspelled and all – it should be 'Acqua').

Melbourne City Baths   SWIMMING
(Map p216; www.melbournecitybaths.com.au; 420 Swanston St, Melbourne; casual swim adult/child/family $5.50/2.60/12, gym $20; ⊘6am-10pm Mon-Thu, 6am-8pm Fri, 8am 6pm weekends) The City Baths first opened in 1860 and were intended to stop people bathing in the seriously polluted Yarra River. Enjoy a swim in the 1903 heritage-listed building.

👉 Tours

🚶 Aboriginal Heritage Walk   INDIGENOUS
(☑9252 2429; www.rbg.vic.gov.au; Royal Botanic Gardens; adult/child/$25/10; ⊘11am Tue & Thu & first Sun of month) The Royal Botanic Gardens are on a traditional camping and meeting place of the original owners, and this tour takes you through their story – from songlines to plant lore, all in 90 fascinating minutes.

MELBOURNE FOR CHILDREN

» **Children's Garden** (p211) Has natural tunnels in the rainforest, a kitchen garden and water-play areas.

» **Collingwood Children's Farm** (p210) Old MacDonald has nothing on this farm; this one has an organic, wholesome vibe and a bunch of farm animals (usually) happy to be made a fuss of.

» **ACMI** (p203) Free access to computer games and movies may encourage square eyes, but it's a great spot for a rainy day.

» **Melbourne Zoo** (p210) Roar 'n' Snore packages take you behind the scenes.

» **National Sports Museum** (p209) Just walking in will get your junior champion's heart rate up.

» **Melbourne Museum** (p210) The Children's Museum has hands-on exhibits that make kids squeal.

Sunset Eco Penguin Tour WILDLIFE
(☏0416 184 994; www.supb.com.au; $130)
See St Kilda's penguin colony while you navigate your paddle board standing up (a lesson is included).

FREE **City Circle trams** TRAM
(www.metlinkmelbourne.com.au) Free W-class trams trundle around the city perimeter from 10am to 6pm daily.

FREE **Melbourne City Tourist Shuttle** CITY
(www.thatsmelbourne.com.au; ☺9am-4.30pm) This shuttle takes about 1½ hours round trip and takes passengers to sights including Melbourne Museum, the MCG (on non-sporting days) and the Docklands.

Melbourne by Foot WALKING
(☏0418 394 000; www.melbournebyfoot. com; tours $29) Take a couple of hours out with Dave and experience a mellow, informative walking tour that covers lane art, politics, Melbourne's history and diversity.

FREE **Greeter Service** CITY
(☏9658 9658; Melbourne Visitor Centre, Federation Sq) This free two-hour 'orientation tour' departs from Fed Sq daily at 9.30am (bookings required).

Hidden Secrets Tours WALKING
(☏9663 3358; www.hiddensecretstours.com; tours $70-145) Offers a variety of walking tours covering everything from lanes and arcades, wine, architecture, coffee and cafes, and vintage Melbourne.

Real Melbourne Bike Tours CYCLING
(☏0417 339 203; www.rentabike.net.au; tours including lunch adult/child $110/79) Offers four-hour cycling tours covering the CBD, parts of the Yarra and Fitzroy.

✦ Festivals & Events

Melbourne isn't fussy about when it gets festive. Winter chills or summer's swelter are no excuse, with Melburnians joining like-minded types at outdoor festivals, in cinemas, performance spaces or sporting venues year-round.

January

Australian Open TENNIS
(www.australianopen.com; National Tennis Centre, Melbourne Park) The world's top tennis players and huge, merry-making crowds descend for Australia's Grand Slam tennis championship.

Midsumma Festival ARTS
(www.midsumma.org.au) Melbourne's annual gay and lesbian arts festival features more than 100 events from mid-January to mid-February, with a Pride March finale.

Big Day Out MUSIC
(www.bigdayout.com) The national rock-fest comes to town at the end of January.

Chinese New Year CULTURAL
(www.melbournechinatown.com.au; Little Bourke St, Chinatown) Melbourne has celebrated the Chinese lunar new year since Little Bourke St became Chinatown in the 1860s.

February

St Kilda Festival NEIGHBOURHOOD
(www.stkildafestival.com.au; Acland & Fitzroy Sts, St Kilda) This week-long festival ends in a suburb-wide street party on the final Sunday.

Melbourne Fashion Festival FASHION
(www.mff.com.au) This style-fest features salon shows and parades showcasing established designers' ranges.

Melbourne Food & Wine Festival

FOOD, WINE

(www.melbournefoodandwine.com.au) Market tours, wine tastings, cooking classes and presentations by celeb chefs take place at venues across the city.

March

Moomba CULTURAL

(www.thatsmelbourne.com.au; Alexandra Gardens, Birrarung Marr & Docklands) A waterside festival famous locally for its wacky Birdman Rally, where competitors launch themselves into the Yarra in homemade flying machines.

Australian Formula One Grand Prix

CAR RACING

(www.grandprix.com.au; Albert Park) The 5.3km street circuit around normally tranquil Albert Park Lake is known for its smooth, fast surface. The buzz, both on the streets and in your ears, takes over Melbourne for four days of rev-head action.

April

International Comedy Festival COMEDY

(www.comedyfestival.com.au) An enormous range of local and international comic talent hits town with four weeks of laughs.

May

Melbourne Jazz JAZZ

(www.melbournejazz.com) International jazz cats head to town and join locals for gigs at Hamer Hall, the Regent Theatre and the Palms at Crown Casino.

July

Melbourne International Film Festival FILM

(www.melbournefilmfestival.com.au) This midwinter movie love-in brings out black-skivvy-wearing cinephiles in droves.

August

Melbourne Writers Festival LITERATURE

(www.mwf.com.au) Beginning in the last week of August, the writers' festival features forums and events at various venues.

September

AFL Grand Final AFL FOOTBALL

(www.afl.com.au; MCG) It's easier to kick a goal from the boundary line than to pick up random tickets to the Grand Final, but it's not hard to get your share of finals fever anywhere in Melbourne (particularly at pubs).

Melbourne Fringe Festival ARTS

(www.melbournefringe.com.au) The Fringe showcases experimental theatre, music and visual arts.

October

Melbourne International Arts Festival ARTS

(www.melbournefestival.com.au) Held at various venues around the city, this festival features a thought-provoking program of Australian and international theatre, opera, dance, visual art and music.

November

Melbourne Cup HORSE RACING

(www.springracingcarnival.com.au) Culminating in the prestigious Melbourne Cup, the Spring Racing Carnival is as much a social event as a sporting one. The Cup, held on the first Tuesday in November, is a public holiday in Melbourne.

December

Boxing Day Test CRICKET

(www.mcg.org.au; MCG) Boxing Day is day one of Melbourne's annually scheduled international Test cricket match, drawing out the cricket fans. Expect some shenanigans from Bay 13.

Sleeping

Stay in the CBD for good access to the main sights, or spread your wings and get to know an inner-city suburb such as funky Fitzroy, seaside St Kilda or smart South Yarra.

CENTRAL MELBOURNE

Melbourne Central YHA HOSTEL $

(Map p216; 9621 2523; www.yha.com.au; 562 Flinders St; dm/d $32/100; @🛜) This heritage building has been totally transformed by the YHA gang; expect a lively reception, handsome rooms, and kitchens and common areas on each of the four levels. Entertainment's high on the agenda, there's a fab restaurant (Bertha Brown) on the ground floor and a grand rooftop area.

Medina Executive Flinders Street APARTMENTS $$

(Map p216; 8663 0000; www.medina.com.au; 88 Flinders St; apt from $165; ❄) These cool monochromatic serviced apartments are extra-large and luxurious. Ask for one at the front for amazing parkland views or get glimpses into Melbourne's lanes from the giant timber-floored studios, all boasting full kitchens.

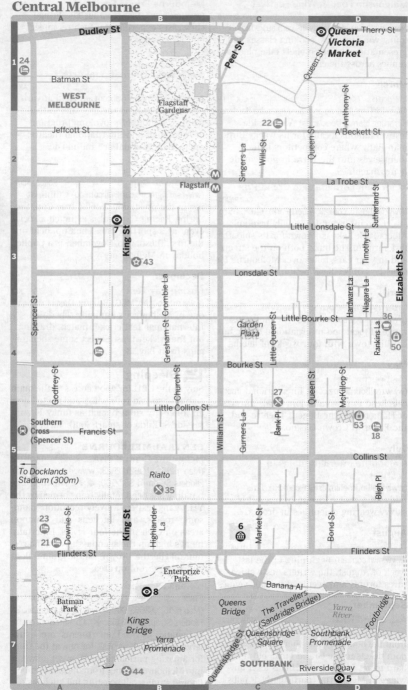

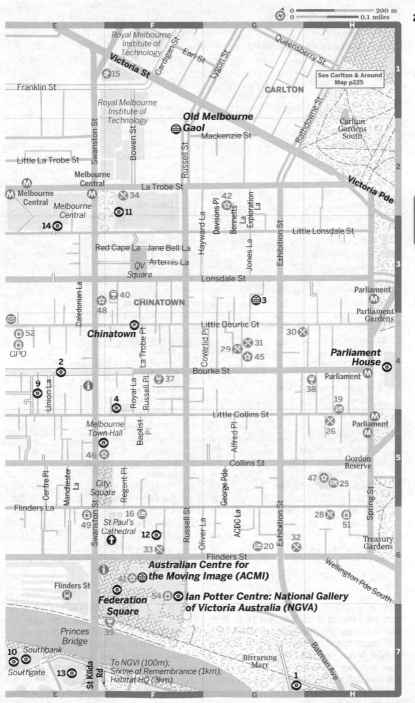

0   200 m
0   0.1 miles

Royal Melbourne Institute of Technology

Queensberry St

Victoria St

☉15

Franklin St

Cardigan St
Earl St
Lygon St

CARLTON

See Carlton & Around
Map p225

Royal Melbourne Institute of Technology

Old Melbourne
🏛 Gaol

Mackenzie St

Carlton Gardens South

Rathdowne St

Little La Trobe St

Swanston St
Bowen St
Russell St

Victoria Pde

Ⓜ Melbourne Central

Ⓜ Melbourne Central
Melbourne Central

Ⓜ

La Trobe St

☒34

☉11

42
Davisons Pl
Bennetts
La Exploration La

Little Lonsdale St

14☉

Red Cape La   Jane Bell La
QV
Square
Artemis La

Hayward La
Jones La
Exhibition St

Lonsdale St

☆40
48
CHINATOWN

Caledonian La

🏛3

Parliament

Parliament Gardens

✉
🔒52
🔒
GPO

Chinatown ☉

La Trobe Pl

Little Bourke Ct

Coverlid Pl

29☒☒31
☆45

30☒

Parliament House ☉

Ⓜ

2☉

9☉
Union La

ⓘ

Royal La
Russell Pl

☒37

Bourke St

Parliament Ⓜ
38

19
🛏

4☉

Baptist Pl

Little Collins St

Alfred Pl

☒
26

Ⓜ
Parliament

Ⓜ

Melbourne Town Hall ☉
46☆

City Square

Regent Pl

Collins St

Gordon Reserve

47☆🛏25

Spring St

Flinders La

Centre Pl
Manchester La

Swanston St

George Pde
Exhibition St

28☒🔒
51

Treasury Gardens

49🔒
St Paul's Cathedral ✝

16🛏
12☉
33☒

Russell St
Oliver La
ACDC La

20🛏

32☒

Flinders St

ⓘ
Australian Centre for
41☉🏛 the Moving Image (ACMI)

Flinders St
🚇

54🔒☉ Ian Potter Centre: National Gallery
of Victoria Australia (NGVA)

Federation ☉
Square

39

Princes Bridge

10☉ Southbank
☉☉
Southgate   13☉

St Kilda Rd

To NGVI (100m);
Shrine of Remembrance (1km);
Habitat HQ (3km)

Birrarung Marr

Wellington Pde South

Batman Ave

1☉

MELBOURNE CENTRAL MELBOURNE

Central Melbourne

Nomad's Industry HOSTEL $
(Map p216; ☎9328 4383; www.nomadshostels.com; 198 A'Beckett St; dm $28-36, d $125; @🛜) Flashpacking hits Melbourne's CBD with this smart hostel boasting a mix of four- to 14-bed dorms (groups can take hold of a four-bed dorm with en suite). There's a rooftop area and plenty of gloss (especially in the girls-only 'Princess Wing').

Adelphi Hotel HOTEL $$
(Map p216; ☎8080 8888; www.adelphi.com.au; 187 Flinders Lane; r from $185; ❄@🛜🏊) This discreet Flinders Lane property, designed by Denton Corker Marshall in the early '90s, was one of Australia's first boutique hotels. The cosy rooms with original fittings have stood the test of time and its pool, which juts out over Flinders Lane, has sparked imitators.

Robinsons in the City
BOUTIQUE HOTEL **$$**

(Map p216; ☏9329 2552; www.ritc.com.au; 405 Spencer St; r from $185 including full breakfast; ❄️🛜) Robinsons is a gem with six large rooms and warm service. The building is a former bakery, dating from 1850, but it's been given a modern, eclectic look. Bathrooms are not in the rooms; each room has its own in the hall.

Sofitel
HOTEL **$$$**

(Map p216; ☏9653 0000; www.sofitelmelbourne.com.au; 25 Collins St; r from $270; ❄️@🛜) Guestrooms at the Sofitel start on the 36th floor, so you're guaranteed views that will make you giddy. The rooms are high-international style, opulent rather than minimal, and though the hotel entrance, with its superb IM Pei–designed ceiling, is relentlessly workaday, you'll soon be a world (or at least 36 floors) away. No35 is an excellent restaurant on level (you guessed it) 35.

Alto Hotel on Bourke
HOTEL **$$**

(Map p216; ☏9606 0585; www.altohotel.com.au; 636 Bourke St; r/apt from $160/190; ❄️@🛜) This environmentally minded hotel has water-saving showers, energy-efficient light globes, double-glazed windows that open, and in-room recycling is promoted. Rooms are also well equipped, light and neutrally decorated.

Causeway 353
HOTEL **$$**

(Map p216; ☏9660 8888; www.causeway.com.au; 353 Little Collins St; r from $150, including breakfast; ❄️@🛜) Who needs a view when you've got laneway location? Causeway 353's breakfast is in a cafe on a bustling laneway, and you'll be more than relaxed after a night in its simple, stylish rooms, which feature long and dark timber bedheads, king-sized beds and smart leather furniture.

Pensione Hotel
HOTEL **$**

(Map p216; ☏9621 3333; www.pensione.com.au; 16 Spencer St; r from $100, ❄️@🛜) With refreshing honesty, the Pensione Hotel names some rooms a 'petit double' but what you don't get in size is more than made up for in spot-on style, room extras and super-reasonable rates.

City Centre Hotel
HOTEL **$**

(Map p216; ☏9654 5401; www.citycentrebudgethotel.com.au; 22 Little Collins St; s/d/f $70/90/130; @🛜) Intimate, independent and inconspicuous, this 38-room budget hotel is a find. It's located at the city's prettier end, down a 'Little' street, up some stairs, inside an unassuming building. All rooms share bathroom facilities but the fresh rooms are light-filled with working windows; there's also free wi-fi and a laundry.

FITZROY & AROUND

TOP CHOICE Brooklyn Arts Hotel
BOUTIQUE HOTEL **$$**

(Map p223; ☏9419 9328; www.brooklynartshotel.com; 48-50 George St, Fitzroy; r from $135; 🛜) There are seven very different rooms in this unique, character-filled hotel. Owner Maggie has put the call out for artistic people and they've responded by staying, so expect lively conversation around the continental breakfast. Rooms are clean, quirky, colourful and beautifully decorated; one even houses a piano.

Tyrian Serviced Apartments
APARTMENTS **$$$**

(Map p223; ☏9415 1900; www.tyrian.com.au; 91 Johnston St; r from $200; ❄️🛜) These spacious, self-contained modern apartments have a certain Fitzroy celeb appeal, which you'll feel from the moment you walk down the dimmed hallway to reception. Big couches, flat-screen TVs and balconies add to the appeal.

Home @ The Mansion
HOSTEL **$**

(Map p223; ☏9663 4212; www.homemansion.com.au; 80 Victoria Pde, East Melbourne; dm $28-34, d $90; @🛜) This grand-looking heritage building houses 92 dorm beds and a couple of doubles, all of which are light and bright and have lovely high ceilings. There are two small PlayStation and TV-watching areas, a courtyard out the front and a sunny kitchen.

Nunnery
HOSTEL **$**

(Map p223; ☏9419 8637; www.nunnery.com.au; 116 Nicholson St, Fitzroy; dm/s/d including breakfast $30/75/110; @🛜) The Nunnery oozes atmosphere, with sweeping staircases and many original features; the walls are dripping with religious works of art and ornate stained-glass windows. You'll be giving thanks for the big comfortable lounges and communal areas.

SOUTH YARRA, PRAHRAN & WINDSOR

TOP CHOICE Punthill Apartments South Yarra
APARTMENTS **$$**

(Map p228; ☏1300 731 299; www.punthill.com.au; 7 Yarra St, South Yarra; rooms from $180; ❄️🛜) It's the little things – like a blackboard and chalk in the kitchen for messages, and individually wrapped liquorice allsorts by the bed – that make this a great choice. The bright rooms have laundry facilities and those with

GAY & LESBIAN MELBOURNE

Melbourne's gay and lesbian community is well integrated into the general populace but clubs and bars are found in two distinct locations: Abbotsford/Collingwood and Prahran/South Yarra. Commercial Rd, which separates the latter two suburbs, is home to numerous gay clubs, cafes and businesses. It's more glamorous than the 'north side', which is reputedly more down to earth and a little less pretentious.

The **Midsumma Festival** (www.midsumma.org.au; ☉mid-Jan–early Feb) has a diverse program of cultural, community and sporting events.

MCV (www.mcv.net.au) is a free weekly newspaper, and gay and lesbian community radio station **JOY 94.9 FM** (www.joy.org.au) is another important resource for visitors and locals.

Drinking & Nightlife

Xchange Hotel
CLUB

(Map p228; www.xchange.com.au; 119 Commercial Rd, South Yarra; ☉4pm-1am Mon-Thu, 2pm-3am Fri-Sun) A brand-new fit-out has added girly 'Pamela's Place' and transformed the 'Boom Boom Room' into an arena-style, multilevel dance floor.

Glasshouse Hotel
PUB

(www.glass-house.com.au; 51 Gipps St, Collingwood; ☉5pm-late Wed, noon-late Fri & Sun, 4pm-late Sat) Caters to a mostly lesbian crowd with entertainment including live bands, drag kings and DJs.

Peel Hotel
CLUB

(www.thepeel.com.au; cnr Peel & Wellington Sts, Collingwood; ☉9pm-late Thu-Sat) Features a mostly male crowd dancing to house music, retro and commercial dance.

Sleeping

169 Drummond
GUESTHOUSE $$

(Map p225 (☎9663 3081; www.169drummond.com.au; 169 Drummond St, Carlton; d $135-145) A privately owned guesthouse in a renovated, 19th-century terrace in the inner north, one block from vibrant Lygon St.

balconies come complete with their own (tin) dog on fake grass.

Art Series (The Olsen)
BOUTIQUE HOTEL $$$

(Map p228; ☎9040 1222; www.artserieshotels.com.au/olsen; 637 Chapel St, South Yarra; r from $200; ✴@☎✺) This new hotel honouring artist John Olsen is where international celebs are staying these days, and we think we know why. The staff are attentive. The modern glam foyer is beaut. The open-plan rooms are delightful. Oh, and the hotel's pool juts out over Chapel St. You never know who you'll bump into in the lift.

Art Series (The Cullen)
BOUTIQUE HOTEL $$

(Map p228; ☎9098 1555; www.artserieshotels.com.au/cullen; 164 Commercial Rd, Prahran; r from $169; ✴@☎) Expect visions of Ned Kelly shooting you from the glam opaque room/bathroom dividers in this new and lively hotel resplendent in the works of Sydney artist Adam Cullen. Borrow the 'Cullen Car' ($60 per day) or Kronan bike ($5 per hour) and let the whole of Melbourne know where you're staying.

Lyall
HOTEL $$$

(Map p228; ☎9868 8222; www.thelyall.com; 14 Murphy St, South Yarra; r from $270; ✴@☎) The Lyall is tucked away in a leafy residential street. The spacious rooms are well appointed, with little luxuries including gourmet cheese in the minibar, laundry facilities, and, in some, televisions in the bathrooms.

Back of Chapel
HOSTEL $

(Map p228; ☎9521 5338; www.backofchapel.com; 50 Green St, Windsor; dm $20-28, d $60-80, including breakfast; @) This clean backpacker place in an old Victorian terrace has its own bar (claiming to have the cheapest drinks in Melbourne), and is literally 20 steps away from buzzing Chapel St. Television is a feature (there are two biggies) and new bathrooms and a bunch of freebies (breakfast, for one) add appeal.

Hotel Claremont GUESTHOUSE $
(Map p228; 9826 8000, 1300 301 630; www.
hotelclaremont.com; 189 Toorak Rd, South Yarra;
dm/s/d including breakfast $34/69/79; @🛜) In a
large heritage building dating from 1868, the
Claremont is good value, with comfortable
rooms, high ceilings and shared bathrooms.
Don't expect fancy decor: it's simply a clean,
welcoming cheapie.

ST KILDA & AROUND

Prince HOTEL $$$
(Map p232; 9536 1111; www.theprince.com.au; 2
Acland St, St Kilda; r including breakfast from $260;
❄@🛜) The Prince has a suitably dramatic
lobby and the rooms are an interesting mix
of the original pub's proportions, natural
materials and a pared-back aesthetic. Larger
rooms and suites feature some key pieces
of vintage modernist furniture. On-site 'fa-
cilities' take in some of the city's most men-
tioned: bars, band rooms and even a wine
shop downstairs.

Base HOSTEL $
(Map p232; 8598 6200; www.basebackpackers.
com; 17 Carlisle St, St Kilda; dm/r from $30/110;
❄@🛜) Accor spin off Base has streamlined
dorms, each with en suite, or slick doubles.
There's a 'sanctuary' floor for female travel-
lers, and a bar and live-music nights to keep
the good-time vibe happening.

Habitat HQ HOSTEL $
(9537 3777; www.habitathq.com.au; 333 St
Kilda Rd; dm $30-$38, d $139, all incl breakfast;
❄@🛜) There's not much that this new
hostel doesn't have. Tick off open-plan
communal spaces, a beer garden, a travel
agent and a pool table, for starters.

✖ Eating
Go beyond the boundaries for Melbourne's
best food: once rugged Collingwood now
heaves with food bloggers, Brunswick is
home to boutique eateries, and CBD venues
are raising the lunchtime bar. Don't miss St
Kilda for its consistently good old-timers.

CENTRAL MELBOURNE

TOP CHOICE Cumulus Inc MODERN AUSTRALIAN $$
(Map p216; www.cumulusinc.com.au; 45
Flinders Lane; mains $21-38; ⊗breakfast, lunch &
dinner Mon-Sat) One of Melbourne's best for
breakfasts, lunches and dinners; it gives you
that wonderful Andrew McConnell style
along with really reasonable prices. The focus is on beautiful produce and simple but
artful cooking: from breakfasts of sardines

and smoked tomato on toast at the marble
bar to suppers of freshly shucked clair de
lune oysters tucked away on the leather
banquettes.

Vue de Monde FRENCH, MODERN AUSTRALIAN $$$
(Map p216; 9691 3888; www.vuedemonde.com.
au; 430 Little Collins St; lunch/dinner menus gour-
mands from $100/150; ⊗lunch & dinner Tue-Fri,
dinner Sat) Melbourne's favoured spot for oc-
casion dining is in the throes of relocating
to the old 'observation deck' of the **Rialto**,
so its view will finally match its name. It'll
no doubt be the usual fantastic French cui-
sine thanks to visionary Shannon Bennett.
Book ahead. Remaining at the old barrister's
chambers will be **Bistro Vue** (9691 3838)
and **Cafe Vue** (⊗Mon-Fri 7am-4pm).

Movida SPANISH $$
(Map p216; 9663 3038; www.movida.com.au; 1
Hosier Lane; tapas $4-6, raciones $10-17; ⊗lunch &
dinner) Movida is nestled in a cobbled laneway emblazoned with one of the world's
densest collections of street art; it doesn't
get much more Melbourne than this. Line
up along the bar, cluster around little window tables or, if you've booked, take a table
in the dining area. **Movida Next Door** (next
door!) is the perfect place for a pre-show
beer and tapas.

Flower Drum CHINESE $$$
(Map p216; 9662 3655; www.flower-drum.com;
17 Market Lane; mains $35-55; ⊗lunch Mon-Sat,
dinner daily) Flower Drum continues to be
Melbourne's most celebrated Chinese res-
taurant. The finest, freshest produce pre-
pared with absolute attention to detail keeps
this Chinatown institution booked out for
weeks in advance. The sumptuous but os-
tensibly simple Cantonese food is delivered
with the slick service you'd expect in such
elegant surrounds.

HuTong Dumpling Bar CHINESE $
(Map p216; 14-16 Market Lane; mains $12)
HuTong's windows face out on famed
Flower Drum, and its reputation for divine
dumplings including *shao-long bao,* means
it's just as hard to get a lunchtime seat here.
Watch the chefs make the delicate dump-
lings, then hope they don't watch you mak-
ing a mess of them (there are step-by-step
instructions for eating them on the table).
Also in Prahran (see Map p228).

Little Press & Cellar GREEK $$$
(Map p216; 72 Flinders St; mains $35-49; ⊗7am-
late Mon-Fri, noon-late weekends) It may not be

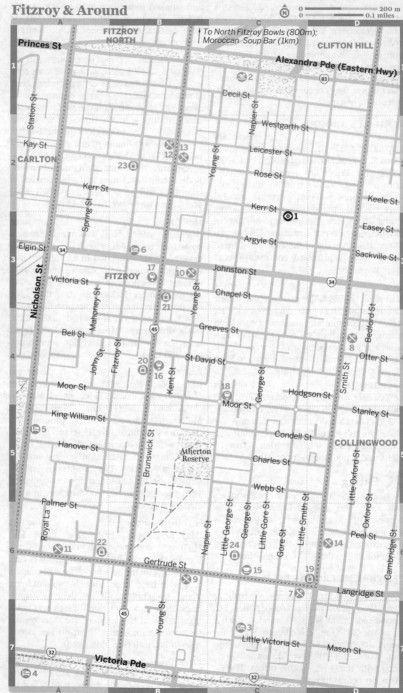

FITZROY
NORTH

Princes St

CLIFTON HILL

To North Fitzroy Bowls (800m);
Moroccan Soup Bar (1km)

Alexandra Pde (Eastern Hwy)

Cecil St

Westgarth St

Napier St

Leicester St

Young St

Rose St

CARLTON

Station St

Kay St

Kerr St

Keele St

Spring St

Kerr St

Easey St

Argyle St

Sackville St

Elgin St

FITZROY

Johnston St

Chapel St

Victoria St

Mahoney St

Young St

Greeves St

Bell St

John St

Fitzroy St

St David St

George St

Moor St

Kent St

Hodgson St

Moor St

Stanley St

King William St

Condell St

COLLINGWOOD

Smith St

Bedford St

Otter St

Hanover St

Charles St

Atherton
Reserve

Webb St

Brunswick St

Palmer St

Napier St

Little George St

George St

Little Gore St

Gore St

Little Smith St

Little Oxford St

Oxford St

Peel St

Royal La

Gertrude St

Cambridge St

Langridge St

Young St

Little Victoria St

Mason St

Victoria Pde

Nicholson St

as large as the Press Club next door, but this 'little press' gives you a taste of George Calombaris' style at a bargain price. Consider its Monday-to-Friday express lunch menu, which fires off three Greek dishes for $34, but don't miss the 'little snack' of taramasalata with hot chips ($13.50).

Gingerboy ASIAN FUSION **$$**
(Map p216; ☑9662 4200; www.gingerboy.com.au; 27-29 Crossley St; small dishes $13-16, large dishes $30-36; ☺lunch & dinner Mon-Fri, dinner Sat) Brave the aggressively trendy surrounds and weekend party scene, as talented Teague Ezard does a fine turn in flash hawker cooking. Flavours pop in dishes such as scallops with green chilli jam or coconut kingfish with peanut-and-tamarind dressing. There are two dinner sittings, and bookings are required.

Bar Lourinhã TAPAS **$$**
(Map p216; ☑9663 7890; www.barlourinha.com.au; 37 Little Collins St; tapas $9-20 ☺lunch & dinner Mon-Fri, Sat dinner) Matt McConnell's wonderful northern Spanish-Portuguese specialities have the swagger and honesty of an Iberian shepherd, but with a cluey, metropolitan touch. Start light with the melting, zingy kingfish pancetta and finish with the hearty house-made chorizo or baked *morcilla* (blood sausage).

FITZROY & AROUND

TOP CHOICE **Cutler & Co** MODERN AUSTRALIAN **$$$**
(Map p223; ☑9419 4888; www.cutlerandco. com.au; 55 Gertrude St, Fitzroy; ☺lunch Fri & Sun,

dinner Tue-Sun) Hyped for all the right reasons, this is Andrew McConnell's latest restaurant, and though its decor might be a little over the top, its attentive, informed staff and joy-inducing meals (suckling pig is a favourite) have quickly made this one of Melbourne's best.

St Jude's Cellar MODERN AUSTRALIAN **$$**
(Map p223; www.stjudescellars.com.au; 389-391 Brunswick St, Fitzroy; mains around $22-26; ☺breakfast Sat & Sun, lunch & dinner Tue-Sun) A cavernous warehouse space has been given a clever, cool and humanising fit-out while not losing its airy industrial feel. The restaurant stretches out from behind the shopfront cellar, affording respite from the Brunswick St hustle. Mains include mussels and leek in Coldstream cider and goat ragout, but try the innovative desserts, too.

Moroccan Soup Bar
NORTH AFRICAN, VEGETARIAN **$$**
(☑9482 4240; 183 St Georges Rd, North Fitzroy; banquets $18; ☺6pm-10pm Tue-Sun) Prepare to queue before being seated by stalwart Hana, who will then go through the menu verbally. Best bet is the banquet, which, for three courses, is tremendous value. The sublime chickpea bake has locals queuing with their own pots and containers to nab some to take away. It's an alcohol-free zone, but (shhh) there's a cute bar next door.

Cavallero MODERN AUSTRALIAN **$**
(Map p223; www.cavallero.com.au; 300 Smith St, Collingwood; mains $10-25; ☺breakfast, lunch &

Fitzroy & Around

dinner Tue-Sun) A supersmart, subtle fit-out lets the charm of this grand Victorian shopfront shine. Served under the gaze of a deer's head, morning coffee and brioche make way for fancy toasties and pinot gris then shared plates galore and cocktails.

Charcoal Lane AUSTRALIAN $$
(Map p223; 9418 3400; www.charcoallane. com.au; 136 Gertrude St, Fitzroy; mains $17-35; lunch & dinner Tue-Sat) This training restaurant for Aboriginal and disadvantaged young people is one of the best places to try native flora and fauna; menu items include wallaby tartare and native peppered kangaroo.

Commoner MODERN BRITISH $$
(Map p223; 9415 6876; www.thecommoner.com. au; 122 Johnston St, Fitzroy; mains $13-30; lunch Sat & Sun, dinner Wed-Sun) If you need to be convinced of this off-strip restaurant's serious intent, the woodfired goat or pork it offers up come Sunday lunch should do it. On Sunday nights there's no menu, you just get fed.

Birdman Eating TAPAS $
(Map p223; www.birdmaneating.com.au; 238 Gertrude St, Fitzroy; mains $8-18) Popular? You bet. It's named after the infamous 'Birdman Rally' held during Melbourne's Moomba festival; you'll be glad you don't have to hurl yourself off a bridge to sit pretty on Gertrude St and eat up Welsh rarebit or dip into leek pate.

Wabi Sabi Salon JAPANESE $
(Map p223; www.wabisabi.net.au; 94 Smith St, Collingwood; dishes $3-20; lunch & dinner Mon-Sat) Expect kooky Japanese decor and delish Japanese cuisine, including bento boxes that change daily (you choose meat, fish or veg and the Japanese chefs do the rest).

Vegie Bar VEGETARIAN $
(Map p223; www.vegiebar.com.au; 380 Brunswick St, Fitzroy; mains $7-15; lunch & dinner) Delicious thin-crust pizzas, tasty curries and seasonal broths can be eaten sitting by fab Brunswick St itself, or in the cavernous, shared-table space inside.

CARLTON & AROUND

Rumi MIDDLE EASTERN $$
(9388 8255; 116 Lygon St, Brunswick East; mains $17-22; dinner Tue-Sun) A fabulously well-considered place that serves up a mix of traditional Lebanese cooking and contemporary interpretations of old Persian dishes. The *sigara boregi* (cheese and pine-nut pastries) are a local institution and tasty mains such as meatballs are balanced with a large and interesting selection of vegetable dishes.

Bar Idda ITALIAN $$
(9380 5339; www.baridda.com.au; 132 Lygon St, Brunswick East; mains $18; dinner Tue-Sat) The diner-style table coverings give little clue to the tasty morsels this Sicilian restaurant serves. Shared plates are the go and range from pistachio-crumbed lamb loin to vegetarian layered eggplant.

Hellenic Republic GREEK $$
(9381 1222; www.hellenicrepublic.com.au; 434 Lygon St, Brunswick East; mains $21-32; breakfast, lunch & dinner Sat & Sun, lunch Fri-Sun, dinner Mon-Sun) The Iron Bark grill at George Calombaris' northern outpost works overtime grilling up pitta, king prawns, local calamari and snapper and luscious lamb.

ST KILDA & AROUND

TOP CHOICE Attica CONTEMPORARY $$$
(9530 0111; www.attica.com.au; 74 Glen Eira Rd, Ripponlea; 8-course tasting menus $144; dinner Tue-Sat) Staking its claim to fame by being the only Melbourne restaurant to make it onto San Pellegrino's Best Restaurant list in 2010, Attica is a suburban restaurant that serves Ben Shewry's creative dishes dégustation-style. Expect small portions of texture-oriented delight, such as potatoes cooked in earth.

Stokehouse MODERN AUSTRALIAN $$$
(Map p232; 9525 5555; www.stokehouse.com. au; 30 Jacka Blvd, St Kilda; mains upstairs $28-32, downstairs $10-20; lunch & dinner) Two-faced Stokehouse makes the most of its beachfront position, cleverly catering to families and drop-ins downstairs, and turning on its best upstairs for finer diners. It's a fixture on the Melbourne dining scene and known for its seafood, service and the bay views on offer. Book for upstairs.

Cicciolina MODERN MEDITERRANEAN $$
(Map p232; www.cicciolinastkilda.com.au; 130 Acland St, St Kilda; mains $19-40; lunch & dinner) This warm room of dark wood, subdued lighting and pencil-sketches is a St Kilda institution. The inspired mod-Med menu is smart and generous, and the service warm. It doesn't take bookings; eat early or while away your wait in the moody little back bar. Check out its new restaurant, Ilona Staller (282 Carlisle St), in nearby Balaclava.

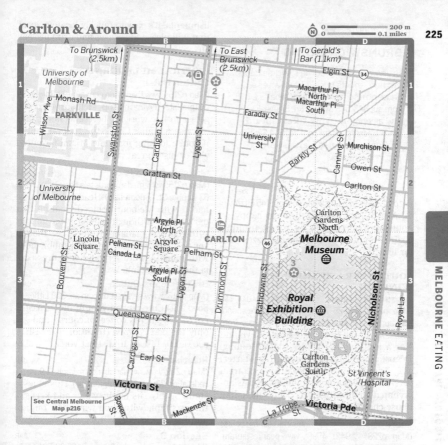

Lentil as Anything   VEGETARIAN $

(Map p232; www.lentilasanything.com; 41 Blessington St, St Kilda; prices at customers' discretion; ⏱lunch & dinner) Choosing from the always-organic, no-meat menu is easy. Deciding how much you would like to pay can be hard. This unique not-for-profit operation provides training and educational opportunities for marginalised people, as well as offering tasty, if not particularly notable, vegetarian food. There are other branches that are located at the **Abbotsford Convent** (Map p204; 1 St Heliers St, Abbotsford) and on Barkly St, Footscray.

Café di Stasio   ITALIAN $$

(Map p232; ☎9525 3999; www.distasio.com.au; 31a Fitzroy St, St Kilda; mains $27-43; ⏱lunch & dinner) Capricious white-jacketed waiters, a tenebrous Bill Henson photograph and a jazz soundtrack set the mood. The Italian menu has the appropriate drama and grace.

Carlton & Around

Claypots   SEAFOOD $$

(Map p232; 213 Barkly St; mains $25-$35; ⏱lunch & dinner) A local favourite, Claypots serves up seafood in its namesake. Get in early to both get a seat and ensure the good stuff is still available, as hot items go fast.

DON'T MISS

BRUNSWICK EATING

Brunswick is Melbourne's Middle Eastern hub, and its busy **A1 Lebanese Bakehouse** (www.a1lebanesebakery.com.au; 643-645 Sydney Rd, Brunswick) and alcohol-free **Tiba's Restaurant** (www.tibasrestaurant.com.au; 504 Sydney Rd, Brunswick; closed Tue) are worth a trip in themselves.

Banff
PIZZA $

(Map p232; www.banffstkilda.com.au; 145 Fitzroy St; mains $9) It's not just the daily happy hour that keeps Banff's Fitzroy St–fronting chairs occupied, it's also the $9 pizzas ($5 for lunch).

SOUTH YARRA, PRAHRAN & WINDSOR

Jacques Reymond　　MODERN AUSTRALIAN $$$

(Map p228; ✆9525 2178; www.jacquesreymond.com.au; 78 Williams Rd, Prahran; 3 courses from $98; ⊘lunch Thu-Fri, dinner Tue-Sat) Reymond was a local pioneer of dégustation dining. Dégustation plates are now entrée (starter) size, and there's an innovative vegetarian version. Expect a French-influenced, Asian-accented menu with lovely details including house-churned butter.

Pearl　　MODERN AUSTRALIAN $$$

(Map p228; ✆9421 4599; www.pearlrestaurant.com.au; 631-633 Church St, Richmond; mains $35-48; ⊘lunch & dinner) Owner-chef Geoff Lindsay proclaims himself 'a fifth-generation Aussie boy who is seduced by ginger, chilli and palm sugar, Turkish delight, chocolate and pomegranate'. We're seduced too: his exquisitely rendered food really does epitomise Modern Australian cooking. The space is slick but comfortable, though service can be lax.

Outpost　　CAFE $$

(Map p228; http://outpostcafe.com.au; 9 Yarra St, South Yarra; mains $14) Of the St Ali coffee realm, this mighty-busy cafe has a range of different rooms to dine and converse in. Our pick? The one where you get to watch the food (including items such as shaved Italian black truffle) being prepared.

🍴 Drinking

Melbourne's bars are legendary, and from laneway hideaways to brassy corner establishments, it's easy to quickly locate a 'local' that will please the senses and drinking palate.

CENTRAL MELBOURNE

Carlton Hotel　　BAR

(Map p216; www.thecarlton.com.au; 193 Bourke St; ⊘4pm-late) Over-the-top Melbourne rococo gets another workout here and never fails to raise a smile. Check the rooftop **Palmz** if you're looking for some Miami-flavoured vice or just a great view.

Madame Brussels　　BAR

(Map p216; www.madamebrussels.com; Level 3, 59-63 Bourke St; ⊘noon-1am) Head here if you've had it with Melbourne moody and all that dark wood. Although named for a famous 19th-century madam, it feels as though you've fallen into a camp '60s rabbit hole, with much Astroturfery and staff dressed à la the country club.

Brother Baba Budan　　CAFE

(Map p216; www.sevenseeds.com.au; 359 Little Bourke St) Cute city outpost of indie roasters St Ali. There's coffee, of course, and only the odd *ruglach* (traditional Jewish cookie) or biscuit to distract you.

Riverland　　BAR

(Map p216; www.riverlandbar.com; Vaults 1-9, Federation Wharf; ⊘7am-midnight) This bluestone beauty sits by the water and keeps things simple with good wine, beer on tap and bar snacks.

Section 8　　BAR

(Map p216; www.section8.com.au; 27-29 Tattersalls Lane; ⊘8am-late Mon-Fri, noon-late Sat & Sun) The latest in shipping-container habitats; come and sink a Mountain Goat with the after-work crowd, who make do with packing cases for decor.

EAST MELBOURNE & RICHMOND

TOP CHOICE Der Raum　　BAR

(www.derraum.com.au; 438 Church St, Richmond; ⊘5pm-late) The name conjures up images of a dark Fritz Lang flick and there's definitely something noir-ish about the space and the extreme devotion to hard liquor.

Mountain Goat Brewery　　BREWERY

(www.goatbeer.com.au; cnr North & Clark Sts, Richmond; ⊘from 5pm Wed & Fri only) This local microbrewery is set in a massive beer-producing warehouse; enjoy its range of beers while nibbling on pizza.

FITZROY & AROUND

Little Creatures Dining Hall   BEER HALL
(Map p223; www.littlecreatures.com.au; 222 Brunswick St, Fitzroy; 🛜) With free wi-fi, community bikes and a daytime kid-friendly groove, this vast drinking hall is the perfect place to spend up big on pizzas and enjoy local wine and beer.

Naked for Satan   BAR
(Map p223; www.nakedforsatan.com.au; 285 Brunswick St; ⊘noon until late) Vibrant, loud and reviving an apparent Brunswick St legend (a man nicknamed Satan who would get down and dirty, naked because of the heat, in an illegal vodka distillery under the shop), this place packs a punch both with its popular *pintxos* (tapas; $2) and cleverly named beverages.

De Clieu   CAFE
(Map p223; 187 Gertrude St, Collingwood) From the folk who brought coffee-mad-Melbourne Seven Seeds comes De Clieu, a funky little cafe with polished-concrete floors and a sense of humour.

Napier Hotel   PUB
(Map p223; www.thenapierhotel.com; 210 Napier St, Fitzroy; ⊘3-11pm Mon-Thu, 1pm-1am Fri & Sat, 1-11pm Sun) The Napier has stood on this corner for over a century; many pots have been pulled as the face of the neighbourhood changes.

CARLTON & AROUND

Gerald's Bar   WINE BAR
(386 Rathdowne St, Carlton North; ⊘5-11pm Mon-Sat) Wine by the glass is democratically selected at Gerald's and they spin some fine vintage vinyl from behind the curved wooden bar. This place won bar of the year in 2010.

ST KILDA & AROUND

Carlisle Wine Bar   WINE BAR
(137 Carlisle St, Balaclava; ⊘brunch Sat & Sun, dinner daily) Locals love this often rowdy, wine-worshipping former butcher shop. The staff will treat you like a regular and find you a glass of something special, or effortlessly throw together a cocktail amid the weekend rush.

George Public Bar   BAR
(Map p232; www.georgepublicbar.com.au; Basement, 127 Fitzroy St, St Kilda) Behind the crumbling paint and Edwardian arched windows of the George Hotel, there's the Melbourne Wine Room and a large front bar that keeps the after-work crowd happy. In the bowels of the building is the George Public Bar, often referred to as the Snakepit.

☆ Entertainment

Nightclubs

alumbra   NIGHTCLUB
(www.alumbra.com.au; Shed 9, Central Pier, 161 Harbour Esplanade, Docklands; ⊘4pm-late Fri-Sun) Great music and a stunning location will impress – even if the Bali-meets-Morocco follies of the decorator don't.

Revolver Upstairs   NIGHTCLUB
(Map p228; www.revolverupstairs.com.au; 229 Chapel St, Prahran; ⊘noon-4am Mon-Thu, 24hr Fri-Sun) Rowdy Revolver can feel like an enormous version of your own lounge room, but with 54 hours of nonstop music come the weekend, you're probably glad it's not.

Brown Alley   NIGHTCLUB
(Map p216; www.brownalley.com; cnr King & Lonsdale Sts; ⊘Mon-Fri 11.30am-late, Sat & Sun 6pm-late) This historical pub hides away a fully fledged nightclub with a 24-hour licence. It's enormous, with distinct rooms that can fit up to 1000 people.

Cinemas

Cinema multiplexes are spread throughout Melbourne city, and there are quite a few treasured independent cinemas in both the CBD and surrounding suburbs. Grab a choc-top (ice cream dipped in chocolate) and check out the following:

Astor   CINEMA
(Map p228; www.astor-theatre.com; cnr Chapel St & Dandenong Rd, St Kilda)

Cinema Nova   CINEMA
(Map p225; www.cinemanova.com.au; 380 Lygon St, Carlton)

Kino Cinemas   CINEMA
(Map p216; www.palacecinemas.com.au; Collins Pl, 45 Collins St)

Imax   3-D CINEMA
(Map p225; www.imaxmelbourne.com.au; Melbourne Museum, Carlton Gardens)

Palace Como   CINEMA
(Map p228; www.palacecinemas.com.au; cnr Toorak Rd & Chapel St, South Yarra)

Outdoor cinemas are popular in summer; check the websites for seasonal opening dates and program details:

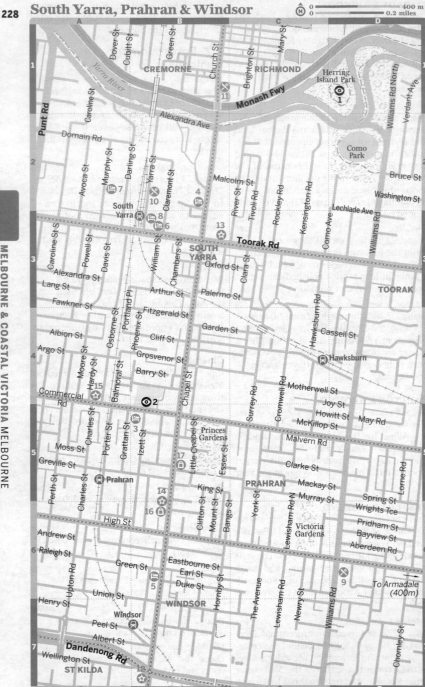

0 400 m
0 0.2 miles

Moonlight Cinema OUTDOOR CINEMA
(www.moonlight.com.au; Gate D, Royal Botanic
Gardens Melbourne, Birdwood Ave, South Yarra)

Rooftop Cinema OUTDOOR CINEMA
(Map p216; www.rooftopcinema.com.au; Level 6,
Curtin House, 252 Swanston St, Melbourne)

St Kilda Openair Cinema OUTDOOR CINEMA
(Map p232; www.stkildaopenair.com.au; St Kilda
Sea Baths, 10-18 Jacka Blvd, St Kilda)

Theatre
Melbourne's theatre scene is not limited to
one particular area: individual companies
and theatres are spread across town. Try
Half Tix Melbourne (Map p216; www.halftix
melbourne.com; Melbourne Town Hall; ⊙10am-2pm
Mon, 11am-6pm Tue-Fri, 10am-4pm Sat) for cheap
tickets to the theatre. You need to front up
at the Half Tix office in person on the day
with cash.

Melbourne Theatre Company THEATRE
(MTC; ☑8688 0800; www.mtc.com.au; 140
Southbank Blvd, Southbank) Melbourne's major theatrical company stages around 15
productions annually, ranging from contemporary and modern (including many new
Australian works) to Shakespearean and
other classics.

Malthouse Theatre THEATRE
(☑9685 5111; www.malthousetheatre.com.au;
113 Sturt St, South Melbourne) The Malthouse
Theatre Company often produces the most
exciting theatre in Melbourne.

Live Music
Northcote Social Club LIVE MUSIC
(☑9489 3917; www.northcotesocialclub.com; 301
High St, Northcote) This is one of Melbourne's
best live-music venues, with a stage that's

seen plenty of international folk just one al-
bum out from star status. Its home-grown
line-up is also notable. If you're just after a
drink, the front bar buzzes every night of the
week, or there's a large deck out the back for
lazy afternoons. A perfect, and well-loved,
local.

Bennetts Lane LIVE MUSIC
(Map p216; www.bennettslane.com; 25 Bennetts
Lane, Melbourne; ⊙8.30pm-late) Bennetts Lane
has long been the boiler room of Melbourne
jazz. It attracts the cream of local and international talent and an audience that knows
when it's time to applaud a solo. Beyond
the cosy front bar, there's another space reserved for big gigs.

Esplanade Hotel LIVE MUSIC
(Map p232; http://espy.com.au; 11 The Esplanade,
St Kilda; ⊙noon-late Mon-Fri, 8am-late weekends)
Rock-pigs rejoice. The Espy remains gloriously shabby and welcoming to all. Bands
play most nights and there's a spruced-up
kitchen out the back. And for the price of
a pot of beer you get front-row seats for the
pink-stained St Kilda sunset.

Ding Dong Lounge LIVE MUSIC
(Map p216; www.dingdonglounge.com.au; 18 Market Lane, Melbourne; ⊙7pm-late Wed-Sat) Ding
Dong walks the rock-and-roll walk and is
a great place to see a smaller touring act
or catch local bands.

Toff in Town LIVE MUSIC
(Map p216; ☑9639 8770; www.thetoffintown.
com; Level 2, Curtin House, 252 Swanston St,
Melbourne; ⊙5pm-late Sun-Thu, noon-late Fri) An
atmospheric venue well suited to cabaret
but also works for intimate gigs by rock
gods, avant-folksters or dance-hall queens.

MELBOURNE'S BEST MARKETS

Meet local artists or stock up on fantastic original pieces at one of the following weekend markets.

Rose Street Artists' Market (Map p223; www.rosestmarket.com.au; 60 Rose St, Fitzroy; ⊙11am-5pm Sat &Sun) One of Melbourne's best and most popular art-and-craft markets is just a short stroll from Brunswick St.

Camberwell Sunday Market (www.sundaymarket.com.au; Station St, Camberwell; admission gold coin donation; ⊙7am-12.30pm Sundays),Located behind the corner of Burke and Riversdale Rds, this is where Melburnians come to offload their unwanted items and antique-hunters come to find them.

Esplanade Market (Map p232; www.esplanademarket.com; Upper Esplanade, btwn Cavell & Fitzroy Sts, St Kilda; ⊙10am-5pm Sun),Fancy shopping with a seaside backdrop? At this market, a kilometre of trestle tables joined end to end carry individually crafted products from toys to organic soaps to large metal sculptures of fishy creatures.

Dance

Australian Ballet   BALLET
(⌨1300 369 741, 9669 2700; www.australianballet.com.au; 2 Kavanagh St, Southbank) Based in Melbourne and now more than 40 years old, the Australian Ballet performs traditional and new works at the Victorian Arts Centre.

Chunky Move   DANCE
(www.chunkymove.com; 111 Sturt St, Southbank) Melbourne-based Chunky Move performs 'genre-defying' dance around the world and, when at home, at the Malthouse Theatre.

🔒 Shopping
CENTRAL MELBOURNE

Captains of Industry   BESPOKE CLOTHING
(Map p216; www.captainsofindustry.com.au; Level 1, 2 Somerset Pl) Where can you get a haircut, a bespoke suit and pair of shoes made in the one place? Here. The hard-working folk at Captains also offer homey breakfasts and thoughtful lunches.

Counter   CRAFT, DESIGN
(Map p216; www.craftvic.org.au; 31 Flinders Lane) The retail arm of Craft Victoria, Counter showcases the handmade. Its range of jewellery, textiles, accessories, glass and ceramics bridges the art/craft divide and makes for some wonderful mementoes of Melbourne.

Alice Euphemia   FASHION, JEWELLERY
(Map p216; Shop 6, Cathedral Arcade, 37 Swanston St, Melbourne) Art-school cheek abounds in the labels sold here and jewellery similarly sways between the shocking and exquisitely pretty.

NGV shop at the Ian Potter Centre   GALLERY STORE
(Map p216; www.ngv.vic.gov.au; Federation Sq) This museum space has a wide range of international design magazines, a kids section and the usual gallery standards. Also at **NGV International**.

FITZROY & AROUND

Crumpler   ACCESSORIES
(Map p223; www.crumpler.com.au; cnr Gertrude & Smith Sts, Fitzroy) Crumpler's bike-courier bags started it all. Its durable, practical designs can now be found around the world, and it makes bags for cameras, laptops and MP3 players as well as its original messenger style.

Little Salon   CRAFT, FASHION
(Map p223; www.littlesalon.com.au; 71 Gertrude St, Fitzroy) Part art gallery and part retail outlet, this little store is hipster heaven. Wearable art pieces, including bags woven from seatbelts, knitted corsages and button bracelets, share space here with decorative items for your wall or shelf. Also in Melbourne (Map p216; 1/353 Little Collins St).

TOP CHOICE **Third Drawer Down**   DESIGN
(Map p223; www.thirddrawerdown.com; 93 George St, Fitzroy) This seller-of-great-things makes life beautifully unusual by stocking everything from sesame-seed grinders to beer-o'clock beach towels and 'come in, we're closed' signs.

CARLTON & AROUND

Readings   BOOKS
(Map p225; www.readings.com.au; 309 Lygon St, Carlton) A potter around this defiantly pros-

pering indie bookshop can occupy an entire afternoon if you're so inclined. There's a dangerously loaded (and good-value) specials table, switched-on staff and everyone from Lacan to *Charlie & Lola* on the shelves.

SOUTH YARRA, PRAHRAN & WINDSOR

Chapel Street Bazaar   COLLECTABLES
(Map p228; 217-223 Chapel St, Prahran) Calling this a 'permanent undercover collection of market stalls' won't give you any clue to what's tucked away here. This old arcade is a retro-obsessive riot. It doesn't matter if Italian art glass or Noddy egg cups are your thing, you'll find it here.

Fat   FASHION, ACCESSORIES
(Map p228; www.fat4.com; 272 Chapel St, Prahran) The Fat girls' empire has changed the way Melbourne dresses, catapulting a new generation of designers into the city's consciousness, including Claude Maus and Dress Up. There are also branches in Melbourne (Map p216; GPO, 250 Bourke St, Melbourne) and Fitzroy (Map p223; 209 Brunswick St, Fitzroy).

ST KILDA & AROUND

Brotherhood of St Laurence VINTAGE, FASHION
(Map p232; 82a Acland St, St Kilda) This op shop features the most retro of welfare organisation Brotherhood of St Laurence's 26-odd op shops. There's a similar branch in Fitzroy, called **Hunter Gatherer** (Map p223; 274 Brunswick St, Fitzroy).

Dot & Herbey   FASHION, ACCESSORIES
(Map p232; www.dotandherbey.com; 229 Barkly St, St Kilda) Grandma Dot and Grandpa Herb smile down upon this tiny corner boutique from a mural-sized photo, right at home among the vintage floral fabrics and retro style.

ℹ Information

Dangers & Annoyances

There are occasional reports of alcohol-fuelled violence in some parts of Melbourne's CBD, in particular King St.

Travelling on public transport without a valid ticket is taken very seriously by ticket inspectors.

Emergency

For police, ambulance or fire emergencies dial ☑000.
Centre Against Sexual Assault (CASA; ☑1800 806 292)
Poisons Information Centre (☑13 11 26)

Translating & Interpreting Service (☑13 14 50) Available 24 hours.

Internet Access

Wi-fi is available free at central CBD spots including Federation Square. Hotels often charge between $3 and $20 per hour for wi-fi access. If you don't have a laptop or smartphone, there are plenty of internet cafes around Melbourne with terminals (from $2 per hour).

Internet Resources

Lonely Planet's website (www.lonelyplanet.com) has useful links. Other online resources:
That's Melbourne (www.thatsmelbourne.com.au) Downloadable maps, info and podcasts from the City of Melbourne.
Three Thousand (www.threethousand.com.au) A weekly round-up of (groovy) local goings-on.
Visit Victoria (www.visitvictoria.com.au) Highlights events in Melbourne and Victoria.

Media

Melbourne's broadsheet the *Age* (www.theage.com.au) covers local, national and international news. The *Herald Sun* (www.heraldsun.com.au) does the same in tabloid form. *Broadsheet* (www.broadsheet.com.au) is available from cafes.

Music is covered in free street magazines *Beat* (www.beat.com.au) and *Inpress* (www.streetpress.com.au).

Medical Services

Visitors from Belgium, Finland, Italy, Ireland, Malta, the Netherlands, New Zealand, Sweden and the UK have reciprocal health-care agreements with Australia and can access cheaper health services through **Medicare** (☑13 20 11; www.medicareaustralia.gov.au).

Travel Doctor (TVMC; ☑9935 8100; www.traveldoctor.com.au; Level 2, 393 Little Bourke St) specialises in vaccinations. There's another branch at Southgate (☑9690 1433; 3 Southgate Ave, Southgate).

Royal Melbourne Hospital (☑9342 7666; www.rmh.mh.org.au; 300 Grattan St, Parkville) is a public hospital with an emergency department.

Tambassis Pharmacy (☑9387 8830; cnr Sydney & Brunswick Rds, Brunswick) and **Mulqueeny Midnight Pharmacy** (☑9510 3977; cnr High St & Williams Rd, Prahran) are pharmacies open until midnight.

Money

There are ATMs throughout Melbourne. Bigger hotels offer a currency-exchange service, as do most banks during business hours. There's a bunch of exchange offices on Swanston St.

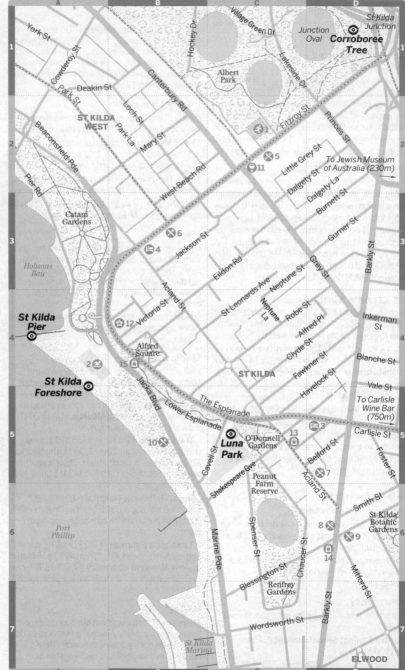

Post

Melbourne GPO (Map p216; cnr Little Bourke & Elizabeth Sts; ⊙8.30am-5.30pm Mon-Fri, 9am-5pm Sat)

Tourist Information

Melbourne Visitor Centre (MVC; Map p216; ☑9658 9658; Federation Sq; ⊙9am-6pm)

❶ Getting There & Away

Air

Two airports – Avalon and Tullamarine – serve Melbourne, though at present only domestic airlines **Tiger** (☑9335 3033; www.tigerairways .com) and **Jetstar** (☑13 15 38; www.jetstar. com) operate from Avalon. These two airlines also fly to and from Tullamarine, in addition to the domestic and international flights offered by **Qantas** (☑13 13 13; www.qantas.com) and **Virgin Blue** (☑13 67 89; www.virginblue.com.au).

There is a **left-luggage facility** (International Arrivals; $15 per 24hr; ⊙5.30am-12.30am) in Terminal 2 at Tullamarine Airport.

Regional Express (☑13 17 13; www.regional express.com.au) has services from Melbourne to Portland.

Boat

Spirit of Tasmania (☑1800 634 906; www. spiritoftasmania.com.au) crosses the Bass Strait between Melbourne and Devonport, Tasmania. It has services that run at least nightly; there are also day sailings during peak season. It takes 11 hours and departs from Station Pier, Port Melbourne (Map p204).

Bus, Car & Motorcycle

Southern Cross Station (Map p216; www. southerncrossstation.net.au) is the main terminal for interstate bus services.

V/Line (www.vline.com.au) Services around Victoria.

Firefly (www.fireflyexpress.com.au) To/from Adelaide and Sydney.

Greyhound (www.greyhound.com.au) Australia-wide.

There is a **left-luggage facility** ($12 per 24hr) at Southern Cross Station.

Train

Interstate trains arrive and depart from Southern Cross Station.

❶ Getting Around

To/From the Airport

TULLAMARINE AIRPORT There are no trains or trams to Tullamarine Airport. Taxis charge from $40 for the trip to Melbourne's CBD, or you can catch **Sky Bus** (☑9335 3066; www.skybus.com. au; adult/child one-way $16/6), a 20-minute express bus service to/from Southern Cross Station.

Part of the main route into Melbourne from Tullamarine Airport is a toll road run by **CityLink** (☑13 26 29; www.citylink.com.au). If you're driving you'll need to buy a Tulla Pass ($4.65). If you have more time and less money, take the exit ramp at Bell St then head up Nicholson St to the CBD.

AVALON AIRPORT Sita Coaches (www. sitacoaches.com.au; one-way to/from Avalon Airport $20; 50min) meets all flights flying into

PLAYING HOOKIE

Many of the city's intersections require you to make a right-hand turn from the left lane so you don't block oncoming trams. When you see a 'Right Turn from Left Only' sign, get in the left lane and wait with your right indicator on; when the light turns green in the street you want to turn into, hook right and complete your turn.

and out of Avalon. It departs from Southern Cross Station; check website for times. No pre-booking required.

Bicycle

Melbourne Bike Share (www.melbournebikeshare.com.au; ☑1300 711 590) began in 2010 and has had a slow start, mainly blamed on Victoria's compulsory helmet laws. Subsidised safety helmets are now available at 7Eleven stores around the CBD ($5 with a $3 refund on return). Each first half-hour of hire is free. Daily ($2.50) and weekly ($8) subscriptions require a credit card and $300 security deposit.

Car & Motorcycle

CAR HIRE Rental-car agencies:

Avis (☑13 63 33; www.avis.com.au)

Budget (☑1300 362 848; www.budget.com.au)

Europcar (☑1300 131 390; www.europcar.com.au)

Hertz (☑13 30 39; www.hertz.com.au)

Rent a Bomb (☑9696 7555; www.rentabomb.com.au)

Thrifty (☑1300 367 227; www.thrifty.com.au)

CAR SHARING Two car-sharing companies operate in Melbourne: **Go Get** (☑1300 769 389; www.goget.com.au) and **Flexi Car** (☑1300 363 780; www.flexicar.com.au). You rent the cars by the hour or the day and prices include petrol. Both have joining fees (around $30) and Go Get has a fully refundable security deposit of $500, while Flexi Car has an annual insurance fee of $70. The cars are parked in and around the CBD in designated 'car share' car parks. Car sharing costs around $10 per hour depending on the plan you choose.

PARKING 'Grey ghosts' (parking inspectors) are particularly vigilant in the CBD; most of the street parking is metered and if you overstay your metered time you'll probably be fined (between $60 and $119). Also keep an eye out for Clearway zones. There are plenty of parking garages in the city; rates vary.

Motorcyclists are allowed to park on the footpath.

TOLL ROADS Motorcycles travel free on CityLink; car drivers will need to purchase a pass if they are planning on using one of the two toll roads (CityLink or EastLink, which runs from Ringwood to Frankston).

Public Transport

Flinders Street Station (Map p216) is the main metro train station connecting the city and suburbs. The City Loop runs under the city, linking the four corners of town.

An extensive network of tramlines covers every corner of the city, running north–south and east–west along most major roads. Trams run roughly every three minutes Monday to Friday, every 10 minutes on Saturday, and every 20 minutes on Sunday. Check **Metlink** (www.metlink.com.au) for more information. Also worth considering is the free City Circle tram, which loops around town.

TRAM ROUTE	TRAM NO/S
Carlton	1, 96
Collingwood	86
Docklands	30, 48, 86
Fitzroy	86, 96, 112
North Carlton	1, 96
Northcote	86
North Melbourne	55, 68
Parkville/Brunswick	19
Prahran	72, then 78/79 along Chapel St
Richmond	45, 70, 75, 109
South Melbourne	1/109/112 or light rail 96
South Yarra	72
St Kilda	16/67/112 or light rail 96
Toorak	8

TICKETING The **myki** (www.myki.com.au) transport system covers Melbourne's buses, trams and trains and uses a 'touch on, touch off' system. Myki cards ($10 full fare) are available online; from Flinders Street Station; the **MetShop** (☑13 16 38); and the **myki discovery centre** at Southern Cross Station.

You need to top your myki card with cash at machines located at most stations (or online, though it can take 24 hours to process). If you're only in town for a few days, short-term tickets can be bought from machines on buses, trains and trams, though fares are slightly more expensive than using a myki. Using myki, Zone 1 ticket fares are $3.02/6.04 for a two-hour/daily, while short-term tickets are $3.80/7.00.

Taxi

Melbourne's taxis are metered and require an estimated prepaid fare when hailed between 10pm and 5am. You may need to pay more or get a refund depending on the final fare. Toll charges are added to fares.

AROUND MELBOURNE

The Dandenongs

On a clear day, you can see the Dandenong Ranges from Melbourne – conversely you can watch the sun set over the city from the lookout at the summit of 633m Mt Dandenong. A 35km day trip east of the city, there's good bushwalking and wildlife-spotting in the hills, or just go for a drive and stop for lunch at the quaint little villages of Olinda, Sassafras, Kallista and Emerald, where tea and scones is just about *de rigueur*.

A restored steam train, perennially popular Puffing Dilly (0754 6800; www.puffing billy.com.au; Old Monbulk Rd, Belgrave; Belgrave-Gembrook return adult/child/family $52/26/105) toots its way through the Dandenongs, with six departures during holidays, and three or four on other days. Nearby, Trees Adventure (9752 5354; www.treesadventure.com. au; Old Monbulk Rd; 2hr session adult/child/family $16/32/95; 11am-5pm Mon-Fri, 9am-5pm Sat & Sun) is a blast of tree-climbs, flying foxes and obstacle courses in a stunning patch of old-growth forest boasting sequoia, mountain ash and Japanese oak trees.

Dandenong Ranges National Park has many great walking tracks. The Ferntree Gully Area has the popular 1000 Steps Track up to One Tree Hill picnic ground (two hours return).

Sherbrooke Forest has a towering cover of mountain ash trees and is home to kookaburras, currawongs and honeyeaters.

Drive up to SkyHigh Mt Dandenong (9751 0443; www.skyhighmtdandenong.com.au; Observatory Rd, Mt Dandenong; vehicle entry $5; 9am-10pm Mon-Fri, 8am-10pm Sat & Sun) for amazing views over Melbourne and Port Phillip Bay from the highest point in the Dandenongs.

The Dandenong Ranges & Knox visitors centre (9758 7522; www.dandenongranges tourism.com.au; 1211 Burwood Hwy, Upper Ferntree Gully; 9am-5pm) is outside the Upper Ferntree Gully train station.

Queenscliff

POP 3300

Historic Queenscliff is a lovely spot, popular with daytripping and overnighting Melburnians who come for fine food and wine, boutique shopping and leisurely walks along the beach. The views across the Port Phillip Heads and Bass Strait are glorious and a new observation tower by the ferry terminal shows the town and surrounds off beautifully.

Sights & Activities

The Bellarine Rail Trail runs adjacent to the historic railway and is a 34km rail trail that is popular with cyclists, joggers and walkers.

Bellarine Peninsula Railway HISTORIC RAILWAY (5258 2069; www.bpr.org.au; Queenscliff train station; return adult/child/family $20/12/50; trips 11.15am, 1.40pm & 2.45pm Sun year-round, Tue & Thu school holidays, daily 26 Dec-9 Jan, Tue-Thu, Sat & Sun mid–late Jan) A group of cheerful volunteer steam-train tragics keep the trains plying the 1¾-hour return journey to Drysdale.

Sea-All Dolphin Swims SIGHTSEEING (5258 3889; www.dolphinswims.com.au; Larkin Pde; sightseeing adult/child $70/60, 3½hr snorkel $130/115; 8am & 1pm Sep-May) Look at or swim with seals and dolphins.

Festivals & Events

Queenscliff Music Festival MUSIC (5258 4816; www.qmf.net.au) Held on the last weekend in November, this festival features Australian musos with a folksy, bluesy bent.

DON'T MISS

LOAM

Don't be surprised if you're handed a home-grown beetroot or a sprig of local salt bush to smell – award-winning restaurant Loam (5251 1105; 650 Andersons Rd, Drysdale; lunch Thu-Sun, dinner Fri & Sat) is all about stripping food back. Aaron and Astrid Turner's dream restaurant is a success story hidden in the Bellarine hinterland near Queenscliff – book months in advance.

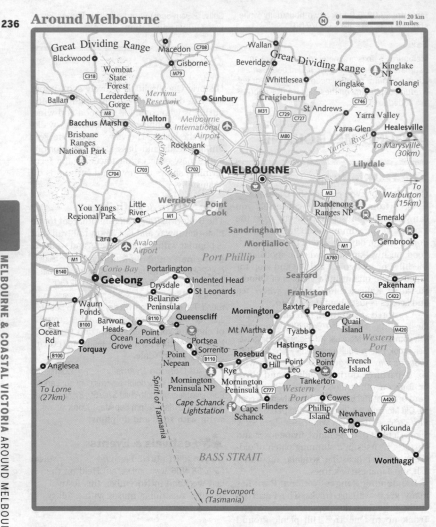

ℹ Information

Queenscliff visitors centre (☎5258 4843; www.queenscliffe.vic.gov.au; 55 Hesse St; ⊙9am-5pm; @) Internet access $6 per hour (also available next door at the library).

ℹ Getting There & Away

It's possible to catch a **V/Line** (☎13 61 96; www. vline.com.au) train from Melbourne to Geelong ($6.20, one hour), then a **McHarry's** (☎5223 2111; www.mcharrys.com.au) bus to Queenscliff ($3.20, 50 minutes). Alternatively, catch the ferry from Sorrento.

Mornington Peninsula

The Mornington Peninsula – the boot-shaped bit of land between Port Phillip and Western Port Bays – has been Melbourne's summer playground since the 1870s, when paddlesteamers ran down to Portsea. Today, the calm 'front beaches' on the Port Phillip Bay side are still a big magnet for family holidays at the bayside towns of Mornington, Rosebud, Dromana, Rye, Blairgowrie and Sorrento. The rugged ocean 'back beaches' facing Bass Strait offer challenging surfing and stunning walks along the coastal strip, part of Mornington Peninsula National Park.

Don't overlook a trip to the peninsula's interior, where much of the undulating farmland has been replaced by vineyards and orchards – foodies love this region, where a winery lunch is a real highlight – but it still retains lovely stands of native bushland.

❶ Information

Mornington Peninsula visitors centre (☑1800 804 009, 5987 3078; www.visit morningtonpeninsula.org; 359b Nepean Hwy, Dromana; ◷9am-5pm) The main visitor information centre for the peninsula can book accommodation and tours.

Mornington visitors centre (☑5975 1644; www.visitmorningtonpeninsula.org; 320 Main St; ◷9am-5pm) Conveniently located in Mornington.

❶ Getting There & Around

Met trains (buy a Zones 1 & 2 ticket) run from Flinders St Station to Frankston station. **Portsea Passenger Service** (☑5986 5666; www.grenda.com.au) bus 788 runs from Frankston to Portsea ($5, 1½ hours) via Mornington, Dromana and Sorrento.

Inter Island Ferries (☑9585 5730; www.interislandferries.com.au; return adult/child/ bike $21/10/8) runs between Stony Point and Cowes (Phillip Island) via French Island.

Queenscliff–Sorrento Car & Passenger Ferries (☑5258 3244; www.searoad.com.au; one-way foot passenger adult/child $9/7, 2 adults & car standard/peak $58/64; ◷hourly) sails between Sorrento and Queenscliff.

SORRENTO & PORTSEA
POP 1500

Historic Sorrento is the standout town on the Mornington Peninsula for its beautiful limestone buildings, ocean and bay beaches and buzzing seaside summer atmosphere. This was the site of Victoria's first official European settlement, established by an expedition of convicts, marines, civil officers and free settlers that arrived from England in 1803.

Grand 19th-century buildings include the **Sorrento Hotel** (1871), the **Continental Hotel** (1875) and **Koonya** (1878).

There are plenty of swimming and walking opportunities along Sorrento's wide, sandy beaches and bluffs. At low tide, the rock pool at the back beach is a safe spot for adults and children to swim and snorkel and the surf beach here is patrolled in summer.

LIQUID LUNCH

The Mornington Peninsula has developed into one of Victoria's great cool-climate wine regions. Most of the peninsula's 50-plus wineries are in the hills between Red Hill and Merricks and many have excellent cafes or restaurants attached. Some wineries to consider:

Montalto (☑5989 8412; www.montalto.com.au; 33 Shoreham Rd, Red Hill South; ◷cellar door 11am-5pm, lunch daily, dinner Fri & Sat) One of the Mornington Peninsula's best winery restaurants, and the Pinot Noir and Chardonnay here are terrific.

Port Phillip Estate (☑5989 4444; www.portphillipestate.com.au; 263 Red Hill Rd, Red Hill South; ◷cellar door 11am-5pm, lunch Wed-Sun, dinner Fri & Sat) Home of Port Phillip Estate and Kooyong wines, this award-winning winery has an excellent, breezy restaurant.

Red Hill Estate (☑5989 2838; www.redhillestate.com.au; 53 Shoreham Rd, Red Hill South; ◷cellar door 11am-5pm, lunch daily, dinner Fri & Sat) Red Hill Estate's signature Pinot and sparkling wines are outstanding, while Max's Restaurant is one of the best on the peninsula.

Ten Minutes by Tractor (☑5989 6080; www.tenminutesbytractor.com.au; 1333 Mornington-Flinders Rd, Main Ridge; ◷cellar door 11am-5pm, lunch Wed-Sun, dinner Thu-Sat) Another outstanding restaurant and a fine range of Pinot Noir, Chardonnay and Pinot Gris. The unusual name comes from the three vineyards, which are each 10 minutes apart by tractor.

T'Gallant (☑5989 6565; www.tgallant.com.au; 1385 Mornington-Flinders Rd, Main Ridge; ◷lunch) Pioneered luscious Pinot Gris in Australia and produces the country's best. There's fine dining at La Baracca Trattoria, casual dining and pizza in Spuntino's Bar, and live music on weekends.

FRENCH ISLAND

It's only a 15-minute ferry ride from Stony Point on the Mornington Peninsula, but French Island feels a world away – it's two-thirds national park, virtually traffic-free and there's no mains water or electricity. The main attractions are bushwalking and cycling, taking in wetlands, one of Australia's largest **koala colonies**, and a huge variety of birds.

The island served as a penal settlement for prisoners serving out their final years from 1916 and you can still visit the original prison farm. A major industry here from 1897 to 1963 was chicory (a coffee substitute); visit the old **kilns** on Bayview Rd, where fourth-generation local Lois will whip you up chicory coffee or Devonshire tea in her rustic cafe.

The ferry docks at Tankerton, from where it's around 2km to the licensed **French Island General Store** (☑5980 1209; Lot 1, Tankerton Rd, Tankerton; bike hire $25; ⏾8am-6pm, from 9am Sun), which also serves as post office, tourist information, bike-hire centre and has accommodation ($110 per person). Bikes can also be hired at Tankerton Jetty.

French Island Biosphere Bus Tours (☑5980 1241, 0412 671 241; www.frenchisland tours.com.au; half-day adult/child $18/10, full day $38/22; ⏾Tue, Thu, Sun, plus Sat during school holidays) runs informative half-day tours with morning or afternoon tea. The full-day tour includes lunch.

You can camp for free at the basic **Fairhaven Camping Ground**, but bookings (through Parks Victoria) are essential.

Inter Island Ferries (☑9585 5730; www.interislandferries.com.au; adult/child/bike return $21/10/8) runs a service between Stony Point and Tankerton (10 minutes, at least two daily, four on Tuesday, Thursday, Saturday and Sunday), continuing on to Phillip Island. You can reach Stony Point directly from Frankston on a Metlink train.

Only 4km further west, tiny **Portsea** also has good back beaches and diving and watersports operators.

The small **Sorrento visitors centre** (☑5984 5678; 2 St Aubins Way) is on the main street.

☞ Tours

Two established operators run popular dolphin- and seal-swimming cruises from Sorrento Pier.

Moonraker Charters WILDLIFE
(☑5984 4211; www.moonrakercharters.com.au; adult/child sightseeing $55/44, dolphin & seal swimming $115/105)

Polperro Dolphin Swims WILDLIFE
(☑5988 8437; www.polperro.com.au; adult/child observers $55/35, all swimmers $125)

🛏 Sleeping & Eating

Sorrento Beach House YHA HOSTEL $
(☑5984 4323; www.sorrento-beachhouse.com; 3 Miranda St; dm/d $40/90; @) This purpose-built hostel that is situated in a quiet but central location maintains a relaxed atmosphere. The back deck and garden is a great place to catch up with other travellers. Staff can organise horseriding, snorkelling and diving trips.

Portsea Hotel HOTEL $$
(☑5984 2213; www.portseahotel.com.au; Point Nepean Rd; s/d from $65/110, with bathroom from $125/160) This iconic, half-timber pub is Portsea's pulse, with a great lawn and terrace area looking out over the bay. There's an excellent bistro (mains $20 to $28) and old-style accommodation (most rooms have shared bathroom) that increases in price based on sea views and season.

Carmel of Sorrento GUESTHOUSE $$
(☑5984 3512; www.carmelofsorrento.com.au; 142 Ocean Beach Rd; d $150-220, self-contained units from $220; ❋) This lovely old limestone heritage house right in the centre of Sorrento has been tastefully restored in period style and neatly marries the town's history with contemporary comfort.

Baths MODERN AUSTRALIAN, FISH AND CHIPS $$
(☑5984 1500; www.thebaths.com.au; 3278 Point Nepean Rd; mains $26-32; ⏾lunch & dinner, fish & chippery noon-8pm) The waterfront deck of the former sea baths is the perfect spot for lunch or a romantic sunset dinner overlooking the jetty and the Queenscliff ferry. The menu has some good seafood choices and there's a popular takeaway fish and chippery at the front.

Sorrento Foreshore Reserve

CAMPGROUND **$**

(✆5986 8286; Nepean Hwy; unpowered/powered sites $25/30, high season $40/45) Hilly, bush-clad sites between the bay beach and the main road into Sorrento.

Smokehouse

PIZZA **$$**

(✆5984 1246; 182 Ocean Beach Rd; mains $17-32; ⊙dinner Wed-Mon) Gourmet pizzas and pastas are the speciality at this local family favourite. Innovative toppings and the aromas wafting from the wood-fired oven are a winner.

POINT NEPEAN & MORNINGTON PENINSULA NATIONAL PARKS

The peninsula's tip is marked by the scenic **Point Nepean National Park** (✆5984 4276; Point Nepean Rd, Portsea), originally a quarantine station and army base. There are long stretches of traffic-free road for excellent cycling, and walking trails leading to beaches. You can hire bikes at the visitor centre ($20 per day) or take the Point Transporter (adult/child/family return $8.70/6/22.90), a hop-on, hop-off bus service that departs the visitor centre six times daily.

Mornington Peninsula National Park covers the dramatic sliver of coastline between Portsea and Cape Schanck, where rugged ocean beaches are framed by cliffs and bluffs. You can walk all the way from Portsea to Cape Schanck (26km, eight hours) along a marked trail.

Built in 1859, **Cape Schanck Lightstation** (✆5988 6184; 420 Cape Schanck Rd, Cape Schanck; museum only adult/child/family $12/8/34, museum & lighthouse $15/12/40, parking $4.50; ⊙10.30am-4pm) is a photogenic working lighthouse, with a kiosk, museum, information centre and regular guided tours. You can stay at **Cape Schanck B&B** (✆5988 6184; www.austpacinns.com.au; d from $150) in the limestone Keeper's Cottage.

The Great Ocean Road (B100) is one of Australia's most famous road-touring routes. It takes travellers past world-class surfing breaks, through pockets of rainforest, calm seaside towns and under koala-filled tree canopies. It shows off heathlands, dairy farms and sheer limestone cliffs and gets you up close and personal with the dangerous crashing surf of the Southern Ocean. Walk it, drive it, enjoy it.

Geelong

POP 216,000

Geelong is a confident town proud of its two icons: Geelong Football Club (aka the Cats) and the Ford Motor Company. The Cats have had a fair run in the AFL recently, winning the Grand Final in 2007 (for the first time in 44 years) and again in 2009, while Ford, Geelong's other blue-and-white icon, continues to make manufacturing Geelong's largest employer.

The Wathaurong people – the original inhabitants of Geelong – called the area Jillong. Today's Geelong has a new bypass, so travellers can skip the city and head straight to the Great Ocean Road, however there are plenty of reasons to stop.

◉ Sights & Activities

Wander Geelong's revamped **waterfront**, and locate Jan Mitchell's 111 **painted bollards**. At **Eastern Beach**, stop for a splash about at the art deco **bathing pavilion**, opposite the promenade.

FREE **Geelong Art Gallery**

ART GALLERY

(www.geelonggallery.org.au; Little Malop St; ⊙10am-5pm) This gallery houses more than 4000 works – its Australian collection is strong and includes Frederick McCubbin's *A Bush Burial* (1890).

GREAT OCEAN ROAD TOURS

The following tours depart from Melbourne and often cover the Great Ocean Road in a day:

Adventure Tours (✆1800 068 886; www.adventuretours.com.au)

Autopia Tours (✆9391 0261; www.autopiatours.com.au)

Go West Tours (✆1300 736 551; www.gowest.com.au)

Goin South (✆1800 009 858; www.goinsouth.com.au)

Otway Discovery (✆9654 5432; www.otwaydiscovery.com.au)

Ride Tours (✆1800 605 120; www.ridetours.com.au)

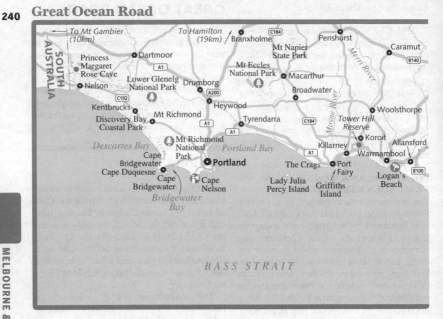

National Wool Museum
MUSEUM

(www.nwm.vic.gov.au; 26 Moorabool St; adult/child/family $7.50/4/20; ⊙9.30am-5pm) This museum showcases the history, politics and heritage of wool growing in a lovely 1872 bluestone building.

Geelong Helicopters
HELICOPTER FLIGHTS

(✆0422 515 151; www.geelonghelicopters.com.au; flights adult/child $45/35) Operates from the waterfront.

Bay City Seaplanes
SEAPLANE FLIGHTS

(✆0438 840 205; www.baycityseaplances.com.au; flights from $35 per person) Operates from the waterfront.

Sleeping

Gatehouse on Ryrie
GUESTHOUSE $

(✆0417 545 196; www.gatehouseonryrie.com.au; 83 Yarra St; d including breakfast $75-120; @🖦) This is the best choice for budget travellers; it was built in 1897, has timber floorboards throughout, spacious rooms and a communal kitchen and lounge area. Upstairs rooms share bathrooms.

Haymarket
BOUTIQUE HOTEL $$$

(✆5221 1174; www.haymarkethotel.com.au; 244 Moorabool St; d including breakfast from $200; 🖦) Luxurious rooms in this historic building are furnished with French antiques matching the building's age (1855). The six bedrooms have modern en suites, flat-screen TVs with cable TV, and the ground floor's 'honesty bar' is a refreshing and swanky sight. It's a kid-free zone.

✕ Eating

Go!
CAFE $

(www.cafego.com.au; 37 Bellarine St; mains from $8; ⊙breakfast & lunch Mon-Sat) Go! is a fun cafe that serves great food in a riot of colour and amusement. The covered courtyard out the back is huge and welcoming, and staff could not be sweeter.

Mr Hyde
CAFE, BAR $$

(www.myhyde.com.au; 11 Malop St; mains $15-23; ⊙breakfast, lunch & dinner Tue-Sun) This vast old bank building is filled with booths, secret rooms and stunning bathrooms. Dinner offers mezze-style dishes (such as falafel-encrusted lamb cutlets) and a range of Turkish pizzas. Breakfast includes herb omelette and organic granola.

Le Parisien
FRENCH $$$

(✆5229 3110; www.leparisien.com.au; 15 Eastern Beach Rd; mains $40-45; ⊙lunch & dinner) Feast on classic French cuisine *à l'Australienne* (try the kangaroo fillet with bush-tomato chutney) right on the water.

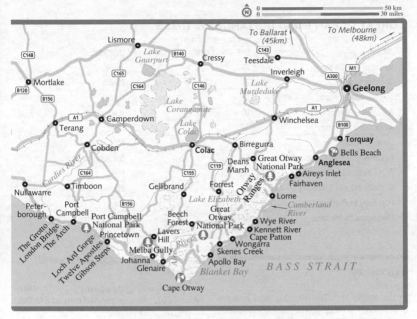

Drinking & Entertainment

CQ   COCKTAIL BAR
(City Quarter; www.thecityquarter.com.au; Cunningham Pier; ⊘afternoon-late Thu-Sun) The redevelopment of Cunningham Pier has brought a restaurant, cafe and boutique bar to this stunning location. Climb the sweeping steps to CQ, and check out its smart fit-out while you enjoy the superb cocktail menu and tapas selection.

❶ Information

Geelong & Great Ocean Road visitors centre (www.greatoceanroad.org; Princes Hwy, Little River; ⊘9am-5pm) Located at the service station in Little River, about 20km from Geelong.

National Wool Museum visitors centre (www.visitgreatoceanroad.org.au; 26 Moorabool St; ⊘9am-5pm)

❶ Getting There & Away

Air

Jetstar (☑13 15 38; www.jetstar.com.au) and **Tiger** (☑9335 3033; www.tigerairways.com) airlines run domestic services from nearby Avalon Airport.

Bus

Avalon Airport Shuttle (☑5278 8788; www.avalonairportshuttle.com.au) meets flights at Avalon Airport and travels to Geelong ($17, 35 minutes) and Lorne ($70, 1¾ hours)

Gull Airport Service (☑5222 4966; www.gull.com.au; 45 McKillop St) has 14 services a day between Geelong and Melbourne Airport ($30, 1¼ hours).

McHarry's Buslines (☑5223 2111; www.mcharrys.com.au) offers frequent bus services that run to Torquay as well as the Bellarine Peninsula.

V/Line (☑13 61 96; www.vline.com.au) has regular bus services that run between Geelong and Apollo Bay ($13, 2½ hours, two to four daily) via Torquay ($3.50, 25 minutes) and Lorne ($8.50, 1½ hours). On Monday, Wednesday and Friday there is also a bus service that continues out further to Port Campbell ($24, four hours) and Warrnambool ($27, six hours).

Car

The 25km Geelong Ring Rd runs from Corio to Waurn Ponds, bypassing Geelong entirely. To get to the city stay on the Princes Hwy (M1).

Train

V/Line (☑13 61 96; www.vline.com.au) runs from **Geelong train station** (☑5226 6525; Gordon Ave) to Melbourne's Southern Cross station ($9, one hour, frequent). Trains also head to Warrnambool ($19, 2½ hours, three daily).

GREAT OCEAN ROAD DISTANCES & TIMES

ROUTE	DISTANCE (KM)	DURATION
Melbourne to Geelong	75	1hr
Geelong to Torquay	21	15min
Torquay to Anglesea	16	15min
Anglesea to Aireys Inlet	10	10min
Aireys Inlet to Lorne	22	15min
Lorne to Apollo Bay	43	1hr
Apollo Bay to Port Campbell	88	1hr 10min
Port Campbell to Warrnambool	66	1hr
Warrnambool to Port Fairy	28	20min
Port Fairy to Portland	71	1hr
Melbourne to Portland	440	6hrs, 25min

Torquay

POP 15,700

In the 1960s and '70s Torquay was just another sleepy seaside town. Back then surfing in Australia was a decidedly countercultural pursuit, and its devotees were crusty hippie drop-outs living in clapped-out Kombis, smoking pot and making off with your daughters. Since then surfing has become unabashedly mainstream and a huge transglobal business. The town's proximity to world-famous Bells Beach and status as home of two iconic surf brands – Ripcurl and Quicksilver, both initially wetsuit makers – ensures Torquay is the undisputed capital of Australian surfing.

Sights & Activities

Surfworld Museum　　　　　MUSEUM
(www.surfworld.org.au; adult/child/family $10/6/20; 9am-5pm) Embedded at the rear of the **Surf City Plaza** is this homage to Australian surfing, with shifting exhibits, a theatre and displays of old photos and monster balsa mals.

Spring Creek Horse Rides　　HORSE RIDING
(5266 1541; www.springcreekhorserides.com.au; 245 Portheath Rd, Bellbrae; 1hr/2hr $35/60) Guided horse rides through Spring Creek Valley.

Two-hour surfing lessons start at $50:
Go Ride A Wave　　　　　SURFING
(1300 132 441; www.gorideawave.com.au; 1/15 Bell St, Torquay; 9am-5pm) Has another

branch at Anglesea (143b Great Ocean Rd, Anglesea).

Torquay Surfing Academy　　SURFING
(5261 2022; www.torquaysurf.com.au; 34a Bell St, Torquay; 9am-5pm)

Westcoast Surf School　　　SURFING
(5261 2241; www.westcoastsurfschool.com; 9am-5pm in summer)

Sleeping

Bellbrae Harvest　　APARTMENTS $$$
(5266 2100; www.bellbraeharvest.com.au; 45 Portreath Rd; d $200) Far from the madding crowd, here are three separate (and stunning) split-level apartments looking onto a dam. Expect rainwater shower heads, kitchenettes, huge flat-screen TVs and lots and lots of peace.

Bells Beach Lodge　　　HOSTEL $
(5261 7070; www.bellsbeachlodge.com.au; 51-53 Surfcoast Hwy; dm/d $25/65; @) This grungy budget option is on the highway and has shared facilities and surfboard and bike hire. It's especially popular during events and caters for large groups (can be noisy!).

Torquay Foreshore Caravan Park
CAMPGROUND, CABINS $
(5261 2496; www.torquaycaravanpark.com.au; unpowered sites $30-50, d cabins $75-250) Just behind Back Beach, this is the largest camping ground on the Surf Coast. It has good facilities and new premium-priced cabins with sea views.

✗ Eating

Moby CAFE $
(41 The Esplanade; mains $9-16; ⊙breakfast & lunch) This old weatherboard place on the Esplanade harks back to a time when Torquay was simple. That's not to say that its meals are not complicated; fill up on linguini or honey-roasted lamb souvlaki.

Scorched MODERN AUSTRALIAN $$
(☑5261 6142; www.scorched.com.au; 17 The Esplanade; mains $26-36; ⊙lunch Fri-Sun, dinner Wed-Sun) Overlooking the waterfront, with classy understated decor and windows that open right up to let the sea breeze in, this might be the swankiest restaurant in Torquay. Try the seasonal grazing plate.

❶ Information

Torquay visitors centre (www.greatocean road.org; Surf City Plaza, Beach Rd; ☻) Torquay has a well-resourced tourist office next to the Surfworld Museum.

❶ Getting There & Away

McHarry's Buslines (☑5223 2111; www.mc harrys com au) runs buses hourly from 9am to 9pm from Geelong to Torquay ($3.20, 30 minutes). **V/Line** (☑13 61 96; www.vline.com.au) has daily buses from Geelong to Torquay ($3.20, 30 minutes, four daily Monday to Friday, two on weekends).

By car, Torquay is 15 minutes south of Geelong on the B100.

Torquay to Anglesea

About 7km from Torquay is **Bells Beach**. The powerful point break at Bells is part of international surfing folklore (it's here, in name only, that Keanu Reeves and Patrick Swayze had their ultimate showdown in the film *Point Break*). It's notoriously inconsistent, but when the long right-hander is working it's one of the longest rides in the country. Since 1973, Bells has hosted the **Rip Curl Pro** (www.aspworldtour. com) every Easter – *the* glamour event on the world-championship ASP World Tour. The Rip Curl Pro regularly decamps to Johanna, two hours west, when fickle Bells isn't working.

Nine kilometres southwest of Torquay is the turn-off to spectacular **Point Addis**, 3km down this road. It's a vast sweep of pristine 'clothing-optional' beach that attracts surfers, hang-gliders and swimmers. There's a signposted **Koorie Cultural Walk**, a 1km

circuit trail to the beach through the **Ironbark Basin** nature reserve.

The **Surf Coast Walk** (www.surfcoast.vic. gov.au/walkingtracks.htm) follows the coastline from Jan Juc to near Aireys Inlet, and can be done in stages – the full route takes 11 hours. It's marked on the *Surf Coast Touring Map*, available from tourist offices.

Anglesea

POP 2300
Anglesea's **Main Beach** is the ideal spot to learn to surf, while sheltered **Point Roadknight Beach** is good for kiddies. Check out the resident kangaroo population at the town's golf course, or hire a paddleboat and cruise up the Anglesea River.

✗ Activities

Go Ride A Wave SURFING
(☑1300 132 441; www.gorideawave.com.au; 143b Great Ocean Rd; ⊙9am-5pm) Rents out kayaks and surfboards and runs two-hour surfing lessons (from $75).

⊨ Sleeping

Anglesea Overboard COTTAGE $$
(☑5289 7424; www.overboardcottages.com.au; 39c O'Donohue Rd; d from $195; ❊) This one-bedroom cottage has ocean views, a spa and a wood fire for those chilly winter nights. Designed for couples, but accepting babies and dogs (check first), there's also one in Aireys Inlet. Minimum two-night stay.

Anglesea Backpackers HOSTEL $
(☑5263 2664; www.angleseabackpackers.com; 40 Noble St; dm/d $35/95) This simple backpacker place (just two dorm rooms and one triple) is clean, bright and welcoming, and in winter the fire glows warmly in the living room.

Rivergums B&B B&B $$
(☑5263 3066; www.anglesearivergums.com.au; 10 Bingley Pde; d $100-160; ❊) Tucked by the river with tranquil views, this B&B has two spacious, tastefully furnished rooms (a self-contained bungalow and a room attached to the house).

✗ Eating

River Vu MODERN AUSTRALIAN $$
(113 Great Ocean Rd; mains $21-38; ⊙breakfast, lunch & dinner Tue-Sun) It's changed its name a fair few times, but this incarnation offers

a simple menu with generous servings. The tables on the front deck make for fine evening alfresco dining.

Red Till
CAFE $

(143a Great Ocean Rd; ⊗breakfast & lunch Sat-Mon & Thu, daily in summer) This cafe, on the outskirts of town, does coffee and retro decor as well as its Melbourne peers do – only the pace of life is different.

ℹ Information

Visitors Centre (16/87 Great Ocean Rd; ⊙9am-5pm Sep-May, 10am-4pm Jun-Aug) Located opposite Angahook Cafe, this new information centre sits beside an equally new barbecue area.

ℹ Getting There & Away

V/Line has services linking Anglesea with Geelong ($4.80, 45 minutes).

The new Geelong bypass has reduced the time it takes to drive from Melbourne to Anglesea to around 75 minutes.

Aireys Inlet

POP 1200

Aireys Inlet is home to glorious stretches of beach, including horse-friendly **Fairhaven** and hang-glider hot spot **Moggs Creek**.

The 34m-high **Split Point Lighthouse** and its keepers' cottages were built in 1891. The lighthouse is still operational (tours run until 3pm) and there's a sweet cafe near its base.

◉ Sights & Activities

Blazing Saddles
HORSE RIDING

(☑5289 7322; www.blazingsaddlestrailrides.com.au; Lot 1 Bimbadeen Dr; 1¼-/2¼hr rides $40/65) Hop on a horse and head into the bush or along the stunning beach.

🛏 Sleeping

Cimarron B&B
B&B $$

(☑5289 7044; www.cimarron.com.au; 105 Gilbert St; d $185; 🛜) This house was built in 1979 from local timbers using only wooden pegs and shiplap joins, and is an idyllic getaway with views over Point Roadknight. It's rustic yet sophisticated. There are two unique, loft-style doubles with vaulted timber ceilings and a denlike apartment. Out back, it's all state park and wildlife. Cimarron is a gay friendly accommodation option but not a child-friendly one.

Lightkeepers Inn
MOTEL $$

(☑5289 6666; www.lightkeepersinn.com.au; 64 Great Ocean Rd; d $110; 🛜✎) Expect clean motel rooms with extra-thick walls for peace and quiet. Trevor runs the place and has an excellent knowledge of local walks and mountain-biking opportunities.

🍴 Eating

A La Grecque
GREEK $$$

(☑5289 6922; www.alagreque.com.au; 60 Great Ocean Rd; mains $28-36; ⊗breakfast, lunch & dinner Wed-Sun, daily in summer) This modern Greek taverna is outstanding and serves mezze including cured kingfish with apple, celery and a lime dressing and mains such as chargrilled king prawns with fresh oregano. The verandah is an ideal spot to lunch mid-drive.

Lorne

POP 1000

Lorne has an incredible natural beauty; tall gumtrees line its hilly streets and Loutit Bay gleams irresistibly.

Lorne gets busy; in summer you'll be competing with day trippers for restaurant seats and boutique bargains, but, thronged with tourists or not, Lorne is a lovely place to hang out.

◉ Sights & Activities

Qdos Art Gallery
GALLERY

(☑5289 1989; www.qdosarts.com; 35 Allenvale Rd; ⊙8.30am-6pm Thu-Mon, daily school holidays) Qdos, tucked in the hills behind Lorne, always has something arty in its galleries, and sculptures dot its lush landscape. Its cafe fare is nothing but delicious and you can stay the night in one of the luxury Zen tree houses ($200 per night, two-night minimum, no kids).

Erskine Falls
WATERFALL

Head out of town to see this lovely waterfall. It's an easy walk to the viewing platform or 250 (often slippery) steps down to its base, from which you can explore further or head back on up.

🎉 Festivals & Events

Falls Festival
MUSIC

(www.fallsfestival.com; tickets $350) A three-day knees-up over New Year's on a farm out of town. A top line-up of rock and indie groups; tickets include camping.

📛 Sleeping

There's often a minimum two-night stay on weekends in Lorne, and high-season rates can be nearly double winter prices. For other options, ask the visitors centre.

Chapel COTTAGES $$$
(📞5289 2622; thechapellorne@bigpond.com; 45 Richardson Blvd; d $200; ❋) Outstanding – this contemporary two-level bungalow has been lifted from the pages of a glossy magazine, with tasteful Asian furnishings, splashes of colour and bay windows that open into the forest. It's secluded and romantic, with double shower and complimentary robes.

Allenvale Cottages COTTAGES $$
(📞5289 1450; www.allenvale.com.au; 150 Allenvale Rd; d from $175) These four self-contained early-1900s timber cottages, which each sleep four (or more), have been luxuriously restored. They're 2km northwest of Lorne, arrayed among shady trees and green lawns, complete with bridge and babbling brook. It's ideal for families.

Great Ocean Road Cottages & Backpackers YHA HOSTEL $
(📞5289 1070; www.yha.com.au; 10 Erskine Ave; tents $25, dm $20-30, d $55-75, cottages $170) Tucked away in the bush among the cockatoos and koalas, this two-storey timber lodge has spacious dorms, bargain tents with beds already set up, and top-value doubles. The more expensive A-frame cottages sleep up to six with kitchens and en suites.

Lorne Foreshore Caravan Park
CAMPGROUND $
(📞1300 736 533; www.lornecaravanpark.com.au; 2 Great Ocean Rd; powered sites $30-50, d cabins from $60) Book here for Lorne's five caravan parks. Of these, Erskine River Park is the prettiest; on the left-hand side as you enter Lorne, just before the bridge. Book well ahead for peak-season stays.

🍴 Eating

Ba Ba Lu Bar SPANISH $$$
(www.babalubar.com.au; 6a Mountjoy Pde; mains $32-42; ⊘breakfast, lunch & dinner) It's all a bit Spanish at Ba Ba Lu Bar, what, with its wintery paella nights and Chilean singers popping in for a gig in summer. The menu has inspired tapas and plenty of meat-based mains, and the bar kicks on into the wee hours.

Kafe Kaos CAFE $
(www.kafekaos.com.au; 52 Mountjoy Pde; lunches $8-15; ⊘breakfast & lunch) Bright and perky, Kafe Kaos typifies Lorne's relaxed foodie philosophy – barefoot patrons in boardies or bikinis tucking into first-class panini, bruschettas, burgers and chips.

Bottle of Milk BURGERS $
(52 Mountjoy Pde; burgers from $8.50; ⊘breakfast, lunch & dinner) Sit back on one of the old school chairs at this cool version of a diner, and tuck into a classic burger stacked with fresh ingredients.

🛈 Information

Lorne visitors centre (📞1300 891 152; www.visitsurfcoast.com.au; 15 Mountjoy Pde; ⊘9am-5pm) Stacks of information, helpful staff and an accommodation booking service.

Cumberland River

Just 7km southwest of Lorne is **Cumberland River**. There's nothing here – no shops or houses – other than the wonderful **Cumberland River Holiday Park** (📞5289 1790; www.cumberlandriver.com.au; Great Ocean Rd; unpowered sites $37, en suite cabins from $105). This splendidly located bushy camping ground is next to a lovely river and high craggy cliffs that rise on the far side.

Wye River
POP 140

The Great Ocean Road snakes spectacularly around the cliffside from Cumberland River before reaching this little town with big ideas.

Wye River Foreshore Camping Reserve (📞5289 0412; sites $30; ⊘Dec-Apr) offers powered beachside sites during summer.

TOP CHOICE **Wye General** (www.thewyegeneral. com; 35 Great Ocean Rd; dinners $15-26; ⊘breakfast & lunch daily, dinner Fri & Sat in winter, daily in summer) cafe has marched into

---

HARD YAKKA

The first sections of the Great Ocean Road were constructed by hand (using picks, shovels and crowbars) by returned WWI soldiers. Work began in September 1919 and the road between Anglesea and Apollo Bay was completed in 1932.

town and there's nothing general about it. From homemade sourdough to perfect coffee, this smart indoor/outdoor joint has polished concrete floors, timber features and an impressive confidence.

Kennett River

Just 5km along from Wye River is **Kennett River**, which has some truly great **koala-spotting** in the town itself, and you'll also spot the furry creatures above the Great Ocean Road towards Apollo Bay. In town, just behind the caravan park, walk 200m up Grey River Rd and you'll see bundles of sleepy koalas clinging to the branches. **Glow-worms** light up the same stretch at night (take a torch).

The friendly **Kennett River Holiday Park** (☑1300 664 417, 5289 0272; www.kennettriver.com; unpowered/powered sites $29/35, d cabins from $105; @☞) is a bush park with free wireless internet and free barbecuse. There are plans afoot for a camp kitchen.

Apollo Bay

POP 1800

Apollo Bay is synonymous with music festivals, the Otways and lovely beaches, and it's one of the least claustrophobic hamlets along the Great Ocean Road.

Majestic rolling hills provide a postcard backdrop to the town, while broad, white-sand beaches dominate the foreground. It's an ideal base for exploring magical Cape Otway and Otway National Park.

◉ Sights & Activities

Mark's Walking Tours   TOURS
(☑0417 983 985; www.greatoceanwalk.asn.au/markstours; 2-3hr tours adult/child $50/15) Take a walk around the area with local Mark Brack, son of the Cape Otway Lighthouse keeper. He knows this stretch of coast, its history and ghosts better than anyone around. His daily tours include shipwreck tours, historical tours, glow-worm tours and Great Ocean Walk tours. Minimum two people.

Community Market   MARKET
(www.apollobay.com/market_place; ☉8.30am-4.30pm Sat) This market is held along the main strip and is the perfect spot for picking up local apples, locally made souvenirs and just-what-you've-always-wanted table lamps made from tree stumps.

Apollo Bay Surf & Kayak   OUTDOOR ACTIVITIES
(☑0405 495 909; www.apollobaysurfkayak.com.au; 2hr tour $65) Head out to an Australian fur seal colony on a two-seated kayak. Tours depart from Marengo beach and are suitable for children over 12.

Otway Expeditions   OUTDOOR ADVENTURE
(☑5237 6341; http://otwayexpeditions.tripod.com; argo rides from $45) Take a dual-suspension bike through the Otways (minimum six people), or go nuts in an amphibious all-terrain 8x8 argo buggy.

✦ Festivals & Events

Apollo Bay Music Festival   MUSIC FESTIVAL
(☑5237 6761; www.apollobaymusicfestival.com; weekend pass adult/youth/under 13yr $162/90/free) Held over a weekend in early April, this three-day festival features classical, folk, blues, jazz, rock and some edgy contemporary sounds too. The town truly comes alive.

⌂ Sleeping

YHA Eco Beach   HOSTEL $
TOP CHOICE (☑5237 7899; 5 Pascoe St; dm $32-38, d $88-95, f $109-145; ❋@) Even if you're not on a budget this three-million-dollar, architect-designed hostel is an outstanding place to stay. Its eco-credentials are too many to list here, but it's a wonderful piece of architecture with great lounge areas, kitchens, TV rooms, internet lounge and rooftop terraces.

Nelson's Perch B&B   B&B $$
(☑5237 7176; www.nelsonsperch.com; 54 Nelson St; d $160; ❋@☞) Nelson's looks fresher than some of the town's weary B&Bs. There are three rooms, each with a courtyard, and free wireless internet.

Surfside Backpackers   HOSTEL $
(☑5237 7263; www.surfsidebackpacker.com; cnr Great Ocean Rd & Gambier St; dm $23-30, d $60) So, the rooms are a little cramped, but the lounge is blessed with large windows looking out onto the ocean, making this homey place worthwhile.

✕ Eating

The **Apollo Bay Fishermen's Co-operative** (Breakwater Rd; ☉10am-4pm) sells fresh fish and seafood from the wharf.

Vista   SEAFOOD $$
(www.thevistaseafoodrestaurant.com; 155 Great Ocean Rd, mains $25-35; ☉dinner) This is fab, upmarket dining on the main drag. Spend

hours cracking a locally caught crab, supported in your endeavours by local wine.

Café Nautigals
CAFE $

(1/57-59 Great Ocean Rd; mains $14-16; ⊗breakfast & lunch daily, dinner in summer; @) A baby stack of pancakes and a coffee will use up a tenner, which is not bad in anyone's books.

La Bimba
MODERN AUSTRALIAN $$$

(125 Great Ocean Rd; mains $25-45; ⊗breakfast, lunch & dinner Wed-Mon) This upstairs Mod Oz restaurant is outstanding – definitely worth the splurge. It's a warm, relaxed smart-casual place with views, friendly service and a good wine list.

⊕ Information

Great Ocean Road visitors centre (☑5237 6529; 100 Great Ocean Rd; ⊗9am-5pm) Has an impressive 'eco-centre' with displays on Aboriginal history, rainforests, shipwrecks and the building of the Great Ocean Road.

Parks Victoria (☑5237 2500; www.parkweb. vic.gov.au; cnr Oak Ave & Montrose St; ⊗8am-4.30pm Mon-Fri)

Around Apollo Bay

Seventeen kilometres past Apollo Bay is **Maits Rest Rainforest Boardwalk**, an easy 20-minute rainforest-gully walk, while inland, 5km from Beech Forest, is the **Otway Fly** (☑5235 9200; Phillips Track; www.otwayfly. com; adult/child/family $22/9.50/55; ⊗9am-4.30pm). It's an elevated steel walkway in the forest canopy with a wavy lookout tower.

Cape Otway

Cape Otway is the second most southerly point of mainland Australia (after Wilsons Promontory) and one of the wettest parts of the state. This coastline is particularly beautiful, rugged and dangerous. More than 200 ships came to grief between Cape Otway and Port Fairy between the 1830s and 1930s, which led to the 'Shipwreck Coast' moniker.

The turn-off for Lighthouse Rd, which leads 12km down to the lighthouse, is 21km from Apollo Bay. The **Cape Otway Lighthouse** (☑5237 9240; www.lightstation.com; adult/child/family $17/8/42; ⊗9am-5pm) is the oldest surviving lighthouse on mainland Australia and was built in 1848 by more than 40 stonemasons without mortar or cement.

GREAT OCEAN WALK

The multiday **Great Ocean Walk** (www.greatoceanwalk.com.au) starts at Apollo Bay and runs all the way to the Twelve Apostles. It's possible to start at one point and arrange a pick-up at another (there are few public transport options). You can do shorter walks or the whole 104km trek over six days. Designated (and free) camp sites are spread along the Great Ocean Walk. **Walk 91** (☑5237 1189; www.walk91.com. au) arranges transport, equipment hire and can take your backpack to your destination for you. **GOR Shuttle** (☑5237 9278; 0428 379 278) is a recommended shuttle service for luggage and walkers; it will pick you up when your walking's done.

🛏 Sleeping

Blanket Bay
CAMPGROUND $

(☑13 19 63; www.parkweb.vic.gov.au; sites $20) Blanket Bay is serene (depending on your neighbours) and the nearby beach is beautiful. It's not really a secret; in fact it's so popular from Christmas to late January that sites must be won by ballot (held in October). Other sites nearby include **Parker Hill**, **Point Franklin** and **Crayfish Beach**. Contact **Parks Victoria** (☑13 19 63; www.parkweb. vic.gov.au) for bookings.

🌱 Great Ocean Ecolodge
ECOLODGE $$$

(☑5237 9297; www.capeotwaycentre.com; 635 Lighthouse Rd, s/d from $160/320) Pre-book a room at this ecolodge and check out the native animals, as the attached Cape Otway Centre for Conservation Ecology also serves as an animal hospital for a menagerie of local fauna. The luxurious en suite rooms in the post-and-beam, solar-powered, mudbrick homestead have bush-view decks and the centre offers guided walking tours and eco activities.

Lighthouse Keeper's Residence
B&B $$$

(Cape Otway Lighthouse; www.lightstation.com; d from $200) There is a range of options at this windswept spot; you can book out the whole Head Lightkeeper's House (sleeping 16), or the smaller Manager's B&B (sleeping two).

Bimbi Park
CAMPGROUND, CABINS $$

(☑5237 9246; www.bimbipark.com.au; Manna Gum Dr; unpowered sites low/high season $20/30, powered sites $30/35, d cabins $60-180)

Down a dirt road 3km from the lighthouse, this horse-riding ranch has bush sites, fancy (and not-so-fancy) cabins and horse rides ($45 per hour).

Cape Otway to Port Campbell National Park

After Cape Otway, the Great Ocean Road levels out and enters the fertile Horden Vale flats, returning briefly to the coast at tiny Glenaire. Then the road returns inland and begins the climb up to Lavers Hill. On overcast or rainy days the hills here can be seriously fog-bound, and the twists and turns can be challenging when you can't see the end of your car bonnet.

Six kilometres north of Glenaire, a 5km detour goes down Red Johanna Rd, winding through rolling hills and grazing cows to the wild thrashing surf of Johanna Beach (forget swimming). The world-famous Rip Curl Pro surfing competition relocates here when Bells Beach isn't working.

🛏 Sleeping

Johanna Campground   CAMPGROUND
(Parks Victoria; ☎13 19 63; www.parkweb.vic.gov.au; sites free) This campground is situated on a protected grassy area between the dunes and the rolling hills. Book ahead, but there are no fees due or permits required. There's an ablutions facility, but fires are banned and you'll need to bring in your own drinking water.

Boomerangs   APARTMENTS **$$$**
(☎5237 4213; www.theboomerangs.com; cnr Great Ocean & Red Johanna Rds; d from $230) These boomerang-shaped cabins have vaulted ceilings, jarrah floorboards, leadlighting, spas and commanding views of the Johanna Valley. The on-site owners are lovely.

Port Campbell National Park

The road levels out after leaving the Otways and enters narrow, relatively flat scrubby escarpment lands that fall away to sheer, 70m cliffs along the coast between Princetown and Peterborough – a distinct change of scene. This is Port Campbell National Park, home to the Twelve Apostles; it's the most famous and most photographed stretch of the Great Ocean Road. For aeons, waves and tides have crashed against the soft limestone rock, eroding, undercutting and carving out a fascinating series of rock stacks, gorges, arches and blowholes.

The **Gibson Steps**, hacked by hand into the cliffs in the 19th century by local landowner Hugh Gibson (and more recently replaced by concrete steps), lead down to feral Gibson Beach, an essential stop. This beach, and others along this stretch of coast, are not suitable for swimming because of strong currents and undertows – you can walk along the beach, but be careful not to be stranded by high tides or nasty waves. The lonely **Twelve Apostles** are rocky stacks that have been abandoned to the ocean by retreating headland. Today, only seven apostles can be seen from the viewing platforms. The understated roadside **lookout** (Great Ocean Rd; ⊙9am-5pm), 6km past Princetown, has public toilets and a cafe. Helicopters zoom around the Twelve Apostles, giving passengers an amazing view of the rocks. **12 Apostles Helicopters** (☎5598 6161; www.12apostleshelicopters.com.au) is just behind the car park at the lookout; it offers a 10-minute tour covering attractions such as the Twelve Apostles, Loch Ard Gorge, Sential Rock and Port Campbell from $95 per person.

Nearby **Loch Ard Gorge** is where the Shipwreck Coast's most famous and haunting tale unfolded when two young survivors of the wrecked iron clipper *Loch Ard* made it to shore (see p250).

Port Campbell

POP 400

This small, windswept town is poised on a dramatic, natural bay, eroded from the surrounding limestone cliffs, and almost perfectly rectangular in shape. It's a friendly spot with some great bargain accommodation options, and makes an ideal spot for debriefing after the Twelve Apostles. The tiny bay has a lovely sandy beach, the only safe place for swimming along this tempestuous coast.

⊙ Sights & Activities

There is stunning **diving** in the kelp forests, canyons and tunnels of the **Arches Marine Sanctuary** and to the *Loch Ard* wreck. There are shore dives from **Wild Dog Cove** and **Crofts Bay**. A 4.7km **Discovery Walk**, with signage, gives an introduction to the

The Twelve Apostles are not 12 in number, and, from all records, never have been. From the viewing platform you can clearly count seven Apostles, but maybe some obscure others? We consulted widely with Parks Victoria officers, tourist office staff and even the cleaner at the lookout, but it's still not clear. Locals tend to say 'It depends where you look from', which, really, is true.

The Apostles are called 'stacks' in geologic lingo, and the rock formations were originally called the 'Sow and Piglets'. Someone in the '60s (nobody can recall who) thought they might attract some tourists with a more venerable name, so they were renamed 'the Apostles'. Since apostles tend to come by the dozen, the number 12 was added some time later. The two stacks on the eastern (Otway) side of the viewing platform are not technically Apostles – they're Gog and Magog (picking up on the religious nomenclature yet?).

So there aren't 12 stacks; in a boat or helicopter you might count 11. The soft limestone cliffs are dynamic and changeable, constantly eroded by the unceasing waves – one 70m-high stack collapsed into the sea in July 2005 and the Island Archway lost its archway in June 2009. If you look carefully at how the waves lick around the pointy part of the cliff base, you can see a new Apostle being born. The labour lasts many thousands of years.

area's natural and historical features. It's just out of town on the way to Warrnambool.

Port Campbell Touring Company TOURS
(☑5598 6424; www.portcampbelltouring.com.au; half-day tours $65) Runs Apostle Coast tours, a Loch Ard evening walk and fishing trips to Crofts Bay.

Port Campbell Boat Charters TOURS
(☑5598 6411) Runs diving, scenic and fishing tours.

🛏 Sleeping & Eating

Port Campbell Guesthouse GUESTHOUSE $
(☑0407 696 559; www.portcampbellguesthouse.com.au; 54 Lord St; guesthouse/flashpackers per person $35/38) It's great to find a home away from home, and this property close to town has a cosy house with four bedrooms out back and a separate motel-style 'flashpackers' section up front. Great for families.

✐ Port Campbell Hostel HOSTEL $
(☑5598 6305; www.portcampbellhostel.com.au; 18 Tregea St; dm/d $25/70; ☎) This brand-new, purpose-built double-storey backpacker place has rooms with western views, a huge shared kitchen and an even bigger lounge/bar area. It's big on recycling and the toilets are ecofriendly, too. Hang out in the lounge and read the days' papers or get involved with a *Mills & Boon*.

Room Six RESTAURANT $$
(28 Lord St; mains $15-30; ☺breakfast, lunch & dinner Fri-Wed) Come here for delightful dinners

(featuring all the good seafood of the area) or a simple snack during the day. Although this place is only new, its ambience suggests a lovely maturity.

12 Rocks Cafe Bar CAFE $
(19 Lord St; mains $8-15; ☺breakfast, lunch & dinner) Watch flotsam wash up on the beach from this busy place, which has the best beachfront views. Try a local Otways beer with a pasta or seafood main, or just duck in for a coffee.

ℹ Information

Port Campbell visitor centre (☑1300 137 255; www.visit12apostles.com.au; 26 Morris St; ☺9am-5pm) Stacks of regional and accommodation information and interesting shipwreck displays – the anchor from the *Loch Ard*, salvaged in 1978, is out the front.

ℹ Getting There & Away

V/Line (☑13 61 96; www.vline.com.au) buses leave Geelong on Monday, Wednesday and Friday and travel through Port Campbell ($24, four hours) and on to Warrnambool ($27, six hours).

Port Campbell to Warrnambool

The Great Ocean Road continues west of Port Campbell, passing more rock stacks. The next one is the **Arch**, offshore from Point Hesse.

Nearby is **London Bridge**...fallen down! Now sometimes called London Arch, it was once a double-arched rock platform linked to the mainland. Visitors could walk out across a narrow natural bridge to the huge rock formation. In January 1990, the bridge collapsed, leaving two terrified tourists marooned on the world's newest island – they were eventually rescued by helicopter. Nearby is the **Grotto**.

The **Bay of Islands** is 8km west of tiny **Peterborough**, where a short walk from the car park takes you to magnificent lookout points.

You can't help but notice the acres and acres of farming land here, and if you're driving keep an eye out for milk trucks pulling slowly into and out of farms. Slightly tacky **Cheese World** (www.cheeseworld.com. au; Great Ocean Rd, Allansford; ⊙9.30am-5pm Mon-Fri, 9am-4pm Sat, 9am-3pm Sun) is opposite the area's main dairy factory, and has a museum, restaurant, cheese cellar and tasty (and cheap) milkshakes. It's 12km before Warrnambool.

The Great Ocean Road ends near here where it meets the Princes Hwy, which continues through the traditional lands of the Gunditjmara people into South Australia.

Warrnambool

POP 28,100

Warrnambool was originally a whaling and sealing station – now it's booming as a major regional commercial and whale-watching centre. Its historic buildings, waterways and tree-lined streets are attractive, and there's a large student population who attend the Warrnambool campus of Deakin University.

The major housing and commercial development around the fringes of the city look much like city suburbs anywhere in Australia, but the regions around the waterfront have largely retained their considerable historic charm.

◉ Sights & Activities

Southern right whales come to mate and nurse their bubs in the waters off Logan's Beach from July to September, breaching and fluking off **Logan's Beach Whale-Watching Platform**. It's a major tourist drawcard, but sightings are not guaranteed.

Flagstaff Hill
Maritime Village REPLICA MARITIME VILLAGE
(⊘1800 556 111; www.flagstaffhill.com; Merri St; adult/child/family $16/7/39; ⊙9am-5pm) This major tourist attraction is modelled on an early Australian coastal port. See the cannon and fortifications, built in 1887 to withstand the perceived threat of Russian invasion, and **Shipwrecked** (adult/child/family $26/14/67), an engaging sound-and-laser show of the *Loch Ard*'s plunge. Grab a meal at Pippies by the Bay while you're here.

FREE **Warrnambool Art Gallery**
ART GALLERY
(www.warrnambool.vic.gov.au; 165 Timor St; ⊙10am-5pm Mon-Fri, noon-5pm Sat & Sun) Head here to see the permanent Australian collection, which includes such notable painters as Tom Roberts, James Gleeson and Arthur Boyd.

Rundell's Mahogany
Trail Rides HORSE RIDING
(⊘0408 589 546; www.rundellshorseriding.com. au; 2hr beach ride $65) Get to know some of Warrnambool's quiet beach spots by horseback.

THE WRECK OF THE LOCH ARD

The Victorian coastline between Cape Otway and Port Fairy was a notoriously treacherous stretch of water in the days of sailing ships, due to hidden reefs and frequent heavy fog. More than 80 vessels came to grief on this 120km stretch in just 40 years.

The most famous wreck was that of the iron-hulled clipper *Loch Ard*, which foundered off Mutton Bird Island at 4am on the final night of its long voyage from England in 1878. Of 37 crew and 19 passengers on board, only two survived. Eva Carmichael, who couldn't swim, clung to wreckage and was washed into a gorge, where apprentice officer Tom Pearce rescued her. Tom heroically climbed the sheer cliff and raised the alarm but no other survivors were found. Eva and Tom were both 19 years old, leading to speculation in the press about a romance, but nothing actually happened – they never saw each other again and Eva soon returned back to Ireland (this time, perhaps not surprisingly) via steamship.

🛌 Sleeping

Hotel Warrnambool   PUB $$
(☎5562 2377; www.hotelwarrnambool.com.au;
cnr Koroit & Kepler Sts; d with/without bathroom
$140/110; ❄@) Recent renovations in this
historic 1894 pub have done wonders with
the rooms, which have plasma TVs and
access to a kitchenette and lounge. Some
have bathrooms and balconies. Downstairs
is one of the friendliest pub-eateries in
town.

**Warrnambool Beach
Backpackers**   HOSTEL $
(☎5562 4874; www.beachbackpackers.com.au; 17
Stanley St; dm/d $28/80; ❄@) Close to the sea,
this former museum has a huge living area
with a bar, internet access, kitchen and free
pick-up. Its rooms, however, could do with a
freshen up. It's a good place to seek casual
employment.

Atwood Motor Inn   MOTEL $$
(☎5562 7144; www.atwoodmotorinn.com.au; 8
Spence St; d from $105; ❄🅿) Expect spacious
motel-style rooms with flat-screen TVs and
bathrooms big enough to wash a (small)
whale in. The standard doubles are the
smallest, but are still comfortable.

🍴 Eating & Drinking

Donnelly's Restaurant   MODERN AUSTRALIAN $$
(78 Liebig St; mains $24-31; ⊙lunch & dinner Tue-
Sun, daily in summer) This smart restaurant
makes a big deal of its steaks and seafood,
and it's no wonder: both are as local as
you can get and very satisfying.

Wyton   CAFE $
(www.wytonevents.com; 91 Kepler St; mains $12;
⊙breakfast Mon-Sat, lunch Mon-Fri) Come here
for sophisticated breakfasts, excellent cof-
fee and healthy lunches (including spiced
carrot and risoni pasta) that you can take
away.

Pippies by the Bay   MODERN AUSTRALIAN $$
(Flagstaff Hill Maritime Village, Merri St; mains
$28-32; ⊙lunch & dinner daily, breakfast Sat
& Sun) A fine restaurant in the Flagstaff
Hill visitors centre; make an evening of
it with a meal and show, or just pop in
for a weekend breakfast and admire the
view.

ℹ Information

Warrnambool Library (25 Liebig St; ⊙9.30am-
5pm Mon-Tue, to 6pm Wed-Fri, 10am-noon Sat)
Free internet access.

Warrnambool visitors centre (www.visit
warrnambool.com.au; Merri St; ⊙9am-5pm)
Signposted off the Princes Hwy (A1) in the
Flagstaff Hill complex, it produces a bike map
and several walking maps. There's also internet
access here ($10 per hour) and bicycle hire
($30 per day).

ℹ Getting There & Away

Bus

Three buses a week (Monday, Wednesday and
Friday) travel from Geelong along the Great
Ocean Road to Warrnambool ($27, six hours).
There are around 10 **V/Line** (☎13 61 96; www.
vline.com.au) buses a day to Port Fairy ($3.50,
30 minutes) and three continue on to Portland
($9.50, 1½ hours). There's a bus on Monday,
Wednesday and Friday to Apollo Bay ($15.80, 3½
hours). **Christians Bus Co** (☎5562 9432) runs
services on Tuesday, Friday and Saturday to Port
Fairy ($3.30, departing 8am).

Train

V/Line (☎13 61 96; www.vline.com.au; Merri St)
trains run to Melbourne ($26, 3¼ hours, three
or four daily).

Tower Hill Reserve

Tower Hill, 15km west of Warrnambool, is
a vast caldera born in a volcanic eruption
35,000 years ago. Aboriginal artefacts un-
earthed in the volcanic ash show that Indigenous people lived in the area at the time.
The Worn Gundidj Aboriginal Cooperative
operates the **Tower Hill Natural History
Centre** (www.worngundidj.org.au; ⊙9am-5pm
Mon-Fri, 10am 4pm Sat, Sun & public holidays). It's
one of the few places where you'll spot wild
emus, kangaroos and koalas hanging out
together.

There are excellent day walks, including
the steep 30-minute **Peak Climb** with spectacular 360-degree views.

Port Fairy

POP 2600

This seaside township at the mouth of the
Moyne River was settled in 1835, and the
first arrivals were whalers and sealers.
Port Fairy still has a large fishing fleet and
a relaxed, salty feel, with its old bluestone
and sandstone buildings, whitewashed cottages, colourful fishing boats and tree-lined
streets. The town is very much a luxury tourist destination and is home to art galleries,
antique shops and boutiques.

THE MAHOGANY SHIP

The Mahogany Ship is said to be a Portuguese vessel that ran aground off Warrnambool in the 1500s – there have been alleged sightings of the elusive wreck sitting high in the dunes dating back to 1846. Portuguese naval charts from the 16th century known as the Dieppe Maps are said to depict parts of Australia's southern coastline, including Armstrong Bay 6km west of Warrnambool, and this has further fuelled the Mahogany Ship legend. Alternative theories claim that the Mahogany Ship was an even earlier Chinese junk. For more than 150 years people have been trying to find the remains of the Mahogany Ship – some say it's buried deep in the dunes or was swallowed by the sea. There's no direct evidence that the ship ever existed, but every decade or so it all rises to the surface again at the locally held Mahogany Ship Symposium.

◉ Sight & Activities

The visitors centre has brochures and maps that show the popular **Shipwreck Walk** and **History Walk**. On Battery Hill there's a lookout point, and cannons and fortifications positioned here in the 1860s. Down below there's a lovely one-hour walk around Griffiths Island where the Moyne River empties into the sea. The island is connected to the mainland by a footbridge, and is home to a protected **muttonbird colony** (they descend on the town each October and stay until April) and a modest lighthouse.

✮✮ Festivals & Events

Port Fairy Folk Festival   FOLK FESTIVAL
(www.portfairyfolkfestival.com; tickets $195) Australia's premier folk-music festival is held on the Labour Day long weekend in early March. Book accommodation early.

🛏 Sleeping

Pelican Waters Holiday Park   BOUTIQUE ACCOMMODATION **$**
(☑5568 1002; www.pelicanwatersportfairy.com.au; 34 Regent St; cabins/carriages from $100) Why stay in a hotel when you can sleep in a train? This beautifully presented property has cabins as well as two two-bedroom converted Melbourne train carriages.

Port Fairy YHA   HOSTEL **$**
(☑5568 2468; www.portfairyhostel.com.au; 8 Cox St; dm $26-30, d/f/2-bed apt from $75/115/200; @🛜) In the rambling (former) 1844 home of merchant William Rutledge, this friendly and well-run hostel has a large kitchen, pool table and free cable TV.

Daisies by the Sea B&B   B&B **$$**
(☑5568 2355; www.port-fairy.com/daisiesbythe sea; 222 Griffiths St; d from $160) Nod off to the sound of crashing waves just 50m from your door in these two cosy beachfront suites, 1.5km from town.

✗ Eating

TOP CHOICE **Merrijig Inn**   MEDITERRANEAN **$$$**
(☑5568 2324; www.merrijiginn.com; cnr Campbell & Gipps Sts; 5 courses $90) This is superb dining and the menu changes according to what's seasonal. You might get duck breast, leg in brik pastry, baby beetroot, pickled rose, rhubarb and chard one day, and yabbies with asparagus, almonds and nasturtium the next.

Rebecca's Cafe   CAFE **$**
(70-72 Sackville St; mains $9-16; ⊘breakfast & lunch) Excellent for breakfast and light lunches, Rebecca's has interesting items on the menu including rich wild-rice porridge topped with rhubarb as well as the usual cakes, muffins, slices, scones and biscuits.

Hub   CAFE **$**
(cnr Bank & Sackville Sts; mains $14; ⊘breakfast, lunch & dinner; 🛜) On weekends this corner cafe is packed with people enjoying spicy gourmet breakfasts featuring locally made chorizo sausage, and good old bacon and eggs. The menu steps up a notch for mostly seafood dinners.

❶ Information

Port Fairy visitors centre (☑5568 2682; www.visitportfairy-moyneshire.com.au; Bank St; ⊘9am-5pm) Can recharge your mobile phone's battery while providing spot-on information.

❶ Getting There & Away

V/Line (☑13 61 96; www.vline.com.au) buses run three times daily on weekdays (twice on Saturday and once on Sunday) to Portland ($6.50, one hour) and 10 times daily to Warrnambool ($3.50, 30 minutes).

Port Fairy is 20 minutes west of Warrnambool on the A1.

Portland

POP 9800

There's a charm to largish Portland; it has historic houses, a bunch of ghost stories and is a short distance from a lovely lighthouse. It's also the start and end of the Great Southwest Walk.

This was Victoria's first European settlement, and became a whaling and sealing base in the early 1800s. Blessed Mary MacKillop, Australia's first saint, arrived here from Melbourne in 1862 and founded Australia's first religious order.

🛏 Sleeping & Eating

TOP CHOICE **Annesley House**   BOUTIQUE HOTEL **$$**
(☑0429 852 235; www.annesleyhouse. com.au; 60 Julia St; d from $135) This recently restored former doctor's mansion (c 1878) has six very different self-contained rooms, some featuring claw-foot baths and lovely views. All feature a unique sense of style. Highly recommended.

Claremont Holiday Village   CABINS **$**
(☑5523 7567; www.holidayvillage.com.au; 37 Percy St; unpowered/powered sites from $26/35, cabins from $70; ☻) This central caravan park has decent facilities including a large camp kitchen. The cheaper cabins have shared bathrooms.

Deegan Seafoods   FISH AND CHIPS **$**
(106 Percy St; mains $10 ☻lunch & dinner) This fish-and-chip shop serves up some of the freshest fish in Victoria.

ℹ Information

Parks Victoria (☑5522 3454; www.parkweb. vic.gov.au; 8-12 Julia St; ☻8am-4.30pm Mon-Fri)

Portland visitors centre (☑5523 2671; www. greatoceanroad.org; Lee Breakwater Rd; ☻9am-5pm) In the impressive-looking Maritime Discovery Centre.

ℹ Getting There & Away

V/Line (☑13 61 96; www.vline.com.au) buses connect Portland with Port Fairy three times daily and once on Sunday ($6.50, 55 minutes) and Warrnambool ($9.50, 1½ hours).

Nelson

POP 230

Tiny Nelson is the last vestige of civilisation before the South Australian border – just a general store, pub and a handful of accommodation places. It's a popular holiday and fishing spot at the mouth of the **Glenelg River**, which flows through **Lower Glenelg National Park**. Note that Nelson uses South Australia's 08 telephone area code. Why? We dunno!

◉ Sights & Activities

Glenelg River Cruises   TOUR
(☑08-8738 4191; cruises adult/child $30/10) Cruises depart Nelson daily (except Thursday and Monday) at 1pm for a leisurely 3½-hour cruise to the **Princess Margaret Rose Cave** (☑08-8738 4171; www.princessmargaret rosecave.com; adult/child/family $14/9/32), but tickets for the cave tour cost extra. If you travel to the cave on your own it's about 17km from Nelson, towards the border.

Nelson Boat & Canoe Hire   BOATING
(☑08-8738 4048; www.nelsonboatandcanoehire. com.au) This outfit can rig you up for

---

DON'T MISS

CAPE BRIDGEWATER

Cape Bridgewater is a 21km detour off the Portland–Nelson Rd. The stunning 4km arc of **Bridgewater Bay** is perhaps one of Australia's finest stretches of white-sand surf beach, backed by pristine dunes. The wind farm–lined road continues on to **Cape Duquesne**, where walking tracks lead to a **Blowhole** and the **Petrified Forest** on the clifftop. A longer two-hour return walk takes you to a **seal colony** where you can see dozens of fur seals sunning themselves on the rocks.

Stay at friendly **Sea View Lodge B&B** (☑5526 7276; www.hotkey.net.au/~seaviewlodge; Bridgewater Rd; d from $140) or **Cape Bridgewater Holiday Camp** (☑5526 7247; www. capebridgewatercoastalcamp.com.au; Blowhole Rd; unpowered sites/dm/houses $15/30/150), which has sparkling dorms, self-contained houses and a huge camp kitchen. The holiday camp also runs fun **Seals by Sea tours** (adult/child $30/20).

GREAT SOUTHWEST WALK

This 250km signposted loop begins and ends at Portland's information centre, and takes in some of the south-west's most stunning natural scenery, from the remote, blustery coast, through the river system of the Lower Glenelg National Park and back through the hinterland to Portland. The whole loop would take at least 10 days, but it can be done in sections. Maps are available from the Portland visitors centre and the Parks Victoria and visitors centre in Nelson. See www.greatsouth westwalk.com.

serious river-camping expeditions – canoe hire costs from $60 a day. It also has paddleboats for hire ($20 for 30 minutes).

🛏 Sleeping

There are nine **camp sites** between Nelson and Dartmoor along the Glenelg River that are popular with canoeists but are also accessible by road, with rain-fed water tanks, toilets and fireplaces (BYO firewood). Camping permits are issued by Parks Victoria in Nelson. Forest Camp South is the nicest of these, right on the river, rich in bird life and accessible from the Portland–Nelson Rd.

Nelson Hotel   PUB $
(📞08-8738 4011; www.nelsonhotel.com.au; Kellett St; d/apt from $40/135; ⊙lunch & dinner) This hotel has a dusty stuffed pelican above the bar and a few vegetarian meals on the fishy menu (mains $17 to $30). The quarters are plain but adequate with shared facilities, and the attached apartment/studio is great.

ℹ Information

Parks Victoria & Nelson visitors centre
(📞08-8738 4051; nelsonvic@hotkey.net.au; ⊙9am-5pm; @) Just before the Glenelg River bridge.

GIPPSLAND & THE SOUTHEAST COAST

It may not be as well known as the Great Ocean Road to the west, but Victoria's southeast coast boasts easily the state's best beaches, impossibly pretty lakeside villages and Victoria's finest coastal national parks, typi-

fied by the glorious Wilsons Promontory. This region of eastern Victoria is known as Gippsland (named for former New South Wales Governor George Gipps), and while most travellers head for the coast between Phillip Island and Mallacoota, it also encompasses a vast inland area of farmland, power stations, High Country foothills and forest wilderness.

A trip through Gippsland could mean swimming, surfing, fishing, camping and boating along the coast – much of it practically deserted for a good part of the year (yes, it's busy during summer holidays!); penguin- and wildlife-spotting; cycling from town to town on the network of rail trails; feasting on the freshest seafood; or packing the rucksack and hiking boots and heading into the most remote wilderness national parks in the state.

Phillip Island
POP 7500

Famous for the Penguin Parade and Grand Prix racing circuit, Phillip Island attracts a curious mix of surfers, petrolheads and international tourists making a beeline for those little penguins.

But the little island has plenty more to offer. At its heart, 100-sq-km Phillip Island is still a farming community, but along with the penguins, there's a large seal colony, abundant bird life around the Rhyll wetlands, and a koala colony. The rugged south coast has some fabulous surf beaches and the summer swell of tourists means there's a swag of family attractions, plenty of accommodation, and a buzzing cafe and restaurant scene in the island capital, Cowes. Visit in winter, though, and you'll find a very quiet place where the local population of farmers, surfers and hippies go about their business.

⊙ Sights & Activities

A **Three Parks Pass** ($36/18/90 adult/child/family) gives access to the Penguin Parade, Koala Conservation Centre and Churchill Island, or you can buy tickets for each attraction individually.

Penguin Parade   WILDLIFE
(📞5951 2800; www.penguins.org.au; Summerland Beach; adult/child/family $21/11/53; ⊙10am-nightfall) The Penguin Parade attracts more than 500,000 visitors a year. Amphitheatres hold up to 3800 people who coo over the penguins as they emerge from the sea after

sunset and waddle up the beach to their nesting areas. Bring warm clothing. There are a variety of specialised tours (adult $40-75) where you can be accompanied by rangers or see penguins from the vantage of a Skybox (an elevated platform). There's also a cafe and interpretive centre at the complex.

Nobbies Centre   WILDLIFE
(Ventnor Rd; tours adult/child $10/5; ☺10am-8pm Dec-Feb, to 5pm Mar-May, 11am-4pm Jun-Aug, 11am-6pm Sep-Nov) The Nobbies are a rock formation on the island's southwest tip. The Nobbies Centre offers great views, kids' entertainment and lots of interactive displays including underwater cameras. Beyond the Nobbies are Seal Rocks, inhabited by Australia's largest fur-seal colony.

Motor Racing Circuit   MOTOR SPORT
(☎5952 9400; www.phillipislandcircuit.com.au; Back Beach Rd; ☺9am-5.30pm) Even when the motorbikes aren't racing, revheads love the motor racing circuit. From the visitor centre there are guided circuit tours (adult/child/family $19/10/44; ☺tours 11am & 2pm), or check out the History of Motorsport Museum (adult/child/family $13.50/6/30). The more adventurous can cut laps of the track with a racing driver in hotted-up V8s ($295, bookings essential), or drive yourself in a go-kart around a scale replica of the track with Champ Karts (per 10/20/30min $29/53/68).

Phillip Island
Chocolate Factory   CHOCOLATE FACTORY
(☎5956 6600; www.phillipislandchocolatefactory.com.au; 930 Phillip Island Rd, Newhaven; factory tours adult/child/family $12/8/36; ☺9am-5pm) Offers free samples of handmade Belgian chocolate, a walk-through tour of the chocolate-making process, and a remarkable gallery of chocolate sculptures, from Michelangelo's *David* to an entire model chocolate village!

Beaches   BEACHES
Excellent surf beaches bring day-tripping board riders from Melbourne, while there are calmer kid-friendly beaches on the island's north side, including Cowes. The island's south-side ocean beaches include spectacular Woolamai, which has rips and currents and is only suitable for experienced surfers. Beginners and families can go to Smiths Beach, where Island Surfboards (☎5952 3443; www.islandsurfboards.com.au; 225 Smiths Beach & 147 Thompson Ave, Cowes; 2hr lesson $55) offers surfing lessons and hires out gear (boards $40 per day).

Churchill Island   HISTORIC FARM
(☎5956 7214; off Phillip Island Rd; adult/child/family $11/6/26.50; ☺10am-4.30pm) Connected by a bridge to Phillip Island, this is an historic working farm.

Koala Conservation Centre   WILDLIFE
(☎5951 2800; www.phillipislandguide.com/koala; Phillip Island Rd; adult/child/family $11/6/26.50; ☺10am-5pm) From the elevated treetop boardwalks here you can watch koalas in a natural environment, chewing eucalyptus leaves and dozing.

Phillip Island Wildlife Park   WILDLIFE
(☎5952 2038; www.piwildlifepark.com.au; Phillip Island Rd; adult/child/family $15/8/40; ☺10am-5pm) About 2km south of Cowes, this park has more than 100 Australian native wildlife species.

☞ Tours

Go West   DAY TOURS
(☎1300 736 551; www.gowest.com.au; 1-day tours $125) One-day tour from Melbourne that includes lunch and iPod commentary in several languages. Includes entry to the Penguin Parade.

Wildlife Coast Cruises   WILDLIFE
(☎1300 763 739, 5952 3501; www.wildlifecoastcruises.com.au; Rotunda Bldg, Cowes Jetty; tours $35-70; ☺Nov-May) Runs a variety of cruises including seal-watching, twilight and cape cruise; also a half-day cruise to French Island (adult/child $75/55) and full day to Wilsons Promontory ($190/140).

✷ Festivals & Events

Pyramid Rock Festival   MUSIC
(www.thepyramidrockfestival.com; New Year) This huge event coincides with New Year

> **DON'T MISS**
>
> ## CAPE NELSON LIGHTHOUSE
>
> Cape Nelson Lighthouse is a wonderful spot for a bite to eat and some stunning views. Isabella's Cafe (☺10am-4pm) takes pride of place at its blustering base and offers excellent deli-style food within its thick bluestone walls. Lighthouse tours (adult/child $15/10; ☺10am & 2pm) get you high up, while those wanting to stay a while can book into a self-contained assistant lighthouse keepers' cottage (www.capenelsonlighthouse.com.au; d from $180).

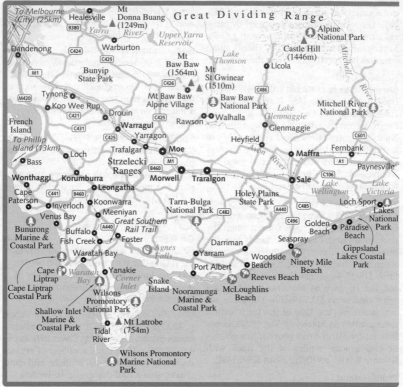

festivities and features some of the best Aussie bands.

Australian Motorcycle Grand Prix
MOTORCYCLE RACING

(www.motogp.com.au; Oct) The island's biggest event – three days of bike action in October.

🛏 Sleeping

Most of the accommodation is in and around Cowes, although there are a few places in Rhyll and Newhaven, and B&Bs and numerous caravan parks are scattered around the island.

Surf & Circuit Accommodation
APARTMENTS $$

(☎5952 1300; www.surfandcircuit.com; 113 Justice Rd, Cowes; apt $135-380; ❋🐾) Ideal for families or groups, these eight spacious, modern and comfortable two- and three-bedroom units accommodate up to six and 10 people. They

have kitchens and lounges with plasma TVs and patios, and some have spas. Outside there are barbecue areas, a tennis court and a playground.

Amaroo Park YHA
HOSTEL $

(☎5952 2548; www.yha.com.au; 97 Church St, Cowes; unpowered sites $30, dm/d/f from $30/95/135; @🛜❋) In a shady bush setting, the Amaroo Park YHA is a lovely old-style guesthouse with a communal kitchen and barbecue areas, bar, lounge and TV room. There are en suite cabins and camp sites outside.

Island Accommodation
HOSTEL $

(☎5956 6123; www.theislandaccommodation.com. au; 10-12 Phillip Island Tourist Rd, Newhaven; dm $30-36, d $155; ❋🛜) Part of the Islantis Wave complex in Newhaven, this brand-spanking-new backpacker place is perfect for surfers wanting to be close to the action at Woolamai. It's simple but spotless, with a rooftop deck and kitchen.

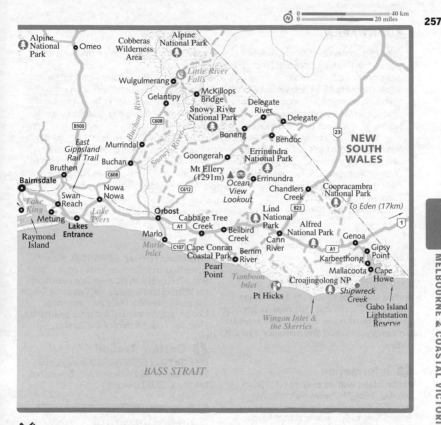

✖ Eating & Drinking

Most of the eateries are in Cowes – the Esplanade and Thompson Ave are crowded with fish-and-chip shops, cafes and take-aways – but there are a few more gems scattered around the island.

COWES

Infused   MODERN AUSTRALIAN **$$**
(☎5952 2655; www.infused.com.au; 115 Thompson Ave, Cowes; mains $25-38; ☺lunch & dinner Wed-Mon) Infused's groovy mix of timber, stone and lime-green decor makes a relaxed place to enjoy a beautifully presented lunch or dinner, or just a late-night cocktail. The eclectic Mod Oz menu is strong on seafood and moves from freshly shucked oysters to Asian curries and Black Angus rib eye.

Hotel   PUB **$$**
(☎5952 2060; www.hotelphillipisland.com; 11-13 The Esplanade, Cowes; mains $10-28; ☺lunch & dinner) So cool that it only goes by its first name (like Cher...), this breezy corner pub is all leather, sleek lines and big windows. The menu is honest and good value, with all-day tapas plates, pizza and the standards of steak and chicken parma.

Madcowes   CAFE-DELI **$**
(☎5952 2560; 17 The Esplanade, Cowes; mains $7-17; ☺breakfast & lunch) This stylish cafe-foodstore looks out to the main beach and cooks up some of the heartiest breakfasts and light lunches on the island. Try the ricotta hotcakes or the grazing platter, and browse the selection of wine and produce.

CAPE WOOLAMAI

White Salt   FISH AND CHIPS **$**
(☎5956 6336; 7 Vista Pl; fish from $5, meal packs from $20; ☺lunch & dinner Fri-Sun, from 4.30pm Wed & Thu) White Salt serves the best fish and chips on the island – selected fish fillets and hand-cut chips, tempura prawns

KOONWARRA

But a blip on the South Gippsland Hwy, culinary Koonwarra has made a name for itself thanks to a fine food store and an organic cooking school.

Koonwarra Food, Wine & Produce Store (☑5664 2285; cnr South Gippsland Hwy & Koala Dr; mains $6-34; ☺breakfast & lunch daily, dinner Fri; ☑) serves simple food with flair using organic, low-impact suppliers and products. The store stocks local wines and produce such as sauces, preserves and pâtés made on site. It also has wine and cheese tasting on weekends ($5) and a lovely shady garden area outside.

Peaceful Gardens Organic Cooking School (☑5664 2480; Koala Dr; half-/full-day from $70/130, children's half-day $30-50) is Victoria's first organic-certified cooking school, which carries the motto 'organic, seasonal, local'. It offers a wonderful selection of short courses, including making cakes, bread, preserves and traditional pastries and pasta. All of the courses use produce from the owners' farm. Full-day classes are offered for children.

Koonwarra also has a day spa and several good wineries nearby.

and marinated BBQ octopus salad with corn, pesto and lemon.

Curry Leaf INDIAN $
(☑5956 6772; 9 Vista Pl; mains $12-18; ☺dinner Wed-Mon, lunch Fri-Sun; ☑) This cheery Indian restaurant and takeaway is popular for its piquant meat, seafood and vegetarian curries, samosas and aromatic biryani dishes.

ⓘ Information

Phillip Island visitors centres (☑1300 366 422, 5956 7447; www.visitphillipisland. com; 895 Phillip Island Tourist Rd, Newhaven; ☺9am-5pm, to 6pm during school holidays) The main visitor centre for the island is on the main road in at Newhaven, and there's a smaller centre at Cowes (cnr Thompson & Church Sts, Cowes).

Waterfront Internet Service (☑5952 3312; Shop 1/130 Thompson Ave, Cowes; ☺9am-5pm Mon-Fri, 10am-1pm Sat) Internet access is $6 per hour.

ⓘ Getting There & Away

By car, Phillip Island can only be accessed across the bridge at San Remo to Newhaven. From Melbourne take the Monash Fwy (M1) and exit at Pakenham, joining the South Gippsland Hwy at Koo Wee Rup.

Bus

V/Line (☑13 61 96; www.vline.com.au) has train/bus services from Melbourne's Southern Cross station via Dandenong station or Koo Wee Rup ($10.40, 2 hours). There are no direct services.

Ferry

Inter Island Ferries (☑9585 5730; www. interislandferries.com.au; return adult/child/bike $21/10/8) runs between Stony Point on the Mornington Peninsula and Cowes via French Island (45 minutes). There are two sailings Monday and Wednesday, and three on Tuesday, Thursday, Friday, Saturday and Sunday.

ⓘ Getting Around

Ride On Bikes (☑5952 2533; www.rideon bikes.com.au; 43 Thompson Ave, Cowes; half-/full-day $25/35) Bike hire.

South Gippsland

South Gippsland has plenty of gems along the coast between Inverloch and Wilsons Promontory – Venus Bay, Cape Liptrap Coastal Park and Waratah Bay are all worthy of exploration. Inland among the farming communities and vineyards are some beautiful drives through the Strzelecki Ranges, the Great Southern Rail Trail cycle path, and trendy villages like Koonwarra and Fish Creek.

INVERLOCH

Fabulous surf, calm inlet beaches and outstanding diving and snorkelling make Inverloch and the surrounding Bass Coast along the road to Cape Paterson a popular destination. Even with the inevitable holiday crowds it manages to maintain a down-to-earth vibe. Pencil in the popular Inverloch Jazz Festival (www.inverlochjazzfest.org.au) on the Labour Day long weekend each March.

You can take lessons with **Learn to Surf Offshore Surf School** (☎5674 3374; www.surfingaustralia.com.au; 32 Park St; 2hr lesson $45) at the main surf beach at Inverloch. Everything is provided – you just need to book and turn up at the beach.

SEAL Diving Services (☎5174 3434; www.sealdivingservices.com.au; 7/27 Princes Hwy, Traralgon) offers shore dives at Cape Paterson and boat dives in the nearby Bunurong Marine & Coastal Park.

Sleeping & Eating

Inverloch Foreshore Camping Reserve   CAMPING $
(☎5674 1447; www.inverlochholidaypark.com.au; cnr The Esplanade & Ramsay Blvd; unpowered/powered sites from $26/30) Just back from the inlet beach, camping is a pleasure here with shade and privacy.

Tomo   JAPANESE $$
(☎5674 3444; www.tomo-modern-jp.com; 23 A'Beckett St; sushi from $4, mains $21-39; ⊙lunch & dinner Tue-Sun, daily in summer) Modern Japanese cuisine prepared to perfection. Start with tender sushi or sashimi, but don't miss the *gyoza* (dumplings) or tempura tiger prawns.

Red Elk Bar & Café   CAFE $
(☎5674 3264; 27 A'Beckett St; mains $12-20; ⊙breakfast & lunch) In a weatherboard corner cottage, this new cafe and bar is a buzzing place for coffee, a hearty breakfast or weekend live music.

ⓘ Information

Inverloch visitors centre (☎1300 762 433; www.visitbasscoast.com; 39 A'Beckett St; ⊙9am-5pm; @) Helpful staff can make accommodation bookings for free.

Bunurong Environment Centre & Shop (☎5674 3738; www.sgcs.org.au; cnr The Esplanade & Ramsay Blvd; ⊙10am-4pm Fri-Mon, daily during school holidays) Plenty of books and brochures on environmental and sustainable-living topics. Also here is a Shell Museum ($2) with more than 6000 shells.

ⓘ Getting There & Away

V/Line (☎13 61 96; www.vline.com.au) trains depart daily from Melbourne's Flinders St and Southern Cross stations for Dandenong, connecting with buses to Inverloch ($13.70, 3 hours). A quicker option (2 hours) is the V/Line coach with a change at Koo Wee Rup.

FISH CREEK
Travellers in the know have been stopping for a bite to eat at quirky Fish Creek on their way to the coast or the Prom for years, and these days it has developed into a bohemian little artists community with craft shops, galleries, studios, bookshops and some great cafes.

Celia Rosser Gallery (☎5683 2628; www.celiarossergallery.com; Promontory Rd; ⊙10am-4pm Fri-Mon) is a bright art space featuring the works of renowned botanical artist Celia Rosser, and various visiting artists. The attached **Banksia Café** has a sunny deck.

The art deco **Fish Creek Hotel** (☎5683 2416; Old Waratah Rd; mains $16-30; ⊙lunch & dinner), universally known as the Fishy Pub (but also called the Promontory Gate Hotel), is an essential stop for a beer or bistro meal, and there's motel accommodation at the back.

Wilsons Promontory National Park

If you like wilderness bushwalking, stunning coastal scenery and secluded white-sand beaches, you'll absolutely love this place. 'The Prom', as it's affectionately known, is one of the most popular national parks in Australia and our favourite coastal park.

Wilsons Promontory was an important area for the Kurnai and Boonwurrung Aborigines, and middens have been found in many places, including Cotters and Darby Beaches, and Oberon Bay. The southernmost part of mainland Australia, the Prom once formed a land bridge that allowed people to walk to Tasmania.

Tidal River, 30km from the park entry, is the hub, and home to the Parks Victoria office, a general store, cafe and accommodation. The wildlife around Tidal River is remarkably tame: kookaburras and rosellas lurk expectantly (resist the urge to feed

GREAT SOUTHERN RAIL TRAIL

This 49km **cycle and walking path** (www.railtrails.org.au) follows the old rail line from Leongatha to Foster, passing through the villages of Koonwarra, Meeniyan, Buffalo and Fish Creek – all good places to stop and refuel. The trail meanders through farmland with a few gentle hills, trestle bridges and occasional views of the coast and Wilsons Prom.

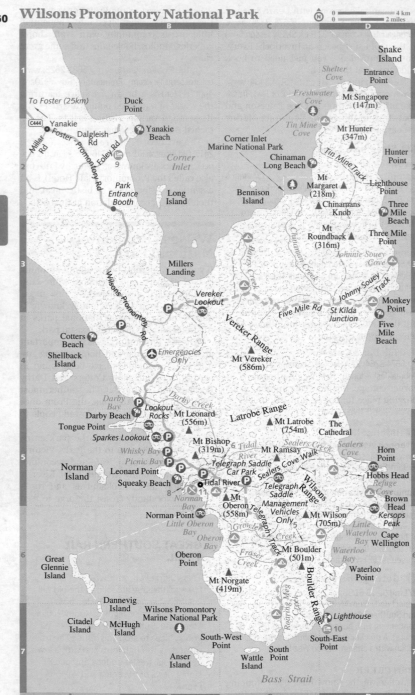

them), and wombats nonchalantly waddle out of the undergrowth.

Although there's a staffed **entry station** (⏱9am-sunset) where you receive a ticket, entry is free. There's no fuel available at Tidal River.

🏃 Activities

There's more than 80km of marked **walking trails** here, taking you through forests, marshes, valleys of tree ferns, low granite mountains and along beaches backed by sand dunes. Even nonwalkers can enjoy much of the park's beauty, with car park access off the Tidal River road leading to gorgeous beaches and lookouts.

Swimming is safe from the beautiful beaches at **Norman Bay** (Tidal River) and around the headland at **Squeaky Beach** – the ultra-fine quartz sand here really does squeak beneath your feet!

If you're travelling light, you can hire camping equipment, including tents, stoves, sleeping bags and backpacks, from **Wilsons Prom Hiking Hire** (☑5678 1152; 3670 Prom Rd, Yanakie).

👉 Tours

Hiking Plus   HIKING
(☑0418 341 537; www.hikingplus.com; 3-/5-day tour $1100/1800) This tour company organises fully catered and guided hikes to the Prom from nearby Foster. Packages include a two- to three-day hike, meals, a massage and spa, and you need only carry a light pack.

Bunyip Tours   DAY TOURS
(☑1300 286 947, 9650 9680; www.bunyiptours. com; day tour $120) One-day guided tour

Wilsons Promontory NP

to the Prom from Melbourne, with the option of staying on another two days to explore by yourself.

First Track Adventures   OUTDOOR ACTIVITIES
(☑5634 2761; www.firsttrack.com.au) This Yarragon-based company organises customised bushwalking, rockclimbing and abseiling trips to the Prom.

🛏 Sleeping

Nothing beats a night at the Prom. The main accommodation base is at Tidal River, but there are 11 bush-camping (outstation) areas around the Prom, all with pit or compost toilets, but no other facilities; carry in your own drinking water. Overnight hikers need camping permits (adult/child $8/4 per night), which must be booked ahead through Parks Victoria.

TIDAL RIVER
Situated on Norman Bay and a short walk to a stunning beach, accommodation at Tidal River is justifiably popular. Book well in advance through **Parks Victoria** (☑1800 350 552, 13 19 63; www.parkweb.vic.gov.au), especially for weekends and holidays.

Lorikeet Units & Cabins   CABINS $$
(d $110-172, extra adult $23) The spacious and private self-contained cabins sleep up to six people and have large, sliding glass doors and decking, and overlook the bush or river. The Lorikeet Units are equally comfortable, sleeping up to four people.

Wilderness Retreat   SAFARI TENTS $$$
(d $250, extra person $20) Squirreled away in bushland at Tidal River, these are the most expensive tents on the Prom! The luxury safari tents, with their own deck, sleep up to four people and are pretty cool, with en suite, queen-sized beds, heating and a communal tent kitchen.

Lighthouse Keepers' Cottages   COTTAGES $
(8-bed cottages per person $51-83) These isolated, heritage-listed 1850s cottages with thick granite walls are a real getaway, attached to a working lightstation on a pimple of land that juts out into the wild ocean. Kick back after the 19km hike here and watch ships or whales passing by. The cottages have shared facilities, including a fully equipped kitchen.

Camp Sites   CAMPGROUND $
(unpowered sites per car & 3 people $20-24, powered sites per vehicle & up to 8 people $44-52) Tidal River has 480 camp sites, but only 20 powered sites. For the Christmas

TOP PROM WALKS

The Prom's delights are best discovered on foot. From November to Easter a free shuttle bus operates between the Tidal River visitors' car park and the Telegraph Saddle car park (a nice way to start the Prom Circuit Walk). Here are six of the best:

Great Prom Walk This is the most popular long-distance hike, a moderate 45km circuit across to Sealers Cove from Tidal River, down to Refuge Cove, Waterloo Bay, the light-house and back to Tidal River via Oberon Bay. Allow three days, and coordinate your walks with tide times, as creek crossings can be hazardous.

Sealers Cove Walk The best overnight hike, this two-day walk starts at Telegraph Saddle and heads down Telegraph Track to stay overnight at beautiful Little Waterloo Bay (12km, 4 hours). The next day walk on to Sealers Cove via Refuge Cove and return to Telegraph Saddle (24km, 7 hours).

Lilly Pilly Gully Nature Walk An easy 5km (two-hour) walk through heathland and euca-lypt forests, with lots of wildlife.

Mt Oberon Summit Starting from the Mt Oberon car park, this moderate-to-hard 7km (2 hours) walk is an ideal introduction to the Prom, with panoramic views from the sum-mit. The free Mt Oberon shuttle bus can take you to the Telegraph Saddle car park and back.

Little Oberon Bay An easy-to-moderate 8km (three-hour) walk over sand dunes cov-ered in coastal tea trees with beautiful views over Little Oberon Bay.

Squeaky Beach Nature Walk Another easy 5km return stroll through coastal tea trees and banksias to a sensational white-sand beach.

school holiday period there's a ballot for sites (apply online by 31 July at www.parkweb.vic.gov.au).

Park Huts HUTS $
(4-/6-bed $65/100) If you're travelling tent-free, these cosy wooden huts are a decent budget option, with bunks and kitchenettes.

YANAKIE & FOSTER
The tiny, dispersed settlement of Yanakie of-fers the closest accommodation outside the park boundaries – from cabins and camping to luxury cottages. Foster, the nearest main town, has a backpacker hostel and several motels.

Black Cockatoo Cottages COTTAGES $$
(☑5687 1306; www.blackcockatoo.com; 60 Foley Rd, Yanakie; d $160) You can take in glorious views of the national park without leaving your very comfortable bed – or without breaking the bank – in these private, stylish, black-timber cottages. There are three mod-ern cottages and a three-bedroom house.

Prom Coast Backpackers HOSTEL $
(☑5682 2171; www.yha.com.au; 40 Station Rd, Foster; dm/d/f from $30/70/90; @) This comfy little 10-bed YHA cottage in Foster is the closest backpacker hostel to the park. The owners also run the motel next door.

✗ Eating
The General Store in Tidal River stocks gro-cery items and some camping equipment, but if you're hiking it's cheaper to stock up in Foster. The **Prom Café** (⊘breakfast, lunch & dinner; mains $12-22) is open daily for takeaway food, and serves breakfast, light lunches and bistro-style meals on weekends and holidays.

ℹ Information
Parks Victoria (☑1800 350 552, 13 19 63; www.parkweb.vic.gov.au; Tidal River; ⊘8.30am-4.30pm) The helpful visitor centre books all park accommodation, including per-mits for camping away from Tidal River.

ℹ Getting There & Away
There's no direct public transport between Mel-bourne and the Prom, but the **Wilsons Promon-tory Bus Service** (Moon's Bus Lines; ☑5687 1249) operates from Foster to Tidal River (via Fish Creek) on Friday at 4.30pm, returning on Sunday at 4.30pm (adult/child $8/4). This service connects with the V/Line bus from Mel-bourne at Fish Creek.

V/Line (☑13 61 96; www.vline.com.au) buses from Melbourne's Southern Cross Station travel direct to Foster ($16.60, three hours, four daily).

Gippsland Lakes

The beautiful Gippsland Lakes form the largest inland waterway system in Australia, with the three main interconnecting lakes – Wellington, King and Victoria – stretching from Sale to beyond Lakes Entrance. The lakes are actually saltwater lagoons, separated from the ocean by the Gippsland Lakes Coastal Park and the narrow coastal strip of sand dunes that is known as Ninety Mile Beach.

SALE

POP 13,300

Gateway to the Gippsland Lakes, Sale has plenty of accommodation, shops, restaurants and pubs, making it a good town-sized base for exploring the Ninety Mile Beach.

The **Sale Wetlands Walk** (4km, 1 hours) is a pleasant wander around Lake Gutheridge and adjoining wetlands and incorporates an Indigenous Art Trail commemorating the importance of the wetlands to the local Gunai/Kurnai population. **Sale Common**, a 300-hectare wildlife refuge with bird hides, an observatory, waterhole, boardwalks and other walking tracks, is part of an internationally recognised wetlands system.

FREE **Gippsland Art Gallery** (☑5142 3372; www.wellington.vic.gov.au/gallery; Civic Centre, 68 Foster St; ☺10am-5pm Mon-Fri, noon-4pm Sat & Sun) exhibits work by locally and nationally renowned artists and hosts touring exhibitions.

🍴 Sleeping & Eating

Free camping is permitted (no facilities) in the Lake Wellington wetlands area (excluding Sale Common), as long as you're at least 20m away from the water.

Cambrai Hostel HOSTEL $
(☑5147 1600; www.maffra.net.au/hostel/backpackers.htm; 117 Johnson St, Maffra; dm/d $25/60; @) In nearby Maffra, this relaxed hostel is a budget haven and one of the few true backpacker places in Gippsland. It has a licensed bar, open fire and pool table in the cosy lounge, as well as a tiny self-catering kitchen

---

WORTH A TRIP

WALHALLA

Ensconced high in the green hills and forests of West Gippsland, 46km northeast of Moe, tiny Walhalla is one of the state's best-preserved and most charming historic gold-mining towns. Stringer's Creek runs through the centre of the township – an idyllic valley encircled by a cluster of sepia-toned historic buildings set into the hillsides.

Walhalla Historical Museum (☑5165 6250; www.walhalla.org.au; admission $2; ☺10am-4pm), in the old post office, also acts as an information centre and books the popular two-hour **ghost tours** (www.walhallaghosttour.info; adult/child $25/18) on Friday and Saturday nights.

A star attraction is the scenic **Walhalla Goldfields Railway** (☑9513 3969; www.walhallarail.com; return adult/child/family $18/13/40; ☺from Walhalla Station 11am, 1pm & 3pm, from Thomson Station 11.40am, 1.40pm & 3.40pm Wed, Sat & Sun, public holidays), a 20-minute ride between Walhalla Station and Thomson Station through forested gorge country and over restored trestle bridges.

Relive the mining past with guided tours of the **Long Tunnel Extended Gold Mine** (☑5165 6259; off Walhalla-Beardmore Rd; tours adult/child/family $19.50/13.50/49.50; ☺tours 1.30pm Mon-Fri, noon, 1.30pm & 3pm Sat & Sun, public & school holidays), which explores Cohens Reef, once one of Australia's top reef-gold producers.

Camp for free at **North Gardens**, with toilets and barbecues, at the north end of the village, or anywhere along Stringer's Creek. Walhalla also has a handful of B&Bs and cottages.

The rebuilt historic **Walhalla Star Hotel** (☑5165 6262; www.starhotel.com.au; Main Rd; B&B d $219, including dinner $319; ✳) offers stylish boutique accommodation with king-size beds and sophisticated designer decor making good use of local materials such as corrugated-iron water tanks. There are good breakfasts, coffee and cake at the attached **Greyhorse Café** (meals from $5; ☺11am-2pm).

and clean, cheerful rooms. The owners can sometimes arrange work in the region.

bis cucina CAFE-RESTAURANT **$$**
(☎5144 3388; www.biscucina.com.au; 100 Foster St; breakfast & lunch $12-23, dinner $23-36; ☺breakfast & lunch daily, dinner Fri, Sat & show nights) At the Wellington Entertainment Centre, the modern Australian cuisine and Mediterranean influences make this a good choice for serious foodies, a preshow meal, or just a coffee or lazy breakfast.

❶ Information
Wellington visitor information centre
(☎1800 677 520; www.tourismwellington.com.au; 8 Foster St; ☺9am-5pm; @) Internet facilities and a free accommodation booking service.

❶ Getting There & Away
V/Line (☎13 61 96; www.vline.com.au) has train and train/bus services between Melbourne and Sale ($20.40, three hours, six daily) via Traralgon.

NINETY MILE BEACH
To paraphrase the immortal words of Crocodile Dundee: that's not a beach...*this* is a beach. Isolated Ninety Mile Beach is a narrow strip of sand backed by dunes and lagoons and stretching unbroken for more-or-less 90 miles (150km) from near McLoughlins Beach to the channel at Lakes Entrance – arguably Australia's longest single beach. The area is great for surf-fishing, camping and long beach walks, though the crashing surf can be dangerous for swimming, except where patrolled at Seaspray, Woodside Beach and Lakes Entrance.

Between Seaspray and Lakes Entrance, the **Gippsland Lakes Coastal Park** is a protected area of low-lying coastal shrub, banksias and tea trees, bursting with native wildflowers in spring. Permits for remote camping can be obtained from **Parks Victoria** (☎13 19 63; www.parkweb.vic.gov.au).

For a retro blast, head to **Seaspray** (population 190), which has somehow escaped the rampant development along the coast and is packed full of old holiday shacks – it's how Victorian coastal towns used to be in the 1970s.

On the road between Seaspray and Golden Beach, there are free **camp sites**, nestled back from the beach and shaded by tea tree – it's hard to get a spot over summer but at other times it's supremely peaceful. Some sites have barbecues and pit toilets, but you need

to bring your own water and firewood. Hot showers are available at **Golden Beach** ($2).

Loch Sport (population 780) is a small, bushy town sprawling along a narrow spit of land with a lake on one side and the ocean on the other. There are some good swimming areas here for children. The **Marina Hotel** (☎5146 0666; Basin Blvd, Loch Sport; mains $16-28 ☺lunch & dinner), perched by the lake and marina, has a friendly local-pub vibe, superb sunset views and decent seafood dishes on the bistro menu.

LAKES NATIONAL PARK
This narrow strip of coastal bushland surrounded by lakes and ocean is a beautiful and quiet little spot to set up camp.

Banksia and eucalypt woodland abound with areas of low-lying heathland and some swampy salt-marsh scrub. In spring the park is carpeted with native wildflowers and has one of Australia's best displays of native orchids. A loop road through the park provides good vehicle access, and there are well-marked walking trails. **Point Wilson**, at the eastern tip of the mainland section of the park is the best picnic spot and a popular gathering place for kangaroos. Industrial-strength mosquito repellent is a must here.

Emu Bight Camp Site (sites per 6 people $14.50) is the only camping area in the park, with pit toilets and fireplaces available; BYO water.

Bairnsdale
POP 11,290
Bairnsdale is East Gippsland's commercial hub and the turn-off for the Great Alpine Rd north to Omeo or south to Paynesville and Raymond Island. It's a bustling sort of town with a sprinkling of attractions, but most travellers are merely passing through on the way to the coast or the mountains.

❍ Sights & Activities
Krowathunkoolong Keeping Place INDIGENOUS CULTURAL CENTRE
(☎5152 1891; 37-53 Dalmahoy St; adult/child/family $6/4/15; ☺9am-5pm Mon-Fri) This stirring and insightful Koorie cultural exhibition space explores Gunai/Kurnai life from the Dreaming until after white settlement. The exhibition traces the Gunai/Kurnai clan from their Dreaming ancestors, Borun the pelican and his wife Tuk the

musk duck, and covers life at Lake Tyers Mission, east of Lakes Entrance, now a trust privately owned by Aboriginal shareholders. The massacres of the Kurnai during 1839–49 are also detailed.

MacLeod Morass Boardwalk   WILDLIFE
On the edge of town (signposted from the highway at the roundabout as you arrive in Bairnsdale from the west), this internationally recognised wetland reserve has walking tracks and bird hides.

FREE East Gippsland Art Gallery   ART GALLERY
(☑5153 1988; www.eastgippslandartgallery.org.au; 2 Nicholson St; ☺10am-4pm Tue-Fri, to 2pm Sat) This bright, open space has regular exhibitions, which mostly show the work of East Gippsland artists.

St Mary's Church   CHURCH
(Main St) This church is worth a look inside for its ornate Italian frescos on the ceiling and walls.

🛏 Sleeping & Eating

Mitchell Gardens Holiday Park   CARAVAN PARK $
(☑5152 4064, www.mitchellgardens.com.au; unpowered/powered sites from $23/26, d cabins $56-140; ✳✳) East of the town centre on the banks of the Mitchell River, this is a friendly, shady park. The deluxe cabins have a lovely outlook over the Mitchell River.

Grand Terminus Hotel   PUB $$
(☑5152 4040; www.grandterminus.com.au; 98 McLeod St; mains $13-26; ☺lunch & dinner) This corner pub serves bistro meals, while the upstairs en suite rooms (singles/doubles $65/75) are excellent value.

River Grill   MODERN AUSTRALIAN $$
(☑5153 1421; 2 Wood St; mains $25-36; ☺lunch & dinner Mon-Sat) Fine dining with flair comes to Bairnsdale in the form of rustic River Grill, offering contemporary food with a Mediterranean touch.

ℹ Information
Bairnsdale visitors centre (☑1800 637 060, 5152 3444; www.discovereastgippsland.com.au; 240 Main St; ☺9am-5pm; @) Next to St Mary's Church; free accommodation booking service.

ℹ Getting There & Away
Bairnsdale is the last stop on the Gippsland rail line. **V/Line** (☑13 61 96; www.vline.com.au) runs trains between Melbourne and Bairnsdale ($25, 3½ hours, three daily). Buses continue on to Lakes Entrance ($5.60, 40 minutes, three daily) and Orbost ($13.70, 1¼ hours, one daily).

Metung
POP 730

Curling around Bancroft Bay, little Metung is one of the prettiest towns on the Gippsland Lakes – besotted locals call it the

---

WORTH A TRIP

PAYNESVILLE & RAYMOND ISLAND

Paynesville, 16km south of Bairnsdale, is a relaxed little lakes town where life is all about the water. A good reason to detour down here is to take the flat-bottom ferry on the five-minute hop across to Raymond Island for some koala-spotting in a natural environment. There's a large colony of koalas here, mostly relocated from Phillip Island in the 1950s. The vehicle/passenger ferry operates every half-hour from 7am to 11pm and is free for pedestrians and bicycles.

Several operators hire out boats. **Aquamania** (☑0417 163 365; www.aquamania.com.au) organises boat tours, waterski and wakeboard instruction and operates a water taxi.

The popular **Paynesville Jazz Festival** (www.paynesvillejazzfestival.com.au) happens on the last weekend in February.

Over on Raymond Island, **Cafe Espas** (☑5156 7275; Raymond Island Foreshore; mains $29-35; ☺lunch Fri-Sun; dinner Fri & Sat) has a real island vibe with a well-prepared global menu from Thai seafood salad to paella, and the owner's artworks on the walls.

Perched over the water and with an alfresco deck, **Fisherman's Wharf Pavilion** (☑5156 0366; 70 The Esplanade; lunch $8-24, dinner $24-45; ☺breakfast & lunch Wed-Sun, dinner Wed-Sat) is a sublime place for breakfast of pancakes or quiche for lunch on a sunny day. By night it's a fine-dining steak and seafood restaurant, using fresh, local produce.

EAST GIPPSLAND RAIL TRAIL

The **East Gippsland Rail Trail** (www.eastgippslandrailtrail.com) is a 97km walking/cycling path along the former railway line between Bairnsdale and Orbost, passing through Bruthen, Nowa Nowa and close to a number of other small communities. The trail passes through undulating farmland, temperate rainforest, the Colquhoun Forest and some impressive timber bridges. On a bike the trail can comfortably be done in two days, but allow longer to explore the countryside and perhaps detour on the Gippsland Lakes Discovery Trail to Lakes Entrance. Arty Nowa Nowa is a real biking community, with a new mountain-bike park and trails leading off the main rail trail. There are plans to extend the trail from Orbost down to Marlo along the Snowy River.

If you don't have your own bike, **Snowy River Cycling** (☑0428 556 088; www.snowyrivercycling.com.au) offers self-guided tours with a bike (from $30), map and transfers ($25), plus luggage transport. It also runs guided cycle adventures.

Gippsland Riviera and with its absolute waterfront location and unhurried charm it's hard to argue.

Getting out on the water is easy enough: **Riviera Nautic** (☑5156 2243; www.rivieranautic.com.au; 185 Metung Rd; motor boat per day $140, yachts from $1210 for 2 days) hires out boats and yachts for cruising, fishing and sailing on the Gippsland Lakes. At the visitor centre, **Slipway Boat Hire** (☑5156 2969) has small motor boats for hire from $55 for an hour to $165 a day, including fuel.

If you'd rather take it easy, cruise on board the **Director** (☑5156 2628; www.thedirector.com.au; 2½hr cruise adult/child/family $45/10/105; ⊙3pm Tue, Thu & Sat) to Ninety Mile Beach and back.

At high noon pelicans fly in like divebombers for fish issued outside the Metung Hotel. Pelicans can tell time – or at least know when to get a good free feed.

🛏 Sleeping & Eating

The only budget accommodation is at the Metung Hotel. The nearest camping is up the road at Swan Reach.

McMillans of Metung   RESORT $$$
(☑5156 2283; www.mcmillansofmetung.com.au; 155 Metung Rd; cottages $145-440, villas $185-415; ❋🛜🏊) This swish lakeside resort has won stacks of tourism awards for its complex of English-country-style cottages, set in three hectares of manicured gardens, modern villas, private marina and spa centre.

Metung Hotel   PUB $
(☑5156 2206; www.metunghotel.com.au; 1 Kurnai Ave; mains $20-32; ⊙lunch & dinner) You can't beat the location overlooking Metung Wharf, and the big windows and outdoor timber decking make the most of the water views. The bistro serves top-notch pub food. The hotel also has the cheapest rooms in town, with basic doubles for $85 and a bunkroom for $30 per person.

Metung Galley   CAFE-RESTAURANT $$
(☑5156 2330; www.themetunggalley.com.au; 50 Metung Rd; lunch $10-22, dinner $21-31; ⊙breakfast & lunch daily, dinner Wed-Mon) Felicity and Richard's city hospitality experience shines through in this friendly, innovative cafe, serving up beautifully presented, quality food using local produce such as fresh seafood and Gippsland lamb. Recently expanded into new premises, they've also added a wine bar, and a deli and provedore across the road.

Metung Holiday Villas   CABINS $$
(☑5156 2306; www.metungholidayvillas.com; cnr Mairburn & Stirling Rds; cabins $110-160; ❋🏊) Metung's former caravan park has reinvented itself as a minivillage of semi-luxury cabins and one of the best deals in Metung.

❶ Information

Metung visitors centre (☑5156 2969; www.metungtourism.com.au; 3/50 Metung Rd; ⊙9am-5pm) Accommodation booking and boat-hire services.

Lakes Entrance

POP 4100

With the shallow Cunninghame Arm waterway separating town from the crashing ocean beaches, Lakes Entrance basks in an undeniably pretty location, but in holiday season it's a packed-out tourist town with a graceless strip of motels, caravan parks, minigolf courses and souvenir shops lining the Esplanade. Still, the bobbing fishing boats, fresh seafood, endless beaches and cruises out to Metung and Wyanga Park Winery should easily win you over. There's plenty here for families and kids, and out of season there's an unhurried pace and accommodation bargains.

The town is named for the channel, artificially created in 1889 to provide ocean access from the lakes system and creating a harbour for fishing boats.

◉ Sights & Activities

Beaches & Lakes   BEACHES, LAKES
A long footbridge crosses the Cunninghame Arm inlet from the east of town to the ocean and Ninety Mile Beach. From December to Easter, paddle boats, canoes and sailboats can be hired by the footbridge on the ocean side. This is also where the **Eastern Beach Walking Track** (2.3km, 45 minutes) starts, taking you through coastal scrub to the entrance itself.

To explore the lakes, three operators along Marine Pde (on the back side of the town centre) offer boat hire (hire per 1/4/8hr $50/90/150).

Lookouts   LOOKOUTS
On the Princes Hwy on the western side of town, Kalimna Lookout is a popular viewing spot with coin-operated binoculars. For an even better view of the ocean and inlet (and a quieter location), take the road directly opposite to Jemmy's Point Lookout.

Surf Shack   SURFING
(☑5155 4933; 507 The Esplanade; 2hr lesson $50) Surfing lessons (gear provided) are run by the at nearby Lake Tyers Beach.

☞ Tours
Several companies offer cruises on the lakes:

Lonsdale Cruises   ECO CRUISE
(☑5155 2889; Post Office Jetty; 3hr cruise adult/child/family $45/25/99; ☺1pm) Scenic eco

cruises out to Metung and Lake King on a former Queenscliff–Sorrento passenger ferry.

Peels Lake Cruises   LUNCH CRUISE
(☑5155 1246; Post Office Jetty; 4hr Metung lunch cruise adult/child $48/13) This long-running operator has daily lunch cruises aboard the *Stormbird* to Metung at 11am.

🎣 Sea Safari   MARINE LIFE
(☑5155 5027; www.lakes-explorer.com.au; Post Office Jetty; 1-/2-hr cruise $12/20) These safaris aboard the *Lakes Explorer* have a focus on research and ecology, identifying and counting seabirds, testing water for salinity levels and learning about marine life.

🛏 Sleeping
Lakes Entrance has stacks of accommodation, much of it your typical motels, holiday apartments and caravan parks squeezed cheek-by-jowl along the Esplanade. Prices more than double during holiday periods (book ahead), but there are good discounts out of season.

Déjà Vu   B&B $$$
(☑5155 4330; www.dejavu.com.au; 17 Clara St; d $165-300; ✻☒) This imposing, sandstone-coloured, modern home has been built on the slope of a hill to maximise water views, and the lush native garden ensures privacy. Choose from the views of the designer ocean-view apartments, the waterfront boathouse, or B&B studios.

Riviera Backpackers YHA   HOSTEL $
(☑5155 2444; www.yha.com.au; 660-71 The Esplanade; YHA members dm/s/d $23/35/50; @☒) This well-located YHA has clean rooms in old-style brick units, each with two or three bedrooms and an en suite. There's a big communal kitchen, and lounge with pool table and internet access.

WINING, DINING & CRUISING
One of the great cruises from Lakes Entrance is the lunch or dinner trip out to Wyanga Park Winery (☑5155 1508; www.wyangapark.com.au; 222 Baades Rd; lunch/dinner cruise $50/75) aboard the *Corque*. The boat departs daily from the Post Office Jetty in Lakes Entrance for a lunch cruise at 11am, returning at 3pm. The 50-minute cruise through the lakes includes wine tasting and commentary. At the rustic winery – Gippsland's oldest and beautifully situated overlooking the North Arm – you can sample a range of wines, including the delectable frozen muscat, and sit down to a meal at Henry's Café. On Thursday, the cruise goes via Metung. On Friday and Saturday nights there's a dinner cruise departing at 5.30pm, which includes a three-course meal – great value.

Lakes Entrance

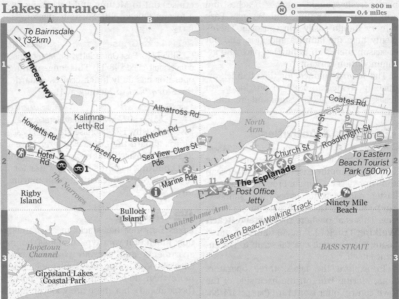

Lakes Entrance

Kalimna Woods COTTAGES **$$**
(☎5155 1957; www.kalimnawoods.com.au; Kalimna Jetty Rd; d $125-220; ❄) Retreat 2km from the town centre to Kalimna Woods, set in a large rainforest-and-bush garden, complete with friendly resident possums and birds. These self-contained country-style cottages with either spa or wood fire are spacious, private and cosy.

Eastern Beach Tourist Park CARAVAN PARK **$**
(☎5155 1581; www.easternbeach.com.au; 42 Eastern Beach Rd; unpowered/powered sites from $24/29, cabins $110-240; @☎) Most caravan parks in Lakes pack 'em in, but this one

has space, grassy sites and a great location away from the hubbub of town in a bush setting that has a wonderful location that is set back from Eastern Beach. A walking track leads you into town and takes about 30 minutes.

Lazy Acre Log Cabins CABINS **$$**
(☎5155 1323; www.lazyacre.com; 35 Roadknight St; d/f $105/125; ❄☎❄) Choose from small timber cabins that are self-contained and shaded with old gumtrees. Lazy Acre has friendly staff and is a relaxed place to stay. Accommodation rates double during the peak holiday periods.

Eating & Drinking

With the largest fishing fleet in Victoria, Lakes Entrance is the perfect place to indulge in fresh seafood. You can sometimes buy shellfish (prawns, bugs etc) straight from local boats (look for signs) or try Ferryman's. **Omega 3** (Shop 5, Safeway Arcade, Church St; ☉9am-5pm) is the shopfront for the local Fishermen's Co-op, so the seafood is always fresh.

The best cafe strip is on the Esplanade and around the corner on Myer St, right opposite the Cunninghame Arm footbridge.

Ferryman's Seafood Cafe SEAFOOD $$
(☑5155 3000; www.ferrymans.com.au; Middle Harbour, The Esplanade; lunch $14-22, dinner $25-42; ☉brunch, lunch & dinner) It's hard to beat the ambience of dining on the deck of this floating cafe-restaurant, which will fill you to the gills with fish and seafood preparations, including good old fish and chips. Downstairs you can buy fresh seafood, including prawns and crayfish, from 8.30am to 5pm.

Six Sisters & a Pigeon CAFE $
(☑5155 1144; 567 The Esplanade; meals $7-17; ☉breakfast & lunch Tue-Sun; ☑) The name alone should guide you to this quirky licensed cafe on the Esplanade opposite the footbridge. Good coffee, all-day breakfasts – Mexican eggs, French toast or Spanish omelette – and lunches of focaccias, baguettes and light mains with an Asian-Italian influence.

Pinocchio Inn ITALIAN $
(☑5155 2565; 569 Esplanade; pizza & pasta $12-25; ☉dinner) When you've had enough seafood and only pizza will do, Pinocchio's is a long-running place in the cafe strip. It's also a bar but offers BYO wine for diners – good value.

Waterwheel Beach Tavern PUB $$
(☑5156 5855; www.waterwheeltavern.com; 577 Beach Rd, Lake Tyers; mains $18-32; ☉lunch & dinner) It's worth the trip out to Lake Tyers, 10 minutes' drive from Lakes Entrance, for a beer at this beachside pub. The setting is superb and the bistro food is classy but unpretentious – Tuesday is steak night, Wednesday parma night.

Miriam's Restaurant STEAKHOUSE $$
(☑5155 3999; cnr The Esplanade & Bulmer St; mains $16-34; ☉dinner) The upstairs dining room at Miriam's overlooks the Esplanade, and the Gippsland steaks, seafood dishes and casual cocktail-bar atmosphere are excellent.

❶ Information

The Hub (☑5155 4247; cnr Myer St & The Esplanade; ☉9.30am-5pm Mon-Fri, 10am-2pm Sat; internet per hr $5; @☎) Internet cafe in a quirky, aroma-scented fashion shop.

Lakes Entrance Library (☑5153 9500; 18 Mechanics St; ☉8.30am-5pm Mon-Fri; @) Free internet access.

Lakes Entrance visitors centre (☑1800 637 060, 5155 1966; www.discovereastgippsland. com.au; cnr Princes Hwy & Marine Pde; ☉9am-5pm) Free booking service that organises accommodation and tours. Also check out www.lakesentrance.com.

❶ Getting There & Away

V/Line (☑13 61 96; www.vline.com.au) runs a train/bus service from Melbourne to Lakes Entrance via Bairnsdale ($28.50, 4½ hours, three daily).

Buchan

POP 330

The sleepy village of Buchan in the foothills of the Snowy Mountains is famous for the spectacular and intricate limestone cave system at the **Buchan Caves Reserve**, open to visitors for almost a century. Underground rivers cutting through ancient limestone rock formed the caves and caverns, and they provided shelter for Aboriginal people as far back as 18,000 years ago. **Parks Victoria** (☑5162 1900; www.parks.vic.gov.au; tours adult/child/family $14.50/8.50/40.50; ☉10am, 11.15am, 1pm, 2.15pm & 3.30pm Oct-Easter, 11am, 1pm & 3pm Easter-Sep) runs guided caves tours daily, alternating between Royal and Fairy Caves. Tours to both caves cost $22/12.50/60.50 adult/child/family. The rangers also offer hard-hat guided tours to the less-developed Federal Cave during high season. The reserve itself is a pretty spot with shaded picnic areas, walking tracks and grazing kangaroos.

❍ Sleeping

Buchan Caves Reserve CAMPGROUND, CABINS $
(☑5162 1900; www.parks.vic.gov.au; Buchan Caves Reserve; unpowered/powered sites $18/24, d cabins $77, wilderness retreats d $150; ☒) You can stay right by the caves at this serene Parks Victoria camping ground, edged by state forest. There are a couple of standard cabins, plus safari-style tents providing a 'luxury' wilderness experience.

Interested in doing some volunteer work? National parks and organic farms are two options for travellers.

Parks Victoria (☑13 16 93; www.parkweb.vic.gov.au) operates a program for volunteers at Wilsons Promontory National Park, Buchan Caves Reserve, Cape Conran and Croajingolong National Park during the Christmas and Easter holidays. Volunteers act as campground hosts for a minimum of two weeks and are involved in the day-to-day operations of the park assisting visitors and rangers. Volunteers camp for free; tents can be provided. Apply through Parks Victoria.

Willing Workers on Organic Farms (WWOOF; ☑5155 0218; www.wwoof.com.au; 2615 Gelantipy Rd, W Tree) is a national organisation with its base in East Gippsland. Volunteers work on organic farms that are members of the WWOOF association, in exchange for their meals and accommodation.

Buchan Lodge   HOSTEL **$**
(☑5155 9421; www.buchanlodge.com.au; 9 Saleyard Rd; dm $20) A short walk from the town centre and just by the river, this welcoming pine-log backpacker place is great for lounging about and taking in the country views. Big country-style kitchen, convivial lounge and campfires out the back.

❶ Getting There & Away

Buchan is an easy drive 56km north of Lakes Entrance. **Buchan Bus 'n' Freight** (☑5155 0356) operates a service on Wednesday and Friday from Bairnsdale to Buchan ($16.50, one hour, three weekly), linking with the train from Melbourne. At other times you'll need your own transport.

Orbost & Marlo

POP 2100

The town of **Orbost** services the surrounding farming and forest areas. Most travellers whiz through as the Princes Hwy passes just south of the town, while the Bonang Rd heads north towards the Snowy River and Errinundra National Parks. Marlo Rd follows the Snowy River south to Marlo and continues along the coast to Cape Conran.

Orbost visitor information centre (☑5154 2424; cnr Nicholson & Clarke Sts; ☺9am-5pm) is in the historic 1872 Slab Hut. The impressive **Orbost Exhibition Centre** (☑5154 2634; www.orbostexhibitioncentre.org; Clarke St; adult/child $4/free; ☺10am-4pm Mon-Sat, 1-4pm Sun), next to the visitor centre, showcases works by local timber artists.

Just 15km south of Orbost, **Marlo** is a sleepy beach town at the mouth of the Snowy River. It's a lovely spot and the road continues on to Cape Conran before rejoining the highway. Aside from the gorgeous coast, the main attraction here is the **PS Curlip** (☑5154 1699; www.paddlesteamercurlip.com.au; adult/child/family $25/15/60; ☺11.30am & 2.30pm Wed-Sun), a recreation of an 1890 paddle steamer that once chugged up the Snowy River to Orbost. Buy tickets at the general store in town.

You can't beat an afternoon beer on the expansive wooden verandah of the **Marlo Hotel** (☑5154 8201; www.marlohotel.com.au; 17 Argyle Pde; d $140, with spa $130-160). The boutique rooms here are above average for a pub and the restaurant serves local seafood such as gummy shark and king prawns (mains $14 to $30).

Cape Conran Coastal Park

This blissfully undeveloped part of the coast is one of Gippsland's most beautiful corners, with long stretches of remote white-sand beaches. The 19km coastal route from Marlo to Cape Conran is particularly pretty, bordered by banksia trees, grass plains, sand dunes and the ocean.

Good walks include the nature trail, which meets up with the East Cape Boardwalk, where signage gives you a glimpse into how Indigenous people lived in this area. Following an Indigenous theme, take the West Cape Rd off Cape Conran Rd to **Salmon Rocks**, where there's an Aboriginal shell midden dated at more than 10,000 years old.

Cabbage Tree Palms, a short detour off the road between Cape Conran and the Princes Hwy, is Victoria's only stand of native palms – a tiny rainforest oasis.

🛏 Sleeping

Parks Victoria (📞5154 8438; www.conran.net.au) runs three excellent accommodation options in Cape Conran Coastal Park, including foreshore **camp sites** ($18-24), **cabins** ($96-145 for up to 4 people) and **safari tents** ($150).

West Cape Cabins   CABINS **$$**
(📞5154 8296; www.westcapecabins.com; 1547 Cape Conran Rd; d/f $175/250) Crafted from locally grown or recycled timbers, these self-contained cabins a few kilometres from the park are a work of art. The timbers are all labelled with their species, and even the queen-size bed bases are made from tree trunks. The large outdoor spa baths add to the joy.

Mallacoota

POP 980

Isolated Mallacoota is a real gem – Victoria's most easterly town but an easy detour if you're heading along the coastal route between Melbourne and Sydney. It's snuggled on the vast Mallacoota Inlet and surrounded by the tumbling hills and beachside dunes of beautiful Croajingolong National Park. Those prepared to come this far are treated to long, empty ocean surf beaches, tidal river mouths and swimming, fishing and boating on the inlet. At Christmas and Easter Mallacoota is a busy family holiday spot but most of the year it's pretty quiet and very relaxed.

👁 Sights & Activities

Gabo Island   ISLAND
On Gabo Island, 14km offshore from Mallacoota, the windswept 154-hectare **Gabo Island Lightstation Reserve** is home to seabirds and one of the world's largest colonies of little penguins – far outnumbering those on Phillip Island. Whales, dolphins and fur seals are regularly sighted off shore. The island has an operating **lighthouse**, built in 1862 and the tallest in the southern hemisphere, and you can stay in the old keepers' cottages here (contact Parks Victoria). **Mallacoota Air Services** (📞0408 580 806; return per 3 adults or 2 adults & 2 children $300) offers fast access to the island on demand, or you can get there by boat with Wilderness Coast Ocean Charters.

Mallacoota Hire Boats   BOAT HIRE
(📞0438-447 558; Main Wharf, cnr Allan & Buckland Drs; motor boats per 2-/4-/6hr $60/100/140) One of the best ways to experience the beauty of Mallacoota and its estuarine waters is by boat. This outfit is centrally located and hires out canoes and boats. No licence required; cash only.

Walks   WALKING
There are plenty of great short walks around the town, the inlet, and in the bush. It's an easy 4km walk or cycle around the inlet to Karbeethong. From there the **Bucklands Jetty to Captain Creek Jetty Walk** (one-way 5km, one hour) follows the shoreline of the inlet past the Narrows. The **Mallacoota Town Walk** (7km, five hours) loops round Bastion Point, and combines five different walks.

Beaches   BEACHES
For good surf, head to **Bastion Point** or **Tip Beach**. There's swimmable surf and some sheltered waters at **Betka Beach**, which is patrolled during Christmas school holidays.

🚌 Tours

Wilderness Coast Ocean Charters   WILDERNESS
(📞5158 0701, 0417 398 068; wildcoast@dragnet.com.au) Runs day trips to Gabo Island ($60, minimum eight people; $60 each way if you stay overnight) and may run trips down the coast to view the seal colony off Wingan Inlet if there's enough demand.

MV Loch-Ard   WILDLIFE
(📞5158 0764; Main Wharf; adult/child 2hr cruise $28/10, 3hr cruise $38/12) Runs several inlet cruises from the Main Wharf, with wild-life-spotting and a twilight cruise.

Porkie Bess   CRUISES, FISHING
(📞5158 0109, 0408 408 094; 2hr cruise $25, fishing trip $50) A 1940s wooden boat offering fishing trips and cruises around the lakes, and ferry services for hikers ($20 per person, minimum four). Departs Karbeethong Jetty.

🛏 Sleeping

During Easter and Christmas school holidays you'll need to book well ahead and expect prices to be significantly higher.

Adobe Mudbrick Flats   GUESTHOUSE **$**
(📞5158 0329; www.adobeholidayflats.com.au; 17 Karbeethong Ave; d $75, q $90-140) A labour of love by Margaret and Peter Kurz, these unique mudbrick flats in Karbeethong, a few kilometres north of Mallacoota, are something special. With an emphasis on recycling and ecofriendliness, there's solar hot

SNOWY RIVER & ERRINUNDRA NATIONAL PARKS

These two isolated wilderness parks north of Orbost occupy most of Victoria's eastern corner between the alpine country and the coast. The parks are linked in the north by the partially unsealed MacKillops Rd, making it possible to do a driving loop from Buchan to Orbost. In dry weather it's passable to conventional vehicles but check road conditions with Parks Victoria.

Snowy River National Park

Northeast of Buchan, this is one of Victoria's most isolated and spectacular national parks, dominated by deep gorges carved through limestone and sandstone by the Snowy River on its route from the Snowy Mountains in New South Wales to its mouth at Marlo. The entire 1145-sq-km park is a smorgasbord of unspoiled, superb bush and mountain scenery, ranging from alpine woodlands and eucalypt forests to rainforests. Abundant wildlife includes the rare brush-tailed rock wallaby.

On the west side of the park, the views from the well-signposted clifftop lookouts over **Little River Falls** and **Little River Gorge**, Victoria's deepest gorge, are awesome. From there it's about 20km to **McKillops Bridge**, a huge bridge spanning the Snowy River, making it possible to drive across to Errinundra National Park. The hilly and difficult **Silver Mine Walking Track** (15km, six hours) starts at the eastern end of the bridge.

There's free camping at a number of basic sites around the park, but the main site is McKillops Bridge, a beautiful spot with toilets and fireplaces.

Karoonda Park (☎5155 0220; www.karoondapark.com; 3558 Gelantipy Rd; dm/s/d $30/50/70, cabins per 6 people $115; ✳@☒), 40km north of Buchan on the road to Snowy River National Park, has comfortable backpacker and cabin digs. Activities available include abseiling, horse riding, wild caving, white-water rafting, mountain-bike hire and farm activities.

Errinundra National Park

Errinundra National Park contains Victoria's largest cool-temperate rainforest but the forests surrounding the park are a constant battleground between loggers, and environmentalists who are trying to protect old-growth forests.

The national park covers an area of 256 sq km and has three granite outcrops that extend into the cloud, resulting in high rainfall, deep, fertile soils and a network of creeks and rivers that flow north, south and east. This is a rich habitat for native birds and animals, which include many rare and endangered species such as the potoroo.

You can explore the park by a combination of scenic drives, and short and medium-length walks. **Mt Ellery** has spectacular views; **Errinundra Saddle** has a rainforest boardwalk; and from **Ocean View Lookout** there are stunning views down the Goolengook River as far as Bemm River.

Frosty Hollow Camp Site (sites free) is the only camping area within the national park, on the eastern side. There are also free camping areas on the park's edges – at Ellery Creek in Goongerah, and at Delegate River.

Jacarri (☎5154 0145; www.eastgippsland.net.au/jacarri; cnr Bonang Hwy & Ellery Creek Track, Goongerah; d/f $80/90) is a gorgeous little eco-cottage on an organic farm. It's solar-powered, has a slow-combustion stove for heating and cooking, and sleeps four.

Tours

Gippsland High Country Tours (☎5157 5556; www.gippslandhighcountrytours.com.au) offer easy, moderate and challenging five- to seven-day hikes in Errinundra, Snowy River and Croajingolong National Parks.

Snowy River Expeditions (☎5155 0220; www.karoondapark.com/sre; Karoonda Park, Gelantipy; tours per day from $85) is an established company running adventure tours including one-, two- and four-day rafting trips on the Snowy. Half- or full-day abseiling or caving trips are also available.

water and guests are encouraged to compost their kitchen scraps. Birds, lizards and possums can be hand-fed right outside your door. The array of whimsical apartments is comfortable, well equipped and incredibly cheap.

Mallacoota Foreshore Holiday Park CAMPGROUND $
(☑5158 0300; www.mallacootaholidaypark.com.au; cnr Allan Dr & Maurice Ave; unpowered/powered sites $12/18, peak season from $27/32; ☎) Curling around the waterfront, the grassy sites here morph into one of Victoria's most sociable and scenic caravan parks, with sublime views of the inlet and its resident population of black swans and pelicans. No cabins, but the best of Mallacoota's many parks for campers.

Karbeethong Lodge GUESTHOUSE $$
(☑5158 0411; www.karbeethonglodge.com.au; 16 Schnapper Point Dr; d $75-220) It's hard not to be overcome by a sense of serenity as you rest on the broad verandahs of this early 1900s timber guesthouse, which has uninterrupted views over Mallacoota Inlet.

Mallacoota Wilderness Houseboats HOUSEBOATS $$
(☑0409 924 016; www.mallacootawilderness houseboats.com.au; Karbeethong Jetty; 4 nights midweek from $750, one week $1200-1600) These six-berth houseboats are not luxurious but they are the perfect way to explore Mallacoota's waterways.

Mallacoota Hotel Motel MOTEL $$
(☑5158 0455; www.mallacootahotel.com.au; 51-55 Maurice Ave; motel s/d from $75/95, d/tw units $115/125; ☀☎) The neat, good-value motel units next to the hotel orbit a lawn area and swimming pool. There's a range of standard rooms, but all with mod cons.

✖ Eating & Drinking

Most visitors consider the best eating to be the fish you catch yourself; otherwise there are a few good places along Maurice Ave.

Lucy's ASIAN $
(☑5158 0666; 64 Maurice Ave; dishes $10-20; ☀8am-9pm; ☺) Lucy's is popular for the delicious and great-value homemade rice noodles with chicken, prawn or abalone, as well as dumplings. It's also a good place for breakfast on the side deck.

Croajingolong Cafe CAFE $
(☑5158 0098; Shop 3, 14 Allan Dr; mains $5-14; ☀breakfast & lunch Tue-Sun; ☎) Overlooking

the inlet, this is the place to spread out the newspaper over coffee, baguettes or a pancake breakfast.

Mallacoota Hotel PUB $$
(☑5158 0455; 51-55 Maurice Ave; mains $17-30; ☀lunch & dinner) The local pub bistro serves hearty meals from its varied menu, with reliable favourites such as chicken parmagiana and Gippsland steak. Bands play here regularly in summer.

❶ Information

Mallacoota visitors centre (☑5158 0800; www.visitmallacoota.com.au; Main Wharf, cnr Allan & Buckland Dr; ☀10am-4pm) Operated by friendly volunteers.

❶ Getting There & Away

Mallacoota is 23km southeast of Genoa (on the Princes Hwy). From Melbourne, take the train to Bairnsdale, then the V/Line bus to Genoa ($26.70, 3 hours, one daily). **Mallacoota-Genoa Bus Service** (☑0408 315 615) meets the V/Line coach on Monday, Thursday and Friday, plus Sunday during school holidays, and runs to Mallacoota ($3.40, 30 minutes).

Croajingolong National Park

Croajingolong is one of Australia's finest coastal wilderness national parks, recognised by its listing as a World Biosphere Reserve by Unesco (one of 12 in Australia). For remote camping, bushwalking, fishing, swimming and surfing, this one is hard to beat, with unspoiled beaches, inlets, estuaries and forests. The park covers 87,500 hectares, stretching for about 100km from Bemm River to the New South Wales border. The five inlets – Sydenham, Tamboon, Mueller, Wingan and Mallacoota (the largest and most accessible) – are popular canoeing and fishing spots.

The **Wilderness Coast Walk**, only for the well prepared and intrepid, starts at Sydenham Inlet by Bemm River and heads along the coast to Mallacoota. **Thurra River** is a good starting point, making the walk an easy-to-medium hike (59km, five days) to Mallacoota.

Point Hicks was the first part of Australia to be spotted by Captain Cook and the *Endeavour* crew in 1770, and was named after his first Lieutenant, Zachary Hicks. There's a **lighthouse** (☑5158 4268; www.pointhicks.com.au; ☀tours 1pm Fri-Mon) here, open for tours and accommodation in the old cottages. You can still see remains of the SS *Saros,* which ran ashore in 1937, on a short walk from the lighthouse.

Access roads of varying quality lead into the park from the Princes Hwy. Apart from Mallacoota Rd, all roads are unsealed and can be very rough in winter, so check road conditions with Parks Victoria before venturing on, especially during or after rain.

🛏 Sleeping

Thanks to their remoteness, the park's camping grounds are surprisingly quiet, and bookings only need to be made for the Christmas and Easter holiday periods, when sites are issued on a ballot system. There are four designated camp sites: Wingan Inlet and Shipwreck Creek can be booked through **Parks Victoria** (☑13 19 63; sites $17); Thurra River and Mueller Inlet through

Point Hicks Lighthouse (☑5158 4268; www. pointhicks.com.au; sites $20). Shipwreck is the most accessible, 15km from Mallacoota, while Wingan has the prettiest setting.

Point Hicks Lighthouse   COTTAGES **$$** (☑5158 4268, 5156 0432; www.pointhicks.com.au; bungalow $100-120, cottage $330) This remote lighthouse has two comfortable, heritage-listed cottages, and one double bungalow, that originally housed the assistant lighthouse keepers. The cottages sleep six people and have sensational ocean views and wood fires.

❶ Information

Parks Victoria (☑13 19 63, Cann River 5158 6351, Mallacoota 5161 9500; www.parkweb. vic.gov.au) Contact offices in Cann River or Mallacoota for information on road conditions, overnight hiking, camping permits and track notes.

Brisbane & the Gold Coast

Best Places to Eat

- » E'cco (p291)
- » Ortiga (p292)
- » Mondo Organics (p294)
- » Oskars (p320)
- » Elephant Rock Café (p320)

Best Places to Stay

- » Treasury (p287)
- » Portal (p287)
- » Limes (p289)
- » Komune (p322)

Why Go?

Boasting 35 beaches and 300 sunny days a year, the Gold Coast promises its four million annual visitors a taste of the quintessential Aussie lifestyle of sun, surf and fun. The beaches are spectacular, with excellent surfing at Burleigh Heads, Currumbin, Kirra and Duranbah; and there's never a dull moment, whether you're joining the brash party scene of Surfers Paradise, island exploring on lovely Moreton Bay or simply soaking up the seaside charm of towns strung south along the coast. In the lush, subtropical hinterland, Lamington and Springbrook National Parks have rainforest walks, waterfalls and cosy mountain retreats.

Gateway to the Gold Coast is Brisbane, an easygoing city with a vibrant arts scene, burgeoning nightlife and first-rate dining. Brisbanites make good use of the temperate climate and lovely riverside setting, with weekends spent jogging, cycling, kayaking and rock-climbing, wandering through outdoor markets or dining and drinking at lovely open-air spots all across town.

When to Go

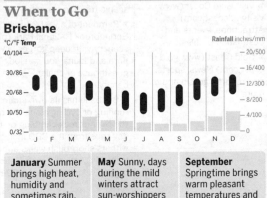

Brisbane

January Summer brings high heat, humidity and sometimes rain.

May Sunny, days during the mild winters attract sun-worshippers from across the globe.

September Springtime brings warm pleasant temperatures and lively festivals.

TOP TIP

Brisbane has great food markets, with delicacies, live music and big crowds (go early). The top two are the bimonthly Jan Power's Farmers Market (p302) and the Saturday West End Market (p302).

Fast Facts

» Population: 2.3 million
» Area: 6150 sq km
» Telephone Code: 07

Planning your Trip

» Book your accommodation at http://hotels.lonelyplanet.com or www.wotif.com.

» Think about how you'll be getting around the region and hire a car or check bus and train schedules (www.translink.com.au).

Resources

» Our Brisbane (www.ourbrisbane.com) Great all-round site on Brisbane.

» Visit Gold Coast (www.visitgoldcoast.com) Attractions, events and destination profiles.

» Gold Coast (www.goldcoast.com) News, sports, surf reports, gossip and more.

Island Dreaming

Known for big-city allure and great beaches, Brisbane and the Gold Coast also have some fantastic island settings where long lovely shorelines and bushland interiors are ripe for exploring. Moreton Island has sandy tracks but no roads, so you'll need a 4WD to discover this idyllic subtropical island (you can also join a day or overnight tour). North Stradbroke has paved roads and more services, with options for diving, snorkelling, surfing and sea kayaking. You may want your own wheels to visit the island's pristine lakes. South Straddie is car-free, making for a peaceful getaway. All of the islands have bushwalking and magnificent whale-watching in season (June to November), so don't forget your binoculars.

DON'T MISS

The heady Gold Coast has some of the most inviting sun-drenched shores along the East Coast. Party-loving Surfers Paradise has a pretty beach and good surf, but for more relaxing beaches head further south. Burleigh Heads has white-sand beaches backed by photogenic rocky headland and amazing surfing. Coolangatta and neighbouring Tweed Heads are also charming seaside villages, with long beach walks, friendly locals and an easygoing pace. If you're not a surfer, but keen to give it a go, there are plenty of places where you can learn along the Gold Coast, including laid-back Currumbin Alley, an ideal place for beginners.

Outdoor Adventures

» The 200-sq-km Lamington National Park (p325), with its subtropical rainforests, steep cliffs and wildlife-filled valleys, has superb bushwalking. Serious hikers can tackle the 24km Border Trail, linking two sections of the park. There's also a scenic tree-top canopy walk.

» Remnant of a vast 23-million-year-old shield volcano, Springbrook National Park (p324) has lush subtropical scenery with deep gorges, awe-inspiring waterfalls and rich flora and fauna. You can lodge in a woodland-surrounded guesthouse or chalet – a fine base to take in the park's beauty.

» Brisbane has its own share of outdoor adventure, from running or cycling along the riverside paths to kayaking on the river or rock-climbing on the Kangaroo Point Cliffs. Easy day trips from the CBD include Mt Coot-tha Reserve (p282) with its short bush walks and lovely views over town. The trails of D'Aguilar Range National Park (p283) provide more rugged wilderness, just a 30-minute bus ride from town.

Getting There & Away

Air

Brisbane Airport (http://bne.com.au) 16km northeast of the city

Gold Coast Airport (http://goldcoastairport.com.au) In Coolangatta, 25km south of Surfers Paradise.

Bus

Long-distance buses stop at the **Brisbane Transit Centre** (www.brisbanetransitcentre.com.au) on Roma St in the CBD, and at bus transit centres in Southport, Surfers Paradise and Coolangatta. **Greyhound Australia** (☑1300 473 946; www.greyhound.com.au) and **Premier Motor Service** (☑13 34 10; www.premierms.com.au) provide services from Brisbane or the Gold Coast to Byron Bay (from $30, 2½ to four hours), Sydney (from $150, 15 to 18 hours) and beyond.

Getting Around

To/From the Airport

Airtrain (☑3215 5000; www.airtrain.com.au; per adult/child $15/7.50; ⊗6am-7.30pm) Zips from Brisbane airport to Fortitude Valley, Central Station and Brisbane Transit Centre. There are also half-hourly services to Brisbane Airport from Gold Coast TransLink train stops.

Coachtrans (☑3358 9700; www.coachtrans.com.au; per adult/child $15/8) Operates a shuttle between the Brisbane Airport and any hotel in the CBD. It also travels from Brisbane Airport to anywhere on the Gold Coast (one way $43.50).

Gold Coast Tourist Shuttle (☑1300 655 655, 5574 5111; www.gcshuttle.com.au; adult/child/family $18/9/45) Meets every flight into Coolangatta Airport and operates door-to-door transfers to most Gold Coast accommodation.

Bus

Greyhound Australia (☑1300 473 946; www.greyhound.com.au) Has frequent services between Gold Coast and Brisbane ($20, 1½ hours).

Surfside Buslines (☑13 12 30; www.translink.com.au) Runs a frequent service up and down the Gold Coast Hwy from Tweed Heads, stopping at Dreamworld, Sanctuary Cove and Paradise Point.

Coachtrans (www.coachtrans.com.au) Runs shuttle services between Brisbane and Tweed Heads, with stops along the way, including Dreamworld, Movie World and Wet'n'Wild. Coachtrans also has services that run between Brisbane City to Surfers ($32, 1½ hours) or to the theme parks.

Taxi

Ring ☑13 10 08 or ☑13 19 24 for taxi services in Brisbane; on the Gold Coast call ☑13 10 08.

Train

TransLink train services connect Brisbane with Helensvale (zone 12, one-way $12.40, one hour), Nerang (zone 13, one-way $12.90, 65 minutes) and Robina (zone 15, one-way $15.10, 71 minutes) stations roughly every half-hour. **Surfside Buslines** (☑13 12 30; www.surfside.com.au) runs regular shuttles from the train stations down to the theme parks, Surfers ($4 to $5) and beyond.

BRISBANE

One of Australia's fastest-growing cities, Brisbane is home to subtropical gardens, a laid-back attitude, an outdoor lifestyle, first-rate restaurants, iconic heritage buildings and a fantastic arts scene. The city's heart and soul is scenic Brisbane River, which is both a blessing (open-air waterfront cafes, bars and restaurants, riverside paths) and a curse (when in 2011, the flooded river left a heart-breaking swath of devastation).

Brisbane has a temperate climate, making it easy to forget you're in Australia's third-largest city where the high-rises still compete with a verdant spread of trees. A smorgasbord of cultural offerings makes the city Queensland's epicentre for the arts with world-class galleries, museums, theatres, art-house cinemas, live-music venues and events. Adding to the appeal is Brisbane's superb dining scene with chefs catering to a truly global palate.

East of the city, the islands of Moreton Bay make an idyllic getaway, with great bushwalking, surfing and sea kayaking. There are fine dive sites off North Stradbroke and snorkelling amid the Tangalooma Wrecks just off Moreton Island.

◉ Sights

Most of Brisbane's major sights are in the CBD or inner-city suburbs. A walk through the city centre will reveal Brisbane's colonial history and architecture, while a ferry ride or bridge walk across the river lands you in South Bank, home to stellar art museums and peaceful parkland (complete with attractive artificial swimming lagoons). Chinatown and Brunswick St, both in Fortitude Valley, provide healthy doses of dining, nightlife, shopping and gallery-hopping.

Brisbane & the Gold Coast Highlights

① Strolling through the tropical foliage at Brisbane's City Botanic Gardens (p278)

② Wandering the enormous floors of the world-class Gallery of Modern Art (p279)

③ Booking a table at one of Brisbane's best restaurants in New Farm (p293)

④ Taking in the heady bar and club scene in Brisbane's Fortitude Valley (p295)

⑤ Pumping into party overdrive in heady Surfers Paradise (p311)

⑥ Beating the heat at Streets Beach in the South Bank Parklands (p279)

⑦ Bushwalking through deep gorges and towering rainforests in Springbrook National Park (p324) and Lamington National Park (p325)

⑧ Catching a boat (or bus) to go koala-cuddling at Lone Pine Koala Sanctuary (p283)

⑨ Exploring the pristine islands of Moreton Bay (p303)

⑩ Surfing the breaks and soaking up the famous Gold Coast sunshine at Coolangatta (p321)

CITY CENTRE

City Hall
HISTORIC BUILDING

(Map p284; between Ann & Adelaide Sts; admission free) This historic sandstone building overlooks King George Sq. Built in 1930, it has an observation platform up in the bell tower, which affords brilliant views across the city. At research time, City Hall was undergoing extensive restoration and remained closed to visitors.

Museum of Brisbane
MUSEUM

(Map p284; 157 Ann St; admission free; ☺10am-5pm) Around the corner from City Hall, this museum illuminates the city from a wide variety of viewpoints, with interactive exhibits that explore both social history and the current cultural landscape.

Treasury Building
HISTORIC BUILDING

(Map p284) At the western end of the Queen St Mall is the magnificent Italian Renaissance-style Treasury Building. Behind the lavish facade you won't find pin-striped bureaucrats and tax collectors, but rather spruikers and an entirely different kind of money spinner: Brisbane's 24-hour casino. Opposite the casino across a grassy plaza stands the equally gorgeous former **Land Administration Building**, which has been converted to a five-star hotel.

Parliament House
HISTORIC BUILDING

(Map p284; cnr Alice & George Sts; admission free) Further south along George St is Parliament House, dating from 1868, where you can sign up for a free guided tour (between 9am and 4pm Monday to Friday).

City Botanic Gardens
GARDEN

(Map p284; Albert St; ☺24hr) Brisbane's Botanic Gardens are right on the river and are a mass of green lawns, towering Moreton Bay figs, bunya pines, macadamia trees and other tropical flora, descending gently from the Queensland University of Technology (QUT) campus. Its lawns are popular with lunching office workers, joggers and picnickers.

QUT Art Museum
MUSEUM

(Map p284; 2 George St; admission free; ☺10am-5pm Tue, Thu & Fri, 10am-8pm Wed, noon-4pm Sat & Sun) In the grounds of QUT, this art museum has regularly changing exhibits of contemporary Australian art and works by Brisbane art students. Next door is the former **Old Government House**, a beautiful colonnaded building dating from 1860 and now the home of the National Trust.

Commissariat Stores Building

HISTORIC BUILDING

(Map p284; 115 William St; adult/child $5/2.50; ⊙10am-4pm Tue-Fri) Built by convicts in 1829, the Commissariat Stores Building is one of Brisbane's oldest and houses a museum devoted to Brisbane's convict and colonial history.

SOUTH BANK

TOP CHOICE **Cultural Centre**   CULTURAL CENTRE
On South Bank, just over Victoria Bridge from the CBD, the Cultural Centre is the epicentre of Brisbane's cultural confluence. It's a huge compound that includes a concert and theatre venue, four museums and the Queensland State Library.

Queensland Museum

(Map p282; www.southbank.qm.qld.gov.au; cnr Grey & Melbourne Sts; admission free; ⊙9.30am-5pm) This museum occupies imaginations with all manner of curiosities. Queensland's history is given a once-over with an interesting collection of exhibits, including a skeleton of the state's own dinosaur, *Muttaburrasaurus*; and the *Avian Cirrus*, the tiny plane in which Queensland's Bert Hinkler made the first England to Australia solo flight in 1928.

The museum also houses the **Sciencentre** (adult/child/family $12/9/40), with over 100 hands-on, interactive exhibits that delve into life science and technology in fun, thought-provoking ways.

Queensland Art Gallery

(Map p282; www.qag.qld.gov.au; Melbourne St, South Brisbane; admission free; ⊙10am-5pm Mon-Fri, 9am-5pm Sat & Sun) Inside an austere chunk of concrete, the Queensland Art Gallery houses a fine permanent collection, mostly of domestic and European artists. The Australian art dates from the 1840s to the 1970s, and you can view works by celebrated masters including Sir Sidney Nolan, Arthur Boyd, William Dobell and George Lambert.

Gallery of Modern Art

(Map p282; Stanley Place; admission free; ⊙10am-5pm Mon-Fri, 9am-5pm Sat & Sun) This massive gallery displays Australian art from the 1970s to today in a variety of changing exhibitions and media: painting, sculpture and photography sit alongside video, installation and film.

South Bank Parklands   PARK

(Map p282; admission free; ⊙dawn-dusk) This beautiful swath of green park, skirting the western side of the Brisbane River, suffered damage during the 2011 Brisbane Flood. South Bank's ferry docks were washed away and riverside sections of the Parklands were inundated, but restoration of these facilities proceeded quickly. A good thing, as this popular spot is home to cultural attractions, fine eateries, small rainforests, hidden lawns and gorgeous flora. The standout attractions here are **Streets Beach**, a funky artificial

---

BRISBANE IN...

Two Days

Start with breakfast in Brisbane's bohemian **West End**, and then saunter across to **South Bank Parklands**. Take in an exhibit at the **Cultural Centre**, then head to a riverside eatery. Take a stroll (or a swim) at **Streets Beach** and explore the parklands. Afterwards, jump on a ferry to the **Brisbane Powerhouse** in New Farm for a bite or perhaps a show.

On day two head downtown for a gander at the mix of old and new architecture, visiting **City Hall**, **King George Square** and the **Treasury Building**, before strolling through the lush **City Botanic Gardens**. Finish the day with a brew at the **Belgian Beer Cafe** and a banquet in Fortitude Valley's **Chinatown**.

Four Days

On day three check out cafe culture in **New Farm**, then delve into the shopping or gallery scene in nearby Fortitude Valley. Spend the afternoon exploring **Mt Coot-tha Reserve** and the **Brisbane Botanic Gardens**. Then head back to **Fortitude Valley** for fine dining, and work it all off in one of the Valley's late-night bars and clubs.

On day four take a cruise upriver to **Lone Pine Koala Sanctuary**. Recount the day's events over a beer at the **Breakfast Creek Hotel** and then gravitate to Paddington for cocktails and a bite at the **Lark**.

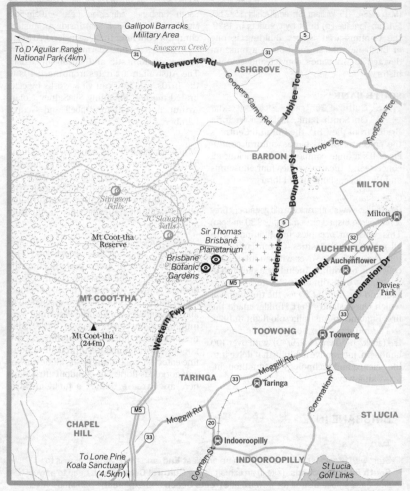

BRISBANE & THE GOLD COAST BRISBANE

beach resembling a tropical lagoon, and, behind the beach, **Stanley Street Plaza**, a renovated section of historic Stanley St, with shops, cafes and a tourist information centre.

The South Bank parklands are within easy walking distance of the city centre, but CityCat and Inner City Ferries stop here if you'd like to go by boat. Alternatively, you can get here by bus or train from Roma St or Central station.

Queensland Maritime Museum   MUSEUM
(Map p282; Sidon St, South Brisbane; adult/child $8/3.50, dry dock $4/2; ⊙9.30am-4.30pm) On

the eastern edge of the parklands is a museum with a wide-ranging display of maritime adventures (and misadventures) along the coast. It's worth shelling out a little extra to tour the dry dock – the museum highlight is clambering around the fascinating rooms of the HMAS *Diamantina*, a restored 1944 navy frigate.

Wheel of Brisbane   FERRIS WHEEL
(Map p282; www.thewheelofbrisbane.com.au; Russell St, South Brisbane; adult/child $15/10; ⊙11am-9pm) A Ferris wheel in the parklands offering a 360-degree panorama of the city from its 60m heights; rides last around 15

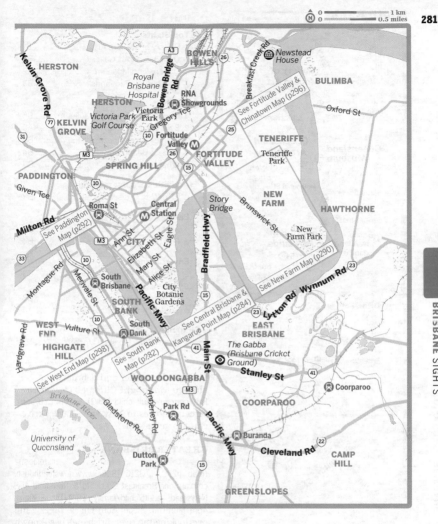

minutes and include audio commentary of Brisbane sights.

FORTITUDE VALLEY & NEW FARM

For over a decade the alternative neighbourhoods of Fortitude Valley and nearby New Farm have been the hub of all things contemporary and cool, thanks to a confluence of artists, restaurateurs and various fringe types flocking to the area. Brisbane's very own **Chinatown** is small (with most of the action on Duncan St) but exhibits the same flamboyance and flavour as its counterparts in Sydney and Melbourne.

Institute of Modern Art ART GALLERY
(Map p296; www.ima.org.au; ⏱11am-5pm Tue-Sat, to 8pm Thu) This is one of the top galleries in Brisbane and the second-oldest contemporary art space in the country. Its industrial exhibition rooms showcase cutting-edge works from Australia and beyond, and multimedia works (sound art, music, moving images) are an important part of the repertoire. It's housed inside the **Judith Wright Centre for Contemporary Arts** (Map p296; ☎3872 9000; www.judithwrightcentre.com.au; 420 Brunswick St, Fortitude Valley), which is another

Between December and February, the alfresco **Moonlight Cinemas** (www.moonlight.com.au; adult/child $15/11; ⊙7pm Wed-Sun) screens movies in New Farm Park. Arrive early to get a spot.

GREATER BRISBANE

Newstead   HISTORIC SITE
(Map p280; ☑3216 1846; www.newsteadhouse.com.au; cnr Breakfast Creek Rd & Newstead Ave, Newstead; adult/child/family $6/4/15; ⊙10am-4pm Mon-Thu, 2-5pm Sun) On a breezy hill overlooking the river, Brisbane's best-known heritage site dates from 1846 and is beautifully fitted out with Victorian furnishings, antiques, clothing and period displays. It's surrounded by manicured gardens and has superb water vistas. It's located north of the centre, in Newstead Park. On Sundays, Devonshire tea is served on the veranda.

Mt Coot-tha Reserve   NATURE RESERVE
A short drive or bus ride from the city, this huge bush reserve and parkland (Map p280) has an excellent botanic garden, a planetarium, eateries and a superb lookout over the city. On a clear day you can see the Moreton Bay islands. The lookout is accessed

excellent venue for live performance of all genres.

Other galleries in the area:

Suzanne O'Connell Gallery (Map p290; www.suzanneoconnell.com; 93 James St; ⊙11am-4pm Wed-Sat)

Fireworks Gallery (www.fireworksgallery.com.au; 52 Doggett St, Newstead; ⊙10am-6pm Tue-Fri, 10am-4pm Sat)

Jan Murphy Gallery (Map p296; ☑3254 1855; 486 Brunswick St; ⊙10am-5pm Tue-Sat)

Philip Bacon Galleries (Map p296; ☑3358 3555; 2 Arthur St; ⊙10am-5pm Tue-Sat)

via Samuel Griffith Dr and has wheelchair access.

Just north of the road to the lookout, on Samuel Griffith Dr, is the turn-off to **JC Slaughter Falls**, reached by a short walking track, plus a 1.5km **Aboriginal Art Trail**, which takes you past eight art sites with works by local Aboriginal artists.

The pleasant **Brisbane Botanic Gardens** (Map p280; admission free; ⊙8am-5pm, free guided walks 11am & 1pm Mon-Sat) has a plethora of mini ecologies, which include cactus, Japanese and herb gardens, rainforests and arid zones, making you feel like you're traversing the globe's landscape in all its vegetated splendour.

Also within the gardens, the **Sir Thomas Brisbane Planetarium** (⊙10am-4pm Tue-Fri, 11am-7.30pm Sat, 11am-4pm Sun) is Australia's largest planetarium. There's a great observatory here and the shows inside the **Cosmic Skydome** (adult $7-14, child $7-9) will make you feel like you've stepped on board the *Enterprise*. Outside show times, you can explore the small space museum.

To get here via public transport, take bus 471 from Adelaide St, opposite King George Sq ($3.90, 25 minutes, hourly Monday to Friday, five services Saturday and Sunday). The bus drops you off in the lookout car park and stops outside the Brisbane Botanic Gardens en route.

D'Aguilar Range National Park

NATURE RESERVE

Brisbanites suffering from suburban malaise satisfy their wilderness cravings at this 50,000-hectare park in the D'Aguilar Range, 10km north of the city centre. There are **walking trails** ranging from a few hundred metres to 13km, including the 6km Morelia Track at Manorina day-use area and the 5km Greene's Falls Track at Mt Glorious.

At the park entrance the **Walkabout Creek Visitor Centre** (camping permits ☑13 74 68; www.derm.qld.gov.au; 60 Mt Nebo Rd) has information about camping (per person $5.15) and maps of the park. If you plan to camp, keep in mind that these are remote, walk-in, bush-camp sites.

Beside the visitors centre is **Walkabout Creek** (adult/child/family $6/3/15), a wildlife centre where you can see a resident platypus up close, as well as turtles, green tree frogs, lizards, pythons and gliders. There's also a small but wonderful walk-through aviary. It's an outstanding alternative to a zoo.

To get here, catch bus 385 ($5.30, 30 minutes), which departs from Roma St Station hourly from 10.22am to 3.22pm (services start at 8.47am on weekends). The bus stops outside the visitors centre, and the last departure back to the city is at 4.48pm (3.53pm on weekends).

Lone Pine Koala Sanctuary

NATURE RESERVE

(☑3378 1366; Jesmond Rd, Fig Tree Pocket; adult/child/family $30/21/80; ⊙8.30am-5pm) A 35-minute bus ride south of the city centre, Lone Pine Koala Sanctuary is set in attractive parklands beside the river. It is home to 130 or so koalas, as well as kangaroos, possums and wombats. The koalas are undeniably cute and most visitors readily cough up the $16 to have their picture taken hugging one.

To get here catch bus 430 ($4.70, 43 minutes, hourly), which leaves from the Queen Street bus station. Alternatively, **Mirimar II** (☑1300 729 742; www.miramar.com; incl park entry per adult/child/family $55/33/160) cruises to the sanctuary along the Brisbane River from North Quay, next to Victoria Bridge. It

BRISBANE SIGHTS

WHEN IT RAINS, IT POURS

Wild weather in the Sunshine State in December 2010 and January 2011 caused major flooding throughout Queensland with many towns inundated and isolated throughout the state. Brisbane did not escape the onslaught, recording its biggest flood since 1974. The usually placid Brisbane River became a swirling torrent of brown water sweeping boats, pontoons and other debris downstream towards the sea. Floodwater streamed into the CBD's riverfront areas while in low-lying suburbs only rooftops remained above the waterline. More than 30,000 homes were affected by the floods. Popular attractions such as South Bank Parklands and the Riverside Centre were also affected, while the Riverwalk, the section of floating walkway of the Riverside path, was destroyed. Along the riverfront, the city's ferry terminals suffered substantial damage, with many docks swept away, disrupting Brisbane's busy ferry services. After the clean-up, restoration and reconstruction of damaged areas proceeded rapidly. In many parts of the city, little evidence remains of the 2011 floods.

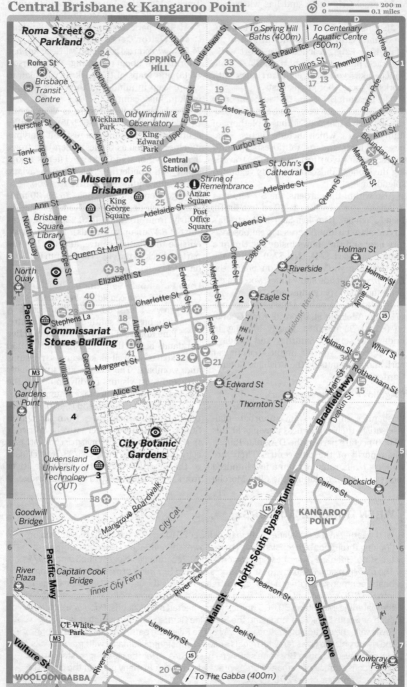

BRISBANE ACTIVITIES

departs daily at 10am, returning from Lone Pine at 1.45pm.

🏃 Activities

Cycling

Brisbane has over 900km of bike trails, including scenic routes that follow the Brisbane River. Pick up free maps at the **Transport Information Centre** (cnr Ann & Albert Sts, Brisbane). You can rent bikes from **Valet Cycle Hire** (Map p284; ☏04-0800 3198; www.cyclebrisbane.com; cnr Edward & Alice Sts; per hr/2hr/day $18/24/42) and **Bicycle Revolution** (Map p298; www.bicyclerevolution.org.au; 294 Montague Rd, West End; per day/week $35/150).

Brisbane also has a bike-sharing program **City Cycle** (www.citycycle.com.au), but you'll need a helmet, and it's not cheap for long rentals. The subscription cost per day/three months is $11/28 plus usage fees (free the

first half hour, then $2.20/6/11 per additional 30/60/90 minutes). To use the service, you'll need to reserve a bike online.

Rock Climbing & Abseiling

Riverlife Adventure Centre

ROCK CLIMBING, KAYAKING

(Map p284; ☏3891 5766; www.riverlife.com.au; Naval Stores, Kangaroo Point) A good one-stop shop for a wide range of activities is Riverlife, located near the **Kangaroo Point cliffs**. It offers rock climbing ($45 per session), abseiling (rapelling, $39) and kayaking instruction ($39), and hires out bicycles (per 90 minutes/four hours $15/30), kayaks (per 90 minutes $25) and in-line skates (per 90 minutes/four hours $20/40).

Adventures Around Brisbane

ROCK CLIMBING

(☏1800-689-453; www.adventuresaroundbrisbane.com.au; climbing $35) Introductory

RIVERSIDE PATH

One of the best ways to see the city is to stroll, cycle or jog along the riverside path. You can plot a day out following one side of the river and head back on the other side. Don't miss a stroll through the South Bank Parklands and up to Kangaroo Point, passing below the rock-climbing cliffs (a good pit stop is the Cliffs Cafe). Nearly every bridge has a separate pedestrian lane separate from traffic, including the Story Bridge, which has magnificent views of the city centre. Frequent ferry docks means you can always hop on a boat when you're ready to call it a day.

courses are run for rock-climbing at the cliffs, abseiling, as well as climbs to Glass House Mountains and Mt Tinbeerwah.

Adventure Seekers ROCK CLIMBING
($1300 855 859; www.adventureseekers.com.au; ½-day climb or abseil $110) Runs half-day abseiling and rock climbing (separately) at Kangaroo Point.

Swimming

There are several good swimming pools in Brisbane, including **Centenary Aquatic Centre** (400 Gregory Tce, Spring Hill; adult/child $5/4; ⊙5.30am-7pm Mon-Fri, 7am-4pm Sat & Sun), **Spring Hill Baths** (14 Torrington St, Spring Hill; adult/child $4.50/3.20; ⊙6.30am-7pm Mon-Thu, to 6pm Fri, 8am-5pm Sat, 8am-1pm Sun) and the **Streets Beach** lagoon at the South Bank parklands.

Skydiving & Ballooning

You can take tandem skydiving jumps with the **Brisbane Skydiving Centre** ($1300 788 555; www.jumpthebeachbrisbane.com.au; tandem skydive from $310), or go on ballooning adventures with **Fly Me to the Moon** ($3423 0400; www.flymetothemoon.com.au; Mon-Fri $300, Sat & Sun $350).

☞ Tours

City Sights Tour CITY
(day tickets per adult/child $25/20) This hop-on-hop-off shuttle bus takes in 19 of Brisbane's major landmarks. Tours depart every 45 minutes between 9am and 3.45pm from Post Office Sq on Queen St. The same ticket covers you for unlimited use of CityCat ferry services.

Ghost Tours GHOST
($3344 7265; www.ghost-tours.com.au; walking/coach tour $25/75) This tour company hosts guided 90-minute walking tours or 2½-hour bus tours of Brisbane's haunted heritage: murder scenes, cemeteries, eerie arcades and the infamous Boggo Rd Gaol.

Story Bridge Adventure Climb ADVENTURE
(Map p284; ☑1300 254 627; www.storybridgeadventureclimb.com.au; 170 Main St, Kangaroo Point; adult/child from $89/76) Story Book gives bridge climbers 2½ hours of exhilarating (or terrifying) views over Brisbane and beyond, to the Glass House Mountains in the north and Gold Coast hinterland to the south, from the upper reaches of the city's premier bridge.

Castlemaine-Perkins XXXX Brewery BEER
(Map p292; ☑3361 7597; www.xxxxalehouse.com.au; cnr Black & Paten Sts; adult/child $22/15; ⊙hourly 11am-4pm Mon-Fri & 6pm Wed, 12.30pm, 1pm & 1.30pm Sat) Adult entry to this famous brewery includes four ales to quench your thirst at the end of the tour, so it's a good idea to leave the car at home. The brewery also offers weekend beer and barbecue tours, which include lunch ($35). It's a 20-minute walk west from the transit centre, or you can take the train to Milton station. Wear enclosed shoes.

Kookaburra River Queens CRUISE
(☑3221 1300; www.kookaburrariverqueens.com; lunch/dinner cruises per person from $49/75) Kookaburra runs lunch or dinner cruises up and down the river in restored wooden paddle steamers, usually departing from the Eagle St Pier. At the time of research, the cruise was temporarily operating from Bretts Wharf due to Brisbane Flood damage to the pier. Check the departure point when booking.

River City Cruises CRUISE
(Map p282; ☑0428-278 473; www.rivercitycruises.com.au; South Bank Parklands; adult/child/family $25/15/60) Has 1½-hour cruises with commentary, departing from South Bank at 10.30am and 12.30pm (plus 2.30pm during summer).

Festivals & Events

For further information about festivals and events, check out www.ourbrisbane.com/whatson.

Chinese New Year Always a popular event in the Valley in January/February.

Tropfest (www.tropfest.com) Nationwide short-film festival telecast live at South Bank in mid-February.

Paniyiri Festival (www.paniyiri.com) Greek cultural festival with dancing, food and music. Held in late May at Musgrave Park in West End.

Brisbane Pride Festival (www.pridebrisbane.org.au) Brisbane's fabulously flamboyant gay and lesbian celebration, held in June.

Queensland Music Festival (http://qmf.org.au) Outstanding celebration of the world of music, held over 17 days in July in odd-numbered years.

'Ekka' Royal National Agricultural (RNA) Show (www.ekka.com.au) The country comes to town in early August with competitions, wood chopping and rides.

Brisbane Festival (www.brisbanefestival.com.au) Brisbane's major festival of the arts, with buskers, performances, music and concerts held in September. See the boxed text (p287) for more information.

Valley Fiesta (www.valleyfiesta.com.au) Food and music festival held in Chinatown and Brunswick St Mall in mid-September.

Brisbane International Film Festival (www.biff.com.au) Ten days of quality films in November.

Sleeping

Brisbane has an excellent selection of accommodation options that will suit any budget. The inner suburbs have their own distinct flavours. Spring Hill, just north of the CBD, is quiet and within easy striking distance of downtown and Fortitude Valley. Petrie Tce and Paddington, just west of the city centre, combine trendy restaurants and lively bars. Staying in the alternative neighbourhoods of Fortitude Valley and nearby New Farm places you next door to Chinatown and in the city's best nightlife. West End, south of the river, has a decidedly chilled-out, slightly bohemian atmosphere and some great cafes and restaurants.

CITY CENTRE

TOP CHOICE **Treasury** LUXURY HOTEL $$$
(Map p284; 3306 8888; www.treasurybrisbane.com.au; 130 William St; r $200-349; ✳@) Brisbane's classiest hotel is in the beautifully preserved former Land Administration Building. Every room is unique and awash with heritage features, with high ceilings, framed artwork on the walls and polished wood furniture and elegant furnishings.

Portal BOUTIQUE HOTEL $$$
(Map p284; 3009 3400; www.portalhotel.com.au; 52 Astor Tce; d from $160; ✳🛜) Behind the ultramodern black-and-white facade, Portal has contemporary rooms with a nice overall design and thoughtful touches (original artwork in each room, iPod docking stations, free wi-fi). There's also a women-only floor. The downside: some rooms are quite

---

BRISBANE FOR CHILDREN

One of the best attractions for children is the **Cultural Centre** (p279). Here the Queensland Museum runs some fantastic, hands-on programs for little tackers during school holidays. The incorporated Sciencentre is made for inquisitive young minds and will keep them inventing, creating and discovering for hours. The Queensland Art Gallery has a Children's Art Centre in which it runs regular programs throughout the year

The **South Bank Parklands** (p279) has the safe and child-friendly Streets Beach and a scattering of jungle-gym playgrounds with rubber surfaces. There are more imaginative playgrounds in the **Roma Street Parkland** (Map p284).

C!RCA (Map p296; 3852 3110; www.circa.org.au; 420 Brunswick St; per day $80) offers action-packed 'circus classes' (tumbling, balancing, jumping, trapeze work) for budding young performers at the Judith Wright Centre in Fortitude Valley.

The river is a big plus. Many children will enjoy a river-boat trip, especially if it's to **Lone Pine Koala Sanctuary** (p283) where they can cuddle up to one of the lovable creatures.

Daycare or babysitting options include **Dial an Angel** (1300 721 111; www.dialanangel.com) and **Care4Kidz** (www.careforkidz.com.au/brisbane/babysitting.htm).

Brisbane's streets become a hurly-burly of colour, flair, flavour and fireworks during the city's biggest arts event of the year – the Brisbane Festival (formerly known as Riverfest; www.brisbanefestival.com.au). Running over three weeks in September, the festival is one of Australia's biggest with over 300 performances and 60-odd events, bringing 2000-plus artists from across the globe. Art exhibitions, dance, theatre, opera, symphonies, circus performers and vaudeville all add to the eclectic scene, with street events and free concerts around town.

The festival is opened each year with a bang – literally. Staged over the Brisbane River, with vantage points from South Bank, the city and West End, Riverfire is a massive fireworks show with dazzling visual choreography and a synchronised soundtrack.

small. The bar-restaurant on the ground floor is an atmospheric spot for a drink.

Urban Brisbane BOUTIQUE HOTEL $$$
(Map p284; 3831 6177; www.hotelurban.com.au; 345 Wickham Tce; d from $170;) Fresh from a $10 million makeover in 2008, the Urbane Brisbane has stylish rooms kitted out in masculine tones with balconies and high-end fittings (supercomfortable beds, oversized LCD TVs, fluffy bathrobes). There's a heated outdoor pool and a bar with live music on Friday nights.

Stamford Plaza Brisbane HOTEL $$$
(Map p284; 3221 1999; www.stamford.com.au; cnr Edward & Margaret Sts; r from $225;) At the southern end of the city, the Stamford has a historic facade in front of a modern tower. The indulgent rooms have antique touches, large beds and plenty of atmosphere. On site is a gym, an art gallery, a hair-and-beauty salon, a bar and several restaurants.

M on Mary APARTMENTS $$
(Map p284; 3503 8000; www.monmary.com.au; 70 Mary St; apt from $170;) Handily located a few blocks from the botanical gardens, this 43-storey building has modern, comfortably furnished one- and two-bedroom apartments. The best apartments have balconies. Some have poor layouts and are gloomy.

Annie's Inn B&B $
(Map p284; 3831 8684; www.babs.com.au/annies; 405 Upper Edward St; s/d without bathroom $68/78, d $88) In a central location within walking distance of the CBD, this budget-minded B&B has simple rooms with thin walls, tiny wash basins and frilly curtains and duvets. It can be noisy in the morning.

Tinbilly HOSTEL $
(Map p284; 1800 446 646, 3238 5888; www.tinbilly.com; 466 George St; dm $22-30; d $100;) Tinbilly has a clean, modern interior and excellent facilities. The popular bar is one big party place – with live bands, DJs and open-mic nights.

Inchcolm Hotel HOTEL $$$
(Map p284; 3226 8888; www.theinchcolm.com.au; 73 Wickham Tce; r $160-250;) This elegant heritage hotel retains elements from its early-20th-century past, but the rooms have been renovated extensively. Those in the newer wing have more space and light, while rooms in the older wing have more character. There's also a rooftop pool and in-house restaurant.

Acacia Inner-City Inn B&B $
(Map p284; 3832 1663; www.acaciainn.com; 413 Upper Edward St; s/d without bathroom $75/85, d $100) This well-maintained B&B has small, motel-style rooms in a functional environment. The singles are fairly snug, but the doubles have more space and it's clean throughout. All rooms come with TVs and bar fridges. It's a great set-up for the price and location.

Explorers Inn HOTEL $$
(Map p284; 3211 3488; www.explorers.com.au; 63 Turbot St; d from $100;) A modern hotel with very friendly management and a supreme city-centre location. The downside: the rooms are extremely small, but clean and well maintained, and all with en-suite. Not recommended for those seeking space.

X-Base Brisbane Central HOSTEL $
(Map p284; 1800 242 273, 3211 2433; www.stayatbase.com; 398 Edward St; dm $27-32, s/d $50/80;) This colossal backpacker

institution has basic rooms set in a heritage building across from Central Station. There's a rooftop terrace with views over the CBD, and a bar on the ground floor. It has a second branch on 214 Elizabeth St.

PETRIE TERRACE

Aussie Way Backpackers
HOSTEL $
(Map p292; ☑3369 0711; 34 Cricket St, Petrie Tce; dm/s/d without bathroom $28/55/68; ❋@) Set in a picturesque, two-storey timber Queenslander, Aussie Way feels more like a guesthouse than hostel with spacious, nicely furnished rooms and a pleasant outdoor area. No children.

Brisbane City YHA
HOSTEL $
(Map p292; ☑3236 1004; www.yha.com.au; 392 Upper Roma St, Petrie Tce; dm $32-40, tw & d $83-100; ❋@❅❄) This clean and well-run hostel has a rooftop pool and sundeck with river views. Rooms range from three-bed to 10-bed dorms, and there's a cafe-bar on-site where you can meet other travellers. Several other hostels are along this street.

SPRING HILL

Spring Hill Terraces
GUESTHOUSE $$
(☑3854 1048; www.springhillterraces.com; 260 Water St, Spring Hill; budget/standard r $85/110, studio/terrace unit $130/160; ❋@❅❄) Offering good old-fashioned service, Spring Hill has motel-style rooms and roomier terrace units with balconies and leafy courtyards. It's set amid greenery within 10 minutes' walk of the Valley.

Dahrl Court
APARTMENTS $$
(Map p284; ☑3830 3400; www.dahrlcourt.com.au; 45 Phillips St, Spring Hill; apt from $155; ❋❅) Tucked into a quiet, leafy pocket of Spring Hill, this boutique complex offers good value for its roomy accommodation. The sizeable apartments are fully self-contained with kitchens and heritage aesthetics throughout (two with balconies).

Kookaburra Inn
GUESTHOUSE $
(Map p284; ☑3832 1303; www.kookaburra-inn.com.au; 41 Phillips St; s/d without bathroom $55/72; ❋❅@) This small and friendly two-level guesthouse has simple rooms with a wash basin and fridge and shared clean bathrooms. There's a lounge, guest kitchen and an outdoor patio. Overall, it's a good budget option for those looking to escape the dormitory experience.

FORTITUDE VALLEY

Limes
BOUTIQUE HOTEL $$$
(Map p296; ☑3852 9000; www.limeshotel.com.au; 142 Constance St; d from $229; ❋@❅❄) A stylish accommodation newcomer to the Valley, Limes Hotel has handsomely outfitted rooms that make good use of tight space – each guestroom has plush furniture, kitchenettes and thoughtful extras, including iPod docks, free wi-fi and a free gym pass. Check out the rooftop bar – it's smashing.

Bunk Backpackers
HOSTEL $
(Map p296; ☑3257 3644; www.bunkbrisbane.com.au; cnr Ann & Gipps Sts; dm $15-33, s/d $65/75; ❋@❅❄) This party-minded hostel has generous dorms with bathrooms, good mattresses, gleaming kitchens and funky decor. It's steps to Brisbane's best nightlife, and weekends are noisy. There's also a fabulous bar (Birdee Num Num), swimming pool and spa.

City Palms Motel
MOTEL $
(☑3252 1338; www.citypalmsmotel.com; 55 Brunswick St; d from $90; ❋) Fringed by palm trees on busy Brunswick St, this little motel has cool, dark rooms with kitchenettes. Some rooms are in better shape than others. It's a decent location if you want to be close to the Valley, but can be noisy – so request a room at the back.

NEW FARM

Bowen Terrace
GUESTHOUSE $
(Map p290; ☑3254 0458; www.bowentceaccommodation.com; 365 Bowen Tce; dm/s/d $35/60/85, deluxe r $99-145; @❄) A beautifully restored Queenslander, this guesthouse is tucked away in a quiet area of New Farm. The friendly owners have installed a TV and bar fridge in every room and there's a lovely back deck overlooking the pool. Excellent value for money.

Allender Apartments
APARTMENTS $$
(Map p290; ☑3358 5832; www.allenderapartments.com.au; 3 Moreton St; studio/one-bedroom apt $130/160; ❋❅) Allender's studios and one-bedroom apartments are a mixed bag. In the plain yellow-brick building are simply furnished but clean rooms that are in need of an update. More attractive are the heritage apartments that are located in the adjoining Fingal House, a 1918 Queenslander with polished wood floors, oak furniture and access to a private verandah or courtyard.

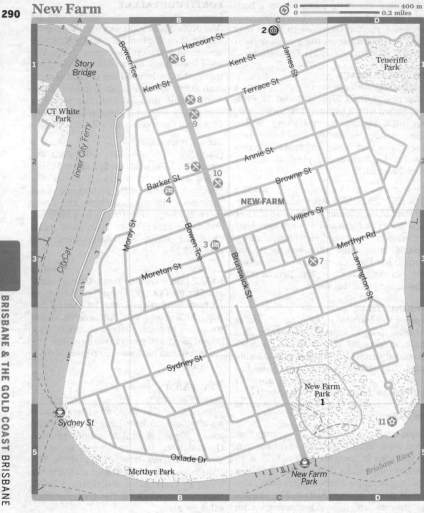

WEST END

Edmondstone Motel   MOTEL **$$**
(Map p298; ☎3255 0777; www.edmondstonemotel.com.au; 24 Edmondstone St, South Brisbane; s/d $109/119; 🐾@🛜🏊) A 10-minute walk from both the South Bank parklands and West End, the Edmondstone Motel has small, comfortable rooms with new mattresses, kitchenette and LCD TV. Most have a small balcony, and there's a small pool and barbecue.

Brisbane Backpackers Resort   HOSTEL **$**
(Map p298; ☎3844 9956; www.brisbanebackpackers.com.au; 110 Vulture St, West End; dm $25-32, d/tr $99/120; 🐾@🏊) The best feature of this popular hostel is the pool and spa, with a tiled outdoor area and a bar. The rooms are basic but generally well maintained. It's a short stroll to the bars and cafes of West End.

KANGAROO POINT

Il Mondo   HOTEL **$$**
(Map p284; ☎3392 0111; www.ilmondo.com.au; 25 Rotherham St; r/apt $160/250; 🐾@🏊) In a fine location near the Story Bridge, this boutique hotel has handsome three- and four-star rooms with a contemporary, minimalist

New Farm

⊙ **Sights**

🛏 **Sleeping**

🍴 **Eating**

Drinking

🎭 **Entertainment**

Shopping

design, high-end fixtures and plenty of space. The cheaper options are standard hotel rooms while the more expensive are self-contained apartments.

Queensland Motel   HOTEL **$**
(Map p284; ☑3391 1061; www.queenslandmotel.id.au; 777 Main St; d/tr $98/109; ❋🛜🌊) The nicely maintained Queensland Motel offers large, brightly coloured rooms with good beds. Try to get a room on the top floor where you'll be greeted by rustling palm trees while enjoying coffee on the balcony.

OUTER BRISBANE

Fern Cottage   B&B **$$**
(☑3511 6685; www.ferncottage.net; 89 Fernberg Rd, Paddington; s/d $115/140; ❋@) Fern Cottage is a beautifully renovated Queenslander with a splash of Mediterranean ambience. The rooms are cushy and there's a lush garden retreat out the back with a shady balcony.

Newmarket Gardens Caravan Park
    CAMPGROUND **$**
(☑3356 1458; www.newmarketgardens.com.au; 199 Ashgrove Ave, Ashgrove; powered/unpowered sites $33/31, cabins $95-116; ❋@) This clean site doesn't have many trees, but it is just

4km north of the city centre, accessible by several bus routes and train (Newmarket station).

🍴 Eating

In the Valley you'll find inexpensive cafes and a smorgasbord of Asian flavours, thanks to Chinatown. Nearby, stylish New Farm has great dining with a large selection of multicultural eateries and award-winners. West End is a distinctly cosmopolitan corner, with trendy cafes and eclectic cuisine.

CITY CENTRE

E'cco   MODERN AUSTRALIAN **$$$**
(Map p284; ☑3831 8344; 100 Boundary St; mains $43; ⊙lunch Tue-Fri, dinner Tue-Sat) One of the finest restaurants in the state, award-winning E'cco is a must for any culinary aficionado. Masterpieces on the menu include milly hill lamb rump with baby beetroot, roast pumpkin, blue cheese and pine nuts. The interior is suitably swish and you'll need to book well in advance.

Cha Cha Char   STEAK **$$$**
(Map p284; ☑3211 9944; Eagle St Pier; mains $30-50; ⊙lunch Mon-Fri, dinner daily) Wallowing in awards, this long-running favourite serves Brisbane's best steaks, along with first-rate seafood and roast game meats. The elegant semicircular dining room has floor-to-ceiling windows with waterfront views.

Embassy Hotel   PUB FARE **$**
(Map p284; 188 Edward St; mains $10-18; ⊙lunch & dinner) With red tones, cubed seating and polished wood, this groovy hotel dishes out some excellent pub nosh and is popular with city folk and travellers alike.

🌿 Bleeding Heart Gallery   CAFE **$**
(Map p284; www.bleedingheart.com.au; 166 Ann St; mains $6-8; ⊙8am-5pm Mon-Fri; 🛜) Set back from busy Ann St in a charming, two-storey Queenslander with verandah, this spacious cafe and gallery has a bohemian vibe and hosts art openings, occasional concerts and other events.

Java Coast Cafe   CAFE **$**
(340 George St; mains $9-14; ⊙7.30am-3.30pm Mon-Fri) Head to the peaceful back garden with its fountain, subtropical plants and Buddha statues for a quick escape from the bustling CBD. Good coffee, teas, plus sandwiches, salads and light meals with Asian accents.

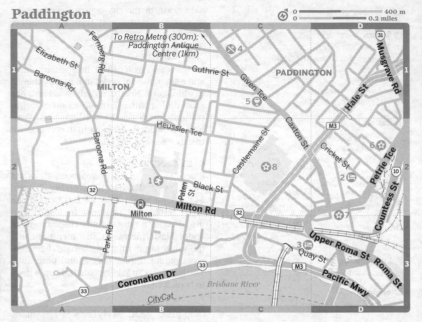

0 400 m
0 0.2 miles

Paddington

FORTITUDE VALLEY & CHINATOWN

Ortiga   SPANISH $$$
(Map p296; ☑3852 1155; 446 Brunswick St; sharing plates $18-36; ◯dinner Tue-Sun) One of Brisbane's best new restaurants, Ortiga opened in 2010 to much fanfare. You can dine in the stylish upstairs tapas bar with rustic wood tables or head to the elegant subterranean dining room where chefs work their magic in an open kitchen. Top picks include *cochinillo* (slow-cooked suckling pig), *pulpo a gallega* (Galician-braised octopus) and whole slow-cooked lamb shoulder.

Vietnamese Restaurant   VIETNAMESE $$
(Map p296; 194 Wickham St; mains $8-15; ◯lunch & dinner) Aptly if unimaginatively named, this is indeed *the* place in town to eat Vietnamese, with exquisitely prepared dishes served to an always crowded house. The real delights are to be found on the 'Authentic Menu'. The shredded beef in spinach rolls is tops, as is any dish containing the word 'sizzling'. BYO and licensed.

Kuan-Yin Tea House   VEGETARIAN $
(Map p296; 198 Wickham St; mains $8-10; ◯11.30am-5pm Mon & Sat, 11.30am-7pm Wed-Fri, to 3pm Sun) Kuan-Yin is a small, warmly lit BYO place with wood panelling and a bamboo-lined ceiling, where a wide cross-section of Brisbanites come for flavourful vegetarian noodle soups, dumplings and mock-meat rice dishes. Great tea selection.

Garuva   FUSION $$
(Map p296; ☑3216 0124; 324 Wickham St; mains $24; ◯dinner) Garuva's rainforested foyer leads to tables with cushioned seating concealed by silk curtains. There's a rather

Arabian Nights feel to the place, with dim lighting, loungey beats and subdued banter (more raucous on weekends). Plates are meant for sharing and lean towards Asian fusion – sweet-potato and bean curry, warm Thai beef salad, coconut prawns. Hunt out the cool, hidden cocktail bar.

Spoon Deli   CAFE $$
(Map p296; 22 James St; breakfast $10-15, mains $14-21; ⊙5.30am-7pm Mon-Fri, to 6pm Sat & Sun) Inside James St market, this upmarket deli serves deliciously rich pasta, salads, soup and colossal panini and focaccias. The fresh juices are a liquid meal in themselves. Diners munch their goodies amid the deli produce at oversized square tables or low benches skirting the windows, which flood the place with sunlight. You'll feel hungry as soon as you walk in.

Cafe Cirque   CAFE $$
(Map p290; 618 Brunswick St; breakfast mains $14-17; ⊙8am-4pm) One of the best breakfast spots (served all day) in town, the buzzing Cafe Cirque serves rich coffees and daily specials, along with open-faced sandwiches and gourmet salads for lunch.

Flamingo   CAFE $
(Map p296; 5b Winn St; mains $9-15; ⊙7.30am-4pm) Tucked down a tiny lane off Ann St, the Flamingo is a buzzing little cafe with black and pink walls, a boho vibe and cheerfully profane wait staff.

Self-Catering

James St Market (Map p296; James St, Fortitude Valley) is pricey, but the quality is excellent and there's a good seafood shop here.

There's a great produce market inside McWhirters Marketplace (Map p296; cnr Brunswick & Wickham Sts). The Asian supermarkets in Chinatown mall also have an excellent range of fresh vegies, Asian groceries and exotic fruit.

NEW FARM

Anise   FRENCH $$$
(Map p290; ☑3358 1558; 697 Brunswick St; mains $36-42; ⊙5pm-1am Sun-Wed, noon-1pm Thu-Sat) This dapper 21-seat restaurant and wine bar features an award-winning menu of seasonally inspired Gallic fare. Patrons plant themselves around the narrow bar and feast on *amuse-bouches* (hors d'oeuvres) like oysters and Alsace foie gras, followed by grass-fed black Angus beef, fresh fish of the day or slow-braised spring lamb.

Watt   MODERN AUSTRALIAN $$$
(Map p290; ☑3358 5464; Brisbane Powerhouse; mains $24-34; ⊙lunch Tue-Sun, dinner Tue-Sat, breakfast Sat & Sun) On the lower level of the Powerhouse Arts precinct, Watt serves award-winning Modern Australian fare. Start with the Queensland spanner crab or crispy-duck salad before moving on to lamb striploin, seafood pasta or the daily catch perfectly grilled.

Cafe Bouquiniste   CAFE $
(Map p290; 121 Merthyr Rd; mains $8-10; ⊙8am-5.30pm) Set in the front room of a charming Queenslander, this tiny cafe and bookseller has oodles of charm, if not much space. The coffee is fantastic, service is friendly, and the prices are right for the breakfast fare, toasted sandwiches, savoury tarts and cakes.

Himalayan Cafe   NEPALESE $
(Map p290; ☑3358 4015; 640 Brunswick St; mains $15-23; ⊙dinner Tue-Sat; ☑) Set in a sea of prayer flags and colourful cushions, this friendly, unfussy restaurant serves authentic Tibetan and Nepalese fare such as *momo cha* (steamed dumplings), Sherpa chicken (curry and sour cream) and tender *fhaiya darkau* (lamb with vegies, coconut milk and spices). It gets rave reviews and kids are welcome.

Wok on Inn   ASIAN FUSION $
(Map p290; 728 Brunswick St; mains $11-14; ⊙lunch Sun-Fri, dinner daily) With a lovely shaded front courtyard, this industrious and popular noodle bar is the New Farm spot for some fast noodles. Choose your noodle, your cooking style (including Mongolian) and your meat/veg combo. Regular $7.50 lunch special.

BurgerUrge   BURGERS $
(Map p290; 542 Brunswick St; mains $9-13; ⊙lunch Fri-Sun, dinner Tue-Sun) Among the city's best burgers, with a wealth of options: lamb, chicken avocado bacon, classic beef, and vegie options (grilled tofu, portabello, eggplant and goat's cheese). Good milkshakes too.

PADDINGTON

Lark   MODERN AUSTRALIAN $$
(Map p292; ☑3369 1299; 267 Given Tce; small plates $8-26; ⊙4pm-midnight Tue-Thu, noon-midnight Fri-Sun) In a converted colonial-style cottage, the Lark is an award-winning restaurant that's praised for both its inventive fusion fare and its artfully prepared cocktails. Share plates from the 'grazing' (tapas) menu like Wagyu sliders, followed

BRISBANE EATING

PHILIP JOHNSON: HEAD CHEF AT E'CCO

Kitchens are great. There's always a melting pot of ideas – you work with different chefs, and things evolve over the years.

Claim to Fame

Winning *Gourmet Traveller*'s Restaurant of the Year award in 1997. Some people say that's what helped put Brisbane's restaurant scene on the map. I hate to look at it like that, but I think the rest of the country took notice: 'there must be some decent places to eat up there in Brisbane'. A well-known food critic said you couldn't eat north of Paddington – as in Paddington, Sydney. That changed a bit that year.

Cooking style

Modern Australian, it has Italian influences, and there's always a bit of Asian in it owing to our proximity, plus a bit of Mediterranean.

Dining scene in Brisbane

It's amazing. Brisbane is a city that has grown up in the last 15 years. I think for years we were considered to be playing second fiddle to Sydney and Melbourne; now I think we have great restaurants with top quality and service.

Other favourite restaurants

Something casual I love is **Alto** at the Powerhouse. **Ortiga** has just opened and it's fantastic.

by yoghurt-baked barramundi or tempura prawns with wakame salad.

SOUTH BANK & KANGAROO POINT

Ahmet's TURKISH **$$**
(Map p282; ✆3846 6699; 164 Grey St; mains $20-28; ◷lunch & dinner) On restaurant-lined Grey St, Ahmet's serves delectable Turkish fare amid a riot of colours. The *pide* (oven-baked Turkish pizza) here is sublime. There's belly dancing on Friday and Saturday nights, plus live 'gypsy-jazz' playing on Thursday nights.

Piaf FRENCH **$$**
(Map p282; ✆3846 5026; 186 Grey St; mains $22; ◷7am-late) A laid-back bistro with a loyal following, Piaf serves a small selection (just five mains and a few salads and lighter meals) of good-value contemporary fare.

Cliffs Cafe MODERN AUSTRALIAN **$**
(Map p284; 3 River Tce; mains $12-17; ◷7am-5pm) A steep climb up from Kangaroo Point park, this cliff-top cafe has superb views over the river. Cyclists, joggers, young families – all are welcome at this casual open-air spot, where thick burgers, battered barramundi and chips, salads, desserts and good coffee are among the standouts.

WEST END

Mondo Organics MODERN AUSTRALIAN **$$**
(Map p298; ✆3844 1132; 166 Hardgrave Rd; mains $26-38; ◷lunch Fri-Sun, dinner Wed-Sat, breakfast Sat & Sun) Using the highest-quality organic and sustainable produce, Mondo Organics earns high marks for its delicious seasonal menu. Recent hits include pumpkin, leek and ricotta tortellini, lamb rack with wild mushroom risotto, and ocean trout with shaved fennel and saffron-infused mashed potatoes.

Gunshop Cafe MODERN AUSTRALIAN **$$**
(Map p298; ✆3844 2241; 53 Mollison St; mains $24-33; ◷7am-2pm Mon, 7am-late Tue-Sat, 7am-12.30pm Sun) A beautiful repurposing of a former gunshop with exposed brick walls, sculptural-like ceiling lamps and an inviting back garden. The locally sourced menu changes daily, with favourites like eggs Benedict with vodka-cured ocean trout, grass-fed rib fillet with roast mushrooms and grilled emperor with braised leek and bacon.

Caravanserai TURKISH **$$**
(Map p298; ✆3217 2617; 1-3 Dornoch Tce; mains $25-33; ◷lunch Thu-Sun, dinner Tue-Sun) Richly woven tablecloths, red walls and candlelit tables create a warm and inviting

atmosphere at this standout Turkish restaurant. Meze platters are great for sharing (with humus, baba ganoush, artichokes, dolma and more). Dine on the back verandah for pleasant river views.

Kafe Meze GREEK **$$**
(Map p298; ☑3844 1720; 56 Mollison St; mains $27-29; ⊘lunch & dinner) This indoor-outdoor Greek restaurant delivers fresh flavours and tastes of the Mediterranean. Tapas-style is a good way to sample a range of dishes, like grilled haloumi, marinated octopus, calamari and tzatziki with pita bread.

Three Monkeys CAFE **$**
(Map p298; 58 Mollison St; mains $12-15; ⊘9.30am-10pm) This laid-back bohemian teahouse is steeped in pseudo-Moroccan decor and ambience. Low lighting, rustic wood furnishings and tiny nooks make a fine setting for delicious cake and coffee – or heartier pizzas, focaccia and panini. There's also a courtyard in the back.

Black Star CAFE **$**
(Map p298; 44 Thomas St; ⊘7am-3pm Mon, 7am-5pm Tue-Fri, to late Sat, 8am-3pm Sun) A neighbourhood favourite, West End's most popular roastery has excellent coffee, outdoor tables, all-day breakfast and live music on Saturday nights.

🍷 Drinking

The prime drinking destination in Brisbane is Fortitude Valley, with its lounges, live-music bars and nightclubs. New Farm also has fine nightlife, while the CBD attracts a bottoms-up after-work crowd. West End has some fine bars, attracting a mostly neighbourhood crowd.

CITY CENTRE
Belgian Beer Cafe BAR
(Map p284; cnr Mary & Edward Sts, Brisbane; ⊘noon-late) Tin ceilings, wood-panelled walls and globe lights lend an old-fashioned charm to the front room of this buzzing space, while out the back, the inviting split-level beer garden provides a laid-back setting for sampling fine brews (including 30-plus Belgian beers) and high-end bistro fare.

Moo Moo RESTAURANT-WINE BAR
(Map p284; cnr Margaret & Edwards Sts, Brisbane; ⊘6pm-midnight Mon-Sat) Inside the heritage Port Office building, this stylish high-end Grill restaurant has an inviting open-air lounge on the lane out the back, with trickling fountain and fairy lights.

Port Office Hotel BAR
(Map p284; cnr Margaret & Edward Sts) The industrial edge of this renovated city pub is spruced up with swaths of dark wood and jungle prints. Pull up a stool or find a bench early and settle in for the evening, when a mixed crowd usually descends.

FORTITUDE VALLEY
Press Club COCKTAIL BAR
(Map p296; www.thepressclub.net.au; 339 Brunswick St; ⊘5pm-late Thu-Sat) The Press Club is an elegant spot of amber hues, leather sofas and ottomans, glowing chandeliers and fabric-covered lanterns, giving it a touch of Near Eastern glamour. Live music happens on Thursdays – jazz, funk, rockabilly – while DJs spin on weekends.

La Ruche COCKTAIL BAR
(Map p296; 680 Ann St) French for 'the hive', La Ruche is indeed a buzzing place, where a well-dressed crowd banters over nicely mixed cocktails and tasty bistro-style tapas plates. The main room channels *Alice in Wonderland* with wildly sculpted chandeliers and elegantly mismatched furniture, while there's a spacious (smokers') courtyard in the back and a small, cosy retreat upstairs.

Cloudland COCKTAIL BAR
(Map p296; 641 Ann St, Fortitude Valley; ⊘11.30am-late Wed-Sun) Like stepping into a cloud forest (or at least the Ann St version of it), this sprawling, multilevel space has a huge open plant-filled lobby with retractable roof, a wall of water and wrought-iron birdcage-like nooks sprinkled about; you'll also find a rooftop garden and a cellar bar.

Alloneword BAR
(Map p296; www.alloneword.com.au; 188 Brunswick St) On a seedy stretch of Brunswick St, this underground spot is the antidote to sleek cocktail bars taking over the Valley. The front room is pure whimsy: vintage wallpaper, velvety banquettes and a mirrored ceiling, while the back patio has graffiti murals and DJs.

Sky Room COCKTAIL BAR
(Map p296; Level 2, 234 Wickham St; ⊘5pm-late Wed-Sun) The Sky Room is a rambling lounge of plants, lime-green couches and chairs, a long wooden bar and a balcony complete with flickering tiki torches. DJs play a mix

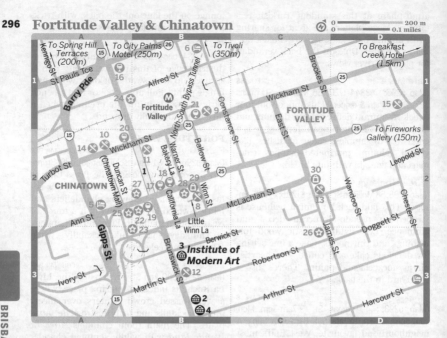

Fortitude Valley & Chinatown

of old-school rock. Bottled beer is served in a brown paper bag.

Bowery
COCKTAIL BAR

(Map p296; 676 Ann St) Exposed brick walls, gilded mirrors and antique chandeliers lend a classy, old-fashioned vibe to this long narrow bar. The cocktails are top-notch (and priced accordingly), and there's a tiny patio in the back. There's live jazz Tuesday to Thursday and DJs spin on weekends.

WEST END

Lychee Lounge
COCKTAIL BAR

(Map p298; 94 Boundary St, West End) Sink into the lush furniture and stare up at the macabre dolls'-head chandeliers at this exotic oriental lounge-bar, with mellow beats, mood lighting and an open frontage to Boundary St.

Lock 'N' Load
BAR, RESTAURANT

(Map p298; www.locknloadbistro.com.au; 142 Boundary St, West End; ☺10am-late) This classic all-wood two-storey gastro-pub gathers a friendly mixed crowd most nights. Bands play on the small front stage, and there's a leafy garden in the back.

NEW FARM & BREAKFAST CREEK

Alto Bar
BAR, RESTAURANT

(Map p290; www.brisbanepowerhouse.org; Brisbane Powerhouse, New Farm) Inside the arts-loving Brisbane Powerhouse, this open, upstairs bar has an enormous balcony overlooking the river that makes a mighty fine vantage point, no matter the weather. There's a full menu of creative Australian cooking, and always something happening at the Powerhouse.

Breakfast Creek Hotel
BAR, RESTAURANT

(2 Kingsford Smith Dr; ☺lunch & dinner) In a great rambling building dating from 1889, this historic pub is a Brisbane institution. Built in French Renaissance style, the pub encompasses various bars (including a beer garden and an art deco 'private bar' where you can still drink draught beer tapped from a wooden keg). The stylish, modern Substation No 41 bar serves boutique beers and cocktails.

KANGAROO POINT & SOUTH BANK

Story Bridge Hotel
BAR

(Map p284; 200 Main St, Kangaroo Point) This beautiful old pub beneath the bridge at Kangaroo Point is the perfect place for a pint after a long day exploring. There are several different spaces, including a traditional bistro, an alfresco drinking, snacking

spot and the popular Outback Bar – a casual beer garden that hosts live jazz on Sundays (from 3pm).

☆ Entertainment

Brisbane pulls almost of the international bands heading to Oz and the city's clubs have become nationally renowned. There's also plenty of theatre. Pick up copies of the free entertainment papers **Time Off** (www.timeoff.com.au), **Rave** (www.ravemag.com.au) and **Scene** (www.scenemagazine.com.au) from any cafe in the Valley.

The *Courier-Mail* also has daily arts and entertainment listings, and a comprehensive 'What's On In Town' section each Thursday. The city council also publishes a bimonthly *Live* guide, listing arts and culture events, many free.

Ticketek (☑13 28 49; http://premier.ticketek.com.au) is an agency that handles phone bookings for many major events, sports and performances.

To ensure you can get into Brisbane's nightspots, carry proof of age and (especially if you're male) avoid wearing tank tops, shorts or thongs (flip-flops). It's also best not to rock up in a big group of guys.

Nightclubs

Brisbane is proud of its nightclub scene – most clubs are open Thursday to Sunday nights, are adamant about ID and charge between $7 and $25 cover. The alternative scene is centred on the Valley, and attracts a mixed straight and gay crowd.

Monastery
NIGHTCLUB

(Map p296; ☑3257 7081; 621 Ann St, Fortitude Valley) Monastery really does look like a monastery with its ethereal lighting, tall stained-glass window panels and heavy chandeliers – apart from the heaving, sweaty hordes churning up the dance floor.

Family
NIGHTCLUB

(Map p296; ☑3852 5000; 8 McLachlan St, Fortitude Valley) One of Brisbane's best nightclubs, Family exhilarates dance junkies every weekend on four levels with two dance floors, four bars, four funky themed booths and a top-notch sound system.

Uber
NIGHTCLUB

(Map p298; ☑3846 6680; 100 Boundary St, West End) Uber is a bit decadent like an old-style boutique hotel, with its brushed steel and polished dark wood. The music varies but weekends are dedicated to pure main-room

house. There's a fine 'beer boutique and bistro' – called Archive – on the lower level.

Beat MegaClub   NIGHTCLUB
(Map p296; ☎3852 2661; 677 Ann St, Fortitude Valley) Five dance floors, six bars and hardcore techno equals the perfect place for dance junkies who like their beats hard. It's popular with the gay and lesbian crowd, with regular drag performances.

Live Music

Hi-Fi   ROCK
(Map p298; www.thehifi.com.au; 125 Boundary St, West End) In 2009, Melbourne's popular rock venue opened an outpost in Brisbane's hipster-loving West End. The modern, minimalist space has unobstructed sight lines and a decent line-up of local and international talent (hosting the likes of the Bronx, Guttermouth, Concrete Blonde and the Charlatans).

Zoo   ECLECTIC
(Map p296; www.thezoo.com.au; 711 Ann St, Fortitude Valley; ⊙Wed-Sat) The long queues at Zoo start early for a good reason: whether you're into hard rock, hip-hop, acoustic, reggae or electronic soundscapes, Zoo has a gig for you. It's one of your best chances to hear some raw local talent.

Brisbane Jazz Club   JAZZ
(Map p284; ☎3391 2006; www.brisbanejazzclub.com.au; 1 Annie St, Kangaroo Point) Beautifully sited overlooking the river, this tiny club has been a beacon for jazz purists since 1972. The space is small and intimate, and anyone who's anyone in the jazz scene plays here when they're in town. Sets happen Thursday to Sunday nights; there's usually a cover charge of $15 to $20.

X&Y Bar   ECLECTIC
(Map p296; ☎3257 1259; www.xandybar.com.au; 648 Ann St, Fortitude Valley) This welcoming

and unpretentious bar aims to attract an eclectic crowd owing to its nondiscriminatory door policy. It features a mix of live music (mostly indie rock) and DJs, and there's always something going on.

Tivoli   ECLECTIC
(☑3852 1711; www.thetivoli.net.au; 52 Costin St, Fortitude Valley) Artists such as Nick Cave and Noel Gallagher have graced the stage at this elegant old art deco venue built in the early 20th century. As it hosts a range of touring acts, you're likely to see quality comedy here too. All tickets are sold through Ticketek.

Cafe Checocho   ACOUSTIC
(Map p298; 69 Hardgrave Rd, West End; ⊙3-10pm Mon, 10am-10pm Tue-Sat; ☎) Serving up chess, coffee and chocolate (che-co-cho), this charming, lived-in cafe also has live music most nights (jazz, blues, world).

Music Kafe   ROCK
(Map p298; www.themusickafe.com; 185 Boundary St, West End) Live music most days with blues, rock, jazz and folk, plus open-mic nights (currently Wednesdays).

Cinemas

There are open-air movies screened over summer in the South Bank Parklands and in New Farm Park.

Palace Centro   CINEMA
(Map p296; www.palacecinemas.com.au; 39 James St, Fortitude Valley) In the Valley, Palace Centre screens art-house films and has a Greek film festival at the end of November.

Palace Barracks   CINEMA
(Map p292; www.palacecinemas.com.au; Petrie Tce) Near Roma St Station, the Palace

shows a mix of Hollywood and alternative fare.

South Bank Cinema   CINEMA
(Map p282; www.cineplex.com.au; cnr Grey & Ernest Sts, South Bank) The cheapest cinema for mainstream flicks; tickets cost about a third less than at other places.

Brisbane City Myer Centre   CINEMA
(Map p284; Level 3, Myer Centre) On Queen St Mall; also shows mainstream blockbusters.

Performing Arts

Brisbane is well stocked with theatre venues, most of them located at South Bank. For bookings at the Queensland Performing Arts Centre and all South Bank theatres, contact **Qtix** (☑13 62 46; www.qtix.com.au).

Queensland Performing Arts Centre   THEATRE, LIVE MUSIC
(QPAC; Map p282; ☑3840 7444; www.qpac.com.au; Cultural Centre, Grey St, South Bank) This centre consists of three venues and features concerts, plays, dance and performances of all genres. Catch anything from flamenco to *West Side Story* revivals.

Brisbane Powerhouse   THEATRE, LIVE MUSIC
(Map p290; ☑3358 8600; www.brisbanepowerhouse.org; 119 Lamington St, New Farm) The former 1940 power station continues to bring electricity to the city – albeit in the form of nationally acclaimed theatre, music and dance productions. There are loads of happenings at the Powerhouse – many free – and the venue, with its several bar-restaurants, enjoys a beautiful setting overlooking the Brisbane River.

GAY & LESBIAN BRISBANE

While Brisbane can't compete with the prolific gay and lesbian scenes in Sydney and Melbourne, what you'll find here is quality rather than quantity.

Most action, centred in Fortitude Valley, is covered by the fortnightly Q News (www.qnews.com.au). Queensland Pride (www.queenslandpride.gaynewsnetwork.com.au), another gay publication, takes in the whole of the state.

Major events on the year's calendar include the Queer Film Festival (www.bqff.com.au), held in April, which showcases gay, lesbian, bisexual and transgender films and videos; and the Brisbane Pride Festival (www.pridebrisbane.org.au) in June. Pride attracts up to 25,000 people every year, and peaks during the parade held mid-festival.

Brisbane's most popular gay and lesbian venue is the Wickham Hotel (Map p296; cnr Wickham & Alden Sts, Fortitude Valley), a classic old Victorian pub with good dance music, drag shows and dancers. The Wickham celebrates the Sydney Mardi Gras and the Pride Festival in style and grandeur.

Other good options include gay-friendly **Beat MegaClub** (p298) and the popular club **Family** (p297), which hosts 'Fluffy', Brisbane's biggest gay dance party, on Sundays. Sportsman's Hotel (Map p284; 130 Leichhardt St, Spring Hill) is another fantastically popular gay venue, with a different theme or show for each night of the week.

Queensland Conservatorium   LIVE MUSIC
(Map p282; ☎3735 6111; www.griffith.edu.au/concerts; 140 Grey St, South Bank; ☻Mar-Oct) Located south of the Queensland Performing Arts Centre, the Conservatorium hosts opera, as well as national and international artists playing classical, jazz, rock and world music. Many concerts that are held at the conservatorium are free.

Metro Arts Centre   THEATRE
(Map p284; ☎3002 7100; www.metroarts.com.au; Level 2, 109 Edward St) This progressive venue hosts community theatre, local dramatic pieces, dance and art shows.

QUT Gardens Theatre   THEATRE
(Map p284; ☎3138 4455; www.gardenstheatre.qut.com; QUT, 2 George St) This university theatre plays host to touring national and international productions as well as performances from the university's dramatic, musical and dance companies.

Brisbane Arts Theatre   THEATRE
(Map p292; ☎3369 2344; www.artstheatre.com.au; 210 Petrie Tce) Amateur theatre performances along the lines of Shakespeare and Dickens are held here.

Sit Down Comedy Club   COMEDY
(Map p292; ☎3369 4466; www.standup.com.au; Paddo Tavern, Given Tce, Paddington) There are a few comedy venues, the most prominent being this well-established one at the Paddo Tavern.

Sport

Like most other Australians, Brisbanites are sports-mad. You can see interstate cricket matches and international test cricket at the Gabba (Brisbane Cricket Ground; Map p280; www.thegabba.org.au; 411 Vulture St) in Woolloongabba, south of Kangaroo Point. If you're new to the game, try and get along to a 20/20 match, which is cricket in its most explosive form. The cricket season runs from October to March.

During the other half of the year, rugby league is the big spectator sport. The Brisbane Broncos play home games at Suncorp Stadium (Map p292; www.suncorpstadium.com.au; 40 Castlemaine St, Paddington).

Once dominated by Victorian teams, the Australian Football League (AFL) has been challenged by the Brisbane Lions (www.lions.com.au), who have tasted success in recent years. You can watch them live at a home game at the Gabba between March and September. Queensland's newest AFL team, the Gold Coast Suns (www.goldcoastfc.com), took to the field in 2011. Their home games are held in Metricon Stadium in the Gold Coast suburb of Carrara.

🛍 Shopping

Brisbane is home to splendid riverside markets, eye-catching boutiques and galleries, and one-of-a-kind shops selling everything from indie fashions to indigenous artwork, with vintage apparel, new and used books, rare vinyl and much more.

Paddington Antique Centre ANTIQUES
(167 Latrobe Tce, Paddington) The city's biggest antique emporium houses over 50 dealers selling all manner of treasure/trash from the past. Clothes, jewellery, dolls, books, artwork, lamps, musical instruments, toys and more.

Blonde Venus CLOTHING
(Map p296; 707 Ann St, Fortitude Valley) One of the top boutiques in Brisbane, Blonde Venus has been around for 20-plus years, stocking a well-curated selection of both indie and couture labels. Other great boutiques line this street.

Record Exchange MUSIC
(Map p284; Level 1, 65 Adelaide St, Brisbane) Record Exchange is home to an astounding collection of vinyl, plus CDs, DVDs, posters and other memorabilia.

Archives Fine Books BOOKS
(Map p284; 40 Charlotte St) You could get lost in here for hours, with its fantastic range of secondhand books.

Avid Reader BOOKS
(Map p298; www.avidreader.com.au; 193 Boundary St, West End) Diverse selection, excellent cafe and frequent readings and other events.

Folio Books BOOKS
(Map p284; www.foliobooks.com.au; 80 Albert St) Small bookshop with eclectic offerings.

World Wide Maps & Guides BOOKS
(Map p284; Shop 30, Anzac Sq Arcade, 267 Edward St; ⊙closed Sun) Good assortment of travel guides and maps.

ℹ Information

Emergency
Ambulance (⌨000, 1300 369 003)

Fire (⌨000, 3247 5539)

Lifeline (⌨13 11 14)

Police (⌨000) City (⌨3224 4444; 67 Adelaide St); Headquarters (⌨3364 6464; 200 Roma St); Fortitude Valley (⌨3131 1200; Brunswick St Mall)

RACQ (⌨13 19 05, breakdown 13 11 11) City (GPO Bldg, 261 Queen St); St Pauls Tce (300 St Pauls Tce) Roadside service.

Internet Access

Wireless internet access is widely available at many hotels and cafes in the city, though it's rarely free.

State Library of Queensland (South Bank; ⊙10am-8pm Mon-Thu, to 5pm Fri-Sun; 🛜) Quick 20-minute terminals or free wi-fi.

Brisbane Square Library (266 George St; 🛜) Free internet terminals and wi-fi access.

Medical Services
Pharmacy on the Mall (141 Queen St)

Royal Brisbane & Women's Hospital (⌨3636 8111; cnr Butterfield St & Bowen Bridge Rd, Herston; ⊙24hr casualty ward)

Travel Clinic (⌨1300 369 359, 3211 3611; 1st fl, 245 Albert St)

Travellers' Medical & Vaccination Centre (TMVC; ⌨3815 6900; 75 Astor Tce, Spring Hill)

Money
There are foreign-exchange bureaus at Brisbane Airport's domestic and international terminals, as well as ATMs. ATMs are prolific throughout Brisbane.

American Express (⌨1300 139 060; Shop 3, 156 Adelaide St)

Travelex (⌨3210 6325; Shop 149f, Myer Centre, Queen St Mall)

Post
Australia Post (⌨13 13 18; 261 Queen St; ⊙7am-6pm Mon-Fri) Has poste restante.

Tourist Information
Brisbane Visitor Information Centre (Map p284; ⌨3006 6290; Queen St Mall; ⊙9am-5.30pm Mon-Thu, to 7pm Fri, to 4.30pm Sat, 9.30am-4pm Sun) Located between Edward and Albert streets. Great one-stop info counter for all things Brisbane.

Queensland Parks & Wildlife (⌨1300 130 372; Level 3, 400 George St; ⊙8.30am-4.30pm Mon-Fri) Pick up maps, brochures and books on national parks and state forests, as well as camping information and Fraser Island permits.

South Bank Visitors Centre (Map p282; www.visitsouthbank.com.au; Stanley St Plaza, South Bank Parklands; ⊙9am-5pm)

BRISBANE OPEN AIR

For six weeks in March and April each year, the South Bank Parklands hosts **Brisbane Open Air** (www.brisbaneopenair.com.au), which brings a line-up of film screenings and live bands to the Rainforest Green. Live acoustic or DJ sets kick off around 5.45pm, with films starting at dusk, around 6.45pm. Buy tickets online to avoid sell-outs and arrive early to snag a seat. Food and alcohol are sold at stands on the green.

MARKET-LOVERS' GUIDE TO BRISBANE

James St Market
FOOD

(Map p296; James St, Fortitude Valley; ⊘8.30am-6pm) Paradise for gourmands, this small but beautifully stocked market has gourmet cheeses, a bakery/patisserie, fruits, vegetables, and lots of gourmet goodies. The fresh seafood counter serves excellent sushi and sashimi.

Jan Power's Farmers Market
FOOD

(Map p290; Brisbane Powerhouse, 119 Lamington St, New Farm; ⊘7am-noon every 2nd & 4th Sat of the month) Don't miss this excellent and deservedly popular farmers' market if it's on when you're in town: over 120 stalls selling fresh produce, local wines, jams, juices, snacks (waffles, sausages, desserts, coffees) and much more. The Citycat takes you there.

West End Markets
FOOD

(Map p298; Davies Park, cnr Montague Rd & Jane St; ⊘6am-2pm Sat) This sprawling flea market has loads of fresh produce, herbs, flowers, organic foodstuffs, clothing and bric-a-brac. It's an apt representation of the diverse West End and a good place for noshing, with stalls selling a wide range of cuisines; there's also live music in the park.

South Bank Lifestyle markets
FOOD

(Map p282; Stanley St Plaza, South Bank; ⊘5-10pm Fri, 10am-5pm Sat, 9am-5pm Sun) These popular markets have a great range of clothing, craft, art, handmade goods and souvenirs.

ℹ Getting There & Away

For more details on planes, trains and buses, see p277. The Brisbane Transit Centre (Map p284), 500m northwest of the city centre, is the main terminus and booking point for all long-distance buses and trains, as well as train services.

Air

Brisbane's main airport is about 16km northeast of the city centre, and has separate international and domestic terminals almost 3km apart, linked by the **Airtrain** (www.airtrain.com.au; tickets $5), which runs every 15 to 30 minutes.

Bus

Bus companies have booking desks on the 3rd level of the Roma St Transit Centre. **Greyhound Australia** (☑1300 473 946; www.greyhound.com.au) and **Premier Motor Service** (☑13 34 10; www.premierms.com.au) are the big carriers. The Sydney–Brisbane run costs between $90 and $200, and takes 16 to 17 hours.

Sample times and prices heading north:

DESTINATION	DURATION	ONE-WAY FARE
Cairns	29-34hr	$310-360
Hervey Bay	5½hr	$50-75
Noosa Heads	2½hr	$21-35
Mackay	16½-22hr	$200-230
Rockhampton	11-14hr	$138-170
Townsville	23hr	$265-300

Car & Motorcycle

There are five major routes, numbered from M1 to M5, into and out of the Brisbane metropolitan area. If you're just passing through, take the Gateway Motorway (M1) at Eight Mile Plains, which bypasses the city centre to the east and crosses the Brisbane River at the Gateway Bridge ($3 toll).

HIRE All of the major companies – **Hertz** (☑13 30 39), **Avis** (☑13 63 33), **Budget** (☑1300 362 848), **Europcar** (☑13 13 90) and **Thrifty** (☑1300 367 227) – have offices at the Brisbane Airport terminals and throughout the city.

Smaller rental companies in Brisbane:

Abel Rent A Car (☑1300 13 14 29; 3832 3666; www.abel.com.au; Roma St Transit Centre)

Ace Rental Cars (☑1800 620 408; www.acerentals.com.au; 330 Nudgee Rd, Hendra)

East Coast Car Rentals (☑1800 028 881; www.eastcoastcarrentals.com.au; 76 Wickham St, Fortitude Valley)

Train

Brisbane's main station for long-distance trains is the Brisbane Transit Centre. For reservations and information, visit the **Queensland Rail Travel Centre** (☑13 16 17; www.queenslandrail.com.au) Central Station (Ground fl, Central Station, 305 Edward St); Roma St (Roma St Transit Centre).

Long-distance services:

CountryLink (☑13 22 32; www.countrylink.nsw.gov.au) Has a daily service between Brisbane and Sydney (economy/1st class $92/130,

14½ hours). Northbound services run overnight; southbound services run during the day.

Spirit of the Outback (economy seat/economy sleeper/1st-class sleeper $190/250/385, 24 hours) Brisbane–Longreach via Rockhampton ($190/250/385, 10 hours) twice weekly.

Sunlander ($219/279/430, 31 hours) Departs Tuesday, Thursday and Sunday for Cairns via Townsville.

Tilt Train (business $328, 24 hours) Brisbane–Cairns train leaves Brisbane at 6.25pm Monday and Friday, returning from Cairns at 9.15am Wednesday and Sunday.

❶ Getting Around

Car & Motorcycle

Brisbane's peak hour is a very bad time to drive. There is free two-hour parking on many streets in the CBD and in the inner suburbs, but the major thoroughfares become clearways (ie parking is prohibited) during the morning and afternoon rush hours. Parking is free in the CBD during the evening.

Public Transport

Brisbane boasts an excellent public transport network. Obtain bus, train and ferry info at the **Transit Information Centre** (Map p284; www.translink.com.au; cnr Ann & Albert Sts).

Fares on buses, trains and ferries operate on a zone system. There are 23 zones in total, but the city centre and most of the inner-city suburbs fall within Zone 1, which means most fares will be $3.90/2 per adult/child. To save money (around 30% off individual fares), purchase a **Go Card** ($5), which is sold (and recharged) at transit stations and newsagents.

BOAT The 2011 Brisbane Flood damaged a number of pontoons and ferry terminals along the Brisbane River. Limited CityCat and City Ferry services resumed operating soon after but many ferry terminals remained off-line at the time of research. It is anticipated most, if not all, services will be operating by mid-late 2011. Check with **TransLink** (☑13 12 30; www.translink.com.au) for updates to services and timetables.

Resumption of normal services would see the blue CityCat catamarans run every 20 to 30 minutes between 5.45am and 11pm between University of Queensland in the west and Bretts Wharf in the east. Stops include North Quay (for Queen St Mall), South Bank, Riverside (for the CBD) and New Farm Park.

The Inner City Ferries zigzag back and forth across the river between North Quay, near the Victoria Bridge, and Mowbray Park. There are also several cross-river ferries; most useful is the Eagle St Pier to Thornton St (Kangaroo Point) service.

Like all public transport, fares are based on zones. Most stops you'll need will be city-based and therefore in Zone 1.

BUS The Loop, a free bus that circles the city area and stops at QUT, the Queen St Mall, City Hall, Central Station and Riverside, runs every 10 minutes on weekdays between 7am and 6pm.

The main stop for local buses is in the basement of the Myer Centre. You can also pick up most of the useful buses from the colour-coded stops along Adelaide St, between George and Edward Sts.

Useful buses include 195, 196, 197 and 199 to Fortitude Valley and New Farm, which leave from Adelaide St between King George Sq and Edward Sts.

TRAIN The fast TransLink network has seven lines, which run as far as Nambour, Cooroy and Gympie in the north (for the Sunshine Coast), and Nerang and Robina in the south (for the Gold Coast). Other useful routes include Rosewood (for Ipswich) and Cleveland (for the North Stradbroke Island ferry).

The **Airtrain** (www.airtrain.com.au) service integrates with the TransLink network in the CBD and along the Gold Coast line. All trains go through the Brisbane Transit Centre and Central Station in the city, and Brunswick St Station in Fortitude Valley.

Trains run from around 4.30am until about 11.30pm (10pm on Sundays).

MORETON BAY ISLANDS

The patch of water lapping at Brisbane's urban edges is packed full of marine life including whales, dolphins and dugongs. Moreton Bay also has a bunch of startlingly beautiful islands that are very accessible from the mainland. North Stradbroke Island, with its nonchalant holiday air, and Moreton Island, a stunning patch of wilderness on Brisbane's doorstep, are two of the best.

North Stradbroke Island

Brisbanites are lucky to have such a brilliant holiday island on their doorstep. A mere 30-minute ferry ride from Brisbane's seaside suburb of Cleveland, this sand island has a string of glorious powdery white-sand beaches. Inland are two glittering lakes carved out of the surrounding bushland, and back along the coast quality accommodation and dining options await.

Sights & Activities

Straddie's best beaches for both surfing and swimming are around Point Lookout, where there's a series of points and bays around the headland and long stretches of white sand.

If you're not so keen on the surf, there are some great walks, including the scenic 30-minute saunter around the North Gorge, on the headland at Point Lookout; porpoises, dolphins, manta rays and in season (June to November) whales can be spotted from up here. Straddie also has some inland lakes worth exploring. If you don't have your own vehicle, you can take a tour or hire a bike, but be warned that there are some punishing hills. Both Brown Lake and Blue Lake are accessed via the sealed Mining Company Rd from Dunwich. The turn-off to Brown Lake is reached first after about 3km; the lake is a short distance down a dirt track. The water is indeed brown, and shallow to boot, but it's a decent spot for a picnic and popular with young families.

Blue Lake, accessed from a car park a further 5km along the road, is a different proposition altogether. The centrepiece of Blue Lake National Park, it's reached via a beautiful and winding 2.1km walking track. The lake itself is small, crystal clear and very deep – the bottom drops away quickly and a little alarmingly right by the shore – but it's a serene and very beautiful spot.

The eastern beach, known as Eighteen Mile Beach, is open to 4WD vehicles and campers and finishes up at the popular fishing spot of Jumpinpin on the island's southern tip. Straddie Super Sports (☎3409 9252; Bingle Rd) hires out fishing gear from $25 per day. Manta Lodge & Scuba Centre (☎3409 8888; www.mantalodge.com.au; 1 East Coast Rd), based at the YHA, offers snorkelling for $85 inclusive of a two-hour boat trip; two-tank dives run $185.

Straddie Adventures (☎3409 8414; www.straddieadventures.com.au; 112 East Coast Rd, Point Lookout) offers sea-kayaking trips (including snorkelling stops $60) around Straddie, and sandboarding ($30), which is like snowboarding, except on sand.

Tours

A number of tour companies offer tours of the island. Generally the 4WD tours take in a strip of the eastern beach and several freshwater lakes.

North Stradbroke Island 4WD Tours & Camping Holidays 4WD
(☎3409 8051; straddie@ecn.net.au) Generally, half-day tours cost $35/20 per adult/child.

Straddie Kingfisher Tours 4WD, FISHING
(☎3409 9502; www.straddiekingfishertours.com.au; adult/child $79/59) Operates six-hour 4WD and fishing tours; also has whale-watching tours in season.

Sleeping

Most accommodation is at Point Lookout, which is strung along 3km of coastline on the northern shore of the island.

Pandanus Palms Resort APARTMENTS $$
(☎3409 8106; www.pandanus.stradbrokeresorts.com.au; 21 Cumming Pde; apt $245-315; ☷) Perched high above the beach, with a thick tumble of vegetation beneath, the large two-bed townhouses here are a good size and boast modern furnishings; the best face the ocean, with private yards and barbecues. Excellent restaurant on-site.

Straddie Views B&B $$
(☎3409 8875; www.northstradbrokeisland.com/straddiebb; 26 Cumming Pde; r from $150) Several spacious and comfortably furnished suites are available in this friendly B&B run by a Straddie couple. Breakfast is served on the upstairs deck with fantastic water views.

Stradbroke Island Beach Hotel HOTEL $$
(☎3409 8188; www.stradbrokeislandbeachhotel.com.au; East Coast Rd; d $230-310; ☒☷) Straddie's only hotel has an intriguing modern design, with 12 cool, inviting rooms in muted colour schemes, each with high-end fixtures and a balcony. The open bar downstairs with outdoor beer garden is a delight, and there's also a restaurant and spa.

Anchorage on Straddie APARTMENTS $$
(☎3409 8266; www.anchorage.stradbrokeresorts.com.au; East Coast Rd; 2 nights $235-400; ☷) The friendly managers of these large self-contained apartments with balconies keep the place shipshape and there's a boardwalk from the hotel grounds straight to the beach. For sea views, ask for a room on the third level.

Manta Lodge YHA HOSTEL $
(☎3409 8888; www.mantalodge.com.au; 1 East Coast Rd; dm/d $30/78; @☷) This large well-kept hostel near the beach has excellent facilities, including a dive school on the doorstep. There are four-, six- and eight-bed dorms and the owners are happy to close off

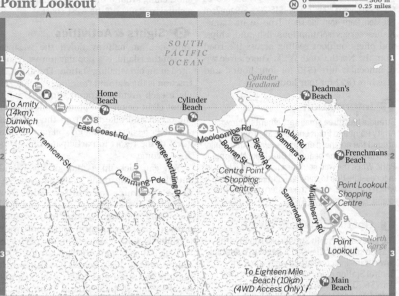

small dorms to couples or friends who don't want to share, and just charge a bit extra.

Straddie Holiday Parks　　CAMPGROUND **$**
(☑1300 551 253; unpowered/powered sites $35/40, cabins $109-165) There are seven camping grounds on the island operated by this outfit, but the most attractive are those grouped around Point Lookout. The **Adder** **Rock Camping Area** and the **Thankful Rest Camping Area** both overlook lovely Home Beach, while the **Cylinder Beach Camping Area** sits right on one of the island's most popular beaches. There are also several cheaper sites (from $15 per night) accessible by 4WD only. Book well in advance.

✗ Eating

There are a couple of general stores selling groceries in Point Lookout, but it's worth bringing basic supplies.

TOP **Amis**　　MODERN AUSTRALIAN **$$**
CHOICE
(☑3409 8600; 21 Cummings Pde, Pandanus Palms Resort; mains $28-36; ☺dinner Wed-Sun) Combining north African and Asian accents with fresh local produce, Amis is one of Straddie's best. Standouts include Queensland kangaroo loin fillet, chargrilled prawns on bamboo, fish of the day and crispy duck confit.

Look　　MODERN AUSTRALIAN **$$**
(☑3415 3390; 29 Mooloomba Rd; lunch mains $12-18, dinner mains $25-30; ☺breakfast & lunch daily, dinner Thu-Sat) This seems to be the hub of Point Lookout during the day, with funky tunes in the background and great outdoor seating with breezy water views. It's an elegant but relaxed affair.

BRISBANE & THE GOLD COAST NORTH STRADBROKE ISLAND

Fishes SEAFOOD **$$**
(15 Mooloomba Rd; mains $15-20; ⊙9am-7pm Sat-Mon, 9am-4pm Tue-Thu) True to its name, Fishes serves scrumptious fish and chips, and offers outdoor seating across the road from the North Gorge Walk. There's free wi-fi, binocular hire ($10 for four hours) and bike hire ($22 for four hours).

ℹ Information

Straddie has three small settlements, Dunwich, Amity Point and Point Lookout, all grouped around the northern end of the island. In the hilly central area is the beautiful Blue Lake National Park. While the wild southern half of the island is inaccessible due to mining, Eighteen Mile Beach, which runs clear down the eastern edge of the island, is accessible to 4WDs.

ℹ Getting There & Away

The gateway to North Stradbroke Island is the seaside suburb of Cleveland. Regular **TransLink** (www.translink.com.au) services run from Central Station or Roma St to Cleveland station ($6.70, one hour) and buses to the ferry terminals meet the trains at Cleveland station (10 minutes).

Stradbroke Ferries (☑3488 5300; www. stradbrokeferries.com.au) operates to Dunwich almost every hour from about 6am to 6pm ($19 return, 25 minutes). It also has a slightly less frequent vehicle ferry (per vehicle including passengers return $135, 40 minutes).

Gold Cat Stradbroke Flyer (☑3286 1964; www.flyer.com.au) runs an almost-hourly catamaran service from Cleveland to One Mile Jetty ($19 return, 25 minutes), 1km north of central Dunwich.

ℹ Getting Around

Local buses (☑3409 7151) meet the ferries at Dunwich and One Mile Jetty and run across to Point Lookout ($9.50 return). The last bus to Dunwich leaves Point Lookout at about 6.45pm, later on Friday.

Moreton Island

You don't need to head north to find a patch of island paradise in Queensland. Thick foliage tumbles down to white-sand beaches along the coast of Moreton Island. Largely undeveloped, most of the island is national park with walking trails, and the bird life is prolific. The water itself is a patchy jade and indigo colour, and once you're in it, crystal clear, as you'll discover if you go diving or snorkelling around the Tangalooma Wrecks, a shipwreck just off the west coast.

◉ Sights & Activities

Tangalooma, halfway down the western side of the island, is a popular tourist resort sited at an old whaling station. The main attraction is the **dolphin feeding**, which takes place each evening around sunset. Usually about eight or nine dolphins swim in from the ocean and take fish from the hands of volunteer feeders. Although you have to be a guest of the resort to participate, onlookers are welcome.

You can pick up a map of the island showing walking trails at the **Marine Research & Education Centre**, which has a display on the diverse marine and bird life of Moreton Bay. Walking trails include a desert trail (two hours) and a bushwalk (1½ hours), both leaving from the resort, as well as a longer walk to Water Point (four hours) on the East Coast. It's also worth making the strenuous trek to the summit of Mt Tempest, 3km inland from Eagers Creek, but you'll need transport to get to the start.

Several rental outfits in the resort hire out snorkelling gear so you can explore the Tangalooma Wrecks. If you prefer to view things from on top of the water, you'll also find kayaks and catamarans for hire.

About 3km south and inland from Tangalooma is an area of bare sand known as the **Desert**, while the **Big Sandhills** and the **Little Sandhills** are towards the narrow southern end of the island. The biggest lakes and some swamps are in the northeast.

⎔ Tours

Tangatours (Tangalooma Wild Dolphin Resort; ☑1300 652 250, 3637 2000; www.tangalooma. com) Offers 1½-hour snorkelling trips around the Tangalooma Wrecks ($35) and diving trips.

Micat (☑3909 3397; www.micat.com.au; 1-day tours adult/child from $155/95, 2-day camping tours from $299) Offers tours of the island with heaps of activities thrown in, including snorkelling, sand-boarding and bushwalking.

Moreton Bay Escapes (☑1300 559 355; www.moretonbayescapes.com.au; 1-day tours adult/child from $165/125, 2-day camping tours $249/149) Runs similar itineraries to Moreton Bay Escapes.

Sunrover Expeditions (📞1800 353 717, 3203 4241; www.sunrover.com.au; adult/child $120/100) A friendly and reliable 4WD-tour operator with good day and camping tours.

🛏 Sleeping

There are a few holiday flats and houses for rent at Kooringal, Cowan Cowan and Bulwer. To browse listings, go to www.moreton island.com.au.

Tangalooma Wild Dolphin Resort
HOTEL, APARTMENTS $$$

(📞1300 652 250, 3637 2000; www.tangalooma. com; 1-night package from $310; ❄@☰) This beautifully sited but ageing resort is the only formal set-up on the island. There's a plethora of options available, starting with pretty bland hotel-style rooms. A step up are the units and suites, where you'll get beachside access and rooms kitted out in cool, contemporary decor with good facilities. Look for online deals through www.wotif.com. The resort has several eating options.

National Park camping grounds
CAMPGROUND

(DERM office 📞1300 130 372; level 3, 400 George St, Brisbane CBD; sites per person/family $6/21) There are 10 national park camping grounds, all with water, toilets and cold showers; of these, five are on the beach. For information and camping permits, book online (www.derm.qld.gov.au), contact the Brisbane DERM office or call 📞13 74 68. Camping permits must be arranged before you get to the island.

ℹ Information

Apart from the Tangalooma resort, the only other settlements are Bulwer near the northwestern tip, Cowan Cowan between Bulwer and Tangalooma, and Kooringal near the southern tip. The shops at Kooringal and Bulwer can be expensive, so bring what you can from the mainland.

ℹ Getting There & Around

Boat

A number of ferries operate from the mainland. The **Tangalooma Flyer** (📞3268 6333; www. tangalooma.com/tangalooma/transport; per adult/child return day trip $40/25, or from $80/40), a fast catamaran operated by the resort, sails to the resort on Moreton Island daily from a dock at Holt St, off Kingsford Smith Dr (in Eagle Farm). A bus ($10) to the flyer departs from the Roma St Transit Centre at 9am. You can use the bus for a day trip (it returns at 9am

and 4pm daily as well as at 2pm on Saturday and Sunday) or for camping drop-offs. Bookings are necessary. The trip takes 1¼ hours.

The **Moreton Venture** (📞3909 3333; www. moretonventure.com; adult/child/vehicle & 2 passengers return $50/35/190; ⏱8.30am Wed-Mon) is a vehicle ferry that runs from Howard-Smith Dr, Lyton, at the Port of Brisbane, to Tangalooma. It leaves the island at 3.30pm daily, as well as at 10.30am on Friday, and 1pm and 4.30pm on Sunday. On Tuesday it travels to and from Bulwer.

The new vehicle ferry **Amity Trader** (📞0487 227 437; www.amitytrader.com; vehicle & passengers return $100) sails between Amity and Kooringal on Moreton Island's southern tip. Call for times and to reserve a spot.

Car & Motorcycle

Moreton Island has no paved roads, but 4WD vehicles can travel along the beaches and a few cross-island tracks – seek local advice about tides and creek crossings before venturing out. You can get Queensland Parks & Wildlife Service (QPWS) maps from the vehicle-ferry offices or the Information desk at the Marine Research & Education Centre at Tangalooma. Vehicle permits for the island cost $40 and are available through the ferry operators, online (www.derm. qld.gov.au) or at a DERM office (in Brisbane: level 3, 400 George St). Note that ferry bookings are *mandatory* if you want to take a vehicle across.

GOLD COAST

Behind the long, unbroken ribbon of sand of some of the world's best surfing beaches is a shimmering strip of high-rises, eateries, bars and theme parks that attracts a perpetual stream of sun-loving holidaymakers. The undisputed capital is Surfers Paradise where the dizzying fun sucks you into a relentless spin and spits you back out exhausted. But the brash commercialism and nonstop pace won't appeal to everyone. The hype diminishes drastically outside the epicentre, Broadbeach's beach-chic and Burleigh Heads' seaside charm mellowing into Coolangatta's laid-back surfer ethos.

Southport & Main Beach

📞07 / POP 24,100

Sheltered from the ocean by a long sandbar, known as the Spit, and the Broadwater estuary, Southport is a relatively quiet residential enclave 4km north of Surfers Paradise. There's not much to do here and it's a long way from the beach but it can be a good base if you want to escape the frenzy of Surfers.

Main Beach, just south of Southport, marks the gateway to the Spit and the high-rise tourist developments. The Spit runs 3km north, dividing the Broadwater from the South Pacific Ocean. The ocean side of the Spit is relatively untouched, backed by a long strip of natural bushland, and has excellent beaches and surf. At the southern end of the Spit is the Sea World theme park, while the upmarket shopping complex of Marina Mirage is near Mariner's Cove and the marina, the departure point for cruises and other water-based activities.

🏃 Activities

Mariner's Cove is the place to book all water activities. The easiest way to sift through the plethora of operators is to book at the **Mariner's Cove Tourism Information & Booking Centre** (☎5571 1711; Mariner's Cove; ☻8.30am-4.30pm). There are several recommended activities companies:

Australian Kayaking Adventures KAYAKING
(☎0412 940 135; www.australiankayakingadventures.com.au; half-day tours to South Stradbroke Island $85)

GC Hovercraft Tours & Watersports
HOVERCRAFT RIDES
(☎1300 559 931; www.goldcoasthovercraft.com; 30min ride adult/child/family $55/40/150, 45min ride $60/45/170)

Gold Coast Helitours HELICOPTER FLIGHTS
(☎5591 8457; www.goldcoasthelitours.com.au; Mariner's Cove Marina) Range of heli flights. Opt to skydive from 10,000ft.

Jet Ski Safaris JETSKIING
(☎5526 3111; www.jetskisafaris.com.au) Tours from 40 minutes ($70) to 2½ hours ($160) around islands and mangroves; overnight camping ($325) on South Stradbroke Island.

Paradise Jet Boating JETBOATING
(☎1300 538 2621, 5526 3190; Mariner's Cove Marina; 45min rides $63) Serious speed, spins and beach-blasting on a jet boat reaching 85km/h.

Tall Ship SAILING
(☎5532 2444; www.tallship.com.au; Mariner's Cove Marina; full-day cruises adult/child from $129/79) Cruises to South Stradbroke Island on yachts dressed up to look like tall ships. Combine parasailing with a tall-ship experience for $50.

🛶 Tours

Broadwater Canal Cruises RIVER CRUISE
(☎0410 403 020; Mariner's Cove; 2hr cruise adult/child $35/18; ☻10.30am & 2pm) Cruises to Tiki Village Wharf in Surfers Paradise.

Wyndham Cruises RIVER CRUISE
(☎5539 9299; www.wyndhamcruises.com.au; 2hr cruise adult/child/family $45/25/115) Cruise around the Broadwater.

🛏 Sleeping

Palazzo Versace RESORT $$$
(☎1800 098 000, 5509 8000; www.palazzoversace.com; Sea World Dr, Main Beach; d $480-585, ste/condos from $685/1300; ❄@☰) The Palazzo is quite simply pure extravagance, from the sumptuous rooms to the equally indulgent restaurants and bars. Everything, from the pool furniture to the buttons on the staff uniforms, has Donatella Versace's glamorous mark on it.

Sheraton Mirage Resort & Spa RESORT $$$
(☎1800 073 535, 5591 1488; www.starwoodhotels.com/sheraton; Sea World Dr, Main Beach; d from $215, ste $500-650; ❄@☰) If you must have direct beach access this is the only five-star resort on the coast that will do. The rooms are classy and spacious. Spa aficionados will get their fix at the Golden Door Spa & Health Club at Mirage Resort.

Harbour Side Resort MOTEL $$
(☎5591 6666; www.harboursideresort.com.au; 132 Marine Pde, Southport; studio $90, 1-/2-bedroom apt $120/160; ❄@☰) Disregard the overwhelming brick facade and busy road; within this sprawling property you will find pastel-hued units with oodles of room. The kitchens are very well equipped and the complex also has a laundry and tennis courts.

Surfers Paradise YHA at Main Beach
HOSTEL $
(☎5571 1776; www.yha.com.au/hostels; 70 Sea World Dr, Main Beach; dm/d & tw $25/$69.50; @) In a great position overlooking the marina, here you only have to drop over the balcony to access the plethora of water sports, cruises and tours on offer. There's a free shuttle bus, barbecue nights every Friday, and the hostel is within staggering distance of the Fisherman's Wharf Tavern.

Also recommended:

Trekkers HOSTEL $
(☎1800 100 004, 5591 5616; www.trekkersbackpackers.com.au; 22 White St, Southport; dm/d &

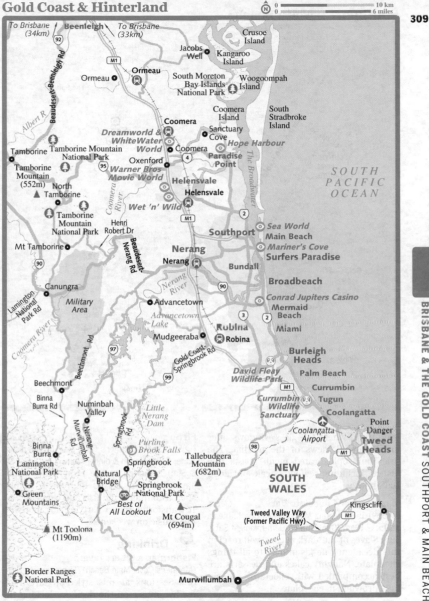

tw \$27/70; @⏰) A friendly, homey hostel in a quiet street.

Main Beach Tourist Park CARAVAN PARK **\$\$**
(☎5667 2720; www.gctp.com.au/main; Main Beach Pde, Main Beach; unpowered/powered sites from \$33/36, cabins from \$140; ❄⏰) Popular with families.

✖ Eating

The cheapest place to eat is the food court in the Australia Fair Shopping Centre.

Saks ITALIAN **\$\$\$**
(☎5591 2755; Marina Mirage, 74 Sea World Dr, Main Beach; mains \$30-50; ⏱lunch & dinner) Head straight for the deck in this popular Italian

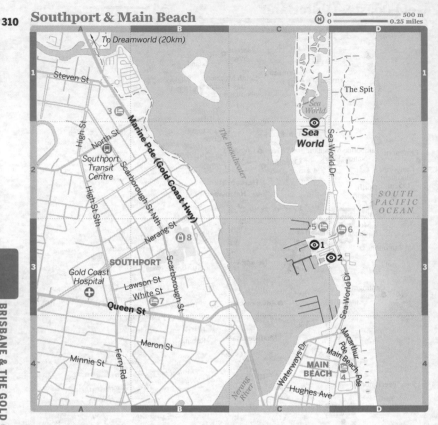

restaurant, where tall glass windows offer uninterrupted views of the marina. The brief but sophisticated menu boasts fine dishes, including seafood, steak and good Italian fare.

Max Brenner Chocolate Bar   CAFE **$**
(📞5591 1588; Marina Mirage, Main Beach; meals $5-15; 🕐10am-10pm Mon-Fri, 9am-midnight Sat & Sun) Slaves of the 'dark master' will revel in this decadent cafe given over to all things chocolate. Naughty cakes and desserts are best accompanied with 'choctails' – mocktails drowned in chocolate.

Sunset Bar & Grill   MODERN AUSTRALIAN **$$**
(📞5528 2622; Marina Mirage, Main Beach; dishes $8-25; 🕐7am-6pm) If your wallet has taken a beating at the exclusive boutiques in the mall, you'll be glad to find this little place right on the water. Steaks, burgers and seafood dishes are all reasonably priced.

Fisho's   SEAFOOD **$**
(📞5571 0566; Mariner's Cove, Main Beach; dishes under $13; 🕐lunch & dinner Mon-Fri, breakfast Sat & Sun) Attached to the Fisherman's Wharf Tavern, Fisho's serves up reliable staples such as burgers, and fish and chips for $15. It transforms into a partying hot spot with live music on weekends.

🍷 Drinking

Fisherman's Wharf Tavern   PUB
(Mariner's Cove, Main Beach) The famous Sunday Sessions at this styled-up tavern offer live music on the deck overlooking the Broadwater.

❶ Getting There & Away

Coaches stop at the Southport Transit Centre on Scarborough St, between North and Railway Sts. Catch local Surfside buses from outside the Australia Fair Shopping Centre on Scarborough St.

South Stradbroke Island

This narrow, 20km-long sand island is largely undeveloped, and a tranquil contrast to the mainland sprawl of the Gold Coast tourist strip. At the northern end, the narrow channel separating it from North Stradbroke Island is popular for fishing, while at the southern end the tip of the Spit is only 200m away. There are two resorts, a camping ground and plenty of bush, sand and sea to satisfy anglers, surfers, bushwalkers and kayakers. Cars aren't permitted on the island so you'll have to walk or cycle to get around.

The **Couran Cove Island Resort** (☑1800 268 726, 5509 3000; www.couran.com; d from $260; ✱✼) is an exclusive luxury resort with all guests' rooms perched on the water's edge. There are four restaurants to choose from, a day spa, a private marina and guided nature walks. Rates don't include ferry transfers (adult/child $50/25 return) from Hope Harbour at the northern end of the Gold Coast. Ferries leave at 11am, 2.30pm and 6pm and return at 9.30am, 1pm, 5pm and 7pm.

For something less extravagant, you can head to the **Couran Point Island Beach Resort** (☑5501 3555; www.couranpoint.com. au; d from $150; ✼), which has colourful and comfortable hotel rooms, and slightly larger units with kitchenettes. All rates include use of nonmotorised facilities but do not include ferry transfers (adult/child $25/10 return). Day-trippers can access the resort facilities (adult/child/family $55/25/150, includes bistro lunch). The ferry leaves Marina Mirage daily at 10am and returns at 4pm.

Surfers Paradise

☑07 / POP 18,510

Sprouting out of the commercial heart of the Gold Coast is the signature high-rise settlement of Surfers Paradise. Here the pace is giddy and frenetic, a brash pleasure dome of nightclubs, shopping and relentless entertainment. Surfers is the acknowledged party hub of the Gold Coast, happily catering to all demographics, from 40-somethings getting squiffy on martinis to Gen Ys dropping pills on the dance floor and schoolies cutting loose on the beach. With so much bling and glitz in your face, be prepared to part with your cash. About the only time you won't is if one of the famous 'meter maids' – pretty young things in gold-lamé bikinis – feeds your expired parking meter.

The density of towering high-rises shades the beach from mid-afternoon so if you're after a suntan or a relaxing beach holiday, head further south.

⊙ Sights

QDeck   LOOKOUT
(☑5582 2713; Q1 Bldg, Hamilton Ave; adult/child/family $19/11/49; ⊙9am-9pm Sun-Thu, to midnight Fri & Sat) Surfers' sights are usually spread across beach towels but for a spectacular 360-degree panorama of the Gold Coast and hinterland zip up to the QDeck. On a clear

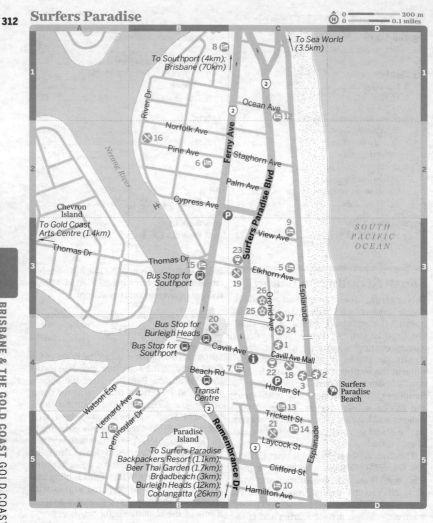

day you can see north to Brisbane and south to Byron Bay.

Infinity   MAZE
(☎5538 2988; www.infinitygc.com.au; Chevron Renaissance, cnr Surfers Paradise Blvd & Elkhorn Ave; adult/child/family $24.90/16.90/69.90; ⏱10am-10pm) The kiddies will like Infinity, a walk-through maze cleverly disguised by an elaborate sound and light show.

Gold Coast Art Gallery   ART GALLERY
(☎5581 6567; www.gcac.com.au; Gold Coast Arts Centre, 135 Bundall Rd; ⏱10am-5pm Mon-Fri, 11am-5pm Sat & Sun) About 1.5km inland,

this gallery displays excellent temporary exhibitions.

🏃 Activities
Surfing & Kayaking
Behind the seemingly impenetrable wall of high-rises, the beach here has enough swell to give beginners a feel for the craft of surfing. Surf schools charge between $40 and $50 for a two-hour lesson.

Brad Holmes Surf Coaching   SURFING
(☎5539 4068, 0418 757 539; www.bradholmes surfcoaching.com; 90min lessons $75)

Cheyne Horan School of Surf SURFING
(☏1800 227 873, 0403 080 484; www.cheyneh
oran.com.au; The Esplanade; 2hr lessons $45)

Go Ride a Wave SURFING
(☏1300 132 441, 5526 7077; www.gorideawave.
com.au; Cavill Ave Mall; surfing & kayaking 2hr
lessons from $55; ⊙9am-5pm)

Splash Safaris Sea Kayaking KAYAKING
(☏0407 741 748; half-day tours $85)

Airborne Activities
Champagne breakfast follows a flight over
the Gold Coast hinterland.

Balloon Aloft BALLOON FLIGHTS
(☏5578 2244; www.balloonaloft.net; 1hr flights
adult/child $310/195)

Balloon Down Under BALLOON FLIGHTS
(☏5593 8400; www.balloondownunder.com.au; 1hr
flights adult/child $310/200)

Adrenalin Action

Movie Stunt Experience STUNTS
(☏0415 999 626; www.moviestuntexperi
ence.com; half-/full day $149/$299; pick up &
drop-off free) You can be an action hero
for the day, choosing whether to abseil
commando-style through windows, fly on
wires, jump from buildings or even be set
on fire.

Jetboat Extreme JETBOATING
(☏5538 8890; www.jetboatextreme.com.au; 1hr
rides adult/child $50/35) Slides and spins
across the water in a turbo-charged, twin-
jet-powered, custom-built jet boat.

Whale-watching

Whales in Paradise WHALE-WATCHING
(☏3880 4455; www.whalesinparadise.com; adult/
child $95/60; Jun-Nov) Leaves central Surfers
for 3½ hours of whale-watching action.

Horse Riding

Gumnuts Horseriding HORSE RIDING
(☏5543 0191; www.gumnutsfarm.com.au; Bid-
daddaba Creek Rd; adult/child $110/75) Damper,
billy tea, lunch and transfers to accommodation throughout the Gold Coast.

Numinbah Valley Adventure Trails
HORSE RIDING
(☏5533 4137; www.numinbahtrails.com; adult/
child $75/65) Three-hour horse-riding treks
through beautiful rainforest and river
scenery in the Numinbah Valley, 30km
south of Nerang.

⌲ Tours
A kitschy way to explore Surfers is on the
AquaDuck (☏5539 0222; www.aquaduck.
com.au; 7a Orchid Ave; adult/child $35/26), a

GOLD COAST IN...

One Day

On day one take your pick of being dunked, rolled or spun a thousand different ways at one of the **Gold Coast theme parks** (p314). After freshening up, and dinner at one of the alfresco restaurants in Circle on Cavill, it's time to hit the party scene big time. Fortunately, nearly all of Surfers' **nightclubs** (p317) are within stumbling distance of each other on Orchid Ave.

Two Days

For water-sports action hit Mariner's Cove at **Main Beach** (p308) but surfers will want to ride the coast's legendary waves at **Burleigh Heads** (p319) or **Coolangatta** (p321). Have lunch at **Oskars** (p320) overlooking Burleigh's beautiful beach, then spend the afternoon getting friendly with Australia's native critters at **Currumbin Wildlife Sanctuary** (p319). Tonight, try your luck at **Jupiters Casino** (p317).

Three Days

On day three take a leisurely drive into the hinterland. To browse the arts and crafts cottage set, head to **Tamborine Mountain** (p314) where a Devonshire tea is mandatory. Serious hikers will prefer the walks in **Springbrook** (p324) or **Lamington National Parks** (p325).

semi-aquatic bus (or a boat on wheels) that moves effortlessly from the road to the river and back again.

You can also access the Gold Coast hinterland with a number of tour operators from Surfers Paradise. See p323 for more information.

✨ Festivals & Events

Big Day Out   MUSIC
(www.bigdayout.com) Huge international music festival in late January.

Quicksilver Pro-Surfing Competition
                                           SURFING
See some of the world's best surfers out on the waves in mid-March.

Surf Life-Saving Championships   SURF LIFE-SAVING
Also in mid-March, expect to see some stupidly fit people running about wearing very little.

Gold Coast International Marathon   MARATHON
In July.

Coolangatta Gold   IRONMAN
October.

Schoolies   SCHOOLIES
Mid-November to mid-December. Generally involves lots of alcohol and unruly behaviour.

🛏 Sleeping

Surfers is riddled with self-contained units. In peak season, rates skyrocket and there's usually a two- or three-night minimum stay. Low-season rates are quoted here.

The **Gold Coast Accommodation Service** (☎5592 0067; www.goldcoastaccommodationservice.com; Shop 1, 1 Beach Rd) can arrange and book accommodation and tours.

Vibe Hotel   BOUTIQUE HOTEL **$$**
TOP CHOICE (☎5539 0444; www.vibehotels.com.au; 42 Ferny Ave; d from $140; ❄@☱) You won't miss this chocolate and lime-green high-rise situated on the Nerang River, a vibrant gem among Surfers Paradise's bland offering of hotels and apartments. The rooms are styled in subtle-chic and the poolside is the perfect spot for sundowners. The aqua-view rooms have superb views over the river.

Q1 Resort   APARTMENTS **$$$**
(☎1300 792 008, 5630 4500; www.q1.com.au; Hamilton Ave; 1-/2-/3-bedroom apt from $252/340/500; ❄@☱) Spend a fantastic night in the world's second-tallest residential tower. This stylish 80-storey resort is a modern structure that combines metal, glass and fabulous wrap-around views. All units have glass-enclosed balconies. Facilities are great and include a lagoon-style pool, a fitness centre and a day spa.

Surfers International Apartments

APARTMENTS $$

(☑1800 891 299, 5579 1299; www.surfers-inter national.com.au; 7-9 Trickett St; 1-/2-bedroom apt 3-night minimum stay from $450/630; @▣) This high-rise, just off the beach, has large, comfortable apartments with full ocean views. The complex comes with a small gym and a rooftop pool. This is a good option, close to everything.

Chateau Beachside

APARTMENTS $$

(☑5538 1022; www.chateaubeachside.com.au; cnr Elkhorn Ave & The Esplanade; d/studio/1-bedroom apt $145/160/175, minimum 2-night stay; ✳@▣) Right in the heart of Surfers, this seaside complex is an excellent choice. All the newly renovated studios and apartments have ocean views and the 18m pool is a bonus.

Marriott Resort

RESORT $$$

(☑5592 9800; www.marriott.com.au; 158 Ferny Ave; d/ste from $295/640; ✳@🛜▣) Just north of the centre, this resort is ridiculously sumptuous, from the sandstone-floored foyer with punkah-style fans to the lagoon-style pool, complete with artificial white-sand beaches and a waterfall.

Trickett Gardens Holiday Inn

APARTMENTS $$

(☑5539 0988; www.trickettgardens.com.au; 24-30 Trickett St; s/d $150/185; ✳▣) This friendly low-rise block is great for families, with a central location and well-equipped, self-contained units. It's so tranquil it's hard to believe you're close to Surfers' frantic action.

Olympus

APARTMENTS $$

(☑5538 7288; www.olympusapartments.com. au; 62 The Esplanade; d $130-180; @🛜▣) Just 200m north of Elkhorn Ave and opposite the beach, this high-rise block has well-kept, spacious apartments with one or two bedrooms.

Sleeping Inn Surfers

HOSTEL $

(☑1800 817 832, 5592 4455; www.sleepinginn.com. au; 26 Peninsular Dr; dm $22-26, d with/without bathroom $78/68; @▣) The newly renovated rooms are comfortable and all dorms have their own ensuite and well-equipped kitchen. Request the four-bed dorm if you don't want to share the bathroom with a large number of people. Free limo pick-up from the transit centre.

Surfers Paradise Backpackers Resort

HOSTEL $

(☑1800 282 800, 5592 4677; www.surfersparadise backpackers.com.au; 2837 Gold Coast Hwy; dm/d $23/74; @🛜▣) This purpose-built hostel, with sauna, tennis court, pool room and bar, has newly renovated rooms and self-contained apartments. It's family friendly, offers good security, free laundry facilities and a free courtesy bus to and from the transit centre.

Backpackers in Paradise

HOSTEL $

(☑5538 4344; www.backpackersinparadise.com; 40 Peninsular Dr; dm/d from $20/65; @▣) The mini-cinema is a major drawcard in this party hostel. The rooms and bathrooms were all undergoing much-needed renovations at the time of research which should lift its standards and make this a comfortable hostel. The on-site convenience store is a bonus. It's about 1.5km from the town centre.

Also recommended:

Surf 'n' Sun Backpackers

HOSTEL $

(☑1800 678 194, 5592 2363; www.surfnsun-goldcoast.com; 3323 Surfers Paradise Blvd; dm/d $25/65; @🛜▣) Looking dowdy, worn and tired, this is still a friendly family-run business and is close to Surfers' beach and bars.

Cheers Backpackers

HOSTEL $

(☑1800 639 539, 5531 6539; www.cheersback packers.com.au; 8 Pine Ave; dm $22-32, d $60-90; @▣) Definitely a party hostel but watch out for the grotty bathrooms.

✖ Eating

Self-caterers will find supermarkets in **Centro Surfers Paradise** (Cavill Ave Mall), **Chevron Renaissance Shopping Centre** (cnr

---

ℹ SCHOOLIES ON THE LOOSE

Every year in November, hundreds of teenagers flock to Surfers Paradise to celebrate the end of their high-school education in a month-long party that's become known as 'schoolies week'. It's an anything-goes affair, with drunk and drug-addled teens a common sight in the streets and pubs of Surfers. Although the local authorities have stepped in to regulate the excesses, unruly behaviour is still the norm. Avoid schoolies week if possible (unless you've just finished school!).

For more information visit www. schoolies.com.

Elkhorn Ave & Gold Coast Hwy) and Circle on Cavill (cnr Cavill & Ferny Ave).

Baritalia
ITALIAN $$

(☑5592 4700; Shop 15, Chevron Renaissance Bldg, cnr Elkhorn Ave & Surfers Paradise Blvd; mains $10-25; ⊘breakfast, lunch & dinner) The perfect spot for people-watching, this alfresco Italian-style bar and restaurant has rustic wooden benches and an atmosphere to match. The coffee is *perfetto*, and the good-value Friday-night special includes a plate of pasta or risotto with a glass of wine.

Kamikaze Teppanyaki
JAPANESE $$

(☑5592 0888; Circle on Cavill, Surfers Paradise Blvd; dishes $8-27; ⊘lunch & dinner) This very popular alfresco Japanese restaurant dishes up teppan vegetables, steamed rice, kamikaze salad, miso soup, and ginger and sesame sauce with every main meal.

Bumbles Café
CAFE $$

(☑5538 6668; 21 River Dr; dishes $11-25; ⊘7am-4pm) One of the few tranquil spots in Surfers, this cute cafe is located in a quiet nook opposite the Nerang River. The menu isn't extensive but has some interesting global temptations.

Surfers Sandbar
MODERN AUSTRALIAN $$

(cnr Elkhorn Ave & The Esplanade; dishes $8-20; ⊘breakfast, lunch & dinner) The ocean views give this cafe, bar and restaurant the edge over most Surfers' eateries. The menu gravitates towards burgers, beer-battered fish and chips, and light seafood meals but forgo the rather impersonal indoor restaurant and dine alfresco. Or just order a coldie and enjoy the sea breeze.

Fishnets Café
SEAFOOD $

(Circle on Cavill, 3/38 Surfers Paradise Blvd; dishes $7-13; ⊘lunch & dinner) Forget the paper plates and plastic cutlery – the fish and chips, octopus salad and fresh fish fillets at this outdoor eatery in the heart of the Circle are excellent value.

Central Lounge Bar & Restaurant
FUSION $$

(☑5592 3228; 27 Orchid Ave; mains lunch $11-20, dinner $20-32; ⊘lunch Fri-Sun, dinner Tue-Sun) This central restaurant and lounge bar is a cool place to indulge in a long lunch. Tables and chairs spill into the centre of the mall so passers-by can watch you having a good time. Salads, steaks and beer-battered fish and chips are on offer. The resident DJ creates a fusion of cool tunes to smooth you into the weekend club scene.

Beer Thai Garden
THAI $$

(☑5538 0110; cnr Chelsea Ave & Gold Coast Hwy; mains $15-25; ⊘dinner) Reputed to dish up the best *pad Thai* on the coast, this lovely restaurant brims with atmosphere. Two glitzy elephants flank the entrance, and soft lighting makes the most of the outdoor Thai garden bar. Good value and easy on the pocket. It's south down the Gold Coast Hwy.

Tandoori Place
INDIAN $$

(☑5538 0808; Aegean Resort, Laycock St; mains $15-25; ⊘lunch & dinner) An Indian restaurant that boasts a swag of awards and is highly recommended by locals has to be a winner. On the extensive menu you'll find seafood, poultry, lamb, beef and hot, hot, *hot* vindaloo roo.

♇ Drinking

Beer Garden
BAR

(Cavill Ave Mall) A very popular watering hole, the upstairs Beer Garden isn't a garden but a huge barnlike affair overlooking Cavill Ave. It's the place to start a night of clubbing.

Clock Hotel
PUB

(cnr Elkhorn Ave & Surfers Paradise Blvd) From the bar inside you won't see the parade of Aussie icons (kangaroo, emu, swagman and koala) emerging from the clock tower on the hour, every hour, but you'll certainly hear the bells tolling...time for another cocktail... or wine...or beer...

☆ Entertainment

Orchid Ave is Surfers' main bar and night-club strip. Cover charges are usually between $10 and $20 and Wednesday and Saturday are generally the big party nights.

Take the hassle out of your big night out with Wicked Club Crawl (☑5580 8422; www.wickedclubcrawl.com.au; tickets $30-50) or Plan B Party Tours (☑0400 685 501; www.planbtours.com; tickets $30). Every Wednesday, Friday and Saturday the teams organise a club crawl to five or six nightclubs (including free entry for the rest of the week), a free drink and pizza at each venue, party games and loads of fun.

Backpackers Big Night Out (www.goldcoastbackpackers.net; tickets $30) hosts a similar club crawl on Wednesdays and Saturdays, exclusively for backpackers. A party bus picks you up from your hostel and that's when the party begins. Tickets are available only through Gold Coast Association hostels and get you free entry into four nightclubs, a free drink and pizza at each venue, and other goodies.

Nightclubs

Vanity
NIGHTCLUB

(26 Orchid Ave) Formerly the Bedroom, Vanity is one of the hottest clubs in town, priding itself on beautiful people and upmarket glam.

Sin City
NIGHTCLUB

(22 Orchid Ave) A newcomer on the party scene, this Las Vegas–style nightclub is the place to be seen.

Cocktails & Dreams
NIGHTCLUB

(15 Orchid Ave) One of the oldest clubs in town, it still draws a regular crowd of party animals.

❶ Information

Gold Coast Information & Booking Centre (☑5538 4419; Cavill Ave Mall; ◷8.30am-5pm Mon-Fri, to 5pm Sat, 9am-4pm Sun) Information booth; also sells theme-park tickets.

Our High Speed Internet (☑5504 7992; 3063 Surfers Paradise Blvd; ◷9am-11pm)

Post office (☑13 13 18; Shop 165, Centro Surfers Paradise, Cavill Ave Mall; ◷9am-5.30pm Mon-Fri, to 12.30pm Sat)

Surfers Paradise Day & Night Medical Centre (☑5592 2299; 3221 Surfers Paradise Blvd; ◷7am-11pm)

Travellers Central (☑5538 3274; www.travellerscentral.com.au; Surfers Paradise Transit Centre, cnr Beach Rd & Remembrance Dve; ◷9am-7pm) Help with accommodation and tours for travellers of all budget ranges.

❶ Getting There & Away

The transit centre is on the corner of Beach Rd and Remembrance Dve. All the major bus companies have desks here. For more information on buses and trains, see p277.

❶ Getting Around

Car hire costs around $30 to $50 per day. Some of the many operators:

Avis (☑13 63 33, 5539 9388; cnr Ferny & Cypress Aves)

Budget (☑1300 362 848, 5538 1344; cnr Ferny & Palm Aves)

Getabout Rentals (☑5504 6517; Shop 9, The Mark, Orchid Ave) Also rents out scooters and bikes and organises motorcycle tours of the Broadwater area (from $60 for 30 minutes to $280 per half-day).

Red Back Rentals (☑5592 1655; Transit Centre, cnr Beach & Cambridge Rds)

Red Rocket Rent-A-Car (☑1800 673 682, 5538 9074; Centre Arcade, 16 Orchid Ave) Also rents out scooters (per day $30) and bicycles (per day $12).

Broadbeach

☑07 / POP 3780

Boutique shops and fashionable cafes line the Broadbeach streets while open stretches of green parkland separate the fine sandy beach from the esplanade. This is where Gold Coast locals wine and dine, and for a taste of the stylish beach-and-sun lifestyle it's exquisite.

◉ Sights & Activities

Conrad Jupiters Casino
CASINO

(☑5592 8100; www.conrad.com.au; Gold Coast Hwy; admission free; ◷24hr) Hundreds of thousands of optimistic gamblers filter through this mammoth temple to Mammon every year and leave with their pockets slightly lighter and their addiction briefly sated. Also here is **Jupiters Theatre** (☑1800 074 144), with live music and glamorous dinner shows.

🛏 Sleeping

Wave
APARTMENTS $$$

(☑5555 9200; www.thewavesresort.com.au; 89-91 Surf Pde; r $225-550, minimum 3-night stay; ❇◉🅿❄) You can't miss this spectacular high-rise with its wave-inspired design towering over Broadbeach's glam central. These luxury apartments make full use of the coast's spectacular views, especially from the sky pool on the 34th floor.

Hi-Ho Beach Apartments
APARTMENTS $$

(☑5538 2777; www.hihobeach.com.au; 2 Queensland Ave; 1-/2-bedroom apt $150/180; ❄) A great choice for location, close to the beach and Broadbeach's cafe scene. Standard apartments are looking weary but the renovated superior and executive apartments are very comfortable.

✗ Eating

Broadbeach's culinary scene is a class above Surfers'.

1two3
MEDITERRANEAN $$

(☑5538 4123; Phoenician Bldg, 90 Surf Pde; dishes $10-30; ◷breakfast, lunch & dinner) This new concept Mediterranean dining and lounge bar offers three portion sizes with every dish – taster, entree and main. Great

GOLD COAST THEME PARKS

Test your lung capacity (or better yet, the kids') on the thrilling rides and swirling action at the five American-style theme parks just north of Surfers. Discount tickets are sold in most of the tourist offices on the Gold Coast; the 3 Park Super Pass (adult/child $177/115) covers entry to Sea World, Movie World and Wet'n'Wild. Be aware that most parks do not allow visitors to bring their own food and drink onto the premises.

Con-x-ion (☎5556 9888; www.con-x-ion.com) operates shuttle service to the five different theme parks.

Dreamworld
THEME PARK

(☎5588 1111; www.dreamworld.com.au; Pacific Hwy, Coomera; adult/child $72/47; ☺10am-5pm) Skip breakfast if you plan on tackling the Big 6 Thrill Rides, which include the Claw, a giant pendulum that swings you nine storeys high at 75km/h, and the Giant Drop, a terminal-velocity machine where you free-fall from 38 storeys. It's not all rides, though – there's an interactive tiger show and an IMAX theatre. A two-day world pass (adult/child $99/69) lets you jump between Dreamworld and WhiteWater World as often as you like.

WhiteWater World
THEME PARK

(☎5588 1111; www.whitewaterworld.com.au; Pacific Hwy, Coomera; adult/child $45/30; ☺10am-4pm) Next door to Dreamworld, this aquatic theme park is the place to take the kids on a hot summer day. There's the Hydrocoaster (a rollercoaster on water) and the Green Room, where you'll spin in a tube through a tunnel then drop 15m down a green water funnel. Get caught in the Rip or splash around in the surging swells in the Cave of Waves.

Sea World
THEME PARK

(☎5588 2222, show times 5588 2205; www.seaworld.com.au; Sea World Dr, Main Beach; adult/child $75/50; ☺10am-5pm) See Australia's only polar bears in this aquatic park, along with dugongs, sharks and performing seals and dolphins. There are dizzying rides, of course, but for a unique hands-on experience book an Animal Adventure with a marine-mammal trainer.

Warner Bros Movie World
THEME PARK

(☎5573 8485; www.movieworld.com.au; Pacific Hwy, Oxenford; adult/child $75/50; ☺10am-5pm) 'Hollywood on the Gold Coast' boasts more movie-themed rides than movie-set action but the kids will love meeting their favourite movie legends and Looney Tunes characters.

Wet'n'Wild
THEME PARK

(☎5573 2255; www.wetnwild.com.au; Pacific Hwy, Oxenford; adult/child $55/35; ☺10am-5pm Feb-Apr & Sep-Dec, to 4pm May-Aug, to 9pm 27 Dec–25 Jan) If the beach is too sedate, this colossal water-sports park offers plenty of creative ways to get wet. You can launch from a 15m-high platform in a tube and blast down a 40m tunnel, or swirl through the Black Hole, or zoom down Mammoth Falls in a big rubber ring.

concept, great atmosphere and live music every night.

Moo Moo
STEAKHOUSE $$$

(☎5539 9952; Broadbeach on the Park, 2685 Gold Coast Hwy; mains $30-60; ☺lunch & dinner) A mecca for serious carnivores, Moo Moo's signature dish is a 1kg Wagyu rump steak rubbed with spices, char-grilled until smoky then roasted, and carved at the table. Vegetarians will be happy with the pasta dishes on the menu.

Manolas Brothers Deli
DELI $

(19 Albert Ave; dishes $8-25; ☺breakfast & lunch, deli 7am-6pm) Cosmopolitan delicacies fill every nook and cranny on the ceiling-high shelves in this sumptuous gourmet deli-cafe. Park yourself at the massively long central table to better salivate over the juicy olives, antipasti, imported cheeses and decadent homemade cakes and biscuits.

Koi

FUSION $$

(☑5570 3060; Wave Bldg, cnr Surf Pde & Albert Ave; mains $24-40; ☺breakfast, lunch & dinner) For serious people-watching, morning lattes or sunset cocktails, this cruisy cafe and lounge bar is the happening place to be in. Gourmet pizzas and tapas rub shoulders with an interesting contemporary menu where seafood features prominently. Live music on Sunday afternoons draw the après-beach crowd.

Burleigh Heads & Currumbin

☑07 / POP 7610 & 2650

In the chilled-out surfie town of Burleigh Heads, cheery cafes and beachfront restaurants overlook a gorgeous stretch of white sand and a beautiful, tiny national park on the rocky headland. Burleigh is legendary among surfers for the spectacular barrel of its right-hand break off the headland. The strong rip and jagged rocks make this one for experienced surfers only.

Learner surfers should head to Currumbin Alley, located 6km south of Burleigh. Currumbin is a sleepy little town, and a great spot for a relaxing family holiday, especially as the kids can swim in the calm waters of Currumbin Creek.

◉ Sights

Burleigh Heads National Park is crisscrossed with a number of walking tracks. Look out for the basalt columns poking through the forest – they hold considerable cultural significance to the local Kombumerri people.

Currumbin Wildlife Sanctuary WILDLIFE PARK

(☑5534 1266; www.cws.org.au; Gold Coast Hwy, Currumbin; adult/child $49/31; ☺8am-5pm) See Australian native animals in natural bush and rainforest habitats. Tree kangaroos, koalas, emus, wombats and other cute-and-furries are joined daily by flocks of brilliantly coloured rainbow lorikeets, which take great delight in eating out of your hand. There are informative and interactive shows throughout the day (did you know the scrub python can swallow prey four times the size of its head?), and there is also an Aboriginal dance show. One of the best ways to see the sanctuary is on a Wildnight Tour (adult/child $89/59), when the native nocturnal animals go about their business.

David Fleay Wildlife Park WILDLIFE PARK

(☑5576 2411; West Burleigh Rd; adult/child/senior/ family $17.10/7.95/10.30/43.45; ☺9am-5pm) Run by the Queensland Environmental Protection Agency, this park has 4km of walking tracks that are dispersed through mangroves and rainforest. There are also plenty of educational and informative shows that run throughout the day. The park is named after its founder, Australian naturalist David Fleay, the first person to breed the platypus in captivity (at Healesville Sanctuary in Victoria). The park runs a research and breeding program for rare and endangered species, although no platypus has successfully been bred here.

🏃 Activities

The right-hand point break at Burleigh Heads is the best wave here, but it's usually crowded with pro surfers. There are plenty of other waves to practise on along the beach.

🛏 Sleeping

Hillhaven Holiday Apartments

APARTMENTS $$

(☑5535 1055; www.hillhaven.com.au; 2 Goodwin Tce, Burleigh Heads; d $170, minimum 3-night stay; ☀) The pick of these upmarket apartments is the gold deluxe room at $300 per night. Situated on the headland adjacent to the national park, these apartments have a grand view of Burleigh Heads. There's no through traffic so it's ultraquiet yet only 150m to the beach and cafe scene.

Burleigh Palms Holiday Apartments

APARTMENTS $$

(☑5576 3955; www.burleighpalms.com; 1849 Gold Coast Hwy, Burleigh Heads; 1-bedroom apt per night/week from $130/550, 2-bedroom apt from $160/660; ☀) Even though they're on the highway, these large and comfortable self-contained units are close to the beach and are solid value. The owner is a mine of information and is happy to organise tours and recommend places to visit.

Burleigh Beach Tourist Park

CARAVAN PARK $

(☑5667 2750; www.goldcoasttouristparks.com.au; Goodwin Tce, Burleigh Heads; unpowered/powered sites $29/36, cabins from $115; ❄@🛜☀) This council-run park is snug, but it's in a great spot. Get in quick to bag a shady site. The good news is that you can stumble to the beach and the barbies are free. Rates are for two people.

Also recommended:

Wyuna APARTMENTS **$$**
(☑5535 3302; www.wyunaapartments@bigpond.
com; 82 The Esplanade, Burleigh Heads;
2-bedroom apt per week from $640; ☞) Old-
fashioned apartments opposite the beach.

Tallebudgera Creek Tourist Park
CARAVAN PARK **$**
(☑5667 2700; www.goldcoasttouristparks.com.
au; 1544 Gold Coast Hwy, Burleigh Heads; unpow-
ered/powered sites $29/36, cabins from $115;
❈@☞≋) Large sprawling park on Tal-
lebudgera Creek.

✕ Eating

Oskars SEAFOOD **$$$**
(☑5576 3722; 43 Goodwin Tce, Burleigh Heads;
dishes $20-50; ☺lunch & dinner) One of the
Gold Coast's finest, this elegant restaurant
(right on the beach) constantly lands a cov-
eted place on best-dining lists from all quarters, and for good reason. Against elevated,

sweeping views of the coastline you'll dine
on a changing selection of seafood dishes.

Elephant Rock Café MODERN AUSTRALIAN **$$**
(☑5598 2133; 776 Pacific Pde, Currumbin; mains
$16-34; ☺breakfast & lunch daily, dinner Tue-Sat) A
cool cafe specialising in Mod Oz and 'gour-
met vegetarian' cuisine (gluten sufferers
will want to head here), this trendy place
morphs from beach-chic by day to ultrachic
at night. You can watch the moon rise over
the ocean from the top deck or just enjoy the
sound of waves lapping the beach.

Mermaids on the Beach MEDITERRANEAN **$$$**
(☑5520 1177; 31 Goodwin Tce, Burleigh Heads;
mains $23-36; ☺breakfast, lunch & dinner) Mer-
maids is another gem directly on the white
sands of Burleigh Heads. Have the fruit
platter for breakfast and for dinner sample
interesting Mediterrasian dishes like prawn
and lemon tortellini. Outside meal hours
this is a snappy beach bar.

Burleigh Heads

Zullaz   FUSION **$$**

(☑5535 3511; 50 James St; mains $11-28; ☺lunch Fri, dinner Tue-Sat) The menu is as exotic as the decor in this funky bar-cum-restaurant. The Polynesian, Moroccan and Indian dishes sound tantalising but be brave and order the Jamaican goat curry. Cocktails are just as exotic.

Govinda's   INDIAN **$**

(20 James St; dishes $7-13; ☺11.30am-8pm) You can't go wrong with a large combo of three dishes for just $13 at this tiny Indian restaurant. Zero atmosphere but your taste buds won't complain.

Also recommended:

Bluff Café   CAFE **$$**

(1/66 Goodwin Tce; dishes $10-30; ☺breakfast, lunch & dinner) A popular and breezy cafe opposite the beach.

Fishmongers   SEAFOOD **$**

(9 James St, Burleigh Heads; dishes $8-17; ☺lunch & dinner) Unpretentious fish-and-chip shop delivers the goods.

❶ Information

QPWS Information Centre (QPWS; ☑5535 3032; 1711 Gold Coast Hwy; ☺9.30am-3pm Mon & Wed, 9am-3pm Tue, Thu & Fri, 9am-noon Sat & Sun) At the northern end of Tallebudgera Creek.

Coolangatta

☑07 / POP 4870

Coolangatta is a laid-back seaside resort on Queensland's southern border, proud of its good surf beaches and tight community. With a sleek makeover transforming the esplanade, this once-sleepy town is now the pick of the Gold Coast. If you want to bypass the glam and party scene, catch the best waves on the coast, or just kick back on the beach, you've found the spot. North of the point, Kirra has a beautiful long stretch of beach with challenging surf. Heading south, there are good views down the coast from Point Danger, the headland at the end of the state line.

🏃 Activities

The most difficult break here is Point Danger, but Kirra Point often goes off and there are gentler breaks that are located down at Greenmount Beach and Rainbow Bay. You can learn to surf with **Walkin' on Water** (☑5534 1886, 0418 780 311; www.walkinonwater. com; 2hr group lesson per person $40). Former professional surfer and Australian surfing team coach Dave Davidson promises to get you up and surfing in your first lesson when you take classes at **Gold Coast Surf Coaching** (☑0417 191 629).

Cooly Surf (☑5536 61470; cnr Marine Pde & Dutton St; ☺9am-5pm) hires out high-performance surfboards as well as malibu surfboards (half/full day $30/45) and stand-up paddleboards ($40/55).

Cooly Dive (☑5599 4104; www.coolydive. com.au; cnr McLean & Musgrave Sts; ☺8am-6pm) offers guided dives ($180), snorkelling courses ($85) and PADI dive courses.

Coolangatta Whale Watch (☑5599 4104; www.coolangattawhalewatch.com.au; cnr McLean & Musgrave Sts; 3hr cruise adult/child $85/60; ☺8am-6pm) runs cruises from June to the end of October.

Get high with **Gold Coast Skydive** (☑5599 1920; Coolangatta Airport; tandem jumps from $325).

☞ Tours

Catch-A-Crab   RIVER CRUISE

(☑5599 9972; www.catchacrab.com.au; adult/child $55/36) Half-day tours along the Terranora Inlet of the Tweed River include mud-crab catching (try to say that in a hurry), fishing, pelican feeding and, if the tides permit, yabbie hunting.

Rainforest Cruises   RIVER CRUISE

(☑5536 8800; www.goldcoastcruising.com) Cruises range from crab catching to surf 'n' turf lunches and rainforest cruises along the Tweed River. Cruises start from $35 for two hours.

Coolangatta

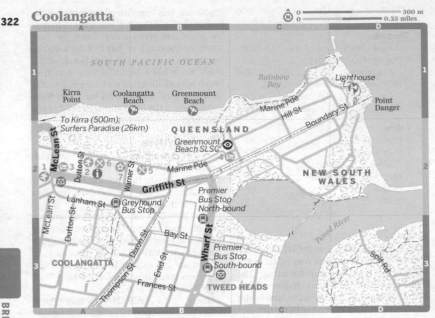

Coolangatta

Activities, Courses & Tours

Sleeping

Eating

Entertainment

🛏 Sleeping

TOP CHOICE **Komune**　　　　　BOUTIQUE HOTEL **$$**
(📞5536 6764; www.komuneresorts.com;
146 Marine Pde, Coolangatta; dm from $45, 2-bed-
room apt $220, penthouse $695, penthouse &
Sky-House party room $1500, breakfast included;
@🛜🏊) The beach-funk decor, tropical pool-
side, and a 'no shirt, no shoes, no problem'
mantra makes this the ultimate surf retreat.
The new concept in accommodation –
from budget dorms (including a girls-only
dorm), self-contained apartments and a hip
penthouse begging for a party – attracts a
broad range of travellers, and fosters eclectic
friendships. With superb ocean views, great
staff and a cosy outdoor movie *sala,* you
won't want to leave.

Coolangatta Sands Hostel　　　HOSTEL **$**
(📞5536 7472; www.coolangattasandshostel.com.
au; cnr Griffith & McLean Sts; dm from $30, d $72)
Above the Coolangatta Sands Hotel and
directly opposite the beach, this clean, airy
and pleasant hostel is a good choice. The
Queenslander balcony has comfortable
daybeds to catch the sea breeze. As well as
a free shuttle to and from the airport, there
are plenty of incentives – free surf lessons
and free trips to Nimbin, Mt Warning and
Byron Bay.

Meridian Tower　　　　　APARTMENTS **$$**
(📞1300 785 599, 5536 9400; www.meridiantower.
com.au; 6 Coyne St, Kirra; 1-/2-bedroom apt per
week from $795/910; ❄@🏊) This tall tower
block (the first in Kirra), opposite the beautiful Kirra beach, has spacious and airy fully
self-contained apartments with large north-
facing balconies. There's a spa, sauna and
tennis courts. Outside peak season, shorter
stays are available.

Coolangatta YHA HOSTEL $
(☎5536 7644; www.coolangattayha.com; 230 Coolangatta Rd, Bilinga; dm $25-32, s $38-42, d $60-67, all incl breakfast; @☎☒) A looong 4km haul from the bustle, this well-equipped YHA is favoured by surf junkies (of all vintages) who overdose on the excellent breaks across the road. You can also hire boards ($25 per day) and bikes. Courtesy transfers from Coolangatta are available.

Kirra Vista Holiday Units APARTMENTS $$
(☎5536 7375; www.kirravista.com.au; 12-14 Musgrave St, Kirra; d $150; ☒) Forget the drab exterior; the renovated units in this small complex are a welcome surprise. All rooms have ocean views but be sure to book the renovated units.

Kirra Beach Tourist Park CARAVAN PARK $
(☎5667 2740; www.goldcoasttouristparks.com.au; Charlotte St, Kirra; unpowered/powered sites $29/34, cabins from $115; ☒@☎☒) This large council-run park has plenty of trees and a well-stocked open-air camp kitchen. The modern self-contained cabins are good value. There's also a TV room, barbecues, and volleyball and basketball courts. Rates are for two people.

🍴 Eating & Drinking
Marine Pde is lined with alfresco cafes and restaurants.

Bread'n'butter TAPAS $$
(☎5599 4666; 76 Musgrave St, Kirra; tapas $14-19; ☺dinner nightly, lunch Sat & Sun) Head upstairs to the balcony where mood lighting and chill tunes make this Spanish tapas bar perfect for a drink or a light meal. The pizzas are tasty and the tapas are huge. On Friday and Saturday nights, a DJ turns upstairs into a lively bar scene.

Mist MODERN AUSTRALIAN $$$
(☎5536 8885; cnr Douglas & Musgrave Sts, Kirra; tapas $10-23, mains $36-42; ☺breakfast, lunch & dinner) The Mod Oz cuisine is creative, innovative and sassy; the curtained alcoves, arty chandeliers and eclectic decor is stylish beach-chic. Cocktails are spot-on but tapas servings can be a bit light.

Bellakai MODERN AUSTRALIAN $$
(☎5531 5177; Marine Pde; meals $12-30; ☺breakfast, lunch & dinner) This casual and relaxed cafe has great ocean views to complement a menu based on fresh local produce. At night soft candlelight adds a touch of romance to the restaurant's crisp white decor. Meals can be inconsistent but the coffee is excellent.

Also recommended:

Earth'n'Sea Pizza & Pasta PIZZA $$
(☎5536 3477; Marine Pde, Coolangatta; mains $17-33; ☺lunch & dinner) Voted Best Pizza Restaurant on the Gold Coast.

Grill'd BURGERS $
(Showcase on the Beach, Marine Pde; burgers $9-13; ☺11am-10pm) Burgers of every description, including low-fat and vegan.

☆ Entertainment
Coolangatta Hotel PUB
(cnr Marine Pde & Warner St) One of the hottest spots on the Gold Coast, the 'Cooly' has legendary Sunday sessions, and the Balcony nightclub attracts some of the biggest acts in the music industry.

❶ Information
Coolangatta visitors centre (☎5569 3380; Shop 22, Showcase on the Beach, Griffith St; ☺8.30am-5pm Mon-Fri, 9am-3pm Sat, 9am-noon Sun)

Post office (☎13 13 18; cnr Griffith St & McLean St)

❶ Getting There & Away
The **Greyhound** (☎1300 473 946; www.greyhound.com.au) bus stop is in Warner St while **Premier** (☎13 34 10; www.premierms.com.au) coaches stop in Wharf St. See p277 for further information.

GOLD COAST HINTERLAND

Inland from the surf, sand, and half-naked bods on the Gold Coast beaches, the densely forested and unspoiled mountains of the McPherson Range feel like a million miles away. The range forms a natural barrier between the eastern coastline and the rolling green hills of the Darling Downs, and the national parks here are a subtropical paradise of rainforests, waterfalls, numerous walking tracks, panoramic lookouts and amazing wildlife.

☞ Tours
The only way to access the hinterland without your own wheels is on a tour.

Australian Day Tours SCENIC TOUR
(☎1300 363 436; www.daytours.com.au) Largest operator with a variety of tours.

Tour Gold Coast   GLOW-WORM TOUR
(☏5532 8687; www.tourgc.com.au; adult/child $90/45, incl dinner $110/55) Runs glow-worm night tours to Natural Bridge.

Bushwacker Ecotours   ECOTOUR
(☏3720 9020; www.bushwacker-ecotours. com.au; day trips adult/child $115/95) Has an extensive array of ecotours to the hinterland.

Scenic Hinterland Day Tours   SCENIC TOUR
(☏5531 5536; day trip incl wine tasting adult/child $89.90/59.90) Includes wine tasting at O'Reilly's Canungra Valley Vineyards.

Springbrook National Park

An excellent winding drive up from the Gold Coast beaches takes you into a *Jurassic Park* ecosystem of lush subtropical rainforests where closed canopies high overhead protect an amazing array of endangered and protected flora and fauna. The 3425-hectare Springbrook National Park consists of three reserves: Springbrook Plateau, Mt Cougal and Natural Bridge.

Like the rest of the McPherson Range, the Springbrook area is a remnant of the huge shield volcano that dominated the region 23 million years ago. From Best of All Lookout (reached via Lyrebird Ridge Rd) you can see the once-buried volcanic plug, Mt Warning (1156m), in NSW. The southern cliffs of Springbrook and Lamington continue into NSW arcing around in a giant circle, outlining the rim of the ancient volcanic crater.

The park is a mix of subtropical warm and cool temperate rainforest and open eucalypt forest. Hikers will want to make full use of the extensive walking tracks showcasing the weird world of strangler figs, vines, epiphytes, glow-in-the-dark mushrooms and worms, colourful wildlife and spectacular waterfalls and gorges. But be prepared: at 900m the national park can be up to 5°C cooler than the lowlands.

Each section of the park is reached by a long access road, and there are no shortcuts between the sections, so make sure you get on the right road. Coming from Nerang, take Springbrook Rd for the Springbrook section and the Nerang–Murwillumbah Rd for the Natural Bridge section. Take the Currumbin Creek Rd from Currumbin for Mt Cougal.

As well as stargazing you can pick up hiking maps from the Springbrook Research Observatory (☏5533 5055; www.springbrookobservatory.com.au; 2337 Springbrook Rd; adult/child $15/8; ☉7pm, by appointment), an unofficial information centre.

SPRINGBROOK PLATEAU

The village of Springbrook is balanced right on the edge of the plateau, with numerous waterfalls tumbling down to the coastal plain below. The 'town' is actually a series of properties stretched along a winding road. Understandably, lookouts are the big attraction here, and there are several places where you can get the giddy thrill of leaning right out over the edge.

At Gwongorella Picnic Area, just off Springbrook Rd, the lovely Purling Brook Falls drop 109m into the rainforest. There are two easily accessed lookouts with views of the lush canopy and towering falls, and a number of walking trails including a 6km-return walk to Waringa Pool, a beautiful swimming hole.

The national park information centre is at the end of Old School Rd. A little further south Canyon Lookout affords jagged views through the valley all the way to the coast. This is also the start of a 4km circuit walk to Twin Falls and the 17km Warrie Circuit.

At the end of Springbrook Rd, the pleasant Goomoolahra Picnic Area has barbecues beside a small creek. A little further on, there's a great lookout point beside the falls with views across the plateau and all the way back to the coast.

True to its name, the Best of All Lookout offers spectacular views from the southern edge of the plateau to the flats below. The 350m trail from the car park to the lookout takes you past a clump of mighty Antarctic beech trees. Take time to admire the gnarled and twisted roots of these ancient giants. You'll only find them around here and in northern NSW.

🛏 Sleeping

Most guesthouses are along or signposted off Springbrook Rd.

TOP CHOICE **Mouses House**   BOUTIQUE COTTAGES **$$$**
(☏5533 5192; www.mouseshouse.com.au; 2807 Springbrook Rd; 2 nights from $395, 1-night stay $240 Sun-Fri) These ultraprivate fairy-tale cottages are the ultimate romantic mountain hideaway. Soft lighting along rainforest boardwalks leads to 12 enchanted A-frame red-cedar chalets hidden in the magical misty wood. Each has a double spa and a wood fire. Breakfast, lunch and dinner hampers are available on request.

TAMBORINE MOUNTAIN

A mountaintop rainforest community just 45km inland from the Gold Coast beaches, Tamborine Mountain has cornered the chocolate, fudge and craft cottage industries in a big way. Of the three satellite suburbs (Eagle Heights, North Tamborine and Mt Tamborine), **Gallery Walk** in Eagle Heights is the place to stock up on homemade jams and all things artsy-craftsy but wherever you are on Tamborine Mountain a Devonshire tea is never too far away.

As well as housing a bevy of artists and musicians, Tamborine Mountain is home to Queensland's oldest national park. The **Tamborine Mountain National Park** is actually 13 sections of land that stretch across the 8km plateau, offering tumbling cascades and great views of the Gold Coast. Most of the national parks surround North Tamborine and some of the best spots are **Witches Falls, Curtis Falls, Cedar Creek Falls** and **Cameron Falls**.

To get to Tamborine Mountain, turn off the Pacific Hwy at Oxenford or Nerang. The **visitor information centre** (☑5545 3200; Doughty Park; ☺10am-4pm Mon-Fri, 9.30am-4pm Sat & Sun) is located in North Tamborine. Have lunch at the **St Bernards Hotel** (☑5545 1177; 101 Alpine Tce, Mt Tamborine; mains $20-32; ☺lunch & dinner), a rustic old mountain pub with a large deck that has commanding views of the gorge.

There are plenty of romantic weekend hideaways in the rainforest including **Songbirds Rainforest Retreat** (☑5545 2563; www.songbirds.com.au; Tamborine Mountain Rd, North Tamborine; villas per night from $425). Each of the six luxurious Southeast Asian–inspired villas has a double spa bath with rainforest views.

English Gardens BOUTIQUE COTTAGES **$$**
(☑5533 5244; www.englishgardens.com.au; 2932 Springbrook Rd; cottages from $160) Next to Goomoolahra Falls are two quaint cottages set within beautiful landscaped gardens. Meandering pathways, terraced cascades, rose arches and babbling creeks are picture-pretty. There's also a **teahouse** (☺10.30am-5.30pm) in the grounds.

Springbrook Mountain Manor
GUESTHOUSE **$$**
(☑5533 5344; www.springbrookmountainmanor.com.au; 2814 Springbrook Rd; r from $175) This stately manor gives you a taste of Tudor-style accommodation. It's set on 10 hectares of landscaped gardens, and you can play golf, croquet and tennis and even try your hand at archery. The rooms are heavy with brocade and period furniture.

Rosellas at Canyon Lookout MOTEL **$**
(☑5533 5090; www.springbrookrosellas.com.au; 8 Canyon Pde; s/d from $80/95) This basic motel is across the road from the Lookout.

Settlement Camp Ground CAMPGROUND **$**
(☑13 74 68; www.derm.qld.gov.au; Carrick's Rd; camp sites per person $5.15) This rather uninspiring camping ground devoid of trees and showers is the only camping ground at Springbook. It does have toilets and barbecues.

✗ Eating

Dancing Waters Café CAFE **$**
(☑5533 5335; 33 Forestry Rd; dishes $8-17; ☺10am-4pm) Next to the car park for Purling Brook Falls is a simple tearoom with healthy salads and light meals.

Gourmet Galah CAFE **$**
(☑5533 5126; 1924 Springbrook Rd; mains $6-22; ☺9.30am-4.30pm Thu-Mon) Either cosy up by the fire indoors or enjoy the sunny landscaped gardens while you devour a Devonshire tea or tuck into a more substantial lunch.

Lamington National Park

Australia's largest remnant of subtropical rainforest covers the deep valleys and steep cliffs of the McPherson Range, reaching elevations of 1100m on the Lamington Plateau. The 200-sq-km Lamington National Park is a Unesco World Heritage site and has over 160km of walking trails.

The two most popular and accessible sections of the park are **Binna Burra** and **Green Mountains**, both reached via Canungra. Binna Burra can also be reached from Nerang. Both roads twist and snake their way up the mountain, cutting through encroaching forest and open grazing land. It's a spectacular drive, particularly along the Green Mountain Rd, and well worth the effort.

At Green Mountains, be sure to walk the excellent **tree-top canopy walk** along a series of rope-and-plank suspension bridges 15m above the ground. Serious hikers can tackle the 54km **Great Walk** which starts at Green Mountains, passes through Binna Burra and ends at the **Settlement Camp Ground** on the Springbrook Plateau. The first 24km from Green Mountains to Binna Burra is also known as the **Border Trail**.

Walking trail guides are available from the **ranger stations** (Binna Burra ☑5533 3584; ☺9am-3.30pm Sat & Sun; Green Mountains ☑5544 0634; ☺9-11am & 1-3.30pm Mon-Fri).

Binna Burra Mountain Lodge (☑1300 246 622, 5533 3622; www.binnaburralodge.com.au; Binna Burra Rd, Beechmont; unpowered/powered sites $24/30, safari tents from $55, d incl breakfast with/without bathroom $250/190) is an excellent mountain retreat with rustic log cabins and camp sites surrounded by forest. **O'Reilly's Rainforest Guesthouse** (☑1800 688 722, 5502 4911; www.oreillys.com.au; Lamington National Park Rd; guesthouse s/d from $163/278, villas 1-/2-bedroom from $400/435, minimum 2-night stay; @☎) at Green Mountains was built in 1926. The guesthouse is looking dated and faded but still manages to retain its old-world rustic charm – and sensational views.

Noosa & the Sunshine Coast

Includes »

Why Go?

The laid-back beach-chic culture of the Sunshine Coast turns lazy summer holidays into treasured memories of melting ice creams, sand between your toes and fish and chips on the beach. The natural, unaffected charm of this strip of coastline is one of its greatest attractions.

From the tip of Bribie Island, the 'Sunny Coast' stretches north for 100 golden kilometres to the Cooloola Coast, just beyond the exclusive, leafy resort town of Noosa. The coast is perfect for surfing and swimming, and Mooloolaba with its popular beach, outdoor eateries and cafes is a firm favourite with holidaying Australian families.

Forming a stunning backdrop to this spectacular coastline are the ethereal Glass House Mountains and the forested folds and ridges, gorges and waterfalls, lush green pastures and quaint villages of the Blackall Range.

Best Places to Eat

» Spirit House Restaurant (p347)
» Humid (p334)
» Berardo's (p333)
» Wasabi (p334)

Best Places to Stay

» Secrets on the Lake (p348)
» Islander Noosa Resort (p333)
» Hidden Valley B&B (p347)

When to Go

Noosa

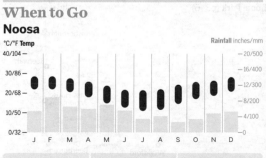

May Satisfy indulgent gustatory cravings at the Noosa Food & Wine Festival

August–September Noosa's streets fill with music during the four-day Noosa Jazz Festival

December Celebrate the end of the year, eclectically at the Woodford Folk Festival

Noosa & the Sunshine Coast Highlights

1. Hiking the coastal track at **Noosa National Park** (p329)

2. Sampling gourmet beach fare in one of Noosa's **swish restaurants** (p333)

3. Surfing, sunning and lapping up the beach-cafe scene in **Mooloolaba** (p339)

4. Visiting the wild critters at **Australia Zoo** (p336)

5. Finding funky treasures at the **Eumundi markets** (p347)

6. Donning flares, kaftans and wild, new-age hippie-chic at the wonderfully eclectic **Woodford Folk Festival** (p349)

7. Hiking to the summit of Mount Beerwah in the ethereal **Glass House Mountains National Park** (p336)

8. Canoeing and exploring the Cooloola Section of the **Great Sandy National Park** (p346)

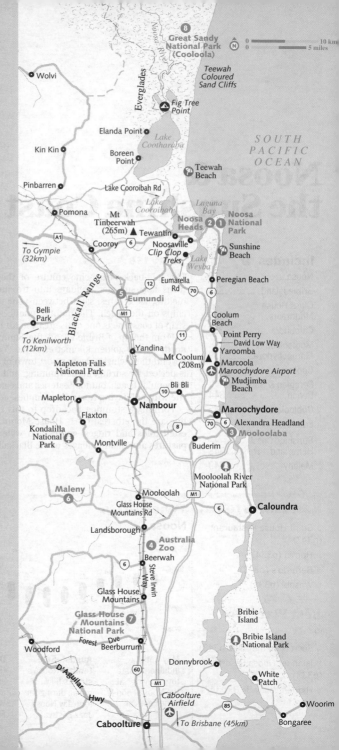

ℹ️ Getting There & Away

Air

The Sunshine Coast's airport (Sunshine Coast Airport) is at Mudjimba, 10km north of Maroochydore and 26km south of Noosa. **Jetstar** (☎13 15 38; www.jetstar.com.au) and **Virgin Blue** (☎13 67 89; www.virginblue.com.au) have daily flights from Sydney and Melbourne. **Tiger Airways** (☎03-9335 3033; www.tigerairways.com) has less frequent flights from Melbourne.

Bus

Greyhound Australia (☎1300 473 946; www.greyhound.com.au) has several daily services from Brisbane to Caloundra ($30, two hours), Maroochydore ($30, two hours) and Noosa ($32, 2½ hours). **Premier Motor Service** (☎13 34 10; www.premierms.com.au) also services Maroochydore and Noosa from Brisbane.

Veolia (☎1300 826 608; www.vtb.com.au) has an express service from Brisbane to Noosa (one way/return $25/46) twice daily.

ℹ️ Getting Around

Several companies offer transfers from Maroochydore Airport and Brisbane to points along the coast. Fares from Brisbane cost $40 to $50 for adults and $20 to $25 for children. From Sunshine Coast Airport fares are around $15 to $25 per adult and $7 to $12 per child. The following are recommended:

Col's Airport Shuttle (☎5450 5933; www.airshuttle.com.au)

Henry's (☎5474 0199; www.henrys.com.au)

Noosa Transfers & Charters (☎5450 5933; www.noosatransfers.com.au)

Sun-Air Bus Service (☎1800 804 340, 5477 0888; www.sunair.com.au)

The blue minibuses run by **Sunbus** (☎13 12 30) buzz frequently between Caloundra and Noosa. Sunbus also has regular buses from Noosa across to the train station at Nambour ($5, one hour) via Eumundi.

Noosa

☎07 / POP 9110

Gorgeous Noosa is a stylish resort town with a stunning natural landscape of crystalline beaches and tropical rainforests. Designer boutiques and swish restaurants draw beach-elite sophisticates, but the beach and bush are still free, so glammed-up fashionistas simply share the beat with thongs, boardshorts and bronzed bikini bods baring their bits.

Noosa is undeniably developed but its low-impact condos and chichi landscape have been cultivated without losing sight of simple seaside pleasures. On long weekends and school holidays, however, bustling Hastings St becomes a slow-moving file of traffic.

Noosa has an amazing number of roundabouts and it's easy to get lost. Broadly speaking, Noosa encompasses three zones: Noosa Heads (around Laguna Bay and Hastings St), Noosaville (along the Noosa River) and Noosa Junction (the administrative centre).

◉ Sights

One of Noosa's best features, the lovely **Noosa National Park** (Map p330), covering the headland, has fine walks, great coastal scenery and a string of bays with waves that draw surfers from all over the country. The most scenic way to access the national park is to follow the boardwalk along the coast from town. Pick up a walking track map from the **QPWS centre** (Map p330; ☎5447 3243; ⊙9am-3pm) at the entrance to the park. Sleepy koalas are often spotted in the trees near Tea Tree Bay and dolphins are commonly seen from the rocky headlands around Alexandria Bay, an informal nudist beach on the eastern side.

For a panoramic view of the park, walk or drive up to **Laguna Lookout** (Map p330) from Viewland Dr in Noosa Junction.

🏃 Activities

Surfing & Water Sports

With a string of breaks around an unspoilt national park, Noosa is a fine place to catch a wave. Generally the waves are best in December and January but Sunshine Corner, at the northern end of Sunshine Beach, has an excellent year-round break, although it has a brutal beach dump. The point breaks around the headland only perform during the summer, but when they do, expect wild conditions and good walls at Boiling Point and Tea Tree on the northern coast of the headland. There are also gentler breaks on Noosa Spit at the far end of Hastings St, where most of the surf schools do their training.

Kite-surfers will find conditions at the river mouth and Lake Weyba are best between October and January, but on windy days the Noosa River is a playground for serious daredevils.

Recommended companies:

Merrick's Learn to Surf   SURFING
(☎0418 787 577; www.learntosurf.com.au; surfing 2hr lesson $60) Holds 1-, 3- and 5-day surfing programs.

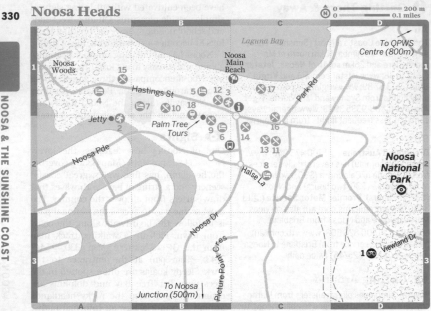

Adventure Sports Noosa KITESURFING
(Map p332; ☑5455 6677; www.kitesurfaustralia.
com.au; 203 Gympie Tce, Noosaville; kitesurfing
2½hr lesson $150, stand-up paddleboarding 2hr
$50) Also hires kayaks (half day $35) and
bikes (two hours $19).

Go Ride A Wave SURFING
(☑1300 132 441; www.gorideawave.com.au; 2hr
surf lesson $60, 2hr surfboard hire $25, 1hr stand-
up paddleboard hire $25)

Noosa Longboards SURFING
(Map p330; ☑5447 2828; www.noosalongboards.
com; 255 Hastings St, Noosa; 2hr surfing lesson
$60, surfboard hire $35/50, bodyboard hire per
day $10)

Canoeing & Kayaking
The Noosa River is excellent for canoeing;
it's possible to follow it up through Lakes Cooroibah and Cootharaba and through the Cooloola Section of Great Sandy National Park.

Noosa Ocean Kayak Tours KAYAKING
(☑0418 787 577; www.learntosurf.com; 2hr tours
$66, kayak hire per day $55) Tours around
Noosa National Park and along the Noosa
River.

Kayak Noosa KAYAKING
(Map p332; ☑0448 567 321; www.kayaknoosa.
com; 194 Gympie Tce, Noosaville; 2hr sunset kayak
$60, half-/full-day guided kayak tour $95/155)
Tours around Noosa National Park. Also
hires out kayaks (two hours single/double
$25/40).

Adventure Activities

Noosa Ocean Rider SPEEDBOAT
(Map p332; ☑0438 386 255; cnr Gympie Tce
& Weyba Rd, Noosaville; 1hr $70) Thrills and
spills on a very fast and powerful speedboat.

Noosa Bike Hire & Tours MOUNTAIN-BIKING
(☑5474 3322; www.bikeon.com.au; tours $95)
Half-day mountain-bike tours along the
Noosa Trail Network and along the Noosa
Enduro 100km course.

Cruises

Gondolas of Noosa GONDOLA CRUISE
(Map p330; ☑0412 929 369; www.gondolasof
noosa.com; Sheraton Jetty, Noosa) Romantic
and moonlit cruises along the Noosa River
leave from the Sheraton Jetty. Prices start
from $150 for an hour.

Noosa Ferry RIVER CRUISE
(Map p330; ☑5449 8442; Sheraton Jetty, Noosa)
This ferry service has informative 90-
minute round-trip cruises that run to
Tewantin from the Sheraton Jetty.

Horse Riding & Camel Safaris

Clip Clop Treks   HORSE RIDING
(☑0429 051 544; www.clipcloptreks.com.au;
Eumarella Rd, Lake Weyba; 2hr rides $90) This
trek outfit offers horse rides around (and
in) Lake Weyba and the surrounding bush.
For more information on horse rides and
camel rides on the beach and in the bush,
see p345.

☞ Tours

Fraser Island

A number of operators offer trips to Fraser
Island via the Cooloola Coast.

Fraser Island Adventure Tours   4WD TOUR
(☑5444 6957; www.fraserislandadventuretours.
com.au; day tour $170) Has won several in-
dustry awards for its day tour to Eli Creek
and Lake McKenzie, which packs as much
punch as a two-day tour.

Trailblazer Tours   4WD TOUR
(☑1800 639 518, 5499 9595; www.trailblazer-
tours.com.au; 3-day safaris per person $330)
This tour company operates small group
tours and can pick up and drop off passengers at either Noosa or Rainbow
Beach. It also offers two-day safaris for a
cost of $260. Popular with backpackers.

Discovery Group   4WD TOUR
(☑5449 0393; www.thediscoverygroup.com.
au; day tour adult/child $169/115, 2-day tour per
person $360) Visit the island in a big black
4WD truck. There's a guided rainforest
walk at Central Station that visits Lakes
Birrabeen and McKenzie.

For more information about tours to Fraser Island, see p361.

If you're cashed up and want to do it the
spectacular way, **Air Fraser Island** (☑1800
247 992; www.airfraserisland.com.au) and **Sunshine Aviation** (☑5450 5665; www.sunshinea
viation.com.au) offer fly/drive packages including flights to Fraser Island and 4WD hire
for self-guided day trips. Tours cost $250 to
$300 per person.

Everglades

The passage of the Noosa River that cuts
into the Great Sandy National Park is poet-
ically known as the 'river of mirrors' or the
Everglades. It's a great place to launch a
kayak and camp along the many **national
park campgrounds** (www.derm.qld.gov.
au; per person/family $5.15/20.60) along the
riverbank.

Otherwise, take a tour:

Discovery Group   BOAT CRUISE
(☑5449 0393; www.thediscoverygroup.com.au; day
tour adult/child $155/105) Includes a 4WD trip
along the coloured sands and a boat cruise
in the Everglades. On Wednesday and Saturday, visit the Eumundi markets and cruise
the Everglades in the afternoon (per person
$125).

Kanu Kapers   KAYAKING
(☑5485 3328; www.kanukapersaustralia.com; 11
Toolara St, Boreen Point; per person from $145,
overnight trip $145) Guided or self-guided
kayaking trips into the Everglades. Kayak
hire per day from $65.

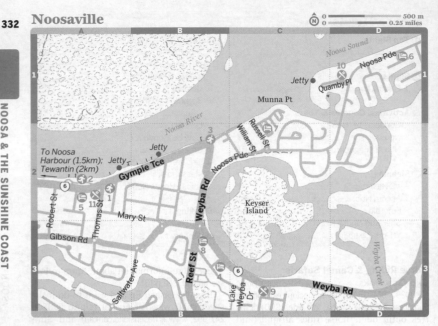

Noosaville

◎ Activities, Courses & Tours

◎ Sleeping

◎ Eating

Scenic Tours
The Eumundi markets are popular on Wednesdays and Saturdays. Companies that throw in an extra dash of pizzazz:

On the Prowl Surf n Adventures   SCENIC
(☑0450 279 623; www.ontheprowl.com.au; per person $59) Follow a stint at the Eumundi markets with two hours of surfing, kayaking or wake-boarding. After lunch, swim in the hinterland waterfalls before stopping for a beer on the way home.

Boomerang Tours   SCENIC
(☑1800 763 077; per person $59) Following the 'hippie trail' visiting Eumundi markets, Kondalilla Falls, Montville and Mary Cairncross Reserve. Includes sausage-sizzle lunch.

✵ Festivals & Events

Noosa Festival of Surfing   SURFING
(www.usmevents.com.au/noosasurf) A week of longboard action in March.

Noosa Food & Wine Festival
    GASTRONOMIC
(☑5447 5666; www.noosafoodandwine.com.au) A three-day tribute to all things of gastronomic and culinary delight in May.

Noosa Jazz Festival   MUSIC
(☑5449 9189; www.noosajazz.com.au) Four-day event in late August to early September.

Noosa Long Weekend   CULTURAL
(☑5474 9941; www.noosalongweekend.com) Ten-day festival of arts, culture, food and fashion in June/July.

Noosa Triathlon   TRIATHLON
(☑5449 0711; www.usmevents.com.au) Triathlon and week-long sports festival in early November.

🛏 Sleeping

With the exception of backpackers' hostels, accommodation prices can rise by 50% in busy times and 100% in the December to January peak season. During these times most places require a minimum two- or three-night stay. Low-season rates are quoted.

For an extensive list of private holiday rentals good for three nights or more, try **Accom Noosa** (Map p330; ☑1800 072 078; www.accomnoosa.com.au; Shop 5, Fairshore Apartments, Hastings St, Noosa Heads).

Islander Noosa Resort　　RESORT $$
(Map p332; ☑5440 9200; www.islandernoosa.com.au; 187 Gympie Tce, Noosaville; 2-/3-bedroom villa $178/205; ✺⊛🖢🖥) Set on 4 acres of lush tropical gardens, with a central tropical pool and wooden boardwalks meandering through the trees to your comfortable bungalow, this resort is excellent value. It's bright and cheerful and packs a cocktail-swilling, island-resort ambience.

#2 Hastings St　　APARTMENTS $$$
(Map p330; ☑5448 0777; www.2hastingsst.com.au; 2 Hastings St, Noosa Heads; units from $225; ✺🖢) These two-bedroom, two-bathroom units at the Noosa Woods end of Hastings St are great value for four people. Units overlook the river or the woods and you're within a short walk of everything.

Sheraton Noosa Resort　　RESORT $$$
(Map p330; ☑5449 4888; www.starwoodhotels.com/sheraton; 14 16 Hastings St, Noosa Heads; r $255; ✺🖢) As expected, this five-star hotel has tastefully decorated rooms with suede fabrics, fabulous beds, balconies, kitchenettes and spas. The hotel houses the popular Cato's as well as a day spa.

YHA Halse Lodge　　HOSTEL $
(Map p330; ☑1800 242 567, 5447 3377; www.halselodge.com.au; 2 Halse Lane, Noosa Heads; members/nonmembers dm $29/32, d $78/86; meals $10-15; 🖢🖥) Elevated from Hastings St by a steep driveway, this splendid colonial-era timber Queenslander is a legend on the backpacker route. There are three- and six-bed dorms as well as doubles and a lovely wide verandah. The bar is a mix-and-meet bonanza and serves great meals.

Emerald　　APARTMENTS $$$
(Map p330; ☑1800 803 899, 5449 6100; www.emeraldnoosa.com.au; 42 Hastings St, Noosa Heads; 1-bedroom apt from $255; ✺🖢🖥) The stylish Emerald has indulgent rooms bathed in ethereal white and sunlight. Expect clean,

crisp edges and exquisite furnishings. All one-, two- and three- bedroom apartments are fully self-contained, but ask for a balcony with a view.

Anchor Motel Noosa　　MOTEL $$
(Map p332; ☑5449 8055; www.anchormotelnoosa.com.au; cnr Anchor St & Weyba Rd, Noosaville; r from $115; ✺🖢🖥) There's no escaping the nautical theme in this colourful motel. Blue-striped bedspreads, porthole windows and marine motifs will have you wearing stripes and cut-offs while grilling prawns on the barbie.

Noosa Parade Holiday Inn　　APARTMENTS $$
(Map p332; ☑5447 4177; www.noosaparadeholidayinn.com; 51 Noosa Pde, Noosa Heads; r $125; ✺🖢🖥) Not far from Hastings St, these large, bright apartments are good value. The pleasant and cool interiors are clad in bold colours and face away from the street and passing traffic.

Noosa River Retreat　　APARTMENTS $$
(Map p332; ☑5474 2811; www.noosariverretreat.net; cnr Weyba Rd & Reef St, Noosaville; studio $110; ✺🖢🖥) Your buck goes a long way at this orderly complex with spick, span and spacious units. Onsite are a central barbecue and laundry and the corner units are almost entirely protected by small, native gardens.

Nomads Backpackers　　HOSTEL $
(Map p330; ☑5447 3355; www.nomadshostels.com; 44 Noosa Dr, Noosa Junction; dm from $26; 🖢🖥) One of the Nomad chain, this hostel has the usual trademarks: popular bar, central location and party atmosphere. You can't get less than an eight-bed dorm, but you'll be partying so hard it won't matter. There's a tour desk on site.

Noosa River Caravan Park　　CARAVAN PARK $
(Map p332; ☑5449 7050; Russell St, Noosaville; unpowered/powered sites $31/39; 🖥) On the banks of the Noosa River, this park has the closest camping facilities to Noosa, but although it's in a pretty spot, the regulations might make you think twice before pitching your tent.

🍴 Eating

You can eat well for around $10 at the **Bay Village Shopping Centre food court** (Map p330; Hastings St, Noosa Heads). Self-caterers can stock up at the Noosa Fair Shopping Centre in Noosa Junction.

TOP CHOICE **Berardo's**　　MODERN AUSTRALIAN $$$
(Map p330; ☑5447 5666; Hastings St; mains $30-42; ◔dinner) Beautiful Berardo's is culinary Utopia, from the sun-dappled

setting swimming in elegance to the heavenly food. Soft music from the grand piano and delicate dishes made from fresh local produce will have you swooning in gustatory ecstasy.

Humid
MODERN AUSTRALIAN $$

(Map p332; ☑5449 9755; 195 Weyba Rd, Noosaville; mains $25-30; ☺lunch & dinner Wed-Sun) It might feel as though you're eating inside a designer warehouse in this high-ceilinged, two-storey restaurant, but the food begs to differ. The Italian influences are subtle and classy, with Humid consistently rated among the best restaurants in Noosa.

Berardo's on the Beach
MODERN AUSTRALIAN $$

(Map p330; ☑5448 0888; On the Beach, Hastings St; mains $20-36; ☺breakfast, lunch & dinner) Reminiscent of the French Riviera, this stylish bistro is only metres from the waves. Classy without being pretentious, this is Noosa in a seashell. The Mod Oz menu uses local produce with a focus on seafood.

Wasabi
JAPANESE $$

(Map p332; ☑5449 2443; 2 Quamby Pl, Noosaville; mains $20-33; ☺dinner Tue-Sun, lunch Fri & Sat) The must-try is this award-winning Japanese restaurant's signature dish, *hiramasa ponzu*: kingfish sashimi slices on a long glass plank, drizzled with toasted sesame seeds, fried ginger chips, sliced green onions and citrusy soy ponzu dressing.

Cafe Le Monde
MODERN AUSTRALIAN $$

(Map p330; Hastings St; mains $15-28; ☺breakfast, lunch & dinner) There's not a fussy palate or dietary need that isn't catered for on Cafe Le Monde's enormous menu. The large, open-air patio buzzes with diners digging into burgers, seared tuna steaks, curries, pastas, salads and plenty more. Come for daily happy hour drinks between 4pm to 6pm.

Lindoni's
ITALIAN $$$

(Map p330; ☑5447 5111; Hastings St; mains $20-50; ☺dinner) Behind the gothic candelabra guarding the entrance, this romantic Italian restaurant has a Mediterranean courtyard for intimate candlelit dining. The cuisine favours the lighter southern Italian style – think Positano and the Amalfi coast – with lashings of *amore*.

Aromas
CAFE $

(Map p330; 32 Hastings St; mains $10-28; ☺breakfast, lunch & dinner) This European-style cafe is unashamedly ostentatious with chandeliers, faux-marble tables and cane chairs deliberately facing the street so patrons can ogle the passing foot traffic. There's the usual array of panini, cakes and light meals, but most folk come for the coffee and the atmosphere.

Gaston
MODERN AUSTRALIAN $$

(5/50 Hastings St; mains $17-25; ☺breakfast, lunch & dinner) This casual alfresco bar and bistro is highly recommended by the locals. It's also a great place to watch the passing parade of beautiful people.

Bistro C
MODERN AUSTRALIAN $$

(Map p330; ☑5447 2855; On the Beach, Hastings St; mains $25-35; ☺breakfast, lunch & dinner) The menu at this yuppie beachfront brasserie is an eclectic blend of everything that seems like a good idea at the time. The legendary egg-fried calamari is still popular.

Ricky's River Bar & Restaurant
MODERN AUSTRALIAN $$$

(Map p332; ☑5447 2455; Noosa Wharf, 2 Quamby Pl, Noosaville; mains $30-40; ☺lunch & dinner) An elegant restaurant on the water.

Thomas Corner
MODERN AUSTRALIAN $$

(Map p332; cnr Thomas St & Gympie Tce, Noosaville; mains $15-31; ☺lunch & dinner) A casual but chic newcomer to Noosaville's 'Eat Street'.

Noosa Heads SLSC
PUB FARE $$

(Map p330; Hastings St; mains $10-28; ☺breakfast Sat & Sun, lunch & dinner daily) Perfect beach views from the deck.

Massimo's
GELATI $

(Map p330; Hastings St; gelati $2-4; ☺9am-10pm) Definitely one of the best gelaterias in Queensland.

🍷 Drinking

Zachary's
BAR

(Map p330; 30 Hastings St, Noosa Heads) This shabby-chic, second-storey 'gourmet pizza bar' is a favourite meeting place and night-starter.

KB's
BAR

(44 Noosa Dr, Noosa Junction) Noosa's backpackers and other free spirits start their nightly revelry at this popular hostel bar. Live rock fills every crevice several nights a week.

Cato's
COCKTAIL BAR

(Map p330; 16 Hastings St) As well as a decadent cocktail list, Cato's, at the Sheraton Noosa Resort, boasts over 30 wines by the glass.

Information

Noosa visitors centre (☑5430 5020; www.visitnoosa.com.au; Hastings St; ◷9am-5pm)

Palm Tree Tours (☑5474 9166; www.palm-treetours.com.au; Bay Village Shopping Centre, Hastings St; ◷9am-5pm) Very helpful tour desk. Can book tours, accommodation and bus tickets.

Post office (91 Noosa Dr)

Urban Mailbox (Ocean Breeze, Noosa Dr, Noosa Heads; per 15min $3; ◷8am-8pm) Superexpensive internet access.

Getting There & Away

Long-distance bus services stop at the bus stop that is located near the corner of Noosa Dr and Noosa Pde (Map p330). **Greyhound Australia** (☑1300 473 946; www.greyhound.com.au) has several daily bus connections from Brisbane ($32, 21/2 hours) while **Premier Motor Service** (☑13 34 10; www.premierms.com.au) has one ($23, 2½ hours). **Veolia** (☑1300 826 608; www.vtb.com.au) has an express service from Brisbane to Noosa (one way/return $25/46) twice daily.

At the time of research, a new transit centre was under construction in Noosa Dr, Noosa Junction. Once completed, long-distance buses will arrive there.

Sunbus (☑13 12 30) has frequent services to Maroochydore ($5, one hour) and the Nambour train station ($5, one hour).

Getting Around

Bicycle

Noosa Bike Hire & Tours (☑5474 3322; www.bikeon.com.au; per 4hr/day $29/39) hires bicycles from several locations in Noosa including Nomads Backpackers (p333). Alternatively, bikes are delivered to and from your door for free.

Boat

Noosa Ferry (☑5449 8442) operates ferries between Noosa Heads and Tewantin (one way adult/child/family $13/4.50/30, all-day pass $19.50/5.50/45, 30 minutes). Tickets include onboard commentary.

Bus

During the peak holiday seasons – 26 December to 10 January and over Easter – there are free shuttle buses every 10 to 15 minutes between Weyba Rd, just outside Noosa Junction, travelling all the way to Tewantin and stopping just about everywhere in between. Sunbus has local services that link Noosa Heads, Noosaville, Noosa Junction and Tewantin.

Car

Car rental starts from around $60 per day.

Avis (☑5447 4933; Shop 1, Ocean Breeze Resort, cnr Hastings St & Noosa Dr, Noosa Heads)

Budget (☑5474 2820; 52 Mary St, Noosaville)

Hertz (☑5447 2253; 12 Eenie Creek Rd, Noosaville)

Thrifty (Accom Noosa, Shop 5, Fairshore Apartments, Hastings St, Noosa Heads)

Bribie Island

☑07 / POP 15,920

This slender island at the northern end of Moreton Bay is popular with young families, retirees and those with a cool million or three to spend on a waterfront property. It's far more developed than Stradbroke or Moreton Islands, but the Bribie Island National Park on the northwestern coast has some beautifully remote national park camping areas (www.derm.qld.gov.au; per person/family $5.15/20.60). Note that access is by 4WD only.

There's no 4WD hire on the island and 4WD permits (per week/year $37.65/117.60) can

---

UNEXPECTED TREASURE: ABBEY MUSEUM

The impressive art and archaeology collection in the Abbey Museum (☑5495 1652; www.abbeytournament.com; 1 The Abbey Pl; adult/child $8.80/5; ◷10am-4pm Mon-Sat) spans the globe and would be at home in any of the world's famous museums. Once the private collection of Englishman John Ward, the pieces include neolithic tools, medieval manuscripts and even an ancient Greek foot-guard (one of only four worldwide), and will have you scratching your head in amazement. The church has more original stained glass from Winchester Cathedral than what is actually left in the cathedral. In July, you can make merry at Australia's largest medieval festival held on the grounds.

The Abbey Musuem is on the road to Bribie Island, 6km from the Bruce Hwy turn-off, where you'll find the Caboolture Warplane Museum (☑5499 1144; Hangar 104, Caboolture Airfield, McNaught Rd; adult/child/family $8/5/18; ◷9am-3pm), with its collection of restored WWII warplanes, all in flying order.

DON'T MISS

CREATURE FEATURE: AUSTRALIA ZOO

Just north of Beerwah is one of Queensland's, if not Australia's, most famous tourist attractions. **Australia Zoo** (✆5494 1134; www.australiazoo.com.au; Steve Irwin Way, Beerwah; adult/child/family $49/29/146; ☺9am-4.30pm) is a fitting homage to its founder, zany celebrity wildlife enthusiast, Steve Irwin. As well as all things slimy and scaly, the zoo has an amazing wildlife menagerie complete with a Cambodian-style Tiger Temple, the Asian-themed Elephantasia and the famous crocoseum. There are macaws, birds of prey, giant tortoises, snakes, otters, camels and more crocs and critters than you can poke a stick at. Plan to spend a full day at this amazing wildlife park.

Various companies offer tours from Brisbane and the Sunshine Coast (see p348). The zoo operates a free courtesy bus from towns along the coast, as well as from the Beerwah train station (bookings essential).

be purchased online (www.derm.qld.gov.au). You can also purchase permits at **Bribie Passage Kiosk & Boat Hire** (✆5497 5789; 23 Kalmakuta Dr, Sandstone Point; ☺6am-4pm Mon-Fri, 5.30am-5.30pm Sat & Sun). **Bribie Island visitors centre** (✆3408 9026; www.bribie.com.au; Benabrow Ave, Bellara; ☺9am-4pm Mon-Fri, to 3pm Sat, 9.30am-1pm Sun) has more information.

Inn Bongaree (✆3410 1718; www.innbongaree.com.au; 25 Second Ave, Bongaree; s/d $50/65) is a great budget option, or you can stay at **Sylvan Beach Resort** (✆3408 8300; www.sylvanbeachresort.com.au; d from $170; ✴@⊠), with comfortable self-contained units across the road from the beach.

Bribie Island SLSC (✆3408 4420; Rickman Pde; mains $10-25; ☺lunch & dinner), at the southern end of the beach, serves up good ol' Aussie tucker.

Frequent Citytrain services run from Brisbane to Caboolture where a Trainlink bus connects to Bribie Island.

Glass House Mountains

The ethereal volcanic crags of the Glass House Mountains rise abruptly from the subtropical plains 20km northwest of Caboolture. In Dreaming legend, these rocky peaks belong to a family of mountain spirits. It's worth diverting off the Bruce Hwy onto the slower Steve Irwin Way (formerly the Glass House Mountains Rd) to snake your way through dense pine forests and green pastureland for a close-up view of these spectacular volcanic plugs.

The **Glass House Mountains National Park** is broken into several sections (all within cooee of Beerwah) with picnic grounds and lookouts but no camping grounds. The peaks are reached by a series of sealed and unsealed roads known as Forest Dr, which heads inland from Steve Irwin Way. For more information, visit the **QPWS** (✆5494 0150; Bells Creek Rd, Beerwah).

◉ Sights & Activities

A number of signposted walking tracks reach several of the peaks, but be prepared for some steep and rocky trails. **Mt Beerwah** (556m) is the most trafficked but has a section of open rock face that may increase the anxiety factor. The walk up **Ngungun** (253m) is more moderate and the views are just as sensational, while **Tibrogargan** (364m) is probably the best climb with a challenging scramble and several amazing lookouts from the flat summit. Rock climbers can usually be seen scaling Tibrogargan, Ngungun and Beerwah (for climbing information visit www.qurank.com). **Mt Coonowrin** (aka 'crook-neck'), the most dramatic of the volcanic plugs, is closed to the public.

⊨ Sleeping & Eating

With only basic accommodation available, the Glass House Mountains are best visited as a day trip.

Glasshouse Mountains Holiday Village
CARAVAN PARK **$**
(✆5496 9338; www.glasshousemountainsholiday village.com.au; 778 Steve Irwin Way, Glass House Mountains; unpowered/powered sites $25/35, cabins from $110; ✴⊠) This park has comfortable, self-contained cabins, pretty sites and spectacular mountain views. Facilities include barbecues, a tennis court and a small cafe.

Glasshouse Mountains Tavern PUB FARE $$
(10 Reed St, Glasshouse Mountains; mains $15-25; ⊙lunch & dinner) This welcoming pub cooks up good pub nosh. The open fire keeps things cosy during winter and a peppering of outdoor seating is great for a midday middy on sunny days.

Caloundra

☑07 / POP 20,140

Straddling a headland at the southern end of the Sunshine Coast, Caloundra is slowly shedding its staid retirement-village image without losing its sleepy seaside charm. Excellent fishing in Pumicestone Passage (the snake of water separating Bribie Island from the mainland) and a number of pleasant surf beaches make it a popular holiday resort for both families and water-sports fans.

◉ Sights & Activities

Caloundra's beaches curve around the headland so you'll always find a sheltered beach no matter how windy it gets. **Bulcock Beach**, just down from the main street and pinched by the northern tip of Bribie Island, captures a good wind tunnel, making it popular with kite-surfers. There's a lovely promenade on the foreshore that extends around to **Kings Beach**, where there's a kiddie-friendly interactive water feature and a free saltwater swimming pool on the rocks. The coastal track continues around the headland towards **Currimundi**. Depending on the conditions, **Moffat Beach** and **Dickey Beach** have the best surf breaks.

Q Surf School SURFING
(☑0404 869 622; www.qsurfschool.com; 1hr lesson $45, 3 lessons $120) Also offers stand-up paddleboarding (one-hour lesson $55).

Blue Water Kayak Tours KAYAKING
(☑5494 7789; www.bluewaterkayaktours.com; full-/half-day tours $150/75, minimum 4 people) Kayak across the channel to the northern tip of Bribie Island National Park.

Caloundra Cruise BOAT CRUISE
(☑5492 8280; www.caloundracruise.com; Maloja Jetty; adult/child/family $20/10/45; 2½hr eco-explorer cruise adult/child $44/20) Cruise into Pumicestone Passage.

Sunshine Coast Skydivers SKYDIVING
(☑5437 0211; www.sunshinecoastskydivers.com.au; dives from $220) If you're mad enough to step out of a plane, this company will allow you to film the process.

Queensland Air Museum MUSEUM
(☑5492 5930; www.qam.com.au; Caloundra Airport; adult/child/family $10/6/24; ⊙10am-4pm) Plenty of planes to keep budding aviators happy for hours.

🛏 Sleeping

There are plenty of high-rise apartments to choose from in Caloundra. There's often a minimum three- to five-night stay in high season, and high-season rates are quoted.

Rolling Surf Resort APARTMENTS $$$
(☑5491 9777; www.rollingsurfresort.com; Levuka Ave, Kings Beach; 1-/2-bedroom apt $240/400; ✳@🛜🏊) This ultrachic resort directly on the beach has *très* modern furnishings, fantastic views and a heated pool. Be king of Kings Beach in the three-bedroom penthouse suite. In high season, there's a minimum five-night stay.

Caloundra Backpackers HOSTEL $
(☑5499 7655; www.caloundrabackpackers.com.au; 84 Omrah Ave; dm/d $28/65; @🛜) A newcomer to Caloundra; the dorms here are adequate, plus there's a comfy lounge and two decent kitchens. You also get free bike, surfboard and stand-up paddleboard hire.

Dicky Beach Family Holiday Park
CARAVAN PARK $
(☑5491 3342; www.dicky.com.au; 4 Beerburrum St, Dicky Beach; unpowered/powered sites $32/35, cabins from $90; ✳🛜🏊) You can't get any closer to one of Caloundra's most popular beaches. The brick cabins are as ordered and tidy as the grounds and there's a small swimming pool for the kids. Rates are for two people.

City Centre Motel MOTEL $$
(☑5491 3301; 20 Orsova Tce; d $100-119; ✳) The closest motel to the city centre holds no surprises. It's a small complex and the rooms, although basic, are comfortable.

🍴 Eating

The newly spruced-up Bulcock Beach esplanade has a number of alfresco cafes and restaurants, all with perfect sea views.

La Dolce Vita ITALIAN $$
(☑5438 2377; Shop 1, Rumba Resort, Esplanade, Bulcock Beach; mains $20-35; ⊙breakfast, lunch & dinner) This modern Italian restaurant has a stylish black-and-white theme but it's best to sit outdoors behind the large glass windowed booth for alfresco dining with gorgeous sea views. Try the *gambari alio olio*

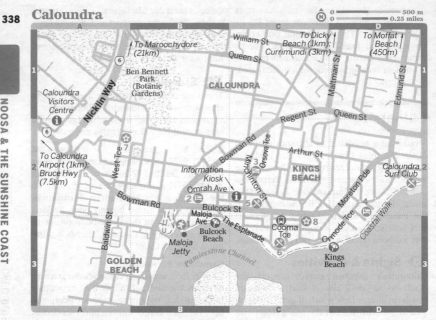

Caloundra

pepperoncini (prawns with garlic, oil and chilli).

Saltwater@Kings CAFE $$
(☑5437 2260; 8 Levuka Ave, Kings Beach; mains $16-35; ☺breakfast, lunch & dinner) The playful menu that is on offer at this casual beachside cafe promises nude oysters, spiced chook salad and a range of 'voluptuous dishes'. It's perfect for lunch straight off the beach.

Chilli Jam Cafe CAFE $
(51 Bulcock St; mains $8-14; ☺breakfast & lunch) A friendly couple from Yorkshire runs this popular cafe where you can devour a range of gourmet sandwiches, wraps, salads and burgers.

☆ Entertainment

CBX PUB
(12 Bulcock St) Queensland's only beer exchange hovers somewhere between an RSL and a surf club. In fact, the bar works like a stock exchange, with beer prices rising and falling depending on demand. Live bands and DJs on weekends make this the local party scene.

Caloundra RSL CLUB
(19 West Tce) Some RSLs are small and unassuming affairs – not this one. With enough flamboyance to outdo Liberace, Caloundra's award-winning RSL has a number of restaurants and bars including the groovy 1970s-style Lava Lounge Bar. The glitzy atmosphere can be a little overwhelming.

❶ Information

Caloundra visitors centre (☑1800 644 969; 7 Caloundra Rd; ☺9am-5pm) On the roundabout at the entrance to the town. There's also an information kiosk in the main street.

Hotspot Internet Cafe (☎5499 6644; Shop 8, 51 Bulcock St; per hr $6; ⊙9am-5pm Mon-Fri, to 3pm Sat)

ⓘ Getting There & Away

Greyhound (☎1300 473 946; www.greyhound. com.au) buses from Brisbane ($32, two hours) stop at the **bus terminal** (☎5491 2555; Cooma Tce). **Sunbus** (☎13 12 30) has frequent services to Noosa ($5.80, 1½ hours) via Maroochydore ($3.20, 50 minutes).

Mooloolaba & Maroochydore

☎07 / POP 10,250 / 16,360

Mooloolaba has seduced many a 'sea-changer' with its sublime climate, golden beach and cruisy lifestyle. The locals here are proud of their surfing roots and relaxed beach culture. Just take a morning walk on the foreshore and you'll find walkers and joggers, suntans and surfboards, and a dozen genuine smiles before breakfast.

Mooloolaba and Maroochydore, along with Alexandra Headland and Cotton Tree, form the Maroochy region. While Maroochydore takes care of the business end, Mooloolaba steals the show. Eateries, boutiques and pockets of low-rise resorts and apartments have spread along the Esplanade, transforming this once-humble fishing village into one of Queensland's most popular holiday destinations. In summer, Maroochy bursts with families indulging in good fishing and surf beaches, but it quickly reverts back to the tranquil epitome of coastal Oz for the remainder of the year.

◉ Sights & Activities

There are good surf breaks along the strip – one of Queensland's best for longboarders is the **Bluff**, the prominent point at Alexandra Headland. The beach breaks from Alex to Maroochydore are consistent even in a southerly, while **Pincushion** (Map p340) near the Maroochy River mouth can provide an excellent break in the winter offshore winds.

Diving for the wreck of the sunken warship, the **ex-HMAS Brisbane**, is also incredibly popular. Sunk in July 2005, the wreck lies in 28m of water and its funnels are only 4m below the surface.

Underwater World   OCEANARIUM
(Map p342; the Wharf, Mooloolaba; www.underwaterworld.com.au; adult/child/family $32/22/90; ⊙9am-5pm) Here, in the largest tropical oceanarium in the southern hemisphere, you can swim with seals, dive with sharks or simply marvel at the ocean life outside the 80m-long transparent underwater tunnel. There's a touch tank, seal shows and educational spiels to entertain both kids and adults.

Scuba World   DIVING
(☎5444 8595; www.scubaworld.com.au; The Wharf, Mooloolaba; dives from $99; ⊙9am-5pm Mon-Sat, 10.30am-4pm Sun) Arranges shark dives (certified/uncertified divers $195/225) at Underwater World, coral dives off the coast and a wreck dive of the *Brisbane*. PADI courses available.

Robbie Sherwell's XL Surfing Academy
                SURFING
(☎5478 1337; www.robbiesherwell.com.au; 1hr lesson private/group per person $95/45) Get your toes wet.

Suncoast Kiteboarding   KITEBOARDING
(0412 985 858; www.suncoastkiteboarding.com. au; 2hr lesson $180) At Cotton Tree, Noosa and Caloundra.

Sunreef   DIVING
(☎5444 5656; www.sunreef.com.au; 110 Brisbane Rd, Mooloolaba; PADI Open Water Diver course $595) Offers two dives ($145) on the wreck of the sunken warship, the ex-HMAS *Brisbane*. Also runs night dives on the wreck.

Hire Hut   WATER SPORTS
(☎5444 0366; www.oceanjetski.com.au; The Wharf, Parkyn Pde, Mooloolaba) Hires kayaks (two hours $25), stand-up paddleboards (two hours $35), jet skis (one hour $100) and boats (per hour/half day $42/75).

Sunshine Coast Bike & Board Hire
                SPORTING HIRE
(☎0439 706 206; www.adventurehire.com.au) Hires out bikes/kayaks/surfboards for $30/40/25.

Swan's Boat Hire   BOAT HIRE
(☎5443 7225; 59 Bradman Ave, Maroochydore; half/full day $146/226; ⊙6am-6pm) On the Maroochy River. Also hires out kayaks (one hour/half day $20/60).

☞ Tours
Boat Cruises

Steve Irwin's Whale One   WHALE WATCHING
(Map p342; ☎1300 27 45 39; www.whaleone.com. au; adult/child/family $135/75/330) Sunrise whale-watching cruises in September and October.

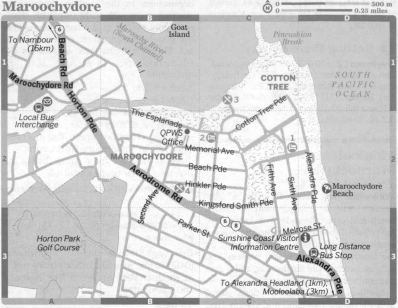

Canal Cruise

BOAT CRUISE

(Map p342; 5444 7477; www.mooloolaba
canalcruise.com.au; The Wharf, Mooloolaba; adult/
child/family $18/6/45; 11am, 1pm & 2.30pm)
These boat trips cruise past the glitterati
canal houses located along the Mooloolah
River.

Cruiz Away River Tours

BOAT CRUISE

(Map p342; 5444 7477; www.cruisemooloolaba.
com.au; The Wharf, Mooloolaba; ecotours adult/
child $39/27, sunset cruises $30) Birdwatching
and nature cruises on the Mooloolah River
National Park.

Kayaking

Aussie Sea Kayak Company KAYAKING

(Map p342; 0407 049 747; www.ausseakayak.
com.au; The Wharf, Mooloolaba; 4hr tour/2hr
sunset paddle $65/45) Kayaking around
Mooloolaba and Noosa Everglades, plus
multiday trips to North Stradbroke, Fraser
and Moreton Islands.

Fraser Island

Fraser Island Adventure Tours 4WD

(5444 6957; www.fraserislandadventuretours.
com.au; day tour $170) Offers excellent day
tour to Eli Creek and Lake McKenzie.

🛏 Sleeping

During school holidays, rates can double
and most places require a minimum two-
or three-night stay. Low-season prices are
quoted.

Landmark Resort RESORT $$

(Map p342; 1800 888 835, 5444 5555; www.
landmarkresort.com.au; cnr Esplanade & Burnett St,
Mooloolaba; studio/1-bedroom apt from $175/195;
❋@🛜🏊) Nothing compares to the ocean
views from these breezy apartments. The re-
sort sits above Mooloolaba's trendy eateries
and is only 20m from the beach. There's a
heated lagoon-style pool and a rooftop spa
and barbecue.

Seamark on First APARTMENTS $$$

(Map p342; 5457 8600; www.seamarkresort.com.
au; 29 First Ave, Mooloolaba; 1-bedroom apt from
$180; ❋🛜🏊) One street back from Mooloo-
laba's fashionable Esplanade, this stylish
and modern resort is bright, airy and spacious. Most apartments have ocean views –
sit on the balcony and watch the moon rise
over the water. There's a two-night minimum stay.

Kyamaba Court Motel MOTEL $$

(Map p342; 5444 0202; www.kyambacourtmotel.
com.au; 94 Brisbane Rd, Mooloolaba; d Mon-Fri $95,
Sat $130; ❋🛜🏊) Although this motel is on

Maroochydore

a busy road, it also fronts the canal where you can lounge around in comfort while throwing a few shrimps on the barbie. The rooms are large, comfortable and clean. It's a short walk into town and to the beach. Great value.

Coral Sea Apartments   APARTMENTS $$
(Mapp340;☑54792999;www.coralsea-apartments. com; 35-7 Sixth Ave, Maroochydore; 1-/2-bedroom apt from $160/190; ✹@✖) These yawning two- and three-bedroom apartments occupy a lovely spot close to Maroochy Surf Club and the beach. Inside you'll find tasteful decor and the balconies are plenty big and breezy.

Alexandra Beach Resort   RESORT $$
(Map p340; ☑5475 0600; www.breakfreealex andrabeach.com.au; cnr Alexandra Pde & Pacific Tce, Alexandra Headland; studio/1-bedroom apt $170/199; ✹@🛜✖) Directly opposite the beach, these large and comfy apartments open onto either a courtyard or a balcony, but can be quite noisy. The 150m tropical-lagoon pool comes with a pool bar! Two-night minimum stay.

Mooloolaba Beach Backpackers
                            HOSTEL $
(Map p342; ☑5444 3399; www.mooloolababack packers.com; 75 Brisbane Rd, Mooloolaba, dm/d $28/70; @🛜✖) Some dorms have en suites, some don't, and although the rooms look a bit tired, the amount of freebies (bikes, kay-aks, surfboards, stand-up paddleboards and breakfast) more than compensate. Besides, it's only 500m from the beachside day- and night-life.

Cotton Tree Beach House Backpackers
                            HOSTEL $
(Map p340; ☑5443 1755; www.cottontreeback packers.com; 15 Esplanade, Cotton Tree; dm/d $26/55) The vibe is as warm as the brightly painted common-room walls and the atmo-sphere as laid-back as the fat Lab lolling on the sofa. Opposite a park and a river,

this renovated century-old Queenslander is clean and homey and oozes charm along with free surfboards, kayaks and bikes.

Mooloolaba Beach Caravan Park
                   CARAVAN PARK $
(Map p342; ☑1800 441 201, 5444 1201; www.ma roochypark.qld.gov.au; Parkyn Pde, Mooloolaba; powered sites from $35) This little beauty fronts lovely Mooloolaba Beach. It also runs a tiny van site at the northern end of the Espla-nade, with the best location and views of any accommodation in town. Prices are for two people.

✖ Eating

ᵀᴼᴾ **Bella Venezia**   ITALIAN $$$
(Map p342; ☑5444 5844; 95 Esplanade, Mooloo-laba; mains $25-38; ⊘lunch & dinner) This un-derstated yet casually chic restaurant, with a funky wine bar, spreads across an arcade cul-de-sac. The menu is extensive and exclu-sively Italian and includes exquisite dishes such as Moreton Bay bug ravioli.

Boat Shed   SEAFOOD $$
(Map p340; ☑5443 3808; Esplanade, Cotton Tree; mains $25-35, ⊘lunch daily, dinner Mon-Sat) A shabby-chic gem on the banks of the Ma-roochy River, great for sunset drinks be-neath the sprawling cotton tree. Seafood is the star of the menu and a must-try is the coconut-battered prawns with roasted banana and caramelised rum syrup. After dinner, roll back to the outdoor lounges for dessert and some seriously romantic star-gazing.

India Today   INDIAN $$
(Map p340; ☑5452 7054; 91 Aerodrome Rd, Ma roochydore; mains $15-22; ⊘lunch Thu, Fri & Sat, dinner nightly) You can't miss the masses of fairy lights decorating this restaurant on Maroochydore's main drag. Be prepared for the brightly and chaotically coloured visual feast of Indian cloths, textiles, paintings and wall hangings waiting inside. The butter chicken with the chef's special sauce is deli-cious.

Nude   CAFE $
(Map p342; Shop 3, Mooloolaba Esplanade, Mooloo-olaba; dishes $6-18; ⊘breakfast & lunch) Occu-pying the prime position on the esplanade, this casual alfresco cafe is the ideal spot for people-watching and for ocean views with your latte. Salads, wraps, gourmet sand-wiches and naughty cakes will satisfy post-swimming munchies.

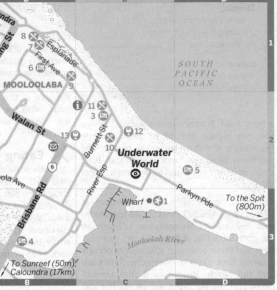

Via Italia
ITALIAN **$$**

(Map p342; ☎5477 7343; Shop 13, Peninsular Apartments, Esplanade, Mooloolaba; mains $17-25; ☺breakfast, lunch & dinner) This stylish but casual outdoor restaurant opposite the beach is in the thick of the action. Come for a sundowner at the central bar. The gourmet pizzas will tempt you to linger on.

Karma Waters
MODERN AUSTRALIAN **$$**

(Map p342; Mantra, Esplanade, Mooloolaba; mains $21-32; ☺breakfast, lunch & dinner) Another outdoor eatery along the lively esplanade, Karma Waters dishes up Mod Oz cuisine with a Portuguese influence. The influence isn't always apparent but the meals are tasty. Try the seared Atlantic salmon with lemon-caper butter sauce.

Thai Seasons
THAI **$**

(Map p342; ☎5444 4611; 10 River Esplanade, Mooloolaba; mains $10-12; ☺dinner) Affectionately known as 'dirty Thai', but don't be put off by the plastic outdoor setting and grubby exterior. Although you have to grab your own cutlery, this unpretentious restaurant dishes out the best Thai food in town. If it's crowded, order takeaway and head for the picnic tables overlooking Mooloolaba's main beach.

🍷 Drinking

Mooloolaba SLSC
SURF CLUB

(Map p342; Esplanade, Mooloolaba; ☺10am-10pm Sun-Thu, to midnight Fri & Sat) A traditional Aussie icon, the surf club somehow seamlessly morphs from a midweek, good-value family outing to a weekend singles pick-up joint where local bands play '80s dance music every Friday night. The floor-to-ceiling windows on the deck provide stunning views.

Soave
BAR

(17-19 Brisbane Rd, Mooloolaba) The place to meet for after-work drinks or to fuel up for a Friday night on the town. The gourmet pizza menu is matched with an impressive cocktail list.

Fridays
NIGHTCLUB

(Map p342; The Wharf, Parkyn Pde, Mooloolaba; ☺Tue-Sat) Loud, tacky and incredibly popular with backpackers and locals.

ℹ️ Information

The Mooloolaba Esplanade seamlessly morphs into Alexandra Pde along the beachfront at Alexandra Headland ('Alex' to the locals), then flows into Aerodrome Rd and the main CBD of Maroochydore. Cotton Tree is at the mouth of the Maroochy River.

Email Central Internet Lounge (19 The Esplanade, Cotton Tree; per hr $5; ⊙9am-8pm)

Sunshine Coast Visitor Information Centre (☑1800 644 969, 5478 2233; www.maroochytourism.com; ⊙9am-5pm) Maroochydore (cnr Sixth Ave & Melrose Sts, Maroochydore); Mooloolaba (cnr Brisbane Rd & First Ave, Mooloolaba); Sunshine Coast Airport (Friendship Dr, Marcoola)

Post office Mooloolaba (☑13 13 18; cnr Brisbane Rd & Walan St); Maroochydore (Sunshine Plaza, Horton Pde)

QPWS office (Map p340; ☑5443 8940; 29 The Esplanade, Cotton Tree; ⊙8.30am-4.30pm Mon-Fri)

⊙ Getting There & Away

Long-distance buses stop in front of the Sunshine Coast Visitor Information Centre in Maroochydore. **Greyhound Australia** (☑1300 473 946; www.greyhound.com.au) and **Premier Motor Services** (☑13 34 10; www.premierms.com. au) run to and from Brisbane. **Veolia** (☑1300 826 608; www.vtb.com.au) has a direct service from Brisbane to Underwater World (one-way/return $23/42).

⊙ Getting Around

Sunbus (☑13 12 30) has frequent services between Mooloolaba and Maroochydore ($2) and on to Noosa ($5, one hour). The local bus interchange is at the Sunshine Plaza.

Coolum

☑07 / POP 7180

Coolum is one of the Sunshine Coast's hidden treasures. Rocky headlands create a number of secluded coves before spilling into the fabulously long stretch of golden sand and rolling surf of Coolum beach. With its budding cafe society, within easy reach of the coast's hot spots, it's an attractive escape from the more popular and overcrowded holiday scene at Noosa and Mooloolaba.

⊙ Sights & Activities

For outstanding views of the coast, a hike to the top of **Mt Coolum**, south of town, is worth the sweat factor. For information on how to get there, try the **visitors centre** (David Low Way; ⊙9am-5pm Mon-Fri, 10am-4pm Sat).

  Coolum Surf School (☑5446 5279; www. coolumsurfschool.com.au; 2hr lesson $50, 3-/5-day package $135/180) gets you standing on a board and also hires out stand-up paddleboards (24 hours $50).

  Skydive Ramblers (☑5446 1855; www. skydiveforfun.com; jumps from 10,000/14,000ft $350/399) will throw you out of a plane at a ridiculous height. Savour the coastal view before a spectacular beach landing.

⊨ Sleeping

Beach Retreat   APARTMENTS **$$**
(☑5471 7700; www.beachretreatcoolum.com; 1750 David Low Way; d from $250 minimum 2 nights; ❄@⊚❄) With ocean views and within walking distance of the esplanade eateries, these spacious apartments are in a great location. The central pool area is handy for rough beach weather. Standby one-night rates are available.

Villa Coolum   MOTEL **$**
(☑5446 1286; www.villacoolum.com; 102 Coolum Tce, Coolum Beach; r $79-99; ❄) Hidden behind a leafy verandah, these modest

bungalows have spacious motel-style rooms fronting a long balcony. The refurbished rooms are good value.

Coolum Beach Caravan Park
CARAVAN PARK $

(☑1800 461 474, 5446 1474; www.maroochypark. qld.gov.au; David Low Way, Coolum; unpowered/powered sites $32/35; ☎) This adequate park is nudged onto a grassy plot in front of the beach, just across the road from Coolum's main strip.

✖ Eating

The newly refurbished esplanade has sprouted a string of outdoor cafes and restaurants. It's fun to wander the strip before deciding where to eat.

My Place
MEDITERRANEAN $$

(☑5446 4433; David Low Way; mains $17-25; ⊙7am-11pm) Opposite the boardwalk and boasting sensational ocean views, My Place can't be beaten for sunset cocktails, tapas specials or summer alfresco dining.

Castro's Bar & Restaurant
ITALIAN $$

(☑5471 7555; cnr Frank St & Beach Rd; mains $15-30; ⊙dinner) All radicals will be satisfied with dishes such as tempura-battered wild barramundi fillet, Tuscan fish stew, Middle Eastern seared salmon and wood-fired pizza.

Raw Energy
CAFE $

(David Low Way; mains $6-14; ⊙breakfast & lunch) Après surf, tuck into a raw energy lunch where the menu reeks of salads, tofu and all things healthy.

Peregian & Sunshine Beach

☑07 / POP 2800 & 2360

Fifteen kilometres of uncrowded, unobstructed beach stretches north from Coolum to Sunshine Beach and the rocky northeast headland of Noosa National Park. Peregian clusters around a small village square that plays host to only a few cafes and restaurants – its lack of nightlife can be a drawcard for families that visit here on holidays. This is the place for you to indulge in long solitary beach walks, excellent surf breaks, fresh air and plenty of sunshine – and it is not uncommon to see whales breaking offshore.

A little further north, the laidback latte ethos of Sunshine Beach attracts Noosa locals escaping the summer hordes. Beach walks morph into bush walks over the headland; a postprandial stroll through the Noosa National Park takes an hour to reach Alexandria Bay and two hours to Noosa's Laguna Bay. Road access to the park is from McAnally Dr or Parkedge Rd.

◎ Sights & Activities

The Peregian Originals (www.eastcoasto riginals.org.au) is a changing line-up of both popular and obscure local, national and international bands. Attracting earth mothers and surfers as well as lovers of good music, these free Sunday-afternoon sessions (held on the first and third Sundays of each month) located in the park in front of the Peregian SLSC have become a summer classic. Check the website for performance dates and details.

Learn to surf with Wavesense (☑0414 369 076; www.wavesense.com.au), an excellent outfit that has been twice voted Surfing Australia Surf School of the Year.

🛏 Sleeping

It's hard to book anything less than a two-night stay in Sunshine Beach's holiday apartments.

Dolphins Beach House
HOSTEL $

(☑5447 2100; www.dolphinsbeachhouse.com; 14 Duke St, Sunshine Beach; dm $24-26, d $65-75; @☎) This cosy backpacker hostel is nestled in a patch of tropical gardens, and reflects the Asian and Mexican influences of its well-travelled owner. The rooms are basic and clean, there's plenty of kitchen space, it's close to cafes and the beach and is only a short bus ride to Noosa. Don't come looking for party central (there's no bar), but instead chill out before rejoining the frenzy of the backpacker trail.

Andari
APARTMENTS $$$

(☑5474 9996; www.andari.com.au; 19-21 Belmore Tce, Sunshine Beach; 2-bedroom apt $200; ☀☎) This quiet retreat of townhouses is set in shady, subtropical gardens. The apartments are light and airy, overlook the beach and are a short stroll to cafes and restaurants.

Pacific Blue Apartments
APARTMENTS $$

(☑5448 3611; www.pacificblueapartments.com. au; 236 David Low Way, Peregian Beach; r from $130; ☀) Close to the pub and the beach, Pacific Blue has cheerful two-bedroom units, all self-contained and with a healthy dose of space.

Sunshine Beach

✗ Eating

Embassy XO   MEDITERRANEAN **$$**
(☎5455 4460; cnr Duke & Bryan Sts, Sunshine Beach; mains $15-25; ⊙lunch & dinner) This chic bistro wine bar is an innovative concept for the Sunshine Coast. Select a bottle of wine from the boutique cellar and enjoy a casual meal in the adjoining bistro. Upstairs, there's a classy cocktail bar and fine-dining restaurant (mains $32 to $36) serving Modern Asian cuisine.

Wahoo   SEAFOOD **$$**
(218 David Low Way, Peregian Beach; mains $16-23; ⊙lunch daily, dinner Wed-Sat) Located on the edge of the square, this casually cool, two-storey restaurant has an excellent selection of seafood. The Asian influence extends to the decor. Settle down for a long lunch under the giant pandanus tree.

Baked Poetry Cafe   CAFE **$**
(218 David Low Way, Peregian Beach; dishes $10-16; ⊙breakfast & lunch) This minibakery and cafe is a famous instituation for its great coffee and German sourdough bread. The *eier im glass* is a Frankfurt breakfast special where your soft-boiled eggs arrive in a glass alongside a plate of bacon, grilled tomato and cheese.

☕ Drinking

Marble Bar Bistro   BAR
(40 Duke St; tapas $12-19; ⊙noon-late) Kick back in a cushioned lounge or perch yourself at one of the marble benches at this cruisy cocktail and tapas bar sans door or walls. Pizzas are popular.

Cooloola Coast

Stretching for 50km between Noosa and Rainbow Beach, the Cooloola Coast is a remote strip of long sandy beach backed by the Cooloola Section of the Great Sandy National Park. Although it's undeveloped, the 4WD and tin-boat set flock here in droves so it's not always as peaceful as you might imagine. If you head off on foot or by canoe along the many inlets and waterways, however, you'll soon escape the crowds.

From the end of Moorindil St in Tewantin, the Noosa North Shore Ferry (☎5447 1321; pedestrians/cars one way $1/6; ⊙5.30am-12.20am Fri & Sat, to 10.20pm Sun-Thu) shuttles across the river to Noosa North Shore. If you have a 4WD, you can drive along the beach to Rainbow Beach (and on up to Inskip Point to the Fraser Island ferry), but you'll need a permit (www.derm.qld.gov.au; per day/week/month $10/25/40). You can also buy a permit from the Noosa visitors centre (☎5430 5020; www.visitnoosa.com.au; Hastings St; ⊙9am-5pm) but it'll cost extra. Check the tide times!

On the way up the beach, you'll pass the Teewah coloured sand cliffs, estimated to be about 40,000 years old.

LAKE COOROIBAH

A couple of kilometres north of Tewantin, the Noosa River widens into Lake Cooroibah. If you take the Noosa North Shore Ferry, you can drive up to the lake in a conventional vehicle and camp along sections of the beach.

Camel Company Australia   CAMEL RIDES
(☎0408 710 530; www.camelcompany.com.au; Beach Rd, North Shore, Tewantin; 1hr rides adult/child $60/45, 2hr rides $80/60) Has beach camel rides.

Noosa Horseriding   HORSE RIDING
(☎0438 710 530; www.noosahorseriding.com.au; 1-/2-/half-day rides $65/95/195) Has rides in the beach and the bush.

THE HEAD IN THE SEA

Along the Maroochy coast, you'll see a small rocky island a little way offshore of Mud-jimba, near Coolum. Mudjimba Island is also known to locals as 'Old Woman Island', but according to Aboriginal legend, this rocky outcrop is in fact the head of a mighty warrior, Coolum. It seems Coolum and Ninderry were two warriors in love with the same woman, Maroochy. Ninderry kidnapped her, Coolum rescued her, and in retaliation Ninderry knocked off his head.

This, of course, angered the gods who promptly turned Ninderry into a rock and Coolum into a mountain. From where it was catapulted 1km into the sea, Coolum's head became Mudjimba Island. Maroochy, grief-stricken, fled into the mountains and wept a river of tears – the Maroochy River. And where the old woman of 'Old Woman Island' came from is anybody's guess.

Noosa Equathon   HORSE RIDING
(☏5474 2665; www.equathon.com; 1½hr beach ride $85; 1hr beach & bush ride $110) Offers multiday rides.

Noosa North Shore Retreat   CARAVAN PARK
(☏5447 1225; www.noosanorthshoreretreat.com. au; Beach Rd; unpowered/powered sites from $15/24, r from $145, cabins from $65; ✷@✷) A sprawling park in a great location on Lake Coorooibah, with a variety of sleeping options. There's a minimum two-night stay on weekends.

LAKE COOTHARABA & BOREEN POINT

Cootharaba is the biggest lake in the Cooloola Section of Great Sandy National Park, measuring about 5km across and 10km in length. On the western shores of the lake and at the southern edge of the national park, Boreen Point is a relaxed little community with several places to stay and to eat. The lake is the gateway to the Noosa Everglades, offering bushwalking, canoeing and bush camping.

Kanu Kapers (☏5485 3328; www.kanukaper saustralia.com; 11 Toolara St, Boreen Point; kayak hire per day $65) offers guided or self-guided kayaking trips (one-/two-day trip $145/395) into the Everglades.

The **Discovery Group Canoe Safari** (☏5449 0393; www.thediscoverygroup.com.au; 3-day & 2-night self-guided canoe trip $135, 3-day camping safari $139) includes transfers, canoe hire and camping gear for self-guided trips.

On the river, the quiet and simple **Boreen Point Camping Ground** (☏5485 3244; Dun's Beach, Teewah St, Boreen Point; unpowered/powered sites $15/22) is dominated by large gums and native bush. Take a right turn off Laguna St onto Vista St and bear right at the lake. Rates are for two people.

Apollonian Hotel (☏5485 3100; Laguna St, Boreen Point; mains $10-24; ◷lunch & dinner) is a gorgeous old pub with sturdy timber walls, shady verandahs and a beautifully preserved interior. Come for the famous Sunday spit-roast lunch.

From Boreen Point, an unsealed road leads another 5km to Elanda Point.

GREAT SANDY NATIONAL PARK – COOLOOLA SECTION

The Cooloola Section of Great Sandy National Park covers more than 54,000 hectares from Lake Cootharaba north to Rainbow Beach. It's a varied wilderness area with long sandy beaches, mangrove-lined waterways, forest, heath and lakes, all featuring plentiful bird life, including rarities such as the red goshawk and the grass owl, and lots of wildflowers in spring.

The Cooloola Way, from Tewantin up to Rainbow Beach, is open to 4WD vehicles unless there's been heavy rain – check with the rangers before setting out. Most people prefer to bomb up the beach, though you're restricted to a few hours either side of low tide. You'll need a permit (www.derm.qld.gov.au; per day/week/month $10/25/40). Make sure you check the tides as many a 4WD has met a wet end at high tide.

Although there are many 4WD tracks to lookout points and picnic grounds, the best way to see Cooloola is by boat or canoe along the numerous tributaries of the Noosa River. Boats can be hired from Tewantin and Noosa (along Gympie Tce), Boreen Point and Elanda Point on Lake Cootharaba.

There are some fantastic walking trails starting from Elanda Point on the shore of Lake Cootharaba, including the 46km Cooloola Wilderness Trail to Rainbow Beach and a 7km trail to an unstaffed QPWS information centre at Kinaba.

The **QPWS Great Sandy Information Centre** (☑5449 7792; 240 Moorindil St, Tewantin; ☺8am-4pm) can provide information on park access, tide times and fire bans within the park. The centre also issues car and camping permits for both Fraser Island and the Great Sandy National Park, but these are best booked online at www.derm.qld.gov.au.

The park has a number of camping grounds, many of them along the river. The most popular (and best-equipped) camping grounds are **Fig Tree Point** (at the northern end of Lake Cootharaba), Harry's Hut (about 4km upstream) and Freshwater (about 6km south of Double Island Point) on the coast. You can also **camp** (per person/family $5.15/20.60) at designated zones on the beach if you're driving up to Rainbow Beach. Apart from Harry's Hut, Freshwater and Teewah Beach, all sites are accessible by hiking or river only.

Eumundi

☑07 / POP 490

Sweet little Eumundi is a quaint highland village with a quirky New-Age vibe greatly amplified during its famous market days. The historic streetscape blends well with modern cafes, unique boutiques, silversmiths, craftsmen and body artists doing their thing. Once you've breathed Eumundi air, don't be surprised if you feel a sudden urge to take up beading or body painting.

◎ Sights & Activities

The **Eumundi markets** (☺6.30am-2pm Sat, 8am-1pm Wed) attract thousands of visitors to their 300-plus stalls and have everything from hand-crafted furniture and jewellery to homemade clothes and alternative healing booths.

The town's other claim to fame is Eumundi Lager, originally brewed in the Imperial Hotel. Nowadays it's made down at Yatala on the Gold Coast but you can still sample it on tap at the **Imperial Hotel** (Memorial Dr).

Beautiful glass sculptures and other works of art are on display at **Tina Cooper Glass** (☑5442 8110; www.tinacooper.com; 106

Memorial Dr; ☺9am-4pm Sat-Wed, 10am-3pm Thu, 11am-3pm Sun). On Saturdays you can see glass-blowing artists at work.

Murra Wolka Creations (☑5442 8691; www.murrawolka.com; 39 Memorial Dr; ☺9am-4.30pm Mon-Fri) is Aboriginal-owned and -operated. Here you can buy boomerangs and didgeridoos hand-painted by Indigenous artists.

About 10km northwest of Eumundi, the little village of **Pomona** sits in the shadow of looming Mt Cooroora (440m) and is home to the wonderful **Majestic Theatre** (☑5485 2330; www.majestictheatre.com.au; 3 Factory St, Pomona; ☺Tue-Fri), one of the only places in the world where you can see a silent movie accompanied by the original Wurlitzer organ soundtrack. For a step back in history, catch a **screening** (tickets $15, meal deal $27; ☺7.30pm) of the iconic *The Son of the Sheikh* on the first Thursday of each month.

🛏 Sleeping & Eating

Hidden Valley B&B   B&B $$
(☑5442 8685; www.eumundibed.com; 39 Caplick Way, r $175-195, 🐾🖥) This not-so-hidden retreat is on 1.5 hectares of land, only 400m from Eumundi on the Noosa road. Inside this attractive Queenslander, you can choose a themed room to match your mood: Aladdin's Cave, the Emperors Suite or the Hinterland Retreat. All have private balcony and attention to detail.

Harmony Hill Station   B&B $$
(☑5442 8685; www.eumundibed.com; 81 Seib Rd; carriage $150; 🐾) Perched on a hilltop in a 5-hectare property, this restored and fully self-contained 1912 purple railway carriage is the perfect place to relax or romance. Share the grounds with grazing kangaroos, watch the sunset from Lover's Leap, share a bottle of wine beneath a stunning night sky...or even get married (the owners are celebrants!).

TOP CHOICE **Spirit House Restaurant**   ASIAN $$$
(☑5446 8994; 20 Ninderry Rd, Yandina; mains $28-36; ☺lunch daily, dinner Wed-Sat) This legendary restaurant is at Yandina, 11km south of Eumundi. The subtropical surrounds create an authentic Southeast Asian setting, while the kitchen concocts divine Thai-infused innovations. Order the shared dining plates ($10) to sample all the exquisite offerings.

WORTH A TRIP

MONTVILLE & KENILWORTH

It's hard to imagine that the chintzy mountain village of Montville with its fudge empo-riums, Devonshire tearooms and cottage crafts began life under the dramatic name of Razorback – until you arrive at the town's spectacular ridge-top location 500m above sea level. To work off that excess fudge, take a pleasant rainforest hike to Kondalilla Falls in Kondalilla National Park, 3km northwest of town. After a refreshing swim in the rock pool at the head of the falls, check for leeches!

Secrets on the Lake (☑5478 5888; www.secretsonthelake.com.au; 207 Narrows Rd; midweek/weekend from $200/250; ✿) is a romantic hideaway where boardwalks through the foliage lead to magical, wooden treehouses with sunken spas, log fires and stunning views of Lake Baroon.

From Montville, head to the tiny village of Mapleton and turn left on the Obi Obi Rd. After 18km, you reach Kenilworth, a small country town in the pretty Mary River Valley. Kenilworth Country Foods (☑5446 0144; 45 Charles St; ⊙9am-4pm Mon-Fri, 10.30am-3pm Sat & Sun) is a boutique cheese factory with creamy yoghurt and wickedly good cheese. If you plan to camp in the Kenilworth State Forest or Conondale National Park you'll need a permit (☑13 74 68; www.derm.qld.gov.au; per person $5.15).

Otherwise, head northeast on the Eumundi–Kenilworth Rd for a scenic drive through rolling pastureland dotted with traditional old farmhouses and floods of jacarandas. After 30km you reach the Bruce Hwy near Eumundi.

Azzurro ITALIAN $$
(69 Memorial Dr; mains $13-28; ⊙breakfast Wed, Sat & Sun, lunch Tue-Sun, dinner Wed-Sat) Recommended by the locals, this breezy Italian restaurant has simple panini and salads as well as delicious sounding dishes like roasted ducks breast with wilted radicchio and wild mushroom risotto.

Sala Thai THAI $
(☑Memorial Dr; dishes $10-16; ⊙lunch & dinner Tue-Sun) This excellent Thai restaurant dishes up consistently good quality meals and comes highly recommended by the locals. Enough said.

Drinking

Joe's Waterhole PUB
(www.musicliveatjoes.com; Memorial Dr) Built in 1891, this old pub has weathered the century to attract big-name national and international musicians. Check the website for details.

ℹ Information

Discover Eumundi Heritage & Visitors Centre (☑5442 8762; Memorial Dr; ⊙10am-4pm Mon-Fri, 9am-3pm Sat, 10am-2pm Sun) Also houses the museum (admission free).

ℹ Getting There & Away

Sunbus (☑13 12 30) runs hourly from Noosa Heads ($3.20, 40 minutes) and Nambour

($4.10, 30 minutes). A number of tour operators (p332 and p348) visit the Eumundi markets on Wednesdays and Saturdays.

SUNSHINE COAST HINTERLAND

Reaching to heights of 400m and more, the Blackall Range forms a stunning backdrop to the Sunshine Coast's popular beaches a short 50km away. A relaxed half- or full-day circuit drive from the coast follows a winding road along the razorback line of the escarpment, passing through quaint mountain villages and offering spectacular views of the coastal lowlands. The villages (some suffering an overdose of kitschy craft shops and Devonshire tearooms) are worth a visit, but the real attraction is the landscape, with its lush green pastures and softly folded valleys and ridges, and the waterfalls, swimming holes, rainforests and walks in the national parks. Cosy cabins and B&Bs are popular weekend retreats, especially during winter.

☞ Tours

Plenty of tour companies operate through the hinterland and will pick up from anywhere along the Sunshine Coast.

Boomerang Tours SCENIC
(☑1800 763 077; per person $59) Following the 'hippie trail', visiting Kondalilla Falls,

Montville Mary Cairncross Reserve as well as the Eumundi markets. Includes sausage-sizzle lunch.

Storeyline Tours SCENIC
(☑5474 1500; www.storeylinetours.com.au; adult/child $90/55) Runs small-group tours to Montville and nearby rainforests and trips to the Glass House Mountains.

Off Beat Rainforest Tours SCENIC
(☑5473 5135; www.offbeattours.com.au; adult/child $155/100) Four-wheel drive ecotours to Conondale National Park including morning tea, a gourmet lunch and transfers.

Maleny

☑07 / POP 1300

Perched high in the heart of the rolling green hills of the Blackall Range, Maleny is an intriguing melange of artists, musicians and creative souls, the ageing hippie scene, rural 'tree-changers' and cooperative ventures. Its quirky bohemian edge underscores a thriving commercial township that has well and truly moved on from its timber and dairy past without yielding to the tacky heritage developments and ye olde tourist-trap shoppes that have engulfed nearby mountain villages. The town has a strong community and amazing support for local 'co-ops' and environmental concerns.

There's a small **visitors centre** (☑5499 9033; www.tourmaleny.com.au; 23 Maple St; ⊙10am-3pm) at the Maleny Community Centre.

Mary Cairncross Scenic Reserve (☑5499 9907; Mountain View Rd) is a pristine rainforest shelter spread over 52 hectares southeast of town. Walking tracks snake through the rainforest and there's a healthy population of bird life and unbearably cute pademelons.

🛏 Sleeping

Maleny Lodge Guest House B&B $$
(☑5494 2370; www.malenylodge.com; 58 Maple St; s $155-180, d $180-205; ☎☒) This rambling B&B boasts myriad gorgeous rooms with cushy, four-poster beds and lashings of stained wood and antiques. There's an open fire for cold winter days and an open pool house for warm summer ones. Prices include breakfast.

Relax at the Cabin BOUTIQUE CABIN $$$
(☑5499 9377; www.kingludwigs.com.au; cabins $350) Only 3km from Maleny, this secluded cabin is set in pine forest on 8 hectares of land. The spa, fireplace and large, comfy bed dominate the living room and a wall of glass doors opens onto a wide timber deck. Your favourite wines, a range of beers and a welcoming cheese platter greet your arrival.

Morning Star Motel MOTEL $$
(☑5494 2944; www.morningstarmotel.com; 2 Panorama Pl; r $88-110) The rooms at this comfortable and clean motel have outstanding coastal views and deluxe suites have spas. Wheelchair accessible.

🍴 Eating

Up Front Club CAFE $
(31 Maple St; dishes $10-20; ⊙breakfast, lunch & dinner) This cosy cafe injects funk by the bucketful into Maleny's main strip, with organic breads and tofu and tempeh salads. Live music takes to the stage Friday to Sunday nights and you'll catch anything from reggae to a bout of folk.

WOODSTOCK DOWN UNDER

The famous **Woodford Folk Festival** features a huge diversity of over 2000 national and international performers playing folk, traditional Irish, Indigenous and world music, as well as buskers, belly dancers, craft markets, visual-arts performances, environmental talks and a visiting squad of Tibetan monks. The festival is held on a property near the town of Woodford from 27 December to 1 January each year. Camping grounds are set up on the property with toilets, showers and a range of foodie marquees, but prepare for a mud bath if it rains. The festival is licensed so leave your booze at home.

Tickets cost around $97 per day ($116 with camping) and can be bought online, at the gate or the **festival office** (☑5496 1066). Check www.woodfordfolkfestival.com for the program.

Woodford is 35km northwest of Caboolture. Shuttle buses run regularly from the Caboolture train station to and from the festival grounds.

Terrace   INTERNATIONAL **$$$**

(☎5494 3700; cnr Mountain View & Maleny-Landsborough Rds; mains $25-50; ⊙lunch & dinner) One of Queensland's best, this award-winner serves delectable seafood and has spectacular views of the Glass House Mountains. If you're ravenous, try the Moreton Bay bugs, king prawns, salmon and barramundi served on a sizzling granite tile with root vegetables and polenta salad.

Monica's Cafe   CAFE **$**

(11/43 Maple St; mains $10-20; ⊙breakfast & lunch) Snazzy Monica's blackboard menu promises innovative dishes and has gluten-free options available. Sit outside to soak up the town's cruisy vibe or alternatively, take a seat at the long wooden table located indoors. There's also a cosy nook you'll discover if you venture upstairs.

Fraser Island & the Fraser Coast

Best Places to Eat

» Waterview Bistro (p361)
» Cafe Tapas (p358)
» Black Dog Cafe (p357)

Best Places to Stay

» Kingfisher Bay Resort (p369)
» Debbie's Place (p359)
» Beachfront Tourist Parks (p356)

Why Go?

Fraser Island, the world's largest sand island, is a natural paradise sculpted by wind and surf. It's a mystical land of giant dunes, ancient rainforests, luminous lakes and endemic wildlife that includes Australia's purest strain of dingo.

Across the calm waters of the Great Sandy Strait, the mellow coastal community of Hervey Bay is the gateway to Fraser Island. From July to October, migrating humpback whales stream into the bay for a few days before continuing on to Antarctica. Further south, tiny Rainbow Beach is a laidback seaside village and an alternative launch pad to Fraser Island. Fishing, swimming, boating and camping are hugely popular along this entire stretch of coastline.

Inland, dry bushland and agricultural fields surround old-fashioned country towns steeped in history. Bundaberg, the largest city in the region, overlooks a sea of waving cane fields that gives birth to its famous liquid-gold rum, a fiery, gut-churning spirit guaranteed to scramble a few brain cells!

When to Go

Bundaberg

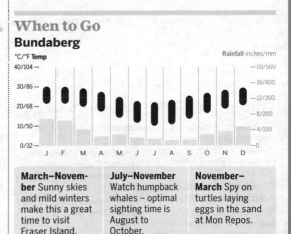

March–November Sunny skies and mild winters make this a great time to visit Fraser Island.

July–November Watch humpback whales – optimal sighting time is August to October.

November–March Spy on turtles laying eggs in the sand at Mon Repos.

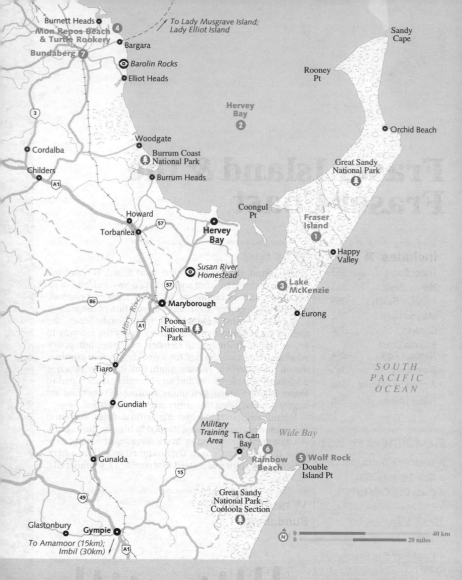

Fraser Island & the Fraser Coast Highlights

① Cruising up the beach 'highway', hiking through the rainforest and camping under the stars on **Fraser Island** (p368)

② Watching the whales play in **Hervey Bay** (p353)

③ Cooling off in the pristine, clear-blue water of the white sand–fringed freshwater **Lake**

McKenzie (p369) on Fraser Island

④ Witnessing turtles take their first flipper-stumble down the beach at **Mon Repos** (p365)

⑤ Diving with sharks at **Wolf Rock** (p359) off Rainbow Beach

⑥ Copping an eyeful of the coloured sand cliffs at **Rainbow Beach** (p359)

⑦ Sampling 'liquid gold' at the rum distillery in **Bundaberg** (p365)

Getting There & Away

Air

Qantas (☑13 13 13; www.qantas.com.au) flies to Bundaberg and Hervey Bay to/from Brisbane. **Virgin Blue** (☑13 67 89; www.virginblue.com.au) has direct flights to Hervey Bay from Sydney.

Bus

Greyhound Australia (☑1300 473 946; www.greyhound.com.au) and **Premier Motor Service** (☑13 34 10; www.premierms.com.au) both have regular coach services along the Bruce Hwy with stops at all the major towns. They also detour off the highway to Hervey Bay and Rainbow Beach.

Train

Queensland Rail (☑13 22 32, 1300 13 17 22; www.traveltrain.com.au) has frequent services between Brisbane and Rockhampton passing through the region. Choose between the high-speed *Tilt Train* or the more sedate *Sunlander*. For details see the Getting There & Away sections of the relevant towns and cities.

FRASER COAST

The Fraser Coast runs the gamut from coastal beauty, beachfront national parks and tiny seaside villages to agricultural farms and sugarcane fields surrounding old-fashioned country towns.

Hervey Bay

POP 41,225

Named after an English Casanova, it's no wonder that Hervey Bay's seductive charms are difficult to resist. Attractive features such as a warm subtropical climate, long sandy beaches, calm blue ocean and a relaxed and unpretentious local community lure all sorts of travellers to its shores – from backpacking travellers to families and sea-changing retirees. Throw in the chance to see majestic humpback whales frolicking in the water and the town's convenient access to the World Heritage–listed Fraser Island, and it's easy to understand how this once sleepy fishing village seduces you without even trying.

Don't bother packing a surfboard, though: Fraser Island shelters Hervey Bay from the ocean surf and the sea here is shallow and completely flat – perfect for kiddies and postcard summer-holiday pics.

◉ Sights

Reef World   AQUARIUM
(☑4128 9828; Pulgul St, Urangan; adult/child $18/9, shark dives $40; ◷9.30am-4pm) A small aquarium stocked with some of the Great Barrier Reef's most colourful characters, including a giant 18-year-old groper. You can also take a dip with lemon, whaler and other non-predatory sharks.

Vic Hislop's Great White Shark & Whale Expo   SHARK EXHIBIT
(553 The Esplanade, Urangan; adult/child $15/7; ◷8.30am-5.30pm) For an informative, but slightly kitschy, peek at what hides beneath the sea visit the acclaimed Sharkman's collection of all things Jaws-like. If the newspaper clippings of gruesome shark attacks don't make you shudder maybe the 5.6m frozen Great White in the freezer will!

Wetside   PARK
(Esplanade, Scarness; ◷noon-5pm Mon, 10am-5pm Tue, Thu & Sun, to after sunset lightshow Fri & Sat) On a hot day the kids will want to flock to this wet spot on the foreshore. There's plenty of shade, fountains, tipping buckets and a boardwalk with water intotainment (you'll learn such gems as your brain and a beef steak have almost the same amount of water). Wetside is open most afternoons and longer on weekends, with an after-sunset lightshow on Fridays and Saturdays. Opening hours vary so check the website for current details.

🏃 Activities

Whale-watching

Whale-watching tours operate out of Hervey Bay every day (weather permitting) during the annual migrations between late July and early November. Sightings are guaranteed from August to the end of October (with a free return trip if the whales don't show). Off season, many boats offer dolphin-spotting tours. Boats cruise from Urangan Harbour out to Platypus Bay and then zip around from pod to pod to find the most active whales. Most vessels offer half-day tours for around $115 for adults and $60 for children, and most include breakfast or lunch. Tour bookings can be made through your accommodation or the information centres.

Some recommended operators:

Spirit of Hervey Bay   WHALE-WATCHING
(☑1800 642 544; www.spiritofherveybay.com; ◷8.30am & 1.30pm) The largest vessel with the greatest number of passengers.

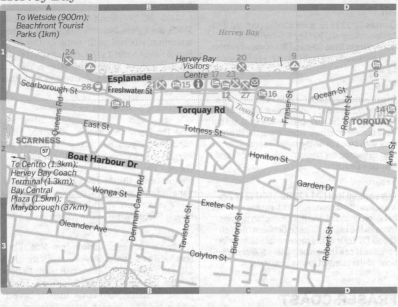

Hervey Bay

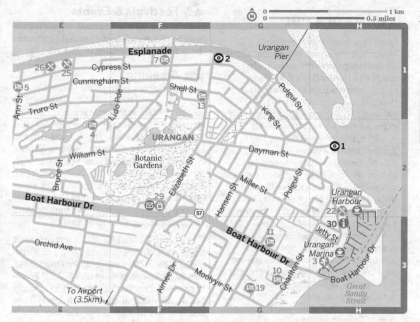

That's Awesome WHALE-WATCHING
(☎1800 653 775; www.awesomeadventure.com.
au; ⊙7am, 10.30am, 2.30pm) This rigid inflatable boat speeds out to the whales faster than any other vessel.

MV Tasman Venture WHALE-WATCHING
(☎1800 620 322; www.tasmanventure.com.au; ⊙8.30am & 1.30pm)

Blue Dolphin Marine Tours WHALE WATCHING
(☎4124 9600; www.bluedolphintours.com.au; ⊙7.30am)

Freedom Whale Watch WHALE-WATCHING
(☎1300 879 960; www.freedomwhalewatch.com.
au; adult/child $120/80; ⊙9.30am)

Fishing

MV Fighting Whiting FISHING
(☎4124 6599; www.fightingwhiting.com.au; adult/child/family $70/35/170)

MV Princess II FISHING
(☎4124 0400; adult/child $130/85)

Cruises

Freedom Whale Watch BOAT CRUISE
(☎1300 879 960; www.freedomwhalewatch.
au; adult/child $80/50) Cruise across the bay to a pearl farm and watch demonstrations on seeding, opening and setting a pearl.

Krystal Klear BOAT CRUISE
(☎4128 9800; 5hr tour adult/child $90/50)
Cruise on a 40ft glass-bottomed boat. Includes snorkelling, coral viewing and an island barbecue.

Water Sports

Aquavue WATER SPORTS
(☎4125 5528; www.aquavue.com.au; The Esplanade, Torquay) Hires out SeaKarts/kayaks per hour $50/20 and jet skis $50 per 15 minutes). Guided Fraser Island jet ski tour $320.

Enzo's on the Beach WATER SPORTS
(☎4124 6375; 351a The Esplanade, Scarness; 2hr lesson $130), Kitesurfing (1½-hour lesson $130), paddleboarding (per hour/two hours $30/40). Also hires out kayaks and surfskis.

Scenic Flights

Air Fraser Island SCENIC FLIGHT
(☎1800 247 992, 4125 3600; www.airfraserisland.
com.au) Scenic flights over Fraser Island from $70.

MI Helicopters SCENIC FLIGHT
(☎1800 600 345; www.mihelicopters.com.au)
Scenic flights from 10 minutes ($95) to one hour.

A WHALE OF A TIME

Every year, from August to early November, thousands of humpback whales (Megaptera novaeangliae) cruise into Hervey Bay's sheltered waters for a few days before continuing their arduous migration south to the Antarctic. Having mated and given birth in the warmer waters off northeast Australia, they arrive in Hervey Bay in groups of about a dozen (known as pulses), before splitting into smaller groups of two or three (pods). The new calves utilise the time to develop the thick layers of blubber necessary for survival in icy southern waters, by consuming around 600L of milk daily.

Viewing these majestic creatures is simply awe-inspiring. Showy aqua-acrobats, you'll see humpbacks waving their pectoral fins, tail slapping, breaching or simply 'blowing', and many will roll up beside the whale-watching boats with one eye clear of the water making those on board wonder who's actually watching whom.

Fraser Coast Microlites SCENIC FLIGHT
(☑1300 732 801; flights per 20/30/45/70min $75/120/175/230) Ditch the metal shell.

Other Activities

Hervey Bay Skydivers SKYDIVING
(☑1300 558 616, 4183 0119; www.herveybayskydivers.com.au) Tandem skydives for $250 from 10,000ft and $270 from 14,000ft. Add an extra $30 for skydives over the beach.

Susan River Homestead HORSE RIDING
(☑4121 6846; www.susanriver.com; Hervey Bay-Maryborough Rd; 2hr ride $85) Horse-riding packages (adult/child $220/165) include accommodation, all meals and use of the on-site swimming pool and tennis courts.

☞ Tours

Besides tours to Fraser Island (p361), you can fly to Lady Elliot Island (p367).

Tory's Tours SIGHTSEEING
(☑4128 6500; www.torystours.com.au; adult/child $99/85) On Mondays and Fridays, visits the Bundaberg Rum Distillery (p365). Every Wednesday, feed the dolphins on a trip to Tin Can Bay.

✹✹ Festivals & Events

Hervey Bay Whale Festival WHALE FESTIVAL
(www.herveybaywhalefestival.com.au) Celebrates the return of the whales in August.

🛏 Sleeping

The Quarterdecks Harbour Retreat
APARTMENTS $$
(☑4197 0888; www.quarterdecksretreat.com.au; 80 Moolyyir St, Urangan; 1/2/3-bedroom villas $150/195/225; ✳🛜🛋) These excellent villas are stylishly furnished with a private courtyard, all the mod cons you could wish for and little luxuries like fluffy bathrobes. Backing onto a nature reserve, it's quiet apart from the wonderful bird life and only a cooee from the beach. The accommodation and tour packages are great value.

Beachfront Tourist Parks CARAVAN PARK $
(Pialba ☑4128 1399, Scarness ☑4125 1578, Torquay ☑4128 1274; www.beachfronttouristparks.com.au; unpowered/powered sites $23/31) Fronting onto Hervey Bay's exquisitely long sandy beach, all three of these shady parks have the best ocean views. The Torquay site is smack bang in the heart of the action.

Australis Shelly Bay Resort APARTMENTS $$
(☑4125 4533; www.shellybayresort.com.au; 466 The Esplanade, Torquay; 1/2-bedroom units $125/170; ✳@🛋) The bold, cheerful self-contained units at this complex are clean and spacious. All rooms have water views, and with the beach just across the road, this is one of the best options in town. There's also an Indian restaurant on site.

Bay B&B B&B $$
(☑4125 6919; www.baybedandbreakfast.com.au; 180 Cypress St, Urangan; s $75, d $135-150; ✳@🛋) This great value B&B is run by a friendly, well-travelled Frenchman. Guest rooms are in a comfy annexe out the back, and breakfast is served on an outdoor patio in a tropical garden surrounded by birds and masses of greenery. Families can take over the separate fully self-contained unit.

Colonial Village YHA HOSTEL $
(☑1800 818 280; www.cvyha.com; 820 Boat Harbour Dr, Urangan; unpowered/powered sites $18/24; dm/d/cabins from $20/54/85; ✳@🛋) This excellent YHA is set on eight hectares of tranquil bushland, close to the marina and only 50m from the beach. It's a lovely spot, thick with ambience, possums and parrots. Facilities include a spa, tennis and basketball courts and a funky bar.

Alexander Lakeside B&B
B&B $$

(☑4128 9448; www.herveybaybedandbreakfast.com.au; 29 Lido Pde, Urangan; r $135-165; ✳🛉🛜) In a quiet street, this warm and friendly B&B offers lakeside indulgence where turtles come a-visiting in the morning. There's a heated lakeside spa, two spacious rooms with ensuites and two luxury self-contained suites. Guests also have access to a kitchen and laundry.

La Mer Beachfront Apartments
APARTMENTS $$

(☑1800 100 181, 4128 3494; www.lamer.com.au; 396 The Esplanade, Torquay; 1/2 bedrooms from $150/200; ✳🛉🛜) With colours this bold, you'll think you're in the Med. The rainbow scheme continues indoors but it's actually quite pleasant. The apartments are large, comfortable and have fully equipped kitchens. Choose between poolside or beachfront units.

Next Backpackers
HOSTEL $

(☑4125 6600; www.nextbackpackers.com.au; 10 Bideford St, Torquay; dm $20-32, d $69; ✳@🛜) Having won a swag of awards, you'd expect this modern hostel to be a cut above the usual suspects. With polished wooden floors, ultraclean roomy rooms and a well-equipped stainless-steel kitchen, it certainly is. There's a 'girls only' dorm and a bar open until midnight.

Nomads
HOSTEL $

(☑4125 3601; www.nomadshostels.com; 408 The Esplanade, Torquay; dm/d from $18/60; ✳@🛉🛜) This sprawling complex opposite the beach has all bases covered. Low-level housing clusters around the colonial-style bar, pool and shady barbecue area. The tour desk can organise packages (with a free night if you book the half-day whale-watching tour) and self-drive Fraser Island tours to their permanent camp site on Fraser Island.

Grange Resort
RESORT $$$

(☑4125 2002; www.thegrange-herveybay.com.au; cnr Elizabeth & Shell Sts, Urangan; 1/2-bedroom villas $195/225; ✳🛉🛜) Reminiscent of a stylish desert resort with fancy split-level condos and filled with life's little luxuries, this place is close to the beach and to town.

Arlia Sands Apartments
APARTMENTS $$

(☑4125 4360; www.arliasands.com.au; 13 Ann St, Torquay; 1/2 bedrooms $135/145; ✳🛉) This refurbished series of units contains plush furniture and spacious modern bathrooms. It's off the main drag yet close to the beach and shops and is *trés* quiet.

Boat Harbour Resort
APARTMENTS $$

(☑4125 5079; www.boatharbourresort.net; 651-652 Charlton St, Urangan; r $115-135; ✳🛉🛜) Close to the Urangan marina, these timber studios and cabins are set on attractive grounds. The studios have sizeable decks out the front and the roomy villas are great for families.

Also recommended:

Fraser Roving
HOSTEL $

(☑1800 989 811, 4125 6386; www.fraserroving.com; 412 The Esplanade, Torquay; dm $23-25, d with/without bathroom $60/65; @🛉) Fraser's party vibe continues undiminished.

Palace Backpackers
HOSTEL $

(☑1800 063 168, 4124 5331; www.palaceadventures.com; 184 Torquay Rd, Scarness, dm/d $25/55; ✳@🛉) Dorms in self-contained units set in tropical gardens.

Happy Wanderer Village
CARAVAN PARK $

(☑4125 1103; www.happywanderer.com.au; 105 Truro St, Torquay; unpowered/powered sites from $30/35, cabins/villas from $64/121; ✳🛉🛜) A large park with good tent sites.

🍴 Eating

Self-caterers can stock up at the supermarkets inside the Centro, Urangan Central and Bay Central Plaza shopping centres.

Black Dog Cafe
TOP CHOICE · FUSION $$

(☑4124 3177; 381 The Esplanade, Torquay; mains $14-33; ⊙lunch & dinner) The ambience is funk, the menu is Zen and the East-meets-West dishes feature sushi, Japanese soup, fresh burgers, curries, club sambos and seafood salads, enough to tame any black dog.

Enzo's on the Beach
CAFE $

(351a The Esplanade, Scarness; mains $8-20; ⊙6.30am-5pm) A shabby-chic outdoor cafe with a superb beachfront location where you can dine on focaccias, wraps, healthy salads and light meals, or just sip a coffee and wallow in the perfect ocean views.

Raging Bull Stonegrill
STEAKHOUSE $$

(☑4194 6674; 486 The Esplanade, Torquay; mains $20-40; ⊙dinner) This interactive dining experience, whereby a slab of meat, chicken or fish cooks on a hot rock on your plate, will make carnivores feel righteously healthy. Don't forget to eat your greens.

Pier Restaurant
SEAFOOD $$

(☑4128 9699; 573 The Esplanade, Urangan; mains $20-40; ⊙dinner Mon-Sat) Although sitting opposite the water, the Pier makes little use of its ocean views, but this à la carte restaurant has an interesting seafood menu (crocodile and Hervey Bay scallops) and is deservedly popular.

Cafe Tapas
TAPAS $$

(417 The Esplanade, Torquay; tapas $7; ⊙lunch & dinner) This slick venue has funky artwork, dim lighting, red couches and low tables flickering with coloured lights. Come for Asian-inspired tapas, and linger longer for drinks and music.

Aquavue
CAFE $

(415 The Esplanade, Torquay; mains $8-13; ⊙breakfast & lunch) Another outdoor cafe on the beachfront offering unbeatable sea views and the usual assortment of sandwiches and light meals. There are plenty of water toys for hire.

Cafe Balaena
CAFE $$

(Shop 7, Terminal Bldg, Buccaneer Ave, Urangan; mains $10-25; ⊙breakfast & lunch daily, dinner Thu-Mon) This waterfront cafe at the marina provides expansive views, atmosphere with a decidedly laidback twist and wallet-friendly prices. The menu ranges across the board with a good dose of seafood.

Simply Wok
ASIAN $$

(417 The Esplanade, Torquay; mains $14-25; ⊙breakfast, lunch & dinner) Noodles, stirfries, seafood and curries will satisfy any cravings for Asian cuisine, and there's an all-you-can-eat hot buffet for $15.90.

Drinking

Hoolihan's
PUB

(382 The Esplanade, Scarness) Like all good Irish pubs, Hoolihan's is wildly popular, especially with the backpacker crowd.

Information
Hervey Bay covers a string of beachside suburbs – Point Vernon, Pialba, Scarness, Torquay and Urangan – but behind the flawless beachfront and pockets of sedate suburbia, the outskirts of town dissolve into an industrial jungle.

Hervey Bay Visitor Information Centre (☎1800 811 728, 4125 9855; www.herveybaytourism.com.au; cnr Urraween & Maryborough Rds; ⊙9am-5pm) Helpful and professional tourist office on the outskirts of town.

Hervey Bay Visitors Centre (☎1800 649 926, 4124 4050; 401 The Esplanade, Torquay; internet per hr $4; ⊙8.30am-8.30pm Mon-Fri, 9am-6.30pm Sat & Sun) Privately run booking office with internet access. Very friendly. Call anytime.

Post office (☎4125 1101; 414 The Esplanade, Torquay) Branches also at Pialba and Urangan.

Whale Watch Tourist Centre (☎1800 358 595, 4128 9800; Urangan Marina, Urangan; ⊙7.30am-6pm) At the marina; it's privately run and has good information on whale-watching tours.

Getting There & Away

Air
Hervey Bay airport is off Booral Rd, Urangan, on the way to River Heads.

Qantas (☎13 13 13; www.qantas.com.au) has several daily flights to/from Brisbane. **Virgin Blue** (☎13 67 89; www.virginblue.com.au) flies daily from Sydney.

Boat
Boats to Fraser Island leave from River Heads, about 10km south of town, and Urangan Marina. Most tours leave from Urangan Harbour.

Bus
Buses depart **Hervey Bay Coach Terminal** (☎4124 4000; Central Ave, Pialba). **Greyhound Australia** (☎1300 473 946; www.greyhound.com.au) and **Premier Motor Service** (☎13 34 10; www.premierms.com.au) have several services to/from Brisbane ($75, 5½ hours), Maroochydore ($50, 3½ hours), Bundaberg ($24, 1½ hours) and Rockhampton ($95, six hours).

Tory's Tours (☎4128 6500; www.torystours.com.au) has twice daily services to Brisbane airport ($65).

Wide Bay Transit (☎4121 3719) has hourly services from Urangan Marina (stopping along The Esplanade) to Maryborough ($8, one hour) every weekday, with fewer services on weekends.

Trainlink buses connect Maryborough West train station with the Coach Terminal ($8, 45 minutes).

Getting Around

Car
Plenty of choice makes Hervey Bay the best place to hire a 4WD for Fraser Island:

Aussie Trax (☎1800 062 275; 56 Boat Harbour Dr, Pialba)

Fraser Magic 4WD Hire (☎4125 6612; www.fraser-magic-4wdhire.com.au; 5 Kruger Crt, Urangan)

Hervey Bay Rent A Car (☎4194 6626) Also rents out scooters (from $30 per day).

Safari 4WD Hire (☎1800 689 819, 4124 4244; www.safari4wdhire.com.au; 102 Boat Harbour Dr, Pialba)

Rainbow Beach

POP 999

Gorgeous Rainbow Beach is a tiny town at the base of the Inskip Peninsula with spectacular multicoloured sand cliffs overlooking its rolling surf and white sandy beach. Still relatively untouched, the town's friendly locals, relaxed vibe and convenient access to Fraser Island (only 10 minutes by barge) and the Cooloola section of the Great Sandy National Park has made this a rising star of Queensland's coastal beauty spots.

◉ Sights

The town is named for the **coloured sand cliffs**, a 2km walk along the beach. The cliffs arc their red-hued way around Wide Bay, offering a sweeping panorama from the lighthouse at Double Island Point to Fraser Island in the north.

A 600m track along the cliffs at the southern end of Cooloola Dr leads to the **Carlo Sandblow**, a spectacular 120m-high dune.

🏃 Activities

Bushwalking & Camping

The Cooloola section of the **Great Sandy National Park** (p346) has a number of national park camp sites (www.derm.qld.gov.au; per person/family $5.15/20.60) including a wonderful stretch of beach camping along Teewah Beach. Book camping and **4WD permits** (per day/week/month $10/25/40) online.

Bushwalking tracks in the national park (maps from the QPWS office) include the 46.2km **Cooloola Wilderness Trail**, which starts at Mullens car park (off Rainbow Beach Rd) and ends near Lake Cooloola.

Camping on the beach is one of the best ways to experience this part of the coast, but if you don't have camping gear **Rainbow Beach Hire-a-Camp** (☑5486 8633; www.rainbow-beach.org) can hire out equipment, set up your tent and camp site, organise camping permits and break camp for you when you're done.

Diving

Wolf Rock, a congregation of volcanic pinnacles off Double Island Point, is regarded as one of Queensland's best scuba-diving sites. The endangered grey nurse shark is found here all year round.

Wolf Rock Dive Centre DIVING
(☑5486 8004; www.wolfrockdive.com.au; double dive charter from $160) Offers adrenalin dives to experienced divers at Wolf Rock.

Kayaking & Canoeing

Rainbow Beach Dolphin View Sea Kayaking KAYAKING
(☑0408 738 192; 4hr tour per person $85; kayak hire per half-day $65) Offers kayaking safaris.

Carlo Canoes CANOEING
(☑5486 3610; per half/full day $30/45)

Skydiving & Paragliding

Skydive Rainbow Beach SKYDIVING
(☑0418 218 358; www.skydiverainbowbeach.com; 8000ft/10,000ft/14,000ft dives $260/295/334) Lands on the beach.

Rainbow Paragliding PARAGLIDING
(☑5486 3048, 0418 754 157; www.paraglidingrainbow.com; glides $150) Tandem glides above the Carlo Sandblow.

Surfing

There's a good surf break at Double Island Point.

Rainbow Beach Surf School SURFING
(☑0408 738 192; rainbowbeachsurf@hotmail.com; 2hr session $55; board hire per day $40)

☞ Tours

Surf & Sand Safaris SCENIC TOUR
(☑5486 3131; www.surfandsandsafaris.com.au; adult/child $70/35) 4WD tours through the national park and along the beach to the coloured sands and lighthouse at Double Island Point.

Dolphin Ferry Cruise BOAT CRUISE
(☑0428 838 836; www.dolphinferrycruise.net.au; 3hr cruise adult/child $30/15; ⊘7.20am & 9.30am) Cruise across the inlet to Tin Can Bay to hand-feed Mystique, a wild Indo-Pacific humpback dolphin who makes regular breakfast visits to the Tin Can Bay marina.

🛏 Sleeping

TOP CHOICE **Debbie's Place** B&B $
(☑5486 3506; www.rainbowbeachaccommodation.com.au; 30 Kurana St; d/ste from $79/89, 3-bedroom apt from $99; ✳) Inside this beautiful timber Queenslander dripping with pot plants, the charming rooms are fully self-contained and have private entrances and verandahs. The effervescent Debbie is a mine of information and makes this a cosy home away from home.

SAND SAFARIS: EXPLORING FRASER ISLAND

The only way to explore Fraser Island is with a 4WD vehicle. For most travellers, there are three transport options: tag-a-long tours, organised tours or 4WD hire.

Tag-a-Long Tours

The original self-drive tours where 4WD convoys headed off for a three-day, two-night camping safari were incredibly popular with backpackers. However, due to a spate of fatal vehicular accidents on Fraser Island in the past few years, new laws have changed the original self-drive tours into tag-a-long tours where a maximum of five vehicles follow a lead vehicle with an experienced guide and driver. Rates hover around $300-320 and exclude food, fuel and alcohol.

Advantages – flexibility; you can make new friends fast.

Disadvantages – if your group doesn't get along it's a loooong three days. Inexperienced drivers get bogged in sand all the time but this can be part of the fun.

 Recommended operators:

» **Colonial Village YHA** (☑1800 818 280, 4125 1844; www.cvyha.com) Hervey Bay.

» **Dingo's Backpacker's Resort** (☑1800 111 126, 5486 8200; www.dingosatrainbow.com) Rainbow Beach.

» **Fraser Roving** (☑1800 989 811, 4125 6386; www.fraserroving.com.au) Hervey Bay.

» **Nomads** (☑1800 354 535, 4125 3601; www.nomadshostels.com) Hervey Bay.

» **Next Backpackers** (☑4125 6600; www.nextbackpackers.com.au) Hervey Bay.

» **Pippies Beach House** (☑1800 425 356, 5486 8503; www.pippiesbeachhouse.com.au) Rainbow Beach.

Organised Tours

Most organised tours cover the highlights: rainforests, Eli Creek, Lakes McKenzie and Wabby, the coloured Pinnacles and the *Maheno* shipwreck.

Advantages – minimum fuss, expert commentary.

Disadvantages – during peak season you could share the experience with 40 others.

Rainbow Ocean Palms Resort
APARTMENTS **$$$**
(☑5486 3211; www.rainbowoceanpalms.com; 105 Cooloola Dr; 1-bedroom apt from $200, 2-bedroom apt from $300; ✻☒) Making the most of the panoramic ocean views, these luxury apartments have a modern, contemporary design and feature loads of glass, light and space. It overlooks the national park and you can see the ocean from your spa. The excellent Waterview Bistro is next door.

Pippies Beach House
HOSTEL **$**
(☑1800 425 356, 5486 8503; www.pippiesbeach house.com.au; 22 Spectrum St; dm/d $24/65; ✻@☒) With only 12 rooms, this small, superchilled hostel is the place to relax between surfing, diving and bushwalking. It's clean and the bathrooms are large. Take a Fraser Island trip with Pippies and you get two nights free accommodation at the hostel. Other bonuses include free breakfasts

and water toys, and plenty of space in the garden for tents and vans.

Dingo's Backpacker's Resort
HOSTEL **$**
(☑1800 111 126, 5486 8222; www.dingosatrainbow. com; 20 Spectrum Ave; dm/d $22/65; ✻@☒) The vivacious English manager is still here and keeps the bar hopping in this party hostel. There's live music every Wednesday and Saturday night, a Balinese-style gazebo for recovery, free tours to Carlo Sandblow, free pancake breakfasts and cheap meals every night.

Rainbow Sands Holiday Units
MOTEL **$$**
(☑5486 3400; 42-46 Rainbow Beach Rd; d $95, 1-bedroom apt $125; ✻☎☒) This low-rise, palm-fronted complex has standard motel rooms with poolside glass doors and bar fridges, and self-contained units with full laundries for comfortable longer stays.

Fraser's on Rainbow
HOSTEL **$**
(☑1800 100 170, 5486 8885; www.frasersonrain bow.com; 18 Spectrum St; dm/d from $25/65;

Among the many operators:

» **Footprints on Fraser** (☑1300 765 636; www.footprintsonfraser.com.au; 4/5-day walk $1375/1825) Highly recommended guided walking tours of the island's natural wonders.

» **Cool Dingo Tours** (☑1800 072 555, 4194 9222; www.cooldingotour.com; 2/3-day tour $328/405) Overnight at lodges with option to stay extra nights on the island. Party in the Dingo Bar!

» **Kingfisher Bay Tours** (☑1800 072 555, 4120 3333; www.kingfisherbay.com; Fraser Island; day tours adult/child $169/99) Ranger-guided ecotours.

» **Fraser Explorer Tours** (☑1800 249 122; 4194 9222; www.fraserexplorertours.com.au; 1/2-day tours $175/312) Highly recommended.

» **Fraser Experience** (☑1800 689 819, 4124 4244; www.fraserexperience.com; 2-day tours $295) Small groups and more freedom with the itinerary.

4WD Hire

You can hire a 4WD from Hervey Bay, Rainbow Beach and even on Fraser Island. All companies require a hefty bond, usually in the form of a credit-card imprint, which you *will* lose if you drive in salt water – don't even think about running the waves!

A driving-instruction video will usually be shown when planning your trip. Fraser has had some nasty accidents, often due to speeding, and new laws restrict the speed limit to 80km/hr on the beach and 30km/hr inland. Note that there is a maximum limit of eight passengers to a hire 4WD vehicle. Seatbelts are mandatory, or face fines of up to $300.

Rates for multiday rentals start at around $150 a day and most companies also rent camping gear.

Advantages – complete freedom to roam the island and escape the crowds.

Disadvantages – you may find you have to tackle beach and track conditions even experienced drivers find challenging.

See p358 and p362 for rental companies in Hervey Bay and Rainbow Beach. On the island, **Kingfisher Bay 4WD Hire** (☑4120 3366) hires out 4WDs from $280 per day.

@☀) Roomy dorms in a converted motel and a popular outdoor bar.

Rainbow Beach Holiday Village CARAVAN PARK $
(☑1300 366 596, 5486 3222; www.beach-village.com; 13 Rainbow Beach Rd; unpowered/powered sites from $27/34, cabins from $90; ❄☀) Popular beachfront park.

✗ Eating

Self-caterers will find a supermarket on Rainbow Beach Rd.

TOP CHOICE **Waterview Bistro** MODERN AUSTRALIAN $$
(☑5486 8344; Cooloola Dr; mains $26-35; ☺breakfast & lunch Sun, lunch & dinner Wed-Sat) Sunset drinks are a must at this swish restaurant with sensational views of Fraser Island from its hilltop perch. The small menu changes regularly and offers carnivores and vegetarians alike something delicious to complement the view.

Rainbow Beach Hotel PUB FARE $$
(1 Rainbow Beach Rd; mains $20-35; ☺lunch & dinner) The spruced-up pub carries on the plantation theme with ceiling fans, palm trees, timber floors and cane furnishings. The restaurant is bright, airy and serves up traditional pub grub. Scope the street scene from the upstairs balcony.

❶ Information

QPWS office (☑5486 3160; Rainbow Beach Rd; ☺8am-4pm)

Rainbow Beach visitors centre (☑5486 3227; 8 Rainbow Beach Rd; ☺7am-5pm)

Shell Tourist Centre (☑5486 8888; Rainbow Beach Rd; ☺8am-5pm) At the Shell service station; tour bookings and barge tickets for Fraser Island.

Tribal Travel (☑1800 559 987; www.tribaltravel.com.au; Rainbow Beach Rd; ☺7am-7pm summer, 9am-7pm winter)

ℹ Getting There & Around

Greyhound (☑1300 473 946; www.greyhound.com.au) has several daily services from Brisbane ($65, five hours), Noosa ($33, 2½ hours) and Hervey Bay ($30, 90 minutes). **Premier Motor Service** (☑13 34 10; www.premierms.com.au) has less-expensive services. **Cooloola Connections** (☑5481 1667; www.coolconnect.com.au) runs a shuttle bus to Rainbow Beach from Brisbane Airport ($110, three hours) and Sunshine Coast Airport ($65, two hours). **Polley's Coaches** (☑5480 4500) has buses from Gympie ($15, 1¾ hours).

Most 4WD-hire companies will also arrange permits, barge costs (per vehicle $90 return) and hire out camping gear. Some recommended companies:

All Trax 4WD Hire (☑5486 8767; Rainbow Beach Rd) At the Shell service station.

Rainbow Beach Adventure Centre 4WD Hire (☑5486 3288; www.adventurecentre.com.au; Rainbow Beach Rd; ⊘7am-5pm)

Safari 4WD (☑1800 689 819, 5486 8188; 3 Karoonda Ct)

Maryborough

POP 21,500

Born in 1847, Maryborough is one of Queensland's oldest towns, and its port was the first shaky step ashore for thousands of 19th-century free settlers looking for a better life in the new country. Heritage and history are Maryborough's fortes, the pace of yesteryear reflected in its beautifully restored colonial-era buildings and gracious Queenslander homes.

This big old country town is also the birthplace of PL Travers, creator of everyone's favourite umbrella-wielding nanny, Mary Poppins.

◉ Sights

Portside   HISTORIC SITE
In the historic port area beside the Mary River, Portside has 13 heritage-listed buildings, parklands and museums. Today's tidy colonial-era buildings and landscaped gardens paint a different story from Maryborough's once-thriving port and seedy streets filled with sailors, ruffians, brothels and opium dens. The **Portside Centre** (☑4190 5730; cnr Wharf & Richmond Sts; ⊘10am-4pm Mon-Fri, to 1pm Sat & Sun), located in the former **Customs House**, has interactive displays on Maryborough's history. Part of the centre but a few doors down, the **Bond Store**

Museum also highlights key periods in Maryborough's history. Downstairs is the original packed-earth floor and even some liquor barrels from 1864.

Mary Poppins statue   MONUMENT
On the street in front of the neoclassical **former Union Bank** (birthplace of *Mary Poppins* author, PL Travers) is a life-size statue of the acerbic character Travers created rather than the saccharine Disney version.

Brennan & Geraghty's Store   MUSEUM
(64 Lennox St; adult/child/family $5.50/2.50/1350; ⊘10am-3pm) This National Trust–classified store traded for 100 years before closing its doors. The museum is filled with tins, bottles and packets, including early Vegemite jars and curry powder from the 1890s, all crammed onto the ceiling-high shelves. Look for the 1885 tea packet from China, the oldest item in the store.

Maryborough Military & Colonial Museum   MUSEUM
(106 Wharf St; adult/child $5/2; ⊘9am-3pm) Check out the only surviving three-wheeler Girling car, originally built in London in 1911. There's also a replica Cobb & Co coach and one of the largest military libraries in Australia.

Queens Park   PARK
With a profusion of glorious trees, including a banyan fig that's more than 140 years old, this is a pleasant spot for a picnic.

🏃 Activities

On a **Tea with Mary** (☑1800 214 789, 4190 5730; per person $12.50) tour of the historic precinct, a costumed guide spills the beans on the town's past. Free **guided walks** (⊘9am Mon-Sat) depart from the City Hall every morning and take in the town's sites.

Otherwise, **Maryborough Riverboat Cruises** (☑4123 1523; www.maryboroughrivercruise.com; 1hr tour $20, 2hr lunch cruise $35; ⊘10am, noon & 2pm Tue-Sun) provide informed commentaries as you cruise along the Mary River.

On the last Saturday of each month, you can get spooked on a torch-lit tour of the city's grisly murder sites, opium dens, haunted houses and cemetery with **Ghostly Tours & Tales** (☑1800 214 789, 4190 5742; tour & progressive dinner $75).

🛏 Sleeping

Eco Queenslander RENTAL HOUSE $$
(📞0438 195 443; www.ecoqueenslander.
com; 15 Treasure St; house $120-140) Bypass the
impersonal motels and get your own cosy
home. You won't want to leave this lovely
converted Queenslander with comfy lounge,
full kitchen, laundry and a cast iron bathtub.
Eco features include solar power, rainwater
tanks, energy efficient lighting and bikes for
you to use.

McNevin's Parkway Motel MOTEL $$
(📞1800 072 000, 4122 2888; www.mcnevins.com.
au; 188 John St; r from $110; ❈@🅿🛜🏊) This well-
run complex is popular with business folk but
the fresh, light motel rooms are comfortable,
regardless of your reason for staying. The
smart executive suites are a step up in style
and price, with separate bedrooms and spas.

Arkana Motel MOTEL $
(📞4121 2261; www.arkanamotel.com.au; 46
Ferry St; r from $90; ❈🅿🛜) Just out of the
town centre, this good-value motel has no
surprises and is a reasonably comfortable
option.

🍴 Eating

The Basement TAPAS $ **363**
(📞4121 0002; 389 Kent St; tapas $9; ⏱4.30pm-
midnight Thu-Sat) Descend the stairs to this
ultra-chic underground tapas bar with its
mood lighting, leather lounges and high-
set steel benches and you'll think you've
stepped into the big city. This is the in-place
for after-work drinks and Mediterrasian-
inspired tapas.

The Port Residence MODERN AUSTRALIAN $$
(📞4123 5001; Customs House, Wharf St; mains
$15-30; ⏱breakfast, lunch & dinner Thu-Sun) An
elegant restaurant and tea room in the old
Customs House residence. Light meals and
traditional Aussie favourites like scones and
tea are served on the shady verandah, which
has lovely views over the Mary River Park-
lands.

Toast CAFE $
(199 Bazaar St; dishes $5-10; ⏱6am-4pm Mon-
Sat, 7am-10pm Fri & Sat) Stainless-steel fit-
tings, polished cement floors and coffee
served in paper cups stamp the metro-chic
seal on this groovy cafe.

GOLD, WOOD, STEAM & SONG: GYMPIE & THE MARY VALLEY

Gympie's gold once saved Queensland from near-bankruptcy, but that was in the 1860s
and not much has happened here since. History buffs will find a large collection of mining
equipment and functioning steam-driven engines at the **Gympie Gold Mining & His-
torical Museum** (📞5482 3995; 215 Brisbane Rd; adult/child/family $10/5/25; ⏱9am-4pm).
Of greater interest is the **Woodworks Forestry & Timber Museum** (📞5483 7691; cnr
Fraser Rd & Bruce Hwy; adult/student $10/5; ⏱10am-4pm Wed-Sun) on the Bruce Hwy south
of town. The highlight of the museum (and perhaps the lowlight of the logging industry)
is a cross-section of a magnificent kauri pine that lived through the Middle Ages, Colum-
bus' discovery of America and the industrial revolution, only to be felled in the early 20th
century.

After the summer rains, the Mary Valley around here is lush and scenic. If you don't
have a car, explore the valley on a 1923 steam train, the **Valley Rattler** (📞5482 2750;
www.thevalleyrattler.com; half-day tours per adult/child $20/10, day tours $47/23.50). It leaves
from the old Gympie train station on Tozer St every Wednesday and Sunday morning at
10am and chugs through the pretty Mary Valley to the tiny township of Imbil 40km away.
The return trip takes 5½ hours. On Saturday, half-day tours (⏱9.30am, 11.30am, 1.45pm)
only go as far as Amamoor, 20km away.

Amamoor is the site of the annual **Muster** (www.muster.com.au), a six-day country
music hoedown held annually in August.

Gympie Cooloola Tourism (📞1800 444 222, 5482 5444; www.cooloola.org.au); Matilda
(Matilda Service Centre, Bruce Hwy; ⏱9am-5pm); Lake Alford (Bruce Hwy, Gympie; ⏱9am-
4.30pm) has a wealth of information on sights and activities along the entire Fraser Coast.

Greyhound (📞1300 473 946; www.greyhound.com.au) and **Premier** (📞13 34 10; www.
premierms.com.au) have numerous daily services to Gympie from Brisbane, Noosa, Bund-
aberg and Hervey Bay. **Traveltrain** (📞1300 131 722; www.traveltrain.com.au) operates the
Tilt Train (Sunday to Friday) and the *Sunlander* (three services a week), from Brisbane to
Gympie on their way to Rockhampton and Cairns.

Muddy Waters Cafe SEAFOOD $$
(☑4121 5011; 71 Wharf St; mains $15-32; ⊘breakfast & lunch Tue-Sat, dinner Thu-Sat) The shady riverfront deck and the summery menu at this classy cafe will keep you happy with tempting seafood dishes such as Heineken-battered barramundi and salt-and-pepper squid.

☆ Entertainment
The strikingly contemporary **Brolga Theatre** (☑4122 6060; 5 Walker St) hosts musical and theatrical events.

❶ Information
The **Maryborough/Fraser Island visitors centre** (☑1800 214 789, 4190 5742; City Hall, Kent St; ⊘9am-5pm Mon-Fri, to 1pm Sat & Sun) in the 100-year-old City Hall is extremely helpful and has free copies of comprehensive self-guided walking tours.

❶ Getting There & Away
Both the *Sunlander* ($60, five hours, three weekly) and the *Tilt Train* ($60, 3½ hours, Sunday to Friday) connect Brisbane with the Maryborough West station, 7km west of the centre. There's a shuttle bus into town from the main bus terminal beside the Maryborough train station on Lennox St.

Greyhound Australia (☑1300 473 946; www.greyhound.com.au) and **Premier Motor Service** (☑13 34 10; www.premierms.com.au) have buses to Gympie ($30, one hour), Bundaberg ($40, three hours) and Brisbane ($64, 4½ hours).

Wide Bay Transit (☑4121 3719) has hourly services between Maryborough and the Urangan Marina in Hervey Bay ($8, one hour) every weekday, with fewer services on the weekend. Buses depart Maryborough from outside the City Hall in Kent St.

Childers
POP 1350

Surrounded by lush green fields and rich red soil, Childers is a charming little town, its main street lined with tall, shady trees and lattice-trimmed historical buildings. Backpackers flock here for fruit picking and farm work, although, sadly, Childers is best remembered for the 15 backpackers who perished in a fire in the Palace Backpackers Hostel in June 2000.

◉ Sights & Activities
There is a moving memorial, with poignant images of the backpackers who perished, at the **Childers Palace Memorial & Art Gallery** (72 Churchill St; ⊘9am-4pm Mon-Fri, to 3pm Sat & Sun).

The **Old Pharmacy** (90 Churchill St; ⊘9am-3.30pm Mon-Fri) operated as a pharmacy from 1894 to 1982. The original chemist also worked as the town dentist, vet, optician and local photographer.

The lovely, 100-year-old **Federal Hotel** has batwing doors, while a bronze statue of two fighting pig dogs sits outside the **Grand Hotel**.

On the last Sunday in July, Childers' main street is swamped with street performers, musicians, dancers and food-and-craft stalls during its annual **Festival of Cultures**, which draws over 50,000 people.

🛏 Sleeping & Eating
For warm, country hospitality, the cute cane-cutter cottages at **Mango Hill B&B** (☑4126 1311; www.mangohillcottages.com; 8 Mango Hill Dr; s/d $90/120; ✱), 4km south of town, are decorated with handmade wooden furniture, country decor and comfy beds that ooze charm and romance.

Childers Tourist Park & Camp (☑4126 1371; 111 Stockyard Rd; unpowered/powered sites $24/25, on-site vans $66) is a good choice for working backpackers, although it's out of town and you'll need a car.

Kapé Centro (65 Churchill St; mains $9-15; ⊘breakfast & lunch) in the old post office building dishes up light meals, salads and pizzas.

On your way out of town, take a detour to **Mammino's** (115 Lucketts Rd; ⊘9am-5pm) for wickedly delicious, homemade macadamia-nut ice cream. Lucketts Rd is off the Bruce Hwy just south of Childers.

❶ Information
Childers Visitors Information Centre (☑4130 4660; ⊘9am-4pm Mon-Fri, to 3pm Sat & Sun) Beneath the Childers Palace Memorial & Art Gallery.

❶ Getting There & Away
Childers is 50km southwest of Bundaberg. **Greyhound Australia** (☑1300 473 946) and **Premier Motor Service** (☑13 34 10) both stop at the Shell service station north of town and have daily services to/from Brisbane ($75, 6½ hours), Hervey Bay ($18, one hour) and Bundaberg ($18, 1½ hours).

Burrum Coast National Park

The Burrum Coast National Park covers two sections of coastline on either side of the little holiday community of Woodgate, 37km east of Childers. The Woodgate section of the park begins at the southern end of The Esplanade, and has attractive beaches, abundant fishing and a QPWS camping ground (per person/family $5.15/20.60) at Burrum Point, reached by a 4WD-only track. Several walking tracks start at the camping ground or Acacia St in Woodgate. There are more isolated bush-camping areas in the Kinkuna section of the park, a few kilometres north of Woodgate, but you'll need a 4WD to reach them. Book camping permits online at www.derm.qld.gov.au.

Woodgate Beach Tourist Park
CARAVAN PARK **$**
(✆4126 8802; www.woodgatebeachtouristpark.com; 88 The Esplanade; unpowered/powered sites $27/29, cabins $85-95, beachfront villas $110; ❄@) Close to the national park and opposite the beach.

Bundaberg

POP 46,961

Boasting a sublime climate, coral-fringed beaches and waving fields of sugarcane, 'Bundy' should feature on the Queensland tourist hit parade. But this old-fashioned country town feels stuck in a centuries-old time warp and nothing much seems to happen here. The pleasant main strip is a wide, palm-lined street and the surrounding countryside forms a picturesque chequer-board of rich red volcanic soil, small crops and sugarcane stretching pancake-flat to the coastal beaches 15km away. Born out of these cane fields is the famous Bundaberg Rum, a potent, mind-blowing liquor bizarrely endorsed by a polar bear but as iconically Australian as Tim Tams and Vegemite.

Hordes of backpackers flock to Bundy for fruit-picking and farm work; other visitors quickly pass through on their way to family summer holidays at the nearby seaside villages.

◉ Sights

Bundaberg Rum Distillery
RUM DISTILLERY
(✆4131 2999; www.bundabergrum.com.au; Avenue St; self-guided tour adult/child $15/7.50; ⏰9am-3.30pm Mon-Fri, to 2.30pm Sat & Sun; tours adult/child $25/12.50) Bundaberg's biggest claim to fame is the iconic Bundaberg Rum – you'll see the Bundy Rum polar bear on billboards all over town. Tours follow the rum's production from start to finish and include a tasting.

Hinkler Hall of Aviation
MUSEUM
(✆4130 4400; www.hinklerhallofaviation.com; Botanic Gardens, Mt Perry Rd; adult/child/family $15/10/40; ⏰9am-4pm) Situated within the grounds of the Botanic Gardens, this modern museum has multimedia exhibits, a flight simulator and informative displays that chronicle the life of Bundaberg's famous son and pioneer aviator, Bert Hinkler, who made the first solo flight between England and Australia in 1928.

Alexandra Park & Zoo [FREE]
PARK
(Quay St) Beside the Burnett River, this is a lovely sprawling park with plenty of shady trees, flower beds and swathes of green lawn for a lazy picnic. There's also a small zoo at the park with kangaroos, wallabies, birds and deer.

Bundaberg Barrel
BREWERY
(✆4154 5480; www.bundaberg.com; 147 Bargara Rd; adult/child $12.50/5.50;

TURTLE TOTS

Mon Repos 15km northeast of Bundaberg, is one of Australia's most accessible turtle rookeries. From November to late March, female loggerheads lumber laboriously up the beach to lay eggs in the sand. About eight weeks later, the hatchlings dig their way to the surface, and under cover of darkness emerge en masse to scurry as quickly as their little flippers allow down to the water.

The **Mon Repos visitors centre** (✆4159 1652; ⏰7.30am-6pm Mon-Fri) has information on turtle conservation and organises nightly tours (adult/child $10/5.25) from 7pm during the season. Bookings are mandatory and can be made through the Bundaberg visitors centre (p368) or online at www.bookbundabergregion.com.au. Alternatively, take a turtle-watching tour with **Foot Prints Adventures** (✆4152 3659; www.footprintsadventures.com.au; adult/child incl transfers $48/30).

Bundaberg

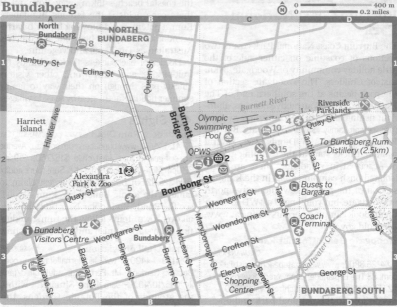

Bundaberg

⊙9am-4.30pm Mon-Sat, 10am-3pm Sun)
Bundaberg Ginger Beer is not quite as
famous as Bundy Rum, probably because
it's nonalcoholic. Visit the Barrel to see
how the ginger is mushed, crushed,
brewed and fermented.

Bundaberg Regional Arts Gallery
ART GALLERY
(☑4130 4750; www.brag-brc.org.au; 1 Barolin
St; ⊙10am-5pm Mon-Fri, 11am-3pm Sat & Sun)
This small (and vividly purple) gallery has
surprisingly good exhibitions.

🏃 Activities
Diving
About 16km east of Bundaberg, the small
beach hamlet of Bargara has good diving
and snorkelling at Barolin Rocks and in the
Woongarra Marine Park.

Dive Musgrave
DIVING
(☑1800 552 614; www.divemusgrave.com.au; 239
Bourbong St; per person $698)

Bundaberg Aqua Scuba
DIVING
(☑4153 5761; www.aquascuba.com.au; Shop 1, 66
Targo St; diving courses from $265)

☞ Tours

Lady Elliot Island ISLAND TOUR
(☎1800 072 200, 5536 3644; www.ladyelliot.com.
au; adult/child $299/162) Fly to Lady Elliot
Island, spend five hours on the Great Barrier Reef and use the resort's facilities.

Bundaberg Ferry Company RIVER CRUISE
(☎4152 9188; 3 Quay St; 2½hr tours per adult/
child/family $25/13/70; ⊙9.30am Wed & Fri,
1.30pm Tue, Fri, Sat & Sun) The *Bundy Belle,*
an old-fashioned ferry, chugs at a pleasant
pace to the mouth of the Burnett River.

🛏 Sleeping

There are plenty of midrange motels on the
Bundaberg–Childers Rd into town. Bundaberg's hostels cater to working backpackers,
and most can arrange harvest work; stays
of one week or longer are the norm. Check
the hostels carefully before deciding as standards vary considerably.

Inglebrae B&B $$
(☎4154 4003; www.inglebrae.com; 17 Branyan St; r
incl breakfast $110-140; ❄) For old-world Eng-
lish charm in a glorious Queenslander, this
delightful B&B is just the ticket. Polished
timber and stained glass seep from the en-
trance into the rooms, which come with
high beds and small antiques.

Quality Hotel HOTEL $$
(☎4155 8777; www.burnettmotel.com.au; 7 Quay
St; r $185-200; ❄🛜🏊) This modern pit stop
is popular with conferences and travelling
business folk, but the good facilities and dé-
cor set it apart from just about every other
option in town. The rooms are quite stylish
and there's a gym, a sauna and a licensed
restaurant and cocktail bar overlooking the
Burnett River.

Cellblock Backpackers HOSTEL $
(☎1800 837 773, 4154 3210; cnr Quay & Maryborough Sts; dm per night/week from $27/160, d $66;
❄@🏊) This arresting hostel in Bundy's
heritage-listed former lock-up is a swish resort with plasma-screen TVs, a trendy pool
bar and clean, modern facilities. The seven
restored jail cells (grab the padded cell!) lack
windows and are a tad claustrophobic, but
they're great for couples.

Feeding Grounds Backpacker HOSTEL $
(☎4152 3659; www.footprintsadventures.com.au;
4 Hinkler Ave; dm $30) The smallest hostel in
Bundaberg is a friendly, family-run affair in
a converted and extended house. It's a bit
cramped, although a new purpose-built hos-

tel was under construction in the backyard
at the time of research. The environmentally
conscious owner of the hostel runs Footprints Adventures turtle tours (see p365).
Combined accommodation and tour packages are available.

Bundaberg Spanish Motor Inn MOTEL $$
(☎4152 5444; www.bundabergspanishmotorinn.
com; 134 Woongarra St; s/d $85/95; ❄🐾🛜)
In a quiet side street off the main drag,
this Spanish hacienda-style motel is great
value. All units are self-contained and all
rooms overlook the central pool.

✕ Eating

Les Chefs INTERNATIONAL $$
(☎4153 1770; 238 Bourbong St; mains $27; ⊙lunch
Tue-Fri, dinner Mon-Sat) One for the carnivores,
this upmarket, intimate restaurant goes
global, treating diners to duck, veal, seafood,
chicken and beef dishes à la Nepal, Mexico,
France, India and more. It's immensely popular so make a reservation.

Spinnaker Restaurant & Bar
MODERN AUSTRALIAN $$
(☎4152 8033; 1A Quay St; dishes $10-40; ⊙lunch
Tue-Fri, dinner Tue-Sat) With a picturesque
perch above the Burnett River, this is a great
choice for a long lunch or an intimate din-
ner, or just a sundowner at the bar while
nibbling on tapas.

Spicy Tonight FUSION $
(☎4154 3320; 1 Targo St; dishes $12-20; ⊙lunch
& dinner Mon-Sat) Bundaberg's spicy little
secret combines Thai and Indian cuisine
with hot curries, vindaloo, tandoori and a
host of vegetarian dishes.

Indulge CAFE $
(80 Bourbong St; dishes $9-16; ⊙breakfast &
lunch) Delicious pastries.

Teaspoon CAFE $
(10 Targo St; mains $5-10; ⊙8am-5pm Mon-Sat)
Great coffee.

☕ Drinking & Entertainment

Central Hotel PUB
(18 Targo St) Strut your stuff on the dance
floor at Bundy's hottest nightclub. Pretty
young things and backpackers crowd in
here every weekend.

ℹ Information

Bundaberg Email Centre (☎4153 5007; 197
Bourbong St; per hr $4; ⊙10am-10pm) Internet
access.

Bundaberg visitors centre (☑1300 722 099, 4153 8888; www.bundabergregion.info; 271 Bourbong St; ☺9am-5pm)

Cosy Corner Internet Cafe (☑4153 5999; Barolin St; per hr $4; ☺8am-7pm Mon-Fri, 9am-5pm Sat, 11am-5pm Sun)

Post office (☑4151 6708; cnr Bourbong & Barolin Sts)

QPWS (☑4131 1600; 46 Quay St)

❶ Getting There & Around

Air
Bundaberg's **Hinkler Airport** (Takalvan St) is about 4km southwest of the centre. There are several daily flights to Brisbane with **Qantaslink** (☑13 13 13; www.qantas.com.au).

Bus
The coach terminal is on Targo Street. Both **Greyhound Australia** (☑1300 473 946; www.greyhound.com.au) and **Premier Motor Service** (☑13 34 10; www.premierms.com.au) have daily services connecting Bundaberg with Brisbane ($95, seven hours), Hervey Bay ($24, 1½ hours), Rockhampton ($75, four hours) and Gladstone ($50, 2½ hours).

Local bus services are handled by **Duffy's Coaches** (☑4151 4226). It has numerous services every weekday to Bargara ($5, 35 minutes), leaving from the back of Target on Woongarra St and stopping around town.

Train
Queensland Rail's (www.traveltrain.com.au) *Sunlander* ($68, seven hours, three weekly) and *Tilt Train* ($68, five hours, Sunday to Friday) travel from Brisbane to Bundaberg on their respective routes to Cairns and Rockhampton.

Around Bundaberg

In many people's eyes, the beach hamlets around Bundaberg are more attractive than the town itself. Some 25km north of the centre is **Moore Park** with wide, flat beaches. To the south is the very popular **Elliot Heads** with a nice beach, rocky foreshore and good fishing. Locals and visitors also flock to Mon Repos (p365) to see baby turtles hatching from November to March.

BARGARA
POP 5525

Some 16km east of Bundaberg, the cruisy beach village of **Bargara** is a picturesque little spot with a good surf beach, a lovely esplanade and a few snazzy cafes. Recent years have seen a few high-rises sprout up along the foreshore but the effect is relatively low-key. Families find Bargara attractive for its clean beaches and safe swimming, particularly at the 'basin', a sheltered artificial rock pool.

In a great location opposite the esplanade, **Kacy's Bargara Beach Motel** (☑1800 246 141, 4130 1111; www.bargaramotel.com.au; cnr See & Bauer Sts; d from $119, 2-bedroom apt from $199; ❋❄❅❆) offers a range of accommodation from pleasant motel rooms to self-contained apartments. Downstairs is the tropically themed **Kacy's Restaurant and Bar** (mains $12-32; ☺breakfast & dinner daily, lunch Fri-Sun).

FRASER ISLAND

The local Aborigines call it K'Gari or 'paradise'. Sculpted from wind, sand and surf, the striking blue freshwater lakes, crystalline creeks, giant dunes and lush rainforests of this gigantic sandbar form an enigmatic island paradise unlike any other in the world. Created over hundreds of thousands of years from sand drifting off the East Coast of mainland Australia, Fraser Island is the largest sand island in the world (measuring 120km by 15km) and the only place where rainforest grows on sand.

Inland, the vegetation varies from dense tropical rainforest and wild heath to wetlands and wallum scrub, with 'sandblows' (giant dunes over 200m high), mineral streams and freshwater lakes opening on to long sandy beaches fringed with pounding surf. The island is home to a profusion of bird life and wildlife, while offshore waters teem with dugong, dolphins, sharks and migrating humpback whales.

Once exploited for its natural resources, sand and timber, Fraser Island joined the World Heritage list in 1992. At present, the northern half of the island is protected as the Great Sandy National Park while the rest of the island comprises state forest, crown land and private land.

This island utopia, however, is marred by an ever-increasing volume of 4WD traffic tearing down the beach and along sandy inland tracks. With over 350,000 people visiting the island each year, Fraser can sometimes feel like a giant sandpit with its own peak hour and congested beach highway.

❂ Sights & Activities

Starting at the island's southern tip, where the ferry leaves for Inskip Point on the main-

The Fraser Island Great Walk is a stunning way to experience this enigmatic island. The trail undulates through the island's interior for 90km from Dilli Village to Happy Valley. Broken up into seven sections of around six to 16 kilometres each, plus some side trails off the main sections, it follows the pathways of Fraser Island's original inhabitants, the Butchulla people. En route, the walk passes underneath the rainforest canopies, circles around some of the island's vivid lakes and courses through shifting dunes.

Pick up the *Fraser Island Great Walk* brochure from a QPWS office or download it from www.derm.qld.gov.au for updates on the track's conditions.

land, a high-tide access track cuts inland, avoiding dangerous Hook Point, and leads to the entrance of the Eastern Beach's main thoroughfare. The first settlement is **Dilli Village**, the former sand-mining centre; **Eurong**, with shops, fuel and places to eat, is another 9km north. From here, an inland track crosses to Central Station and Wanggoolba Creek (for the ferry to River Heads).

Right in the middle of the island is the ranger centre at **Central Station**, the starting point for numerous walking trails. From here you can walk or drive to the beautiful **McKenzie**, **Jennings**, **Birrabeen** and **Boomanjin Lakes**. Lake McKenzie is spectacularly clear and ringed by white-sand beaches, making it a great place to swim, but Lake Birrabeen sees fewer tour and backpacker groups.

About 4km north of Eurong along the beach, a signposted walking trail leads across sandblows to the beautiful **Lake Wabby**, the most accessible of Fraser's lakes. An easier route is from the lookout on the inland track. Lake Wabby is surrounded on three sides by eucalypt forest, while the fourth side is a massive sandblow that encroaches on the lake at about 3m a year. The lake is deceptively shallow and diving is very dangerous.

As you drive up the beach, you may have to detour inland to avoid Poyungan and Yidney Rocks during high tide before you reach **Happy Valley**, with places to stay, a shop and bistro. About 10km north is **Eli Creek**, a fast-moving, crystal-clear waterway that will carry you effortlessly downstream. About 2km from Eli Creek is the rotting hulk of the **Maheno**, a former passenger liner blown ashore by a cyclone in 1935 as it was being towed to a Japanese scrap yard.

Roughly 5km north of the *Maheno* you'll find the **Pinnacles**, an eroded section of coloured sand cliffs, and about 10km beyond, **Dundubara**, with a ranger station and

excellent camping ground. Then there's a 20km stretch of beach before you come to the rock outcrop of **Indian Head**. Sharks, manta rays, dolphins and (during the migration season) whales can often be seen from the top of this headland.

Between Indian Head and Waddy Point, the trail branches inland, passing **Champagne Pools**, which offer the only safe saltwater swimming on the island. There are good camping areas at **Waddy Point** and **Orchid Beach**, the last settlement on the island.

Many tracks north of this are closed for reasons of environmental protection.

On the island, you can take a scenic flight with **MI Helicopters** (☎1800 600 345, 4125 1599; www.mihelicopters.com.au; 25min flight $240), based at Kingfisher Bay Resort, or with **Air Fraser** (☎1800 600 345, 4125 3600; 10min flights from $70).

🍴 Sleeping & Eating

Kingfisher Bay Resort　ECORESORT **$$**
(☎1800 072 555, 4194 9300; www.kingfisherbay.com; Kingfisher Bay; d $160, 2-bedroom villa $198; ❂@≋) This elegant ecoresort has hotel rooms with private balconies and sophisticated two- and three-bedroom timber villas that are elevated to limit their environmental impact. The villas and spacious holiday houses are utterly gorgeous and some even have spas on their private decks. There's a three-night minimum stay in high season. The resort has restaurants, bars and shops and operates two different ranger-guided, eco-accredited tours of the island (daily, adult/child $169/99).

Sailfish on Fraser　APARTMENTS **$$$**
(☎4127 9494; www.sailfishonfraser.com.au; Happy Valley; d from $230-250, extra person $10; ≋) Any notions of rugged wilderness and roughing it will be forgotten quick smart at this plush, indulgent retreat. These two-bedroom

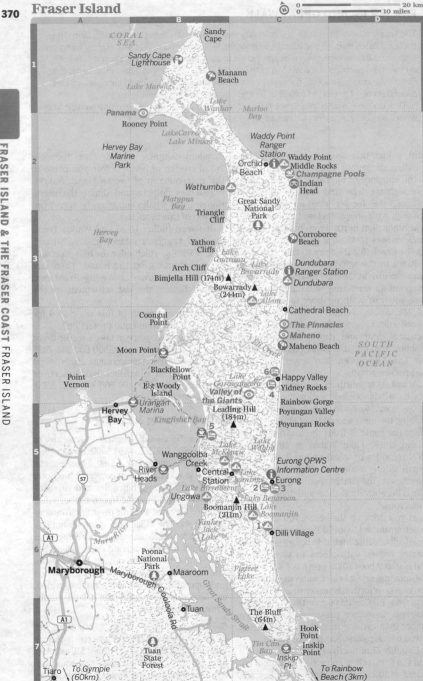

CORAL SEA

Sandy Cape

Sandy Cape Lighthouse

Manann Beach

Lake Maring

Lake Wanhar

Marloo Bay

Panama

Rooney Point

LakeCarree
Lake Minkar

Waddy Point Ranger Station

Hervey Bay Marine Park

Orchid Beach

Waddy Point

Middle Rocks

Champagne Pools

Wathumba

Indian Head

Platypus Bay

Great Sandy National Park

Triangle Cliff

Hervey Bay

Yathon Cliffs

Lake Guanan

Corroboree Beach

Arch Cliff
Bimjella Hill (174m)

Lake Bowarrady

Dundubara Ranger Station

Bowarrady (244m)

Dundubara

Lake Allom

Coongul Point

Cathedral Beach

The Pinnacles

Maheno

Moon Point

Maheno Beach

SOUTH PACIFIC OCEAN

Point Vernon

Blackfellow Point

Lake Guruwangera

Happy Valley

6

Big Woody Island

Valley of the Giants

Yidney Rocks

4

Urangan Marina

Leading Hill (184m)

Rainbow Gorge

Hervey Bay

Kingfisher Bay

Poyungan Valley

Poyungan Rocks

5

Wanggoolba Creek

Lake McKenzie

Lake Wabby

River Heads

Central Station

Lake Jennings

Eurong QPWS Information Centre

Ungowa

2

Eurong

3

Lake Birrabeen

Boomanjin Hill (211m)

Lake Benaroon

Lake Boomanjin

1

Dilli Village

A1

Yankee Jack Lake

Mary River

Poona National Park

Maryborough

Maaroom

Maryborough Cooloola Rd

Figtree Lake

Great Sandy Strait

A1

Tuan

The Bluff (64m)

Hook Point

Tuan State Forest

Tin Can Bay

Inskip Point

Tiaro

To Gympie (60km)

Inskip Pt

To Rainbow Beach (3km)

0   20 km
0   10 miles

Fraser Island

apartments (which sleep up to six people) are cavernous and classy, with wall-to-wall glass doors, spas, mod cons, mod furnishings and an alluring pool.

Fraser Island Beachhouses RENTAL HOUSE $$ (☑1800 626 230, 4127 9205; www.fraserisland-beachhouses.com.au; Eurong Second Valley; studio per 2 nights $300, 2-bedroom house per 2 nights from $700; ☒) Another luxury option, this complex contains sunny, self-contained units kitted out with polished wood, cable TVs and ocean views. Rates start with studios and climb to $900 for two-bedroom beachfront houses.

Eurong Beach Resort RESORT $$ (☑1800 111 808, 4120 1600; www.eurong.com.au; Eurong; r $140, 2-bedroom apt $199, mains $17.50-50; ⊙breakfast, lunch & dinner; ✳@☒) Bright, cheerful Eurong is the main resort on the East Coast and the most accessible for all budgets. At the cheaper end of the market are simple motel rooms, while comfortable, fully self-contained apartments are good value for families. On site is a restaurant, a bar, two pools and tennis courts.

Fraser Island Wilderness Retreat HOSTEL $ (☑4127 9144; Happy Valley; dm $30; mains $20-25; ⊙lunch & dinner; @☎☒) This wilderness-retreat-turned-backpackers has dorms that sleep up to six in nine timber lodges. The cabins cascade down a gentle slope amid plenty of tropical foliage and there's a bistro and bar on site.

Camping

Supplies on the island are limited and costly. Before arriving, stock up well and be prepared for mosquitoes and March flies.

Camping permits are required at QPWS camping grounds and any public area (ie along the beach). The most developed **QPWS camping grounds** (per person/family $5.15/20.60) with coin-operated hot showers, toilets and BBQs are at Waddy Point, Dundabara and Central Station. Campers

with vehicles can also use the smaller camping grounds with fewer facilities at Lake Boomanjin, Ungowa and Wathumba on the western coast. Walkers' camps are set away from the main campgrounds along the Fraser Island Great Walk trail (p369). The trail map lists the camp sites and their facilities. Camping is permitted on designated stretches of the eastern beach, but there are no facilities. Fires are prohibited except in communal fire rings at Waddy Point and Dundubara – bring your own firewood in the form of untreated, milled timber.

Dilli Village Fraser Island CAMPGROUND $ (☑4127 9130; Dilli Village; unpowered sites/bunk-rooms/cabins $20/40/100) Managed by the University of the Sunshine Coast, Dilli Village offers good sites on a softly sloping camping ground. The facilities are as neat as a pin and the cabins are ageing but accommodating.

ℹ Information

A 4WD is necessary if you're driving on Fraser Island. General supplies and expensive fuel are available from stores at Cathedral Beach, Eurong, Kingfisher Bay, Happy Valley and Orchid Beach. Most stores stock some camping and fishing gear, and those at Kingfisher Bay, Eurong, Happy Valley and Orchid Beach sell alcohol. There are public telephones at these locations and at most camping grounds.

The main ranger station, **Eurong QPWS Information Centre**, (☑4127 9128) is at Eurong. Others can be found at **Dundabara** (☑4127 9138) and **Waddy Point** (☑4127 9190). Office hours vary.

The **Fraser Island Taxi Service** (☑4127 9188) operates all over the island. A one-way fare from Kingfisher Bay to Eurong costs $80.

If your vehicle breaks down, call **Fraser Island Breakdown** (☑4127 9173) or the **tow-truck service** (☑4127 9449, 0428 353 164), both based in Eurong.

Permits

You must purchase permits from **QPWS** (☑13 74 68; www.derm.qld.gov.au) for vehicles (per month/year $39.40/197.20) and camping (per person/family $5.15/20.60) before you arrive. Permits aren't required for private camping grounds or resorts. Permit issuing offices:

Bundaberg QPWS Office (☑4131 1600; 46 Quay St)

Great Sandy Information Centre (☑5449 7792; 240 Moorinidil St, Tewantin; ⊙8am-4pm) Near Noosa.

Marina Kiosk (☑4128 9800; Buccaneer Ave, Urangan Boat Harbour, Urangan; ⊘6am-6pm)

Maryborough QPWS (☑4121 1800; 20 Tennyson St; ⊘8.30am-5pm Mon-Fri)

Rainbow Beach QPWS (☑5486 3160; Rainbow Beach Rd)

River Heads Information kiosk (☑4125 8485; ⊘6.15-11.15am & 2-3.30pm) Ferry departure point at River Heads, south of Hervey Bay.

❶ Getting There & Away

Air

Air Fraser Island (☑1800 247 992, 4125 3600; www.airfraserisland.com.au) charges from $125 for a return flight (20 minutes each way) to the island's eastern beach, departing Hervey Bay airport.

Boat

Several large vehicle ferries connect Fraser Island to the mainland. Most visitors use the two services that leave from River Heads (about 10km south of Hervey Bay) or from Inskip Point near Rainbow Beach.

Fraser Island Barges (☑1800 227 437, 4194 9300; www.fraserislandferry.com.au; vehicle & 4 passengers return $150, additional passengers $11) makes the 30-minute crossing from River Heads to Wanggoolba Creek on the western coast of Fraser Island. It departs daily from River Heads at 8.30am, 10.15am and 4pm and returns from the island at 9am, 3pm and 5pm. The same company also operates a service from the Urangan Marina in Hervey Bay to Moon Point on Fraser Island, but car-hire companies won't allow you to drive their cars here so it's limited to car owners and hikers. Rates are the same as for the service from River Heads to Wanggoolba Creek. Pedestrian fare is $36 return.

Kingfisher Vehicular Ferry (☑1800 072 555, 4194 9300; www.fraserislandferry.com; pedestrian adult/child return $50/25, vehicle & 4 passengers return $150, additional passengers $11) operates a vehicle and passenger ferry for the 50-minute crossing from River Heads to Kingfisher Bay, departing daily at 6.45am, 9am, 12.30pm, 3.30pm, 6.45pm and 9.30pm and returning at 7.50am, 10.30am, 2pm, 5pm, 8.30pm and 11pm.

Coming from Rainbow Beach, the operators **Rainbow Venture & Fraser Explorer** (☑4194 9300; pedestrian/vehicle return $10/80) and **Manta Ray** (☑5486 8888; vehicle return $90) both make the 15-minute crossing from Inskip Point to Hook Point on Fraser Island continuously from about 7am to 5.30pm daily.

The Great Barrier Reef

Gateways to the Reef »
Top Reef Encounters »
Nature's Theme Park »
The Perfect Reef Trip »

A diver explores the wonderland of Kelso Reef (p24)

Gateways to the Reef

There are numerous ways to approach Australia's massive undersea kingdom. You can head to a popular gateway town and join an organised tour, sign up for a multiday sailing trip exploring less-travelled outer fringes of the reef, or fly out to a remote island, where you'll have the reef largely to yourself.

Port Douglas

1 An hour's drive north of Cairns, Port Douglas (p468) is a laid-back beach town with dive boats heading out to more than a dozen sites, including pristine outer reefs such as the Agincourt Reef.

Townsville

2 Australia's largest tropical city (p425) is far from the outer reef (2½ hours by boat) but has some exceptional draws: access to Australia's best wreck dive, an excellent aquarium and marine-themed museums, plus multiday live-aboard dive boats departing from here.

Cairns

3 The most popular gateway to the reef, Cairns (p449) has dozens of boat operators offering both day trips and multiday reef explorations on live-aboard vessels. For the uninitiated, Cairns is a good place to learn to dive.

The Whitsundays

4 Home to turquoise waters, coral gardens and palm-fringed beaches, the Whitsundays (p407) have many options for reef-exploring: base yourself on an island, go sailing or stay on Airlie Beach and island-hop on day trips.

Southern Reef Islands

5 For an idyllic getaway off the beaten path, book a trip to one of several remote reef-fringed islands (p387) on the southern edge of the Great Barrier Reef. You'll find fantastic snorkelling or diving right off the island.

Clockwise from top left

1. A windswept vista at Port Douglas (p468) 2. Townsville's marina (p425) 3. Cairns' northern beaches (p461)

Top Reef Encounters

Donning a mask and fins and getting an up-close look at this marine wonderland is one of the best ways to experience the Great Barrier Reef. You can get a different view aboard a glass-bottomed boat tour, on a scenic flight or on a land-based reef walk.

Semisubmersibles

1 A growing number of reef operators (especially around Cairns) offer semi-submersible or glass-bottomed boat tours, which give cinematic views of coral, rays, fish, turtles and sharks – without ever getting wet.

Scenic Flights

2 Get a bird's-eye view of the vast coral reef and its cays and islands from a scenic flight. You can sign up for a helicopter tour (such as those offered from Cairns) or a seaplane tour (particularly memorable over the Whitsundays).

Diving & Snorkelling

3 The classic way to see the Great Barrier Reef is to board a catamaran and visit several different coral-rich spots on a long day trip. Nothing quite compares to that first underwater glimpse, whether diving or snorkelling.

Sailing

4 You can escape the crowds and see some spectacular reef scenery aboard a sailboat. Experienced mariners can hire a bareboat, others can join a multiday tour – both are easily arranged from Airlie Beach (p412), near the Whitsundays.

Reef Walking

5 Many reefs of the southern Great Barrier Reef are exposed at low tide, allowing visitors to walk on the reef top (on sandy tracks between living coral). This can be a fantastic way to learn about marine life, especially if accompanied by a naturalist guide.

Clockwise from top left

1. Anemone fish 2. Seaplane on Hayman Island (p420)
3. Snorkelling the reef (p26)

MICHAEL AW / LONELY PLANET IMAGES ©

DAVID WALL / LONELY PLANET IMAGES ©

2

Nature's Theme Park

Home to some of the greatest biodiversity of any ecosystem on earth, the Great Barrier Reef is a marine wonderland. It's home to 30-plus species of marine mammals along with countless species of fish, coral, molluscs and sponges. Above the water, 200 bird species and 118 butterfly species have been recorded on reef islands and cays.

Commonly encountered fish species include dusky butterfly fish, which are a rich navy blue, with sulphur-yellow noses and back fins; large and lumbering graphic turkfish, with luminescent pastel coats; teeny neon damsels, with darting flecks of electric blue; and six-banded angelfish, with blue tails, yellow bodies and tiger stripes.

The reef is also a haven to many marine mammals, such as whales, dolphins and dugongs. Dugongs are listed as vulnerable, and a significant number of them live in Australia's northern waters; the reef is home to around 15% of the global population. Humpback whales migrate from Antarctica to the reef's warm waters to breed between May and October. Minke whales can be seen off the coast from Cairns to Lizard Island in June and July. Porpoises and killer and pilot whales also make their home on the reef.

One of the reef's most-loved inhabitants is the sea turtle. Six of the world's seven species (all endangered) live on the reef and lay eggs on the islands' sandy beaches in spring or summer.

1

3

Clockwise from top left
1. A school of barracuda **2.** Nesting turtle **3.** Giant soft coral, Coral Sea

The Perfect Reef Trip

A Two-Week Itinerary

Along with experiencing the majesty of the Great Barrier Reef on snorkelling and diving trips, this itinerary includes a sailing excursion around coral-trimmed cays, rainforest walks and idyllic stays on tropical islands fronting white-sand beaches.

» After arriving in Bundaberg, take a seaplane to **Lady Elliot Island** (p388), an island resort with superb snorkelling and diving.

» Head north to the **Town of 1770** (p382) and day-trip out to **Lady Musgrave Island** (p388), for semisubmersible coral-viewing, plus snorkelling or diving in a pristine blue lagoon.

» Continue to **Airlie Beach** (p412) and book a two-night sailing cruise exploring the Whitsundays' white-sand beaches and coral gardens.

» Back at Airlie, board a catamaran to **Hardy Reef**, a spectacular 13km-long reef with a suspended lagoon and 'waterfalls' that drain it.

» Go north to **Townsville** (p425), visiting the excellent Reef HQ aquarium; if you're an experienced diver, book a trip on a live-aboard boat to dive the *Yongala*.

» Unwind on **Mission Beach** (p440), with rainforest walks, and overnight on nearby **Dunk Island** (p445), which has good bushwalking, swimming and snorkelling.

» Head to **Cairns** (p449), and take day trips to stunning **Green and Fitzroy Islands** (p463), both with rainforest and fringing coral.

» Pretty **Port Douglas** (p468) is next. From here visit the Agincourt Reef, home to excellent diving and snorkelling sites.

» If time and money allow, add on a trip to **Lizard Island** (p484), gateway to some of Australia's best diving sites.

Above

1. Idyllic Lady Musgrave Island (p388) 2. Rainforest trek to Mt Kootaloo, Dunk Island (p445)

Capricorn Coast & the Southern Reef Islands

Best Places to Eat

» Shio Kaze (p393)

» Ferns Hideaway (p394)

» Tree Bar (p384)

» Saigon Saigon (p390)

» The Deck (p384)

Best Places to Stay

» Svendsen's Beach (p396)

» Waterpark Farm (p395)

» Surfside Motel (p393)

» Criterion Hotel (p390)

» Agnes Water Beach Caravan Park (p384)

Why Go?

The stretch of coastline that straddles the tropic of Capricorn is one of the quietest and loveliest lengths of the East Coast. While local families flock to the main beaches during school holidays, the scene is uncrowded for most of the year, and even in high season you needn't travel far to find a deserted beach.

The stunning powdery white sand and aqua-blue waters of the Capricorn Coast fit the picture-postcard image superbly. The pristine islands of the southern Great Barrier Reef offer some of the best snorkelling and diving in Queensland, and the opportunities for wildlife spotting – from turtle hatchlings to passing whales – are plentiful. Unspoilt beaches and windswept national parks can be found along the entire coastline.

Inland, you'll find bustling Rockhampton – Capricornia's economic hub and the capital of cattle country, with steakhouses aplenty.

When to Go
Rockhampton

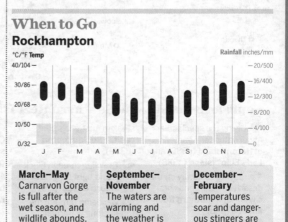

March–May
Carnarvon Gorge is full after the wet season, and wildlife abounds.

September–November
The waters are warming and the weather is relatively mild.

December–February
Temperatures soar and dangerous stingers are out.

Agnes Water & Town of 1770

⚑ 07 / POP 1620

Surrounded by national parks and the Pacific Ocean, the twin coastal towns of Agnes Water and Town of 1770 are among Queensland's most appealing seaside destinations. The tiny settlement of Agnes Water has a lovely white-sand beach, the east coast's most northerly surf beach, while the even tinier Town of 1770 (little more than a marina!) marks Captain Cook's first landing in Queensland. The 'Discovery Coast' is popular for surfing, boating, and fishing away from the crowds. To get here, turn east off the Bruce Hwy at Miriam Vale, 70km south of Gladstone. It's another 57km to Agnes Water and a further 6km to the Town of 1770.

Capricorn Coast & the Southern Reef Islands Highlights

① Diving the spectacular underwater coral gardens of **Heron Island** (p388) and **Lady Elliot Island** (p388)

② Playing castaway on the deserted islands and coral cays of the **Southern Reef Islands** (p387)

③ Tucking into a huge steak in Australia's beef capital, **Rockhampton** (p389)

④ Crawling through black holes and tight tunnels in the **Capricorn Caves** (p391)

⑤ Canoeing through the forest along Waterpark Creek in **Byfield** (p394)

⑥ Surfing and chilling at Queensland's most northerly surf beach, **Agnes Water** (p382)

⑦ Claiming a tropical beach for the day on **Great Keppel Island** (p395)

Sights

Miriam Vale Historical Society Museum
MUSEUM

(☑4974 9511; Springs Rd, near cnr Captain Cook Dr, Agnes Water; adult/child $3/free; ⊙1-4pm Mon & Wed-Sat, 10am-4pm Sun) The museum displays a small collection of artefacts, rocks and minerals, as well as extracts from Cook's journal and the original telescope from the first lighthouse built on the Queensland coast.

Activities & Tours

The action around here happens on and in the water. Agnes Water is Queensland's northernmost **surf beach**. A surf life-saving club patrols the main beach and there are often good breaks along the coast. If you're looking for boating, Round Hill Creek at the Town of 1770 is a calm anchorage. There's also good **fishing** and **mudcrabbing** upstream, and the southern end of the Great Barrier Reef is easily accessible from here. Charter boats are available for fishing, surfing, snorkelling and diving trips to the Reef.

Lady Musgrave Cruises
BOAT TOURS

(☑4974 9077; www.1770reefcruises.com; 1770 Marina, 535 Captain Cook Dr, 1770; adult/child $175/85) Has excellent day trips to Lady Musgrave Island aboard the *Spirit of 1770*. It takes 1¼ hours to get there and five hours is spent at the island and its stunning blue lagoon. Coral viewing in a semisubmersible, lunch, morning and afternoon tea, snorkelling and fishing gear are provided on the cruises, which depart the Town of 1770 marina every morning at 8am. For an extra cost you can go diving. Island camping transfers are also available for $320 per person.

1770 UnderSea Adventures
DIVING, SNORKELLING

(☑1300 553 889; www.1770underseaadventures.com.au) It offers a range of dive courses, and Great Barrier Reef and wreck dives ($160 including snorkel gear and meals, plus $25 per dive and $30 for diving-gear rental).

Reef 2 Beach Surf School
SURFING

(☑4974 9072, 0402 328 515; www.reef2beachsurf.com; 1/10 Round Hill Rd, Agnes Water) Learn to surf on the gentle breaks of the main beach with this highly acclaimed surf school. A three-hour group surfing lesson is $17 per person, and surfboard hire is $20 for four hours.

1770 Liquid Adventures
KAYAKING

(☑0428 956 630, www.1770liquidadventures.com.au) Run by the same outfit as Lazy Lizard, it runs a spectacular twilight kayak tour. For $40 you get a lesson in sea kayaking, riding the waves just off 1770, before retiring to the beach for drinks and snacks as the sun sets – keep an eye out for dolphins. You can also rent kayaks for $40 per half day.

Scooteroo
MOTORCYCLE RENTALS

(☑4974 7697; www.scooterootours.com; 21 Bicentennial Dr, Agnes Water; 3hr chopper ride $55; ⊙pick-ups at around 2:45pm) Straddle a chopper and cover the back roads around Agnes Water in the coolest way possible. On the 60km tour you ride the mean beast along back-country roads for scenic views of the coast and hinterland, with plenty of kangaroo and wallaby sightings thrown in. All you need is a car licence as the machines are fully automatic and you don't have to worry about changing gears. Wear long pants and closed-in shoes.

1770 Larc Tours
ADVENTURE TOURS

(☑4974 9422; www.1770larctours.com.au) From the Town of 1770 marina, this outfit runs fun full-day tours in its amphibious vehicles. The tours take in Middle Island, Bustard Head and Eurimbula National Park, and operate Monday, Wednesday and Saturday. It costs $148/88 per adult/child, including lunch. It also runs daily one-hour sunset cruises (adult/child $35/16) and sandboarding safaris (Thurs and Sun, $85 per person). Larc Tours also runs the **MV James Cook** (www.1770jamescook.com.au), a 14m vessel that sleeps up to 10 people for tours of up to seven days.

ThunderCat 1770
SPEED BOATING

(☑0427-177 000; adult/child $85/65) Adrenalin junkies will love the wave jumping in a surf racing boat this joint offers. The action is toned down slightly on the Action Adventurer and even more so on the Wilderness Explorer tours, where you visit secluded beaches, learn some local history and explore 1770's pristine waterways and national park coastline. Tours and activities can be tailored and combined to include diversions like tube riding and even wearable 'sumo suits' that have swimmers spinning like crazy as they are towed behind boats.

Wyndham Aviation
FLIGHTS

(1¼hr flight per person $85) A flight over the headland in a Skyhawk three-seater Cessna light aircraft is another popular activity.

From your aerial viewpoint you can often spot dolphins and turtles swimming in the water and you get to land on a secluded beach. Book flights through your accommodation.

Lazy Lizard Surf School SURFING
(☎0488 177 000, www.lazylizardsurfschool.com.au) The Lazy Lizard offers lessons for smaller groups (up to 12 people, $33 for ½ day).

Dive 1770 DIVING
(☎4974 9359; www.dive1770.com) It offers courses (PADI Open Water $250) and Great Barrier Reef dives (from $30).

1770 Marina Café BOAT RENTAL
(☎4974 9227) This cafe hires out aluminium dinghies (half/full day $65/95).

Hooked on 1770 (☎4974 9794) BOAT RENTAL
Hooked on 1770 has full- and half-day fishing and scenic charters starting from $55 per person.

🛌 Sleeping

TOP CHOICE **Agnes Water Beach Caravan Park**
CARAVAN PARK/CABINS $
(☎4974 9132; www.agneswaterfirst point.com.au; Jeffrey Court, Agnes Water; unpowered sites $30, powered sites $35-59, en-suite cabins $120-$250) This park has tented cabins on stilts that must offer some of the best-value beachfront rooms around. Each cabin comes with its own deck, equipped with gas barbecue. The camp's toilet and shower facilities are clean and new.

Sandcastles 1770 Motel & Resort
MOTEL, RESORT $$
(☎4974 9428; www.sandcastles1770.com.au; 1 Grahame Colyer Dr, Agnes Water; motel r from $120, villas & beach-home apt from $160-650; ❄@☒) Set on 4 hectares of landscaped gardens and subtropical vegetation, Sandcastles has a range of accommodation options from motel-style rooms to luxury beach-home apartments and villas. The funky one- to four-bedroom Balinese-themed villas are large and airy and open on to a central courtyard, and some have private pools. There's also a popular restaurant, Kahunas, on-site and a small cafe that is open for breakfast and lunch.

Cool Bananas HOSTEL $
(☎4974 7660; www.coolbananas.net.au; 2 Springs Rd, Agnes Water; dm $26; @) This funky Balinese-themed backpackers has roomy six- and eight-bed dorms, open and airy communal

areas, and is only a five-minute walk to the beach and shops. Otherwise, you can laze the day away in a hammock in the tropical gardens.

1770 Southern Cross Tourist Retreat
HOSTEL $
(☎4974 7225; www.1770southerncross.com; 2694 Round Hill Rd, Agnes Water; dm/d incl breakfast $25/75, 2 night minimum stay; @☒) This excellent backpackers' retreat is set on 6.5 hectares of bushland, 2.5km out of town. The double rooms and the three- and four-bed dorms are in clean, airy timber cabins (all with en suites), there's an open-air meditation area, an ultracool communal chill-out zone, kangaroos in the grounds, and a free shuttle bus to town. Bikes are lent for free or you can hire a scooter, and you can swim or fish in the lake. Highly recommended.

Sovereign Lodge BOUTIQUE HOTEL $$
(☎4974 9257; www.1770sovereignlodge.com; 1 Elliot St, Town of 1770; d $165-280; ❄☒) This lovely boutique accommodation has a range of immaculate self-contained rooms, some with excellent views from its hilltop perch. There's also a Balinese 'Body Temple' here where you can be massaged, wrapped in clay, rubbed with hot rocks and scrubbed with salt.

1770 Camping Grounds CARAVAN PARK $
(☎4974 9286; www.1770campinggrounds.com; Captain Cook Dr, Town of 1770; unpowered/powered sites $33/38) A large but peaceful park with sites right by the beach and plenty of shady trees. Prices are for two people.

🍴 Eating

TOP CHOICE **Tree Bar** MODERN AUSTRALIAN $$
(☎4974 7446; 576 Captain Cook Dr, Town of 1770; mains $14-38; ☺breakfast, lunch & dinner) This little salt-encrusted waterfront diner has plenty of charm and an atmospheric bar. Seafood is a prime offering.

Deck MODERN AUSTRALIAN $$
(☎4974 9157; 584 Captain Cook Drive, Town of 1770; mains $20-30; ☺dinner Tue-Sun) Locally caught seafood is served inside or alfresco among the palms, accompanied by delicious sides or nestled in perfectly cooked pasta. Great service and candlelit tables make this a romantic option.

Kahunas Pizza Bar & Grill
MODERN AUSTRALIAN $$
(☎4974 9428; 1 Grahame Colyer Dr, Agnes Water; mains $15-38; ☺dinner) At Sandcastles, Kahu-

nas is a popular choice, especially for beer and pizza on a hot night. There's plenty of meat on the grill and an excellent seafood plate.

Yok Attack THAI **$$**
(☎4974 7454; Endeavour Plaza, cnr Captain Cook Dr & Round Hill Rd, Agnes Water; mains $17-25; ☺lunch & dinner Thu-Tue) This simple Thai restaurant is very popular with the locals and is highly recommended.

❶ Information

The **Agnes Water visitors centre** (☎4902 1533; 3 Captain Cook Dr, Agnes Water; ☺8.30am-5pm Mon-Fri, 9am-5pm Sat & Sun) is opposite Endeavour Plaza. Next door, the **Agnes Water Library** (☎4902 1515; 3 Captain Cook Dr, Agnes Water; ☺9am-4.30pm Mon-Fri) has free internet access – half an hour, booked in advance.

The **Hub CaféCentre** (☎4974 7460; Endeavour Plaza, cnr Captain Cook Dr & Round Hill Rd, Agnes Water) serves some of the best coffee in town, with half an hour's worth of internet (otherwise $5 an hour) thrown in for free.

❶ Getting There & Away
Bus

Only one of several daily **Greyhound** (☎13 20 30; www.greyhound.com.au) buses detours off the Bruce Hwy to Agnes Water; the direct bus from Bundaberg ($24, 1½ hours) arrives opposite Cool Bananas at 6.10pm. Others, including **Premier Motor Service** (☎13 34 10; www.premierms.com.au), drop passengers at Fingerboard Rd.

Eurimbula & Deepwater National Parks

South of Agnes Water is Deepwater National Park, an unspoiled coastal landscape with long sandy beaches, freshwater creeks, good fishing spots and two camping grounds. It's also a major breeding ground for loggerhead turtles, which dig nests and lay eggs on the beaches between November and February. You can watch the turtles laying and see hatchlings emerging at night between January and April, but you need to observe various precautions outlined in the QPWS park brochure (obtainable at the office in Town of 1770).

The northern park entrance is 8km south of Agnes Water and is only accessible by 4WD. It's another 5km to the basic camping ground at Middle Rock (no facilities) and

a further 2km to the Wreck Rock camping ground and picnic area, with rain and bore water and composting toilets. Wreck Point can also be accessed from the south by 2WD vehicles via Baffle Creek.

The 78-sq-km Eurimbula National Park, on the northern side of Round Hill Creek, has a landscape of dunes, mangroves and eucalypt forest. There are two basic camping grounds, one at Middle Creek with toilets only and the other at Bustard Beach with toilets and limited rainwater. The main access road to the park is about 10km southwest of Agnes Water.

Middle Rock in Deepwater and Middle Creek in Eurimbula have self-registration stands but you must obtain permits for the other camping grounds from the QPWS (☎13 74 68; www.qld.gov.au/camping).

Gladstone
☎07 / POP 28,810

On first impression, the industrial town of Gladstone, with its busy port, power station and alumina refineries, is rather uninspiring. Sometimes first impressions are right. There's little to keep you in town – head straight for the marina, the main departure point for boats to the southern coral cay islands of Heron, Masthead and Wilson on the Great Barrier Reef. What little action there is can be found at the port end of Gondoon St.

◉ Sights & Activities

If you have some time to spare before or after island hopping, drive up to the **Auckland Point Lookout** for views over Gladstone harbour, the port facilities and shipping terminals. A brass tablet on the lookout maps the harbour and its many islands.

The **Toondoon Botanic Gardens** (☎4971 4444; Glenlyon Rd; admission free; ☺9am-6pm Oct-Mar, 8.30am-5.30pm Apr-Sep), about 7km south of town, comprise 83 hectares of rainforest, lakes and Australian native plants. There's a visitors centre, an orchid house, and free one-hour guided tours between February and November (tours can be booked at the gardens or visitors centre). The gardens have wheelchair access.

If you are in the area, **market days** (ask the visitors centre for dates) at the **Calliope River Historical Village** (☎4975 7428; Dawson Hwy, Calliope; admission $2; ☺8am-4pm), 26km south of Gladstone, are hugely popular. Held six times a year, the 200-plus

ART DETOUR

Cedar Galleries (☑4975 0444; www. cedargalleries.com.au; Bruce Hwy; ⊙9am-4pm Thu-Sun) is a tranquil artists' bush retreat where you can watch painters and sculptors at work in the hand-built slab-hut studios. To unleash your creative genius you can take **art & craft classes** with visiting artists (call ahead to book in) or just browse the gardens and the gallery. There's also a cafe, a beautiful handcrafted wedding chapel, a kids' jumping castle, a herd of friendly alpacas and a winery cellar door but no accommodation, although aspiring artists are welcome to pitch a tent or sleep on the floor. If you're here on the last Sunday of the month you can watch local musicians do their thing at the monthly Sunday Sessions (admission $12, includes barbecue dinner).

This unique artists' colony (114km south of Gladstone) is signposted off the Bruce Hwy, 7km southeast of Calliope.

stalls offering arts, crafts, clothes, jewellery and local produce attract over 3000 people. While here you can wander around the historical village's restored heritage buildings, including an old pub (licensed on market days), church, schoolhouse and a slab hut.

Created by the construction of the Awoonga Dam in 1984, Lake Awoonga is a popular recreational area 30km south of Gladstone. Backed by the rugged Castle Tower National Park, the lake, which is stocked with barramundi, has a scenic setting with landscaped picnic areas, a cafe, barbecues, walking trails and bird life. You can hire canoes, boats and fishing gear from the Lake Awoonga Caravan Park (☑4975 0155; www.lakeawoongscaravanpark.com.au; Lake Awoonga Rd, Benaraby; unpowered/powered sites $20/29, cabins from $75). Prices are for two people.

☞ Tours

Gladstone's big-ticket industries, including the alumina refineries, aluminium smelter, power station and port authority, open their doors for free **industry tours**. The one- or 1½-hour tours start at different times on different days of the week depending on the industry. Book at the visitors centre.

Fishing, diving and sightseeing cruises to the Swains and Bunker Island groups are the speciality of the 20m MV Mikat (☑4972 3415; www.mikat.com.au). Cruises are a minimum of three days with all meals catered, and there's a licensed bar on board. Capricorn Star Cruises (☑4978 0499) and Rob Benn Charters (☑4972 8885) also offer charter trips with fishing, diving, snorkelling and reef-viewing.

🛏 Sleeping

Auckland Hill B&B   B&B $$$
(☑4972 4907; www.ahbb.com.au; 15 Yarroon St; s/d incl breakfast $230/260; ❇❊) This sprawling, comfortable Queenslander has six spacious rooms with king-sized beds. Each is differently decorated: there is a spa suite and one with wheelchair access. Breakfasts are hearty and the mood is relaxed.

Gladstone Backpackers   HOSTEL $
(☑4972 5744; www.gladstonebackpackers.com; 12 Rollo St; dm/d $25/65;@❊) This fairly central hostel has recently undergone renovations with more to come. It's a friendly, family-run place in an old Queenslander, with a large kitchen, clean bathrooms and an airy outside deck. There's free use of bicycles and free pick-ups from the marina, bus, train and airport. You're sure to feel like part of the family by the time you leave.

Barney Beach Caravan Park   CARAVAN PARK $
(☑4972 1366; barneybeach.com.au; 10 Friend St; powered sites $37, cabins $150-205; ❇@❊) About 2km east of the city centre and close to the foreshore, this is the most central of the caravan parks. It's large and tidy, with a good camp kitchen and excellent self-contained accommodation. There are complimentary transfers to the marina for guests visiting Heron Island. Prices for cabins are for two people. Buslink Queensland runs buses here; see p392.

Harbour City Motel   MOTEL $$
(☑4976 7100; 20-24 William St; s/d $115/125) If you must stay in Gladstone, this is a decent motel in the centre of town. The large rooms have modern bathrooms and the motel has a licensed steakhouse.

🍴 Eating & Drinking

Tables on Flinders   SEAFOOD $$
(☑4972 8322; 2 Oaka La; mains $20-39; ⊙lunch Tue-Fri, dinner Tue-Sat) This delightful, cosy restaurant specialises in seafood and does it well. Tasty mud crabs are served steamed

with hot butter, or with garlic cream or Singapore-style chilli. The quality, prices and ambience draw visiting suits and romantic couples.

Library Square Brasserie
MODERN AUSTRALIAN **$$**
(☎4972 8611; 56 Goondoon St; mains $22-30; ⊗lunch Mon-Fri, dinner Mon-Sun) The varied menu at this local favourite can be enjoyed at outside tables that take in the live music on show in the square on Thursday and Friday nights.

Gladstone Yacht Club
PUB FARE **$**
4972 8611; 1 Goondoon St; mains $12-24; ⊗lunch & dinner) The yacht club is a popular place to wine and dine on a budget, and with good reason. The steak, chicken, pasta and seafood are tasty and generous, there are daily buffet specials and you can eat on the deck overlooking the water.

ⓘ Information
Gladstone City Library (☎4976 6400; 39 Goondoon St; ⊗9.30am-5.45pm Mon-Fri, to 7.45pm Thu, 9am-4.30pm Sat) Free internet access but you must book in advance.

Post office (☎13 13 18; Valley Shopping Centre, Goondoon St)

QPWS (☎4971 6500; 3rd fl, 136 Goondoon St; ⊗8.30am-4.30pm Mon-Fri) Provides information on all the southern Great Barrier Reef islands, as well as the area's mainland parks.

Visitors centre (☎4972 9000; Bryan Jordan Dr; ⊗8.30am-5pm Mon-Fri, 9am-5pm Sat & Sun) Located at the marina, the departure point for boats to Heron Island.

ⓘ Getting There & Away

Air
Qantaslink (☎13 13 13; www.qantas.com.au) has several daily flights between Brisbane and Gladstone (70 minutes) and two flights a day between Rockhampton and Gladstone (25 minutes). The airport is 7km from the centre.

Boat
Curtis Ferry Services (☎4972 6990; www.curtisferryservices.com.au) has regular services to Curtis Island (p387) five days per week. The service leaves from the Gladstone marina and stops at Farmers Point on Facing Island en route. Transport to North West and Masthead Islands can be arranged on request.

You can also access the islands with various charter operators (p386).

If you've booked a stay on Heron Island, the resort operates a launch (adult/child $110/55,

two hours), which leaves the Gladstone marina at 11am daily.

Bus
Greyhound Australia (☎13 20 30; www.greyhound.com.au) has several coach services from Brisbane ($105, 10½ hours), Bundaberg ($45, 1½ hours) and Rockhampton ($34, 2½ hours). The terminal for long-distance buses is at the Mobil 24 Hour Roadhouse, on the Dawson Hwy, about 200m southwest of the centre.

Train
Queensland Rail (☎1800 872 467, 3235 1122; www.queenslandrail.com.au) has frequent north- and southbound services passing through Gladstone daily. The *Tilt Train* stops in Gladstone from Brisbane ($108, 6½ hours) and Rockhampton ($34, one hour). The more sedate *Sunlander* and *Spirit of the Outback* trains take far longer.

Southern Reef Islands

If you've ever had 'castaway' dreams of tiny coral atolls fringed with sugary white sand and turquoise-blue seas, you've found your island paradise in the southern Great Barrier Reef Islands. From beautiful Lady Elliot Island, 80km northeast of Bundaberg, secluded and uninhabited coral reefs and atolls dot the ocean for about 140km up to Tryon Island, east of Rockhampton.

Several cays in this part of the Reef are excellent for snorkelling, diving and just getting back to nature – though reaching them

---

WORTH A TRIP

CURTIS ISLAND

Curtis Island, just across the water from Gladstone, can't be confused with a resort island. Apart from swimming, fishing and curling up with a good book, its only real drawcard is the annual appearance of rare flatback turtles on its eastern shores between November and January. Camping permits can be booked via **QPWS** (☎13 74 68; www.qld.gov.au/camping) and rental accommodation can be found by calling **Capricorn Lodge** (☎4972 0222; lodgings from around $100). **Curtis Ferry Services** (☎4972 6990; www.curtisferryservices.com.au; return adult/child/family $30/22/84) connects the island with Gladstone on Monday, Wednesday, Friday, Saturday and Sunday.

is generally more expensive than reaching islands nearer the coast. Some of the islands are important breeding grounds for turtles and seabirds, and visitors should be aware of precautions to ensure the wildlife's protection, outlined in the relevant QPWS information sheets.

Camping is allowed on Lady Musgrave, Masthead and North West national park islands, and campers must be totally self-sufficient. Numbers are limited, so it's advisable to apply well ahead for a camping permit. Contact QPWS (☎13 74 68; www.qld.gov.au/camping; permits per person/family $5.15/20.60).

Access is from Town of 1770 and Gladstone.

LADY ELLIOT ISLAND

On the southern frontier of the Great Barrier Reef, Lady Elliot is a 40-hectare vegetated coral cay popular with divers, snorkellers and nesting sea turtles. The island is a breeding and nesting ground for many species of tropical seabirds but its stunning underwater landscape is the main attraction. Divers can walk straight off the beach to explore an ocean-bed of shipwrecks, coral gardens, bommies (coral pinnacles or outcroppings) and blowholes, and abundant marine life including barracuda, giant manta rays and harmless leopard sharks.

Lady Elliot Island is not a national park, and camping is not allowed. Your only option is the low-key Lady Elliot Island Resort (☎1800 072 200; www.ladyelliot.com.au; per person from $160-326). Accommodation at this no-frills resort is in basic tent cabins, simple motel-style units, or more expensive two-bedroom self-contained suites. Rates include breakfast and dinner, snorkelling gear and some tours; note that a three-night minimum applies over Christmas and New Year.

The only way to reach the island is in a light aircraft. Seair (book through the resort) flies guests to the resort from Bundaberg and Hervey Bay return for $254/136 per adult/child. You can also visit the island on a day trip from Bundaberg and Hervey Bay for $300/170 (the price includes a range of tours and activities as well as lunch and snorkelling gear).

LADY MUSGRAVE ISLAND

Wannabe castaways look no further – this is the perfect desert island! This tiny, 15-hectare cay 100km northeast of Bundaberg sits on the western rim of a stunning, turquoise-blue reef lagoon renowned for its safe swimming, snorkelling and diving. A squeaky, white-sand beach fringes a dense canopy of pisonia forest brimming with roosting bird life, including terns, shearwaters and white-capped noddies. Birds nest from October to April while green turtles nest from November to February.

The uninhabited island is part of the Capricornia Cays National Park and there is a QPWS camping ground on the island's west side. The camping ground has bush toilets but little else and campers must be totally self-sufficient, even bringing their own water. Numbers are limited to 40 at any one time, so apply well ahead for a permit with the QPWS (☎13 74 68; www.qld.gov.au/camping). Online bookings can be made – search under Capricornia Cays National Park. Don't forget to bring a gas stove as fires are not permitted on the island.

Day trips to Lady Musgrave depart from the Town of 1770 marina (see p383).

HERON & WILSON ISLANDS

With the underwater reef world accessible directly from the beach, Heron Island is famed for superb scuba diving and snorkelling, although you'll need a fair amount of cash to visit. A true coral cay, it is densely vegetated with pisonia trees and surrounded by 24 sq km of reef. There's a resort and research station on the northeastern third of the island; the remainder is national park.

Heron Island Resort (☎4972 9055, 1800 737 678; www.heronisland.com; s/d incl buffet breakfast from $399/479) has comfortable accommodation that is suited to families and couples; the Point Suites have the best views. Meal packages are extra, and guests will pay $200/100 per adult/child for launch transfer, or $440/270 for helicopter transfer. Both are from Gladstone.

Wilson Island (www.wilsonisland.com; s/d from $671/918), also part of a national park, is an exclusive wilderness retreat with six permanent tents and solar-heated showers. There are excellent beaches and superb snorkelling. The only access is from Heron Island and to get here, you'll need to buy a combined Wilson-Heron package and spend at least two nights on Wilson Island. Transfers between Wilson and Heron are included in the tariff.

Rockhampton

📞 07 / POP 74,500

If the wide-brimmed hats, cowboy boots and V8 utes don't tip you off, the large bull statues around town let you know you're in the 'beef capital' of Australia. With over 2.5 million cattle within a 250km radius of Rockhampton, it's no surprise the smell of bulldust hangs thick in the air. This sprawling country town is the administrative and commercial centre of central Queensland, its wide streets and fine Victorian-era buildings reflecting the region's prosperous 19th-century heyday of gold and copper mining and the beef-cattle industry.

Straddling the tropic of Capricorn, 'Rocky' marks the start of the tropics; lying 40km inland and lacking coastal sea breezes, summers here can be unbearably hot and humid. Rocky has a smattering of attractions but is best seen as the gateway to the coastal gems of Yeppoon and Great Keppel Island. Stay in the old part of town to enjoy some charming walks along the Fitzroy.

👁 Sights & Activities

Botanic Gardens   GARDEN

(📞4922 1654; Spencer St; admission free; ⊙6am-6pm) Just south of town, these gardens are a beautiful oasis, with impressive banyan figs, tropical and subtropical rainforest, landscaped gardens and lily-covered lagoons. The formal Japanese garden is a zen-zone of tranquillity, the **cafe** (⊙8am-5pm) serves tea and cakes under a giant banyan fig, and the **zoo** (⊙8.30am-4.30pm) has koalas, wombats, dingoes and a walk-through aviary.

Quay Street   STREET

In town, wander down this historic streetscape, with its grand sandstone Victorian-era buildings dating back to the gold-rush days. You can pick up leaflets that map out walking trails around the town from the visitors centres.

Rockhampton City Art Gallery   ART GALLERY

(📞4927 7129; 62 Victoria Pde; admission free; ⊙10am-4pm Tue-Fri, 11am-4pm Sat & Sun) Boasting an impressive collection of Australian paintings, this gallery includes works by Sir Russell Drysdale, Sir Sidney Nolan and Albert Namatjira. Contemporary Indigenous artist Judy Watson also has a number of works on display. The permanent collection is supplemented by innovative temporary exhibitions, for which there are varying admission charges.

Dreamtime Cultural Centre   CULTURAL CENTRE

(📞4936 1655; www.dreamtimecentre.com.au; Bruce Hwy; adult/child $13.50/6.50; ⊙10am-3.30pm Mon-Fri, tours 10.30am & 1pm) About 7km north of town, this rewarding Aboriginal and Torres Strait Islander heritage display centre provides a fascinating insight into local Indigenous history. The centre is set on 30 acres of natural bushland and ancient tribal sites, and features sandstone displays of the archaeology and mythology of the Aboriginal people. The recommended 90-minute tours include boomerang throwing.

Kershaw Gardens   GARDEN

(📞4936 8254; via Charles St; admission free; ⊙6am-6pm) Just north of the Fitzroy River, this excellent botanical park is devoted to Australian native plants. Its attractions include artificial rapids, a rainforest area, a fragrant garden and heritage architecture.

Heritage Village   MUSEUM

(📞4936 1026; Bruce Hwy; adult/child/family $7.70/4.50/22.70; ⊙9am-4pm) This active museum of replica historic buildings set in lovely landscaped gardens, 10km north of the city centre, even has townspeople at work in period garb. There's also a visitors centre here.

Mt Archer   MOUNTAIN

As a backdrop to the city, this mountain rises 604m out of the landscape northeast of Rockhampton, offering stunning views of the city and hinterland from the summit, especially at night. It's an environmental

---

ℹ️ **STINGERS**

The potentially deadly chironex box jellyfish and irukandji, also known as sea wasps or 'marine stingers', occur in Queensland's coastal waters north of Agnes Water (occasionally further south) from around October to April, and swimming is not advisable during these times. Fortunately, swimming and snorkelling are usually safe around the reef islands throughout the year; however, appearances of the rare and tiny (1cm to 2cm across) irukandji have been recorded on the outer Reef and islands. For more information on stingers and treatment, see p514.

park with walking trails weaving through eucalypts and rainforest abundant in wildlife. Rockhampton City Council publishes a brochure to the park, available from the visitors centres.

Archer Park Station & Steam Tram Museum
MUSEUM

(☑4922 2774; Denison St; adult/child/family $6.60/4.50/15; ☉9am-4pm Sun-Fri) This museum is housed in a former train station built in 1899. Through photographs and displays it tells the station's story, and that of the unique Purrey steam tram.

☞ Tours

Little Johnny's Tours and Rentals
SIGHTSEEING

(☑0414 793 637; www.littlejohnnystours.com) Runs trips to many nearby attractions like Byfield and the Capricorn Caves (p391), and also does minibus runs between Rockhampton Airport and Yeppoon.

Capricorn Coast Trail Rides
HORSE-RIDING

Runs horse-riding tours (p393) through local bushland.

☆ Festivals & Events

Beef Australia
FOOD

(www.beefaustralia.org) Held every three years (the next one will be in May 2012), this is a huge exposition of everything beefy.

Jazz on Quay Festival
JAZZ

(www.jassonquay.com.au) In September.

⌴ Sleeping

The northern and southern approach roads to Rocky are lined with numerous motels but if you want to stroll the elegant palm-lined streets overlooking the Fitzroy, choose somewhere in the old centre, south of the river.

Criterion Hotel
HOTEL, PUB $

TOP CHOICE (☑4922 1225; www.thecriterion.com.au; 150 Quay St; r $55-80, motel r $125-150; ✱) The Criterion is Rockhampton's grandest old pub, with an elegant foyer and function room, a friendly bar and a great bistro (Bush Inn). Its top two storeys have dozens of period rooms, some of which have been lovingly restored; although the rooms have showers, the toilets are down the hall. If you're not into period rooms, the hotel also has a number of 4.5-star motel rooms.

Rockhampton YHA
HOSTEL $

(☑4927 5288; www.yha.com.au; 60 MacFarlane St; dm $22, d $50-67; ✱@✉) The Rocky YHA is well looked after, with a spacious lounge and dining area and a well-equipped kitchen. It has six- and nine-bed dorms as well as doubles and cabins with bathrooms, and there's a large patch of lawn to toss a ball around. The hostel arranges tours, has courtesy pick-ups from the bus station, and is an agent for Premier and Greyhound buses.

Denison Hotel
BOUTIQUE HOTEL $$

(☑4923 7378; www.denisonhotel.com.au; 233 Denison St; r $165-200; ✱@) This freshly renovated 1885 Victorian home is an easy walk from Quay St. Its stately rooms come with four-poster beds and plasma TVs, and the hotel's Rolls-Royce can pick you up from the airport or station.

Southside Holiday Village
CARAVAN PARK, CABINS $

(☑1800 075 911, 4927 3013; www.sshv.com.au; Lower Dawson Rd; unpowered/powered/ensuite sites $25/32/42, cabins $62-102; ✱✉✉) This is one of the city's best caravan parks. It has neat, self-contained cabins and villas with elevated decking, large grassed campsites, a courtesy coach and a good kitchen. Prices are for two people. It's about 3km south of the centre.

✗ Eating & Drinking

Saigon Saigon
ASIAN FUSION $$

TOP CHOICE (☑4927 0888; www.saigonbytheriver. com; Quay St, near cnr Denham St; mains $15-20; ☉lunch & dinner Wed-Mon) This two-storey bamboo hut overlooks the Fitzroy River and serves pan-Asian food with local ingredients like kangaroo and crocodile served in a sizzling steamboat (preorder required for these exotic treats). If you're not up for reptile, try the crispy chicken or the king prawns.

Criteron Hotel
PUB FARE, STEAKHOUSE $$

(☑4922 1225; Criterion Hotel, 150 Quay St; dishes $10-40; ☉lunch & dinner) The Criterion's front bar is a friendly place to grab a beer, while its Bush Inn restaurant has a Western theme with stone floors, wooden booths and tables, and huge steaks – like the $38 Kilo Challenge. There are plenty of non-steak options, including slabs of barra, chicken dishes and pizzas. Regular live music later in the week.

In the Berserker Ranges, 24km north of Rockhampton near the Caves township, the amazing **Capricorn Caves** (☑4934 2883; www.capricorncaves.com.au; Caves Rd; adult/child $26/13; ☺9am-4pm) are not to be missed. These ancient caves honeycomb a limestone ridge, and on a guided tour through the caverns and labyrinths you'll see cave coral, stalactites, dangling fig-tree roots, and little insectivorous bats. The highlight of the one-hour 'cathedral tour' is the beautiful natural rock cathedral where a recording of 'Amazing Grace' is played to demonstrate the cavern's incredible acoustics. Every December, traditional Christmas carol singalongs are held in the cathedral. Also in December, around the summer solstice (1 December to 14 January), sunlight beams directly through a 14m vertical shaft into Belfry Cave, creating an electrifying light show. If you stand directly below the beam, reflected sunlight colours the whole cavern with whatever colour you're wearing.

Daring spelunkers can book a two-hour 'adventure tour' ($60) which takes you through tight spots with names such as 'Fat Man's Misery'. You must be at least 16 years old for this tour.

The Capricorn Caves complex has barbecue areas, a pool, kiosk, and **accommodation** (unpowered/powered sites $27/32, cabins from $160).

Pacino's ITALIAN $$
(☑4922 5833; cnr Fitzroy & George Sts; mains $19-39; ☺dinner Tue-Sun) This stylish Italian restaurant oozes Mediterranean warmth with its wooden tables and potted fig trees. A class act for an intimate dinner of delicious Italian cooking featuring favourites like osso bucco and pasta cooked a dozen different ways.

Cassidy's SEAFOOD, STEAKHOUSE $$
(☑4927 5322; www.98.com.au; 98 Victoria Pde; mains $18-46 ☺breakfast Mon-Sun, lunch Mon-Fri & dinner Mon-Sat) One of Rocky's finest, this licensed dining room features modern Australian versions of kangaroo, steak, lamb and seafood. Sit inside or on the terrace overlooking the Fitzroy River.

Thai Tanee THAI $$
(☑4922 1255; cnr William & Bolsover Sts; mains $15-28; ☺dinner) This unpretentious restaurant, recommended by the locals for consistently good Thai food, has a yum cha special for Sunday brunch.

Heritage Hotel PUB $
(☑4927 6996; cnr William & Quay St; meals $7-21) This pub with iron-lattice balconies has a cocktail lounge with river views and outdoor tables. The menu includes pizzas, burgers and lamb shank pie as well as the ubiquitous steak.

☆ Entertainment

Great Western Hotel PUB
(☑4922 3888; www.greatwesternhotel.com.au; 39 Stanley St) Looking like a spaghetti-western film set, this 116-year-old pub is home to Rocky's cowboys and 'gals. Out the back there's a rodeo arena where every Wednesday (which is also two-for-one meal night in the bistro) and Friday night you can watch cowboys being tossed in the air by bucking bulls and broncos. Touring bands occasionally rock here; you can get tickets online.

Stadium CLUB
(☑4927 9988; 234 Quay St; admission after 10pm $12; ☺late Fri & Sat) Next door to the Heritage, this is the place most partygoers head after the pubs. It's a large, flashy club with a sporty theme – you dance on a mini basketball court.

Pilbeam Theatre THEATRE
(☑4927 4111; Victoria Pde) This plush 967-seat theatre is located in the Rockhampton Performing Arts Complex and hosts national and international acts. Its Italian restaurant is recommended by locals.

❶ Information

Capricorn visitors centre (☑4921 2311; Gladstone Rd; ☺9am-5pm) Helpful centre on the highway beside the tropic of Capricorn marker, 3km south of the centre. Its sister branch is the **Rockhampton visitors centre** (☑4922 5339; 208 Quay St; ☺8.30am-4.30pm Mon-Fri, 9am-4pm Sat & Sun) in the beautiful former Customs House in central Rocky.

CQ Net(☑4922 5988; 29 William St; ☺9am-3.30pm & 5pm-late Mon, Tue, Thu & Fri; per hr $5) Internet access.

Post office (☑13 13 18; 150 East St; ☺9am-5pm Mon-Fri)

RINGERS & COWBOYS: FARM STAYS

Kick up some red dust on a fair-dinkum Aussie outback cattle station and find out the difference between a jackeroo, a ringer, a stockman and a cowboy. On a farm stay, you'll be immersed in the daily activities of a working cattle station, riding horses and motorbikes, mustering cattle, fencing, and cooking damper and billy tea over a campfire. Before you know it you'll find yourself looking for a ute and a blue dog to go with your RM Williams boots and Akubra hat.

Myella Farm Stay (✆4998 1290; www.myella.com; Baralaba Rd; 3/7 days including meals & activities $360/750, day trips $110; ✳@✉), 125km southwest of Rockhampton, gives you a taste of the outback on its 10.5-sq-km farm. The package includes bush explorations by horseback, motorcycle and 4WD, all meals, accommodation in a renovated homestead with polished timber floors and a wide veranda, farm clothes and free transfers from Rockhampton. You get to help care for orphaned joeys at the station's kangaroo rehab centre.

Kroombit Park covers 2 hectares of eucalypt bushland on the 40-sq-km **Lochenbar Cattle Station** (✆4992 2186; www.kroombit.com.au; dm $27, d with/without bathroom $68/84, 2-day/2-night package incl dm, meals & activities $280 per person; ✳@✉). There are several farm stay packages to choose from and you can pitch a tent or stay in bush-timber or upmarket cabins. While soaking up the Aussie experience you can learn to crack a whip, throw a boomerang or loop a lasso, and earn your spurs on a mechanical bucking bull. Rates include meals and pick-up from nearby Biloela.

Queensland Parks & Wildlife Service (QPWS; ✆4936 0511; 61 Yeppoon Rd, North Rockhampton) About 7km northwest of central Rockhampton.

Rockhampton library (✆4936 8265; 232 Bolsover St; ☺9.15am-5.30pm Mon, Tue & Fri, 1-8pm Wed, 9.15am-8pm Thu, 9.15am-4.30pm Sat) Free internet access, but you need to book.

ℹ Getting There & Away

Air

Qantas, Tiger Airways and Virgin Blue connect Rockhampton with various cities.

Bus

Greyhound Australia (✆13 20 30; www.greyhound.com.au) has regular services from Rocky to Mackay ($60, four hours), Brisbane ($114, 11 hours) and Cairns ($178, 18 hours). All services stop at the **Mobil roadhouse** (91 George St). **Premier Motor Service** (✆13 34 10; www.premierms.com.au) operates a Brisbane-Cairns service, stopping at Rockhampton.

Paradise Coaches (✆4933 1127) makes the run from Rocky to Emerald ($48, four hours) daily. Services leave from the Mobil roadhouse.

Young's Bus Service (✆4922 3813) to Yeppoon ($12.10, 45 minutes) includes a loop through Rosslyn Bay and Emu Park. Young's also has buses to Mt Morgan ($12.10, 50 minutes), Monday to Friday. Buses depart the Kern Arcade in Bolsover St.

Train

Queensland Rail (✆1800 872 467, 3235 1122; www.queenslandrail.com.au) runs the *Tilt Train*, which connects Rockhampton with Brisbane (from $119, 7½ hours, Sun-Fri) and Cairns (from $266, 16 hours, twice weekly). The slower *Sunlander* also connects Brisbane with Rockhampton three times per week, and has a sleeper service between Rockhampton and Cairns (sleepers from $252, 20 hours). The *Spirit of the Outback* also connects Rockhampton with Brisbane (from $119), Emerald ($65, five hours, twice weekly) and Longreach ($130, 14 hours, twice weekly). The train station is 450m southwest of the city centre.

ℹ Getting Around

Rockhampton airport is 5km south of the centre. **Sunbus** (✆4936 2133) runs a reasonably comprehensive city bus network operating all day Monday to Friday and Saturday morning. All services terminate in Bolsover St, between William and Denham Sts, and you can pick up a timetable at the visitors centre. There's also a taxi service in town, **Rocky Cabs** (✆13 10 08).

Yeppoon

✆07 / POP 13,290

Pretty little Yeppoon is a small seaside town with a long beach, a calm ocean and an attractive hinterland of volcanic outcrops, pineapple patches and grazing lands. The handful of quiet streets, sleepy motels and beachside cafes attracts Rockhamptonites beating the heat, and tourists heading for Great Keppel Island only 13km offshore.

Sights & Activities

About 15km north of Yeppoon, **Cooberrie Park** (☑4939 7590; www.cooberriepark.com.au; Woodbury Rd; adult/child/family $25/15/65; ☉10am-3pm) is a small wildlife sanctuary on 2 hectares of bushland. You can see kangaroos, wallabies and peacocks wandering freely through the grounds. You can also feed the critters (with the park's prepackaged food) and, for an extra cost, hold a furry koala or some slithering reptiles.

Funtastic Cruises (☑0438 909 502; www.funtasticcruises.com; full-day cruise adult/child $90/75) operates full-day snorkelling trips to Middle Island on board its 17m catamaran, with a two-hour stopover on Great Keppel Island, morning and afternoon tea, and all snorkelling equipment included. It can also organise camping drop-offs to islands en route. **Sail Capricornia** (☑0402-102 373; www.keppelbaymarina.com.au; full-day cruise incl lunch adult/child $115/75) offers snorkelling cruises on board a 12m yacht, as well as sunset and overnight cruises.

These activities, as well as the ferry to Great Keppel Island, depart from the Keppel Bay Marina at Rosslyn Bay, just south of Yeppoon.

You can see the local sights on horseback with **Capricorn Coast Trail Rides** (☑0413 483 850/4939 2611; www.cctrailrides.com.au), offering one- and two-hour rides ($40/70) on weekends, as well as occasional longer rides. They set out from the Oaks Caltex service station, about halfway along the Yeppoon to Rockhampton road.

Sleeping

There are beaches, caravan parks, motels and holiday units along the 19km coastline running south from Yeppoon to Emu Park, where you'll find the nearest backpackers. A fairly complete listing can be found at www.yeppooninfo.com.au.

| TOP CHOICE | Surside Motel | MOTEL $ |

Surfside Motel (☑4939 1272; 30 Anzac Pde; r $90/95; ❄@⊛⊛) Across the road from the beach and close to town, this 1950s strip of lime-green motel units epitomises summer holidays at the beach. And it's terrific value – the rooms are spacious and unusually well equipped, complete with toaster, hair dryer and free wi-fi.

While Away B&B B&B $$
(☑4939 5719; www.whileawaybandb.com.au; 44 Todd Ave; s/d incl breakfast $115/140; ❄) With four good-sized rooms and an immaculately clean house with wheelchair access, this B&B is a perfect, quiet getaway – note that there are no facilities for kids. There are complimentary nibbles, tea, coffee, port and sherry as well as generous breakfasts.

Beachfront 55 APARTMENTS $$
(☑4939 1403; www.beachfront55.com.au; 55 Todd Ave; units $139, villa from $285; ❄) North of town, these very comfortable, fully self-contained units each come with a private barbecue and courtyard. There's also a large villa that comfortably sleeps six: with a private pool and garden view, it also has ocean glimpses, but is very close to the manager's quarters.

Rydges Capricorn Resort RESORT $$$
(☑1800 075 902, 4925 2525; www.capricornresort.com; Farnborough Rd; d $179-350; ❄⊛⊛) This is a large and lavish golf resort about 8km north of Yeppoon. Its accommodation ranges from standard hotel rooms through to plush self-contained apartments, and there's a huge pool, a gym and several bars and restaurants – locals rave about the sushi. Package deals are available, and booking online gets you the best deal. The resort's two immaculate golf courses are open to the public at $80 for 18 holes, which includes a motorised buggy. Club hire costs another $15.

Beachside Caravan Park CARAVAN PARK $
(☑4939 3738; Farnborough Rd; unpowered/powered sites $21/26-29) This basic but neat little camping park north of the town centre boasts an absolute beachfront location. It has good amenities and grassed sites with some shade but no cabins or on-site vans. Rates are for two people.

Eating & Drinking

| TOP CHOICE | Shio Kaze | JAPANESE $$ |

Shio Kaze (☑4939 5575; 18 Anzac Pde; meal about $50 for 2; ☉lunch & dinner Wed-Sun) This highly recommended place offers delicious, fresh sushi. The menu selection is great value and meals are served overlooking the beach. Bring your own alcohol.

Thai Take-Away THAI $$
(☑4939 3920; 24 Anzac Pde; mains $12-20; ☉dinner) A deservedly popular Thai BYO restaurant where you can sit outside on the sidewalk, catch a sea breeze, and satisfy those chilli and coconut cravings. There's a

large selection of seafood dishes and snappy service.

Shore Thing BREAKFAST, SANDWICHES $
(☑4939 1993; 6 Normanby St; mains under $14; ☺breakfast & lunch) A breezy little cafe on the main street dishing up sandwiches, focaccias, wraps and big breakfasts.

Strand Hotel PUB
(☑4939 1301; 2 Normanby St, cnr Anzac Pde) The battered old Strand has live music every weekend. The pub serves $10 counter meals at lunch and dinner daily, but is especially known for its Sunday evening *parrilla*, an Argentine-style barbecue with music to match.

☆ Entertainment

Footlights Theatre Restaurant (☑4939 2399; www.footlights.com.au; 123 Rockhampton Rd; dinner & show $90) hosts a three-course meal and a two-hour comedy-variety show every Friday and Saturday night.

The **Little Theatre** (www.yeppoonlittletheatre.org.au; 64 William St) puts on occasional amateur productions. Tickets available at Yellow Door (p394)

ℹ Information

The **Capricorn Coast visitors centre** (☑1800 675 785, 4939 4888; www.capricorncoast.com.au; Scenic Hwy; ☺9am-5pm), beside the Ross Creek roundabout at the entrance to the town, has plenty of information on the Capricorn Coast and Great Keppel Island, and can book accommodation and tours.

Yellow Door (☑4939 4805; 11 Normanby St) sells new and used books and CDs, and runs a book exchange. It also has internet access for $5 per hour, while the **Yeppoon library** (☑4939 3433; 78 John St) has free internet access.

ℹ Getting There & Away

Yeppoon is 43km northeast of Rockhampton. **Young's Bus Service** (☑4922 3813, www.youngsbusservice.com.au) runs frequent buses from Rockhampton ($12 one way) to Yeppoon and down to the Keppel Bay marina.

If you're heading for Great Keppel or the Reef, some ferry operators will transport you between your accommodation and Keppel Bay marina. Otherwise, if you're driving, there's a free day car park at the marina. For secure undercover parking, the **Great Keppel Island Security Car Park** (☑4933 6670; 422 Scenic Hwy; per day from $12) is located on the Scenic Hwy south of Yeppoon, close to the turn-off to Keppel Bay marina.

Around Yeppoon

The drive south from Yeppoon and Rosslyn Bay passes three fine headlands with good views: **Double Head**, **Bluff Point** and **Pinnacle Point**. After Pinnacle Point, the road crosses Causeway Lake, a saltwater inlet where you can hire fishing boats, bait and tackle for a spot of estuary fishing. Emu Park (population 2967), 19km south of Yeppoon, is the second-largest township on the coast, but there's not much here, apart from more good views and the **Singing Ship memorial** to Captain Cook – a curious monument of drilled tubes and pipes that emit mournful whistling and moaning sounds in the breeze. Emus Beach Resort (☑4939 6111; www.emusbeachresort.com; 92 Pattinson St; dm $24-27, d/tr/q $75/95/100) is a superlative backpackers, with a pool, kitchen, barbecue and a travel booking service; it also offers tours to the local crocodile farm. Otherwise, Bell Park Caravan Park (☑4939 6202; bellpark@primus.com.au; Pattinson St; unpowered/powered sites $18/22, cabins $84) has spacious sites, clean amenities and comfortable cabins a stone's throw from the beach.

Emu Park Pizza & Pasta (☑4938 7333; Hill St; pizzas $10-22; ☺dinner) is an unprepossessing restaurant but the pizzas attract locals from Yeppoon.

Fifteen kilometres along the Emu Park–Rockhampton road, the Koorana Crocodile Farm (☑4934 4749; www.koorana.com.au; Coowonga Rd; adult/child $22/11; ☺tours 10.30am & 1pm) can only be explored via the informative guided tours. Get there early to sample croc kebabs, croc ribs or a croc pie at the restaurant.

Byfield

Tiny Byfield consists of a general store, a school and a cluster of houses but the main attractions in this largely undeveloped region are the gorgeous Byfield National Park and State Forest. The park is a pleasant 40km drive north from Yeppoon through the pine plantations of the Byfield State Forest, with turn-offs along the way to various picnic areas. North of Byfield, the Shoalwater Bay military training area borders the forest and park, and is strictly off limits.

The Byfield National Park and State Forest form the Byfield Coastal Area, a wild and scenic region of rocky headlands, long sandy beaches, massive dunes, heathland, forest, mangrove-lined estuaries, rainforested creeks and granite mountains. The main waterway, Waterpark Creek, supplies Rockhampton's town water, and is a magnificent place to go canoeing. There are five **camping grounds** (🖉13 74 68; www.qld.gov.au/camping; per person/family $4.50/18) to choose from: Upper Stoney Creek, Red Rock, Waterpark Creek, Nine Mile Beach and Five Rocks, all of which must be prebooked. Both Nine Mile Beach and Five Rocks are on the beach and you'll need a 4WD to access them. When conditions are right, there's decent surf at Nine Mile.

Nob Creek Pottery (🖉4935 1161; 216 Arnolds Rd; admission free; ◑9am-5pm), just south of Byfield, is a unique working pottery and gallery nestled in leafy rainforest where you can see the potters at work. The giant kiln here resembles an enormous sleeping dragon, the gallery showcases hand-blown glass, woodwork and jewellery, and the handmade ceramics are outstanding.

Waterpark Farm (🖉4935 1171; www.waterparkecotours.com; 201 Waterpark Creek Rd; 2-3hr tours $25; cabin $110; ✲) runs excellent ecotours in an electric-powered boat so you can experience the rainforest in complete silence. The tour also includes a horse-drawn carriage ride of a working tea-tree plantation, demonstration of tea-tree-oil distillation, a safari bus trip to the farm's historic sites, and morning tea. If you find it hard to leave the genuine hospitality on offer, there's a fully self-contained timber cabin on the 97-hectare farm where you can swing in a hammock, swim in the creek, or just relax in the outdoor hot tub.

TOP CHOICE **Ferns Hideaway** (🖉4935 1235; www.fernshideaway.com.au; 67 Cahills Rd; unpowered sites $24, d $150; ✲🐾), signposted just north of Byfield, is a secluded bush oasis in immaculate gardens that offers canoeing and nature walks. The timber homestead has a quality à la carte **restaurant** (mains $18-32; ◑lunch & afternoon tea Wed-Sun, dinner Sat, breakfast Sun) featuring live music on weekends. Nestled among the trees are cosy self-contained cabins with wood fires; there are also double rooms with shared facilities, or you can camp, with hot showers included in the tariff. The camping rate is for two people. Restaurant patrons and those staying on site have free access to all facilities, including canoes.

The **Byfield General Store & Café** (🖉4935 1190; 223 Byfield Rd; ◑8am-6pm Wed-Mon, to 2pm Tue) has basic grocery supplies and a simple courtyard cafe serving pies, sandwiches and highly recommended burgers. You can get fuel here and also some very good information about the national park.

Great Keppel Island

Great Keppel Island is a stunningly beautiful island with rocky headlands, forested hills and a fringe of powdery white sand lapped by clear azure waters. Numerous 'castaway' beaches ring the 14-sq-km island, while natural bushland covers 90% of the interior. A string of huts and accommodation options sits behind the trees lining the main beach but the developments are low key and relatively unobtrusive. Only 13km offshore, and with good snorkelling, swimming and bush walking, Great Keppel is an easily accessible, tranquil island retreat.

The sprawling Great Keppel Island Resort was once the centre of activity here, but it closed suddenly in 2008, leaving an increasingly dilapidated shell, and making for a much quieter island. The resort isn't set to reopen any time soon.

◉ Sights

The beaches of Great Keppel rate among Queensland's best. Take a short stroll from **Fisherman's Beach**, the main beach, and you'll find your own deserted stretch of white sand. There is fairly good coral and excellent fish life, especially between Great Keppel and Humpy Island to the south. A 30-minute walk south around the headland brings you to **Monkey Beach**, where there's good snorkelling. A walking trail from the southern end of the airfield takes you to **Long Beach**, perhaps the best of the island's beaches.

There are several bush-walking tracks from Fisherman's Beach; the longest and perhaps most difficult leads to the 2.5m 'lighthouse' near **Bald Rock Point** on the far side of the island (three hours return).

You can see an **underwater observatory** off Middle Island, close to Great Keppel. A confiscated Taiwanese fishing junk was sunk next to the observatory to provide a haven for fish.

🏃 Activities

The **Watersports Hut** on the main beach hires out snorkelling equipment, kayaks and catamarans, and runs banana rides. You can buy drinks and ice creams here, at the

Sandbar, and watch the sun set over the water.

Keppel Reef Scuba Adventures (☑4939 5022, 0408 004 536; www.keppeldive.com; Putney Beach) offers introductory dives for $200, snorkelling trips (per person $50), and also hires out snorkelling gear (per day $15).

☞ Tours

Freedom Fast Cats (☑1800 336 244, 4933 6244) operates a coral cruise to the best location of the day (depending on tides and weather), which includes viewing through a glass-bottomed boat and fish feeding. The cruise costs $63/42 per adult/child and leaves from Keppel Bay marina. Freedom also runs full-day cruises (adult/child $130/85) including coral viewing, fish feeding, snorkelling, boom netting and a barbecue lunch, as well as wave-jumping, thrill-seeking trips on the fast boat *Wild Duck* (35-minute ride adult/child $25/20).

🛏 Sleeping

Without Great Keppel Island Resort, accommodation options are somewhat limited. Holiday homes can be rented through the **Capricorn Coast visitors centre** (☑1800 675 785, 4939 4888; www.capricorncoast.com. au; Scenic Hwy, Yeppoon; ☺9am-5pm) in Yeppoon. Six- and eight-bedroom homes can be rented in their entirety or the rooms can be rented as individual motel-style suites.

TOP **Svendsen's Beach**   CABINS **$**
CHOICE (☑4938 3717; www.svendsensbeach. com; Svendsen's Beach; cabins $285 for 3 nights, minimum 3-night stay) This secluded boutique castaway retreat has two luxury tent-bungalows on separate elevated timber decks overlooking lovely Svendsen's Beach. The environmentally friendly operation has solar heating, wind generators, rainwater tanks and an ecofridge, and the communal beach-kitchen has a barbecue and stove-top. The artistic owner has fashioned decorative wooden sculptures and furnishings including a quaint candlelit bush-bucket shower. It's the perfect place for snorkelling, bush-walking and romantic getaways. Transfers from the ferry drop-off on Fisherman's Beach are included in the tariff.

Great Keppel Island Backpackers & Holiday Village   HOSTEL, CABINS **$**
(☑4939 8655; www.gkiholidayvillage.com.au; dm $35, s/d tents $85, cabins with bathroom $140, 2-bedroom houses from $220) This village offers various types of good budget accommodation (including four-bed dorms and cabins that sleep three people). It's a friendly, relaxed place with shared bathrooms and a decent communal kitchen and barbecue area. Snorkelling gear

Great Keppel Island

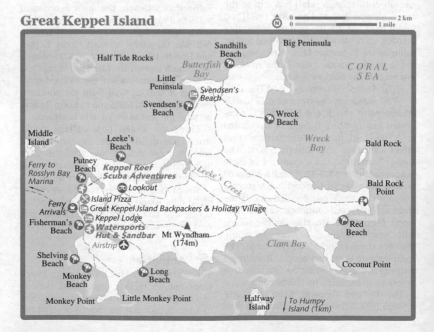

LYNDIE MALAN: RETREAT OWNER

Lyndie Malan sailed into Svendsen's Beach on Great Keppel Island 20 years ago and fell in love with the place...and a modern-day Robinson Crusoe, Carl Svendsen, who has lived there his entire life. The pair are fierce protectors of the island's natural environment and they run a boutique ecotourist retreat at Svendsen's Beach. Here are Lyndie's tips:

Great Keppel's most spectacular walk

From Svendsen's, take the circuit up the ridge towards the lighthouse, then cut down the spur to Wreck Beach and back via Butterfish Bay.

Best snorkelling spots

Wreck Beach at the northern end, or Butterfish Bay.

Favourite secret swimming spot

Secret Beach – yes! It's really called that! Ask for directions...

Great Keppels' most adorable animal

Flatback turtle hatchlings – they're very cute!

Its most dangerous beast

Mosquitoes – they are the world's most dangerous.

is free and the village runs motorised canoe trips around Middle Island ($30 per person).

Keppel Lodge GUESTHOUSE **$$**
(☑4939 4251; www.keppellodge.com.au; Fisherman's Beach; s/d $90-100/110-130, each additional person $50) A pleasant open-plan house with four large bedrooms (with bathrooms) branching from a large communal lounge and kitchen. The house is available in its entirety – ideal for a group booking – or as individual motel-type suites.

✖ Eating

Self-caterers will need to bring all their supplies, as there are no grocery stores, and only one restaurant, on the island.

Island Pizza PIZZA **$**
(☑4939 4699; The Esplanade; dishes $6-30) This friendly place prides itself on its gourmet pizzas with plenty of toppings. The pizzas are rather pricey but still tempting. Hot dogs and pasta are also available. Check blackboard for opening times.

❶ Getting There & Away

Freedom Fast Cats (☑1800 336 244, 4933 6244, www.freedomfastcats.com) departs from the Keppel Bay marina in Rosslyn Bay (7km south of Yeppoon) for Great Keppel Island each morning, returning that same afternoon (call ahead for precise times). The return fare is

$49/41/29/127 per adult/concession/child/family. If you've booked accommodation on the island, check that someone will meet you on the beach to help with your luggage.

Other Keppel Bay Islands

Great Keppel is the largest of 18 stunning continental islands dotted around Keppel Bay, all within 20km of the coast. Unlike coral cay islands, which are formed by the build-up of tiny fragments of coral, algae and other reef plants and animals, continental islands were originally rocky outcrops of the mainland ranges.

These beautiful islands feature clean beaches and clear water ranging from pale turquoise through to deep indigo blue. Several have fringing coral reefs excellent for snorkelling or diving. You can visit **Middle Island**, with its underwater observatory, or **Halfway** and **Humpy Islands** if you're staying on Great Keppel. Some of the islands are national parks where you can maroon yourself for a few days of self-sufficient camping.

To camp on a national-park island, you need to take all your own supplies, including water. Camper numbers on each island are restricted. For information and permits call the **QPWS** (☑13 74 68, www.qld.gov.au/camping).

Whitsunday Coast

Includes »

Best Places to Eat

» Bommie Restaurant (p420)

» Alain's Restaurant (p415)

» Fish D'vine (p414)

Best Places to Stay

» Qualia (p420)

» Paradise Bay (p417)

» Hayman Island Resort (p420)

» Platypus Bushcamp (p406)

» Water's Edge Resort (p412)

Why Go?

Opal-jade waters and white sandy beaches fringe the forested domes of the stunning subtropical archipelago of the Whitsunday Islands. Sailing through the calm waters of the Coral Sea is simply magical, but there are many ways to savour the island's natural beauty: camping in secluded bays as a modern-day castaway, lazing in a tropical island resort, snorkelling or diving the pristine coral reef.

The gateway to the islands, Airlie Beach, is a vibrant backpacker hub with a continual parade of changing faces and a throbbing nightlife. South of Airlie, overlooking a sea of waving sugar cane, Mackay is the region's major centre, a typical Queensland coastal town with pleasant palm-lined streets. It's a handy base for trips to Finch Hatton Gorge and Eungella National Park – lush, green hinterland oases where platypuses play in the wild.

When to Go

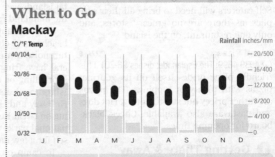

Mackay

°C/°F Temp — Rainfall inches/mm

June–October
The perfect time to enjoy sunny skies, calm days, mild weather and stinger-free seas.

August Sailboats skim across the water, and parties are held during Airlie Beach Race Week.

September–October Optimal conditions for kayaking around the islands.

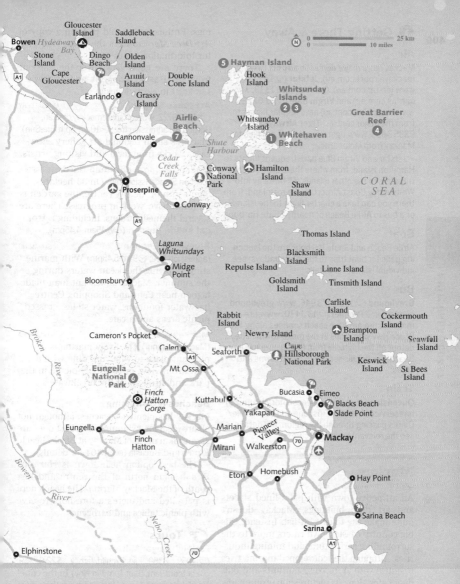

Whitsunday Coast Highlights

1 Being dazzled by the bright-white silica sand at stunning **Whitehaven Beach** (p421)

2 Sailing through the magnificent aquamarine waters of the **Whitsunday Islands** (p407)

3 Camping under the stars, hiking nature trails and making

like an island castaway in the **Whitsunday Islands National Park** (p409)

4 Diving and snorkelling the fringing reefs or the outer **Great Barrier Reef** (p408)

5 Sipping cocktails by the pool at the luxurious tropical island resort of **Hayman Island** (p420)

6 Waiting patiently for a glimpse of a shy platypus and walking in the misty rainforest at **Eungella National Park** (p405)

7 Getting wet, swilling beer and partying hard in fun-lovin' **Airlie Beach** (p412)

ℹ Getting There & Away

Air

Mackay has a major domestic **airport** (www. mackayairport.com.au). **Jetstar** (☑13 15 38; www.jetstar.com.au), **Qantas** (☑13 13 13; www. qantas.com.au) and **Virgin Blue** (☑13 67 89; www.virginblue.com.au) have regular flights to/ from the major centres. **Tiger Airways** (☑03-9335 3033; www.tigerairways.com.au) flies to Mackay from Melbourne.

Jetstar and Virgin Blue have frequent flights to Hamilton Island, from where there are boat/air transfers to the other islands. All three fly into Whitsunday Coast Airport on the mainland; from there you can take a charter flight to the islands or a bus to Airlie Beach or nearby Shute Harbour.

Boat

Airlie Beach and Shute Harbour are the launching pads for boat trips to the Whitsundays; see individual islands for details.

Bus

Greyhound (☑1300 473 946; www.greyhound. com.au) and **Premier** (☑13 34 10; www.pre mierms.com.au) have coach services along the Bruce Hwy with stops at the major towns. They detour off the highway from Proserpine to Airlie Beach. For details see the relevant towns and cities.

Train

Queensland Rail (www.queenslandrail.com.au) has services between Brisbane and Townsville/ Cairns passing through the region. For details see the relevant towns and cities.

Mackay

☑07 / POP 66.880

An attractive town with palm-lined streets and art deco buildings, Mackay doesn't quite make the tourist hit list. Instead, this big country coastal town caters more to the surrounding agricultural and mining industries. Although the redeveloped marina tries to entice with al fresco restaurants and outdoor cafes along its picturesque promenade, Mackay is more a convenient base for excursions out of town. It's only a 1½-hour drive to the Whitsundays, a short flight to pretty Brampton Island and a scenic drive among the sugar-cane fields to Pioneer Valley and Eungella National Park.

◉ Sights & Activities

Mackay's impressive **art deco architecture** owes much to a devastating cyclone in 1918, which flattened many of the town's build-

ings. Enthusiasts should pick up a copy of *Art Deco Mackay* from the Town Hall Visitor Information Centre.

There are good views over the harbour from **Mt Basset Lookout** and at **Rotary Lookout** in North Mackay.

Artspace Mackay   ART GALLERY
(☑4961 9722; www.artspacemackay.com.au; Gordon St; admission free; ⊙10am-5pm Tue-Sun) Mackay's small regional art gallery showcases works from local and visiting artists.

Mackay Regional Botanic Gardens GARDEN
(Lagoon St; admission free) On 33 hectares, 3km south of the city centre, the garden is an impressive 'work in progress'. There are several themed gardens, including a **tropical shade garden** (⊙8.45am-4.45pm).

Bluewater Lagoon   SWIMMING
(admission free; ⊙9am-5.45pm) With marine stingers plying the ocean waters during the summer, Mackay's pleasant man-made lagoon near Caneland Shopping Centre has water fountains, water slides, grassed picnic areas and a cafe.

Mackay Marina   MARINA
(Mackay Harbour) The lively marina is a pleasant place to wine and dine with a waterfront view, or to simply picnic in the park and stroll along the breakwater.

Beaches & Swimming

Mackay has plenty of beaches, although not all are ideal for swimming. The best ones are about 16km north of Mackay at Blacks Beach, Eimeo and Bucasia (see p404 for details).

The best option near town is **Harbour Beach**, 6km north of the centre and just south of the Mackay Marina. The beach here is patrolled and there's a foreshore reserve with picnic tables and barbecues.

☞ Tours

Farleigh Sugar Mill   INDUSTRIAL
(☑4959 8360; adult/child/family $22/12/59; ⊙2hr tours 9am, 11am, 1pm Jun-Nov) In the cane-crushing season, you can see how the sweet crystals are made. Learn all about the history, production and technology, but dress prepared for a working mill: long sleeves, long pants, enclosed shoes.

Jungle Johno Eco Tours   SCENIC
(☑4944 1230; tours $75) The elusive platypus is the pot of gold at the end of this rainbow. You'll be taken deep into the national park to spot these shy, amphibious creatures in their natural habitat. You'll also get to swim

under crystal-clear waterfalls and spot other wildlife like kingfishers, turtles and water dragons. Operating from the Gecko's Rest hostel, these seven-hour day trips include Finch Hatton Gorge and are a good way to see the best bits of Eungella and surrounds in one day.

Reeforest Adventure Tours SCENIC
(📞1800 500 353, 4959 8360; www.reeforest.com) The day-long Platypus & Rainforest Eco safari (per person $145) explores Finch Hatton Gorge and visits the platypuses of Broken River. It includes lunch at a secluded bush retreat near the gorge and an interpretive walk. The tour also departs from Airlie Beach ($145).

★✿ Festivals

Wintermoon Festival MUSIC
(www.wintermoonfestival.com) Features local and interstate musicians. May/June.

🛏 Sleeping

There are plenty of motels strung along busy Nebo Rd, south of the centre. The budget options (around $75 for a double) post their prices out front and tend to suffer from road noise.

Clarion Hotel Mackay Marina HOTEL $$$
(📞4955 9400; www.mackaymarinahotel.com; Mulherin Dr, Mackay Harbour; d $245-445; ❋@🅿🖳) The Clarion is the darling of the rapidly developing marina precinct. All rooms have spacious showers and balconies and all the mod cons you'd expect of a hotel of international standing. Couples should try the Pamper Package ($455), which includes sparkling wine and chocolates, a 30-minute massage, hot breakfast and noon checkout in a spa suite.

Coral Sands Motel MOTEL $$
(📞4951 1244; www.coralsandsmotel.com.au; 44 Macalister St; s/d $110/120; ❋🅿🖳) One of Mackay's better midrange options, the Coral Sands boasts ultra-friendly management and large rooms in a central location. The pool looks like it has seen better days, but with the river, shops, pubs and cafes so close to your doorstep, you won't care.

Mackay Grande Suites HOTEL $$$
(📞4969 1000; www.mackaygrandesuites.com.au; 9 Gregory St; r $205, 1-bedroom apt from $245; ❋@🖳) Mackay's long awaited addition to the city centre's top end doesn't disappoint with its stylish decor and modern amenities.

Lash out and try the spa suite ($310-390) with its huge plasma TV and balcony with panoramic vistas.

Gecko's Rest HOSTEL $
(📞4944 1230; www.geckosrest.com.au; 34 Sydney St; dm/s/d $24/55/90; ❋@) Bustling and busy, Gecko's almost bursts at the seams with adventurous travellers. The place is looking slightly grubby but the four-bed dorms each have a small fridge. There's a large kitchen and huge rooftop balcony area. Jungle Johno Eco Tours runs from here.

International Lodge Motel MOTEL $$
(📞4951 1022; internationallodge@bigpond.com; 40 Macalister St; r from $105; ❋🛜) Hidden behind an unimpressive facade are clean, bright and cheerful motel rooms. This is a good-value option close to the city's restaurants and bars.

Mid City Motor Inn MOTEL $$
(📞4951 1666; stay@midcitymotel.com.au; 2 Macalister St; r $114-180; ❋@🛜🖳) Looking tired but comfortable, this motel is in a superb location beside the river promenade, a short stroll from the town centre.

🍴 Eating

Burp Eat Drink MODERN AUSTRALIAN $$$
(📞4951 3546; www.burp.net.au; 86 Wood St; mains $32 40; ⊙lunch & dinner Tue-Fri, dinner Sat) A swish Melbourne-style restaurant in the tropics, Burp has a small but tantalising menu. The contemporary dishes include an interesting assortment of sharing plates such as Japanese eggplant stuffed with prawns and oyster sauce.

Fish D'vine SEAFOOD $$
(📞4953 4442; www.fishdvine.com.au; Sydney St; mains $12-25; ⊙lunch & dinner) This original concept fish cafe and rum bar serves up fresh fish in various guises as well as all things nibbly from Neptune's realm. If you don't want to sample one of the 100 rums on offer, there are plenty of other potent beverages.

Oscar's on Sydney FUSION $
(📞4944 0173; cnr Sydney & Gordon Sts; mains $10-21; ⊙breakfast & lunch) The delicious *poffertjes* (authentic Dutch pancakes with traditional toppings) are still going strong at this very popular corner cafe, but don't be afraid to give the other dishes a go.

Kevin's Place ASIAN $$
(📞4953 5835; cnr Victoria & Wood Sts; mains $18-25; ⊙lunch & dinner Mon-Fri, dinner Sat)

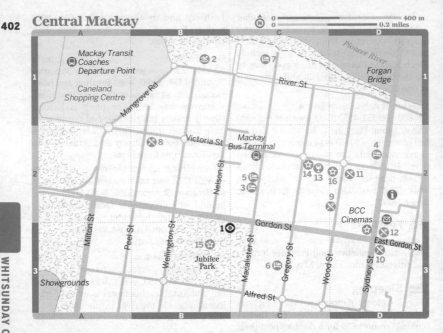

Sizzling, spicy Singaporean dishes and efficient, revved-up staff combine with the building's colonial ambience and the tropical climate to create a Rafflesesque experience.

Angelo's on the Marina ITALIAN $$
(☑4955 5600; www.angelosonthemarina.com. au; Mulherin Dr, Mackay Marina; mains $20-30; ☺lunch & dinner daily, breakfast Sat & Sun) Marina views with your pasta.

Austral Hotel PUB FARE $$
(☑4951 3288; www.theaustralhotel.com.au; 189 Victoria St; mains $17-31, steaks $23-41; ☺lunch & dinner) Great steaks.

🍷 Drinking

Gordi's Cafe & Bar PUB
(85 Victoria St) Good for people watching.

Satchmo's at the Reef BAR
(Mulherin Dr, Mackay Harbour) A classy wine-and-tapas bar full of boaties. Live music Sunday afternoon.

☆ Entertainment
Nightclubs

The Code NIGHTCLUB
(99 Victoria St; www.thecodenightclub.com.au; ☺10pm-3am) Don your glad rags to sassy into this classy nightclub.

Platinum Lounge NIGHTCLUB
(83 Victoria St; ☺7pm-3am Wed-Sat, 5pm-2am Sun) Most popular nightclub in town.

Theatre

Mackay Entertainment & Convention Centre THEATRE
(☑4961 9777; Alfred St; ☺box office 9am-5pm Mon-Fri, 10am-1pm Sat) Live performances.

❶ Information

The train station, airport, botanic gardens and visitors centre are about 3km south of the city centre. Mackay Harbour, 6km northeast of the centre, is dominated by a massive sugar terminal, while the adjacent marina has a select offering of waterfront restaurants.

Mackay City Library (☑4961 9387; Gordon St; ☺9am-5pm Mon & Fri, 10am-6pm Tue, 10am-8pm Thu, 9am-3pm Sat) Internet access.

Mackay Queensland Parks & Wildlife Service (QPWS; ☑4944 7800; www.derm.qld.gov.au; 30 Tennyson St)

Mackay visitors centre (☑4944 5888; www. mackayregion.com; 320 Nebo Rd; ☺8.30am-5pm Tue-Fri, 9am-5pm Mon, 9am-4pm Sat & Sun)

Post office (Sydney St) Near the corner of Gordon St.

Town Hall Visitor Information Centre (☑4951 4803; townhall@mackayregion.com; 63 Sydney St; ⊙9am-5pm Mon-Fri, to noon Sat & Sun)

ⓘ Getting There & Away

Air
The airport is about 3km south of the centre of Mackay.

Jetstar (☑13 15 38; www.jetstar.com.au), **Qantas** (☑13 13 13; www.qantas.com.au) and **Virgin Blue** (☑13 67 89; www.virginblue. com.au) have flights to/from Brisbane. **Tiger Airways** (☑03-9335 3033; www.tigerairways. com.au) has direct flights between Mackay and Melbourne.

Bus
Buses stop at the **Mackay Bus Terminal** (☑4944 2144; cnr Victoria & Macalister Sts; ⊙7am-6pm Mon-Fri, to 4pm Sat), where tickets can also be booked. **Greyhound** (☑1300 473 946; www.greyhound.com.au) travels up and down the coast. Sample one-way adult fares and journey times: Airlie Beach ($35, two hours), Townsville ($95, 6½ hours), Cairns ($170, 13 hours), Rockhampton ($75, 4½ hours), Hervey Bay ($155, 11 hours) and Brisbane ($200, 17 hours).

Premier (☑13 34 10; www.premierms.com. au) is less expensive than Greyhound but has less services.

Train
Queensland Rail (☑13 22 32, 1300 13 17 22; www.traveltrain.com.au) has several services stopping at Mackay on its way between Brisbane and Townsville/Cairns. The speedy *Tilt Train* departs at 6.50am on Tuesday and Saturday heading to Cairns ($190, 12 hours) via Townsville ($110, 5½ hours), and 8.50pm on Sunday

and Wednesday heading to Brisbane ($240, 13 hours). Fares shown are adult business class.

The *Sunlander* departs at 2.25am, heading to Cairns on Monday and Wednesday and 5.35am on Friday. Brisbane-bound, it departs Mackay at 11.30pm on Tuesday, Thursday and Saturday. Adult fares between Mackay and Brisbane (17 hours) are $160/220 in seat/sleeper berths.

ⓘ Getting Around

Avis (☑4951 1266; www.avis.com.au), **Budget** (☑4951 1400; www.budget.com.au), **Europcar** (☑4952 6269; www.europcar.com.au), **Hertz** (☑4951 3334; www.hertz.com.au) and **Redspot** (☑4998 5799; www.redspotcars.com.au) have counters at the airport.

Mackay Transit Coaches (☑4957 3330) has several services around the city, and connects the city with the harbour and northern beaches; pick up a timetable from one of the visitors centres. Routes begin from Caneland Shopping Centre and there are many signposted bus stops, but you can hail a bus anywhere along the route as long as there is room for it to pull over. There's a free service on Sunday, running to all the major tourist sights. Signal for the driver to pull over anywhere along the route on Gordon St and Nebo Rd.

For a taxi, call **Mackay Taxis** (☑13 13 08). Count on about $20 for a taxi from either the train station or the airport to the city centre.

Around Mackay

SARINA
☑07 / POP 3290
In the foothills of the Connors Range, Sarina is a service centre for the surrounding sugarcane farms and home to CSR's Plane Creek sugar mill and ethanol distillery.

The **Sarina Tourist Art & Craft Centre** (☎4956 2251; Railway Sq, Bruce Hwy; ⊙9am-5pm) showcases locally made handicrafts and assists with information. Next door, there's a small **museum** (adult/child $4/1; ⊙9.30am-2pm Tue, Wed & Fri).

Sarina Sugar Shed (☎4943 2801; www. sarinasugarshed.com.au; Railway Sq; adult/child $18/9; ⊙tours 9.30am, 10.30am, noon & 2pm Mon-Sat) is the only miniature sugar-processing mill and distillery of its kind in Australia. After the tour, enjoy a complimentary tipple at the distillery.

The town centre straddles the Bruce Hwy. The **Tramway Motel** (☎4956 2244; 110 Broad St; s/d $100/105; ❋🐾❂) , north of the centre, has clean, bright rooms. For a dining experience with a difference, head to the **Diner** (11 Central St; mains $4-6; ⊙4am-6pm Mon-Fri, to 10am Sat), a rustic roadside shack that has served tucker to truckies and cane farmers for decades. To find it, take the turn-off to Clermont in the centre of town and look for the tin shack on your left, just before the railway crossing.

AROUND SARINA

There are a number of low-key beachside settlements a short drive east from Sarina. Clean, uncrowded beaches and mangrove-lined inlets provide excellent opportunities for relaxing, fishing, beachcombing and spotting wildlife such as nesting marine turtles.

Sarina Beach

On the shores of Sarina Inlet, this laid-back coastal village boasts a long beach, a general store/service station and a boat ramp at the inlet.

Fernandos Hideaway (☎4956 6299; www. sarinabeachbb.com; 26 Captain Blackwood Dr; s/d $100/130-140; ❋❂) is a Spanish hacienda-style B&B perched on a rugged headland. It offers magnificent coastal views and absolute beachfront. In the living room there's a stuffed lion, a suit of armour and an eclectic assortment of souvenirs from the eccentric owner's global travels.

Sarina Beach Motel (☎4956 6266; sarbeach@mackay.net.au; The Esplanade; d $100-135; ❋❂) is located at the northern end of the Esplanade. Most rooms have beach frontage.

Armstrong Beach

Armstrong Beach Caravan Park (☎4956 2425; 66 Melba St; unpowered/powered sites $25/30) is a situated a few kilometres south-

east of Sarina. Prices at this coastal van park are for two people.

Mackay's Northern Beaches

The coastline north of Mackay is made up of a series of headlands and bays sheltering small residential communities with holiday accommodation.

At **Blacks Beach**, the beach extends for 6km, so stretch those legs and claim a piece of Coral Sea coast for a day. Of the several accommodation options, **Blue Pacific Resort** (☎1800 808 386, 4954 9090; www.bluepacificresort.com.au; 26 Bourke St, Blacks Beach; studios $155, 1-/2-bedroom units $175/225; ❋🐾❂) has bright, cheerful units directly on the beach. All rooms have self-catering facilities.

Close by is **Seawinds Caravan Park** (☎4954 9334; seawinds16@bigpond.com; unpowered sites $21-25, powered sites $29-31, cabins $82-101; ❋@❂), with tent sites overlooking a gloriously long stretch of beach.

At the north end of Blacks Beach, stay at the four-star **Dolphin Heads Resort** (☎1800 075 088, 4954 9666; www.dolphinheadsresort.com.au; Beach Rd, Dolphin Heads; d $180-220; ❋@🐾❂), with 80 comfortable, motel-style units overlooking an attractive (but rocky) bay.

North of Dolphin Heads is **Eimeo**, where the **Eimeo Pacific Hotel** (Mango Ave, Eimeo) crowns a headland commanding magnificent Coral Sea views. It's a great place for a beer.

Bucasia is across Sunset Bay from Eimeo and Dolphin Heads, but you have to head all the way back to the main road to get up there. **Bucasia Beachfront Caravan Resort** (☎4954 6375; www.bucasiabeach.com.au; 2 The Esplanade; unpowered sites $27, powered sites $28-37, villa $160; ❂) has camp sites, but they aren't on the beach, although the small, comfortable villa is a short stroll across a swathe of lawn to the beach.

Pioneer Valley

Travelling west, Mackay's urban sprawl gives way to the lush greenness of beautiful Pioneer Valley, where the unmistakable smell of sugar cane wafts through your nostrils as loaded cane trains busily work their way along the roadside. The first sugar cane was planted here in 1867 and today almost the entire valley floor is planted with the stuff.

The route to Eungella National Park, the Mackay-Eungella Rd, branches off the Peak Downs Hwy about 10km west of Mackay and follows the river through vast fields of cane to link up with the occasional small town or steam-belching sugar mill.

About 17km west of Mirani is the **Pinnacle Hotel** (Eungella Rd, Pinnacle; mains $10-20). The pub has an outdoor cafe, and live music on Sunday afternoons.

Another 10km further down the road is the turn-off for Finch Hatton Gorge, part of Eungella National Park, and 1.5km past the turn-off is the pretty township of **Finch Hatton**.

From Finch Hatton, it's another 18km to Eungella, a quaint mountain village overlooking the valley. The last section of this road climbs suddenly and steeply with several incredibly sharp corners – towing a large caravan is not recommended.

Eungella

Pretty little Eungella (*young*-gluh, meaning 'land of clouds') sits perched on the edge of the Pioneer Valley. There's a **general store** with snacks, groceries and fuel, plus a couple of accommodation and eating options.

Eungella Mountain Edge Escape (☑4958 4590; www.mountainedgeescape.com.au; 1-/2-bedroom cabins $115/135; ✷) has three self-contained wooden cabins perched on the edge of the escarpment, with superb views of the valley below.

Eungella Chalet (☑4958 4509; www.eungellachalet.com.au; 1-/2-bedroom cabins $115/135; ✷) exudes a rustic charm in a once-grand kind of way. The chalet is perched on the edge of a mountain and the views are spectacular. The cabins are large and spacious but furnishings are quite dated. There's a small bar, the dining room has fantastic views and there's live music most Sunday afternoons.

Eungella Holiday Park (☑0437 479 205; www.eungella.com; unpowered/powered sites $20/22, cabins $85-120) is a small and very basic camping ground located just north of the township, right on the edge of the escarpment. You'll need to self-register on arrival. Prices are for two people.

It's worth stopping in for lunch at the interesting **Hideaway Cafe** (☑4958 4533; Broken River Rd; dishes $4-10; ☺9am-4pm), which may or may not be open. If it's open sit on the picturesque little balcony and enjoy a decent home-cooked dish.

Stunning Eungella National Park is 84km west of Mackay, covering nearly 500 sq km of the Clarke Range and climbing to 1280m at Mt Dalrymple. The mountainous park is largely inaccessible, except for the walking tracks around Broken River and Finch Hatton Gorge. The large tracts of tropical and subtropical vegetation have been isolated from other rainforest areas for thousands of years and now boast several unique species.

Most days of the year, you can be pretty sure of seeing a platypus or two in the Broken River. The best times are the hours immediately after dawn and before dark, but you must remain patiently silent and still. Platypus activity is at its peak from May to August, when the females are fattening themselves up in preparation for gestating their young. Other river life you're sure to see are the large northern snapping turtles, and brilliant azure kingfishers flitting above the feeding platypuses.

BROKEN RIVER

There's a **QPWS information office** (☑4958 4552; ☺8am-4pm), picnic area and **kiosk** (☺9.30am-5.30pm Wed-Mon) near the bridge over the Broken River, 5km south of Eungella. A **platypus-viewing platform** has been built near the bridge and bird life is prolific. There are some excellent walking trails between the Broken River picnic ground and Eungella. Maps are available from the information office, which unfortunately is rarely staffed.

For accommodation, you have the choice of camping or cabins. **Broken River Mountain Resort** (☑4958 4000; www.brokenrivermr.com.au; d $105-160; ✷@☎✱) has comfortable cedar cabins ranging from small, motel-style units to a large self-contained lodge sleeping up to six. There's a cosy guest lounge with an open fire and the friendly **Possums Table Restaurant & Bar** (mains $21-37; ☺breakfast & dinner). The resort organises several (mostly free) activities for its guests, including spotlighting, birdwatching and guided walks, and can organise shuttle transfers for longer walks.

Fern Flat Camping Ground (per person/family $5.15/20.60) is a lovely place to camp, with shady sites adjacent to the river where the platypuses play. This is a walk-in camping ground and is not vehicle accessible. Camp sites are about 500m past the information centre and kiosk and you need to self-register.

Crediton Hall Camping Ground (per person/family $5.15/20.60), 3km after Broken River, is accessible to vehicles. Turn left into Crediton Loop Rd and turn right after the Wishing Pool circuit track entrance.

FINCH HATTON GORGE

About 27km west of Mirani, just before the town of Finch Hatton, is the turn-off to Finch Hatton Gorge. The last 2km of the 10km drive from the main road are on unsealed roads with several creek crossings that can become impassable after heavy rain. A 1.6km walking trail leads to **Araluen Falls**, with its tumbling waterfalls and swimming holes, and a further 1km hike takes you to the **Wheel of Fire Falls**, another cascade with a deep swimming hole.

A fun and informative way to explore the rainforest here is to glide through the canopy on a cable with **Forest Flying** (☎4958 3359; www.forestflying.com; rides $60).

The following places are signposted on the road to the gorge.

Platypus Bushcamp (☎4958 3204; www.bushcamp.net; Finch Hatton Gorge; camp sites $10, dm/d $35/100) is a totally amazing, true bush retreat hand-built by Wazza, the eccentric owner. The basic huts have barely-there walls, with the rainforest at your fingertips. A creek with platypuses and great swimming holes runs next to the camp, and the big open-air communal kitchen-eating area is the heart of the place. There are wonderful hot bush showers and a cosy stone hot tub. Bring your own food and linen. WWOOFers welcome.

The only luxury accommodation in Eungella National Park is the **Rainforest B&B** (☎4958 3099; www.rainforestbedandbreakfast. com.au; 52 Van Houweninges Rd; cabin per night $300). There's a touch of Balinese to this rainforest retreat with its garden sculptures, wooden cabin and romantic decor.

The self-contained cabins at **Finch Hatton Gorge Cabins** (☎4958 3281; www.finch hattongorgecabins.com.au; d $95, extra person $20; ✱) are quite basic but have wonderful views of the forest.

❶ Getting There & Away

There are no buses to Eungella or Finch Hatton, but Reeforest Adventure Tours and Jungle Johno Eco Tours both run day trips from Mackay and will drop off and pick up those who want to linger

(see p400), although tours don't run every day and your stay may be longer than intended.

Cumberland Islands

There are about 70 islands in the Cumberland group (including Brampton Island), which is sometimes referred to as the southern Whitsundays. The islands are all designated national parks except for Keswick, St Bees and part of tiny Farrier Island. Although these lands are accessible, access can be difficult.

BRAMPTON ISLAND

Brampton Island proudly announces that there are no daytrippers (except on Sundays) to interrupt the peace and solitude. It's a classy resort popular with couples, honeymooners and those wanting a relaxed island experience. It's definitely not a party island and kids are not catered for.

Brampton Island Resort (☎1300 134 044, 4951 4499; www.bramptonholidays.com.au; s $290-640, d $310-660; ✱@✱) has four grades of room depending on the view and facilities. Naturally, rates increase the closer you get to the ocean, but the premium ocean views are stunning and even the standard rooms are classy. The Bluewater Restaurant serves a buffet breakfast and lunch and a scrumptious à la carte dinner as well as beach barbecues. Prices are often much cheaper if you book a five-night package or wait for standby rates.

Island transfers by either helicopter or launch from Mackay are organised through the resort when booking accommodation.

OTHER CUMBERLAND ISLANDS

If you have your own boat or can afford to charter a boat or seaplane, most other islands in the Cumberland Group and the Sir James Smith Group to the north are also beautiful national parks.

Camp-site availability, bookings and permits for **Carlisle**, **Scawfell** and **Goldsmith Islands** and others are done online at www. derm.qld.gov.au, at the Mackay QPWS (p402) or the Mackay visitors centre (p402).

Carlisle Island can be reached from Brampton Island via the sand spit at low tide or by chartering a boat at Brampton resort. Scawfell and Goldsmith Islands are reached by charter boat, which can be organised through the Mackay visitors centre.

Cape Hillsborough National Park

Despite being so easy to get to, this small coastal park, 58km north of Mackay, feels like it's at the end of the earth. Ruggedly beautiful, it takes in the rocky, 300m-high Cape Hillsborough and Andrews Point and Wedge Island, which are joined by a causeway at low tide. The park features rough cliffs, a broad beach, rocky headlands, sand dunes, mangroves, hoop pines and rainforest. Kangaroos, wallabies, sugar gliders and turtles are common, and the roos are likely to be seen on the beach in the evening and early morning. There are also the remains of Aboriginal middens and stone fish traps, accessible by good walking tracks. On the approach to the foreshore area, there's also an interesting boardwalk leading out through a tidal mangrove forest.

Smalleys Beach Campground (sites per person/family $5.15/20.60) is a small, pretty and grassed camping ground hugging the foreshore and jumping with kangaroos. There's no self-registration here, so you'll need to book a permit (☎13 74 68; www. derm.qld.gov.au).

Cape Hillsborough Nature Resort (☎4959 0152; www.capehillsboroughresort.com.au; unpowered/powered sites $25/30, r $95, cabins $65-120; @☀) is in a quiet spot on a long stretch of beach. Motel-style rooms are large but basic and the beach huts on the foreshore are looking tired and run-down. The caravan sites are a better option.

THE WHITSUNDAYS

The Whitsunday group of islands off the northeast Queensland coast is, as the cliché goes, a tropical paradise. The 74 islands that make up this stunning archipelago are really the tips of mountain tops jutting out from the Coral Sea, and from their sandy fringes the ocean spreads towards the horizon in beautiful shades of crystal, aqua, blue and indigo. Sheltered by the Great Barrier Reef, there are no crashing waves or deadly undertows, and the waters are perfect for sailing.

Of the numerous stunning beaches and secluded bays, Whitehaven Beach stands out for its pure white silica sand. It is undoubtedly the finest beach in the Whitsundays, and possibly one of the finest in the world.

Airlie Beach, on the mainland, is the coastal hub and major gateway to the islands. Only seven of the islands have tourist resorts – catering to every budget and whim from the basic accommodation at Hook Island to the exclusive luxury of Hayman Island. Most of the islands are uninhabited, and several offer the chance of back-to-nature beach camping and bushwalking.

🏃 Activities
Sailing
What could be better than sailing from one island paradise to another? There are plenty of **sailing tours** (p410) itching to get your landlubber feet on deck, but if you've got salt water in your veins, a **bareboat charter** might be more your style. No, there are no bare butts involved, although since a bareboat charter means you rent a boat without skipper, crew or provisions, you could conceivably bare whatever bits you want. You don't need formal qualifications to hire a boat but you (or one of your party) have to prove you can competently operate a vessel.

Expect to pay between $500 to $800 a day in the high season (September to January) for a yacht comfortably sleeping four to six people. A booking deposit of $500 to $750 and a security bond of between $200 and $2000 is payable before departure and refunded after the boat is returned undamaged. Bedding is usually supplied and provisions can be provided at extra cost. Most companies have a minimum hire period of five days.

It's worth asking if the company belongs to the Whitsunday Bareboat Operators Association, a self-regulatory body that guarantees certain standards. Also check that the latest edition of David Colfelt's *100 Magic Miles* (see p410) is stowed on board.

There are a number of bareboat charter companies around Airlie Beach:

Charter Yachts Australia (☎1800 639 520; www.cya.com.au; Abel Point Marina)

Cumberland Charter Yachts (☎1800 075 101; www.ccy.com.au; Abel Point Marina)

Queensland Yacht Charters (☎1800 075 013; www.yachtcharters.com.au; Abel Point Marina)

Whitsunday Escape (☎1800 075 145, 4946 5222; www.whitsundayescape.com; Abel Point Marina)

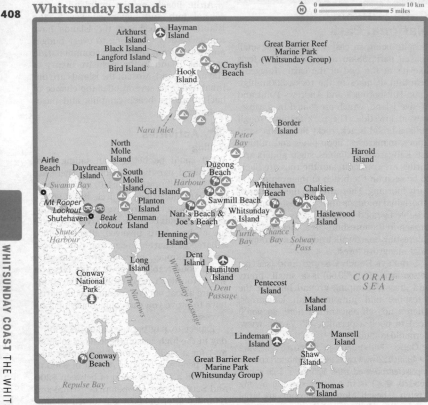

Whitsunday Rent A Yacht (☑1800 075 000; www.rentayacht.com.au; Trinity Jetty, Shute Harbour)

If you want to know why those old salts at the bar keep smiling into their drinks, learn to sail:

Whitsunday Marine Academy (☑1800 810 116; www.explorewhitsundays.com; 4 The Esplanade) Run by Explore Whitsundays.

Whitsunday Sailing Club (☑4946 6138; www.whitsundaysailingclub.com.au; Airlie Point)

Diving

The ultimate diving experience to be had here is on the actual **Great Barrier Reef** at places such as Black, Knuckle, Fairy, Bait and Elizabeth Reefs. However, the fringing reefs around the islands (especially on their northern tips) is often more colourful and abundant than most of the walls on the outer reef, and there's usually a greater variety of softer coral.

Costs for open-water courses with several ocean dives start at around $500 and generally involve two or three days' tuition on the mainland, with the rest of the time diving in the Great Barrier Reef Marine Park. Check that the Great Barrier Reef Marine Park levy and any other additional costs are included in the price.

A number of **sailing cruises** (p410) include diving as an optional extra. Prices start from $75 for introductory or certified dives. The two main island ferry operators, **Fantasea** (☑4967 5455; www.fantasea.com. au) and **Cruise Whitsundays** (☑4946 4662; www.cruisewhitsundays.com), offer dives on day trips to the reef.

Most of the **island resorts** also have dive schools and free snorkelling gear.

Kayaking

Paddling serenely in search of an island with dolphins and turtles as company is one of the best ways to experience the Whitsundays. **Salty Dog Sea Kayaking** (☑4946 1388; www.saltydog.com.au) offers guided tours and kayak rental. Half-/full-day tours from Shute Harbour cost $70/125. There are also overnight trips ($365) and a brilliant six-day expedition, suitable for beginners ($1500), that covers about 15km to 20km per day. Kayak rental costs $50/60 for a half-/one-day single kayak and $80/90 for a double.

The **Ngaro Sea Trail** combines kayaking trails with island bushwalks. Pick up the guide *Whitsunday National Park Islands and Ngaro Sea Trail* from the QPWS office to plan your itinerary.

⛵ Tours

Not everyone has the time or the money to sail, and therefore must rely on the faster catamarans to whisk them to several different islands on a day trip.

Most day trips include activities such as snorkelling or boom netting with scuba diving as an optional extra. Children generally pay half fare. Most of the cruise operators run out of Abel Point Marina but those that run from Shute Harbour do coach pick-ups from Airlie Beach and Cannonvale. You can take a public bus to Shute Harbour.

Following are some of the day trips on offer; bookings can be made at any Airlie Beach tour agent:

Cruise Whitsundays CRUISES
(☑4946 4662; www.cruisewhitsundays.com; Shingley Dr, Abel Point Marina; full-day adventure cruise adult/child $199/95) As well as operating as an island ferry, Cruise Whitsundays offers trips to Daydream and Long Islands, plus it runs a catamaran out to a pontoon moored at Knuckle Reef Lagoon. Alternatively, hop on and off the islands at leisure with a daily Island Hopper pass (adult/child $79/49). It also operates a popular day trip aboard the *Camira* (adult/child $165/85 including lunch and all drinks), a catamaran that takes in Whitehaven Beach.

Voyager 3 Island Cruise CRUISES
(☑4946 5255; www.wiac.com.au; Shute Harbour Rd; adult/child $140/80) A good-value day cruise that includes snorkelling at Hook Island, beachcombing and swimming at Whitehaven Beach, and checking out Daydream Island.

Ocean Rafting BOAT TRIP
(☑4946 6848; www.oceanrafting.com; adult/child/family $120/78/360) Visit the 'wild' side of the islands in a very fast, big yellow speedboat. Swim at Whitehaven Beach,

view Aboriginal cave paintings at Nara Inlet or snorkel the reef at Mantaray Bay and Border Island.

Fantasea CRUISES
(☑4967 5455; www.fantasea.com.au; Shute Harbour) Another large tour operator in Airlie Beach, Fantasea offers high-speed catamaran cruises to its Reefworld pontoon on the Great Barrier Reef (adult/child/family $225/102/589). An overnight 'Reefsleep' costs from $460.

Big Fury CRUISES
(☑4948 2201; Abel Point Marina; adult/child/family $130/70/350) This small operator allows a maximum of 35 passengers and speeds out to Whitehaven Beach on an open-air sports boat followed by lunch and then some snorkelling at a secluded reef nearby.

Scenic Flights

Air Whitsunday SCENIC FLIGHT
(☑4946 9111; www.airwhitsunday.com.au; Terminal 1, Whitsunday Airport) Offers a range of tours, including day trips to Hayman Island ($195).

HeliReef SCENIC FLIGHT
(☑4946 9102; www.avta.com.au) Scenic helicopter flights.

Aviation Adventures SCENIC FLIGHT
(☑4946 9988; www.av8.com.au; 2927 Shute Harbour Rd) Scenic helicopter flights.

🛏 Sleeping

Resorts

Rates quoted are standard, but hardly anyone pays them. Most travel agents can put together a range of discounted package deals combining air fares, transfers, accommodation and meals.

Camping

QPWS (www.derm.qld.gov.au) manages the **Whitsunday Islands National Park** camping grounds on several islands for both independent campers as well as groups on commercial trips. Camping permits (per person/family $5.15/20.60) are available online, from the Whitsunday QPWS office and from the Whitsunday Information Centre in Proserpine.

The national parks leaflet, *Whitsunday National Park Islands and Ngaro Sea Trail,* describes the various sites, and provides detailed information on what to take and do. You must be self-sufficient and are

SAILING THE WHITSUNDAYS

Dream of an island holiday and alongside the swaying palms, sand-fringed bays and calm blue seas, there's usually a white sailboat skimming lightly across the water. In the Whitsundays, it isn't hard to put yourself in the picture, but with the plethora of charters, tours, and specials on offer, deciding how to go about it can be confusing. Before booking, compare what you get for the price you pay. Cheaper companies often have crowded boats, bland food and cramped quarters. If you're flexible with dates, last-minute stand-by rates can considerably reduce the price and you'll also have a better idea of weather conditions.

Aside from day trips, most overnight sailing packages are for three days and two nights or two days and two nights. Again, check what you pay for. Some companies set sail in the afternoon of the first day and return by mid-morning of the last, while others set out early and return late. Also be sure about what you're committing to – don't set sail on a party boat if you're after a chilled-out cruise.

Most vessels offer snorkelling on the fringing reefs, where the softer coral is often more colourful and abundant than on the outer reef. Check if snorkel equipment, stinger suits and reef taxes are included in the package. Diving usually costs extra.

Once you've decided what suits, book at one of the many booking agencies in town such as **Whitsundays Central Reservation Centre** (☑1800 677 119, 4946 5299; www.airliebeach.com; 259 Shute Harbour Rd) or a management company such as **Whitsunday Sailing Adventures** (☑4940 2000; www.whitsundaysailing.com; 293 Shute Harbour Rd) or **Explore Whitsundays** (☑4946 4999; www.explorewhitsundays.com; 4 The Esplanade).

Some recommended sailing trips:

Camira
(day trip $165) One of the world's fastest commercial sailing catamarans is now a lilac-coloured Whitsunday icon. This good-value day trip includes Whitehaven Beach, snorkelling, morning and afternoon tea, a barbecue lunch, and all refreshments (including wine and beer).

Maxi Action Ragamuffin
(day trip $156) Choose between a cruise to Whitehaven Beach (Thursday and Sunday) or snorkelling at Blue Pearl Bay (Monday, Wednesday, Friday and Saturday). Diving ($90) is an option on the Blue Pearl Bay cruise.

advised to take 5L of water per person per day plus three days' extra supply in case you get stuck. You should also have a fuel stove as wood fires are banned on all islands.

Get to your island with **Whitsunday Island Camping Connections – Scamper** (☑4946 6285; www.whitsundaycamping.com.au), which leaves from Shute Harbour and can drop you at South Molle, Denman or Planton Islands ($65 return); Whitsunday Island ($105 return); Whitehaven Beach ($155 return); and Hook Island ($160 return). Camping transfers also include complimentary snorkelling gear and water containers. You can also hire camp kits ($40 per night) and a food drop-off service can be provided at extra cost.

ℹ️ Information

Airlie Beach is the mainland centre for the Whitsundays, with a bewildering array of accommodation options, travel agents and tour operators. Shute Harbour, about 12km east of Airlie,

is the port for some day-trip cruises and island ferries, while most of the yachts and other cruise companies berth at Abel Point Marina about 1km west of Airlie Beach.

QPWS (☑4967 7355; www.derm.qld.gov.au; cnr Shute Harbour & Mandalay Rds; ☺9am-4.30pm Mon-Fri) Situated 3km west of Airlie Beach.

Whitsunday Information Centre (☑1300 717 407, 4945 3711; www.whitsundaytourism.com) On the Bruce Hwy at the southern entry to Proserpine.

Maps & Books

David Colfelt's *100 Magic Miles of the Great Barrier Reef – The Whitsunday Islands* has been referred to as the 'bible to the Whitsundays'. It contains an exhaustive collection of charts with descriptions of boat anchorages in the area, articles on the islands and resorts and features on diving, sailing, fishing, camping and natural history.

Two of the best maps to this region are the Travelog *Great Barrier Reef* map, with a *Whit-*

Derwent Hunter

(3-day/2-night trip from $590) A very popular sailing safari on a timber gaffe-rigged schooner. Its a good option for couples and those wanting to experience nature and the elements.

Whitsunday Magic

(3-day/3-night trip from $779) This beautiful three-masted schooner is the largest vessel sailing the Whitsundays and cruises to the outer reef. One of the more upmarket tours.

Wings 2

(2-day/2-night trip from $475) Comfortable, well-maintained fast cat for those wanting to sail, dive and make new friends.

Solway Lass

(3-day/3-night trip from $549) Get more bang for your buck. You get a full three days on this 28m tallship – the only authentic tallship in Airlie Beach. It's a popular choice for backpackers.

Pride of Airlie

(3-day/2-night trip $349) The original party boat, the *Pride of Airlie* is still exactly that: a raucous booze cruise popular with young backpackers. Nights are spent at Adventure Island Resort on South Molle Island.

Crewing

Adventurous types might see the 'Crew Wanted' ads posted in backpackers or at the marina and yacht club and dream of hitching a ride on the high seas. In return for a free bunk, meals, and a sailing adventure, you get to hoist the mainsail, take the helm and clean the head. You could have the experience of a lifetime – whether good or bad depends on the vessel, skipper, other crew members (if any) and your own attitude. Think about being stuck with someone you don't know on a 10m boat several kilometres from shore before you actually find yourself there. For safety reasons, let someone know where you're going, with whom and for how long.

sunday Passage map on the reverse side, and Sunmap's *Australia's Whitsundays*.

🛈 Getting There & Around

Air

The two main airports for the Whitsundays are at Hamilton Island (see p420) and Proserpine (see p411). The Whitsunday airport, near Airlie Beach, has regular flights from the mainland to the islands by light plane, seaplane and helicopter.

Boat

Cruise Whitsundays (☏4946 4662; www. cruisewhitsundays.com) provide ferry transfers to Daydream, Long and South Molle Islands and to the Hamilton Island airport. **Fantasea** (☏4946 5111; www.fantasea.com.au) provides ferry transfers to Hamilton Island – see the individual islands for details.

Bus

Greyhound (☏1300 473 946; www.greyhound. com.au) and **Premier** (☏13 34 10; www.premier

ms.com.au) detour off the Bruce Hwy to Airlie Beach. **Whitsunday Transit** (☏4946 1800; www.whitsundaytransit.com.au) connects Proserpine, Cannonvale, Abel Point, Airlie Beach and Shute Harbour.

Whitsundays 2 Everywhere (☏4946 4940; www.whitsundays2everywhere.com.au) operate airport transfers from both Whitsunday Coast (Proserpine) and Mackay airports to Airlie Beach.

Proserpine

☏07 / POP 3250

Proserpine airport decided to change its name to Whitsunday Coast, no doubt in an effort to spruce up its image, but there's still no reason to linger in this industrial sugar-mill town, which is the turn-off point for Airlie Beach and the Whitsundays. However, it's worth stopping at the helpful **Whitsunday Information Centre** (☏1300 717 407, 4945 3711; www.whitsundaytourism.com; Bruce

TOP 3 BEACHES

If the Whitsundays has some of Australia's finest beaches, and Australian beaches are some of the best in the world, then beach connoisseurs have hit the jackpot. Although there are plenty of secluded, postcard-perfect, sandy bays in this tropical paradise, the following are reasonably accessible for most tour companies (see p410 and p409).

» **Whitehaven Beach** (p408) With azure-blue waters lapping the pure-white, silica sand, Whitehaven on Whitsunday Island is absolutely stunning.

» **Chalkies Beach** Opposite Whitehaven Beach, on Haslewood Island, this is another pure-white, silica-sand beach. As it's not on the usual tourist circuit, charter a boat and make like a castaway.

» **Langford Island** At high tide, Langford is a thin strip of sand on the rim of a coral-filled turquoise lagoon.

Hwy; ◷9am-5pm Mon-Fri, 10am-4pm Sat & Sun) just south of town for information about the Whitsundays and surrounding region.

Shoppers of eclectic jewellery, zany clothing and homewares will want to detour into town to **Colour Me Crazy** (☑4945 2698; 2B Dobbins Lane; ◷8.30am-5.30pm Mon-Fri, to 3.30pm Sat, 9.30am-2.30pm Sun).

Whitsunday Coast Airport is 14km south of town, serviced from Brisbane and some other capitals by **Jetstar** (☑13 15 38; www.jetstar.com.au) and **Virgin Blue** (☑13 67 89; www.virginblue.com.au).

In addition to meeting all planes and trains, **Whitsunday Transit** (☑4946 1800) has six scheduled bus services running daily from Proserpine to Airlie Beach. One way/return from the airport costs $15/28, and from the train station it's $8.20/15.20.

Airlie Beach

☑07 / POP 6770

Airlie Beach should be a picturesque little town. As the mainland gateway to the magnificent Whitsunday Islands, it's framed by a backdrop of soft hills with a tropical lagoon and a landscaped foreshore, and white yachts gracing the aqua-blue ocean just metres offshore. Sadly, the pretty esplanade is hidden behind the tacky main drag, a busy and unattractive road, but the heart and soul of the action. And action there is aplenty! After a day sailing to the islands, the bustling backpacker set fills the street, partying hard, fast and frequently. Although at times it seems there's nary an Aussie accent to be heard, look around – cruising yachties, couples and families have just as much fun, just not as loud.

Abel Point Marina, where the Cruise Whitsunday island ferries depart and where many of the cruising yachts are moored, is about 1km west along a pleasant boardwalk, and Shute Harbour, where the Fantasea island ferries depart, is about 12km east. The new marina precinct at the Shute Harbour end of town was under construction at the time of writing, but by the look of the works going on, it's bound to be big.

🏃 Activities

There are seasonal operators in front of the Airlie Beach Hotel that hire out jet skis, catamarans, windsurfers and paddle skis. For details on sailing, diving and kayaking around the islands, see p407.

Jump out of a plane with **Tandem Skydive Airlie Beach** (☑4946 9115; www.skydiveairliebeach.com.au; from $249).

☞ Tours

Fawlty's 4WD Tropical Tours SCENIC (☑4946 6665; adult/child $65/50) Day tour to rainforest and Cedar Creek Falls.

🛌 Sleeping

Airlie Beach is a backpacker haven, but with so many hostels, standards vary and bedbugs are a common problem. Most of the resorts have package deals and stand-by rates that are much cheaper than their regular ones. The new marina development in Boathaven Bay has spoilt the view for some of the prestigious resorts and apartments on the hill. Until the development is complete, look elsewhere for ocean views.

TOP CHOICE **Water's Edge Resort**

APARTMENTS $$$

(☑4948 4300; www.watersedgewhitsundays.com.au; 4 Golden Orchid Dr; 1-bedroom apt $210-260, 2-bedroom apt $275-345; ❄❀) The reception area immediately tells you that you're on holiday, as its open-air plan and gently revolving ceiling fans stir the languid, tropical heat. In the rooms, soft colours, cane headboards and shutters sealing off the bedroom from the living space immediately put your mind at ease.

Waterview   APARTMENTS **$$**
(☑4948 1748; www.waterviewairliebeach.com.au; 42 Airlie Cres; studio/1-bedroom unit from $135/149; ✳🛜) An excellent choice for location and comfort, this boutique accommodation overlooks the main street and has gorgeous views of the bay. The rooms are modern, airy and spacious and have kitchenettes for self-caterers.

Coral Sea Resort   RESORT **$$$**
(☑1800 075 061, 4946 1300; www.coralsearesort. com; 25 Ocean View Ave; d $220-370, 1-bedroom apt $330, 2-bedroom apt $350-400; ✳@🛜☀) At the end of a low headland overlooking the water, just west of the town centre, Coral Sea Resort has one of the best positions around. Many rooms have stunning views.

Airlie Waterfront B&B   B&B **$$$**
(☑4946 7631; www.airliewaterfrontbnb.com.au; cnr Broadwater Ave & Mazlin St; d $259-285; ✳@) Absolutely gorgeous views and immaculately presented from top to toe, this sumptuously furnished B&B oozes class and is a leisurely five-minute walk into town along the boardwalk. Some rooms have a spa.

Bush Village Budget Cabins   CABINS **$**
(☑1800 8098 256, 4946 6177; www.bushvillage. com.au; 2 St Martins Rd; dm from $30, d $93; ✳@☀) These boutique backpacker cabins have undergone a revamp and are now the best budget accommodation in town. Dorms and doubles are in 17 self-contained cabins set in leafy gardens. There's off-street parking, it's close to the supermarket and it offers a courtesy bus into town.

🌿Whitsunday Organic B&B   B&B **$$**
(☑4946 7151; www.whitsundaybb.com.au; 8 Lamond St; s/d $155/210) Rooms are comfortable, but it's the organic garden walk and the orgasmic three-course organic breakfasts (included in the rates; nonguests $22.50) that everyone comes here for. You can book a healing essential-oil massage, meditate in the garden tepee or just indulge in all things organic.

Nomads Backpackers   HOSTEL **$**
(☑4999 6600; www.nomadsairliebeach.com; 354 Shute Harbour Rd; dm/d $28/90; ✳@🛜☀) The newest hostel to open in the heart of Airlie,

Nomads is the pick of the lot. Set on 7½ acres in the centre of town, the rooms are clean and bright. The camping sites out the back are in a good, shady spot (away from the noisy main street), all dorm rooms are en-suited (and beds have reading lights!), and private rooms have TV, fridge and kitchenette. There's a large kitchen and a small bar in the complex.

Airlie Beach Hotel   HOTEL **$$**
(☑1800 466 233, 4964 1999; www.airliebeach hotel.com.au; cnr The Esplanade & Coconut Grove; s/d $129/139, apt $179-289; ✳🛜☀) The motel units are looking decidedly shabby but the sea-facing apartments are clean and spacious. With three restaurants on site and a perfect downtown location, you could do far worse than stay here.

Club Crocodile   RESORT **$$**
(☑1800 075 151, 4946 7155; www.oceanhotels.com. au; Shute Harbour Rd, Cannonvale; dm from $30, s/d $120/140; ✳☀) Favoured by tour groups and families, Club Croc, 2km west of Airlie, has opened up budget options for backpackers. The motel-style units are looking worn and tired but they overlook an attractive central courtyard featuring a tropical pool, fountains, a tennis court, restaurants and a bar.

Beaches Backpackers   HOSTEL **$**
(☑1800 636 630; 4946 6244; www.beaches. com.au; 356 Shute Harbour Rd; dm/d $25/85; ✳@🛜☀) You must at least enjoy a drink at the big open-air bar, even if you're not staying here. Although it's busy, Beaches doesn't try to outdo Magnums in the boisterous stakes, but it comes close anyway.

Magnums Backpackers   HOSTEL **$**
(☑1800 624 634, 4946 1199, www.magnums.com. au; 366 Shute Harbour Rd; camp/van sites $22/24, dm/d/cabins $19/56/25; ✳@🛜) A loud party bar, loads of alcohol and a bevy of pretty young things…it must be Magnums. Forget

---

SUMMER STING: WHERE TO SWIM?

The presence of marine stingers means swimming in the sea isn't advisable between October and May unless you wear a stinger suit. In Airlie Beach, the gorgeous lagoon on the foreshore provides year-round safe swimming, so beach babes can show off their itty-bitty bikinis without getting stung.

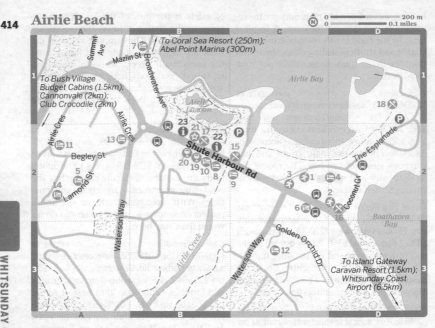

the tent sites close to the bar – you won't sleep unless you're comatose. Once you get past the hectically busy reception, you'll find simple dorms in a tropical garden setting. There's a small breakfast room but no kitchen to speak of.

Flametree Tourist Village CARAVAN PARK $
(☑4946 9388; www.flametreevillage.com.au; Shute Harbour Rd; unpowered/powered sites $21/29, cabins from $77; ❄@≋) The spacious sites are scattered through lovely, bird-filled gardens and there's a good camp kitchen and barbecue area. It's 6.5km west of Airlie.

Sunlit Waters APARTMENTS $$
(☑4946 6352; www.sunlitwaters.com; 20 Airlie Cres; studios from $92, 1-bedroom apt $115; ❄≋) One of the best-value options in Airlie Beach, these large studios have everything you could want, including a self-contained kitchenette and stunning views from the long balconies.

Airlie Beach Motor Lodge MOTEL $$
(☑1800 810 925, 4946 6418; www.airliebeach motorlodge.com.au; 6 Lamond St; d $130-140, 2-bedroom apt $240; ❄⑈≋) Comfortable, renovated units behind a drab exterior.

Backpackers by the Bay HOSTEL $
(☑1800 646 994, 4946 7267; www.backpack ersbythebay.com; 12 Hermitage Dr; dm/d & tw $28/70; ❄@≋) Quiet and homey. Once the new marina is finished, the views will be back.

Airlie Beach YHA HOSTEL $
(☑1800 247 251, 4946 6312; airliebeach@yha. com.au; 394 Shute Harbour Rd; dm $26.50, d $69.50-77.50; ❄@≋) Central and reasonably quiet.

Island Gateway Caravan Resort
CARAVAN PARK $
(☑4946 6228; www.islandgateway.com.au; Shute Harbour Rd, Jubilee Pocket; unpowered/powered sites $30/37, cabins $80-135, chalets $145-225; ❄⑈≋) This large park is located 1.5km east of Airlie.

✗ Eating

Fish D'vine SEAFOOD $$
TOP CHOICE (☑4948 0088; www.fishdvine.com.au; 303 Shute Harbour Rd; mains $10-25; ⊙lunch & dinner) Of course, rum and fish – what a perfect combination! But somehow this quirky concept has taken off like a storm. Maybe those early rum-drinking buccaneers were onto something. Fish D'vine serves dishes from Neptune's realm that will keep you happy and the selection of over 100 different rums is bound to unleash your inner pirate.

Alain's Restaurant   FRENCH $$$
(☑4946 5464; www.alainsrestaurant.com.au; 44 Coral Esplanade, Cannonvale; mains $25-35; ☺dinner Thu-Sat) For fine dining, you can't go past this intimate French restaurant opposite Cannonvale beach. White linen, silverware and soft candlelight add up to romance. Indulge in the six-course table d'hôte menu and you'll have time to ask about that Citroen parked in the corner.

Deja Vu   FUSION $$$
(☑4948 4309; www.dejavurestaurant.com.au; Golden Orchid Dr; lunch mains $15-21, dinner mains $27-40; ☺lunch Wed-Sun, dinner Wed-Sat) Rated as one of Airlie's best, this Polynesian-themed restaurant concocts dishes with Asian and Mediterranean influences. Be sure to while away a few hours at the long Sunday lunch (eight courses per person $39.50).

Village Cafe   CAFE $
(www.villagecafe.com.au; 351 Shute Harbour Rd; mains $10-21; ☺breakfast, lunch & dinner) Always busy with hungover backpackers and those after good coffee, the breakfasts at this popular cafe are just the tonic to get the day started. For lunch or dinner, order a 'hot rock' ($26 to $34) and watch your protein of choice cook to perfection on a volcanic rock that's been heated for 12 hours. Divine.

Whitsunday Sailing Club   PUB FARE $$
(☑4946 7894; www.whitsundaysailingclub.com.au; Airlie Point; mains $14-32; ☺lunch & dinner)

Choose not to sit inside at this club – the sailing-club terrace is a great place for a meal, a drink and wonderful ocean views. Choose from the usual steak and schnitzel culprits.

Marino's Deli   DELI $
(☑4946 4207; 269 Shute Harbour Rd; dishes $6-15; ☺11am-8pm Mon-Sat) Great takeaway pasta and antipasto offerings.

Self-Catering
If you're preparing your own food, there's the small **Airlie Supermarket** (277 Shute Harbour Rd) in the centre of town and a larger one in Cannonvale, about 2km west of town.

🍷 Drinking
Airlie Beach is a drinking town with a sailing problem. The bars at **Magnums** and **Beaches**, the two big backpackers in the centre of town, are always crowded, and everyone starts their night at one or both of them.

Uber   BAR
(www.uberairliebeach.com; 350 Shute Harbour Rd; ☺2pm-11pm Tue-Thu, to 2am Fri & Sat) Classy and uber-cool.

Paddy's Shenanigans   BAR
(352 Shute Harbour Rd; ☺5pm-3am) Proudly encourages the Irish penchant for hard drinking.

☆ Entertainment

Mama Africa NIGHTCLUB
(263 Shute Harbour Rd; ⊙10pm-5am) Just a stumble across the road from the main party bars, this African-style safari nightclub throbs a beat that both hunter and prey find hard to resist.

ⓘ Information

The main drag is stacked with privately run tour agencies. Check out their noticeboards for stand-by rates on sailing tours and resort accommodation. Internet access is widely available: many hostels have terminals and there are several internet cafes.

Airlie Beach visitors centre (✆4946 6665; 277 Shute Harbour Rd)

Post office (✆13 13 18; Cannonvale Shopping Centre; ⊙9am-5pm Mon-Fri, to 12.30pm Sat)

QPWS (✆4967 7355; www.derm.qld.gov.au; cnr Shute Harbour & Mandalay Rds; ⊙9am-4.30pm Mon-Fri)

ⓘ Getting There & Away

Air

The closest major airports are Whitsunday Coast (Proserpine) and Hamilton Island.

Whitsunday airport (✆4946 9933), a small airfield 6km east of Airlie Beach, is midway between Airlie Beach and Shute Harbour. Half a dozen different operators are based here and you can take a helicopter, light plane or seaplane out to the islands or the Reef.

Boat

Transfers between Abel Point Marina and Daydream, Long and South Molle Islands are provided by **Cruise Whitsundays** (✆4946 4662; www.cruisewhitsundays.com). It also runs airport transfers from Abel Point Marina to Hamilton Island. Transfers between Shute Harbour and Hamilton Island are provided by **Fantasea** (✆4946 5111; www.fantasea.com.au) – see the Getting There & Away sections for the individual islands for details.

Bus

Greyhound (✆1300 473 946; www.greyhound. com.au) and **Premier Motor Service** (✆13 34 10; www.premierms.com.au) buses detour off the Bruce Hwy to Airlie Beach. There are buses between Airlie Beach and all the major centres along the coast, including Brisbane ($230, 19 hours), Mackay ($38, two hours), Townsville ($58, 4½ hours) and Cairns ($140, 11 hours).

Long-distance buses stop on The Esplanade, between the sailing club and the Airlie Beach Hotel. Any of the booking agencies along Shute Harbour Rd can make reservations and sell bus tickets.

Whitsunday Transit (✆4946 1800) connects Proserpine (Whitsunday Coast Airport), Cannonvale, Abel Point, Airlie Beach and Shute Harbour. Buses operate from 6am to 10.30pm.

ⓘ Getting Around

Airlie Beach is small enough to cover by foot. Most cruise boats have courtesy buses that will pick you up from wherever you're staying and take you to either Shute Harbour or Abel Point Marina. To book a taxi, call **Whitsunday Taxis** (✆13 10 08) – there's a taxi rank opposite Magnums on Shute Harbour Rd.

There are several car-rental agencies in town:

Avis (✆4946 6318; www.avis.com.au; 366 Shute Harbour Rd)

Europcar (✆4946 4133; www.europcar.com. au; 398 Shute Harbour Rd)

Fun Rentals (✆4948 0489; www.funrentals. com.au; 344 Shute Harbour Rd)

Hertz (✆4946 4687; www.hertz.com.au; Shute Harbour Rd)

Conway National Park

The mountains of this national park and the Whitsunday Islands are part of the same coastal mountain range. Rising sea levels following the last ice age flooded the lower valleys, leaving only the highest peaks as islands, now cut off from the mainland.

The road from Airlie Beach to Shute Harbour passes through the northern section of the park. Several **walking trails** start from near the picnic and day-use area. About 1km past the day-use area, there's a 2.4km walk up to the **Mt Rooper lookout**, with good views of the Whitsunday Passage and islands. Further along the main road, towards Coral Point and before Shute Harbour, there's a 1km track leading down to **Coral Beach** and **The Beak lookout**. This track was created with the assistance of the Giru Dala, the traditional custodians of the Whitsunday area, and a brochure available at the start of the trail explains how the local Aborigines use plants growing in the area.

To reach the beautiful **Cedar Creek Falls**, turn off the Proserpine to Airlie Beach road on to Conway Rd, 18km southwest of Airlie Beach. It's then about 15km to the falls; the roads are well signposted. This is a popular picnic and swimming spot – when there's enough water, that is!

Long Island

Underrated Long Island has the best of everything. Although the romantic Pepper's Palm Bay Resort has closed, honeymooners and couples can snuggle up at Paradise Bay while the more casual atmosphere at Long Island Resort will suit families. The island is about 9km long but not much more than 1.5km wide, and a channel only 500m wide separates it from the mainland. Daytrippers can use the facilities at Long Island Resort.

Activities

The beaches on Long Island are among the best in the Whitsundays and there are 13km of walking tracks with some fine lookouts. Campers can stay at Sandy Bay's national park campsite (per person/family$5/21).

Sleeping & Eating

Paradise Bay　　　　　RESORT $$$
(4946 9777; www.paradisebay.com.au; 3-night packages per person from $1800) This secluded lodge on Paradise Bay consists of 10 waterfront bungalows made from Australian hardwood, with high cathedral ceilings. The bungalows are positioned to make the most of the sea breezes and the resort uses solar power, natural gas and collected rainwater. The entire complex aims to consume less energy than the average suburban home while still maintaining its standards of 'eco-luxury'. The maximum number of guests is just 20 and there are no phones, no TV and no kids allowed. All meals, beer, wine and soft drinks are included in the tariff. Also, there's a three-night minimum stay, no day visitors and no motorised water sports, so you're guaranteed peace and tranquillity. The tariff is inclusive of helicopter transfers from Hamilton Island, sailing tours and activities.

Long Island Resort　　　　RESORT $$
(1800 075 125, 4946 9400; www.oceanhotels.com.au/longisland; d incl all meals $260-380; ❄@❀) A resort for everyone – yep, the kids are more than welcome here. Sitting on Happy Bay at the north of the island, Long Island Resort is a comfortable, midrange place with three levels of accommodation, the best being those on the beachfront. There are some fabulous short walks and plenty of activities to keep all age groups busy. The resort is currently undergoing much-needed renovations.

Getting There & Around

Cruise Whitsundays (4946 4662; www.cruisewhitsundays.com) connects Long Island Resort to Abel Point Marina by frequent daily services. The direct trip takes about 20 minutes, and costs $30/20 per adult/child.

Hook Island

The 53-sq-km Hook Island, second-largest of the Whitsundays, is predominantly national park and rises to 450m at Hook Peak. There are a number of good beaches dotted around the island, and some of the region's best diving and snorkelling locations. The resort itself is a no-frills, budget place. Many travellers come here enticed by the low prices and have left disappointed because it's not what they expect. If you want five-star luxury, don't come to Hook Island...try Hayman instead!

There are national-park **camping grounds** (per person/family $5.15/20.60) at Maureen Cove, Steen's Beach, Bloodhorn Beach, Curlew Beach and Crayfish Beach. Although basic, they provide some wonderful camping opportunities.

Hook Island Wilderness Resort (4946 9380; www.hookislandresort.com; camp sites per person $20, d $120, d without bathroom $100; ❄❀) has seen better days – amenities and rooms are basic and maintenance is an issue. The simple, adjoining units each sleep up to six or eight people and the bathrooms are *tiny*. Private rooms have no en suite, the barbecues are out of action and the camp kitchen isn't much better. On the plus side, the camp sites have a superb beachfront location and there's great snorkelling just offshore from the resort. So if snorkelling is your main priority and you don't mind roughing it, this place might just do.

Transfers are arranged when you book your accommodation; return transfers are by regular tour boat. The **Voyager** does a daily three-island cruise (Hook Island, Whitehaven Beach and Daydream; see p409) and can drop you off at Hook ($40), but you'll have to complete the three-island cruise on the return at a cost of $120. With enough notice, the resort can organise a more economical option. **Whitsunday Island Camping Connections – Scamper** (4946 6285; www.whitsundaycamping.com.au) can organise drop offs to the camping grounds for around $160 return.

South Molle Island

South Molle Island offers an impressive array of short or long walks through gorgeous rainforest, making it an ideal destination for those wanting to put their legs to good use. The decidedly nonglitzy resort has a nine-hole golf course, a gym and tennis and squash courts, plus a wide range of watersports gear available for day trippers to hire.

Largest of the Molle group of islands at 4 sq km, South Molle is virtually joined to Mid Molle and North Molle Islands. Apart from the resort area and golf course at Bauer Bay in the north, the island is all national park and is crisscrossed by 15km of walking tracks, with some superb lookout points. The highest point is Mt Jeffreys (198m), but the climb up **Spion Kop** will reward you with fantastic sunset views. The track to Spion Kop passes an ancient Ngaro stone quarry – look out for an area of shattered rock spilling down the hillside.

There are national park **camping grounds** (per person/family $6/21) at Sandy Bay in the south and at Paddle Bay near the resort.

Adventure Island Resort (⚡1800 466 444; www.koalaadventures.com; dm from $49-100, d $180-240, minimum 3 nights; ✳@🌀), formerly known as South Molle Island Resort, is far from luxurious and in dire need of a spruceup. The rooms are clean, comfortable and functional – pretty much your basic motel style. The bungalows on the beachfront are the best option, each with its own spa and balcony to catch the sea breeze. There are also four-, five- and six-share dorm rooms with en suites.

Attracting a more adventurous, young-at-heart crowd, Adventure Island is *the* party 'island' but there are plenty of daytime activities to keep you busy, including archery, bushwalking, fish feeding, sailing, paddling and snorkelling.

Make the most of the Adventure Island experience by cruising on the *Pride of Airlie*, which stops at South Molle for two nights on its three-day trip. The journey (per person $349) also includes Whitehaven Beach, and you can extend the sailing trip by opting to stay for two extra nights at the resort for only $49 per night. Book through **Koala Adventures** (⚡1800 466 444; www.koalaadventures.com).

Cruise Whitsundays (⚡4946 4662; www.cruisewhitsundays.com) has connections to South Molle via Daydream Island from Abel Point Marina (adult/child $30/20).

Daydream Island

Gorgeous little Daydream Island, just over 1km long and 200m wide, would be dreamy if it wasn't always so busy. The closest resort to the mainland, it's a very popular day-trip destination suitable for everybody, especially busy families, swinging singles and couples looking for a romantic island wedding.

The large **Daydream Island Resort & Spa** (⚡1800 075 040, 4948 8488; www.daydreamisland.com; 3-night packages $900-2500; ✳🌀🌀) is surrounded by beautifully landscaped tropical gardens, with a stingray-, shark- and fish-filled lagoon running through it. It has tennis courts, a gym, catamarans, windsurfers, three swimming pools and an open-air cinema, all included in the tariff so you won't have time for daydreaming. There are five grades of accommodation and most package deals include a buffet breakfast. There's also a club with constant activities to keep children occupied, and they'll love the **stingray splash** ($38) and fish-feeding sessions held at the small coral-reef pool near the main atrium. The resort occupies the entire island, so it's not the place to head if you're seeking isolation.

Cruise Whitsundays (⚡4946 4662; www.cruisewhitsundays.com; one way adult/child $30/20) connects Daydream Island to Abel Point Marina by frequent daily services. **Voyager** (⚡4946 5255; adult/child $140/80) visits Daydream on its daily three-island cruise to Hook Island, Whitehaven Beach and Daydream Island.

Hamilton Island

⚡07 / POP 1840

Hamilton can come as quite a shock for the first-time visitor, with swarms of people and heavy development making it seem like a busy town rather than a resort island. Although this is not everyone's idea of a perfect getaway, it's hard not to be impressed by the sheer range of accommodation options, restaurants, bars and activities – the great thing about Hamilton is that there's something for everyone. The sheer size means there are plenty of entertainment possibilities, so it's also an interesting day trip from Shute Harbour as you can use some of the resort facilities, including tennis courts, squash courts, a gym, a golf driving range and a minigolf course.

Only seven of the islands have resorts, but each has its own unique flavour and style. Depending on whether you want to romance, party or pamper, check the list below or you might end up with a carrot instead of a squiffy umbrella in your cocktail.

...for ecotourism

» **Paradise Bay** (p417) is an exclusive eco-resort with an environmental conscience. It has just 10 simple bungalows and implements 'Earth-kind' sustainable operations without compromising on luxury.

...for luxury

» **Qualia** (p420) on Hamilton Island is divine. Guests stay in luxurious pavilions among the trees and feast on Coral Sea views from their own private plunge pool.

» **Hayman Island Resort** (p420) epitomises old-fashioned pampering and luxury with a focus on sensory and gustatory indulgence and impeccable service. It also has a whopping big pool.

...for families

» **Daydream Island Resort & Spa** (p418) is always buzzing with activity. There's fun stuff for all age groups on and off the water. With a kiddies club, an open-air cinema and plenty of restaurants, cafes and a pool bar, you won't be bored.

» **Long Island Resort** (p417) is decidedly less glitzy, but still has plenty of activities to keep the kids busy while you laze on the beach or lounge beside the pool with pink cocktail in hand.

» **Club Med** (p421) on Lindeman Island has its famous kids' club with a limitless choice of kiddie activities.

...for romance

» **Paradise Bay** (p417), also on Long Island, is not only an eco-resort, it's a favourite honeymoon hotspot. It's exclusive and intimate but don't expect glitzy-glam – this is simple nature-based elegance.

...for fun

» **Adventure Island Resort** (p418) on South Molle Island carries the Airlie Beach party crowd into the wee hours. With DJs, hot bands and full moon parties, good times are as far as the next drink away. The island has fantastic bushwalks to cure those nasty hangovers so, come nightfall, you can start all over again.

From **Catseye Beach**, in front of the resort, you can hire windsurfers, catamarans, jet skis and other equipment, and go parasailing or waterskiing.

A few dive shops by the harbour organise dives and certificate courses; you can take a variety of cruises to other islands and the outer reef. Half-day fishing trips cost around $125 per person with fishing gear supplied.

Before leaving the marina, go down to **Foots Artwork** (☑4946 8308; www.foot.com. au). The beautiful marble and bronze sculptures of mermaids, dolphins, marine creatures and fantasy creations are fascinating.

There are a few **walking trails** on the island, the best being from behind the Reef View Hotel up to Passage Peak (230m) on the northeastern corner of the island. Hamilton also has day care and a Clownfish Club for kids.

🛏 Sleeping

Hamilton Island Resort (☑137 333, 4946 9999; www.hamiltonisland.com.au; ❄@🛜🏊) has options ranging from hotel rooms to self-contained apartments and penthouses. The rates listed in the following reviews are for one night, although almost everyone stays for at least three when the cheaper package deals come into effect. All bookings need to be made through the central reservations number.

Qualia
RESORT $$$

(d $1450-3500) The newest, most luxurious resort in the Whitsundays is set on 30 acres. Modern villas appear like heavenly tree houses in the leafy hillside. The resort has a private beach, two restaurants and two swimming pools.

Beach Club
RESORT $$$

(d $700) Flanking the main resort complex, the Beach Club has five-star rooms with absolute beachfront positions.

Whitsunday Holiday Apartments
APARTMENTS $$$

(d $385) Serviced one- to four-bedroom apartments.

Palm Bungalows
CABINS $$$

(d $315) These attractive individual units behind the resort complex are closely packed but buffered by lush gardens. Each has a double and single bed and a small patio.

Self-Catering Accommodation
APARTMENTS $$$

(d $380-2000) Self-contained units with a four-night minimum stay.

Reef View Hotel
HOTEL $$$

(d from $385) Four-star hotel; large, ugly, 20 storeys, popular with families.

✖ Eating

The main resort complex has a number of restaurants, but the marina also offers plenty of choice. There's also a supermarket/ general store for self-caterers.

Bommie Restaurant
MODERN AUSTRALIAN $$$

(☑4948 9433; Hamilton Island Yacht Club; mains $20-45; ☺dinner) This fine-dining restaurant at the stunning new yacht club has superb water views. The menu isn't extensive but there's a unique twist on its mouth-watering selections. There's also a cafe on the deck.

Romano's
ITALIAN $$$

(☑4946 8212; Marina Village; mains $28-40; ☺dinner Wed-Sun) This relaxed and popular Italian restaurant has a large enclosed deck built right out over the water.

Manta Ray Cafe
CAFE $$

(☑4946 8213; Marina Village; mains $17-30; ☺lunch & dinner) The food is popular here because it's simple and very tasty, with the wood-fired gourmet pizzas a favourite.

Mariners Seafood Restaurant
SEAFOOD $$$

(☑4946 8628; Marina Village; mains $38-47; ☺di-nner) In a big, enclosed veranda overlooking the harbour, stylish Mariners is both licensed and BYO. While the emphasis is on seafood, grills are also available.

Marina Tavern
PUB FARE $

(☑4946 8839; Marina Village; mains $14-20; ☺lunch & dinner) Formerly the yacht club, this busy harbourside pub affords wonderful views of the marina. It's a great place for a decent pub feed or a drink.

☆ Entertainment

Some of the bars in the resort and harbourside offer nightly entertainment, and there's always Boheme's NightClub (Marina Village; ☺9pm-late Thu-Sat).

❶ Getting There & Away

Air

Hamilton Island airport is the main arrival centre for the Whitsundays. Jetstar (☑13 15 38; www. jetstar.com.au) has flights to/from Brisbane, Sydney and Melbourne. Virgin Blue (☑13 67 89; www.virginblue.com.au) has flights to/from Brisbane.

Boat

Fantasea (☑4946 5111; www.fantasea.com. au) connects Hamilton Island marina (adult/ child $125/62) and airport ($49/27) to Shute Harbour by frequent daily services. Cruise Whitsundays (☑4946 4662; www.cruisewhit-sundays.com) connects Hamilton Island airport and Abel Point Marina in Airlie Beach (adult/ child $59/37).

❶ Getting Around

There's a free shuttle-bus service operating around the island from 7am to 11pm.

Everyone hires a golf buggy (per one/two/ three hours $45/55/60, all day $65) to whiz around the island. They are available from the office near reception or from the Charter Base near the ferry terminal.

Hayman Island

The most northern of the Whitsunday group, Hayman is just 4 sq km in area and rises to 250m above sea level. It has forested hills, valleys and beaches and a luxury five-star resort.

An avenue of stately 9m-high date palms leads to the main entrance of Hayman Island Resort (☑1800 075 175, 4940 1234; www.hayman.com.au; r $595-3900 incl breakfast; ❄@☒), with its hectare of swimming pools, landscaped gardens and grounds, an impressive collection of antiques and arts and exclusive boutiques. The resort's original '80s-style architectural design and furnishings have recently undergone a makeover with emphasis on light and space. Pool access rooms open directly onto the fabulous pool (and stepladders from your balcony into the water), and, with the introduction of eight contemporary and stylish beachfront villas, Hayman is definitely one of the most luxurious resorts on the Great Barrier Reef.

Guests flying to Hamilton Island are met by Hayman staff and escorted to one of the resort's fleet of luxury cruisers (one way adult/child $290/145) for a pampered transfer to the resort. **Air Whitsunday Seaplanes** (☑4946 9111) provides a seaplane charter service from Hamilton Island (per plane $1590).

Flying is the only way to do day trips to Hayman. Check out **Air Whitsunday Seaplanes** (☑4946 9111; per person $195).

Lindeman Island

Sitting snugly at the southern end of the Whitsundays, pretty little Lindeman Island will appeal to families and Club Med devotees. While the resort is a little dated in appearance, a vibrant, youthful atmosphere seems to radiate from everywhere you go. The 8-sq-km island is mostly national park but those who don't have – or don't want to share the island with – lots of kids should look elsewhere.

Club Med (☑1800 258 2633, 4946 9333; www.clubmed.com; 3-night full-board packages per 2 people $1788; ✳☲) is all hustle and bustle. The staff ensure there are plenty of activities to keep you entertained, and the famous kids' club may well ensure you don't see the little ones all day (good news for most parents!). The accommodation serves a purpose, but don't expect luxury. Unless you want to hoof it up a mountain of steps, splash out a bit and ask for a resort-side room.

Club Med has its own launch, included in your package, that connects with flights from Hamilton Island.

Whitsunday Island

Whitehaven Beach, on Whitsunday Island, is a pristine 7km-long stretch of dazzling white silica sand bounded by lush tropical vegetation and a brilliant blue sea. From Hill Inlet at the northern end of the beach, the swirling pattern of pure, white sand through the turquoise and aquamarine water paints a magical picture. There's excellent snorkelling from its southern end. Whitehaven is one of Australia's most beautiful beaches.

There are national-park camping grounds at Dugong, Nari's and Joe's Beaches in the west; at Chance Bay in the south; at the southern end of Whitehaven Beach; and Peter Bay in the north.

Other Whitsunday Islands

The northern islands are undeveloped and seldom visited by cruise boats or water taxis. Several of these – Gloucester, Saddleback, Olden and Armit Islands – have national-park camping grounds. The **QPWS office** (☑4946 7022; www.derm.qld.gov.au), 3km south of Airlie Beach, can issue camping permits and advise you on which islands to visit and how to get there.

Bowen

☑07 / POP 7850

Bowen is a classic reminder of the typical small Queensland coastal towns of the 1970s: wide streets, low-rise buildings, wooden Queenslander houses and laid-back, friendly locals. The foreshore, with its newly landscaped esplanade and picnic tables and barbecues is a focal point. Although the town itself holds little of interest to travellers, except those keen on fruit-picking between April and November, there are some stunning beaches and bays northeast of the town centre.

🛏 Sleeping & Eating

Coral Cove Apartments   APARTMENTS $$$
(☑4791 2000; www.coralcoveapartments.com.au; Horseshoe Bay Rd; 1-/2-/3-bedroom apt $250/340/360) These swish apartments have a modern contemporary edge with masses of windows and glass doors to take in the stunning ocean view. They're spacious, ultra-comfortable and all rooms have king beds.

Aussiemates Backpackers   HOSTEL $
(☑4786 3100; aussiemates@live.com; dm/d per week $160/190) In a lovely old Queenslander in the centre of town, this family-run and ultra-friendly hostel is like a home away from home. It's clean, freshly painted and has a large upstairs veranda overlooking the main street. Weekly rates include transfers to working farms.

The Cove ASIAN FUSION **$$**
(☎4791 2050; Coral Cove Apartments, Horseshoe Bay Rd; mains $15-25; ☺lunch & dinner Tue-Sun) The spectacular views of the Coral Sea from the timber deck demand a long lunch, or at least a sunset drink before dinner. The menu features an interesting fusion of Chinese and Malay dishes.

Also recommended:

360 on the Hill CAFE **$**
(☎4786 6360; Flagstaff Hill; mains $6-16; ☺breakfast & lunch daily, dinner Fri) On top of Flagstaff Hill with amazing views.

❶ Information

Tourism Bowen (☎4786 4222; www.tourismbowen.com.au; ☺8.30am-5pm Mon-Fri, 10.30am-5pm Sat & Sun) About 7km south of Bowen on the Bruce Hwy.

There's also an **information booth** (☎4786 2602; Santa Barbara Pde; ☺10am-5pm Mon-Fri, 10.30am-5pm Sat & Sun) in town.

❶ Getting There & Away

Bus

Long-distance bus services stop outside **Bowen Travel** (☎4786 2835; 40 William St) where you can book and purchase tickets for bus journeys. **Greyhound Australia** (☎1300 473 946; www.greyhound.com.au) and **Premier** (☎13 34 10; www.premierms.com.au) are two companies that have frequent bus services running to/from Airlie Beach ($28, 1½ hours) and Townsville ($50, four hours).

Townsville to Innisfail

Best Places to Eat

» A Touch of Salt (p429)
» Man Friday (p434)
» Monsoon Cruising (p447)
» Benny's Hot Wok (p429)

Best Places to Stay

» Elandra (p442)
» Noorla Heritage Resort (p436)
» Sanctuary (p443)
» Reef Lodge (p428)

Why Go?

In between the tourist magnets of Cairns to the north and Airlie Beach to the south, Townsville is a real, living, breathing city with a pulse. Yet although North Queensland's largest urban centre is often bypassed by visitors, it has a surprising number of attractions of its own: a palm-lined beachfront promenade, gracious 19th-century architecture and a host of cultural and sporting venues and events. And Magnetic Island's national park, walking trails and wildlife are just offshore.

To the north of Townsville, through cane fields and laid-back tropical coastline known as the Cassowary Coast, Cyclone Yasi carved a path of destruction in February 2011, mainly around Mission Beach, Tully and Cardwell. However, most services, attractions and national parks should be open by the time you read this. Charters Towers and Ravenswood, inland to the southwest, offer an accessible slice of the dusty outback, while boats make the short crossing to forested Hinchinbrook and Dunk Islands.

When to Go

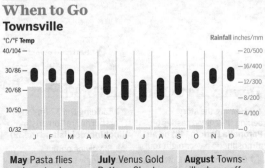

Townsville

May Pasta flies and music plays during Ingham's Australian-Italian Festival.

July Venus Gold Battery, Charters Towers, cranks into action during the town's Gold Fever Festival.

August Townsville shows off its cultural side during the Australian Festival of Chamber Music.

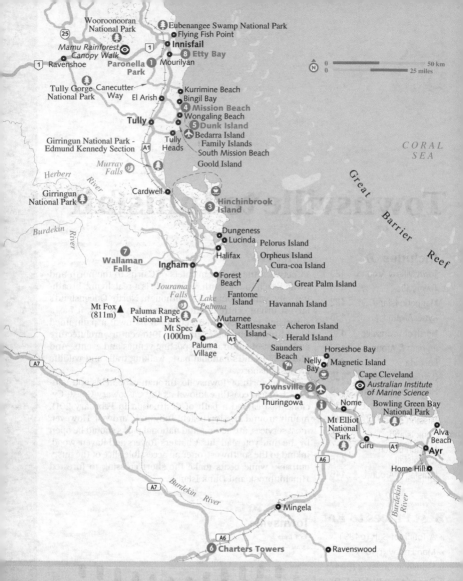

Townsville to Innisfail Highlights

❶ Hearing the story behind the ruined castles of **Paronella Park** (p445) on an atmospheric day or night tour

❷ Cheering on the Cowboys, North Queensland's revered National Rugby League team or National Basketball League team, the Crocodiles, in **Townsville** (p427)

❸ Tackling the 32km-long Thorsborne Trail on pristine **Hinchinbrook Island** (p439)

❹ Skydiving onto a reassuringly soft, sandy landing at **Mission Beach** (p440)

❺ Searching out a secluded beach to yourself on idyllic **Dunk Island** (p445)

❻ Watching a *Ghosts After Dark* outdoor film screening in the outback gold-rush town of **Charters Towers** (p437)

❼ Photographing Australia's highest single-drop waterfall, **Wallaman Falls** (p436)

❽ Watching wild cassowaries wander along the beach at picturesque **Etty Bay** (p445)

TOWNSVILLE & AROUND

North Queensland's largest city is an ideal base for coastal, inland and offshore day trips.

Townsville

📍07 / POP 181,743

Excellent museums, a huge aquarium, world-class diving, two major sporting teams, vibrant nightlife and a stunningly landscaped waterfront esplanade – that's a pretty impressive list for a capital city, let alone a regional centre. Townsville has a lively student population and some 70% of the Australian Army is based here. And then there's the climate. With an average of 320 days of sunshine per year, undercover seating at its stadium was considered unnecessary because of the minimal rainfall during the rugby league season.

Not content to stand still, central Townsville is in the final stages of a major refurbishment that showcases its 19th-century buildings.

◉ Sights & Activities

The compact city centre is easy to get about on foot.

The Strand   PARKS

Stretching 2.2km, Townsville's waterfront is interspersed with parks, pools, cafes and playgrounds – with hundreds of palm trees providing shade. Walkers and joggers take to the path from first light while beachgoers take over by midmorning and evening strollers are at it by late afternoon. Its golden-sand beach is patrolled and protected by two stinger enclosures.

At the northern tip is the **rock pool** (admission free; ⊘24hr), an enormous artificial swimming pool surrounded by lawns and sandy beaches. Alternatively, head to the chlorinated safety of the heritage-listed, Olympic-sized swimming pool, **Tobruk Memorial Baths** (www.townsville.qld.gov.au; The Strand; adult/child $3/2; ⊘5.30am-7pm Mon-Thu, to 6pm Fri, 7am-4pm Sat, 8am-5pm Sun).

Kids will revel at the brilliant little **water playground** (admission free; ⊘10am-8pm Dec-Mar, to 6pm Sep-Nov, Apr & May, to 5pm Jun-Aug). Water is pumped through all sorts of tubes, culminating with a big bucket filling and then dumping its load onto the squealing little ones below.

Castle Hill   WALKS

The striking 286m-high red hill (an isolated pink granite monolith) that dominates Townsville's skyline offers stunning views of the city and of Cleveland Bay. Walk up via the rough 'goat track' (2km one way) from Hillside Cres. If that sounds too energetic, drive via Gregory St up the narrow, winding 2.6km Castle Hill Rd. At the car park up top, a signboard details short trails leading to various lookout points.

Reef HQ   AQUARIUM

(📍4750 0800; www.reefhq.com.au; Flinders St E; adult/child $24.75/12.10; ⊘9.30am-5pm) Townsville's excellent aquarium is a living reef on dry land. A staggering 2.5 million litres of water flow through the coral-reef tank, home to 130 coral and 120 fish species. The backdrop of the predator exhibit is a replica of the bow of the SS *Yongala*, which sank in 1911 off the coast of Townsville during a wild cyclone with 125 passengers and wasn't located until 1958. Kids will love seeing, feeding and touching turtles at the **turtle hospital**. Talks and tours throughout the day focus on different aspects of the reef and the aquarium.

Adjacent to the aquarium, you can continue to experience life underwater without getting wet at the **IMAX cinema** (adult/child/concession $14/9/12; ⊘10.30am-4.30pm). Its 18m-high screen and surround sound are enough to turn people into plankton.

Combined aquarium and IMAX admission is $38.05/20.65 per adult/child.

Museum of Tropical Queensland   MUSEUM

(www.mtq.qld.gov.au; 70-102 Flinders St E; adult/child $13.50/8; ⊘9.30am-5pm) Not your ordinary, everyday museum, the Museum of Tropical Queensland reconstructs scenes using detailed models with interactive displays. At 11am and 2.30pm, you can load and fire a cannon, 1700s-style; galleries include the kid-friendly MindZone science centre and displays on North Queensland's history from the dinosaurs to the rainforest and reef.

Botanic Gardens   GARDENS

(admission free; ⊘sunrise-sunset) Townsville's botanic gardens are spread across three locations: each has its own character, but all have tropical plants and are abundantly green. Closest to the centre, the formal, ornamental **Queens Gardens** (cnr Gregory & Paxton Sts) are 1km northwest of town at the base of Castle Hill.

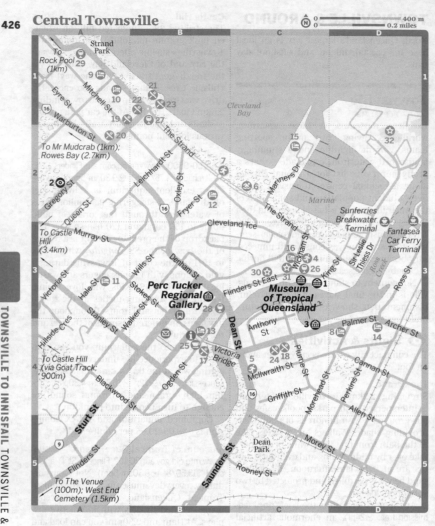

N
0   400 m
0   0.2 miles

Billabong Sanctuary   SANCTUARY
(www.billabongsanctuary.com.au; Bruce
Hwy; adult/child $30/19; ☺8am-5pm; ☒) Just
17km south of Townsville, this eco-certified
wildlife park offers up-close-and-personal
(but not *too* up-close-and-personal) encounters with Australian wildlife – from
dingoes to cassowaries – in their natural
habitat. You could easily spend all day at
the 11-hectare park, with feedings, shows
and talks every half-hour or so. Transfers
are available from Townsville with **Abacus
Tours** (☏4775 5544; adult/child $50/30 incl
park entry).

FREE **Cultural Centre**   CULTURAL CENTRE
(☏4772 7679; www.cctownsville.com.au;
2/68 Flinders St E; ☺9.30am-4.30pm) Showcases the history, traditions and customs
of the Wulgurkaba and Bindal people. Call
for guided-tour times.

Perc Tucker Regional Gallery   ART GALLERY
(www.townsville.qld.gov.au; cnr Denham &
Flinders Sts; admission free; ☺10am-5pm Mon-
Fri, to 2pm Sat & Sun) Contemporary art gallery in a stately 1885-built former bank.
Exhibitions focus on North Queensland
artists.

Townsville Maritime Museum MUSEUM
(www.townsvillemaritimemuseum.org.au; 42-68 Palmer St; adult/child $6/3; ⊙10am-4pm Mon-Fri, noon-3pm Sat & Sun) One for maritime buffs, with a gallery dedicated to the wreck of the *Yongala* and exhibits on northern Queensland's naval industries.

North Queensland Military Museum MUSEUM
(www.army.gov.au; Mitchell St, Kissing Point; admission by donation; ⊙9am-12.30pm Mon, Wed & Fri, 10am-2pm Sun) Military paraphernalia displayed in the old gun stores in the grounds of the Jezzine Army Barracks. Bring photo ID.

Skydive Townsville SKYDIVING
(☑4721 4721; www.skydivetownsville.com.au; tandem jumps $395-445) Hurl yourself from a perfectly good plane and land right on the Strand.

☞ Tours

Several companies operate Great Barrier Reef trips and dive courses – see p430. See p454 for details of cruises aboard the *Coral Princess* between Townsville and Cairns.

Kookaburra Tours DAY TOURS
(☑0448 794 798; www.kookaburratours.com.au) Highly recommended day trips in Townsville and further afield, with enthusiastic, informed commentary. Options include 'Heritage and Highlights' city tours (adult/child $40/18), Wallaman Falls (adult/child $125/55), rainforest tours in Mount Spec National Park (adult/child $125/55) and Aboriginal cultural tours (adult/child $140/65).

Townsville Ghost Tours GHOST TOURS
(☑0404 453 354; www.townsvilleghosttours.com.au) Five spooky options, from city haunts aboard the 'ghost bus' (from $65) to an overnight trip to Ravenswood ($295 including meals and accommodation).

✬ Festivals & Events

The city has a packed calendar of festivals and events, including home games of its revered sporting teams: the **North Queensland Cowboys** (☑4773 0700; www.cowboys.com.au; ⊙season Mar-Sep) National Rugby League team; and the **Crocodiles** (☑4778 4222; www.crocodiles.com.au; ⊙season mid-Oct–Apr) National Basketball League team. If you don't believe how popular basketball can be

CYCLONE YASI

When Tropical Cyclone Yasi began to form in the Coral Sea early in 2011, residents of North Queensland prepared for the worst. Coming almost five years after the destructive Cyclone Larry, many feared Category 5 Yasi would be even more damaging, prompting thousands of residents between Cairns and Townsville to evacuate.

The cyclone hit the coast around Mission Beach early on 3 February, with winds estimated at up to 300km/h ripping through the hardest-hit towns of Tully and Cardwell and islands including Dunk, Bedarra and Hinchinbrook.

Hundreds of homes along the coast between Innisfail and Ingham were severely damaged, banana plantations and cane fields flattened and areas of national park rainforest pummelled, but fortunately there were no deaths or serious injuries. Cairns was spared the full brunt of the cyclone as it veered southwest before hitting the coast, while Townsville suffered only superficial damage.

Despite the estimated $800 million bill, recovery should be swift and travellers won't notice too many changes. At the time of writing, most national parks between Cairns and Townsville – including Hinchinbrook Island, Dunk Island, Goold Island, Orpheus Island, Girringun and Eubenangee Swamp – were either closed or partially closed while rangers assessed damaged and made access and walking trails safe. All are expected to be open by the time you're reading this. Contact the **Department of Environment & Resource Management** (DERM; ☑13 74 68; www.derm.qld.gov.au) for information.

in Australia, you will when you see locals driving around with croc tails hanging out of their car boots.

Other highlights:

Townsville 400   MOTOR SPORTS
(www.v8supercars.com.au) V8 Supercars roar through a purpose-built street circuit each year in mid-July during the V8 Supercar Championship.

Australian Festival of Chamber Music
     MUSIC
(www.afcm.com.au) Townsville gets cultural during this internationally renowned festival each September. Spin-off events include the Taste of Townsville food and wine festival.

🛌 Sleeping

You wouldn't think a city of Townsville's size could fill to capacity, but it does during festivals and events so book ahead. Midrange motels and self-catering units stretch along the Strand, while international chains and backpacker places cluster in the city centre and around Palmer St.

Historic Yongala Lodge Motel   MOTEL **$$**
(☑4772 4633; www.historicyongala.com.au; 11 Fryer St; motel $99-110, 1-bed apt $115-120, 2-bed apt 150-160; ✳🛜🎐) Built in 1884, these historic premises reside in a quiet side street, a short stroll from the Strand and city centre. Sympathetically modern motel rooms and apartments are built around the original heritage

building, which now houses an excellent **restaurant** (mains $20-38; ⊙dinner Mon-Sat) serving classy Greek cuisine.

Reef Lodge   HOSTEL **$**
(☑4721 1112; www.reeflodge.com.au; 4 Wickham St; dm $22-26, d $76, without bathroom $62; ✳@🎐) The cruisy atmosphere at Townsville's best hostel extends from Buddhist sculptures and hammocks strewn through the garden to an outdoor 'cinema' with swinging lounges and over 1200 DVDs, plus a games room with a minigym and retro video game machine (with Space Invaders, Frogger, Pacman... very cool).

Coral Lodge B&B   B&B **$**
(☑4771 5512; www.corallodge.com.au; 32 Hale St; downstairs s/d $65/70, upstairs s/d $80/85; ✳) If you're looking to stay in a charmingly old-fashioned Aussie home, this century-old property can't be beat. Upstairs self-contained units are like having your own apartment while downstairs guest rooms share bathrooms. Breakfast is available for an extra $5 per person. The welcoming owners will pick you up from the bus, train and ferry.

Holiday Inn   HOTEL **$$**
(☑4772 2477; www.townsville.holiday-inn.com; 334 Flinders St; d $114-199; ✳🛜🎐) Dubbed the 'sugar shaker' (for reasons that are immediately obvious), this 20-storey, 1976-built circular building (the city's tallest) is a Townsville

icon. Its 199 rooms are much more contemporary than the exterior suggests, and there's a great rooftop pool and unrivalled views over the city.

Adventurers Resort
HOSTEL $

(4721 1522; www.adventurersresort.com; 79 Palmer St; dm/s/d $25/45/55; ❄@🛜🏊) Roomy, multilevel dorms await at this motel-style complex, which puts on regular falafel nights, theme parties and has its own egg-laying chicken. The highlight is the panoramic rooftop pool and barbecue area. Vans can park up for $5 per night, including full use of the hostel's facilities.

Aquarius on the Beach
HOTEL $$

(1800 622 474, 4772 4255; www.aquariuson-thebeach.com.au; 75 The Strand; d $125-145; ❄@🛜🏊) The full-width balcony views from all 130 apartments impress almost as much as the size of this place, the tallest building on the Strand. Don't be put off by the dated facade – this is one of the better places around, especially the refurbished 'executive rooms' (tiles instead of carpets, flat-screens instead of hefty TVs).

Hotel M
HOTEL $$$

(1800 760 144; www.oakshotelsresorts.com; 81 Palmer St; d $144-189; ❄🛜🏊) Built in 2009, this 11-storey hotel has space-agey rooms with metallic and lime colour schemes, kitchens and laundries, and a gym, plus glittering skyline views from higher-priced rooms.

Beach House Motel
MOTEL $$

(4771 6683; www.orchidguesthouse.com.au; 34 Hale St; dm $26, s $70, without bathroom $50, d $80, without bathroom $60; ❄) Sky-blue, '60s-style motel that's a good option if you just want a clean, comfortable, well-equipped room and friendly service without unnecessary trimmings.

Rowes Bay Caravan Park
CARAVAN PARK $

(4771 3576; www.rowesbaycp.com.au; Heatley Pde, Rowes Bay; unpowered/powered sites $25/33, cabins from $95, without bathroom from $65; villas $98; ❄@🛜🏊) Leafy park directly opposite Rowes Bay's beachfront. Brand-new villas are smaller than cabins but spiffier.

Orchid Guest House
GUEST HOUSE $

(4721 1333; www.beachhousemotel.com.au; 66 The Strand; d $99-118; ❄🛜🏊) A guest house in every sense, with free pick-ups and laundry facilities, cosy, old-fashioned rooms and guaranteed peace and quiet thanks to a no-noise policy after 10pm.

Mariners North
APARTMENTS $$$

(4722 0777; www.marinersnorth.com.au; 7 Mariners Dr; 2-/3-bed apt from $250/390; ❄🛜🏊) Townsville's only absolute oceanfront accommodation. Self-contained apartments have generous living areas, big bathrooms and brilliant balconies overlooking Cleveland Bay. Minimum stay two nights.

🍴 Eating

Palmer St is Townsville's premier dining strip, offering a diverse range of cuisines: wander along and take your pick. Perpendicular to the Strand, Gregory St has a clutch of cafes and takeaway joints. Many of Townsville's bars and pubs also serve food – see p430.

A Touch of Salt
MODERN AUSTRALIAN $$$

(4724 4441; www.atouchofsalt.com.au; cnr Stokes & Ogden Sts; mains $30-36; ⊙lunch Thu & Fri, dinner Tue-Sat) Delectable seafood is accompanied by an extensive wine list and genuinely good service. Even the pies, such as lamb, green pea and mint or peppered beef with hand-cut chips, are gourmet; desserts include twice-baked cheese soufflé. When we visited, the same team was putting the finishing touches on a Palmer St tapas and wine bar, the Salt Cellar (4724 5866; www.thesaltcellar.com.au; 13 Palmer St; ⊙dinner Mon-Sat).

Benny's Hot Wok
ASIAN $$

(4724 3243; www.bennyshotwok.com.au; 17-21 Palmer St; mains $14-29; ⊙lunch Fri & Sun, dinner daily) Outdoor seating, savvy staff and a good wine list set the scene for some of the finest pan-Asian cuisine in North Queensland from freshly made sushi and sashimi to

---

ⓘ DANGER: STINGERS & CROCS

From around late October to May, swimming in coastal waters is inadvisable due to the presence of box jellyfish, Irukandji and other marine stingers.

Saltwater crocodiles inhabit the mangroves, estuaries and open water. Warning signs are posted around the waterways where crocodiles might be present.

GREAT BARRIER REEF TRIPS FROM TOWNSVILLE

The Great Barrier Reef lies further offshore than from Cairns and Port Douglas, hence fuel costs push up the prices. On the upside, it's less crowded (and suffers fewer effects from crowds). Trips from Townsville are dive-oriented; if you just want to snorkel, take a day trip that just goes to the reef – the *Yongala* is for diving only. The *Yongala* is considerably closer to Alva Beach near Ayr, so if your main interest is wreck diving, you may want to consider a trip with Alva Beach–based Yongala Dive (p436).

The visitor centre has a list of Townsville-based operators offering Professional Association of Diving Instructors (PADI)–certified learn-to-dive courses with two days' training in the pool, plus at least two days and one night living aboard the boat. Prices start at about $615; you'll need to obtain a dive medical, which they can arrange (around $50).

Adrenalin Dive
DIVING

(☑4724 0600; www.adrenalinedive.com.au; 9 Wickham St) Day trips to the *Yongala* (from $220) and Wheeler Reef (from $280), both including two dives. Also offers snorkelling (from $180) on Wheeler Reef as well as live-aboard trips and dive certification courses.

Remote Area Dive
DIVING

(RAD; ☑4721 4424; www.remoteareadive.com; 16 Dean St) Runs day trips (from $220) to Orpheus and Pelorus Islands. Also live-aboard trips and dive courses.

Salt Dive
DIVING

(☑4721 1760; www.saltdive.com.au; 2/276 Charters Towers Rd, Hermit Park) *Yongala* and reef-diving day trips (from $199) aboard a fast boat; dive courses available.

Peking duck rolls, steaming laksas, and sizzling Mongolian lamb, as well as create-your-own stir fries.

Cafe Bambini
CAFE $

(http://cafebambini.com.au; 47 Gregory St; mains $11.50-20; ⏰5.30am-5pm Mon-Fri, 6.30am-4pm Sat & Sun; ☑) Spawning five branches around town at last count, this local success story cooks up the best breakfasts in Townsville: lambs fry and bacon, smashed avocado on multigrain, and pork, apple and sage sausages. Lunches have international flavours, from smoked salmon with pappadums to French steak sandwiches.

Jamaica Joe's
JAMAICAN $$

(☑4724 1234; www.jamaicajoes.com; The Strand, opposite Gregory St; mains $17-43; ⏰lunch & dinner) The best time to head to this funky Caribbean diner/bar is on Sunday afternoons, when entertainment includes live music and DJs spinning old-school reggae vinyl. But it's a worthy dining option any time for dishes like Jamaican goat curry.

Mr Mudcrab
SEAFOOD $

(www.mrmudcrab.com.au; 1 Rose St; dishes $3-10; ⏰8am-8pm) If mud crab's on offer here, you know it's fresh – Mr Mudcrab refuses to get it in frozen. This excellent seafood shop sells fresh catches to cook yourself, as well as fish and chips (with homemade tartare sauce) and yummy daily-baked seafood pies.

Cbar
CAFE $$

(www.cbar.com.au; The Strand, opposite Gregory St; mains $16-26; ⏰7am-10pm; ☑) Your best bet if you're hungry outside regular dining hours, serving full meals throughout the day from coconut prawns with mango salsa to Moroccan-style beef tajines.

Harold's Seafood
SEAFOOD $

(cnr The Strand & Gregory St; meals $4-10; ⏰lunch & dinner) This takeaway joint has bug burgers of the Moreton Bay variety.

Souvlaki Bar
GREEK $

(Shop 3 & 4, 58 The Strand; mains $6.50-17.50; ⏰10.30am-9pm Mon-Fri, to 10pm Sat & Sun) Grab a big Greek breakfast of bacon, eggs, sausage, souvlaki, grilled tomatoes, haloumi and pita bread.

Bountiful Thai
THAI $

(Shop 1/52 Gregory St, North Ward; mains $13-21; ⏰lunch Mon-Fri, dinner daily) Pokey little takeaway whipping up noodle and rice dishes, curries and soups in huge portions and quick time.

❦ Drinking & Entertainment

It must be the sunny climate because Townsville sure loves a sip. Most nightlife concentrates around Flinders St East, while Palmer

St and the Strand offer lower-key spots. Check listings in Friday's edition of the *Townsville Bulletin* newspaper. Opening hours tend to vary according to the season and the crowds, and nightclubs generally stay open until 5am.

Coffee Dominion
CAFE
(www.coffeedominion.com.au; cnr Stokes & Ogden Sts; ☺6am-5pm Mon-Wed, to 5.30pm Thu & Fri, 7am-1pm Sat & Sun) If you drop by between 8am and 11.30am on weekdays, you can watch – and smell – this eco-conscious establishment roasting beans from the Atherton Tableland to Zambia. If you don't find a blend you like, invent your own and they'll grind it fresh.

TOP CHOICE The Brewery
MICROBREWERY
(www.townsvillebrewery.com.au; 252 Flinders St; ☺Mon-Sat) Brews made on-site at Townsville's stunningly restored 1880s former post office, with paisley wallpaper, original fireplaces and exposed brickwork, include local favourite Townsville Bitter (midstrength lager) and a seasonal brew (ask what's on tap). Soak them up with a meal at its refined restaurant (mains $17-36; ☺lunch & dinner Mon-Sat).

Watermark Hotel
BARS
(www.watermarktownsville.com.au; 72 74 The Strand) *The* place to be seen in Townsville. Well, if it's good enough for Missy Higgins and Silverchair, then it's good enough for the rest of us. Some serious Sunday sessions take place in the tavern bar, while there's also a more upmarket bar and an excellent Mod Oz restaurant (mains $28 36; ☺breakfast Sun, lunch & dinner daily).

Seaview Hotel
PUB
(www.seaviewhotel.com.au; cnr The Strand & Gregory Sts) Renowned for its Sunday sessions in the huge concrete beer 'garden', the Seaview serves ice-cold schooners and has live music and entertainment. Its immense restaurant (mains $21-44; ☺lunch & dinner) serves steaks on a par with the size of the premises.

Molly Malones
PUB
(www.mollymalonesirishpub.com.au; 87 Flinders St E) This boisterous Irish pub stages live music on Friday and Saturday nights, or you can shake it on the dance floor of its adjacent nightclub, The Shed (☺8pm-5am Tue, Fri & Sat).

Consortium
NIGHTCLUB
(www.consortiumtownsville.com.au; 159 Flinders St E; ☺9am-5am Tue & Thu-Sun) Resident DJs, DJ comps and events like 'fetish and fantasy' balls make this big-city-style venue Townsville's hippest nightclub.

Flynns
LIVE MUSIC
(www.flynnsirishbar.com; 101 Flinders St E; ☺5pm-late Tue-Sun) A jolly Irish pub that doesn't try too hard to be Irish. Wildly popular for its $8 jugs and live music every night except Wednesdays, when karaoke takes over.

The Venue
LIVE MUSIC
(www.thevenuetownsville.com.au; 719 Flinders St W) Multilevel place with regular gigs by Aussie acts (Grinspoon et al) and four bars.

Jupiters Casino
CASINO
(www.jupiterstownsville.com.au; Sir Leslie Thiess Dr) For a waterside flutter.

🛍 Shopping

Cotters Market
MARKET
(www.townsvillerotarymarkets.com.au; Flinders St; ☺8.30am-1pm Sun) Around 200 craft and food stalls, as well as live entertainment.

Strand Night Market
MARKET
(www.townsvillerotarymarkets.com.au; The Strand; ☺5-9.30pm 1st Fri of month May-Jun & Sep-Dec, 2nd Fri of month Jul & Aug) Browse the stalls on the Strand for curios, crafts and knick-knacks.

ℹ Information

Internet Access
Internet Den (☑4721 4500; 265 Flinders St; per 90 min $5; ☺8am-10pm) More than just a full-service internet cafe (with super-fast computers), this home-from-home has a dedicated room for reading, storytelling and Indigenous art workshops, and traveller friendly services like luggage storage.

Post
Post office (Post Office Plaza, Shop 1, Sturt St)

Tourist Information
Visitor Information Centre (☑4721 3660; www.townsvilleonline.com.au; cnr Flinders & Stokes Sts; ☺9am-5pm) Extensive visitor information on Townsville, Magnetic Island and nearby national parks. There's another branch on the Bruce Hwy 10km south of the city.

Department of Environment & Resource Management (DERM; ☑13 74 68; www.derm.qld.gov.au; 1-7 Marlow St)

ℹ Getting There & Away
Air
From **Townsville Airport** (www.townsvilleairport.com.au), **Virgin Blue** (☑13 67 89; www.

virginblue.com.au), **Qantas** (☎13 13 13; www.qantas.com.au) and **Jetstar** (☎13 15 38; www.jetstar.com) to Cairns, Brisbane, the Gold Coast, Sydney, Melbourne, Mackay and Rockhampton, with connections to other major cities. **Strategic Airlines** (☎13 53 20; www.flystrategic.com.au) runs a twice-weekly direct service to/from Bali.

Boat

See p435 for ferries to/from Magnetic Island.

Bus

Greyhound Australia (☎1300 473 946, 4772 5100; www.greyhound.com.au) has three daily services to Brisbane ($270, 23 hours), Rockhampton ($149, 12 hours), Airlie Beach ($71, 4½ hours), Mission Beach ($63, 3¾ hours) and Cairns ($83, six hours). Buses pick up and drop off at Townsville's Sunferries passenger ferry terminal (p435).

Premier Motor Service (☎13 34 10; www.premierms.com.au) has one service a day to/from Brisbane and Cairns, stopping in Townsville at Townsville's Fantasea car ferry terminal (p435).

Car

Major car-rental agencies are represented in Townsville and at the airport.

Train

Townsville's **train station** (Charters Towers Rd) is 1km south of the centre.

The Brisbane-Cairns *Sunlander* travels through Townsville three times a week. Journey time between Brisbane and Townsville is 24 hours (one-way from $190); contact **Queensland Rail** (☎1800 872 467; www.traveltrain.com.au).

❶ Getting Around

To/From the Airport

Townsville airport is 5km northwest of the city centre at Garbutt. A taxi to the centre costs about $20. The **Airport Shuttle** (☎4775 5544; one-way/return $10/18) services all arrivals and departures, with pick-ups and drop-offs throughout the central business district (bookings essential).

Bus

Sunbus (☎4725 8482; www.sunbus.com.au) runs local bus services around Townsville, including the Redbus service – a dedicated loop stopping at key tourist attractions in the city. Fares start from $1.60. Route maps and timetables are available at the visitor information centre.

Taxi

Taxis congregate outside the Sunbus **bus interchange** (cnr Flinders & Stokes Sts), or call **Townsville Taxis** (☎13 10 08).

Magnetic Island
☎07 / POP 2107

'Maggie', as she's affectionately called, is a 'real' island. Permanent residents live and work here and some even make the daily commute to Townsville. Over half of this mountainous, triangular-shaped island's 52 sq km is national park, with scenic walks and abundant wildlife, including one of Australia's largest concentrations of wild koalas. Stunning beaches offer adrenalin-pumping water sports or just the chance to bask in the sunshine, and the granite boulders, hoop pines and eucalypts are a change from your typical tropical-island paradise.

◉ Sights & Activities

There's one main road across the island, which goes from Picnic Bay, past Nelly and Geoffrey Bays, to Horseshoe Bay. Local buses ply the route regularly.

PICNIC BAY

Since the ferry terminal was relocated to Nelly Bay, Picnic Bay now resembles a ghost town. Shopfronts have been abandoned as businesses suffered. But that curious, elegant bird, the curlew, has made it its own, and there's a stinger enclosure and twinkling night-time views of Townsville from the jetty.

NELLY BAY

Crowds swarm off the ferry and onto the bustling marina at the newly developed Nelly Bay terminal. This is where your holiday on Magnetic will begin, but it's the total opposite to what you'll probably experience during your stay here.

That said, Nelly Bay has a wide range of eating and sleeping options and a decent beach. There's a children's playground towards the northern end of the beach and good snorkelling on the fringing coral reef.

ARCADIA

Arcadia village has the island's major concentration of shops, eateries and accommodation. Its main beach, Geoffrey Bay, has a reef at its southern end (DERM discourages reef walking at low tide). By far its prettiest beach is Alma Bay cove, with huge boulders tumbling into the sea. There's plenty of shade, along with picnic tables and a children's playground here.

If you head to the end of the road at Bremner Point, between Geoffrey Bay and

Alma Bay, at 5pm you can have wild rock wallabies – which have become accustomed to being fed at the same time each day – literally eating out of your hand.

RADICAL BAY & THE FORTS

Townsville was a supply base for the Pacific during WWII, and the forts were strategically designed to protect the town from naval attack. If you're going to do just one walk, then the **forts walk** (2.8km, 1½ hours return) is a must. It starts near the Radical Bay turn-off, passing lots of ex-military sites, gun emplacements and false 'rocks'. At the top of the walk is the observation tower and command post, which have spectacular coastal views, and you'll almost certainly spot koalas lazing about in the treetops. Return the same way or continue along the connecting paths, which deposit you at Horseshoe Bay (you can catch the bus back).

HORSESHOE BAY

Horseshoe Bay, on the north coast, is Maggie's water-sports hub. Its crescent-shaped, golden-sand beach is easily the best of the island's accessible beaches, and has a stinger enclosure.

Blast about on Horseshoe Bay aboard a **jet ski** (⊉4758 1100; Horseshoe Bay beach; 2-seater jet ski per 15/30/60mins $50/90/165; ⊙closed Tue & Thu, daily during school holidays).

Magnetic Island Hire Boats (⊉4778 5327) rents boats (per day $220 plus fuel) that can carry up to eight people – great for fishing and snorkelling trips.

Bungalow Bay Koala Village has a **wildlife park** (adult/child $19/10; ⊙2hr tours 10am, noon & 2.30pm), where you can cuddle koalas.

Pick up local arts and crafts at Horseshoe Bay's **market** (⊙9.30am-2pm last Sun of month), which sets up along the beachfront.

Tours

Diving

At Base Backpackers in Nelly Bay, **Reef Safari** (⊉4778 5777; www.reefsafari.com; 1 Nelly Bay Rd, Nelly Bay) runs four-day open-water courses from $299 in addition to advanced courses, introductory dives and certified dives.

Pleasure Divers   DIVING
(⊉1800 797 797, 4778 5788; www.pleasuredivers.com.au; 10 Marine Pde, Arcadia) Adjacent to Magnums in Arcadia, this outfit offers bargain-priced three-day PADI open-water courses from $339, as well as advanced courses and *Yongala* wreck dives.

Tropicana Tours   ISLAND TOURS
(⊉4758 1800; www.tropicanatours.com.au; full-day tours adult/child $198/99) If you're time poor, this full-day tour with guides takes in the island's best spots in its stretch 4WD. Enjoy close encounters with wildlife, lunch at a local cafe and a sunset cocktail (all included in the price). Shorter tours are available.

Horseshoe Ranch   HORSE RIDING
(⊉4778 5109; www.horseshoebayranch.com.au; 38 Gifford St, Horseshoe Bay) Popular two-hour rides ($100) take you through bushland to the beach, where you can swim your horse. Also 3½-hour rides ($130), plus pony rides (20 minutes, $20) for kids.

Providence V   SAILING
(⊉4778 5580; www.providencesailing.com.au) Six-hour sailing trips aboard a 62-foot gaff rigged schooner (including snorkelling gear) for $129, or 2½-hour champagne sunset cruises.

Magnetic Island Sea Kayaks   KAYAKING
(⊉4778 5424; www.seakayak.com.au; 93 Horseshoe Bay Rd; tours from $60) Eco-oriented morning tours to Balding Bay (from $85, including breakfast) and sunset tours (from $60, including drinks). Also rents out kayaks (single/double per day $75/150).

Reef EcoTours   SNORKELLING
(⊉0419 712 579; www.reefecotours.com) One-hour guided snorkelling tour (adult/child $80/70) with a marine biologist. Good for families.

Sleeping

Much of the accommodation on the island is holiday rental cottages – contact **First National Real Estate** (⊉4778 5077; 21 Marine Pde, Arcadia) or **Smith & Elliott** (⊉4778 5570; 4/5 Bright Ave, Arcadia).

PICNIC BAY

Tropical Palms Inn   MOTEL $$
(⊉4778 5076; www.tropicalpalmsinn.com.au; 34 Picnic St; s/d $100/110; ❋ ☀) With a terrific little swimming pool right outside your front door, the self-contained motel units here are bright and comfortable. Reception hires 4WDs (from $75 per day).

NELLY BAY

TOP CHOICE **Base Backpackers**   HOSTEL $
(⊉1800 242 273, 4778 5777; www.stayatbase.com; 1 Nelly Bay Rd; camping per person $10,

dm $24-30, d from $120, without bathroom from $65; @🛜🏊) Famous for its wild full-moon parties, no matter when you're here you can feel the energy pumping through this huge backpackers resort. Some of its A-frame cabins are oceanfront; facilities include a massive waterside deck and adjoining cafe (mains $7-16; 🕑lunch & dinner; 🅿). Great-value package deals available.

Shambhala Retreat UNITS **$$**
(🛜0448 160 580; www.shambhala-retreat-magnetic-island.com.au; 11-13 Barton St; d $110; 🚫🏊) Feel the serenity... these three tropical-hued units have Buddhist wall hangings and books scattered about and their own tree-screened patios attracting local wildlife. Two have outdoor courtyard showers, and all have fully equipped kitchens, large bathrooms and laundry facilities. The saltwater pool's scarcely bigger than a puddle, but the property is entirely green powered. Minimum stay is two nights.

Peppers Blue on Blue Resort HOTEL **$$$**
(🛜4758 2400; www.peppers.com.au/blue-on-blue; 123 Sooning St; d/1-/2-bed apt from $229/321/379; 🚫🛜🏊) A glinting vision of glass-and-steel alongside the ferry terminal, the island's ritziest resort has citified rooms and apartments, a day spa and the casually chic **Boardwalk Restaurant & Bar** (mains $24.50-32; 🕑breakfast, lunch & dinner; 🅿), opening onto an enormous deck.

ARCADIA

Arcadia Beach Guest House GUESTHOUSE **$$**
(🛜4778 5668; www.arcadiabeachguesthouse.com.au; 27 Marine Pde; dm $30, safari tent $50, d $120-150, without bathroom $80-100; 🚫🛜🏊) Super-friendly owners have created a stunningly different place to stay, with bright, beachy rooms named after Magnetic Island's bays and coves. You can turtle-spot from the balcony, and rent a canoe, a Moke or a 4WD. Free ferry pick-ups.

Magnums on Magnetic HOSTEL **$**
(🛜1800 663 666, 4778 5177; www.magnums.com.au; 7 Marine Pde; dm $20-24, d $75-85; 🚫@🏊) Fresh from a facelift, Magnums tries its best to trade off the success of its namesake at Airlie Beach. All dorms and doubles have en suites; make sure you ask for one with an ocean view. Doubles come with a small fridge and TV. The hub of Arcadia bay is the on-site bistro and bar, the **Island Tavern** (mains $19.50-28; 🕑lunch & dinner), which keeps punters happy with $10 jugs, cane-

toad races every Wednesday night and large swimming pool accessible to the public.

HORSESHOE BAY

Bungalow Bay Koala Village HOSTEL **$**
(🛜1800 285 577, 4778 5577; www.bungalowbay.com.au; 40 Horseshoe Bay Rd; unpowered/powered sites per person $12.50/15, dm $30, d $90, without bathroom $74; 🚫@🏊) Not only a resort-style, YHA-associated hostel but a nature wonderland (with its own wildlife park). Less than five minutes' walk from the beach, A-frame bungalows are strewn throughout leafy grounds backing onto national park. Cool off at the breezy outdoor bar, go coconut bowling on Thursdays, or tuck into a curry at the on-site **restaurant** (mains $15.50-24; 🕑lunch & dinner).

Shaws on the Shore APARTMENTS **$$$**
(🛜4778 1900; www.shawsontheshore.com.au; 7 Pacific Dr; 1-/2-/3-bedroom apt $195/270/325; 🚫🛜🏊) Natural light floods these sparkling apartments, with balconies overlooking the bay. Larger apartments have big bathrooms plus en suites off the master bedroom.

🍴 Eating & Drinking

Oh, Maggie. You might have natural beauty in spades, but (with a few exceptions) your culinary skills aren't much. Sure, everything has to be brought over from the mainland, but still, it's surprisingly hard to find a decent meal on the island.

Several hotels and hostels have restaurants and bars that are at least as popular with locals as they are with guests and visitors. Opening hours can fluctuate according to the season and the crowds.

PICNIC BAY

Picnic Bay Hotel PUB **$$**
(Picnic Bay Mall) Settle in for a drink with Townsville's city lights sparkling across the bay. Its **R&R Cafe Bar** (mains $10.50-26; 🕑lunch & dinner) has an all-day grazing menu and huge salads, including Cajun prawn.

NELLY BAY

Man Friday MEXICAN **$$**
TOP CHOICE (🛜4778 5658; 37 Warboy St; mains $14-38.50; 🕑dinner Wed-Mon; 🅿) Easily the best Mexican food on Maggie (and no, it's not the only Mexican food on Maggie), which, along with other imaginative international dishes, is served in a rustic, fairy-lit garden. Bring your own wine (it's unlicensed) but book ahead or risk missing out.

The Terrace
MEDITERRANEAN $$

(☎4778 5200; www.allseasons.com.au; 61 Mandalay Ave; mains $22-44; ⊘lunch Sat & Sun, dinner Mon-Sat; 🛜) Overlooking the pool of the dated All Seasons Hotel (so dated, in fact, that it won't be too long before it's retro-cool again), the Terrace is one of the better places on the island to dine on the likes of panroasted duck or oven-baked spring lamb on kumara mash.

Fat Possum Cafe
CAFE $

(55 Spooning St; mains $7-17; ⊘breakfast & lunch; 🖋) Aptly named for the well-fed possums scampering around the island, and the best pickings on the specials board; Sunday's $15 all-you-can-eat breakfast buffet is something of a village social event.

ARCADIA

Butler's Pantry
CAFE $

(Shop 2-3/5 Bright Ave; mains $15-21; ⊘breakfast & lunch Wed-Mon; 🖋) The island's best brekkies are served at this bang-up-to-date gourmet grocery store/cafe, including pancakes, eggs every-which-way and stacks of veggie options. Great lunches too, from Thai fish cakes to Greek lamb salad, and attentive service.

caffè dell' isola
ITALIAN $$

(Shop 1, Arcadia Village; mains $15-26; ⊘breakfast & lunch Tue, Thu & Sun, breakfast, lunch & dinner Wed, Fri & Sat, daily during school holidays) The Italian radio station reverberating through the outdoor courtyard attests to the authenticity of the crisp-crust pizzas here (as does the menu that reads 'please do not even ask for pineapple'). No credit cards.

Arcadia Night Market
MARKET $$

(Hayles Ave, Arcadia; ⊘5-8pm Fri) Small but lively night market next door to the RSL, with sizzling Indonesian food and seafood to cook up yourself.

HORSESHOE BAY

Marlin Bar
PUB $$

(3 Pacific Dr; mains $15.50-24; ⊘lunch & dinner) You can't leave Maggie without enjoying a cold one by the window as the sun sets across the bay at this busy seaside pub. The meals are on the large side and (surprise!) revolve around seafood. Great value.

Barefoot
MODERN AUSTRALIAN $$

(☎4758 1170; www.barefootartfoodwine.com.au; 5 Pacific Dr; mains $16-30; ⊘lunch & dinner Thu-Mon) Dine on artichoke risotto with truffle oil or Egyptian-spiced kangaroo burgers at this restaurant/art gallery.

ℹ Information

There's no official visitor information centre on Magnetic Island, but Townsville's visitor information centre has comprehensive info and maps and can help find accommodation. Maps are also available at both ferry terminals in Townsville and at the terminal at Nelly Bay.

ATMs are scattered throughout the island, although there are no banks. The **post office** (Sooning St, Nelly Bay) also has an ATM.

ℹ Getting There & Away

All ferries arrive and depart Maggie from the terminal at Nelly Bay.

Sunferries (☎4726 0800; www.sunferries.com.au) operates a frequent passenger ferry between Townsville and Magnetic Island (adult/child return $29/14.50), which takes around 20 minutes. Ferries depart Townsville from the Sunferries Breakwater Terminal at 2/14 Sir Leslie Thiess Dr.

Fantasea (☎4796 9300; www.magneticislandferry.com.au; Ross St, South Townsville) operates a car ferry crossing eight times daily (seven on weekends) from the south side of Ross Creek, taking 35 minutes. It costs $164 (return) for a car and up to three passengers, and $26/15.50 (adult/child return) for foot passengers only. Bookings are essential and bicycles are transported free.

Both Townsville terminals have car parking.

ℹ Getting Around
Bicycle

Magnetic Island is ideal for cycling although some of the hills can be hard work. Most places to stay rent bikes for around $15 a day and a number of places offer them free to guests.

Bus

The **Magnetic Island Bus Service** (☎4778 5130) ploughs between Picnic Bay and Horseshoe Bay at least 18 times a day, meeting all ferries and stopping at major accommodation places. A hop-on, hop-off day pass costs $6.

Moke & Scooter

Moke and scooter rental places abound around the island. You'll need to be over 21, have a current international or Australian driver's licence and leave a credit-card deposit. Scooter hire starts at around $30 per day. Try **MI Wheels** (☎4778 5491; 138 Sooning St, Nelly Bay) for a classic Moke or 'topless' (open-topped) car, or **Roadrunner Scooter Hire** (☎4778 5222; 3/64 Kelly St, Nelly Bay) for scooters and trail bikes.

Ayr & Around

📞07 / POP 8093

On the delta of the mighty Burdekin River 90km southeast of Townsville, Ayr is the major commercial centre for the rich farmlands of the Burdekin Valley. The town and its surrounds are devoted to the production and harvesting of sugar cane, melons and mangoes. Find out more at the **Burdekin visitor centre** (📞4783 5988; www.burdekintourism.com. au; Plantation Park, Bruce Hwy; ☉9am-4pm) on the southern side of town.

Yongala Dive (📞4783 1519; www.yongaladive.com.au; 56 Narrah St, Alva Beach) does dive trips ($220 including gear) out to the *Yongala* wreck from Alva Beach, 17km northeast of Ayr. It only takes 30 minutes to get out to the wreck from here, instead of a 2½-hour boat trip from Townsville. Book ahead for backpacker-style accommodation at its onshore **dive lodge** (dm/d $27/65; @), with free pick-ups from Ayr.

NORTH OF TOWNSVILLE

As you leave Townsville, you also leave the Dry Tropics. The scorched-brown landscape slowly gives way to sugarcane plantations lining the highway and tropical rainforest shrouding the hillsides.

Waterfalls, national parks and small villages hide up in the hinterland, including **Paluma Range National Park** (part of the Wet Tropics World Heritage Area); DERM offices and visitor centres in the area have leaflets outlining walking trails, swimming holes and camping grounds.

The area north of Townsville was hardest hit by Cyclone Yasi in February 2011 (and by Cyclone Larry in 2006), with damage to the coastline, islands, national parks and farmland.

Ingham & Around

📞07 / POP 6127

Laid-back Ingham is the proud guardian of the 120-hectare **Tyto wetlands** (Tyto Wetlands Information Centre; 📞4776 4792; www. hinchinbrooknq.com.au; cnr Cooper St & Bruce Hwy; ☉8.45am-5pm Mon-Fri, 9am-4pm Sat & Sun), which has 4km of walking trails and attracts around 230 species of birds, including far-flung guests from Siberia and Japan, as well as hundreds of wallabies at dawn and dusk. From the visitor centre, a wheelchair-accessible boardwalk leads across the lagoon to the stylish cafe/restaurant **Pepper for Passion @ Tyto** (📞4776 6212; 24-30 Macrossan Ave; mains $16.50-25; ☉10am-4pm Mon-Thu, to 9pm Fri & Sat, 8am-4pm Sun; ⓐ).

Ingham is the jumping-off point for a trip out to magnificent **Wallaman Falls**, the longest single-drop waterfall in Australia at 305m. Located in **Girringun National Park**, 51km southwest of the town (sealed except for 10km), the falls look their best in the Wet, though are spectacular at any time, with camping and walking trails nearby – pick up a leaflet from the Tyto Wetlands Information Centre.

Mungalla Station (📞4777 8718; www. mungallaaboriginaltours.com.au; Forrest Beach, Allingham; 2hr tours adult/child $40/10), located 15km east of Ingham, runs insightful Aboriginal-led tours, including boomerang throwing and stories from the local Nywaigi culture. Definitely book in for a traditional **Kup Murri** ($80/20, including tour) lunch of meat and vegies that are wrapped in banana leaves and cooked underground in an earth 'oven'. If you have a self-contained caravan or a campervan, you can **camp** (per van $10) overnight.

In mid-May the **Australian Italian Festival** (www.australianitalianfestival.com.au) celebrates the fact that 60% of Ingham residents are of Italian descent, with pasta flying, wine flowing and music playing over three days.

TOP CHOICE **Noorla Heritage Resort** (📞4776 1100; www.hotelnoorla.com.au; 5-9 Warren St; unpowered/powered sites $15/22, dm $28, d $139, without bathroom $89; ❄🛜🏊) was once the domain of Italian cane cutters. These days, Ingham's wonderful 1920s art deco guesthouse has magnificently restored high-ceilinged rooms, plus cheaper container-style rooms in the garden. A photo montage of local stories lines the walls, bringing its history to life, as do the stories told around its aqua-tiled, guest-only bar.

A main-street icon with a statue of a mounted horseman on the roof, good old Aussie pub **Lees Hotel** (📞4776 1577; www. leeshotel.com.au; 58 Lannercost St; s/d $55/65; ❄🛜) occupies the site of the Day Dawn Hotel of 'Pub Without Beer' fame (based on the poem by 1882-born Ingham native, poet Dan Sheahan, which was the inspiration for late Australian country-music icon Slim Dusty's 1956 song, 'Pub With No Beer'). The en suite rooms, while not flash, are perfectly accept-

You don't have to venture too far inland for a taste of the dry, dusty Queensland outback – a stark contrast to the verdant coast. This detour is easily accessible on a day trip from Townsville, but it's worth staying overnight if you can.

Along the Flinders Hwy, a turn-off at Mingela, 88km southwest of Townsville, leads 40km south to the tiny gold-mining village of **Ravenswood** (population 150), with a couple of gorgeous turn-of-the-20th-century pubs with basic (share bathroom) accommodation.

A further 47km west along the Flinders Hwy from Mingela is the historic gold-rush town of **Charters Towers** (population 7979). The 'towers' are its surrounding tors (hills). William Skelton Ewbank Melbourne (WSEM) Charters was the gold commissioner during the rush, when the town was the second-largest, and wealthiest, in Queensland. With about 100 mines, some 90 pubs and a stock exchange, it became known simply as 'the World'.

Today, a highlight of a visit to the Towers is strolling past its glorious facades recalling the grandeur of those heady days, and listening to locals' ghost stories.

History oozes from the walls of the 1890 **Stock Exchange Arcade**, next door to the **Charters Towers visitor centre** (☑4752 0314; www.charterstowers.qld.gov.au; 74 Mosman St; ⊙9am-5pm). The visitor centre has a free brochure outlining the **One Square Mile Trail** of the town centre's beautifully preserved 19th-century buildings. The centre books all tours in town, including the **Venus Gold Battery** (Millchester Rd; tours adult/child $12/6; ⊙10am-3pm), where gold-bearing ore was crushed and processed, and which cranks into action during mid-July's **Gold Fever Festival**.

Come nightfall, panoramic **Towers Hill**, the site where gold was first discovered, is the atmospheric setting for a free **open-air cinema** showing the 20-minute film *Ghosts After Dark* – check seasonal screening times with the visitor centre.

In-town accommodation includes the period furniture–filled former pub, the **Royal Private Hotel** (☑4787 8688; 100 Mosman St; d $90 115, s/d without bathroom $45/55; ❄️🛜). A venture to Charters Towers is incomplete without scoffing one of the award-winning pies at **Towers Bakery** (114 Gill St; pies $3.90-4.30; ⊙5am-3pm Mon-Fri, to 1pm Sat).

Greyhound Australia (☑1300 473 946; www.greyhound.com.au) has four weekly services between Townsville and Charters Towers ($36, 1¾ hours).

The **Queensland Rail** (☑1300 131 722; www.traveltrain.com.au) *Inlander* train runs twice weekly between Townsville and Charters Towers ($28, three hours).

able, and it serves decent meals (mains $10-27.50; ⊙lunch & dinner Mon-Sat) and, yes, beer.

Greyhound Australia (☑1300 473 946; www.greyhound.com.au; Townsville/Cairns $39/63) and **Premier** (☑13 34 10; www.premierms.com.au; Townsville/Cairns $26/34) buses stop in Ingham on their Cairns–Brisbane runs.

Ingham sits along the **Queensland Rail** (☑1300 131 722; www.traveltrain.com.au) Brisbane–Cairns train line.

Lucinda

☑07 / POP 448

The big reason camera-wielding tourists head to little Lucinda, 27km northeast of Ingham, is to snap a photo of its 5.76km-long jetty. The roofed structure, with a continuous conveyor belt running its length, is the world's longest bulk sugar-loading jetty, allowing enormous carrier ships to dock. Public access is off limits but it's an impressive sight nonetheless.

Offshore, Hinchinbrook Island is seemingly within touching distance. You can take a four-hour cruise along the Deluge Inlet or a 2½-hour tour along the channel with **Hinchinbrook Wilderness Safaris** (☑4777 8307; www.hinchinbrookwildernesssafaris.com.au; inlet/channel cruise $80/60), which also offers transfers to Hinchinbrook for hikers to/from the southern end of the Thorsborne Trail.

Fishing is a popular pastime at Lucinda. Pick up bait and tackle (and great seafood) at the **Lucinda Jetty Store & Take-Away** (☑4777 8280; 2 Rigby St; mains $15.50-19.50; ⊙6am-7pm). Friendly staff have an encyclopedic knowledge of the jetty's operations and the sweetest fishing spots.

Ingham's Tyto Wetlands Information Centre can help book accommodation in Lucinda, or head 1.5km up the road to **Hinchinbrook Marine Cove** (☑4777 8377; www.hinchin-

DON'T MISS

MANGO MANIA

Frosty Mango (✆4770 8184; www.frostymango.com.au; Bruce Hwy, Mutarnee; dishes $6-15; ⏰8am-6pm; 🅿) Break your journey 70km north of Townsville for everything and anything to do with mangoes: fresh-squeezed mango juice, mango muffins with mango jam and cream, mango trifle and scrumptious mango ice cream, as well as fresh-picked fruit from just $1. Hot dishes include jackfruit curry.

brookmarinecove.com.au; Dungeness; d $125, cabin $150-195; ✳✳), overlooking a busy little fishing port, with airy, contemporary rooms and cabins, as well as a **cafe** (dishes $5-15; ⏰7am-6pm Mon-Fri, 6am-6pm Sat & Sun) and **restaurant** (mains $22-30; ⏰dinner Wed-Sat). It also rents out **houseboats** (from $415 for 2 days/1 night) to cruise the waters at your own pace (no boat licence required).

Cardwell & Around

✆07 / POP 1250

Most of the Bruce Highway runs several kilometres inland from the coast, so it comes as something of a shock to see the sea lapping right next to the road as you pull into the small town of Cardwell – the closest access point to Hinchinbrook Island. Poor Cardwell took a beating from Cyclone Yasi, with many of the town's older homes smashed and the new marina switched to spin cycle.

⊙ Sights & Activities

Girringun National Park NATIONAL PARK
From the town centre, the **Cardwell Forest Drive** is a scenic 26km round trip through the national park, with lookouts, walking tracks and picnic areas signposted along the way. There are super swimming opportunities at **Attie Creek Falls**, as well as the aptly named **Spa Pool**, where you can sit in a hollow in the rocks as water gushes over you.

Cardwell's visitor centre has brochures detailing other walking trails and swimming holes in the park.

FREE **Historic Cardwell Post Office & Telegraph Station** MUSEUM
(53 Victoria St; ⏰10am-1pm Mon-Fri, 9am-noon Sat) Check out the original postal room

and old telephone exchange at this 1870-built wooden building, which has survived cyclones and termites.

Girringun Aboriginal Art Centre GALLERY
(http://girringunaboriginalart.com.au; 235 Victoria St; ⏰8.30am-5pm Mon-Thu, to 2pm Fri) Traditional woven baskets are among the works for sale at this corporation of Aboriginal artists.

🛌 Sleeping & Eating

Mudbrick Manor B&B $$
(✆4066 2299; www.mudbrickmanor.com.au; Lot 13 Stony Creek Rd; s/d $90/120; ✳✳) Hand-built from mud bricks, natural timber and stone, this family home has huge, beautifully appointed rooms grouped around a fountained courtyard. Rates include hot breakfast; book at least a few hours ahead for delicious three-course dinners (per person $30).

Beachcomber CARAVAN PARK $
(✆4066 8550; www.cardwellbeachcomber.com.au; 43a Marine Pde; unpowered/powered sites $25/30, motel d $75-100, cabins & studios $90-110; ✳@🛰✳) There's a happy holiday vibe at this large park, where accommodation includes snazzy new studios with timber decks and bright, tropical cafe. Its licensed **restaurant** (mains $24.40-36.50; ⏰breakfast daily, lunch & dinner Mon-Sat) is the best in town, serving the likes of rosemary-crusted lamb, slow-roasted pork, and sweet-and-sour flathead, plus pizzas.

Kookaburra Holiday Park CARAVAN PARK $
(✆4066 8648; www.kookaburraholidaypark.com.au; 175 Bruce Hwy; unpowered/powered sites $22/29, dm/s/d $25/45/50, cabins $65, en suite units $85-105; ✳@✳) Well-run park that lends guests fishing rods, prawn nets and crab pots to catch dinner.

Cardwell Central Backpackers HOSTEL $
(✆4066 8404; www.cardwellbackpackers.com.au; 6 Brasenose St; dm $20; @🛰✳) Friendly hostel with partitioned dorms in former squash courts with high ceilings. Caters mostly to banana and prawn workers (management helps find work), but accepts overnighters. Free internet and pool table.

ℹ Information

The **DERM Rainforest & Reef Centre** (✆4066 8601; www.derm.qld.gov.au; Bruce Hwy; ⏰8.30am-5pm Mon-Fri, 9am-3pm Sat & Sun Apr-Oct, to 1pm Sat & Sun Nov-Mar; @), next to Cardwell's jetty, has an interactive rainforest display and detailed info on Hinchinbrook Island and other nearby national parks.

Getting There & Away

Greyhound Australia (☎1300 473 946; www.greyhound.com.au; Cairns/Townsville $47/49) and **Premier** (☎13 34 10; www.premierms.com.au; Cairns/Townsville $30/26) buses on the Brisbane–Cairns route stop at Cardwell.

Cardwell is on the Brisbane–Cairns train line; contact **Queensland Rail** (☎1300 131 722; www.traveltrain.qr.com.au) for details.

Boats depart for Hinchinbrook Island from Port Hinchinbrook Marina, 2km south of town.

Hinchinbrook Island

Its resort might have closed, but Australia's largest island national park remains a holy grail for walkers. Granite mountains rise dramatically from the sea; rugged Mt Bowen (1121m) is the 399-sq-km island's highest peak. The mainland side is dense with lush tropical vegetation, while long sandy beaches and tangles of mangrove curve around the eastern shore. Hinchinbrook's rainforest sustained a considerable amount of damage during Cyclone Yasi. The island was closed at the time of writing but should be reopened by the time you read this.

Hinchinbrook's highlight is the **Thorsborne Trail** (also known as the East Coast Trail), a 32km coastal track from Ramsay Bay past Zoe Bay, with its beautiful waterfall, to George Point at the southern tip. **DERM campsites** (☎13 74 68; www.derm.qld.gov.au; per person $5.15) are interspersed along the route. It's recommended that you take three nights to complete the challenging trail; return walks of individual sections are also possible. A maximum of 40 walkers are allowed to traverse the trail at any one time. DERM recommends booking a year ahead for a place during the high season and six months ahead for other dates. Cancellations are not unheard of, so it's worth asking if you've arrived without a booking.

Cardwell's Rainforest & Reef Centre stocks the imperative *Thorsborne Trail* brochure and screens the 15-minute *Without a Trace* video, which walkers are required to view.

Hinchinbrook Island Ferries (☎4066 8585; www.hinchinbrookferries.com.au) runs a service from Cardwell's Port Hinchinbrook Marina to Hinchinbrook's Ramsay Bay boardwalk (one way $85, 1½ hours). It also operates a five-hour **day tour** (adult/child $99/50; ⏲daily Easter-Sep, Wed, Fri & Sun Oct-Easter), including a cruise between Goold and Garden Islands, spotting dolphins, dugongs and turtles and docking at Ramsay Bay boardwalk for a walk on the 9km-long beach and picnic lunch.

Thorsborne Trail walkers can pick up a one-way transfer back to the mainland with **Hinchinbrook Wilderness Safaris** (☎4777 8307; www.hinchinbrookwildernesssafaris.com.au; one way $50) from George Point at the southern end of the trail.

Tully

☎07 / POP 2457

A 7.9m **golden gumboot** at the entrance to Australia's wettest town boasts that Tully received 7.9m of rain in 1950. Climb the spiral staircase to the viewing platform up top to get a sense of just how much that is! All that rain ensures plenty of raftable rapids on the nearby Tully River – see p440.

The **Tully Visitor & Heritage Centre** (☎4068 2288; Bruce Hwy; ⏲8.30am-4.45pm Mon-Fri, 9am-3pm Sat & Sun) has a brochure outlining a self-guided **heritage walk** around town, with 17 interpretative panels including one dedicated to Tully's UFO sightings, and **walking trail** maps for the nearby national parks.

Book at the visitor centre for 90-minute **Tully Sugar Mill Tours** (adult/child $12/8; ⏲daily late Jun-early Nov). Tour times depend on seasonal conditions; wear closed shoes and a shirt with sleeves.

Practically all accommodation in Tully is geared for banana workers, with cheap weekly rates and help finding farm work – try the excellent **Banana Barracks** (☎4068 0455; www.bananabarracks.com; 50 Butler St; dm without/with bathroom $24/26, bungalows $60; @🛜🏊) bang in the town centre, which is also the hub of Tully's nightlife, with an on-site **nightclub** (⏲Thu, Fri & Sat).

Tully's pubs serve hearty meals (except Sundays), while **Joe's Pizza Parlour** (☎4068 1996; 46 Butler St; pizzas $11.30-21; ⏲dinner, days vary) has steaming, thick-crust old-school pizzas.

Greyhound Australia (☎1300 473 946; www.greyhound.com.au, Cairns/Townsville $22/54) and **Premier** (☎13 34 10; www.premierms.com.au; Cairns/Townsville $26/30) buses stop in town on the Brisbane–Cairns route. Tully is also on the Queensland Rail (☑1300 131 722; www.traveltrain.qr.com.au) Brisbane–Cairns train line.

Mission Beach

☑07 / POP 2594

Less than 30km east of the Bruce Hwy's rolling sugar-cane and banana plantations, the hamlets that make up greater Mission Beach are hidden amongst World Heritage rainforest. The rainforest extends right to the Coral Sea, giving this 14km-long palm-fringed stretch of secluded inlets and wide, empty beaches the castaway feel of a tropical island.

Cyclone Yasi made landfall at Mission Beach, stripping much of the rainforest and vegetation bare. However, the communities here certainly recovered quickly – within two weeks, water and power was restored and most businesses and tourist operators were running normally.

Although collectively referred to as Mission Beach or just 'Mission', the area comprises a sequence of individual hamlets strung along the coast. **Bingil Bay** lies 4.8km north of **Mission Beach proper** (sometimes called North Mission). **Wongaling Beach** is 5km south; from here it's a further 5.5 kilometres south to **South Mission Beach**. Most amenities are in Mission prop-

er and Wongaling Beach; South Mission Beach and Bingil Bay are mainly residential.

One of the closest access points to the Great Barrier Reef, and the gateway to Dunk Island, walking tracks fan out around Mission Beach, with Australia's highest density of cassowaries (around 40) roaming the rainforest.

◉ Sights & Activities

Adrenalin junkies flock to Mission Beach for extreme and water-based sports, including white-water rafting on the nearby Tully River. And, if you've got your own board, Bingil Bay is one of the rare spots inside the reef where it's possible to surf, with small but consistent swells of around 1m.

Stinger enclosures at Mission Beach and South Mission Beach provide safe year-round swimming.

Skydiving   SKYDIVING

Mission Beach is one of the most popular spots in Queensland for skydiving. Two outfits will take you up: **Jump the Beach** (☑1800 444 568; www.jumpthebeach.com.au; 9000/11,000/14,000ft tandem dives $249/310/334) and **Skydive Mission Beach** (☑1800 800 840; www.skydivemissionbeach.com; 9000/11,000/14,000ft tandem dives $249/310/334). Both use the soft sand to cushion your landing.

Calypso Dive & Snorkel   DIVING

(☑4068 8432; www.calypsodive.com; Wongaling Beach Rd, Wongaling Beach) Calypso runs reef dives (from $264, including gear), wreck dives of the *Lady Bowen* ($245), and three-day PADI open-water courses ($625). Alternatively, you can snorkel the reef ($169) or take a **jet-ski tour** around Dunk Island (from $224).

Spirit of the Rainforest   CULTURAL TOURS

(☑4088 9161; www.echoadventure.com.au; 4hr tour adult/child $80/60; ◷Tue, Thu & Sat) Local Aboriginal guides offer a unique insight into the ancient rainforest, creeks, waterholes and waterfalls around Mission Beach, including plant and animal life, and Dreaming stories. Prices include pick-ups from Mission Beach.

Mission Beach Adventure Centre

WATER SPORTS

(☑0429 469 330; www.missionbeachadventurecentre.com.au; Seaview St, Mission Beach) This little hut by the beach runs the gamut of water and beach sports, including kayak hire (single/double per hour $15/30), three-hour

---

DON'T MISS

TULLY RIVER RAFTING

The Tully River provides thrilling white water year-round thanks to the country's highest rainfall and the river's hydroelectric floodgates. Rafting trips are timed to coincide with the daily release of the floodgates, resulting in grade-four rapids, with stunning rainforest scenery as a backdrop.

Day trips with **Raging Thunder Adventures** (☑4030 7990; www.ragingthunder.com.au/rafting.asp; standard/'xtreme' trip $185/215) or **R'n'R White Water Rafting** (☑4041 9444; www.raft.com.au; $185) include a barbecue lunch and transport from Tully or nearby Mission Beach. It only costs an extra $10 for transfers from Cairns and as far north as Palm Cove, but you'll save yourself several tedious hours' return bus ride if you pick up a trip here.

Looking like something out of *Jurassic Park,* a flightless prehistoric bird struts through the rainforest. It's as tall as a grown man, has three razor-sharp, dagger-style clawed toes, a bright-blue head, red wattles (the lobes hanging from its neck), a helmet-like horn and shaggy black feathers similar to an emu's. Meet the cassowary, an important link in the rainforest ecosystem. It's the only animal capable of dispersing the seeds of more than 70 species of trees whose fruit is too large for other rainforest animals to digest and pass (which acts as fertiliser). You're most likely to see cassowaries in the wild around Mission Beach, Etty Bay and the Cape Tribulation section of the Daintree National Park. They can be aggressive, particularly if they have chicks. Do not approach them; if one threatens you, don't run – give the bird right-of-way and try to keep something solid between you and it, preferably a tree.

There are thought to be between 1500 and 2500 cassowaries in the wild north of Queensland. An endangered species, the cassowary's biggest threat is loss of habitat, and most recently the cause has been natural. Tropical Cyclone Yasi stripped much of the rainforest around Mission Beach bare, threatening the struggling population with starvation. The birds are also exposed to the elements and more vulnerable to dog attacks and being killed by cars as they venture out in search of food. A conservation effort was launched soon after Cyclone Yasi hit in February 2011, with remote feeding stations established at some 80 locations around Mission Beach, Tully, Cardwell and Etty Bay, as well as aerial food drops. Experience suggests it will take the rainforest at least 12 months to sufficiently recover as a food resource.

Next to the Mission Beach visitor centre, there are cassowary conservation displays at the **Wet Tropics Environment Centre** (☑4068 7197; www.wettropics.gov.au; Porter Promenade, Mission Beach; ◷10am-4pm, hrs can vary), staffed by volunteers from the **Community for Cassowary & Coastal Conservation** (C4; www.cassowaryconservation.asn. au). Proceeds from gift-shop purchases go towards buying cassowary habitat. The website www.savethecassowary.org.au is also a good source of info. **Rainforest Rescue** (www.rainforestrescue.org.au) is a conservation NGO working with government authorities in the campaign to save the cassowary.

kayak tours ($60), stand-up board hire (per hour $15), and, when the wind's up, blokarting (per half-hour/hour $30/50). Its **cafe** (dishes $5-8.50) is famed for its hot dogs.

Walking
WALKS

Rainforest walks are your best chance to spot a cassowary, especially early morning. The visitor centre stocks walking guides detailing trails in the area.

Coral Sea Kayaking
KAYAKING

(☑4068 9154; www.coralseakayaking.com; half-/ full-day tours $77/128) Paddle over to Dunk Island for the day or bob around the coastline for half a day.

Fishin' Mission
FISHING

(☑4088 6121; www.fishinmission.com.au; half-/ full-day tours $130/190) Half-day island fishing trips and full-day reef fishing trips with local anglers.

Mission Beach Tropical Fruit Safari
FOOD TASTING

(☑4068 7099; www.missionbeachtourism.com; Mission Beach Visitor Centre, Porter Promenade;

admission $4; ◷1-2pm Mon & Tue) Tastings and presentations of tropical fruits from the surrounding region.

🎊 Festivals & Events

Markets
MARKETS

Local arts, crafts, jewellery, tropical fruit, homemade gourmet goods and more overflow from stalls at the **Mission Beach Markets** (opposite Hideaway Holiday Village caravan park; ◷1st & 3rd Sun of month). An even bigger range of goods, including handmade log furniture, is for sale at the **Mission Beach Rotary Market** (Marcs Park, Cassowary Dr, Wongaling Beach; ◷last Sun of month Apr-Nov).

Mission Beach Film Festival
FILM

(www.missionbeachfilmfestival.com.au) Outdoor screenings, guest speakers, Q&A panels and short film comps over three days in mid-September.

Mission Evolve Music Fest
MUSIC

(www.missionevolvemusicfest.com) Two days of live music in mid-October featuring blues,

N
0   1 km
0   0.5 miles

Clump Pt
Jetty
To Dunk
Island
Clump Pt
Alexander Dr
Boyett Rd
Mission
Beach
Endeavour Ave
Porter Prm
Licuala
State
Forest
El Arish - Mission Beach Rd
MISSION
BEACH
To Bruce Hwy (13km);
El Arish (13km)
Seaview St
Seaview St
Pacific Pde
Stinger
Enclosure
CORAL
SEA
Causeway Dr
Conch St
To Wongaling
Beach (3km)

roots, soul, funk and other musos from around Far North Queensland.

🛏 Sleeping

Holiday house and apartment rentals proliferate throughout the area – the visitor centre has a list of booking agents. Hostels have courtesy bus pick-ups.

SOUTH MISSION BEACH

Elandra RESORT $$$
TOP CHOICE
(☑4068 8154; www.elandraresorts.com; 1 Explorer Dr; d $270, ste $370-520; ❈@🛜🏊) Mission's most upmarket resort isn't snooty in the slightest, with a breezy, beachy vibe. All 52 contemporary rooms at this secluded piece of paradise front the ocean and most have balconies to take full advantage of the views. Interiors have sparing African and Asian decor (headdresses, carvings and raised soapstone basins), and the huge Dunk Island–facing decked pool area houses

the Elandra's fabulous restaurant and cocktail bar.

WONGALING BEACH

Hibiscus Lodge B&B B&B $$
(☑4068 9096; www.hibiscuslodge.com.au; 5 Kurrajong Close; r $95-120; ❈🏊) Wake to the sound of birds chirping and, more than likely, spot a cassowary or two during breakfast on the rainforest-facing deck of this lovely B&B. Each of its three rooms have en suites; you can play croquet on the pitch out front.

Scotty's Mission Beach House HOSTEL $
(☑1800 665 567, 4068 8676; www.scottysbeachhouse.com.au; 167 Reid Rd; dm $24-29, d $71, without bathroom $61; ❈@🛜🏊) Clean, comfy rooms (including girls-only dorms with Barbie-pink sheets) are grouped around Scotty's grassy pool area – a great spot for catching some rays. Out front, **Scotty's Bar & Grill** (mains $10-30; ☺dinner), open to non-

Mission Beach

Activities, Courses & Tours

guests, has something happening virtually every night, from fire-twirling shows to pool comps and live music.

Licuala Lodge B&B $$
(☑4068 8194; www.licualalodge.com.au; 11 Mission Circle; s/d $99/130; 🕸🖼) State-of-the-art B&B with a guest kitchen, complimentary beer, soft drinks and fruit juices, and a resident teddy bear in each of its five rooms.

Absolute Backpackers HOSTEL $
(☑4068 8317; www.absolutebackpackers.com. au; Wongaling Beach Rd; dm $22-26, d $56; 🕸@🛜🖼) Well-managed, relaxed hostel with a hammock-festooned pool area, airy rooms, music piped into the bathrooms and a 24-hour kitchen. You can BYO drinks onto the premises.

MISSION BEACH
Mission Beach Ecovillage CABINS $$
(☑4068 7534; www.ecovillage.com.au; Clump Point Rd; d $145-190; 🕸🛜🖼) It's not eco-certified, but with its own banana and lime trees scattered around its tropical gardens and a direct path through the rainforest to the beach, this 'ecovillage' makes the most of its environment. Higher-priced bungalows have spas, and there's a brilliant free-form pool and licensed **restaurant** (mains $18.50; ⊙dinner Tue-Sat).

Castaways Resort & Spa RESORT $$
(☑1800 079 002, 4068 7444; www.castaways. com.au; Pacific Pde; d $145-185, 1-/2-bedroom unit $205/295; 🕸@🛜🖼) Castaways' cheapest rooms don't have balconies, so it's worth splashing out a bit more for one of the 'Coral Sea' rooms with an extended deck and day bed. Even the units are small, but perks include two elongated pools, a luxurious **spa** (www.driftspa.com.au) and live entertainment at its **bar/restaurant** (mains $12-32; ⊙breakfast, lunch & dinner).

Sejala on the Beach CABINS $$$
(☑4088 6699; http://missionbeachholidays.com. au/sejala; 26 Pacific Pde; d $239; 🕸🖼) Three huts (go for the two facing the beach) with rainforest showers, decks with private BBQs and loads of character.

Rainforest Motel MOTEL $$
(☑4068 7556; www.missionbeachrainforestmotel. com; 9 Endeavour Ave; s/d $89/109; 🕸@🛜🖼) If only all motels could be like this. Set back from the road, these immaculate, tiled rooms come with coffee infusions and quality shampoos, with free bikes available.

Hideaway Holiday Village CARAVAN PARK $
(☑1800 687 104, 4068 7104; http://mission-beachhideaway.com.au; 58-60 Porter Promenade; unpowered/powered sites $29/35, cabins $105, without bathroom $85; 🕸@🛜🖼) Shady, central park backing onto rainforest and overlooking the beach. Grassy sites and cabins are well spaced and amenities are in tip-top condition.

Mission Beach Retreat HOSTEL $
(☑4088 6229; www.missionbeachretreat.com. au; 49 Porters Promenade; dm $21-24, d $56; 🕸@🛜🖼) Escape the party scene at this intimate 35-bed beachfront backpacker spot.

BINGIL BAY
Sanctuary CABINS $
(☑4088 6064, 1800 777 012; www.sanctu-aryatmission.com; 72 Holt Rd; dm $35, s/d huts $65/70, s/d cabins $145/160; ⊙mid-Apr-mid-Dec; @🛜🖼) Reached by a steep 600m-long rainforest walking track from the car park (4WD pick-up available), you can sleep surrounded only by flyscreen on a platform in simple huts, or opt for en suite cabins whose glass-walled showers have floor-to-ceiling rainforest views. About 95% of the land is set aside for conservation; in addition to walks you can take a yoga class ($15), indulge in a massage (per hour $80), and cook in the

self-catering kitchen or dine on wholesome fare at the **restaurant** (mains $18.50-32.50; ⊛breakfast, lunch & dinner; ⊘). Eco-initiatives include its own sewerage system, rainwater and biodegradable detergents. Not suitable for kids under 11.

Treehouse HOSTEL $
(⊘4068 7137; www.treehousehostel.com.au; Frizelle Rd; unpowered sites $12, dm/d $25/55; @⊛⊘⊛) Musical instruments and no TV set the chilled-out scene at this timber pole-framed YHA-associated hostel high in the rainforest.

🍴 Eating & Drinking

The majority of bars and/or restaurants are clustered in Mission Beach proper along Porter Promenade and its adjoining spider's web of tiny walkways and arcades. There's a small supermarket here, and a huge Woolworths supermarket at Wongaling Beach, which also has a handful of eateries, bars and bottle shops.

SOUTH MISSION BEACH

Elandra MODERN AUSTRALIAN $$$
(⊘4068 8154; www.elandraresorts.com; 1 Explorer Dr; mains $28-42; ⊛breakfast, lunch & dinner; ⊘) Even if you can't afford a room at the Elandra resort, don't miss chef Kurt Goodban's stunning cuisine, such as wattle seed–spiced kangaroo or coconut-dusted squid with pawpaw and mango. Goodban uses local and/or organic produce and makes his own jams and pastries. If that's still beyond your budget, at least stop by for a sunset Mission Rumble cocktail of Frangelico, banana liqueur, banana ice cream and honey.

WONGALING BEACH

Cafe Rustica ITALIAN $$
(⊘4068 9111; Wongaling Beach Rd; mains $18-22; ⊛lunch Sun, dinner Wed-Sun; ⊘) Book ahead to dine on nearly a dozen authentic Italian pastas and almost two dozen types of traditional crispy-crusted pizzas accompanied by Italian wines in this contemporary corrugated-iron beach shack. Delicious desserts include homemade gelato. (Bring a torch, though, as its mood lighting is seriously dim.)

Spicy Thai Hut THAI $$
(⊘4068 9111; Shop 5, 2042 Tully Mission Beach Rd; mains $16-25; ⊛dinner Wed-Sun; ⊘) Mission Beach's best Thai is served up to eat in or take-away from this hip newcomer. Soups, stir fries and salads are all made fresh;

choose whether you want your curry mild, moderate or 'damn hot!'.

MISSION BEACH

TOP CHOICE **New Deli** CAFE $
(Shop 1, 47 Porter Promenade; mains $7.50-15.50; ⊛9.30am-6pm Sun-Fri; ⊘) Tuck into blueberry pancakes or smoked salmon and brie bagels for breakfast, or zucchini and fetta tart for lunch. Or stock up on goodies for a gourmet picnic at this aromatic gourmet deli/cafe where most produce is organic and everything is homemade, including scrumptious biscuits.

Early Birds Cafe CAFE $
(Shop 2, 46 Porter Promenade; mains $6-14.50; ⊛6am-3pm; ⊘) Early Birds' all-day tropical Aussie Brekkie of bacon and eggs, grilled tomato and local banana, toast, and tea or coffee goes down a treat after a morning swim.

Friends MODERN AUSTRALIAN $$
(⊘4068 7107; Porter Promenade; meals $6-14; ⊛dinner Fri-Tue) Fine dining (minus the dress code) with an elegant atmosphere and short, inventive, Mediterranean-accented menu. Vegetarians will struggle. Call for seasonal changes.

Coffee Tree CAFE $
(Shop 3, 47 Porter Promenade; dishes $3.50-6; ⊛9.30am-5pm Tue-Sun) Strong espresso, handmade chocolates and a tantalising array of cakes.

BINGIL BAY

Bingil Bay Cafe CAFE $$
(29 Bingil Bay Rd; mains $13.50-22; ⊛breakfast, lunch & dinner; ⊘) A lavender-painted landmark, this retro corner store has been transformed into a groovy licensed cafe with original aqua tiles, burgundy leather seats salvaged from vintage train carriages, and a menu spanning felafel wraps to fish and chips, German sausages with sauerkraut to seafood linguine. Groceries and ice creams to take to the beach are available on one side.

ℹ️ Information

The efficient **Mission Beach visitor centre** (⊘4068 7099; www.missionbeachtourism.com; Porters Promenade; ⊛9am-4.45pm Mon-Sat, 10am-4pm Sun; @) has reams of info in multiple languages.

Internet cafes with tour-booking desks include **Intermission@the Beach** (David St, Mission Beach; per 20min/hr $2/5; ⊛8.30am-6pm

Mon-Sat) and **Mission Beach Information Station** (www.missionbeachinfo.com; 4 Wongaling Shopping Ctr, Cassowary Dr, Wongaling Beach; per 20min/hr $2/5; ⊘9am-7pm).

ⓘ Getting There & Around

Greyhound Australia (☑1300 473 946; www.greyhound.com.au, Cairns/Townsville $21/40) and **Premier** (☑13 34 10; www.premierms.com.au, Cairns $19, Townsville $46) buses stop in Wongaling Beach next to the giant 'big cassowary'. **Sun Palm** (☑4087 2900; www.sunpalmtransport.com) has daily services that run to Cairns and Cairns airport ($49) as well as Innisfail and Tully.

The hail-and-ride **Mission Impossible Beach Shuttle** (www.calypsocoaches.com.au; day pass $8; ⊘Mon-Sat) runs roughly every hour between Bingil Bay and South Mission Beach, and also serves Tully (one way $10); the visitor centre has timetables.

Sugar Land Car Rentals (☑4068 8272; www.sugarland.com.au; 30 Wongaling Beach Rd, Wongaling Beach; ⊘8am-5pm) rents small cars from $59 per day.

Mission Beach Adventure Centre (p440) rents bikes (per half/full day $10/20).

Call ☑13 10 08 for a taxi.

Dunk Island

The water surrounding Dunk Island, just 4.5 kilometres southeast of Mission Beach proper, seems too blue to be true. It's the first thing you notice when you step off the ferry and onto the long jetty. As you make your way to terra firma and peer over the edge of the old wooden structure, myriad fish swarm below as if they take it upon themselves to be the island's unofficial welcoming party (and also offer fantastic fishing). Known to the Djiru Aboriginal people as Coonanglebah (the island of peace and plenty), Dunk is pretty much your ideal tropical island.

Dunk Island was severely battered by Cyclone Yasi in February 2011 and the resort was closed. At the time of writing, no bookings were being taken until at least late August. It's likely that there will be no regular day trips out to the island until the resort reopens – call ahead or check with the Mission Beach visitor centre for updates.

Walking trails crisscross (and almost circumnavigate) the island. There's good **snorkelling** over bommies at Muggy Muggy and great **swimming** at Coconut Beach.

Day-trippers can utilise a limited number of the resort's facilities with a **day pass** (adult/child $40/20), including a two-course lunch at one of the resort's excellent **cafes**.

The standard beachfront rooms at family-friendly **Dunk Island Resort** (☑4068 8199, reservations 1300 384 403, 4047 4740; www.dunk-island.com; s/d from $386/375 incl breakfast, lunch & dinner; ❋@◉⬙⬚) are just as nice as the more expensive beachfront suites. Permits for the **DERM campground** (☑13 74 68; www.derm.qld.gov.au; per person $5.15) need to be organised through the resort.

Air transfers to/from Cairns (adult/child return $390/290, 45 minutes, two daily) can be booked through the resort.

Calypso (☑4068 8432; www.calypsoadventures.com.au; adult/child same-day return $40/20, one way $25/12.50), departing from Mission Beach's Clump Point jetty, and **Mission Beach Dunk Island Water Taxi** (☑4068 8310; Banfield Pde, Wongaling Beach; adult/child return $35/18), departing from Wongaling Beach, make the 20-minute trip to Dunk Island. Calypso also operates an amphibious marine craft, **Sealegs** (adult/child return $30/15), which can pick up from a dozen departure points along Mission's beachfront and drop you over on Dunk.

Mission Beach to Innisfail

The road north from Mission Beach rejoins the Bruce Hwy at **El Arish** (population 232), home to not much bar a golf course and the memorabilia- and character-filled **El Arish Tavern** (38 Chauvel St), built in 1927.

From El Arish, you can take the more direct route north by continuing straight along the Bruce Hwy, with turn-offs leading to beach communities, including exquisite **Etty Bay**, surrounded by rocky headlands and rainforest, with cassowaries roaming along the shore, a large stinger enclosure and a simple but superbly sited caravan park.

Alternatively, detour west via the Old Bruce Hwy, also known as the **Canecutter Way** (www.canecutterway.com.au). At the tiny township of **Mena Creek** are the enchanting ruins of two once-grand castles at the five-hectare **Paronella Park** (☑4065 0000; www.paronellapark.com.au; Japoonvale Rd; adult/child $34/17; ⊘9am-7.30pm). Built in the 1930s to bring a whimsical entertainment centre to the area's hard-working folk, today the mossy Spanish ruins have an almost medieval feel, and walking trails lead through rambling gardens past a waterfall and swimming hole. Take the 45-minute daytime tour and/or one-hour night tour to hear the full, fascinating story. Admission includes both tours, as well as one night at its powered **campground**, or book in to one of the newly constructed timber **cabins** (d $75; 图), which share a brand-new bathroom block. Tickets to Paronella Park are valid for one year.

Innisfail & Around

📞07 / POP 8262

Just 80km south of the mayhem of Cairns, at the confluence of the North and South Johnstone Rivers, Innisfail is a buzzing regional hub with a real community feel and some gorgeous art deco architecture (Australia's largest concentration, no less).

Beachside Flying Fish Point is 8km northeast of Innisfail's town centre, while national parks, including the Mamu Rainforest Canopy Walkway, are within a short drive.

⊙ Sights & Activities

Johnstone River Crocodile Farm

CROCODILE FARM

(www.crocpark.com.au; Flying Fish Point Rd; adult/child $28/14; ⊙8.30am-4.30pm, feeding times 11am & 3pm) At this breeding facility for handbags and steak, frequent half-hour tours let you watch guides sit on one-tonne, 5m-long Gregory – the farm's fattest reptile – and meet its oldest, 90-year-old Johnny. Don't get so attached that you don't taste the croc skewers at the kiosk!

Wooroonooran National Park   NATIONAL PARK

The **Palmerston (Doongan) section** of Wooroonooran National Park is home to some of the oldest continually surviving rainforest in Australia; DERM has details of campgrounds and walking trails.

🌿**Mamu Rainforest Canopy Walkway**

NATURE WALK

(www.derm.qld.gov.au/mamu; Palmerston Hwy; adult/child $20/10; ⊙9.30am-5.30pm, last entry 4.30pm) About 27km along the Palmerston Hwy (signposted 4km northwest of Innisfail), this canopy-level rainforest walkway gives you eye-level views of the fruits, flowers and birds, and a bird's-eye perspective from its 100-step, 37m-high tower. Sustainable materials used in its construction include decking made from over 900,000 re-cycled 2L plastic milk bottles. Allow at least an hour to complete the 2.5km, wheelchair-accessible circuit.

The Palmerston Hwy continues west to Millaa Millaa, passing the entrance to the Waterfalls Circuit (p467).

Art Deco Architecture   ARCHITECTURE, WALKS

(www.artdeco-innisfail.com.au) Following a devastating 1918 cyclone, Innisfail rebuilt in the art deco style of the day, and 2006's Cyclone Larry resulted in many of these striking buildings being refurbished. Pick up a free **town walk brochure** from the visitor centre, detailing over two dozen key points of interest.

✱✲ Festivals & Events

Foodie fun during the four-day **Feast of the Senses** (www.feastofthesenses.com.au) in March includes food stalls and celebrity chefs.

⊨ Sleeping & Eating

Innisfail's hostels primarily cater to banana pickers who work the surrounding plantations; several offer weekly rates only (around $175 for a week's dorm accommodation); the visitor centre has a list.

Barrier Reef Motel   MOTEL $$

(⊇4061 4988; www.barrierreefmotel.com.au; Bruce Hwy; s/d $100/110, units $130-150; 图@全全) The best place to stay in Innisfail, this comfortable motel next to the visitor centre has 41 airy, tiled rooms with large bathrooms. If you're self-catering, book into one of the units with kitchenettes; otherwise head to the **restaurant** (mains $28-30.50; ⊙breakfast & dinner; 🅟) or just have a drink at the bar.

Codge Lodge   HOSTEL $

(⊇4061 8055; www.codgelodge.com; 63 Rankin St; dm $33; 图@全全) Housed in an atmospheric turn-of-the-20th-century Queenslander, with a wide timber verandah and rambling corridors, this cheerful hostel has plenty of farm workers bunking down for an extended stay, but also welcomes overnight travellers. Staff organise regular excursions (swimming, walks, fishing and crabbing).

Flying Fish Point Tourist Park

CARAVAN PARK $

(⊇4061 3131; www.ffpvanpark.com.au; 39 Elizabeth St, Flying Fish Point; unpowered/powered sites $26/31, dm $30, cabins & villas $85-105, without bathroom $50-65; 图@全全) Fish right off the beach across the road from this first-rate park, or organise boat rental through the friendly managers.

ROBERT STEPHENS: RANGER, MAMU RAINFOREST CANOPY WALKWAY

Mamu's origins?

Several sites had been under consideration for a rainforest walkway, then [Cyclone] Larry came along; he'd done the hard work for us, all the clearing – we just came in and cleaned it up. The construction helped inject money back into the Innisfail area. We planted 7000 trees, and another couple of thousand since it opened.

Relationship with the Ma:Mu people?

Ma:Mu represents five separate clans, including Waribara, whose land we're on; we've found quite a few artefacts here. We've got a traditional owner on staff and part of every entry fee goes back to the traditional owners. Long-term, it's anticipated the Ma:Mu people will take over from DERM and generate income and jobs from the project.

Typical tasks?

Weed and feral animal control, track and infrastructure maintenance, recording photo databases and assisting visitors. Previously I was a zoo keeper, so it's similar in terms of public awareness and education. I want to make a difference, fixing the problems of the past to preserve native species.

Job highlight?

I walk this track every day and see stuff on a daily basis that I haven't seen before. There's so much diversity.

Monsoon Cruising CAFE $
(☎0427 776 663; 1 Innisfail Wharf; mains $10-14; ⊙10am-5pm Wed-Sun year-round weather permitting; ⊉) Everything is locally sourced and/or organic aboard this moored cruiser – from bread baked fresh on the boat to black tiger prawns straight off the trawlers.

Flying Fish Point Cafe CAFE $
(9 Elizabeth St, Flying Fish Point; mains $13-19; ⊙7.30am-8.30pm; ⊉) You're doing well if you can finish the huge seafood baskets of battered and crumbed fish, barbecued calamari, wonton prawns, tempura scallops and more.

Oliveri's Continental Deli DELI $
(www.oliverisdeli.com.au; 41 Edith St; sandwiches $7.50-8.50; ⊙8.30am-5.30pm Mon-Fri, to 1pm Sat; ⊉) An Innisfail institution for decades, with over 60 varieties of European cheese, ham and salami and awesome sandwiches.

Roscoe's ITALIAN $$
(☎4061 6888; 3b Ernest St; mains $22-36, buffets $24-38.50; ⊙lunch & dinner) Hugely popular local haunt for its enormous buffets, complete with homemade desserts like tiramisu.

Innisfail Fish Depot SEAFOOD $
(51 Fitzgerald Esplanade; ⊙7.30am-6pm Mon-Fri, 8am-4pm Sat, 10am-4pm Sun) Fresh-as-it-gets fish to throw on the barbie and organic cooked prawns by the bagful (per kilo $18).

ⓘ Information

The **visitor centre** (☎4061 2655; www.innis-failtourism.com.au; cnr Eslick St & Bruce Hwy; ⊙9am-5pm Mon-Fri, 9.30am-12.30pm Sat, 10am-1pm Sun; ⊕) gives out discount vouchers for many of the area's attractions.

ⓘ Getting There & Away

Bus services operate once daily with **Premier** (☎13 34 10; www.premierms.com.au; Townsville/Cairns $52/19) and five times daily with **Greyhound Australia** (☎1300 473 946; www.greyhound.com.au; Townsville/Cairns $70/32) from Innisfail to Townsville (4½ hours) and Cairns (1½ hours). **Sun Palm** (☎4087 2900; www.sunpalmtransport.com) runs to Cairns ($35), including Cairns airport, and south as far as Tully ($25).

Innisfail is on the Cairns–Brisbane train line; contact **Queensland Rail** (☎1300 131 722; www.traveltrain.com.au) for information.

Cairns & the Daintree Rainforest

Why Go?

Cairns has a heady reputation as Australia's reef-diving capital, with dazzling marine life and coral-fringed islands a short boat ride offshore, and as tropical North Queensland's party central. Yet lush rainforest, waterfalls, volcanic-crater lakes and beach communities lie just beyond the city limits, as do the Atherton Tableland's gourmet food producers, farms and orchards.

The dramatic coastal drive winding from Cairns to the ritzy resort town of Port Douglas is the start of the Far North experience. But it's past the Daintree River that the adventure really begins. The magnificent Daintree National Park stretches up the coast, its rainforest tumbling right onto white-sand beaches. Further north, the Bloomfield Track from Cape Tribulation to Cooktown is one of Australia's great 4WD journeys.

The entire region is impressively – and at times overwhelmingly – geared for tourism. The only limitations are your budget and your imagination (not necessarily in that order!).

Best Places to Eat

» Mojo's (p474)
» Yorkeys Knob Boating Club (p461)
» Julaymba Restaurant (p480)
» Zinc (p472)

Best Places to Stay

» Crater Lakes Rainforest Cottages (p468)
» Tropic Days (p455)
» Sebel Reef House (p462)
» Mungumby Lodge (p482)

When to Go?

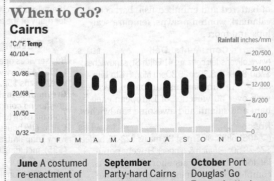

Cairns

°C/°F Temp

40/104 —
30/86 —
20/68 —
10/50 —
0/32 —

J F M A M J J A S O N D

Rainfall inches/mm
— 20/500
— 16/400
— 12/300
— 8/200
— 4/100
— 0

June A costumed re-enactment of Cook's landing is the centrepiece of the Cooktown Discovery Festival.

September Party-hard Cairns parties even harder during the Cairns Festival.

October Port Douglas' Go Troppo festival embraces the creativity of living in the tropics.

CAIRNS

POP 147,118

Cairns has come a long way from struggling cane town to international resort city. It may not have a beach, but the mudflats and mangroves along the Esplanade foreshore have been replaced with a multimillion-dollar development of parks and the dazzling saltwater lagoon, with top-quality restaurants overlooking the marina. And if you do want some sand, it's a short local bus ride or easy drive to the Cairns' Northern Beaches.

Old salts claim Cairns has sold its soul, but it has an infectious holiday vibe. The CBD (central business district) is more board shorts than briefcases – a mini-urban jungle of tour shops, booking agents, car-hire agents and internet cafes.

For many visitors, this is the end of the line on the East Coast jaunt (or the start for those flying into Cairns' international airport), and the city is awash with bars and nightclubs, as well as accommodation and eateries in all price ranges. It's a perfect place to meet other travellers, and to kick off your Far North experience.

Sights

Cairns Foreshore & Lagoon   SWIMMING
In the absence of a beach, sunbathers flock to Cairns' shallow but spectacular saltwater swimming lagoon (admission free; 6am-10pm Thu-Tue, noon-10pm Wed) on the city's reclaimed foreshore. The artificial 4800-sq-metre lagoon is patrolled by lifeguards and illuminated at night.

Northwest from the lagoon, the boardwalk promenade, stretching for almost 3km, has picnic areas, free barbecues and playgrounds lining the foreshore.

Reef Teach   INTERPRETIVE CENTRE
(4031 7794; http://reefteach.wordpress. com; 2nd fl, Main St Arcade, 85 Lake St; adult/child $15/8; lectures 6.30-8.30pm Tue-Sat) Before heading out to the reef, take your knowledge to greater depths at this excellent and informative centre, where marine experts explain how to identify specific types of coral and fish and how to treat the reef with respect.

Flecker Botanic Gardens   GARDEN
(4044 3398; www.cairns.qld.gov.au; Collins Ave, Edge Hill; admission free; 7.30am-5.30pm Mon-Fri, 8.30am-5.30pm Sat & Sun) These beautiful tropical gardens are an explosion of greenery and rainforest plants. Pick up a walks brochure from the information centre

(8.30am-5pm Mon-Fri) or ask about free guided walks. There's a great cafe here and an outdoor cinema (admission $10; 3rd Wed of month May-Nov) screening classic films.

Tanks Arts Centre   GALLERY
(4032 2349; www.tanksartscentre.com; 46 Collins Ave, Edge Hill; gallery 10am-4pm Mon-Fri) Three gigantic, ex-WWII fuel-storage tanks have been transformed into studios, galleries, showcasing local artists' work and an inspired performing-arts venue. There's a lively market day (last Sun of month Apr-Sep).

Cairns Regional Gallery   GALLERY
(www.cairnsregionalgallery.com.au; cnr Abbott & Shields Sts; adult/child under 16 $5/free; 10am-5pm Mon-Sat, 1-5pm Sun) In a colonnaded 1936-built heritage building, exhibitions at Cairns' acclaimed regional gallery reflect the consciousness of the tropical north region, with an emphasis on local and Indigenous works. The cafe-restaurant out front is excellent.

Tjapukai Cultural Park   CULTURAL CENTRE
(4042 9900; www.tjapukai.com.au; Kamerunga Rd, Smithfield; adult/child $35/18; 9am-5pm) Allow at least three hours at this Indigenous-owned cultural extravaganza. It incorporates the Creation Theatre, which tells the story of creation using giant holograms and actors, a Dance Theatre and a gallery, as well as boomerang- and spear-throwing demonstrations and turtle-spotting during a canoe ride on the lake. A fireside corroboree is the centrepiece of the Tjapukai by Night (adult/child $99/50; 7-10pm) dinner-and-show deal.

The park is about 15km north of the city centre, just off the Captain Cook Hwy near the Skyrail terminal; transfers are available (extra charge).

Centre of Contemporary Arts   GALLERY, THEATRE
(CoCA; 4050 9401; www.coca.org.au; 96 Abbott St; 10am-5pm Tue-Sat) CoCA houses the KickArts (www.kickarts.org.au) galleries of local contemporary visual art, as well as the Jute Theatre (www.jute.com.au) and the End Credits Film Club (www.endcredits.org.au).

Activities

Tour operators run adventure-based activities from Cairns, most offering transfers to/from your accommodation – see p453.

Great Adventures   BOAT TOURS
(4044 9944; www.greatadventures.com.au; 1 Spence St; adult/child $75/37.50) Runs day

Cairns & the Daintree Rainforest Highlights

1 Diving, snorkelling and swimming among the fish, turtles and anemones in the multicoloured corals of the Great Barrier Reef from Cairns (p453) or Port Douglas (p469)

2 Taking an Aboriginal guided walk and swimming in the crystal-clear waters of Mossman Gorge (p474)

3 Riding the Skyrail cable car through the rainforest to the market town of Kuranda (p464) and returning to Cairns by Scenic Railway

4 Barra fishing, barbecuing or simply watching the sun set during a cruise on Lake Tinaroo (p468)

CORAL SEA

To Lizard Island Group (80km)

Nob Pt

Endeavour River National Park

Endeavour Falls

Cooktown

Mt Cook National Park

Archer Pt

Trevathen Falls

Black Mountain National Park

Rossville

Helenvale

Lion's Den Hotel

Cedar Bay (Mangkal-Mangkalba) National Park

Annan River Gorge

Annan River

Endeavour River

Developmental Rd

Quinkan Reserve

Lakeland

Palmer River

Palmer River Roadhouse

Cooktown Developmental Rd

Peninsula Developmental Rd

McLeod River

Daintree National Park

Daintree Village

Daintree River

Mossman Gorge

Mossman

Miallo

Newell Beach

Port Douglas

Wonga Beach

Snapper Island National Park

Low Isles

Cow Bay

Thornton Beach

Myall Beach

Cape Tribulation

Emmagen Beach

Daintree National Park - Cape Tribulation Section

Bloomfield Track

Ayton

Wujal Wujal

Bloomfield Falls

Bloomfield River

Hope Islands

Endeavour Reef

Agincourt Reefs

Tongue Reef

Great Barrier Reef

N

0   25 km
0   10 miles

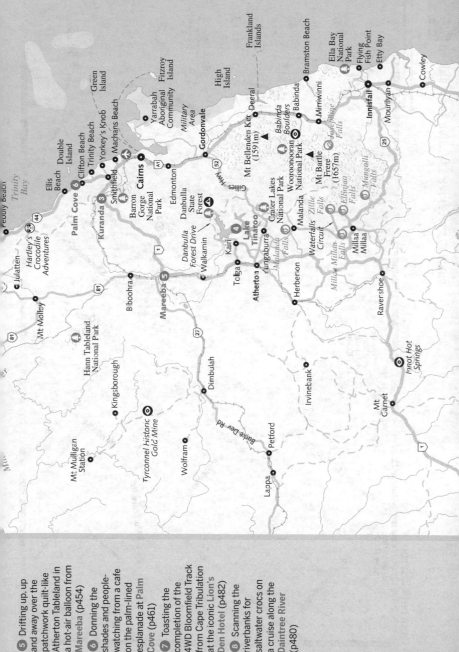

5 Drifting up, up and away over the patchwork quilt-like Atherton Tableland in a hot-air balloon from Mareeba (p454)

6 Donning the shades and people-watching from a cafe on the palm-lined esplanade at Palm Cove (p461)

7 Toasting the completion of the 4WD Bloomfield Track from Cape Tribulation at the iconic Lion's Den Hotel (p482)

8 Scanning the riverbanks for saltwater crocs on a cruise along the Daintree River (p480)

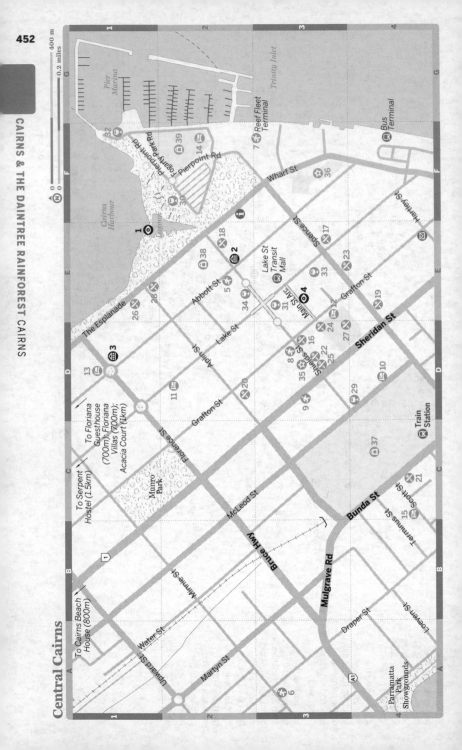

Central Cairns

trips to Green Island, off Cairns, with optional glass-bottomed boat and semisubmersible tours.

AJ Hackett Bungy & Minjin   BUNGY JUMPING
(☎1800 622 888; www.ajhackett.com; McGregor Rd, Smithfield; bungy jump/minjin swing $139/89, bungee & minjin swing combo $194; ⊙10am-5pm) Bungy jump from the purpose-built tower or swing from the trees on the minjin (a harness swing). All rates also include transfers.

🏃 Tours

A staggering 600-plus tours bus, boat, fly and drive out of Cairns each day. The following is but a taste of what's on offer. See p463 for tours to Green, Fitzroy and the Frankland Islands.

Great Barrier Reef

Reef trips generally include transport, lunch and snorkelling gear. Many have diving options including introductory dives requiring no prior experience. When choosing a tour, consider the vessel (catamaran or sailing ship), its capacity (from six to 300 people), what extras are offered and the destination. The outer reefs are more pristine; inner reef areas can be patchy – showing signs of damage from humans, coral bleaching and crown-of-thorns starfish. Of course, companies that are only licensed to visit the inner reef have cheaper tours; in most cases you pay for what you get.

In addition to day trips, a number of operators also offer multiday live-aboard trips, which include specialised dive opportunities, such as night diving. Dive course companies (p454) also offer tours.

Several dive boats offer helmet diving (from $140), which involves 'walking' on a submerged platform. Hoses attached to the helmet deliver air, so you can breathe normally – this option is ideal for nonswimmers, kids over 12 and anyone who doesn't like to get their hair wet.

Cod Hole, near Lizard Island, is one of Australia's premier diving locations, so extended live-aboard trips are mainly for keen certified divers.

Coral Princess
CRUISES
(☑1800 079 545, 4040 9999; www.coralprincess.com.au) Three-night cruises (from $1496 per person, twin share) between Cairns and Townsville, and four-night Cairns to Lizard Island return (from $1896).

Passions of Paradise
DIVING
(☑1800 111 346; www.passions.com.au; adult/child $139/89) Sexy sailing catamaran taking you to Michaelmas Cay and Paradise Reef for snorkelling or diving.

Silverswift
DIVING
(☑4044 9944; www.silverseries.com.au; adult/child from $167.50/125.50) Popular catamaran snorkelling/diving three outer reefs.

Sunlover
DIVING
(☑4050 1333; www.sunlover.com.au; adult/child from $180/65) Fast catamaran to a pontoon on the outer Moore Reef. Options include semisubmersible trips and helmet diving. Good for families.

Vagabond
YACHT
(☑4031 9959; www.vagabond-dive.com; 2-day tours from $290) Luxury yacht for 11 guests.

Taka Dive
DIVING
(☑4051 8722; www.takadive.com.au; 319 Draper St; 4/5/7-day tours from $1290/1610/2650) Dives the Cod Hole and the remote Os-

prey Reef. Also speciality courses, such as underwater photography.

Scenic Flights

Cairns Heliscenic
SCENIC FLIGHTS
(☑4031 5999; www.cairns-heliscenic.com.au; Pier Marketplace; 15/30-min flight per person from $220/295) Helicopter flights.

White-Water Rafting
The excitement level of white-water rafting down the Barron, Russell and North Johnstone Rivers is hitched to the season (the wetter the weather, the whiter your water). The Tully River has rapids year-round – see p440.

Trips are graded according to the degree of difficulty, from armchair rafting (Grade 1) to white knuckle (Grade 5).

Foaming Fury
WHITE-WATER RAFTING
(☑1800 801 540, 4031 3460; www.foamingfury.com.au) Full-day trips on the Russell River ($139); half-day on the Barron ($124), with options for kids aged over 10.

Ballooning & Skydiving

Hot Air Cairns
BALLOONING
(☑4039 9900; www.hotair.com.au; 30-min flight from $215)

Raging Thunder
BALLOONING
(☑4030 7990; www.ragingthunder.com.au; 30-min flight from $225)

Skydive Cairns
SKYDIVING
(☑1800 444 568; 4031 5466; www.skydivecairns.com.au; 59 Sheridan St; tandem jumps from

---

DIVE COURSES

Cairns is the scuba-diving capital of the Great Barrier Reef and a popular place to attain Professional Association of Diving Instructors (PADI) open-water certification. There's a plethora of courses on offer, from budget four-day courses that combine pool training and reef dives to five-day courses that include two days' pool theory and three days' living aboard a boat, diving less-frequented parts of the reef.

All operators require you to have a dive medical certificate, which they can arrange for around $50. Many operators also offer advanced courses for certified divers. Dive schools include the following:

Cairns Dive Centre
DIVING
(☑1800 642 591; 4051 0294; www.cairnsdive.com.au; 121 Abbott St) One of the cheapest operators, affiliated with Scuba Schools International (SSI) rather than PADI. There are live-aboard tours (two/three days $355/470) and day tours ($120).

Deep Sea Divers Den
DIVING
(☑1800 612 223, 4046 7333; www.diversden.com.au; 319 Draper St) Long-established school running multiday live-aboard courses and trips from $570.

Pro-Dive
DIVING
(☑1800 353 213; 4031 5255; www.prodivecairns.com; cnr Grafton & Shields Sts) One of Cairns' most experienced operators, offering a comprehensive, five-day learn-to-dive course incorporating a three-day live-aboard trip ($825).

9000ft $249) Licensed skydivers can jump solo for $50.

Atherton Tableland

Food Trail Tours FOOD
(☑4041 1522; www.foodtrailtours.com.au; adult/child from $154/77; ☺Mon-Sat) Taste your way around the Tableland visiting farms producing macadamias, tropical-fruit wine, cheese, chocolate and coffee.

On the Wallaby ACTIVITIES, NATURE
(☑4033 6575; www.onthewallaby.com; day/overnight tours $99/169) Excellent activity-based tours including cycling, hiking and canoeing.

Uncle Brian's Tours NATURE
(☑4033 6575; www.unclebrian.com.au; tour $109; ☺Mon-Wed, Fri & Sat) Lively small-group day trips covering forests, waterfalls and lakes.

Cape Tribulation & the Daintree

Billy Tea Bush Safaris ECOTOUR
(☑4032 0077; www.billytea.com.au; day trips adult/child $170/120) Exciting day ecotours to Cape Trib.

Tropics Explorer NATURE
(☑1800 801 540; www.tropicsexplorer.com.au; day tours from $119) Fun Cape Trib trips; overnight tours available.

Cooktown & Cape York

Adventure North Australia CULTURAL
(☑4053 7001; www.adventurenorthaustralia.com; 1-day tour $235) 4WD trips to Cooktown via the Bloomfield Track. Also multiday, fly-drive and Aboriginal cultural tours.

Undara Lava Tubes

Undara Experience ACTIVITIES, NATURE
(☑4097 1411; www.undara.com.au; 2-day tour adult/child $389/270) Coach tours to the world's longest continuous (though fragmented) lava tubes, staying in converted railway carriages.

✯✯ Festivals & Events

The regional **Cairns Festival** (www.festivalcairns.com.au) takes over the city for three jam-packed weeks in September each year with a packed program of performing arts, music, visual arts and family events, such as sand sculpting.

🛏 Sleeping

Cairns is a backpacker hotspot, with around 40 hostels, ranging from intimate converted

ⓘ DANGER: STINGERS & CROCS

From around late October to May, swimming in coastal waters is inadvisable due to the presence of box jellyfish, Irukandji and other marine stingers.

Saltwater crocodiles inhabit the mangroves, estuaries and open water. Warning signs are posted around the waterways where crocodiles might be present.

houses to hangar-sized resorts. The city's wealth of self-contained accommodation works well for groups or families, while dozens of virtually identical motels line up along Sheridan St. Most tour operators also pick up and drop off at Cairns' Northern Beaches accommodation.

TOP CHOICE **Tropic Days** HOSTEL $
(☑1800 421 521, 4041 1521; www.tropicdays.com.au; 28 Bunting St; camping/tent/dm $11/16/26, d $64-74; ❉@☏☲) Tucked behind the Showgrounds (with a courtesy bus into town), Cairns' best hostel is a haven of tropical gardens with hammocks, plus there's a pool table, spice-stocked kitchen, bunk-free dorms and a chilled vibe. Doubles share spotless bathrooms. Even nonguests can book for Monday night's croc, emu and roo barbecue ($12 including a didgeridoo show)

Floriana Guesthouse GUEST HOUSE $$
(☑4051 7886; www.florianaguesthouse.com; 183 The Esplanade; s $69, d $79-120; ❉@☏☲) Run by charismatic jazz musician Maggie, Cairns-of-old still exists at this old-fashioned guest house, which retains its original polished floorboards and Art Deco fittings. The swirling staircase leads to 10 individually decorated rooms. Some have bay windows with window seats, others have balconies, and all come with en suites.

Shangri-la HOTEL $$$
(☑4031 1411; www.shangri-la.com; Pierpoint Rd; r from $270; ❉@☏☲) In an unbeatable waterfront setting, towering over the marina, Shangri-la is Cairns' top hotel, a super-swish five-star that ticks all the boxes for location, views, facilities (including a gym and pool bar) and attentive service. The Horizon Club rooms are top notch.

Floriana Villas APARTMENTS **$$**
(☎4041 2637; www.florianavillas.com.au; 187-189
The Esplanade; 1/2-bedroom apt $140/180; ❄️❤️🛜🏊) Built by a Maltese family in the 1940s, this distinctive complex has been converted into enormous, contemporary self-contained apartments. There's free bike hire, a shaded pool with spa jets and a landscaped barbecue area. Minimum stay three nights.

Hotel Cairns HOTEL **$$$**
(☎4051 6188; www.thehotelcairns.com; cnr Abbott & Florence Sts; d $195-265; ❄️❤️🛜) There's a real tropical charm to this sprawling bone-white hotel, built in a traditional Queenslander plantation style. Rooms have an understated elegance and the huge 'tower' rooms and suites offer luxury touches, such as wicker chaise longues and private balconies. The bar has nightly piano and double bass performances.

Reef Palms APARTMENTS **$$**
(☎1800 815 421, 4051 2599; www.reefpalms.com.au; 41-47 Digger St; apt $125-145; ❄️@❤️🛜🏊) The crisp, white interiors of Reef Palms' apartments will have you wearing your sunglasses inside. All rooms have kitchen facilities; larger ones include a lounge area and a spa. Good for couples and families.

Serpent Hostel HOSTEL **$**
(☎1800 666 237, 4040 7777; www.serpenthostel.com; 341 Lake St; dm $24-28, d $55, en suite d $65-75; ❄️@❤️🛜🏊) About 2km north of the centre, this spiffing Nomads resort (*not* to be confused with Cairns' Nomads Esplanade) is a good-time backpacker bubble with a huge pool, beach volleyball, a sports bar, free evening meals and a free shuttle bus into town.

Acacia Court HOTEL **$$**
(☎1300 850 472; www.acaciacourt.com; 223-227 The Esplanade; d $120-145; ❄️❤️🛜🏊) A stroll along the foreshore from town, this waterfront high-rise's beachy touches, including bright aqua bedspreads and a choice of ocean or mountain views, make it great value for money. Most rooms have private balconies and its famed buffet restaurant Charlie's is downstairs.

Gilligan's HOSTEL **$**
(☎4041 6566; www.gilligansbackpackers.com.au; 57-89 Grafton St; dm $26-32, d $130; ❄️@❤️🛜🏊) The 'G spot' is pricey, impersonal and very loud, but all rooms at this flashpacker resort have en suites and most have balconies; higher-priced rooms come with fridges and TVs. It has several bars plus nightly entertainment, such as jelly wrestling; a beauty salon; and a gym to work off all that beer.

Travellers Oasis HOSTEL **$**
(☎4052 1377; www.travellersoasis.com.au; 8 Scott St; dm $26, s $45, d $64-74; ❄️❤️🛜🏊) Soulful 50-bed hang-out with handmade timber furniture, bunk-free dorms and a brand-new barbecue area. Private rooms share squeaky-clean bathrooms.

Cairns Holiday Park CARAVAN PARK **$**
(1800 259 977; 4051 1467; www.cairnscamping.com.au; 12-30 Little St; unpowered/powered/en suite sites $32/39/50, cabins/en suite cabins $60/85; ❄️@❤️🛜🏊) The closest caravan park to central Cairns, 3.5km north of the city centre, with recently overhauled facilities and free internet.

Cairns Girls Hostel HOSTEL **$**
(☎4051 2767; www.cairnsgirlshostel.com.au; 147 Lake St; dm/tw $20/48; @❤️) Sorry, boys! This white-glove-test-clean, female-only hostel is one of the most accommodating budget stays in Cairns.

Cairns Beach House HOSTEL **$**
(☎1800 229 228; 239 Sheridan St; dm $13-20, d $50; ❄️@❤️🛜🏊) Party spot with surprisingly quiet dorms and doubles (share bathroom) and freebies, including evening meals.

Cairns Central YHA HOSTEL **$**
(☎4051 0772; www.yha.com.au; 20-26 McLeod St; dm $27-36; ❄️@❤️🛜) Bright, spotless and professionally staffed.

✖️ Eating

Cairns' status as an international city is reflected in its multicultural restaurants, which often incorporate a tropical Aussie twist. Along the waterfront outside the **Pier Marketplace**, half a dozen international restaurants share a boardwalk overlooking the marina – just wander along and take your pick.

If you want something cheap and quick, the Night Markets, between the Esplanade and Abbott St, have a busy Asian-style food court.

Some pubs dish up amazingly cheap meals to the thrifty backpacker hordes and they're not half bad.

Cairns' main food market is **Rusty's Markets** (Grafton St, between Shields & Spence Sts; ⏰5am-6pm Fri, 6am-3pm Sat, 6am-2pm Sun).

TOP CHOICE **Ochre** MODERN AUSTRALIAN **$$$**
(☎4051 0100; www.ochrerestaurant.com.au; 43 Shields St; mains $30-36; ⏰lunch Mon-

Fri, dinner nightly; ♨) In an ochre- and plum-toned dining room, the changing menu at this innovative restaurant utilises native Aussie fauna (such as croc with native pepper or roo with quandong chilli glaze) and flora (from sides, such as wattle seed damper loaf with peanut oil and native dukka, to desserts, such as lemon myrtle panna cotta). If you can't decide, try a tasting plate ($23 to $36) or go all-out with a six-course tasting menu ($90, with wines $130).

Green Ant Cantina
MEXICAN $$
(☎4041 5061; www.greenantcantina.com; 183 Bunda St; mains $17-40; ☉dinner) Behind the railway station, this funky little slice of Mexico is worth seeking out for its homemade quesadillas, enchiladas and Corona-battered tiger prawns. Great cocktail list and cool tunes (including an open-mic night on Sundays).

Charlie's
SEAFOOD $$
(www.acaciacourt.com; 223-227 The Esplanade; buffet $29; ☉dinner) It's not the fanciest place in town, but Charlie's, at the Acacia Court, is legendary for its nightly all-you-can-eat seafood buffet. Fill your plate over and over with prawns, oysters, clams or hot food and eat out on the poolside terrace. Great cocktails too.

Fusion Organics
CAFE $
(www.fusionorganics.com; cnr Grafton & Aplin Sts; dishes $4-20; ☉7am-4pm Mon-Fri, to 1pm Sat; ♨) In the wicker-chair-strewn corner courtyard of an historic 1921 redbrick former ambulance station, Indian chefs spice up Fusion's organic, allergy-free fare, such as quiches, frittata, corn fritters and filled breads. Healthy brekkie options include buckwheat waffles and pick-me-up 'detox' juices.

Marinades
INDIAN $$
(☎4041 1422; 43 Spence St; mains $14-30; ☉lunch & dinner Tue-Sun) The pick of Cairns' Indian restaurants for its long, *long* menu of aromatic dishes, such as lobster marinated in cashew paste and Goan prawn curry, and for the restrained decor in its dining room.

Cherry Blossom
JAPANESE $$$
(☎4052 1050; www.cherryblossom.com.au; cnr Spence & Lake Sts; mains $29-53; ☉lunch Tue-Fri, dinner Mon-Sat) This first-floor restaurant is reminiscent of an Iron Chef cook-off, with two chefs working at opposite ends of the restaurant floor. Book ahead for sushi, teppanyaki and plenty of theatre.

First House
VIETNAMESE $$
(☎4051 5153; 55 Spence St; mains $11-20; ☉11am-9pm) Serving continuously throughout the day (a rarity for Cairns restaurants), this small, simple spot is a good bet if you like pork, which appears in virtually every dish. Unlicensed but BYO.

Meldrum's Pies in Paradise
BAKERY $
(97 Grafton St; pies $5-6; ☉7am-5pm Mon-Fri, to 2.30pm Sat; ♨) A Cairns institution, Meldrum's bakes some 40 inventive varieties of the humble Aussie pie – from chicken and avocado to pumpkin gnocchi or tuna mornay.

Raw Prawn
SEAFOOD $$$
(☎4031 5400; www.rawprawnrestaurant.com.au; The Esplanade Centre, The Esplanade; mains $29-40; ☉lunch & dinner) Fine-dining affair especially renowned for its seafood platters ($54 to $90 per person). The priciest include succulent mud crab.

Dolce & Caffe
CAFE $$
(Shop 1, Mantra Esplanade, Shields St; dishes $6-19; ☉6am-4.30pm Mon-Sat, 7am-4.30pm Sun; ♨) A local fave for its sublime coffee and super-fresh salads.

La Fettuccina
ITALIAN $$
(☎4031 5959; www.lafettuccina.com; 41 Shields St; mains $25-30; ☉dinner) Homemade sauces are a speciality at this small, atmospheric Italian restaurant. Try for a seat on the tiny, internal wrought-iron mezzanine balcony. Licensed and BYO.

Vanilla Gelateria
ICE CREAM $
(cnr Esplanade & Aplin Sts; cone or cup $4-6; ☉9.30am-11pm) Icy concoctions, such as Toblerone, lemon, lime and bitters – even Red Bull!

Self-Catering
Try Rusty's Markets or Cairns Central Shopping Centre.

Asian Foods Australia (101-5 Grafton St) sells food products from all over Asia.

🍸 Drinking & Entertainment
The number of places to go out for a drink is intoxicating. Most venues are multipurpose, offering food, alcohol and some form of entertainment. Some, such as Gilligan's, are attached to hostels, but are equally popular with locals, and you can always find a beer garden or terrace to enjoy balmy evenings. Nightclubs generally close at 3am or later and cover charges usually apply.

The website www.entertainmentcairns. com and the free *Backpacker Xpress* magazine list the hotspots.

TOP CHOICE **Salt House** BAR
(www.salthouse.com.au; 6/2 Pierpoint Rd; ⊙9am-2am) Next to Cairns' new yacht club, Salt House's sleek nautical design has seen it become the city's most sought-after bar since it opened a couple of years ago. Actually, it's two bars: the luxury-yacht-styled Sailing Bar, with live music, and the Balinese-influenced Deck Bar, with killer cocktails and DJs hitting the decks.

Vibe Bar & Lounge BAR
(www.vibebarcairns.com; 39 Lake St; ⊙10.30am-1am Mon-Thu, to 5am Fri, noon-5am Sat, 5am-3am Sun) Walk through the unassuming street entrance to the cathedral-like back room with funky artworks adorning the walls and couches in the corners. The dance floor cranks from 9pm nightly. Gay-friendly.

Pullman Reef Hotel Casino CASINO
(www.reefcasino.com.au; 35-41 Wharf St; ⊙9am-3am Sun-Thu, to 5am Fri & Sat) Cairns' casino has table games (blackjack, roulette, baccarat et al), as well as hundreds of bling-bling poker machines; four restaurants; four bars including **Vertigo Bar & Lounge**, with free live music; a pumpin' nightclub, **Velvet Underground** (www.myspace.com/clubvelvetunderground), which also hosts ticketed shows; and a mini-zoo on the roof, **Cairns Wildlife Dome** (www.cairnsdome.com.au; adult/child $22/11; ⊙9am-6pm).

Pier Bar & Grill BAR
(www.pierbar.com.au, Pier Point Rd; ⊙11.30am-late) A local institution for its waterfront location and well-priced meals. The Sunday session is a must.

Grand Hotel PUB
(33 McLeod St; ⊙11am-1am) This laidback local is worth a visit just so that you can rest your beer on the bar – an 11m-long carved crocodile!

12 Bar Blues LIVE MUSIC
(62 Shields St; ⊙7pm-late Tue-Sun) Intimate bar with jazz, blues and swing.

PJ O'Briens BAR
(www.pjobriens.com.au; cnr Lake & Shields St; ⊙daily until late) It has sticky carpets and the smell of stale Guinness, but Irish-themed PJ's packs 'em in with party nights, pole dancing and dirt-cheap meals.

Woolshed Chargrill & Saloon BAR
(24 Shields St; ⊙daily until late) Another backpacker magnet, where a young crowd of travellers and dive instructors gets hammered and dances on tables.

🔒 Shopping

Cairns offers the gamut of shopping, from high-end boutiques like Louis Vuitton to garishly kitsch souvenir barns. You'll have no trouble finding a box of macadamia nuts, emu or crocodile jerky, fake designer sunglasses and tropical-fish fridge magnets.

The huge **Cairns Central Shopping Centre** (www.cairnscentral.com.au; McLeod St; ⊙9am-5.30pm Mon-Wed & Fri & Sat, to 9pm Thu, 10am-4.30pm Sun) has a couple of supermarkets plus a huge range of speciality stores selling everything from books to bikinis.

Head to the **Night Markets** (The Esplanade; ⊙4.30pm-midnight) and **Mud Markets** (Pier Marketplace; ⊙Sat morning) if your supply of 'Cairns Australia' T-shirts is running low, or you need your name on a grain of rice.

ℹ Information

Internet Access

Most tour-booking agencies and accommodation places have internet access, and dedicated internet cafes are clustered along Abbott St between Shields and Aplin Sts.

Money

Major banks have branches with ATMs throughout central Cairns. Most banks exchange foreign currency. There are private currency-exchange bureaux along the Esplanade that are open longer hours.

American Express (63 Lake St) In Westpac Bank.

Post

Main post office (www.auspost.com; 13 Grafton St) Handles poste restante. There are branches in Orchid Plaza and in Cairns Central Shopping Centre.

Tourist Information

Despite the glut of tourist information and commercial tour-booking agents that call themselves 'information centres' and brandish an 'i' symbol (white on a blue background, with an upright 'i'), the only officially accredited visitor information centre (represented by a yellow, italicised '*i*' on a blue background) is the government-run **Cairns & Tropical North Visitor Information Centre** (☑4051 3588; www.tropicalaustralia.com.au; 51 The Esplanade; ⊙8.30am-6.30pm). In addition to impartial advice, the centre books accommodation and tours and houses an interpretive centre. It also distributes the *Welcome to Cairns* directory and map and is the main point of contact for the wider region stretching north to Cape York and south to Mission Beach.

Other useful contacts:

Cairns Discount Tours (☑4055 7158; www.cairnsdiscounttours.com.au) Knowledgeable booking agent for day trips and tours, specialising in last-minute deals.

Far North Queensland Volunteers (☑4041 7400; www.fnqvolunteers.org; 68 Abbott St) Arranges volunteer positions with nonprofit community groups.

Department of Environment & Resource Management (DERM; ☑13 74 68; www.derm.qld.gov.au; 5B Sheridan St) Information on national parks and state forests, walking trails and camping permits.

❶ Getting There & Away

Air

International routes from **Cairns Airport** (www.cairnsairport.com) include **Jetstar** (www.jetstar.com.au) to Auckland, Singapore, Tokyo and Osaka; **Cathay Pacific** (www.cathaypacific.com) to Hong Kong; and **Air New Zealand** (www.airnewzealand.com) to Auckland.

Domestically, Jetstar (☑13 15 38), **Qantas** (☑13 13 13; cnr Lake & Shield Sts, City Place; www.qantas.com.au) and **Virgin Blue** (☑13 67 89; www.virginblue.com.au) fly to major destinations including Brisbane (two hours), Sydney (four hours), Melbourne (five hours), Adelaide (four hours) and Darwin (two hours). Perth and Hobart usually require a change in Sydney or Melbourne.

Skytrans (☑1800 818 405, 4046 2462; www.skytrans.com.au) services Cape York with regular flights to Cooktown, Coen, Bamaga and Lockhart River, as well as Burketown and Normanton in the Gulf and Mount Isa and Cloncurry.

Hinterland Aviation (☑4035 9323; www.hinterlandaviation.com.au) has one to four flights daily except Sunday to/from Cooktown (one-way $150, 40 minutes).

Bus

Cairns is the hub for Far North Queensland buses.

Greyhound Australia (☑1300 473 946; www.greyhound.com.au; Reef Fleet Terminal) has four daily services down the coast to Brisbane ($310, 29 hours) via Townsville ($81, six hours), Airlie Beach ($139, 11 hours) and Rockhampton ($215, 18 hours). Bus passes can reduce costs.

Premier (☑13 34 10; www.premierms.com.au; departs Stop D, Lake St) also runs one daily service to Brisbane ($205, 29 hours) via Innisfail ($19, 1½ hours), Mission Beach ($19, two hours), Tully ($26, 2½ hours), Cardwell ($30, three hours), Townsville ($55, 5½ hours) and Airlie

Beach ($90, 10 hours). Cheaper bus passes are available.

TransNorth (☑4061 7944; www.transnorthbus.com; departs 46 Spence St) has two to five daily bus services connecting Cairns with the Tableland, serving Kuranda ($4, 30 minutes, five daily), Mareeba ($16.80, one hour), Atherton ($22, 1¾ hours), and Ravenshoe ($33, 2½ hours).

John's Kuranda Bus (☑0418-772 953; $4, 30 min; departs Lake St Transit Centre) runs a service between Cairns and Kuranda two to five times daily.

Sun Palm (☑4087 2900; www.sunpalmtransport.com) runs two northern services from Cairns to Cape Tribulation ($78, three hours) via Port Douglas ($35, 1½ hours) and Mossman ($40, 1¾ hours), with additional services direct to Port Douglas; and south to Mission beach ($49, two hours).

Country Road Coachlines (☑4045 2794; www.countryroadcoachlines.com.au) runs a daily bus service between Cairns and Cooktown ($75) on either the coastal route (Bloomfield Track) or inland route (via Mareeba), depending on the day of departure and the condition of the track.

Car & Motorcycle

All the major car rental companies have branches in Cairns and at the airport, with discount car and campervan rental companies proliferating throughout town. Daily rates start at around $45 for a late-model small car and around $80 for a 4WD. If you're in for the long haul, check out the noticeboard on Abbott St for used campervans and ex-backpackers' cars.

Choppers Motorcycle Tours & Hire (☑0408-066 024; www.choppersmotorcycles.com.au; 150 Sheridan St) Hire a Harley from $160 to $250 a day, or smaller bikes from $95 a day. Also offers motorcycle tours, from one hour to a full-day ride to Cape Trib.

Train

The *Sunlander* departs Cairns' **train station** (Bunda St) on Tuesday, Thursday and Saturday for Brisbane (one-way from $219, 31½ hours).

The Scenic Railway (p466) runs daily to/from Kuranda. Contact **Queensland Rail** (☑1800 872 467; www.traveltrain.com.au).

❶ Getting Around

To/From the Airport

The airport is about 7km north of central Cairns, and many accommodation places offer courtesy pick-ups. **Sun Palm** (☑4087 2900; www.sunpalmtransport.com; adult/child $10/5) meets all incoming flights and runs a shuttle bus to the

GORDONVALE

Gordonvale (population 4420), 24km south of Cairns, is a delightfully old-fashioned community, with a disproportionate number of timber pubs set around its central park, an enormous sugar mill – and the dubious honour of being the first place where cane toads were released in 1935. It's backed by the looming 922m peak **Walsh's Pyramid**, one of the world's highest free-standing natural pyramids. A hard-going but worthwhile walking track (6km return, six hours) runs from the base to the summit. Start out early and take plenty of water.

CBD. **Black & White Taxis** (☑13 10 08) charges around $26.

Bicycle

Bike hire is available from some accommodation places, or try the following:

Bike Man (☑4041 5566; www.bikeman.com.au; 99 Sheridan St; $20/60 per day/week) Hire, sales and repairs.

Cairns Bicycle Hire (☑4031 3444; www.cairnsbicyclehire.com.au; 47 Shields St; per day/week from $15/45, scooters from $85 per day) Groovy bikes and scooters.

Bus

Sunbus (☑4057 7411; www.sunbus.com.au) runs regular services in and around Cairns from the Lake St Transit Centre, where schedules are posted. Useful routes include Flecker Botanic Gardens/Edge Hill and Machans Beach (bus 7), Holloways Beach and Yorkeys Knob (buses 1c, 1d and 1h), Trinity Beach, Clifton Beach and Palm Cove (buses 1N, 1X, 2, 2A). Most buses heading north go via Smithfield. All are served by the (almost) 24-hour night service (N) on Friday and Saturday. Heading south, bus 1 runs as far as Gordonvale.

Taxi

Black & White Taxis (☑131 008) has a rank near the corner of Lake and Shields Sts, and one on McLeod St outside Cairns Central Shopping Centre.

AROUND CAIRNS

The city and its northern beaches have plenty to keep you entertained, but its islands and highlands make great side trips.

Babinda & Around

South of Cairns, a lush pocket of rainforest offers a rewarding trip for walkers and wildlife watchers. The surrounding towns and settlements also provide fascinating windows onto the area's heritage.

BABINDA
POP 1167

On the Bruce Hwy, 60km south of Cairns, Babinda is a small working-class town that leads 7km inland to a mythical rainforest and boulders, where a fast-running creek rushes between 4m-high granite rocks. It's croc-free, though beware of surging water after heavy rain and take care on the slippery rocks at any time. The point where swimming is out of bounds, downstream from the main pool, is clearly signposted – numerous drownings have occurred here over the years.

Just before the picnic area at the car park is the free **Boulders Camping Ground** (two night maximum) with toilets, cold showers and free barbecues. There are just five sites, with a maximum of five people per site.

South of the Boulders, 3.3km from the town centre, you can kayak the clear waters of Babinda Creek almost all the way back to town with **Babinda Kayak Hire** (☑4067 2678; www.babindakayakhire.com.au; 330 Stager Rd; per half-day/day $35/50). Prices include pick-ups.

Around the corner from the **visitor centre** (☑4067 1008; www.cairnsgreatbarrierreef.org.au; cnr Munro St & Bruce Hwy; ◎9am-4pm), the Aboriginal art gallery, **Babinda Heritage Blessing** (☑4067 2333; 29-33 Munro St; ◎8am-5pm Mon-Fri, to 4.30pm Sat, 3-5pm Sun) is operated by artists Judy Ross-Kelly and Mat Kadir, who can teach you to make your own didgeridoo ($200). The day includes lunch, a trip to the Boulders, Dreaming stories, as well as transfers from Cairns.

WOOROONOORAN NATIONAL PARK

Part of the Wet Tropics World Heritage Area, the rugged tropical rainforest in the **Josephine Falls section** of Wooroonooran National Park covers the foothills and creeps to the peak of Queensland's highest mountain, Mt Bartle Frere (1657m). It provides a shielded and exclusive environment for a number of plant and animal species. The car park for Josephine Falls – a spectacular series of waterfalls and pools – is signposted

6km off the Bruce Hwy, about 10km south of Babinda, followed by a steep but paved 600m walk through the rainforest and along a mossy creek. Beware: the rocks connecting the pools are slippery and can be treacherous, and the flow can be powerful after rain, when flash flooding can occur.

The falls are at the foot of the Bellenden Ker Range. The **Mt Bartle Frere Summit Track** (15km, two days return) leads from the Josephine Falls car park to the summit. Don't underestimate this walk: the ascent is for fit and well-equipped walkers only, and rain and cloud can close in suddenly. Get a trail guide from the visitors centre or contact **Department of Environment & Resource Management** (DERM; ☑13 74 68; www.derm.qld.gov.au). **Camping** (per person $5.15) is permitted along the trail; book ahead.

For the Palmerston (Doongan) section of Wooroonooran National Park, see p446.

Cairns' Northern Beaches
☑07

A string of independent communities cling to the 26km stretch of coast north of Cairns, each separated by the twists and turns of the coastline and reached by signposted turnoffs from the Captain Cook Hwy.

YORKEYS KNOB
The most appealing of Cairns' Northern Beaches, Yorkeys is a sprawling, low-key settlement on a white-sand beach. In the crescent-shaped Half Moon Bay is the marina, supporting 200 bobbing boats.

Kite Rite (☑0409 283 322; www.kiterite.com.au; Shop 1, 471 Varley St; per hr $79) offers kite- and windsurfing instruction, including gear hire, and a two-day certificate course ($499).

A block or so back from the beach, **Villa Marine** (☑4055 7158; www.villamarine.com.au; 8 Rutherford St; d $119-159; ❋ 🛜 ⛱) is the best-value spot in Yorkeys. Friendly owner Peter makes you feel at home in the retro-style, single-storey self-contained apartments arranged around a pool.

TOP CHOICE **Yorkeys Knob Boating Club** (☑4055 7711; www.ykbc.com.au; 25-29 Buckley St; mains $17.50-28.50; ⊙lunch & dinner daily, breakfast Sat & Sun; ☑) is a diamond find. Yorkeys' boat club serves up some of the freshest seafood in North Queensland (which is really saying something!). Go for the cod if it's on the menu, or the cooked-to-perfection calamari, order a schooner (or two – there's a local courtesy bus) and take a seat on the deck and dream about sailing away on one of the luxury yachts moored out front.

TRINITY BEACH & AROUND
High-rise developments detract from Trinity Beach's long stretch of sheltered white sand, but holidaymakers love it – turning their backs to the buildings and focusing on what is one of Cairns' prettiest northern beaches.

Self-contained apartments are just footsteps from the beach at **Castaways** (☑4057 6699; www.castawaystrinitybeach.com.au; cnr Trinity Beach Rd & Moore St; 1-/2-bed apt $132/165; ❋⛱), which has three pools, spas, tropical gardens and good stand-by rates.

TOP CHOICE **L'Unico Trattoria** (☑4057 8855; www.lunico.net.au; 75 Vasey Esplanade; mains $22-44; ⊙lunch & dinner, breakfast Sat & Sun; ☑) opens to a wraparound wooden deck. The stylish Italian cuisine at this beachside find includes veal medallions in marsala sauce, homemade four-cheese gnocchi and wood-fired pizzas, along with specials, such as scallops in creamy chilli sauce and a stellar wine list.

PALM COVE
More intimate than Port Douglas and much more upmarket than its southern neighbours, Palm Cove is essentially one big promenade along Williams Esplanade, with a gorgeous stretch of white-sand beach and top-notch restaurants luring sunlovers out of their luxury resorts.

WORTH A TRIP

BRAMSTON BEACH

About 6km south of Babinda, turn east at tiny Mirriwinni down a 17km road winding through rolling cane fields and rainforest to one of North Queensland's undiscovered gems, peaceful Bramston Beach (population 300).

Overlooked by most tourists, this long stretch of coarse golden sand is practically deserted and undeveloped compared to beaches north of Cairns. A stinger net is erected during summer; there's beachfront camping, a stylish little motel, and a great cafe, which also rents bikes to explore the surrounding national park.

⊙ Sights & Activities

Beach strolls, shopping and leisurely swims will be your chief activities here but there's no excuse for not getting out on the water.

Palm Cove Watersports   KAYAKING
(☑0402 861 011; www.palmcovewatersports.com) Organises 1½-hour early-morning sea-kayaking trips ($56) and half-day paddles to Double Island (adult/child $96/68), offshore from Palm Cove. It also runs a half-day hike to Lake Placid and the Barron Gorge (adult/child $92/72).

Beach Fun & Co   WATER SPORTS
(☑0411-848 580l www.tourismpalmcove.com) Hires catamarans ($50 per hour), jet skis (per 15 minutes single/double $60/80), paddle boats ($30) and boogie boards ($10), and organises jet ski tours around Double Island and Haycock Island (single/double from $120/180). Fishing boats start from $100 per two hours.

🛏 Sleeping

Most of Palm Cove's accommodation has a minimum three nights' stay.

TOP CHOICE Sebel Reef House   HOTEL $$$
(☑1800 079 052, 4055 3633; www.reefhouse.com.au; 99 Williams Esplanade; d from $299; ❉@🛜☒) Once the private residence of an army brigadier, the Sebel is more intimate and understated than most of Palm Cove's resorts. The whitewashed walls, wicker furniture and big beds romantically draped in muslin all add to the air of refinement. The Brigadier's Bar works on a quaint honesty system; complimentary punch is served by candlelight at twilight.

Peppers Beach Club & Spa   HOTEL $$$
(☑1300 987 600, 4059 9200; www.peppers.com.au; 123 Williams Esplanade; d from $290; ❉@🛜☒) Step through the opulent lobby at Peppers and into a wonder-world of swimming pools – there's the sand-edged lagoon pool and the leafy rainforest pool and swim-up bar, plus tennis courts and spa treatments. Even the standard rooms have private balcony spas, and the penthouse suites (from $540) have their own rooftop pool. Service exceeds even the highest expectations.

Palm Cove Camping Ground CAMPGROUND $
(☑4055 3824; 149 Williams Esplanade; unpowered/powered sites $16.50/23) Council-run beachfront camping ground near the jetty, with a barbecue area and laundry. No cabins but the only way to do Palm Cove on the cheap!

Silvester Palms   APARTMENTS $$
(☑4055 3831; www.silvesterpalms.com; 32 Veivers Rd; 1-/2-/3-bed apt $110/130/190; ❉🛜☒) These bright self-contained apartments are an affordable alternative to Palm Cove's city-sized resorts. Good for families.

✕ Eating & Drinking

Palm Cove has some fine restaurants and cafes strung along the Esplanade. All of the resort hotels have swish dining options open to non-guests.

TOP CHOICE Beach Almond   MODERN ASIAN $$$
(☑4059 1908; www.beachalmond.com; 145 Williams Esplanade; mains $14-39.50; ⊙lunch & dinner) A rustic beach house near the jetty is the setting for Palm Cove's most inspired dining. Black pepper prawns, ginger pork belly, Singaporean mud crab and Balinese barra are among the fragrant, freshly prepared innovations.

Nu Nu   MODERN AUSTRALIAN $$$
(☑4059 1880; www.nunu.com.au; 123 Williams Esplanade; mains $31-47; ⊙breakfast, lunch & dinner) With one of the highest profiles on the coast, you'll need to book way ahead at the retro Nu Nu, which specialises in 'wild foods' like beet-poached Angus tenderloin or roast chicken with leatherwood honey grilled figs.

The Surf Club Palm Cove   LICENSED CLUB $
(☑4059 1244; www.thesurfclubpalmcove.com; 135 Williams Esplanade; meals $14.50-27.50; ⊙dinner) A great local for a drink in the sunny garden bar and bargain-priced seafood plus decent kids meals.

El Greko   GREEK $$
(☑4055 3690; www.elgrekostaverna.com.au; Level 1, Palm Cove Shopping Village, 117 Williams Esplanade; mains $22-34; ⊙dinner; 🖉) Souvlaki, spanakopita and mousaka are among the staples at this lively taverna. Good mezze platters; belly dancing on Friday and Saturday nights.

Apres Beach Bar & Grill   BISTRO $$
(☑4059 2000; http://apresbeachbar.com.au; 119 Williams Esplanade; mains $23-39; ⊙breakfast, lunch & dinner) The most happening place in Palm Cove, with a zany interior of old motorcycles, racing cars and a biplane hanging from the ceiling, and regular live music.

ⓘ Information

Commercially run tour-booking companies are strung along Williams Esplanade; Cairns & Tropical North Visitor Information Centre (p458) can help with bookings.

The two-storey, ice cream-coloured **Paradise Village Shopping Centre** (113 Williams Esplanade) has a post office (with internet access, per hr $4), small supermarket and newsagent.

ELLIS BEACH

Ellis Beach is the last of the northern beaches and the closest to the highway, which runs right past it. The long-sheltered bay is a stunner, with a palm-fringed, patrolled swimming beach and stinger net in summer. This is where the coastal drive to Port Douglas really gets interesting.

[TOP CHOICE] **Ellis Beach Oceanfront Bungalows** (🖉1800 637 036, 4055 3538; www.ellisbeach.com; Captain Cook Hwy; unpowered sites $26, powered sites $32-38, cabins $85, en suite bungalows $149-185; ✳@) offers camping and cabins, including contemporary bungalows, all of which enjoy widescreen ocean TV at this palm-shaded beachfront park. Paradise, except when the horse flies are out in force.

Across the road, **Ellis Beach Bar 'n' Grill** (Captain Cook Hwy; mains $8-24; ⊙breakfast, lunch & dinner) has good food, live music some Sunday afternoons and, best of all, pinball.

Daily events at **Hartley's Crocodile Adventures** (🖉4055 3576; www.crocodileadventures.com; adult/child $32/16; ⊙8.30am-5pm) include tours of this croc farm, along with feedings, 'crocodile attack' shows, and boat cruises on its lagoon.

Islands off Cairns

A short skim across the water the islands off Cairns make for great day trips or longer sojourns.

GREEN ISLAND

Green Island's long, dog-legged jetty heaves under the weight of boatloads of day trippers. This beautiful coral cay is only 45 minutes from Cairns and has a rainforest interior with interpretive walks, a fringing white-sand beach and snorkelling just offshore. You can walk around the island in about 30 minutes.

The island and its surrounding waters are protected by their national- and marine-park status. **Marineland Melanesia** (www.marinelandgreenisland.com; adult/child $17/8) has an aquarium with fish, turtles, stingrays and crocodiles, as well as a collection of Melanesian artefacts.

Luxurious **Green Island Resort** (🖉1800 673 366; 4031 3300; www.greenislandresort.com.au; ste $570-670; ✳@✳) has stylish split-level suites, each with its own private balcony. Island transfers are included. It is partially open to day trippers (who are able to use a separate pool), so even if you are not staying at the resort, you can enjoy the restaurants, bars, ice-cream parlour and watersports facilities.

Great Adventures (🖉4044 9944; www.greatadventures.com.au; 1 Spence St, Cairns; adult/child $75/37.50) and **Big Cat** (🖉4051 0444; www.greenisland.com.au; adult/child from $75/37.50) is an operation that runs day trips, with optional glass-bottomed boat and semi-submersible tours.

Alternatively, sail to the island aboard **Ocean Free** (🖉4052 1111; www.oceanfree.com.au; adult/child from $135/90), spending most of the day offshore at Pinnacle Reef, with a short stop on the island.

FITZROY ISLAND

A steep mountaintop rising from the sea, Fitzroy Island has coral-strewn beaches, woodlands and walking tracks, and Australia's last staffed lighthouse. The most popular snorkelling spot is around the rocks at Nudey Beach (1.2km from the resort), which, despite its name, is not clothing-optional, so bring your togs.

You can pitch a tent at the **Fitzroy Island Camping Ground** (🖉4044 3044; $28), run by Cairns Regional Council. It has showers, toilets and barbecues; advance bookings are essential.

Refurbished accommodation at the **Fitzroy Island Resort** (🖉4044 6700; www.fitzroyisland.com; studio/cabin $195/299, 1-/2-bed ste $350-515 ✳✳) ranges from sleek studios and beachfront cabins through to a decadent-and-then-some penthouse ($1899). Its restaurant, bar and kiosk are open to day trippers.

Raging Thunder (🖉4030 7900; www.ragingthunder.com.au; Reef Fleet terminal, Cairns; adult/child $58/31.50) runs day trips from Cairns.

FRANKLAND ISLANDS

If the idea of hanging out on one of five uninhabited coral-fringed islands with excellent snorkelling and stunning white sandy beaches appeals – and if not, why not? – cruise out to the Frankland Group National Park.

Camping is available on High or Russell Islands, which both feature rainforest areas. Contact the DERM (☎13 74 68; www.derm.qld.gov.au) office in Cairns for advance reservations and seasonal restrictions, in case you were getting any ideas about dropping out of life for a while.

Frankland Islands Cruise & Dive (☎4031 6300; www.franklandislands.com.au; adult/child from $136/84) runs excellent day trips, which include a cruise down the Mulgrave River, snorkelling gear and lunch. Guided snorkelling tours with a marine biologist and diving packages are also offered. Transfers for campers to/from Russell Island are available. Boats depart from Deeral; transfers from Cairns and the Northern Beaches cost $16 per person.

You'll need to organise your own boat or charter to reach High Island.

Atherton Tableland

Climbing back from the coast between Innisfail and Cairns is the fertile food bowl of the region, the Atherton Tableland. Quaint rural towns, ecowilderness lodges and luxurious B&Bs are sprinkled between patchwork fields, pockets of rainforest, spectacular lakes and waterfalls, and Queensland's highest mountains: Bartle Frere (1657m) and Bellenden Ker (1591m).

Four main roads lead in from the coast: the Palmerston Hwy from Innisfail, the Gillies Hwy from Gordonvale, the Kennedy Hwy from Cairns, and Rex Range Rd between Mossman and Port Douglas.

The following section follows the Kennedy Hwy from Cairns and heads south before looping up along the Gillies Hwy back to Cairns.

ⓘ Getting There & Around

There are bus services to the main towns from Cairns (generally three services on weekdays, two on Saturday and one on Sunday), but not to the smaller towns or all the interesting areas *around* the towns, so it's worth bringing or hiring your own wheels.

Trans North (☎0400 749 476; www.transnorthbus.com) has regular bus services connecting Cairns with the Tableland, departing from 46 Spence St and running to Kuranda ($4, 30 mins), Mareeba ($16.80, one hour), Atherton ($22, 1¾ hours), Herberton ($28, two hours, three per week). John's Kuranda Bus (☎0418 772 953; www.kuranda.org) runs a service between Cairns and Kuranda two to five times daily

($4, 20 mins). Kerry's (☎0427 841 483) serves Ravenshoe ($33, 2½ hours). Buses depart from Cairns' Lake St Transit Centre.

KURANDA
POP 1428

Hidden in the rainforest, the artsy, alternative market town of Kuranda is the Tableland's most popular day trip.

⊙ Sights & Activities

Walking trails wind around the village – the visitor centre has maps.

Markets   MARKETS

With revamped boardwalks terraced in the rainforest and wafting incense, the Kuranda Original Rainforest Markets (www.kurandaoriginalrainforestmarket.com.au; Therwine St; ⊙9am-3pm) first opened in 1978 and are still the best place to see artists, such as glassblowers at work, pick up hemp products and sample local produce, such as honey and fruit wines.

Across the road, the Heritage Markets (www.kurandamarkets.com.au; Rob Veivers Dr; ⊙9am-3pm) overflow with souvenirs and crafts, such as ceramics, emu oil, jewellery, clothing (lots of tie-dye) and pistachio-nut figurines.

The New Kuranda Markets (www.kuranda.org; 21-23 Coondoo St; ⊙9am-4pm), the first you come to if you're walking up from the train station, are essentially just an ordinary group of shops.

Djurri Dadagal Art Enterprises
ART GALLERY

(DDAE; ☎0428 645 945; 9 Coondoo St; ⊙9.30am-3.30pm) Many of the authentic paintings, artefacts, screen prints and textiles at this central Indigenous art cooperative run by community leader and proprietor Wanegan (Glenis Grogan) are produced on site by local artists.

Kuranda Riverboat   BOAT CRUISE

(☎4093 7476; www.kurandariverboat.com.au; adult/child $15/7; ⊙hourly 10.30am-2.30pm) One of the most relaxing ways to see the Barron River is aboard a 45-minute cruise. The departure dock is behind the train station, over the footbridge; buy tickets on board.

Wildlife Sanctuaries & Zoos   ZOO

There's loads of wildlife in Kuranda, in zoos and sanctuaries as well as the rainforest; the visitor centre has a comprehensive list.

If you can wake 'em from their gum-leaf coma, you can cuddle a koala (there are wombats and wallabies too) at the Koala

WANEGAN (GLENIS GROGAN): PROPRIETOR, DJURRI DADAGAL ART ENTERPRISES (DDAE)

Background?

I'm a nurse/midwife and worked in academia. I set up the gallery in 2007 to stop the exploitation of our cultural products.

How many artists are involved?

About 100. One lady still knows how to weave baskets traditionally used for fishing. She's keeping the culture alive by teaching younger ones to find the pandanus leaves, then cleaning, cutting, soaking, preparing and weaving them. My elderly uncle is teaching someone to make boomerangs. I love to paint; I also work with dancers and musicians.

Gallery philosophy?

To be more than just a gallery: profits go back to the community, including a healing centre using Aboriginal ways, helping people overcome transgenerational grief, loss and trauma and helping them understand how they got so far removed from tribal culture.

Is exploitation of Aboriginal art still a big problem?

Yes! Places sell 'Aboriginal' souvenirs made by non-Indigenous artists, including from overseas; they don't pay artists what their work is worth...there's no legislation in this country to prevent it. I couldn't just complain and not do anything, so the gallery is my 'doing'. It's all self-funded. Discerning visitors want to know what they're buying.

Gardens (www.koalagardens.com; adult/child $16/18; ☺9am-4pm). The **Australian Butterfly Sanctuary** (www.australianbutterflies.com; 8 Rob Veivers Dr; adult/child $18/9; ☺9.45am-4pm) is a fluttering butterfly aviary where you can see butterflies being bred in the lab and take a free 30-minute tour on request. **Birdworld** (www.birdworldkuranda.com; adult/child $16/8; ☺9am-4pm) is an expansive aviary displaying free-flying native and exotic birds. Combination tickets for all three cost $42/21 per adult/child.

The **Cairns Wildlife Safari Reserve** (www.cairnswildlifesafarireserve.com.au; Kennedy Hwy; adult/child $28/14; ☺9am-4.30pm), which isn't located in Cairns but 9km west of Kuranda, is as close as you'll get to an African safari in Queensland. Lions, cheetahs, hippos, rhinos and the odd tiger and bear roam the free-range zoo. Don't stick your fingers outside the cage when a pride of lions prowl around during **Breakfast with the Beasts** (adult/child $49.50/29.50; ☺7.30-10.30am)! Feedings and talks take place during the day.

🛏 Sleeping & Eating

Kuranda Hotel Motel　　　　MOTEL $$
(☎4093 7206; www.fireflykuranda.com.au; cnr Coondoo & Arara Sts; d $100-120; ❊❄) Locally known as the 'bottom pub' (and rebadging its accommodation section as 'Firefly'), the back of the Kuranda Hotel Motel has spacious '70s-style motel rooms with exposed brick and tinted crinkle cut glass, enhanced with eye-catching artworks, quality linens and groovy light fittings.

Kuranda Rainforest Park　　CARAVAN PARK $
(☎4093 7316; www.kurandarainforestpark.com.au; 88 Kuranda Heights Rd; unpowered/powered sites $26/28, backpacker rooms s/d $30/55, en suite cabins $90-110; ☎❄) This excellent, well-tended park lives up to its name, with grassy camping sites enveloped in rainforest. The basic but cosy private 'backpacker rooms' open onto a tin-roofed timber deck, cabins come with poolside or garden views, and there's a Sri Lankan **restaurant** (mains $14-36; ☺dinner Wed-Sun; ☎✍) on site. It's a 10-minute walk from town via a forest trail.

TOP CHOICE **Kuranda Coffee Republic**　　CAFE $
(www.kurandacofferepublic.com.au; 10 Thongon St; coffee $1-5.50; ☺8am-4pm Mon-Fri, 9am-4pm Sat & Sun) Food is basically limited to biscotti, but who cares when the coffee's this good? You can see – and smell – the locally grown beans being roasted on site. The three days leading up to the full moon is the only roasting time for its Full Moon Roast infused with vanilla pod.

Frogs
CAFE $$

(www.frogsrestaurant.com.au; 11 Coondoo St; mains $14-32; ⊙10am-3pm Sun-Wed, to 7pm Thu-Sat; @🛜🐾) Barra, prawns and a brilliant brekkie omelette (which they'll cook up at any time of day, if you ask nicely) are the staples of this breezy, family-run cafe. In the back garden, Aboriginal dance shows (admission by donation; ⊙1pm) take place daily, weather permitting.

German Tucker
GERMAN $

(☎4057 9688; Therwine St; dishes $6-10; ⊙10am-2.30pm) Emu, crocodile or kangaroo sausages with sauerkraut? German Tucker serves extreme Australiana/traditional German fare and German beer.

Annabel's Pantry
PIES $

(Therwine St; pies $4.10-4.50; ⊙breakfast & lunch; 🐾) With around 25 pie varieties, including kangaroo, and spinach-and-feta rolls, Annabel's is great for lunch on the run.

❶ Information

The **Kuranda visitor centre** (☎4093 9311; www.kuranda.org; ⊙10am-4pm) is centrally located in Centenary Park.

❶ Getting There & Away

The Skyrail and Scenic Railway between Kuranda and Cairns are themselves big attractions and most people go up one way and down the other. Otherwise, it's only a 20-minute drive or cheap bus ride to/from Cairns.

Kuranda Scenic Railway (☎4036 9333; www.ksr.com.au; Cairns train station, Bunda St; adult/child $45/23; return $68/34) winds 34km from Cairns to Kuranda station on Arara St twice daily through picturesque mountains and 15 tunnels.

At 7.5km, **Skyrail Rainforest Cableway** (☎4038 1555; www.skyrail.com.au; adult/child one way $42/21, return $61/30.50; ⊙9am-5.15pm) is one of the world's longest gondola cableways. The Skyrail runs from the corner of Kemerunga Rd and the Cook Hwy in the northern Cairns suburb of Smithfield (15 minutes' drive north of Cairns) to Kuranda (Arara St), taking 90 minutes and including two stops along the way. Combination Scenic Railway and Skyrail deals are available. Only daypacks are allowed on board; advance bookings are recommended.

MAREEBA
POP 6806

Adjoining its excellent little museum, the **Mareeba Heritage Museum & Tourist Information Centre** (☎4092 5674; www.mareeba-heritagecentre.com.au; Centenary Park, 345 Byrnes St; admission free; ⊙8am-4pm) has info on the area's **military museums, wetlands**, and its **whisky and tropical wine producers**, which can be visited. A growing number of food producers have also opened their doors for tours, such as Bruno Maloberti's entertaining tours of his **North Queensland Gold Coffee Plantation** (☎4093 2269; www.nqgoldcoffee.com.au; Dimbulah Hwy; tours $5; ⊙8am-5pm).

Mareeba is a hot-air ballooning mecca – see p454 for operators, which you can link up with here.

July's **Mareeba Rodeo** (www.mareebarodeo.com.au) is one of Australia's biggest and best, with bull and bronco riding, a 'beaut ute' muster and boot scootin' country music.

ATHERTON & AROUND
POP 6247

From the panoramic lookout of Hallorans Hill, the farmland surrounding the unofficial 'capital' of the Tableland looks like an earthy-coloured patchwork quilt. More than 500 Chinese migrants came to the region in search of gold in the late 1800s, but all that's left at **Atherton Chinatown** (www.nationaltrustqld.org; 86 Herberton Rd; adult/child $10/5; ⊙11am-4pm Wed-Sun) is the Hou Wang Temple. Museum admission includes a guided tour.

Atherton Tableland Information Centre (☎4091 4222; www.athertoninformationcentre.com.au; cnr Main St & Silo Rd; ⊙9am-5pm) has info on visiting the area's food producers.

Built in the early 1940s, the grand Art Deco 'BV', aka the **Barron Valley Hotel** (☎4091 1222; www.bvhotel.com.au; 53 Main St; s/d $40/60, en suite s/d $60/75, mains $12-30; ❄🛜) has tidy budget pub rooms; the menu includes giant steaks.

MILLAA MILLAA
POP 250

The dairy community of Millaa Millaa is the gateway to the Tableland from the south and the closest village to the Waterfalls Circuit (p467). Information is available at www.millaamillaa.com.au.

The village's heart is its only pub, the **Millaa Millaa Hotel** (☎4097 2212; 15 Main St; s/d $70/80, mains $14.50-26; ⊙restaurant lunch & dinner Mon-Sat), which serves mountain-sized meals and has six spick-and-span motel units. Publican Terry organises regular events, such as gumboot throwing.

TOP CHOICE **Falls Teahouse & B&B** (☎4097 2237; www.fallsteahouse.com.au; Palmerston Hwy; s/d $65/110, meals $7-16;

WATERFALLS CIRCUIT

Passing some of the Tableland's most picturesque waterfalls, this 15km circuit makes for a leisurely drive or cycle. Enter by taking Theresa Creek Rd, 1km east of Millaa Millaa on the Palmerston Hwy. Surrounded by tree ferns and flowers, the **Millaa Millaa Falls**, 1.5km along, are easily the best for swimming and have a grassy picnic area. The star of Qantas ads, the spectacular 12m falls are reputed to be the most photographed in Australia. **Zillie Falls**, 8km further on, are reached by a short walking trail that leads to a lookout peering down on the falls from above. The next, **Ellinjaa Falls**, have a 200m walking trail down to a rocky swimming hole at the base of the falls. A further 5.5km down the Palmerston Hwy there's a turn-off to **Mungalli Falls**.

⊙10am-5pm) Even the bread is homemade in the country-style kitchen here, along with dishes, such as pan-fried barra and Ray's famed pies with local beef. The back verandah overlooks rolling farmland, and its three guest rooms are individually furnished with period fittings. It's at the intersection of the Millaa Millaa Falls turn-off.

Mungalli Creek Dairy (www.mungallicreek dairy.com.au; 254 Brooks Rd; mains $15.50-16.50; ⊙10am-4pm Mar-Jan) About 6km southeast of the village, you can tuck into free tasting platters of yoghurt and cheese at this biodynamic dairy, or order them cooked in dishes, such as three-cheese pie followed by a sinful Sicilian cheesecake (with chocolate, on a cinnamon base).

MALANDA & AROUND
POP 1928

Milk has flowed through the proverbial veins of Malanda since 500 cattle made the 16-month overland journey from New South Wales in 1908. There's still a working dairy here, and the town is surrounded by lush rainforest and shady, croc-free swimming spot, **Malanda Falls**.

Guided rainforest walks ($15, by appointment) led by members of the Ngadjonji community can be organised through Malanda's visitor centre (☑4096 6957; www.malandafalls. com; ⊙9.30am-4.30pm). A new centre is currently being built next to the falls after a fire destroyed the previous building; in the meantime, it's housed at the **Malanda Dairy Centre** (8 James St; ⊙9.30am-3pm, closed 3 weeks in Oct). The centre can tell you more than you ever wanted to know about cows on 40-minute **factory tours** ($10.50/6.50; ⊙10am & 11am Mon-Fri); its licensed **cafe** (mains $12-18; ☑) is the best place to eat in town.

Lined with black-and-white photos, the enormous, 1911-built **Malanda Hotel** (cnr James & Edith Sts; mains $13-26; ⊙breakfast, lunch & dinner) is the largest wooden structure in the southern hemisphere.

Australia's largest tea plantation, **Nerada Tea** (☑4096 8328; www.neradatea.com.au; Glen Allyn Rd; ⊙9am-4pm) runs **factory tours** (adult/child $13/6; ⊙on request). It's 6km southeast of Malanda.

YUNGABURRA
POP 1200

Home to a shy colony of platypus (the jury is still out on the plural – some experts say platypode!), tiny Yungaburra is one of the unassuming gems of the Tableland. Queensland's largest National Trust village with 18 heritage-listed buildings, quaint chocolate-box-pretty architecture, central location and boutique accommodation have made it a popular weekend retreat for those in the know.

The 500-year-old **Curtain Fig** tree, signposted 3km out of town, is a must-see for its aerial roots that hang down to create an enormous feathery curtain.

Day trippers descend on the village to hunt through crafts and food products at the vibrant **Yungaburra Markets** (www.yungaburramarkets.com; Gillies Hwy; ⊙7.30am-noon 4th Sat of month). In late October, the **Yungaburra Folk Festival** features music, workshops, poetry readings and kids' activities.

TOP CHOICE **On the Wallaby** (☑4095 2031; www.onthewallaby.com; 34 Eacham Rd; camping/dm/d $10/24/55; @) is a homey hostel with handmade timber furniture and mosaics, spotless rooms – and no TV! Nature-based **tours** ($30) include night canoeing; tour packages (p455) and transfers (one-way $30) are available from Cairns.

B&Bs in the village include the 1911-built **Williams Lodge** (☑4095 3449; www.williams lodge.com; Cedar St; d $180-285; ❋@🛜🏊), with original period furniture and four-poster beds (some rooms with spa baths). Under 12s aren't allowed.

Yungaburra's **visitor centre** (☑4095 2416; www.yungaburra.com; Cedar St; ☺10am-6pm; ◉) has a complete list, including beautiful retreats in the surrounding countryside.

LAKE TINAROO

Also known as Tinaroo Dam, Lake Tinaroo was originally created for the Barron River hydroelectric power scheme. When it was filled in 1959, the village of Kulara was submerged below water, with residents relocated to Yungaburra and the surrounding area.

Barramundi fishing is legendary in the croc-free artificial lake and is permitted year-round. Head out for a fish, a barbie or simply a glass of wine during a sunset cruise aboard a super-comfy 'floating lounge room' skippered by **Lake Tinaroo Cruises** (☑0457 033 016; www.laketinaroocruises.com.au; 2hr/half-/full-day boat charter $240/380/550). Rates are for the whole boat (up to 12 people).

The **Danbulla Forest Drive** winds its way through rainforest and softwood plantations along the north side of the lake. It's 28km of unsealed but well-maintained road. There are five **DERM campgrounds** (☑13 74 68; www.derm.qld.gov.au; per person $5.15) in the Danbulla State Forest. All have water, barbecues and toilets; advance bookings essential.

CRATER LAKES NATIONAL PARK

Part of the Wet Tropics World Heritage area, the two mirror-like, croc-free crater lakes of **Lake Eacham** and **Lake Barrine** are nestled among rainforest. Walking tracks fringe both lakes, which are easily reached by sealed roads off the Gillies Hwy. Camping is not permitted.

The **Lake Barrine Rainforest Tea House** (☑4095 3847; www.lakebarrine.com.au; Gillies Hwy; mains $7.50-16.50; ☺breakfast & lunch) sits out over the lakefront; book downstairs for 45-minute **lake cruises** (adult/child $16/8; ☺4 daily).

Stop in Lake Eacham's **Rainforest Display Centre** (McLeish Rd; ☺9am-1pm Mon, Wed & Fri) at the rangers' station for information on the history of the timber industry and rebuilding of the rainforest.

TOP CHOICE **Crater Lakes Rainforest Cottages** (☑4095 2322; www.crater-lakes.com.au; Eacham Close, off Lakes Dr; d $230; ❋◉) has four individually themed timber cottages – 'Bali', 'beach shack', 'Tuscany' and 'pioneer'. Ideally spaced in its own private patch of rainforest, each is a romantic hideaway filled with candles, fresh flowers and logs for the wood stoves, with spa baths, fully fitted kitchens and breakfast hampers with bacon, eggs and chocolates, and fruit to feed the birds.

PORT DOUGLAS TO THE DAINTREE

Be pampered in Port Douglas, explore the wilderness of the Daintree Rainforest, or journey to frontier-like Cooktown.

Port Douglas

POP 3000

Port Douglas is the flashy playground of tropical northern Queensland. Like a spoilt child, it thumbs its nose at Cairns by being more sophisticated, more intimate and (perhaps most of all) by having a beautiful, white-sand beach right on its doorstep. The Great Barrier Reef is less than an hour offshore.

From the Captain Cook Hwy, a 6km stretch along a low spit of land passes swanky village-sized resorts and golf courses to the township. A purpose-built holiday hub, there's a happy, relaxed vibe and clearly plenty of money floating around. Yet Port Douglas (or just 'Port') retains an endearing character, with all the comforts of a big city condensed into a surprisingly small town. Just don't forget there's more to explore further north!

◉ Sights

Although the town itself is short on sights, there are a few you shouldn't miss.

Four Mile Beach   BEACH
Backed by palms, this broad band of squeaky white sand reaches as far as your squinting eyes can see. In front of the surf life-saving club is a swimming enclosure patrolled and protected with a stinger net during summer.

For a fine view over Four Mile Beach, follow Wharf St and the steep Island Point Rd to **Flagstaff Hill Lookout**.

Wildlife Habitat Port Douglas NATURE RESERVE
(☑4099 3235; www.wildlifehabitat.com.au; Port Douglas Rd; adult/child $30/15; ☺8am-5pm) There's no shortage of wildlife tourist parks in north Queensland, but this one is up there with the best. The sanctuary endeavours to keep and showcase native animals in enclosures that closely mimic their natural environment – wetlands, grasslands and rainforest – but also allow you to get up

close to koalas, kangaroos, crocs, tree kangaroos and much more; take your time as your ticket is valid for three days. It's 4km from town; head south along Davidson St.

Come early to have **Breakfast with the Birds** (adult/child incl. park entry $44/22; ⊘8-10.30am) or book in for **Lunch with the Lorikeets** (adult/child $44/22; ⊘noon-2pm).

Court House Museum MUSEUM
(www.douglas-shire-historical-society.org; 18 Wharf St; admission $2; ⊘10am-3pm Tue, Thu, Sat & Sun) Small but absorbing local history museum housed in Port Douglas' 1879-built former courthouse.

St Mary's by the Sea CHURCH
(6 Dixie St) Worth a peek inside (when it's not overflowing with wedding parties), this quaint, nondenominational, white timber church was built in 1911 and relocated to its seaside position in 1989.

🏃 Activities

What Port Douglas lacks in sights, it makes up for with a smorgasbord of activities and tours. The Sheraton Mirage and Sea Temple resorts have prestigious (and pricey) golf courses.

FREE **Port Douglas Yacht Club** SAILING
(www.portdouglasyachtclub.com.au; Spinnaker Close) Already been to the reef? Port's yacht club offers free sailing with club members every Wednesday afternoon. You might have to do some sweet-talking if places are limited but it's a great way to get out on the water and meet some locals.

Ballyhooley Steam Railway MINIATURE TRAIN
(www.ballyhooley.com.au; adult/child day pass $8/4; ⊘Sun) Kids will get a kick out of this cute, miniature steam train. Every Sunday (and some public holidays), it runs from the little station at Marina Mirage to St Crispins station at 11am, 1pm and 2.30pm, stopping at Dougies, Mirage Country Club and Rydges Sabaya Resort. A round trip takes about one hour; discounts are available for shorter sections. Buy tickets onboard.

WindSwell KITE SURFING
(☏0427 498 042; www.windswell.com.au; Four Mile Beach; 2hr lesson from $100) At the beach's southern end.

Port Douglas Boat Hire BOAT HIRE
(☏4099 6277; pdboathire@bigpond.com; Berth C1, Marina Mirage) Rents dinghies (per hour $31) and canopied, family-friendly pontoon boats (per hour $41) plus fishing gear.

☞ Tours

Port Douglas is a hub for tours, and many based out of Cairns also pick up from Port Douglas, including some white-water rafting and hot-air ballooning trips. Conversely, many of the following tours departing from Port Douglas also offer pick-ups from Cairns and Cairns' Northern Beaches.

Great Barrier Reef

The outer reef is closer to Port Douglas than it is to Cairns, and the unrelenting surge of visitors has had a similar impact on its condition here. You will still see colourful corals and marine life, but it is patchy in parts. Access to the majority of spots that operators visit takes around an hour from Port Douglas.

Most day tours depart from Marina Mirage. Tour prices include reef tax, snorkelling, transfers from your accommodation, lunch and refreshments. An introductory, controlled scuba dive, with no certification or experience necessary, costs around $240, with additional dives around $40; certified divers will pay around $250 for two dives with all gear included.

Several operators visit the Low Isles: a small, idyllic group of islands surrounded by beautiful coral reef just 15km offshore, offering your best chance for spotting turtles.

Operators include the following:

Quicksilver REEF TOURS
(☏4087 2100; www.quicksilver-cruises.com; adult/child $205/105) Major operator with fast cruises to Agincourt Reef. If you don't want to get your hair wet, try an 'ocean walk' helmet dive ($142) on a submerged platform, with hoses attached to your helmet so you can breathe normally (great for non-swimmers and kids over 12). Also offers scenic helicopter flights from the pontoon on the reef ($148, minimum two passengers).

Sailaway SAILING
(☏4099 4772; www.sailawayportdouglas.com; adult/child $190.50/120.50) Popular sailing and snorkelling trip (maximum 27 passengers) to the Low Isles that's great for families. Also offers 90-minute twilight sails ($50 Monday to Friday) off the coast of Port Douglas.

Haba REEF TOURS
(☏4098 5000; www.habadive.com.au; adult/child $181/105) Long-standing local dive company; 25-minute glass bottom boat tours (adult/child $16/8) available.

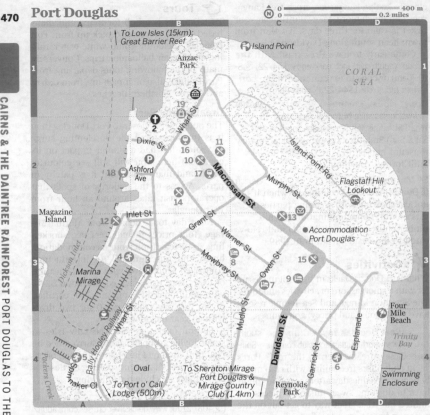

Poseidon

REEF TOURS

(4099 4772; www.poseidon-cruises.com.au; adult/child $196/136) Friendly family-owned and operated luxury catamaran with trips to Agincourt Reef.

Reef Dive School

DIVING

(4099 6980; www.reefdiveschool.com; 4- to 5-day open water courses from $550) Friendly instruction; also offers advanced courses.

Reef Sprinter

SNORKELLING

(4099 3175; www.reefsprinter.com.au; adult/child $100/80) Take this superfast 15-minute trip to the Low Isles for some speed snorkelling (that means you won't suffer from any seasickness!). Reef Sprinter departs from a docking point located beside the On the Inlet restaurant.

The Daintree & Around

See p453 for 4WD tours from Cairns via Port Douglas to Cooktown and Cape York.

Reef and Rainforest Connections

DAINTREE

(4099 5333; www.reefandrainforest.com.au) Runs a flagship Cape Trib and Mossman Gorge trip (adult/child $163/105).

Fishing

Reef-, river- and land-based fishing charters operate regularly out of Port Douglas. Fishing gear and bait is included.

Fishing Port Douglas

FISHING TOURS

(4099 4058; www.fishingportdouglas.com.au) Fishing on the river (share/sole charter per day $200/800) and reef (share/sole charter per day $225/3200).

River Cruises & River Snorkelling

Lady Douglas

RIVER CRUISES

(4099 1603; www.ladydouglas.com.au; 1½hr cruises adult/child $30/15) Lovely paddlewheeler running croc-spotting morning, afternoon and sunset cruises along the Dickson Inlet.

Back Country Bliss Adventures

SNORKELLING

(☑4099 3677; www.backcountryblissadventures.com.au; trips $80) Drift with the current along the river, spotting turtles and freshwater fish. Kid-friendly.

Scenic Flights

GBR Helicopters HELICOPTER FLIGHTS

(☑4099 6030; www.gbrhelicopters.com.au; Port Douglas Rd; flights $359-529) Reef and/or rainforest flights.

✦ Festivals & Events

Port Douglas Carnivale CARNIVAL

(http://carnivale.com.au) It's not Rio, but Port Douglas' 10-day Carnivale in late May includes a colourful street parade, live music, and food and wine galore.

Go Troppo Arts Festival ARTS

(www.go-troppo-arts-festival.com) Pottery workshops, painting classes, storytelling and more in late October.

⌷ Sleeping

Befitting a holiday town, Port Douglas is swimming in accommodation, mainly in self-contained apartments or upmarket resorts (mostly located a few kilometres from the centre on the way into town).

TOP CHOICE Pink Flamingo RESORT $$

(☑4099 6622; www.pinkflamingo.com.au; 115 Davidson St; r $125-195; ❄@☎☒) Flamboyant fuchsia-, purple- and orange-painted rooms opening to private walled courtyards (with hammocks, outdoor baths and outdoor showers) and a groovy mirror-balled al fresco bar make the Pink Flamingo Port Douglas' hippest digs. Outdoor movie nights screen under the palms; tone your abs in the gym or rent a bike for a spin around town. Gay-owned, gay-friendly and all-welcoming (except for kids).

Hibiscus Gardens RESORT $$$

(☑1800 995 995, 4099 5315; www.hibiscusportdouglas.com.au; 22 Owen St; d from $205; ❄@☒) Balinese influences of teak furnishing and fixtures, bi-fold doors and plantation shutters – as well as the occasional Buddha – give this stylish resort an exotic ambience. The in-house day spa, specialising in Indigenous healing techniques and products, has a local reputation as the best (of many) places to be pampered in town.

Dougies HOSTEL $

(☑1800 996 200, 4099 6200; www.dougies.com.au; 111 Davidson St; tent sites per person $12, dm/safari tent/d $26/23/75; ❄@☎☒) At this laid-way-back hostel, it's easy to hang about the sprawling grounds in a hammock by day and move to the bar at night. If you do decide to leave the premises for a bit, rent bikes and/or fishing gear from the reception area, which also stocks groceries. Free pickup from Cairns on Monday, Wednesday and Saturday.

Sheraton Mirage Port Douglas RESORT $$$

(☑4099 5888; www.starwoodhotels.com; Davidson St; d from $329; ❄@☎☒) Not to be confused with the separately located Marina Mirage,

Port Douglas' original luxury resort is surrounded by five acres of swimmable lagoons. There's no doubt it's past its prime but it still has its own beachfront, golf course, childcare facilities, a shuttle service into town, tennis courts and a gym.

Sea Temple Resort & Spa RESORT $$$
(☎1800 833 762, 4084 3500; www.mirvachotels.com.au; Mitre St; d from $309; ✱@🛈🛜🌊) Port Douglas' most luxurious five-star, with a championship links golf course set in lush, tropical gardens near the southern end of Four Mile Beach. Rooms range from spa studios to the opulent 'swim out' penthouse with direct access to the lagoon pool.

Pandanus Caravan Park CARAVAN PARK $
(☎4099 5944; Davidson St; unpowered/powered sites $30/35, cabins with/without en suite $95/72; ✱@🛈🛜🌊) Five minutes' stroll from the beach, this large, shady park has a good range of cabins and free gas barbecues.

Port Douglas Motel MOTEL $
(☎4099 5248; www.portdouglasmotel.com; 9 Davidson St; d $96; ✱🌊) No views but bright rooms and a great location.

ParrotFish Lodge HOSTEL $
(☎1800 995 011, 4099 5011; www.parrotfishlodge.com; 37-39 Warner St; dm $25-33, d/en suite d $85/95; ✱@🌊) Energetic backpackers with extreme beach decor and lots of freebies, including pick-ups from Cairns.

Lychee Tree APARTMENTS $$
(☎4099 5811; www.lychee-tree.com.au; 95 Davidson St; 1/2-bed apt $155/180; ✱🌊) These family-friendly, single-storey, self-contained apartments have full laundries. Minimum two-night stay.

Port o' Call Lodge HOSTEL $
(☎4099 5422; www.portocall.com.au; cnr Port St & Craven Cl; dm $35, d $99-119; ✱@🛈🛜🌊) This low-key solar- and wind-powered, YHA-associated hostel has all en suite rooms and a good-value bistro.

✕ Eating

For a town its size, Port Douglas has some of the most sophisticated dining north of Noosa. Chairs and tables spill out of cafes, and candlelit gardens are a romantic setting for lingering dinners. Advance reservations are recommended and essential for really popular places.

Duck down tiny Grant St for juice bars, pie shops, pizzerias and more.

Beach Shack MODERN AUSTRALIAN $$
(☎4099 1100; www.the-beach-shack.com.au; 29 Barrier St, Four Mile Beach; mains $21-30; ⊙dinner; 🚸) There'd be an outcry if this locals' favourite took its macadamia-crumbed eggplant (with grilled and roast veggies, goat's cheese and wild rocket) off the menu. But it's the setting that makes it really worth heading to the southern end of Four Mile Beach: a lantern-lit garden with sand underfoot. Good reef fish, sirloins and blackboard specials, too.

Zinc MODERN AUSTRALIAN $$
(☎4099 6260; www.zincportdouglas.com; 53-61 Macrossan St; mains $25-34; ⊙7am-midnight) Over 70 wines (40 by the glass) and 110 spirits and liqueurs set Zinc apart from its neighbours – as do dishes, such as pan-seared bugs with apple- and vanilla-scented sweet potato purée and candied cashews. Don't leave without checking out the floor-to-ceiling, fish-filled aquarium in the bathrooms!

On the Inlet SEAFOOD $$
(☎4099 5255; www.portdouglasseafood.com; 3 Inlet St; mains $22-39.50; ⊙lunch & dinner) Jutting out over Dickson Inlet, tables spread out along a huge deck where you can await the 5pm arrival of George the grouper, who comes to feed most days. Take up the bucket of prawns and a drink deal for $18 from 3.30pm to 5.30pm, or choose your own crayfish and mud crabs from the live tank. Great service, cool atmosphere.

Nautilus MODERN AUSTRALIAN $$$
(☎4099 5330; www.nautilus-restaurant.com.au; 17 Murphy St, enter via Macrossan St; mains $33-55; ⊙dinner) A hidden pathway leads through tropical gardens to intimate white-cloth tables amid tall palms at this decades-old fine-dining institution. Seafood is a speciality, such as wok-tossed mud crab with kaffir lime and lemongrass laksa. The pièce de résistance is the six-course chef's tasting menu ($110; $160 with paired wines). Children under eight aren't accepted.

Re:hab CAFE $
(www.beijaflordesign.com.au; 7/42 Macrossan St; ⊙8am-6pm; @🛜) Coffee is literally an art form at this chilled cafe–local art gallery, with astoundingly intricate designs etched in the froth of its fresh-roasted brews. Home-baked cakes, muffins and slices, and a zen little courtyard out back.

Four Mile Seafood & Takeaway BURGERS **$**
(Four Mile Beach Plaza, Barrier St, Four Mile Beach; dishes $5.50 14; ☺9am-8pm Mon-Sat, 11am-8pm Sun) This takeaway joint offers some winning combos, such as fresh coral trout with avocado.

Self-catering
Stock up on supplies at the large Coles Supermarket (11 Macrossan St) in the Port Village shopping centre. For locally caught seafood, including prawns, mud crabs and a big range of fish, head to Seafood House (11 Warner St; ☺9am-6pm).

♉ Drinking & Entertainment
Drinking and dining go hand in hand in Port Douglas and the local clubs and hotels all serve up inexpensive pub-style meals. Even before the cutlery is packed away, many restaurants are inviting places for a drink.

[TOP CHOICE] Tin Shed BAR
(www.thetinshed-portdouglas.com.au; 7 Ashford Ave) Port Douglas's Combined Services Club is a locals' secret. This is a rare find: bargain dining on the waterfront, and even the drinks are cheap. Sign in, line up and grab a table on the river- or shore-fronting deck.

Iron Bar PUB
(5 Macrossan St) A bit of whacky outback shearing-shed decor never goes astray in Queensland. After polishing off your Don Bradman eye fillet (the steaks are named after famous Aussies), head upstairs for a flutter on the cane-toad races ($5). Usually the latest closer in town.

Court House Hotel PUB
(www.at-the-courty.com; cnr Macrossan & Wharf Sts; mains $15-25; ☺lunch & dinner) Commanding a prime corner location, the 'Courty' is a lively local, with cover bands on weekends.

Port Douglas Yacht Club BAR
(www.portdouglasyachtclub.com.au; Spinnaker Close) Another local favourite, there's a spirited nautical atmosphere at Port's yacht club. Inexpensive meals are served nightly.

🔒 Shopping
Port Douglas Markets MARKETS
(Anzac Park, end of Macrossan St; ☺8am-1.30pm Sun) These markets are treasure without the trash. Only wares that are made by the stall holders or their families – including arts, crafts and jewellery, plus locally produced tropical fruits and the like – are allowed to be sold here. Make sure you arrive early before it all sells.

❶ Information
There's no 'official' (ie non-commercial) tourist information centre in Port Douglas; the government-run Cairns & Tropical North Visitor Information Centre (p458) covers Port Douglas and the Daintree region and can make bookings.

Along Macrossan St, internet cafes charge around $5 per hour. The main post office is on Owen St.

❶ Getting There & Away
For more information on getting to Cairns, see p459.

Coral Reef Coaches (☎4098 2800; www.coralreefcoaches.com.au) connects Port Douglas with Cairns ($36, 1¼ hours) via Cairns airport and Palm Cove.

Sun Palm (☎4087 2900; www.sunpalmtransport.com) has frequent daily services between Port Douglas and Cairns ($35, 1½ hours) via the northern beaches and the airport, and up the coast to Mossman ($10, 20 minutes), Daintree village and the ferry ($20, one hour) and Cape Tribulation ($48, three hours).

Airport Connections (☎4099 5950; www.tnqshuttle.com; $36; ☺3.20am-5.20pm) runs an hourly shuttle-bus service between Port Douglas, Cairns' northern beaches and Cairns airport, continuing on to Cairns' CBD.

Country Road Coachlines (☎4069 5446; www.countryroadcoachlines.com.au) has a bus service between Port Douglas and Cooktown on the coastal route via Cape Tribulation three times a week ($63), weather permitting.

❶ Getting Around
Bicycle
Port Douglas Bike Hire (☎4099 5799; www.portdouglasbikehire; cnr Wharf & Warner Sts; per day $19).

Bus
Sun Palm (☎4087 2900; www.sunpalmtransport.com; ☺7am-midnight) Runs in a continuous loop every half-hour from Wildlife Habitat Port Douglas to the Marina Mirage, stopping regularly en route. Flag down the driver at marked bus stops.

Car & Motorcycle
Port Douglas has plenty of small, local car-hire companies as well as major international chains. With the exception of the Daintree Wild Zoo, it's the last place before Cooktown where you

THE BAMA WAY

From Cairns to Cooktown, you can see the country through Aboriginal eyes along the **Bama Way** (www.bamaway. com.au). Bama (pronounced Bumma) means 'person' in the Kuku Yalanji and Guugu Yimithirr languages, and highlights include tours with Aboriginal guides, such as the Walker Family tours (p481) on the Bloomfield Track, and Willie Gordon's enlightening Guurrbi Tours (p483) in Cooktown. Pick up a Bama Way map from visitor centres.

can hire a 4WD. Expect to pay around $65 a day for a small car and $130 a day for a 4WD, plus insurance.

Latitude 16 (☑4099 4999; www.latitude16. com.au; 54 Macrossan St) Also rents open-sided Mokes (per day from $49).

Taxi
Port Douglas Taxis (☑13 10 08) offers 24-hour service and has a rank on Warner St.

Mossman
POP 1740

After the holiday hype of Port Douglas, Mossman – only 20km north – is a pleasant, unpretentious cane town with a working sugar mill and cane trains to prove it. Mossman should be an obligatory stop to visit Mossman Gorge (and Mojo's restaurant!), and it's also a good place to fill up the tank and stock up on supplies if you're heading north.

◉ Sights & Activities

Mossman Gorge   NATIONAL PARK
In the southeast corner of Daintree National Park, 5km west of Mossman town, Mossman Gorge forms part of the traditional lands of the Kuku Yalanji Indigenous people. Carved by the Mossman River, the gorge is a boulder-strewn valley where sparkling water washes over ancient rocks. **Walking tracks** loop along the river to a refreshing **swimming hole** – take care as the currents can be swift. There's a picnic area here but no camping. The complete circuit back to the entrance takes about an hour.

To truly appreciate the gorge's cultural significance, book in for one of the 1½-hour Indigenous-guided **Kuku-Yalanji Dream-**time Walks (adult/child $39/22; ☺9am, 11am, 1pm & 3pm Mon-Fri) through the cultural and visitor centre, **Mossman Gorge Gateway** (☑4098 2595; www.yalanji.com.au; ☺8.30am-5pm Mon-Fri).

Janbal Gallery   GALLERY
(☑4099 5599; www.janbalgallery.com.au; 5 Johnston Rd; ☺Tue-Sat or by appointment) Browse and buy the art at this Aboriginal-run gallery, or create your own under the guidance of its artist in residence, Binna. Art classes include painting an A4 canvas (adult/child $65/30, two hours), a boomerang ($48/30, one hour), painting (and playing) a didgeri-doo ($165/80, three hours), and one-on-one lessons, while learning about Indigenous reef and rainforest heritage.

Mossman Sugar Mill Tours   TOUR
(☑4030 4190; www.mossag.com.au; Mill St; adult/child $25/15; ☺11am & 1.30pm Mon-Fri Jul-Oct) With all the cane fields around, you're probably curious by now to know how all that giant tropical grass gets turned into sugar. During crushing season, tours reveal all. Wear closed shoes; kids under five aren't allowed.

🛏 Sleeping & Eating

Silky Oaks Lodge   CABINS $$$
(☑4098 1666; www.silkyoakslodge.com.au; Finlayvale Rd; treehouse/river house from $598/798; ❄@🛜🏊) This international resort woos honeymooners and soothes stressed-out execs with languorous hammocks, spa treatments and designer polished-timber cabins complete with aromatherapy oil burners. Its stunning **Treehouse Restaurant & Bar** (mains $34-38; ☺breakfast, lunch & dinner) is open to interlopers.

[TOP CHOICE] **Mojo's**   INTERNATIONAL $$
(☑4098 1202; www.mojosbarandgrill.com. au; 41 Front St; mains $24-29; ☺lunch Mon-Fri, dinner Mon-Sat; ☑) Save yourself a round-the-world plane ticket: French-Australian team Remi Pougeard-Dulimbert and Michael Hart (who caters every two years for the summer and winter Olympics) are the creative force behind exquisite dishes, such as feather-light gnocchi with blue cheese and caramelised pear, spicy samosas with tamarind chutney, soft-shell prawn tacos, and a *divine* scallop pie, followed by their 'Flaming Mojo' chocolate fondue with Bundy rum. Incredible value and well worth the trip from Port Douglas (or Paris, or anywhere, actually).

ⓘ Information

DERM (☑4098 2188; www.derm.qld.gov.au); Centenary Bldg, 1 Front St; ◷8am-4pm Mon-Fri) has information on the Daintree National Park up to and beyond Cape Tribulation.

ⓘ Getting There & Away

Sun Palm (☑4087 2900; www.sunpalmtransport.com) has three daily buses between Mossman and Cairns ($70, 1¾ hours), via Cairns airport, and Port Douglas ($10, 20 minutes) on its run to Cape Trib.

Mossman to the Daintree

Travelling north from Mossman, it's 26km through cane fields and farmland before the crossroads to either Daintree village or the Daintree river ferry, with some worthwhile stops en route.

Five kilometres from Mossman you'll come to the first 2.5km-long palm-fringed stretch of sand, **Newell Beach**. It's a small community where lazing around or fishing for dinner off the beach take priority.

About 8km northwest of Mossman, follow the turn-off to Miallo in the **Whyanbool Valley**. Highlights of this hidden, fertile haven include the horticultural gardens and orchards of **High Falls Farm** (☑4098 8231; www.highfallsfarm.com.au; Old Forestry Rd, Miallo; mains $12-20; lunch Fri-Tue, breakfast & lunch Sun Jun-Oct; ☑); ask about self-guided orchard tours and tropical fruit tastings.

The turn-off to **Wonga Beach**, 22km north of Mossman, leads to this peaceful 7km ribbon of beach backed by palms and Calophyllum trees. **Wonga Beach Horse Rides** (☑4098 7583; www.beachhorserides.com.au; group rides $115) offers three-hour morning and afternoon rides along the beach.

Back on the main road about 5km north of Wonga Beach, en route to the intersection to Daintree village or the Daintree River ferry, the wildlife at **Daintree Wild Zoo** (☑4098 7272; 2054 Daintree Rd; www.daintreewild.com.au; adult/child $26/13; ◷8.30am-4.30pm) includes fresh and saltwater crocs, roos, dingoes and a cacophony of birds. It also has cosy farm-stay accommodation, a BYO restaurant and tours from Cairns and Port Douglas, with various package deals available, and can arrange good deals on 4WD rental for the Bloomfield Track.

THE DAINTREE

The Daintree represents many things: a river, a rainforest national park, a reef, a village, and the home of its traditional custodians, the Kuku Yalanji people. It encompasses the coastal lowland area between the Daintree and Bloomfield Rivers, where the rainforest meets the coast. It's an ancient but fragile ecosystem, once threatened by logging and development but now largely protected as a World Heritage area.

The Daintree was named after British-born geologist, gold prospector and photographer Richard Daintree (1832–78), the first government geologist for North Queensland, whose pioneering work included geological surveys as well as the collection of plant specimens.

Daintree River to Cape Tribulation

Part of the Wet Tropics World Heritage area, the region from the Daintree River north to Cape Tribulation is extraordinarily beautiful and famed for its ancient rainforest, sandy beaches and rugged mountains.

Cow Bay and Cape Tribulation are loosely termed 'villages', but the length of Cape Tribulation Rd is scattered with places to stay and eat. There is no mains power north of the Daintree River – electricity is supplied by generators or, increasingly, solar power. Shops and services are limited, and mobile phone reception is largely nonexistent out here.

The lovable cable ferry, the **Daintree River ferry** (car/motorcycle/bicycle & pedestrian one way $12/5/1; ◷6am-midnight, no bookings), carries you and your vehicle across the river every 15 minutes or so.

COW BAY & AROUND

On the steep, winding road between Cape Kimberley and Cow Bay is the **Walu Wugirriga (Alexandra Range) lookout**, with an information board and sweeping views over the range and the Daintree River inlet that are especially breathtaking at sunset.

🏛 **Daintree Discovery Centre** (☑4098 9171; www.daintree-rec.com.au; Tulip Oak Rd; adult/child $28/14; ◷8.30am-5pm) The **aerial walkway** at this award-winning rainforest interpretive centre takes you high into the forest canopy, including climbing up a 23m-high tower

DAINTREE NATIONAL PARK: THEN & NOW

The greater Daintree Rainforest is protected as part of Daintree National Park. The area has a controversial history: despite conservationist blockades, in 1983 the Bloomfield Track was bulldozed through lowland rainforest from Cape Tribulation to the Bloomfield River, and the ensuing international publicity led indirectly to the federal government to nominate Queensland's wet tropical rainforests for World Heritage listing. The move drew objections from the Queensland timber industry and the state government but, in 1988, the area was inscribed on the World Heritage List, resulting in a total ban on commercial logging in the area.

World Heritage listing doesn't affect land ownership rights or control and, since the 1990s, efforts have been made by the Queensland State Government and conservation agencies to buy back and rehabilitate freehold properties, adding them to the Daintree National Park and installing visitor interpretation facilities. Sealing the road to Cape Tribulation in 2002 opened the area to rapid settlement, triggering the buy-back of hundreds more properties. Coupled with development controls, these efforts are now bearing the fruits of forest regeneration. Check out **Rainforest Rescue** (www.rainforest rescue.org.au) for more information.

Biodiversity

Far North Queensland's Wet Tropics area has amazing pockets of biodiversity. The Wet Tropics World Heritage Area stretches from Townsville to Cooktown and covers 894,420 hectares of coastal zones and hinterland, diverse swamp and mangrove-forest habitats, eucalypt woodlands and tropical rainforest. It covers only 0.01% of Australia's surface area, but has:

» 36% of all the mammal species

» 50% of the bird species

» around 60% of the butterfly species

» 65% of the fern species.

Making a Difference

Increased tourism is undoubtedly having an impact on the Daintree area. When visiting, leave only footsteps behind: take your rubbish with you, stick to designated trails and watch out for wildlife on the roads.

Other ways to help preserve this impossibly beautiful part of the world:

» Check whether tour companies have ecocertification (www.ecotourism.org.au).

» Use natural, chemical-free toiletries.

» Ask about volunteer opportunities to clean up beaches or monitor wildlife, or contact Austrop (Bat House; p479) to assist with forest rehabilitation and planting.

» Consider donating to a not-for-profit environment group, such as Rainforest Rescue, the Wilderness Society or the Australian Conservation Foundation.

» Choose accommodation that encourages recycling and reduces energy and water consumption.

(used to study carbon levels). There are a few short interpretive walks – including superb life-size sculptures of now-extinct giant wombats, echidnas and more, hidden among the foliage – and a small theatre running films on cassowaries, crocodiles, conservation and climate change. Tickets are valid for seven days, with good rates for families.

Daintree Rainforest Retreat (☎4098 9101; www.daintreeretreat.com. au; 1473 Cape Tribulation Rd; d $121-149, family $190-210; ※) Set back from the main road amid rainforest, these boutique motel rooms have striking tropical colour schemes and glossy woodwork. Some have kitchenettes, or you can dine at its onsite restaurant, **Tree Frogs** (mains $15-36; ⊘dinner Mon-Sat), which is also open to nonguests.

TOP CHOICE Jambu (www.daintreecoffeecompany.com.au; 335 Cape Tribulation Rd; mains $9.50-15; ☺breakfast & lunch; ☑) is a funky little find dishing up 12-inch wraps, fantastic burgers including tofu with homemade peanut sauce, rib steak, and reef fish, as well as boutique Australian beers, such as Little Creatures, and its own Daintree Coffee Company brews served in 10 different styles (espresso, ristretto, affogato et al).

The Cow Bay Hotel (☑4098 9011; Cape Tribulation Rd; s/d $77/99, mains $12-25; ☺lunch & dinner), adjacent to the turn-off to the beach, is the only real pub in the whole Daintree region.

Floravilla Ice Cream Factory (☑4098 9016; Bailey Creek Rd; ice creams $5; ☺8am-5.30pm), next door to the pub, has at least 26 flavours of organic ice cream.

Along the sealed Buchanan Creek Rd (often called Cow Bay Rd, or simply 'the road to the beach'), the YHA-associated Crocodylus Village (☑4098 9166; www.crocodyluscapetrib.com; Buchanan Creek Rd; dm $25, d en suite $85; @☎☒) has a restaurant (mains $15; ☺dinner) and bar that are open to the public, as well as activities including half-day kayaking trips ($65) and adventurous two-day sea-kayaking tours to Snapper Island ($220; ☺Mon, Wed & Fri).

Laid-back Epiphyte B&B (☑4098 9039; www.rainforestbb.com; 22 Silkwood Rd; s/d/cabin $70/95/140) is situated on a lush 3.5-hectare property with individually styled rooms of varying sizes but all with en suites and their own verandahs. Even better is the spacious, super-private cabin that has a patio, kitchenette and sunken bathroom. From the front deck of the house you can kick back with views of imposing Thornton Peak (1975m). Rates include breakfast.

The best-value accommodation in the area, hands-down, is at Daintree Rainforest Bungalows (☑4098 9229; www.daintreerainforestbungalows.com; Lot 40 Spurwood Rd; d $90). Its free-standing wooden cabins are simple but stylish, with violet- and lilac-toned fabrics, en suites and covered decks overlooking the rainforest. Minimum stay is two nights.

Of course, Cow Bay's real highlight lies at the end of the road, where the beautiful white-sand **Cow Bay Beach** rivals any coastal paradise.

Daintree Ice Cream Company (☑4098 9114; Lot 100 Cape Tribulation Rd; ice cream $5; ☺11am-5pm) Back on the main road, there are no agonising decisions at this all-natural ice-cream producer – you get a cup of four exotic flavours that change daily. Work it off on a 20-minute orchard walk.

Just south of Cooper Creek, Rainforest Village (☑4098 9015; ☺7am-7pm) sells groceries, ice and fuel, and has a small camping ground (unpowered/powered sites $24/32) with hot showers and a camp kitchen.

Also known as Jungle Bugs & Butterflies, the Daintree Entomological Museum (☑4098 9045; www.daintreemuseum.com.au; Turpentine Rd; adult/child $10/5; ☺10am-4pm) displays a large private collection of local and exotic bugs, butterflies and spiders pinned inside large glass cases. There are a few live exhibits of giant cockroaches and a butterfly enclosure.

Book ahead for a walk with Cooper Creek Wilderness (☑4098 9126; www.ccwild.com; Cape Tribulation Rd; guided walks $45). Bring your togs for the day walks (departing 9am, 2pm & 3pm), which take you through Daintree rainforest and include a dip in Cooper Creek. Night walks (departing at 8pm) focus on spotting nocturnal wildlife. There's also a full day tour including lunch and a river cruise ($130).

Cape Tribulation Wilderness Cruises (☑4033 2052; www.capetribcruises.com; Cape Tribulation Rd; adult/child $25/18) has one-hour mangrove cruises where you can go in search of crocodiles.

At magnificent crescent-shaped Thornton Beach, the licensed Cafe on Sea (Cape Tribulation Rd; mains $12-20; ☺9am-4pm) is only a towel-length back from the sand.

Cape Tribulation

This little piece of paradise retains a frontier quality, with low-key development, road signs alerting drivers to cassowary crossings and crocodile warnings that make beach strolls that little bit less relaxing.

The rainforest tumbles right down to two magnificent, white-sand beaches – Myall and Cape Trib – separated by a knobby cape. The village of Cape Tribulation marks the end of the road, literally, and the beginning of the 4WD-only coastal route along the Bloomfield Track.

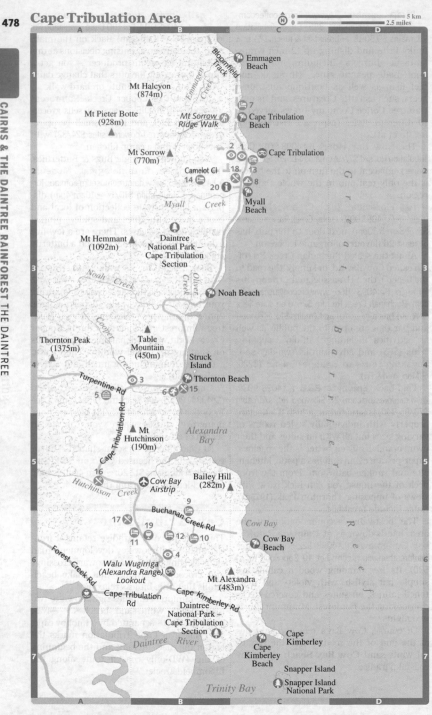

Sights & Activities

Beaches & Waterholes SWIMMING, WALKS
Long walks on the stunning swathes of **Cape Tribulation Beach** or **Myall Beach** are a favourite pastime and you can swim safely outside stinger season, though heed any warning signs and local advice about croc sightings. A couple of boardwalks run through the mangroves.

Alternatively, take a dip in the crystal-clear, croc-free **swimming hole** (admission by gold coin donation) adjacent to Mason's Store.

Ocean Safari REEF TRIPS
(☑4098 0006; www.oceansafari.com.au; adult/child $108/69; ☺9am & 1pm) The Great Barrier Reef is just half an hour offshore, but at the time of writing Ocean Safari was the only outfit offering trips to the reef. Prices include snorkelling gear; there's a maximum of 25 people, so book ahead.

Jungle Surfing FLYING FOX
(☑4098 0043; www.junglesurfing.com.au; $90) Get right up into the rainforest on an exhilarating zipline flying fox through the rainforest canopy, stopping at five tree platforms. Tours depart eight times daily from Cape Tribulation Pharmacy (next to the IGA supermarket); it's not possible to self-drive to the property, and spectators aren't allowed.

The same outfit also runs guided **night walks** ($40; ☺7.30pm), during which zany

biologist-guides help shed light on the dark jungle. Rates include pick-ups throughout Cape Trib.

Cape Trib Exotic Fruit Farm FRUIT FARM
(☑4098 0057; www.capetrib.com.au; tastings $20; ☺2pm) Bookings are essential for tours of these magnificent tropical orchards and a tasting of 10 of the 100-plus seasonal organic fruits grown here using permaculture methods. It also has a couple of stunning private cabins.

Bat House CONSERVATION CENTRE
(☑4098 0063; Cape Tribulation Rd; www.austrop.org.au; admission $2; ☺10.30am-3.30pm Tue-Sun) A nursery for injured or orphaned fruit bats (flying foxes), run by conservation organisation Austrop, which also welcomes forest rehabilitation and planting volunteers for a minimum of one week (on-station bunk room accommodation and meals included).

Mt Sorrow WALKING
Serious, fit walkers should lace up early for the Mt Sorrow Ridge Walk (7km, five to six hours return); it's strenuous but worth it. The start of the marked trail is about 150m north of the Kulki picnic area car park, on your left.

Tours

Cape Trib Horse Rides HORSE RIDING
(☑1800 111 124; 4098 0030; per person $95; ☺8am & 1.30pm) Leisurely rides along the beach.

WORTH A TRIP

DAINTREE VILLAGE

You may be racing to the beaches of Cape Trib, but it's worth taking the 20km detour to tiny Daintree village (population 130). While neither the village nor the surrounding countryside are part of the Wet Tropics World Heritage Area, there are still pockets of untouched rainforest.

Croc-spotting cruises on the Daintree River are the village's main attraction. Numerous operators run trips – try **Crocodile Express** (☑4098 6120; www.daintreeconnection. com.au; Daintree Village; 1hr cruise adult/child $25/13; ☉daily from 8.30am), or **Daintree River Wild Watch** (☑4098 7068; www.daintreeriverwildwatch.com.au; 2hr cruise adult/child $50/35), which has informative sunrise bird-watching cruises and sunset photography nature cruises.

Daintree Eco Lodge & Spa (☑4098 6100; www.daintree-ecolodge.com.au; 20 Daintree Rd; d $550-598; ❋@☎☀) The 15 boutique 'banyans' (pole cabins; 10 with private spas) sit high in the rainforest canopy a few kilometres south of Daintree Village. Even the day spa is eco-minded, with its own range of organic, Indigenous-inspired products and treatments. Nonguests are welcome at its superb **Julaymba Restaurant** (mains $29-32; ☉breakfast, lunch & dinner), utilising local produce, including indigenous berries, nuts, leaves and flowers. Don't miss a Flaming Green Ant cocktail!

No fuel is available in Daintree village.

Cape Tribulation Kayaks   KAYAKING
(☑4098 0077; www.capetribcamping.com.au; 2hr tours $60) Runs guided kayaking trips and rents kayaks (single/double kayak per hour $20/30).

D'Arcy of the Daintree   4WD
(☑4098 9180; darcyofdaintree@yahoo.com.au) Entertaining 4WD trips up the Bloomfield Track as far as Cooktown (adult/child $185/90) and down Cape Tribulation Rd (adult/child from $55/35). Free pick-ups from Cape Trib and Cow Bay.

Mason's Tours   WALKING, 4WD
(☑4098 0070; www.masonstours.com.au, Mason's Store, Cape Tribulation Rd) Interpretive walks lasting two hours (adult/child $49/40) or a half-day ($70/55), and a croc-spotting night walk ($49). Also 4WD tours up the Bloomfield Track (from $135/114).

🛏 Sleeping & Eating

Restaurants at Cape Trib's resorts are all open to nonguests.

TOP CHOICE **Cape Trib Exotic Fruit Farm Cabins**   CABINS **$$**
(☑4098 0057; www.capetrib.com.au; d $180) Right on the burbling World Heritage creek boundary, amid the orchards of Cape Trib Exotic Fruit Farm, this pair of timber pole cabins are far enough apart that you feel like you're alone in the forest. With exposed timber floors, ceilings and huge decks, simple but elegant cabins are equipped with electric Eskies. Rates include breakfast hampers filled with tropical fruit from the farm. Minimum stay is two nights.

Rainforest Hideaway   B&B **$$**
(☑4098 0108; www.rainforesthideaway.com.au; 19 Camelot Close; d $95-135) This colourful B&B has been single-handedly built by its owner, artist and sculptor 'Dutch Rob' – even the furniture and beds are handmade. A sculpture trail winds through the property; rates include breakfast.

Cape Trib Beach House   HOSTEL **$**
(☑4098 0030; www.capetribbeach.com.au; dm $26-32, d $75, cabins $130-230; ❋@☀) Rainforest huts at this low-key beachfront property house dorms through to en suite timber cabins. There's a tidy communal kitchen as well as an open-deck licensed **restaurant** (mains $11.50-26.50; ☉breakfast, lunch & dinner).

PK's Jungle Village   HOSTEL **$**
(☑4098 0040; www.pksjunglevillage.com; unpowered sites per person $15, dm $25, budget cabin s/d $48/70, en suite cabin d $125; ❋@☎☀) PK's is a longstanding backpacker hub. You can reach Myall Beach by boardwalk, and its **Jungle Bar** (dishes $5-18; ☉restaurant lunch & dinner, bar noon-midnight) is the entertainment epicentre of Cape Trib.

Mason's Store & Cafe   CAFE **$**
(Cape Tribulation Rd; mains $12; ☉10am-4pm Sun-Thu, to 7pm Fri & Sat) Laid-back cafe

dishing up good fish and chips and huge steak sandwiches. The store sells limited groceries and takeaway alcohol.

Cape Tribulation Camping CAMPGROUND$
(☑4098 0077; www.capetribcamping.com.au; unpowered/powered sites $30/40, safari huts s/d $45/70; @) Sociable beachfront spot with a nightly communal fire and friendly managers and kayaking guides.

Whet Restaurant & Cinema
MODERN AUSTRALIAN $$
(☑4098 0007; 1 Cape Tribulation Rd; mains $27.50-33; ⊙lunch & dinner) Cape Trib's coolest address, with passable but overhyped food – perhaps because it's the only place you can get a meal much after 8pm. Call for film screening times.

IGA GROCERIES $
(PK's Jungle Village; ⊙8am-6pm) The Daintree's largest supermarket.

❶ Information

Stop in at **Mason's Store** (☑4098 0070; Cape Tribulation Rd; ⊙8am-6pm; @) for info on the region, including Bloomfield Track conditions.

NORTH TO COOKTOWN

There are two routes to Cooktown from the south: the coastal route from Cape Tribulation via the 4WD-only Bloomfield Track, and the inland route, which is sealed all the way via Peninsula Developmental Rd and Cooktown Developmental Rd.

Inland Route

The inland route skirts along the western side of the Great Dividing Range for 332km (about 4½ hours' drive) from Cairns to Cooktown.

The historical township of **Mt Molloy** (population 275) marks the start of the Peninsula Developmental Rd, about 40km north of Mareeba. Since its heady gold- and copper-mining days, the town centre has shrivelled to comprise a pub, bakery, post office and cafe. The road continues north via **Mt Carbine**, and all that's left of a once thriving mining town, to the **Palmer River**, where you'll find fuel, camping and meals.

It's another 15km to **Lakeland**, a hamlet at the junction of the Peninsula Developmental Rd and the Cooktown Developmental Rd. Head west and you're on your way

to Laura and Cape York (4WD and forward planning are essential); continue straight northeast and you've got another 80km to Cooktown.

Some 30km shy of Cooktown, the staggering **Black Mountain National Park**, with thousands of stacked, square, black granite boulders formed 260 million years ago, marks the northern end of the Wet Tropics World Heritage Area.

Coastal Route

The legendary 4WD-only Bloomfield Track from Cape Tribulation to Cooktown traverses creek crossings, diabolically steep climbs and patchy surfaces. It can be impassable for many weeks on end during the Wet, and even in the Dry you should check road conditions locally, as creek crossings are affected by tide times. The track runs for around 80km before linking up with the sealed Cooktown Developmental Rd 30km south of Cooktown.

Forged as far back as 1968, for many years the contentious track was little more than a remote walking track – see p476. Some locals are seeking its staged closure over the next decade or so.

It's 5km from Cape Trib to **Emmagen Creek**, from where the road climbs and dips steeply and turns sharp corners. This is the most challenging section of the drive, especially after rain. The road then follows the broad Bloomfield River before crossing it 30km north of Cape Trib.

Turn left immediately after the bridge to see the **Bloomfield Falls**. Crocs inhabit the river and the site is significant to the Indigenous **Wujal Wujal** community, located just north of the river. Residents of Wujal Wujal, the **Walker Family** (☑4060 8069; www. bamaway.com.au; adult/child $15/8; ⊙by reservation) runs highly recommended half-hour **walking tours** of the falls and surrounding forest.

About 5km north of Wujal Wujal, the **Bloomfield Track Takeaway & Middleshop** (☑4060 8174; dishes &7-28; ⊙8am-10pm Tue-Sat, to 8pm Sun & Mon) serves pizzas and burgers and has fuel, fishing tackle and groceries.

North of Bloomfield, several walks begin from **Home Rule Wilderness Cabins** (☑4060 3925; www.home-rule.com.au; Rossville; unpowered sites per adult/child $10/5, r adult/child $25/15), at the end of a bumpy 3km driveway.

Spotless facilities include a communal kitchen; meals are available as well as canoe hire. Home Rule is ground zero for the weekend-long **Wallaby Creek Festival** (www.wallabycreekfestival.org.au; ⊘Sep), with roots and blues music on two stages, alternative workshops and family events.

It's only another 9km to the welcoming sight of the **Lion's Den Hotel** (☑4060 3911; www.lionsdenhotel.com.au; Helenvale; unpowered/powered sites $20/26, s/d $40/50, d safari tents $70; ☀). This iconic watering hole with genuine corrugated, graffiti-covered decor dates back to 1875 and still attracts a steady stream of travellers and local characters. There's fuel and ice-cold beer, and its **restaurant** (mains $18-23; ⊘breakfast, lunch & dinner) serves up excellent pub grub.

Mungumby Lodge (☑4060 3158; www.mungumby.com; Helenvale; s/d $260/279; ⊛☀) David Attenborough recently came to film at this verdant oasis 5km east of the Bloomfield Track – you'll see why as you explore its surrounding rainforest walks and nearby waterfall. En suite bungalows are scattered among the lawns and mango trees. Rates include breakfast; lunch, dinner and nature tours are available.

About 4km north, the Bloomfield Track meets the sealed Cooktown Developmental Rd, from where it's a dust-free 28km to Cooktown.

Cooktown

POP 2093

At the southeastern edge of Cape York Peninsula, Cooktown is a small place with a big history: for thousands of years, Waymbuurr was the place the local Guugu Yimithirr and Kuku Yalanji people held as a meeting ground, and it was here that on 17 June 1770, Lieutenant (later Captain) Cook beached his bark, the *Endeavour*, on the banks of its estuary at Waymbuurr. The *Endeavour* had earlier struck a reef offshore from Cape Tribulation, and Cook and his crew spent 48 days here while they repaired the damage – making it the site of Australia's first, albeit transient, non-Indigenous settlement.

The inland route from Mareeba was finally sealed all the way in 2005, and tourism is now a growing industry. It's still remote territory, though, and still firmly believes that happiness is a fishing rod and an Esky full of beer.

⊙ Sights & Activities

Cooktown hibernates during summer, ie the Wet (locals call it 'the dead season'), and many attractions and tours close or have reduced hours. The main street, Charlotte St, has some beautiful 19th-century buildings.

Nature's Powerhouse & Botanic Gardens
GALLERIES
(☑4069 6004; www.naturespowerhouse.com.au; Walker St; galleries adult/child $3.50/free; ⊘9am-5pm) This environment interpretive centre is home to two excellent galleries: the **Charlie Tanner Gallery**, with pickled and preserved creepy-crawlie exhibits; and the **Vera Scarth-Johnson Gallery**, displaying botanical illustrations of the region's native plants.

The centre doubles as Cooktown's official visitor centre, with brochures outlining some of the area's excellent walking trails. Its **Verandah Cafe** (mains $9-16; ⊘10am-2.30pm; ⊘) serves dishes, such as gado gado with coconut damper.

Nature's Powerhouse is at the entry to Cooktown's 62-hectare **Botanic Gardens** (unrestricted access). Filled with native and exotic tropical plants, including rare orchids, the gardens are among Australia's oldest and most magnificent.

James Cook Museum MUSEUM
(www.nationaltrustqld.org; cnr Helen & Furneaux Sts; adult/child $10/3; ⊘9.30am-4pm) Built as a convent in 1889, Cooktown's finest historical building houses well-preserved and presented relics from Cook's time in the town, including journal entries and the cannon and anchor from the *Endeavour*, retrieved from the sea floor in 1971, and displays on the area's Indigenous culture.

Bicentennial Park & Around MONUMENTS
Bicentennial Park is home to the much-photographed bronze **Captain Cook statue**. Nearby, the **Milbi Wall (Story Wall)** is a 12m-long mosaic that spans creation stories to European contact with the local Gungarde (Guugu Yimithirr) Indigenous people, WWII and recent attempts at reconciliation. Sitting just out in the water from Bicentennial Park is the **rock** marking the spot where Cook ran aground and tied up to a tree (part of the original tree is on display at the James Cook Museum).

Cooktown's **wharf** is one of Queensland's sweetest fishing spots.

Although the reef is not far away, there are no regularly scheduled dive or snorkelling trips. Water-based tours depart from the wharf.

» **Guurrbi Tours** (☑4069 6259; www.guurrbitours.com; 2/4hr tours $95/120, self-drive $65/85; ☺Mon-Sat) Nugal-warra family elder Willie Gordon runs revelatory tours that use the physical landscape to describe the spiritual landscape. The morning Rainbow Serpent tour involves some walking, bush tucker and rock-art sites, including a birthing cave. The afternoon Great Emu tour is shorter and visits three rock-art sites. Self-drivers meet near the Hopevale Aboriginal Community.

» **Catch-a-Crab** (☑4069 6289; cook.cac@bigpond.com; adult/child $100/50) Local seafood supplier Nicko runs river tours on the Endeavour and Annan Rivers in search of mud crabs. Great for kids and very popular – book ahead.

» **Cooktown Barra Fishing Charters** (☑4069 5346; www.cooktownbarracharters. com; half/full day $100/200) Also runs croc-spotting, bird-watching, mud-crabbing and ecotours.

» **Cooktown Tours** (☑1300 789 550; www.cooktowntours.com) Two-hour town tours (adult/child $55/33) and half-day trips to Black Mountain and the Lion's Den Hotel (adult/child $110/77).

» **Cooktown Cruises** (☑4069 5712; www.cooktowncruises.com; 2hr cruise adult/child $55/35; ☺Tue-Sun Jun-Sep, 3 days per week Apr-Jun & Oct-Dec) Scenic cruises up the Endeavour River.

Grassy Hill WALKS
By the time you're reading this, a winding road in the shape of the rainbow serpent (a sacred being in Indigenous Dreaming stories) will snake all the way up to the top of Grassy Hill Lookout, with 360-degree views of the town, river and ocean. Otherwise, the steep 15-minute walk up is especially worthwhile at sunrise. Cook climbed this hill looking for a passage out through the reefs.

Another walking trail (800m one-way; 25 minutes) leads from the summit down to the beach at Cherry Tree Bay.

✵ Festivals & Events

The **Cooktown Discovery Festival** (www.cooktowndiscoveryfestival.com.au; ☺early Jun) is held over the Queen's Birthday weekend to commemorate Captain Cook's landing in 1770 with a costumed re-enactment and fancy dress grand parade, as well as Indigenous workshops and a traditional corroboree.

🛏 Sleeping & Eating

Cooktown has plenty of accommodation, including several caravan parks, but book ahead in the Dry.

Sovereign Resort Hotel HOTEL $$
(☑4043 0500; www.sovereign-resort.com.au; cnr Charlotte & Green Sts; d $170-185, 2-bed apt $210; ✳@🛜❄) Cooktown's swishest digs are right on the main street, with a warren of breezy, tropical-style rooms with wooden-slat blinds and tile floors. Kick back in the landscaped garden pool area, the smart **Balcony Restaurant** (mains $23.50-30.50; ☺breakfast & dinner) and low-key **Cafe-Bar** (mains $11-21.50; ☺11am-8pm; @🖉).

Pam's Place & Cooktown Motel MOTEL $
(☑4069 5166; www.cooktownhostel.com; cnr Charlotte & Boundary Sts; dm/s/d $28/50/55, motel d $90; ✳@🛜❄) Cooktown's YHA-associated hostel is everything a backpackers should be: welcoming and cosy, with sociable common areas, spotless facilities and a leafy garden. Spiffy new motel units still have a faint scent of fresh paint. The friendly managers can help find harvest work.

Endeavour Falls Tourist Park CARAVAN PARK $
(☑4069 5431; www.endeavourfallstouristpark. com.au; Endeavour Valley Rd; unpowered/powered sites $24/28, cabins $115; ✳❄) Situated 32km northwest on the road to Hopevale (15km unsealed), this well-run, peaceful park backs onto the Garden of Eden-like Endeavour Falls (with a resident croc – don't swim!). Its well-stocked shop serves **takeaways** (dishes $6.50-13.50) and has fuel.

Seaview Motel MOTEL $$
(☑4069 5377; seaviewmotel@bigpond.com.au; 178 Charlotte St; d $99-155, townhouse $220;

⊛⊠) Awesomely located opposite the wharf, with modern rooms (some with private balconies).

Restaurant 1770 MODERN AUSTRALIAN **$$**
(☑4069 5440; 7 Webber Esplanade; mains $20.50-32; ⊘breakfast, lunch & dinner; ☑)
Opening onto a romantic waterside deck, fresh fish takes top billing, but save space for mouth-watering desserts, such as white chocolate mud cake.

Cooktown Bowls Club LICENSED CLUB **$$**
(☑4069 5819; Charlotte St; mains $14-25; ⊘lunch Wed-Fri, dinner daily) Big bistro meals. Join in social bowls on Wednesday and Saturday afternoon and barefoot bowls on Wednesday evening.

Gill'd & Gutt'd FISH & CHIPS **$**
(☑4069 5863; Fisherman's Wharf, Webber Esplanade; mains $7-12; ⊘lunch & dinner) Fish and chips the way it should be – fresh and right on the waterside wharf.

❶ Information

The website www.cooktownandcapeyork.com has information on the town and surrounding areas.

Cooktown DERM (☑13 74 68; www.derm.qld.gov.au; Webber Esplanade; ⊘9am-3pm Mon-Fri). Information and camping permits for national parks, including Lizard Island.

Nature's Powerhouse (☑4069 6004; www.naturespowerhouse.com.au; Walker St; ⊘9am-5pm) Incorporates the visitor information centre.

❶ Getting There & Around

Cooktown's airfield is 10km west of town along McIvor Rd. **Hinterland Aviation** (☑4035 9323; www.hinterlandaviation.com.au; one-way $150) has one to four flights daily except Sunday to/from Cairns (one-way $150, 40 minutes).

Country Road Coachlines (☑4045 2794; www.countryroadcoachlines.com.au) runs a daily bus service between Cairns and Cooktown ($75) on either the coastal route (Bloomfield Track, via Port Douglas) or inland route (via Mareeba), depending on the day of departure and the condition of the track.

The Sovereign Resort Hotel rents out 4WDs from $120 per day.

For a taxi call ☑4069 5387.

Lizard Island

The five islands of the Lizard Island Group cluster just 27km off the coast about 100km from Cooktown. Known to the Indigenous Dingaal people as Jiigurru, the continental main island, Lizard Island, has a dry, rocky, mountainous terrain and spectacular fringing reef for snorkelling and diving. Most of the island is national park, with plenty of wildlife – including 11 different species of lizard – and 24 glistening white beaches.

Accommodation is either five-star luxury at *ultra*-exclusive **Lizard Island Resort** (☑1300 863 248; www.lizardisland.com.au; Anchor Bay; d from $1700; ⊛@⊜⊠), or – conversely – bush camping at the island's **DERM campsite** (☑13 74 68; www.derm.qld.gov.au; per person $5.15). Bring all supplies as there are no shops on the island.

Flying is the easiest way to reach Lizard Island; book all air transfers to/from Cairns (return $530) through the resort. Flight time is one hour.

Daintree Air Services (☑1800 246 206; 4034 9300; www.daintreeair.com.au) has full-day tours from Cairns at 8am ($690). The trip includes lunch, snorkelling gear, transfers and a local guide.

Understand East Coast Australia

>

population per sq km

SYDNEY | MELBOURNE | BRISBANE

≈ 337 people

East Coast Australia Today

Floods & Fires

The end of 2010 brought record rainfall to much of the East Coast, particularly NSW and Queensland. Farmers initially welcomed the announcement that the 10-year drought was over, then saw their crops waterlogged and destroyed. As the rains continued, things grew progressively worse, and by early 2011, flood waters had inundated dozens of towns, affecting 1 million sq km – roughly the size of France and Germany combined. Brisbane, Australia's third-largest city, suffered devastation on 11 January when the Brisbane River broke its banks and water levels reached above 4m, flooding vast stretches of the city.

When the waters finally subsided they left 35 people dead and over 30,000 homes and businesses destroyed or damaged. Australian Treasurer Wayne Swan described the floods as the 'most costly economic disaster in our history', costing the nation $5.6 billion. Coal production, crop losses and a hit to tourism would all take their toll.

The south also suffered from flooding in early 2011, with more than 50 communities in western and central Victoria affected. Some 1700 properties were flooded, fields were inundated and thousands of livestock were lost – placing an economic cost to agriculture upwards of $1.5 billion.

Victoria's floods followed roughly two years after an even worse natural disaster. The tragic bushfires of 7 February 2009 (dubbed 'Black Saturday') claimed 173 lives. Caused by a record-breaking heatwave, the fires destroyed some 4500 sq km and caused over $1 billion in damage.

Reef or Madness

For many climatologists these events were just part of the growing evidence that the effects of human-induced climate change were wreaking havoc on weather patterns in Australia – among other places.

Top Films

Australia (2008) Baz Luhrmann's epic set against the backdrop of WWII and beautifully shot in NSW and Queensland.
Ned Kelly (2003) An entertaining portrait of the legendary bushranger.

The Castle (1997) Hilarious comedy that gleefully plays with Aussie stereotypes.
Picnic at Hanging Rock (1975) Haunting film about schoolgirls 'absorbed' into the mysterious Australian landscape.

Top Musicians

Powderfinger Five platinum albums; retired in 2010.
Slim Dusty The twanging NSW legend – great road music.
Christine Anu Torres Strait Island singer who blends Creole-style rap and Islander chants with English.

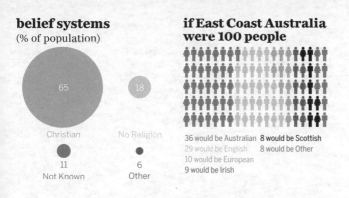

belief systems
(% of population)

65 Christian

18 No Religion

11 Not Known

6 Other

if East Coast Australia were 100 people

36 would be Australian
29 would be English
10 would be European
9 would be Irish
8 would be Scottish
8 would be Other

Climate change remains a hot topic in Australia these days (no pun intended) – particularly when it comes to Queensland's biggest tourist attraction. As sea temperatures continue to rise, marine researchers predict disastrous consequences for the Great Barrier Reef. Some estimates place the near-total devastation of the reef within the next 50 years. This destruction is unthinkable on many fronts – not least of which is the catastrophic economic consequences: the Great Barrier Reef generates an estimated $4 billion in annual tourism revenue.

Economic Stability

Natural disasters aside, Australia has done quite well on the economic front. The commodities-powered country was one of the only OECD nations to avoid recession during the global financial crisis. Unemployment was expected to reach 8% to 10% during the GFC, but didn't even reach 6%, in part owing to a shrewd $50 billion stimulus project, which helped offset the faltering world economy. The GFC occurred while Kevin Rudd was prime minister, though he has since been superseded by Julia Gillard. In 2010, unemployment fell to 5% and GDP grew by over 3%, led by NSW, Victoria and pre-flood-stricken Queensland, Australia's three largest economies.

Despite the seemingly harsh, dramatic environment, Australia remains a desirable destination among expats and immigrants, and the nation boasts one of the world's highest living standards. In the UN's Human Development Index, Australia consistently appears in the world's top five countries for its high levels of education, healthcare, democratic freedoms, safety and security, and life expectancy. Australians enjoy a high per-capita income and Melbourne, Sydney and Brisbane often appear in top spots among the world's most liveable cities lists.

Top Albums

Back in Black – AC/DC
Diesel & Dust – Midnight Oil
Circus Animals – Cold Chisel
Neon Ballroom – Silverchair
Kick – INXS
Woodface – Crowded House
The Boatman's Call – Nick Cave & the Bad Seeds

Key Aussie Slang

Aussie salute action of brushing flies away from your face
rough as guts very rough, uncivilised
blow-in unexpected guest
perve to look at lustfully
yapping/verbal diarrhoea incessant talk

gutless wonder coward
tinnie a can of beer
pissed as a fart/parrot/newt;
legless extremely drunk
like a stunned mullet in a state of complete confusion
looks like a dog's breakfast is in a dreadful mess

Quality-of-living indexes notwithstanding, some Australians remain anxious about the future. House prices have soared in the last 30 years, with many Aussies overextending themselves or being left behind in the widespread dream to own a house with a bit of land. Some economists even warned of a serious sub-prime crisis in coming years – like the one in the US that sparked the global financial crisis – with home values overinflated by 20% or more in some places.

A Nation for All

Australia has come a long way since suffering the anti-immigrant slurs of One Nation party founder Pauline Hanson (who in 1996 famously said that Australia was at risk of being 'swamped by Asians'). Most Aussies have rejected the xenophobic White Australia policy of the past, but are still coming to grips with the dark legacy of abuse inflicted upon the Indigenous population. In 2008, Prime Minister Kevin Rudd opened the door to reconciliation when he issued a comprehensive and moving apology for wrongs of the past, and announced a call for bipartisan action to improve the lives of Indigenous Australians. Rudd's apology was particularly directed to the stolen generations (Indigenous children taken from their parents and placed with white families during the 19th and 20th centuries).

Rudd's speech resonated in many parts of Australia, and local governments have since launched their own initiatives – like Queensland's Reconciliation Plan, which set goals for improving relationships, nurturing respect and creating more opportunities in higher education and in the workforce. These were important steps, Rudd hailed, on the road to 'truly reconcile and together build a great nation'.

Top Books

The Secret River Kate Grenville's tale of convicts, compromises and Indigenous people
The Tree of Man Profound story of early pioneers living in the bush, by Patrick White
Johnno David Malouf's coming-of-age tale in 1940s Brisbane

Aussie Inventions

refrigeration James Harrison built the first mechanical refrigeration plant in the 1850s
electric drill patented by Melburnian Arthur James in 1889
two-stroke lawn mower developed in 1930; featured in Sydney Olympic Games

Giant Objects

Big Banana – Coffs Harbour, NSW
Big Wine Bottle – Pokolbin, Hunter Valley, NSW
Big Guitar – Tamworth, NSW
Big Koala – Phillip Island, Victoria
Big Mango – Bowen, QLD

History

Michael Cathcart
Michael Cathcart presents history programs on ABC TV, is a broadcaster on ABC Radio National and teaches History at the Australian Centre, University of Melbourne.

Intruders

By sunrise, the storm had passed. Zachary Hicks was keeping sleepy watch on the British ship *Endeavour* when suddenly he was wide awake. He summoned his captain, James Cook, who climbed into the brisk morning air to a miraculous sight. Ahead of them lay an uncharted land of wooded hills and gentle valleys. It was 19 April 1770. In the coming days, Cook began methodically to draw the first European map of Australia's eastern coast. He was mapping the end of Aboriginal supremacy.

Convicts

Eighteen years later, in 1788, the English were back to stay. They numbered 751 ragtag convicts and children, and around 250 soldiers, officials and their wives. This motley 'First Fleet' was under the command of a humane and diligent naval captain, Arthur Phillip. By a small cove, in the idyllic lands of the Eora people, Phillip established a British penal settlement. He renamed the place after the British Home Secretary, Lord Sydney.

Robert Hughes' bestseller, *The Fatal Shore* (1987), depicts convict Australia as a terrifying 'Gulag' where Britain tormented rebels, vagrants and criminals. But other historians point out that powerful men in London saw transportation as a scheme for giving prisoners a new and useful life. Indeed, with Phillip's encouragement, many convicts soon earned

Vestiges from a convict past

» Hyde Park Barracks Museum, Sydney

» St Thomas Anglican Church, Port Macquarie, NSW

» Trial Bay Gaol, Trial Bay, NSW

» Commissariat Stores Building, Brisbane

» Heritage Centre, Maryborough

TIMELINE

60,000 BC	43,000 BC	6000 BC
Although the exact start of human habitation in Australia is still uncertain, according to most experts this is when Aborigines settled in the continent.	A group of original Australians sits down in the Nepean Valley near current-day Sydney and makes some stone tools. Archaeological sites like this have been found across Australia.	Rising water levels due to global warming force many Indigenous groups off their fertile flatlands homes along the coasts. Sections of land rivalling today's New South Wales in area are lost.

Little is known about how the first people came to Australia. Even the dates are broadly debatable and seem measured more in geological rather than human terms: 50,000 to 70,000 years ago. What is known is that people came to the continent from Asia during times when the Earth was much cooler and water levels much lower. This made it possible for them to walk across Torres Strait from New Guinea. Migrations are thought to have occurred at various times since, with the last major one 5000 years ago. By Cook's arrival in 1770, the continent had a rich and varied culture of Indigenous communities.

Best History Encounters

» The Rocks Discovery Museum, Sydney

» Cadman's Cottage, Sydney

» Melbourne Museum, Melbourne

» Immigration Museum, Melbourne

» Newstead House, Brisbane

» Queensland Maritime Museum, Brisbane

» Historical Museum, North Stradbroke

» Mossman Gorge, Queensland

» National Gallery of Australia, Canberra

their 'ticket of leave', a kind of parole that gave them the freedom of the colony and the right to seek work on their own behalf.

However, the convict system could also be savage. Women (who were outnumbered five to one) lived under constant threat of sexual exploitation. Female convicts who offended their gaolers languished in the depressing 'female factories'. Male reoffenders were cruelly flogged, and could even be hanged for minor crimes, such as stealing. In 1803 English officers established a second convict settlement at Hobart in Van Diemen's Land (later called Tasmania). Soon male reoffenders filled the grim prison at Port Arthur on the beautiful and wild coast. Others endured the senseless agonies of Norfolk Island in the remote Pacific.

At first Sydney and these smaller colonies depended on supplies brought in by ship. Anxious to develop productive farms, the government granted land to soldiers, officers and emancipated convicts. After 30 years of trial and error, their farms began to flourish. The most irascible and ruthless of these landholders was John Macarthur. Along with his spirited wife Elizabeth, Macarthur pioneered the breeding of merino sheep on his verdant property near Sydney.

Rum

John Macarthur was also a leading member of the Rum Corps, a clique of powerful officers which bullied successive governors and grew rich by controlling much of Sydney's trade, notably rum. But its racketeering was ended in 1810 by a tough new governor named Lachlan Macquarie. Under Macquarie's administration the major roads of modern-day Sydney were constructed, some fine public buildings built (many designed by talented convict architect Francis Greenway) and the foundations for a more civil society were laid.

Macquarie also championed the rights of freed convicts, granting them land and appointing several to public office. But this tolerance

3000 BC	**AD 1607**	**1770**	**1776**
The last known large immigration to the continent from Asia occurs (at least until about 1970). Over 250 languages are spoken among the myriad groups living in Australia.	Spanish explorer Luis Torres manages to sail between Australia and New Guinea and not discover the rather large continent to the south. The strait bears his name today.	English captain James Cook maps Australia's East Coast in the scientific ship *Endeavour*. He then runs aground on the Great Barrier Reef near a place he names Cape Tribulation.	The 13 British colonies in the US declare independence, leaving the King's government without a place to ship undesirables and convicts. Authorities turn their attention to the vast Australian continent.

was not shared by the 'exclusives'. These large landholders, middle-class snobs and senior British officials observed a rigid expatriate class system. They shunned ex-prisoners, and scoffed at the distinctive accent and the easy-going manners of these new Australians.

By now word was reaching England that Australia offered cheap land and plenty of work, and adventurous migrants took to the oceans in search of their fortunes. At the same time, the British government transported more and more prisoners. In 1825 a party of soldiers and convicts established a penal settlement in the territory of the Yuggera people, close to modern-day Brisbane. Before long this hot, fertile region attracted free settlers, who were soon busy farming, grazing, logging and mining on Aboriginal land.

Sheep

In the cooler grasslands of Tasmania, the sheepmen were also thriving, and they too were hungry for new pastures. In 1835 an ambitious young squatter named John Batman sailed to Port Phillip Bay on the mainland. On the banks of the Yarra River, he chose the location for Melbourne, famously announcing that 'This is the place for a village'. Batman then worked a staggering swindle: he persuaded local Aborigines to 'sell' him their traditional lands (a whopping 2500 sq km) for a crate of blankets, flour, knives and knick-knacks. Back in Sydney, Governor Burke declared the contract void, not because it was unfair, but because the land officially belonged to the British Crown. Burke proved his point by granting Batman some prime acreage near Geelong.

Land

Each year, settlers pushed deeper into the Aboriginal territories in search of pasture and water for their stock. These men became known as squatters (because they 'squatted' on Aboriginal lands), and many held this territory with a gun. In the USA the conflict between settlers and the Indigenous people formed the basis for a rich mythology known as 'the Wild West'. But in Australia the conflict has largely passed from white memory, so white historians now disagree about the extent of the violence. However, Aborigines still recount how their waterholes were poisoned and their people massacred. Some of the most bitter struggles occurred in the remote mining districts of central Queensland. In Tasmania the impact of settlement was so devastating that today, no 'full blood' Aborigines survive; all of the island's Aborigines are of mixed heritage.

On the mainland many of the squatters reached a truce with the defeated tribes. In remote regions it became common for Aborigines to take low-paid jobs on farms, working on sheep and cattle stations as drovers, rouseabouts, shearers and domestics. In return, those lucky enough to be

Reading Australian History

» *Fatal Shore*, Robert Hughes

» *History of Queensland*, Raymond Evans

» *Burke's Soldier*, Alan Atwood

» *True History of the Kelly Gang*, Peter Carey

» *Birth of Melbourne*, Tim Flannery

Before Europeans arrived, Australia contained an estimated 750,000 Indigenous people, scattered among 600 to 700 Aboriginal nations. Among them, they spoke at least 250 indigenous languages and dialects.

1788	1824	1835	1844–45
The Eora people of Bunnabi discover they have new neighbours; 11 ships arrive bearing soldiers and convicts, and drop anchor in what the new arrivals call Botany Bay.	The government establishes the brutal penal colony of Moreton Bay, a place of blood, sweat and tears. A second penal colony, Brisbane, follows two years later.	John Batman arranges the 'purchase' of 2500 sq km from Aborigines of the Dutigalla tribe for flour and trinkets. Melbourne is established on the north bank of the Yarra River.	The first guidebook to Australia is written in the form of a journal by Ludwig Leichhardt. It chronicles his party's exploration from Brisbane almost to Darwin. In 1848, he vanishes without a trace.

working on their traditional lands adapted their cultures to the changing circumstances. This arrangement continued in outback pastoral regions until after WWII.

Gold & Rebellion

Transportation of convicts to eastern Australia ceased in the 1840s. This was just as well: in 1851 prospectors discovered gold in New South Wales and central Victoria. The news hit the colonies with the force of a cyclone. From every social class, young men and some adventurous women headed for the diggings. Soon they were caught up in a great rush of prospectors, entertainers, publicans, sly-groggers, prostitutes and quacks from overseas. In Victoria the British governor was alarmed – both by the way the Victorian class system had been thrown into disarray, and by the need to finance law and order on the goldfields. His solution was to compel all miners to buy an expensive monthly licence, in the hope that the lower orders would return to their duties in town.

But the lure of gold was too great. In the reckless excitement of the goldfields, the miners initially endured the thuggish troopers who enforced the government licence. But after three years the easy gold at Ballarat was gone, and miners were toiling in deep, water-sodden shafts. They were now infuriated by a corrupt and brutal system of law that held them in contempt. Under the leadership of a charismatic Irishman named Peter Lalor, they raised the flag of the Southern Cross and swore to defend their rights and liberties. They armed themselves and gathered inside a rough stockade at Eureka, where they waited for the government to make its move.

In the predawn of Sunday 3 December 1854, a force of troopers attacked the stockade. In 15 terrifying minutes, they slaughtered 30 miners and lost five soldiers. The story of the Eureka Stockade is often told as a battle for nationhood and democracy – as if a true nation must be born out of blood. But these killings were tragically unnecessary. The eastern colonies were already in the process of establishing democratic parliaments, with the full support of the British authorities. In the 1880s Lalor himself became speaker of the Victorian Parliament.

The gold rush also attracted boatloads of prospectors from China. The Chinese prospectors endured constant hostility from whites, and were the victims of ugly race riots on the goldfields at Lambing Flat (now called Young) in NSW in 1860–61. Chinese precincts developed in the backstreets of Sydney and Melbourne and, by the 1880s, popular literature indulged in tales of Chinese opium dens, dingy gambling parlours and oriental brothels. But many Chinese went on to establish themselves in business and particularly in market gardening. Today the busy China-

Sydney's Mint and Parliament House were originally wings of the infamous Rum Hospital, which was built by two Sydney merchants in 1816 in return for a monopoly on the rum trade.

1846	**1871**	**1891**	**1901**
Sole survivor of a shipwreck off Queensland, Jemmy Morrill is rescued by Aboriginal people. He lives with them 17 years, and later plays a key role in improving European-Aboriginal relations.	Aboriginal stockman Jupiter discovers gold in Queensland and the rush is on. Within 10 years Brisbane has made its fortune from both gold and wool.	A shearers' strike around Barcaldine, Queensland, establishes a labour legend; the confrontation leads to the birth of the Australian Labor Party.	The Australian colonies federate; a new national Parliament meets in Melbourne. The White Australia policy is passed, which bans non-Europeans from immigrating.

Describing the history of European exploration in Australia is to delve into a world of tragic misadventure, where prized attributes like courage and common sense are regularly trumped by breathtaking ignorance and blinding hubris.

The Great Northern Expedition was an attempt to cross Australia from Melbourne to the Gulf of Carpentaria, and was funded by the colonial government. Despite a sad lack of experience, Robert O'Hara Burke was chosen to lead the 19-man expedition with William 'Jack' Wills his deputy. As 10,000 onlookers cheered them on, the group set off for the 3200km journey from Melbourne in August 1860. They were spectacularly unprepared – bringing with them such ephemera as heavy wooden tables, rockets, flags and a Chinese gong, as well as two years' worth of rations. All in all, they brought more than 20 tonnes of supplies, loaded onto 26 camels, 23 horses and six wagons. Overburdened, they moved at a snail's pace, taking nearly two months to cover some 750km (the mail run took about 10 days), and the road was littered with discarded items. They also reached the hottest parts of Australia in the middle of summer. With temperatures soaring above 50°C, the group ran into serious troubles – equipment malfunctions, incessant quarrelling, resignations and dismissal of expedition members.

Growing frustrated, Burke split the group and made a dash for the coast with three others (Wills, Charles Gray and John King) in December. The main group stayed behind, ordered by Burke to wait three months before returning south. Burke calculated he could make it to the coast and back in two months. In fact it took over four months, and when they finally came near the coast, mangrove swamps prevented them from actually reaching the ocean. They returned to base camp (Gray died along the way), only to discover the group had packed up and headed south just hours earlier. The three then set off for a pastoral settlement near Mt Hopeless. Burke and Wills perished. King was rescued by Aborigines and nursed back to health. He was the only expedition member to make the full crossing and return alive.

towns of Sydney and Melbourne, and the ubiquitous Chinese restaurants in country towns, are reminders of Chinese vigour.

Gold and wool brought immense investment and gusto to Melbourne, Sydney and a swath of Queensland. By the 1880s they were stylish modern cities, with gaslights in the streets, railways and that great new invention: the telegraph. In fact, the southern capital became known as 'Marvellous Melbourne', so opulent were its theatres, hotels, galleries and fashions.

Meanwhile, the huge expanses of Queensland were remote from the southern centres of political and business power. It was a tough, raw frontier colony, in which money was made by hard labour – in mines, in the forests and on cattle stations. In the coastal sugar industry, southern

1915

In line with Australia's close ties to Britain, Australian and New Zealand troops (the Anzacs) join the Allied invasion of Turkey at Gallipoli. The Anzac legend is born.

1918

The Great War ends. Out of a country of 4.9 million, 320,000 were sent to war in Europe and almost 20% were killed. Cracks appear in Australian–British relations.

1928

Reverend John Flynn starts the Royal Flying Doctor Service in Cloncurry, Queensland – an invaluable service that now has networks around the country.

» Anzac Bridge, Sydney

CAROL WILEY/LONELY PLANET IMAGES ©

investors grew rich on a plantation economy that exploited tough Pacific Island labourers (known as 'Kanakas'), many of whom had been kidnapped from their islands.

Many white Queenslanders still embody the gritty, independent, egalitarian yet racist attitudes that were the key elements of the so-called 'Australian legend'. The legend reached its classic form at the end of the 19th century, when nationalist writers idealised 'the bush', its people and their code of 'mateship'. The great forum for this bush nationalism was the massively popular *Bulletin* magazine. Its politics were egalitarian, democratic, republican...and white.

But while writers were creating national legends the politicians of Australia were devising the framework for a national constitution.

Nationhood

On 1 January 1901 Australia became a federation. When the bewhiskered members of the new national Parliament met in Melbourne, their first aim was to protect the identity and values of a European Australia from an influx of Asians and Pacific Islanders. Their solution was what became known as the White Australia policy. It became a racial tenet of faith in Australia for the next 70 years. For those who were welcome to live in Australia (ie whites), this was to be a model society, nestled in the skirts of the British Empire.

Just one year later, white women won the right to vote in federal elections. In a series of radical innovations, the government introduced a broad social welfare scheme and protected Australian wage levels with import tariffs. Its mixture of capitalist dynamism and socialist compassion became known as 'the Australian settlement'.

Meanwhile, most Australians lived on the coastal 'edge' of the continent. So forbidding was the arid inland that they called the great dry Lake Eyre 'the Dead Heart' of the country. It was a grim image. But one prime minister, the dapper Alfred Deakin, was determined to overcome the tyranny of the climate. Back in the 1880s, Deakin championed a scheme by two Canadian engineers to develop irrigated farming on the Murray River at Mildura. The region developed a prosperous grape and dried-fruit industry. (Today this massively productive region is facing an ecological crisis, as salinity and overuse threaten to kill the Murray River.)

War & the Great Depression

Living on the edge of this forbidding land, and isolated from the rest of the world, most Australians took comfort from the idea that they were still a part of the British Empire. When war broke out in Europe in 1914, thousands of Australian men rallied to the Empire's call. They had their first taste of death on 25 April 1915, when the Australian and New Zea-

Written in 1895 by 'Banjo' Paterson, 'Waltzing Matilda' is widely regarded as Australia's unofficial national anthem. Some say the song paid homage to striking sheep shearers during the 1890s labour uprisings.

Lake Burley Griffin in Canberra honours the Chicago architect hired to design the new Australian capital in 1912. Much of Griffin's striking and radical design was never implemented.

1929	1937	1941	1950s–1960s
The Great Depression: thousands go hungry as the economy crashes. Unemployment peaks at 28% in 1932 – one of the highest rates in the industrialised world (second only to Germany).	Cane toads are released into the wild to control pests damaging Queensland's sugar cane fields. The action proves disastrous, creating a plague that spreads to other states.	The Japanese bomb Townsville. The war in the Pacific is on. Hundreds of thousands of Australian troops pour out to battlefields worldwide. Thousands of American troops pour in and drink a lot of beer.	The post-war boom is on as Queensland experiences strong growth in manufacturing and other industries. Affordable housing is the norm with rampant construction in the suburbs.

land Army Corps (the 'Anzacs') joined British and French troops in an assault on the Gallipoli Peninsula in Turkey. It was eight months before the British commanders acknowledged that the tactic had failed, but by then 8141 young Australians were dead. Soon the Australian Imperial Force was fighting in the killing fields of Europe. By the time the war ended, 60,000 Australian men had been slaughtered. Ever since, on 25 April, Australians have gathered at war memorials around the country and at Gallipoli for the sad and solemn services of Anzac Day.

Australia careered wildly through the 1920s, continuing to invest in immigration and growth, until the economy collapsed into the abyss of the Great Depression in 1929. Unemployment brought its shame and misery to one in three houses. For those who were wealthy – or who had jobs – the Depression was hardly noticed. In fact, the fall in prices actually meant that the purchasing power of their income was enhanced.

Heroes

In the midst of the hardship, sport brought escape to a nation in love with games and gambling. Champion racehorse Phar Lap won an effortless and graceful victory in the 1930 Melbourne Cup (the horse race that stops a nation). In 1932 the great horse travelled to the racetracks of America where he mysteriously died. In Australia the gossips insisted that the horse had been poisoned by envious Americans. And the legend was established of a sporting hero cut down in his prime.

The year 1932 also saw accusations of treachery on the cricket field. The English team, under its aloof captain Douglas Jardine, employed a violent new bowling tactic known as 'Bodyline'. Jardine's aim was to unnerve Australia's star batsman, the devastating Donald Bradman. The bitterness of the tour became part of the Australian legend. And Bradman batted on – achieving the unsurpassed career average of 99.94 runs.

That same year, the radical premier of NSW, Jack Lang, officiated at the opening of the great Sydney Harbour Bridge. Before anyone knew what was happening, a man in military uniform rode forward on a skittish horse, drew a sabre and cut the ceremonial ribbon in the name of the King. He was Francis de Groot, a member of the fascist New Guard, who accused Lang of being a closet communist. The bridge survived the controversy to become a great symbol of hope and optimism, uniting a divided city.

WWII

As the economy began to recover, the whirl of daily life was hardly dampened when Australian servicemen sailed off to Europe for a new war, in 1939. Though Japan was menacing, Australians took it for granted that the British navy would keep them safe. In December 1941 Japan bombed the US Fleet at Pearl Harbor. Weeks later the 'impregnable' British naval base

Peter Weir's epic film *Gallipoli* (1981) shows the utter brutality and senselessness of WWI, through the eyes of two young mates (played by Mark Lee and a young Mel Gibson).

HISTORY HEROES

The legendary racehorse Phar Lap was stuffed and is an exhibit at the Melbourne Museum, revered by some and reviled by others. You'll have to go to Canberra (the National Museum of Australia) to see his heart; New Zealand (where he was foaled) has his skeleton.

1956	1962	1965	1969
The Summer Olympics are held in Melbourne – the first time the games are held in southern hemisphere. Australia performed brilliantly – placing third in medal ranking behind the USSR and the USA.	Indigenous Australians gain the right to vote in federal elections – but they have to wait until 1967 to receive full citizenship, which happens overwhelmingly in a nationwide referendum.	Merle Thornton and Rosalie Bogner chain themselves to a Brisbane bar to protest against men-only public bars. Their action marked the early beginnings of the feminist movement in Australia.	Setting the political scene in Queensland for the next 21 years, Joh Bjelke-Petersen becomes premier. His political agenda was widely described as development at any price.

in Singapore crumbled, and soon thousands of Australians and other Allied troops were enduring the savagery of Japan's prisoner-of-war camps.

As the Japanese swept through Southeast Asia and into Papua New Guinea, the British announced that they could not spare any resources to defend Australia. But the legendary US commander General Douglas MacArthur saw that Australia was the perfect base for American operations in the Pacific. In a series of savage battles on sea and land, Allied forces gradually turned back the Japanese advance. Importantly, it was the USA, not the British Empire, that came to Australia's aid. The days of the British alliance were numbered.

Avian Cirrus, Bert Hinkler's tiny plane that made the first England-to-Australia solo flight, is on display at the Queensland Museum in Brisbane.

Peace, Prosperity & Multiculturalism

As the war ended, a new slogan rang through the land: 'Populate or Perish!' The Australian government embarked on an ambitious scheme to attract thousands of immigrants. With government assistance, people flocked from Britain and from non-English-speaking countries. They included Greeks, Italians, Slavs, Serbs, Croatians, Dutch, Poles, Turks and Lebanese among others. These 'new Australians' were expected to assimilate to a suburban stereotype known as 'the Australian way of life'.

This was the great era of the nuclear family in which Australians basked in the prosperity of a 'long boom'. Many migrants found jobs in manufacturing, where companies such as General Motors and Ford operated with generous tariff support. At the same time, there was growing world demand for Australia's primary products: metals, wool, meat and wheat. In time, Australia even became a major exporter of rice to Japan.

Patrick White's *Voss* (1957) is inspired by the Prussian explorer Leichhardt's story. *Voss* is both a psychological tale, a love story and an epic journey over the Australian desert. It's revered by many as the great Australian novel.

This era of growth and prosperity was dominated by Robert Menzies, the founder of the modern Liberal Party and Australia's longest-serving prime minister. Menzies had an avuncular charm, but he was also a vigilant opponent of communism. As the Cold War intensified, Australia and New Zealand entered a formal military alliance with the USA – the 1951 Anzus security pact. And when the USA hurled its righteous fury into a civil war in Vietnam, Menzies committed Australian forces to the conflict. The following year Menzies retired, leaving his successors a bitter legacy. The antiwar movement split Australia.

There was a feeling among artists, intellectuals and the young that Menzies' Australia had become a dull, complacent country, more in love with American popular culture and British high arts than with its own talents and stories. Australia, they said, had 'an inferiority complex'. In an atmosphere of youth rebellion, and newfound nationalism, Australians began to embrace their own history and culture. The arts blossomed. Universities flourished. A distinctive Australian film industry made iconic movies, mostly funded by government subsidies.

At the same time, increasing numbers of white Australians believed that

1970s	1972	1975
Inflation, soaring interest rates and rising unemployment bring the golden post-war days to an end. As house prices skyrocket, home ownership remains out of reach for many.	The Aboriginal Tent Embassy is erected on the lawns of Parliament House in Canberra. Over the next decades it serves as a reminder that Indigenous peoples have been denied sovereignty to their land.	The Great Barrier Reef Marine Park is created. It later becomes a World Heritage Site, which angers Queensland Premier Joh Bjelke-Petersen, who intended to explore for oil on the reef.

DAVID WALL/LONELY PLANET IMAGES ©

» Great Barrier Reef (p373)

TERRA NULLIUS TURNED ON ITS HEAD *ALAN MURPHY*

In May 1982 Eddie Mabo led a group of Torres Strait Islanders in a court action to have traditional title to their land on Mer (Murray Island) recognised. Their argument challenged the legal principle of *terra nullius* (literally, 'land belonging to no one') and demonstrated their unbroken relationship with the land over a period of thousands of years. In June 1992 the High Court found in favour of Eddie Mabo and the Islanders, rejecting the principle of *terra nullius* – this became known as the Mabo decision. The result has had far-reaching implications in Australia ever since, including the introduction of the Native Title Act in 1993.

Eddie Mabo accumulated more than 20 years' experience as an indigenous leader and human-rights activist. He had 10 children and was often unemployed, and he established a Black Community School, the first institution of its kind in Australia. He was also involved in indigenous health and housing. In the late 1960s he worked as a gardener at James Cook University, returning there in 1981 to a conference on land rights, where he delivered a historic speech which culminated in the landmark court case.

Unfortunately Eddie Mabo died of cancer six months before the decision was announced. After a customary period of mourning he was given a king's burial ceremony on Mer, reflecting his status among his people – such a ritual had not been performed on the island for some 80 years.

the Aborigines had endured a great wrong that needed to be put right – and from 1976 until 1992, Aborigines won major victories in their struggle for land rights. Australia's imports with China and Japan increased – and the White Australia policy became an embarrassment. It was officially abolished in the early 1970s, and Australia became a leader in the campaign against the racist 'apartheid' policies of white South Africa.

By the 1970s, more than one million migrants had arrived from non-English-speaking countries, filling Australia with new languages, cultures, foods and ideas. At the same time, China and Japan began to outstrip Europe as Australia's major trading partners. As Asian immigration increased, Vietnamese communities became prominent in Sydney and Melbourne. In both those cities a new spirit of tolerance and diversity known as 'multiculturalism' became a particular source of pride.

To see some of the immigrant faces of today's Australia, catch the train in Sydney out to Cabramatta, where you can get caught up in a market swirl that could be the heart of Hanoi or Shanghai.

1992	2008	2009	2011
After 10 years in the courts, the landmark Mabo decision is delivered by the High Court. Effectively, this gives recognition to Indigenous land rights across the country.	On behalf of parliament, Prime Minister Kevin Rudd delivers a moving apology to Aborigines for laws and policies that 'inflicted profound grief, suffering and loss'.	A record-breaking heatwave and high winds create conditions for the catastrophic 'Black Saturday Bushfires' that rage in Victoria. Over 170 people die; property damages are around $1 billion.	Powerful floods inundate vast areas of Queensland (including Brisbane), killing 35 people and causing billions of dollars in damages. Cyclone Yasi follows weeks later, devastating parts of north Queensland.

Environment

Tim Flannery
Tim Flannery is a scientist, explorer and writer. He has
written several award-winning books, including *The Future
Eaters*, *Throwim Way Leg* (an account of his work as a
biologist in New Guinea) and *The Weather Makers*. He lives
in Sydney where he is a professor in the faculty of science at
Macquarie University.

The first platypus
sent to England
for study was
dismissed as a
hoax. Evidently
a critter with a
duck's bill and a
beaver's tail that
also laid eggs yet
suckled its young
was considered
an impossibility.

Australia's plants and animals are just about the closest things to alien
life you are likely to encounter on Earth. That's because Australia has
been isolated from the other continents for a very long time – at least
45 million years. The other habitable continents have been able to exchange various species at different times because they've been linked
by land bridges. Just 15,000 years ago it was possible to walk from the
southern tip of Africa right through Asia and the Americas to Tierra del
Fuego. Not Australia, however. Its birds, mammals, reptiles and plants
have taken their own separate and very different evolutionary journey,
and the result today is the world's most distinct – and one of its most
diverse – natural realms.

The first naturalists to investigate Australia were astonished by what
they found. Here the swans were black – to Europeans this was a met-
aphor for the impossible – while mammals such as the platypus and
echidna were discovered to lay eggs. It really was an upside-down world,
where many of the larger animals hopped, where each year the trees
shed their bark rather than their leaves, and where the 'pears' were made
of wood.

If you are visiting Australia for a short time, you might need to go
out of your way to experience some of the richness of the environment.
That's because Australia is a subtle place, and some of the natural environment – especially around the cities – has been damaged or replaced
by trees and creatures from Europe. Places like Sydney, however, have
preserved extraordinary fragments of their original environment that
are relatively easy to access. Before you enjoy them though, it's worthwhile understanding the basics about how nature operates in Australia.
This is important because there's nowhere like Australia, and once you
have an insight into its origins and natural rhythms, you will appreciate
the place so much more.

The website of
the Australian
Museum (www.
australianmu-
seum.net.au)
holds a wealth of
info on Australia's
animal life from
the Cretaceous
period till now.
Kids will love the
online games,
fact files and
movies.

A Unique Environment

There are two really big factors that go a long way towards explaining
nature in Australia: its soils and its climate. Both are unique. Australian
soils are the more subtle and difficult to notice of the two, but they have
been fundamental in shaping life here. On the other continents, in recent geological times processes such as volcanism, mountain building
and glacial activity have been busy creating new soil. Just think of the

UNESCO WORLD HERITAGE SITES

Australia is home to 18 Unesco World Heritage sites, over a dozen of which are listed for their outstanding significance to the natural world. Top picks from the East Coast include the following:

» **Blue Mountains** The sandstone plateaus, escarpments and gorges near Sydney provide dramatic views and great bushwalks (to spy some of 400 native animal species); it's also home to extraordinarily rich plant species, including the ancient Wollemi pine that dates back to the age of the dinosaurs.

» **Fraser Island** The world's largest sand island and home to a diversity of fragile and complex ecosystems, including coloured sand cliffs, freshwater lakes and rainforests growing right in sand.

» **Gondwana Rainforests** Straddling Queensland and New South Wales are these temperate and unique rainforests, including the world's most extensive sub-tropical rainforest. Includes Lamington and Main Range National Parks.

» **Great Barrier Reef** Comprising 3000 individual reefs and home to a staggering array of aquatic life, the Great Barrier Reef is one of the world's most diverse ecosystems.

» **Wet Tropics** Spanning 9000 sq km of Queensland's northern coast and harbouring the highest concentration of primitive flowering plant families in the world (creating a near-perfect record of plant-life evolution on Earth). Includes Daintree, Barron Gorge and Wooroonooran National Parks.

glacier-derived soils of North America, north Asia and Europe. They feed the world today, and were made by glaciers grinding up rock of differing chemical composition over the last two million years. The rich soils of India and parts of South America were made by rivers eroding mountains, while Java in Indonesia owes its extraordinary richness to volcanoes.

All of these soil-forming processes have been almost absent from Australia in more recent times. Only volcanoes have made a contribution, and they cover less than 2% of the continent's land area. In fact, for the last 90 million years, beginning deep in the age of dinosaurs, Australia has been geologically comatose. It was too flat, warm and dry to attract glaciers, its crust too ancient and thick to be punctured by volcanoes or folded into mountains. Look at Uluru (Ayers Rock) and Kata Tjuta (the Olgas). They are the stumps of mountains that 350 million years ago were the height of the Andes. Yet for hundreds of millions of years they've been nothing but nubs.

Under such conditions no new soil is created and the old soil is leached of all its goodness by the rain, and is blown and washed away. Even if just 30cm of rain falls each year, that adds up to a column of water 30 million kilometres high passing through the soil over 100 million years, and that can do a great deal of leaching! Almost all of Australia's mountain ranges are more than 90 million years old, so you will see a lot of sand here, and a lot of country where the rocky 'bones' of the land are sticking up through the soil. It is an old, infertile landscape, and life in Australia has been adapting to these conditions for aeons.

Australia's misfortune in respect to soils is echoed in its climate. In most parts of the world outside the wet tropics, life responds to the rhythm of the seasons – summer to winter, or wet to dry. Most of Australia experiences seasons – sometimes very severe ones – yet life does not respond solely to them. This can clearly be seen by the fact that although there's plenty of snow and cold country in Australia, there are almost no trees that shed their leaves in winter, nor do any Australian animals hibernate. Instead there is a far more potent climatic force that Australian life must obey: El Niño.

National Parks

» New South Wales: www.environment.nsw.gov.au/national-parks

» Victoria: www.parkweb.vic.gov.au

» Queensland: www.derm.qld.gov.au/parks_and_forests

RESPONSIBLE BUSHWALKING

You can help preserve the ecology and beauty of Australia by keeping in mind the following when you're out hiking:

» Don't pee or poo within 100m of any water sources. Doing so can lead to the transmission of serious diseases, and it also pollutes precious water supplies.

» Wash at least 50m from any water sources, and use a biodegradable detergent.

» Don't cut wood for fires in popular bushwalking areas as this can cause rapid deforestation. Instead, use a stove that runs on kerosene, methylated spirits or some other liquid fuel. Avoid stoves powered by disposable butane gas canisters.

» Stick to existing tracks when you're walking, as hillsides and mountain slopes are prone to erosion.

Australia is currently moving north at a rate of 73 millimetres per year. According to NASA, in 250 million years, Australia will collide with Asia as Africa smashes into Europe – all of which will create the new supercontinent of Pangaea Ultima.

The cycle of flood and drought that El Niño brings to Australia is profound. Our rivers – even the mighty Murray River, the nation's largest river, which runs through the southeast – can be miles wide one year, yet you can literally step over their flows the next. This is the power of El Niño, and its effect, when combined with Australia's poor soils, manifests itself compellingly. As you might expect from this, relatively few of Australia's birds are seasonal breeders, and few migrate. Instead, they breed when the rain comes, and a large percentage are nomads, following the rain across the breadth of the continent.

So challenging are conditions in Australia that its birds have developed some extraordinary habits. The kookaburras, magpies and blue wrens you are likely to see – to name just a few – have developed a breeding system called 'helpers at the nest'. The helpers are the young adult birds of previous breedings, which stay with their parents to help bring up the new chicks. Just why they should do this was a mystery, until it was realised that conditions in Australia can be so harsh that more than two adult birds are needed to feed the nestlings. This pattern of breeding is very rare in places like Asia, Europe and North America, but it is common in many Australian birds.

Australia is, of course, famous as the home of the kangaroo (roo) and other marsupials. Unless you visit a wildlife park, such creatures are not easy to see as most are nocturnal. Their lifestyles, however, are exquisitely attuned to Australia's harsh conditions. Have you ever wondered why kangaroos, alone among the world's larger mammals, hop? It turns out that hopping is the most efficient way of getting about at medium speeds. This is because the energy of the bounce is stored in the tendons of the legs – much like in a pogo stick – while the intestines bounce up and down like a piston, emptying and filling the lungs without needing to activate the chest muscles. When you travel long distances to find meagre feed, such efficiency is a must.

Marsupials are so energy-efficient that they need to eat one-fifth less food than equivalent-sized placental mammals (everything from bats to rats, whales and ourselves). But some marsupials have taken energy efficiency much further. If you visit a wildlife park or zoo you might notice that faraway look in a koala's eyes. It seems as if nobody is home – and this in fact is near the truth. Several years ago biologists announced that koalas are the only living creatures that have brains that don't fit their skulls. Instead they have a shrivelled walnut of a brain that rattles around in a fluid-filled cranium. Other researchers have contested this finding, however, pointing out that the brains of the koalas examined for the study may have shrunk because these organs are so soft. Whether soft-brained or empty-headed, there is no doubt that the koala is not the

Of Australia's enormous 7.4 million sq km of landmass, only about 6.5% is arable – which is roughly the size of Spain.

Einstein of the animal world, and we now believe that it has sacrificed its brain to energy efficiency. Brains cost a lot to run – our brains typically weigh 2% of our body weight, but use 20% of the energy we consume. Koalas eat gum leaves, which are so toxic that koalas use 20% of their energy just detoxifying this food. This leaves little energy for the brain, and living in the treetops where there are so few predators means that they can get by with few wits at all.

The peculiar constraints of the Australian environment have not made everything dumb. The koala's nearest relative, the wombat (of which there are three species), has a large brain for a marsupial. These creatures live in complex burrows and can weigh up to 35kg, making them the largest herbivorous burrowers on Earth. Because their burrows are effectively air-conditioned, they have the neat trick of turning down their metabolic activity when they are in residence. One physiologist, who studied their thyroid hormones, found that biological activity ceased to such an extent in sleeping wombats that, from a hormonal point of view, they appeared to be dead! Wombats can remain underground for a week at a time, and can get by on just a third of the food needed by a sheep of equivalent size. One day, perhaps, efficiency-minded farmers will keep wombats instead of sheep. At the moment, however, that isn't possible; the largest of the wombat species, the northern hairy-nose, is one of the world's rarest creatures, with only around 100 surviving in a remote nature reserve in central Queensland.

Among the more common marsupials you might catch a glimpse of in the national parks around Australia's major cities are the species of antechinus. These nocturnal, rat-sized creatures lead an extraordinary life. The males live for just 11 months, the first 10 of which consist of a concentrated burst of eating and growing. Like teenage males, the day

Pizzey and Knight's *Field Guide to Birds of Australia* is an indispensable guide for birdwatchers and anyone else even peripherally interested in Australia's feathered tribes. Knight's illustrations are both beautiful and helpful in identification.

ENVIRONMENT A UNIQUE ENVIRONMENT

THE GREAT BARRIER REEF

The world's largest and best-known reef system stretches some 2300km from south to north, beginning near Bundaberg and continuing the length of Queensland almost to Papua New Guinea. The Great Barrier Reef is made up of about 2900 separate fringing reefs (which form an outer ribbon parallel to the coast and dot the lagoons around the islands and the mainland) and barrier reefs (which are further out to sea). The 'real' reef, or outer reef, is at the edge of the Australian continental shelf. The biological diversity here is truly astounding, with over 1500 species of fish; 400 types of coral; 4000 breeds of clams and other molluscs; 800 echinoderms, including sea cucumbers; 500 varieties of seaweed; 1500 different sponges; 30-plus species of marine mammals; 200 bird species; and 118 species of butterflies. Six of the planet's seven species of sea turtles breed here.

The 900 islands dotting the reefs also play an important role in the ecosystem. Some are home to lush rainforests and mangroves, and key habitats for both nesting seabirds and sea turtles. Other islands are little more than sandy deserts that get washed away during fierce storms.

Unlike mainland Australia, the reef is relatively young (geologically speaking). It first formed around 500,000 years ago, but has gone through dramatic changes – growing and receding on Australia's continental shelf – in response to changing sea levels. The present structure of the reef is only about 6000 to 8000 years old, growing atop fossil remains of reefs formed during eras of higher sea levels.

One of the most spectacular sights of the Barrier Reef occurs for a few nights after a full moon in late spring or early summer each year, when vast numbers of corals spawn at the same time. The tiny bundles of sperm and eggs are visible to the naked eye, and together they look like a gigantic underwater snowstorm. Many other reef organisms reproduce around this time, giving their spawn a greater chance of surviving predators.

Damage to Australia's environment has been inflicted in several ways, the most important being the introduction of pest species, destruction of forests, overstocking rangelands, inappropriate agriculture and interference with water flows.

Beginning with the escape of domestic cats into the Australian bush shortly after 1788, a plethora of vermin – from foxes to wild camels and cane toads – have run wild in Australia, causing extinctions in the native fauna. One out of every 10 native mammals living in Australia prior to European colonisation is now extinct, and many more are highly endangered.

The destruction of forests has also had a profound effect on the environment. Most of Australia's rainforests have suffered clearing, while conservationists fight with loggers over the fate of the last unprotected stands of 'old growth'.

In terms of financial value, just 1.5% of Australia's land surface provides over 95% of its agricultural yield, and much of this land lies in the irrigated regions of the Murray-Darling Basin. This is Australia's agricultural heartland, yet it too is under severe threat from salting of soils and rivers. Irrigation water penetrates into the sediments laid down in an ancient sea, carrying salt into the catchments and fields.

Despite the enormity of the biological crisis engulfing Australia, governments and the community have been slow to respond. The establishment of **Landcare** (www. landcareaustralia.com.au), an organisation enabling people to effectively address local environmental issues, and the expenditure of over $2 billion through the federal government initiative **Caring for our Country** (www.nrm.gov.au) have been important national initiatives.

Individuals are also banding together to help. Groups such as **Bush Heritage Australia** (www.bushheritage.org.au) and **Australian Wildlife Conservancy** (AWC; www. australianwildlife.org) allow people to donate funds and time to conserving native species. Some such groups have been spectacularly successful; AWC, for example, already manages many endangered species over its 25,000-sq-km holdings.

Renewable energy, sustainable agriculture and water use lie at the heart of solving these problems, and Australians are only now developing the road map to sustainability that they so desperately need if they are to have a long-term future on the continent.

comes when their minds turn to sex, and in the antechinus this becomes an obsession. As they embark on their quest for females they forget to eat and sleep. Instead they gather in logs and woo passing females by serenading them with squeaks. By the end of August – just two weeks after they reach 'puberty' – every male is dead, exhausted by sex and by carrying around swollen testes. This extraordinary life history may also have evolved in response to Australia's trying environmental conditions. It seems likely that if the males survived mating, they would compete with the females as they tried to find enough food to feed their growing young. Basically, antechinus dads are disposable. They do better for antechinus posterity if they go down in a testosterone-fuelled blaze of glory.

The Australian Conservation Foundation (ACF; www.acfonline. org.au) is Australia's largest nongovernment organisation involved in protecting the environment.

One thing you will see lots of in Australia are reptiles. Snakes are abundant, and they include some of the most venomous species known. Where the opportunities to feed are few and far between, it's best not to give your prey a second chance, hence the potent venom. Around Sydney and other parts of Australia, however, you are far more likely to encounter a harmless python than a dangerously venomous species. Snakes will usually leave you alone if you don't fool with them. Observe, back quietly away and don't panic, and most of the time you'll be OK.

Some visitors mistake lizards for snakes, and indeed some Australian lizards look bizarre. One of the more abundant is the sleepy lizard. These creatures, which are found throughout the southern arid region, look like animated pine cones. They are the Australian equivalent of tortoises, and are harmless. Other lizards are much larger. Unless you visit the Indonesian island of Komodo you will not see a larger lizard than the desert-dwelling perentie. These beautiful creatures, with their leopard-like blotches, can grow to more than 2m long, and are efficient predators of introduced rabbits, feral cats and the like.

Current Environmental Issues

Headlining the environmental issues facing Australia's fragile landscape at present are climate change, water scarcity, nuclear energy and uranium mining. All are interconnected. For Australia, the warmer temperatures resulting from climate change spell disaster to an already fragile landscape. A 2°C climb in average temperatures on the globe's driest continent will result in an even drier southern half of the country and greater water scarcity. Scientists also agree that hotter and drier conditions will exacerbate bushfire conditions and increase cyclone intensity, two natural phenomena that have cost lives and a great deal of money to the Australian public.

Australia is a heavy greenhouse-gas emitter because it relies on coal and other fossil fuels for its energy supplies. The most prominent and also contentious alternative energy source is nuclear power, which creates less greenhouse gases and relies on uranium, in which Australia is rich. But the radioactive waste created by nuclear power stations can take thousands of years to become harmless. Moreover, uranium is a finite energy source (as opposed to yet-cleaner and renewable energy sources such as solar and wind power), and even if Australia were to establish sufficient nuclear power stations now to make a real reduction in coal dependency, it would be years before the environmental and economic benefits were realised.

Uranium mining itself also produces polarised opinions. Because countries around the world are also looking to nuclear energy, Australia finds itself in a position to increase exports of one of its top-dollar resources. But uranium mining in Australia has been met with fierce opposition for decades, not only because the product is a core ingredient of nuclear weapons, but also because much of Australia's uranium supplies sits beneath sacred Indigenous land. Supporters of increased uranium

Megafauna – large animal species – once flourished in Australia, but became extinct around the time humans arrived (40,000–60,000 BC).

OF WHALES & HUMANS

NSW's Aboriginal Yuin people have long considered orcas (killer whales) to be ancestral beings. Pods of orcas would use Twofold Bay to herd and trap larger migrating whales in the shallows. Aboriginal elders would perform rites on the beach, begging the orcas for a share of the bounty. Amazingly, the orcas would oblige. After consuming the lips and tongue of their victim, they would leave the carcass behind.

After 1830, the relationship was taken up a notch. The Davidson whaling station (p159) employed many local Aboriginals, which was rare for the times. When the orca pod caught sight of a migrating whale, one of their number would head off to alert the whalers. The crew would then race out to the tired and harried victim and finish it off with a handheld harpoon. Keeping their half of the bargain, the whalers would anchor the dead whale and leave it overnight. By the next morning the orcas would have removed the tongue and lips and the contract was complete.

This all came to an end in 1900 when an orca beached itself on Aslings Beach during a hunt. With the rest of the pod looking on and as the whalers rushed to the orca's assistance, a vagrant walked up to the beached animal and killed it. After that, only a few of the older orcas, including Old Tom – whose skeleton is on display at Eden's Killer Whale Museum (p158) – continued to hunt with the whaling crews. Shortly after this the last of the Yuin community left Eden for Wallaga Lake.

mining and export suggest that the best way to police the use of uranium is to manage its entire life cycle; that is, to sell the raw product to international buyers, and then charge a fee to accept the waste and dispose of it. Both major political parties consider an expansion of Australia's uranium export industry to be inevitable for economic reasons.

Watching Wildlife

For those intrigued by the diversity of tropical rainforests, Queensland's World Heritage sites are well worth visiting. Birds of paradise, cassowaries and a variety of other birds can be seen by day, while at night you can search for tree kangaroos (yes, some kinds of kangaroo do live in the treetops). In your nocturnal wanderings you are highly likely to see curious possums, some of which look like skunks, and other marsupials that today are restricted to a small area of northeast Queensland. Fossils from as far afield as western Queensland and southern Victoria indicate that such creatures were once widespread.

The fantastic diversity of Queensland's Great Barrier Reef is legendary, and a boat trip out to the reef from Cairns or Port Douglas is unforgettable. Just as extraordinary but less well known is the diversity of Australia's southern waters.

If your visit extends only as far as Sydney, however, don't give up on seeing Australian nature. The Sydney sandstone – which extends approximately 150km around the city – is one of the most diverse and spectacular regions in Australia. In springtime, spectacular red waratahs abound in the region's parks, while the woody pear (a relative of the waratah) that so confounded the early colonists can also be seen, alongside more than 1500 other species of flowering plants. Even in a Sydney backyard you're likely to see more reptile species (mostly skinks) than can be found in all of Great Britain – so keep an eye out!

Australian icon Steve Irwin died while shooting *Ocean's Deadliest*, a 2007 documentary he produced with Philippe Cousteau, Jr. It features all sorts of deadly critters from Queensland's waters but not the ray that stung Irwin.

Food & Wine

Born in convict poverty and raised on a diet heavily influenced by Great Britain, Australian cuisine has come a long way in the last 20 years. Australia is now one of the most dynamic places in the world to have a meal, thanks to a diverse expatriate community, ever-inventive chefs and an open-minded public. Restaurant-goers face dizzying choices when it comes to dining. Culinary riches come from every corner of the globe, with Vietnamese, Indian, Thai, Italian, Spanish, Greek and Japanese making up just a small part of the Australian culinary experience.

Sydney and Melbourne – even Brisbane and Canberra – have established themselves as food-loving cities worthy of touring gourmands. Fantastic food markets, award-winning chefs, stylish dining rooms and great cafe culture make for some fine culinary exploring. Outside the capitals the restaurant density decreases, but there are still some gems. All along the coast, you'll find incredible seafood from humble fish-and-chips shops to fine-dining restaurants overlooking the ocean; or head to wharves and markets for the freshest catch, which you can grill up yourself, Aussie style. The vineyards of the Mornington Peninsula and Hunter Valley (which is also home to great restaurants) provide the chance to sample some of the nation's finest quaffs. Byron Bay and Noosa are both renowned for unique and innovative cuisine, and both even have their own cookbooks. Wherever you roam, from the scenic Blue Mountains to Newcastle, Townsville and Cairns, you won't be far from a fine meal.

Australia has readily embraced the moniker Modern Australian, or 'Mod Oz', to describe the nation's cuisine. If it's a melange of East and West, it's Modern Australian. If it's not authentically French or Italian, it's Modern Australian – a sometimes challenging attempt to classify the unclassifiable. Dishes aren't usually too fussy and the flavours are often bold and imaginative.

Local Delicacies

Australia's best food comes from the sea. Nothing compares to this continent's seafood, harnessed from some of the purest waters you'll find. Right along the coast, even a simple dish of fish and chips (and that includes the takeaway variety) is superfresh and cooked with care.

Connoisseurs prize Sydney rock oysters (a species living along the New South Wales coast) and sea scallops from Queensland. Rock lobsters are fantastic and fantastically expensive, and mud crabs, despite the name, are a sweet delicacy. Another odd-sounding delicacy is 'bugs' – like shovel-nosed lobsters without a lobster's price tag; try the Balmain and Moreton Bay varieties. Yabbies, the smaller cousins of crayfish, can be found throughout the southeast. Prawns are also incredible, particularly the sweet school prawns or the eastern king (Yamba) prawns found along northern NSW.

You'll find thousands of recipes and cooking videos, tips and techniques on www.lifestylefood.com.au. All the classics are here, including pavlova, lamingtons, roasts, salt and pepper squid, scones on the damper and loads of fast and easy recipes (the 'quickies in the kitchen' series).

The Cook's Companion by Stephanie Alexander is the bible of Australian cooking, with nearly 1000 recipes across 12 different chapters. Encyclopedic in scope but highly readable, this 1000-page tome explores not just recipes but culinary history and ingredients, while spicing things up with touches of folklore and literary quotations.

COFFEE TALK

In terms of coffee, Australia has phenomenal options, with Italian-style espresso machines in virtually every cafe, boutique roasters all the rage and, in urban areas, the expertly trained barista (coffee maker) virtually the norm. You'll find the best coffee in Melbourne, where everyone has their preferred bean and blend and will probably also be on first-name terms with a local barista. You'll also find excellent cafes in Sydney and Brisbane, and plenty of fine spots in smaller towns as well. Melbourne's cafe scene rivals the most vibrant in the world; the best way to immerse yourself is by wandering the city centre's cafe-lined lanes.

Top Foodie Sites

» www.urbans poon.com: restaurant reviews countrywide

» grabyourfork. blogspot.com: gastronomic journeys around Sydney

» www. melbournegas tronome.com: in-depth restaurant/ bar reviews

» www.eating brisbane.com: the Bris-vegas eating scene

Add to that countless wild fish species and we've got one of the greatest bounties on earth. In fact, the Sydney Fish Market (p59) trades in several hundred species of seafood every day, second only to Tokyo.

Aussies love their seafood, but they've not lost their yen for a hefty chunk of steak. Rockhampton is the beef capital of Australia and visiting carnivores would be foolish not to cut into a sizzling steak. Lamb from Victoria's lush Gippsland is also highly prized. While sizzling steaks and roast lamb remain staples, they are now done with tandoori, Greek or Provençal flavourings...as well as just as chops or steak.

Australia's size and diverse climate – from the tropical north to the temperate south – mean that there's an enormous variety of produce on offer. Queensland's fertile fields are decorated with rolling banana and mango plantations, quilted orchards and vast seas of sugar cane (used to make the amber-hued Bundaberg rum). In summer, mangoes are so plentiful that Queenslanders actually get sick of them. The macadamia, a native nut with a smooth, buttery flavour, grows throughout southeastern Queensland and some Queenslanders use it in everything – tossed in salads, crushed and frozen in ice cream and stickily petrified in gooey cakes and sweets.

There's a small but brilliant farmhouse-cheese movement, hampered by the fact that all the milk must be pasteurised. Despite that, the results can be great. Keep an eye out for goat's cheese from Gympie and anything from the boutique Kenilworth Country Foods company (p348).

Tasting Tours

The vine-covered Hunter Valley produces far more than just wine. Among the rolling hillsides, you'll find farmhouse cheeses, smoked fish and meats, seasonal produce (figs, citrus, peaches, avocados), Belgian-style chocolate, boutique beer, olives and much more. For a memorable assemble-your-own picnic, it doesn't get much better than this.

The total at the bottom of a restaurant bill is all you really need to pay. It should include 10% GST, and no 'optional' service charge added. Waiters are paid a reasonable salary, so they don't rely on tips to survive. Increasingly though, people leave a few coins in a cafe and up to 15% at high-end places.

In the Atherton Tableland in North Queensland, you can get a first-hand look at the nation's best coffee-growing plantations. Even better, you'll get to sample the good stuff – not just the incredibly rich, freshly made coffee, but also the coffee liqueur and dark-chocolate-coated coffee beans.

Further north, the Daintree offers gustatory temptations of a different sort. You can sample delectable ice cream made from freshly picked fruits grown in the surrounding orchards, or feast on tropical fruits grown at the Cape Trib Exotic Fruit Farm.

Wine Country

The oldest wine region in Australia, the Hunter Valley (p109) first had vines in the 1830s and has grown to international renown in the last half-century. Located a few hours north of Sydney, the Valley is home to over 120 wineries, with a mix of boutique, family-run outfits and large-scale commercial vintners. Top tipples include a lively unwooded Semillon, considered among the best in the world. Shiraz here is also world-class. Other popular varieties produced here include Chardonnay, Verdelho, Cabernet Sauvignon and Merlot.

Melbourne itself is surrounded by superb wine-growing regions – all with distinct climates and soils. Beginning at Melbourne's suburban fringe, the Yarra Valley is a patchwork of vines, and it's here that you'll find the glamorous big boys of the industry, Chateau Yering and Domaine Chandon, with fruity unwooded Pinot Noirs, peachy Chardonnay and crisp sparkling standouts. Further south, the hills and valleys of the Mornington Peninsula hide a wealth of viticultural riches, including beautiful early ripening Pinot Noirs, subtle honeyed Chardonnay and Pinot Gris, as well as fragrant Italian varietals such as Arneis and Pinot Grigio.

There's even a wine region in Queensland (the Granite Belt), which has slowly been carving out a name for itself in recent years, buoyed by an excellent showing at international awards shows. The neighbouring

FARMERS MARKETS

Beloved by many locals, the farmers market is a great destination to sample the culinary riches of the region, support local growers in the process and enjoy the congenial air (live music, friendly banter, free food sampling) that often pervades these places. You'll find fruits, veggies, seafoods, meats, baked breads and pastries and much more in these and other markets scattered across East Coast Australia. For more options, visit the **Australian Farmers Market Association** (www.farmersmarkets.org.au) website.

NSW

For a complete rundown of the many markets in northern NSW, see p191.

» **Sydney** (p49) In addition to Sydney's legendary fish market (p60), you'll find lively farmers markets in the Rocks (Friday and Saturday), Bondi Junction (Thursday), Darlinghurst (www.sydneysustainablemarkets.org; Saturday) and Manly (www.manlymarkets.com.au; Saturday).

» **Byron Bay**(p161) A community treasure on Thursday mornings.

» **Nimbin** (p174) One of NSW's free-spirited best, with live music and a sea of (largely organic) produce.

» **Bellingen** (p191) Over 250 stalls, live music and family entertainment make this a top monthly market.

» **Bangalow** (p173) A Saturday market in the charming hinterland town.

Victoria

Melbourne is synonymous with magnificent markets. These are great places to start the gourmand's journey:

» **Queen Victoria Market** (p206) Legendary market over 130 years old.

» **Prahran Market** (p211) One of Melbourne's finest produce markets.

» **Abbotsford Convent** (p209) Once-monthly slow-food market.

» **Ceres** (p210) Twice-weekly organic market in a park setting.

Queensland

Brisbane has a fine array of markets, including magnificent waterfront favourites in New Farm and West End (p302). Other Queensland hits:

» **Surfers Paradise** (p311; www.yourlocalmarkets.com.au) One of the Gold Coast's biggest, with 80-plus stalls; held on Sundays.

» **Noosa** (p329; www.noosafarmersmarket.com.au) A splendid Sunday market that brings a huge number of vendors.

WINE TIPS

The *Australian Wine Annual* by Jeremy Oliver is a must-read for those who want the low down on the Aussie wine scene. Oliver profiles more than 300 wineries, with notes on thousands of wines. His picks – wine of the year, top 100 and best under $20 – make a handy cheat sheet when selecting a bottle.

towns of Stanthorpe and Ballandean, two hours southwest of Brisbane, are gateways to this charming region.

Most wineries are open to visitors, with free tastings, though some keep limited hours (opening only on weekends). See p109 for a list of top wineries in the region.

For something completely different, don't miss a chance to taste the 'tropical wines' produced in north Queensland and made from plum, mango and passionfruit among others.

Beer, Breweries & Bundaberg

There's a wide array of beer available in bottle shops, pubs, bars and restaurants. The standby options (ice-cold Carlton, VB, XXXX and Tooheys) are fine on a hot summer's day, but for something more flavourful, look to the growing number of microbreweries.

A few labels to look out for include the following:

» **James Squire** A Sydney brewer with a wide distribution and a range of craft beers; the IPA is superb.

» **St Arnou** A micro-micro brewery in NSW; it has an excellent Belgian-style white beer, St Cloud.

» **Northern Rivers Brewing Co** A full range of craft beers come from this small brewery near Byron Bay; Ruby Raspberry is a popular postbeach treat.

» **Mountain Goat** Brewed right in the Melbourne suburb of Richmond, the Hightale Ale is an English-style ale that makes a perfect pint.

» **Piss** A beer from Victoria that takes the piss out of piss... Once you're past the puns, it's an excellent, rich lager.

» **Blue Sky Brewery** This award-winning Cairns brewery produces a crisp lager (the FNQ) and a traditional Czech-style Pilsner, as well as cider and stout.

» **Burkes Brewing Company** In North Brisbane, Burkes is best known for its Hemp Premium Ale, a golden beer with a touch of sweetness; it's brewed (legally, apparently) through hemp filters.

» **Mt Tamborine Brewery** (www.mtbeer.com) Producing some of Queensland's best microbrews, the top picks include Belgian-style ale, a hops-loving IPA and a rich imperial stout.

In addition, for a new appreciation of Queensland's favourite beverage, head to Brisbane's XXXX (pronounced 'four-ex') brewery (p286), which has been around since 1924. It's much maligned elsewhere in the country, but the locals swear by it. The widely bandied joke is that Queenslanders call it XXXX because they don't know how to spell 'beer'.

Sport

If Australia had a national religion, Catholics and Anglicans might vie for top honours, but as any Aussie can tell you, standing in a church singing gentle hymns will never hold a candle to gathering in grandstands and roaring for the home team. In Australia the passion for sport flows deep, and it's undoubtedly the nation's great uniter (and depending on which team you're following, the great *divider* as well).

All three East Coast states can stake legitimate claims to the title of Australia's sporting mecca (even Canberra has pro teams and more than its fair share of sports-mad residents). The object of passion, however, varies from state to state. In NSW and Queensland it's the gladiatorial arena of rugby ('thugby'), while down south, Victoria is a smouldering cauldron of Aussie Rules football ('aerial ping pong'). Cricket ('watching paint dry') is a nationwide obsession in summer. But these sports are hardly the only games in town. Australians love all sport, from basketball and motor sports to tennis, soccer, horse racing, netball, surfing, even bull-riding – when competition is afoot, the roaring crowds will appear (case in point: Brisbane's Australia Day Cockroach Races attract upwards of 7000 cheering fans each year).

Given the great sanctity of sport, there are a few important rituals that accompany the event. These are the unspoken rules of watching Australian sport. If attending a match, dress in your team's colours. Dress your children in the team's colours as well and take them to games as soon as they're born in order to indoctrinate them as early as possible. Discuss the sport at every opportunity, before, after and during play. And, of course, the drinking of beer while watching is highly encouraged. If unable to attend in person, go to your mate's place – the one who has the largest TV screen would be a good choice – or head to the pub. Make sure the fridge is stocked and the coffee table littered with snacks. The wearing of the team's colours and the incessant chatter about the game apply here as well.

Australians may have made an art form of watching sport, but they're even better at playing it. The national rugby union team, the Wallabies, has won the William Webb Ellis trophy (or Rugby World Cup trophy) with sufficient frequency for Australians to refer to it as 'Bill'. In rugby league (more on the differences to follow), they do even better, having won the World Cup nine times (by contrast, Great Britain, the next best team, has won it only three times). The Australian cricket team has long dominated the sport, having won the World Cup a record four times. It was ranked number one for the better part of the last decade, and is known to have some of the most formidable players in the game.

Although Australia is a relatively small nation, its inhabitants constantly vie for kudos by challenging well-established opponents around the globe in just about any sporting event there is. They've hosted the Summer Olympics twice (Melbourne in 1956, Sydney in 2000) and have placed fourth, fourth and sixth in the last three Summer Olympics –

CRICKET HEROES

The first Australian cricket team to tour England was 100% Victorian Aboriginal – in 1868. The subsequent 'whiteness' of the sport in Australia meant that this achievement was unheralded until recently.

An oft-repeated quote is 'Rugby [union] is a hooligan's game played by gentlemen. Football is a gentlemen's game played by hooligans.' Others have added that 'Rugby league is a hooligan's game played by hooligans.'

FOOTY LINGO

» **Avagoyermug!** 'Have a go, you mug!' – Traditional rallying call, also used at cricket matches

» **Carn!** 'Come on', as in 'Carn the Saints!'

» **Chewie on ya boot** Aimed at distracting a footballer on the verge of kicking a goal (chewie is chewing gum)

» **Got coat-hangered** Was hit by a straight arm

» **Got dragged** Was taken off the field by the coach

» **Had a blinder** Played really well

» **Drop kick** Not a field manoeuvre but a term of verbal abuse; a deadbeat, a loser

Note that 'rooting' for the home team will always elicit a smile among Aussies; around these parts, 'rooting' is a rather coarse term for 'having sex'. To 'barrack for', on the other hand, means to cheer on a team.

laying claim to one of the highest medal rankings per capita of any nation competing.

Footy

Australian Rules football, the only sport that matters to Victorians, is commonly referred to as Aussie Rules or, more simply, 'footy'. Melbourne is the spiritual home of this strange hybrid sport (a sort of cross between rugby and Gaelic football), from where the **Australian Football League** (AFL; www.afl.com.au) administers the national competition. Traditionally, most big games are played at the Melbourne Cricket Ground (MCG; p209). During the season (March to September), Victorians go footy-mad, entering tipping competitions, discussing groins and hamstrings and savouring the latest in loutish behaviour (on and off the field). It all culminates on the last Saturday in September when Melbourne hosts the AFL grand final – the whole city goes wild. Some 100,000 fans pack the MCG with millions more watching on TV.

Originally exclusive to Victoria, the AFL is overrepresented in Melbourne (home to nine of the 16 teams) and there are no teams from Tasmania, the Northern Territory (NT) or the Australian Capital Territory (ACT). However, some teams – notably Essendon, Richmond and Port Adelaide – run Indigenous programs designed to promote the sport in communities across the country, and all teams recruit Indigenous players, praising their unique vision (kicking into a space for a teammate to run into) and skills.

The most spectacular aspects of the game are the long kicking, the high marking and the brutal collisions. Crowd participation is high, with 'Carn the [insert team nickname]' and 'Baaalll... You're joking umpire' voiced times 50,000, merging into a roar that upsets dogs in suburban backyards for kilometres around.

> Russell Crowe spent part of his childhood in Sydney. Today he's part-owner of the Rabbitohs, the 100-year-old South Sydney team in the National Rugby League.

Rugby

While Melburnians refuse to acknowledge it (or do so with a scowl akin to that directed at an unfaithful spouse), there are other versions of 'footy'. The National Rugby League (the 13-a-side version) is the most popular sporting competition north of the Murray River and a 'real man's game' as far as NSW and Queensland are concerned. The competition, which also runs from March to September, features 16 teams – 10 from NSW, three from Queensland, and one each from ACT, New Zealand and Victoria. The latter (a Melbourne team) has historically done well, winning grand finals in 2007 and 2009. However, it was later discovered to have grossly violated the league's salary caps and was stripped of its titles – much to the delight of most NSW residents.

One of the most anticipated events in the league calendar (apart from the grand final in September) is the State of Origin series held in June or July, when all-star players from Queensland take on their counterparts from NSW in an explosive state-against-state rivalry. At last count, NSW – known as the Blues (or Cockroaches) – had suffered a long run of humiliating defeats (five in a row from 2006 to 2010) to their Queensland arch-rivals, the Maroons (or Cane Toads).

Rugby union (the 15-a-side variant, run by the Australian Rugby Union) is almost as popular, especially since turning professional in the mid-1990s. Historically, union was an amateur sport played by upper-class blokes from prestigious British public school systems, while rugby league was associated with working-class communities of northern England. The ideological divide carried over to Australia, where it has remained to a large degree over the past century.

It's said by some cynics that more Australians know cricket legend Don Bradman's Test batting average (99.94) than know the year Captain Cook first bobbed around the coast (1770).

BRADMAN'S AVERAGE

Survival Guide

Deadly & Dangerous

Home to bushfires, treacherous surf, blazing heat, jellyfish, snakes, spiders, sharks, crocodiles, ticks and mosquitos, Australia certainly has its share of hazards. Thankfully, the real threat to travellers is greatly exaggerated – and those who take basic precautious are unlikely to encounter serious problems. For info on road hazards and outback travel see p532.

Bushfires

Bushfires happen every year in Australia. In hot, dry, windy weather, be extremely careful with any naked flame, and don't throw live cigarette butts out of car windows. On a day of total fire ban it is forbidden even to use a camping stove in the open.

If you're out in the bush and you see smoke, even at a great distance, take it seriously. Go to the nearest open space, downhill if possible. A forested ridge is the most dangerous place to be. Bushfires move very quickly and change direction with the wind. Last but not least, always take seriously the advice of authorities and follow their warnings, regulations and instructions.

Environmental Hazards

Coral Cuts

Coral can be extremely sharp; you can cut yourself by merely brushing against the stuff. Thoroughly clean cuts and douse with antiseptic to avoid infection.

Heat Sickness

Very hot weather is common in Australia and can lead to heat exhaustion or more severe heatstroke (resulting from extreme fluid depletion). When arriving from a temperate or cold climate, remember that it takes two weeks to acclimatise.

Unprepared travellers die from dehydration each year in outback Australia. To survive, follow these rules:

» Carry sufficient water for any trip, including extra in case of breakdown.

» Always let someone know where you are going and when you expect to arrive.

» Carry communications equipment of some form.

» If in trouble, stay with the vehicle rather than walking for help.

» When out bushwalking, always stay hydrated and carry water with you at all times, even on short hikes.

Sunburn & Skin Cancer

Australia has one of the highest rates of skin cancer in the world. Monitor exposure to sunlight closely. Ultraviolet (UV) exposure is greatest between 10am and 4pm, so avoid skin exposure during these times. Wear a wide-brimmed hat and a long-sleeved shirt with a collar, and always use 30+ sunscreen, applied 30 minutes before exposure, and repeated regularly to minimise sun damage.

Drowning

Around 80 people a year drown on Australia's beaches, where pounding surf and rips (strong currents) can create serious hazards. If you happen to get caught in a rip and are being taken out to sea, swim parallel to the shore – don't try to swim back against the rip, you'll only tire yourself.

BASIC REEF SAFETY RULES

» Don't touch any marine life.

» Wear shoes with strong soles when walking near reefs.

» Don't eat fish you don't know about or can't identify.

» Don't swim in murky water; try to swim in bright sunlight.

Critters that Bite & Sting

Stingers & Marine Animals

Marine spikes and poisonous spines, such as those found on sea urchins, catfish, stingrays, scorpion fish and stonefish, can cause severe local pain. If this occurs, immediately immerse the affected area in hot water (as hot as can be tolerated) and seek medical care.

Blue-ringed octopuses and Barrier Reef cone shells can be fatal, so don't pick them up. If someone is stung, apply a pressure bandage, monitor breathing carefully and conduct mouth-to-mouth resuscitation if breathing stops. Seek immediate medical care.

Marine stings from jellyfish, such as the potentially deadly box jellyfish and Irukandji, also occur in Australia's tropical waters. It's unwise to swim north of Agnes Water between November and May unless there's a stinger net. 'Stinger suits' (full-body Lycra swimsuits) prevent stinging, as do wetsuits. Swimming and snorkelling are usually safe around Queensland's reef islands throughout the year; however, the rare and tiny (1cm to 2cm across) Irukandji has been recorded on the outer reef and islands.

If you are stung, wash skin with vinegar to prevent further discharge of remaining stinging cells, followed by rapid transfer to a hospital. Do not attempt to remove the tentacles.

Mosquitoes

Mozzies can be a problem just about anywhere in Australia. Malaria is not present in Australia, although dengue fever is a danger in northern Queensland, particularly during the wet season (November to April). This viral disease is spread by a species of mosquito that feeds primarily during the day. Most people recover in a few days, but more severe forms of the disease can occur.

To minimise bites:

» Wear loose, long-sleeved clothing.

» Apply repellent with minimum 30% DEET on exposed skin.

» Wear Permethrin-impregnated clothing.

» Use mosquito coils.

» Sleep under ceiling fans set to high speed.

Sharks & Crocodiles

The risk of a shark attack is low. Check the local risks with surf life-saving groups.

The risk of crocodile attack in tropical Far North Queensland is real, but it is entirely avoidable with common sense. Crocs aren't a risk in Victoria, New South Wales or southern Queensland (south of Rockhampton). 'Salties' are estuarine crocodiles that can grow to 7m. They inhabit coastal waters and are mostly seen in the tidal reaches of rivers, though on occasion they're spotted on beaches and in freshwater lagoons. Always heed any advice, such as crocodile warning signs, that you might come across. Don't assume it's safe to swim if there are no signs: if you're not sure, don't swim.

If you're away from popular beaches anywhere north of Mackay, avoid swimming in rivers, waterholes and in the sea near river outlets. Don't clean fish or prepare food near the water's edge, and camp at least 50m away from waterways. Crocodiles are particularly mobile and dangerous around breeding season (October to March).

Snakes

Australian snakes have a fearsome reputation owing to the potency of their venom, but pose small actual risk to travellers. Snakes are usually timid in nature and in most instances will move away if disturbed. They are endowed with only small fangs, making it easy to prevent bites to the lower limbs (where 80% of bites occur) by wearing protective clothing (such as gaiters) around the ankles when bushwalking. If bitten, apply an elastic bandage (as one would a sprained ankle; you can improvise with a T-shirt). Wrap firmly – but not tight enough to cut off the circulation – around the entire limb, and immobilise with a splint or sling; then seek immediate medical attention. Don't use a tourniquet, and *don't* try to suck out the poison!

Spiders

Australia has poisonous spiders, although deaths are extremely rare. Common species:

» Redback: bites cause increasing pain followed by profuse sweating. Apply ice and transfer to hospital.

» Whitetail (brown recluse): blamed for causing slow-healing ulcers; if bitten, clean wound and seek medical assistance.

» Huntsman: large, tarantula-like spider with a painful but harmless bite.

Ticks

The common bush tick (found all along the eastern coast) can be dangerous if left lodged in the skin because the toxin the tick excretes can cause partial paralysis and, in theory, even death. Check your body every night (and that of children and dogs) if walking in tick-infested areas. Remove by dousing a tick with methylated spirits or kerosene and levering it out intact.

Tick typhus cases have been reported in Australia. A week or so after being bitten a dark area forms around the bite, followed by a rash and possible fever, headache and inflamed lymph nodes. The disease is treatable with antibiotics (doxycycline).

Directory A–Z

Accommodation

The East Coast is a route that is well trodden with plenty of accommodation options to suit all budgets. Endowed with Australia's largest cities and most famous holiday resorts, the coast boasts abundant hotels, motels, guesthouses, B&Bs, hostels, pubs and caravan parks with camp sites. There are also less conventional possibilities, such as farmstays, houseboats and yachts. The listings in the accommodation sections of this guidebook are in order of preference, from most to least desirable.

Prices

In this guide, budget accommodation ($) is any place that charges less than $100 per double. Midrange listings ($$) run $100 to $180 per double, while the top end ($$$) features places charging more than $180 per double. Prices rise by about 25% during school and public holidays, during breaks around Easter and Christmas, and during the high season – which coincides with the summer months (December to February) anywhere south of Queensland.

In Queensland, particularly in the tropical north, the high season runs from June to September, when the weather is mild and the beaches are free of stingers.

Booking online

Useful websites for discounted or last-minute accommodation:

Wotif.com (www.wotif.com.au)

Lastminute.com (www.au.lastminute.com)

Quickbeds.com (www.quickbeds.com.au)

B&Bs

Bed-and-breakfast (B&B) options include restored miners' cottages, converted barns, rambling old houses, upmarket country manors, beachside bungalows and simple bedrooms in family homes. Tariffs are typically in the $100 to $180 (per

double) bracket, but can be much higher.

Local tourist offices can usually give you a list of available options. Good online information:

B&B and Farmstay NSW & ACT (www.bedandbreakfastnsw.com.au)

B&B and Farmstay Far North Queensland (www.bnbnq.com.au)

B&B Australia (www.babs.com.au)

B&B and Farmstay Victoria (www.accommodationgetawaysvictoria.com.au)

OZ Bed and Breakfast (www.ozbedandbreakfast.com)

Camping

If you want to explore the East Coast on a shoestring, camping is the way to go. Camping in national parks can cost from nothing to $14 per person – nights spent around a campfire under the stars are unforgettable. Tent sites at private camping and caravan parks cost around $20 to $30 per couple per night, and a few dollars more with electricity. Many of these outfits also hire out cabins with kitchenettes (running from $60 to $100 per night).

National parks and their camping areas are administered by each state. Contact details include:

New South Wales www.environment.nsw.gov.au

Queensland www.derm.qld.gov.au

Victoria www.parkweb.vic.gov.au

If you intend to do a lot of caravanning or camping, it's not a bad idea to join one of the major chains, such as **Big**

BOOK YOUR STAY ONLINE

For more accommodation reviews by Lonely Planet authors, check out hotels.lonelyplanet.com/East Coast Australia. You'll find independent reviews, as well as recommendations on the best places to stay. Best of all, you can book online.

4 Holiday Parks (www.big4. com.au), which will give you discounts on accommodation.

Note that all camping and cabin rates quoted throughout this guide are for two people.

Farmstays

Many coastal and hinterland farms offer a bed for the night and the chance to see rural Australia at work. At some you sit back and watch other people raise a sweat, while others like to get you involved in day-to-day activities. Check out options at www.babs.com.au under family holidays/farmstays. For travellers who don't mind getting their hands dirty, there's Willing Workers on Organic Farms (WWOOF; www.wwoof.com.au). Regional and town tourist offices should also be able to tell you what's available in their area.

Hostels

The hostel or 'backpackers' is a highly social, low-cost fixture of the East Coast accommodation scene. There is a staggering number, ranging from family-run places in converted houses to huge, custom-built resorts replete with bars, nightclubs and a party attitude. Standards range from outstanding to awful, and management from friendly to scary.

Dorm beds typically cost $20 to $30, with single rooms sometimes available (around $60) and doubles costing $70 to $100.

Useful organisations with annual memberships ($37 to $43) that yield lodging and other discounts:

Nomads Backpackers (www.nomadsworld.com)

VIP Backpacker Resorts (www.vipbackpackers.com) Membership ($43 for 12 months) entitles you to various discounts.

YHA (www.yha.com.au)

A warning for Australian and Kiwi travellers: some hostels

will only admit overseas backpackers, mainly because they've had problems with local males staying overnight and harassing travellers. Fortunately, it's only a rowdy minority that makes trouble, and often hostels will only ask for identification in order to deter potential troublemakers.

Hotels & Motels

There are many excellent four- and five-star hotels and quite a few lesser places. The best tend to have a pool, restaurant or cafe, room service and various other facilities. We quote 'rack rates' (official advertised rates) throughout this book, but often hotels and motels offer regular discounts and special deals – particularly if you browse online.

For comfortable midrange accommodation that's available all over the state, motels (or motor inns) are the places to stay. Prices typically run between $80 and $130 for a room.

Pubs

For the budget traveller, rooms in pubs (more formally known as public houses) aka hotels, aka 'the local', can be a good option. In the cities they are less attractive, and the rooms are either noisy or run down, or both. In the country, however, pubs usually make for a convenient and often interesting choice. In tourist areas some of these pubs have been restored as they are often in outstanding heritage buildings, but generally the rooms remain small and old-fashioned, with a long amble down the hall to the bathroom. Never book a room above the bar if you're a light sleeper.

Pubs usually have single/ double/twin rooms with shared facilities from around $50/80/80, obviously more if you want a private bathroom. The website www. pubstay.com.au lists an array of the better places.

Rental Accommodation

Rental accommodation is found in the form of holiday flats (in tourist areas) and serviced apartments (in cities). A holiday flat is much like a motel unit but has a serviceable kitchen. Holiday flats are often rented on a weekly basis; expect to pay anywhere from $90 to $180 per night for a one-bedroom flat. Ask a local real-estate agent about holiday rentals. If you want to stay for a longer period, the first place to look for a shared flat or a room in the cities is the classified-advertisements sections of daily newspapers. Wednesday and Saturday are the best days for these ads. Noticeboards at universities, hostels and cafes are also good places to look for flats and houses to share or rooms to rent. Keep in mind that some long-term lodgings require deposits (or bonds) and don't come furnished.

Useful websites:

Couch Surfing (www.couch-surfing.com) Hooks you up with spare couches and new friends around the world.

Domain.com.au (www. domain.com.au) Lists holiday and long-term rentals.

Flatmate Finders (www. flatmatefinders.com.au) Good site for long-term share accommodation in Sydney and Melbourne.

Sleeping with the Enemy (www.sleepingwiththeenemy. com) Another good site for long-term accommodation (one-month minimum) in Sydney and Cairns.

Business Hours

Reviews in this book don't list operating hours unless they deviate from the following normal opening times:

Restaurants noon-2.30pm & 6.30-9pm

Cafes 8am-5pm

Shops 9am-5pm Mon-Fri, 9am-1pm Sat
Shopping centres 9am-9pm
Supermarkets 9am-8pm
Pubs & bars noon-2am
Nightclubs 11pm-4am Thu-Sat
Banks 9.30am-4pm Mon-Fri
Post offices 9am-5pm Mon-Fri

Children
Practicalities
All cities and major towns have public rooms where parents can breast-feed or change nappies (diapers). While many Australians have a relaxed attitude about breastfeeding or nappy changing in public, others frown upon it.

Most motels supply cots; many also have playgrounds and swimming pools, as well as child-minding services. Many B&Bs, on the other hand, market themselves as child-free sanctuaries.

If you want to leave Junior behind for a few hours, licensed child-care agencies have places set aside for casual care, and many of the larger hotels have contacts.

Concessions for children apply for such things as accommodation, admission fees, and air, bus and train transport, with some discounts as high as 50% of the adult rate. However, the definition of 'child' can vary from under 12 to under 18 years.

Medical services and facilities in Australia are of a high standard, and items such as baby food, formula and disposable nappies are widely available in urban centres. For an extra cost, major car-hire companies will supply and fit child safety seats for you (under new-ish national laws, safety restraints are now compulsory for all children up to seven years old).

Sights & Activities
There's plenty to keep kids occupied along the East Coast. Theme parks such as Sea World and Movie World on the Gold Coast are popular, but there are many cheaper and free options as well. Useful websites:
New South Wales www.sydneyschild.com.au
Victoria www.melbourneschild.com.au
Queensland www.brisbaneschild.com.au

Discount Cards
The **International Student Identity Card** (ISIC; www.isic.org), available to full-time students worldwide, yields discounts on accommodation, transport and admission to various attractions. Seniors also net discounts on transport and sights.

Electricity

240v/50hz

Gay & Lesbian Travellers
The East Coast of Australia – Sydney especially – is a popular destination for gay and lesbian travellers. Certain areas are the focus of the gay and lesbian communities: Cairns and Noosa in Queensland; Sydney's Oxford St and Kings Cross; the Blue Mountains, Hunter Valley and the NSW north-coast hinterland; and the Melbourne suburbs of Prahran, St Kilda and Collingwood are all popular areas. As well as Sydney's Mardi Gras in February to early March, there's Melbourne's Midsumma Festival in January and February.

In general, Australians are open-minded about homosexuality, but the further out of the big towns and cities you get, the more likely you are to run into homophobia.

Australia's gay community produces a wide range of publications, including *DNA*, *Lesbians on the Loose* and the art magazine *Blue*.

Useful websites:
Gay & Lesbian Tourism Australia (Galta; www.galta.com.au) General info
Pink Board (www.pinkboard.com.au) Sydney-based, with useful forums.

Health
Although there are plenty of hazards in Australia (see p514), few travellers should experience anything worse than an upset stomach or a bad hangover and, if you do fall ill, the standard of hospitals and health care is high.

Availability & Cost of Health Care
Australia has an excellent health-care system, with a mixture of privately run medical clinics and hospitals, and a system of government-funded public hospitals. Medicare covers Australian residents for some health-care costs. Visitors from countries with which Australia has a reciprocal health-care agreement (New Zealand, the UK, the Netherlands, Sweden, Finland, Italy, Malta and Ireland) are eligible for benefits to the extent specified under

the Medicare program. If you are from one of these countries, check the details before departure. For further information visit www.health. gov.au.

In remote locations there may be significant delays in emergency services reaching you in the event of serious accident or illness – do not underestimate the vast distances between most major outback towns. An increased level of self-reliance and preparation is essential; consider taking a wilderness first-aid course, such as that offered by **Equip Wilderness First Aid Institute** (www.equip.com.au); take a comprehensive first-aid kit that's appropriate for the activities planned and ensure that you have adequate means of communication. Built-up areas have extensive mobile-phone coverage, but radio communications are important for remote areas. The Royal Flying Doctor Service provides a back-up for remote communities.

Chemists (Pharmacies) & Prescription Medication

Over-the-counter medications are available at chemists (pharmacies) throughout Australia. These include painkillers, antihistamines, and skin-care products. You may find that medications readily available over the counter in some countries are only available in Australia by prescription. These include the oral contraceptive pill,

some medications for asthma and all antibiotics. If you take medication on a regular basis, bring an adequate supply and ensure you have details of the generic name as brand names may differ between countries.

Health Insurance

Health insurance is essential for all travellers. While health care in Australia is of a high standard and not expensive by international standards, costs can build up if you require medical care. Find out in advance if your insurance plan will make payments directly to providers or reimburse you later for overseas health expenditures. If your health insurance doesn't cover you for medical expenses abroad, consider purchasing some extra insurance; see the Insurance section for more information.

Recommended Vaccinations

Proof of yellow-fever vaccination is required only from travellers entering Australia within six days of having visited a yellow-fever–infected country. For a full list of these countries, visit the website of the **World Health Organization** (WHO; www.who.int) or the **Centers for Disease Control and Prevention** (CDC; wwwnc.cdc.gov/travel).

The WHO recommends that all travellers be vaccinated for diphtheria, tetanus, measles, mumps, rubella, chickenpox and polio, and hepatitis B, regardless of their destination.

Tap Water

Tap water is generally quite safe to drink – but not always delicious. In recent years, there have been rare failures of water-treatment plants in small communities and remote areas. It never hurts to enquire locally about tap water safety. The website **Water Alerts** (www.freewater alerts.com) lists areas with problematic drinking water around Australia. Water taken directly from streams, rivers and lakes should be treated before drinking.

Further Reading

Lonely Planet's *Healthy Travel Australia, New Zealand & the Pacific* is a handy, pocket-sized guide packed with useful information, including pretrip planning, emergency first aid, immunisation and disease information and what to do if you get sick on the road. *Travel with Children*, from Lonely Planet, also includes advice on travel health for younger children.

Insurance

Don't underestimate the importance of a good travel-insurance policy that covers theft, loss and medical problems. Most policies offer lower and higher medical-expense options; the higher ones are chiefly for countries that have extremely high medical costs, such as the USA. There is a wide variety of policies available, so compare the small print.

Some policies specifically exclude designated 'dangerous activities,' such as scuba diving, parasailing, bungee jumping, motorcycling, skiing and even bushwalking. If you plan on doing any of these things, make sure the policy you choose fully covers you for your activity of choice.

See the Health Insurance section for further information. For information on car insurance, see p531.

TRAVEL HEALTH WEBSITES

It's usually a good idea to consult your government's travel-health website before departure, if one is available.

Australia www.smartraveller.gov.au
Canada www.hc-sc.gc.ca
UK www.fco.gov.uk
USA www.cdc.gov

Internet Access

Most East Coast towns have places where you can access the internet, usually for about $6 to $8 an hour. In really popular places, you'll find access in convenience stores, travel agencies, visitors centres and more. Hostels almost always have internet access. Libraries offer free access. Places offering internet access are identified in this book with an internet symbol (@).

Wireless Access

Wireless access is widespread, and common in cities and large towns. We've indicated places that offer access (either free or paid) by the ☎ symbol. Unfortunately, free access is rare and most hotspots require you to buy credit (with a credit card) before use – though some hotels, motels and caravan parks may provide free access (others charge as much as $20 for 24 hours). Most libraries offer free wi-fi access.

Telstra, Optus, Vodaphone and other big carriers sell mobile broadband devices with a USB connection that works with most laptops and allows you to get online just about anywhere in the country. Prices are around $80 for 30 days of access, with up to 2GB of data.

Legal Matters

Drinking & Driving

Australia is very strict when it comes to drinking and driving or driving while under the influence of drugs. There is a significant police presence on the roads, and police have the power to stop you and ask to see your licence (you're required to carry it), check your vehicle for road-worthiness, and ask you to take a breath test for alcohol. The legal limit is 0.05 blood alcohol content. If you're over, you'll be in seri-

ous trouble, facing a fine of anywhere from a few hundred dollars to $3300 and suspension of your licence.

Drugs & Overstaying a Visa

First offenders caught with small amounts of illegal drugs are likely to receive a fine rather than go to jail, but the recording of a conviction against you may affect your visa status. Speaking of which, if you remain in Australia beyond the life of your visa, you will officially be an 'overstayer' and could face detention and expulsion, and then be prevented from returning to Australia for up to three years.

Maps

You'll find plenty of maps available when you arrive in Australia. Visitors centres usually have free maps of the region and towns, although quality varies. Automobile associations (p529) are a good source of reliable road maps. City street directories, such as those produced by Ausway, Gregory's and UBD, are very useful but they're expensive, bulky and usually only worth getting if you intend to do a lot of driving in one city.

For bushwalking and other activities that require large-scale maps, the topographic sheets put out by Geoscience Australia (☎1800

TAX REFUNDS

If you purchase new or secondhand goods with a total minimum value of $300 from any one supplier no more than 30 days before you leave Australia, you are entitled under the Tourist Refund Scheme (TRS) to a refund of any GST paid (usually 10%). The scheme only applies to goods you take with you as hand luggage or wear onto the plane or ship. Also note that the refund is valid for goods bought from more than one supplier, but only if at least $300 has been spent at each. For more information, contact the **Australian Customs Service** (www.customs.gov.au).

---

800 173; www.ga.gov.au) are the ones to get. Many of the more popular sheets are usually available over the counter at outdoor-equipment shops.

Money

In this book all prices given in dollars refer to Australian dollars. Exchange rates are listed on the inside front cover.

ATMs are prominent throughout Australia and are the best way to get local currency. MasterCard and Visa are widely accepted. You can use debit cards at most retail outlets, which carry Eftpos (Electronic Funds Transfer at Point of Sale) facilities.

You can change foreign currency or travellers cheques at most banks, and at foreign exchange counters such as Travelex or Amex, found in major cities. American Express, Thomas Cook and other well-known travellers cheques are all widely accepted.

Tipping is not common in Australia.

Photography & Video

Digital cameras and gear are widely available at electronics shops and department stores across the state. For tips on shooting images, see Lonely Planet's *Travel Photography: A Guide To Taking Better Pictures*.

Entering the Region

Before embarking on a trip to Australia, make sure you have your visa in order. Arriving in Australia is a straightforward affair – just be mindful of not bringing in any food or contraband. If you plan to drive in Australia, you can use your own foreign driving licence, as long as it's in English – if not you'll need an international licence along with it.

Customs Regulations

For comprehensive information on customs regulations, contact the **Australian Customs Service** (www.customs.gov.au).

There's a duty-free quota of 2.25L of alcohol, 250 cigarettes and dutiable goods up to the value of $900 per person.

Prohibited goods include drugs (all medicines must be declared) and food – Australia is very strict on this, so declare all food items, even leftover edibles taken from the plane.

Embassies & Consulates

The **Department of Foreign Affairs & Trade** (www.dfat.gov.au) lists all foreign missions in Australia. In addition to Canberra-based embassies below, some countries have diplomatic offices in Brisbane, Melbourne and Sydney.

Canada (☑02-6270 4000; www.australia.gc.ca; Commonwealth Ave, Canberra)
France (☑02-6216 0100; www.ambafrance-au.org; 6 Perth Ave, Yarralumla, ACT)
Germany (☑02-6270 1911; www.canberra.diplo.de; 119 Empire Circuit, Yarralumla, ACT)
Ireland (☑02-6273 3022; canberraembassy@dfa.ie; 20 Arkana St, Yarralumla, ACT)
Netherlands (☑02-6220 9400; www.netherlands.org.au; 120 Empire Circuit, Yarralumla, ACT)
New Zealand (☑02-6270 4211; www.nzembassy.com/australia; Commonwealth Ave, Canberra)
UK (☑02-6270 6666; www.ukinaustralia.fco.gov.uket; Commonwealth Ave, Yarralumla, ACT)
USA (☑02-6214 5600; www.canberra.usembassy.gov; 21 Moonah Pl, Yarralumla, ACT)

Practicalities

» DVDs use the PAL system.
» Plugs have angled pins: voltage is 220V to 240V; 50Hz.

Cheap, disposable underwater cameras are widely available at most beach towns. These are OK for snapshots when snorkelling or shallow diving and can produce reasonable results in good conditions, but without a flash the colours will be washed out. These cameras won't work below about 5m because of the water pressure. If you're serious about underwater photography, good underwater cameras with flash units can be hired from many of the dive shops along the coast.

As in any country, politeness goes a long way when taking photographs; ask before taking pictures of people. Aboriginal people generally do not like to have their photographs taken, even from a distance.

Post

Australia Post (www.auspost.com.au) is efficient. Posting standard letters or postcards within the country costs 60c. International rates for airmail letters up to 50g cost $2.20. Postcards cost $1.45.

Public Holidays

Public holidays vary quite a bit from state to state. The following is a list of the main national and state public holidays; for precise dates (which may vary from year to year), check locally.

National

New Year's Day 1 January
Australia Day 26 January
Easter (Good Friday to Easter Monday) March/April
Anzac Day 25 April
Queen's Birthday Second Monday in June
Christmas Day 25 December
Boxing Day 26 December

New South Wales

Bank Holiday First Monday in August
Labour Day First Monday in October

Queensland

Labour Day First Monday in May

» Top newspapers include the national *Australian*, the *Sydney Morning Herald*, Melbourne's *Age* and Brisbane's *Courier-Mail*.

» The metric system is used for weights and measures.

» Free-to-air TV channels include the government-sponsored, ad-free ABC, multicultural SBS, and three commercial stations – Seven, Nine and Ten – plus additional digital channels.

Visas

All visitors to Australia need a visa. Only New Zealand nationals are exempt: they receive a 'special category' visa on arrival.

Visa application forms are available from Australian diplomatic missions overseas, travel agents and the website of the **Department of Immigration and Citizenship** (www. immi.gov.au). For working holiday visas, see p525.

SHORT-TERM TOURIST VISAS

For stays of less than three months, the most straightforward visa is the short-term tourist visa. Where to apply, and how much it costs depends on your citizenship.

Visitors from the USA, Canada, Japan, South Korea, Hong Kong, Singapore, Malaysia and Brunei should apply through the **ETA, the Electronic Travel Authority** (www.eta. immi.gov.au). The cost is $20, and approval is rapid – usually within 12 hours.

Visitors from the UK and Europe should apply for the **eVisitor** (www.immi.gov.au). This visa is free and can be rapidly obtained online.

OTHER VISAS

If you are from a country not covered by the ETA or the eVisitor, or you want to stay longer than three months, you'll need to apply for a **Tourist Visa, subclass 676**. Standard visas (which cost $105) allow one entry (or in some cases multiple entries) and stays of up to three, six or 12 months.

VISA EXTENSIONS

Visitors are allowed a maximum stay of 12 months, including extensions. Visa extensions are made through the Department of Immigration and Citizenship; apply two or three weeks before your visa expires. The non-refundable application fee is currently $255.

RNA Show Day (Brisbane) August

Victoria

Labour Day Second Monday in March

Melbourne Cup Day First Tuesday in November

School Holidays

Key times when prices are highest and much accommodation is booked out well in advance:

Christmas holiday season (mid-December to late January)

Easter (March/April)

Shorter (two-week) school-holiday periods generally fall in mid-April, late June to mid-July, and late September to mid-October.

Safe Travel

Australia is a relatively safe place to visit, but it's better to be sure and take reasonable precautions.

Don't leave hotel rooms or cars unlocked, and don't leave your valuables unattended or visible through a car window. Sydney, the Gold Coast, Cairns and Byron Bay all get a dishonourable mention when it comes to theft, so keep a careful eye on your belongings in these areas. Make use of lockers or hotel safes.

Some pubs in Sydney and other cities popular with travellers carry posted warnings about drugged drinks, after several reported cases in the past few years of women accepting a drink from a stranger only to later fall unconscious and be sexually assaulted. Women are advised to refuse drinks offered by strangers in bars and to drink bottled alcohol rather than from a glass.

Telephone

To make a reverse-charge (collect) call within Australia, dial ☏1800-REVERSE (1800 738 3773) from any public or private phone.

Toll-free numbers (prefix ☏1800) can be called free of charge. Calls to numbers beginning with ☏13 or ☏1300 are charged at the rate of a local call.

Mobile Phones

Local numbers with the prefix ☐04xx belong to mobile phones. Coastal cities and towns get good reception, but service can be haphazard or non-existent in the interior.

Australia's digital network is compatible with GSM 900 and 1800 (used in Europe), but generally not with networks in the USA or Japan. It's easy and cheap enough to get connected short-term, as the main service providers (Telstra, Optus and Vodafone) all have prepaid mobile systems.

To get connected, just buy a starter kit, which may include a phone or, if you have your own phone, a SIM card (under $10) and a prepaid charge card. Purchase recharge cards at convenience stores and newsagents.

Phone Codes

To call overseas from Australia, dial ☐0011 or ☐0018, the country code and the area code (without the initial 0). So, for a London number you'd dial ☐0011-44-171, then the number.

If dialling Australia from overseas, the country code is ☐61 and you need to drop the 0 (zero) in the area code.

Useful area codes in Australia:

STATE/ TERRITORY	AREA CODE
ACT	☐02
NSW	☐02
VIC	☐03
QLD	☐07

Phonecards

Purchase phonecards at newsagents and post offices (for $10, $20, $30 etc). You can use them with any public or private phone by dialling a toll-free access number and then the PIN on the card. Some public phones also accept credit cards.

Time

Australia is divided into three time zones:

Eastern Standard Time (Greenwich Mean Time + 10 hours) Queensland, New South Wales, Victoria and Tasmania

» Central Standard Time (half-hour behind Eastern Standard Time) Northern Territory, South Australia

» Western Standard Time (two hours behind Eastern Standard Time) Western Australia

Note that Queensland remains on Eastern Standard Time all year, while most of Australia switches to daylight-saving time over the summer.

Tourist Information

Tourist information is provided in Australia by various regional and local offices, details of which are given in the relevant city and town sections throughout this book. Each state has a government-run tourist organisation ready to inundate you with information. Useful websites:

Tourism New South Wales (www.visitnsw.com)

Tourism Queensland (www. queenslandholidays.com.au)

Tourism Victoria (www. visitvictoria.com)

The **Australian Tourism Commission** (ATC; www.aust ralia.com) is the government body charged with luring foreign visitors; the website has information in eight languages. For ATC branches in other countries visit www. tourism.australia.com.

Travellers with Disabilities

Disability awareness in Australia is reasonably high. Legislation requires that new accommodation must meet accessibility standards and tourist operators must not discriminate.

Reliable information is the key ingredient for travellers with disabilities, and the best place to start is the **National Information Communication & Awareness Network** (Nican; ☐/TTY 02-6241 1220, TTY 1800 806 769; www.nican. com.au). It's an Australia-wide directory providing information on access, accommodation, sporting and recreational activities, transport and specialist tour operators.

The website of the **Australian Tourist Commission** (ATC; www.australia.com) publishes detailed, downloadable information for people with disabilities, including travel and transport tips and contact addresses of organisations in each state.

Other organisations with information for travellers with disabilities:

Accessible Tourism Website (www.australiaforall.com) Good site for tourists with disabilities to obtain accessibility information.

Ambleside Tours (☐03-9720 9800; www.ambleside tours.com) Offers fully escorted tours around Melbourne and Victoria.

National Disability Service (☐07-3357 4188; www.nds. org.au) The national industry association for disability services; a good place to start for information.

Wheelchair Accessible Sydney (☐0419-017-085; www.wheelchairs.sydney. net) Offers accessible tours around Sydney, the Hunter Valley and the Blue Mountains.

Wheelie Easy (☐07-4091 4876; www.wheelieeasy.com. au) This company runs specialised tours in the Far North Queensland for travellers with impaired mobility. Also has useful information about Cairns.

Volunteering

There are a lot of opportunities to volunteer your time and expertise in Australia. Useful resources:

Conservation Volunteers Australia (www.conservationvolunteers.com.au) Organises practical conservation projects, such as tree planting, walking-track construction and flora and fauna surveys.

Go Volunteer (www.govolunteer.com.au) National website listing volunteer opportunities.

i-to-i (www.i-to-i.com) Conservation-based volunteer holidays in Australia.

Volunteering Australia (www.volunteeringaustralia.org) Support, advice and volunteer training.

Willing Workers on Organic Farms (WWOOF; www.wwoof.com.au) Work on a farm in return for bed and board.

Women Travellers

Australia is generally a safe place for women travellers, although the usual sensible precautions apply. It's best to avoid walking alone late at night in any of the major cities and towns. And if you're out on the town, always keep enough money aside for a taxi back to your accommodation. Lone women should be wary of staying in basic pub accommodation unless it looks safe and well managed.

Work

New Zealanders can work in Australia without having to apply for a special visa or permit, but other short-term visitors can only work in Australia if they have a Working Holiday Makers (WHM) visa. Major tourist centres, such as the resort towns along the Queensland coast and the ski fields of Victoria and NSW, are all good prospects for casual work during peak seasons.

Seasonal fruit-picking (harvesting) relies on casual labour, and there is something to be picked, pruned or farmed somewhere in Australia all year round. It's hard work that involves early-morning starts, and you're usually paid by how much you pick (per bin/bucket); expect to earn around $10 to $15 an hour to start with, more when you get quicker at it.

Other options for casual employment include factory work, labouring, bar work and waiting on tables. People with computer, secretarial, nursing and teaching skills can find work temping in the major cities by registering with a relevant agency. See the websites below for contact details of some agencies.

Information

Backpacker accommodation, magazines and newspapers are good resources for local work opportunities.

Useful websites:

Career One (www.careerone.com.au) General employment site, good for metropolitan areas.

Face2Face Fundraising (www.face2facefundraising.com.au) Fund-raising jobs for charities and not-for-profits.

Good Cause (www.goodcause.com.au) Fund-raising jobs for charities and not-for-profits.

Harvest Trail (www.jobsearch.gov.au/harvesttrail) Harvest jobs around Australia.

Seek (www.seek.com) General employment site, good for metropolitan areas.

Workabout Australia (www.workaboutaustralia.com.au) By Barry Brebner; it gives a state-by-state breakdown of seasonal work opportunities.

Working Holiday Visas

Visitors aged 18 to 30 years old from Canada, Denmark, France, Germany, Hong Kong, Ireland, Japan, Korea, the Netherlands, Sweden, the UK, the USA and a handful of other countries are eligible for a Working Holiday visa, which allows you to visit for up to 12 months and gain casual employment. Working Holiday visa–holders may be eligible to apply for a second 12-month WH visa if they have done at least three months' 'specified work' (including harvest work, fishing, pearling, mining, construction) in regional Australia. Note that US citizens must apply for a different visa (subclass 462) than those from other countries (subclass 417). Visa holders are only supposed to work for any one employer for a maximum of six months. There is an application fee of $235, and visas can be applied for online (www.immi.gov.au) or at Australian diplomatic missions abroad. For more information go online (www.immi.gov.au).

TAXES

If you have a WHM visa, you should apply for a tax file number (TFN). Without it, tax will be deducted from any wages you receive at the maximum rate (around 47%). Apply for a TFN online via the ATO (www.ato.gov.au); it takes about four weeks to be issued. The office can provide additional info about paying taxes and refunds.

Transport

GETTING THERE & AWAY

This section covers how to get to and from major cities along the East Coast for visitors to Australia. Flights, tours and rail tickets can be booked online at lonely planet.com/bookings.

Air

International

The high season for flights into Australia is roughly over the country's summer (December to February), with substantially lower prices over the shoulder months (October/November and March/April). The low season generally tallies with the winter months (June to August), when you can pay as little as 50% of the high-season fare.

Many international flights head to Sydney, Melbourne or Brisbane, though Cairns and Coolangatta airport on the Gold Coast also receive international flights.

Brisbane Airport (http://bne.com.au)

Cairns Airport (www.cairns airport.com)

Gold Coast Airport (www.goldcoastairport.com.au)

Melbourne Airport (www.melbourneairport.com.au)

Sydney Airport (aka Kingsford Smith Airport; www.sydneyairport.com.au)

Australia's national carrier is **Qantas** (www.qantas.com), which has an exemplary safety record.

Tickets

Round-the-world tickets can be a good option for getting to Australia.

For online bookings:

Airbrokers (www.airbrokers.com) US company specialising in round-the-world tickets.

Cheap Flights (www.cheapflights.com) Flight searches from the US and other regions.

Cheapest Flights (www.cheapestflights.co.uk) Cheap worldwide flights from the UK.

Kayak (www.kayak.com) Best site in the US for finding flight deals.

Opodo (www.opodo.com) Has localised French, German and UK sites.

Orbitz (www.orbitz.com) Excellent site for web-only fares for US airlines.

Travel Online (www.travelonline.co.nz) Good place to check worldwide flights from New Zealand.

Travel.com.au (www.travel.com.au) Good Australian site.

Roundtheworld.com (www.roundtheworldflights.com) Build your own multi-flight trip from the UK.

Zuji (www.zuji.com.au) Good Asia–Pacific–based site.

CLIMATE CHANGE & TRAVEL

Every form of transport that relies on carbon-based fuel generates CO_2, the main cause of human-induced climate change. Modern travel is dependent on aeroplanes, which might use less fuel per kilometre per person than most cars but travel much greater distances. The altitude at which aircraft emit gases (including CO_2) and particles also contributes to their climate change impact. Many websites offer 'carbon calculators' that allow people to estimate the carbon emissions generated by their journey and, for those who wish to do so, to offset the impact of the greenhouse gases emitted with contributions to portfolios of climate-friendly initiatives throughout the world. Lonely Planet offsets the carbon footprint of all staff and author travel.

GETTING AROUND

Air

East Coast Australia is well serviced by airlines, big and small.

Jetstar (☎13 15 38; www.jetstar.com.au) Budget offshoot of Qantas; has extensive service.

Qantas/QantasLink (☎13 13 13; www.qantas.com.au) Service across Australia.

Tiger Airways (☎03-9335 3033; www.tigerairways.com) Budget airline with Melbourne as a hub. Serves a swath of East Coast destinations, from Mackay to Canberra.

Virgin Blue (☎13 67 89; www.virginblue.com.au) Has service throughout Australia.

Limited regional service:

Hinterland Aviation (☎07-4035 9323; www.hinterlandaviation.com.au) Flies Monday to Saturday between Cairns and Cooktown.

Regional Express (Rex; ☎13 17 13; www.regionalexpress.com.au) Connects Melbourne, Sydney and Townsville with small regional airports.

Skytrans (☎1300 759 872; www.skytrans.com.au) Serves northern Queensland, flying from Cairns to Bamaga (tip of Australia) and Mt Isa among other obscure locations.

Bicycle

Whether you're hiring a bike to ride around a city or wearing out your chain wheels on a long-distance haul, the East Coast is a great place for cycling. There are bike paths in most major cities, and in the country you'll find thousands of kilometres of good roads. In many areas along the coast, the countryside is flat or composed of gently rolling hills.

Much of eastern Australia was settled on the principle of not having more than a day's horse ride between pubs, so it's possible to plan even ultralong routes and still get a shower at the end of each day. Most cyclists carry camping equipment but it's feasible to travel from town to town staying in hostels, hotels or caravan parks.

No matter how fit you are, water is vital. Dehydration is no joke and heatstroke can be life threatening (see p514). It can get very hot in summer, and you should take things easy. Wear a helmet with a peak (or a cap under your helmet) and plenty of sunscreen, avoid cycling in the middle of the day and drink lots of water. Remember that it can get very cold in the mountains, so pack appropriately. In the south, be aware of the blistering hot 'northerlies' that can make a northbound cyclist's life hell in summer.

Bicycle helmets are compulsory, as are white front lights and red rear lights for riding at night. Most good-sized towns will have a shop stocking at least basic bike parts.

Information

The national cycling body is the **Bicycle Federation of Australia** (www.bfa.asn.au). Each state and territory has a touring organisation with heaps of cycling information:

ACT www.pedalpower.org.au
New South Wales www.bicyclensw.org.au
Queensland www.bq.org.au
Victoria www.bv.com.au

For more information, see Lonely Planet's *Cycling Australia*.

Purchase & Hire

Few outfits hire out bikes for longer than a day or two so, if you're coming to tour, it makes sense to bring your own.

If you prefer to buy a reliable new road cycle or mountain bike in Australia, your absolute bottom-level starting point is around $500. All the requisite on-the-road equipment, such as panniers, helmet etc, will run upwards of $1700.

Good sites for reselling your bike include **Trading Post** (www.tradingpost.com.au), **Gumtree** (www.gumtree.com.au) and **Bike Exchange** (www.bikeexchange.com.au).

The rates charged by most outfits for renting road or mountain bikes (not including

QANTAS AIRPASS

International travellers planning to visit more than a few destinations in Australia should have a look at the Qantas **Aussie Airpass**, allowing travel to up to three cities for a heavily discounted price. The Qantas **Walkabout Pass** allows visitors to custom-make an itinerary, visiting major destinations at set prices across the country. The catch is that the itinerary must include a Qantas international flight, and all itineraries must be booked together.

The fee structure places all flights into three zones: flights within one zone are US$59 for each leg of the journey; flights between zones cost US$119. One zone comprises Queensland, New South Wales, South Australia, Tasmania and ACT. Zones two and three include Western Australia and Northern Territory. See www.qantas.com.au for more information.

BIKE MELBOURNE & BRISBANE

Both Melbourne and Brisbane have inexpensive bike-sharing schemes that allow speedy access to a bike all across town. Basically, you pay a one-time fee and then check out a bike at one of dozens of stations. Bikes are free for the first half-hour (and you can ride all day for free, as long as bikes are returned within half-hour intervals). After the first half-hour, prices rise exponentially. The other catch: you must wear a helmet or risk a hefty fine. In Melbourne, inexpensive helmets are available from some retail outlets or vending machines at Southern Cross Station and Melbourne University. For details, including a list of places that sell helmets, go online:

Melbourne (www.melbournebikeshare.com.au)
Brisbane (www.citycycle.com.au)

the discounted fees offered by budget accommodation places to their guests) are anywhere from $10 to $15 per hour and $20 to $45 per day. Security deposits can range from $50 to $200, depending on the rental period.

Bus

East Coast Australia's bus network is reliable, but not the cheapest for long hauls. Most buses have air-con, toilets and videos, and all are smoke-free zones. Small towns eschew formal bus terminals for a single drop-off/pick-up point, usually outside a post office or shop.

Bus Companies & Routes

Greyhound Australia (1300 473 946; www.greyhound.com.au) Has the most extensive nationwide network.

Premier Motor Service (13 34 10; www.premierms.com.au) Greyhound's main competitor on the East Coast. It has fewer daily services but usually costs a little less.

Smaller operators:

Firefly Express (1800 631 164; www.fireflyexpress.com.au) Connects Sydney with Melbourne and Canberra.

V/Line (13 61 96; www.vlinepassenger.com.au) Operates coach and train services in Victoria.

Countrylink (13 22 32; www.countrylink.nsw.gov.au) Operates coach and train services in NSW.

Coachtrans (07-3358 9700; www.coachtrans.com.au) Serves Queensland's Gold Coast and Sunshine Coast.

Backpacker Buses

Several party tour buses operate along the coast, stopping at sights and pubs along the way and checking into hostels each night. These trips are economically priced and can be more fun than conventional buses: the buses are usually smaller and you'll meet other travellers – but you may not see much of Australia except through the bottom of a glass.

Discounts for students carrying cards, and members of hostel organisations are available.

Oz Experience (1300 300 028; www.ozexperience.com) Covers central, northern and eastern Australia.

Bus Passes

Bus passes are a good option if you plan plenty of stopovers. You should book or phone at least a day ahead to reserve a seat if you're using any of the following passes:

Greyhound (13 14 99; www.greyhound.com.au) offers many money-saving passes, and it's worth checking its website. A few options:

Kilometre Pass Gives you go-anywhere flexibility, plus the choice to backtrack; choose from 500km ($105) up to 20,000km ($2239).

Mini Traveller Pass Allows up to 90 days to travel from Cairns to Sydney ($360) or Melbourne ($417), stopping as often as you like.

Explorer Pass Set routes along East Coast and beyond, including the Central Coaster between Sydney and Brisbane ($211).

Premier (13 34 10; www.premierms.com.au) offers several passes for travel along the East Coast. A six-month pass between Melbourne and Cairns costs $320.

Classes

There are no separate classes on buses, and the vehicles of the different companies all look pretty similar and are equipped with air-con, toilets and videos. Smoking isn't permitted on Australian buses.

Costs

Following are the average, one-way bus fares on some East Coast routes.

ROUTE	FARE	DURATION (HOURS)
Melbourne–Canberra	$60-85	9
Melbourne–Sydney	$60-110	12
Sydney–Byron Bay	$90-145	13
Sydney–Brisbane	$90-160	16
Brisbane–Airlie Beach	$180-240	20
Brisbane–Cairns	$310-360	29
Townsville–Cairns	$50-85	5½

Reservations

During summer, school holidays and public holidays, you should book well ahead, especially on intercity services. At other times you should have few problems getting onto your preferred service.

Reserve at least a day in advance if you're using a travel pass.

Car & Motorcycle

The best way to see the East Coast is by car – it's certainly the only way to get to those interesting out-of-the-way places without taking a tour.

Diesel and unleaded fuel is available from service stations. LPG (gas) is also available in populated areas but not always at more remote service stations. On main East Coast highways there's usually a small town or a petrol station roughly every 50km or so.

Motorcycles are popular, as the climate is just ideal for bikes for much of the year. Bringing your own motorcycle into Australia will entail an expensive shipping exercise, valid registration in the country of origin and a *Carnet de Passages en Douanes*. This is an internationally recognised customs document that allows you to import your vehicle without paying customs duty or taxes. To get one, apply to a motoring organisation or association in your home country. You'll also need a rider's licence and a helmet. A fuel range of 350km will easily cover fuel stops up the East Coast and, for that matter, around the continent. The long, open roads are really made for large-capacity machines above 750cc.

Automobile Associations

For emergency breakdown services, touring maps and detailed guides to accommodation and camp sites, it's wise to join an automobile association. The national

Australian Automobile Association (www.aaa.asn.au) is the umbrella organisation for the various state associations.

The state organisations have reciprocal arrangements with other states and with similar organisations overseas – including AAA in the USA and RAC or AA in the UK. Bring proof of membership with you.

The main state associations:

NSW & ACT NRMA (☎13 21 32; www.nrma.com.au)
Queensland RACQ (☎13 19 05; www.racq.com.au)
Victoria RACV (☎13 72 28; www.racv.com.au)

Driving Licence

You can use your home country's driving licence in Victoria, NSW and Queensland, as long as it is written in English (if it's in another language, a certified translation must be carried) and carries your photograph for identification. ACT also requires an international driving permit.

Car Hire

There are plenty of car-rental companies ready and willing to put you behind the wheel. Between a group, car hire can be reasonably economical. The main thing to remember is distance – if you want to travel far, you need unlimited kilometres.

Major companies:
Avis (☎13 63 33; www.avis.com.au)

Budget (☎1300 362 848; www.budget.com.au)
Hertz (☎13 30 39; www.hertz.com.au)
Thrifty (☎1300 367 227; www.thrifty.com.au)

These companies have offices or agents in most major towns. There are also numerous local firms that are sometimes cheaper but may have restrictions.

The big firms sometimes offer one-way rentals, which may not cost extra.

The major companies offer a choice of deals, either unlimited kilometres or 100km or so a day free plus so many cents per kilometre over this. Daily rates are typically from $50 a day for a small car, from $75 or $80 a day for a medium car, or from $85 to $100 a day for a big car, not including insurance. Booking online can often save quite a bit.

You must be at least 21 years old to hire from most firms; if you're under 25 you may only be able to hire a small car or may have to pay a surcharge.

4WD & CAMPERVAN

Having a 4WD enables you to get right off the beaten track and out to some of the natural wonders that most travellers miss. Something small, such as a Suzuki, costs around $120 per day; for a Toyota Land Cruiser you're looking at around $170, which should include

---

SHARE A RIDE

Jayride (www.jayride.com.au) is a new ride-sharing organisation that helps link locals and travellers with drivers heading where they want to go. It's not unlike couchsurfing for the road community – you can offer or share a ride, meet new people and feel good about reducing your carbon footprint. As with hitch-hiking, there are potential risks involved with taking or giving a lift. After connecting with your prospective car-mate online, it's wise to meet in a public place before hitting the road. If anything seems off, don't hesitate to back out.

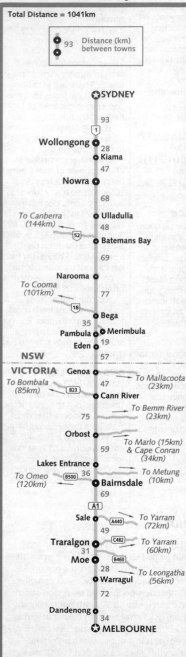

Sydney to Melbourne via the Princes Hwy

Total Distance = 1041km

⊙ 93 ⊙ Distance (km) between towns

⊙ **SYDNEY**

93
[1]

Wollongong ⊙
28
Kiama ⊙
47

Nowra ⊙

68

Ulladulla ⊙
48
To Canberra (144km) — [52]
Batemans Bay ⊙

69

Narooma ⊙
To Cooma (101km) — 77
[18]
Bega ⊙
35
Pambula ⊙ ⊙ **Merimbula**
19
Eden ⊙
NSW
57
VICTORIA   **Genoa** ⊙ → To Mallacoota (23km)
To Bombala (85km) — [B23]   47
Cann River ⊙
→ To Bemm River (23km)
75
Orbost ⊙
→ To Marlo (15km) & Cape Conran (34km)
59
Lakes Entrance ⊙ → To Metung (10km)
To Omeo (120km) — [B500] 36
Bairnsdale ⊙
69
[A1]
Sale ⊙ [A440] → To Yarram (72km)
49
Traralgon ⊙ [C482] → To Yarram (60km)
31
Moe ⊙ [B460]
28 → To Leongatha (56km)
Warragul ⊙
72
Dandenong ⊙
34
⊙ **MELBOURNE**

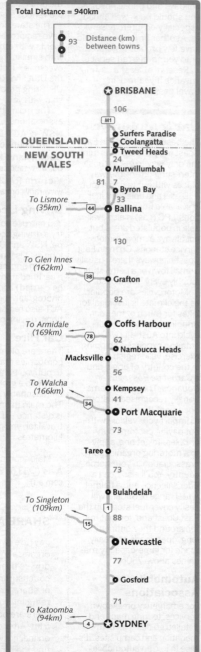

Sydney to Brisbane via the Pacific Hwy

Total Distance = 940km

⊙ 93 ⊙ Distance (km) between towns

⊙ **BRISBANE**

106
[M1]
QUEENSLAND   ⊙ Surfers Paradise
⊙ Coolangatta
NEW SOUTH   ⊙ Tweed Heads
WALES   24
⊙ Murwillumbah
81   7
⊙ Byron Bay
To Lismore (35km) — [44]   33
Ballina ⊙

130

To Glen Innes (162km) — [38]   ⊙ **Grafton**

82

To Armidale (169km) — [78]   ⊙ **Coffs Harbour**
62
⊙ Nambucca Heads
Macksville ⊙
56
To Walcha (166km) — [34]   ⊙ **Kempsey**
41
⊙ ⊙ **Port Macquarie**

73

Taree ⊙

73

⊙ **Bulahdelah**
To Singleton (109km) — [1]
[15]   88

⊙ **Newcastle**

77

⊙ **Gosford**

71
To Katoomba (94km) — [4] ⊙ **SYDNEY**

Brisbane to Cairns via the Bruce Hwy

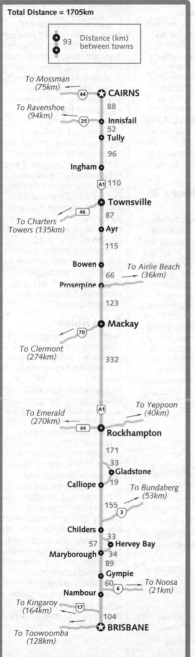

Total Distance = 1705km

93 | Distance (km) between towns

To Mossman (75km)

44 ☆ CAIRNS

88

To Ravenshoe (94km)

25 ● Innisfail

52

● Tully

96

Ingham ●

A1 110

● Townsville

A6 87

To Charters Towers (135km)

● Ayr

115

Bowen ●

66 — To Airlie Beach (36km)

Proserpine ●

123

● Mackay

70

To Clermont (274km)

332

To Emerald (270km)

A1

A4

To Yeppoon (40km)

● Rockhampton

171

33

● Gladstone

Calliope ● 19

To Bundaberg (53km)

155

3

Childers ●

33

57 ● Hervey Bay

Maryborough ● 34

89

● Gympie

60 6 — To Noosa (21km)

Nambour ●

To Kingaroy (164km)

17

104

☆ BRISBANE

To Toowoomba (128km)

insurance and some free kilometres (typically 100km per day; unlimited kilometres is common in the far north and outback though). Check the insurance conditions carefully, especially the excess, as they can be onerous.

Hertz, Budget and Avis have 4WD rentals. Specialist rental firms:

Britz Australia (☎1800 331 454; www.britz.com.au)

Camperman Australia (☎1800 216 223; www.camper manaustralia.com.au) Rents campervans.

Wicked Campervans (☎1800 246 869; www.wicked-campers.com.au) Has vehicles emblazoned with profane commentary.

Insurance

In Australia, third-party personal injury insurance is included in the vehicle-registration cost, ensuring that every registered vehicle carries at least minimum insurance. We recommend extending that minimum to at least third-party property insurance – minor collisions can be amazingly expensive.

When it comes to hire cars, understand your liability in the event of an accident. You can pay an additional daily amount to the rental company which will reduce your liability in the event of an accident from upwards of $3000 to a few hundred dollars. Check with your credit-card company as many provide this coverage for free with use of your card.

Purchase

If you plan to stay several months with plenty of driving, buying is much cheaper than renting. Reliability is all-important. It's also wise to buy a locally manufactured vehicle, such as a Holden Commodore or Ford Falcon, or one of the mainstream VW, Toyota, Mitsubishi or Nissan campervans.

Sydney is a particularly good place to buy cars from backpackers who have finished their trips. Try hostel noticeboards or at car markets.

When you buy or sell a car, every state has its own regulations, particularly with rego (registration). In Victoria, for example, a car has to have a compulsory safety check (Road Worthy Certificate; RWC) before it can be registered in the new owner's name.

Note that it's much easier to sell a car in the same state that it's registered in, otherwise you (or the buyer) must re-register it in the new state, and that's a hassle.

Before you buy any vehicle, have it thoroughly checked by a competent mechanic. The state automobile associations have lists of reputable mechanics.

Contact the relevant state office of the Register of Encumbered Vehicles (REVS), where you can find out if the car you're buying is fully paid up and owned by the seller. Call and ask for a REVS check.

NSW & ACT (✆13 32 20; www.revs.nsw.gov.au)

QLD (✆13 13 04; www.fairtrading.qld.gov.au)

VIC (✆13 11 71; www.vicroads.vic.gov.au)

BUY-BACK DEALS
One way of getting around the hassles of buying and selling a vehicle privately is to enter into a buy-back arrangement with a car or motorcycle dealer. One company that specialises in buy-back on cars and campervans is **Travellers Autobarn** (✆1800 674 374; www.travellers-autobarn.com.au), which has offices in Brisbane, Cairns, Melbourne and Sydney and offers a range of vehicles.

Road Conditions & Hazards
Australia has few multi-lane highways, although there are stretches of divided road (four or six lanes) in some particularly busy areas such as the toll roads of Sydney, Melbourne and Brisbane. Two-lane roads however, are the only option for many routes.

You don't have to get far off the beaten track to find yourself on dirt roads. The problem here is that if you have a hire car, the company's insurance won't cover you unless you've hired an expensive 4WD.

ANIMAL HAZARDS
Kangaroos are common hazards on country roads. If you're travelling at any sort of speed, hitting one can make a real mess of your car, not to mention the kangaroo. They are most active at dawn and dusk, and often travel in groups. Many Australians avoid travelling altogether after dark in country areas because of the hazards posed by animals.

If you are travelling at night and a large animal appears in front of you, hit the brakes (if there isn't a car right behind you), dip your lights (so you don't continue to dazzle and confuse it) and only swerve if it's safe to do so. Numerous travellers have been killed in accidents caused by swerving to miss animals. It's better to damage your car and perhaps kill the animal than cause the death of yourself and your passengers and other motorists on the road.

Road Rules
Australians drive on the left-hand side of the road and all cars are right-hand drive. An important road rule is 'give way to the right' – at roundabouts and unmarked intersections, you must give way to vehicles entering the intersection from your right.

The general speed limit in built-up areas is 60km/h, although this has been reduced to 50km/h on many residential streets. Near schools, the limit is 40km/h in the morning and afternoon. On the open highway it's usually 100km/h or 110km/h. Keep an eye out for signs. The police have speed radar and cameras, and are very fond of using them in strategically concealed locations.

Seatbelt usage is compulsory. Children up to the age of seven years must be belted into an approved safety seat.

TOLL ROADS

There are a handful of toll roads on the East Coast, and since toll booths have largely disappeared from the landscape, you'll need to make sure you pay the toll online or face a hefty fine – whether you're travelling in your own vehicle or in a rental. Most toll roads are located on major freeways around Melbourne, Sydney and Brisbane. You usually have two or three days to pay after driving the toll road.

In NSW, you can pay for the toll by signing up for an e-pass online: www.roam.com.au, www.myRTA.com, or www.roamexpress.com.au.

In Victoria, you can register for a Melbourne Pass, available on www.citylink.com.au, which allows you to pay for your tolls online.

In Queensland, pay for tolls through Go Via (www.govia.com.au).

DRINK-DRIVING

Along the East Coast, drink-driving is a real problem, especially in country areas. Serious attempts are being made to reduce the road toll, and random breath tests are not uncommon in built-up areas. If you're caught with a blood-alcohol level of more than 0.05% be prepared for a hefty fine and the loss of your licence.

PARKING

One of the big problems with driving around big cities like Sydney and Melbourne (or popular tourist towns like Byron Bay) is finding somewhere to park. Even if you do find a spot there's likely to be a time restriction, a meter (or ticket machine) or both. Parking fines range from about $50 to $120 and if you park in a clearway your car will be towed away or clamped – look for signs.

In the cities there are large car parks where you can park all day for $20 to $40.

Hitching

Hitching is never entirely safe in any country in the world, and we don't recommend it. Travellers who decide to hitch should understand that they are taking a small but potentially serious risk. People who do choose to hitch will be safer if they travel in pairs and let someone know where they are planning to go.

In Australia, the hitching signal can be a thumbs up, but a downward-pointed finger is more widely understood.

Local Transport

Brisbane, Melbourne and Sydney have public-transport systems utilising buses, trains, ferries and/or trams. Larger regional towns and cities along the East Coast have their own local bus systems. These usually operate from the main train station, or, where there isn't one, from the main long-distance coach terminal. Sizeable towns also have taxis. There's almost no service north of Cairns so your only option is to join a tour or hire a car (Cairns is one of the last places heading north to arrange car hire).

Train

Train travel is a comfortable option for short-haul sectors along the East Coast – but it's also a few dollars more than travelling by bus and it may take a few hours longer. XPT stands for Express Passenger Train. These NSW trains link Sydney with Melbourne, Brisbane, Dubbo, Grafton and Casino.

Rail services within each state are run by that state's rail body, either government or private.

CityRail (☑13 15 00; www.cityrail.info) Covers the NSW coast around Sydney and as far north as Newcastle; also to the Blue Mountains.

CountryLink (☑13 22 32; www.countrylink.info) In NSW, operates from Sydney south to Canberra and Melbourne and along the coast north to Brisbane (but *not* Byron Bay).

Queensland Rail (☑13 12 30; www.queenslandrail.com.au) Operates various train services from Brisbane to Cairns.

V/Line (☑13 61 96; www.vline.com.au) Has train services in Victoria.

Costs

Children can travel for reduced fares; purchasing fares in advance saves you 30% to 50%. First class costs about 40% more than economy. Discounted tickets usually require advance purchase. Australian and foreign students (with an ISIC) get a 50% discount on economy fares. Some standard one-way train fares:

ROUTE	FARE	DURATION (HOURS)
Sydney–Melbourne	$130	11
Sydney–Canberra	$60	4½
Sydney–Brisbane	$130	14½
Brisbane–Cairns	$230	31

Reservations & Classes

During national holidays, school holidays and weekends it can be a good idea to book a seat. You can do this at railway stations or through the railway companies. Many discount fares require you to reserve well in advance.

Extra-cost sleeper service is available between Melbourne, Sydney, Brisbane and Cairns. Some trains also carry 1st-class seats.

Train Passes

Coverage of the East Coast by rail isn't bad. Several useful passes are sold. **Rail Australia** (www.railaustralia.com.au) has information on passes available from the various rail companies.

Austrail Flexipass Allows travel across Australia over a six-month period: $890 if purchased outside Australia, $990 within Australia. It is only sold to non-Australians.

Backtracker Unlimited travel on Countrylink trains linking Sydney with Canberra, Melbourne and Brisbane. It costs $220 for 14 days, $251 for one month and $275 for three months (your best value). It is only sold to non-Australians.

East Coast Discovery Pass Allows travel with unlimited stops over a designated route in one direction in a six-month period. The entire Melbourne to Cairns route costs $451. You can buy shorter segments, such as Sydney to Brisbane ($130).

behind the scenes

SEND US YOUR FEEDBACK

We love to hear from travellers – your comments keep us on our toes and help make our books better. Our well-travelled team reads every word on what you loved or loathed about this book. Although we cannot reply individually to postal submissions, we always guarantee that your feedback goes straight to the appropriate authors, in time for the next edition. Each person who sends us information is thanked in the next edition – and the most useful submissions are rewarded with a free book.

Visit **lonelyplanet.com/contact** to submit your updates and suggestions or to ask for help. Our award-winning website also features inspirational travel stories, news and discussions.

Note: We may edit, reproduce and incorporate your comments in Lonely Planet products such as guidebooks, websites and digital products, so let us know if you don't want your comments reproduced or your name acknowledged. For a copy of our privacy policy visit lonelyplanet.com/privacy.

OUR READERS

Many thanks to the travellers who used the last edition and wrote to us with helpful hints, useful advice and interesting anecdotes:

Alexander Backes, Meredith Bambrick, David Barker, Thoralf Bock, Louise Botterill, Jane L Brown, Gillon Campbell, Alexandra Cantwell, Catsuris Carole, Brittany Dahl, Stuart Davie, John Dunbar, Joe Fletcher, Rebecca Fletcher, Lucas George, Juliette Giannesini, Katherine Golding, Charles Ingrao, Louise Keevill, Tracy Kingstone, Fran Lax, Kelly Maloney, Heather McNeill, Alex Murden, Nick Pond, Janneke Pot, Martin Reisser, Charlotte Rowley, Mark Simons, Petrina Slaytor, Dominik Spoden, Rebecca Tofield, Sophie Trenear

AUTHOR THANKS

Regis St Louis

Thanks to the many Brisbanites who shared tips and insight into their lovely city. I'd also like to thank master chef Philip Johnson and the many winemakers who plied me with viticultural insight (plus wine) in the Granite Belt, and the many helpful Queenslanders elsewhere in the state. At LP, thanks to Maryanne Netto for inviting me on board and my co-authors for all their hard work. Special thanks to Cassandra and daughters Magdalena and Genevieve for a memorable stay in Brisbane. Hugs and handshakes to Leonie and Col for providing a home away from home, and to Tim, Leone, Nadina, August and Luca for all their hospitality.

Jayne D'Arcy

Thanks to *M* magazine colleagues Miranda Tay, Dani Valent, James Smith and Penny Modra. Thanks Blakey, Nat, Keshia, Cecilia and the Humes. Thanks Denis from Seaview Lodge: what a welcome sight your B&B's lights were through the fog. Thanks Sharik Billington for your amazing support and our preppie, Miles, for reminding me how great the Great Ocean Road is (those seals!). Thanks Mum, Dad and Kate for Miles-sitting. Cheers to Paul Harding and Donna Wheeler, and big thanks to Maryanne Netto.

Sarah Gilbert

Thanks to Misha, Jamie, Elijah and Zeke for the fine hospitality. Thanks to my LP colleagues, particularly Regis and Maryanne. Thanks to Kyles, Mel, Pen, Bill, BJ, Ports, Jane and the rest for generating all those happy Canberra memories. I'll always be grateful to my loving and beloved parents, Danny and Kathleen, and my brother and sister James and Mary. Thanks most of all to Nico for his company on the road, and in life.

Paul Harding

Firstly, thanks to my wife Hannah and my beautiful daughter, Layla, who came into the world just before I started working on this book. On the road, many people helped with ideas and advice and the occasional place to stay – you know who you are. Thanks to Jayne D'Arcy for such dedication and the debriefing session in Melbourne. Big thanks at Lonely Planet to Maryanne Netto for your help and faith, as well as Liz, David and the rest of the crew.

Catherine Le Nevez

Cheers to the countless locals, tourism professionals and fellow travellers who provided insider tips, invaluable insights and great times during my journey throughout Far North Queensland. Thanks especially to Robert Stephens at Mamu and Wanegan (Glenis Grogan) in Kuranda, as well as Colin and family, everyone at Bramston Beach and, of course, to Julian. Thanks too to Maryanne for signing me up, and to Regis and all at LP. As ever, *merci surtout* to my family.

Virginia Maxwell

Many thanks to Maryanne Netto, Regis St Louis, Elizabeth Maxwell, Matthew Clarke, Bridget Smyth, Christopher Procter, Phil Learoyd, Helen Campbell, Stephen Alexander, Peter Handsaker and Max Handsaker.

Olivia Pozzan

At Lonely Planet, thanks to Maryanne for the opportunity to again research and write about this land I love so much. Thanks also to Regis and my co-authors. A huge thanks to everyone I met, especially in the Whitsundays where tourism officials and operators went out of their way to show me the beauty of the islands. A special thank you to Tony – serendipity at work? And a very heartfelt thanks to Andrew for making my trip fun and memorable.

Penny Watson

Thanks always and ever to Pippy and our new sidekick Digby. You are my two favourite people. Also to the folk who looked after us on the way: Kekky and Gaga; Jojo Mcharg; JJ and Sar Quigley; Jem Norris and Ali & Ferg McPhee. We love you.

ACKNOWLEDGMENTS

Climate map data adapted from Peel MC, Finlayson BL & McMahon TA (2007) 'Updated World Map of the Köppen-Geiger Climate Classification', *Hydrology and Earth System Sciences*, 11, 163344.

Cover photograph: Looking out to the city skyline from South Head, Sydney, Carol Wiley, Lonely Planet Images. Many of the images in this guide are available for licensing from Lonely Planet Images: www.lonelyplanet images.com.

THIS BOOK

This is the 4th edition of East Coast Australia. The 1st edition was published in 2002, the result of work led by Verity Campbell. The 2nd edition was coordinated by Lindsay Brown, and the 3rd edition by Ryan Ver Berkmoes. Regis St Louis was the coordinating author on this edition, joined by co-authors Jayne D'Arcy, Sarah Gilbert, Paul Harding, Catherine Le Nevez, Virginia Maxwell, Olivia Pozzan and Penny Watson; see Our Writers (p544) to find out which destinations they covered. Dr Tim Flannery wrote the Environment chapter and Dr Michael Cathcart wrote the History chapter, with sidebars and boxed texts in both chapters added by Regis St Louis. This guidebook was commissioned in Lonely Planet's Melbourne office, and produced by the following:

Commissioning Editor
Maryanne Netto

Coordinating Editors
Susie Ashworth, Alison Ridgway

Coordinating Cartographer
Corey Hutchison

Coordinating Layout Designer
Kerrianne Southway

Managing Editor
Liz Heynes

Managing Cartographer
David Connolly

Managing Layout Designer Chris Girdler

Senior Editor
Anna Metcalfe

Assisting Editors Elizabeth Anglin, Elisa Arduca, Andrew Bain, Adrienne Costanzo, Jackey Coyle, Andrea Dobbin, Carly Hall, Kim Hutchins, Bella Li, Simon Sellars

Assisting Cartographer
Tom Webster

Cover Research
Naomi Parker

Internal Image Research
Aude Vauconsant

Thanks to Helen Christinis, Ryan Evans, Jane Hart, Laura Jane, Lisa Knights, Annelies Mertens, Susan Paterson, Gerard Walker, Jeanette Wall, Celia Wood

index

000 Map pages
000 Photo pages

how to use this book

These symbols will help you find the listings you want:

⊙	Sights	🎊	Festivals & Events	☆	Entertainment
🏃	Activities	🛏	Sleeping	🛍	Shopping
🥢	Courses	✗	Eating	ℹ	Information/Transport
☞	Tours	🍷	Drinking		

Look out for these icons:

TOP CHOICE	Our author's recommendation
FREE	No payment required
🌱	A green or sustainable option

Our authors have nominated these places as demonstrating a strong commitment to sustainability – for example by supporting local communities and producers, operating in an environmentally friendly way, or supporting conservation projects.

These symbols give you the vital information for each listing:

♫	Telephone Numbers	🛜	Wi-Fi Access	🚌	Bus
⊙	Opening Hours	🏊	Swimming Pool	⛴	Ferry
P	Parking	🥗	Vegetarian Selection	Ⓜ	Metro
⊖	Nonsmoking	🍴	English-Language Menu	Ⓢ	Subway
✳	Air-Conditioning	👪	Family-Friendly	⊖	London Tube
@	Internet Access	🐾	Pet-Friendly	🚋	Tram
				🚆	Train

Reviews are organised by author preference.

Map Legend

Sights
⊙	Beach
⊙	Buddhist
⊙	Castle
⊙	Christian
⊙	Hindu
⊙	Islamic
⊙	Jewish
⊙	Monument
⊕	Museum/Gallery
⊙	Ruin
⊙	Winery/Vineyard
⊙	Zoo
⊙	Other Sight

Activities, Courses & Tours
⊙	Diving/Snorkelling
⊙	Canoeing/Kayaking
⊙	Skiing
⊙	Surfing
⊙	Swimming/Pool
⊙	Walking
⊙	Windsurfing
⊙	Other Activity/Course/Tour

Sleeping
⊙	Sleeping
⊙	Camping

Eating
⊗	Eating

Drinking
⊙	Drinking
⊙	Cafe

Entertainment
⊙	Entertainment

Shopping
⊙	Shopping

Information
⊙	Post Office
⊙	Tourist Information

Transport
⊙	Airport
⊗	Border Crossing
⊗	Bus
⊕	Cable Car/Funicular
⊙	Cycling
⊙	Ferry
Ⓜ	Metro
⊙	Monorail
P	Parking
Ⓢ	S-Bahn
⊙	Taxi
⊕	Train/Railway
⊙	Tram
⊙	Tube Station
①	U-Bahn
•	Other Transport

Routes
	Tollway
	Freeway
	Primary
	Secondary
	Tertiary
	Lane
	Unsealed Road
	Plaza/Mall
	Steps
)≡(	Tunnel
	Pedestrian Overpass
	Walking Tour
	Walking Tour Detour
	Path

Boundaries
	International
	State/Province
	Disputed
	Regional/Suburb
	Marine Park
	Cliff
	Wall

Population
⊙	Capital (National)
◉	Capital (State/Province)
⊙	City/Large Town
•	Town/Village

Geographic
⌂	Hut/Shelter
⊙	Lighthouse
⊙	Lookout
▲	Mountain/Volcano
⊙	Oasis
⊙	Park
)(	Pass
⊙	Picnic Area
⊙	Waterfall

Hydrography
	River/Creek
	Intermittent River
	Swamp/Mangrove
	Reef
	Canal
	Water
	Dry/Salt/Intermittent Lake
	Glacier

Areas
	Beach/Desert
+ + +	Cemetery (Christian)
× × ×	Cemetery (Other)
	Park/Forest
	Sportsground
	Sight (Building)
	Top Sight (Building)

Catherine Le Nevez

Townsville to Innisfail, Cairns & the Daintree Rainforest Catherine's first writing for Lonely Planet was on Queensland while completing her Doctorate of Creative Arts in Writing, during a 65,000km lap-and-a-half of the continent, including driving through two cyclones. Since then, Catherine has authored or co-authored more than two dozen guidebooks worldwide, including Lonely Planet's *Australia* and *Queensland & the Great Barrier Reef* guides. She jumped at the chance to return to tropical paradise for this assignment.

Virginia Maxwell

Sydney & the Central Coast, This is Sydney colour section Virginia worked for many years as a publishing manager at Lonely Planet's Melbourne headquarters before deciding that she would be happier writing guidebooks than commissioning them. Since then, she has written about destinations across the world for a host of international guidebooks, magazines and websites. Though based in Melbourne, she has lived in Sydney and refuses to engage in the age-old Melbourne vs Sydney game of one-upmanship, being equally happy and at home in both.

Olivia Pozzan

Brisbane & the Gold Coast, Noosa & the Sunshine Coast, Fraser Island & the Fraser Coast, The Whitsundays Raised on the Fraser Coast in the Sunshine State, Olivia had a coastal upbringing that shaped a life-long addiction to gorgeous beaches. Her bikini collection graced every sandy shore from the northern Reef to the Gold Coast. After years of travelling the globe, Olivia had a craving for sand between her toes that drew her back to Queensland, where she lives on the glorious Sunshine Coast. Olivia revisited her favourite coastal hot spots while researching this book.

Penny Watson

Canberra & Southern NSW, Byron Bay & Northern NSW Penny is a trained journalist and full-time professional travel writer. She grew up in regional NSW and has since become an expert on its varied landscapes, in particular its beachy borders. *East Coast Australia* is Penny's third title covering this beautiful strip of coastline. As a Hong Kong resident, the opportunity to return home and explore some more is always too tempting to ignore.

Contributing Authors

Dr Tim Flannery wrote the Environment chapter. Tim is a scientist, explorer and writer. He has written several award-winning books including *The Future Eaters, Throwim Way Leg* and *The Weather Makers*. He lives in Sydney where he is a professor in the faculty of science at Macquarie University.

Dr Michael Cathcart wrote the History chapter. Michael teaches history at the Australian Centre, the University of Melbourne. He is well known as a broadcaster on ABC Radio National and has presented history programs on ABC TV. His most recent book is *The Water Dreamers* (2009), a history of how water shaped the history of Australia.

OUR STORY

A beat-up old car, a few dollars in the pocket and a sense of adventure. In 1972 that's all Tony and Maureen Wheeler needed for the trip of a lifetime – across Europe and Asia overland to Australia. It took several months, and at the end – broke but inspired – they sat at their kitchen table writing and stapling together their first travel guide, *Across Asia on the Cheap*. Within a week they'd sold 1500 copies. Lonely Planet was born.

Today, Lonely Planet has offices in Melbourne, London and Oakland, with more than 600 staff and writers. We share Tony's belief that 'a great guidebook should do three things: inform, educate and amuse'.

OUR WRITERS

Regis St Louis

Coordinating Author, Brisbane & the Gold Coast Regis' love of Australia has taken him all along the coast, through the captivating markets of Melbourne, along Sydney's scenic headlands and through the rainforests and tropical islands of Queensland. On his most recent trip, he watched whales off North Stradbroke Island, introduced his daughters to cuddly koalas at Lone Pine Sanctuary and enjoyed a bit of mayhem during the lively Brisbane Festival. Regis has contributed to more than 30 Lonely Planet titles, including the latest *Queensland & Great Barrier Reef* guide. When not travelling the world, he splits his time between New York City and Sydney.

Jayne D'Arcy

Melbourne & Coastal Victoria Growing up in the Victorian seaside suburb of Frankston had its advantages for Jayne; it motivated her to catch the Met through all three zones to hang out in Prahran's Greville St, Fitzroy's Brunswick St, St Kilda and the Queen Vic market. After a longish spell working in community radio in East Timor, she finally settled with her family in Melbourne's vibrant north. When she's not riding her 1970s folding bike around North Fitzroy or pretending to renovate, Jayne writes for *The Age*. Jayne has contributed to eight Lonely Planet guides.

Sarah Gilbert

Canberra & Southern NSW, Capricorn Coast & the Southern Reef Islands Sarah was born in rural New South Wales, raised in Sydney, studied at the Australian National University in Canberra and has since lived in Amsterdam, New York and Buenos Aires. As a writer, she cut her teeth on the Big Apple's tabloids before moving home to work in TV current affairs. She has contributed to several Lonely Planet guides and is now based in Sydney once more, making her living as a freelance writer and a researcher for film and TV. She is currently writing her first book of non-fiction.

Paul Harding

Melbourne & Coastal Victoria Melbourne-born but country-raised, Paul spent childhood summers in the Gippsland Lakes, and later plenty of road trips up the East Coast of Australia. He's since seen (and written about) a good part of the world, but still calls this part of Australia home. For this edition, Paul travelled the length and breadth of beautiful Gippsland, occasionally finding time to down the notebook and hit the beach. A freelance writer and photographer, Paul has contributed to more than 30 Lonely Planet guides, including numerous Australian titles.

OVER PAGE MORE WRITERS

Published by Lonely Planet Publications Pty Ltd
ABN 36 005 607 983
4th edition – Aug 2011
ISBN 978 1 74179 471 7
© Lonely Planet 2011   Photographs © as indicated 2011
10 9 8 7 6 5 4 3 2 1
Printed in China